CURRENT RESEARCH IN PHOTOSYNTHESIS

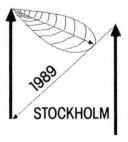

Current Research in Photosynthesis

Volume II

Proceedings of the VIIIth International Conference on Photosynthesis
Stockholm, Sweden, August 6–11, 1989

edited by

M. BALTSCHEFFSKY
Department of Biochemistry,
University of Stockholm,
Stockholm, Sweden

KLUWER ACADEMIC PUBLISHERS
DORDRECHT / BOSTON / LONDON

Library of Congress Cataloging in Publication Data

International Congress on Photosynthesis (8th : 1989 : Stockholm,
  Sweden)
    Current research in photosynthesis : proceedings of the VIIIth
  International Congress on Photosynthesis, Stockholm, Sweden, August
  6-11, 1989 / edited by M. Baltscheffsky.
        p.   cm.
    ISBN 0-7923-0587-6 (set)
    1. Photosynthesis--Congresses.   2. Photosynthesis--Research-
  -Congresses.   I. Baltscheffsky, Margareta.   II. Title.
  QK882.I55   1989
  581.1'3342--dc20   89-48127

ISBN 0-7923-0588-4 (Vol. I)
ISBN 0-7923-0589-2 (Vol. II)
ISBN 0-7923-0590-6 (Vol. III)
ISBN 0-7923-0591-4 (Vol. IV)
ISBN 0-7923-0587-6 (Set)

Published by Kluwer Academic Publishers,
P.O. Box 17, 3300 AA Dordrecht, The Netherlands.

Kluwer Academic Publishers incorporates
the publishing programmes of
D. Reidel, Martinus Nijhoff, Dr W. Junk and MTP Press.

Sold and distributed in the U.S.A. and Canada
by Kluwer Academic Publishers,
101 Philip Drive, Norwell, MA 02061, U.S.A.

In all other countries, sold and distributed
by Kluwer Academic Publishers Group,
P.O. Box 322, 3300 AH Dordrecht, The Netherlands.

GENERAL CONTENTS

CONTENTS TO VOLUME II

4. Prokaryotic Antennae Systems

5. Eukaryotic Antennae Systems

6. Photoinhibition

7. Photosystem I

XX

PREFACE

These four volumes with close to one thousand contributions are the proceedings from the VIIIth International Congress on Photosynthesis, which was held in Stockholm, Sweden, on August 6-11, 1989. The site for the Congress was the campus of the University of Stockholm. This in itself was an experiment, since the campus never before had been used for a conference of that size. On the whole, it was a very sucessful experiment. The outcome of a congress depends on many contributing factors, one major such factor being the scientific vigour of the participants, and I think it is safe to say that the pariticipants were vigourous indeed. Many exciting new findings were presented and thoroughly dicussed, indoors in the discussion sessions as well as outdoors on the lawns. For the local organizing committee it was very rewarding to participate in these activities, and to watch some of our younger colleagues for the first time being subjected to the impact of a large international congress. The stimulating effect of this event on the local research atmosphere has been substantial.

As was the case with the proceedings from both the 1983 and 1986 Congresses these proceedings have been compiled from camera ready manuscripts, and the editing has mainly consisted of finding the proper place for each contribution and distributing the manuscripts into four volumes with some internal logic in each. In this I have had the invaluable help from Dr. Åke Strid, to whom I am indeed very thankful. The professional and unfailing support of our publisher, Ir. Ad. C. Plaizier, is also gratefully acknowledged.

The scientific programme for the Congress was put together by the Swedish Organizing Committee, with important input from the International Committee on Photosynthesis, and I thank my fellow-organizers for their competent and valuable work. The practical arrangements for the Congress were very well handled by Congrex AB, and I would like to specially mention Anette Lifors and Christel Bomgren for their enthusiastic help. The Congress would not have functioned without strong local support, foremost that of Professor Bertil Andersson and Dr. Stenbjörn Styring from the Department of Biochemistry, but also from all the students who were most helpful in uncounted numbers of ways, before, during and after the Congress.

Finally I thank all those who financially contributed to the Congress. Without their support there would not have been any Photosynthesis Congress in Sweden.

Stockholm in October 1989   Margareta Baltscheffsky

ACKNOWLEDGEMENTS

The Swedish Organizing Committee wishes to thank the following sponsors for their financial Support of the Congress.

Sponsors

Astra AB, Sweden
Pharmacia AB, Sweden
Scandinavian Airlines System, Sweden
Sparbankernas Bank, Sweden
Stiftelsen Kempes Minne, Sweden
Stiftelsen Lantbruksforskning, Sweden
Strålfors AB, Sweden
Swedish Council for Forestry and Agricultural Research
Swedish Natural Science Research Council
The City of Stockholm
The Nobel Foundation, Sweden

Exhibitors

ADC. The Analytical Development Company Ltd, UK
BIOMONITOR SCI, Sweden
HANSATECH Ltd., UK
LI-COR Inc., USA
QA-DATA, Finland
SKYE INSTRUMENTS LTD, UK
TECHTUM INSTRUMENT AB, Sweden
WALZ, Mess-und Regeltechnik, FRG

Swedish Organizing Committee

Chairperson: Margareta Baltscheffsky, University of
Stockholm

Per-Åke Albertsson	Lund University
Bertil Andersson	University of Stockholm
Carl-Ivar Brändén	The Swedish University of Agricultural Sciences
Petter Gustafsson	Umeå University
Anders Kylin	Lund University
Christer Sundqvist	Gothenburg University
Jan-Eric Tillberg	University of Stockholm
Tore Vänngård	Gothenburg University
Gunnar Öquist	Umeå University

International Committee on Photosynthesis

C. Arntzen	USA
M. Baltscheffsky	Sweden (Chairperson)
J. Biggins	USA
G. Farquhar	Australia
G. Forti	Italy
R. Van Grondelle	The Netherlands
H. Heldt	FRG
P. Horton	UK
R. Malkin	USA
P. Mathis	France
I. Ohad	Israel
K. Satoh	Japan
Y.K. Shen	PR of China
V. Shuvalov	USSR
R. Vallejos	Argentina

SPEECH HELD AT THE OPENING OF THE VIIIth INTERNATIONAL
CONGRESS ON PHOTOSYNTHESIS STOCKHOLM, AUGUST 6th, 1989

BENGT GÖRANSSON
MINISTRY OF EDUCATION, 103 33 STOCKHOLM, SWEDEN

I consider it a great honour to extend to the delegates to this
congress the greetings of the Government of Sweden. Welcome to
Sweden and welcome to our capital. I would like to take this opportunity to share with you a number of personal reflections.

Photosynthesis is a good example of a science which enjoys rapid
development and whose practical application extends to ever wider
areas. It provides, to my mind, evidence of the role which highly
qualified and at the same time highly theoretical research plays in
changing and developing our lives and our society. Earlier societies
were much more static in character, the individual relied on well
established patterns for economic activity and survival. Ways of
life, attitudes, values and interests all built on traditions established by earlier generations. Today we live more like the sailor
who when he sails on open sea, must rely on the discoveries made by
the researcher/navigator on the basis of his experience and knowledge.

The researcher is to a very great extent our navigator, our path-
finder. The fact that he is also more and more of a theoretician is
of no small importance - this makes for greater demands on basic
theoretical education. It also calls for greater effort in providing
the wider public with sufficient popularized knowledge in order to
ensure that the insights and directions developed by the theoretical
researcher can be usefully exploited.

I would like to be concrete on this particular point. With mounting
concern I have observed how here in Sweden, as in many other countries, while basic schooling for the majority of our citizens has
improved there has been an increase in various types of what can
only be described as occult trends. A lack of faith in the future
together with a strong mistrust not only in the political establishment but also in the intellectual establishment to which the world
of research belongs, - these are far from uncommon today. To put it

more provocatively I might say that only those who know next to
nothing about the subject they express their opinions on, are
accepted as authorities.

A lack of faith in the future is dangerous for mankind. It is
dangerous because it is, paradoxically enough, often combined with
an unlimited exaggeration of the level of development we now enjoy
and of the capacity of the human brain that we judge ourselves to
possess. Those who do not think that we can solve the different problems we face today with tomorrow's discoveries and with the help of
tomorrow's people appear to believe that we in our own time, have
reached the final frontiers of knowledge.

Just as dangerous is the naive belief in the future or in progress,
especially that which is based on the belief that development is
automatic, that we have no cause to worry. In reality development
and change come about through the persistant pursuit of knowledge,
through the demanding job of fitting together various bits of knowledge, of matching ideas to ideas. The foundations of a positive
and productive belief in the future are to be found in the belief
that there are always new possibilities combined with the hard work
of winning new knowledge.

In creating a positive and productive belief in the future we have
good reason to consider more closely the research being carried out
in the field of photosynthesis. The experience gained in this field
gives us hope that we will be able to solve the global problems
affecting our environment, our future production of the necessities
of life and the possibility of finding a cure for serious diseases.
The global solutions will also be solutions to the problems faced by
the individual. The importance of the results of research in the
field of photosynthesis go far beyond the confines of the
researcher's world. Those aspects of research on photosynthesis
which have a bearing on the question of energy lead to an increased
interest on the part of government bodies and of business interests.
The nature of research calls for interdisciplinary cooperation and
important contributions are made by such groups as programmers and
technicians to the work of the researcher. This means that the need
to promote the exchange of ideas and experiences, such as take place
at congresses and conferences, is very great. The fact that representatives for science and research from university departments and
research institutions all over the world meet and confer, becomes an
event of decisive importance. I would therefore like to express my
gratitude and appreciation to you all for attending this congress.
I am of course delighted at the fact that our Swedish representives
in this field of scientific research have been entrusted with the
task of organizing the congress.

I would like to pursue my line of thinking further. In pointing to the paradoxical conflict between highly qualified and highly developed research on the one hand and the trend towards more occult interests on the other, I have done so because I think it is of vital importance that we combat the latter. Getting the researcher to step outside his isolation in the world of "interdisciplinary science" is not enough. It is vital that a broad section of the public should be given the opportunity to share the knowledge gained by research. A society in which the reseacher is isolated because of his research and knowledge and possibly regarded as a "deus ex machina", a wizard who can do things we others cannot do, such a society will never liberate itself from the threats posed by occultist movements. These threats are all the more dangerous because of the effects that they can have on wider relationships in society. A democratic social order rests ultimately on the fact that the citizens know enough about what happens in their community to feel secure. The ignorant and insecure citizen, who through lack of understanding is manipulated or feels manipulated becomes all too easily a victim of antidemocratic forces and campaigns. This gives me special cause to appeal to you as representatives for a highly specialized science, to give some consideration to what is often called popular science. I trust that the exchange of experience at the congress will in some way be made available for larger sections of the public. A quick glance through a Swedish school book shows that photosynthesis is far from being among the easiest of scientific topics and I regret to add that any student who satisfies himself with the contents of the school book will hardly broaden his knowledge of photosynthesis. What is important is that this broader knowledge is accessible to the average interested member of the public. (In this context it would be interesting to speculate on the causes of the chlorophyll hysteria of the nineteen fifties - you all remember the toothpaste with chlorophyll - was it in part due to a lack of understanding of man's own capacity in the field of photosynthesis?)

My personal wish, if you allow me to voice it, is that this congress and its work will stimulate popular education to take up popular science in the best sense of the term.

I would like to wish you all a fruitful congress week, a week that will benefit your scientific endeavours and ultimately, benefit humanity. It goes without saying, though I very much enjoy saying it - that I wish each and every one of you a pleasant stay in our summer clad Sweden and in Stockholm which I trust will show you the very best it has to offer the visitor from home or abroad.

Dear guests and congress participants!
I have used my privilege as invited minister by making these comments. I now turn to my official and ceremonial duty and declare the VIIIth International Congress on Photosynthesis opened.

ANALYSIS OF PHYCOBILISOME AND PHOTOSYSTEM I COMPLEXES OF CYANOBACTERIA

DONALD A. BRYANT, ERHARD RHIEL, ROBERT DE LORIMIER, JIANHUI ZHOU,
VERONICA L. STIREWALT, GAIL E. GASPARICH, JAMES M. DUBBS, AND WILLIAM
SNYDER, DEPT. OF MOLECULAR AND CELL BIOLOGY, THE PENNSYLVANIA STATE
UNIVERSITY, UNIVERSITY PARK, PA 16802 USA

1. PHYCOBILISOMES

Phycobilisomes (PBS) are supramolecular, multiprotein complexes
which function as the light-harvesting antennae for Photosystem II (PS
II) in the cyanobacteria, the chloroplasts of red algae, and the cyanelles of phylogenetically ambiguous flagellates such as Cyanophora paradoxa (1). PBS occur as highly ordered arrays on the stromal surfaces
of the thylakoids; each is believed to interact with two or more PS II
reaction centers. PBS are predominantly composed of phycobiliproteins,
a family of water-soluble proteins that carry linear tetrapyrrole chromophores (phycobilins; see 2). Each phycobiliprotein consists of two
dissimilar subunits, denoted α and β, each of which carries 1-4 chromophores. The fundamental structural unit of the phycobiliproteins is
the $(\alpha\beta)_3$ trimer, a torroidal molecule about 11 nm indiameter and 3-3.5
nm in thickness with a central cavity about 3.5 nm in diameter (3, 4).
Face-to-face stacking of two trimers produces $(\alpha\beta)_6$ hexamers which are
11 X 6 nm. The assembly of larger substructures and PBS themselves
requires the participation of a second class of proteins, the so-called
"linker polypeptides," which are absolutely required for the assembly
of higher order structures (see below; also see 1, 2). The linker polypeptides probably fill the central cavity of the phycobiliprotein tor-
roids and participate in the tail-to-tail joining of pairs of hexamers.
Linker polypeptides also are required for the rod-to-core joining of
phycocyanin (PC) to allophycocyanin (AP; see below) and in the PBS-to-
PS II joining interaction (1, 2, 5). The linker polypeptides generally
do not carry chromophores, but they effect spectral changes in a subset
of the phycobilin chromophores which contributes to the unidirectional
flow of light energy from the PBS to the PS II reaction center (see 1,
2, 6).

Although PBS occur in several structural variants, hemidiscoidal PBS
are by far the most common. These structures are composed of either
eight or nine cylindrical substructures which can be placed into two
functionally defined categories. The "peripheral rods" are cylinders
11 nm in diameter of variable length (6-40 nm) and composition. These
structures may be exclusively composed of the phycobiliprotein phycocyanin (PC, λmax 620 nm), but may additionally contain phycoerythrin
(PE, λmax 560 nm) and phycoerythrocyanin (PEC, λmax 570 nm) when pro-

duced (1, 2, 6, 7). The phycobiliprotein components of the peripheral rods are only assembled in the presence of the appropriate linker polypeptides (see Table 1). The "core substructure" is largely comprised of allophycocyanin (AP) and structurally related proteins (see Table 1). Depending upon species, the two, or more commonly three, core cylinders (11 X 14 nm) are either aligned side-by-side or stacked to form a pyramidal structure. The peripheral rods are attached to two of the three lateral surfaces of the core, while the third surface contacts the PS II reaction centers at the thylakoid surface. The "asymmetric" third surface is postulated to be differentiated due to the presence of the minor AP-related subunits of the core (see 2, 6, 8). These minor components are also proposed to play important roles in the energy transfer pathway to chlorophyll (as terminal energy acceptors in the PBS) and in the attachment of the PBS to the thylakoid surface (5, 8).

For the past several years we have been studying aspects of the structure, function; and assembly of PBS components via genetic analyses in the unicellular, marine cyanobacterium Synechococcus sp. PCC 7002. Additionally, we have been studying the effects of light intensity, light wavelength, and nutrient availability on the expression of genes encoding PBS, PS I, and PS II components in Synechococcus sp. PCC 7002 and Pseudanabaena sp. PCC 7409, a filamentous, non-heterocystous cyanobacterium which undergoes complementary chromatic adaptation.

The PBS of Synechococcus sp. PCC 7002 are comprised of only eleven structural polypeptides (9); these polypeptides and the gene loci which encode them are listed in Table 1 along with other pertinent information. As shown in Table 1, each of the eleven genes has been cloned, sequenced, and mutagenized. Additionally, analyses of the transcripts produced from these gene loci have been performed by Northern-blot hybridization, primer extension, and S1 nuclease protection. The eleven structural genes are organized into six transcriptional units: cpcBAC-DEF; cpcG; apcABC; apcD; apcE; and apcF (Two of the genes, cpcE and cpcF, in the first transcriptional unit do not encode structural components of the PBS, but are required for the proper attachment of the phycocyanobilin chromophore to the cpcA gene product (8).).

The cpcBACDEF transcripts have two major 5' endpoints as determined by S1 nuclease protection mapping and primer extension (9). These endpoints occur at -322 bases and -160 bases relative to the cpcB translational start codon. Two mRNA species are detected for each of the following transcriptional units: cpcBA; cpcBAC; cpcBACD; cpcBACDE; and possibly cpcBACDEF. In each case the size difference between the two RNA species is compatible with the hypothesis that these mRNAs have the same 3' endpoints and the two 5' endpoints mentioned. The intergenic regions cpcA-cpcC, cpcC-cpcD, and cpcD-cpcE each have the potential to form complex secondary structures (with roughly equivalent energies of formation). These structures possibly function as mRNA stabilizers, as transcription terminators, or as both. Immediately 5' to the endpoint at -322 bases are sequence motifs (TTTAAA--17 bp--TAACAT) which closely resemble the consensus promoter for the sigma-70 form of RNA polymerase

TABLE 1. Composition of phycobilisomes of Synechococcus sp. PCC 7002

Subunit	Copies/PBS[a]	Gene Locus	Length[b]	Cloned	Sequenced	Mutants[c]
		PERIPHERAL RODS:				
α^{PC}	72	cpcA	162	+	+	D, I
β^{PC}	72	cpcB	172	+	+	D, I
LR33	6	cpcC	290	+	+	I
LR9	6	cpcD	80	+	+	D, I
LR29	6	cpcG	248	+	+	D
		CORES:				
α^{AP}	32	apcA	161	+	+	D, I
β^{AP}	34	apcB	161	+	+	D, I
α^{AP-B}	2	apcD	161	+	+	I
β^{18}	2	apcF	169	+	+	D
LC8.5	6	apcC	67	+	+	I
LCM99	2	apcE	886	+	+	I

[a] Copies per phycobilisome. Numbers reflect measured values for the ratio AP:PC, and the relative ratios of the linker polypeptides. The actual numbers for the αAP-B and β18 subunits could be slightly higher than listed. These numbers reflect the composition of an idealized PBS as predicted by the model of Glazer (2) for a PBS with a tricylindrical core with a 1:2 ratio of AP:PC. Data from (10).

[b] Length, in amino acids, of the deduced translation product of the gene

[c] D, deletion; I, insertion.

in E. coli. In fact, primer extension analysis of RNA from E. coli cells harboring a cpcB-lacZ translational fusion indicates that this promoter is recognized in E. coli (9). Hence, these results provide strong evidence in support of the notion that Synechococcus sp. PCC 7002 has an RNA polymerase, one form of which has a sigma factor with promoter recognition properties similar to those of the major form of RNA polymerase in E. coli. The sequences immediately 5' to the second endpoint do not resemble those of any known procaryotic promoter and an equivalent 5' endpoint was not observed with RNA isolated from E. coli cells harboring the cpcB-lacZ fusion. Although an endonucleolytic processing event cannot yet be excluded as a possibility, support for the secondary promoter concept is found by comparing the 5' flanking sequences of this endpoint with those of several other transcriptional units including psaAB and apcABC. These comparisons and others suggest that Synechococcus sp. PCC 7002 probably has multiple forms of RNA polymerase whose promoter recognition is governed by alternative sigmas.

None of the genes encoding peripheral rod components is apparently required for core assembly. Although intact cores were not isolated from mutants devoid of PC (cpcBA deletion) or the rod linker of 29 kDa (cpcG deletion), the growth rates of these mutants and their fluorescence properties indicate that intact cores probably are assembled in vivo (8; J. Zhou, unpublished). The cpcC gene product, the PC-associated rod linker of 33 kDa, is required for the attachment of the core-distal PC hexamer to the core-proximal hexamer (8, 11). The cpcD gene product, the PC-associated rod linker of 9 kDa, is probably associated with the core-distal PC trimer (8, 12). The absence of this polypeptide in a cpcD insertion mutant greatly increased the heterogeneity of peripheral rod lengths on the PBS (12). The cpcG gene product, the 29 kDa PC-associated rod linker, is required for the attachment of the peripheral rods to the PBS; in a cpcG deletion mutant, no cores with attached PC could be isolated (J. Zhou, V. Stirewalt, and D. A. Bryant, unpublished). The loss of PC, actually through deletion or functionally through assembly defects, greatly reduces the growth rate of Synechococcus sp. PCC 7002, and the effect on the growth rate is greater as the light intensity is reduced (8).

Although all mutations in genes encoding components of the peripheral rods produce detectable effects on the assembly and growth rate of Synechococcus sp. PCC 7002, the same is not true of mutations affecting core components. Mutations in the apcD and apcF genes, encoding the αAP-B subunit and the AP-β-like polypeptide β18, produced no obvious phenotype. The growth rate of such mutants is equivalent to that of the wild-type at both high and low light intensities (8). Moreover, the PBS produced by such mutants are largely equivalent to the wild-type in stability and energy transfer properties (13; J. Zhou, unpublished). In contrast, a mutation in apcC, the gene encoding the AP-associated core linker of 8.5 kDa, causes the cells to produce PBS which are less stable than those of the wild-type and which are slightly impaired in energy transfer properties (13). These lesions together produce an increase of about 30% in the doubling time of the mutant relative to the wild-type (8). Finally, mutations in apcA, apcB, apcAB, or apcE completely prevent the assembly of PBS or significant substructures thereof; moreover, the doubling times of such mutants are much larger (6-12 X) than those of the wild-type (8).

The apcE gene product, which is the core-linker phycobiliprotein of 99 kDa, plays critical roles in PBS assembly and function (5). Two copies of this polypeptide occur in each PBS (10; see 2, 6). The LCM99 polypeptide is believed to be the "terminal" energy acceptor in the PBS and hence plays an important role in energy transfer to chlorophyll a in the PS II antenna (5). Additionally, this polypeptide is believed to play a role in attaching PBS to the thylakoid membrane (5). The apcE gene of Synechococcus sp. PCC 7002 predicts a protein of 886 amino acids which has at least four functionally discernable domains. The first domain (about 220 aa) encodes a typical phycobiliprotein; this region shares sequence similarity with all known phycobiliprotein subunits. This part of the molecule includes a typical chromophore binding domain,

although the position of the chromophore-binding cysteine is altered
relative to that of all other known phycobiliproteins (see 8 for discussion). This domain also includes a 50-60 aa insertion, relative to
other phycobiliproteins, which might play a role in attaching the PBS to
the thylakoid. The remainder of the apcE gene product consists of three
similar domains of approximately 220 aa each. Each of these domains
consists of a conserved sequence of about 120 aa, which is additionally
homologous to the conserved domains of the cpcC and cpcG gene products,
and a non-conserved spacer. Since the cpcC gene product can be defined
as a tail-to-tail joining linker, we postulate that each of the three
conserved domains of the LCM99 polypeptide plays a similar role in the
core. There are six "AP hexamer equivalents" in the core of a tricylindrical PBS and six such joining domains. Thus, a third major role of
the LCM99 polypeptide is to provide the scaffolding upon which the entire core substructure is assembled (for further discussion, see 8).

Northern-blot hybridization analyses and lacZ translational fusions
(to cpcB and apcA) have been employed to assess the expression of these
transcriptional units during nutrient starvation conditions and under
different light intensities. Transcript abundance for the four monocistronic loci encoding PBS components is not greatly affected by nitrogen or carbon starvation (9). However, the cpcBACDEF and apcABC operons
are severely affected; after five hours of nitrogen starvation, their
mRNAs fall to barely detectable levels. Transcripts encoding PC appear
to increase as the light intensity decreases (9). Finally, the ratio
of AP:PC varies as a function of light intensity; this variation is also
apparently regulated by adjusting the relative amounts of the transcripts encoding these proteins (R. de Lorimier, unpublished).

The genes encoding the PE subunits (cpeB and cpcA) and two PCs
(cpcB1A1EF and cpcB2A2) of Pseudanabaena sp. PCC 7409 have been cloned
and sequenced and their transcripts analyzed (J. Dubbs, unpublished).
Transcripts from the cpeBA genes are found in cells grown in green light
but not in cells grown in red light, while transcripts from cpcB2A2 are
found in cells grown in red light but not in cells grown in green light.
Transcripts from the cpcB1A1EF locus are found in cells grown in both
red and green light. The cpeBA promoter has been mapped by S1 nuclease
protection and by primer extension; gel-shift experiments with a 170 bp
DNA fragment encoding this promoter suggest that a protein found in the
extracts of cells grown in red light specifically binds to this DNA
fragment (J. Dubbs, unpublished). This result suggests that cpeBA
transcription is specifically repressed during growth of cells in red
light. Attempts to localize the binding sequence by DNA footprint analyses are in progress; similar experiments are also in progress with the
cpcB2A2 promoter.

2. PHOTOSYSTEM 1.

The cyanobacterial PS I complex is compositionally and functionally
similar to the PS I core reaction centers of higher plants (1). Interest in the PS I complex of the cyanobacteria has increased markedly for

three reasons. Firstly, the PS I complexes of two thermophilic cyanobacteria have been crystalized (14, 15). Secondly, removal of the small
polypeptides of the PS I complex and reconstitution of the complex has
been achieved (16). Thirdly, cyanobacterial PS I is amenable to analyses by molecular genetics.

The PS I complexes of two Synechococcus sp. strains, PCC 7002 and
PCC 6301, were recently shown to be composed of eight polypeptides (17).
In addition to the psaA and psaB products, which are quite similar to
their higher plant homologs (18), immunoblotting demonstrated structurally related homologs of the psaC, psaD, and psaF gene products of plants
(17). The psaD and psaF gene products were shown to be functionally
homologous as well by cross-linking to ferredoxin (psaD) and cytochrome
c553 (psaF). The psaC product of Synechococcus sp. PCC 6301 can be replaced with the spinach protein with no detectable effect upon the electron transport properties of the complex (16).

We have been studying PS I structure and function by a molecular
genetics approach. For these studies we have largely employed the unicellular, marine cyanobacterium Synechococcus sp. PCC 7002 and the filamentous, heterocystous cyanobacterium Nostoc sp. PCC 8009. Although
genetic analyses are more easily accomplished in the Synechococcus sp.,
since the strain if efficiently transformed, this organism has extremely
limited heterotrophic growth potential (doubling time about 75-100 h).
On the other hand, genetic analyses are potentially possible in the Nostoc sp. via the more complex conjugation system of Wolk and coworkers;
moreover, this species has a reasonable growth rate in the dark (about
20 h). Because each system presents certain limitations, we have chosen
to work on the genes encoding the two complexes in parallel. However, it
should be noted that some problems associated with PS I analysis by genetics may also be circumvented by the route of reconstitution using proteins over-expressed in E. coli.

The PS I complexes of both species were purified, and low-molecular
mass polypeptides were isolated from each by preparative electrophoresis
and subjected to amino-terminal amino acid sequencing. Partial sequences
were obtained for the psaC, psaD, psaE, and putative psaF gene products
from Synechococcus sp. PCC 7002; partial sequences for the psaD and psaE
gene products of Nostoc sp. PCC 8009 were also determined (19). The
putative psaF product of Nostoc sp. was blocked.

The psaC genes of Synechococcus sp. PCC 7002, Nostoc sp. PCC 8009,
and of the cyanellar genome of Cyanophora paradoxa were cloned by heterologous hybridization using the tobacco chloroplast gene as probe. The
psaC genes of the two cyanobacterial species produce rather abundant,
monocistronic mRNAs. The deduced amino acid sequences of the three gene
products are shown below; each predicts a protein of 81 aa. The amino-
terminal methionine is cleaved from the Synechococcus sp. PCC 7002 protein, as is the case in higher plants. The cyanobacterial and cyanellar
psaC products are greater than 90% homologous in sequence to their chloroplast homologs. This high degree of sequence conservation explains the

```
PCC 7002 psaC:  MSHSVKIYDTCIGCTQCVRACPLDVLEMVPWDGCKAGQIASSPRTEDCVGCKRCET
                ACPTDFLSIRVYLGAETTRSMGLAY
PCC 8009 psaC:  MSHTVKIYDTCIGCTQCVRACPTDVLEMVPWDGCKAAQIASSPRTEDCVGCKRCET
                ACPTDFLSIRVYLGAETTRSMGLAY
C. para. psaC:  MAHTVKIYDTCIGCTQCVRACPTDVLEMVPWDGCRANQIASAPRTEDCVGCKRCES
                ACPTDFLSIRVYLGAETTRSMGLGY
PCC 7002 psaE:  MAIERGSKVKILRKESYWYGDVGTVASIDKSGIIYPVIVRFNKVNYNGFSGSAGGL
                NTNNFAEHELEVVG
PCC 8009 psaE:  MVQRGSKVRILRPESYWFQDVGTVASVDQSGIKYPVIVRFEKVNYSGINTNNFAED
                ELVEVEAPKAKPKK
PCC 6301 psaE:  MAIARGDKVRILRPESYWFNEVGTVASVDQSGIKYPV-VVRFEKVNYNGFSGSDGG
                VNTNNFAEAELQVVAAAAKK
PCC 8009 psaD:  MAEQLSGKTPLFAGSTGGLLTKANVEEKYAITWTSPKAQVFELPTGGAATMNQGEN
                LLYLARKEQGIALGGQLRKFKITDYKIYRIFPNGETTFIHPADGVFPEKVNEGREK
                VRFVPRRIGQNPSPAQLKFSGKYTYDA
```

effectiveness of the spinach protein in reconstituting electron transport properties to depleted core complexes from Synechococcus sp. PCC 6301 (16).

The psaD gene of Nostoc sp. PCC 8009 was cloned by low-stringency heterologous hybridization using probes derived from the tomato psaD cDNA (20) and the Synechococcus sp. PCC 6301 psaD gene (J. Omaha and A. N. Glazer, personal communication). The Nostoc sp. gene predicts a protein (above) which is rather similar to the psaD gene products of plants and other cyanobacteria (17, 20). The Nostoc sp. PCC 8009 gene is transcribed as a monocistronic transcript; the sequences flanking the gene were not closely related to those flanking the Synechocystis sp. PCC 6803 gene (21). Cloning and characterization of the psaD gene of Synechococcus sp. PCC 7002 is in progress.

The psaE gene of Synechococcus sp. PCC 6301 was cloned using a synthetic oligonucleotide based upon the amino acid sequence determined by Alhadeff et al. (22). This gene, in turn, was used to clone the genes from both Nostoc sp. PCC 8009 and Synechococcus sp. PCC 7002 (see above). The psaE products share considerable homology to the psaE (Subunit IV) polypeptides of spinach, barley, and Chlamydomonas reinhardtii (23, 24, 25). The psaE product does not have a secretion sequence and hence predicts a stromal polypeptide, as do the psaC and psaD genes. The psaE genes are transcribed as monocistronic mRNAs of about 350 bases. The spinach cDNAs encoding the psaF and psaG gene products have been employed as probes in low-stringency hybridization experiments with genomic Southern blots carrying endonuclease digests of Synechococcus sp. PCC 7002 DNA. No hybridization was observed at low stringency zith the psaG probe (probe from 26). The psaF probe (26) hybridized strongly at low stringency to multiple DNA fragments; however, at higher stringency only one major hybridizing fragment was observed for most digests. These results are in agreement with the observation of Wynn et al. (17) that the cyanobacterial PS I complex has a subunit with structural and funational homology to the psaF gene product of spinach.

The psaE gene of Synechococcus sp. PCC 7002 was insertionally inactivated by cloning the aph gene in both orientations into a unique BamHI site near the 5' end of the gene. These constructions were used to transform the cyanobacterium and kanamycin-resistant transformants were selected and streak-purified. Southern-blot hybridizations revealed the transformants to be homozygous; the unique psaE gene was clearly inactivated. The growth rate of the mutants was indistinguishable from that of the wild-type. Further detailed analyses of the PS I complexes are being determined in collaboration with Dr. John Golbeck and coworkers. Preliminary results indicate that the psaE polypeptide is absent from the purified complexes as exptected; hozever, the chl/P700 values for the mutants are similar to those of the wild-type (J. Golbeck, personnal communication). Hence, the psaE polypeptide probably does not play a role in chlorophyll binding. The electron transport properties of the mutant PS I complexes do not appear to be significantly different from those of the wild-type.

REFERENCES

1 Bryant, D.A. (1987) in Photosynthetic Picoplankton (Platt, T. and Li, W.K.W., eds.), Canadian Bulletin of Fisheries and Aquatic Sciences, Vol. 214, pp. 423-500, Dept. Fisheries and Oceans, Ottawa, Canada
2 Glazer, A.N. (1985) Ann. Rev. Biophys. Biophys. Chem. 14, 47-77
3 Bryant, D.A., Glazer, A.N., and Eiserling, F.A. (1976) Arch. Microbiol. 110, 61-75.
4 Schirmer, T., Bode, W., and Huber, R. (1987) J. Mol. Biol. 196, 677-695
5 Gantt, E. (1988) in Light)Energy Transduction in Photosynthesis: Higher Plant and Bacterial Models (Stevens, S.E.Jr., and Bryant, D.A., eds.), pp. 91-101, Am. Soc. Plant Physiol., Rockville
6 Glazer, A.N. (1989) J. Biol. Chem. 264, 1-4
7 Zuber, H. (1987) in The Light Reactions (Barber, J., ed.), pp. 197-259, Elsevier, Amsterdam
8 Bryant, D.A. (1988) in Light-Energy Transduction in Photosynthesis: Higher Plant and Bacterial Models (Stevens, S.E.Jr., and Bryant, D.A., eds.), pp. 62-90, Am. Soc. Palnt Physiol., Rockville
9 Gasparich, G.E. (1989) Ph. D. Dissertation, The Pennsylvania State University
10 Bryant, D.A., de Lorimier, R., Guglielmi, G., and Stevens, S.E.Jr. (1989) Arch. Microbiol., submitted
11 de Lorimier, R., Guglielmi, G., Bryant, D.A., and Stevens, S.E.Jr. (1989) Arch. Microbiol., submitted
12 de Lorimier, R., Bryant, D.A., and Stevens, S.E.Jr. (1989) Biochim. Biphys. Acta, submitted
13 Maxson, P., Sauer, K., Zhou, J., Bryant, D.A., and Glazer, A.N. (1989) Biochim. Biophys. Acta, in press
14 Ford, R.C., Picot, D., and Garavito, R.M. (1987) EMBO J 6, 1581-1586
15 Ford, R.C. (1989) Nature 337, 510-511
16 Golbeck, J.H., Mehari, T., Parrett, K., and Ikegami, I. (1988) FEBS Lett. 240, 9-14
17 Wynn, R.M., Omaha, J., and Malkin, R. (1989) Biochemistry 28, 5554-5560
18 Cantrell, A. and Bryant, D.A. (1987) Plant Mol. Biol. 9, 453-468

19 Rhiel, E., and Bryant, D.A. (1988) in Light-Energy Transduction in Photosynthesis: Higher Plant and Bacterial Models (Stevens, S.E.Jr. and Bryant, D.A., eds.), pp. 320-323, Am. Soc. Plant Physiol., Rockville

20 Hoffman, N.E., Pichersky, E., Malik, V.S., Ko, K., and Cashmore, A.R. (1988) Plant Mol. Biol. 10, 435-455.

21 Reilly, P., Hulmes, J.D., Pan, Y.-C.E., and Nelson, N. (1988) J. Biol. Chem. 263, 17658-17662

22 Alhadeff, M., Lundell, D.J., and Glazer, A.N. (1988) Arch. Microbiol. 150, 482- 488

23 Munch, S., Ljungberg, U., Steppuhn, J., Schneiderbauer, A., Nechushtai, R., Beyreuther, K., and Hermann, R.G. (1988) Curr. Genet. 14, 511-518

24 Okkels, J.S., Jepsen, L.B., Honberg, L.S., Lehmbeck, J., Scheller, H.V., Brandt, P., Hoyer-Hansen, G., Stummann, B., Henningsen, K.W., von Wettstein, D., and Moller, B.L. (1988) FEBS Lett. 237, 108-112

25 Franzen, L.-G., Frank, G., Zuber, H., and Rochaix, J.-D. (1989) Plant Mol. Biol. 12, 463-474

26 Steppuhn, J., Hermans, J., Nechushtai, R., Ljungberg, U., Thummler, F., Lottspeich, F., and Herrmann, R.G. (1988) FEBS Lett. 237, 218-224

ACKNOWLEDGEMENTS

The research described from the laboratory of D.A.B. was supported by grants GM31625 from the National Institutes of Health (Public Health Service), DMB-8504294 from the National Science Foundation, and 83-CRCR-1-1336 from the U.S. Department of Agriculture.

PHOTOPHYSICS AND PHOTOBIOLOGY OF THE CAROTENOID SINGLET STATE

Tomas Gillbro[1], Per-Ola Andersson[1] and Richard J. Cogdell[2].

[1]Department of Physical Chemistry, Umeå University, S-901 87
Umeå, Sweden.
[2]Department of Botany, University of Glasgow, Glasgow, G 12 8QQ
Scotland.

1. INTRODUCTION

Carotenoids have two important functions in photosynthetic light-harvesting systems. One function is to protect the organism from harmful singlet oxygen. The second is to absorbe light in the blue part
of the solar spectrum and transfer the excitation energy to chlorophyll
or bacteriochlorophyll chromophores. For both biological processes an
understanding of the photophysics of carotenoids is of primary importance.

Carotenoids can be regarded as linear polyenes of intermediate length.
Theoretical quantum chemical calculations have shown that in linear
polyenes there are two low-energy excited state of different symmetry,
i.e. $1B_u$ and $2A_g$ (1). The allowed transition is $1A_g \longrightarrow 1B_u$. It has
also been proposed that the forbidden $2A_g$-state should be placed below the $1B_u$-state. One strong argument for this bas been the weak $1B_u$
$\longrightarrow 1A_g$ fluorescence in combination with a rather efficient ($\approx 70\%$)
energy transfer process. In this contribution we present detailed information on carotenoid fluorescence and the non-radiative processes from
the $1B_u$ and $2A_g$-states in vitro as well as in vivo systems.

2. MATERIALS AND METHODS

The carotenoid spheroidene used in this work was extracted from Rhodobacter spheroides and purified by chromography. Lycopene was obtained
from Sigma. A Spex Fluorolog spectrometer was used for recording fluorescence spectra and anisotropies. The time-resolved picosecond experiments were performed with the pump-probe technique. The source of
the picosecond pulses was a cavity-dumped synchronously pumped dye
laser with rhodamin 110. The solvents used where of spectroscopic
grade. Samples containing the antenna complex B880 were prepared from
the purple bacterium Rhodospirillum rubrum and the B800-850 antenna
was isolated from Rhodobacter spheroides.

M. Baltscheffsky (ed.), Current Research in Photosynthesis, Vol. II, 11–16.
© 1990 *Kluwer Academic Publishers. Printed in the Netherlands.*

Lycopene

Spheroidene

OCH₃

3. RESULTS AND DISCUSSION

3.1 Fluorescence and excitation spectra

We have recently reported fluorescence from several carotenoids, including β-carotene, spheroidenone, spirilloxanthin and rhodopin(2). In
this work we present new results on lycopene and spheroidene. Spheroidene has been chosen because it is the carotenoid in the B800-850 antenna complex of <u>Rhodobacter spheroides</u>, while lycopene due to its linear symmetric structure should be a good model for linear polyene.

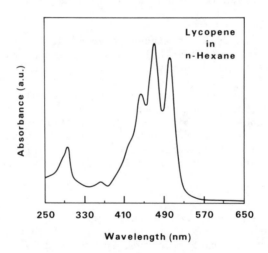

Figure 1. Absorption spectrum of lycopene i n-hexane.

In Fig. 1 we show the absorption spectrum of lycopene i n-hexane.
We can clearly see three optical transitions in the region 250-500 nm.
The strong transition beeing $1A_g$ --->$1B_u$. At 360 nm the weak so-called
"cis"-peak can be observed. In Fig. 2 we show two fluorescence spectra
of lycopene obtained with excitation at 364 and 470 nm, respectively.
We notice that the spectra are not identical. This means that also the
weak "cis"-transition is emitting. This can bee most clearly see in

the excitation spectrum recorded at an emission wavelength of 560 nm
(Fig.3). In the excitation spectrum. The "cis"-peak is of the same
magnitude as the allowed transition. This means that the fluorescence
quantum yield is higher when the "cis" transition is excited, due to
slower non-radiative processes. The excitation anisotropy in the same
figure is 0.35 at 470 nm and decays to 0.0 at 360 nm. This shows that
the "cis" and the $1B_u \longrightarrow 1A_g$ transitions are not exactly perpendicular
but rather at an angle of ca 55°.

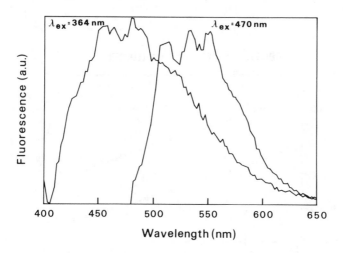

Figure 2. Fluorescence spectra of lycopene in n-hexane excited at
364 and 470 nm, respectively.

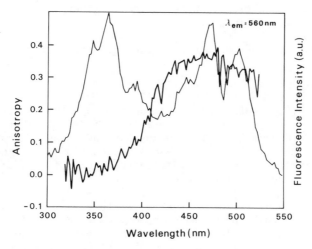

Figure 3. Excitation spectrum and anisotropy of lycopene i n-hexane.
Emission wavelength 560 nm.

3.2 Fluorescence spectral shift and quantum yield

We mentioned above that the lowest excited state is supposed to be the forbidden $2A_g$-state. It might thus be possible that this is the emitting state (Kasha´s rule). We have tested this possibility by observing the absorption and fluorescence spectral shifts in several non-polar solvents with different polarizabilities. Fig. 4 show the results for spheroidene i n-hexane/CS_2 mixtures and in CS_2 at different temperatures.

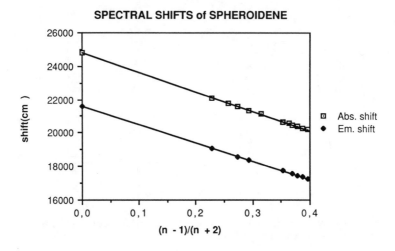

Figure 4. Absorption and fluorescence maxima of spheroidene in n-hexa-
         ne-CS_2 solvent mixtures.

According to theory (3) we would expect the shift to follow the eqv.

$$\Delta \nu = k \; \frac{n^2 - 1}{n^2 + 2} \; |\mu|^2$$

where n is the index of refraction, k a constant and μ the transition dipol. Our results show that the shifts of the $1B_u$ <---$1A_g$ absorption and the emission are parallel. This means that the emission has to be the $1B_u$ ---> $1A_g$ transition. The $2A_g$ ---> $1A_g$ transition has a much smaller transition dipol which would give rise to a very small spectral shift according to the eqvation above.

The fluorescence quantum yield of several carotenoids in different solvents has been found to be about 10^{-4} in most case. From this low quantum yield combined with a calculated radiative lifetime of ca l ns we expect the lifetime of the $1B_u$ state to be about 100fs.This implies a very efficient non-radiative relaxation to a low-lying state.According to the "energy-gap law" (4) the rate constant for the radionless transitions depend on exp $(-\Delta E)$. Since the energy levels $1B_u$ and $2A_g$ should have different solvent shifts, the energy difference, ΔE, should decrease as the polarizability of the solvent is increased. The result should be a low quantum yield (ϕ_F) at high polarizability. Table 1 below thus strongly support the presence of $2A_g$ below $1B_u$.

Table 1. Fluorescence quantum yield of spheroidene in different solvents.

solvent:	n-hexane	CCl_4	CS_2
$\phi_F(\times 10^4)$:	7.7	4.4	1.1
n:	1.37	1.46	1.63

3.3 Ground state recovery

The estimated lifetime of $1B_u$ is 100 fs(τ_{nr}). Absorption experiments with picosecond time-resolution have shown, however, that typical ground state recovery times (τ_g) are about 10 ps (2,6). This is again a strong indirect evidence for a state between $1B_u$ and the ground state. We can thus give the scheme in Fig. 5 for the lowest states.

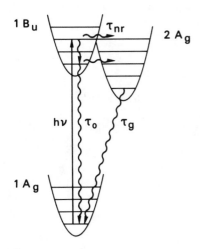

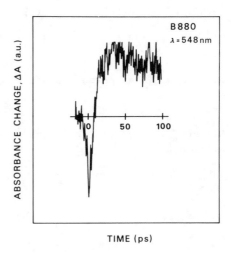

Figure 5. Schematic energy level diagram of a carotenoid.

Figure 6. Absorption recovery kinetics of the carotenoid - bacteriochlorophyll energy transfer in B 880 complexes at 548 nm.

3.4 Energy transfer in light-harvesting systems

In order to compare our in vitro fluorescence data with carotenoid fluorescence in vivo we have studied the fluorescence of spheroidene in the B800-850 complex from R. spheroides. The quantum yield was found to be $2 \cdot 10^{-4}$, in good agreement with results obtained in solvents with high polarizability, e.g. CS_2. It thus seems unlikely tht the energy is transfered directly from the carotenoid $1B_u$ state to bacteriochlorophyll. Ground state recovery experiments have shown that the energy is transferred in a few picoseconds. In Fig. 6 the kinetic curve at 548 nm showing the energy transfer in the B880 complex of Rsp. rubrum is displayed. The transfer time is estimated to be 1-3 ps. i.e. it competes with the 10 ps ground state recovery lifetime observed in vitro (2,5,6).

The Förster dipole-dipole mechanism for energy transfer from the forbidden $2A_g$ level seems to be ruled out. Therefore we have used Dexter´s electron-exchange model (7). With reasonable coupling parameters we have estimated the distance between the carotenoid and bacteriochlrophyll to be 4-5 Å.

REFERENCES

1. Tavan, P. and Schulter, K.   (1987) Phys. Rev. B. 36:4337-4358.

2. Gillbro, T. and Cogdell, R.J.   (1989) Chem. Phys. Letters 158:312-316.

3. Basu, S.   (1964) Advan. Quantum. Chem. 1:145-167.

4. Engelman, R. and Jortner, J.   (1970) Mol. Phys. 18:145-164.

5. Gillbro, T., Cogdell, R.J. and Sundström, V.   (1988) Febs. Letters 235:169-172.

6. Wasielewski, M.R. and Kispert, L.D. (1986) Chem. Phys. Letters 128:238-243.

7. Dexter, D.L. (1953) J. Chem. Phys. 21:836-850.

EFFICIENCY AND KINETICS OF ENERGY TRANSFER IN CHLOROSOME ANTENNAS FROM GREEN PHOTOSYNTHETIC BACTERIA

ROBERT E. BLANKENSHIP, JIAN WANG, TIMOTHY P. CAUSGROVE AND DANIEL C. BRUNE
Department of Chemistry and Center for the Study of Early Events in Photosynthesis, Arizona State University, Tempe, Arizona 85287-1604 USA

1. INTRODUCTION

Green photosynthetic bacteria are anoxygenic prokaryotes that contain a light gathering antenna complex known as a chlorosome (for reviews see references 1-2). The chlorosome is an ellipsoidal structure of dimensions approximately 100 nm x 30 nm x 12 nm in the green gliding bacterium *Chloroflexus aurantiacus* and somewhat larger in the green sulfur bacteria such as *Chlorobium vibrioforme*. The chlorosome is bounded by an envelope thought to be a lipid monolayer with some associated proteins. It is attached to the cytoplasmic side of the inner cell membrane, with additional membrane-bound antenna complexes and reaction centers embedded within the membrane (Fig. 1). Chlorosomes contain approximately 10,000 molecules of bacteriochlorophyll *c*, *d* or *e* and smaller amounts of BChl *a* and carotenoids.

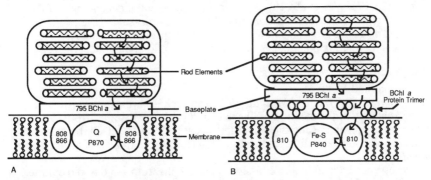

FIGURE 1   Schematic models of chlorosomes from the green gliding bacteria, e.g. *Chloroflexus aurantiacus* (A) and the green sulfur bacteria, e.g. *Chlorobium vibrioforme* (B). The numbers refer to wavelength maxima of antenna bacteriochlorophyll complexes. The reaction centers are of the "quinone type" in A, with a Q_A-Q_B acceptor complex and the "Fe-S type" in B, with Fe-S proteins as early electron acceptors. The rod elements probably contain oligomers of bacteriochlorophyll *c*, *d* or *e*, as discussed in the text.

A substantial body of evidence indicates that the pigments in chlorosomes are organized in a manner that is quite different from that observed in most photosynthetic pigment-proteins. Relatively little protein is found in the chlorosome interior and its precise functional role is not yet certain. A variety of evidence, including UV-VIS, IR and resonance Raman spectroscopy on both chlorosomes and model complexes indicates that the BChl *c*, *d* or *e* pigments form what are essentially pigment oligomers, with the pigments in direct van der Waals contact with each other (see papers in references 3-4). A number of possible structural models for the pigment geometry have been proposed, although the precise geometrical arrangement of the pigments is not yet known. A somewhat different view of the pigment organization has been proposed by Zuber and coworkers, although recent sequence data seems to argue against their model (5-6).

Steady-state and time-resolved spectroscopy has been used to follow the flow of excitations from the BChl *c*, *d* or *e* in the interior of the chlorosome, through the baseplate and into the membrane, where the energy is trapped by the reaction center (7-11). The results are consistent with a sequential energy transfer pathway, from the BChl *c*, *d* or *e* in the chlorosome interior to the BChl a 795 pigment in the chlorosome baseplate, to membrane-bound BChl a antenna complexes and finally to the reaction center (Fig. 1). The green sulfur bacteria (Fig. 1B) also contain an additional antenna species, the trimeric water-soluble BChl *a* protein the three dimensional structure of which was determined by Fenna and Matthews (12).

The efficiency of energy collection by chlorosome antenna systems has been studied by several different groups (8,9,13-16). The efficiency of energy collection from *Chloroflexus aurantiacus* chlorosomes has been reported to be 70-100% (8,9,15,16) and is not dependent on the redox potential of the medium, although it is dependent on the state of attachment of the chlorosomes to the cytoplasmic membrane. In contrast, the efficiency of energy collection by chlorosomes from the green sulfur bacteria ranges from 10-100%, with the lower values found at higher redox potentials and the higher values found at lower redox potentials (13, 14, 16). The redox effect on the efficiency of energy collection by chlorosomes appears to be independent of the redox state of the reaction center, because similar redox effects on energy transfer are observed in isolated chlorosomes (16-17). Vos et al. (18) observed a redox potential dependence of the domain size of chlorosomes from *Chlorobium limicola*, as measured by excitation annihilation. This result is consistent with the idea that specific quenchers are present in chlorosomes at high redox potentials and absent at low redox potentials (14, 16, 17).

2. PROCEDURE

2.1 Materials and Methods

Chlorobium vibrioforme f. *thiosulfatophilum* strain 8327 was grown photoautotrophically in the medium of Olson et al. (19). Chlorosomes from *Cb. vibrioforme* were prepared using the chaotropic agent NaSCN to detach them from the membranes of ultrasonically disrupted cells as described by Gerola and Olson (20) for *Cb. limicola*.

For fluorescence excitation and emission spectra, cells from 1-5 day-old cultures suspended in the culture medium or isolated chlorosomes were diluted in 10 mM, pH 8 Tris Cl so that the absorbance at 730 nm was about 0.2 in a 1 cm fluorescence cuvette. Fluorescence spectra were measured on an instrument constructed as described previously (8) using an R 928 photomultiplier as the detector. Absorption spectra were measured on the same instrument, which incorporated an integrating sphere to avoid light-scattering artifacts.

Chlorosome samples for redox titrations were suspended in H_2O containing 50 μM each of the following mediators: N,N,N'N'-tetramethyl-*p*-phenylenediamine (TMPD), sodium 5,5'-indigodisulfonate, 1,4-naphthoquinone, and 2-hydroxy-1,4-

naphthoquinone. $Na_2S_2O_4$ and $K_3Fe(CN)_6$ were added from freshly prepared, anaerobic stock solutions buffered at pH 8 with Tris Cl. Redox potentials were measured against a calomel reference using a platinum redox electrode. The sample cuvette was slowly flushed with nitrogen to maintain anaerobic conditions.

After each addition of dithionite or ferricyanide, the sample was stirred magnetically until a stable redox potential was obtained. A fluorescence emission spectrum, using 460 nm excitation, was then recorded, and the fluorescence intensities at the emission maxima of BChl d (764 nm) and BChl a (812 nm) were noted. The emission intensities at these wavelengths in the initial non-reduced sample were then subtracted to obtain the oxidant-sensitive fluorescence.

Whole cells for fluorescence lifetime measurements were suspended in their growth medium supplemented with pH 8 Tris Cl (10 mM final concentration). *Chlorobium* chlorosome samples were suspended in 10 mM phosphate, pH 7.4 containing 10 mM ascorbate and 2 M NaSCN, which has been reported to stabilize isolated chlorosomes (20). In some experiments on both whole cells and isolated chlorosomes, 50 mM Tris Cl, pH 8 was present to prevent acidification by dithionite added to obtain anaerobic conditions. Samples had an absorbance of about 0.2 at 730 nm in a 1.5 mm pathlength flow cell. The samples were placed in two glass reservoirs, each holding about 150 ml in experiments on whole cells and 20 ml in experiments on chlorosomes. One reservoir was connected to the inlet of the flow cell and the other to the outlet. A second tube from each reservoir connected the two reservoirs via a peristaltic pump that was used to circulate the sample through the reservoirs and the flow cell at a rate of 150 ml/min. To obtain anaerobic, reducing conditions, a weighed amount of solid sodium dithionite was added to one of the reservoirs. The final dithionite concentration was 10 mM.

Fluorescence lifetimes were measured by the time-correlated single photon counting method; a detailed description of the apparatus will appear elsewhere. Briefly, excitation pulses (707-740 nm, ~10 ps duration) were provided by a Nd:YAG-pumped Pyridine 1 dye laser operating at 3.8 MHz. Fluorescence was collected at a right angle to the excitation through a magic angle polarizer and a double monochromator and detected by a cooled red-sensitive micro-channel plate photomultiplier tube. Instrument response functions measured by scattering of the laser pulse exhibited 60-80 ps FWHM (see Fig. 4). Raw data were fit to a sum of exponentials by iterative deconvolution; typical data files were collected to 10,000 counts in the peak channel at 2.0 ps/channel with 2048 channels per data set. Goodness of fit was judged from χ^2, visual inspection of residuals, and autocorrelation of the residuals.

3. RESULTS AND DISCUSSION

Absorption and fluorescence excitation spectra of *Cb. vibrioforme* cells under anaerobic conditions were nearly superimposable (Fig. 2), indicating that excitation transfer from BChl d in the chlorosomes to BChl a (the chromophore fluorescing at 835 nm) was essentially 100% efficient. Aerobic conditions did not affect the absorption spectrum, but caused a 90% decrease in the relative height of the peak at 730 nm (where BChl d absorbs) in the fluorescence excitation spectrum (Fig. 2). Thus aerobic conditions caused the efficiency of excitation transfer from BChl d to BChl a to decrease to about 10%. Similar effects were observed in isolated chlorosomes, in which 835 nm fluorescence comes from BChl a in the chlorosome baseplate (data not shown).

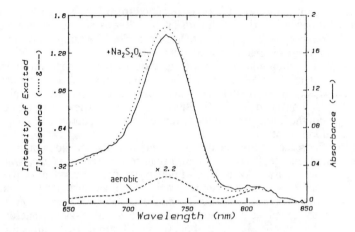

FIGURE 2. Absorption and aerobic and anaerobic (+Na2S2O4) fluorescence excitation spectra of *Cb. vibrioforme* f. *thiosulfatophilum* cells. Fluorescence emission (intensity in arbitrary units) was measured at 835 nm. The spectral bandwidth was 9 nm for both exciting and emitted light. The 3 spectra have been normalized at 810 nm, the approximate absorption maximum of BChl *a* in the membrane. Fluorescence intensities in the excitation spectrum of aerobic cells have been multiplied by 2.2 to compensate for the fact that fluorescence from aerobic cells excited at 810 nm was 2.2 x weaker than fluorescence from anaerobic cells excited at 810 nm.

Further observations on this effect by Wang et al. (16) have shown that cells taken from the culture medium anaerobically and diluted in anaerobic buffer exhibit a 100% efficiency of excitation transfer in the absence of dithionite. They also observed that the intensity of fluorescence from BChl *d* (measured at 760 nm) decreased under aerobic conditions. This suggests that aerobic conditions create quenchers within the chlorosome that compete with excitation transfer for BChl *d* excited states. Wang et al. (16) also found that oxidants other than O_2, such as benzoquinone and $Fe(CN)_6^{3-}$ + TMPD, caused a similar decrease in the efficiency of excitation transfer, indicating that the critical factor is redox potential and not the presence of O_2 *per se*.

The fact that the low fluorescence state is correlated with a low efficiency of energy transfer indicates that quenchers of the BChl *d* excited states are present under these conditions. The opposite pattern, high fluorescence correlated with low energy transfer efficiency, would be observed if, for example, the energy transfer efficiency was modulated by chlorosome detachment rather than induction of quenchers (8).

Figure 3 shows a titration of the dithionite-induced increase in fluorescence as a function of redox potential in the presence of added redox mediators. Similar fluorescence changes were obtained without mediators, but the curve was flattened and exhibited hysteresis in the forward and back titrations. As shown in figure 3, the observed amount of oxidant-sensitive fluorescence was fitted reasonably well by a calculated Nernst curve for a component undergoing a 1-electron oxidation-reduction reaction with a midpoint potential of -168 mV vs NHE. The chemical identity of this component, which apparently quenches BChl *d* excited states in chlorosomes when oxidized, has not yet been determined. One possibility currently under investigation in our laboratory is that the quenching species may be *Chlorobium* quinone (1' oxomenaquinone), which is found only in the green sulfur bacteria (21).

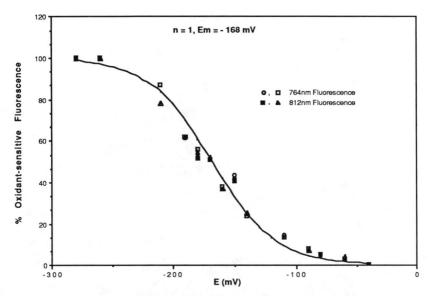

FIGURE 3   Redox titration of oxidant-sensitive fluorescence in isolated *Chlorobium* chlorosomes.
Open symbols, 764 nm fluorescence; □- titration to lower redox potentials by adding dithionite,
O - back titration with ferricyanide. Closed symbols, 812 nm fluorescence; ▲ - titration to lower redox
potentials with dithionite, and ■ - back titration with ferricyanide. The solid line is a calculated Nernst
curve assuming a one-electron change and a midpoint potential of -168 mV. Redox potentials are vs. the
normal hydrogen electrode.

As noted above, *Chlorobium* cells in their normal physiological state in anaerobic
growth medium are in the high-fluorescence state. It is possible that the transformation
under aerobic conditions to a low-fluorescence state, in which excitation transfer from
BChl d to BChl a is inhibited, serves a protective function. Shill and Wood (22) have

shown that reaction centers in membranes from *Cb. limicola* can photoreduce O_2 to O_2^-,
a potentially harmful product. Turning off excitation transfer from the chlorosome to the
reaction center under aerobic conditions would greatly reduce the rate of toxic superoxide
radical formation. Chlorosomes from *Chloroflexus aurantiacus* do not exhibit oxidant-
sensitive changes in fluorescence and excitation transfer efficiency(data not shown). This
observation, together with the quinone type of reaction center found in *Chloroflexus*

which cannot produce O_2^- (23) is consistent with the postulated protective function for
oxidant quenching of chlorosome excited states in *Chlorobium*.

The increased quantum yield of chlorosome fluorescence in *Chlorobium* cells under
anaerobic conditions is reflected in the fluorescence lifetime data shown in figure 4. In
the absence of dithionite (top), the decay was dominated by fast components in
fluorescence from both BChl d (760 nm) and BChl a (820 nm). Much longer
fluorescence lifetimes were observed when 10 mM $Na_2S_2O_4$ was added to the sample
(bottom), in agreement with the increase in steady-state quantum yield.

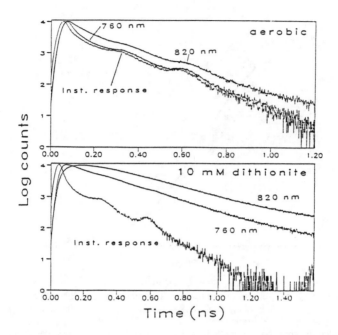

FIGURE 4   Typical fluorescence decay profiles of *Chlorobium* whole cells with excitation at 735 nm and emission at 760 nm and 820 nm. Top: aerobic conditions; bottom: 10 mM Na₂S₂O₄ added.

The fitting parameters for Fig. 4 are listed in Table I along with data from isolated *Chlorobium* chlorosomes and whole cells. Note that in anaerobic *Chlorobium* samples, the major decay times of the 760 nm fluorescence, 68 and 44 ps for cells and chlorosomes respectively, were closely matched by corresponding rise components (negative amplitudes) of 60 and 46 ps in the 820 nm emission. This is direct evidence for sequential energy transfer from BChl *d* to BChl *a* of the baseplate. Such rise components were not observed in the data for aerobic *Chlorobium* samples; it is likely that because these lifetimes were much shorter, the rise components were below the level of detection of the instrument.

TABLE I. Amplitudes and lifetimes (in picoseconds) of fluorescence decay following excitation into chlorosomes of *Chlorobium vibrioforme* measured by single photon counting. Only the two largest-amplitude components are listed for each measurement.

	760 nm				820 nm			
	A_1	τ_1	A_2	τ_2	A_1	τ_1	A_2	τ_2
Whole cells, aerobic	1.00	10	–	–	0.72	15	0.28	57
Whole cells, anaerobic	0.63	68	0.36	201	-0.65	60	0.96	211
Chlorosomes, aerobic	0.96	16	0.04	64	0.78	39	0.21	125
Chlorosomes, anaerobic	0.65	44	0.26	115	-0.43	46	0.60	648

Table I also shows that the fluorescence lifetimes are significantly greater in the 820 nm band for isolated chlorosomes than for whole cells, although they do not approach levels expected on the basis of energy transfer efficiency. For example, the average lifetime of 820 nm emission is about 3 times greater for isolated chlorosomes of *Chlorobium* than for whole cells; this would indicate a maximum transfer efficiency of 75%. Similar behavior is observed in *Chloroflexus*, where the average lifetime increases by only about a factor of 2 (8, Causgrove, Wittmershaus, Brune and Blankenship, unpublished).

4. CONCLUSIONS
The efficiency of energy collection by chlorosome antennas from green sulfur bacteria is strongly dependent on redox potential. The effect, which titrates at $Em = -168$ mV, appears to involve the presence of strongly quenching centers in the chlorosomes at higher redox potentials. This may be a specific control mechanism which protects the cells from photodamage under aerobic conditions.

5. ACKNOWLEDGMENTS
This work was supported by Grant # DE-FG02-85ER-13388 to REB from the Biological Energy Storage Program of the U.S. Department of Energy. This is publication #22 from the Arizona State University Center for the Study of Early Events in Photosynthesis. The Center is funded by U.S. Department of Energy grant #DE-FG02-88ER13969 as part of the USDA/DOE/NSF Plant Science Centers program.

REFERENCES
1   Olson, J. M. (1980) Biochim. Biophys. Acta 594, 33-51.
2   Blankenship, R. E., Brune, D. C. and Wittmershaus, B. P. (1988) in "Light Energy Transduction in Photosynthesis: Higher Plants and Bacterial Models", S. E. Stevens, Jr. and D. A. Bryant, Eds., American Society of Plant Physiologists, Rockville, MD, 32-46.
3   Olson, J. M., Ormerod, J. G., Amesz, J., Stackebrandt, E. and Trüper, H. G., Eds., (1988) "Green Photosynthetic Bacteria", Plenum Press, New York.
4   Scheer, H. and Schneider, S., Eds. (1988) "Photosynthetic Light- Harvesting Systems", Walter de Gruyter, Berlin.
5   Wechsler, T., Suter, F., Fuller, R. C.and Zuber, H. (1985) FEBS Lett. 181, 173-178.

6   Wagner-Huber, R., Brunisholz, R., Frank, G.and Zuber, H. (1988) FEBS Lett.
    239, 8-12.
7   Betti, J.A., Blankenship, R.E., Natarajan, L.V., Dickinson, L.C. and Fuller, R.C.
    (1982) Biochim. Biophys. Acta 680, 194-201
8   Brune, D.C., King, G.H., Infosino, A., Steiner, T., Thewalt, M.L.W. and
    Blankenship, R.E. (1987) Biochem. 26, 8652-8658
9   van Dorssen, R. J. and Amesz, J. (1988) Photosynth. Res. 15, 177-189.
10 Fetisova, Z. G., Freiberg, A. M. and Timpmann, K. E. (1988) Nature 334, 633-
    634.
11 Mimuro, M., Nozawa, T., Tamai, N. Shimada, K., Yamazaki, I., Lin, S., Knox, R.
    S., Wittmershaus, B. P., Brune, D. C. and Blankenship, R. E. (1989) J. Phys.
    Chem., In Press.
12 Fenna, R.E. and Matthews, B.W. (1975) Nature 258, 573-577
13 Fetisova, Z. G. and Borisov, A. Yu. (1980) FEBS Lett. 114, 323-326.
14 Karapetyan, N. V., Swarthoff, T., Rijgersberg, C. P. and Amesz, J. (1980)
    Biochim. Biophys. Acta 593-254-260.
15 Wittmershaus, B. P., Brune, D. C. and Blankenship, R. E. in Ref. 4. pp 543-554.
16 Wang, J., Brune, D.C. and Blankenship, R.E. (1989) submitted to Biochim.
    Biophys. Acta
17 van Dorssen, R.J., Gerola, P.D., Olson, J.M. and Amesz, J. (1986) Biochim.
    Biophys. Acta 848, 77-82
18 Vos, M., Nuijs, A.M., van Grondelle, R., van Dorssen, R.J., Gerola, P.D. and
    Amesz, J. (1987) Biochim. Biophys. Acta 891, 275-285
19 Olson, J.M., Philipson, K.D. and Sauer, K. (1973) Biochim. Biophys. Acta 292,
    57-61
20 Gerola, P.D. and Olson, J.M. (1986) Biochim. Biophys. Acta 848, 69-76
21 Powls, R. and Redfearn, E.R. (1969) Biochim. Biophys. Acta 172, 429-437
22 Shill, D.A. and Wood, P.M. (1985) Arch Microbiol. 143, 82-87
23 Blankenship, R.E. (1985) Photosynth. Res. 6, 317-333

ANTENNA SYSTEMS OF GREEN BACTERIA AND HELIOBACTERIA

J. AMESZ

Department of Biophysics, University of Leiden, P.O. Box 9504, 2300 RA Leiden, The Netherlands

1. INTRODUCTION

According to modern taxonomy, four divisions of photosynthetic bacteria are discerned (1): the purple bacteria, the green sulfur bacteria (Chlorobiaceae), the green filamentous (or gliding) bacteria (Chloroflexaceae) and the heliobacteria. This contribution concerns the antenna properties of the last three groups; groups which have been studied less extensively than the purple bacteria, but which are not less interesting from the scientific point of view.

The green sulfur bacteria are the "classical" green bacteria. They contain relatively large amounts of chlorobium chlorophyll (bacteriochlorophyll c, d or e), in addition to BChl a. The latter pigment is mainly contained in the cytoplasmic membrane, whereas most of the BChl c is situated in the chlorosomes, oblong bodies of several hundred A diameter that are bound to the cytoplasmic membrane. Green sulfur bacteria are strict anaerobes which are found in fresh water as well as in marine habitats.

The green filamentous bacteria were discovered in the early seventies (2). Only one species has been extensively studied so far, *Chloroflexus aurantiacus*, a thermophilic bacterium living in hot springs in various parts of the world. The main pigment of *Cfl. aurantiacus* is BChl c, contained in chlorosomes, whereas the cytoplasmic membrane contains BChl a. Chloroflexus can grow phototrophically as well as heterotrophically in the presence of oxygen.

The heliobacteria are nitrogen fixing, strictly anaerobic phototrophs that were discovered only quite recently (3). Three species are known at present, *Heliobacterium chlorum* (3), *Heliobacillus mobilis* (4) and *Heliospirillum gestii*. The main pigment of heliobacteria is a "new" pigment, BChl g, situated in the cytoplasmic membrane. The heliobacteria do not possess chlorosomes. Although they lack the typical cell wall, on basis of 16S r-RNA sequence analysis they appear to be related to the gram-positive bacteria (1).

2. CHLOROSOMES

The absorption spectra of green sulfur as well as of green filamentous bacteria are dominated by strong absorption bands near 460 and 720-760 nm. These bands belong to BChl c, d or e in the chlorosomes, the major antenna systems in these bacteria. In addition to BChl c chlorosomes of green sulfur bacteria (5-7) as well as those of *Cfl. aurantiacus* (5,8) contain small amounts of BChl *a*, absorbing near 800 nm. Fig. 1 shows the absorption spectrum of isolated chlorosomes of the green sulfur bacterium *Prosthecochloris aestuarii*, measured at low temperature. A minor band near 805 nm can be seen that may be attributed to BChl *a*, present at an amount of approximately 1% of the total BChl in the chlorosome. The excitation spectrum of BChl *a* fluorescence indicates that light energy absorbed by BChl *c* is transferred to BChl *a* with an efficiency of approximately 40% at 4 K (9). Similar results were obtained with chlorosomes of *Chlorobium limicola* (7). In chlorosomes of *Cfl. aurantiacus* the ratio of BChl *c* to BChl *a* is about 25 (8).

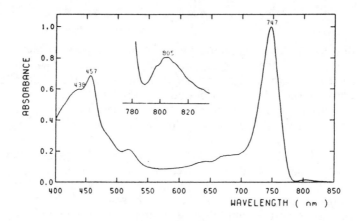

FIGURE 1.   Absorption spectrum of isolated chlorosomes of *P. aestuarii* at 4K. Inset: the region around 800 nm on a 20-fold expanded scale (9).

An obvious role for the BChl *a* in chlorosomes is that of an intermediate for energy transfer from the chlorosome to the membrane. Experiments with Chloroflexus indicate that this is indeed the case. Fluorescence excitation spectra showed that at 4 K the efficiency of energy transfer from BChl *c* to the chlorosomal BChl *a* is 50%, and from the latter pigment to the membrane 30%. Together these efficiencies should result in an efficiency of 15% for energy transfer from BChl *c* to the membrane and, as Fig. 2 shows, this was actually observed experimentally (10).

3.   THE MEMBRANE OF GREEN BACTERIA

The cytoplasmic membrane of *Cfl. aurantiacus* shows a clear similarity to that of purple bacteria. It contains an antenna complex B808-866 (11) which is structurally related to antenna complexes of purple bacteria. Rapid energy transfer occurs from BChl *a* 808 to BChl *a* 866 (12).

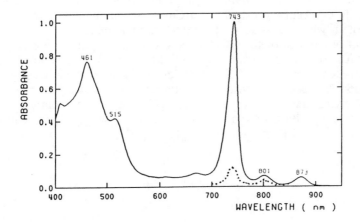

FIGURE 2.   Absorption spectrum of *Cfl. aurantiacus* at 4 K.   The band at
873 nm is due to BChl *a* 866.   The chlorosomal BChl *a* and
BChl *a* 808 contribute about equally to the band at 801 nm.
Dotted line: excitation spectrum of BChl *a* 866 fluorescence,
normalized at 872 nm (10).

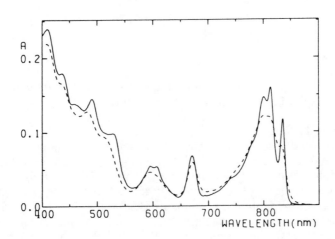

FIGURE 3.   Absorption spectrum of the core complex of *P. aestuarii*,
measured at room temperature (broken line) and at 77 K (14).
The band near 670 nm is due to a BChl *c*-like pigment, the
near-infra red bands are due to BChl *a*.

The structure of the membrane of green sulfur bacteria appears to be fundamentally different. Most of the BChl *a* is contained in a water soluble BChl *a* protein which is attached to, rather than imbedded in the membrane (13). About one-fourth of the BChl *a*, however, forms part of a core complex (Fig. 3), which contains approximately 20 BCls *a* per reaction center (14). The complex also contains about 15 molecules of BChl *c* or a closely related pigment (15). Flash spectroscopic evidence indicates that one of these molecules acts as electron acceptor in the primary charge separation (16,17). The peptide composition of the core complex may suggest a structural relationship to the core of photosystem I of plants (18).

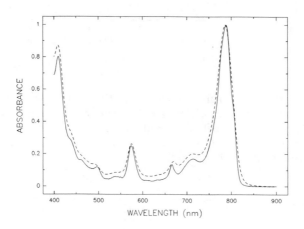

FIGURE 4.   Absorption spectrum of membranes of *H. chlorum* at 100 K (solid line) and at room temperature.

4. HELIOBACTERIA

Fig. 4 shows the absorption spectrum of isolated membranes of *H. chlorum*, measured at 100 K. The bands at 788, 574 and 410 nm are due to Q_y, Q_x, and Soret transitions, respectively, of the main pigment, BChl *g* (19). The major carotenoid, neurosporene (3,20) absorbs at 450-500 nm. The band at 666 nm is due to an as yet unidentified, presumably BChl *c* or Chl *a*-like pigment.

Closer inspection of the near-infra-red absorption band reveals that it can be resolved in at least three components, BChl *g* 778, BChl *g* 793 and BChl g 808. Measurements of fluorescence and of flash-induced absorbance changes show that energy absorbed by the short wave absorbing BChls *g* is rapidly transferred to BChl *g* 808 (20-22). Fig. 5 shows absorbance changes measured at 15 K upon excitation with 25-ps laser flashes (22). At 812 nm a bleaching is observed, caused by the formation of excited singled states of BChl *g* 808, which decays with time constants of 50 and 200 ps. At 793 nm almost all of the bleaching is irreversible at a ns time scale and may be attributed to $P798^+$, the oxidized primary electron donor, while contributions by excited antenna BChl are quite small. This indicates that excitation of short wave BChls is transferred within a few tens of picoseconds to BChl g 808. Energy transfer from the antenna to the reaction center appears to proceed via BChl g 808 (23). Even at 5 K this process appears to be quite efficient, but the mechanism of this seemingly uphill transfer is not clear.

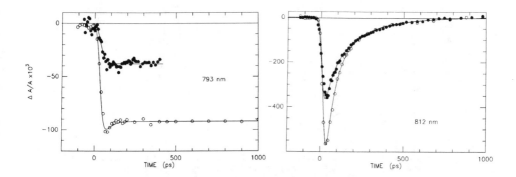

FIGURE 5.   Absorbance kinetics of membranes of *H. chlorum* at 15 K, brought about by 25 ps, 532 nm-laser flashes (22). Flash energy densities 3 mJ cm^{-2} (open circles) and 0.5 mJ cm^{-2} (solid circles). The ratio between the absorbance change and the initial absorbance at the same wavelength is plotted.

A solubilized antenna-reaction center-complex was isolated by detergent treatment of membranes of *H. chlorum* and *Hb. mobilis*, followed by sucrose gradient centrifugation (Van de Meent *et al.*, these Proceedings). The complexes probably contain one complete photosynthetic unit, together with the associated reaction center. The absorption spectra of the complexes from both species were almost indistinguishable from each other, and from those of the membranes used as starting material (Fig. 6). Also the reaction center activity was not changed, as measured by the extent and efficiency of photo-oxidation of P798 in saturating as well as in non-saturating flashes. Fluorescence excitation spectra indicated that the efficiency of energy transfer to BChl g 808 was not affected by the solubilization. These results indicate that the isolated complexes were structurally and functionally intact. The complexes were further purified by size-exclusion HPLC. From the elution volume a molecular weight of approximately 335 kD was determined, of which an estimated 8% may be attributed to the adhering detergent molecules. SDS-PAGE of the purified complexes revealed the presence of a dominant peptide of M_r = 94 kD. Weak and variable bands were seen above 100 kD and in the range 40-90 kD. Peptides of lower molecular weight were not observed. The peptide composition of the complexes thus seems to deviate from that of photosystem I core and of the core complex of green sulfur bacteria, the largest subunits of which are M_r = 65 kD peptides (18,24). These results appear to indicate a basically different structure for the heliobacterial and the other systems.

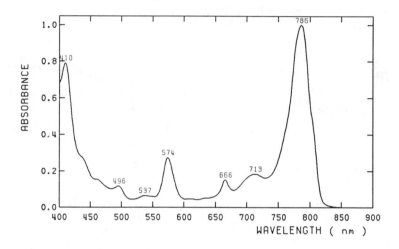

FIGURE 6. Absorption spectrum of the solubilized antenna-reaction center complex of *H. chlorum* at 100 K.

REFERENCES

1   Stackebrandt, E., Embley, M. and Weckesser, J. (1988) in Green Photosynthetic Bacteria (Olson, J.M. Ormerod, J.G., Amesz, J. Stackebrandt, E. and Trüper, H.G., eds.), pp.201-215, Plenum Press, New York
2   Pierson, B.K. and Castenholz, R.W. (1974) Arch. Microbiol. 100, 5-24
3   Gest, H. and Favinger, J.L. (1983) Arch. Microbiol. 136, 11-16
4   Beer-Romero, P. and Gest, H. (1987) FEMS Microbiol. Lett. 44, 109-114
5   Schmidt, K. (1980) Arch. Microbiol. 124, 21-31
6   Gerola, P.D. and Olson, J.M. (1986) Biochim Biophys. Acta 848, 69-76
7   Van Dorssen, R.J., Gerola, P.D., Olson, J.M. and Amesz, J. (1986) Biochim. Biophys. Acta 848, 77-82
8   Betti, J.A., Blankenship, R.E., Natarajan, L.V., Dickinson, L.C. and Fuller, R.C. (1982) Biochim. Biophys. Acta 680, 194-201
9   Van Dorssen, R.J. (1988) Structure and Function of Light-Harvesting Complexes in Photosynthesis, Doctoral Thesis, University of Leiden
10 Van Dorssen, R.J. and Amesz, J. (1988) Photosynth. Res. 15, 177-189
11 Feick, R.G. and Fuller, R.C. (1984) Biochemistry 23, 3693-3700
12 Vasmel, H., Van Dorssen, R.J., De Vos, G.J. and Amesz, J. (1986) Photosynth. Res. 7, 281-294
13 Olson, J.M. (1981) Biochim. Biophys. Acta 549, 33-51

14   Vasmel, H., Swarthoff, T., Kramer, H.J.M. and Amesz, J. (1983) Biochim. Biophys. Acta 725, 361-367
15   Braumann, T., Vasmel, H., Grimme, L.H. and Amesz, J. (1986) Biochim. Biophys. Acta 848, 83-91
16   Nuijs, A.M., Vasmel, H. Joppe, H.L.P., Duysens, L.N.M. and Amesz, J. (1985) Biochim. Biophys. Acta 807, 24-34
17   Shuvalov, V.A., Amesz, J. and Duysens, L.N.M. (1986) Biochim. Biophys. Acta 851, 1-5
18   Hurt, E.C. and Hauska, G. (1984) FEBS Lett. 168, 149-154
19   Brockmann, H. and Lipinski, A. (1983) Arch. Microbiol. 136, 17-19
20   Van Dorssen, R.J., Vasmel, H. and Amesz, J. (1985) Biochim. Biophys. Acta 809, 199-203
21   Nuijs, A.M., Van Dorssen, R.J., Duysens, L.N.M. and Amesz, J. (1985) Proc. Natl. Acad. Sci. USA 82, 6865-6868
22   Van Kan, P.J.M. Aartsma, T.J. and Amesz, J. (1989) Photosynth. Res. in press
23   Smit, H.W.J., Van Dorssen, R.J. and Amesz, J. (1989) Biochim. Biophys. Acta 973, 212-219
24   Malkin, R. (1987) in Topics in Photosynthesis (Barber, J. ed.), Vol. 8, pp. 495-525, Elsevier, Amsterdam.

EFFECT OF PHOSPHOLIPASE A$_2$ ON THE RESPONSIVENESS OF THE ELECTRO-CHROMIC CAROTENOIDS OF *RHODOBACTER SPHAEROIDES* CHROMATO-PHORES

LETICIA M. OLIVERA AND ROBERT A. NIEDERMAN, Department of Molecular Biology and Biochemistry, Rutgers University, P.O. Box 1059, Piscataway, New Jersey 08855-1059, USA.

1. INTRODUCTION

Photosynthetic membrane vesicles (chromatophores) of the purple nonsulfur bacterium *Rhodobacter sphaeroides* contain a carotenoid pool which responds to electrical field alterations with a spectral shift. These field-sensing carotenoids are apparently associated with the B800-850 peripheral light-harvesting complex (1) and are more sensitive to phospholipase A$_2$ (PL'ase A$_2$) treatment than the bulk of the carotenoids (2). The B800-850 light-harvesting complex is composed of bacteriochlorophyll (BChl) and carotenoid molecules in non-covalent association with heterodimers of α- and β-polypeptides. The electrochromic carotenoid pool has been reported, based on spectral deconvolution, to comprise about one third of the total carotenoids in the membrane (3,4). It has been suggested that the field-sensitive carotenoids are located near the cytoplasmic surface since incubation of *R. sphaeroides* chromatophores with PL'ase A$_2$ causes the disappearance of the electrochromic response (5). The observed phospholipase effect could reflect either an increase in the permeability of the membrane to ions or a direct effect upon the local environment of the field-sensing carotenoid pool.

Digestion of the membranes with PL'ase A$_2$ results in the formation of lysophospholipids and free fatty acids. These products affect the fluidity and surface charge of the bilayer, and could result in loss of the ability of the membrane to sustain a potential. The disappearance of the electrochromic response could be related to these changes. In this study, effects of digestion on bilayer composition were determined and correlated to the spectral change. It was shown further that the electrochromic carotenoids lose their ability to sense the field.

2. PROCEDURE

Chromatophores were prepared as described previously (6). Carotenoid absorbance changes were measured at 523 minus 507 nm with a Johnson Foundation DBS-3 double-beam spectrophotometer equipped with a Hamamatsu R928 photomultiplier tube. Measurements of the light-induced bandshift were made with a crossed double-beam apparatus and a xenon-flash lamp as the actinic light source, through a 6-mm Schott RG-9 filter; photomultipliers were protected by 5-mm thick Corning 4-96 blue glass filters. Phospholipids were extracted in butanol (7), and the phospholipid composition was determined from the integrated peak area observed in ^{31}P-NMR (8).

M. Baltscheffsky (ed.), Current Research in Photosynthesis, Vol. II, 33–36.
© 1990 *Kluwer Academic Publishers. Printed in the Netherlands.*

3. RESULTS AND DISCUSSION

During the course of PL'ase A_2 digestion, the valinomycin-K$^+$ induced transient absorbance changes were measured and the amplitudes as well as rate constants of the decay were obtained. This rate constant remained stable at ~0.12 s^{-1} for one h of incubation, indicating that the membrane had not become permeable to cations. After two h the rate of decay accelerated to 0.80 s^{-1}. In contrast, the amplitude of the banshift decreased throughout the incubation (Fig. 1) comprising 45% of the control after one h. This suggests that the electrochromically active chromophores are affected directly by the bilayer perturbation. Further support for the possibility that the PL'ase-induced alteration are confined to this

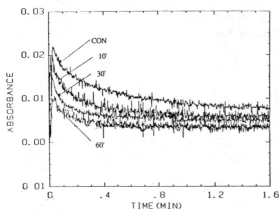

Fig. 1. KCl-valinomycin induced bandshift. Chromatophores, 10 µg Bchl/ml, were incubated with Pl'ase A_2, 0.001U/µg Bchl, in 1 mM CaCl$_2$, 20 mMMOPS, 0.1M NaCl, 1 µM Antimycin A, 1 µM valinomycin at 37° C. To each sample, 12.5 mM KCl was added.

special carotenoid pool was provided from the observation of a decrease in the overall carotenoid absorbance at ~518-520 nm (not shown). This reflected a spectral blue shift and this change was apparently confined to the normally red-shifted field-sensitive species.

The effect of PL'ase A_2 digestion on the light-induced carotenoid bandshift was also examined. The total change in amplitude remained constant for 30 min (Fig. 2), thereafter declining such that at one h it was 40% of the control. The basis for the delay in the amplitude decrease is not understood, but it is possible that this may be related to effects of enzymatic

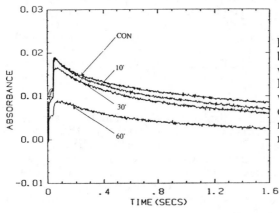

Fig. 2. Light-induced carotenoid bandshift. Measurements were made with a xenon-flash lamp as the actinic light-source. Two flashes 32 ms apart were used. Conditions as in Fig. 1 except that Antimycin A and valinomycin were omitted, and NaCl was replaced by KCl.

digestion on components that are involved in generating the electric field alterations. The decay of the light-induced transients was found to be composed of two phases. The rate constant (k_1) of the first phase remained stable for 30 min, but this phase was not detectable thereafter. The rate of the second phase was stable in the first h of digestion, increasing subsequently, essentially corroborating the results of the decay change measurements of the salt-induced spectral response.

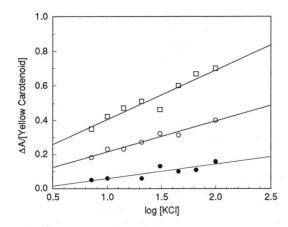

Fig. 3. Relation between carotenoid bandshift and K+ gradients. Chromatophores, 30 μg BChl/ml, were incubated with PL'ase A$_2$, 0.0002 U/ μg BChl, in 1 mM CaCl$_2$, 20 mM MOPS, 0.1 M NaCl, 1 mM Antimycin A, 1 mM valinomycin at 37° C. The concentration of K+ added ranged from 7 to 100 mM. Symbols; , untreated control; o, 10-min digestion; o, 60-min digestion.

The effect of PL'ase A$_2$ on the ability of the carotenoids to sense the field was investigated further in measurements of the relation between the extent of the carotenoid bandshift and the K+ gradient. As shown in Fig. 3, the sensitivity of the carotenoids to increasing diffusion potentials decreased with incubation time (control, 4.9 ΔA/V; 10 min, 3.0 ΔA/V; 60 min, 1.4 ΔA/V) suggesting that the carotenoids are either less responsive to a given field strength or fewer carotenoids can sense the field.

The phospholipid composition of chromatophores treated with PL'ase A$_2$ was determined; three phospholipid classes were detected in the undigested samples (Table 1) which were identified as phosphatidylcholine (PC), phosphatidylethanolamine (PE), and phosphatidylglycerol (PG) by comparing the chemical shifts to those of phospholipid

TABLE 1. PHOSPHOLIPID COMPOSITION OF CHROMATOPHORES DIGESTED BY PHOSPHOLIPASE A$_2$.

				%		
INC. TIME (MIN)	PC	LPC	PE	LPE	PG	LPG
0	31	0	31	0	38	0
10	31	0	26	8	36	0
60	31	0	24	6	39	0
120	35	0	17	11	33	4

standards. The lipid composition of undigested vesicles was in agreement with the results of Onishi and Niederman (9). After 10 min of digestion with phospholipase, lysophosphatidylethanolamine (LPE) was the only detectable lysophospholipid. Two h later, LPE and lysophosphatidylglycerol (LPG) were found. PC was not digested to lysophosphatidylcholine (LPC) by PL'ase A_2 under these conditions, suggesting that it is not available to the enzyme.

Overall, these results suggest that the chromatophore membranes remain impermeable to ions for at least 1 h of PL'ase A_2 digestion since the rate of decay was essentially unchanged for both the salt- and the light-induced spectral changes. During this period, in which PE is the only phospholipid species that is degraded, the field sensing carotenoids become less responsive to the membrane potential.

ACKNOWLEDGEMENTS

This work was supported by National Science Foundation grant DMB85-12587. L. M. O. was supported in part by a fellowship award from the Charles and Johanna Busch Memorial Fund Award to the Rutgers Bureau of Biological Research.

REFERENCES

1. Holmes, N.G., Hunter, C.N., Niederman,R.A. and Crofts, A.R. (1980) FEBS Lett 115, 43-48
2. Symons, M. and Swysen, C. (1983) Biochim. Biophys. Acta 723, 454-457
3. Holmes, N. G. and Crofts, A. R. (1977) Biochim. Biophys. Acta 459,492-505
4. Symons, M., Swysen, C. and Sybesma, C. (1977) Biochim. Biophys. Acta 462, 706-717
5. Swysen, C., Symons, M. and Sybesma, C. (1984) in Advances in Photosynthesis Research (Sybesma, C., ed.), Vol. 2, pp. 3.225-228, Martinus Nijhoff/ Dr. W. Junk Publishers, the Hague. the Netherlands
6. Reilly, P. A. and Niederman, R.A. (1986) J. Bacteriol. 167, 153-159
7. Bjerve, K.S., Daae, L.N.W. and Bremer, J. (1974) Anal. Biochem. 58, 238-245
8. Sotirhos, N., Herslof, B. and Kenne, L. (1986) J. Lipid Res. 27, 386-392
9. Onishi, J. C. and Niederman, R. A. (1982) J. Bacteriol. 149,831-839

BACTERIOCHLOROPHYLL c̲ MONOMERS, DIMERS, AND HIGHER AGGREGATES IN
DICHLOROMETHANE AND CARBON TETRACHLORIDE

J. M. OLSON and J. P. PEDERSEN, INSTITUTE OF BIOCHEMISTRY, ODENSE
UNIVERSITY, CAMPUSVEJ 55, DK-5230 ODENSE M, DENMARK

T. P. CAUSGROVE, D. C. BRUNE and R. E. BLANKENSHIP, DEPARTMENT OF
CHEMISTRY and CENTER FOR THE STUDY OF EARLY EVENTS IN PHOTOSYNTHESIS,
ARIZONA STATE UNIVERSITY, TEMPE, AZ85287, USA

INTRODUCTION
    In green sulfur bacteria and green filamentous bacteria the light-
harvesting function is carried out by chlorosomes, which are
appressed to the inner surface of the cytoplasmic membrane (1). The
absorption spectrum of bacteriochlorophyll (BChl) c̲ in the chlorosome
is red-shifted some 70 nm with respect to that of the monomeric form.
Krasnovskii and Bystrova (2) were among the first to show that
aggregated BChl c̲ in vitro also exhibits a red shift comparable to
that observed in chlorosomes. Smith et al. (3) showed that farnesyl
BChl c̲ extracted from Chlorobium limicola can be induced to form a
748-nm aggregate with an absorption spectrum strikingly similar to the
chlorosome spectrum simply by dissolving BChl c̲ in CH₂Cl₂ and diluting
the mixture in hexane. Similarly Brune et al. (4,5) showed that
stearyl BChl c̲ from Chloroflexus aurantiacus forms a 740-nm aggregate
in hexane. Only chlorophylls containing the 2-hydroxyethyl group are
capable of forming this type of aggregate.
    Caple et al. (6) found that Cb. limicola f. thiosulfatophilum
contains mainly 4 homologs of farnesyl BChl c̲ (F-BChl c̲): the
4-ethyl-5-methyl homolog (EMF-BChl c̲), the 4-ethyl-5-ethyl homolog
(EEF-BChl c̲), the 4-n-propyl-5-ethyl homolog (PEF-BChl c̲), and the
4-isobutyl-5-ethyl homolog (iBEF-BChl c̲).
    In the present study we show that the 748-nm aggregate of Smith et
al. (3) forms spontaneously in CCl₄ only if 4-isobutyl homologs of
BChl c̲ are used.

MATERIALS AND METHODS
    Fast atom bombardment mass spectrometry (7) of chlorophyll samples
(8) was carried out on a Kratos MS50TC mass spectrometer in the
positiveion mode. Absorption spectra were recorded with a Perkin-Elmer
330 spectrophotometer, and fluorescence spectra were recorded with a
Spex Fluorolog 111A. Fluorescence lifetimes were determined by
picosecond single-photon counting as described by Blankenship et al.
(these proceedings). To determine the BChl c̲ concentration in the
various samples of BChl c̲ in CCl₄ or CH₂Cl₂, methanol (1:200) was
added to convert all the BChl c̲ to monomer (BChl·CH₃OH) for which the
absorptivity (ε) at 668 nm in CCl₄ is 76 mM⁻¹cm⁻¹.

M. Baltscheffsky (ed.), Current Research in Photosynthesis, Vol. II, 37–40.
© 1990 Kluwer Academic Publishers. Printed in the Netherlands.

RESULTS AND DISCUSSION

Characterization of the BChl c homologs: The absorption spectra of
the various BChl c fractions in diethyl ether were found to be the
same. In CCl₄ each of the first 3 BChl c fractions (EMF-, EEF-, and
PEF-) showed a peak at 666-675 nm and an aggregate peak at 705-710 nm
(Fig. 1). The last fraction showed a peak at 667 nm and a different
aggregate peak at 744-747 nm (Fig. 2). The last two fractions were
further characterized by mass spectrometry. One fraction showed a main
peak at 821.3 amu corresponding to the positive ion [4-n-propyl-
5-ethyl-BChl c + H]⁺ (821.5 amu), and the other fraction showed two
main peaks at 821.4 and 835.4 amu corresponding to the positive ions
[4-isobutyl-5-methyl (821.5 amu) and 4-isobutyl-5-ethyl (835.5 amu)
BChl c + H]⁺. The two 4-isobutyl homologs were present in roughly
equal amounts in the last fraction, and the mixture is designated as
iBM/EF-BChl c. Only the last two fractions were used in further
experiments.

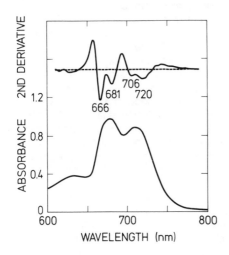 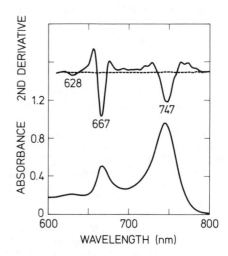

FIGURE 1 (left). Absorption and second derivative spectra of 2.5-μM
PEF-BChl c in CCl₄. Light path = 10 cm.
FIGURE 2 (right). Absorption and second derivative spectra of 16-μM
iBM/EF-BChl c in CCl₄. Light path = 1.0 cm.

Absorption and fluorescence spectra of PEF-BChl c in CCl₄: To detect
possible intermediates in the formation of the 705-710-nm aggregate,
PEF-BCHL c solutions in CCl₄ were prepared over the range of 0.1-770
μM. At ca. 0.1-μM BChl c only the monomer (I$_p$) could be detected. Its
absorption bands were at 434 and 666 nm, and there was a fluorescence
emission at 668 nm. However already at 0.25-μM BChl c there was
evidence of a second species (II$_p$) with absorption at ca. 685 nm and
fluorescence emission at ca. 690 nm. At ca. 2-μM BChl c a third
species (III$_p$) appeared with absorption bands at ca. 455 and 705 nm
and fluorescence emission at ca. 740 nm. At 100 μM, III$_p$ dominated

with an absorption band at 708 nm and fluorescence emission at 740 nm. At 770 μM II_p effectively disappeared from both the absorption and fluorescence spectra. Hyperchromism of the 705-710-nm band of III_p was estimated to be between 30 and 35%.

Absorption and fluorescence spectra of iBM/EF-BChl $\underline{c}$ in CCl_4: For the detection of possible intermediates in the formation of the 743-747-nm aggregate, iBM/EF-BChl $\underline{c}$ solutions in CCl_4 were prepared over the range of 2-360 μM. At ca. 2-μM BChl $\underline{c}$ the absorption bands at 667 and ca. 685 nm and the emission bands at ca. 672 and ca. 690 nm were assigned to I_b and II_b respectively. The prominent emission band at ca. 730 nm indicated the presence of III_b also. At 14-μM BChl $\underline{c}$ absorption bands at ca. 460 and 742 nm signaled the formation of a new species (IV_b) but with no apparent fluorescence emission band corresponding to the 742-nm absorption band. (The ca. 730-nm emission indicated the existence of III_b as a minor component.) At 55 - 106-μM BChl $\underline{c}$ IV_b dominated the absorption spectrum with a peak at 747 nm, and a weak fluorescence emission appeared at ca. 756 nm. Both the absorption and CD spectra were similar to the corresponding spectra of BChl $\underline{c}$ aggregates in CH_2Cl_2/hexane (3,9). Hyperchromism of the 743-747-nm band of IV_p was estimated to be between 30 and 40%.

Second derivative analysis: Derivative absorption spectra were recorded for both 2.5-μM PEF-BChl $\underline{c}$ (Fig. 1) and 16-μM iBM/EF-BChl $\underline{c}$ (Fig. 2) in CCl_4. Clearly shown in Fig. 1 are troughs at 666 and 681 nm due to I_p and II_p and troughs at 706 and 720 nm due to III_p. In Fig. 2 there is one trough at 667 nm due to I_b and another at 747 nm due to IV_b. There is however no well-defined trough at ca. 685 nm that can be assigned to II_b, even though the absorption spectrum shows evidence of an absorption shoulder at about that wavelength. This obvious difference between the second derivative spectra for II_p and II_b indicates an important difference between the absorption spectra of these two dimers.

The second derivative spectrum for 26-μM PEF-BChl $\underline{c}$ in CH_2Cl_2 showed troughs at 667 and 683 nm which were assigned unambiguously to I_p and I_p respectively. The corresponding spectrum for 26-μM iBM/EF-BChl $\underline{c}$ in CH_2Cl_2 had troughs at 668 and 685 nm which appeared to belong to I_b and II_b respectively. II_p is clearly different from II_b in both CH_2Cl_2 and CCl_4. The correct dimer (II_b) is thought to be required to form the 747-nm aggregate.

Dimer and trimer formation in CH_2Cl_2: To study II_p with less interference from higher aggregates PEF-BChl $\underline{c}$ was examined in CH_2Cl_2. Absorption spectra recorded at three different BChl $\underline{c}$ concentrations (2.2, 26, and 195 μM) could be satisfactorily resolved in terms of 4 components assigned as follows: 630 (I_p + II_p + III_p), 667 (I_p), 680 (II_p), and 705 nm (III_p). The log area of the 680-nm component (II_p) was plotted versus the log area of the 667-nm component (I_p), and a slope of 1.9 was found. Similarly the log area of the 705-nm component (III_p) was plotted versus log area 667-nm component, and a slope of 2.7 was found. These slope values are consistent with the assigment of I_p, II_p, and III_p to monomer, dimer, and trimer forms of BChl $\underline{c}$.

Fluorescence lifetimes: A sample of 30-μM PEF-BChl c in CCl₄/heptane (1:1) was excited between 670 and 740 nm at 10-nm intervals and the decay kinetics measured at 758 nm. These kinetics were resolved in terms of 4 components with lifetimes of 0.18, 1.6, 3.2 and 5.6 ns. Based on its excitation spectrum the 3.2-ns component was assigned to the trimer absorbing at ca. 710 nm.

A similar sample in CH₂Cl₂ was excited between 650 and 700 nm at 5-nm intervals and the decay kinetics measured at 706 nm. These kinetics were resolved in terms of 4 components with lifetimes of 0.1, 0.67, 1.8, and 6.4 ns. Based on their excitation spectra the 0.67- and 6.4-ns components were assigned to the dimer (absorbing at 680 nm) and the monomer (absorbing at ca. 665 nm) respectively.

A sample of 20-μM iBM/EF-BChl c in CH₂Cl₂ was also handled in the same way as the sample of PEF-BChl c in CH₂Cl₂. The kinetics were again resolved in terms of 4 components: 0.1, 0.61, 1.5, and 6.1 ns. The excitation spectra again showed that the 0.61- and 6.1-ns lifetimes belonged to the dimer and the monomer respectively.

When 20-μM iBM/EF-BChl c was dissolved in CCl₄/heptane (1:1) and the emission kinetics measured at 765 nm, 4 lifetimes were found: 19 ps, 67 ps, 0.4 ns, and 3.0 ns. From the excitation spectra the 19- and 67-ps lifetimes were assigned to two 743-nm absorbing components, and the 3.0-ns lifetime was assigned to a 710-nm absorbing component.

This is publication no. 24 from the Arizona State University Center for the Study of Early Events in Photosynthesis. The center is funded by U.S. Dept. of Energy grant DE-FG02-88ER13969 as part of the USDA/DOE/NSF Plant Science Centers program.

REFERENCES
1   Olson, J.M. (1980) Biochim. Biophys. Acta 594, 33–51
2   Krasnovsky, A.A. and Bystrova, M.I. (1980) BioSystems 12, 181–194
3   Smith, K.M., Kehres, L.A. and Fajer, J. (1983) J. Am. Chem. Soc.
    105, 1387–1389
4   Brune, D.C., Nozawa, T. and Blankenship, R.E. (1987) Biochemistry
    26, 8644–8652
5   Brune, D.C., King, G.H. and Blankenship, R.E. (1988) in
    Photosynthetic Light-Harvesting Systems (Scheer, H. and Schneider,
    S., eds) pp. 141–151, de Gruyter, Berlin
6   Caple, M.B., Chow, H. and Strouse, C.E. (1978) J. Biol. Chem. 253,
    6730–6737
7   Barber, M., Bordoli, R.S., Sedgwick, R.D. and Tyler, A.N. (1981) J.
    Chem. Soc., Chem. Commun., 325–327
8   Olson, J.M. and Pedersen, J.P. (1988) in Photosynthetic
    Light-Harvesting Systems, (Scheer, H. and Schneider, S., eds) pp.
    365–373, de Gruyter, Berlin
9   Olson, J.M., Gerola, P.D., van Brakel, G.H., Meiburg, R.F. and
    Vasmel, H. (1985) in Antennas and Reaction Centers of
    Photosynthetic Bacteria (Michel-Beyerle, M.E., ed) pp. 67–73,
    Springer-Verlag, Berlin

CONTROL OF BACTERIOCHLOROPHYLL a AND c IN CHLOROFLEXUS AURANTIACUS

Jürgen Oelze, Univ. Freiburg, Institut für Biologie II (Mikrobiologie),
Schänzlestr. 1, D-7800 Freiburg, FRG

1. INTRODUCTION
The thermophilic nonsulfur green bacterium Chloroflexus aurantiacus
forms two types of bacteriochlorophyll (Bchl). Both, photochemical
reaction centers (RC) and one type of light-harvesting complex located
in the cytoplasmic membrane (CM) contain Bchl a, while chlorosomes
attached to the CM contain Bchl c as the sole light-harvesting pigment
(1). It has been reported that as the light intensity decreases, the
specific content of Bchl c increases up to 20-fold, whereas the Bchl a
content increases only slightly (2). More recently, we demonstrated that
the molar ration of Bchl c/Bchl a is modulated by nutritional factors
when C. aurantiacus is grown in a chemostat on the complex medium
usually employed containing yeast extract and casamino acids (2,3). The
present study analyses the effects of defined nutrients on the formation
of Bchls a and c.

2. MATERIALS AND METHODS
C. aurantiacus strain J-10-fl was grown at 56°C on the medium described
in (2) modified as follows; the concentrations of yeast extract and
glycyl-glycine were decreased to 0.025 % and 0.01 % (w/v), respectively.
All sources of inorganic nitrogen were omitted and the concentration of
Fe-ions was increased to 10 μM. Casamino acids were replaced by single
amino acids as indicated.
Chemical analyses were performed as before (3).

3. RESULTS AND DISCUSSION
3.1 In order to test for the effects of defined amino acids on growth
and Bchl synthesis, C. aurantiacus was cultivated at 10,000 lx on the
amino acids as described in Fig. 1. All of the data depicted in Fig. 1
were corrected for a control grown on 0.025 % yeast extract. The results reveal that different amino acids, as the sole carbon and nitrogen sources, supported the syntheses of protein as well as of Bchls a
and c to characteristic extents. Consequently, cultures exhibited different molar ratios of Bchl c/Bchl a, which, however, did not result
from different light conditions because there was no relationship between culture density, i.e. the degree of self-shading and the above
ratio. In the following, the cultures were grown on 5 mM serine.

3.2. Experiments with batch cultures revealed that yeast extract at a
concentration of 0.025 % was optimal for obtaining high ratios of Bchl
c/ Bchl a. This was confirmed by the data depicted in Fig. 2 showing
that during growth in a serine-limited chemostat Bchl c contents were
highest at a supply of 0.025 % yeast extract. Upon increasing the con-

centration to 0.1 % Bchl c contents decreased, and they increased again as the concentration of yeast extract in the feed-medium was lowered to o.025 %.

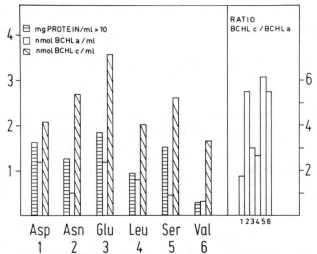

Fig.1. Growth and Bchl formation in batch cultures of C. aurantiacus on different amino acids (5mM). The cultures were grown at 56°C and 10,000 lx for 70 h. All values were corrected for control grown at 0.025 % yeast extract as sole carbon and nitrogen source.

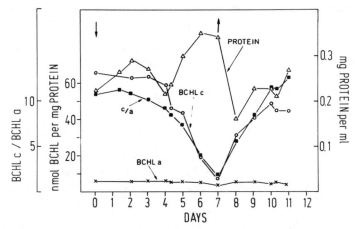

Fig.2. Steady state cell protein and specific Bchl levels in a serine-limited chemostat of C. aurantiacus. Where indicated the concentration of yeast extract in the feed-medium was increased from 0.025 % to 0.1 % (↓) and decreased from 0.1 % to 0.025 % (↑). The cultures were grown at 56 °C, D = 0.075-0.08 h^{-1} and 8,000 lx.

Steady state levels of biomass were highest when the lowest Bchl c
levels were reached. This again excludes an effect of self-shading on
Bchl c synthesis and, because of the constancy of cellular Bchl a
levels, on the ratio of Bchl c/Bchl a. Complete omission of yeast
extract resulted in decreases of both biomasse levels and cellular
Bchl c contents while Bchl a contents remained largely unaffected.

3.3. It has been reported (3) that the ratio of Bchl c/Bchl a decreased in chemostat cultures of C. aurantiacus when the supply
(= dilution rate, D) of complex medium (0.1 % yeast extract plus 0.25 %
casamino acids) was increased. This is accompanied by changes in the
pattern of amino acid consumption (Oelze and Jürgens, unpublished). If,
however, D-values were increased in a serine-limited chemostat, Bchlc
levels increased while steady state biomass and Bchl a levels remained
constant. Consequently, the Bchl c/ Bchl a ratio increased as a response to the rate at which serine was added to the culture.

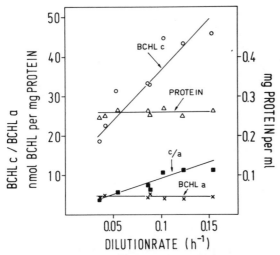

Fig. 3. Steady state cell protein and specific Bchl levels in a serine-
limited chemostat of C. aurantiacus growing at different dilution rates,
56°C and 25,000 lx.

Increasing the dilution rate in light-limited chemostats may decrease
the availability of light within the culture although the external
light conditions are kept constant. In order to exclude this as a
reason for the observed changes in the Bchl c/ Bchl a ratio, the
cultures were adjusted to D of about 0.110 h^{-1} and illuminated at
25,000, 12,000 and 8,000 lx. In spite of this, the Bchl c/ Bchl a ratio
stayed constant at 10-12.

4. CONCLUSIONS: Changes in the Bchl c/ Bchl a ratio result primarily from changes in Bchl c contents. Control of Bchl c levels is obviously a complex process involving the type of the C- and N-source, the rate at which this source is supplied as well as growth factors contained in yeast extract. As far as studied, these factors were more effective in the control of Bchl c than different light intensities.

This investigation was supported by the Deutsche Forschungsgemeinschaft.

REFERENCES
1. Fuller, R.C. and Redlinger, T.E. (1985) in Molecular Biology of the Photosynthetic Apparatus (Steinbeck, K.E., Bonitz, S., Arntzen, C.J. and Bogorad, L., eds.) pp. 155-162, Cold Spring Harbor Laboratory, New York.
2. Pierson, B.K. and Castenholz, R.W. (1974) Arch. Microbiol. 100, 283-305
3. Oelze, J. and Fuller, R.C. (1987) Arch. Microbiol. 148, 132-136

PHYCOCYANIN WITH MODIFIED CHROMOPHORES

FISCHER, R., GOTTSTEIN, J., SIEBZEHNRÜBL, S., SCHEER, H.
Botanisches Institut der Universität, Menzinger Str. 67,
D-8000 MÜNCHEN 19, FRG

1. INTRODUCTION

Phycocyanin plays an important role in collecting light energy and transfering it to the reaction center (1,2). *In vivo*, this chromoprotein is highly aggregated as part of the phycobilisomes (3-5). *In vitro*, in buffers of low ionic strenght, the phycobilisomes dissociate. Under these conditions, phycocyanin of *Mastigocladus laminosus* is aggregated to ring-shaped trimers (αß)$_3$. The α-subunit carries one (α-84) the ß-subunit two covalently linked cyanobilin-chromophores (ß-84 and ß-155) (6,7). These trimers are generally associated with linker-peptides, which can principally function as structural elements, as "terminators" of antenna rod building, but are also involved in fine tuning of the chromophore spectra for optimum energy transfer (3-6). In order to inve-stigate the role of individual chromophores in energy transfer, we are modifying distinct chromophores within energy transfering chromophore ensembles. During such studies, we have now found that chromophore modifications have also a profound influence on protein-chromophore interactions and chromoprotein aggregation. It is this aspect which is presented here.

2. MATERIAL and METHODS

Phycocyanin was isolated according to ref. 8. Subunits were prepared via isoelectric focusing under denaturing, anaerobic conditions (9).

Chromophore modifications: 1) **Reduction with borohydride** (modified from ref. 10). A solution of PC or isolated subunits (chromophore concentra-tion 7-21μM, 0.9M potassium phosphate, pH 7, 8M urea) was treated with NaBH$_4$ (170 mM). After complete reduction (spectrum, ≈45 min) excess reductant was destroyed by glucose. For reoxidation experiments, the samples (100mM potassium phosphate, pH 7, containing 70% ammonium sul-fate to prevent protein degradation) were allowed to stand at room temperature in the dark for up to nine days. This was followed by recom-bination (if not yet done), denaturation (8M urea in 100mM potassium phosphate, pH7) and renaturation as described below. 2) **Photobleaching** of the α-subunit (8μM protein, 100 mM phosphate, 8M urea, pH 7.5) was

carried out with 350 nm light over four periods of 30 min each (11).
3) **Indirect chromophore modification** was done by titration of trimeric
phycocyanin $(\alpha\beta)_3$ with PCMS (para-chloro-mercury-benzenesulfonate) in a
1.1-1.2 fold excess (12).

Recombination: Isolated subunits were modified and then hybridized with
the respective "partners" by dialysis of combined samples containing
5 mM mercaptoethanol, against 100mM potassium phosphate, pH 7 , 25°C
over night, and then with new buffer at 4°C for 5hrs. In control experiments, PC was modified *in toto*. Linker-peptide preparations were also
added in some experiments. The modification and recombination products
were tested by UV-vis-absorption, SDS-PAGE, sedimentation behaviour
(13) and (in some cases) gel-filtration on sephadex-G-75 (Serva, Heidelberg). The chromoprotein bands (which were distinct by their color) were
marked and quantitated by absorption spectroscopy.

concentration of chromophores (μM)	0.025	0.05	0.09	0.12	0.2	0.39
sedimentation						
phycocyanin	93/7	-	-	12/88	8/92	-
phycocyanin + PCMS	92/8	68/32	52/48	45/55	32/68	16/84
gel-filtration						
phycocyanin	-	-	-	2/98	-	-
phycocyanin + PCMS	-	-	-	>4/<96	-	-

Table 1: Influence of the protein-bound mercurial PCMS on the monomer/
trimer $(\alpha\beta)_1/(\alpha\beta)_3$ equilibrium of phycocyanin. Comparison of
two different methods of determination.

3. RESULTS and DISCUSSION

The bilin chromophores of either the α- or the β-subunit of phycocyanin, or both, were (photo)chemically modified and recombined with the
respective missing subunits. The modifications consisted of photobleaching, or reduction of the verdin- to rubin-type chromophore(s). It
was not possible to obtain trimeric phycocyanin $(\alpha\beta)_3$ from such modified
preparations by the recombination procedures used, irrespective of the
modification being done with PC *in toto*, or with isolated subunits which
were then recombined with the complementary subunit containing unmodified chromophores. All products are at most dimeric aggregates (Fig. 1).
Also, addition of a functionally active linker peptide (22 kDa), which

in unmodified samples stabilized trimeric aggregates, did not yield
trimers containing rubin type chromophores. Control experiments showed,
that this was not due to any irreversible modification on the peptide
chain. They were based on the fact that the reduced chromophore(s) were
not stable over longer periods of time under aerobic conditions, but
rather reoxidized to the native dihydrobilin chromophores. Aggregate
analysis of such reoxidation products obtained and with hybrids containing a reduced α-subunit, showed that reoxidation leads to reform-
ation of trimers (Fig. 1).

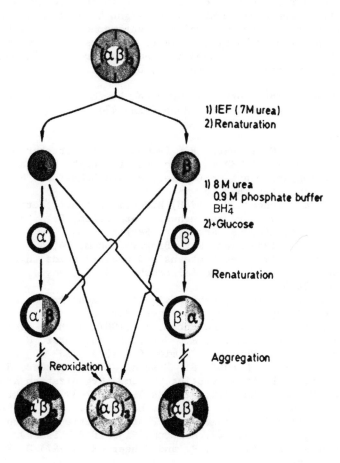

Figure 1: Scheme of the modification procedure at phycocyanin with
borohydride. α and ß are the subunits, "prime" indicates
reduced chromophores; IEF = isoelectric focusing; for more
details see text.

While the chemical modifications tested prevent trimer formation completely, modification with PCMS has only a moderately destabilizing effect on aggregation. The reagent binds to the single free cystein of phycocyanin, near the ß-84-chromophore and quite close to the monomer-monomer $(\alpha\beta)\text{-}(\alpha\beta)$ contact region (7). In the concentration range where the "natural" pigment contains both monomers $(\alpha\beta)_1$ and trimers $(\alpha\beta)_3$, the monomer portion is increased in PCMS titrated samples. This can be concluded from both the sedimentation runs and the gel filtration experiments (Table 1). However, in all tests it was found that the monomer concentration was higher in the sedimentation than in the gel-filtration experiments, which might be a high pressure effect. The desaggregating effect of modified chromophores is reminescent of the situation in phycoerythrocyanin, where a reversible photochemical reaction of the violobilin-chromophore leads to a reversible modulation of the aggregation (see poster Siebzehnrübl et al.).

Acknowledgement: This work was supported by the Deutsche Forschungs-gemeinschaft, Bonn (SFB 143).

REFERENCES
1 Schneider, S., Geiselhart, P., Baumann, F., Siebzehnrübl, S., Fischer, R. and H. Scheer (1988) in Photosynthetic Light Harvesting Systems. Organization and Function (Scheer, H. and Schneider, S., eds.), pp. 469-483, deGruyter, Berlin
2 Sauer, K. and Scheer, H. (1988) Biochim. Biophys. Acta 936, 157-170
3 Gantt, E. (1986) in Photosynthesis (Staehelin, L. A. and Arntzen, C. J., eds.), pp. 260-268, Springer, Berlin
4 Glazer, A. N. (1985) Ann. Rev. Biophys. Chem. 14, 47-77
5 Wehrmeyer, W. (1983) in Proteins and nucleic acids in plant systematics (Jense, U. and Fairbrother, D. E., eds.), pp. 144-167, Springer, Berlin
6 Zuber, H. (1986) in Photosynthesis III (Staehelin, L. A. and Arntzen, C. J., eds.), pp. 238-251, Springer, Berlin
7 Schirmer, T., Bode, W. and Huber, R. (1987) J. Mol. Biol. 196, 677-695
8 Füglistaller, P., Rümbeli, R., Suter, F. and Zuber, H. (1984) Hoppe-Seyler's Z. Physiol. Chemie 365, 1085-1096
9 Schmidt, G., Siebzehnrübl, S., Fischer, R. and Scheer, H. (1988) in Photosynthetic Light Harvesting Systems. Organization and Function (Scheer, H. and Schneider, S., eds.), pp. 77-89, deGruyter, Berlin
10 Kufer, W. and Scheer, H. (1982) Z. Naturforsch. 37c, 179-192
11 Scheer, H. (1987) in Progress in Photosynthesis Research (Biggins, J., ed.), pp. I.1.143-149, Martinus Nijhoff Publishers
12 Siebzehnrübl, S., Fischer, R. and Scheer, H. (1987) Z. Naturforsch. 42c , 258-262
13 Martin, R.G. and Ames, B.N. (1961) J. Biol. Chem. 236, 1372-1379

CAROTENOIDS FROM AN AEROBIC PHOTOSYNTHETIC BACTERIUM,
ERYTHROBACTER LONGUS OCH 101

Shinichi Takaichi[1], Keizo Shimada[2] and Jun-ichi Ishidsu[1]

[1]Biological Laboratory, Nippon Medical School,
 Kosugi-cho 2, Nakahara-ku, Kawasaki 211, JAPAN
[2]Department of Biology, Faculty of Science, Tokyo Metropolitan
 University, Fukasawa 2, Setagaya-ku, Tokyo 158, JAPAN

INTRODUCTION

Erythrobacter species synthesize photosynthetic pigments including
bacteriochlorophyll a and several carotenoids under highly aerobic
conditions, but they can not grow anaerobically even in the light in
contrast to typical photosynthetic bacteria [1].
Carotenoids in aerobically grown cells of Erythrobacter sp. OCh 114
have been identified [2]. Spheroidenone is dominant, and small amounts
of 2,2'-diketospirilloxanthin and OH-spheroidenone are also found. All
of these carotenoids are bound to a photosynthetic reaction center or
light-harvesting complexes, whose properties are similar to those of the
purple photosynthetic bacteria [1].
On the other hand, the carotenoid composition of E. longus is quite
different from that of Erythrobacter sp. OCh 114. About 20 kinds of
carotenoids are found. In vivo, a major carotenoid group with high
polarity is not associated with the light-harvesting complex which is
known to be the sole antenna complex in E. longus and, thus, it does not
function as a light-harvesting pigment [1]. Therefore, identification
of the carotenoids of E. longus should be fruitful for elucidation of
the role of carotenoids in this bacterium and of the phylogenesis of
Erythrobacter species.
In this paper, we report identification of the carotenoids and
preliminary results of the polar carotenoid group in E. longus.

MATERIALS AND METHODS

Biological material. Erythrobacter longus OCh 101 (IFO 14126) was used.
The culture conditions have been described elsewhere [1].
Isolation and purification. Carotenoids were extracted with $CHCl_3$/MeOH
from the wet cells of aerobic or semi-aerobic culture, or from those of
aerobic culture inhibited by DPA or nicotine. The polar carotenoid
group was purified by silica gel column chromatography, SEP-PAK NH_2 and
reversed phase TLC. The others were purified with silica gel and DEAE-
Sepharose CL-6B column chromatography. The purity was analyzed with the
reversed phase HPLC system using water (20-0%, v/v) in methanol as
eluent [3,4].
Spectral analysis. Absorption spectra were obtained by the continuous
monitoring HPLC system equipped with a photodiode array detector.
Molecular weights of the carotenoids and their reduced ($NaBH_4$), acetyl

M. Baltscheffsky (ed.), Current Research in Photosynthesis, Vol. II, 49–52.

TABLE 1. Spectroscopic properties in methanol obtained from the HPLC system, molecular weights (MW) and number of hydroxyl groups (OH) analyzed with the FD-MS of the carotenoids from E. longus

Compound	λ_{max} (nm)	%II/III	%D_B/D_{II}	MW	OH
β-carotene (authentic)	448, 476	25	5	536	0
β-carotene (1)	449, 475	21	8	536	0
β-cryptoxanthin (2)	447, 473	16	9	552	1
zeaxanthin (3)	448, 473	22	6	568	2
caloxanthin (4)	448, 474	29	6	584	3
nostoxanthin (5)	447, 473	22	7	600	4
13-cis-zeaxanthin (6)	442, 468	11	48	568	2
echinenone (7)	462		15	550	0
(reduced)	447, 474	22	8	552	1
rubixanthin (8)	458, 487	41	9	552	1
bacteriorubixanthin (9)	468, 499	46	17	582	1
bacteriorubixanthinal (10)	510		21	596	1
(reduced, cis)	(440),464, 493	37	21	598	2
(reduced, trans)	(440),469, 498	35	12	598	2
phytoene (11)	(275),285,(295)			544	0
lycopene (12)	442, 468, 499	68	10	536	0
anhydrorhodovibrin (13)	454, 481, 513	62	12	566	0
spirilloxanthin (14)	464, 492, 524	64	14	596	0

or trimethylsilyl derivatives were analyzed with the FD-MS [3,4].

RESULTS AND DISCUSSION
About 20 kinds of carotenoids were found in the cells of E. longus from various culture conditions, and 18 of them were identified. All were C_{40}-carotenoids and were divided into three groups; bicyclic, monocyclic and acyclic ones. They are tentatively numbered as indicated in TABLE 1. Compared with the purple photosynthetic bacteria in which only a few kinds of acyclic carotenoids are usually found [5], E. longus showed very wide diversity in its carotenoid composition.

Identification. The retention times on the HPLC system and the Rf-values on silica gel TLC of compounds 1 to 5 and 12 to 14 agreed with those of the known carotenoids from Anacystis nidulans and Chromatium vinosum, respectively. Spectroscopic properties, molecular weights and number of hydroxyl groups, all of which are primary and/or secondary, are shown in TABLE 1. Assignments of ^{1}H-NMR spectra of 1 to 6 and 8 to 11 were made by comparison with the data of typical carotenoids. The CD spectra indicated that the absolute configuration of the hydroxyl groups at C-2 and C-3 were 2R and 3R, respectively. The position of the aldehyde group in 10 was analyzed with the EI-MS spectrum [3,4].

Bicyclic carotenoids. β-Carotene (1) and its hydroxyl derivatives (2 to

FIG 1. Postulated pathway of carotenoid biosynthesis in E. longus

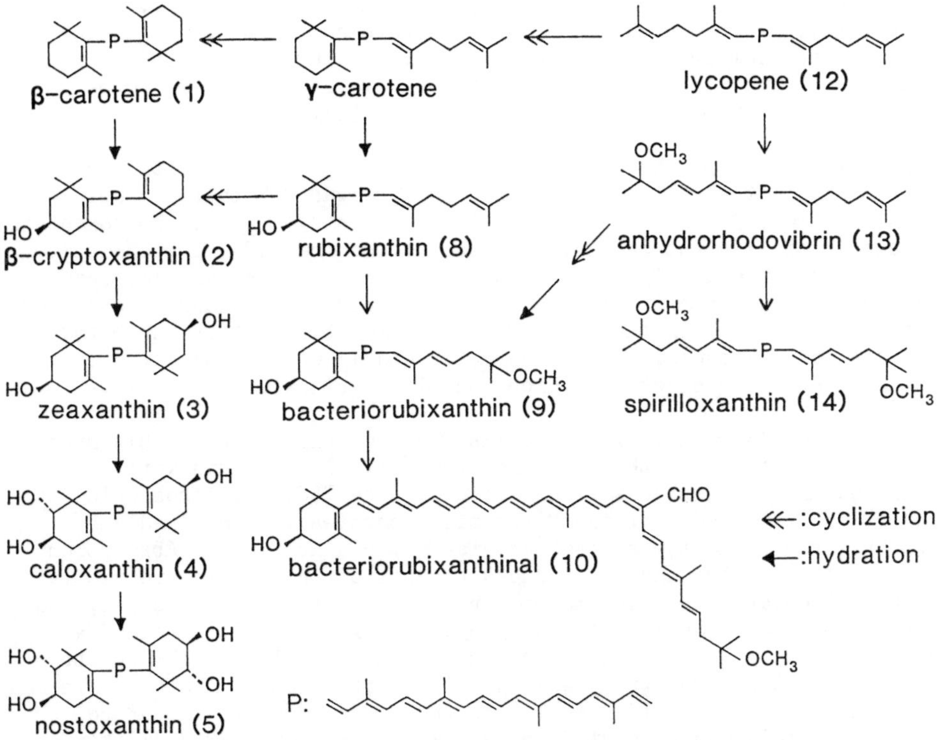

β-carotene (1)   γ-carotene   lycopene (12)
β-cryptoxanthin (2)   rubixanthin (8)   anhydrorhodovibrin (13)
zeaxanthin (3)   bacteriorubixanthin (9)   spirilloxanthin (14)
caloxanthin (4)   bacteriorubixanthinal (10)   ≪:cyclization   ←:hydration
nostoxanthin (5)

6) were identified, which have rarely been found in the purple
photosynthetic bacteria [5], except for a small amount of 1 and 2 in
Rhodomicrobium vannielii [6]. Compounds 1 to 3 are widely distributed
in green plants and algae. However, in phototrophs, 4 and 5 have been
found only in Cyanophyceae [7]. The latter two have also been found in
some aerobic bacteria [8]. The presence of these bicyclic carotenoids
in the purple photosynthetic bacteria seems to be anomalous. This might
indicate a close phylogenetical relationship between E. longus and these
aerobic bacteria. They seem to be synthesized from lycopene (12) by
cyclization and hydration (FIG. 1).

Monocyclic carotenoids. This group has rarely been found in the purple
photosynthetic bacteria [5]. Compounds 9 and 10 are novel ones [3].
The tertiary methoxy and the cross-conjugated aldehyde groups have been
found only in the carotenals of the purple photosynthetic bacteria, and
the position of the aldehyde group in 10 is at C-19' instead of at C-20
as in the known carotenals. The half moieties of their molecules may be
synthesized via a pathway of the normal spirilloxanthin series. The
other half may be formed by cyclization and hydration as in 8 (FIG. 1).

Acyclic carotenoids. This group is widely distributed in the purple
photosynthetic bacteria [5]. The carotenoids of E. longus are

synthesized via asymmetrical ζ-carotene and through a normal
spirilloxanthin series (FIG. 1). As compound 11, phytofluene,
asymmetrical ζ-carotene and neurosporene were not accumulated in the
DPA-inhibited culture, DPA can not inhibit desaturation of the
carotenes. Thus, the biosynthesis of the acyclic ones seems to be
different from that of Erythrobacter OCh 114 [2].

Composition. Except the polar carotenoid group, the composition of
carotenoids in the cells from aerobic culture was 39% bacteriorubixanthinal (10), 31% zeaxanthin (3), 19% caloxanthin (4), 4% nostoxanthin
(5) and 4% cis-zeaxanthin (6). As minor (less than 1%), compounds 1, 2,
9 and 14 were found. Trace amounts of 11, phytofluene, asymmetrical
ζ-carotene, neurosporene, 12 and γ-carotene were also found. Compounds
11 and 7 were found in the cells from semi-aerobic and DPA-inhibited
cultures, respectively. Compounds 8, 12 and 13 were accumulated in a
culture containing nicotine, which inhibits cyclization (FIG. 1).

Polar carotenoid group. In the cells from aerobic culture, this group
comprised about 70% of the total carotenoids. Its members were
separated into three bands with reversed phase TLC. Spectroscopic
properties indicated that the first major carotenoid contained a
carbonyl group, and the second was cis-form of the first. Absorption
spectra of the third and the reduced product of the first were similar
to that of β-carotene. The molecular weight of the first was 596, and
it had two primary and/or secondary hydroxyl groups. It also had a
polar and acidic group, and its pK_a was about 10. The ^{1}H-NMR spectrum
indicated that one end group was identical with that of nostoxanthin and
the other seemed to be identical with that of astacene. Therefore, the
first carotenoid was suggested to be 3,2',3'-trihydroxy-2,3-didehydro-
β,β-caroten-4-one. This carotenoid has not been known at all.
Determination of the structure of other polar carotenoids is under way.

Acknowledgments The authors wish to thank Prof. K. Harashima
(Yachiyo Int. Univ.), Prof. T. Miyazawa, Drs. S. Yokoyama and H. Hayashi
(Univ. Tokyo) and Dr. W. Miki (SUNBOR).

REFERENCES
1 Shimada,K., Hayashi,H. and Tasumi,M. (1985) Arch. Microbiol. **143,**
   244-247
2 Harashima,K. and Nakada,H. (1983) Agric. Biol. Chem. **47,** 1057-1063
3 Takaichi,S., Shimada,K. and Ishidsu,J. (1988) Phytochemistry **27,**
   3605-3609
4 Takaichi,S., Shimada,K. and Ishidsu,J. (1989) Arch. Microbiol.
   submitted
5 Schmidt,K. (1978) in The Photosynthetic Bacteria (Clayton,R.K. and
   Sistrom,W.R. eds.), pp 729-750, Plenum Press
6 Britton,G., Singh,R.K., Goodwin,T.W. and Ben-Aziz,A. (1975)
   Phytochemistry **14,** 2427-2433
7 Liaaen-Jensen,S. (1979) Pure Appl. Chem. **51,** 661-675
8 Kleinig,H., Heumann,W., Meister,W. and Englert,G. (1977) Helv. Chim.
   Acta **60,** 254-258

HPLC ANALYSIS OF THE PIGMENTS OF PURPLE PHOTOSYNTHETIC BACTERIA

ANN E. CONNOR AND GEORGE BRITTON, DEPARTMENT OF BIOCHEMISTRY, UNIVERSITY OF LIVERPOOL, P.O. BOX 147, LIVERPOOL L69 3BX. U.K.

1. INTRODUCTION

High-performance liquid chromatography (h.p.l.c.) is now used extensively to analyse the pigment compositions (carotenoids and chlorophylls) of plants and algae [1]. In spite of the great interest in bacterial photosynthesis and the pigments of photosynthetic bacteria, no widely applicable h.p.l.c. procedures have yet been reported. In this paper, we describe the development and characteristics of a reversed phase procedure suitable for the qualitative and quantitative analysis of the pigment compositions of a wide variety of bacteria, and also comment on a normal, adsorption phase method which will resolve geometrical (Z/E) isomers of carotenoids.

2. PROCEDURE

The h.p.l.c. equipment used consisted of a Waters 600E pumping system and controller with a Waters 990 photodiode array detector. A Spherisorb-ODS2 column (5μm; 25 x 0.46cm) was used with the following solvent programme:

Time (min)	% Solvent A	% Solvent B	Gradient
0-15	23	77	Isocratic
15-30	23-70	77-30	Linear
30-40	70-100	30-0	Linear
40-45	100	0	Purge
45-55	0	100	Equilibrate

Solvent A: ethyl acetate. Solvent B: acetonitrile-water (9:1) containing 0.5% triethylamine. Flow rate 1ml.min^{-1}.

Total lipid samples were obtained rapidly by extraction with acetone-methanol. After evaporation of the solvent the extracts were redissolved in dichloromethane, filtered and 20μl samples injected. Chromatograms were monitored continuously over the wavelength range 275-600nm. Pigments were identified by their retention times and light absorption spectra, determined online. Identifications were confirmed by co-

injection with authentic standards, and by mass
spectrometry.

3.   RESULTS AND DISCUSSION
     With the photosynthetic bacteria, the range of
polarity of the carotenoids present is generally not great
[2].   The main problem lies in the need to resolve
mixtures of carotenoids which contain the same polar
substituent groups (normally HO and MeO) but which differ
in the length of the conjugated polyene chromophore.   The
simple linear solvent gradient that is used routinely to
analyse plant chloroplast pigments is not ideal for this
purpose.   A reversed phase procedure with a C_{18} column and
the more complex gradient programme shown in the table
give good and reproducible resolution of the variety of
carotenoids and bacteriochlorophylls in all the
photosynthetic bacteria that have been examined, namely
Rhodocyclus   gelatinosus,   Rhodobacter   sphaeroides,
Rhodopseudomonas   capsulatus,   Rps.   viridis,   Rps.
acidophila,   Rhodospirillum   rubrum,   Rhodomicrobium
vannielii, Chromatium minutissimum, C. purpuratum.   Some
representative chromatograms are illustrated in Fig. 1
     With this procedure, it is possible to resolve both
the apolar hydrocarbons and carotenoids containing
hydroxy, methoxy and oxo groups, and also to separate
bacteriochlorophylls with different esterifying isoprenoid
sidechains.   The separations achieved are not directly
related to those obtained with a normal, adsorption phase
method such as t.l.c. or h.p.l.c. on silica, in which the
main influence on separation is the presence of polar
substituent groups, and compounds having the same
substituent groups but   differing in the length of the
conjugated polyene chromophore are largely unresolved.
With the reversed phase system, the same general trend is
seen in the absence of other important structural
influences but in reverse order, i.e. the most polar
carotenoids are eluted first and the hydrocarbons latest.
     The degree of unsaturation in the molecule, i.e. the
length of the conjugated polyene chromophore, has a
substantial effect on retention times.   Thus the acyclic
hydrocarbons of the biosynthetic desaturation series,
namely phytoene, phytofluene, tetrahydrolycopene,
neurosporene and lycopene are well resolved, as are
compounds having the same substituent group but different
levels of desaturation, e.g. the 1-hydroxy-derivatives of
these hydrocarbons.   The 1,2-dihydrocarotenes, found in
Rps. viridis are eluted later than their parent
hydrocarbons   e.g.   1,2-dihydroneurosporene   after
neurosporene.

In the case of carotenoids containing polar substituent groups, the main structural feature which influences retention is the presence of an unsubstituted hydrocarbon end-group or half-molecule, which has a strong affinity for the C_{18} hydrocarbon chains of the reversed phase column material, especially when this carotenoid end-group contains a relatively high degree of unsaturation. For example natural 1'-hydroxy-1',2'-dihydrospheroidene, in which a methoxy- and a hydroxy-substituent are located at opposite ends of the molecule, is eluted several minutes earlier than the semi-synthetic 2-hydroxyspheroidene in which both substituents are in one end-group and the other half-molecule remains unsubstitued.

The carotenoids are generally well resolved from the bacteriochlorophylls and bacteriophaeophytins, provided sufficient equilibration time is allowed between injections. Bacteriochlorophylls with different degrees of unsaturation in the esterifying isoprenoid alcohol are well resolved, e.g. that with a geranylgeranyl sidechain is eluted several minutes before the phytyl analogue. This reversed phase h.p.l.c. procedure provides a general method for qualitative and quantitative pigment analysis, is applicable to a wide variety of photosynthetic bacteria, and allows even trace components of complex mixtures to be detected and identified. Only small samples of biological material are required; a full analysis can be obtained from only a few mg of cells in approximately one hour. The method is therefore particularly useful for determining pigment compositions of isolated pigment-protein complexes, and has also been used to study effects of inhibitors or changes in environmental conditions on pigment compositions, and for pigment analyses of mutant strains. The procedure is easily modified by changing the solvent gradient programme to improve the resolution of particularly difficult mixtures of compounds.

Normal, adsorption phase procedures with silica or bonded nitrile columns have also been developed (details not presented here). Some degradation of carotenoids and especially of bacteriochlorophylls may occur on these columns so they are not recommended for accurate quantitative analysis, but they will resolve mixtures of geometrical (Z/E or cis/trans) isomers that are not resolved on the reversed phase column.

With the availability of these h.p.l.c procedures the way is now clear for rapid advances to be made in understanding the distribution and functioning of the

pigments in photosynthetic bacteria as they have with the
photosynthetic pigments of higher plants.

ACKNOWLEDGEMENT
    We thank S.E.R.C. for financial support.

REFERENCES
1. Goodwin, T.W. and Britton, G. (1988) in Plant
    Pigments (Goodwin, T.W., ed.), pp. 61-132, Academic
    Press, London.
2. Schmidt, K. (1978) in The Photosynthetic Bacteria
    (Clayton, R,K. and Sistrom, W.R., eds.), p 729,
    Plenum Press, New York.

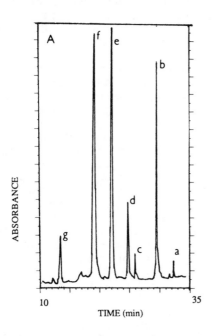
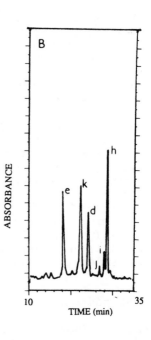

Fig. 1.   Reversed phase HPLC chromatograms of pigment
           extracts of A. _Rhodocyclus_ _gelatinosus_ 151   B.
           Rhodomicrobium _vannielii_ RB4
Pigment   identification: (a)   neurosporene,   (b)
    spheroidene, (c) spheroidenone, (d) spirilloxanthin,
    (e) bacteriochlorophyll (f) hydroxyspheroidene, (g)
    hydroxyspheroidenone   (h)   lycopene   (i)
    bacteriophaeophytin,   (j) anhydrorhodovibrin,   (k)
    rhodopin.

ROLE OF B800-850 LIGHT-HARVESTING PIGMENT-PROTEIN COMPLEX IN THE MORPHOGENESIS OF *RHODOBACTER   SPHAEROIDES* MEMBRANES

JAMES N. STURGIS AND ROBERT A. NIEDERMAN, Department of Molecular Biology and Biochemistry, Rutgers University, Piscataway, NJ 08855-1059, USA

1.   INTRODUCTION

In response to low oxygen tension, the facultative photoheterotrophic bacterium *Rhodobacter sphaeroides* elaborates an extensive intracytoplasmic membrane (ICM) system, consisting of a series of interconnected vesicles, in which the photosynthetic apparatus is localized (1,2). In addition to the photochemical reaction center, this structure contains the B875 and B800–850 light-harvesting bacteriochlorophyll *a* (BChl)-protein complexes which function as core and peripheral antennae, respectively (3). While the core antenna is found in a constant molar ratio to the reaction center of ~25:1, the amount of B800–850 varies with light intensity (4) and under low illumination, can reach levels more than three-fold greater than those of B875. The ICM is continuous with the cytoplasmic membrane (5,6,7), and *in vivo* surface labeling studies have demonstrated that the interior of the ICM is accessible from the periplasmic space (8,9).

The development of the ICM of *R. sphaeroides* has been extensively studied (6) and is thought to proceed from membrane invagination sites that can be isolated in an upper pigmented band by rate-zone sedimentation of French-pressure cell extracts (7,10). Radiolabeling studies in *R. sphaeroides* (7,10,11,12) have suggested that newly synthesized B875-reaction center core particles are assembled preferentially at these sites and are chased into ICM-derived chromatophore vesicles. Moreover, pulse-chase studies in synchronously dividing cells (13) were consistent with the possibility that the addition of B800–850 is a major event in the expansion of the ICM.

In the present study, the effects of the B800-850 antenna on the morphology and physical properties of the ICM were examined in *R. sphaeroides* grown at various light intensities. This permitted a comparison of the membrane maturation process in cells containing a range of levels of this pigment-protein complex. The wild–type strain was employed in order to avoid any pleiotropic effects associated with the use of mutant strains in which the precise nature of the lesion is unknown. A model for the development of the ICM, as well as the role of the B800–850 protein in this process, is also presented.

2.   MATERIALS AND METHODS

R. sphaeroides wild-type strain NCIB 8253 was grown photoheterotrophically at 30°C under various light intensities as described by Holmes *et al.* (14). Near-IR absorption spectra were obtained at 295 K on a Johnson Research Foundation DBS-3 spectrophotometer equipped with a Hamamatsu R-406 photomultiplier tube. Total Bacteriochlorophyll (BChl) was determined in acetone methanol water (7:2:1, vol/vol) using the extinction coefficient of Clayton (15).

3.   RESULTS AND DISCUSSION

R. sphaeroides was grown to a cell density of about $6 \, \mathrm{gl}^{-1}$ at light intensities of ~1000, 300 and 100 Wm^{-2} and extracts prepared from these cells were subjected directly to rate-

M. Baltscheffsky (ed.), Current Research in Photosynthesis, Vol. II, 57–60.

zone sedimentation on sucrose density gradients (Fig.1). In each case, a typical profile of BChl distribution was observed. Although the shape of each gradient was similar, the distances migrated by the chromatophore bands differed significantly, with those derived from cells grown at high, medium and low light intensities sedimenting to positions in the gradient at 1.096, 1.085, and 1.071 g ml^{-1}, respectively. Thus, chromatophores with lower levels of the B800-850 complex sediment more rapidly than those containing higher amounts of this pigment-protein complex. Furthermore, a heterogeneity of the chromatophores derived from each culture was observed; this is shown as a rise in the ratio of B800-850 to antenna BChl across the respective bands, and is most pronounced in the high-light profile.

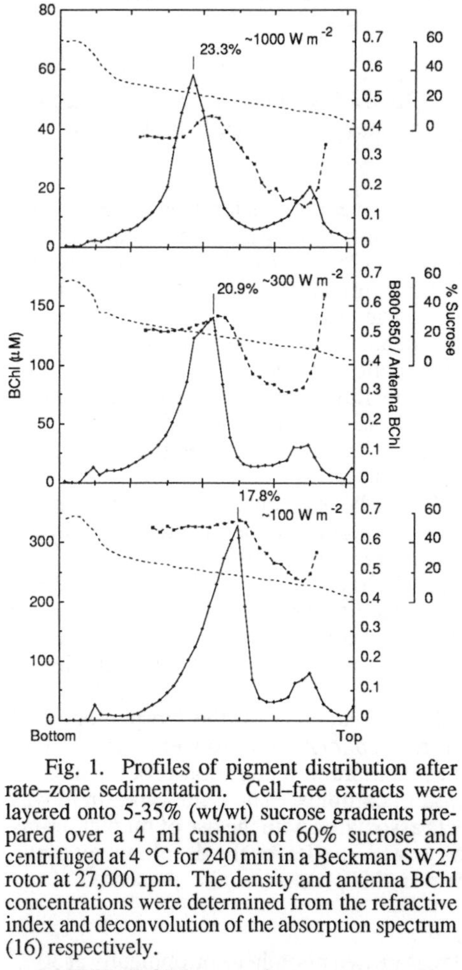

Fig. 1. Profiles of pigment distribution after rate–zone sedimentation. Cell–free extracts were layered onto 5-35% (wt/wt) sucrose gradients prepared over a 4 ml cushion of 60% sucrose and centrifuged at 4 °C for 240 min in a Beckman SW27 rotor at 27,000 rpm. The density and antenna BChl concentrations were determined from the refractive index and deconvolution of the absorption spectrum (16) respectively.

The rate of sedimentation is affected both by the size and density of the sedimenting particle. In order to determine whether the cells grown at the different light intensities give rise to chromatophores of differing sizes, the isolated vesicles were further characterized by gel-exclusion chromatography on Sepharose 2B. The elution profiles (Fig. 2) indicated that the three chromatophore samples showed small differences in relative mobility such that those from high-light cells (1000 Wm^{-2}) eluted with a relative mobility of 1.58 compared to 1.61 and 1.67 for vesicles derived from 300 and 100 Wm^{-2} cultures, respectively. From the molecular exclusion range of Sepharose 2B and the differences in the positions of the chromatophores after rate-zone sedimentation, it can be estimated that under the extremes of high and low light intensity, the size of the isolated chromatophores decreased by about 7%.

These results demonstrate that the size of ICM-derived chromatophore vesicles is dependent upon the amount of B800–850 in the membrane. This is in agreement with previous observations in the mutant strains M21 in which lack of the B800–850 resulted in larger internal membrane structures (17) and NF57 (B875$^-$, reaction center$^-$) where the presence of high levels of oligomeric B800–850 resulted in smaller chromatophores (Sturgis, J.N., Hunter C.N., and Niederman R.A., in preparation). Furthermore, a size and compositional heterogeneity was observed across the chromatophore band after rate-zone sedimentation in which the smaller vesicles in the trailing edge exhibited higher B800–850 levels than the larger structures within the leading edge. This suggests that chromatophores, once formed, are stable and that B800–850 and other integral membrane proteins do not equilibrate across the entire ICM system but are instead restricted to the vesicle into which they were initially incorporated.

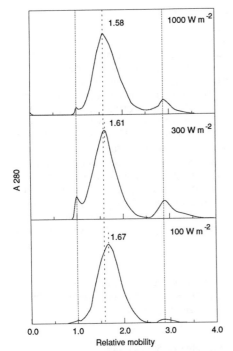

Fig. 2. Gel exclusion chromatography of chromatophore preparations on a Sepharose 2B column. Chromatography was performed essentially as described by Fraker and Kaplan (18). A 0.1 ml sample was loaded onto a 1.7 x 35 cm Sepharose 2B column the flow rate was 11 ml hr⁻¹. Sodium phosphate buffer (100 mM), pH 7.5, containing 10mM EDTA and 0.02% sodium azide was used for both equilibration and elution. The effluent was passed through an LKB 2138 Uvicord S detector to obtain the elution profile. The small amount of material in the void volume apparently represents chromatophore aggregates, while the small peak at the included volume was an artifact caused by refractive index changes upon elution of the sucrose in which the samples were applied.

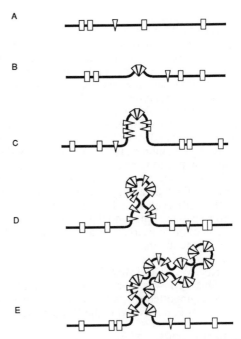

Fig. 3. Model describing the development of ICM system of *R. sphaeroides*. Details are presented in the text. The rectangles represent normal integral membrane protein, while the triangles represent membrane bending integral membrane protein.

In order to explain these results it is proposed that the B800–850 complex belongs to a class of membrane bending proteins that are capable of altering the morphology of the bilayer. The role of such proteins in ICM morphogenesis is illustrated in Fig. 3 and described below. In (A), integral proteins are shown within an initially flat membrane in which local aggregation of special proteins capable of bending the bilayer ultimately leads to the initiation of an invagination (B). This initiation site then elongates into a tubular structure as more components are integrated and is isolatable along with structures A and B in the upper pigmented band seen in Fig. 1 (C). At this stage, the protein constituents can partition between flat regions or bent tubular areas on the basis of their tendency to relax the torsional energy stored in the membrane. It is hypothesized that in those mutants of *R. sphaeroides* in which large tubular structures are seen, notably a number that lack the B800–850 complex (17,19), morphogenesis of internal membranes is arrested in this state. In the next step, as the local concentration of the bending protein in the tubular structure becomes sufficiently high, the proximal end of the tubule constricts to form a vesicle (D) which after cellular disruption gives rise to a chromatophore. This essentially fixes the protein composition, since the constriction introduces an area of membrane that has a large curvature in the direction opposite that of the vesicle. Continuation of this process of elongation and vesicularization generates a chain of structures (E), in which the oldest are distal from, and the youngest proximal to the cytoplasmic membrane.

In the context of this model, it is expected that the components of the photosynthetic unit are all either membrane bending proteins or are associated with them and thus partition into the invaginations; however, for vesicularization to occur, high local concentrations of these proteins are required. For *R. sphaeroides*, it is proposed that this is achieved by the B800–850 complex which is strongly membrane bending and forms large aggregates (20,21) which facilitates accumulation to high local concentrations. This would explain the observed dependence of chromatophore size on B800–850 levels. This proposed role for proteins in membrane morphogenesis provides a framework for understanding a number of important phenomena such as partitioning of proteins and lipids between contiguous areas of bilayer. Segregation of components is observed during chromatophore development; although the ICM and cytoplasmic membrane are continuous (5, 6, 22), their compositions are very different. An efficient mechanism for the partitioning or sorting these proteins must therefore exist. The model proposed here suggests that this role is performed passively as a result of protein structure, and is therefore driven indirectly by the insertion of the protein into the membrane.

ACKNOWLEDGEMENTS

This work was supported by National Science Foundation grant DMB85-12587. J. N. S. was supported in part by a fellowship award from the Charles and Johanna Busch Memorial Fund Award to the Rutgers Bureau of Biological Research.

REFERENCES
1   Brown, A.E., Eiserling, F. A. and Lascelles, J. (1972) Plant Physiol. 50: 743–746
2   Peters, G. A. and Cellarius, R. A. (1972) J. Bioenerg. 3: 345–359
3   Cogdell, R. J. and Thornber, J. P. (1980) FEBS Lett. 122: 1–8
4   Aagaard, J. and Sistrom, W. R. (1972) Photochem. Photobiol. 15, 209-225
5   Drews, G and Oelze, J. (1981) Adv. Microbiol. Physiol. 22: 1–92
6   Kaplan, S. and Arntzen, C. J. (1982) in Photosynthesis (Govindjee ed), Vol. 1, pp 65-151, Academic Press, New York
7   Niederman, R. A., Hunter, C. N., Inamine, G. S. and Mallon, D. E. (1981) in: Photosynthesis (Akoyunoglou, G. ed.), Vol. 5, pp 663–674, Balaban, Philadelphia
8   Inamine, G. S., van Houten, J. and Niederman, R. A. (1984) J. Bacteriol. 158: 425–429
9   Francis, G. A. and Richards, W. R. (1980) Biochemistry 19: 5104–5111
10 Niederman, R. A., Mallon, D. E. and Parks, L. C. (1979) Biochim. Biophys. Acta 555: 210–220
11 Hunter, C. N., Pennoyer, J. D. and Niederman, R. A. (1982) in Cell Function and Differentiation (Akoyunoglou, G., Evangelopoulos, A.E., Georgatsos, J., Palaiologos, G., Trakatellis, A., Tsiganos, C.P. eds.), part B, pp 257-265, Alan R. Liss, New York.
12 Inamine, G.S., Reilly, P. A. and Niederman, R. A. (1984) J. Cell. Biochem. 24: 69–77
13 Reilly, P. A. and Niederman, R. A. (1986) J. Bacteriol. 167:153-159
14 Holmes, N. G., Hunter, C. N., Niederman, R. A. and Crofts, A. R. (1980). FEBS Lett. 115:43–48
15 Clayton, R. (1966) Photochem. Photobiol. 5, 669-677
16 Sturgis, J. N., Hunter, C. N. and Niederman, R. A. (1988) Photochem. Photobiol. 48: 243–247
17 Hunter, C. N., Pennoyer, J. D., Sturgis, J. N., Farrelly, D. and Niederman, R. A. (1988) Biochemistry 27: 3459–3467
18 Fraker, P. J. and Kaplan, S. (1971) J. Bacteriol. 108:465-473.
19 Kiley, P. J., Varga, A. and Kaplan, S. (1988) J. Bacteriol. 170: 1103–1115
20 Broglie, R. M., Hunter, C. N., Delepelaire, P., Niederman, R. A., Chua, N.-H. and Clayton, R. K. (1980) Proc. Natl. Acad. Sci. USA 77, 87-91
21 Westerhuis, W. H. J., Vos, M., van Dorssen, R. J., van Grondelle, R., Amesz, J. and Niederman, R. A. (1987) in Progress in Photosynthesis Research (Biggins, J. ed.), Vol. 1, pp. 29-32, Martinus Nijhoff, Dordrecht, the Netherlands
22 Niederman, R. A. and Gibson, K. D. (1978) in The Photosynthetic Bacteria (Clayton, R.K.and Sistrom, W.R. eds.), pp 79–118, Plenum Publishing Corp., New York

THE PERIPHERAL ANTENNA POLYPEPTIDES OF *RP.PALUSTRIS* :
SYNTHESIS OF MULTIPLE FORMS AND STRUCTURAL VARIABILITY AS A
CONSEQUENCE OF LIGHT INTENSITY.

R.A. Brunisholz[1], M.B. Evans[2], R.J. Cogdell[2], G.Frank[1], H. Zuber[1],
Institute of Mol.Biol.and Biophysik, ETH, Zürich, Switzerland[1], Department.of
Botany, University of Glasgow, UK[2]

INTRODUCTION
Some strains of *Rp. palustris* have been reported to exhibit similar cell-spectral
features in the near-infrared as those of *Rb. sphaeroides* (wild-type) and *Rb.
capsulatus* , indicative of a core antenna (B870) and one single peripheral
antenna (B800-850) [1]. Further investigations on the antenna system of *Rp.
palustris* revealed that certain strains may synthesize spectrally dissimilar
intracytoplasmic membranes[2,3], thus suggesting a similar situation as in *Rp.
acidophila* [4]. In particular the B800-850 complexes from differently cultured
cells (15000lux to 300lux) varied greatly in their absorption characteristics in
the near-infrared; i.e. high light cells synthesize a more standard, sphaeroides-
like B800-850 complex, whereas low light induces a high 800 nm band and a
low 850 nm band. From biophysical studies involving CD spectral analyses
and resonance Raman spectroscopy it has been inferred that the B800-850
complex with a low 850 nm band differs from the 'normal' B800-850 complex
(high 850 nm) from *Rb. sphaeroides* or *Rb. capsulatus* regarding pigment
organization [2,3]. In addition, employing biochemical methods the two
spectrally different peripheral antennae of *Rp. palustris* have been shown to
vary 1.) in their polypeptide composition (only minor differences detected on
SDS-gels) and 2.) in their pigment composition indicating a higher content of
BChl in the low B850 complex [3]. The latter result has been confirmed by
Cogdell et al. (paper in preparation). Recently, protein chemical analyses of
the antennae system of *Rp. acidophila,* strains 7050 and 7750 revealed
antenna complex specific apoproteins for the B800-850 and the B800-820
peripheral antenna system [5,6]. Interestingly, the B800-820 antenna complex
of strain 7750 appears to be composed of one α- and two chemically different
β-polypeptides [5,6]. In this short report we would like to focus on the even
more complex situation in the peripheral antenna systems of *Rp. palustris*
regarding their polypeptide composition.

RESULTS AND CONCLUSIONS
The antenna complexes of *Rp. palustris.*were isolated by sucrose density-
gradient centrifugation of LDAO-solubilised photosynthetic membranes. The

M. Baltscheffsky (ed.), Current Research in Photosynthesis, Vol. II, 61–64.
© 1990 *Kluwer Academic Publishers. Printed in the Netherlands.*

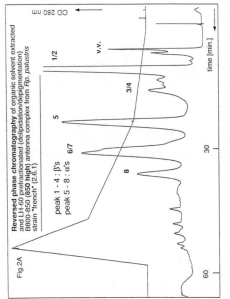

Fig. 2A:

Reversed phase chromatography of organic solvent extracted and LH-60 prefractionated (delipidation/depigmentation) B800-850 (850 **high**) antenna complex from *Rp. palustris* strain "french" (2.6.1)

peak 1 - 4 : β's
peak 5 - 8 : α's

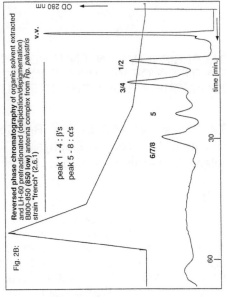

Fig. 2B:

Reversed phase chromatography of organic solvent extracted and LH-60 prefractionated (delipidation/depigmentation) B800-850 (850 **low**) antenna complex from *Rp. palustris* strain "french" (2.6.1).

peak 1 - 4 : β's
peak 5 - 8 : α's

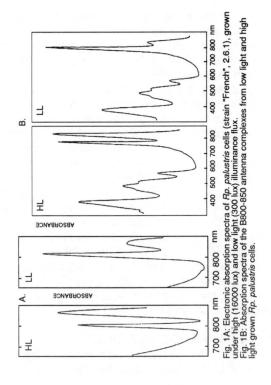

Fig. 1A: Electronic absorption spectra of *Rp. palustris* cells (strain "French", 2.6.1), grown under high (16000 lux) and low light (300 lux) illuminance flux.
Fig. 1B: Absorption spectra of the B800-850 antenna complexes from low light and high light grown *Rp. palustris* cells.

Species (A)

Species (A)	N-terminal (1)	membrane-spanning (2)	C-terminal portion (3)
Rhodobacter sphaeroides B800-850-α 2.4.1	MTNGKIWLVKPTVG	VPLFLSAAVIASVVIHAAVL	TTTWLPAYYQGSAAVAAE
Rhodobacter capsulatus B800-850-α	MNNAKIWTVVKPSTGI	PLILGAVAVAALIVHAG	LLTNTTWFANYWNGNPMATVVAVAPAQ
Rp. acidophila Ac7050 B800-850-α	MNQGKIWTVVNPSVGL	PLLLGSVTVIAILVHAAVL	SHTTWFPAYWQGGLKKAA
Rp. acidophila Ac7050 B800-820-α	MNQGKIWTVVPPAFGL	PLMLGAVAITALLVHAAVL	THTTWYAAFLQGGVKKAA
Rp. acidophila Ac7750 B800-850-α	MNQGKIWTVVPAIGI	PALLGSVTVIAILVHLAIL	SHTTWFPAYWQGGVKKAA
Rp. acidophila Ac7750 B800-820-α	MNQGKIWTVVNPAVGL	PLLLGSVAITALLVHLAVL	THTTWFPAFTQGGLKKAA
Rp. palustris 2.6.1,B800/850-α	MNQARIWTVVKPTVGL	PLLLGSVTVIAILVHFAVL	SHTTWFSKYWNGPA..
Rp. palustris 2.6.1,B800/850-α	MNQGRIWTVVKPTVGL	PLLLGSVAIMVFLVHFAVL	THTTWVAKFMNGKA..
Rp. palustris 2.6.1,B800/850-α	MNQGRIWTVVNPGVGL	PLLLGSVTVIAILVHYAVL	SNTTWFPKYWNGATVAAPAAA...
Rp. palustris 2.6.1,B800/850-α	MNQGRIWTVVPTVGL	PLLLGSVTVIAILVHFAVL	SNTTWFPKYWNGKA..
Rp. palustris LH II a_a(1e5)	MNQARIWTVVKPTVGL	PLLLGSVTVIAILVHFAVL	SHTTWFSKYWNGKAA|IESSVNVG
Rp. palustris LH II a_d(1e5)	MNQGRIWTVVKPTVGL	PLLLGSVAIMVFLVHFAVL	THTTWVAKFMNGKAA|IESSIKAV
Rp. palustris LH II a_b(1e5)	MNQGRIWTVVNPGVGL	PLLLGSVTVIAILVHYAVL	SNTTWFPKYWNGATVAAPAA|PAPAAPAAKK
Rp. palustris LH II a_c(1e5)	MNQGRIWTVVSPTVGL	PLLLGSVAAIAFAVHFAVL	ENTSWVAAFMNGKSVAAAPA|PAAPAAKK

Species (B)

Species (B)	N-terminal(1)	membrane-spanning(2)	C-terminal portion(3)
Rb. sphaeroides B800-850-β 2.4.1	TDDLNKVWPSGLTVAEAEEVHKQLILGTRVF	GGMALIAHFLAAA	ATPWLG
Rb. capsulatus B800-850-β	MTDDKAGPSGLSLKEAEEIHSYLIDGTRVF	GAMALVAHILSAI	ATPWLG
Rp. acidophila Ac7050 B800-850-β	ADDVKGLTGLTAAESELHKHVIDGTRVF	FVIAFAHVLAFAF	SPWLH
Rp. acidophila Ac7050 B800-820-β	AEVLTSEQAELHKHVIDGTRVF	LVIAAIAHFLAFT	LTPWLH
Rp. acidophila Ac7750 B800-850-β	ATLTAEQSELHKYVIDGTRVF	LGLALVAHFIAFS	ATPWLH
Rp. acidophila Ac7750 B800-820-β_1	AVLSPEQSELHKYVIDGARAF	LGIALVAHFLAFS	MTPWLH
Rp. acidophila Ac7750 B800-820-β_2	ADKPLTADQAELHKYVIDGARAF	VAIAAFAHVLAYS	LTPWLH
Rp. palustris 2.6.1 B8/850-β	DKTLTGLTVEESELHKHVIDGTRIF	GAIAIVAHFLAYV	YSPWLH
Rp. palustris 2.6.1 B8/850-β	ADDPNKVWPTGLTIAESELHKHVIDGTRIF	GAIAIVAHFLAYV	YSPWLH
Rp. palustris 2.6.1 B8/850-β	MVDDPNKVWPTGLTIAESELHKHVIDGSRIF	VAIAIVAHFLAYV	YSPWLH
Rp. palustris LH II β_a(1e5)	MA|DKTLTGLTVEESELHKHVIDGTRIF	GAIAIVAHFLAYV	YSPWLH
Rp. palustris LH II β_b(1e5)	MA|DDPNKVWPTGLTIAESELHKHVIDGTRIF	GAIAIVAHFLAYV	YSPWLH
Rp. palustris LH II β_c(1e5)	MVDDSKKVWPTGLTIAESEIHKHVIDGARIF	VAIAIVAHFLAYV	YSPWLH
Rp. palustris LH II β_d(1e5)	MVDDPNKVWPTGLTIAESELHKHVIDGSRIF	VAIAIVAHFLAYV	YSPWLH

Fig. 3: Amino acid sequences of the α-(**A**) and β-(**B**) peripheral antenna polypeptides of *Rb. sphaeroides*, *Rb. capsulatus*, *Rp. acidophila* (strains 7050, 7750) and *Rp. palustris* (strains 2.6.1, ("french") and 1e5). Bold letters indicate transmembrane-located histidines. || indicates lower line of the photosynthetic membrane. | indicates presumable posttranslational enzymatic processing (possibly partial processing)

absorption spectra of the peripheral antenna complexes B800-850 (high) and B800-850 (low) are depicted in Fig. 1B. The antenna apoproteins have been isolated from the purified light-harvesting complexes (or from photosynthetic membranes) by using organic solvent extraction and LH-60 gel-filtration chromatography essentially as described elsewhere [7,8]. Subsequent reversed phase chromatography [9] yielded for the spectrally dissimilar peripheral antenna complexes different polypeptide patterns (Figs. 2A and 2B). According to microsequence analyses at least four α- and three β-polypeptides were identified (Fig. 3). The determined amino acid sequences are compared with those from the peripheral antenna apoproteins from *Rb. sphaeroides, Rb. capsulatus, Rp. acidophila* (strains 7050 and 7750) and with the very recently determined DNA sequences of four α- and four β-peripheral antenna polypeptides of *Rp. palustris* strain1e5, which apparently synthesizes only the B800-850 (high) light-harvesting complex [10]. From our protein-chemical analyses it became evident that some of the α-polypeptides apparently are to some extent posttranslationally processed in their C-terminal part (verified by carboxypeptidase checks and amino acid composition). As indicated in Fig. 3 the β-apoproteins are modified only to a minor degree in their N-termini.

Regarding the variable spectral forms of the peripheral antennae of *Rp. palustris* the question arises, whether these antenna components may, as in the plant system the Chl a/b protein, being involved in regulating the amount of excitation energy to the reaction centre by migrating between the appressed and non-appressed regions of the photosynthetic membrane. Thus, this lateral heterogeneity of light-gathering components may, as in the plant system optimize photon capturing and if necessary, may help to minimize damage to the reaction centers. Whereas in the plant system under certain environmental conditions the different lateral arrangement of the LH-complexes do not invoke harsh spectral variations, the peripheral antenna systems of *Rp. palustris* may vary their typical absorption characteristics in the near-infrared as a consequence of the different microenvironment (different polypeptide pattern).

REFERENCES
[1]   Varga, A.R. and Staehelin, L.A., (1985) *J. of Bacteriol.,* 161, 921.
[2]   Miyazaki, T. and Morita, S. (1981) *Photosynthetica,* 15, 238.
[3]   Hayashi, H., Nakano, M., and Morita, S (1982) *J. Biochem.,* 92, 1805.
[4]   Cogdell, R.J., Durant, I., Valentine, J., Lindsay, J.G., and Schmidt, K. (1983) *Biochim. Biophys. Acta,* 722, 427.
[5]   Brunisholz, R.A. Bissig, I., Niederer, E., Suter, F., and Zuber, H., in *Progress in Photosynthesis,* Biggins, J., Ed., Martinus Nijhoff Publishers, 1987, II.1, 13
[6]   Bissig, I., R.A. Brunisholz, F. Suter, F., Cogdell, R.J., and Zuber, H. (1988) *Z. Naturforschung,* 43c, 77.
[7]   Brunisholz, R.A, Suter, F., and Zuber, H. (1984) *Hoppe-Seyler's Z. Physiol. Chem.,* 365, 675.
[8]   Brunisholz, R.A., Bissig, I., Wagner-Huber, R., Frank, G., Suter, F., Niederer, E., and Zuber, H. (1989) *Z. Naturforschung,* 44c, 407.
[9]   Brunisholz, R.A. and Zuber, H. (1987) *Experientia ,* 43.
[10] Tadros, M.H. and Waterkamp, K. (1989) *The EMBO Journal,* 8, 1303.

COMPARISON OF THE STRUCTURAL SUBUNIT, B820, OF CORE LIGHT-HARVESTING
COMPLEXES OF PHOTOSYNTHETIC BACTERIA.

Barbara A. Heller, Pamela S. Parkes-Loach, Mary C. Chang, and Paul A.
Loach. Department of Biochemistry, Molecular Biology and Cell Biology,
Northwestern University, Evanston, Il 60208 USA

1. INTRODUCTION

    The photoreceptor complexes of Rhodobacter sphaeroides and
Rhodobacter capsulatus have many features in common. Their reaction
centers have about 80 % homology between the amino acid sequences of
their respective L, M, and H polypeptides (1). The electrochemical
and spectroscopic details for the primary photochemical events are nearly
identical (2). Both have a core light-harvesting (LH) complex with a Q_y
band near 875 nm and an accessory LH complex, B800-850, whose amount
varies inversely with the light intensity used for growing the bacteria.
    In our laboratory we have applied to Rb. sphaeroides and Rb.
capsulatus the methodology used for preparation of a structural subunit
of the core LH complex of Rhodospirillum rubrum (3-5). A comparable
structural subunit can be isolated from Rb. sphaeroides and Rb.
capsulatus. The details for the preparation of each will be published
elsewhere.

2. RESULTS AND DISCUSSION

    The structural subunits of the core LH complexes have very
similar absorption and CD spectra (see Figures 1 and 2).

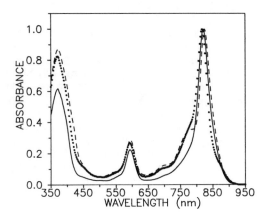

Figure 1. Absorption spectra
of the B820-type complex
prepared from Rs. rubrum (—
), Rb. capsulatus (•••) and Rb.
sphaeroides (---). For
comparison, the spectra were
normalized to a value of one
in their Q_y band.

M. Baltscheffsky (ed.), Current Research in Photosynthesis, Vol. II, 65–68.
© 1990 Kluwer Academic Publishers. Printed in the Netherlands.

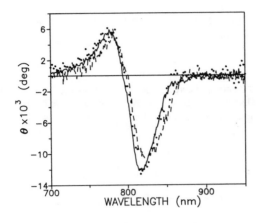

Figure 2. CD spectra of the B820-type complexes whose aborption spectra are given in Figure 1.

As may be noted from Figure 1, the Q_y band is located near 820 nm in each case, but there is some variation. It was found to be at 816, 820, and 825 nm in Rb. capsulatus, Rs. rubrum, and Rb. sphaeroides, respectively. These complexes were accordingly named B816, B820 and B825. The CD spectrum of each has a minimum near the Q_y absorption maximum and a peak near 780 nm. Together with the absorption spectra, this data strongly supports the conclusion that the detailed structural features of each are nearly identical.

The isolated structural subunits can be reversibly dissociated to free BChl a and the alpha and beta polypeptides, as well as reassociated to form a B875-like complex. Furthermore, the separately isolated alpha and beta polypeptides and BChl can be used to reconstitute the subunit structure. Especially interesting is the fact that B816, B820, and B825 may be reconstituted with BChl and their respective beta polypeptides only.

B820 and B825 have comparable stabilities in the dark at room temperature, however, B816 is much less stable. The source of the instability is not in the chromophore since both Rb. sphaeroides and Rb. capsulatus have identical BChl a chromophores containing a phytyl esterifying alcohol. Thus, the differences in polypeptide amino acid sequences must account for the instability.

Although the absorption spectra of B875 from each species are nearly the same, the CD spectra show some significant differences, especially that of Rb. sphaeroides compared with Rs. rubrum and Rb. capsulatus. In Figure 3, the CD spectrum of chromatophores from Rs. rubrum is compared with those from the B800-850-minus mutant of Rb. sphaeroides (puc705-BA) and a B800-850-minus mutant of Rb. capsulatus (MW442).

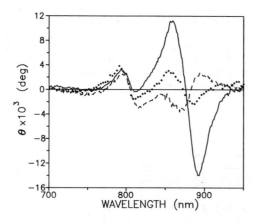

Figure 3. CD spectra of chromatophores of Rs. rubrum (——), the MW442 mutant of Rb. capsulatus (⋯) and the puc705-BA mutant of Rb. sphaeroides (---). All were normalized to a Q_y band absorbance of one.

Although the RC contributes strongly to the spectra between 700 and 850 nm, it is clear that the B875 LH complexes display rather different CD spectra. In spite of the CD spectral variation, each B875 complex seems to function with high efficiency in delivering excitation quanta to the RC.

Because the β-polypeptides are primarily responsible for binding BChl in the structural subunits (see (5) and paper by Parkes-Loach et al., this volume), it is interesting to compare the amino acid sequences of these polypeptides (see Figure 4). Since B816, B820, and B825 have very similar spectral and biochemical behavior, key structural elements must have been conserved. As has been pointed out previously (6), the two histidine residues are conserved as are the hydrophobic stretches of amino acids in the middle of each β-polypeptide which are likely alpha-helical membrane-spanning portions. But what other groups are important in binding BChl? From reconstitution studies using BChl a analogs (see paper by Loach et al. in this volume), three functionalities of the BChl a structure seem to stand out as important elements in protein binding. These were the Mg^{++}, the $C-13^2$ carbomethoxy group and the C-3 acetyl group. The latter two functionalities are presumably involved in accepting hydrogen bonds from the protein. Thus, one might examine the protein structure for functionally conserved amino acids that could provide such hydrogen bonds.

It has been suggested that the histidine closer to the C-terminal end of the polypeptide is a site for coordination to Mg^{++} of BChl (3,7). If this is correct, and the BChl molecule is oriented with five of the six oxygen atoms near the aqueous interface at the C-terminal end (as might be expected from model studies of BChl in monolayers and bilayers), then the amino acid residues near the C-terminus would be required to provide the groups for hydrogen bonding to the $C-13^2$ carbomethoxy group. The only sequences common to all three at the C-terminus that could provide hydrogen bond donors from the side chains are Trp 44 and 47, and Arg 45. Also limited are the possible amino acids that could provide the hydrogen bonding group to the C-3 acetyl carbonyl. Since the latter group would exist somewhere in the middle of the membrane-spanning portion, the only candidate strictly conserved appears to be Ser 25.

The importance of these functionalities can be systematically determined by the combined use of site-directed-mutagenesis and/or chemical modification and reconstitution of the complexes. Such an approach is being undertaken in our laboratory.

Figure 4.   C-terminal amino acid sequences of β-polypeptides.

```
   22  24 |26  28  30  32  34  36 |38  40  42 |44 |46 |48  50  52  54
Rb. capsulatus
 A  V  Y  M  S  G  L  S  A  F  I  A  V  A  V  L  A  H  L  A  V  M  I  W  R  P  W  F
Rb. sphaeroides
 S  V  Y  M  S  G  L  W  P  F  S  A  V  A  I  V  A  H  L  A  V  Y  I  W  R  P  W  F

   21  23 |25  27  29  31  33  35 |37  39  41 |43 |45 |47  49  51  53
Rs. rubrum
 K  I  F  T  S  S  I  L  V  F  F  G  V  A  A  F  A  H  L  L  V  W  I  W  R  P  W  V  P  G  P  N  G  Y  S
```

3.   ACKNOWLEDGEMENTS

We would like to thank Dr. Barry Marrs (Du Pont Corp.) for providing the MW442 mutant of Rb. capsulatus and Dr. Samuel Kaplan (University of Illinois) for providing the puc705-BA mutant of Rb. sphaeroides used in these studies. This research was supported by grants from the U.S. Public Health Service (GM 11741) and the National Science Foundation (DMB-8717997).

REFERENCES
1 Williams, J. C., Steiner, L. A., Feher, G., and Simon, M. I. (1984) Proc. Natl. Acad. Sci. U.S. 81, 7303-7307.
2 Kirmaier, C. and Holton, D. (1987) Photosynthesis Res. 13, 225-260.
3 Loach, P. A., Parkes, P. S., Miller, J. F., Hinchigeri, S. B., & Callahan, P. M. (1985) in Cold Spring Harbor Symposium on Molecular Biology of the Photosynthetic Apparatus (Arntzen, C., Bogorad, L., Bonitz, S., & Steinback, K., Eds.) pp 197-209, Cold Spring Harbor Laboratory, Cold Spring Harbor, NY.
4 Miller, J. F., Hinchigeri, S. B., Parkes-Loach, P. S., Callahan, P.M., Sprinkle, J. R., & Loach P. A. (1987) Biochemistry 26, 5055-5062.
5 Parkes-Loach, P. S., Sprinkle, J. R., & Loach, P. A. (1988) Biochemistry 27, 2718-2727.
6 Zuber, H. (1986) Encyclopedia of Plant Physiol., Vol. 19, Eds. L.A. Staehlin and C.J. Arntzen, Ch 3, pp. 238-251.
7 van Grondelle, R. (1985) Biochim. Biophys. Acta 811, 147-195.

PROBING THE BACTERIOCHLOROPHYLL BINDING SITE REQUIREMENTS OF THE CORE
LIGHT-HARVESTING COMPLEX OF PHOTOSYNTHETIC BACTERIA USING BCHL ANALOGS

Paul A. Loach[1], Tomasz Michalski[2] and Pamela S. Parkes-Loach[1].
[1]Department of Biochemistry, Molecular Biology and Cell Biology,
Northwestern University, Evanston, Il 60208 and [2]Argonne National
Laboratory, Argonne, Il 60439 USA

1. INTRODUCTION
    The methodology developed (1-3) for reconstitution of the light-
harvesting (LH) complex of Rhodospirillum rubrum, B873, and its
structural subunit (B820) has made it possible to begin probing
structural requirements of the bacteriochlorophyll (BChl) binding
site(s). Using the separately-isolated α- and β-polypeptides of R.
rubrum and a series of BChl a analogs, evidence was obtained for the
importance of three functional groups and of the oxidation state of the
macrocyclic ring for B820 and B873 formation, as well as for a role for
the esterifying alcohol (tail) in stabilizing the B820 complex. In this
paper, the results are summarized and the role of the esterifying alcohol
in B820 and B873 formation is discussed. A more detailed account of the
experiments and methodology will be published elsewhere.

2. METHODS
    Two different procedures were used for the reconstitution assay.
In both methods, the α- and β-polypeptides were dissolved in
hexafluoroacetone and then proportioned such that each sample had equal
amounts of each (usually 0.1 - 0.25 mg). The polypeptides were dried
onto the sides of a flask by rotary evaporation. An aerobic dilution
procedure was used when the analog tested was relatively stable and when
it was desired to mix all components in 4.5% n-octyl-β-D-glucopyranoside
(OG). This method has been previously described (3).
    A second procedure was used when samples were unstable in air or
when a higher concentration of components was desired. In this case,
the α- and β-polypeptides were dissolved in 0.5 mL of 4.5% OG in 0.05 M
phosphate buffer, pH 7.5, and 2.0 mL phosphate buffer (no OG) added. For
anaerobic experiments, all the following steps were conducted under
nitrogen. BChl a or an analog was added from an acetone or a pyridine
solution and then additional buffer added until the B820 spectra were
optimal (usually between 0.65 and 0.75% OG). For B873 formation, the
sample was handled as in the first procedure.

M. Baltscheffsky (ed.), Current Research in Photosynthesis, Vol. II, 69–72.
© 1990 *Kluwer Academic Publishers. Printed in the Netherlands.*

3. RESULTS & DISCUSSION

The structure of BChl $\underline{a}$ is shown below with the changes indicated for the analogs tested. The functional groups that have so far been identified as being required for binding are enclosed within the solid ovals. It was expected that Mg^{++} would be a required component, as it provides a site for ligand coordination from the protein. The groups attached to the C-13^2 position seem to be quite important, as the two analogs with changes at that location (pyroBChl $\underline{a}$ and 13^2-hydroxyBChl $\underline{a}$) failed to form red-shifted species. A similar requirement for the C-3 acetyl group was found, as indicated by the lack of formation of red-shifted species with BChl g. Thus, the C-13^2 carbomethoxy group and the C-3 acetyl groups are probably involved in hydrogen bonding to the protein in B820 and B873.

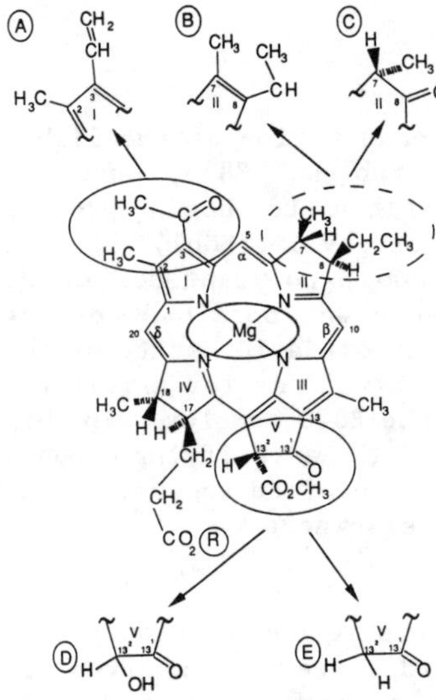

R = farnesyl (f), geranylgeranyl (gg),

or phytyl (p)

BChl a_p = unmodified structure + p;

BChl a_{gg} = unmodified structure + gg;

BChl b_p = C + p;

BChl g_f = A + C + f;

PyroBChl a = E + p;

13^2-OH BChl a = D + p;

Et BChl a = unmodified structure + R = -OCH$_2$CH$_3$;

2-hydroxyethyl pyroBChl a = pyroBChl a + R = -O(CH$_2$)$_2$OH;

Chl a_p = A + B + p;

3-desvinyl-3-acetyl Chl a_p = B + p;

Chl b_p = A + p + B* (where 7-CH$_3$ is replaced by CHO).

The oxidation state of the macrocyclic ring is also important in forming red-shifted species. Three analogs having chlorin oxidation states, 3-acetyl chlorophyll (Chl) $\underline{a}$, Chl $\underline{a}$, and Chl $\underline{b}$, all failed to show spectral red shifts with the protein. The first of these structures is exactly like BChl $\underline{a}$, except for the oxidation of ring II. These results suggest that the more flexible BChl ring system may be required for appropriate binding.

The role of the esterifying alcohol (tail) is especially interesting. BChl $\underline{a}$ with geranylgeranyl (the naturally-occurring esterifying alcohol in $\underline{R}$. $\underline{rubrum}$, BChl $\underline{a}_{gg}$), phytyl (BChl $\underline{a}_p$), or ethyl (BChl $\underline{a}_e$) tails all formed B820 and B873 species. Absorption spectra of the complexes reconstituted with BChl $\underline{a}_e$ are shown in Figure 1. Small differences in λ_{max} were seen in the complexes with the different tails; those of the phytyl and geranylgeranyl derivatives were identical (for spectra of the phytyl derivative, see paper by Parkes-Loach et al., this volume), but BChl $\underline{a}_e$ free in detergent solution and in B820 was several nanometers blue-shifted and, in B873, sometimes was several nanometers red-shifted. All the B873 complexes had comparable stability (measured by following the far-red absorbance of the complex with time), but the B820 prepared with BChl $\underline{a}_e$ was much less stable than that prepared with either BChl $\underline{a}_{gg}$ or BChl $\underline{a}_p$ (see Table 1). The instability of B820 is presumably the result of the equilibrium of the B820 species with the completely-dissociated 777-nm form (3) in which BChl $\underline{a}_e$ is some 100-fold more rapidly degraded than BChl $\underline{a}_{gg}$ or BChl $\underline{a}_p$ (Table 1). Thus, it seems that the tail is important for the overall stability of the B820 complex. The regular spacing of the methyl groups of each of the four isoprenoid units in the phytyl and geranylgeranyl esterifying alcohols may pack well with the α-helical structure of the protein, thus stabilizing the complex.

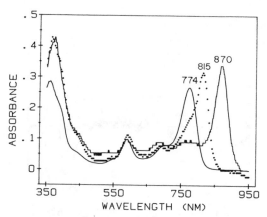

Fig. 1. Absorption spectra of BChl $\underline{a}_e$ (labelled 774), B820 (•••) and B873 (label 870) reconstitued with BChl $\underline{a}_e$.

TABLE 1
STABILITY OF BCHL COMPLEXES

| | $\underline{t}_{1/2}$ | |
	in B820 (min)	in .9%OG (min)
BChl $\underline{a}_{gg}$	1000	>2000
BChl $\underline{a}_p$	1050	>2000
BChl $\underline{a}_e$	35	25

Upon comparing the CD spectra of the B820 and B873 species reconstituted with BChl $\underline{a}_{gg}$, BChl $\underline{a}_p$, or BChl $\underline{a}_e$ (see Figures 2 and 3), an unexpected effect was found regarding the reconstituted B873 complexes. Although the CD spectra of the three reconstituted B820 complexes were nearly identical (Figure 2) and the CD spectra of the reconstituted B873 with the BChl $\underline{a}_p$ or BChl $\underline{a}_e$ were the same, that with BChl $\underline{a}_{gg}$ was different (see Figure 3). In fact, the BChl $\underline{a}_{gg}$ B873 CD was very similar to the in vivo CD of the core LH complex of $\underline{R}$. rubrum chromatophores, whereas the BChl $\underline{a}_p$ and BChl $\underline{a}_e$ spectra appear to be inverted in the Q_y region. Thus, the native tail structure seems to be required in order to appropriately reconstitute B873 of $\underline{R}$. rubrum. Since the absorbance spectra and stability of both the B820 and B873 reconstituted complexes are nearly the same for those made with the phytyl or geranylgeranyl tails, the effect on structure of the three additional double bonds in the geranylgeranyl tail relative to phytyl must be subtle. Because B873 is formed by association of B820 units, the tails of the BChl $\underline{a}$ molecules may be located between such associated units and play an important role in the kind of interaction that occurs between separate chromophores on the surface of these units.

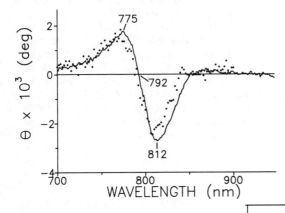

Figure 2. CD spectra of B820 reconstituted with BChl a_e (•••) and BChl a_{gg} (——). B820 reconstituted with BChl a_p (data not shown) was nearly identical to that reconstituted with BChl a_{gg}.

Figure 3. CD spectra of B873 reconstituted with BChl a_{gg} (•••) and BChl a_p (——).

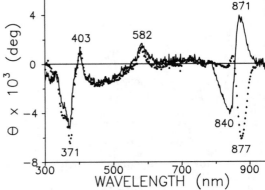

4. ACKNOWLEDGEMENTS

This research was supported by grants to P.A.L. from the U.S. Public Health Service (GM 11741) and the National Science Foundation (DMB-8717997). Part of the work was supported by the U.S. Department of Energy, Office of Basic Energy Sciences, Division of Chemical Sciences under contract W-31-109-Eng-38 (T.J.M.). We would like to express our appreciation to Wendy Bass and Ursula Smith for expert technical assistance.

REFERENCES

1 Loach, P. A., Parkes, P. S., Miller, J. F., Hinchigeri, S. B., & Callahan, P. M. (1985) in Cold Spring Harbor Symposium on Molecular Biology of the Photosynthetic Apparatus (Arntzen, C., Bogorad, L., Bonitz, S., & Steinback, K., Eds.) pp 197-209, Cold Spring Harbor Laboratory, Cold Spring Harbor, NY.
2 Miller, J. F., Hinchigeri, S. B., Parkes-Loach, P. S., Callahan, P.M., Sprinkle, J. R., & Loach P. A. (1987) Biochemistry 26, 5055-5062.
3 Parkes-Loach, P. S., Sprinkle, J. R., & Loach, P. A. (1988) Biochemistry 27, 2718-2727.

RECONSTITUTION OF THE CORE LIGHT-HARVESTING COMPLEX OF PHOTOSYNTHETIC BACTERIA WITH SELECTED POLYPEPTIDES

Pamela S. Parkes-Loach, Barbara A. Heller, Mary C. Chang, Wendy J. Bass, Julie A. Chanatry, and Paul A. Loach
Department of Biochemistry, Molecular Biology, and Cell Biology, Northwestern University, Evanston, IL 60208-3500, USA

1. INTRODUCTION

It is now possible to reconstitute the core light-harvesting complex, B873, of Rhodospirillum rubrum using the α- and β-polypeptides and bacteriochlorophyll (BChl) a that had been separately isolated and purified (1). This ability to put the components of the complex back together allows us to explore structure-function relationships by modifying the component protein and BChl. In this preliminary report we compare the reconstitutions of the B875 complexes from R. rubrum, Rhodobacter capsulatus MW442 (a B800-850⁻ mutant), and Rhodopseudomonas viridis. Hybrid reconstitutions where the α-polypeptide of one bacterium is mixed with the β-polypeptide of another are also described. For this manuscript, B875 refers to the generic core light-harvesting complex or to the core complex of Rb. capsulatus, B873 refers to the core complex of R. rubrum when carotenoids have been removed (B881 is the wild type), and B1015 refers to the core complex of Rps. viridis. B820 is generic for the structural subunit of the core complex.

2. PROCEDURES

The polypeptides were extracted from the bacteria using chloroform-methanol solvents and purified with gel filtration and, in some cases, ion exchange chromatography (1-3). HPLC was used when further purification was required. The identities of the polypeptides were confirmed by N-terminal amino acid sequencing.

The general procedure for reconstitution involved dissolving the polypeptides in hexafluoroacetone and mixing them in a 1:1 ratio (their concentrations were determined by measuring their absorbances at 287 nm). They were then dried onto the sides of a flask and redissolved in phosphate buffer containing 4.5% n-octyl β-D-glucopyranoside (OG). BChl in acetone was added to the solution at this point or after the solution was diluted with buffer to 0.7% OG. B820 usually forms under the latter conditions. To form B875, the samples were either diluted 1:1 with buffer or chilled (4°C, 1 h - overnight). Each system required slight variations in the general procedure. Complex formation was often enhanced by varying the % OG of the buffer, by chilling the sample, or by increasing the concentration of the protein.

M. Baltscheffsky (ed.), Current Research in Photosynthesis, Vol. II, 73–76.
© 1990 Kluwer Academic Publishers. Printed in the Netherlands.

3. RESULTS AND DISCUSSION
3.1. Reconstitution of Core Complexes
    R. rubrum B881-α and -β and BChl a. Reconstitution of the B820
and B873 complexes of R. rubrum from its α- and β-polypeptides has been
previously described (1). The B820 and B873 complexes are readily formed
and are the most stable of the complexes of the three bacteria described
here. They are stable in the cold and dark for months. The CD spectrum
of reconstituted B873 is in-vivo-like (see paper by Loach et al. in these
proceedings).
    Rb. capsulatus B875-α and-β and BChl a. The absorption spectra of
the complexes formed from the Rb. capsulatus (MW442 mutant) B875
polypeptides and BChl a are shown in Figure 1. These complexes are not
as stable as those of R. rubrum and require higher protein concentrations
to form clean B820 (without a large amount of free BChl, the 777-nm
absorbance, remaining). B875 is difficult to form. The B820 CD spectrum
is identical to that of R. rubrum, but the B875 CD spectrum is inverted
in the near infrared relative to that of R. rubrum and relative to the
in vivo spectrum in Rb. capsulatus (data not shown). The B875 CD of R.
rubrum can also be inverted at low concentrations of complex and with
certain procedures (4).

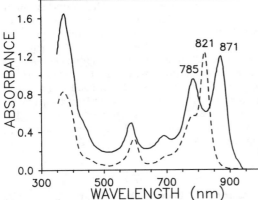

Figure 1. The absorption
spectra of the α- and β-
polypeptides of Rb. capsulatus
and BChl a at 0.8% OG (---,
B820- forming conditions) and
at 0.6% OG, cold (——,
B875-forming conditions). The
latter spectrum was multiplied
by 10 to be on the same scale
as the B820 spectrum. The
absorbance at 785 nm is due to
free BChl a.

    Rps. viridis B1015-α, -β , and -γ and BChl b. The absorption
spectrum of the reconstitututed B890 complex formed with Rps. viridis α-,
β-, and γ-polypeptides and BChl b is shown in Figure 2. This is probably
equivalent to the R. rubrum B820 subunit. Thornber et al. (5) have
described a B880 form of the Rps. viridis light-harvesting complex.
The CD spectrum of the reconstituted B890 is similar to that of R. rubrum
B820 (Figure 2, inset). The B890 complex is very unstable; it forms for
only a few hours in the cold. It degrades to 804 nm upon warming, but
re-forms B890 when chilled again. The BChl b in B890 also degrades
quickly to the oxidized BChl absorbing at 695 nm. This lack of
protection is similar to that seen with R. rubrum B820. The BChl in the
R. rubrum B873 complex is more protected (6). We have not as yet been
able to further red-shift the B890 complex to the in vivo B1015.

3.2. Reconstitution with Mixed Polypeptides
    By mixing polypeptides from different bacteria, various

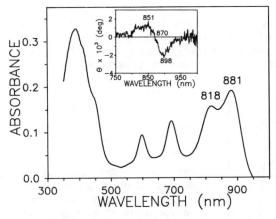

Figure 2. The absorption spectrum of the complex formed with the α-, β-, and γ-polypeptides of Rps. viridis and BChl b at 0.86% OG, cold. Oxidized BChl b is responsible for the absorbance at 695 nm and free BChl b is resposible for the absorbance at 818 nm. Inset: The CD spectrum of the complex.

structure-function questions can be asked. For instance, is the Rb. capsulatus β-polypeptide the best suited for complex formation with its own α-polypeptide? Will the α- and β-polypeptides from different bacteria recognize each other and form stable complexes? In Figure 3 absorption spectra are shown of complexes of: (A) the Rb. capsulatus B875 α- and β-polypeptides, (B) only the B875 β-polypeptide of Rb. capsulatus, (C) the β-polypeptide of Rb. capsulatus and the α-polypeptide of R. rubrum. B875-β alone formed B816, but did not shift to 875 nm.

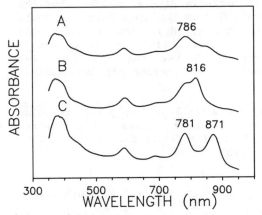

Figure 3. The absorption spectra of (A) Rb. capsulatus B875 α- and β-polypeptides and BChl a, (B) the β-polypeptide alone of Rb. capsulatus and BChl a, and (C) the β-polypeptide of Rb. capsulatus and the α-polypeptide of R. rubrum. All were in 0.7% OG and had been stored cold overnight.

Under these experimental conditions only a small amount of B875 formed with Rb. capsulatus B875-α and B875-β and at B820-forming conditions with these polypeptides, less B820 formed than with B875-β alone (data not shown). The most successful reconstitution was with the Rb. capsulatus β-polypeptide and the R. rubrum α-polypeptide - the hybrid system.

In another experiment, R. rubrum B881-α was reconstituted with the β-polypeptide of Rps. viridis. A large amount of stable B875 formed at B875-forming conditions (Figure 4). It is interesting that this hybrid B875 has the stability and absorption spectrum similar to B873 of R. rubrum and not the instability and greater red shift characteristic of Rps. viridis complexes.

In contrast, some of the hybrid reconstitutions showed inhibition of B820 formation as well as lack of B875 formation (R. rubrum B881-β and Rb. capsulatus B875-α or Rhodopsuedomonas sphaeroides B800-850-α, for example). Thus there can be a lack of appropriate complex formation with some of the hybrid pairs.

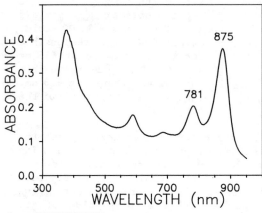

Figure 4. The absorption spectrum of the β-polypeptide of Rps. viridis and the α-polypeptide of R. rubrum at 0.7% OG, cold overnight.

4. CONCLUSIONS

The B820-type of structural subunit of the core complex can be reconstituted in all photosynthetic bacteria studied so far, but the B875-type of complex was more difficult to form (Rb. capsulatus) or would not form under the conditions studied (Rps. viridis). Our initial hybrid reconstitution experiments indicate that, although some hybrid combinations work well (some working better than the in vivo combinations), others lack the specific requirements for association.

5. ACKNOWLEDGEMENTS

We would like to thank Dr. Barry Marrs (Du Pont Corp.) for providing the MW442 mutant of Rb. capsulatus used in these studies. This research was supported by grants from the U. S. Public Health Service (GM 11741) and the National Science Foundation (DMB-8717997).

REFERENCES

1 Parkes-Loach, P.S., Sprinkle, J.R., and Loach, P.A. (1988) Biochemistry 27, 2718-2727
2 Tadros, M.H., Suter, F., Drews, G., and Zuber, H. (1983) Eur. J. Biochem. 129, 533-536.
3 Brunisholz, R.A., Jay, F., Suter, F., and Zuber, H. (1985) Biol. Chem. Hoppe-Seyler 366, 87-98.
4 Miller, J. F., Hinchigeri, S.B., Parkes-Loach, P.S., Callahan, P.M., Sprinkle, J.R., and Loach, P.A. (1987) Biochemistry 26, 5055-5062.
5 Thornber, J.P., Trosper, T.L., and Strouse, C.E. (1978) in The Photosynthetic Bacteria (Clayton, R.K. and Sistrom, W.R., eds.) pp. 113-160, Plenum, New York
6 Callahan, P.M., Cotton, T.M., and Loach, P.A. (1987) in Progress in Photosynthesis Research (Biggins, J., ed.) I.3.325-I.3.328, Martinus Nijhoff, The Netherlands

PHOSPHORYLATION OF THE CHROMATOPHORE MEMBRANES OF RHODOSPIRILLUM RUBRUM
G9 AND ISOLATION OF A B875 PROTEIN KINASE

R. Ghosh, P. Tschopp, S. Eicher, and R. Bachofen, Institute for Plant
Biology, Zollikerstr. 107, CH-8008 Zurich, Switzerland.

1. INTRODUCTION
Protein phosphorylation of light-harvesting complexes has been well-
established as a mechanism for regulating light energy transfer in the
chloroplasts of higher plants [1]. However, only recently has an analogous
phenomenon been implicated for the chromatophore membranes of purple
non-sulfur bacteria [2,3,4]. In particular, Allen and Holmes [4] have
shown that electron transfer within the chromatophore membrane may be
regulated by the degree of phosphorylation of the light harvesting complex
[B875]. The results have been confirmed and a B875-kinase isolated from
the cytoplasmic fraction.

2. MATERIALS AND METHODS
Chromatophores were isolated by French press treatment of washed cells,
followed by low speed centrifugation to yield the crude extract which
was separated by two times high speed centrifugation to yield a pellet
(crude chromatophores) and the water-soluble fraction (supernatant),
containing the water-soluble material. Purified chromatophores were
obtained by sucrose gradient centrifugation of the crude chromatophores.
The phosphorylation assay contained routinely ATP (0.5mM), $MgCl_2$ (20mM),
venturicidin to inhibit ATPase activity (2μg/ml), DBMIB (2,5-Dibromo-3-
methyl-6-isopropyl-p-benzoquinone) an electron transport inhibitor (100μM),
TrisHCl pH 7.5 (50mM), protein (or chromatophores) (30μg), with or without
supernatant (30μg)) and ATP (γ-^{32}P)(25μCi).
Samples were incubated in the light for 30 minutes and then precipitated
with 7% TCA. The pellet was washed once with buffer and then resuspended
in SDS-sample buffer and separated on 15% SDS-PAGE gels. The gels were
stained with Coomassie Blue, dried and autoradiographed at -70°C for 2-
4 days.
The protein kinase was isolated from the supernatant by affinity chromatography on ATP-Sepharose followed by gel filtration. Purity was tested by
2D SDS-PAGE and silver staining and the final isolate proved to contain
practically only a single protein.

3. RESULTS AND DISCUSSION
As seen in figure 1 mainly two polypeptides become phosphorylated under
suitable conditions in the light, one at about 55 kD and one at 6 kD,
the latter being identified as the β subunit of the light-harvesting
complex. As observed by Allen and Holmes [4] the phosphorylation of the
B875 complex depends upon the redox state of the quinone pool. Furthermore
the phosphorylation of B875 β occurs only when the cytochrome b-c1 complex
is oxidized either by potassium ferricyanide or in the presence of DBMIB.

M. Baltscheffsky (ed.), Current Research in Photosynthesis, Vol. II, 77–80.

When the inhibition site of electron transport is after the cytochrome b-cl complex, e.g. by antimycin A, or when the system is reduced by a reductant such as Na-ascorbate or Na-dithionite no phosphorylation of B875 β is observed. This suggest that the redox state of cytochrome b-cl complex is a controlling factor for the kinase activity.

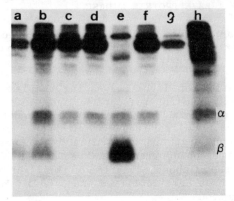

Fig. 1: Effect of various agents on the phosphorylation of the B875 complex in chromatophores. Phosphorylation in the presence of (a) 40μM DCCD (N,N'-Dicyclohexylcarbodiimide, inhibitor of the membrane-bound ATP-ase), (b) 40μm DCCD, (c) 1μM antimycin A (an inhibitor of electron flow between cytochrome b and cytochrome cl), (d) 100μM antimycin A, (e) 100μM DBMIB, (f) 5mM Na-ascorbate (a reductant), (g) 5mM Na-dithionite (a strong reductant) and (h) 5mM potassium ferricyanide (an oxidant and inhibitor of electron transport at the reaction center). All samples except (a) contained 2μg/ml venturicidin.

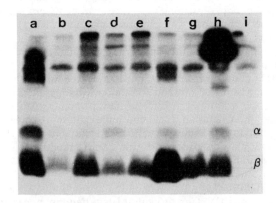

Fig. 2: Substitution of Mg^{++} in the B875 kinase assay by various metal ions. Kinase activity in the presence of: (a) 10mM CuCl$_2$; (b) 10mM CaCl$_2$; (c) 10mM MnCl$_2$; (d) 10mM MgCl$_2$; (e) 5mM MgCl$_2$ and 5mM MnCl$_2$; (f) 10mM ZnCl$_2$; (g) 10mM MgCl$_2$ and after light incubation 10mM ZnCl$_2$; (h) as in (g) but in the presence of 5μg alkaline phosphatase and ZnCl$_2$; (i) control without metal ions.

Fig. 2 demonstrates effects of various metal ions on the activity of
the kinase reaction. Compared with the control in lane (i) metal ions
are essential for kinase activity. Mg^{++}, showing the strongest effect,
however, can be substituted by other divalent cations such as Mn^{++},
Cu^{++} and Zn^{++}, in contrast Ca^{++} is ineffective in replacing Mg^{++}. The
addition of alkaline phosphatase had no effect on B875 phosphorylation.

As seen in fig. 3 only a weak regulatory influence of the levels of ADP
and AMP is observed suggesting that protein phosphorylation is regulated
by another factor than levels of AMP and ADP. Furthermore the presence
of cAMP has no effect on the activity of the enzyme.

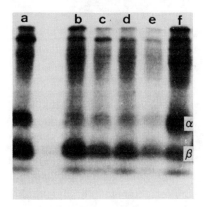

Fig. 3: Regulation of the B875 kinase activity by ADP and AMP. Protein
phosphorylation in the presence of Mg^{++}, DBMIB and (a) 0.1mM ADP, (b)
0.1mM AMP, (c) 0.2mM ADP, (d) 0.2mM AMP, (e) 0.4mM ADP, (f) 0.4mM AMP.

Kinase activity from the cytoplasmic fraction of R. rubrum is observed
with chromatophores, isolated B875 complexes as well as histone V-S
(from calf thymus) as substrates as demonstrated in fig. 4.

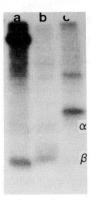

Fig. 4: B875 kinase activity of supernatant fraction using as substrates:
(a) chromatophores, (b) purified B875 complexes, (c) histone V-S.

The B875 kinase activity present in the supernatant fraction was then isolated by affinity chromatography on a Sepharose-ATP column and gel filtration. The purified enzyme was present in only low amounts but rapidly phosphorylated intact chromatophores in the presence of DBMIB or isolated B875 light harvesting complexes, as well as histone V-S (Fig. 5). Its molecular weight was in the range of 18 kD.

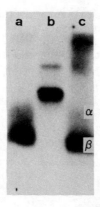

Fig. 5: Substrate specifity of the purified protein kinase: substrate additions (a) purified chromatophores (30μg), (b) isolated B875 complexes (30μg), (c) histone V-S (15μg).

4. REFERENCES

[1] Barber, J. (1982). Influence of surface charges on thylakoid structure and function. Ann. Rev. Plant Physiol. 33: 261-295
[2] Loach, P.A., Parkes, P.S., Bustamante, P. (1984). Regulation of photosynthetic unit structure in Rhodospirillum rubrum whole cells. In Sybesma C. (ed) Adv. Photosynth. Res. vol II. 189-197
[3] Holmes, N.G. and Allen, J.F. (1986). Protein phosphorylation as a control for excitation energy transfer in Rhodospirillum rubrum. FEBS Lett. 200: 144-148
[4] Holmes, N.G. and Allen, J.F. (1988). Protein phosphorylation in chromatophores from Rhodospirillum rubrum. Biochim. Biophys. Acta 935: 72-78

PHOSPHOPROTEINS IN THE PURPLE PHOTOSYNTHETIC BACTERIUM, RHODOSPIRILLUM RUBRUM

ALAN COX AND JOHN F. ALLEN
Department of Pure and Applied Biology, University of Leeds, Leeds LS2 9JT, England.

1. INTRODUCTION

The photosynthetic apparatus of purple photosynthetic bacteria is organised into photosynthetic units (PSU) each consisting of a reaction centre pigment-protein complex with its associated light-harvesting pigment-proteins (1). In what has been described as the cooperative state it is envisaged that excitation energy absorbed by the light-harvesting components of one PSU can be transferred to a neighbouring PSU (2). In the cooperative state (light + Mg^{2+}) increased phoshorylation of the B880- polypeptide of the light-harvesting complex isolated from Rhodospirillum rubrum has been demonstrated and suggested as a possible mechanism for regulating PSU cooperativity (3). In whole cells the phosphorylation of proteins of apparent molecular weight 13 and 10 kDa has also been shown to occur respectively under cooperative (light + Mg^{2+}) and non-cooperative (dark) conditions (4). It has been suggested that these phosphorylated polypeptides may be the B880- and B880- subunits of the light-harvesting complex (4,5). Here we describe experiments designed to evaluate this proposal.

2. MATERIALS AND METHODS

Growth of R.rubrum, sample preparation, SDS-PAGE and autoradiography were performed essentially as described (4). ^{32}P-labelling of whole cells was carried out in the light or dark in medium containg [^{32}P]orthophosphate. Chromatophores were prepared from ^{32}P-labelled cells as previously described (5). Chromatophores for photophosphorylation experiments were resuspended in 20 mM MOPS/20mM NaCl/4mM $MgSO_4$ (pH 7.9).

3. RESULTS AND DISCUSSION.

Incubation of R.rubrum cells with [^{32}P]orthophosphate resulted in a wide variety of proteins being phosphorylated, covering a wide range of molecular

M. Baltscheffsky (ed.), Current Research in Photosynthesis, Vol. II, 81–84.

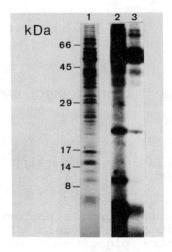 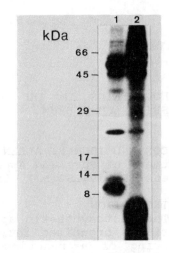

Fig. 1   Fig.2

Figure 1: Lane 1: Whole cell protein from R.rubrum separated by SDS-PAGE and stained with Coomassie blue. Lanes 2 and 3: Autoradiograph showing ^{32}P-labelled protein from R.rubrum incubated with ^{32}P-phosphate for 6 hr in the light (lane 2) or in the dark (lane 3).

Figure 2: Fractionation of light grown ^{32}P-labelled cells. Autoradiograph appearance of soluble fraction (lane 1) and chomatophore fraction (lane 2).

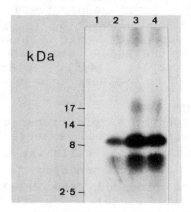

Fig. 3

Figure 3: Protein phosphorylation in chromatophores supplied with [^{32}P]orthophosphate and incubated in the light for 2 hr with various concentrations of ADP, ie. lane 1: 20 mM; lane 2: 200 uM; lane 3: 2 uM; lane 4: 20 nM.

weights. Labelling of proteins in the light (Fig. 1, lane 2) was generally more pronounced than in the dark (Fig. 1, lane 3) but the most striking differences were seen for bands of apparent molecular weight 4, 10, 13 and 22 kDa. Of particular interest are the phosphorylated species of 10 and 13 kDa. Under the conditions employed the 10 kDa protein was strongly labelled in the light whereas the 13 kDa band was weakly labelled , but in the dark neither species was phosphorylated to a detectable level. Both these labelled bands were coincident with Coomassie blue staining bands (Fig. 1, lane 1)

In order to test the proposal that the 10 and 13 kDa phosphoproteins are the subunits of the light-harvesting complex we labelled cells with [^{32}P]orthophosphate in the light and carried out a chromatophore preparation. Samples of soluble components (144,000g supernatent) and chromatophores were analysed by SDS-PAGE and autoradiography. Figure 2, lane 1 shows that the 10 and 13 kDa phosphoproteins were found exclusively in the soluble fraction. This result clearly does not support the suggestion that these phosphoproteins are the light harvesting polypeptides.

We are also evaluating a novel approach to the study of protein phosphorylation reactions in isolated chromatophores. The method involves incubation of chromatophores in the light with [^{32}P]orthophosphate and unlabelled ADP and relies on the ability of chromatophores to synthesize [^{32}P]ATP _in situ_ by photophosphorylation. Figure 3 shows that, surprisigly, the major phosphorylated component observed is a band of 10 kDa. This conflicts with the fractionation experiment data described above and suggests the 10 kDa protein may be associated with the chromatophores. However, it is possible that the 10 kDa phosphorylated band observed here arises from a residual contamination of the chromatophore fraction with some soluble components. In the dark, or in the presence of excess unlabelled phosphate, labelled material was not detected.

In summary, we conclude that the 10 and 13 kDa phosphoproteins of R.rubrum are unlikely to be the subunits of the light-harvesting complex. It appears that both are soluble, cytoplasmic components but it is possible that the 10 kDa protein associates with chromatophores under certain conditions. Consequently, the role of these phosphoproteins in the regulation of PSU cooperativety needs to be re-evaluated.

ACKNOWLEDGEMENTS
    We are grateful to Nicholas Tsinoremas and Michael
Harrison for helpful discussion and to SERC for financial
support.

REFERENCES
1. Drews, G. (1985) Microbiol. Rev. <u>49</u> 59-70
2. Vredenberg, W.J. and Duysens, L.N.M. (1963) Nature <u>197</u>
   355-357.
3. Loach, P.A., Parkes, P.S., and Bustamante, P. (1984) in
   Advances in Photosynthesis Research (Sybesma, C. ed)
   pp 189-197, Martinus Nijhoff/Dr W. Junk, Dordrecht.
4. Holmes, N. G. and Allen, J.F. (1986) FEBS Lett. <u>200</u>
   144-148.
5. Holmes, N.G. and Allen, J.F. Biochim. Biophys. Acta <u>935</u>
   72-78.

INTERACTION OF HYDROPHILIC SUCCINIMIDYL ETHERS WITH
POLYPEPTIDES OF PIGMENT-PROTEIN COMPLEXES IN ASSE-
MBLY A890 FROM SULFUR PHOTOSYNTHETIC BACTERIUM
CHROMATIUM MINUTISSIMUM

Institute of Soil Science and Photosynthesis, USSR Academy of
Sciences, Pushchino, 142292, USSR

Moskalenko A.A., Toropygina O.A. and Erokhin Yu.E.

1. INTRODUCTION

Photosynthetic apparatus of purple sulfur and nonsulfur bacteria is located in pigment-containing membranes (chromatophores).
Depending on bacteria type it can be built of 2-3 types of pigment-protein complexes : two light-harvesting (B800-850 and
B870/890) ones and RC where the primary charge separation takes place /1/. The efficiency of photosynthetic apparatus functioning as a whole is determined not only by the organization of individual complexes but also by the interaction of pigment-protein
complexes. The interaction of the complexes B870(890) and RC is
important for the functioning of not only photosynthetic apparatus
but also of the electron transfer chain sites coupled with it /2/. It
is clear that to identify the arrangement of B890 and RC it is more convinient to study a membrane fragment which is enriched
with these complexes where all side amino groups are available
for the interaction with a cross-linking agent. Earlier we have
shown that a similar fragment, the assembly A890, containing the
pigment-protein complexes B890 and RC and cytochromes can be
isolated from Chr. minutissimum in the native state by electrophoresis with Triton X-100 /3/. The present paper deals with the interaction of DTSSP and DTSSB with polypeptides and subunits of
pigment-protein complexes in the assembly A890 and with the effect of this interaction on the spectral and photochemical properties of the complexes.

2. PROCEDURE

A890 was isolated by the electrophoresis from the chromatophores of Chr. minutissimum treated with 3% Triton X-100 according to /3/. The sample was concentrated up to 60 units of optical density in the long wavelength absorption maximum in 10 mM
Bicin-NaOH buffer(pH 7.8)(30mg/ml protein). DTSSP and DTSSB
was synthetized according to the method described in /4,5/.

Abbreviations : DTSSP - dithio-bis-sulfosuccinimidyl propionate,
DTSSB - dithio-bis-sulfosuccinimidyl butyrate, Chr. - Chromatium,
RC - reaction center, SDS - sodium dodecyl sulfate, PAGE - po-
lyacrylamide gel electrophoresis, kDa - kilodalton.

M. Baltscheffsky (ed.), Current Research in Photosynthesis, Vol. II, 85–88.
© 1990 *Kluwer Academic Publishers. Printed in the Netherlands.*

Before the experiment the sample of A890 was deluted up to a protein concentration of 7.5mg/ml and freshly prepared solution of DTSSP(DTSSB) was added up to a final concentration of 5, 20 and 50 mM. After incubation of sample with the bifunctional cross-linking agent for 5 or 30 min at 0°C the reaction was stopped by the addition of 1M Tris solution up to final concentration of 50mM. The PAGE with Triton X-100, SDS and two-dimensional PAGE were carried out as described /6/. The gel was stayned with coomassie R-250 or argentum ions. For spectral measurements the samples were deluted with distilled water at a ratio of 1:50. The absorption spectra were registered on a spectrophotometer"Specord M-40", photochemical activity – on a phosphoroscopic device.

3. RESULTS AND DICUSSION

It is important that the linking agents interact quickly and under mild conditions with proteins, inducing no notable changes in the structure and spectral characteristics of the pigment-protein complexes under study. High concentrations (20-50 mM) of the cross-linking agents lead to a rapid destruction of the native state of the complex B890 in the assembly A890 and to the appearance of the maximum of monomeric bacteriochlorophyll at 780 nm. Simultaneously, RC photochemical activity decays. Then the incubation period is increased to 30 min, 5mM DTSSP is also capable of destroying pigment-protein complexes in the assembly A890. The results obtained differ from the data of Ludwig and Jay/5/who have found no notable changes in the absorption spectra of pigment-protein complexes under the treatment of membranes from nonsulfur photosynthetic bacterium Rhodopseudomonas viridis containing bacteriochlorophyll "b" with water soluble succinimidyl ethers at a concentration of 8-30mM this can be due to various levels of organization of the samples studied (membranes /5/ and the assembly A890 are investigated in the present work). Further study was carried out at such DTSSP(DTSSB) concentration(5mM, 5 min) which did not induce notable changes in the spectral properties of the pigment-protein complexes in the assembly A890. At first it is necessary to find whether the dimers (or oligomers) of the assembly A890 are formed in the presence of DTSSP (DTSSB). It has been shown by 5% PAGE with Triton X-100 that there is now band corresponding to the dimers A890. During the analysis of the polypeptide content of the assembly A890 treated with DTSSB it has been found that in the presence of the cross-linking agent the intensity of bands of α and β polypeptides from the complex B890 and subunits of the RC complex is decreased and new 37, 38.5, 41.5 and 46.5 kDa bands appear (Fig.1). Special attention should be paid to some peculiarities of the DTSSB interaction with polypeptides of the pigment-protein complexes in the assembly A890. Firstly, There are no bands which correspond to the dimers of the light-harvesting complex polypeptides of $\alpha\alpha$, $\alpha\beta$ and $\beta\beta$ type or their oligomers. Similar dimers were observed when the membranes of nonsulfur bacteria were

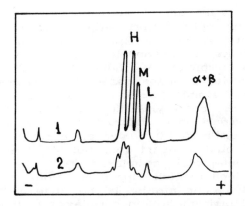
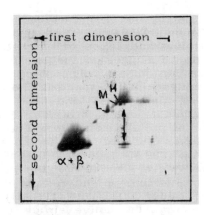

FIGURE 1. PAGE with SDS : control A890(1) and A890 treated
with 5 mM DTSSB(2)

FIGURE 2. Two dimensional PAGE with SDS assembly A890 treated with 5 mM DTSSP

treated with analogous or hydrophobic cross–linking agents /5/.
The cause of the absence of these dimers of the light–harvesting
complex B890 polypeptides is not quite clear, since in the models
which are developed now such complexes consist of 2–3 pairs of
α and β polypeptides /1/, and as it can be expected they will
be linked with each other at first. Secondly, after the treatment of
the assembly A890 with DTSSB no bands with a molecular weight
higher than 50 kDa can be found, i.e. the bands which are dimers or oligomers of the RC subunits. This is in a good accord
with the results obtained by means of hydrophobic imidyl ethers
on chromatophores Chr. minutissimum /6/, but differs from the data obtained on chromatophores or RC from nonsulfur bacteria
where the links between the RC subunits are formed /5,7/.Thirdly,
DTSSB links polypeptides from various pigment–protein complexes
and new bands can be attributed (in accord with a molecular
weight) to the associates of the RC subunits and polypeptides of
the complex B890. It is interesting to note that with the increase
in DTSSB concentration up to 20–50mM during the assembly A890
treatment, i.e. under conditions when the cross–linking agent destroys the native structure of pigment–protein complexes, electropho
retic picture of polypeptide separation is not practically changed.
Probably, at the first stage (1–2 min) DTSSP the cross–linking
agent links proteins and then, at the second stage, destroys the
native structure of the complexes.
   The results of two–dimensional electrophoresis (Fig.2) support
that H and M subunits of the RC are linked with the complex
B890 polypeptides (mainly with α polypeptide) by means of
DTSSP. For more correct determination of the type of the associate formed it is necessary to carry out additional experiments
on individual subunits of the RC and polypeptides of the complex

B890 by using antibodies. This is the aim of our further work. Since DTSSP(DTSSB) links polypeptides from various pigment-protein complexes in the assembly A890 from Chr. minutissimum it can be suggested that similar links are uncapable of stabiliging the structure of pigment-protein complexes. We have studied the changes in the spectral characteristics of the assembly A890 treated with DTSSP and the control sample treated with various agents (heating, pronase, 1% SDS) destroying the spatial structure of protein molecules. The comparison of destruction of the complexes B890 and RC in the assembly A890 treated or untreated with DTSSP indicates that the coupling agent does not stabilize the native structure of the pigment-protein complex.

Summing up the results obtained the following conclusions can be made: 1)DTSSP(DTSSB) at a concentration hagher than 5mM destroys the native structure of pigment-protein complexes in the assembly A890; 2)The treatment of the assembly A890 with DTSSP(DTSSB) does not induce the formation of A890 oligomers; 3)DTSSP(DTSSB) links polypeptides from various pigment-protein complexes, but no links within the limits of one complex are found; 4)The formation of links does not lead to stabilization of the native structure of pigment-protein complexes in the assembly A890.

REFERENCES
1 Drews, G.(1985) Microbiol.Rev. 49, 59-70
2 Jacson, W.J., Prince, R.C. et al.(1986) Biochemistry, 25, 8440-8446
3 Moskalenko, A.A. ,Erokhin, Yu.E. (1974) Microbiologia, 43, 654-658
4 Staros, J.V. (1982) Biochemistry, 21, 3950-3955
5 Ludwig, F.R., Jay, F.A. (1985) Eur. J. Biochem. 151, 83-87
6 Moskalenko, A.A., Toropygina, O.A.(1988) Molek.Biol.(USSR) 22, 944-954
7 Kelly, D.J., Dow, C.S. (1985) J. Cener.Microb. 131,2941-2952

STUDIES ON THE ROD–SUBSTRUCTURE OF THE PHYCOBILISOME FROM THE CYANOBACTERIUM MASTIGOCLADUS LAMINOSUS.

M. Glauser, W. Sidler, G. Frank and H. Zuber
Institut für Molekularbiologie und Biophysik, ETH-Hönggerberg,
CH-8093 Zürich, Schweiz.

INTRODUCTION

Based on earlier studies of the rod and core substructures the following model for the phycobilisome (PBS) of M. laminosus was proposed (1) (Fig. 4.A): the rods consist of one phycoerythrocyanin (PEC) and three phycocyanin (PC) hexamers (disks) connected by noncoloured linker polypeptides of 34.5, 31.5 and 29.5 kDa (app.MW) and of a 8.9 kDa rod-terminator polypeptide located at the PEC hexamer; the PEC-formation increases at lower light intensity; the order of the hexamer-linker complexes in the PBS rods from outside to inside was believed to be

$(\alpha^{PEC}\beta^{PEC})_6 \ L_R^{34.5}$, $(\alpha^{PC}\beta^{PC})_6 \ L_R^{34.5}$, $(\alpha^{PC}\beta^{PC})_6 \ L_R^{31.5}$ and $(\alpha^{PC}\beta^{PC})_6 \ L_{RC}^{29.5}$

although only the first two complexes have been isolated and characterized (2). From the PBS of M. laminosus the complete amino-acid sequences of the phycobiliproteins PEC (α,β), PC (α,β), AP (α,β), $\beta^{16.2}$ as well as from the linker polypeptides $L_C^{8.9}$, $L_R^{8.9}$ are known. Partial amino-acid sequences of the APB α-subunit and the 34.5 kDa PEC and 34.5 kDa PC linker polypeptides have been determined (for a review see Ref. 1.). In this work additional PC-linker polypeptide complexes and PC-linker polypeptide-AP complexes (rod-core complexes) were isolated and characterized which lead to a modified view of the PBS rod structure of M. laminosus (Fig. 4.B). The N-terminal amino-acid sequence of the 29.5 kDa rod-core linker polypeptide, which connects rods with the core, is presented.

RESULTS

The following complexes were isolated after dissociation of freshly prepared PBS from M. laminosus (3) in 5 mM potassium phosphate pH 7.0 by means of ion-exchange chromatography and gelfiltration:

I $(\alpha^{PC}\beta^{PC})_3 \ L_{RC}^{29.5}$, II $(\alpha^{PC}\beta^{PC})_3 \ L_{RC}^{29.5} \ (\alpha^{AP}\beta^{AP})_3 \ L_C^{8.9}$,

III $(\alpha^{PC}\beta^{PC})_6 \ L_{RC}^{29.5} \ (\alpha^{AP}\beta^{AP})_3 \ L_C^{8.9}$, IV $(\alpha^{PC}\beta^{PC})_3 \ L_{RC}^{31.5}$,

V $(\alpha^{PC}\beta^{PC})_3 \ L_{RC}^{31.5} \ (\alpha^{AP}\beta^{AP})_3 \ L_C^{8.9}$, VI $(\alpha^{PC}\beta^{PC})_6 \ L_R^{34.5}$.

M. Baltscheffsky (ed.), Current Research in Photosynthesis, Vol. II, 89–92.
© 1990 *Kluwer Academic Publishers. Printed in the Netherlands.*

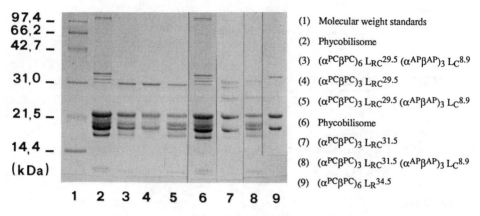

Fig. 1. SDS-PAGE of phycobilisomes and phycocyanin-linker polypeptide complexes. $L_{RC}^{31.5}$ is partly degraded by a natural proteinase.

The 31.5 kDa linker polypeptide of the complexes IV and V was already partly degraded by a natural proteinase (Fig. 1. lanes 7 and 8). The complexes I and II were stable in 5 mM potassium phosphate pH 7.5, the complexes III-VI in 700 mM potassium phosphate pH 7.5. The composition and stoichiometry of these complexes were determined by quantitative scanning of Coomassie blue stained SDS-polyacrylamide gels (SDS-PAGE Fig. 1.), by quantification of the amino-acid yields with HPLC after manual Edman degradation of the whole complexes (4) and by molecular weight determination with sucrose density gradient centrifugation. The results of these experiments show the existence of two rod-core complexes (II and V) with two different linker polypeptides of 29.5 kDa and 31.5 kDa connecting the rod and core components (Fig. 1. lanes 5 and 8). Comparing the absorption (Fig. 2.A, 2.B) and emission spectra (not shown) and the wavelengths of their maxima (Table 1.) the complexes I, IV and II, V show a very similar spectroscopic behaviour indicating quite the same functionality of both 29.5 kDa and 31.5 kDa linker polypeptides within the PBS, although the absorption maxima of the rod-core complexes (II and V) are 1.5 nm respectively 4 nm red-shifted to those of the corresponding PC-linker complexes (I and IV)(Table 1.).

complex	solvent[a]	$\lambda_{A\,max}$(nm)	$\lambda_{F\,max}$(nm)
$(\alpha^{PC}\beta^{PC})_3\,L_{RC}^{29.5}$	I	634.0	648.1
$(\alpha^{PC}\beta^{PC})_3\,L_{RC}^{29.5}\,(\alpha^{AP}\beta^{AP})_3\,L_C^{8.9}$	I	635.5	659.4–661.6[b]
$(\alpha^{PC}\beta^{PC})_6\,L_{RC}^{29.5}\,(\alpha^{AP}\beta^{AP})_3\,L_C^{8.9}$	II	635.0	656.0
$(\alpha^{PC}\beta^{PC})_3\,L_{RC}^{31.5}$	II	632.0	647.7
$(\alpha^{PC}\beta^{PC})_3\,L_{RC}^{31.5}\,(\alpha^{AP}\beta^{AP})_3\,L_C^{8.9}$	II	636.0	659.8–662.5[b]
$(\alpha^{PC}\beta^{PC})_6\,L_R^{34.5}$	II	623.0	647.6

Table 1.

Spectroscopic properties of PC-linker complexes and rod-core complexes.

solvent[a]: I= 5mM potassium phosphate, 1mM sodium azide, 2mM EDTA, 1mM PMSF, pH 7.5; II= 700mM potassium phosphate, 1mM sodium azide, 2mM EDTA, 1mM PMSF, pH 7.5

b : $\lambda_{F\,max}$ depended on the excitation wavelength (590-645 nm)

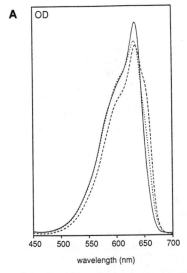 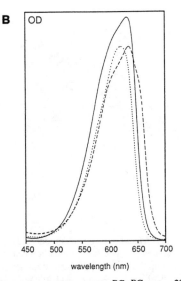

Fig. 2 Absorption spectra of phycocyanin-linker polypeptide complexes. (A) $(\alpha^{PC}\beta^{PC})_3\,L_{RC}^{29.5}$ (——), $(\alpha^{PC}\beta^{PC})_3\,L_{RC}^{29.5}\,(\alpha^{AP}\beta^{AP})_3\,L_C^{8.9}$ (- - -), $(\alpha^{PC}\beta^{PC})_6\,L_{RC}^{29.5}\,(\alpha^{AP}\beta^{AP})_3\,L_C^{8.9}$ (······); (B) $(\alpha^{CP}\beta^{CP})_3\,L_{RC}^{31.5}$ (——), $(\alpha^{CP}\beta^{CP})_3\,L_{RC}^{31.5}\,(\alpha^{AP}\beta^{AP})_3\,L_C^{8.9}$ (- - -), $(\alpha^{CP}\beta^{CP})_6\,L_R^{34.5}$ (······).

The N-terminal sequence of $L_{RC}^{29.5}$ was determined by automatic gas phase Edman degradation and subsequent amino-acid identification on HPLC. This sequence shows nearly no homology to the N-terminal sequences of the other rod linker polypeptides $L_R^{34.5,PC}$ and $L_R^{34.5,PEC}$, which show a significant homology in this region (Fig. 3.), nor to the amino-acid sequences of the phycobiliproteins and small linker polypeptides $L_R^{8.9}$ and $L_C^{8.9}$. This indicates that the three-dimensional structures of the rod-core linkers $L_{RC}^{29.5}$ and $L_{RC}^{31.5}$ might be quite different to those of the other linker polypeptides in the phycobilisomal rod.

$L_{RC}^{29.5}$ — A I P L L Q Y V P S Q N Q R V P G Y T V P N - D T ...
$L_{RC}^{34.5,PC}$ — A I T A A A S R L G T E P F S N A A K I E L R S D A ...
$L_R^{34.5,PEC}$ — >S T S V A E R L A I K D E V D - K K I E L R P N W ...

Fig. 3.   Comparison of the N-terminal amino-acid sequences of the linker polypeptides $L_{RC}^{29.5}$, $L_R^{34.5,PC}$ and $L_R^{34.5,PEC}$. Homologous amino-acid residues are in boxes.

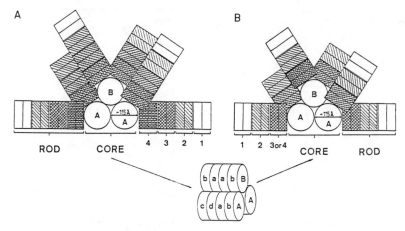

Fig. 4. Previous (A) and updated (B) model of the phycobilisome of *Mastigocladus laminosus*, showing the location and polypeptide composition (phycobiliproteins, linker polypeptides) of the complexes making up the rods and the three-cylinder core. (1) $(\alpha^{PEC}\beta^{PEC})_6 L_R^{34.5} L_R^{8.9}$, (2) $(\alpha^{PC}\beta^{PC})_6 L_R^{34.5}$, (3) $(\alpha^{PC}\beta^{PC})_6 L_R^{31.5}$ for model A and $(\alpha^{PC}\beta^{PC})_6 L_{RC}^{31.5}$ for model B, (4) $(\alpha^{PC}\beta^{PC})_6 L_{RC}^{29.5}$; (a) $(\alpha^{AP}\beta^{AP})_3$, (b) $(\alpha^{AP}\beta^{AP})_3 L_C^{8.9}$, (c) $(\alpha^{APB}\alpha_2^{AP}\beta_3^{AP}) L_C^{8.9}$, (d) $(\alpha^{AP}\beta^{AP})_2 \beta^{16.2} L_{CM}^{89}$.

DISCUSSION

The two isolated rod-core complexes II $(\alpha^{PC}\beta^{PC})_3 L_{RC}^{29.5} (\alpha^{AP}\beta^{AP})_3 L_C^{8.9}$ and V $(\alpha^{PC}\beta^{PC})_3 L_{RC}^{31.5} (\alpha^{AP}\beta^{AP})_3 L_C^{8.9}$ are composed of the same rod and core components but differ in the linker polypeptides, which have different molecular weights (Fig. 1.), different spectroscopic behaviour (Table 1.) and different N-terminal amino-acid sequences (not shown). Based on these results a modified model for the PBS of M. laminosus is proposed (Fig. 4.B), in which the rods consist of only two hexameric PC-disks and both linker polypeptides of 29.5 kDa and 31.5 kDa attach the rods to the core. This model is consistent with the already measured PC:AP ratio of 2:1 in the PBS of M. laminosus (5), with electron micrographs of the PBS (6) and with the presence of two different kinds of core cylinders A and B (Fig. 4.).

REFERENCES

1. Zuber, H. (1987) in The Light Reactions (Barber, J., ed.), pp.197-259, Elsevier, Amsterdam
2. Füglistaller, P., Suter, F. and Zuber, H. (1986) Biol. Chem. Hoppe-Seyler 367, 601-614
3. Füglistaller, P., Rümbeli, R., Suter, F. and Zuber, H. (1984) Hoppe-Seyler's Z. Physiol. Chem. 365, 1085-1096
4. Brandt, W.F. and Frank, G. (1988) Analyt. Biochemistry 168, 314-323
5. Füglistaller, P., Widmer, H., Sidler, W., Frank, G. and Zuber, H. (1981) Arch. Microbiol. 129, 268-274
6. Mörschel, E. and Rhiel, E. (1987) in Membranous Structures pp.209-254

ISOLATION AND CHARACTERIZATION OF THE ALLOPHYCOCYANIN COMPLEXES OF THE CYANOBACTERIUM MASTIGOCLADUS LAMINOSUS

A. Esteban, W. Sidler, G. Frank, P. Füglistaller, R. Rümbeli and H. Zuber.
Institut für Molekularbiologie und Biophysik, ETH-Hönggerberg,
CH-8093 Zürich, Switzerland.

INTRODUCTION

Cyanobacteria contain extramembraneous light-harvesting pigment protein-complexes, the phycobiliproteins. In most of these organisms, three phycobiliproteins (allophycocyanin, C-phycocyanin, phycoerythrin and phycoerythrocyanin) are present and can be distinguished by their absorption and fluorescence spectra. They are aggregated into large light-harvesting antennae, the phycobilisomes, which absorb light energy between 500 nm and 650 nm and transfer the excitation energy to the reaction center in the photosynthetic membrane.

Allophycocyanin from Mastigocladus laminosus is a blue water-soluble pigment protein-complex and a component of the phycobilisome core. The aggregates of core phycobiliproteins are trimeric complexes as shown below:

Protein or complex	$\lambda_{A\ max}$ (nm)	$\epsilon(\lambda_{Amax})$ $(M^{-1}cm^{-1})$	$\lambda_{F\ max}$ (nm)	MG (kDa)
α	615	106 000	642	17.7
β	613	92 000	638	18.0
α^{APB}	645		672	
$\beta^{16.2}$	624	119 000	644	19.4
$(\alpha^{AP}\beta^{AP})$	616	201 000	641	
$(\alpha^{AP}\beta^{AP})_3$	651	745 000	660	
$(\alpha^{AP}\beta^{AP})_3 L_C^{8.9}$	652	1076 000	661	
$(\alpha^{APB}\alpha^{AP}_2 \beta^{AP}_3)L_C^{8.9}$	653	977 000	679	

M. Baltscheffsky (ed.), Current Research in Photosynthesis, Vol. II, 93–96.

Allophycocyanin is composed of two subunits, the α- and the ß-subunit, each with a linear tetrapyrrole, phycocyanobilin, covalently bound to a cystein residue. From the complete amino acid sequence it has been determined that the molecular weight of the α-subunit is 17 700 Da and that of the ß-subunit is 18 000 Da. (Sidler, W., Gysi, J., Isker, E. & Zuber, H. (1981)Hoppe Seyler's Z. Physiol. Chem. 362, 611-628). All core phycobiliproteins and their complexes have been previously isolated and characterized spectroscopically, by SDS-PAGE, ultracentrifugation and by sequence analysis as shown above. (Füglistaller, P., Mimuro, M., Suter, F. & Zuber, H. (1987) Biol. Chem. Hoppe-Seyler 368, 353-367). (Rümbeli, R., Wirth, M., Suter, F. & Zuber, H. (1987) Biol. Chem. Hoppe-Seyler 368, 1-9). (Suter, F., Füglistaller, P., Lundell, D., Glazer, A. & Zuber, H. (1987) Febs Letters 217, 279-282)
For structural investigations (cristallisation experiments) some allophycocyanin complexes were isolated and purified in preparative amounts. Incidentally during these isolation procedures, attention was given to a recently proposed microheterogenity in allophycocyanin trimers (α^{AP}, α^{APB}, α^*, β^{AP}, $\beta^{16.2}$, β^*) (Reuter, W. & Wehrmeyer, W. (1988) Arch. Microbiol. 150, 534-540). We attempted to obtain amino acid sequence data from isolated and separated α^* and β^*-subunits.

METHODS

1) Separation of phycobiliprotein complexes by ion-exchange chromatography

Intact phycobilisomes were dissociated in 5 mM potassium phosphate, 1 mM sodium azide, 2mM EDTA, 1mM Phenylmethane-sulfonyl fluoride (PMSF), pH=7.05. To separate the resulting complex by two different anion-exchange chromatography materials, Cellex-D and Q-Sepharose, a phosphate gradient was used at pH = 7.05 and pH = 8 respectively. (Fuglistaller,P., Suter, F., & Zuber H. (1986) Biol. Chem. Hoppe-Seyler 367, 601-614).Subsequent to chromatographic separation the APC I fractions were pooled.

2) Purification of APC I by Fractogel-DEAE

The fraction APC I from the Cellex-D and Q-Sepharose column was dialysed against 20 mM potassium phosphate, 1mM sodium azide, 2mM EDTA, 1 mM PMSF, pH = 8. The dialysate was applied to a Fractogel-DEAE column (2 x 23.5 cm) which had been equilibrated in the same buffer. After washing with about 30 ml of 20 mM potassium phosphate pH = 8, the column was run with a linear gradient of 100-200 mM sodium chloride, with a total volume of 1000 ml.

The SDS-PAGE of the $(\alpha^{AP}\beta^{AP})_3 L_C^{8.9}$ fraction shows 5 bands instead of the expected 3 bands. The complex was rechromatographed on Fractogel-DEAE under the same conditions.

3) Purification of $(\alpha^{AP}\beta^{AP})_3L_C^{8.9}$ by Mono-Q

The fraction from the Fractogel-DEAE column was dialysed against 20 mM potassium phosphate, 1mM sodium azide, 2 mM EDTA, 1 mM PMSF, at pH = 8. The dialysate was applied to a Mono-Q HR 5/5 from Pharmacia, which had been equilibrated in the same buffer. After washing with about 16 ml of 20 mM potassium phosphate pH = 8, the fractions were eluted with a linear gradient of 20-200 mM potassium phosphate.

The complex was directly used for the isolation of the α^{AP} and $\beta^{AP}-$ subunits by gel filtration on Bio-Gel P60 in 63 mM HCOOH. The resulting two fractions were then identified by amino acid sequencing.

RESULTS AND DISCUSSION

The allophycocyanin complexes were isolated and characterized by an ion-exchange chromatography method and gel filtration. The spectroscopic data of the $(\alpha^{AP}\beta^{AP})_3L_C^{8.9}$ complex obtained are

Complex	$\lambda_{A\,max}$ (nm)	$\lambda_{F\,max}$ (nm)	MG (a) (Da)
$(\alpha^{AP}\beta^{AP})_3L_C^{8.9}$	653	664	148

(a) The molecular weight as determined by gel filtration on Superose 12

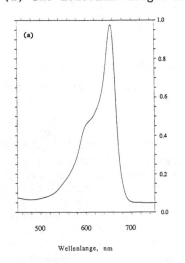

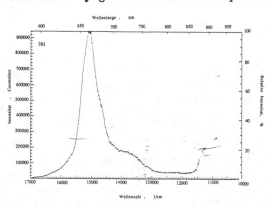

Fig.1 Spectral characteristics of $(\alpha^{AP}\beta^{AP})_3L_C^{8.9}$ in 20 mM potassium phosphate, pH=8
a) Absorptionsspectra
b) Fluorescence-emission spectra

The previously obtained $(\alpha^{AP}\beta^{AP})_3 L_C^{8.9}$ complex by Füglistaller P. et al. and Rümbeli R. et al. showed two phycobiliprotein bands and one linker polypeptide band on SDS-PAGE. Using the new "Mini-Gel Electrophoresis-System" from Bio Rad we obtained higher resolution of the phycobiliprotein bands and we could distinguish four phycobiliprotein bands in the $(\alpha^{AP}\beta^{AP})_3 L_C^{8.9}$ complex, two of them very weak, which remained reproducible after several purification procedures by ion-exchange chromatography.

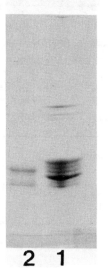

Fig.2 15 % SDS-PAGE after
purification of $(\alpha^{AP}\beta^{AP})_3 L_C^{8.9}$
by ion-exchange
chromatography on Cellex-D, Q-Sepharose,
Fractogel-DEAE and Mono-Q.
Lane (1): Phycobilisome
Lane (2): $(\alpha^{AP}\beta^{AP})_3 L_C^{8.9}$

2 1

Although we isolated the same $(\alpha^{AP}\beta^{AP})_3 L_C^{8.9}$ allophycocyanin complex as obtained by Reuter and Wehrmeyer, complete with corresponding spectroscopic data $\lambda_{A\ max} = 653$ nm and $\lambda_{F\ max} = 664$ nm and four bands on SDS-PAGE, the amino acid sequences of separated α - and β-subunits in 63 mM HCOOH showed the known amino acid sequences of pure α^{AP} - and $\beta^{A\ P}$ chains without any contamination in the first 20 degradation steps. This result may be explained i.) by a post-translatory modification of the protein chains or even protein modification during our purification procedure or ii.) the sequence differences might be located in the region after the first 20 residues. This would require further analysis of tryptic fragments on high-voltage paper electrophoresis (fingerprint-method) or on HPLC and by DNA-sequence analysis of AP-genes. Thus, the question concerning the nature of the additional two weak subunit-bands of the APC-complex identified in SDS-PAGE gels remains to be answered.

STUDIES ON THE PHYCOBILIPROTEIN COMPLEXES FROM THE RED ALGAE
PORPHYRIDIUM CRUENTUM.

W. Sidler, F. Suter, R. Israels and H. Zuber.
Institut für Molekularbiologie und Biophysik, ETH-Hönggerberg,
CH-8093 Zürich, Switzerland.

Introduction

As with cyanobacteria, the red alga Porphyridium cruentum contains large
extramembraneous light-harvesting antennae known as phycobilisomes. The
architecture of some types of phycobilisomes, from cyanobacteria as well
as from the red alga Rhodella violacea, are well known as a result of
electron microscopic studies. The detailed electron microscopic study of
these phycobilisomes has been made possible by their disc-shaped structures (1). The phycobilisome of Porphyridium cruentum is relatively
large (up to $15*10^6$ Da) and its shape has been described as a large
semi-ellipsoid through electron microscopic studies (2). As a result of
its shape and size, detailed insight into the substructures of the P.
cruentum phycobilisome has not been possible through the use of electron
microscopy. Most of the phycobiliproteins of the P. cruentum
phycobilisome have already been isolated and described (3,4). As well,
the linker-polypeptide composition of the whole phycobilisome was been
studied by SDS-polyacrylamide gel electrophoresis (SDS-PAGE). (5). The
assignment however of the different linker-polypeptides to the various
phycobilisome subcomplexes, especially to the core complexes, is not
exactly known. The most abundant phycobiliprotein in the phycobilisome
of P. cruentum is B-phycoerythrin (BPE). It is present as a large com-
plex with the composition $(\alpha\beta)_6\gamma$. The BPE α- and β- polypeptides
correspond to the usual phycobiliprotein subunits with a molecular
weight of 18 and 20 kDa, whereas the γ-polypeptide (30 kDa) is similiar
to the 30 Kda linker-polypeptide family which are mostly buried in the
phycobiliprotein hexamers. The γ-subunits carry four phycobilin
chromophores, two phycoerythrobilins (PEB, λA_{max} 555 nm) and two
phycourobilins (PUB, λA_{max} 499 nm) (6). For this reason these
polypetides are named γ-subunits instead of linker-polypeptides. The
complete amino acid sequences of the α- and β-subunit of BPE have been
established recently by protein sequence analysis (7). Primary structure
information of the γ-subunit is only available from 4 PEB- and PUB-
chromopeptides (6). Redlinger and Gantt (5) found three different γ-
subunits by SDS-PAGE. In order to obtain further sequence data on the γ-
subunits and to elucidate the structural diffrence of the the three γ-
subunits, it is necessary first to isolate the different BPE complexes
and second to separate the γ-subunits from the complexes.

M. Baltscheffsky (ed.), Current Research in Photosynthesis, Vol. II, 97–100.
© 1990 Kluwer Academic Publishers. Printed in the Netherlands.

Phycobiliproteins may be easily obtained in large amounts by ammonium
sulfate precipitation from crude cell extracts followed by ion-exchange
chromatography (IEX) (Fig. 1a). In this study a method for ion-exchange
chromatography is described (Fig. 1a,b) which enables the separation in
one single step of all complexes of the P. cruentum phycobilisome formed
by allophycocyanin (APC), R-phycocyanin (RPC) and phycoerythrin (PE),
with (BPE) or without (bPE) the different ɣ-subunits. However, in order
to determine the linker-polypetide composition of the subcomplexes,
these complexes must be free of contaminating proteins such as RUBISCO
subunits which do not belong to the phycobilisomes. Phycobilisomes have
been isolated by Gantt et al. (2) using an ultracentrifugation method.
This method yields intact and highly pure phycobilisomes. Unfortunately,
this method does not yield the amounts needed for further primary structure analysis of the ɣ-subunits. In this study a method was used which
allowed the preparation of large quantities of phycobilisomes from P.
cruentum. Subsequent to IEX chromatography, following phycobiliprotein
preparation by either ammonium sulfate precipitation of crude cell extract or from dissociated phycobilisomes, the polypeptide patterns from
the fractions eluted by IEX chromatography were compared.

MATERIALS AND METHODS

Phycobilisomes   were prepared by a modified method of Füglistaller et
al. (8) using Triton X-100 for solubilisation of thylakoid membranes and
polyethyleneglycol for precipitaion of the PBS. Proteolytic activity was
inhibited by repeated addition of PMSF at every purification step. Prior
to ion-exchange chromatography the phycobilisomes were dialyzed overnight against 5 mM potassium phosphate buffer pH 7.1 and centrifuged at
20'000 rpm for 30 min. The brownish pellet, containing chlorophyll-
associated material was discarded. The supernatant was applied to an
ion-exchange column as described in Fig. 1b. For the second method,
crude phycobiliprotein extract was obtained by cell disruption on a
Manton Gaulin French Press. Proteolytic activity was also inhibited by
PMSF. Phycobiliproteins were extracted from the centrifuged cell extract
by ammonium sulfate precipitation (60 %). The pellet was dialyzed,
centrifuged and chromatographed as described in Fig. 1 a).
One of the ɣ-subunits was isolated from the hexameric BPE complex by
gel-permeation chromatography in 50% formic acid.

Fig. 1 a-c: Ion-exchange chromatography of phycobiliproteins extracted
from P. cruentum on a Pharmacia XK 26 column (2.6 x 30 cm) containing
220 ml Fractogel TSK DEAE-650 (S) (Merck, Germany) and chromatographed
on an automatic Pharmacia FPLC System at a flow rate of 3.5 ml/min,
using a gradient of 5 mM to 150 mM potassium phosphate pH 7.1; total
volume 1.7 L. Fifteen mL fractions were collected. 1a): Dialyzed ammonium sulfate precipitation. 1b): phycobiliproteins from dialyzed
phycobilisomes. 1c): superposition of a) and b).

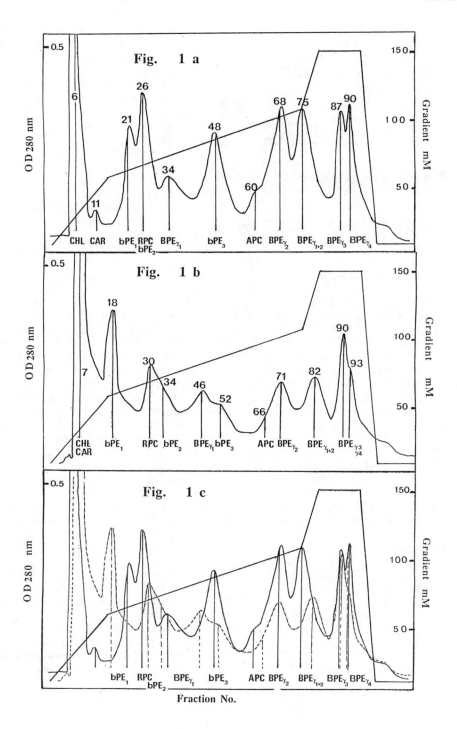

Fig. 1 a

Fig. 1 b

Fig. 1 c

Fraction No.

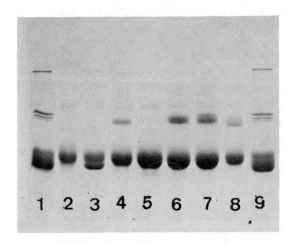

Fig.2: 14 % SDS-PAGE (Mini-Gel, BioRad) of peak fractions from ion-exchange chromatography of phycobiliproteins (Fig. 1a) extracted from P. cruentum: Lane 1: marker,(PBS M. laminosus); lane 2: bPE-1; lane 3: RPC and bPE-2; lane 4: BPE-γ1; lane 5: bPE-3; lane 6: BPE-γ2; lane 7: BPE-γ1+2; lane 8: BPE-γ3; lane 9: marker,(PBS M. laminosus).

RESULTS AND DISCUSSION

Analysis and comparison of the polypeptide pattern of the fractions eluted by ion-exchange chromatography on a Fractogel TSK DEAE column (Fig. 1a-c) by SDS-PAGE (Fig. 2), as well as absorption and fluorescence spectra and sucrose gradient ultracentrifugation (not shown) reveal that the several phycobiliprotein complexes from the P. cruentum phycobilisome were well separated in preparative amounts. Notably, for the first time five BPE complexes were separated differing in the γ-subunit composition, which supports the existence of three γ-subunits (Redlinger and Gantt 1981, ref.5). Phycobiliproteins corresponding to bPE were eluted in three different peaks. The comparison between the PBS- and the ammonium sulfate method show that principally the PBS complexes are eluted in the same order (Fig 1c), beginning with a breakthrough of chlorophyll (CHL) and carotinoid-associated material (CAR).The elution patterns of the BPE complexes are very similar. Differences may also occur due to residual content of detergent and PEG. These BPE complexes and their γ-subunits as well as the bPE fractions will be characterized further.

References

1. Mörschel, E. & Rhiel, E. (1987) in: Membrane structures, pp.209-254.
2. Gantt E. & Lipschultz C.A. (1972) J. Cell Biol. **54**, 313-324.
3. Glazer, A.N. & Hixon, C.S. (1977) J. Biol. Chem. **252**, 32-42.
4. Glazer, A.N. & Hixon, C.S. (1975) J. Biol. Chem. **250**,5487-5495.
5. Redlinger, T. & Gantt, E. (1981) Plant Physiol. **68**, 1375-1379.
6. Lundell, J.D., Glazer, A.N., DeLange, R.J., Brown, D.M., Schoenleber, H., Rapoport, H. (1984) J. Biol. Chem. **259**, 5472-5489.(three papers)
7. Sidler, W., Kumpf, B., Suter, F., Klotz, A.V., Glazer, A.N. and Zuber, H. (1989) Biol. Chem. Hoppe-Seyler **370**, 115-124.
8. Füglistaller, P., Rümbeli, R., Suter, F. & Zuber, H. (1984) Hoppe – Seyler's Z. Physiol. Chem. **365**, 1085-1096.

ROLE OF THE "ANCHOR" POLYPEPTIDE IN THE ARCHITECTURE OF THE
PHYCOBILISOME CORE : A MOLECULAR APPROACH

Véronique Capuano, Nicole Tandeau de Marsac and Jean Houmard,
Physiologie Microbienne, Dept B.G.M., Institut Pasteur,
75724 PARIS Cedex 15, FRANCE

Phycobilisomes (PBsomes) constitute the light-harvesting antennae of cyanobacteria. Most of them are made up of a central three-cylinder core from which six rods radiate (1). However, exceptions have been described: i) *Synechococcus* sp. PCC 6301 and 7942 have hemidiscoidal PBsomes, but the six rods radiate from a core made up of only two cylinders (2); ii) according to the observed ratio of rod phycobiliproteins (PB) versus core PBs, as well as to electron microscopy studies, *Phormidium* sp. PCC 7376 seems to have PBsomes resembling more closely the hemi-ellipsoidal type described for most of the rhodophytes (3); iii) finally, *Gloeobacter violaceus,* which does not have classical thylakoid membranes, harbors very peculiar rod-shaped PBsomes directly attached to the cytoplasmic membrane (4).

Biochemical analyses have demonstrated that proteins are the only components of the PBsomes (2,5). For a given species, changes in the environmental factors have been shown to affect the abundance or the rod substructure of the PBsomes while, in contrast, the core substructure seems insensitive to at least most of the changes (6). Table 1 presents the polypeptide composition of the cores from two different strains; the unicellular and obligate photoautotroph *Synechococcus* sp. PCC 6301, and the filamentous facultative photoheterotroph and chromatic adapter *Calothrix* sp. PCC 7601. In both strains there exist two copies of α^{APB}, $\beta^{18.3}$ and L_{CM} (high molecular weight polypeptide) per PBsome, but the number of α^{AP}, β^{AP} and L_C polypeptides varies (2,7). These quantitative differences result from the presence of the third cylinder, located on top of the two basal ones, and which, by analogy with the biochemical data obtained with other strains, is only composed of α^{AP}, β^{AP} and $L_C^{7.8}$ (8,9). Although the qualitative composition of the cores does not vary, a noticeable difference between the two strains is the size of the L_{CM} (75 kDa vs 92 kDa). The question then arises: "Does the L_{CM} size determine the substructure of the core?".

With this working hypothesis in mind, we started a comparative analysis of the L_{CM} from *Calothrix* sp. PCC 7601 (three cylinder-type core) and *Synechococcus* sp. PCC 6301 (two cylinder-type core). The corresponding gene, *apcE*, has been isolated and characterized from both strains. In each case, as first mentioned by Zilinskas and coworkers (cited in ref. 10) for *Nostoc* sp. strain MAC, the *apcE* genes were found immediately upstream from the *apcABC* operon which encodes the α^{AP}, β^{AP} and L_C core components. The deduced amino acid sequence of the *Synechococcus* sp. PCC 6301 *apcE* gene predicts a polypeptide of M_r 72.4 kDa, in good agreement with the size deduced from SDS-PAGE analysis. The size of the *Calothrix* sp. PCC 7601 L_{CM} , as

M. Baltscheffsky (ed.), Current Research in Photosynthesis, Vol. II, 101–104.
© 1990 *Kluwer Academic Publishers. Printed in the Netherlands.*

Table 1: Protein composition of the phycobilisome cores

copy number/phycobilisome

		Calothrix 7601	Synechococcus 6301
α allophycocyanin	(α^{AP})	32	20
β allophycocyanin	(β^{AP})	34	22
α allophycocyanin B	(α^{APB})	2	2
β-type polypeptide	($\beta^{18.3}$)	2	2
core linker	($L_C^{7.8}$)	6	4
core-membrane linker	(L_{CM})	2	2

deduced from nucleotide sequencing, is 120 kDa while M_r value estimated from SDS gels was about 92 kDa. In the cyanellar genome of *Cyanophora paradoxa*, the *apcE* gene also lies upstream from the *apcAB* gene cluster and encodes a 883 amino acid long polypeptide (M_r 100 kDa) (10).

All the L_{CM} sequences known so far share a similar organization, i. e. a N-terminal biliprotein-like domain followed by at least two, and up to four, rod linker (L_R^{PC})-like domains. The N-terminal domain is about 50 % homologous to every PB subunit (either α or β), but is larger than typical PBs. They have a short N-terminal extension of 16 residues and an insertion of 55, 68 or 70 amino acids (for the cyanelle, *Calothrix* sp. PCC 7601 and *Synechococcus* sp. PCC 6301, respectively) which starts at residue 77 and separates the two homologous regions. We will subsequently refer to this insertion as the PB-loop region. Following the biliprotein domain and another spacing region (Arm 1) are the repeated domains (REPs), each about 120 residues long. Homologies of about 60 % exist between the different REPs within a given L_{CM}, as well as between a REP and the N-terminal domains of the L_R^{PC}. REPs are at variable distance (Arms 2 to 4) from each other. It is worth noting that, with respect to polarity and Pro + Gly content, the amino acid composition of the REPs and of the spacing regions differ. Indeed, the arms contain at least two times more polar than hydrophobic amino acids, while the ratios of polar/hydrophobic residues are of about 1.2 for the REPs (Table 2). In addition, Pro and Gly residues, which are known to be often present in loops of globular proteins, are much more abundant in the spacing arms than in the REPs. It is thus very likely that the REPS represent the domains of interactions between the L_{CM} and the trimers of phycobiliproteins.

The L_{CM}s have long been regarded as representing: (i) The terminal acceptor of the energy transfer chain, because of their spectral properties (9, 11, 12), and (ii) A linker polypeptide which anchors the PBsome on the thylakoid membrane, since their presence was detected after purification both in the PBsome and in the membrane fractions (5). Amino acid sequence analysis indeed reveals that all the L_{CM}s have PB-like and L_R-like domains. However, from sequence data, we could detect neither classical transmembrane elements nor a consensus sequence known to represent potential acylation sites (13) whereby the L_{CM} could be attached to the photosynthetic membrane. These results mean that direct protein-protein interactions between the L_{CM} and components of the photosystem II might ensure the anchoring of the PBsome on the photosynthetic membrane. Gantt and coworkers recently reported that two high

Table 2 : Amino acid composition of the different domains of the L_{CM}

L_{CM} domains		% Amino Acids		
		Polar	Hydrophobic	Pro + Gly
PB domain	*Cal.* 7601	46	32	8
	Syn. 6301	48	34	9
	Cyanelle	49	38	4
PB loop	*Cal.* 7601	40	29	22
	Syn. 6301	42	29	24
	Cyanelle	34	29	24
Arm 1	*Cal.* 7601	52	21	16
	Syn. 6301	56	25	10
	Cyanelle	56	21	10
REP 1	*Cal.* 7601	46	37	11
	Syn. 6301	44	39	9
	Cyanelle	49	35	7
Arm 2	*Cal.* 7601	48	23	21
	Syn. 6301	52	26	15
	Cyanelle	51	25	17
REP 2	*Cal.* 7601	45	39	8
	Syn. 6301	46	40	9
	Cyanelle	43	38	9
Arm 3	*Cal.* 7601	56	27	12
	Cyanelle	59	27	10
REP 3	*Cal.* 7601	43	37	12
	Cyanelle	48	39	7
Arm 4	*Cal.* 7601	57	22	14
REP 4	*Cal.* 7601	45	37	9

molecular weight polypeptides (L_{CM}?), having significant differences in their amino acid composition, could be immunoprecipitated with an antiserum specific for the *Nostoc* sp. L_{CM}[94], both from *Nostoc* sp and *Porphyridium cruentum*. (14) One was obtained from isolated PBsomes and the second from the PBsome-free thylakoid fraction. Interactions between these two molecules might be the clue for the anchoring of the PBsomes.

Overall homology between the three L_{CM} are 74% (6301 vs 7601), 70% (6301 vs cyanelle) and 75% (cyanelle vs 7601). However, these homologies are not evenly distributed. Between these three species, the spacing arms (around 65%), as well as the PB-loop region (about 60%), share less homology than either the PB domains (75%) or the REPs (around 83%). The best homologies are obtained by direct alignment of the sequences. Stated differently, all REP1s are more homologous to each other than REP2 of *Synechococcus* sp. PCC 6301 is to REP3 or to REP4 of *Calothrix* sp. PCC 7601 for example. Similarly, the best homologue of the cyanellar REP3 is REP3 from *Calothrix*. Even the size of the regions which space the different domains is almost perfectly conserved. These observations indicate that all the contacts, if any, between the L_{CM} and the third cylinder in the PBsome most probably occur through the C-terminal part of the L_{CM} . Since *Synechococcus* sp. PCC 6301 cores consist of two cylinders and its L_{CM} has two REPs, it was tempting to correlate REP and cylinder numbers. However, both cyanelles and *Calothrix* sp. PCC 7601 have three-cylinder cores but their L_{CM} have three and four REPs, respectively. Thus, the question of the possible interactions between the L_{CM} and the third cylinder of the PBsome remains open.

In order to define the topology and the functions of the different REPs, we have introduced the *Calothrix apcE* gene into the chromosome of *Synechococcus* sp. PCC 7942. This strain is considered to be almost identical to *Synechococcus* sp. PCC 6301 (15), but has retained its ability to be transformed by DNA. The *Calothrix apcE* gene has been inserted into the *met1* gene of *Synechococcus* sp. PCC 7942 through gene replacement using the platform method developped by J. van der Plas and coworkers (personal communication). Transformants thus obtained harbor two *apcE* gene copies on their genome, the endogenous one and a heterologous copy. Expression of both genes was observed and we are, at present, analyzing the structure and composition of the PBsome in the transformants. Genetic engineering of either one or the other *apcE* gene is now possible and will, no doubt, help in defining the crucial role of the L_{CM} in the assembly and function of the PBsome core substructure.

REFERENCES

1 Bryant, D. A., Guglielmi, G., Tandeau de Marsac, N., Castets, A.-M. and Cohen-Bazire, G. (1979) Arch. Microbiol. 123, 113-127.
2 Glazer, A. N., Lundell, D.J., Yamanaka, G. and Williams, R.C. (1883) Ann. Microbiol. (Inst. Pasteur) 134B, 159-180.
3 Guglielmi, G. and Cohen-Bazire, G. (1984) Protistologica XX, 393-413.
4 Guglielmi, G. Cohen-Bazire, G. and Bryant, D.A. (1981) Arch. Microbiol. 129, 181-189.
5 Tandeau de Marsac, N. and Cohen-Bazire, G. (1977) Proc. Natl. Acad. Sci. USA 74, 1635-1639.
6 Tandeau de Marsac, N. (1983) Bull. Inst. Pasteur 81, 201-254.
7 Tandeau de Marsac, N. Mazel, D., Damerval, T., Guglielmi, G., Capuano, V. and Houmard, J. (1988) Photosynth. Res. 18, 99-132.
8 Anderson, L. K. and Eiserling, F.A. (1986) J. Mol. Biol. 191, 441-451.
9 Glazer, A. N. (1985) Annu Rev. Biophys. Biophys. Chem. 14, 47-77.
10 Bryant, D. A. (1988) In Light-Energy Transduction in Photosynthesis: Higher Plant and Bacterial Models (Stevens, S.E., Jr. and Bryant, D.A., eds.) pp. 62-90, The American Society of Plant Physiologists.
11 Lundell, D. J., Yamanaka, G. and Glazer, A.N. (1981) J. Cell. Biol. 91, 315-319.
12 Mimuro, M. Lipschultz, C. and Gantt, E. (1986) Biochim. Biophys. Acta 852, 126-132.
13 Ferguson, M.A.J. and Williams, A.F. (1988) Annu. Rev. Biochem. 57, 285-320
14 Gantt, E. Cunningham, F.X., Lipschultz, C.A. and Mimuro, M. (1988) Plant Physiol 86, 996-998.
15 Golden, S.S., Nalty, M.S., and Cho, D.-S.C. (1989) J. Bacteriol. 171, 24-29

THE SUPRAMOLECULAR STRUCTURE OF THE LIGHT-HARVESTING SYSTEM OF CYANO-
BACTERIA AND RED ALGAE

W. Lange, G.-H. Schatz*, C. Wilhelm** and E. Mörschel
FB Biologie der Philipps-Universität, D - 3550 Marburg, *MPI für
Strahlenchemie, D - 4330 Mülheim and **Institut für Allgemeine
Botanik D - 6500 Mainz

Introduction
    Phycobilisomes are the major light-harvesting antennae of cyano-
bacteria and red algae. They transfer the absorbed light energy with
high efficiency to photosystem II (PSII). The phycobilisomes are bound
to the external surface of the thylakoids where they are organized to
well aligned arrays (1). They are bound to PSII, as was shown by the
isolation of oxygen-evolving PSII-phycobilisome complexes (2). It was
the aim of our studies to examine the structure and organization of
PSII-phycobilisome complexes of cyanobacteria and red algae.

Results and Discussion
    The thylakoid areas of cyanobacteria are characterized by broad
lanes of densely packed protoplasmic (PF) particles of 7.0 - 9.0 nm. On
the complementary fracture face, rows of well aligned exoplasmic (EF)
particles of the 10 nm size class fit in the particle free grooves
between the PF-particle lanes (3). The minimum centre to centre distance
of these EF-particle rows is 45 nm or more and is thus in register with
the spacing of phycobilisome rows (4).
    The EF-particles of cyanobacteria containing hemi-discoidal phyco-
bilisomes measure 10 x 20 nm and they are aggregated linearly front to
back with their longitudinal faces with a periodicity of 10 nm. Most
particles reveal a central furrow perpendicular to the long axis dividing them into two side by side domains of 10 nm x 10 nm each, suggesting that each particle represents a dimer. Both domains are cleaved
additionally parallel to the longitudinal face of the whole particle.
The structures of the dimers are complementary to the structure of the
two adjacent phycobilisome core cylinders. Freeze-etched thylakoids,
exposing simultaneously phycobilisomes and exoplasmic particles in the
same area, show a direct alignment of both systems; the EF-particle rows
within the membranes correspond to the phycobilisome rows on the surface
of the thylakoids (5). Because phycobilisomes transfer the captured
light energy mainly to photosystem II (6), we proposed that the EF-
particles correspond to PSII particles.
    In order to examine this hypothesis, water splitting PS II particles
were isolated from the cyanobacterium Synechococcus spec. These particles were characterized by Chl/ PSII ratios between 70 to 90 and a

PSII/PSI ratio > 1500. The main pigments were phycocyanin (PC), allo-phycocyanin (AP) and chlorophyll (Chl). When excited at 445 nm the PSII preparations showed a minor fluorescence emission maximum at 660 nm characteristic for allophycocyanin and two major maxima at 685 and 693 nm. The fluorescence at 685 nm was attributed to an interplay of allo-phycocyanin B, the large membrane-phycobilisome linker (Lcm) and a Chl-antenna, whilst the 693 nm fluorescence belonged to a Chl-antenna alone. Most of the light energy captured by phycobilisomes was transferred to the final phycobilisome emitters and the PSII antennae as shown from the emission peak at 685 nm and the shoulder at 692 nm.

The chlorophyll-protein (CP) and polypeptide pattern of PSII complexes were determined by two dimensional gel electrophoresis. Prominent polypeptides could be attributed to the biliprotein subunits of AP (14, 16 kDa) and PC (15, 18 kDa) and at least four phycobilisome-linker polypeptides (29, 31, 34 and 120 kDa. The Chl-proteins were characterized by apoproteins of 47 (CPIIa,b) and 41 (CPIIc) kDa. CP IIa and b were similar in their spectroscopic properties and showed fluorescence maxima at 685 nm and shoulders at 693 nm, whilst CP IIc exhibited only one peak at 686 nm, when excited at 445 nm. Thus the isolated Chl-proteins had similar emission properties as the "in situ" PSII antennae.

The purified PSII complexes were analysed by negative staining electron microscopy after dissociation and purification from bilipro-teins. Two particle classes are distinguished: spherical-ellipsoidal and binary particles. The dominant structures are the binary particles. They measure 22 x 11 nm and are divided perpendicular to their long axis by a lace into two spherical-ellipsoidal parts of about 11 nm. Aggregations of these binary particles to rows also occurred. These binary particles are very similar in their appearance compared to the "in situ" EF-particles. The second particle class is represented by spherical-ellip-soidal particles of about 11 x 14 nm; they are supposed to be the building blocks of the binary particles.

The PSII- complexes were incorporated into phospholipid liposomes and analysed by freeze-fracture techniques.The freeze-fracture particles were randomly distributed and their diameter was about 10.3 nm on the concave and convex fracture faces. Some particles showed a central furrow, that was also present in the EF-particles "in situ"; side by side aggregations of two particles were observed too. With a height of 13-16 nm the particles span the liposome membrane.

From our results we propose that the 10 nm EF-particles correspond to PSII-complexes. In cyanobacteria and red algae with hemi-discoidal phycobilisomes, these PSII complexes are aggregated to dimers, which bind one phycobilisome on top. Each 10 nm particle represents a PSII-complex containing at least the reaction centre complex (RC), the water splitting system, the Chl-antennae with apoproteins of 41 and 47 kDa.

The linker polypeptide (Lcm) is supposed to bind the phycobilisome to the Chl antennae of PSII. Energy is funneled from the terminal emit-ters of the phycobilisome (Lcm, AP B) to the antennae of PSII (CP 41, 47) and from there to the reaction centre.

The arrangement of the EF-particles of red algae containing hemi-ellipsoidal phycobilisomes is similar. However, the EF-particle rows are loosened into packages of particles which are separated normally by

areas of 7-15 nm. Only in short areas, some packages are tightly arranged with nearly no space between them. Each package is composed of two
10 x 20 nm EF-particles, which are aggregated with their long faces.
Each EF-particle corresponds to a dimeric 10 x 10 nm particle as is
observed in well resolved or partially dissociated particles and thus
one particle package contains four 10 nm EF-particles (Fig.1a). This
pattern corresponds well with the pattern of the hemi-ellipsoidal phycobilisomes, which have a basal length of 50 nm, a height of 36 nm and a
width of about 20 nm. They are separated by the same distance as the EF-
particle packages within the rows. The assembly of the EF-particles, and
the fact that phycobilisomes are cleaved parallel to their long axis in
two equivalent halves (Fig. 1b,c), supports the hypothesis that the
hemi-ellipsoidal phycobilisomes are structurally double versions of
hemi-discoidal phycobilisomes (Fig.2). On the average 1439 monomeric,
and on different areas, 375 tetrameric EF-particles/μm^2 were counted.
When these numbers are compared with the phycobilisome number of 366/μm^2,
a 1:1 ratio of tetrameric particles and phycobilisomes is evident.
    The concentration of PSII centres was determined by flash light
induced oxygen evolution (7) and correlated with the amount of AP. A Chl
to PSII ratio of 120 Chl a/PSII was determined. The molar ratio of PSII
to AP was 1:5. Hemi-ellipsoidal phycobilisomes may contain 20-24 moles
of AP. Thus the molar ratio of PSII to AP is 4:20 and consequently a
tetrameric PSII particle package binds one hemi-ellipsoidal phycobilisome. It is supposed that the aggregation of PSII to dimers and tetra-
mers is induced by the phycobilisome structures of the cores. Depending
on the type of phycobilisome, different aggregation patterns are realized.
    When phycobilisome-PSII complexes are tightly packed within their
rows we assume that energy is transferred not only from phycobilisomes
to the underlying PSII particles but also between phycobilisomes and
PSII along the same row resulting in an efficient energy distribution
along the plane of the thylakoid by connecting many PSII reaction centres. In the red alga Porphyridium cruentum only four PSII complexes are
grouped. The rowed PSII-phycobilisome particles imply also a spatial
separation of PSII and PSI equivalent to the lateral heterogeneity of
PSI and PSII in the thylakoid system of grana containing chloroplasts.

REFERENCES
1 Mörschel, E. and Rhiel E. (1987) in Electron Microscopy of Proteins
  (Harris, J. R. and Horne, R. W. eds) Vol. 6. pp.209-254, Academic
  Press, London, New York
2 Clement-Metral, J. C. and Gantt, E. (1983) FEBS Lett. 156, 185-188
3 Giddings, T.H., Wasman C. and Staehelin L. A. (1983) Plant. Physiol.
  71, 409-419
4 Mörschel, E. and Schatz H.-G. (1987) Planta 172, 145-154
5 Mörschel, E. and Mühlethaler K. (1983) Planta 158, 451-457
6 Ley, A. C. (1984) Plant Physiol. 74, 451-454
7 Myers, J. and Graham, J.-R. (1983) Plant Physiol. 71, 440-442

This study was supported by the Deutsche Forschungsgemeinschaft.

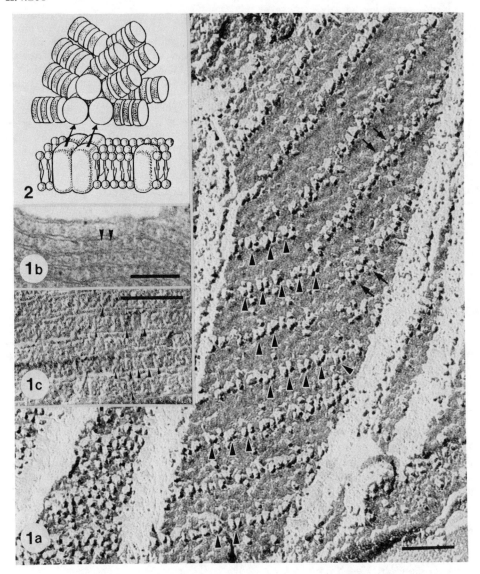

Fig. 1.a) Freeze-fractured thylakoids of <u>Porphyridium</u> <u>cruentum</u>. Arrow-
heads indicate EF-particle clusters. Particle clusters are re-
solved into four 10 nm particles (arrows). Bar: 100 nm.
b,c) Phycobilisomes in profile from the side. The central furrow
is marked. Bars: 200 nm.
Fig. 2.Hypothetical model of a PSII-phycobilisome complex of <u>Porphyri-</u>
<u>dium</u> <u>cruentum</u>. One hemi-ellipsoidal phycobilisome is bound to
four PSII-complexes.

QUANTITATION OF REACTION CENTERS BY HPLC ANALYSIS OF MINOR BUT KEY
CHLOROPHYLL-TYPE PIGMENTS

T. WATANABE and M. KOBAYASHI

Institute of Industrial Science, University of Tokyo, Roppongi,
Minato-ku, Tokyo 106, JAPAN

1. INTRODUCTION

We have developed a rapid, high resolution normal-phase HPLC
technique to quantitate the reaction centers in photosynthetic apparatus based on the amount of the minor but key chlorophyll (Chl)-type
pigments, namely, Chl a', pheophytin (Pheo) a, bacteriopheophytin
(BPheo) a and bacteriochlorophyll (BChl) 663.

In higher plants and cyanobacteria [1], one molecule of Chl a'
(C10-epimer of Chl a, Fig. 1) in PS I and two molecules of Pheo a in
PS II were found, which gave Chl a/P700 and Chl a/P680 stoichiometries consistent with those obtained by flash and/or oxygen evolving
experiments.

The analysis has been extended here to photosynthetic bacteria.
In case of purple nonsulfur bacterium, $Rb.$ $sphaeroides$, twelve independent analyses gave a value BChl a/BPheo $a \simeq 100$, which, in combination with BPheo a/P870 = 2, led to a value of BChl a/P870 $\simeq 200$,
in excellent agreement with the published stoichiometry. Four independent analytical runs on green sulfur bacterium, $Chlorobium$ $limicola$
$f.$ $sp.$ $thiosulfatophilum$, gave a relatively constant value BChl a/
BChl 663 $\simeq 10$; this corresponds to a value of BChl 663/P840 = 7-10
when combined with the stoichiometry BChl a/P840 = 70-100 [2].

2. MATERIALS AND METHODS

Three species of cyano-
bacteria and a purple nonsulfur bacterium were supplied
from Prof. T. Matsunaga, Tokyo
University of Agriculture and
Technology. A green sulfur
bacterium was supplied from Dr.
S. Itoh, National Institute for
Basic Biology. Pigment extrac-
tion/HPLC analysis was performed according to our standard procedure [1].

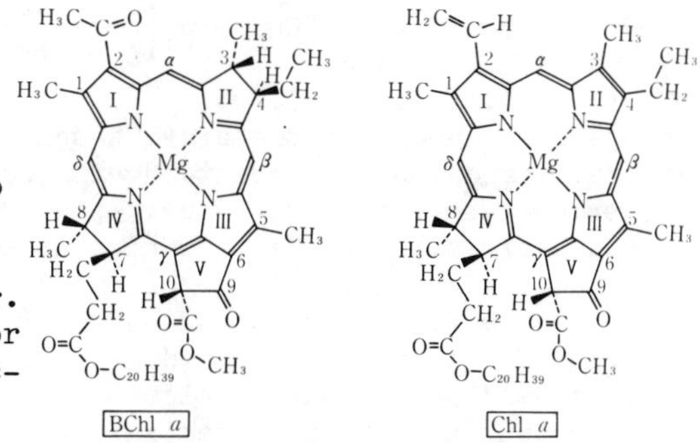

3. RESULTS AND DISCUSSION

Fig. 1 BChl a and Chl a. Replacement of
the central Mg ion with two protons gives
BPheo a and Pheo a respectively.

M. Baltscheffsky (ed.), Current Research in Photosynthesis, Vol. II, 109–112.
© 1990 *Kluwer Academic Publishers. Printed in the Netherlands.*

3.1 The minor Chl-type pigments in higher plants and cyanobacteria

In higher plants four Chl-type pigments, namely, Chl *a*, Chl *b*, Pheo *a* and Chl *a'*, are found [1]. The contents of two minor pigments, Pheo *a* and Chl *a'*, are significantly uniform: the molar ratio of Chl *a*/Chl *a'* and Chl *a*/Pheo *a* in more than 100 leaf tissue samples from 13 different higher plants are:

Chl *a*/Chl *a'* = 460 ± 90   (I),   Chl *a*/Pheo *a* = 120 ± 20   (II)

The fundamental pattern of the HPLC traces for chloroform extracts from cyanobacteria are similar to those from higher plants except that Chl *b* is absent. However, the Chl *a'* and Pheo *a* contents in three species of cyanobacteria are slightly different:

Chl *a*/Chl *a'* = 125 ± 15   (III),   Chl *a*/Pheo *a* = 100 ± 25   (IV)

3.2 Chl *a*/P700 and Chl *a*/P680 stoichiometries determined by HPLC analysis

The presence of two Pheo *a* molecules in PS II has been well established [3], and we recently demonstrated the presence of one Chl *a'* molecule in PS I [1]. Combining Chl *a'*/P700 = 1 with Eqns. (I) and (III), and Pheo *a*/P680 = 2 with Eqns. (II) and (IV), the following photosynthetic unit sizes are obtained:

Chl *a*/P700 = 460 ± 90   (V),   Chl *a*/P680 = 240 ± 40   (VI)

for the 13 higher plants, and

Chl *a*/P700 = 125 ± 15   (VII),   Chl *a*/P680 = 200 ± 50   (VIII)

for the three cyanobacteria. These stoichiometries are consistent with those obtained by other methods, e.g. flash photolysis.

3.3 HPLC analysis of purple nonsulfur bacterium *Rb. sphaeroides*

Fig. 2 shows a typical HPLC trace for chloroform extract from *Rb. sphaeroides*. Besides the major peaks of carotenoids and BChl *a*, two minor peaks of BPheo *a* and 2-desvinyl-2-acetyl Chl *a* (2-2-Chl *a*) are clearly discerned. The authentic BChl *a* (purity above 99.9%, Fig. 3(A)), BChl *a'* (>99.9%, Fig. 3(C)) and BPheo *a* (>99.9%, Fig. 4(D))

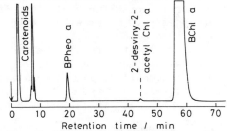

Fig. 2 HPLC trace of *Rb. sphaeroides*.
(λ = 380 nm)

were prepared by means of preparative-scale HPLC [4], and were used as external standards in pigment identification. As is evident in Fig. 4, prime-type pigments, namely, BChl *a'* and BPheo *a'*, are absent in *Rb. sphaeroides*. Ring II of BChl *a* undergoes oxidation very easily, particularly in the presence of oxidants such as 2,3-dichloro-5, 6-dicyanoquinone [5], to give 2-2-Chl *a* (Fig. 4(F)). An equilibrium composition of BChl *a'*/BChl *a* in diethyl ether at 26°C is about 1/3 (Fig. 3(B)), and this value is almost the same as that of Chl *a'*/Chl *a* [6]. The BChl *a'*/BChl *a* epimerization rate in DMF at 25°C is about 7-fold lower than that of Chl *a'*/Chl *a* [6].

3.4 BPheo *a* content and BChl *a*/P870 stoichiometry in *Rb. sphaeroides*

Twelve independent HPLC analyses gave a value:

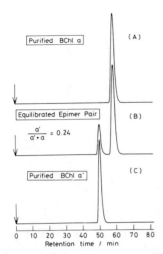

Fig. 3 HPLC traces of purified BChl a(A), BChl a'(C) and equilibrated epimer mixture(B).

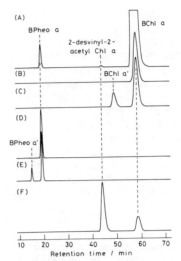

Fig. 4 Identification of components in *Rb. sphaeroides* extract (A).

$$\text{BChl } a/\text{BPheo } a = 100 \pm 7 \qquad\qquad \text{(IX)}$$

this leads, in combination with BPheo a/P870 = 2, to the following value: $\text{BChl } a/\text{P870} = 200 \pm 14$ (X)

A good agreement is seen between the BChl a/P870 molar ratio obtained here and that assayed by flash measurements [7]. The BChl a/2-2-Chl a molar ratio is in a range from 1000 to 3000, consequently 2-2-Chl a/P870 = 1/5-1/15; this indicates that 2-2-Chl a is an artifact produced oxidatively in the course of pigment extraction.

3.5 HPLC analysis of green sulfur bacterium *C. thiosulfatophilum*

An HPLC trace for a chloroform extract from *C. thiosulfatophilum* is displayed in Fig. 5(A). Besides the two major peaks of Chl-type pigments, BChl 663 and BChl a, three minor peaks are detected. These pigments are all Chl-type pigments that can be detected by the present HPLC, except for the BChl cs and BPheo cs eluted at retention times longer than 120 min (not shown in Fig. 5(A)). Fig. 5 clearly shows the absence of prime-type pigments and of BPheo a. The two small peaks just before the peak of 2-2-Chl a have not been identified yet.

3.6 BChl 663 content and BChl 663/P840 stoichiometry in *C. thiosulfatophilum*

BChl 663 with absorption maxima at 663 and 433 nm, like BChl c, was found recently in *Prosthecochloris aestuarii* by means of reversed-phase HPLC [8], and the presence of this pigment in other species of green sulfur bacteria has not been reported. BChl 663 was assayed at an amount of 10-15 molecules per reaction center and was supposed to be a likely candidate for the primary electron acceptor [8]. In our present study the BChl a/BChl 663 molar ratio is 9.5-11.9 (four independent measurements), where the extinction coefficient of BChl 663 is assumed to be equal to that of BChl c. Although we have not measured the BChl *a*/P840 molar ratio in samples used here, the BChl 663/P840 ratio turns out to be ca. 7–10, which corresponds to the Chl *a*/P700 ratio of ether-washed PS I particles [9], on an assumption that the BChl *a*/P840 molar ratio is 70–100. Thus BChl 663s may function as key components in the reaction center. Further studies are required to elucidate the role of BChl 663 in the bacterial photosynthetic apparatus.

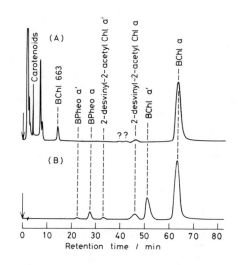

3.7 Summary

The results of the present study are summarized in Table 1. The analytical technique will find further applications in delineating molecular assembly of photosynthetic organs.

Fig. 5 HPLC traces of *C. thiosulfatophilum* (A) and of BPheo a'/a, 2-2-Chl a'/a and BChl a'/a mixture(B).

ACKNOWLEDGMENT: The authors are grateful to Prof. T. Matsunaga and Dr. S. Itoh for supplying us with the samples.

Table 1.   (Bacterio)chlorophyll *a'*, (Bacterio)pheophytin *a* and bacteriochlorophyll 663 in higher palnts, cyanobacteria and photosynthetic bacteria.

Species	$\dfrac{\text{(B)Chl } a}{\text{(B)Chl } a'}$	$\dfrac{\text{(B)Chl } a}{\text{RC*}}$	$\dfrac{\text{(B)Chl } a}{\text{(B)Pheo } a}$	$\dfrac{\text{(B)Chl } a}{\text{RC**}}$	$\dfrac{\text{BChl } a}{\text{BChl } 663}$
Higher plants, 13 species	460 ± 90	460 ± 90	120 ± 20	240 ± 40	—
Cyanobacteria, 3 species	125 ± 15	125 ± 15	100 ± 25	200 ± 50	—
Photosynthetic bacteria					
Rb. sphaeroides	∞	—	100 ± 7	200 ± 14	∞
C. thiosulfatophilum	∞	—	∞	—	10.7 ± 1.2

* RC = P700.   ** RC = P680 or P870.

REFERENCES
1. Kobayashi, M. et al. (1988) *Biochim. Biophys. Acta* 936, 81–89.
2. Amesz, J. (1987) *Photosynthetica* 21, 225–235.
3. Omata, T. et al. (1987) *Biochim. Biophys. Acta* 765, 403–405.
4. Watanabe, T. et al. (1984) *Anal. Chem.* 56, 251–256.
5. Smith, J. R. L. and Calvin, M. (1966) *J. Am. Chem. Soc.* 88, 4500–4506.
6. Watanabe, T. et al. (1987) *Biochim. Biophys. Acta* 892, 197–206.
7. Aagaard, J. and Sistrom, W. R. (1972) *Photochem. Photobiol.* 15, 209–225.
8. Braumann, T. et al. (1986) *Biochim. Biophys. Acta* 848, 83–91.
9. Ikegami, I. and Katoh, S. (1975) *Biochim. Biophys. Acta* 376, 588–592.

A Method for Studying Pigment Organization in Photosynthetic Complexes

H. van Amerongen, M. van Gurp*, F. van Mourik, B. van Haeringen & R. van Grondelle
Dept. of Biophysics, Free University, De Boelelaan 1081, 1081 HV Amsterdam.
* DSM Research, P. O. Box 18, 6160 MD Geleen, The Netherlands

Introduction

The use of polarized light spectroscopy is an important way to study pigment-organization in photosynthetic particles. For instance, linear dichroism (LD) measurements are often used to obtain information about the orientations of absorption transition moment vectors within these particles, which is interesting in view of understanding excitation energy transfer, but it may also lead to knowledge about the pigment organization. To perform LD-measurements, particles are often ordered in biaxially compressed polyacrylamide gels. Knowledge about the average orientation of the particles in the gel is required, to obtain quantitative information about the average transition moment directions. The orientation distribution is often badly known. Mathemetical expressions for rod-like and disc-like particles have been presented by Ganago et al. [1], which relate the amount of gel-compression to the average particle orientation. Recently, we showed that for rod-like chlorosomes of *Chloroflexus aurantiacus*, ordered in gels, the formalism described in [1] does indeed lead to a good estimation of the average orientation [2].Unfortunately, mathematical expressions are not available for particles, which are not rod- or disc-like.

It is described in [3] what kind of information polarized fluorescence measurements on ordered systems may provide. Interpretation of the results is certainly not straightforward but when certain symmetry conditions are fulfilled, average orientations of the dipole moments within the particles can experimentally be obtained as well as the average orientation of the particles in the gel.

We have performed polarized fluorescence measurements on chlorosomes from *Chloroflexus aurantiacus*, both in biaxially compressed gels and uncompressed gels in a 90° fluorescence set-up. These chlorosomes are antenna-systems, containing thousands of BChl c molecules. Assuming a high amount of energy transfer within these chlorosomes, which is in accordance with their biological function and assuming that the transition dipole moments are effectively rotationally symmetrically distributed with respect to the orientation axis (long axis) of the chlorosomes, the average orientation of the chlorosomes and the average orientation of the absorption and emission dipole moments with respect to the orientation axis can be obtained. The results are in very good agreement with results from linear dichroism measurements,

M. Baltscheffsky (ed.), Current Research in Photosynthesis, Vol. II, 113–116.
© 1990 *Kluwer Academic Publishers. Printed in the Netherlands.*

when the theory from [1] is used for the interpretation. The method used, seems to be very promising for the study of particles, which are not rod-like.

Materials and Methods
Similar chlorosome preparations were used as in [2]. Gels were prepared in a similar way as described in [2]. Fluorescence measurements were performed on a home-built fluorimeter ($90°$ set-up) using photon-counting. Light is incident along the x-axis and is polarized either along the y- (horizontal) or z-axis (vertical). Fluorescence light is detected along the y-axis with the polarization direction along the x- (horizontal) or z-axis (vertical). Either an uncompressed gel, or a gel, which is compressed with a factor 1.25 in both the x- and y-direction, is placed in the sample-holder. Both gels contain the same concentration of chlorosomes. The dimensions of the compressed and uncompressed gel are 1 cm along the x- and y-axis. At a certain combination of excitation and emission wavelength, four different fluorescence intensities are measured, corresponding to different combinations of the polarization directions of the excitation and detection beam. From these four intensities I'_{vv}, I'_{vh}, I'_{hv} and I'_{hh} (where v (vertical) and h (horizontal) denote the direction of polarization of the excitation (first index) or emission light (second index)) the corrected intensities I_{vv}, I_{vh}, I_{hv} and I_{hh} must be determined, which are defined in [3]. In other words, the constants c_{vv}, c_{vh} , c_{vh} and c_{hh} have to be determined, which are defined, according to $I'_{vv} = c_{vv}$ I_{vv}, I'_{vh} $= c_{vh}$ I_{vh}, $I'_{hv} = c_{hv}$ I_{hv} and $I'_{hh} = c_{hh}$ I_{hh}. These constants depend on the amount of excitation light and the sensitivity of the apparatus for the fluorescence light. In general they differ for different combinations of polarization directions. Furthermore, they depend on the absorption and fluorescence properties of the gels, containing the chlorosomes. For the corrected intensities the following relations hold [3]:

$$I_{vv} = 1 + 2S_\mu + 2S_v + 4G_0 \tag{1}$$
$$I_{vh} = 1 + 2S_\mu - S_v - 2G_0 \tag{2}$$
$$I_{hv} = 1 - S_\mu + 2S_v - 2G_0 \tag{3}$$
$$I_{hh} = 1 - S_\mu - S_v + G_0 - 3G_2 \tag{4}$$

When there is a large amount of energy transfer between the pigments and when the participating transition moments are effectively rotationally symmetrically distributed with respect to the orientation axis of the chlorosomes, the following relations hold:

$$S_\mu = < P_2 >< P_2(\cos \beta^\mu) > \tag{5}$$
$$S_v = < P_2 >< P_2(\cos \beta^v) > \tag{6}$$
$$G_0 = (1/5 + 2/7<P_2> + 18/35<P_4>)<P_2(\cos \beta^\mu)><P_2(\cos \beta^v)> \tag{7}$$
$$G_2 = (1/5 - 2/7<P_2> + 3/35<P_4>)<P_2(\cos \beta^\mu)><P_2(\cos \beta^v)> \tag{8}$$

$<P_2>$ and $<P_4>$ depend on the angle β between the long axis of the chlorosomes and the z-axis in the gel and they are defined as $<P_2> = 1/2 < 3 \cos^2 (\beta) - 1>$ and $<P_4> = 1/8< 35 \cos^4 (\beta) - 30 \cos^2 (\beta) + 3>$. Both are 0 when the chlorosomes are randomly oriented as is the case in an uncompressed gel. They are both 1 for chlorosomes, ordered perfectly along the z-axis. The brackets <...> denote an average over all chlorosomes orientations.

$<P_2(\cos \beta^\mu)>$ and $<P_2(\cos \beta^v)>$ are defined as $<P_2>$ but β should now be replaced by β^μ and β^v, respectively. β^μ is the angle between the absorption transition dipole moment μ and the long axis of the chlorosome and β^v is defined similarly for the emission transition dipole moment v. In other words, from the intensities I_{vv}, I_{vh}, I_{hv} and I_{hh}, the parameters $<P_2>$, $<P_4>$, $<P_2(\cos \beta^\mu)>$ and $<P_2(\cos \beta^v)>$ can be calculated. Note that in an LD-experiment only the product $<P_2><P_2(\cos \beta^\mu)>$ is determined and an estimation of $<P_2>$ is needed to obtain $<P_2(\cos \beta^\mu)>$. For an uncompressed gel $S_\mu = S_v = 0$ and $G_0 = G_2 = 1/5 <P_2(\cos \beta^\mu)><P_2(\cos \beta^v)> = A/2$, where A is the anisotropy of the fluorescence. Substitution of G_0 and G_2 in equations 1-4 lead to the corrected intensities, and the correction factors c_{vv}, c_{vh}, c_{hv} and c_{hh} can be determined. The same correction factors can be applied for the compressed gel. Although the concentrations of the chlorosomes are the same in the compressed and uncompressed gel, there may exist small differences in the correction factors. To account for these differences, all correction factors are multiplied with a constant C. Note that in an ideal case this constant should be 1. In conclusion, 5 independent parameters can be determined, namely I'_{vv}, I'_{vh}, I'_{hv} and I'_{hh} for the compressed gel and A for an uncompressed gel. These are sufficient to determine the constant C together with the parameters $<P_2>$, $<P_4>$, $<P_2(\cos \beta^\mu)>$ and $<P_2(\cos \beta^v)>$.

Results
We have performed fluorescence depolarization measurements on both compressed and uncompressed gels, containing similar concentrations of chlorosomes. To obtain good results the absorption in the excitation band was kept low, typically 0.05. We excited at 460 nm and detected at 750 nm. Several thousands of counts were needed to minimize statistical errors. To keep the measuring time low, bandwidths of 16 nm were used. The determination of 1 intensity took 30 seconds. To eliminate the effect of fluctuating lamp intensities, 20 series of measurements were performed on both a compressed and an uncompressed gel. One series consists of the determination of 4 intensities for both the uncompressed and the compressed gel. From one series the parameters $<P_2>$, $<P_4>$, $<P_2(\cos \beta^\mu)>$, $<P_2(\cos \beta^v)>$ and the constant C were determined. These led to the following average parameters and standard errors:

$<P_2>$	$<P_4>$	$<P_2(\cos \beta^\mu)>$	$<P_2(\cos \beta^v)>$	C
.28 ± .01	.05 ± .02	.78 ± .02	.88 ± .01	.87 ± .04

There appeared to be a small but significant decrease in the value of C during the measurements. Nevertheless, the values of the other parameters remained the same.

Different measurements with other samples led to similar results, but the value of C varied around 1.

Discussion

It appeared to be possible to determine the parameters $<P_2>$, $<P_4>$, $<P_2(\cos \beta^\mu)>$ and $<P_2(\cos \beta^\mu)>$ very accurately, making the assumptions of effective rotational symmetry of the absorption and emission transition dipole moments and fast, efficient excitation energy transfer between the pigments in the chlorosomes. A correction factor was included to account for small differences between gels. The obtained value of $<P_2>$ is in perfect agreement with the value that can be predicted from the mathematical expressions for rod-like particles in [1] and which is 0.28 at the used degree of compression. Also a value of $<P_4>$ can be calculated from the same expressions and it is 0.09, somewhat different from the obtained value. This difference should not be taken too seriously. It means that the orientation distribution is slightly different from the predicted one, but this does not influence the interpretation of LD-results, which only depend on $<P_2>$. Also the value for $<P_2(\cos \beta^\mu)>$ (460 nm) is in good agreement with results from LD-experiments [2]. The value for $<P_2(\cos \beta^\nu)>$ (750 nm) is similar to $<P_2(\cos \beta^\mu)>$ (740) as determined in [2], which is consistent with the notion that absorption and emission transition dipole moments are more or less parallel. Finally, we must mention that the multiplication of the correction factors c_{vv} etcetera with one constant C is strictly spoken not correct as the intensity of the exciting beam changes differently for horizontally and vertically polarized light throughout the compressed gel as the sample is dichroic. This leads to slightly different values for the determined parameters, and these differences are at most 0.01 for all parameters.

In conclusion, the method of fluorescence depolarization measurements on particles in compressed gels can be performed on chlorosomes and they lead to results, which are in good agreement with the theoretical predictions from [1], and results fromt linear dichroism measurements [2]. The results support the further use of the expressions in [1] for rod-like particles and the method seems very promising for the study of particles, which are not rod- or disc-like. In the future, attention should be paid to getting higher light intensities to reduce the measuring time and to allow the use of smaller bandwidths. However, even with large bandwidths, the method can still be applied to obtain an accurate determination of $<P_2>$, which makes a quantitative interpretation of LD-results possible.

References

[1] Ganago, A. O., Fok, M. V., Abdourakhmanov, I. A., Solov'ev, A. A. & Erokhin, Yu. E. (1980) Mol. Biol. (USSR) 14, 381-389.
[2] van Amerongen, H., Vasmel, H. & R. van Grondelle (1988) Biophysical J. 54, 65-76.
[3] van Gurp, M., van Ginkel, G. & Levine, Y. K. (1988) J. theor. Biol. 131, 333-349.

SPECTRAL SHIFT OF PURPLE BACTERIAL CAROTENOIDS RELATED TO
SOLVENT AND PROTEIN POLARIZABILITY

Per Ola Andersson, Tomas Gillbro,
Department of Physical Chemistry, University of Umeå,
Sweden.
Linda Ferguson, Richard J. Cogdell,
Department of Botany, University of Glasgow, Scotland.

1. INTRODUCTION

When the major light-absorbing pigments in bacterial photosynthesis are non-covalently bound to their apo-protein (antenna apoprotein and reaction center subunits) their absorption spectra
show well-defined red-shifts. The origin of these shifts has been
subject of a lot of conjectures.
There are three general ideas about absorption spectral shifts in
biological systems. (i) Charge induced energy shifts; the visual
protein rhodopsin(1). (ii) Exciton interaction shifts; dimer of
chlorophyll in the reaction center(2). (iii) Dispersion interaction shifts; exists in all systems irrespective of the polar character of the environment and it depends on the polarizability of
the surrounding molecules.
In this study we have investigated the mechanism of the solvent
induced shift in the absorption spectrum of two carotenoids, i.e.
spheroidene and trans-β-carotene. Carotenoids belong to the class
of polyenes and they are essentially hydrophobic. In vivo the carotenoids are non-covalently bound to specific pigment-protein
complexes. Our working model is; the red-shifted spectra of carotenoids in vivo is mainly due to dispersive interactions of the
carotenoid and the surrounding, and consequently the shift is due
to the polarizability of the surrounding medium. The measurements
reported here support this model.

2. MATERIAL AND METHODS

The bacterial carotenoid, spheroidene, was isolated and purified
from Rhodobacter sphaeroides strain 2 4 1. The carotenoid was eluted with diethylether/petroleum ether mixtures and its purity
was confirmed spectrophotometrically and by TLC on silica gel plates. All trans-β-carotene was obtained from Sigma. The β-carotene
molecules were dissolved in unpolar solvents; n-hexane, carbon disulfide and mixtures of these two at different volume ratios. The
absorption measurements were made at room temperature(20-22°C).The
carotenoid spheroidene was dissolved in different unpolar solv-

M. Baltscheffsky (ed.), Current Research in Photosynthesis, Vol. II, 117–120.
© 1990 *Kluwer Academic Publishers. Printed in the Netherlands.*

ents; n-hexane, cyclohexane, carbon tetrachloride, carbon disulfide and two mixtures of carbon disulfide/n-hexane at volume ratios 1/1 and 2/1. Abs.spectra of these samples were made at room
temperature. Measurements of spheroidene in carbon disulfide were
made in the temperature interval of 20 °C to -90 °C. Refractive
index data were taken from Handbook of Chemistry and Physics.

3. RESULTS

In fig. 1 absorption spectra of spheroidene in n-hexane (A), CCl_4
(B) and CS_2 (C), are shown. One notices the red-shift of spheroidene in CCl_4 and in CS relatively the carotenoid in n-hexane. The
refractive indices of the solvents (n(hex)=1.37, n(CCl4)=1.46 and
n(CS2)=1.63) give information about the shifts; the larger refractive index the larger is the red-shift.

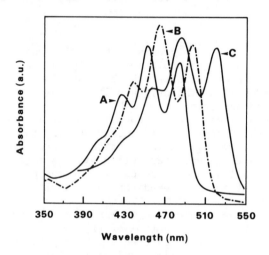

Fig.1. Abs. spect. of spheroidene in n-hexane(A), CCl_4(B) & CS_2(C)

In fig.2 the red-shifts (in cm^{-1}) of spheroidene in different
solvents relative n-hexane ($\Delta\tilde{\nu} = \tilde{\nu}$(hex) - $\tilde{\nu}$(solv)) are plotted
against the refractive index term $(n^2- 1)/(n^2+ 2)$, where n is the
refractive index of the solvent. The shifts were calculated from
the maximum absorbance peak. The circular dots are from measurements of spheroidene in CS_2 with temperatures between -5°C and -99
°C. The refractive index increases linearly with decreasing tempe-
rature. In fig. 2 we see that $\Delta\tilde{\nu}$ is linear function of $(n^2-1)/(n^2 + 2)$. This result agrees with the theoretical models (3,4). The
equation of the line is: $\Delta\tilde{\nu} = -2680 + 11700 (n^2- 1)/(n^2+ 2)$ The
same experiments were done with β-carotene in nonpolar solvents,
which also gave a straight line as a result.
$\Delta\tilde{\nu} = -2690 + 11\ 900 (n^2- 1)/(n^2+ 2)$ (cm^{-1})
In fig.3 abs.spectra of <u>Rhodobacter sphaeroides</u> antenna complex B
800-850 (in Tris-buffer) and of spheroidene in quinoline are
shown. One notice the perfect overlap of absorbance of spheroidene

in vivo and in quinoline.

Spectral Shift of Spheroidene

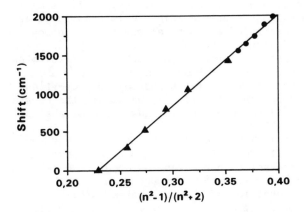

Fig. 2. Spectral shift of spheroidene in different solvents.

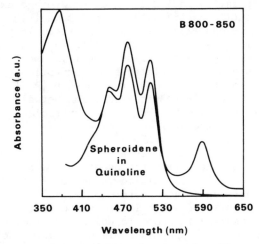

Fig. 3. Absorption spectrum of B800-850 antenna complex (Rb.
       sphaeroides) and spheroidene in quinoline.

4. DISCUSSION

When a carotenoid is transfered from the gas phase to a liquid
medium, the energy difference between the electronic excited state
($1B_u$) and the ground state($1A_g$) decreases, i.e. the abs. max. of
the solute is shifted towards longer wavelengths. This red-shift
is due to the difference between solvent-solute interaction energy
(ΔW) in the ground and in the excited state, i.e. $\tilde{\nu}$(gas)$-$ $\tilde{\nu}$(solv)$=$
$<\Delta W>$/hc, where h is Planck's constant and c is the speed of light.

By using quantum mechanical perturbation theory one can derive a theoretical expression of ΔW. In such a derivation, by S.Basu(4), there are some restrictions: (i) One considers only dilute solutions of solute molecules in solvent environment, which makes the neglect of solute-solute interactions allowed. (ii) Using the Onsager model in which the solute molecule is considered as a point dipole at the centre of a spherical cavity in a homogeneous solvent dielectric. With a nonpolar solute in nonpolar solvents it is only the dispersive interaction which gives rise to ΔW and the shift is given by: $\tilde{\nu}(gas) - \tilde{\nu}(solv) = K \ (n^2 - 1)/(n^2 + 2)$ [1].
Where K is a collection of constants and solute properties. From experimentally absorption data (fig. 2) we obtain the constant, K, and from equation (1) we determine the gas value of absorption maximum ($\tilde{\nu}(gas)$):

Spheroidene : $K = (11 \ 700 \pm 500) \ cm^{-1}$; $\tilde{\nu}(gas) = 24 \ 800 \ cm^{-1}$
β-carotene : $K = (11 \ 900 \pm 500) \ cm^{-1}$; $\tilde{\nu}(gas) = 24 \ 900 \ cm^{-1}$

We conclude that the shift in n-hexane is about 2700 cm^{-1} and in CS_2 about 4100 cm^{-1} to the red of its gas phase value.
An approximately expression of the constant K is(4)

$$K \approx 7.048 \ 10^{15} \ a^{-3} \left[\ |P_{ge}|^2 + \varepsilon \ (\alpha_g - \alpha_e) \ \right] \quad \text{(in cgs units)},$$

Where a is the solute cavity radius and ε is an average excitation energy for the solute. If the transition dipol moment (P_{ge}) of the carotenoid is known, we can calculate the difference in polarizability of the ground($1A_g$) and the excited state($1B_u$), i.e $\alpha_g - \alpha_e$. P_{ge} is determined from the dimensionless quantity, oscillator strength(f), which is easily calculated from absorption spectra. The relationship between f and P_{ge} is, $f = const \ \nu \ |P_{ge}|^2$, where ν refers to the frequency of electronic transition between ground ($1A_g$) and excited state($1B_u$). The results for spheroidene in CS_2 and of β-carotene in n-hexane are:

Spheroidene: $P_{ge} = 12$ D ; $\Delta\alpha = 370$ $\mathring{A}^3$
β-carotene : $P_{ge} = 13$ D ; $\Delta\alpha = 340$ $\mathring{A}^3$

In the calculation of $\Delta\alpha$ the cavity radius of the carotenoid was assumed to be about 10 $\mathring{A}$. The calculated values of P_{ge} and $\Delta\alpha$ are close to literature data on related carotenoids(5).
In fig. 3 the great overlap of spheroidene in a biological system and of spheroidene dissolved in aromatic solvent, quinoline, tells us about the surroundings of spheroidene in Rhodobacter sphaeroides. We suggest that the carotenoids are surrounded by several aromatic amino acids.

REFERENCES :
1 Schulten, K., Dinur, U. and Honig, B. (1980) J. Chem. Phys. 73, 3927-3935
2 Knapp, E. W., Fischer S. F., Zinth, W., Sander M., Kaiser W., Deisenhofer, J. and Michel, H. (1985) P. N. A. S. 82, 8463-8467
3 Andrews, J. R. and Hudson, B. S. (1978) J. Chem. Phys. 68, 4587-4594
4 Basu, S. (1964) Adv. Quantum Chem. 1, 145-169
5 Scmidt, S. and Reich, R. (1972) Bd. 76, 1202-1208

POLARIZED ABSORPTION SPECTRA OF THE B800–850 LIGHT-HARVESTING AND THE RC-B875 REACTION CENTER COMPLEXES FROM PURPLE BACTERIA.

K. Steck, T. Wacker, G. Drews*, N. Gad'on*, R. Cogdell†, W. Welte and W. Mäntele.

Institut für Biophysik und Strahlenbiologie, Albertstr. 23, 7800 Freiburg, *Institut für Biologie II, Schänzlestr. 1, 7800 Freiburg, FRG, †Department of Botany, University of Glasgow, Glasgow G128QQ, UK.

1. CRYSTALLIZATION OF THE B800–850 LIGHT–HARVESTING AND THE RC–B875 REACTION CENTER COMPLEXES.

The B800–850 light harvesting complex of *Rps. acidophila* and the RC–B875 reaction center complex of *Rps. palustris* were crystallized in presence of detergents. The crystals were obtained by vapour diffusion technique using polyethylene glycol 1000 (1,2). For spectroscopic studies, the B800–850 and the RC–B875 complexes were crystallized on thin cover slides, allowing the crystals to grow to sufficient size in two dimensions. Sealed by a second cover slide, the crystals were mounted on a goniometer sample holder in a micro-spectrophotometer (3) built in our laboratory.

The crystals of the B800–850 complex of *Rps. acidophila* as well as the crystals of the RC–B875 complex of *Rps. palustris* typically grow as thin, rectangular platelets with a long edge (y–edge), a small edge (x–edge) and an axis normal to the surface of the platelet (z–edge). The crystals of both complexes show a high degree of dichroism along the x– and y– crystal edges (see Fig. 1.a. and Fig. 1.b.).

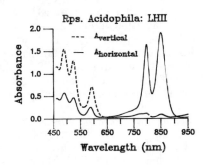

Fig. 1.a.

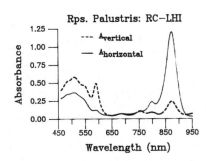

Fig. 1.b.

The Qx transitions of both complexes are aligned preferentially along the vertical (y–) edge and the Qy transitions are correspondingly aligned along the horizontal (x–) edge.

M. Baltscheffsky (ed.), Current Research in Photosynthesis, Vol. II, 121–124.
© 1990 *Kluwer Academic Publishers. Printed in the Netherlands.*

2. SPECTROSCOPIC STUDIES WITH CRYSTALS

The Qx transitions of the B800–850 complex of *Rps. acidophila* show a shift of 5 nm to longer wavelengths for vertical polarized light (see Fig. 2.a.). Due to the overlap of the strong carotenoid absorbance at this polarization, the shift appears reduced and is probably much stronger for the isolated Qx. If a difference spectrum $(A_{vert}-A_{hor})$ is formed, with the horizontal absorbance multiplied by 2.7 to cancel the carotenoid absorbance, it is clearly seen that there are two different and dichroic Qx transition moments corresponding to the bacteriochlorophyll forming the B800 and the B850 pigment of *Rps. acidophila* (see Fig. 2.b.).

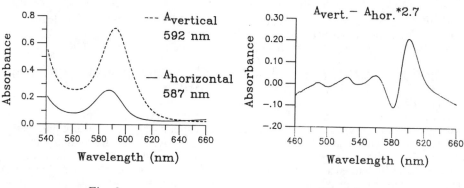

Fig. 2.a.   Fig. 2.b.

In contrast to uniaxially oriented samples, the crystalline state provides a three–dimensional orientation of transition moments. Basically two degrees of order have to be included into the calculations of the arrangement of transition moments. First, the orientation of the transition moments with respect to each other in the complex should be considered. Furthermore crystal symmetry must be applied to the arrangement of transition moments in the complex or in the photosynthetic unit. Crystal forms with a three– or higher–fold symmetry axis randomize even a highly ordered arrangement of transition moments. The final distribution of transition moments results in three absorption main axes, which are perpendicular to each other. The absorption axes, i.e. the normalized absorption axes $A_x+A_y+A_z=1$ can be determined by rotating and tilting the crystal with respect to the incident beam and polarization. For the analysis of those sets of spectra, we have developed an evaluation method combined with a mathematical formalism:

First, the ratio is constructed from the spectra at each rotation angle α or tilt angle β with the help of the linear correlation analysis (K. Fahmy, personal communication): $A(\alpha)/A(\alpha=0)$ $[A(\beta)/A(\beta=0)]$. The ratio of each transition moment as a function of the angle α or β can thus be obtained. This theoretical function can be calculated with the help of the Jones Formalism (4) and this function is necessary for fitting the ratios at $\alpha=90$ and $\beta=90$ degrees to obtain the dichroic ratio A_x/A_y and A_y/A_z. Finally the normalized absorption axes can be determined.

Here we discuss two cases, crystals with high and low dichroism:

2.1. Crystals with high dichroism — Jones Formalism.

The Jones Calculus is based on the physical fact that any optical element will act upon the electric light vector of the incident wave (E_{in}) as a linear operator. The operator is expressed in the convenient form of a two–by–two matrix, whose four matrix elements are, in general, complex.

In almost all cases the examined crystals possessed three optical properties: they were dichroic, birefringent and optically active. Optical activity can be neglected due to the small thickness. The other properties are described in a so–called crystal–matrix, which, in this case, is a diagonal matrix:

$$\{1\} \quad \begin{bmatrix} e^{-\epsilon_x d/2} \cdot e^{-in_x d 2\pi/\lambda} & 0 \\ 0 & e^{-\epsilon_y d/2} \cdot e^{-in_y d 2\pi/\lambda} \end{bmatrix}$$

with ϵ_x, ϵ_y = horizontal and vertical extinction coefficients, n_x, n_y = horizontal and vertical refractive indices and d = thickness of the crystal.

It will then follow, that a complete optical system, consisting of polarizers, rotators, wave plates, crystals, etc. may be represented by a two–by–two matrix. The matrix of the complete system will result by multiplying the matrices of all optical elements in the optical path:

$$\{2\} \quad E_{out} = M_{system} E_{in} = M_{pol} M_{rot} M_{crystal} E_{in}$$

The detected intensity is obtained by calculating $E_{out}^+ E_{out}$ and the angle dependent function can be specified:

$$\{3\} \quad \frac{A(\alpha)}{A(\alpha=0)} = \frac{\log 10\left[\exp(-\epsilon_x d) \cdot \sin^2(\alpha-\varphi) + \exp(-\epsilon_y d) \cdot \cos^2(\alpha-\varphi)\right]}{\log 10\left[\exp(-\epsilon_x d) \cdot \sin^2(\varphi) + \exp(-\epsilon_y d) \cdot \cos^2(\varphi)\right]}$$

with the parameters ϵ_x, ϵ_y, as above, and φ = angle correction.

In the case of strong dichroic and strong absorbing crystals, there is a huge deviation of this formula from the former described function in (5). In Fig. 3.a. the rotation series of the Qx B800 and Qx B850 transitions of *Rps. acidophila* and in Fig. 3.b. the Qy (875nm) transition of *Rps. palustris* are shown. The angle dependent function $A(\alpha)/A(\alpha=0)$ is fitted to the data.

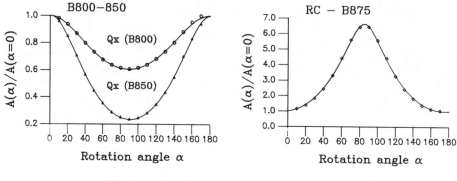

Fig 3.a.   Fig 3.b.

2.2. Crystals with low dichroism.

In the case of crystals with a dichroism smaller than 20%, the logarithm and exponential functions in formula {3} can be developed in power series:

$$\{4\} \qquad \frac{A(\alpha)}{A(\alpha=0)} = \frac{\epsilon_x}{\epsilon_y} - \frac{\epsilon_x - \epsilon_y}{\epsilon_y} \cdot \cos^2(\alpha) \qquad \text{where } \varphi = 0°$$

This simplified formula corresponds to the formula [4] in (5). The angle dependent absorption $A(\alpha, \beta)$ describes here an ellipsoid equation.

In both cases, the normalized absorption axes $A_x + A_y + A_z = 1$ can be determined and involved into the set of equations (5,6), which connect these normalized absorption axes with the corresponding transition moments of a single complex.

REFERENCES:
1   Wacker, T. et al. (1986) FEBS Lett. 197, pp 267–273
2   Cogdell, R. J. et al. (1986) in Antennas and Reaction Centers of Photosynthetic Bacteria (Michel–Beyerle, M.E., ed), pp 88–91, Springer Series in Chem. Phys. 42
3   Mäntele, W. et al. (1988) in The Photosynthetic Bacterial Reaction Center, pp 33–39, NATO ASI Series
4   Jones, R. C. (1941), J. Opt. Soc. Am. 31, pp 488–492
5   Welte, W. et al. (1988) in Photosynthetic Light–Harvesting Systems, pp 201–209, Walter de Gruyter, New York
6   Steck, K. (1987) Diploma Thesis, University of Freiburg

LINEAR DICHROISM AND ORIENTATION OF CHROMOPHORES IN *Nostoc* sp. PHYCOBILISOMES AND THEIR SUBUNITS.

L.J. Juszczak[a], B.A. Zilinskas[b], N.E. Geacintov[a] and J. Breton[c]

[a]Chemistry Department, New York University, New York, NY 10003 (U.S.A.); [b]Department of Biochemistry and Microbiology, Cook College, Rutgers University, New Brunswick, NJ 08903 (U.S.A.); [c]Département de Biologie, C.E.N. de Saclay, 91191 Gif sur Yvette CEDEX (France).

INTRODUCTION

Phycobilisomes (PBS) are supramolecular aggregates of phycobiliproteins (PB proteins), which harvest light energy and deliver this energy to the photosynthetic reaction centers in cyanobacteria. The *Nostoc* sp. hemidiscoidal phycobilisomes grown in cool white fluorescent light has six rods, each consisting of four disks of phycoerythrin (PE) stacked onto two disks of phycocyanin (PC). Each of these disks consists of a trimeric assembly of PB protein complexes. These six rod–like structures are attached to a core consisting of three parallel allophycocyanin (APC) cylinders so that their longitudinal axes are perpendicular to the axes of the APC cylinders. Each of the three APC core cylinders consists of four disk–like assemblies of trimeric APC protein complexes, and the three APC cylinders are stacked so that their ends form a triangle. Linker polypeptides hold the disks together and may also influence the transfer of excitation energy. The PBS are attached by means of a 95 kD colored linker polypeptide to the thylakoid membrane. There is considerable interest in deducing the structure–function relationships which allow for the highly efficient transfer of excitation energy in phycobilisomes. The PE pigments are located at the distal end of the rods, while the PC pigments are located closer to the APC core cylinders. It is well known that the energy transfer sequence involves the PE --> PC --> APC --> chlorophyll *a* pathway. Recent X–ray studies of PC trimer crystals derived from *M. laminosus* [1] has allowed for a detailed appreciation of the influence of orientational and positional parameters on energy transfer pathways in these PB proteins [2].

We have employed linear dichroism methods to study the orientations of the different chromophores in intact phycobilisomes and their subunits oriented in squeezed gelatin gels [3] and in stretched poly(vinyl alcohol) (PVA) films. In this work, we describe the linear dichroism spectra of some of the oriented individual PE, PC and APC subunits, and demonstrate that the linear dichroism spectra of the intact phycobilisomes can be adequately described by a weighted superposition of these individual building blocks. This suggests that there are no marked changes in the orientations of the transition moments of the PE, PC and APC chromophores upon assembly into rods and association of rods with cores to form the intact phycobilisome. In addition, it is shown that chromophores with the higher energy levels tend to be oriented with their transition moments tilted both out of the planes and within the planes of the disks, while the transition moments of the lowest energy APC pigments are all tilted closer to the disk planes. This arrangement of the transition moments of PE and PC apears to favor the absorption of light of different polarizations. The in–disk plane orientations of APC appear to favor the transfer of energy to chlorophyll *a* molecules in the thylakoid membranes whose transition moments tend to be parallel to those of APC [4].

M. Baltscheffsky (ed.), Current Research in Photosynthesis, Vol. II, 125–128.
© 1990 *Kluwer Academic Publishers. Printed in the Netherlands.*

MATERIALS AND METHODS.

Most of the details of sample preparation, description of the linear dichroism apparatus, and preparation of the gels, have been noted elsewhere [3]. The samples were mixed in a 10% (w/v) potassium phosphate buffer solution of gelatin (porcine skin gelatin, 300 Bloom strength, Sigma Chemical Co., St. Louis, Mo.) at 32° C. Cooling to room temperature causes a solidification of the gels, and 1x1x2 cm blocks were used in the linear dichroism experiments. The method of squeezing of the gels, the presumed modes of orientation of the disks, rods and intact phycobilisomes, relative to the direction of the light beam (X) and polarization vectors of the light (E), are shown in Fig. 1. The stretching direction of a PVA film is also shown in Fig. 1B, and the orientations of the PBS subunits are similar in the squeezed gels and in the stretched PVA films under the conditions defined in Fig. 1. The linear dichroism signal (LD) is defined in terms of the absorbances measured with the polarization vectors of the light oriented either parallel ($A_{//}$) or perpendicular ($A_\perp$) to the stretching directions S, where $LD = A_{//} - A_\perp$.

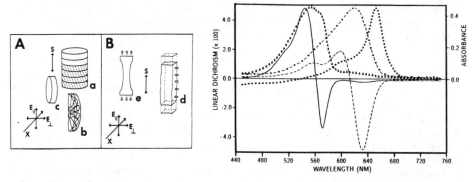

Fig. 1 (left). Presumed modes of orientation of individual rods (a), intact phycobilisomes (b), and disks (c) relative to vector S in squeezed gels (d) or stretched polyvinyl alcohol films (e).

Fig. 2 (right). Absorption and LD spectra of PBS subunits in squeezed gels at room temperature. (———) inverted LD spectrum of PE hexamers; (– – – –) inverted LD spectrum of PC dodecamers; (•••) LD spectrum of APC I (absorption spectrum is similar). Absorption spectra of PE hexamers (▲ ▲ ▲ ▲) and PC dodecamers (– •–•–•–).

RESULTS

The LD spectra of PE hexamers (two stacked disks), PC dodecamers (4 stacked disks), and an APC preparation called APC I [5], are shown in Fig. 2. It should be noted that the LD spectra of the PE and PC preparations shown in Fig. 2 have been inverted, in order to facilitate comparison of the weighted and summed LD spectra of the subunits with the LD spectrum of the intact phycobilisomes shown in Fig. 3. We have previously shown that PBS subunits such as the PE trimer and PC dodecamer orient in the same manner relative to S, i.e., as the disks shown in Fig. 1. However, larger PE/PC subunits consisting of six stacked disks orient as rods [3]. Therefore, the PBS subunits must consist of at least 5–6 disks before they behave like rods in the squeezed gels. The non-inverted LD spectra of PE hexamers are characterized by a positive maximum at 570 nm [3], and a negative LD minimum at 544 nm, while in the case of the PC dodecamers, a positive LD maximum appears at 631 nm, and LD minima are observed at 556 and 598 nm. In the case of APC I, the LD spectrum is entirely positive in sign, and the maximum occurs at 653 nm. The absorption spectra of the PE and PC preparations are also shown in Fig. 2; the maxima are observed at 550 and 618 nm, respectively. However, the absorption spectrum of APC I is not shown, since it is almost identical to the LD spectrum and is also characterized by a maximum at 653 nm.

In general, different APC fractions with different polypeptide compositions can be isolated from dissociated phycobilisomes [5]. Here we focus on the fraction called APC I in which the trimeric disks consist of α and β subunits, each bearing one phycocyanobilin chromophore. In addition, APC I contains a 95 kD colored linker polypeptide, called the terminal emitter, because it receives energy from other APC components and delivers this energy to chlorophyll a in the thylakoid membrane. This terminal emitter is known to be characterized by a long wavelength fluorescence emission band (maximum at 683 nm) in *Nostoc* sp. [6], and thus its absorption maximum is also expected to be located at the long wavelength absorption edge of APC I. The orientation of the transition moment of this terminal emitter relative to those of the other APC molecules and chlorophyll a is of interest. However, there is no long–wavelength structure in the LD spectrum of APC I in squeezed gelatin gels at room temperature (Fig. 2) which could be identified with this terminal emitter.

Because of a reduced overlap of absorption bands of different chromophores whose absorption maxima are located at slightly different wavelengths, it is desirable to measure LD spectra at low temperatures in order to determine the orientation of the terminal emitter linker polypeptide in APC I. Unfortunately, gelatin gels are not suitable for low temperature studies, and we therefore investigated the linear dichroism properties of APC I in stretched PVA films at 100 K (Fig. 4). The maximum in the LD spectrum appears at 653 nm with a prominent shoulder at 677 nm which we attribute to the 95 kD linker polypeptide.

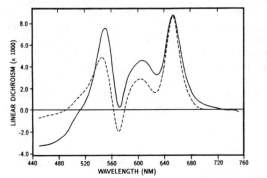 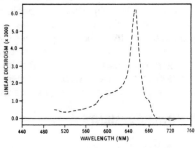

Fig. 3 (left). Individual LD spectra of PE, PC and APC I shown in Fig. 2 multiplied by factors of 0.28, 0.10 and 0.62, respectively and summed to produce a simulated intact PBS spectrum (-------). Linear dichroism spectrum of intact phycobilisomes in squeezed gels measured at room temperature (_____). The two spectra were normalized to one another at 651 nm.

Fig. 4 (right). LD spectrum of *Nostoc* sp. APC I in a stretched polyvinyl alcohol film at 100 K.

DISCUSSION

Reconstituted LD spectrum of PBS from LD spectra of the individual subunits. The individual LD spectra of PE, PC and APC I, as shown in Fig. 2, were multiplied by constant factors and summed to give the overall reconstituted spectrum of phycobilisomes shown in Fig. 3 (dotted line). As a comparison, a measured intact phycobilisome (isolated from *Nostoc* sp. grown in cool white light) LD spectrum is also shown in Fig. 3 (solid line). There is a near-coincidence of the maxima observed at about 550, 606 and 651 nm, and the minima at 572 and 629 nm. The generally lowered LD signals in the simulated LD spectrum can be attributed to variations in the baselines due to light scattering effects observed with the larger intact phycobilisomes. Because the PE and PC are assembled as rods containing six disks in the whole PBS, it was necessary to invert the experimentally observed PE and PC (hexamer and dodecamer, respectively) disk-like LD spectra in order to obtain the simulated whole PBS spectrum. While the APC I LD spectrum was used in this simulation, we have shown that the other APC fractions (APC II and APC III) display very similar LD spectra at room temperature [3]. The fact that the individual APC disks display LD spectra of the same positive sign as the tricylindrical core in the PBS, suggests that the geometry of orientation of the whole PBS shown in Fig. 1A (b) is reasonable. Finally, the near-coincidence of the simulated and observed PBS spectra suggests that there are no significant observable changes in the absorption maxima and orientations of the PE, PC and APC antenna pigments upon assembly of the individual subunits into whole phycobilisomes.

Orientation of transition moments of different chromophores relative to the planes of the disks and energy transfer sequence. We note that in the PE and PC subunits, the shorter wavelength pigment forms are characterized by significant tilts away from the planes of the disks (**negative** LD signals), while the longer wavelength pigment forms are all characterized by tilts closer to the disk planes (**positive** LD). In the APC, all pigment forms, including the terminal emitter are oriented so that the transition moments are oriented close to the planes of the disks (**positive** LD). Thus, it appears that the transition moments of the antenna pigments become progressively more tilted towards the disk planes as the excitation energy flows from higher energy to lower energy pigment forms. Both the APC antenna pigments and the APC I terminal linker are characterized by transition moments which tend to be parallel to the planes of the thylakoid membranes and the transition moments of chlorophyll *a* [4]. This type of orientation is consistent with an efficient absorption and transfer of excitation energy from higher energy accessory pigment forms to lower energy chlorophyll *a* forms.

ACKNOWLEDGEMENTS

This work was supported by grants from the U.S. Department of Agriculture to B.Z. (No. 87-CRCR-1-2318) and to N.E.G. (No. 88-37262-3859).

REFERENCES

[1] Schirmer, T., Bode, W. and Huber, R. (1987) J. Mol. Biol. 196, 677–695.
[2] Sauer, K. and Scheer, H. (1988) Biochim. Biophys. Acta 936, 157–170.
[3] Juszczak, L., Geacintov, N.E., Zilinskas, B.A. and Breton, J. (1988) in Photosynthetic Light Harvesting Systems (Scheer, H. and Schneider, S., eds.), pp. 281–292, W. de Gruyter, Berlin.
[4] Gagliano, A.G., Hoareau, J., Breton, J. and Geacintov, N.E. (1985) Biochim. Biophys. Acta 808, 455–463.
[5] Zilinskas, B.A. (1982) Plant Physiol. 70, 1060–1065.
[6] Mimuro, M., Lipshultz, C.A. and Gantt, E. (1986) Biochim. Biophys. Acta 852, 126–132.

ROLE OF AGGREGATION STATE IN DIRECTED ENERGY TRANSFER WITHIN
THE B875 LIGHT-HARVESTING COMPLEX OF *RHODOBACTER SPHAEROIDES*.

WILLEM H.J. WESTERHUIS, ROLF THEILER AND ROBERT A. NIEDERMAN,
Department of Molecular Biology and Biochemistry, Rutgers University, Piscataway, NJ
08855-1059, USA

1. INTRODUCTION
    The photosynthetic units of *Rhodobacter sphaeroides* consist of photochemical reaction centers together with the B800–850 and B875 light-harvesting pigment-protein complexes. Light energy absorbed by the peripheral B800–850 antenna is transferred to the B875 core complex which surrounds and interconnects the reaction centers and transfers these excitations to the reaction center bacteriochlorophyll *a* (BChl) special pair [1, 2]. A variety of spectroscopic measurements [3-7] have suggested that the B875 complex is spectrally heterogeneous and contains a special BChl component designated as B896 from its apparent position in the red wing of the overall near-IR absorption band [3]. This unique pigment species, whose amplitude was estimated to comprise approximately one-sixth that of the total band [3], is thought to direct excitations from B875 BChls to the reaction center special pair. A recent study of the energy transfer dynamics of detergent solubilized preparations of the B875 complex by picosecond absorption spectroscopy at 77 K [5] has demonstrated that excitations are transferred from B875 to B896 BChls with a half-time of 15 ps and that the excited state of B896 decays with a time constant of 650 ps, in agreement with the measured fluorescense lifetime for the isolated complex [8]. Measurements of induced absorption anisotropy indicated that B896 BChls exist in a highly organized state in the vicinity of the reaction center where they increase the efficiency of the final energy transfer step to the BChl special pair. Assuming a total of 24 B875 BChls per reaction center within the membrane, B896 would be expected to account for 3-4 of these BChl molecules.
    Several explanations for the tight coupling of B896 and B875 BChls have been considered [4]. These include the possibilities that: (i) B896 is intrinsic to the B875 complex and arises from an asymmetry within the basic structural unit such that one of six BChls is in a distinct environment; (ii) two BChl molecules on different B875 units could interact specifically to form B896; (iii) B896 represents a separate pigment-protein complex with highly oriented BChl molecules that is tightly associated with B875; (iv) B896 originates from interactions between the B875 and reaction center complexes. It appears unlikely that B896 represents a distinct complex because much of the spectroscopic evidence for the existence of this component has been obtained with highly purified B875 preparations [3, 5, 6, 8] in which heterogeneities in the primary structures of the B875 apoproteins have not been observed [9]. Moreover, the genes encoding the B875 polypeptides map in a single region of the chromosome together with those that encode the reaction center L and M subunits, and no other sequences, except those that encode for the B800-850 apoproteins, have been found that have the characteristics of antenna protein structural genes [10]. Results presented below with preparations of the B875 complex isolated from mutant strain M2192, which lacks both the reaction center and B800–850 complexes, are not in accord

M. Baltscheffsky (ed.), Current Research in Photosynthesis, Vol. II, 129–132.

with the possibility that B896 arises from B875-reaction center associations. Instead, they imply that oligomerization of B875 units is necessary for the appearance of B896 BChls and that only higher B875 oligomers possess the spectroscopic properties of the functional core antenna in membranes of the wild type.

2. EXPERIMENTAL PROCEDURES

R. sphaeroides mutant strain M21, which lacks the B800–850 antenna complex, was isolated after treatment of wild-type strain NCIB 8253 with N-methyl-N'-nitro-N-nitroso-guanidine [11]. The B800-850 complex has been restored to strain M21 by complementation with the appropriate genes [11]. Strain M2192, which was derived from M21 after insertion of transposon Tn5 into the *pufL* gene [12] encoding subunit L of the reaction center, lacks both the B800-850 and reaction center complexes. These mutants were kindly made available by C. N. Hunter. Membranes were prepared from semiaerobically grown cells by rate-zone sedimentation [13] and were found to consist of open fragments that sedimented in an upper pigmented band. LDS-polyacrylamide gel electrophoresis at 4°C was performed as described previously [13].

Absorption spectra were obtained on a Johnson Research Foundation DBS-3 double-beam scanning spectrophotometer equipped with a Hamamatsu R406 red-sensitive photomultiplier tube. This instrument was modified to allow measurements of fluorescence emission and excitation spectra. Excitation wavelengths were selected with a J-Y H-20 monochromator; the half bandwidth was 16 nm for emission and 4 nm for excitation spectra. Fluorescence was detected at right angles by an EG&G HUV 4000B photodiode through a J-Y H-10 monochromator (half bandwidth 12 nm) for emission spectra or through narrow-bandpass filters (Omega Optical, half bandwidth 10 nm) for excitation spectra. Fluorescence polarization spectra were obtained with linear sheet polarizers (Polaroid, type HR) in both excitation and emission light paths. Fluorescence polarization values are expressed as: $p = (I_{/} - I_{\perp}) / (I_{/} + I_{\perp})$, where $I_{/}$ and $I_{\perp}$ are the relative intensities of fluorescence with polarization either parallel or perpendicular, respectively, to the polarization direction of the excitation light. For measurements at 77 K, the spectrophotometer was equipped with an Oxford Instruments DN1704 liquid nitrogen cryostat.

3. RESULTS AND DISCUSSION

To determine the structural basis for the apparent directed energy transfer from B875 to reaction center BChls via the B896 component, pigmented membranes from the mutant strains were subjected to LDS-polyacrylamide gel electrophoresis. For the B875 protein of strain M21, a number of different aggregates can be isolated by this procedure [13]; these include oligomerization states up to ~8 as well as a trimer of α– and β-subunits containing 6 BChl molecules which is possibly the smallest stable unit. Near-IR absorption and emission spectra obtained at 77 K for this minimal unit (complex 1) as well as a higher aggregate (complex 4) are shown in Fig. 1. The absorption and emmision maxima of complex 1 were at 882 and 900 nm, respectively, while the respective positions for those of complex 4 appeared at 885 and 902 nm. This indicated that the fully red-shifted terminal emitter observed in intact membranes [3] may be confined to only the highest oligomers.

In order to eliminate any possible effects of reaction centers from this analysis, strain M2192 was also examined. After LDS-polyacrlamide gel electrophoresis, the majority of the B875 migrated in large complexes near the top of the gel that probably contain ~20 to 30 BChl molecules, but the apparent $(\alpha\beta)_3$ minimal unit as well as a series of ~10 oligomers of intermediate sizes were also observed (not shown). Fluorescence polarization spectra at 77 K revealed spectral heterogeneity in each of the isolated complexes examined; the spectra obtained with the largest and smallest complexes are shown in Fig. 2. In every case, a strong increase in polarization across the absorption band was observed but this high polarization was shifted markedly to shorter wavelenghts in the smaller complexes. Therefore, the B896 component,which accounts for ~15% of the amplitude of the B875 band in intact membranes [3], is not responsible for the heterogeneity observed in these lower oligomers. Instead, the rise in polarization on the blue side of the absorption band is consistent with an orientation in which ~50% of the transition moments are parallel to that of the emitting species. The remaining transitions, which arise on the blue side of the absorption band, make an angle of ~40-50° with the emitter. On the other hand, the

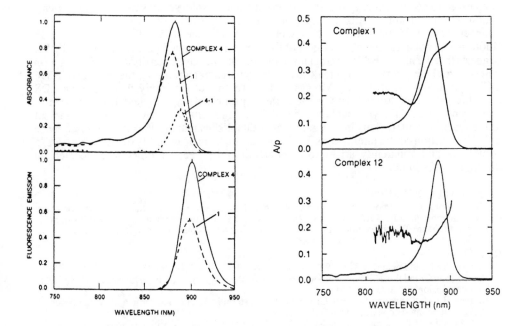

FIGURE 1 (left). Near-IR absorption and fluorescence emission spectra at 77 K of B875 complexes isolated from *R. sphaeroides* mutant strain M21 (B800-850⁻) by LDS-polyacrylamide gel electrophoresis. Complex 1, apparent B875 minimal unit; complex 4, oligomeric B875 complex. The emission spectra (excitation at 590 nm) were not corrected for the response of the measuring system which was essentially flat in the region of the emission bands.

FIGURE 2 (right). Near-IR absorption and fluorescence polarization spectra at 77 K of B875 complexes isolated from *R. sphaeroides* mutant strain M2192 (B800-850⁻, reaction center⁻) by LDS-polyacrylamide gel electrophoresis. Complex 1, apparent B875 minimal unit; complex 12, major, highly oligomeric B875 complex migrating near the top of the gel. The ordinate legend represents the absorbance (A) and fluorescence polarization (p) of the isolated complexes determined as described in the text.

absorption and polarization spectra of the largest complex (Fig. 2) closely resemble those measured at 4 K for membranes from strain M21 [14]; such a steep rise in fluorescence polarization in the red-wing of the near-IR band was interpreted to suggest that all B896 BChls within the complex have approximately the same orientation with their long-wavelength (Q_y) transition moments essentially parallel [3]. At room temperature, a partial depolarization of fluorescence observed in membrane preparations but not in the isolated complex, was ascribed to energy transfer between different complexes. The high polarization at low temperatures in the *in situ* complex was thought to reflect irreversible energy transfer to the long-wavelength BChls [3].

In contrast to these results, a low degree of polarization at 4 K was reported recently for the membranes of strain M2192 [12]; the absence of reaction centers in this strain was considered to result in energy transfer among sufficient B896 species to promote depolarization. Excitation annihilation measurements were consistent with arrays containing ~125 connected B875 BChls persisting at 4 K in these membranes [15]. The finding of a high fluorescence polarization in the largest of the complexes isolated here from strain M2192, suggests that the higher B875 aggregates in the membrane have been dissociated into a form that is nevertheless sufficiently small so that energy transfer among a large number of B896 BChl species does not occur. Moreover, the present results imply that the large LDS complex from this strain may represent the appropriately aggregated B875 system in membranes of the wild type that is capable of directing excitations down an energy gradient to the reaction center. This investigation also establishes that B896 is not a consequence of B875-reaction center interactions, but is instead an intrinsic property of oligomeric B875 complexes and apparently arises from interactions between chromophores located on different B875 units.

ACKNOWLEDGEMENTS
These studies were supported by U.S. National Science Foundation grant DMB85-12587 and Biomedical Research Support grant PHS RR 07058-23. W. H. J. W. and R. T. were recipients of fellowships from the Charles and Johanna Busch Memorial Fund Award to the Rutgers Bureau of Biological Research.

REFERENCES
1 Monger, T.G. and Parson, W.W. (1977) Biochim. Biophys. Acta 460, 393-407
2 Vos, M., van Grondelle, R., van der Kooij, F.W., van de Poll, D., Amesz, J. and Duysens, L.N.M. (1986) Biochim. Biophys. Acta 850, 501-512
3 Kramer, H.J.M., Pennoyer, J.D., van Grondelle, R., Westerhuis, W.H.J., Niederman, R.A. and Amesz, J. (1984) Biochim. Biophys. Acta 767, 335-344
4 van Grondelle, R., Bergström, H., Sundström, V. and Gillbro, T. (1986) Biochim. Biophys. Acta 894, 313-326
5 Bergström, H., Westerhuis, W.H.J., Sundström, V., van Grondelle, R., Niederman, R.A. and Gillbro, T. (1988) FEBS Lett. 233, 12-16
6 Bolt, J.D., Hunter, C.N., Niederman, R.A. and Sauer, K. (1981) Photochem. Photobiol. 34, 653-656
7 Freiberg, A., Godik, V.I., Pullerits, T. and Timpman, K. (1989) Biochim. Biophys. Acta 973, 93-104
8 Sebban, P., Robert, B. and Jolchine, G. (1985) Photochem. Photobiol. 42, 573-578
9 Theiler, R., Suter, F., Pennoyer, J.D., Zuber, H. and Niederman, R.A. (1985) FEBS Lett. 184, 231-236
10 Kiley, P.J. and Kaplan, S. (1988) Microbiol. Rev. 52, 50-69
11 Ashby, M.K., Coomber, S.A. and Hunter, C.N. (1987) FEBS Lett. 213, 245-248
12 Hunter, C.N., van Grondelle, R.and van Dorssen, R.J. (1989) Biochim. Biophys. Acta 973, 383-389
13 Hunter, C.N., Pennoyer, J.D., Sturgis, J.N., Farrelly, D. and Niederman, R.A. (1988) Biochemistry 27, 3459-3467
14 van Dorssen, R. J., Hunter, C. N., van Grondelle, R., Korenhof, A.H. and Amesz, J. (1988) Biochim. Biophys. Acta 932, 179-188
15 Vos, M., van Dorssen, R.J., Amesz, J., van Grondelle, R., and Hunter, C.N. (1988) Biochim. Biophys. Acta 933, 132-140

SPECTROSCOPIC CHARACTERIZATION OF A SUBUNIT FORM OF LIGHT HARVESTING COMPLEX I FROM *RHODOSPIRILLUM RUBRUM* AND *RHODOBACTER SPHAEROIDES*.

R.W. Visschers[a], M.C. Chang[b], F. van Mourik[a], P.A. Loach[b], and R. van Grondelle[a].

a) Dept. of Biophysics, physics laboratory of the Free University, de Boelelaan 1081, 1081 HV Amsterdam, The Netherlands.
b) Dept. of Biochemistry, Molecular Biology and Cell Biology, Northwestern University, Evanston, Illinois 60208, USA.

1.   INTRODUCTION.

The Light Harvesting Antenna of photosynthetic purple bacteria consists of two major types: an inner core (or LH1) antenna, located in the vicinity of of the reaction center, and an outer peripheral antenna (or LH2) surrounding the core antenna. The core antenna complexes usually have an absorbance maximum around 880 nm and are produced in a fixed stochiometry to the photochemical reaction center. The core antenna complexes can be readily extracted from the photosynthetic membranes [1].

In 1987 Miller et. al. [2] succeeded in isolating a subunit form of the core antenna complex of *Rhodospirillum rubrum*. After extracting the carotenoids and titrating the purified complexes with n-octyl-β-D-glucopyranoside (OG) a reversible dissociation of the core antenna was observed. This dissociation is accompanied by a shift in the absorbance maximum from 873 to 820 nm. At even higher concentrations of OG a further shift of the absobance maximum to 777 nm. takes place. Gel filtration experiments showed that the molecular weight of the detergent solubilized B820 form was approximately 55 kD. Assuming that an equal weight of OG is bound this limits the maximum size to an $\alpha_2\beta_2$Bchl$_4$ complex. The B873 particle could be reformed by diluting or removing the OG from the sample. The molecular weight of the B873 particle exceeds 100 kD.

Recently it was found that similar subunit forms could be obtained from the core antenna of both *Rhodobacter sphaeroides* and *Rhodopseudomonas capsulata* []. The B820 subunit form thus seems to be a basic form present in at least three different core antennae. This emphasizes the importance of elucidating the specific conformation of this subunit. We used low temperature fluorescence polarization measurements in combination with other spectroscopic techniques (OD and CD) to obtain information on the specific organization of the bacteriochlorophyll pigments in the subunit forms.

2.   MATERIALS AND METHODS.

The B820 subunit form of LH1 from *Rs. rubrum* was isolated as described in [2]. The B825 subunit form from LH1 from *Rb. sphaeroides* was isolated using a similar method. All low temperature samples where prepared in 50 mM phosphate buffer pH 7.8, containing 50-55% glycerol. The presence of glycerol in the medium affected the dissociation of the B873 into B820 subunits. In general 40-50% more OG was needed to keep the 820 form as compared to samples without glycerol [2]. 77K fluorescence excitation and emission spectra (right angle detection) and CD spectra where measured using a home built spectrophotometer. Fluorescence spectra where corrected for the lampspectrum and wavelength dependence of the detector sensitivity.

3.   RESULTS.

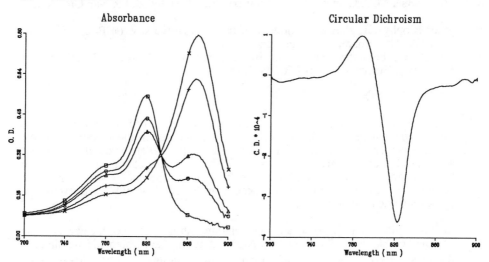

| FIGURE 1. (left) | Near infrared absorption spectra of B873 and the subunit form B820 of LH1 of *Rs. rubrum* that can be obtained by titrating the complex with OG. |
| FIGURE 2. (right) | Low temperature Circular Dichroism spectrum of the B820 subunit of LH1 of *Rs. rubrum*. |

Figure 1 shows the changes in the near infrared absorbance spectrum that can be obtained by titrating *Rs. rubrum* core antenna with OG. Similar effects are observed for the core antenna of *Rb. sphaeroides* with slight changes in the wavelengths of maximal absorbance. In figure 2 the low temperature CD spectrum of the B820 form of *Rs. rubrum* is shown. As in low temperature measurements the bands have sharpened up, revealing that the high energy component is positioned more to the red than the room temperature spectrum suggests.

Figure 3 shows the polarized excitation spectra of the B820 subunit form of *Rs. rubrum* measured at 77K. There is no significant contribution of B777 in the excitation spectra of these particles. A slight depolarization around 790 nm. is clearly present in the polarization curve. The polarization is constant (P=0.43) across the 820 nm. band (apart from the scattering contamination at the red edge). The polarized emission spectrum of the B820 subunit form also shows more negative values when exciting in the Q_x region compared to the B873 form (not shown).

Figure 4 shows the polarized excitation spectra of the B873 form at low temperature. The value of 0.12 for the polarization is in agreement with values reported for LH1 complexes [3]. The fluorescence spectra of the different subunits from *Rb. sphaeroides* all confirmed to the shown spectra of *Rs. rubrum*.. Only a more pronounced increase in the polarization was observed in the red edge of the excitation spectrum of *Rb. sphaeroides* (not shown).

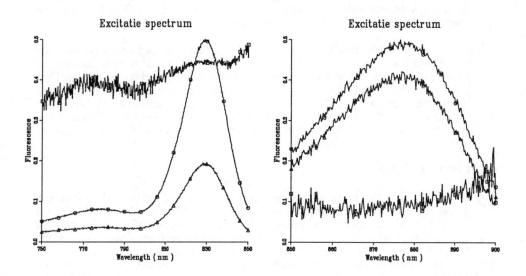

FIGURE 3. (left)   Corrected 77K polarized excitation spectra of B820 subunit form of LH1 from *Rs. rubrum* Detection wavelength 850 nm. Circles: Fluorescence Intensity, detection polarization parallel to incident light, Triangles: Fluorescence Intensity, detection polarization perpendicular to incident light, Squares: Polarization.

FIGURE 4. (right)   idem for the reassociated B873 from *Rs rubrum*, detection wavelength 920 nm.

4.   DISCUSSION.

The absence of a contribution from the B777 form in the fluorescence excitation spectra of the B820 particle clearly demonstrates that the different forms are behaving spectroscopically as distinct particles. This confirms experiments showing that the three different forms are exhibiting different hydrodynamical properties [2,4,5].

Clearly the extreme polarization values found for the B820 subunit of LH1 imposes severe restriction on the construction of models accounting for the spectroscopic properties of this particle. As we did observe even higher polarization values for free bacteriochlorophyll a in 2% OG (p=0.5), the data presented here strongly suggest that the B820 particle consists of an interacting bacteriochlorophyll dimer.

We tentatively ascribe the depolarization observed in the polarized excitation spectrum to the high energy exciton component of this dimer.The contribution of this high energy exciton component to the absorption spectrum can thus be estimated to be in the order of 2%.

To account for the extreme polarization values and the intensity ratio of the high and low energy exciton components, the dimer should be head to tail with an angle between the transition dipoles not larger than 12 degrees. Using model calculations, as in [6], we were able to construct models that produced CD and absorbance spectra in good agreement with our observations (results not shown) .

Reassociation of the B820 form into the B873 form enforces a profound lowering of the polarization value to 0.1 (see figure 3 & 4). This value is indicative of a of number of interacting bacteriochlorophylls with a non-parallel configuration. Thus upon formation of the B873 form the B820 aggregates into larger complexes. This is in agreement with studies showing that the bacteriochlorophylls are more exposed in the B820 form than in the B873 form [4]. We have shown that a circular arrangement of 12 B820 particles can produce CD and OD spectra similar to the ones observed for the B873 form.

5.   CONCLUSIONS.

Since there is a large homolgy between LH1 complexes of different photosynthetic purple bacteria, it is interesting to note that hitherto B820 subunit forms have been isolated from three species. As confirmed by our studies two of these (*Rs. rubrum* and *Rb. sphaeroides*) also exhibit very similar spectral properties.We think that the B820 subunit is a simple building block consisting of an interacting bacteriochlorophyll dimer. In membranes these small building blocks probably aggregate into larger units making up the core antenna whose spectroscopic properties are determined by interaction between these small subunits.

ACKNOWLEDGEMENTS.

The authors acknowledge support from the Dutch Foundation for Biophysics and E.E.C. grant nr. SC1-0004-C

REFERENCES.

1   Picorel, R., B langer, G., & Gingras, G., (1983) *Biochem.* **22**, 2491-2497.
2   Miller, J. F., Hinchigeri, S. B., Parkes-Loach, P. S., Callahan, P. M., Sprinkle, J. R., & Loach, P. A., (1987) *Biochem.* **26**, 5055-5062.
3   Bolt, J. D., Hunter, C. N., Niederman, R. A., & Sauer, K., (1981) *Photochem.and photobiol* . **34**, 653-656.
4   Callahan, P. M., Cotton, T. M., & Loach, P. A., (1987) in *Progr. in Photosynth. res.* (Biggins, J., Ed) Vol. 1, pp I.3.25-I.3.28, Martinus Nijhoff, Dordrecht, The Netherlands.
5   Gosh, R., Rosatzin, Th., & Bachofen, R., (1988) in *Photosynthetic Light-Harvesting Systems* (Scheer, H., & Schneider, S., Eds) pp 93-103, Walter de Gruyter, Berlin, Federal Republic of Germany.
6   Scherz, A., & Parson, W. W., *Biochim.Biophys.Acta* (1984) **766**, 653-655.

A Spectroscopic characterization of the Low-Light B800-850 Light-Harvesting Complex of *Rhodopseudomonas palustris*

Frank van Mourik, Anna M. Hawthornthwaite†, Carine A. Vonk, Richard J. Cogdell† and Rienk van Grondelle.

Dept of Biophysics, Physics Laboratory of the Free University, de Boelelaan 1081, 1081HV Amsterdam (The Netherlands)
†Department of Botany, Glasgow University, Glasgow.

Introduction

In photosynthetic purple bacteria light-energy is absorbed by carotenoid and bacteriochlorophyll (Bchl) molecules, most of which are to be found in the light-harvesting antenna, which forms the major component of the photosynthetic membrane.

Most purple bacteria contain two types of light-harvesting complexes: the LH-1 type of complex, which is produced in a fixed stoichiometry to the amount of reaction centers, and the more variable LH-2.

Most species that contain LH-2 respond to low-light conditions by producing more of the LH-2 complexes. *Rhodopseudomonas palustris* responds to low-light conditions by making a different type of (LH-2) B800-850 light-harvesting complexes [1]. Under high-light conditions *R. palustris* produces light-harvesting complexes that are very similar to the well-characterized complexes of *Rhodobacter sphaeroides*; however, its low-light type B800-850 appears to be rather different.. The main deviation from the 'normal' B800-850 is the fact that the Bchl 850 no longer forms the major component, its "concentration" is apparently halved. The fact that there is less Bchl 850 could have a drastic effect on the transfer rates and efficiencies, which may be compensated by a different organization/aggregation of the complexes.

We have studied the low-light B800-850 complexes (isolated and in membranes) with polarized light spectroscopy (room temperature and 77K CD, LD, absorption and fluorescence depolarization) to get a better understanding of the pigment organization in these complexes.

Materials and Methods

Membranes and B800-850 complexes were isolated as described in [2]. Absorbance spectra were recorded on a Cary 219 spectrophotometer, CD, LD and fluorescence spectra were recorded on a homebuilt spectrophotometer that will be described elsewhere. For LD measurements samples were oriented by biaxial compression in 15 % acrylamide-gels. Low temperature spectra were measured in

M. Baltscheffsky (ed.), Current Research in Photosynthesis, Vol. II, 137–140.
© 1990 *Kluwer Academic Publishers. Printed in the Netherlands.*

50 % glycerol in acrylic, fluorescence cuvettes, 77K CD spectra were recorded in 2 mm quartz cuvettes with a removable cover-plate.

Results

In Fig. 1 the 77K absorption spectra of low-light *Rps. palustris* membranes is shown together with the 77K LD spectrum. The OD spectrum clearly demonstrates the most prominent feature of these low-light complexes: the realtively low amount of B850. In the LD spectum all near-IR bands have a positive LD, whereas the carotenoid bands and the Q_x region have a negative LD signal. Note however that the LD signal of the Q_x region is more complicated than the OD spectrum: at least three Q_x LD bands are required to explain the LD signal in the 570-610 nm region.

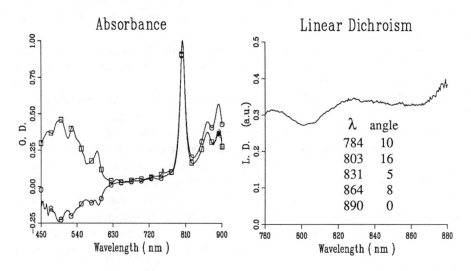

Absorbance	**Linear Dichroism**

Fig. 1: 77K absorption (squares) and LD ((circles, arb. units) of low-light membranes from *R. palustris*.

Fig. 2: LD/A spectrum of the spectra in Fig 1. Inset: calculated angles with the plane of the membrane.

In Fig. 2 the LD/A spectrum of the spectra in fig. 1 is shown for the near-IR region. The angles displayed in the inset were calculated using the formula from [3] for disc-like particles. In the region around 800 nm at least three bands with a different orientation can be distinguished. The LD/A of the B850 is constant over the band (within experimental error). The B880 band shows the maximal LD/A signal, that can be expexted for a perfect in-plane orientation.

In fig. 3 the 77K CD spectrum of low-light B800-850 complexes is shown. Due to the sharpening of the bands the spectrum shows one more band than the spectrum in [4]. The spectrum confirms the complicated nature of the B800 band as already indicated by the LD/A spectrum. The B850 CD is very similar to that of the high-light complex, both in intensity and shape, indicating that the B850 chromophores are organized in a similar way.

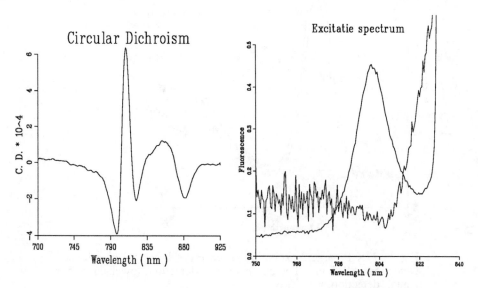

Fig. 3: 77K CD spectrum of low-light B800-850 $OD_{800}=1$.

Fig. 4: 77K excitation spectra of low-light membranes, detection wavelength= 840 nm. Smooth-spectrum vertical exc and detection, noisy spectrum=polarization

In Fig. 4 the excitation spectrum of the B800 emission is shown. The maximal emission uccurs at approx. 835 nm, rather more to the red as compared to the B800-850 from *Rb. sphaeroides*. Upon excitation in the red wing of the B800 band a dramatic increase in the polarization is observed, indicative for a red-shifted transition hidden in the B800 absorption band. The same transition is observed in the CD spectrum at about 822 nm and in the LD/A spectrum.

The polarization of the remaining bands upon 840 nm detection is low and positive. The polarization shows a minimum close to the absorption maximum.

In fig. 5 the polarized excitation spectra of the low-light membranes are shown with fluorescence detected at 915 nm. The polarization spectrum clearly shows that all near-IR transitions have a polarization of approx. 0.1, and slightly higher upon excitation in the B875 band. These results are consistent with the LD/A spectrum.

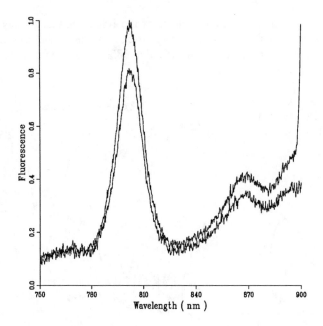

Fig. 5: 77K Polarized excitation spectrum of low-light membranes Detection at 915 nm. Top curve vertical detection, lower curve horizontal detection.

Conclusions.

Low-light B800-850 complexes show a great deal of structural homology with the high-light B800-850, both in the isolated form as in the membranes. Most likely, more B800 chromophores are bound per minimum unit, leading to complicated spectra. The resulting spectral features suggest that exciton interactions between the B800 chromophores dominate. Preliminary pico-second absorption measurements confirm this notion and indicate that energy-transfer from B800 to B850 proceeds via the low-energy exciton state of the B800.

Acknowledgments

This work was supported by the Dutch Foundation for Biophysics, RJC and RvG were supported by a grant from the EEC Grant nr. SC1-0004-C.

References

1) Firsow, N. N., Drews G. (1977) Arch. Microbiol. 115, 299-306

2) Evans M.B., Hawthornthwaite A.M. and Cogdell R.J. (1989) Submitted to *Biochim. Biophys. Acta.*

3) Ganago, A.O., Fok, M. V., Abdourakhmanov, I. A., Solov'ev, A. A. and Erokhin Y. E. (1980) Mol. Biol. (Mosc.) 14:381-389

4) Hayashi H., Nozawa T., Hatano M., Morita S. (1982), *J. Biochem.* 91, 1029-1038

Pigment organization in Bchl-*a*-free and Bchl-*a*-containing Chlorosomes from *Chloroflexus aurantiacus*, studied by absorption dichroism

Frank van Mourik, Kai Griebenow[†], Bart van Haeringen, Alfred R. Holzwarth[†] and Rienk van Grondelle.
Dept. of Biophysics, Physics Laboratory of the Free University, de Boelelaan 1081, 1081 HV Amsterdam (The Netherlands)
[†]Max-Planck-Institut für Strahlenchemie, Mülheim a.d. Ruhr (F.R.G.)

Introduction

Chlorosomes, the major light-harvesting antenna complex of the green bacteria, form a natural model system for the study of energy transfer in large ordered aggregates of chromophores.

In electron microscopic studies the chlorosomes appear as ellipsoid oblong, 100-200 nm long, 30-70 nm wide (species dependent) bodies [1]. A single chlorosome contains up to 10^4 Bchl *c* molecules.

It was believed so far that Bchl *c* was bound to a 5.6 kD protein [3] in a ratio of 5-8 Bchl *c*/polypeptide. However, it has turned out very recently that the Bchl *c* in the interior of chlorosomes is not bound to proteins, instead it forms large protein-free aggregates of interacting chromophores [2]. The Bchl *c* in chlorosomes has many features in common with protein-free aggregates of Bchl *c* in non-polar solvents like CCl_4 and n-hexane [4,5], already indicating that the protein might only play a limited role in the structural organization of the pigments. The outer surface of the chlorosome is formed by a lipid monolayer, that is probably partially replaced by detergent molecules during the isolation procedures. The chlorosome is connected to the cytoplasmatic membrane with a 'baseplate' that contains Bchl *a* and has a function in the process of transferring the energy absorbed by the chlorosome to the membrane part of the photosynthetic apparatus.

Most isolation procedures produce chlorosomes with part of the baseplate, and consequently some Bchl *a*, attached.

Recently, using a new isolation procedure, chlorosomes were prepared that were free of bound Bchl *a* [6]. In order to probe whether the pigment organization of these Bchl *a* free chlorosomes was affected by the isolation procedure we measured Linear Dichroism (LD) and Circular Dichroism (CD) spectra of these chlorosomes.

Materials and Methods

M. Baltscheffsky (ed.), Current Research in Photosynthesis, Vol. II, 141–144.
© 1990 *Kluwer Academic Publishers. Printed in the Netherlands.*

Chlorosomes were isolated as in [6], measurements were performed in 20 mM Tris pH 8.0. For LD measurements chlorosomes were oriented by embedding them in a (15 % w/v, acrylamide:N,N-methylenebisacrylamide = 29:1) poly- acrylamide gel, and subsequently compressing the gel with a compression factor of 1.25 [7].
Absorbance spectra were recorded on a Cary 219 spectrophotometer, CD and LD spectra were recorded on a homebuilt spectrophotometer that will be described elsewhere.

Results

We recorded CD spectra of Bchl *a*-free chlorosomes that were isolated by the GEF procedure, as in [5]. Fig. 1 shows some of the spectra we obtained, using variable concentrations of the detergent LDS. In addition, chlorosomes isolated by various detergents and sucrose density centrifugation were measured.

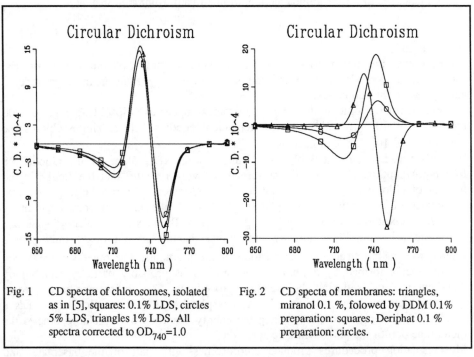

Fig. 1   CD spectra of chlorosomes, isolated as in [5], squares: 0.1% LDS, circles 5% LDS, triangles 1% LDS. All spectra corrected to OD_{740}=1.0

Fig. 2   CD specta of membranes: triangles, miranol 0.1 %, folowed by DDM 0.1% preparation: squares, Deriphat 0.1 % preparation: circles.

The differences between the high (5% !) and the low LDS concentrations are rather small, indicating that LDS is a good detergent for the isolation of chlorosomes. The spectra are very similar to the CD spectrum in [8]. Fig. 2 shows some of the other types of CD spectra we obtained with Bchl *a* containing chlorosomes. Our first idea was that the differences in the CD spectra were the effect of the different isolation procedures. However, it turned out that the CD spectra of different batches of cells/membranes were already different. Apart from the membrane CD spectrum in Fig.2 we also recorded membrane CD spectra that were completely sign-reversed (results not shown). Repeating the same isolation procedures on different batches of cells produced the variety of spectra shown in fig. 1,2.

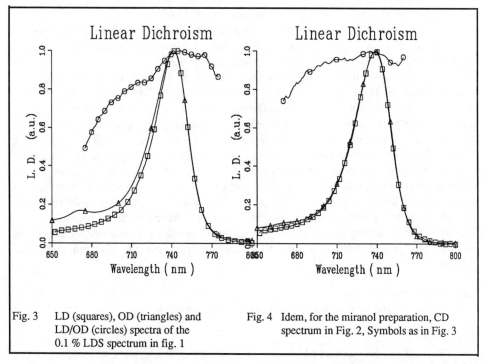

Fig. 3   LD (squares), OD (triangles) and
         LD/OD (circles) spectra of the
         0.1 % LDS spectrum in fig. 1

Fig. 4   Idem, for the miranol preparation, CD
         spectrum in Fig. 2, Symbols as in Fig. 3

Fig. 3 shows the LD spectrum we found for the chlorosomes with the CD spectrum shown in Fig.1. It is clear that the short-wavelenght region of the Bchl c Q_y band has a reduced LD signal. All the samples of Fig. 1 gave similar results. This feature appears to be absent in the spectra shown in Fig. 4. Using the formula derived by Ganago [7] for rod-shaped particles gives angles of approx. 15 degrees between the Bchl c Q_y transition-dipole and the long axis of the chlorosomes (for the maximum in both LD/OD spectra).

Discussion
Olson et al. [3] reported differences between CD spectra for chlorosomes from *Cfl. aurantiacus* and *Chlorobium limicola*. Here we show that spectra similar to both types can be obtained from just *Cfl. aurantiacus*.
Since the CD spectra of the membranes used for the isolation were similar to those of the isolated chlorosomes the differences are not due to the isolation procedure. Growth conditions have been kept as constant as possible, but the species might react to very subtle changes in the light-conditions or the growth medium.
Similar to what was reported in [9] we found high values for the LD of the Bchl c Qy transition, indicating that the average angle of the Q_y transition with the orientation axes of the chlorosome is approx. 15 degrees.

Van Dorssen et al. [8] reported larger angles, but they used a different compression geometry, and much higher compression factors. At these high degrees of compression the chlorosomes might not behave as rigid bodies.

In contrast to their results we did not observe the 725 nm shoulder with a higher degree of orientation in the LD spectrum. Rather, in some samples we found a lower value for the LD in this region, as demonstrated in Fig. 3.

The small angles we find are in good agreement with the high values found for the polarization of the Bchl *c* fluorescence upon excitation in the 740 nm band [8].

We think that the observation of different CD spectra is yet another argument against models in which the organization of the pigments is directed by the structure of the protein. The occurence of the CD spectrum with three bands was correlated with a reduced value of the LD around 720 nm. This could be caused by either a different type of chlorosomes with a blue shifted absorption spectrum, or by different pigment pools within a single chlorosome. Time-resolved fluorescence measurements indicate that we might be dealing with the second possibility, since fast relaxation processes have been observed between different pigment pools [10].

We are currently trying to understand the different spectra we obtained by combined fluorescence polarization, CD and LD measurements on the different types of chlorosomes.

Acknowledgments

FvM was supported by the Dutch Foundation for Biophysics

REFERENCES
1)   Feick, R. R., Fitzpatrick, M., Fuller, R. C. (1982) J. Bacteriol. 150 pp 905-915
2)   Griebenow K., Holzwarth A.R. (1989) in *Molecular Biology of Membrane-Bound Complexes in Phototrophic Bacteria* editor G. Drews.
3)   Wechsler, T., Suter, F., Fuller, R. C., Zuber, H. (1985) FEBS Letters 181, pp 173-178
4)   Olson, J.M., Gerola, P.D., van Brakel, G.H., Meiburg, R., Vasmel, H. (1985) in *Antennas and reaction centers of Photosynthetic Bacteria* (Michel-Beyerle, M. E., Ed.) pp 67-73, Springer-Verlag, West Berlin, Heidelberg, New York, and Tokyo.
5)   Brune, D. C., King, G.H., Blankenship, R.E. (1988) in *Photosynthetic Light-Harvesting Systems* (Scheer, Schneider Ed.) pp 141-151
6)   Griebenow, K., Holzwarth, A.R. (1989) Biochim. Biophys. Acta 973 pp 235-240
7)   Ganago, A.O., Fok, M. V., Abdourakhmanov, I. A., Solov'ev, A. A. and Erokhin Y. E. (1980) Mol. Biol. (Mosc.) 14:381-389
8)   van Dorssen, R.J., Vasmel, H., Amesz, J. (1986) Photosynth. Res. 9, 33-45
9)   van Amerongen, H., Vasmel, H., van Grondelle, R. (1988) Biophys. J. 54 pp 65-76
10) Holzwarth, A. R., Müller, M. G. Griebenow, K. (1989) submitted to *J. Photochem. Photobiol.*

PROPERTIES OF A SOLUBILIZED AND PURIFIED ANTENNA-REACTION CENTER COMPLEX FROM HELIOBACTERIA

E.J. van de Meent, F.A.M. Kleinherenbrink and J. Amesz
Department of Biophysics, Huygens Laboratory of the State University, P.O. Box 9504, 2300 RA Leiden, The Netherlands

1. INTRODUCTION

The heliobacteria are distinguished from other classes of photosynthetic bacteria by the possession of a new type of bacteriochlorophyll, BChl g (1). At present three species have been isolated: *Heliobacterium chlorum* (1), *Heliobacillus mobilis* (2) and *Heliospirillum gestii*. Studies on molecular mechanism of the photosynthetis have been confined so far to *H. chlorum*. The primary electron donor of *H. chlorum*, P-798, is probably a dimer of BChl g (3). Studies of the electron acceptor chain suggested a similarity with green sulfur bacteria and photosystem I. The primary electron acceptor is probably a BChl c or chlorophyll a-like pigment (4), absorbing near 670 nm, and there is evidence that an iron-sulfur center may act as secondary electron acceptor.

This communication reports the isolation and purification of antenna-reaction center complexes from membranes of *H. chlorum* and *Hb. mobilis*. The complexes appear to be functionally and structurally intact. They have an estimated molecular weight of 335 kDa and probably consist of a single photosynthetic unit with the associated reaction center.

2. MATERIALS AND METHODS

H. chlorum and *Hb. mobilis* were grown under nitrogen at 37 °C in medium No. 1552 of the American Type Culture Collection containing 10 mM ascorbate.

Detergent incubation of membranes (A_{788}=10 mm^{-1}) was performed at pH=8.0 with sulphobetaine-12 at a concentration of 1.32 % (w/v) for 30 min at 4 °C in the dark. The incubation mixture was then loaded on a 20 - 55 % (w/v) sucrose gradient containing 0.1 % SB-12 and 0.1 % cholate and centrifuged at 175,000 x g for 16 h.

Size exclusion-HPLC was performed on a TSK G4000 SWG (21.6 x 300 mm) column from LKB with an eluent of pH 6.9 containing 0.1 % SB-12. SDS-PAGE was performed under denaturing conditions. Gels were stained with Coomassie brilliant blue.

3. RESULTS AND INTERPRETATION

Typical results obtained by sucrose gradient centrifugation of membranes of *H. chlorum* and *Hb. mobilis* after incubation with SB-12 are given in Table 1. The upper fraction on top of the gradient probably consisted of free pigment in detergent micelles. The middle fraction, located at approximately 35 % sucrose, consisted of a solubilized pigment-protein complex. The lower fraction presumably consisted of non-solubilized membranes. Similar results were obtained with *H. chlorum* using n-octyl-β-D-glucopyranoside (OGP).

M. Baltscheffsky (ed.), Current Research in Photosynthesis, Vol. II, 145–148.
© 1990 *Kluwer Academic Publishers. Printed in the Netherlands.*

TABLE 1. Fractions obtained after SB-12 solubilization.

The yield is expressed as recovery of BChl g. For each species, the last column gives the activity of P-798 photo-oxidation, as determined from the relative amplitude of the bleaching at 798 nm in a saturating laser-flash.

Material	Heliobacterium chlorum			Heliobacillus mobilis		
	A_{max} (nm)	Yield (%)	$A_{max}/\Delta A_{798}$	A_{max} (nm)	Yield (%)	$A_{max}/\Delta A_{798}$
Membranes	786	−	21	787	−	22
Upper fraction	756	1	300	759	1	270
Middle fraction	785	61	20	786	26	20
Lower fraction	786	38	20	786	73	22

The low-temperature absorption spectra (Fig. 1) of the middle fractions from *H. chlorum* and *Hb. mobilis* were very similar to those of the membranes used as starting material and to each other. Although the Q_y-maxima were shifted by about 1 nm to

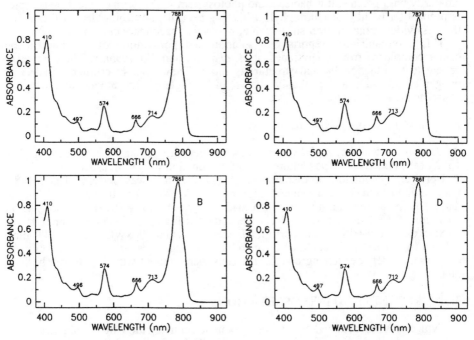

FIGURE 1.   Absorption spectra, measured at 100 K, of membranes and antenna-reaction center complex fractions. A, membranes of *H. chlorum*; B, the antenna-reaction center complex from *H. chlorum* (the"middle fraction"); C, membranes of *Hb. mobilis*; D, the complex from *Hb. mobilis*; 66 % (v/v) glycerol was added to obtain clear samples.

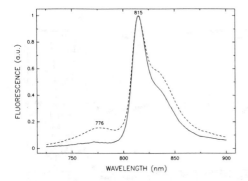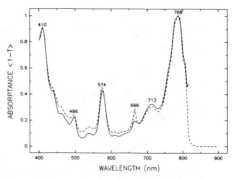

FIGURE 2.   Fluorescence emission spectra at 77 K of the antenna-reaction center complexes from
H. chlorum (solid line) and *Hb. mobilis* (broken line) upon excitation at 575 nm.

FIGURE 3.   Fluorescence excitation spectrum, monitored at 820 nm, (solid line) of the antenna-reaction
center complex from *H. chlorum*, measured at 5 K. The broken line shows the absorptance
(1-T) spectrum. The two spectra are normalized at the Q_y-maxima.

the blue, the three spectral forms of BChl *g*, BChl *g*-778, BChl *g*-793 and BChl *g*-808
(5) were still observed in the same ratio as in the membranes, albeit in a slightly blue
shifted position. The relative height of the band near 670 nm, and the amount of
carotenoid (mainly neurosporene (1,5)) were not significantly changed. The
low-temperature fluorescence spectra of the middle fractions (Fig. 2) were again
similar to those of the membranes. They showed a maximum at 815 nm at 77 K,
indicating that most of the fluorescence originated from BChl *g*-808. Comparison of
the absorptance spectrum with the fluorescence excitation spectrum (Fig. 3) indicated
efficient energy transfer from BChl *g*-778 and BChl *g*-793 to BChl *g*-808. Efficient
energy transfer also occurred from neurosporene to BChl *g*. The efficiency of energy
transfer from the 670-nm pigment to BChl *g* was approximately 50 %. These results
strongly indicate that the structure of the antenna complexes was completely
conserved upon solubilization.

Also the reaction center activity, measured by the yield and extent of
photo-oxidation of the primary electron donor P-798, was completely retained. The
absorbance difference spectra for the complexes from both species and the absorbance
difference spectrum for *H. chlorum* membranes are shown in Fig. 4. The reduction of
P-798+ was slow as compared to membranes but could be speeded up upon addition
of PMS. The absence of a fast decay component showed that the electron acceptor
chain was at least partially intact. Cytochrome *c*-553 photo-oxidation was not
observed, indicating that the cytochrome was either lost or inactivated during the
isolation.

The complexes were further purified by size-exclusion HPLC. In this way colorless material was removed, and from the elution volume a molecular weight of approximately 335 kDa could be estimated for both complexes. The height of the
protein absorbance in the UV as compared to that of other pigment-protein complexes
suggested a BChl *g* content of 10 - 15 % by weight, corresponding to about 40 BChls
per complex. This would indicate that the complexes contain the antenna complement

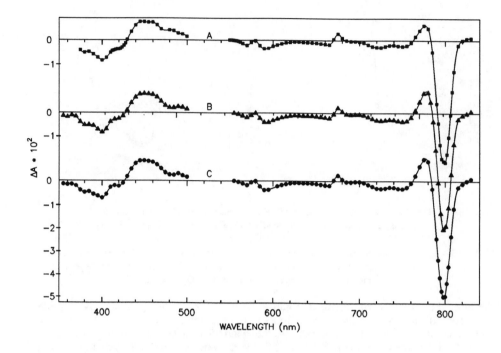

FIGURE 4.   Absorbance difference spectra of (A): membranes of *H. chlorum* (B): the antenna-reaction center complex of *H. chlorum* and (C): the complex from *Hb. mobilis*. The spectra were normalized to an absorbance of 1.0 at the Q_y-maximum for each sample. Actinic flashes were provided by a Q-switched, frequency-doubled Nd-YAG laser (15 ns half width, 532 nm).

of one photosynthetic unit, together with the associated reaction center. SDS-poly-acrylamide gel electrophoresis of the purified complexes revealed the presence of a predominant polypeptide of $M_r = 94$ kDa. The subunit-structure of the complexes thus appears to deviate considerably from that of the core of photosystem I (6), suggesting that there is no clear structural and evolutionary relationship between photosystem I and the photosystem of heliobacteria.

REFERENCES

1   Gest, H. and Favinger, J.L. (1983) Arch. Microbiol. 136, 11-16
2   Beer-Romero, P. and Gest, H. (1987) FEMS Microbiol. Lett. 41, 109-114
3   Prince, R.C., Gest, H. and Blankenship, R.E. (1985) Biochim. Biophys. Acta 810, 377-384
4   Nuijs, A.M., van Dorssen, R.J., Duysens, L.N.M. and Amesz, J. (1985) Proc. Natl. Acad. Sci. USA 82, 6865-6868
5   Van Dorssen, R.J., Vasmel, H. and Amesz, J. (1985) Biochim. Biophys. Acta 809, 199-203
6   Malkin, R. (1987) in The Light Reactions (Barber, J., ed.) pp. 495-525, Elsevier, Amsterdam

EFFECTS OF CONFORMATION AND ENVIRONMENT ON BACTERIOCHLOROPHYLL OPTICAL
SPECTRA: CORRELATIONS OF CALCULATED SPECTRA WITH STRUCTURAL RESULTS

E. GUDOWSKA-NOWAK,* M. D. NEWTON[†] and J. FAJER*, Department
of Applied Science* and The Chemistry Department,[†]
BROOKHAVEN NATIONAL LABORATORY, UPTON, NEW YORK 11973

1. INTRODUCTION
    Recent structural data for (bacterio)chlorophylls and chlorins as
isolated molecules and in proteins have demonstrated the skeletal distortions of the chromophores that can be imposed by crystal packing
and/or protein constraints[1].
    We consider here the possibility that such conformational varia-
tions can affect the highest occupied and lowest unoccupied molecular
orbital levels of the chromophores and thereby modulate their light-
absorption properties.
    We apply the concept to the bacteriochlorophyll (BCHL) a - protein
antenna complex from Prosthecochloris aestuarii, whose structure has
been solved by X-ray diffraction[2] and which exhibits a series of low
energy absorption maxima at low temperatures that range from 793-825
nm[3].
    The seven BCHLs that comprise the BCHL-protein fall into two
distinct conformational classes[2]. INDO/s calculations for the seven
individual BCHLs, based on the crystallographic data, yield absorption
maxima that correlate with the conformational variations and clearly
establish that skeletal variations can influence the optical properties
of the chromophores. Effects of axial ligands, orientations of
substituent groups and neighboring groups are also assessed.
    These calculations and previous results[1] for model porphyrins and
photosynthetic reaction centers suggest that conformational variations
play a significant role in determining optical and redox properties of
porphyrin derivatives and thus may offer attractively simple ration-
ales, in conjunction with additional modulations imposed by protein
residues or solvents, for their properties in vivo and in vitro.

2. METHODS
    The calculations are based on the INDO/s method of Zerner et al.,[4]
and include the lowest 225 singly excited configurations from the
self-consistent field ground state. The calculations utilized the
crystallographic data for P. aestuarii reported by Tronrud et al.[2] For
modifications to the BCHL molecule, the Mg or substituents were
replaced by hydrogens at idealized positions.

M. Baltscheffsky (ed.), Current Research in Photosynthesis, Vol. II, 149–152.
© 1990 Kluwer Academic Publishers. Printed in the Netherlands.

3. RESULTS AND DISCUSSION

Effects of conformation, substituents, ligands, and metal were assessed using models a-d shown in Fig. 1. Results for the Q_y transitions are presented in Table 1 for the 7 BCHLs:

TABLE 1. Calculated first absorption maxima, nm.

BCHL a (Ligand)	model a+L*	model a	model b	model c	model d
1 HIS	769	769	771	725	694
2 H$_2$O	800	795	799	739	732
3 HIS	741	754	768	734	709
4 HIS	842	841	840	788	802
5 LEU	761	786	791	749	719
6 HIS	803	803	808	769	791
7 HIS	842	829	836	793	805

*a+L = model a + ligand shown in first column.

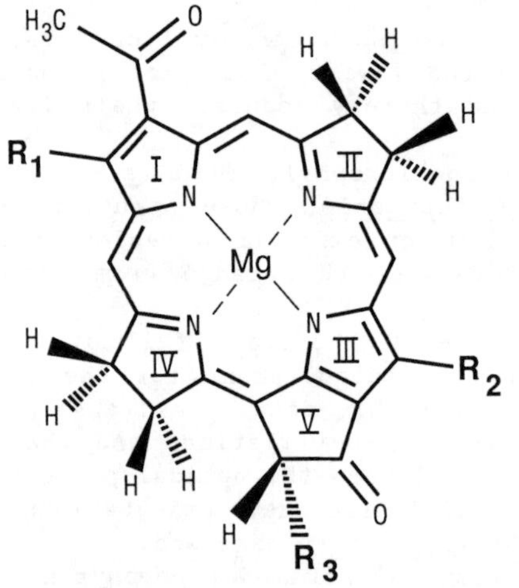

Figure 1.
Models used in the calculations (Coordinates from ref. 2)
(a) $R_1=R_2=CH_3$, R_3=carbomethoxy.
(b) $R_1=R_2=R_3=H$.
(c) $R_1=R_2=R_3=H$; acetyl group on ring I replaced by H.
(d) $R_1=R_2=R_3=H$; Mg replaced by 2H's on rings I and III.

Comparison of models a+L and a yields the effect of the axial ligand bound to the Mg of the BCHLs. The small differences observed are attributable to the nature and configuration of the different ligands present: histidine, H$_2$O, or leucine, and are consistent with experimental results for BCHLs in solution.[5]

Removal of the peripheral carbomethoxy group on ring V has little effect as evidenced by comparison of models a and b.

The crystallographic results show several orientations for the acetyl group on ring I that are reflected in the calculations. Compare models b and c; the acetyl group is removed in c. Maximum interactions are found when the keto group aligns closest to the plane (and π system) of the BCHLs.

The effect of the Mg itself is reflected in the comparison between models b and d. The blue shifts calculated on removal of the Mg are consistent with experimental spectra of BCHL and bacteriopheophytin.[5]

Tronrud et al.[2] noted two distinct types of conformation based on averaging the displacements of the atoms of the π systems (BCHLS 1-3 and 4-7). If this grouping is used, then the conformational effects on the spectra are clearly evident (Table 1, model c).

Additional modulations of the optical spectra by nearby amino acid residues were considered by including the residues surrounding BCHL 6 within 5.5 Å. The Q_y transition is calculated at 740 nm vs 808 nm without the residues (model b). Most of this effect is attributable to an electrochromic shift[6] induced by the positively charged arginine (ARG 90) that lies ~5A from the keto group on ring V. Uncharged aromatic residues cause only small perturbations in the optical spectra.

4. CONCLUSIONS

The calculations of conformational and environmental interactions presented here begin to delineate the factors that control the optical spectra of photosynthetic chromophores in vivo (and in vitro).

The calculations yield a larger spread in optical maxima than observed experimentally.[3] Hole burning experiments for the antenna complex indicate that the BCHLs are excitonically coupled.[7] A standard excitonic model[8] was used to assess the cumulative effects of the aggregation of the 7 BCHLs on the calculated optical spectra. The exciton model, using the results from model a+L, also yielded a larger spread in maxima than observed experimentally. The discrepancies may arise from uncertainties in the crystallographic data[2] for the conformations, orientations of substituents, and the degree of ionization of nearby charged residues. (Future calculations will treat the 7 BCHLs as one supermolecule.) Nonetheless, conformational variations are clearly significant in controlling optical features.

The combination of theoretical and experimental results[1] strongly suggests that conformational variations observed for porphyrin derivatives can provide a mechanism for altering optical and redox properties. Such effects, in combination with additional modulations induced by protein residues (or solvents), thus provide an attractive mechanism for fine-tuning the electronic properties of the chromophores in vitro and in vivo.

ACKNOWLEDGMENTS

We thank M. A. Thompson and M. C. Zerner for the INDO program and L. K. Hanson for discussions. This work was supported by the U.S. Department of Energy, Office of Basic Energy Sciences (M.D.N. and J.F.) and an Exploratory Research grant (E.G.N.).

REFERENCES

1 Barkigia, K.M., Chantranupong, L., Smith, K.M. and Fajer, J. (1988) J. Am. Chem. Soc. 110, 7566, and references therein.
2 Tronrud, D.E., Schmidt, M.F., Matthews, B.W. (1986) J. Mol. Biol., 188, 443.

3 Pearlstein, R.M. (1988) in Photosynthetic Light-Harvesting Systems, (Scheer, H. and Schneider, S., eds.), p. 555, Walter de Gruyter Publishers, Berlin.

4 Edwards, E.D. and Zerner, M.C. (1985) Can. J. Chem. 63, 1763; Thompson, M.A. and Zerner M.C. (1988) J. Am. Chem. Soc. 110, 606.

5 Callahan, P.M. and Cotton, T. M. (1987) J. Am. Chem. Soc. 109, 7001.

6 Hanson, L.K., Fajer, J., Thompson, M.A. and Zerner, M.C. (1987) J. Am. Chem. Soc. 109, 4728.

7 Johnson, S.G. and Small, G.J. (1989) Chem. Phys. Lett. 155, 371.

8 Davydov, A.S. (1962) in Theory of Molecular Excitons, McGraw Hill Publisher, New York.

Temperature dependence of energy transfer from the long wavelength antenna BChl-896 to the reaction center in *Rhodospirillum Rubrum, Rhodobacter Sphaeroides* **(w.t. and M21 mutant) from 77 to 177 K, studied by picosecond absorption spectroscopy.**

Visscher K.J.[a], Bergström H.[b], Sundström V.[b], Hunter C.N.[c] and Van Grondelle R.[a] a) *Department of Biophysics, Physics Laboratory of the Free University, 1081 HV Amsterdam, The Netherlands b) Department of Physical Chemistry, University of Umea, S-90187 Umea, Sweden c) Department of Molecular Biology and Biotechnology, Biochemistry Section, University of Sheffield, Sheffield S10 2TN, United Kingdom*

Introduction

The fast transfer and trapping of excitation energy in photosynthetic bacteria have been intensively studied in recent years. For reviews we refer to (1). Steady-state (2) and time-resolved fluorescence (3) and time-resolved picosecond absorption recovery measurements have led to the formation of the following scheme for energy transfer in *Rhodobacter (Rb.) sphaeroides.* (4,5,6)

$$B\,800{-}850 \xrightarrow{k_3} B\,875 \xrightarrow{k_2} B\,896 \xrightarrow{k_1} RC \qquad (1)$$

At room temperature back transfer rates must be taken into account, but at 77K excitation transfer is unidirectional with $k_3 = 2.5{\times}10^{10}\ s^{-1}$ and $k_2 = 5{\times}10^{10}\ s^{-1}$ (5). The rate constant for transfer from B896 to the reaction center (RC) depends on the photochemical state of the RC. With the bacteriochlorophyll dimer, P, oxidized, i.e. "closed" RC's, $k_1 = 5.5{\times}10^9 s^{-1}$, while recently it was esthablished that with P reduced, k_1 increased to about $2.5{\times}10^{10}\ s^{-1}$ (6).

For *Rhodospirillum (R.) rubrum* , which only contains the LH-1, i.e. B880 + B896, antenna, the scheme simplifies to:

$$B\,880 \xrightarrow{k_2} B\,896 \xrightarrow{k_1} RC \qquad (2)$$

with $k_2 = 5{\times}10^{10}\ s^{-1}$ and $k_1 = 1.3{\times}10^{10}\ s^{-1}$ for open and $7.7{\times}10^9\ s^{-1}$ for closed RC's at 77K (5,6).

The measured rate constants reflect 'average' transfer rates between pigment pools. Transfer rates within an individual pigment-protein complex are considerably faster. For instance, within the B800-850 complex of *Rb. sphaeroides* transfer from $BChl_{800}$ to $BChl_{850}$ takes less than 1 ps at 300 K, but the rate decreases to 1-2 ps at 77 K (4,5). Transfer among identical $BChl_{850}$'s within B800-850 or among identical $BChl_{875}$'s within B875 also proceeds within a time of less than a picosecond, as judged from the strong initial depolarization of the absorption changes (4,5).

The schemes presented above fit to the proposed structural aspects of these systems. In *Rb. sphaeroides* B800-850 is thought to constitute the peripheral part of the antenna, while B875 is supposed to surround and interconnect several reaction centers. In *R. rubrum* the B880 antenna forms a large 'lake-like' arrangement connecting at least 10, but possibly more RC's. At low temperature these large domains appear to break up into smaller fragments and especially excitation annihilation experiments reveal an underlying, more detailed structure.

Special pigments absorbing in the red wing of long-wavelength absorption band purple bacteria were introduced by Borisov et al. (3) We choose to call them B896, where 896 nm reflects their low-temperature (4K) absorption maximum. B896 manifests itself spectroscopically as having strongly anisotropic absorption and emission properties, as the component with the long excited state life time when all RC's are closed (5), and as the component where

M. Baltscheffsky (ed.), Current Research in Photosynthesis, Vol. II, 153–156.
© 1990 *Kluwer Academic Publishers. Printed in the Netherlands.*

preferentially excitons are quenched at high excitation densities (3).
A two-component analysis satisfactorily explains most of the spectroscopic data ((5) assuming a 6:1 ratio for B875:B896 If B896 is a special pigment coupling B875 to the RC the distance between B896 and P must be between 2.6 and 3.1 nm (6).

Energy transfer, as described with the concept of radiationless transitions (7), may show a strong temperature dependence, dependent on the value of the energy difference and coupling energy, and studying the rate of energy transfer as a function of the temperature may yield important information concerning the nature of the coupling. Steady-state fluorescence data on photosynthetic purple bacteria showed a strong increase in the fluorescence yield upon lowering the temperature. For *R. rubrum* this increase started below 100 K., for *Rb. sphaeroides* probably at lower temperatures. Also the dramatic changes in absorption and emission spectra suggest large changes in energy transfer rate constants (2).

To further investigate the properties of B896 we have studied the B896 excited state life time in the presence of open RC's for *R.rubrum, Rb. sphaeroides w.t.* and *Rb. sphaeroides M21* , a mutant lacking the B800-850 complex. As already shown elswhere the B896 excited state decay reflects excitation transfer to P (6). At higher temperatures components due to back transfer to the main antenna may mix in and therefore we have only performed measurements for $T \leq 175K$.

Materials and Methods

To keep the reaction centers 'open' i.e. in a photoactive condition the chromatophore solutions were purged with nitrogen for an hour, after which a 10 - 50 mM sodium-dithionite solution (in 250 mM Tricine) was added to ensure that the first quinone acceptor af the RC, Q_A, is maintained in the reduced state (Q_A^-). Under these conditions illumination of the sample leads to a primary charge separation, but this state will recombine on a nano-second time-scale. At 77 K none of the recombination will occur via the excited singlet state, but at higher temperatures slow emission decay components can be observed due to this recombination (4). However this will not interfere with the measurements of the trapping time reported here, inview of the large difference in time-scales. (≤ 100 ps vs. 10 -20 ns).

Results and Discussion

Performing a one colour picosecond absorption recovery experiment, using excitation wavelengths longer than 905 nm selectively excites the B896 pigment in *Rb. sphaeroides w.t.* (Van Grondelle et al. 1987). Also in *R. rubrum* B896 is preferentially excited, but at 77 K there seems to be more overlap between the B880 and B896 absorption bands (5). This was concluded from a series of one colour anisotropy decay and absorption recovery decay experiments over the wavelength region 850 to 905 nm (5). These experiments showed that the ratio of relative contribution to the observed kinetics of B875 → B896 and B896 → RC peaks at 890 nm. For increasing wavelength the B875 → B986 contribution decreases rapidly and vanishes for wavelength above 905 nm for *Rb. sphaeroides,* while for *R. rubrum* there is still a none neglible B875 excitation even at 905 nm. For these reasons the B896 excited state decay kinetics were measured at 905 nm in *Rb. sphaeroides* , while they were recorded at three independent wavelength in *R. rubrum* , i.e. at 905, 907 and 915 nm. *Rb. sphaeroides M21* was only measured at 877 nm because the sample could not be made concentrated enough. At 877 nm B896 shows a strong excited state absorption while at the same time it is close to the isobestic point for the B880 absorption changes. However, inevitably also a substantial part of the excited state will be due to B880, and because the transfer time from B880 to B896 excited states is approximately 20 ps, the decay time will seem to be faster than the decay of B896 excited states only.

For *R. rubrum* the B896 excited state life time is 76 ps at 77 K; in good agreement with the number obtained by Bergström et al. (6). At 150 K the life time has decreased to 42 ps. At 905 and 907 nm essentially the same lifetimes were observed. For *Rb. sphaeroides* w.t. the B896 excited life time at 77 K is 41 ps, and a very similar number is obtained at 150 K. For *Rb. sphaeroides* M21 at 877 nm the observed decay time is 37 ps at 77 K and 36 ps at 125 K. In all cases the decays could be reasonably well fitted with a single exponent, superimposed on a long-lived component reflecting the formation of the radical pair. The long lived component bas been shown (6) to be due to the formation of P^+I^- by comparing kinetics measured at 790 and 810 nm with results published on pure reaction centers by Shuvalov et al. (8).

The full temperature dependence between 77 K and 177 K of these absorption changes is given in figur . It is seen that below 100 K the B896 excited state lifetime in *R. rubrum* becomes temperature dependent, increasing from a value around 40 ps to between 70 and 80 ps at 77 K. In view of the strong increase in the total fluorescence yield observed by Rijgersberg et al. (2) upon cooling to 4 K it must be concluded that this increase is most likely due to the temperature dependence of the energy transfer step from B896 to the special pair P and not, as suggested by Rijgersberg et al. (2), to the decrease in the Förster rate of the energy transfer among identical BChl molecules.

For *Rb. sphaeroides* w.t. and M21 the absorption changes are virtually temperature independent over the temperature range studied. In fact between 100 K and 175 K the three preparations studied show no temperature dependence and yield very similar B896 excited state life times. The slightly faster value measured for M21 is probably due to mixing in of some B875 decay.

The room temperature trapping times for 'open' and 'closed' reaction centers of *Rb. sphaeroides* and *R. rubrum* have been measured by fluorescence techniques (3) and absorption recovery techniques (4). For a detailed discussion we refer to the latter paper, and only mention the trapping time found for 'open' reaction centers; 60 ps for *R. rubrum* and 100 to 110 ps for *Rb. sphaeroides*. Compared to room temperature the rate of trapping has increased for the three species when measured between 100 K and 175 K. However, this effect is probably due to a delocalization of the excitation density over all the antenna molecules at room temperature. Assuming a 1:1 distribution (4) for the excitation density at 293 K between B896 and B880 in *R. rubrum* , the experimentally measured 60 ps trapping time constant would to first order correspond with a 30 ps trapping time for B896 alone, rather close to the value measured between 100 and 200 K. For *Rb. sphaeroides* w.t. the trapping time increases even further to 80 to 100 ps at room temperature. According to the analysis given by Sundström et al. (4) this is not due to different excitation transfer properties of the LH-1 antenna, but due to a further delocalization of the excitation density over the large B800-850 antenna. For M21, the same argument can be given as for *R. rubrum*. In conclusion, the transfer time from the antenna situated close to the RC to the special pair is the same for these three species, in the 30 to 40 ps time-range, and almost independent of the temperature between 100 K and 293 K. These results indicate that the arrangement af the antenna pigments close to the RC must be very similar in these three systems. For *Rb. sphaeroides* w.t. it was calculated (6) that the closest approach of the antenna to the RC special pair, as reflected by the B896 excited state decay, is between 2.6 and 3.1 nm. This indicates that excitations enter the RC along the short axis of the RC and this is probably also true for the other species (see figure 2).

Acknowledgements

This project was financially supported by the Ducth Foundation of Biophysics, the Swedish Natural Science Research Council and The Magnus Bergval Foundation. Additional financial support received under contract nr. SCI-0004-C of the European Community.

References

1)Van Grondelle R., Sundström V., (1988),excitation energy transfer in photosynthesis. In: Photosynthetic light harvesting systems. Organization and function. Edited by H. Scheer, S. Schneiderm, Walter de Gruyter (Berlin, New York).

2)Rijgersberg C.P., Van Grondelle R. and Amesz J., (1980), Biochimica et Biophysica Acta, 592, 53-64.

3)Borisov A.Yu., Gadonas R.A., Danielius R.V., Piskarkas A.S. and Razjivin A.P., (1982), FEBS Letters, 138, 25-28.

4)Sundström V., Van Grondelle R., Bergström H., Akesson E. and Gillbro T., (1986), Biochimica et Biophysica Acta, 851, 431 - 446.

5)Van Grondelle R., Bergström H., Sundström V. and Gillbro T., (1987), Biochimica et Biophysica Acta, 894, 313 - 326.

6)Bergström H., Van Grondelle R. and Sundström V., (1989), FEBS Letters, submitted for publication.

7)Devault D., (1980), Quantum mechanical tunneling in biological systems. Quarterly Reviews of Biophysics, 13, 387-564.

8)Shuvalov V.A., Shkuropatov A.Ya., Kulakova S.M., Isamailov M.A. and Shkurpatov V.A., (1986), Biochimica et Biophysica Acta, 849, 337-346.

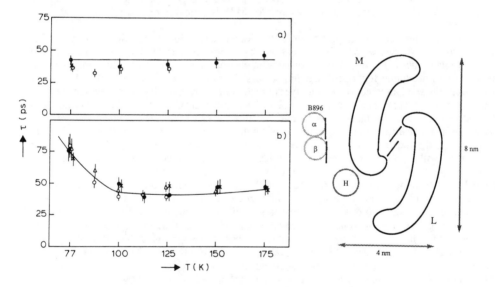

Figure 1: Relation between the absorption recovery lifetimes τ versus temperature. a) for *Rb. sphaeroides* w.t. measured at 905 nm: o and ×, for *Rb. sphaeroides* M21 mutant measured at 877 nm: o and b) for *R. rubrum* measured at 905 nm: o and o, 907 nm × and 915 nm Δ. The bars indicate the standard deviations from averaging 4 to 5 transients.

Figure 2: Top view of reaction center: the M and L proteins with the special pair and the proposed location of the B896 antenna. The proposed site for B896 follows from the calculated distance of B896 to special pair; 2.6 to 3.0 nm.

EXCITATION TRANSPORT AND QUENCHING IN PHOTOSYNTHETIC BACTERIA AT NORMAL
AND CRYOGENIC TEMPERATURES

ARVI FREIBERG, VALENTINA I. GODIK ,TÕNU PULLERITS AND KÕU TIMPMANN
INSTITUTE OF PHYSICS, ESTONIAN ACADEMY OF SCIENCES, 202400 TARTU,
ESTONIA; *) LABORATORY OF MOLECULAR BIOLOGY AND BIOORGANIC CHEMISTRY,
MOSCOW STATE UNIVERSITY, 119899 MOSCOW, USSR

1. INTRODUCTION
     The main principles of a very efficient transport of light excita-
tions   in   photosynthetic   membranes   and   their   utilization   by
photochemically active reaction centres (RC) are already quite well
understood (see, e.g., Ref.1). However, recent spectrally selective
picosecond-time-domain fluorescence kinetics measurements on most simple
photosynthetic organisms, the purple bacteria, have revealed new information (2, 3) that has created a need for further development of the
existing models in order to better adapt them to experiment. In what
follows we have concentrated on the complications connected with the
spectral (and structural) heterogeneity of the light-harvesting antenna.
The influence of the exciting picosecond pulse intensity and the
frequency of successive pulses on excitation quenching kinetics is also
briefly discussed.

2. HETEROGENEITY OF A LIGHT-HARVESTING SYSTEM
     A number of purple photosynthetic bacteria contain light-harvesting
pigment-proteins of spectrally well-resolved types. For example, in
bacteria *Rhodobacter sphaeroides* and *Chromatium minutissimum* pools with
bacteriochlorophyll *a* absorption maxima at 800, 850 and 875 nm can
clearly be defined. The picosecond fluorescence kinetics of these
bacteria versus the emission wavelength has been measured and the
data analyzed by the coupled rate-equations model. Important phenomeno-
logical excitation transport rates between different antenna pigment-
proteins as well as between different pigments within a single B800-850
pigment-protein were revealed (3).
     However, the coupled rate-equations model hiddenly assumes that
pigment molecules inside a certain spectral pool have quite similar
spectral and kinetic qualities and that the rate of excitation migration
within the pool is extremely fast compared to the rate of excitation
transfer from one pool to another. These assumptions, which are in a
reasonable agreement with the room temperature experiment, fail when the
details of low-temperature data are considered. At cryogenic temperatures the inner spectral heterogeneity of antenna pools becomes essential. This has been well documented at 77 K in case of the purple bacte-

M. Baltscheffsky (ed.), Current Research in Photosynthesis, Vol. II, 157–160.
© 1990 *Kluwer Academic Publishers. Printed in the Netherlands.*

rium *Rhodospirillum rubrum* (which is believed to have a single antenna
pool B880) by observing the gradual shortening of the mean fluorescence
decay time at shorter recording wavelengths due to the directed excitation transfer (for experiment, see Ref. 2).

In order to analyze this low-temperature experiment more thoroughly
a two-dimensional random-walk model of excitation transfer with a relatively small number (2-30) of spectrally different light-harvesting
pigment-proteins per RC in the photosynthetic unit (PSU) has been developed. Some other specific features of the model are as follows:

- periodic boundary conditions to take into account the spillover of
  the excitations between PSUs;
- Förster approximation for the pairwise rate of excitation
  transfer between light-harvesting pigment-proteins;
- temperature dependence of energy transfer by vibronic theory
  of spectral lineshapes (for analogy, see Ref.4);
- random orientation of dipole moments.

Figures 1 and 2 demonstrate some of the results of the numerical
calculations for the PSU with 19 antenna pigment-proteins per RC. The

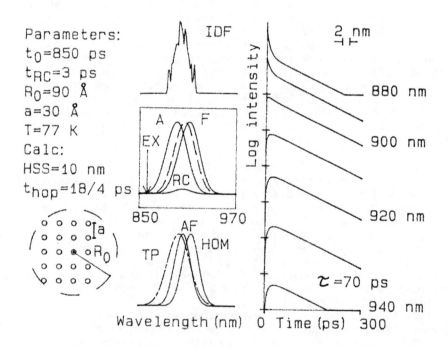

Figure 1. Results of the model calculations of fluorescence decay
in the PSU with an inhomogeneously broadened antenna
and RC in the active state. Temperature 77 K, other
parameters as shown in the picture.

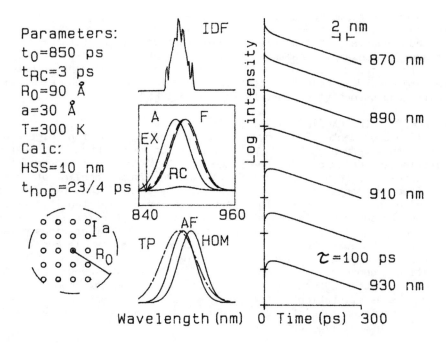

Figure 2. The same as Fig. 1, except T=300 K

model is able to qualitatively repoduce all the main features of the experiment (2) both at room temperature and at 77 K, viz.
- the characteristic dependence of the fluorescence decay on the recording wavelength including a slight time delay of the long-wavelength emission at low temperatures;
- almost no dependence of the fluorescence decay on the recording wavelength at room temperatures;
- an anomalously large shift between the absorption and emission spectra.

All these effects do not appear in case of a spectrally homogeneous antenna (1). Some shortening of the mean decay time is also predicted when the temperature is lowered down to 77 K. This is in line with the theory (4) for homogeneous antenna. According to this theory the transfer rate as a function of temperature may have a maximum at temperatures lower than the room temperature. Preliminary experiment with Rb.sphaeroides seems to confirm these expectations (A.Freiberg et.al., unpublished). However, at liquid helium temperatures there is almost no dependence of fluorescence decay on the RC state. This may be due to substantial conformational changes of the pigment-protein-lipid system at such very low temperatures.

Note that for direct comparison of the calculated decay curves with the experiment the convolution with the apparatus response is needed. Then the peak at shorter wavelengths is lower and broader and the delay at longer wavelengths is less noticeable. A reasonable quantitative agreement between model and experimental decay parameters can be achieved. However, too streightforward interpretation of these results is risky. For example, pairwise hopping parameters depend remarkably on the structure and size of the PSU. Therefore, independent structural data are needed to make quantitative conclusions about the excitation transfer and quenching parameters in the real PSU.

3. EFFECT OF THE EXCITATION INTENSITY

Our measurements (2,3) have been performed by using the picosecond laser with a very high 82 MHz pulse repetition rate. When the average excitation intensity exceeds the value of 0.5-1 W/cm.cm, a shortening of the fluorescence decay time (see Fig.3) and an evident decline of kinetics from exponentiality is observed. An analysis of the experimental data led us to a conclusion that these relatively low-intensity effects are due to the annihilation of the singlet and triplet excitations of the antenna pigments (3). The triplets are generated by previous pulses of the train because the time interval between the pulses is much shorter than the triplet lifetime of the pigments. A more quantitative theoretical approach has revealed a need to take into account also the pigment absorption saturation (L.Valkunas et.al., unpublished). So, to exclude the deterioration of the experimental data by nonlinear effects at MHz repetition rate of picosecond excitation pulses only very moderate pulse intensities can be used.

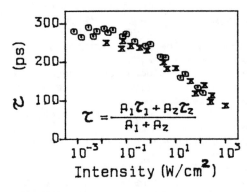

Figure 3.

Dependence of the mean fluorescence decay time of *Chr.minutissimum* (0) and *R.rubrum* (x) chromatophores on excitation light intensity at 786 nm (0) or 762 nm (x) at room temperature. Recording at 910 nm (0) or 900 nm (x) with 4 nm bandwidth

ACKNOWLEDGEMENTS
    The authors thank Dr. L.Valkunas and his colleagues from the Vilnius Institute of Physics for many useful discussions on annihilation.

REFERENCES
1. Pearlstein, R.M. (1982) Photochem.Photobiol. 35, 385-844
2. Freiberg, A., Godik,V.I. and Timpmann, K. (1987) in Progress in Photosynthesis Research (Biggins, J.,ed.), Vol.1, pp.45-48, Martinus Nijhoff, Dordrecht
3. Freiberg,A., Godik,V.I., Pullerits,T. and Timpmann,K. (1989) Biochim.Biophys.Acta 973, 93-104
4. Yomosa, S. (1978) J.Phys.Soc.Japan 45, 967-975

SINGLET-SINGLET ANNIHILATION IN THE ANTENNA OF RHODOSPIRILLUM RUBRUM AT LOW TEMPERATURES

G. DEINUM[a], T.J. AARTSMA[a], R. VAN GRONDELLE[b] and J. AMESZ[a]

[a]Department of Biophysics, Huygens Laboratory, University of Leiden, P.O. Box 9504, 2300 RA Leiden, The Netherlands
[b]Department of Biophysics, Physics Laboratory, Free University, De Boelelaan 1081, 1081 HV Amsterdam, The Netherlands

1. INTRODUCTION.

Photosynthetic antenna pigments serve to absorb light and to transport excitation energy towards the reaction centers. The assembly of a reaction center with surrounding antenna pigments is called a photosynthetic unit, which in the purple bacterium *Rhodospirillum rubrum* contains about 35 antenna bacteriochlorophylls. It is known that in *R. rubrum* many photosynthetic units are clustered together, forming aggregates. Within these aggregates, which are called domains, excitations can be transferred freely from one molecule to another.

Singlet-singlet annihilation can give insight into the size of these domains. For these measurements the fluorescence yield of the antenna BChls is measured as a function of the intensity of a laser excitation pulse. Singlet-singlet annihilation occurs if two singlet excited states accumulate at one molecule, leading to higher excited states. Rapid decay by radiationless processes to the lowest excited state then causes a decrease of the fluorescence yield. An equation relating the fluorescence yield to the number of excitations generated per domain was given by Paillotin et al. (Eqn.20 in (1)). By fitting the experimental data to this equation the domain size and the r-value, twice the rate of mono-excitation decay relative to the annihilation rate per pair of excitations, can be extracted.

The method was applied by Bakker et al. (2) and Vos et al. (3) on *R. rubrum* chromatophores. They obtained domain sizes ≥ 1000 BChls at room temperature. At 4 K however Vos et al. (3) observed less annihilation and concluded that the domain size was reduced to about 150 BChls. They also observed a fluorescence wavelength dependence of the annihilation. We extended their measurements to intermediate temperatures and looked into more detail at the wavelength dependence.

2. MATERIALS AND METHODS.

R. rubrum chromatophores were prepared as described earlier (3). Annihilation measurements with a 25-ps, 532 nm excitation pulse were performed as described by Vos et al. (3).

M. Baltscheffsky (ed.), Current Research in Photosynthesis, Vol. II, 161–164.
© 1990 Kluwer Academic Publishers. Printed in the Netherlands.

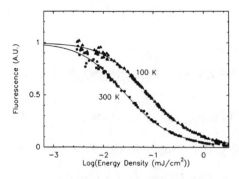

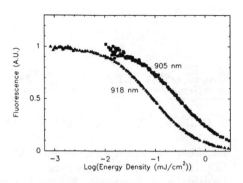

Fig.1. The relative fluorescence yield as a function of the incident energy density of the excitation flash at 300 K (squares) and at 100 K (triangles). The data are fitted with Eqn.20 in (1) with r=2. The curves are normalized at low energy densities.

Fig.2. Annihilation curves at 4 K. Squares: detected at 905 nm; triangles: detected at 918 nm. The data are normalized at low energy densities.

3. RESULTS AND DISCUSSION.

Fig.1 shows the relative fluorescence as a function of the laser pulse energy density at 300 and at 100 K. The measurements were performed at a detection wavelength of 920 nm. At both temperatures the fluorescence can be fitted with r = 2, using Eqn. 20 in (1). However, since r-values larger than 2 can fit the data equally well, only lower limits to the domain sizes of 1000 and 300 can be determined for 300 K and 100 K, respectively. Nevertheless, it can be shown that a considerable change in the average rate of energy transfer between individual BChl molecules must occur in this temperature region. Calculation of the average energy transfer rates (k_h) according to the model of Den Hollander et al. (4) gives 1.0×10^{12} $s^{-1} \leq k_h \leq 2.0 \times 10^{12}$ s^{-1} at 300 K. At 100 K these numbers are 3.0×10^{11} $s^{-1} \leq k_h \leq 5.0 \times 10^{11}$ s^{-1}. Our calculations show that these values are mainly determined by the position of the annihilation curves on the horizontal scale, and do not critically depend on the precise r-values and domain sizes.

Fig.2 shows the results of measurements at 4 K. The measurements were performed at two wavelengths of detection (905 nm and 918 nm). The relative fluorescence as a function of the energy density differs for these wavelengths,

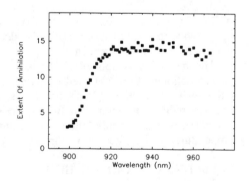

Fig.3. Wavelength dependence of the extent of annihilation (see text) at 4 K.

indicating a spectral inhomogeneity of the antenna. This spectral inhomogeneity was noticeable below approximately 100 K.

At 4 K the wavelength dependence of the extent of annihilation was further studied by recording the fluorescence spectrum at low excitation energy density where no singlet-singlet annihilation occurs and at high excitation energy density where singlet-singlet annihilation is the dominant decay process. The low and high excitation spectrum were obtained by exciting with a xenon flash and with a laser flash with an energy density of 1.0 mJ/cm^2, respectively. The extent of annihilation at high light intensity as a function of emission wavelength, obtained by dividing the first by the second spectrum is shown in Fig. 3. It can be observed that the extent of annihilation increases with wavelength until it reaches a constant level at 920 nm, indicating that the fluorescence above 920 nm originates from one type of pigment. If we assume that the fluorescence spectrum consists of two bands, the data of Fig. 3 can be used to calculate the sizes and shapes of these bands. The bands have a maximum at 918 and 911 nm, respectively. The ratio of the fluorescence yields of the two bands at low excitation density is 11.7 ± 0.8. These bands, which we will call F918 and F911, presumably arise from BChl 880 and BChl 896, respectively (5).

Since the antenna of *R. rubrum* is spectrally inhomogeneous at 4 K, Eqn. 20 in (1), describing the annihilation, is not simply applicable to this system. When analyzing the fluorescence of F911, the pigments emitting at 918 nm can be considered to act as traps and their presence is therefore reflected by the mono-excitation decay. Since energy transfer from BChl 896 to BChl 880 does not take place at 4K (6), Eqn.20 in (1) remains applicable to F911. A correction, however, must be made for the fact that the curve recorded at 905 nm is not entirely due to F911. At low excitation intensity about 25 % of the fluorescence yield originates from F918, as can be calculated from the results in Fig. 3. Applying the correction for the contribution of F918 at 905 nm a domain size of 75 ± 25 BChls was obtained. However, for F911 a correction must also be made for the pulse duration of 25 ps which is of the same order of magnitude as the lifetime of F911. At 77 K the lifetimes of F911 and F918 with closed reaction centers are approximately 20 and 160 ps (7). If we take into account the increase of the total fluorescence yield by a factor of 2.5 to 3 and a ratio of the integrated fluorescence intensities of the two bands of 10 at 4 K, lifetimes of 50 ± 10 ps for F911 and of 500 ± 100 ps for F918 are calculated, respectively. Random walk simulations were used to study the influence of the length of the laser pulse. They showed that, when applying a 25-ps pulse the domain size is overestimated by a factor of

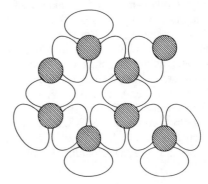

Fig.4. Possible arrangement of BChl 880 (ellipses) and BChl 896 (hatched circles) in the antenna of *R. rubrum*. The ellipses and the hatched circles represent approximately 60 and 20 BChls, respectively.

about 1.3 in this particular case. So we determined the domain size for BChl 880 to be 55 ± 20 BChls.

When correcting the fluorescence originating from BChl 896 for annihilation taking place in BChl 880 a domain size of 21 ± 9 BChls was determined for BChl 896. Since probably only 5-7 BChls 896 are present per reaction center (6), this indicates that each reaction center is closely interconnected with one to four others.

Our results thus indicate that upon cooling down from 300 K to 100 K, a decrease of the average rate of energy transfer in the antenna takes place. A decreasing domain size is not necessary to explain the results in this temperature region. Upon further cooling the antenna of *R. rubrum* is split up into separate BChl 880 and BChl 896 domains, due to inhomogeneities in energy transfer in the antenna.

A model may be constructed where the antenna consists of clusters of about 60 BChls 880 separated by clusters of 20 BChls 896 (Fig. 4). However, it is also possible that the BChl 880 domains are not spatially separated, but physically separated by spectral inhomogeneities within BChl 880. Evidence for such a spectral inhomogeneity involving the presence of long and short wavelength absorbing bacteriochlorophylls was recently obtained from low temperature absorption and flash-induced absorption difference spectra of *Rhodobacter sphaeroides* and *R. rubrum* (7,8). A short-wave BChl might then act as a barrier for energy transfer between BChl 880 clusters at low temperature.

4. REFERENCES.

1 Paillotin, G., Swenberg, C.E., Breton, J. and Geacintov, N.E. (1979) Biophys. J. 25, 513-533.

2 Bakker, J.G.C., van Grondelle, R. and den Hollander, W.T.F. (1983) Biochim. Biophys. Acta 725, 508-518.

3 Vos, M., van Grondelle, R., van der Kooij, F.W., van de Poll, D., Amesz, J. and Duysens, L.N.M. (1986) Biochim. Biophys. Acta 850, 501-512.

4 Den Hollander, W.T.F., Bakker, J.G.C. and Van Grondelle, R. (1983) Biochim. Biophys. Acta 725, 492-507.

5 Van Grondelle, R., Bergström, H., Sundström, V., van Dorssen, R.J., Vos, M. and Hunter, C.N. (1988) in: Photosynthetic Light Harvesting Systems (Scheer, H. and Schneider, S., eds.),pp. 519-530, De Gruyter, Berlin.

6 Kramer, H.J.M., Pennoyer, J.D., van Grondelle, R., Westerhuis, W.H.J., Niederman, R.A. and Amesz, J. (1984) Biochim. Biophys. Acta 767, 335-344.

7 Van Grondelle, R.,Bergström, H., Sundström, V and Gillbro, T. (1987) Biochim. Biophys. Acta 894, 313-326.

8 Van Dorssen, R.J., Hunter, C.N., van Grondelle, R., Korenhof, A.H. and Amesz, J. (1988) Biochim. Biophys. Acta 932, 179-188

TIME-RESOLVED MEASUREMENTS OF FLUORESCENCE FROM THE
PHOTOSYNTHETIC MEMBRANES OF *RHODOBACTER CAPSULATUS* AND
RHODOSPIRILLUM RUBRUM

NEAL WOODBURY AND EDITH BITTERSMANN
Department of Chemistry and Center for the Study of Early Events in Photosynthesis,
Arizona State University, Tempe, AZ 85287, USA.

1. INTRODUCTION

Most current models for energy transfer and trapping in the antenna of purple
nonsulfur bacteria involve excitations visiting many reaction centers before trapping
occurs. This so-called lake model has been supported by a variety of observations
including singlet-singlet annihilation studies (1-3), low intensity picosecond absorption
spectroscopy (4), and fluorescence depolarization studies (5).

In its simplest form, this model makes a clear prediction about the dependence of the
excitation lifetime in the antenna on the fraction of the reaction centers which are closed.
(The term "closed" will be used to refer to reaction centers in which P has been oxidized
to P^+.) When all the reaction centers are open, the excited state of the antenna should
decay with some short lifetime. As reaction centers are closed (by increasing the light
intensity or chemical oxidation) this lifetime should increase monotonically.

This prediction has been tested by Borisov *et al.* (6) using a streak camera to follow
the fluorescence decay of chromatophores (isolated photosynthetic membrane vesicles) of
Rhodospirillum rubrum. *Rs. rubrum* contains no peripheral antenna. Instead, its
antenna seems to consist of an 875 nm absorbing chromophore (B875) and a
chromophore that apparently absorbs at about 905 nm at room temperature (B896, named
for its absorption at 4K) (3,7). Borisov *et al.*, (6) reported a single fluorescence decay
lifetime at all incident light levels which simply increased as the traps were closed (i.e., as
the light level was increased), in good agreement with the prediction of the lake model.

We have repeated and extended these measurements using picosecond resolution
single photon timing techniques. In contrast to the earlier studies, we find that the
increase in the overall decay time of the fluorescence is not only due to an increase in the
initial excitation trapping time but also to a substantial contribution from a second, longer-
lived fluorescence component which grows in as the traps are closed.

2. METHODS

Rhodobacter capsulatus cells lacking the B800/850 antenna complex (strain U43 with
episomal expression of the reaction center and B875 antenna complex) and
Rhodospirillum rubrum cells (strain S1) were grown to late log phase anaerobically in the
light at 30 C and harvested. Cells were either broken using a French press and
chromatophores isolated as described by Woodbury *et al.* (8), or cells were ruptured by
grinding in alumina and chromatophores isolated as described by Jackson and Crofts (9).

M. Baltscheffsky (ed.), Current Research in Photosynthesis, Vol. II, 165–168.
© 1990 *Kluwer Academic Publishers. Printed in the Netherlands.*

The single photon counting apparatus will be described elsewhere. For these experiments, we utilized the laser dye Styryl 9 in a cavity-dumped dye laser synchronously-pumped by a mode-locked Nd YAG laser. Using this instrument we were able to excite the sample between 800 and 890 nm at a repetition rate of 3.8 MHz. The emission was detected with a microchannel plate photomultiplier tube which utilized an S1 photocathode. The detection wavelength was varied between 880 and 940 nm using a monochromator with a 16 nm bandpass. The full-width-at-half-maximum of the instrument response function in this configuration was about 80 ps, measured by detecting scattered light at the excitation wavelength.

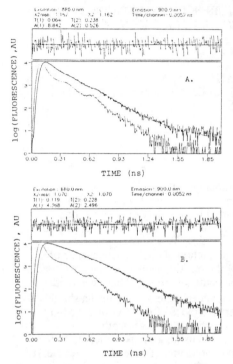

Fig. 1 Time-resolved fluorescence from *Rb. capsulatus* photosynthetic membranes lacking B800/850 antenna complexes. For each decay, an instrument response function is shown as well. (A) Weak measuring beam only. (B) Preillumination with a 532 nm pulse (about 3 mJ) about 50 ms before measurement.

The sample was flowed at a rate of about 5 ml/sec through a cuvette with a 1.5 mm light path. At this flow rate the excited sample volume was completely replaced in less than 1 ms. The optical density of the sample at the excitation wavelength never exceeded 0.1 in the 1.5 mm light path. The excitation beam cross section was about 2 mm^2, and, unless otherwise noted, the intensity was 0.5 mW or less. Decreasing the intensity further had little or no effect on the decay kinetics.

3. RESULTS

3.1 The Fluorescence Decay from Simple Antennae is Not Always Single Exponential. We have used single photon timing measurements to monitor the decay of the excited state of *Rs. rubrum* and mutant *Rb. capsulatus* antennae both of which are thought to contain only B875 and B896 antenna chromophores. The measurements described below were obtained using chromatophores of *Rb. capsulatus*, but qualitatively similar results have been obtained with *Rs. rubrum* chromatophores and whole cells. In contrast with earlier streak camera measurements (Borisov *et al.*, 1985), we have found that as the reaction centers are closed (by increasing the amount of incident light) the fluorescence decay becomes substantially multiphasic (Fig. 1). As Borisov *et al.* (1985) had seen, the fluorescence lifetime with all centers open was 50 to 60 ps, depending on the strain and conditions. In addition to this, however, we observed a small (less than or equal to 5%) component with a lifetime around 200 ps.

3.2 Both Components Change as the Traps are Closed. As the incident light intensity was increased, the lifetime of the shorter component increased by a factor of about 2, plateauing around 120 ps under the conditions of this experiment (Fig. 2A). The initial amplitude of the longer component increased by about seven-fold with increased light intensity, until it was over 30% of the total initial amplitude of the fluorescence (Fig. 2B). (Experiments at slower flow rates indicate that the amplitude of the slower component saturates at about 40%.) Similar results were obtained whether the state of the traps was modulated by increasing the 870 nm measuring light or by using 532 nm preillumination about 50 ms before the fluorescence measurement. Similar kinetics were also seen when a fraction of the traps were closed by chemical oxidation with ferricyanide (data not shown).

3.3 The Two Components Have the Same Spectrum. Preliminary spectral data indicate that the longer-lived kinetic component has a fluorescence spectrum very similar, if not identical, to that of the short component (Fig. 3). Measurements have also been made at several excitation wavelengths including 800 nm (which excites primarily the reaction centers), 860 nm (blue side of the antenna absorption) and 890 nm (red side of the antenna absorption). There did not appear to be any major differences between the lifetimes or relative amplitudes of the short and long components observed at these wavelengths.

4. DISCUSSION

4.1 Fluorescence Quenching When All Traps are Closed is Very Fast. If one assumes that the faster of the two fluorescence components represents excitation trapping in the antenna, then at high light when essentially all reaction centers are closed, excitations in the antenna are still largely quenched within 120 ps. This is only twice the excitation lifetime with all traps open. Even with much higher light levels or chemical oxidation of P, the lifetime of the main fluorescence decay component was never greater than about 150 ps (data not shown). If the intrinsic lifetime of excitation in the antenna were only 150 ps, the yield of photochemistry would not approach the measured value of 90% or more. It seems likely that some quencher is formed as reaction centers are closed, possibly P+ itself.

4.2 The 200 ps Component Could be Due to Delayed Fluorescence. It is interesting that a small amount of the 200 ps component is present even at very low light

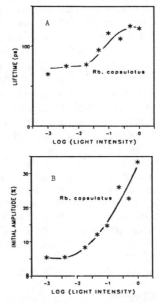

Fig. 2 The lifetime of the shorter fluorescence decay component (A) and the initial amplitude of the longer (200 ps) fluorescence decay component (B) as a function of the relative light intensity of a 532 nm preillumination pulse. The highest light intensity reported corresponds to a pulse of about 3 mJ over a 3-5 ms period.

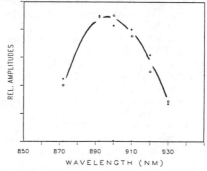

Fig. 3 Spectrum of the short (O) and long (●) components of the fluorescence decay from *Rb. capsulatus* chromatophores (sample and conditions as in Fig. 3B).

intensity. The initial amplitude of this component does not drop below a few percent even when weaker measuring light is used. One possible explanation of this is that the 200 ps component is due to back electron transfer from the state P^+Bph^-. This so-called delayed fluorescence has been observed previously in chromatophores with reduced quinones where P^+Bph^- lives for nanoseconds (8). Both the initial amplitude and the lifetime of the longer-lived fluorescence component observed here agree with what would be expected from previous kinetic and thermodynamic measurements of the electron transfer (8,10). In addition, if the 200 ps component of the fluorescence were due to delayed fluorescence from P^+Bph^-, one would expect an increase in its initial amplitude as the traps were closed. This is primarily due to the fact that the ratio between the number of antenna and the number of open traps accounts for a large fraction of the free energy difference between the excited antenna and P^+Bph^-.

Even if the longer-lived fluorescence component turns out to be unrelated to the trapping process, it is very important to understand just what the two components represent. Numerous measurements of antenna fluorescence have been reported and interpreted assuming that all emitters in a simple antenna system are equilibrated at room temperature on a timescale much faster than trapping, and that trapping results in a state that does not give rise to appreciable fluorescence. If this were true, the fluorescence would be describable as a single kinetic component. Regardless of the source, the fact of the matter is that the fluorescence which arises from the simple antennae of *Rs. rubrum* and *Rb. capsulatus* (lacking the B800/850 antenna) when some of the traps are closed is kinetically heterogeneous. This observation has been made in both whole cells and isolated photosynthetic membranes from two different species of bacteria and cannot be explained without either modifying the lake model for bacterial antenna function or invoking a second process which gives rise to fluorescence in this system.

ACKNOWLEDGEMENTS

This is publication #18 from the Arizona State University Center for the Study of Early Events in Photosynthesis. The Center is funded by U.S. Department of Energy grant #DE-FG02-88ER13969 as part of the USDA/DOE/NSF Plant Science Centers program. N. Woodbury acknowledges support from a Faculty Grant in Aid from Arizona State University.

REFERENCES
1   Vos, M., van Grondelle, R., van der Kooij, F.W., van de Poll, D., Amesz, J. and Duysens, L.N.M. (1986) Biochim. Biophys. Acta 850, 501-512
2   Bakker, J.G.C., van Grondelle. R. and den Hollander, W.T.F. (1983) Biochim. Biophys. Acta 725, 508-518
3   Borisov, A.Yu., Gadonas, R.A., Danielius, R.V., Piskarskas, A.S. and Razjivin, A.P. (1982) FEBS Lett. 138, 25-28
4   Sundstrom, V., van Grondelle, R., Bergstrom, H., Akesson, E., and Gillbro, T. (1986) Biochim. Biophys. Acta 851, 431-446
5   Kramer, H.J.M., Pennoyer, J.D., van Grondelle, R., Westerhuis, W.H.J., Niederman, R.A. and Amesz, J. (1984) Biochim. Biophys. Acta 767, 335-344
6   Borisov, A.Yu., Freiberg, A.M., Godik, V.I., Rebane, K.K. and Timpmann, K.E. (1985) Biochim. Biophys. Acta 807, 221-229
7   van Grondelle, R., Bergstrom, H., Sundstrom, V. and Gillbro, T. (1987) 313-326
8   Woodbury, N.W. and Parson, W.W. (1986) Biochim. Biophys. Acta 850, 197-210
9   Jackson, J.B. and Crofts, A.R. (1968) European J. Biochem. 6, 41-54
10 Parson, W.W. and Ke, B. (1982) in Photosynthesis: Energy Conservation by Plant and Bacteria, vol 1 (Govindjee, ed.) Academic Press, New York pp 331-385

PICOSECOND FLUORESCENCE STUDIES OF *RHODOPSEUDOMONAS VIRIDIS*.

EDITH BITTERSMANN, ROBERT E. BLANKENSHIP AND NEAL WOODBURY
Department of Chemistry and Center for the Study of Early Events in Photosynthesis,
Arizona State University, Tempe, Arizona, 85287-1604, USA.

1. INTRODUCTION

Over the past years a vast amount of information has been gathered on the structure of the reaction center and antenna system of the purple bacterium *R. viridis*. (1,2). However, because of its far red shifted emission maximum (approximately 1030 nm) until recently it was not possible to measure its fluorescence kinetics on a picosecond time scale. We have investigated the energy transfer kinetics of whole cells, chromatophore membranes, photoreceptor units (quantasomes) and reaction centers in a dark adapted state and in the presence of different redox agents, using single photon timing fluorescence techniques.

2. MATERIALS AND METHODS

Chromatophore membranes from *R. viridis* were obtained by breaking the cells in a French press and purifying them on a 10-60 % w/w sucrose gradient. The membranes were kept in 50 mM Tris-buffer at pH 8.0. To isolate the photoreceptor units, also called quantasomes, the membranes were solubilized with 1% Triton X-100 in 100 mM Tris pH 9.0 and put on a sucrose gradient (5-40 % w/w)(3). For the fluorescence experiments the absorbance of the membranes at 1012 nm was ~1.0 for a light path of 1 cm and that of the quantasomes was ~0.6 at 1005 nm. The samples were pumped through a fluorescence cuvette with a pathlength of 1.5 mm and a window of 1.5 x 11 mm at 300 ml/min to avoid photooxidative effects from laser light. Picosecond fluorescence decays were measured with a mode-locked cavity-dumped dye laser system (Coherent) with Rhodamine 6G or with Styryl 9M in a Spectra Physics dye laser. The fluorescence was detected through a monochromator using the single photon timing method with a S1 microchannelplate photomultiplier (Hamamatsu R1564U-05). The width of the laser pulses was 5-15 ps and the instrument response was approximately 60-70 ps FWHM. Data were analyzed in terms of a sum of exponentials. The details of this system will be described elsewhere.

3. RESULTS AND DISCUSSION

The photosynthetic apparatus of *R. viridis* consists of the reaction center surrounded by only one type of antenna, which is organized in rings with a six-fold symmetry axis. These units form large two dimensional sheets in the membrane (2). Consequently, we expected the fluorescence decay in a dark adapted state, with all reaction centers open and

M. Baltscheffsky (ed.), Current Research in Photosynthesis, Vol. II, 169–172.

ready for photochemistry, to be monoexponential. We measured lifetimes of whole cells, membranes, quantasomes and reaction centers. The excitation wavelength was either 600 nm (the Qx band of the antenna) or 830 nm (the Qy band of the reaction center). Due to limitations in our laser system, we were not able to excite the Qy band of the antenna directly. Fluorescence was detected at 1025 nm through a monochromator with 16 nm bandwidth. A representative decay curve is shown in Figure 1.

TABLE 1: Fluorescence lifetimes (τ_i) and relative amplitudes (a_i) of dark adapted cells, membranes, quantasomes and reaction centers of *R. viridis* at different excitation wavelengths (λ_{exc}).

	λ_{exc} (nm)	τ_1 (ps)	a_1	τ_2 (ps)	a_2	τ_3 (ps)	a_3
Whole cells	600	82	.997	726	.003		
	830	83	.988	495	.012		
Membranes	600	75	.982	236	.018		
	830	72	.965	195	.034		
Quantasomes	600	41	.913	142	.086	1000	.001
	830	38	.921	120	.074	422	.005
Reaction centers	830	16	.996	648	.004		

Table 1 shows that in all samples the shortest lifetime component contributed more than 90 % to the initial fluorescence amplitude but none of these samples showed a monoexponential decay. The lifetime of the major component is independent of the excitation wavelength, indicating that the excitation equilibrates on a time scale beyond the time-resolution of our system. This lifetime is 80-85 ps in whole cells of *R. viridis* and is reduced to 70-75ps in chromatophore membranes. Though this reduction is probably within the error of the measurement, it occurred consistently in all direct comparisons. However in the quantasomes it is further reduced by a factor of 2 to 35-45 ps. The 16 ps fluorescence lifetime for the isolated reaction center seems very slow compared to picosecond absorption measurements (4). One possible explanation for this long lifetime might be that our system is not able to resolve a faster lifetime. However, in simulated data a 5 ps decay component could easily be recovered by the analysis program, and we routinely resolve lifetimes in the 10 ps range.

The short lifetime component observed in whole cells of *R.viridis* is somewhat longer than that found with photoelectric measurements (5). A possible reason for that might be a higher light intensity used for the photoelectric as compared to the fluorescence experiments. An increase in the light intensity in our experiments results in a shortening of the lifetimes of both components towards the values found in the photoelectric measurements (cf. Table 2).

In each sample the main lifetime component represents the trapping time of the excitation at the reaction center. Current theory predicts that the trapping time should be directly proportional to the number of antenna molecules per reaction center (6). If the membrane sheets are made up only of arrays of quantasomes, it is difficult to understand why the trapping time drops by a factor of 2 in isolated quantasomes. There is apparently some of the antenna lost during the isolation procedure; the ratio between the absorbance at 1010 nm and at 830 nm drops from 8 to 6 when isolating the quantasomes. However, this does not completely account for the decrease in fluorescence lifetime.

The kinetics measured at different light levels and redox states are compared in Table 2. First, the membranes were exposed to continuous white light and a decay profile was taken. Under these conditions, the lifetimes of both components shorten relative to the dark adapted state, and the relative amplitudes change in favor of the second, longer-lived component so that nearly 1/3 of the initial amplitude is due to this component. This decay is shown in Figure 1.

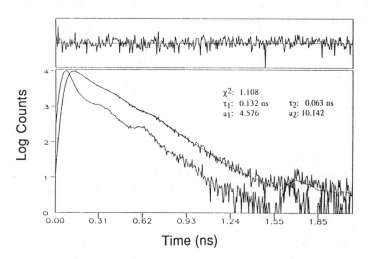

Figure 1: Fluorescence decay curve, instrument response, best fit to the data and weighted residuals of *R. viridis* membranes exposed to continuous white light. λ_{exc} = 830 nm, λ_{em} = 1025 nm.

Next, 20 mM dithionite was added to reduce the quinone acceptors and the sample was again illuminated with strong white light. Under these conditions, the lifetimes lengthened to 160 ps and 250 ps, and the amplitude of the longer component was only 13%. To investigate the influence of $P960^+$ on the fluorescence kinetics of *R. viridis* membranes ferricyanide was added to oxidize P960 and the cytochromes. At this high potential, the lifetime of the main component is shortened to only 50 ps and contributes more than 90% to the initial amplitude.

The appearance of a second fluorescence decay component upon illumination has been observed in other purple non-sulfur bacteria as well, and the possibility that this component is due to delayed fluorescence from P^+Bpheo^- is considered in an accompanying paper (7). The increase in the lifetime of the main fluorescence component from 70 ps to 160 ps in the presence of strong white light and dithionite may be due to a large fraction of the reaction centers in the state P Bpheo Q^- because the quinone is reduced by the dithionite and the bacteriopheophytin is reduced by the strong white light. At this low potential any $P960^+$ is reduced immediately by the reaction center-bound cytochrome and cannot accumulate during continuous illumination. The second lifetime also increased upon dithionite addition, and its contribution is somewhat higher than in the dark adapted state. One possible explanation for this component is fluorescence due to back electron transfer from the M-side bacteriopheophytin. Electron transfer to this bacteriopheophytin in the presence of dithionite and illumination has been documented previously (8). A similar hypothesis has also been proposed by another group (9). The

II.4.**172**

shorter initial trapping time when ferricyanide is used to raise the redox potential may be caused by a reduction in the antenna size (possibly due to oxidation of antenna bacteriochlorophyll b's). This possibility is supported by a bleaching of the absorbance at 1010 nm under these conditions. It is also possible that $P960^+$ is, itself, a quencher. However, if this is true, then it must quench antenna excitation more readily than does P960.

TABLE 2: Fluorescence lifetimes (τ_i) and relative amplitudes (a_i) of *R. viridis* membranes under different light and redox conditions. $\lambda_{exc} = 830$ nm

State	τ_1 (ps)	a_1	τ_2 (ps)	a_2
dark	72	.965	195	.034
white light	63	.681	131	.319
+dithionite+light	163	.869	255	.130
+ferricyanide	53	.903	146	.097

4. ACKNOWLEDGMENT

This publication is #20 from the Arizona State University Center for the Study of Early Events in Photosynthesis. The Center is funded by U.S. Department of Energy grant #DE-FG02-88ER13969 as part of the USDA/DOE/NSF Plant Science Centers program.

REFERENCES
1 Deisenhofer, J., Epp, O., Miki, K., Huber, R. and Michel, H. (1985) Nature 318, 618-624.
2 Stark, W., Kühlbrandt, W., Wildhaber, I., Wehrli, E. and Mühlethaler, K. (1984) EMBO J. 3, 777-783.
3 Jay, F., Lambillotte, M., Stark, W. and Mühlethaler, K. (1984) EMBO J. 3, 773-776.
4 Breton, J., Martin, J.-L., Migus, A., Antonetti, A. and Orszag, A. (1986) Proc. Natl. Acad. Sci. USA 83, 5121-5125.
5 Deprez, J., Trissl, H.W. and Breton, J. (1986) Proc. Natl. Acad. Sci. USA 83, 1699-1703.
6 Pearlstein, R.M. (1982) Photochem. Photobiol. 35, 835-844.
7 Woodbury, N. and Bittersmann, E. (1990) These proceedings.
8 Tiede, D.M., Kellogg, E.C., Kolaczkowski, S., Wasielewski, M.R. and Norris, J.R. (1989) Abstracts of the Thirteenth DOE Photochemistry Research Conference in Silver Creek, Colorado.
9 Hörber, J.K.H., Göbel, W., Ogrodnik, A., Michel-Beyerle, M.E. and Cogdell, R.J. (1981) FEBS Lett. 198, 268-272.

ENERGY TRANSFER DYNAMICS IN THREE LIGHT HARVESTING MUTANTS OF RHODO-
BACTER SPHAEROIDS: A PICOSECOND SPECTROSCOPY STUDY.

Hans Bergström[1], Neil Hunter[2], Rienk van Grondelle[3] and Villy Sundström[1].

[1]Department of Physical Chemistry, University of Umeå, S-901 87 Umeå,
Sweden.
[2]Department of Molecular Biology and Biotechnology University of
Sheffield, U.K.
[3]Department of Biophysics, Physics Laboratory, Free University Amsterdam, The Netherlands.

1. INTRODUCTION

The photosynthetic apparatus of the purple bacterium Rhodobacter sphaeroides is composed of two light harvesting complexes, LH1 and LH2, which
surround and interconnect photochemical reaction centres. Picosecond
absorption spectroscopy with weak picosecond laser pulses is a powerful
technique to probe the excited state dynamics in antenna systems. For
Rb. sphaeroides at 77K the measured picosecond absorption kinetics were interpreted to give the following sequence of energy transfer events
and time constants (1-3).

$$\text{Bchl 800} \xrightarrow[\text{LH2}]{\text{2 ps}} \text{Bchl 850} \xrightarrow{\text{40 ps}} \text{Bchl 875} \xrightarrow[\text{LH1}]{\text{20 ps}} \text{Bchl 896} \xrightarrow{\text{35 ps}} \text{RC}$$

In this paper we have used mutants of Rb. sphaeroides which possess
the following complexes: NF57 (LH2), M21 (LH1 and RC) and M2192 (LH1),
to obtain further information about the composition and possible heterogeneity of the antenna system of purple bacteria. The energy transfer
and trapping dynamics demonstrate the presence of an additional long
wavelength component in the antenna of NF57 and confirm the presence
of Bchl896 as an intrinsic component of LH1.

2. PROCEDURE

The isolation and biochemical characterisation as well as spectral characterisation of mutants NF57, M21 and M2192 have already been described (4-6). Samples were buffered with 50mM Tris pH 8.0 and prepared in
glycerol to give a maximum absorbance of approximately 0.3 mm^{-1}; a gly-
cerol:water ratio of approximately 3:1 ensured that an optically clear
gass was maintained at 77K. Picosecond absorption recovery measurements
were performed at 77K in the 800-900nm region using pump and probe pulses of 10 ps duration as described previously. All results reported here refer to the situaiton of ˉclosedˉ reaction centres, that is no

M. Baltscheffsky (ed.), Current Research in Photosynthesis, Vol. II, 173–176.
© 1990 Kluwer Academic Publishers. Printed in the Netherlands.

charge separation.

3. RESULTS AND DISCUSSION

3.1 Mutant NF57

Isotropic absorption recovery kinetics were measured at a range of wavelengths. It is apparent from Figure 1 that there are two distinct phases of decay: the ratio of relative amplitudes of these phases was observed to be wavelength dependent. From the average of a number of measurements these two components emerge as $\tau_f = 39 \pm 9$ ps and $\tau_s = 300 \pm 50$ ps. The slow component has an isobestic point of 852 nm and represents the decay of the terminal emitter in the light-harvesting complex of this mutant. In Figure 1 we compare the absorption recovery of fast and slow components i NF57 with the monophasic recovery of the isolated LH2 complex: the striking absence of a fast phase for the isolated complex is in agreement with the lack of absorbance on the red side of the 850 nm maximum of this complex at 4K with respect to NF57 (5). Thus we interpret the fast 40 ps component as energy transfer from the main Bch1850 pigment to a minor red-shifted pigment, Bch1870. Previous work on mutant NF57 has shown that the absorption maximum of the additional pigment is 870 nm at 4K and the emission maximum 889 nm (5) Moreover it has been shown that at high excitation densities anni-hilation occurs in these long wavelength pigments which appear to form an aggregate of a least a few Bch1870 molecules (6).

The most straightforward interpretation of the role the pigment identi-fied in mutant NF57 as Bch1870, is that it receives excitations from Bch1850 and transfer them to Bch1875 pigments in LH1. It is not possi-ble to say whether or not Bch1870 forms an obligatory link between LH2 and LH1 or whether energy is also relayed directly from Bch1850 to Bch1875.

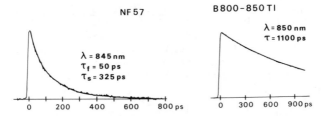

Figure 1. Absorption recovery kinetics of mutant NF57 compared to that of the isolated B800-850 complex.

3.2 Mutant M21

Mutant M21 lacks LH2 and contains the core antenna LH1, together with the reaction centre. From an energy transfer point of view this mutant could be expected to behave similarly to membranes of Rhodospirillum rubrum, which has only one major antenna complex; LH1, containing a minor Bch1896 component (1). The energy transfer kinetics shows

that this comparison is quite realistic: the kinetics observed for
membranes prepared from mutant M21 are very similar to those previously
reported for membranes of <u>Rs. rubrum</u> at 77K. Thus upon excitation of
the main antenna of M21 the excitation energy is transferred to the
red-shifted Bch1896 pigment with a time contains of about 20 ps (see
Figure 2). On a slower time scale $\tau = 170$ ps. the energy is then quenched by the closed reaction centre(P^+). This latter time constant is
also very similar to that observed from <u>Rs. rubrum</u> under similar conditions (2). The relative amplitude of the two decay components exhibits a wavelength depndence which indicates that they arise from pigments with different absorption spectra.

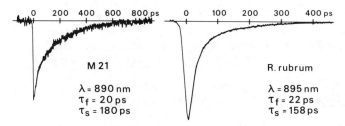

Figure 2. Absorption recovery kinetics of mutant M21 and <u>R. rubrum</u>.

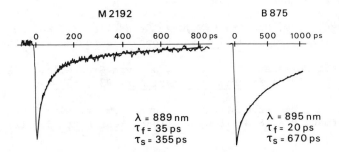

Figure 3. Absorption recovery kinetic of mutant M2192 and isolated
B875 complex.

3.3 Mutant M2192

In this mutant only the core antenna LH1 is present: it is derived from
mutant M21 (4). We have followed the same approach as for the other two
mutants and have attempted to relate observations made on membranes
of the mutant to a previously studied and well known situation. In this
case the isolated LH1 complex of <u>Rb. spheroides</u> (7). The kinetics displayed in Figure 3 exhibit a similar decay pattern for the two preparations and it is clear that the dominatng feature of the kinetics is

the fast energy transfer from Bchl875 to Bchl896 with a time constant of 15-35 ps. The upper limit refers to results for the mutant. It is interesting to note that the domain sizes obtained from singlet-singlet excitation annihilation measurements of M2192 and the isolated LH1 complex (approximately 125 Bchl and 6-8 Bchl, respectively (6) appear to influence the rate of decay measured here ($\tau=35\pm5$ ps and 15 ± 5ps respectively). It is interesting to compare this decay in mutants M2192 and M21; the somewhat longer time constant for the Bchl875 to Bchl896 transfer in M2192 compared to M21 may reflect some changes in the organization of the antenna pigments upon deletion of the reaction centres, or it may suggest that in M21 there is some direct energy transfer from Bchl875 to the special pair of the reaction centre. The results provide more evidence that Bchl896 is an integral part of the LH1 core antenna and plays an important role in energy trapping.

4. REFERENCES

1. Sundström, V., van Grondelle, R., Bergström, H., Åkesson, E. & Gillbro, T.: (1986) Biochim. Biophys. Acta 851, 431-446.

2. van Grondelle, R., Bergström, H., Sundström, V. & Gillbro, T.: (1987) Biochim. Biophys. Acta 894, 313-326.

3. Bergström, H., van Grondelle, R. & Sundström, V.: Febs Lett in press

4. Hunter, C.N., van Grondelle, R. & Olsen, J.D.: (1989) Tibs 14, 72-76 and references therein.

5. van Dorssen, R.J., Hunter, C.N., van Grondelle, R., Korenhof, A.H. & Amersz, J. (1988) Biochim. Biophys. Acta 932, 179-188.

6. Vos, M., van Doressen, R.J., Amesz, J., van Grondelle, R. & Hunter, C.N. (1988) Biochim. Biophys. Acta 933, 132-140.

7. Bergström, H., Westerhuis, W.H.J., Sundström, V., van Grondelle, R., Niederman, R.A. & Gillbro, T. (1988) Febs Lett 233, 12-16.

FLUORESCENCE LIFETIME MEASUREMENTS OF ENERGY TRANSFER IN CHLOROSOMES AND LIVING CELLS OF CHLOROFLEXUS AURANTIACUS OK 70-fl

Marc G. Müller, Kai Griebenow and Alfred R. Holzwarth
Max-Planck-Institut für Strahlenchemie, Stiftstr. 34-36, 4330 Mülheim a. d. Ruhr, FRG

1. INTRODUCTION

The green bacterium Chloroflexus aurantiacus contains three main types of antenna pigments, BChl c_{740}, BChl a_{792} and B806-866. These are functionally coupled to transfer excitation energy from the peripheral antenna complexes located in the chlorosome to the B806-866 and reaction center complex in the cytoplasmatic membrane. The BChl c_{740} pigments are organized within the chlorosome while the BChl a_{792} pigments appear as intermediate pigment pool located between the chlorosome and the membrane. The three pigment groups give rise to spectrally distinct absorption and emission bands in the stationary spectra. This feature allows a detailed study of the energy transfer processes between the pigments. Fluorescence lifetimes of BChl a_{792}-containing chlorosomes and living cells have been measured earlier by Brune et al. (1) and Fetisova et al. (2,3). In the case of intact cells lifetimes of 30 ps and 100 ps for the BChl c fluorescence as well as 100 ps and 350 ps for the BChl a_{792} fluorescence have been observed (2,3). In the case of isolated chlorosomes the BChl c fluorescence was reported to decay with lifetimes below 30 – 50 ps while the BChl a_{792} fluorescence showed lifetimes of 155 ps and 870 ps (1). No risetimes have yet been reported neither in the BChl a_{792} nor in the B806-866 fluorescence. Such risetimes are important to be able to arrive at a kinetic model for the sequence of events and for a scheme of the transfer steps, i.e. either sequentially or perhaps partly parallel.

2. MATERIALS AND METHODS

The cells were grown as described by Griebenow et al. (4). Isolation of BChl a_{792}-containing chlorosomes was carried out by sucrose density gradient centrifugation (SDGC) following the method of Feick et al. (5). Either miranol or deriphat were used as detergent. Fluorescence decays were recorded in a picosecond single-photon timing apparatus under magic angle polarization conditions. A near-infrared sensitive fast microchannel-plate photomultiplier (R2809U-05, Hamamatsu) was installed to provide measurements at detection wavelengths up to 930 nm with a temporal resolution of 3 – 4 ps. All measurements were performed at room temperature upon excitation at 720 nm with a pulse intensity of about 40 nJ/cm^2. The decays were analysed by a global-analysis procedure to calculate the corresponding decay-associated spectra

M. Baltscheffsky (ed.), Current Research in Photosynthesis, Vol. II, 177-180.

(DAS) (6). The intact cells were pumped rapidly through a flow measuring cuvette.

3. RESULTS AND DISCUSSION

3.1. BChl a_{792}-containing chlorosomes

BChl a_{792}-containing chlorosomes prepared either with miranol and with deriphat show similar kinetics and DAS. The observed lifetimes are 11 – 12 ps, 27 – 30 ps, 160 – 210 ps and 310 – 420 ps. For miranol chlorosomes the wavelength dependence of the corresponding amplitudes is plotted as DAS in Fig. 1. The dominant component is the short–lived 11 ps component which has a large positive amplitude in the BChl c fluorescence and a negative amplitude in the BChl a_{792} fluorescence around 805 nm. The two long–lived components show only positive amplitudes with considerable values preferentially in the wavelength range of the BChl a_{792} fluorescence. The 27 ps component is resolved mainly in the BChl c fluorescence. Its amplitude varies with respect to the amplitude of the 11 ps component by a factor of up to two in different preparations. The 11 ps component is clearly associated with the energy transfer BChl c → BChl a_{792} while the long–lived components describe the overall decay of the equilibrated excited states. The origin of the 27 ps component is as yet unclear. It may be concerned with a heterogeneity of the sample due to BChl a_{792}–free chlorosomes.

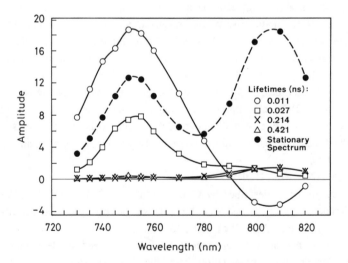

Fig. 1. Decay–associated emission spectra (DAS) of isolated BChl a_{792}-containing chlorosomes as calculated by the global–analysis procedure. Excitation wavelength was 720 nm. The dashed line is the stationary fluorescence spectrum.

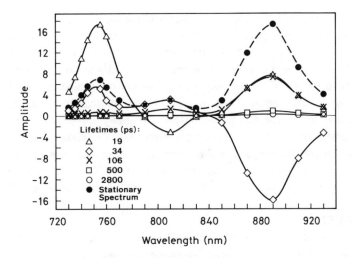

Fig. 2. Decay–associated emission spectra (DAS) of intact cells of C. aurantiacus. Cells were measured at room temperature upon excitation at 720 nm in a flow cuvette. Probably most of the reaction centers are closed under our conditions (7).

3.2. Intact cells of C. aurantiacus

Fig. 2 presents the DAS of intact cells in the detection wavelength range from 730 nm up to 930 nm. The DAS is essentially characterized by three short–lived decay components with lifetimes of about 16 – 19 ps, 32 – 40 ps and 96 – 106 ps. The amplitude of the 19 ps component is positive at wavelengths below 780 nm, negative at wavelengths around 810 nm and again positive at wavelengths above 840 nm. The 34 ps component starts also with positive amplitudes at 730 nm. These remain positive up to 840 nm but fall down to strongly negative values at wavelengths around 890 nm. The 106 ps component shows only positive amplitudes with a maximum at 890 nm. It should be noted that at 890 nm the sum of amplitudes of both the 106 ps component and the 19 ps component equals approximately the amplitude of the 34 ps component but with opposite sign. The DAS can easily be interpreted in terms of an energy transfer chain with two transfer steps each of which is reversible. The first transfer step occurs between the BChl c and the BChl a_{792} pigment pool within 16 – 19 ps. As in the case of chlorosomes this is proven by the corresponding negative amplitude at 810 nm. The second energy transfer step indicated by the negative amplitude of the 34 ps component and by the positive amplitude of the short–lived 19 ps component at 890 nm is the BChl $a_{792} \rightarrow$ B806–866/RC transfer. This transfer occurs within 34 ps after a delay of about 16 – 19 ps. The delay is due to the fact that the BChl a_{792} pigments have to be excited by the first energy transfer step before the second transfer step can start. Therefore we conclude an overall transit time for the excitation energy of about 50 – 55 ps. After $\approx$ 53 ps the population of the excited molecules in the B806–866/RC complex reaches about 90 % of its maximal value. The 106 ps component describes the decay of the equilibrated antenna system probably due to the charge separation process in the reaction center. The 500 ps component is probably also due to a process in the reaction center. The origin of the longest–lived (2.8 ns) component is still unclear. These two long–lived components show very low amplitudes even at 890 nm and their lifetimes vary in different samples by up to 50 %. The data seem to be consistent with a sequential transfer scheme BChl c $\rightarrow$ BChl a_{792} $\rightarrow$ B806–866/RC.

4. ACKNOWLEDGEMENTS

The authors should like to thank Mrs. B. Kalka for valuable assistance. Partial financial support was given by the Deutsche Forschungsgemeinschaft.

REFERENCES

(1) Brune, D.C., King, G.H., Infosino, A., Steiner, T.,
     Thewalt, M.L.W. and Blankenship, R.E. (1987)
     Biochemistry **26**, 8652–8658.

(2) Fetisova, Z.G., Freiberg, A.M. and Timpmann, K.E. (1988)
     in VI Symposium Phototrophic Procaryotes (L.R. Mur
     and T. Burger–Wiersma, eds.), 66.

(3) Fetisova, Z.G., Freiberg, A.M. and Timpmann, K.E. (1988)
     Nature **334**, 633–634.

(4) Griebenow, K. and Holzwarth, A.R. (1989)
     Biochim. Biophys. Acta **973**, 235–240.

(5) Feick, R.G. and Fuller, R.C. (1984)
     Biochemistry **23**, 3693–3700.

(6) Wendler, J. and Holzwarth, A.R. (1987)
     Biophys. J. **52**, 717–728.

(7) Wittmershaus, B.P., Brune, D.C. and Blankenship, R.E. (1988)
     in Photosynthetic Light–Harvesting Systems (H. Scheer and
     S. Schneider, eds.), de Gruyter, Berlin, 543–554.

ENERGY TRANSFER KINETICS IN DIFFERENT CHLOROSOME PREPARATIONS FROM
CHLOROFLEXUS AURANTIACUS

Mette Miller[1], Tomas Gillbro[2] and Raymond P. Cox[1]
[1]Institute of Biochemistry, Odense University, DK-5230 Odense M,
Denmark and [2]Department of Physical Chemistry, Umeå University,
S-901 87 Umeå, Sweden

1. INTRODUCTION
The light-harvesting system of green bacteria consists of BChl c
containing chlorosomes attached to the cell membrane by a baseplate
containing BChl a. The cell membrane contains the B 808-866 antenna
complex and the reaction center. We report here a comparison of the
properties of chlorosome preparations obtained by different treatments.
Energy transfer in these preparations was studied by picosecond
absorbance recovery and steady-state fluorescence measurements. The
results are used to propose a new model for the structure of
chlorosomes.

2. EXPERIMENTAL
Chloroflexus aurantiacus strain OK-70-fl was grown at 55^0C (1).
Chlorosomes were prepared either by breaking the cells in a French press
in the presence of 2 M NaSCN (2) or by treating the broken cells with
0.3% (w/v) Miranol S2M-SF (3).

Picosecond measurements were performed at room temperature at 750 nm and
800 nm, giving preferential excitation of BChl c and a respectively.
Anisotropy measurements were made with the exciting light polarized
parallel or perpendicular to the measuring light. Isotropic measurements
were made with the polarization set to 54.7^0. The excitation intensity
was varied with neutral density filters. Fluorescence spectra and were
measured on a Spex Fluorolog spectrometer. The anisotropy was calculated
from $I_{11}-I_{\perp}/(I_{11}+2I_{\perp})$, where I_{11} and $I_{\perp}$ are the intensity of the
absorbance or fluorescence signal.

3. RESULTS
3.1. Annihilation study.
Since each chlorosome contains large amounts of bacteriochlorophyll c
each pulse can excite more than one BChl c in a given chlorosome,
leading to the annihilation of excitation energy within the BChl
complex (4). This would be observed as a a change in both the absorbance
and fluorescence decay constants and as a decrease of the fluorescence
quantum yield. Since the typical excitation intensities used were 10^{14}
photons cm^{-2} $pulse^{-1}$, some multiple excitation would be expected. We
changed the excitation intensity by an order of magnitude but observed
little effect on the lifetime or quantum yield. The number of BChl c per

M. Baltscheffsky (ed.), Current Research in Photosynthesis, Vol. II, 181–184.
© 1990 *Kluwer Academic Publishers. Printed in the Netherlands.*

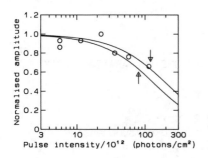 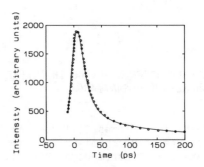

Fig. 1. Effect of pulse intensity on normalised signal intensity. The
   lines represent the expected theoretical curves (4) for domain
   sizes of 20 and 30 BChl molecules. The arrows show the intensity
   at which there is one hit per domain.

Fig. 2. Absorbance recovery kinetics of excited BChl c at 750 nm
   measured with the excitation beam polarized at the "magic
   angle". The fitted curve is drawn through the experimental
   points.

domain was estimated to lie between 20 and 30 (Fig 1). Our conclusion
must be that excitation energy is not free to move over the whole
chlorosome, but is restricted by the size of the BChl c rods. One
possibility is that these rods are individually connected to the BChl a
baseplate and that the coupling between individual rods is poor compared
with the coupling to the baseplate.

3.2 Energy transfer kinetics
On excitation of the main chlorosome absorbtion band at 750 nm (Fig. 2)
a very fast (11 ± 2 ps) absorbance recovery is observed (see Table 1).
This transient comprises about 80% of the total intensity. The second
component (15%-20%) has a decay time of about 30 ps and less than 5% of
the signal is due to more slowly decaying components. With excitation
of the BChl a in the baseplate at 800 nm, two components of similar
amplitude are observed. The fast decay has a lifetime of ca. 30 ps and
the lifetime of the slow component is about 200-300 ps (Table 1).

We interpret these results by the following scheme:

$$
\begin{array}{ccccc}
\text{11 ps} & & \text{30 ps} & & \text{300 ps} \\
\text{BChl c} \longrightarrow & \text{BChl } a_{795} \longrightarrow & \text{BChl } a_{808\text{-}866} \longrightarrow & \text{decay products} \\
 & \text{(baseplate)} & \text{(antenna)} & &
\end{array}
$$

3.3. Anisotropy decay kinetics
The anisotropy data at 750 nm (Table 2) show a decay within <10 ps from
r_0 to 0.2 ± 0.05. If we assume that the BChl c transition dipoles are

TABLE 1. LIFETIMES AND RELATIVE AMPLITUDES FOR THE RELAXATION OF EXCITED
BACTERIOCHLOROPHYLL IN DIFFERENT CHLOROSOME PREPARATIONS

Results are means and standard deviations of 6-8 experiments with SCN
chlorosomes and 3 experiments with Miranol chlorosomes. The experimental
curve was deconvoluted into two or three exponential decays following a
Gaussian pulse.

Sample		Lifetime (ps)			Amplitude (%)		
		T1	T2	T3	A1	A2	A3
SCN	750 nm	11±2	39±11	350±200	76±8	19±8	5±3
Miranol	750 nm	9±1	26±1	380±70	79±4	15±4	6±1
SCN	800 nm	31±8	190±60		46±2	54±3	
Miranol	800 nm	43±23	280±160		44±11	56±11	

TABLE 2. ANISTROPY MEASUREMENTS ON CHLOROSOME PREPARATIONS

Sample		r_∞	r_0	T1 (ps)
SCN, Miranol	750 nm*	0.20±0.05		<10
SCN, Miranol	800 nm	0.13±0.02	0.41±0.05	7.6±1.7

*r_∞ was measured after 40 ps. It was not possible to estimate r_0.

distributed symmetrically about the rod axis at an angle of θ, the
following relation holds: $r = r_0(3\cos^2\theta-1)^2/4$. Inserting $r_0 = 0.40$ and
$r = 0.20 \pm 0.05$ we obtain $\theta = 22^0 \pm 5^0$ (or $\theta = 158^0 \pm 5^0$), i.e. the mean
orientation of the strong BChl c transition is close to the rod symmetry
axis.

At 800 nm we can resolve a 7.6 ± 1.7 ps anisotropy decay (Table 2) that
does not correspond to any component in the isotropic signal. Therefore
this signal probably results from the migration of the excitation energy
in the baseplate. The value for r_∞ of 0.13 ± 0.02 is close to the value
of 0.10 expected if the main BChl a transition is circularly distributed
in the membrane plane ($\theta = 90^0$ in the equation above).

3.4. Steady-state fluorescence.
On excitation of BChl c at 690 nm, we observe fluorescence emission
maxima at 754 and 803 nm in chlorosome preparations prepared with both
thiocyanate and Miranol (Fig. 3). It seems likely that these arise from
the rods and baseplate, respectively. This result shows that there must
be some energy equilibration between the two antenna systems. The
fluorescence anisotropy around 750 nm is 0.18, close to the mean value
of the absorbance isotropy at t = 40 ps. This probably represents the

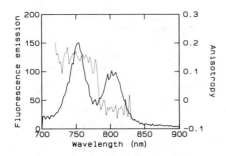 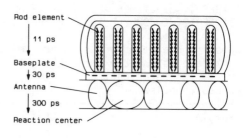

Fig. 3. Fluorescence emission spectrum (solid line) and fluorescence anistropy (dotted line).
Fig. 4. Proposed model for organisation of chlorosomes in *Chloroflexus*.

fluorescence anisotropy of an equilibrated system. The anisotropy of the 800 nm emission is only 0.01, considerably lower than the corresponding absorbtion anisotropy of 0.13. This demonstrates an additional loss of anisotropy on going from the rods to the baseplate.

4. DISCUSSION
The chlorosomes used in these experiments were prepared using either a chaotropic agent (thiocyanate) or a detergent (Miranol). However, the kinetic and spectroscopic properties which we observed are remarkably similar.

Our results suggest a high degree of order for the BChl c transition along the rod axis, and a correspondingly high order of the BChl a transition in the membrane plane. Our observations that excitation of BChl c leads to a lowering of the emission anisotropy of BChl a is difficult to reconcile with the idea that the rod axis is parallel to the plane of the membrane. We propose an alternative model (Fig. 4) in which the rods are attached perpendicular to the membrane baseplate. The annihlation experiments imply that BChl c functions in relatively small units with between 20 and 30 BChl c per unit, which we interpret as representing the number of BChl molecules in the individual rod elements.

ACKNOWLEDGEMENT. This research was supported by the Danish and Swedish Natural Sciences Research Councils.

REFERENCES
1. Cox, R.P., Jensen, M.T., Miller, M. and Pedersen, J.P. (1988) in Green Photosynthetic Bacteria (Olson, J.M., Ormerod J.G, Amesz, J., Stackebrandt, E. and Truper, H.G, eds). pp 15-21 Plenum, New York
2. Gerola, P.D. and Olson, J.M. (1986) Biochim. Biophys. Acta 848, 69-76
3. Feick, R.G. and Fuller, R.C. (1984) Biochemistry 23, 3693-3699
4. Paillotin, G., Swenberg, C.E., Breton, J. and Geactinov, N.E. (1979) Biophys. J. 25, 513-534

EXCITATION TRANSFER AND CHARGE SEPARATION IN HELIOBACTERIUM CHLORUM AT 15 K.

P.J.M. van Kan, T.J. Aartsma and J. Amesz,
Dept. of Biophysics, Huygens Lab., State University,
P.O.Box 9504, 2300 RA Leiden, The Netherlands.

1. INTRODUCTION

The heliobacteria are distinguished from other groups of photosynthetic bacteria by their unusual pigmentation. The first species of this group, *Heliobacterium chlorum*, was discovered about 6 years ago by Gest and Favinger (1). The main pigment of *H. chlorum* and other heliobacteria is Bchl g (2). At low temperature, three different spectral forms can be discerned in the antenna: Bchl g 778, Bchl g 793 and Bchl g 808 (3). Photooxidation of the primary electron donor P_{798} causes a bleaching with a maximum near 798 nm at room temperature (4) and near 793 nm at 5 K (5). This communication presents an analysis of flash-induced absorbance changes at 15 K. Electron transport from P_{798} to the primary electron acceptor was observed at this temperature. The rate of electron transport to the secondary acceptor was found to be 2 - 3 times faster than at 300 K. Significant bleaching of antenna pigments was only observed above 800 nm, indicating that excitation energy is rapidly transferred to the long-wave pigment, Bchl g 808.

2. MATERIALS AND METHODS

H. chlorum was grown anaerobically in medium 112 of the American type culture collection, containing 10 mM ascorbic acid. Membrane fragments were obtained by sonication of the cells and subsequent centrifugation in a buffer containing 10 mM ascorbic acid, 10 mM Tris and 2 mM dithiotreitol (pH=8.0). Glucose, glucose oxidase and catalase were added to maintain anaerobic conditions. For experiments at low temperature 66 % (v/v) glycerol was added. Absorbance differences were measured applying a pump-probe technique with variable delay between pump and probe pulses. For excitation we used 25 ps laser pulses with an energy of up to 10 mJ at 532 nm. The probe pulse was filtered out of a continuum, generated by focusing a 35 ps, 1064 nm pulse in a cuvette containing a H_2O/D_2O-mixture. The time resolution of the apparatus was approximately 35 ps. The kinetic data were fitted with a convolution of a single or bi-exponential decay and an instrument response function represented by a Gaussian of 35 ps FWHM.

M. Baltscheffsky (ed.), Current Research in Photosynthesis, Vol. II, 185–188.
© 1990 *Kluwer Academic Publishers. Printed in the Netherlands.*

3. RESULTS AND INTERPRETATION

Absorbance difference spectra of *H. chlorum* membrane fragments upon 532 nm excitation at 15 K are shown in Fig.1. The difference spectrum measured at 40 ps after the excitation flash shows negative bands near 665, 793 and 812 nm. At 350 ps after the flash the amplitude of the 812 nm band is strongly reduced. We ascribe this band to ground-state depletion of Bchl *g* 808 by the formation of singlet excited states. The band near 793 nm is attributed to photooxidation of P_{798}, the primary donor.

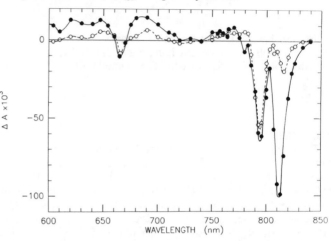

At 350 ps its amplitude is only slightly reduced, and the wavelength of maximum bleaching agrees well with that observed by Smit et al. (5).
Kinetics of the absorbance changes at 793 nm at two different energy densities of excitation are shown in Fig.2. At low energy density, a rapid bleaching occurred to a level which was constant on a nanosecond timescale. At about six times higher flash energy the

FIGURE 1. Absorbance differences at t =40 ps (●) and 350 ps (o) in *H. chlorum* membranes at 15 K. A_{790}= 0.70.

amplitude of the constant component was saturated and an additional transient was observed which decayed with a time constant (1/e) of 30 ps or less. This transient may be caused by the formation of excited Bchl *g* in the antenna.

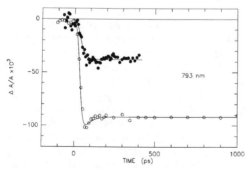

FIGURE 2. Relative absorbance differences at 793 nm vs. time. o : 3 mJ/cm², ● : 0.5 mJ/cm². The fast decay component is fitted with a time constant (1/e) of 30 ps.

The negative band near 665 nm may be ascribed to photoreduction of the primary electron acceptor (4). The kinetics at 668 nm are shown in Fig.3. The decay could be fitted with a single exponential component with a time constant of 300 ± 50 ps. Room temperature kinetics show a 800 ± 50 ps decay.

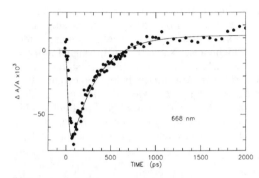

FIGURE 3. Relative absorbance difference vs. time at 668 nm. Energy density 3 mJ/cm², A_{668}= 0.30. The fit has a time constant (1/e) of 300 ps.

The kinetics at 812 nm could be fitted with a bi-exponential decay assuming two components of approximately 50 and 200 ps (Fig.4). The relative amplitudes of these components depended on the energy density of excitation. At 0.5 mJ/cm² these amplitudes were about equal, whereas at 3 mJ/cm² a ratio of 2.5 was needed to obtain a good fit. This suggests that the fast component may be ascribed to excitation annihilation in the antenna. At high energy the maximal amplitude of the absorbance change at 812 nm was about 55 % of the initial absorbance.

4. DISCUSSION

Our results support the concept that the primary charge separation in heliobacteria consists of the transfer of an electron from P_{798} to an acceptor absorbing near 670 nm, which is presumably a Bchl c-like or Chl a-like pigment (6). The decay time of the bleaching at 668 nm is shortened by a factor of 2.5 upon cooling from 300 K to 15 K. This would mean that the second step in the charge separation, electron transfer from the

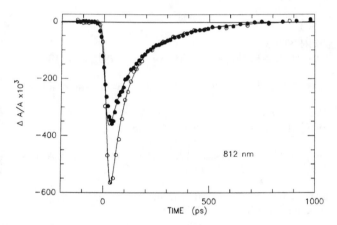

FIGURE 4. Relative absorbance difference vs. time at 812 nm. o : 3 mJ/cm², ● : 0.5 mJ/cm². Fitted with time constants (1/e) of 50 and 200 ps.

pigment absorbing near 670 nm to a subsequent acceptor, is 2.5 times faster at 15 K than at room temperature. The increase in reaction rate may be due to conformational changes and changes in the vibrational modes or frequencies within the pigment-protein complex upon cooling (7). The amplitude of the bleaching at 793 nm was about 3 times larger than at room temperature (4). This factor can only partially be explained by a narrowing of the band of P_{798} upon cooling. The cause of this apparent increase in oscillator strength is not clear.

The bleaching centered at 812 nm may be attributed to the formation of excited singlet states of the long-wave antenna Bchl, Bchl *g* 808. In a high-energy flash its amplitude amounted to more than 50 % of the initial absorbance at this wavelength. This indicates that ground state depletion is the main factor which causes saturation of the signal at high flash energies. The wavelength of maximum bleaching is significantly red-shifted with respect to the absorption maximum of Bchl *g* 808 (3). Apparently at low temperature the excitations are predominantly located on Bchls absorbing at longer wavelength than the 'bulk' Bchl *g* 808 molecules. Absorbance changes that could be attributed to Bchl *g* 778 and Bchl *g* 793 were at least an order of magnitude smaller. This indicates that excitation energy is transferred to Bchl *g* 808 within less than a few tens of picoseconds at 15 K.

ACKNOWLEDGMENTS

We appreciate the help of E.J. van de Meent in providing sample material, and the technical assistance of R.J.W. Louwe. The investigation was supported by the Netherlands Foundation for Biophysics, financed by the Netherlands Organization for Scientific Research (NWO).

REFERENCES

1. Gest H. and Favinger J.L. (1983) Arch. Microbiol. 136, 11-16.

2. Brockmann H. and Lipinski A. (1983) Arch. Microbiol. 136, 17-19.

3. Van Dorssen R.J., Vasmel H. and Amesz J. (1985)
   Biochim. Biophys. Acta 809, 199-203.

4. Nuijs A.M., van Dorssen R.J., Duysens L.N.M. and Amesz J. (1985)
   Proc. Natl. Acad. Sci. USA 82, 6865-6868.

5. Smit H.W.J., van Dorssen R.J. and Amesz J. (1989)
   Biochim. Biophys. Acta 973, 212-219.

6. Michalski T.J., Hunt J.E., Bowman M.K., Smith U., Bardeen K., Gest H., Norris J.R. and Katz J.J. (1987) Proc. Natl. Acad. Sci. USA 84, 2570-2574.

7. Kirmaier C., Holten D. and Parson W.W. (1985)
   Biochim. Biophys. Acta 810, 33-48.

TRIPLETS IN THE ANTENNA AND REACTION CENTRE OF HELIOBACTERIUM CHLORUM AT LOW TEMPERATURE

F.A.M. KLEINHERENBRINK and J. AMESZ

Department of Biophysics, Huygens Laboratory of the State University, P.O. Box 9504, 2300 RA Leiden, The Netherlands

1. INTRODUCTION
    The heliobacteria are a seperate group of photosynthetic bacteria which contain bacteriochlorophyll g as their major pigment (1). Only three species have been isolated so far: *Heliobacterium chlorum*, *Heliobacillus mobilis* and *Heliospirilum gestii*.
    Low temperature measurements show that the antenna of *H. chlorum* is composed of three spectal forms of BChl g, BChl g-778, BChl g-793 and BChl g-808 (2). Experiments on a picosecond timescale show that excitations are rapidly transferred to BChl g-808 even at 15 K (3). At 5 K the efficiency of energy transfer from BChl g-808 to the reaction centre is still high (4).
    Upon excitation with short laser flashes at 5 K absorbance differences have been measured in membrane fragments of *H.chlorum* with decay times of 2.3 ms and approximately 350 μs (4). The 2.3 ms component has its maximum bleaching at 794 nm and reflects the oxidation of the primary donor P-798 and the subsequent recombination with a reduced electron acceptor. The spectrum of the 350 μs component showed negative bands at 794 nm and 812 nm and was ascribed to the formation of triplet states of BChl g. In the present research we examine these absorbance changes more closely and demonstrate that they can be ascribed to triplets both on P-798 in the reaction centre and on BChl g-808 in the antenna.

2. MATERIAL AND METHODS
    Membrane fragments of *H.chlorum* were prepared and low temperature absorbance difference measurements were performed as descibed in (4). Excitation flashes were provided by the frequency doubled output (532 nm) of a Q-switched Nd:YAG-laser (15 ns half-width). The maximum incident energy density on the sample was 10 mJ/cm². Neutral density filters were used to adjust the energy of the laser flash.

3. RESULTS AND INTERPRETATION
    In Fig. 1 kinetics of the flash-induced absorbance changes at 5 K in *H. chlorum* membranes are shown at two different flash energies. It is clear that the rapid transients at 812 nm and 629 nm do not have the same saturation behaviour as the 2.3 ms component at 794 and 812 nm. Fig. 2 shows the energy dependence of the decay components at some typical wavelengths. Photooxidation of P-798, measured by the amplitude of the 2.3 ms component was almost completely saturated at 30% energy. The same applied to the rapid component at 794 nm. At 808 nm (an isosbestic point for P-798 oxidation) a linear dependence without saturation was obtained, indicating that the bleaching at this wavelength must be due to an excited state on the antenna, rather than in the reaction centre. At 629 nm both a saturating and a non saturating rapid component were observed. The difference between the traces at 100% and 30% energy is given in Fig. 3, both at 794 nm and 812 nm. At 794 nm a small signal is seen with the same kinetics as in Fig. 1, but at 812 nm only a rapid decay with a time constant of 400 ± 50 μs is observed, reflecting the lifetime of the antenna triplet.

M. Baltscheffsky (ed.), Current Research in Photosynthesis, Vol. II, 189–192.
© 1990 *Kluwer Academic Publishers. Printed in the Netherlands.*

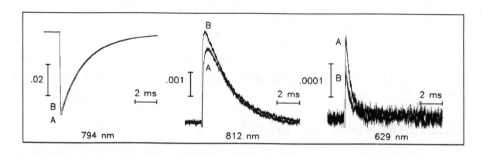

FIGURE 1. *Kinetics of absorbance changes at 5 K in membranes of* H. chlorum *at (A) 100% and (B) 30% laser energy.* $A_{788}=0.67$ *(300 K).*

Triplet-minus-singlet difference spectra for the reaction centre and antenna BChls were obtained from a spectral analysis of the saturating and non-saturating decay components (Fig. 4). The spectrum with the open circles was obtained by subtracting the rapid decay components at 100% and 30% energy, and represents the spectrum of the antenna triplet, with a negative band near 813 nm. Since its difference spectrum is similar to that of singlet excited BChl g-808 (3), we conclude that this triplet is located on BChl g-808. The yield of the antenna triplet formation was approximately 1%, comparable to that found for antenna BChl triplet formation in chromatophores of carotenoid mutants of purple bacteria (5). So far we were not able to detect antenna triplets at room temperature which may be explained by the low fluorescence yield at this temperature (2). The second spectrum of Fig. 4, with a maximum bleaching at 793 nm, was obtained at 30% energy after correction for the small amount of antenna triplet formed under these conditions and may be ascribed to the triplet of P-798. The amplitude at 794 nm of this signal varied between 10% and 30% of the total absorbance change at this wavelength. Its lifetime was found to be 500 ± 50 μs.

The same experiments were done with samples that were frozen under continuous illumination. After turning off the light at low temperature only 30% of the P-798⁺ signal was observed in a flash, indicating that 70% of the reaction centres remained in the oxidized state, in agreement with ESR measurements under similar conditions (6). Fig. 5 shows the results of a spectral analysis similar to that of Fig.4. An additional bleaching was now observed

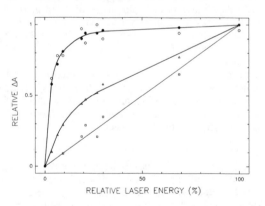

FIGURE 2. *Intensity dependence of the absorbance changes due to oxidation of P-798 measured at 794 nm (●) and due to triplet formation measured at 0.3 ms after a flash and corrected for contribution by P-798⁺ at 794 nm (o), 808 nm (□) and 629 nm (Δ). The absorbance changes were normalized at the maximum value.*

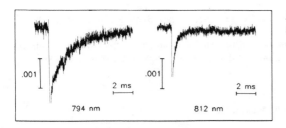

FIGURE 3. Signals obtained by subtracting the absorbance changes at 100% and 30% energy.

near 795 nm (open circles), indicating the formation of a third triplet (with a lifetime of 400 ± 50 µs). Since this triplet did not saturate at high energy, we assume that it is located on BChl g-793 in the antenna.

4. CONCLUSIONS

In membrane fragments of *H. chlorum* that are frozen in the dark triplets are formed upon flash illumination both in the reaction centre and on the antenna. The triplet in the reaction centre is probably located on P-798 and formed by recombination between P-798⁺ and a reduced early acceptor. Its yield of formation varied between about 10 and 30%. The triplet in the antenna is formed with an efficiency of about 1% and on the longest wavelength absorbing component BChl g-808 only, presumably by intersystem crossing. This is in agreement with earlier measurements,

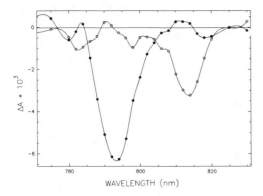

FIGURE 4. Open circles: Absorbance difference spectrum of the antenna triplet signals at 100% energy, calculated by subtracting the rapid components at 100% and 30% energy and extrapolating by means of Fig. 2 (squares). A decay time of 400 µs was assumed. Closed circles: Absorbance difference spectrum of the reaction centre triplet, obtained by plotting the amplitude of the rapid component at 30% energy after correction for the contribution by the antenna triplet. $OD_{788}=0.65$ (300 K).

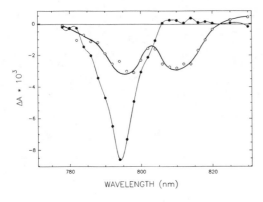

FIGURE 5. Same as Fig. 4, sample frozen under continuous light. $OD_{788}=0.80$ (300 K).

which showed that singlet excitations are rapidly transferred from BChl g-778 and BChl g-793 to BChl g-808 (2,3).

In samples that were frozen under continuous illumination an antenna triplet was also formed on BChl g-793, suggesting that the excitation transfer to BChl g-808 was partially blocked.

REFERENCES

1. Gest, H and Favinger, J.L. (1983) Arch. Microbiol. 136, 11-16

2. Van Dorssen, R.J., Vasmel, H. and Amesz, J. (1985) Biochim. Biophys. Acta 809, 199-203

3. Van Kan, P.J.M., Aartsma, T.J. and Amesz, J. (1989) Photosynth. Res., in the press

4. Smit, H.W.J., Van Dorssen, R.J. and Amesz, J. (1989) Biochim. Biophys. Acta 973, 212-219

5. Monger, T.G., Cogdell, R.J. and Parson, W.W. (1976) Biochim. Biophys. Acta 449, 136-153

6. Brok, M., Vasmel, H., Horikx, J.T.G. and Hoff, A.J. (1985) FEBS Lett. 194, 322-326

EXCITATION ENERGY FLOW IN THE AEROBIC PHOTOSYNTHETIC BACTERIUM,
ERYTHROBACTER sp. OCh 114: A FAST ENERGY TRANSFER FROM B806 TO B870

KEIZO SHIMADA[1], NAOTO TAMAI[2], IWAO YAMAZAKI[2] AND MAMORU MIMURO[3],
[1]DEPT OF BIOLOGY, FACULTY OF SCIENCE, TOKYO METROPOLITAN UNIV., 2-1-1,
SETAGAYA-KU, TOKYO 158; [2]INSTITUTE FOR MOLECULAR SCIENCE AND [3]NATIONAL
INSTITUTE FOR BASIC BIOLOGY, MYODAIJI, OKAZAKI, AICHI 444, JAPAN

1. INTRODUCTION

The aerobic photosynthetic bacterium, Erythrobacter sp. strain OCh 114, has a unique antenna system which consists of two types of complex; B806 and B870 complexes (1,2). Bacteriochlorophyll(Bchl)-forms corresponding to B850 which is common in purple photosynthetic bacteria are absent in this bacterium and, therefore, excitation energy on B806 Bchl is transferred directly to B870. The lower spectral overlap between B806 and B870 suggests lower transfer efficiency when Förster mechanism of excitation energy transfer is assumed (3). Thus the analysis of the transfer process in this bacterium may provide critical information on the transfer mechanism between different classes of antenna complexes.

In Rhodobacter sphaeroides and Rhodospirillum rubrum, a new type of antenna Bchl-form whose energy level is lower than that of the special pair Bchl of the reaction center (RC) has been reported (4-6). Such components should be surveyed in other photosynthetic bacteria to account for the functional role and structural basis for the specific energy level.

Thus we investigated the energy flow in Erythrobacter sp. strain OCh 114 with the time-resolved fluorescence spectroscopy in the picosecond time range. We found fast energy transfer from B806 to B870 (within 6 ps), and also detected the presence of the new type of Bchl-form.

2. MATERIALS AND METHODS

Erythrobacter sp. strain OCh 114 was grown heterotrophically under aerobic condition (2). Cells at late log-growth phase were harvested and suspended in 50 mM Mops buffer (pH 7.5) containing 0.34 M NaCl to make absorbance at 806 nm to be 0.05. Measurements of the time-resolved fluorescence spectroscopy were carried out with the apparatus reported previously (4,7). An S-1 type micro-channel plate photomultiplier (R1564-05U, Hamamatsu Photonics, Japan) was used to detect fluorescence in the near-infrared region, together with the time-correlated single photon counting system. Excitation was at 800 nm with a pulse duration of 6 ps (FWHM). Photon density was 10^8 to 10^9 per cm^2 which is low enough to avoid singlet-singlet annihilation. Time resolution of this set up was 6 ps. Measurements were carried out at 22°C. Deconvolution of the spectra and estimation of lifetimes by convolution calculation with the excitation pulse were carried out as reported (4,8).

M. Baltscheffsky (ed.), Current Research in Photosynthesis, Vol. II, 193–196.

3. RESULTS AND DISCUSSION

The time-resolved fluorescence spectra with the preferential excitation of B806 by the 800 nm light pulse are shown in Fig. 1A after normalization. At 0 ps, the main emission was at 884 nm, and a minor one, around 823 nm. The former originats from B870 and the latter, from B806. It is remarkable that the emission from B870 was dominant even in the initial time range. This clearly indicates that the energy transfer from B806 to B870 occurs within the time resolution of the apparatus (6 ps) in spite of the absence of B850.

In the spectra, time-dependent changes were not drastic. However, the spectrum at 250 ps was different from that at 0 ps in two points; the decrease in the intensity around 823 nm and the increase around 910 nm (Fig. 1, B and C). The latter suggests the spectral heterogeneity of the main emission band; presence of a longer-wavelength component. Based on the observed difference, time-resolved fluorescence spectra were deconvoluted into component bands assuming Gaussian band shape (Fig. 1D). Three major and one minor components were resolved; F823, F883, F907 and F955. F823 and F883 were interpreted to arise from B806 and B870, respectively. F955 may be a vibrational band. F907 is most probably a longer-wavelength component as found in Rb. sphaeroides and Rs. rubrum (4-6). Corresponding absorption maximum was estimated to be at 888 nm based on Stepanov equation as described in (4). This location is close to that in Rb. sphaeroides (890 nm)(4). In the deconvoluted spectra, the relative intensity of F883 to that of F907 became almost constant after about 80 ps from excitation indicating the establishment of the equilibration between the two components.

The rise and decay curves for the three components are shown in Fig. 2. A shift of the time for maximum intensity for each curve is observed indicating sequential energy transfer among these components. Component lifetimes were estimated by convolution calculation assuming exponential decay. In the kinetics of F823, three decay components were necessary for a good fit; 19, 210 and 910 ps with the relative amplitudes of 95.0%, 4.5% and 0.5%, respectively. In the kinetics of F883, no rise terms were found. Essentially, the two decay components were enough for a good fit; 191 ps (90.2%) and 385 ps (9.8%). In the kinetics of F907, on the other hand, a clear rise term was resolved (9 ps). This time probably corresponds to the shift of the equilibration between F883 and F907 as suggested by the time-resolved spectra. Considering the population of Bchl and energy difference between them (see below), the transfer time from B870 to B888 can be estimated to be 3 to 4 ps (cf. ref. 10). In the decay of F907, two components were found; 195 ps (91.0%) and 405 ps (9.0%). The lifetimes of the major decay components of F883 (191 ps) and F907 (195 ps) may correspond to the average trapping time of excitation energy by the closed RC reported for many purple photosynthetic bacteria (approx. 200 ps) (5,6).

Inconsistency between the decay kinetics of F823 and F883 and the absence of the rise term in F883 clearly indicate that the energy transfer between B806 and B870 occurs within the time resolution of the apparatus (6 ps). The 19 ps decay time of F823, therefore, may not reflect the main energy flow but the residual part.

The relative content of B888 was estimated by the method proposed by

Zankel (4,9). After the equilibration between F883 and F907, the ratio
of the fluorescence yield of each component was estimated to be 3.1±0.2.
Then the ratio of B870 to B888 on Bchl basis could be estimated to be
10.0±0.7. In the LH 1 complex, 26±2 Bchls are contained per RC
(Shimada et al., unpublished), which is close to the case of other
purple photosynthetic bacteria (10). Thus, B888 Bchl could be estimated
to be about 2, at most 3 per RC. This number is significantly lower than
that in other purple photosynthetic bacteria (7±1) (4,5). In
Erythrobacter sp. strain OCh 114, therefore, the density of excited
Bchls around RC is not necessarily high even in the equilibrated state.

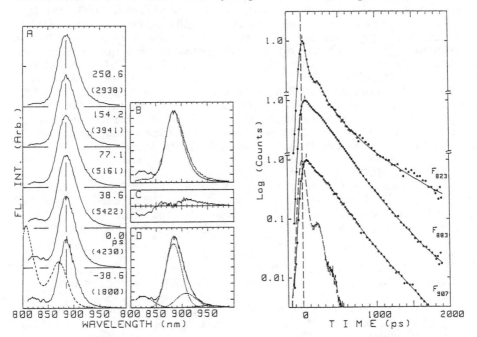

Fig. 1 (A)Time-resolved fluorescence spectra of Erythrobacter sp. OCh
114. Spectra were drawn after normalization to the maximum
intensity of each spectrum. Numbers in parentheses indicate the
maximum number of photons in the spectrum. Absorption spectrum
of the membrane is also indicated by dotted line at the bottom.
(B) Spectra at 0 ps (———) and 250 ps (—·——) are overlapped to
show the differences. (C) Difference spectrum of the two spectra
in (B)(250 ps minus 0 ps) (D) Gaussian deconvolution of the time-
resolved spectrum at 0 ps. (———) the observed spectrum, (—·——)
component bands and (········) sum of the component bands.

Fig. 2 Rise and decay patterns of the fluorescence components resolved
by deconvolution of the spectra as shown in Fig. 1D. Each point
was calculated by the relative height in the spectrum and actual
counts of photons. Broken line; the excitation pulse profile.
The bar over each curve indicates the maximum point of intensity.

The functional role of B888 other than accumulation of excitation energy around RC might be that which associates with the charge separation process and/or structural one in the RC–B870 complex.

According to Forster mechanism (3), very fast energy transfer means stronger interaction between pigments. Compared with the coupling between B800-850 and B875 (4), there is a large energy gap between B806 and B870, and consequent small spectral overlap. At least, therefore, the spatial arrangement of B806 Bchl and B870 Bchl must be suitable for fast energy transfer. In B800-850 of typical photosynthetic bacteria, B850 Bchl is localized near the periplasmic side of the membrane just like B870 Bchl and the special pair Bchl in RC, whereas, B800 Bchl is thought to be located near the cytoplasmic side of the membrane (11). B870 and RC of Erythrobacter sp. strain OCh 114 are very similar to the corresponding complexes of typical photosynthetic bacteria in terms of spectroscopic properties and polypeptide composition (2,12,13). The localization of Bchls in B870 may be, therefore, near periplasmic side. If the localization of B806 Bchl is analogous to B800 Bchl in B800-850, the distance between B806 and B870 Bchls would be too large for the fast energy transfer by the Forster mechanism. Thus, B806 Bchl may be near the periplasmic side just like B850 Bchl. Otherwise, much stronger interaction might be functional between Bchls in different complexes.

4. ACKNOWLEDGEMENTS

The authors thank to the Instrument Center, Institute for Molecular Science for the picosecond spectroscopy. This study is partly supported by a Grant-in-Aid for the Scientific Research from the Ministry of Education, Science and Culture, Japan to KS (60304007) and MM (62540520).

5. REFERENCES

1. Shiba, T. and Shimidu, U.(1982) Int. J. Syst. Bacteriol. 32, 211-217
2. Shimada, K., Hayashi, H. and Tasumi, M.(1985) Arch. Microbiol. 143, 244-247
3. Förster, T.(1948) Ann. Phys. Leipzig. 2, 55-75
4. Shimada, K., Mimuro, M., Tamai, N. and Yamazaki, I.(1989) Biochim. Biophys. Acta 975, 72-79
5. Van Grondelle, R.(1985) Biochim. Biophys. Acta 811, 147-195
6. Van Grondelle, R. and Sundström, V.(1988) in Photosynthetic Light Harvesting Systems (Scheer, H. and Schneider, S. eds.), pp.403-438, Walter de Gruyter, Berlin
7. Yamazaki, I., Tamai, N., Kume, H., Tsuchiya H. and Oba, K.(1985) Rev. Sci. Instrum. 56, 1187-1194
8. Mimuro, M., Yamazaki, I., Itoh, S., Tamai, N. and Satoh, K.(1988) Biochim. Biophys. Acta 933, 478-486
9. Zankel, K.L. (1978) in The Photosynthetic Bacteria (Clayton, R.K. and Sistrom, W.R. eds.), pp. 341-347, Plenum Press, New York
10. Matsuura, K. and Shimada, K.(1986) Biochim. Biophys. Acta 852, 9-18
11. Zuber,H.(1985) Photochem. Photobiol. 42, 821-844
12. Hayashi, H., Shimada, K., Tasumi, M., Nozawa, T. and Hatano, M. (1986) Photobiochem. Photobiophys. 10, 223-231
13. Takamiya, K., Iba, K. and Okamura, K.(1987) Biochim. Biophys. Acta 890, 127-133

EXCITATION ENERGY TRANSFER AMONG PHYCOBILISOMES FROM THE
PHYCOERYTHRIN CONTAINING STRAIN *ANABAENA VARIABILIS* ARM310

P.S. MARUTHI SAI and SUDHA MAHAJAN, SCHOOL OF LIFE SCIENCES,
JAWAHARLAL NEHRU UNIVERSITY, NEW DELHI--110067, INDIA

1. INTRODUCTION

Cyanobacteria, oxygen evolving photosynthetic
prokaryotes use water as an electron donor, harbour phycobilisomes which act as antenna pigments involved in transfer
of excitation energy to chlorophyll *a*. They are composed
of a central core of two or three cylinders to which usually
six rods are connected. The core is composed of allophycocyanin aggregates, while the building blocks of the rods
are hexameric units of phycocyanin. In addition to these,
in some organisms phycoerythrocyanin or phycoerythrin may
be present towards the periphery. There already exist
several spectroscopic studies on the excitation energy
transfer in these systems. It has been possible to follow
the path of excitation energy transfer from higher to lower
energy levels, i.e., from phycoerythrocyanin or phycoerythrin to allophycocyanin via phycocyanin [1]. The energy
transfer occurs on a picosecond (ps)scale in these systems
[2], [3], [4]. In this paper we report ps time resolved
fluorescence kinetics measurements from intact and
dissociated phycobilisomes isolated from *Anabaena variabilis*
ARM310. It is a dark green, filamentous and heterocystous
nitrogen fixing cyanobacterium.

2. PROCEDURE
2.1 Materials and methods
   2.1.1   Organism: *Anabaena variabilis* ARM310 was obtained
           from National facility for Blue Green Algae, Indian
           Agricultural Research Institute, New Delhi. The
           organism was grown on BG-11 medium [5] under con-
           tinuous illumination and constant agitation at
           a temperature of $25 \pm 2^{\circ}$C.
   2.1.2. Experimental: Phycobilisomes were isolated accord-
           ing to [6]. The intact phycobilisomes were
           dissociated against 5mM potassium phosphate buffer
           pH 7.0. Absorption Spectra were recorded on
           Shimadzu UV-visible recording spectrophotometer.
           Static fluorescence excitation and emission
           spectra were recorded on Shimadzu RF-540 recording
           Spectrofluorophotometer. The fluorescence life
           times were measured by the time correlated single
           photon counting set up capable of measuring life

M. Baltscheffsky (ed.), Current Research in Photosynthesis, Vol. II, 197–200.

times down to 20 ps was used for the purpose.
The system broadly consisted of CW mode-locked
Nd-YAG frequency doubled, synchronously pumped
cavity dumped dye laser a time domain Spectrometer, a data acquisition system and a data
analyser. The details of the experimental set
up are published elsewhere [7]. All fluorescence
decays were measured at room temperature.

RESULTS AND DISCUSSION
    The major biliproteins present in the phycobilisomes
of *Anabaena variabilis* ARM310 are phycoerythrin, phycocyanin
and allophycocyanin as evidenced by the absorption spectroscopy [Fig. 1]. Dissociation induced spectral changes
which altered the energy transfer from phycoerythrin to
allophycocyanin. These changes indicating an increase
in the phycoerythrin emission when excited at 545 nm led
to a conclusion that dissociation causes the loss of energy
transfer from phycoerythrin to phycocyanin [Fig. 2]. The
fluorescence decay of intact phycobilisomes is shown in
Fig. 3. For intact phycobilisomes the decays could be
fitted into 3 exponential components with a reasonably
good x^2 of 1.07. But a x^2 of 1.32 for the dissociated
phycobilisomes indicated the need for a four exponential
analysis [Table 1]. The life time of shortest lived

Table 1. Fluorescence decay parameter observed. Samples were excited
         at 580nm and the emission was monitored at 640nm.

Sample	A_1	T_1(ps)	A_2	T_2(ps)	A_3	T_3(ns)	x^2	DWP
Intact phycobilisomes	30.6	104	12.0	820	57.4	1.812	1.08	1.76
Dissociated phycobilisomes	37.4	143	11.8	1392	50.8	1.911	1.36	1.82

A = Amplitude, T = Life time and DWP = Durbin Watson Parameter.

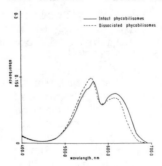

FIGURE 1. Absorption spectra of phycobilisomes.

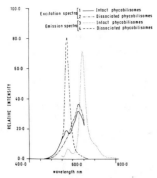

FIGURE 2.
Excitation and Emission
spectra of phycobilisomes.

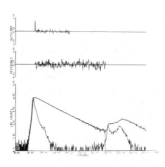

FIGURE 3.
Fluorescence decay profiles
of intact phycobilisomes.

component is attributed to the overall transfer from
C-phycocyanin to the core. The life time of middle
component is attributed to the presence of energetically
uncoupled chromophores. The life time of the longest lived
component is ascribed to the C-phycocyanin emission at
the wavelength of 640 nm. According to [4] the phycocyanin
hexamers could be easily fitted into 3 exponentials due
to higher aggregation which is not true with trimers and
monomers where there was a necessity of 4 exponential
analysis. Since the phycocyanin in intact phycobilisomes
exists in the form of hexamers a fit of 3 exponentials
was sufficient. But in the dissociated phycobilisomes
there is a loss of energy transfer due to the formation
of lower aggregates where there are not enough acceptors
of the excitation energy which might have led to a complex
situation where 3 exponential analysis was insufficient.
The increase in the life time of shortest lived component
confirms the loss of energy transfer in dissociated phycobilisomes. Similarly the increase in the life time of
middle component also strengthens the belief that
dissociated phycobilisomes possess more number of
energetically uncoupled pigments. Further the details
of fluorescence decay kinetics of phycobilisomes and
isolated phycobiliproteins obtained by a global analysis
will be published elsewhere.

4. ACKNOWLEDGEMENTS

We gratefully acknowledge Miss Rajita, Dr. S.Dorai-
swamy and Dr. N.Periasamy, Chemical Physics Group, TIFR,
Bombay for their contribution in the measurements and
analysis of the data on the Laser Spectrofluorometer. P.S.M.
Sai is indebted to Council of Scientific and Industrial
Research, India, for the provision of financial assistance
in the form of a Senior Research Fellowship during the
tenure of this work.

REFERENCES
1 Scheer, H. (1985) in Encyclopedia of Plant Physiology: Photosynthesis III. (Staehelin L. A. and Arntzen C.J., eds.) pp.327-337, Springer-Verlag, Berlin, Heidelberg
2 Porter, G., Tredwell, C.J., Searle, G.F.W. and Barber, J. (1978) Biochim. Biophys. Acta 501, 232-245
3 Grabowsky, J. and Gantt, E. (1978) Photochem. Photobiol. 28, 39-45
4 Holzwarth, A.R., Wendler, J. and Suter, G.W. (1987) Biophys. J. 51, 1-12
5 Stanier, R.Y., Kunisawa, R., Mandel, M. and Cohen-Bazire, G. (1971) Bacteriol. Rev. 35, 2, 171-205.
6 Gantt, E., Lipschultz, C.A., Grabowski, J. and Zimmerman, B.K. (1979) Plant Physiol. 63, 615-
7 Doraiswamy, S., Krishnamoorty G., Periasamy, N. and Venkataraman, B. (1988) Proc. Indian natn. Sci. Acad. 54A, pp. 782-797

SEPARATION OF PS I AND PS II FROM THE PROCHLOROPHYTE
(OXYCHLOROBACTERIUM) P. HOLLANDICA AND THE ROLE OF CHL b.

H.C.P. Matthijs, H. Reith, G.W.M. van der Staay
and L.R. Mur, Laboratorium voor Microbiologie,
Universiteit van Amsterdam, Nieuwe Achtergracht 127,
1018 WS Amsterdam, The Netherlands

1.   INTRODUCTION
     Prochlorophytes have been introduced as a new division
of algae characterized by oxygenic photosynthesis in a
prokaryotic cell with chl a and b (1). The presence of
chl b does not give rise to noticable formation of grana,
at best some pairing of thylakoid membranes can be observed.
Nevertheless, lateral heterogeneity of PS I and II has been
reported in Prochloron and Prochlorothrix hollandica (2,3).
Questions to be answered focus on the potential relatedness
to chloroplasts and thereby also address the role of chl b
in the chl a/b protein complexes. The fluoride and redox
state effected and therefore potentially regulatory phosphorylation of a 29 kDa chl a/b protein (4), may add to the
current disputes on the role of lateral mobility of polypeptide assemblies in chloroplasts and cyanobacteria (5). In a
number of studies a common opinion on the immunological,
pigment compositional and structural non- alikeness of the
chl a/b proteins and LHC II of chloroplasts has been arrived
at (1,2,4,6). It remains to be tested whether these observed
deviations are also reflected in the gene sequences for the
prochlorophytes chl a/b antennae especially with regard to
the diversity of the Cab gene families in chloroplasts (7).

2.   MATERIALS AND METHODS
     Prochlorothrix culture and preparation of thylakoids was
as described before (4,6). Absorbance spectra were obtained
on an Aminco DW 2000 spectrophotometer. Fluorescence spectra
were made on a laboratory assembled instrument. Two phase
partioning separation was done as in (9). Maltoside and
Zwittergent application followed published procedures (6,
10). SDS- PAGE was as in (6). HPLC analysis of chl a and b
was as described in (7). Chl to P_{700} ratios were estimated
from ferricyanide/ ascorbate difference spectra.

3.   RESULTS AND DISCUSSION
     Gradual extraction of chlorophyll- protein assemblies
     with the two phase partioning method gave elution profi-

M. Baltscheffsky (ed.), Current Research in Photosynthesis, Vol. II, 201–204.
© 1990 *Kluwer Academic Publishers. Printed in the Netherlands.*

les as shown in Fig. 1. The data demonstrate the release of a major fraction of chl a enriched complexes, an intermediairy extract with a relatively increased chl b content and finally a fraction with relatively more chl a (relative means with respect to the original thylakoids). Spectral analysis and SDS-PAGE applied to these fractions identified them in the order, PS I enriched complexes, antennae with chlorophyll b and finally, PS II enriched complexes. The isolated antenna fractions (tubes 19 to 22) were poor in reaction centers, contained polypeptides with mass in the area of 29 to 34 kDa but did not contain any appreciable content of polypeptides with mass from 20 to 28 kDa, characteristically the domain of LHC II and I derived polypeptides of chloroplasts. The fractions with PS I and II still contained substantial amounts of chl b and polypeptide bands in the 29 to 34 kDa range. After further purification of the antenna enriched fractions involving hydroxy- apatite chromatography a chl a/b -protein complex with polypeptide bands at 31 kDa and a relatively weak band at 29 kDa on both coommassie and silverstained gels, with a chl a/b ratio of 3.4 + 0.3 (n=5) was obtained. This product demonstrated immunological crossreactivity to the Prochlorothrix antenna present in band CP 5 on non-denaturing LiDS gels of maltoside solubilized thylakoids (6, in cooperation with George S. Bullerjahn, Bowling Green Ohio)and was found structurally different from LHC II as judged from the lack of the chl b trimers in circular dichroism (11). The nature of the antenna associated with PS I, which has been calculated from experimental data like those presented in Fig.1 to make up to as much as 60% of the total chl b content of the Prochlorothrix cells, still remains unknown.

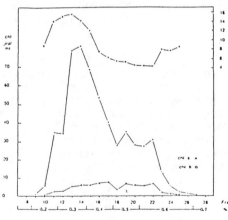

For conclusions on the functional role of the chl a/b antenna complexes one would need to resolve PS I and PS II with the adherent antennae as in-intact as possible from the thylakoid membranes. To reach this goal we have experienced digito-nin, octyl-glucoside, and Zwittergent 8, 10, 12 and 16 to be unappropiate.

Figure 1. Two phase extraction, details are given in the text.

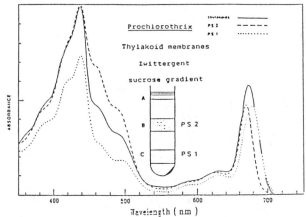

Table 1. Pigment analysis

	chl a/b ratio	chl/P700 ratio
Thylakoids	12	253
band 2	8	> 3800
band 3	53	108

Figure 2. Absorbance spectra of Zwittergent 14 solubilized thylakoid membranes of Prochlorothrix plus the absorbance spectra of isolated PS I and II from sucrose gradients.

Maltoside solubilization as in (7) rendered a PS I complex similar to the Triton X-100 preparation.
In maltoside, PS II was depleted of its antennae (7). Zwittergent 14 was found useful in the separation of PS I and II on sucrose gradients (Fig.2). The lower band with PS I (note its red shifted peak) was depleted of chl b, (a/b ratio >50, Table 1) this however, did not impose a major difference on the fluorescence excitation spectrum, a broad peak at 460 nm (possibly carotenoids) remained present, just as in the maltoside or Triton X-100 extracted material (Fig. 3). The 77K fluorescence emission spectrum of the maltoside (7) and Zwittergent (Fig. 3) acquired preparations were different. Especially the size of the '689' nm peak was smaller in the Zwittergent preparation. From the fluorescence spectra and from HPLC and spectroscopic assay of acetone extracts it was concluded that chl b remained in the Triton X-100 and maltoside acquired preparations of PS I in an antenna which could be detached with Zwittergent 14 (7, Fig. 3, and not shown). Data obtained on the antennae coupled to PS II showed that after solubilization in maltoside, incorporated ^{32}P can be recovered in the 29 kDa polypeptide which runs only in band CP 5 on 'green' gels (6). Its chl a/b ratio was estimated 3 after extraction with isobutanol and HPLC.
    In conclusion, Prochlorothrix hollandica bears chl b about equally distributed over PS I and II.
The PS I antenna remains complexed in Triton X-100 and maltoside but is detached with Zwittergent 14. The PS II antenna can be resolved with maltoside, it has polypeptides of 29 and 31 kDa, the former can be reversibly phosphorylated (4).

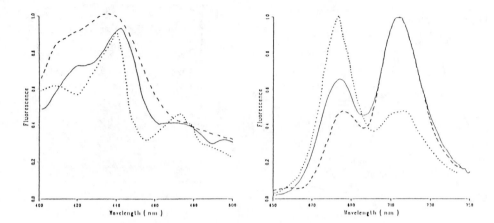

Figure 3. Fluorescence excitation (l) and emission (r)
spectra of isolated preparations of PS I from
Prochlorothrix. maltoside (435), ···············;
Zwtg (435), ───────── ; Zwtg (470), ─ ─ ─ ─ ─

ACKNOWLEDGEMENT
We thank Frank van Mourik (Vrije Universiteit Amster
dam) for help with the fluorescence measurements.
HCPM was supported by a grant of the Dutch Organization
for Scientific Research (NWO).

REFERENCES
1 Prochloron, a microbial enigma (1989) Lewin R.A. and
   Cheng L.A. eds. Chapman and Hall, New York/ London
2 Giddings T.H., Withers N.W. and Steahelin L.A. (1980)
   Proc. Natl. Acad. Sc. USA 77, 352-356
3 Miller K.R., Jacob J.S., Burger-Wiersma T. and Matthijs
   H.C.P. (1988) J. Cell Sc. 91, 577-586
4 Van der Staay G.W.M., Matthijs H.C.P. and Mur L.R. (1989)
   Biochim. Biophys. Acta 975, 317-324
5 Biggins J. and Bruce D. (1989) Photosynth. Res. 20, 1-34
6 Bullerjahn G.S., Matthijs H.C.P., Mur L.R. and
   Sherman L.A. (1987) Eur. J. Biochem. 168, 295-300
7 Matthijs, H.C.P., van der Staay, G.W.M., van Amerongen,
   H., van Grondelle, R. and Garab, G. (1989) Biochim.
   Biophys. Acta 975, 185-187
8 Green B.R. (1988) Photosynth. Res. 15, 3-32
9 Albertsson P.A. and Andersson B. (1981) J. Chrom. 215,
   131-141
10 Dekker, J.P., Boekema, E.J., Witt, H.T. and Rögner, M.
   (1988) Biochim. Biophys. Acta 936, 307-318

HIGH RESOLVED LOW TEMPERATURE SPECTROSCOPY OF PHOTOSYNTHETIC SYSTEMS

J. Hala, J. Dian, O. Prasil*, M. Vacha and K. Vacek
Department of Chemical Physics, Faculty of Mathematics & Physics,
Charles University, 121 16 Prague; Department of Autotrophic Organisms,
Institute of Microbiology, Czechoslovak Academy of Sciences, 379 81
Trebon*, Czechoslovakia

1. INTRODUCTION
   Site selection and hole burning spectroscopy are low temperature
spectroscopic techniques based on the removal of the inhomogeneous
broadening in optical spectra. These spectroscopic techniques, applied
to photosynthetic systems, their subunits and models, represent powerful tools for studying pigment-pigment and pigment-matrix interactions,
as well as energy transfer and electron transport. The digested information obtained from low temperature spectroscopy results on chloro-
phylls and photosynthetic systems can be found in |1|. Most important
results are briefly mentioned below. Conventional low temperature spectra of chlorophylls *in vitro* have shown only broad bands in absorption
and emission. The narrow red laser excitation enables to observe vibra-
tionally resolved site selection spectra in solid solutions |2, 3| and
in polymer foils |4|. The hole burning (HB) effects in absorption (A)
and fluorescence excitation (E) spectra were measured in different ma-
trices including the discussion of HB mechanisms |5, 6, 7|.
   In vivo photosynthetic systems have been widely studied using the
same spectroscopic methods. The site selection technique has brought
positive results on etiolated leaves only |8|. The advantages of laser
selective excitation are lost in most photosynthetic systems due to
strong electron-phonon coupling and efficient transfer of excitation
energy. Nevertheless this technique has succeeded on well defined model
photosynthetic systems, i.e. pigment-polypeptide |9|, pigment-nucleid
acid |10|, pigment-lipide |11| and pigment-quinone |12|. Moreover, the
HB spectra were observed on several *in vivo* green photosystems follow-
ing earlier observations of HB effects on bacterial photosystems |13,
14, 15, 16, 17|. First HB effects were studied in A of green algae |18|
where attempts to determine decay times of PS I and PS II were made.
Further very broad nonphotochemical (NPHB) holes were observed in A of
PS II |19|. The combinations of a narrow hole (~ 0.12 cm^{-1}) and a broad
one (~ 300 cm^{-1}) in A of PS II, resp. core antenna complex are ducu-
mented in |20|, resp. |21|. These works continued in |22, 23| where the
authors offered the complex explanation of both broad and narrow holes
in A together with the discussion of the zero phonon holes and the
vibronic ones. Very interesting persistent spectral hole burning

M. Baltscheffsky (ed.), Current Research in Photosynthesis, Vol. II, 205–208.
© 1990 *Kluwer Academic Publishers. Printed in the Netherlands.*

(PSHB) results were obtained from fluorescence (F) and fluorescence excitation (E) on post etiolated as well as green leaves in |24, 25|. The two level system theory developed for spectral HB is summarised in |26|; moreover strong linear electron-phonon coupling is discussed in |27|.

The aim of this contribution is to present preliminary results of complete A, F and E HB studies of pigment-protein complexes in poly-acrylamide gels obtained from pea leaves including the discussion of HB mechanisms.

2. MATERIALS AND METHODS

Thylakoids were isolated from pea *(Pisum sativum)* leaves largely as described in |28|. Samples were subjected to non-denaturating SDS poly-acrylamide (10 - 20%) gel electrophoresis performed according to |29|. Several pigment-protein complexes were cut out from the gel and stored in glycerol at dry ice temperatures. Pigment-protein complexes were identified according to their position in the gel as PS I oligo, PS I mono, LHC oligo, PS II CP 47, PS II CP 43 and LHC mono.

F and E HB spectra were measured on an apparatus consisting of a pulsed dye laser synchronised with a chopped *cw* Ar-Kr ion laser (676.4 nm line). The luminiscence from the irradiated samples immersed in li-quid helium was spectrally analysed in a double grating monochromator (spectral resolution of $1 - 2$ cm^{-1}) and detected using a photomultiplier along with a boxcar integrator. During A HB measurements a Tungsram lamp (50 - 1000 W) was combined with a monochromator or an interference filter. The Ar-Kr *cw* burning laser beam was cut off using a couple of synchronised choppers (10 - 50 Hz). The detection was performed in a photomultiplier along with a lock-in amplifier or an optical multichan-nel analyser (spectral resolution of $5 - 10$ cm^{-1}). The temperature was kept between $1.5 - 4.2$ K. An extreme care was given to make sure that the whole measured spot on the sample was covered with the burning la-ser beam as well, and to chose the short burn time limit exposition.

3. RESULTS AND DISCUSSION

The red laser (647.1 nm) excited low temperature fluorescence spect-ra of *in vitro* chlorophyll-*a* (Chl-a) in polystyrene and of *in vivo* pigment-protein complexes in polyacrylamide gel show significant dif-ferences between *in vitro* and *in vivo* systems. The *in vitro* systems exhibit vibrationally resolved structure on a broad band fluorescence background. On the other hand no sharp lines are observed in pigment--protein systems due to strong electron-phonon coupling and efficient energy transfer. The wavelengths of zero phonon (0-0) F maxima and the FWHM of these (0-0) F bands well characterize the measured systems as shown in Tab. 1.

The typical PSHB in F spectra of pigment-protein complexes are shown in Fig. 1. The widths of the holes measured at 4.2 K range from 2.1 to 2.8 cm^{-1} for PS II and LHC. The temperature dependence study provides the zero temperature extrapolated value of the width of 1.0 ± 0.5 cm^{-1} which corresponds to the decay time ranging 8 - 18 ps. Note, that this value is smaller than 200 - 400 ps observed in |21| on core antenna C 670 but greater than 1.9 ± 0.2 ps obtained in |29| on PS II. According to these unprecendented F PSHB results one might expect the decay time of this magnitude due to accessory Chl and pheophytin pigments involved in the processes of excitation energy transfer and due to a pigments desaggregation. One must bear in mind the spectral resolution of the applied experimental set up, our limitation in tuning the burning laser out of the wavelength 676.45 nm, as well as additional spectroscopic effects of pigment-proteins in gels (reabsorption, scattering, glass forming ability,...). From this point of view the obtained decay times should be considered as a short time limited value. The hole width measured at 4.2 K on LHC mono was 2.2 cm^{-1} No attention was paid to measurements of very broad (~100 cm^{-1}) HB effects in F spectra.

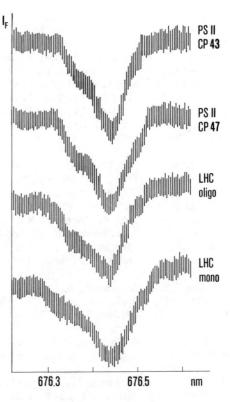

Fig.1 Persistent spectral hole burning fluorescence spectra of the pigment-protein complexes isolated from pea leaves.

The HB effects in A showed transient character (THB). Very broad transient holes (~145 cm-1) were observed in the low temperature A spectra depending on chopper frequency and burning laser intensity. These results are in agreement with the data presented in |19, 23| on PS II. No sharp hole superimposed on the broad hole was observed due to rather low spectral resolution of our A set up. Nevertheless the presented 145 cm^{-1} broad hole in A obtained on *in vitro* Chl-a in polystyrene represents a new argument against the ultrafast (~75 fs) interpretation of very broad holes suggested in |14, 15, 16| measured in A of bacterial reaction centers.

TABLE 1. Low temperature fluorescence (F) data

Measured systems	Chl-a	PS II CP 43	PS II CP 47	LHC oligo	LHC mono	PS I mono	PS I oligo
Wavelengths of 0-0 F maxima in nm	672.0	681.5	685.0	688.0	690.0	718.5	721.5
FWHM of 0-0 F bands in nm	45	18	21	33	30	39	43

REFERENCES
 1 Hala, J. (1989) Low Temperature Optical Spectroscopy of Chlorophyll-like Molecules, Academia, Prague

 2 Fünfschilling, J. and Williams, D.F. (1977) Photochem. Photobiol. 26, 109–113
 3 Avarmaa, R.A. and Mauring, K.K. (1978) Zh. Priklad. Spektrosk. 28, 658–662
 4 Hala, J., Pelant, I., Parma, L. and Vacek, K. (1981) J. Luminisc. 24/25, 803–806
 5 Mauring, K. and Avarmaa, R. (1982) Izv. Akad. Nauk ESSR 31, 155–160
 6 Carter, T.P. and Small, G.J. (1985) Chem. Phys. Lett. 120, 178–182
 7 Carter, T.P. and Small, G.J. (1986) J. Phys. Chem. 90, 1997–1998
 8 Renge, I., Mauring, K.K. and Avarmaa, R.A. (1984) Biochim. Biophys. Acta 766, 501–504
 9 Hala, J., Pelant, I., Ambroz, M., Pancoska, P. and Vacek, K. (1985) Photochem. Photobiol. 41, 643–648
10 Hala, J., Pelant, I., Ambroz, M., Dousa, P. and Vacek, K. (1986) Chem. Phys. Lett. 123, 437–440
11 Fünfschilling, J. and Walz, D. (1983) Photochem. Photobiol. 38, 389–393
12 Hala, J., Vacek, K., Ambroz, M., Grof, K., Pancoska, P. and Pelant, I. (1988) Izv. Akad. Nauk ESSR 37, 186–191
13 Maslov, V., Klevanik, A. and Shuvalov, V. (1984) Biofiz. 29, 156–157
14 Meech, S.R., Hoff, A.J. and Wiersma, D.A. (1985) Chem. Phys. Lett. 121, 287–292
15 Boxer, S.G., Lockhart, D.J. and Middendorf, T.R. (1986) Chem. Phys. Lett. 123, 476–482
16 Boxer, S.G., Middendorf, T.R. and Lockhart, D.J. (1986) FEBS Lett. 200, 237–241
17 Ganago, A., Melkozernov, A. and Shuvalov, V. (1986) Biofiz. 31, 440–443
18 Maslov, V.G., Chunayev, A.S. and Tugarinov, V.V. (1981) Mol. Biol. 15, 1016–1026
19 Vink, K.J., de Boer, S., Plijter, J.J., Hoff, A.J. and Wiersma, D.A. (1987) Chem. Phys. Lett. 142, 433–438
20 Gillie, J.K., Fearey, B.L., Hayes, J.M., Small, G.J. and Goldbeck, J.H. (1987) Chem. Phys. Lett. 134, 316–322
21 Gillie, J.K., Small, G.J. and Goldbeck, J.H. (1989) J. Phys. Chem. 91, 5524–5527
22 Gillie, J.K., Small, G.J. and Goldbeck, J.H. (1989) J. Phys. Chem. 93, 1620–1627
23 Jankowiak, R., Tang, D., Small, G.J. and Seibert, M. (1989) J. Phys. Chem. 93, 1649–1654
24 Mauring, K., Renge, I. and Avarmaa, R. (1987) FEBS Lett. 223, 165–168
25 Renge, I., Mauring, K. and Vladkova, R. (1988) Biochim. Biophys. Acta 935, 333–336
26 Moerner, W.E. ed. (1988) Persistent Spectral Hole-Burning: Science and Applications, Springer-Verlag, Berlin-Heidelberg-New York-London
27 Hayes, J.H., Gillie, J.K., Tang, D. and Small, G.J. (1988) Biochim. Biophys. Acta 932, 287–305
28 Camm, E.L. and Green, B.R. (1982) Arch. Biochem. Biophys. 214, 563–572
29 Laemmli, U.K. (1970) Nature 227, 680–685

THE ROLE OF LIGHT HARVESTING COMPLEX II AND OF THE MINOR CHLOROPHYLL a/b PROTEINS IN THE ORGANIZATION OF THE PHOTOSYSTEM II ANTENNA SYSTEM.

Roberto Bassi and Paola Dainese

Dipartimento di Biologia Universita' di Padova, via Trieste 75 I–35100 Padova ITALY.

1. INTRODUCTION

The pigment portion of Photosystem (PS)I and II in green plants is composed of a chlorophyll(chl) *a* containing core complex and of a light harvesting antenna system containing both chl *a* and chl *b*.

Although major progresses have been recently made, still some basic features of the structural and molecular organization of chl *a/b* binding proteins such as polypeptide and pigment composition are not well defined. In this study we describe the use of improved analytical methods for the isolation and characterization of chlorophyll–proteins. Their use offers new possibilities to investigate the organization of the PSII antenna system.

2. PROCEDURE

The development of analytical non–denaturing electrophoretic procedures (green gels) has been of special importance and recently it has led to the identification of novel chlorophyll binding light harvesting components(1,2). However, LiDS or SDS PAGE are methods based on molecular size and the resolution is limited by the fact that all chl *a/b* binding proteins have polypeptides with similar apparent Mw.

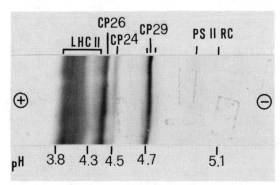

Fig.1: Separation pattern obtained by non–denaturing isoelectrofocussing (pH 3.5–5.5) of 1% dodecylmaltoside solubilized PSII membranes. In the upper line the chlorophyll protein contained in the bands are indicated. In the lower line pH values are indicated. The gel contained 0.06% DM and 2% ampho lytes and was not stained.

To overcome this problem, we have recently used an alternative method, isoelectrofocussing, allowing a separation on the basis of the charge characteristics (pI) of the solubilized complexes. A typical separation is shown in figure 1.

2.1. Materials and methods

Thylakoids and PSII membranes were isolated as previously described (1) from *Zea mays* seedlings. Electrophoresis was as in ref. 1. Gradient centrifugation was as

M. Baltscheffsky (ed.), Current Research in Photosynthesis, Vol. II, 209–216.

in (1), but dodecylmaltoside was used at 1% in solubilization and at 0.06% in the gradient. Run was at 39000 rpm for 24 h. Isoelectrofocussing was as in ref. 3. Western blotting was as in ref. 1. The preparation of antibodies was described in ref. 4.Pigment and protein determination: Protein concentration in solutions was determined by the bicinchoninic acid method (Pierce). Coomassie binding to purified apoproteins was determined as in ref. 5. Gel densitometry was performed with a Shimadzu cromatoscanner. Pigment concentration, chl a/b ratio and chl/carotenoid ratio were determined according to Wellburn and Lichtenthaler (6) In vivo phosphorylation of thylakoid membranes as in ref 7.

3. RESULTS AND DISCUSSION

3.1.Chlorophyll–protein composition of grana membranes: PSII membranes contain three chl *a* binding proteins belonging to PSII reaction centre (RC); these are CP47, CP43 and the D1/D2 heterodimer binding the special chl *a* pair. These subunits bind 23% of the chl present in the grana (see later). At least four chl *a/b* binding proteins are also present: the major Light Harvesting Complex (LHCII) and the minor complexes CP29, CP26 and CP24 that bind respectively 56.7%, 6.6%, 5.9% and 3.3% of the chlorophyll. There is not too much room left for others chlorophyll–proteins although there are evidences for the presence of others immunologically related polypeptides in trace amounts.

LHCII: it binds chl *a* and chl *b* with 1.4 ratio. In *Zea mays* at least six polypeptides can be resolved from this complex by SDS–urea PAGE in the 26 to 30 kDa range. In non denaturing SDS–PAGE, LHCII migrates as a green band of apparent Mw of 64 kDa. Fractionation by IEF resolves several subpopulations in the pH range 3.8 –4.5. They show differences in the polypeptide composition and an aggregation state in detergent solution corresponding to the oligomeric LHCII from green gels. An ecception to this pattern is the most acidic green band (pI=3.8) that migrates faster in the sucrose gradients i.e. at the same density as the minor chlorophyll *a/b* proteins (Fig.2).

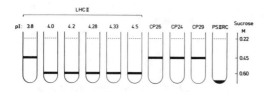

Fig.2:   *Sedimentation   pattern after   sucrose   gradient ultracentrifugation.   The chlorophyll–proteins   were purified   by   non   denaturing IEF   in   the   presence   of   DM (see   fig.1)   and   loaded   on   a 0.1–1   M   sucrose   gradient containing   0.06%   DM   and   5 mM Hepes pH 7.6.*

The reasons for such a large heterogeneity of LHCII are not fully understood but are in part due to different roles in phosphorylation mediated State 1–State 2 transitions.   The more acidic LHCII subpopulations are the most heavily phosphorylated while those with pI=4.3–4.5 carry little or not phosphate groups. Moreover after phosphorylation two LHCII subpopulations desappear from grana stacks and are found in grana membranes (7). Thus at least three forms of LHCII are defined   with respect to phosphorylation behaviour: a mobile phosphorylated form and two non–mobile forms either phosphorylated and non phosphorylated (7). The lower Mw polypeptide of LHCII (26 kDa) is only present in grana confined LHCII and never appears in the complex migrating to stroma membranes (8).

CP26 and CP29: These complexes have a chl *b* content lower than LHCII (chl *a/b* ratio respectively 2.2 and 2.8) and absorbtion peaks red shifted to 676 and 677 nm with respect to LHCII (674.5 nm). SDS–urea PAGE resolves a single 31 kDa polypeptide from CP29 and a doublet (28 and 29 kDa) from CP26. There has been some confusion on the identity of CP26 that has been indicated as a LHCII subset by several authors. The results of the immunological analysis (fig. 3) clearly show that CP26 share epitops with CP29 rather than with LHCII.

CP24: It has a chl *a/b* ratio of 1.6 and a absorbtion peak at 674.5 nm. It contains an apoprotein with apparent Mw of 20 kDa that is immunologically related to CP26 and CP29 although cross reactions can be observed with LHCII as well.

The minor chl *a/b* complexes have the common feature of loosing pigments during purification. However, CP24 preferentially released chl *a* while CP26 and CP29 rather loose chl *b*. The values reported in tab. I were obtained from complexes purified by a single IEF step in the presence of dodecylmaltoside. The use of multistep procedures consistently results into higher chl *a/b* ratios for CP26 and CP29.

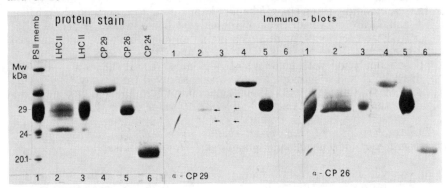

Fig. 3 Immunological assay. Purified chl a/b proteins were separated by SDS–urea PAGE and transferred to nitrocellulose. The filter was assayed with polyclonal antibodies raised against purified CP26 and CP29.

Table I: Characteristics of chlorophyll a/b proteins from maize PSII membranes. Samples were obtained by a single IEF step. Multistep procedures yielded chl a/b ratio values higher for CP26 and CP29, lower for CP24.

	Chl a/b ratio	Chl/protein ratio	red absorption peak (nm)
CP24	1.6+/−0.1	5.1+/−0.2	674.5
CP26	2.2+/−0.1	9.1+/−0.4	676
CP29	2.8+/−0.07	8.2+/−0.3	677
LHCII	1.4+/−0.05	12.3+/−0.4	674.5

3.2: <u>Fractionation of PSII membranes into discrete subsets.</u> The methods of IEF and immunoblotting give us the possibility to separate and identifie chlorophyll–binding proteins both in native conditions, usefull for the study of protein–protein interactions and fully denaturing conditions indispensable when the quantitative relations between apoproteins must be determined. These techniques have been used to analyze the fractions obtained by sucrose gradient ultracentrifugation.

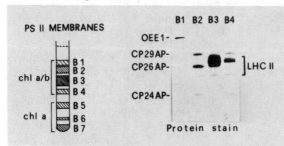

Fig.4: a) separation pattern following sucrose gradient ultracentrifugation of dodecylmaltoside solubilized PSII membranes; b) polypeptide composition of chl a/b containing fractions (bands 1–4).

3.2.1. <u>Fractionation by ultracentrifugation.</u> The separation pattern after ultracentrifugation is shown in figure 4. Besides, sucrose band 1, that mainly contains free carotenoids, three chl a/b bands (bands 2, 3, 4) and three chl a bands (bands 5, 6 and 7) are obtained. Each of the chl a/b bands was analyzed by IEF, SDS–urea PAGE and for its pigment and protein content (Table II). Sucrose band 2 contains the minor chl a/b proteins CP24, CP26 and CP29 besides small amounts of a LHCII subpopulation with characteristically acid pI (pH 3.8– 4.0). Band 3 only contains LHCII and 5 subpopulations can be resolved from it by IEF having pI of 4.2, 4.28, 4.33, 4.40 and 4.45. Band 4 contains CP24 and CP29 bound to a LHCII complex that yields bands at 4.28 and 4.33 pH values after IEF.

Table II:Characteristics of the green bands obtained by sucrose gradient ultracentrifugation of dodecylmaltoside solubilized PSII membranes.

	Chl (%)	Chl a/b ratio	Chl/car ratio	protein (%,w)	chla peak (nm)
B1	1.9	3.8	1.0	3%(*)	669.
B2	17.5	2.2	5.5	18.8	677
B3	46.7	1.4	7.0	37.8	674.5
B4	10.7	1.6	6.3	9.6	676
B5	4.5	>20	6.8	6.0	674
B6	2.1	>20	7.0	3.8	676
B7	16.6	>30	7.7	21.0	674

(*) O.E.E. polypeptides dissociated from PSII RC migrates at this level.

3.2.2 <u>Stoikiometry of chlorophyll binding proteins.</u>
The polypeptide analysis of the bands from sucrose gradient was performed to avoid comigrations with two different gel systems and individual coomassie bands were identified by immunoblotting. Protein content was attributed to individual polypeptides after densitometry and correction was made for the coomassie binding of each purified polypeptide. These results are summarized in Table III and allow the determination of the quantitative relations beetween chlorophyll a/b binding apoproteins in grana membranes.Minor chl a/b proteins are therefore present in PSII membranes in a ratio approaching 1:1:1 and constitute, together 25% of chl a/b binding apoproteins versus over 70% of LHCII.

Table III : relative protein content (%) of chl a/b binding polypeptides in sucrose gradient bands 2, 3 and 4 (containing chlorophyll a/b proteins) from DM solubilized PSII membranes.

	LHCII	CP26	CP29	CP24	others
B2	12	30	31	15	12
B3	100	/	/	/	/
B4	57	/	25	18	/
B2+B3+B4	72.6	8.2	10.7	5.7	2.8
B2+B3+B4(*)	71.4	8.3	9.8	7.8	2.7

(*) *after correction for Mw.*

By combining the data from Table II and III stoikiometry values can be obtained for chl–binding complexes (Table IV).

Table IV: Chlorophyll and protein distribution among chlorophyll–proteins in PSII membranes

	Chl (%)	*chl(moles)*	*protein(%)*	*protein (moles)*
PSII RC	23.2	53(*)	30.7	1(**)
LHCII	56.8	131	48.1	11.8
CP29	6.6	15	7.1	1.6
CP26	5.9	14	5.4	1.4
CP24	3.3	8	3.9	1.4
OTHERS	4.8	9	4.8	/.

(*) *with reference to 230 chl/PSIIRC (McCauley and Melis 1987)*
(**) *assuming 1 PSII RC = 240 kDa.*

3.2.3. A supramolecular antenna complex.

The study of sucrose band 4 provide informations on the interactions between chlorophyll–proteins within the antenna system. This band is obtained by incomplete solubilization of PSII membranes and is present in appreciable amounts only if solubilization time is kept short. As shown in Table II, CP29, CP24 and LHCII are found in this band and the migration rate in the sucrose gradient, higher than that of the individual components, strongly suggests that these are bound to form a supramolecular complex. This is confirmed by running IEF at two detergent concentrations (Fig. 5). At 0.06% DM a single band is obtained, while at 1% DM two LHCII bands as well as a CP24 and a CP29 bands are separated It is worth noticing that in this separation the most acidic LHCII band (pI=4.28) is present in double amounts with respect to the other one (pI=4.33). Stoikiometric determinations in band 4 show that CP29, CP24 and LHCII are present in a minimal molecular ratio of 1:1:3. Fig 5 shows that the minimal number of polypeptides present in the IEF band is three and therefore that the actual stoikiometry of the supramolecular complex in band 4 is 3:3:9 (CP29 : CP24 : LHCII). The LHCII subpopulations belonging to the CP29–CP24–LHCII complex have pI very close to that determined for the mobile LHCII after phosphorylation (7) small differences can be due to the different detergents (OGP vs DM) used in the two experiments.   Moreover CP24 is very similar to LHCI–680 both immunologically and spectroscopically (1) while the latter was found necessary to reconstitute the energy transfer between LHCI and PSI RC (9). The hypothesis that CP29–CP24–LHCII complex isolated in band 4 is actually involved in phosphorylation mediated state transition was tested by studying PSII membranes from phosphorylated thylakoids. In this case band 4 desappears from the sucrose gradient while a subset of it (CP29–CP24) is found to comigrate with band 3. The LHCII subpopulation lacking the 26 kDa polypeptide (pI=4.33) is not present in any of the sucrose gradient bands suggesting its migration to stroma membranes.

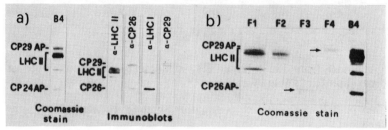

Fig. 5: Analysis of the sucrose band 4. a)immunological analysis of the polypeptides ; b) polypeptide composition (SDS–urea PAGE) of the green fractions (F) 1 to 4 obtained from IEF in 1% DM.

3.2.4: Other biochemical preparations from grana membranes.

The fractionation of grana membranes by various biochemical procedures allow the purification of several PSII–chl a/b subsets others than the CP29–CP24–LHCII complex.   A schematic representation of these preparations is shown in fig.6. Particularly intersting is the preparation (a), obtained by treatment of PSII membranes in high salt conditions, since it demonstrated that CP29 and CP26 are closely bound to CP43 (11,12). Preparation (d) indicates that a LHCII subpopulation is directly bound to CP43 in the absence of CP26 and CP29. Preparation (b) and (c) represent the complex discussed in 3.2.3 obtained from dark adapted and phosphorylated thylakoids.

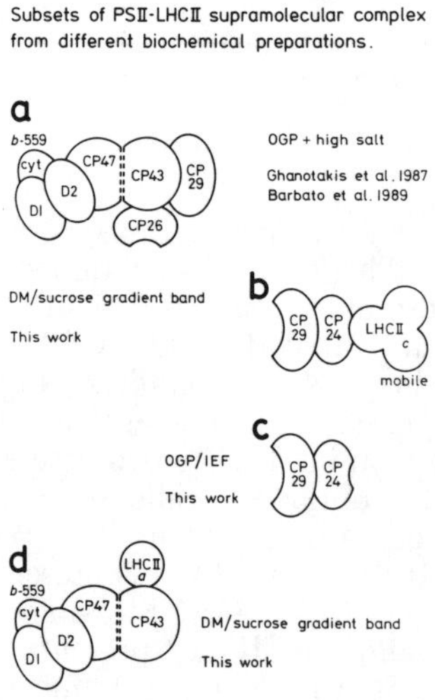

FIG. 6: Schematic representation of the composition of PSII–chl a/b complexes preparations obtained from PSII membranes. See explanation in the text.

3.2.5: A model for chlorophyll–protein organization in PSII membranes.

Fig.8 shows a schematic diagram refining a previous model (1) for the organization of PSII as defined from fractionation and phosphorylation experiments. Similarities can be found with the more simple situation of PSI where a 677 nm absorbing complex (LHCI 730) is tightly bound to PSI RC while LHCI–680 (absorption max = 674 nm) was found indispensable to the energy transfer from LHCII to the PSI–LHCI730 complex (9). Similarly CP24, whose immunological and spectroscopic characteristics are very similar to LHCI–680 (1, 4,10) may have a similar function with respect to the mobile LHCII population. CP26 has properties intermediate between CP29 and CP24 (13) and since it is also closely associated to PSII RC, it probably mediates energy transfer between non mobile non phosphorylatable LHCII and PSII RC. These relations are summarized in fig. 8.

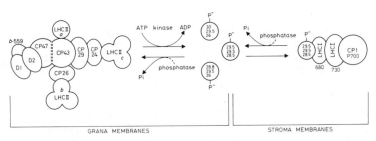

Fig. 7: Diagram illustrating chlorophyll–protein interactions in the membrane plane. This is based on a previous study (1), on the composition of discrete subsets obtained from PSII membranes and on the phosphorylation experiments.

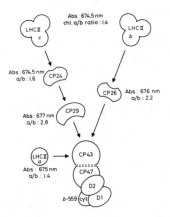

Fig. 8: Hypothetic model for the energy transfer within PSII antenna system. This is based on the interactions between chlorophyll–proteins and on the similarity to the simpler situation of PSI where a complex absorbing at 677 nm (LHCI–730) is closely associated to RC while LHCI–680 (absorbing with a 674 nm peak) mediates energy transfer from mobile LHCII (9).

In the above model different populations of the peripheral antenna (LHCII) transfer energy to PSII RC through intermediate complexes, whose function can be due to their stereochemical characteristics in that the establishment and the rescission of specific protein–protein interactions may be involved as in the case of phosphorylation mediated state 1 – state 2 transition. Spectroscopic characteristics can also be important and the red shift in the absorption spectra of CP26 and CP29 may have a driving function for excitation energy although the differences in energy levels involved are small.

A further consideration can be brought about on the basis of the determined stoikiometry between PSII antenna system components (Table IV). Since there are

1.5 moles of the minor antenna complexes while in the CP29–CP24–LHCII complex they are found in three copies each, then the antenna system stoikiometry must include at least 2 PSII RC units as proposed in fig. 9.

Such a model, although hypothetic, fits the observed stoikiometry and is consistent with the recent data from two dimensional crystals of PSII RC showing a dimeric organization for the complex (14). If we assign to each complex the pigment complement measured (Table I), then an antenna size of 464 chlorophylls is obtained consistently with the spectroscopic determination of 230 chl per PSII RC (15). In this way a chl a/b ratio of 2.28 is obtained versus a measured value for our preparations of 2.3+/−0.05.

Model for the organization of PSII chlorophyll-proteins
based on polypeptide stoikiometry and pigment distribution

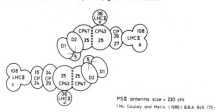

PSII antenna size = 230 chl
(Mc Cauley and Melis (1986) B.B.A. 849, 175-182)

Fig. 9 A model for PSII–chl a/b protein organization in the membrane plane. Two RC complex are needed to fit both the observed stoikiometry between RC and the minor chl a/b complexes.
Numbers indicate the chlorophyll complement of individual complexes as shown in Table I.

1) Bassi, R., Hoyer–Hansen, G., Barbato, R., Giacometti, G.M. and Simpson, D.J. (1987) J. Biol. Chem. 262, 13333–13341.
2) Dunahay, T.G. and Staehelin, L.A. (1986) Plant Physiol 80, 429–434.
3) Dainese, P. Hoyer–Hansen, G.and Bassi, R. (1989) submitted.
4) Di Paolo, M.L., Dal Belin Peruffo, A. and Bassi, R. (1989) submitted.
5) Ball, E.H. (1986) Anal Biochem. 155, 23–27.
6) Wellburn,A.R.and Lichtenthaler,H.K. (1983) Adv.Photosynth.Res. 2, 10–12.
7) Bassi, R., Rigoni, F., Barbato, R. and Giacometti, G.M. (1988) Biochim. Biophys. Acta 936, 29–38.
8) Bassi, R., Giacometti, G.M. and Simpson, D. J. (1988) Biochim. Biophys. Acta 935, 152–165.
9) Bassi, R. and Simpson, D. J. (1987) Eur. J. Biochem. 163, 221–230.
10) Hoyer–Hansen, G., Bassi, R., Honberg, L.S. and Simpson, D.J. (1988) Planta 173, 12–21.
11) Ghanothakis, D.F., Demetriou, D.M. and Yokum, C.J. (1987) Biochim. Biophys. Acta 891, 15–21.
12) Barbato, R., Rigoni, F., Giardi, M.T. and Giacometti, G.M. (1989) FEBS Lett. 251, 147–154.
13) Dainese, P., Di Paolo, M.L., Silvestri, M. and Bassi, R. (1989) These proceedings.
14) Bassi, R., Ghiretti–Magaldi, A., Tognon, G., Giacometti, G.M. and Miller, K. (1989) Eur. J. Cell Biol. in the press.
15) McCauley, S.W. and Melis, A. (1986) Biochim. Biophys. Acta 849, 175–182.

STRUCTURE OF THE LIGHT-HARVESTING CHLOROPHYLL a/b PROTEIN COMPLEX BY HIGH-RESOLUTION ELECTRON CRYSTALLOGRAPHY

Werner Kühlbrandt
European Molecular Biology Laboratory
Postfach 10.2209, Meyerhofstr. 1, D-6900 Heidelberg, F.R.Germany

1. Introduction

High-resolution electron crystallography (1,2) is emerging as an alternative to X-ray crystallography for determining the structure of biological macromolecules at near-atomic resolution. The technique combines electron diffraction, high-resolution electron microscopy and image processing. Crystals for electron crystallography need to be very thin. Crystalline monolayers, often referred to as two-dimensional crystals, are ideal. With membrane proteins, order in two dimensions may be easier to achieve than in three dimensions. Indeed, many membrane proteins tend to form two-dimensional crystals. A well-known example is bacteriorhodopsin which occurs naturally in highly ordered two-dimensional arrays. Two-dimensional crystals can also be grown from purified detergent-solubilized membrane proteins, as is the case with the light-harvesting chlorophyll a/b-protein complex (LHC-II) (3) and bacterial porins (4,5).

LHC-II forms small, partly ordered arrays upon precipitation of the detergent-solubilized complex with mono- and divalent cations. Large two-dimensional crystals form when the rate of precipitation is reduced (3). The structure of these two-dimensional crystals has been determined previously at comparatively low resolution by electron microscopy and image analysis. A study of their surface topography showed that the crystals formed a hexagonal mesh in which only about half of the space was occupied by the complex (6). A three-dimensional map of the LHC-II at 16 Å (1Å = 0.1 nm) was derived from two-dimensional crystals contrasted with negative stain (3). This map showed that the complex was a trimer and that the crystals had p321 symmetry. Very similar crystalline arrays were obtained by incorporating spinach LHC-II into lipid vesicles. Cryo-electron microscopy of these arrays embedded in vitreous ice revealed the structure at low resolution in projection (7) and showed that it was similar, but not identical to the pea complex. A projection map at 7 Å resolution was obtained by electron crystallography of thin three-dimensional crystals of pea LHC-II (8) but these proved to be unsuitable for high-resolution

M. Baltscheffsky (ed.), Current Research in Photosynthesis, Vol. II, 217–222.
© 1990 *Kluwer Academic Publishers. Printed in the Netherlands.*

three-dimensional structure analysis. Electron diffraction of two-dimensional crystals of pea LHC-II at low temperature showed that they were in fact highly ordered and thus provided excellent specimens for high-resolution structure analysis by electron crystallography (9).

2. An outline of the method

2.1 Crystallization
Large (3 - 7 µm diam.) two-dimensional crystals of pea LHC-II form by dialysis of the detergent-solubilized complex at 35 - 40 °C against monovalent cations (3), or upon heating to this temperature in the presence of KCl and glycerol. Addition of lipid is not necessary since the solubilized complex contains approximately 1.3 molecules of thylakoid lipid per molecule of chlorophyll (D.J. Chapman, personal communication).

2.2 Electron diffraction and electron microscopy
The easiest method to assess the quality of two-dimensional crystals is by electron diffraction (10). Special preparation techniques may be necessary to preserve the order of two-dimensional crystals in the electron microscope. For LHC-II, washing with a dilute (0.5 %), buffered (pH 6.0) solution of tannin has proved most successful (9). Cooling the crystals to a temperature below -100 °C is essential to reduce the effect of radiation damage which is severe at room temperature.

High-resolution electron microscopy of specimens cooled with liquid gases requires specially designed high-resolution cold stages. Several instruments exist where high-resolution images of two-dimensional crystals cooled with liquid helium (11) or liquid nitrogen (12,13) can be recorded routinely. The images used in this study were recorded in collaboration with K.H. Downing, Lawrence Berkeley Laboratory, Berkeley, Ca., on an extensively modified JEOL 100B electron microscope equipped with a field emission gun and a liquid nitrogen cooled top entry stage in the laboratory of R.M. Glaeser, University of California, Berkeley, CA. The crystals were imaged in "spot-scan" mode (14,15), whereby a coherent illuminating spot of 100 - 200 nm diameter moves across the crystal in a stepwise fashion, exposing a small area at a time. This mode of illumination reduces beam-induced movements which normally contribute to the blurring of high-resolution features in conventional flood-beam imaging.

2.3 Image processing
An excellent introduction to high-resolution image processing has been given by Henderson et al. (1). Briefly, images are screened by optical diffraction and areas of good crystalline order are digitized on a flat-bed microdensitometer. Typically, image areas measuring 4000 x 4000 to 6000 x 6000 image points are scanned with stepsizes of 7 to 10 µm.

The lattice of a real two-dimensional crystal is never perfect, partly because of physical distortions of the two-dimensional crystals on the carbon support film and, to a lesser extent, because of electron optical distortions introduced by the electron microscope. Both types of distortion cause loss of high-resolution detail if different parts of the image are averaged when its Fourier transform is calculated. The distortions can however be detected by cross-correlation of the image with a small reference area in its centre. Once the distortions are known they can be corrected by re-interpolation of the original digitized image.

A Fourier transform of the distortion-corrected image yields amplitudes and phases of structure factors to high resolution. The phase information is retained since the Fourier transform is generated by computer from an image of the crystal and not by recording a diffraction pattern, as in X-ray crystallography. The phase problem which is the fundamental problem of X-ray crystallography therefore does not arise.

Fourier coefficients at lattice positions with amplitudes significantly above the noise level are selected. The phases are corrected for effects of the contrast transfer function, objective lens astigmatism and beam tilt. Corrected phases from several processed images are merged and combined with electron diffraction amplitudes. Finally, the Fourier coefficients are averaged according to the crystal symmetry. Programs for processing images and electron diffraction patterns were written and kindly made available by R. Henderson and J.M. Baldwin, MRC Laboratory of Molecular Biology, Cambridge.

Inverse Fourier transformation of the corrected, averaged structure factors yields a map which is a projection of the structure onto a plane perpendicular to the incident electron beam, at a resolution determined by the diffraction order of the Fourier terms contributing to it.

3. The structure of LHC-II at 3.7 Å resolution in projection

A projection map of LHC-II at 3.7 Å resolution is shown in Fig. 1. Phases were derived from three processed images and amplitudes were averaged over three electron diffraction patterns. The projection is onto the plane of the two-dimensional crystal which coincides with the plane of the thylakoid membrane. The unit cell ($a = 127$ Å, $\gamma = 120°$) contains two trimers of the complex. One of these is oriented as in the thylakoid membrane, whereas the other is rotated by 180° with respect to an axis in the membrane plane, so that the two trimers appear with opposite hand in projection. Each trimer comprises three LHC-II polypeptides of 25,000 molecular mass, with their associated chlorophylls, xanthophylls and lipids. LHC-II is known to exist as a trimer when solubilized in non-ionic detergents (16) and there is good evidence that the trimeric con-figuration is required for the proper function of the complex (17). The map therefore seems to show the structure of native LHC-II. The projection suggests a division of the trimer into three monomers but the molecular

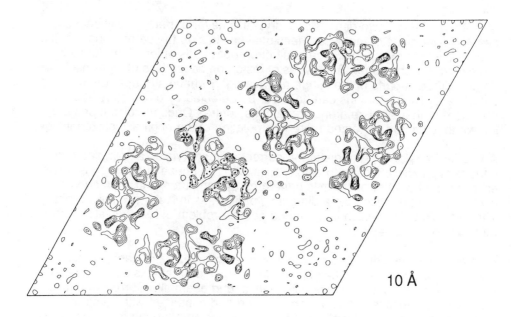

Figure 1   Projection map of one unit cell of two-dimensional crystals of LHC-II at 3.7 Å resolution.

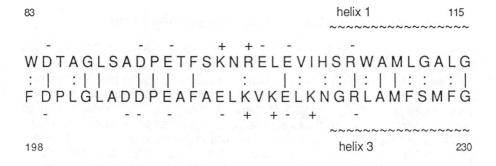

```
83                                                    helix 1              115
                                                      ~~~~~~~~~~~~~~~~~~~~~~~
      -            -   -        + +- -        -
W D T A G L S A D P E T F S K N R E L E V I H S R W A M L G A L G
: |  : | |    | | |  |    :     | :  : : | : | | : :  : |
F D P L G L A D D P E A F A E L K V K E L K N G R L A M F S M F G
-            - -  -      - + +- +      -
                                                      ~~~~~~~~~~~~~~~~~~~~~~~
198                                                   helix 3             230
```

Figure 2   Internal homology within the amino acid sequence of pea LHC-II based on the DNA sequence of the gene (19). Dotted lines indicate similar amino acids (P. Argos, personal communication).

boundary of the monomer cannot be deduced with certainty before tracing the polypeptide chain in a three-dimensional map. Therefore, any other division of the trimer into monomers should be considered as equally likely for the time being.

Most of the contrast in Fig.1 probably arises from the polypeptide which accounts for more than 60 % of the molecular mass of the complex. Judging from the projection map, LHC-II does not resemble the structure of bacterio-rhodopsin (1, 2) or porin (4,5), both of which have been solved by electron crystallography at comparable resolution in projection. In particular, the map shows only one peak that, by comparison with the projection map of bacterio-rhodopsin, has the shape and dimensions expected for a membrane-spanning α-helix running perpendicular to the membrane plane (asterisk in Fig. 1). On this evidence, it would seem that the two other membrane-spanning α-helices that have been predicted from the polypeptide sequence (18,19) either do not run perpendicular to the membrane plane or are obscured by superposition with parts of the complex that project beyond the membrane surface.

A striking feature of the map is the near two-fold symmetry of two regions which appear roughly chevron-shaped in projection (dotted lines in Fig. 1). This suggested the existence of two structural domains within the monomer of possible structural and functional homology. Fig. 2 shows the results of a self-comparison of the amino acid sequence of pea LHC-II (18) which revealed extensive homology between two regions that include the first half of the predicted helices 1 and 3 (19) (P.Rice and P.Argos, personal communication). A similar internal homology has also been found in LHC-II from tomato (20). The significance of this homology is not yet clear but since the domain in question is almost certainly involved in chlorophyll binding it is bound to have implications for the function of LHC-II as a molecular antenna.

The position of individual pigment molecules is not revealed in the projection map. However, since each monomer has to accommodate 15 molecules of chlorophyll (16) and several xanthophylls, it seems likely that at least some of them are contained in the internal space of the trimer. Several small circular centres of density around the periphery of the trimer may represent lipid mole-cules or carotenoids seen end on. The large, almost featureless area in the remainder of the unit cell may be occupied by disordered detergent, tannin or lipid.

The three-dimensional structure analysis of LHC-II by high-resolution electron crystallography of two-dimensional crystals is in progress.

References

1   Henderson, R., Baldwin, J.M., Downing, K.H., Lepault, J. and Zemlin, F. (1986) Ultramicroscopy **19**, 147-178
2   Baldwin, J.M., Henderson, R:, Beckmann, E. and Zemlin, F. (1988) J.Mol.Biol. **202**, 585-591
3   Kühlbrandt, W. (1984) Nature **307**, 478-480
4   Sass, H.J., Massalski, A., Beckmann, E., Büldt, G., Dorset, D., van Heel, M., Rosenbusch, J.P., Zeitler, E. and Zemlin, F. (1988) Proc. 46th Annu. Meet. Electron Micr.Soc.Am. (G.W. Bailey, ed). San Francisco Press, San Francisco,CA., U.S.A.
5   Jap, B.K. (1989) J. Mol. Biol. **205**, 407-419
6   Kühlbrandt, W., Thaler, T and Wehrli, E. (1983) J. Cell Biol. **96**, 1414-1424
7   Lyon, M.K. and Unwin. P.N.T. (1988) J. Cell Biol. **106**, 1515-1523
8   Kühlbrandt, W. (1988) J. Mol. Biol. **202**, 849-864
9   Kühlbrandt, W. and Downing, K.H. (1989) J.Mol.Biol. **207**, 823-828
10 Amos, L.A., Henderson, R. and Unwin, P.N.T (1982) Proc. Biophys. Molec. Biol. **39**, 183-231
11 Dietrich, I., Fox, F., Knapek, E., Lefranc, G., Nachtrieb, K., Weyl, R. and Zerbst, H. (1977) Ultramicroscopy **2**, 241-249
12 Hayward, S.B. and Glaeser, R.M. (1980) Ultramicroscopy **5**, 3-8
13 Henderson, R., Raeburn, C. and Vigers, G., manuscript submitted
14 Downing, K.H. and Glaeser, R.M. (1986) Ultramicroscopy **20**, 269-278
15 Bullough, P. and Henderson, R. (1987) Ultramicroscopy **21**, 223-230
16 Butler, P.J.G. and Kühlbrandt, W. (1988) Proc. Natl. Acad. Sci. USA **85**, 3797-3801
17 Ide, J.P., Klug, D., Kühlbrandt, W., Giorgi, L.B. and Porter, G. (1987) Biochim. Biophys. Acta **893**, 349-364
18 Cashmore, A.R. (1984) Proc. Natl. Acad. Sci. USA **81**, 2960-2964
19 Karlin-Neumann, G.A., Kohorn, B.D., Thornber, J.P. and Tobin, E.M. (1985) J. Mol. Appl. Gen. **3**, 45-61
20 Hoffman, N.E., Pichersky, E., Malik, V.S., Castresana, C., Ko, K., Darr, S.C. and Cashmore, A.R. (1987) Proc. Natl. Acad. Sci. USA **84,** 8844-8848

THE FUNCTIONAL ORGANIZATION OF THE ANTENNA SYSTEMS IN HIGHER PLANTS AND GREEN ALGAE AS STUDIED BY TIME–RESOLVED FLUORESCENCE TECHNIQUES

Alfred R. Holzwarth

Max–Planck–Institut für Strahlenchemie, Stiftstr. 34 – 36, 4330 Mülheim/Ruhr, FRG

1. INTRODUCTION

The excitation energy absorbed by photosynthetic light–harvesting pigments is transported in a series of ultrafast energy transfer steps in a time of tens of picoseconds to special supramolecular structures, the reaction centers, where it is used for photochemical charge separation. The scope of this contribution is focused primarily on a discussion of the progress achieved recently in our understanding of the ultrafast energy transfer and trapping processes in intact systems, i.e. higher plant chloroplasts and green algae. Important insights into these processes have been obtained by the application of ultrafast laser techniques (see (1) for a review). However, over the recent years seemingly conflicting results have been reported by various research groups. On the one hand that may be not very surprising in view of the complexity in the organization of the photosynthetic membranes. On the other hand it should be examined thoroughly whether these contradictory interpretations are really justified by the available data. In order to shed light on these controversial topics I shall try to address the following questions:

i) is the overall exciton decay trap–limited or diffusion–limited,

ii) how many kinetic components can we identify in the exciton decay of intact systems as measured by time–resolved fluorescence methods and what is the origin of these components,

iii) which are appropriate kinetic models to rationalize the observed data,

iv) which of these components are actually due to exciton migration (energy transfer) and which ones reflect reaction center processes, and

v) why did different groups arrive at quite different interpretations of the exciton kinetics?

Before discussing data on intact systems I shall first present some results from isolated photosystem (PS) I and PS II particles. It will become clear from the discussion that the energy transfer processes in the photosystems of oxygen–evolving photosynthesis are intimately related with the primary charge separation processes in the reaction centers.

2. RESULTS AND DISCUSSION

Isolated Photosystem I

Several research groups have measured the Chlorophyll (Chl) fluorescence kinetics of PS I particles from different sources. While in large–size particles (Chl/P700 $\geq$ 100) at least two fast decay components of about 10 – 30 ps and 80 – 150 ps were observed at room temperature the smaller particles showed only one fast decay component in the $\leq$100 ps range whose lifetime was found to be proportional to the antenna size (see (1) for a review). None of these studies reported a risetime (negative amplitude) component in the fluorescence kinetics which would be expected as a direct indication for energy transfer between different Chl pigment pools. A fast rising component at room temperature was found recently for the first time in a PS I preparation from Synechococcus sp. with an antenna size of ~ 100

M. Baltscheffsky (ed.), Current Research in Photosynthesis, Vol. II, 223–230.

Chl/P700 (2). The observation of a riseterm allows for a straightforward interpretation of the data (c.f. Fig. 1). The 37$\pm$3 ps component represents the trap–limited overall exciton decay kinetics by charge separation at P700 while the fast component with negative amplitude at long wavelengths represents the antenna equilibration time between two different pigment pools. Since the latter is by a factor of 3 – 4 faster than the overall exciton decay, the exciton kinetics is clearly trap–limited. This conclusion is not specific to PS I from cyanobacteria. Similar data were found also for a PS I–enriched stroma thylakoid fragment from spinach (2). In analogy to the cyanobacterial system in spinach PS I the fastest component shows again a negative amplitude at long wavelengths due to ultrafast exciton equilibration. The 60 ps and 135 ps components represent the overall exciton trapping times (c.f. Fig. 2). With intact higher plant thylakoids and green algae an ultrafast antenna equilibration component of similar properties as in the isolated systems was also observed (3,4).

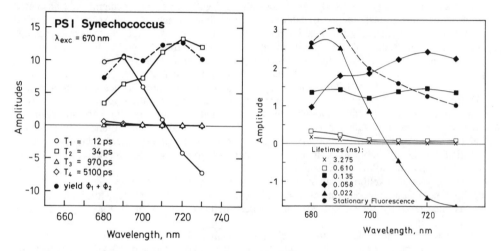

Fig. 1: (left) Decay–associated fluorescence spectra (DAS) of PS I particles from Synechococcus at 5°C upon excitation at 670 nm.
Fig. 2: (right) Decay–associated fluorescence spectra (DAS) of stroma thylakoid PS I particles from spinach (PS I Y100) at 5°C upon excitation at 670 nm. The dashed lines indicate the steady–state emission spectra.

A minimal kinetic scheme employing only two pigment pools to explain the observations for PS I is shown in Fig. 3 (2). The actual situation is likely to be more complex in some cases, however. The finding of a trap–limited kinetics for PS I is in contrast to the hypothesis of Owens et al. (5,6) of a nearly diffusion–limited kinetics. This discrepancy in the interpretations may be due either to a failure of the latter authors to resolve the fast risetime in their samples (which for smaller PS I particles might be actually below 10 ps) or due to structural modifications in the Chl antennae of their PS I particles caused by stripping of a large part of the antenna complexes by detergents. If the latter were the case, the kinetic properties of the smaller antenna size particles would probably not be characteristic for the intact PS I units which are present in higher plants, green algae and cyanobacteria. On the basis of our results we conclude that in general intact PS I shows at least two fluorescence lifetime components at room temperature, i.e. one ultrafast exciton equilibration component with lifetimes $\leq$25 ps and the trap–limited overall exciton decay with lifetimes in the 30 – 150 ps time range, depending on the antenna size and the detailed antenna structure.

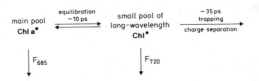

Fig. 3: Kinetic scheme explaining the picosecond fluorescence data from <u>Synechococcus</u> PS I particles. The same scheme holds also for PS I Y100 particles when the corresponding lifetimes are used (c.f. Fig. 2).

Isolated Photosystem II
It has been shown recently that the exciton decay kinetics of PS II both with open (primary quinone Q_A oxidized) or closed (primary quinone reduced) reaction centers is biexponential (7). A kinetic model has been developed which attributes this biexponentiality to the reversible primary charge separation in the reaction centers according to the kinetic scheme shown in   Fig. 4 (8,9). Neither of the two observed fluorescence lifetimes is due to energy transfer in this model. Rather they both reflect the reaction center processes. We call this the "exciton/radical pair equilibrium" model which describes a trap–limited overall kinetics for the excitons, in agreement with the experimental data. The exciton equilibration in the antenna is about an order of magnitude faster than the charge separation processes. For isolated PS II this model has been tested in detail by various independent techniques (9,10) and the rate constants for charge separation, charge recombination, and charge stabilization (for open centers) have been determined. A particularly important parameter in this context which presents a critical test of the model, is the charge separation time for the hypothetical isolated PS II (open) reaction centers, i.e. free from antenna effects. This time was predicted within this model to be ~2.8 ps (9) in excellent agreement with the recently directly measured time of ~3 ps (11).

An alternative model for the PS II exciton kinetics has been developed by Butler and coworkers many years ago (12). This "bipartite model" (Fig. 5) was originally developed to describe steady state fluorescence data only. An extension of this model taking into account heterogeneity in the antenna structure is known as "tripartite model". The bipartite model has been reformulated more recently to describe fluorescence kinetics also and it has been tested on experimental data (13,14).

Both the exciton/radical pair equilibrium model and the bipartite model predict formally the same kinetics and thus both give rise also to a biexponential fluorescence decay. However, the two models are fundamentally different. This difference consists in the entirely different meaning of the rate constants involved and thus in the entirely different origin of the two observed lifetimes. In the bipartite model the biexponentiality is due to the equilibration of the excitons between antenna and reaction center. Thus one of the lifetime components reflects an energy transfer process. In contrast to the exciton/radical pair equilibrium model the bipartite model basically describes a diffusion–limited kinetics. Despite the fact that it formally can describe correctly the observed kinetics, the application of the bipartite model on experimental data leads to physically unreasonable results. First it results in a charge separation time in the reaction centers which is by one to two orders of magnitude too high, as compared to known values (13,14). Second, a drastic change in the energy transfer rate constants between antenna and reaction centers is predicted when closing the reaction centers (14). Such a change in rate constants is unreasonable on physical grounds. Third, it predicts a very slow (up to 500 ps) exciton equilibration time between antenna and reaction centers and/or between different pigment pools which is inconsistent with efficient light–harvesting.

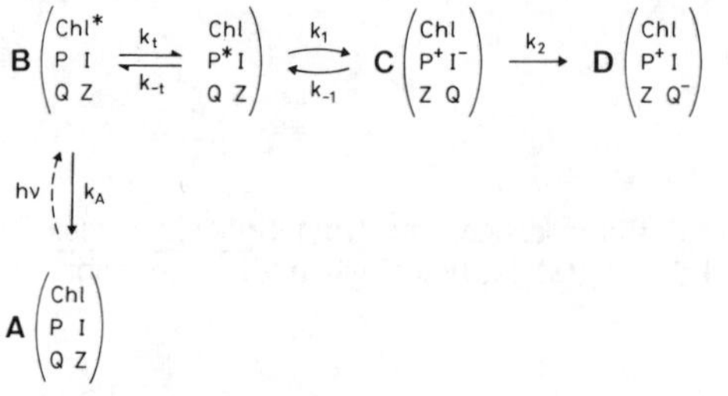

$$B \begin{pmatrix} Chl^* \\ P\ I \\ Q\ Z \end{pmatrix} \underset{k_{-t}}{\overset{k_t}{\rightleftharpoons}} \begin{pmatrix} Chl \\ P^*I \\ Q\ Z \end{pmatrix} \underset{k_{-1}}{\overset{k_1}{\rightleftharpoons}} C \begin{pmatrix} Chl \\ P^+I^- \\ Z\ Q \end{pmatrix} \overset{k_2}{\longrightarrow} D \begin{pmatrix} Chl \\ P^+I \\ Z\ Q^- \end{pmatrix}$$

$$hv \Big\downarrow k_A$$

$$A \begin{pmatrix} Chl \\ P\ I \\ Q\ Z \end{pmatrix}$$

Fig. 4: Kinetic scheme of the "exciton/radical pair equilibrium model" (8,9).

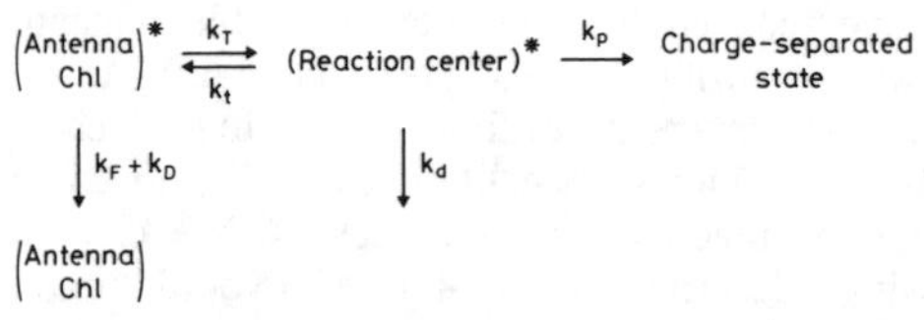

$$\begin{pmatrix} Antenna \\ Chl \end{pmatrix}^* \underset{k_t}{\overset{k_T}{\rightleftharpoons}} (Reaction\ center)^* \overset{k_P}{\longrightarrow} \begin{array}{c} Charge\text{-separated} \\ state \end{array}$$

$$\Big\downarrow k_F + k_D \qquad\qquad \Big\downarrow k_d$$

$$\begin{pmatrix} Antenna \\ Chl \end{pmatrix}$$

Fig. 5: Kinetic scheme of the "bipartite model" (12).

We must therefore exclude the bipartite model as a valid description of the PS II exciton kinetics. In contrast the exciton/radical pair equilibrium model properly describes the experimental data (9). When discussing the kinetics of intact photosynthetic systems it will be important to keep in mind that all fluorescence kinetic measurements up to now have been interpreted – either explicitly or more often implicitly – in terms of either of these two models.

Intact systems
Assuming that the two photosystems behave similarly with respect to their exciton kinetics in the isolated forms and in the intact thylakoids, we can make an estimate for the complexity and number of fluorescence decay components expected for the integral systems. Following the above discussion we expect for PS I at least two components in the range of 10 – 20 ps and $\geq$50 ps. PS II in either of the extreme cases of fully open or fully closed centers is expected to show a biexponential kinetics with lifetimes $\geq$ 100 ps according to the exiton/radical pair equilibrium model. In addition an ultrafast antenna equilibration for either of the two photosystems may be expected. Since there is ample evidence that the PS II pool is heterogeneous, consisting of PS IIα– and PS IIβ–units in higher plants and green algae, this doubles the number of possible PS II components because each of them may have its own set of rate constants and lifetimes. Evidence for this was obtained already in earlier work (15,16). Adding up, we expect a minimum of 4 – 5 components assuming a homogeneous PS II pool only and a maximum of 6 – 7 components in the case of heterogeneous PS II. This estimate holds only for the simplest extreme cases of fully open or fully closed PS II centers. At intermediate cases the kinetics will be even more complex due to the mixing of contributions from open and closed PS II center kinetics.

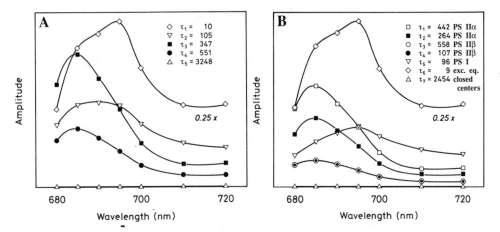

Fig. 6: Decay–associated emission spectra (DAS) of <u>Scenedesmus</u> <u>obl.</u> with open PS II reaction centers (F_o–state). Excitation at 630 nm. (see (19) for more details). The lifetimes are given in ps. (A): Results from the global sums–of–exponentials analysis. (B): Results from the global target analysis of the same data set.

Experimentally, from single–photon timing data of Chl fluorescence, typically 3 or 4 kinetic components have been resolved at either F_o– or F_{max}–conditions (1). This refers to data obtained by either the conventional single–decay analysis methods or the more powerful global analysis method. More recently 5 components have been resolved (17). Even in the latter case the experimentally resolved kinetics is less complex than the theoretically expected one when taking into account the PS II heterogeneity. We suggest that the discrepancy between the actual kinetics and the so far resolvable kinetics for intact systems is the main cause for the discrepancies between the different research groups in the interpretation of the data. In fact comparing the data from all research groups reveals that the actual differences in the data are relatively small (1). They can be explained by slight sample differences, differences in time–resolution of the different instruments and analysis procedures used and also in the signal/noise ratio of the data. We feel that, despite some significant differences in the data, the contradictory interpretations given in the literature by different research groups are not justified. Instead we believe that the differences may in fact be caused by the lack of testing of alternative quantitative kinetic models. In fact most groups preferred a more qualitative interpretation of the data altogether. In view of the complexity of the systems studied, qualitative reasoning alone is clearly insufficient to distinguish between different models, however. A further important aspect concerns the so far employed analysis procedures which do not allow the full resolution of kinetic data of the expected complexity, as can be shown by simulations.

As a possible way out of the dilemma pointed out above we recently employed a new data analysis procedure known as "target analysis" (18). The rational behind this method consists in the replacement of the sum–of–exponentials fitting by a fitting of kinetic models which are described by discrete sets of kinetic parameters, i.e. rate constants. Several different models may be tested against the data for finding out the most appropriate one. The important point is that this method is combined with the advantages of the previously used global analysis procedure. In addition, in view of the complexity of the problem, data with an extremely high signal/noise ratio are absolutely mandatory. We have applied this procedure to the fluorescence kinetic data from both green algae and higher plant chloroplasts. The results (examples are shown in Figs. 6 and 7) are very promising (19).

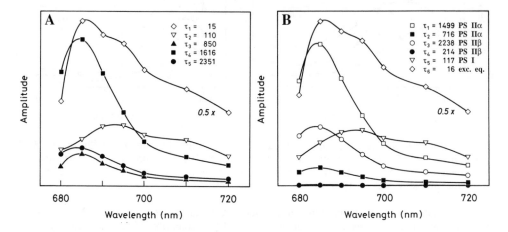

Fig. 7: Decay–associated emission spectra (DAS) of Scenedesmus obl. with closed PS II reaction centers (F_{max}–state). Excitation at 630 nm. (see (19) for more details). The lifetimes are given in ps. (A): Results from the global sums–of–exponentials analysis. (B): Results from the global target analysis of the same data set.

Table 1: Lifetimes τ_i obtained by global target analysis of the fluorescence decays from intact Scenedesmus obl. assuming the heterogeneous exciton/radical pair equilibrium model for PS II. Data are given for open (F_0) and closed (F_{max}) PS II centers.

State	Assignment	τ_1, ns	τ_2, ns
F_0	PS II α	0.26 – 0.33	0.44 – 0.55
	PS II β	0.10 – 0.13	0.53 – 0.57
	PS I	0.094 – 0.096	----
exciton equilibration		0.01 – 0.02	----
F_{max}	α	0.70 – 0.74	1.51 – 1.52
	β	0.12 – 0.15	2.25 – 2.26
	PS I	0.114 – 0.118	----
exciton equilibration		0.01 – 0.02	----

Applying the exciton/radical pair equilibrium model for PS II, the target analysis shows that the PS II pool is indeed heterogeneous. The data obtained from fluorescence lifetimes in this respect are in good agreement with the results of other studies on the α,β–heterogeneity (20). The target analysis predicts about 15 – 20% of all PS II Chls to be organized in PS II β–units in Scenedesmus, which seems to be typical for green algae. Apart from their antenna size α– and β–units differ substantially in their rate constants of charge recombination and charge stabilization... Furthermore β–units are predicted to show a larger F_{max}/F_0–ratio in the fluorescence induction. This is an important result that indicates that the antenna size is neither the only one nor the most important difference between PS IIα– and β–units. The rate constants determined by target analysis for the reaction center processes in α– and β–centers may be useful to elucidate the functional role of these units.

Table 1 collects the lifetimes obtained by global target analysis for the fluorescence kinetics of the green alga Scenedesmus obl.. Figs. 6 and 7 show also the relationship between the set of mixed lifetimes obtained by global lifetime analysis on the one hand and the more resolved set obtained by target analysis on the other hand. From this comparison it can be understood easily why it was not possible in previous work to resolve the components. At least 6 lifetime components could be resolved by target analysis at both F_o– and F_{max}–conditions. Four of them are due to the biexponential PS II kinetics of the heterogeneous PS II pool. These lifetimes change upon closing the PS II centers. The other components are independent of the PS II reaction center state. One of them is due to PS I ($\sim$ 100 ps). Another, ultrafast component (10 – 20 ps) arises from antenna equilibration within both PS I and PS II units.

3. CONCLUSIONS
It is concluded that the exciton kinetics in PS II is now quite well understood. The PS II kinetics is well explained by the exciton/radical pair equilibrium model. Difficulties exist in the analysis of the PS II kinetics in intact systems due to the PS II heterogeneity. These difficulties can be overcome now by global target analysis of high signal/noise ratio data. Our knowledge on the PS I exciton kinetics at present is much less detailed. Further extensive studies on various PS I preparations are still necessary along with the development of appropriate kinetic models. Judging from our data on spinach thylakoids our description of the PS I kinetics in the intact system may be still oversimplified. There exists clear experimental evidence that the overall exciton decay in the antennae of both photosystems is trap–limited and not diffusion–limited.

4. ACKNOWLEDGEMENTS
The work cited from this laboratory has been supported in part by the Deutsche Forschungsgemeinschaft. I thank all my coworkers for their fruitful cooperation. I also should like to thank Prof. K. Schaffner for encouragement and support.

5. REFERENCES
(1)   Holzwarth,A.R., (1989). in: The Chlorophylls, CRC Critical Reviews,
         Uniscience Series (H. Scheer ed.). CRC press, Boca Raton, in press.
(2)   Holzwarth,A.R., Haehnel,W., Ratajczak,R., Bittersmann,E. and Schatz,G.H.,
         (1989). Progr. Photosynth. Res. this volume.
(3)   McCauley,S.W., Bittersmann,E., and Holzwarth,A.R., (1989).
         FEBS Lett. 249: 285–288.
(4)   Bittersmann,E. and Holzwarth,A.R., (1989). Biophys. J. in print.
(5)   Owens,T.G., Webb,S.P., Mets,L., Alberte,R.S., and Fleming,G.R., (1987).
         Proc. Natl. Acad. Sci. USA 84: 1532–1536.
(6)   Owens,T.G., Webb,S.P., Alberte,R.S., Mets,L., and Fleming,G.R., (1988).
         Biophys. J.   53: 733–745.
(7)   Schatz,G.H., Brock,H., and Holzwarth,A.R., (1987).
         Proc. Natl. Acad. Sci. USA 84: 8414–8418.
(8)   Schatz,G.H. and Holzwarth,A.R., (1986). Photosynth. Res. 10: 309–318.
(9)   Schatz,G.H., Brock,H., and Holzwarth,A.R., (1988). Biophys. J. 54: 397–405.
(10)   Leibl,W., Breton,J., Deprez,J., and Trissl,H.–W., (1989).
         Photosynth. Res. in print.

(11) Wasielewski,M.R., Johnson,D.G., Seibert,M., and Govindjee,, (1989).
      Proc. Natl. Acad. Sci. USA 86: 524–528.
(12) Butler,W.L., (1978). Annu. Rev. Plant Physiol. 29: 345–378.
(13) Berens,S.J., Scheele,J., Butler,W.L., and Magde,D., (1985).
      Photochem. Photobiol. 42: 59–68.
(14) Sparrow,R., Evans,E.H., Brown,R.G., and Shaw,D., (1989).
      J. Photochem. Photobiol. B 3: 65–79.
(15) Bittersmann,E., Senger,H., and Holzwarth,A.R., (1987).
      J. Photochem. Photobiol. 1: 247–260.
(16) Wendler,J. and Holzwarth,A.R., (1987). Biophys. J. 52: 717–728.
(17) Roelofs,T.A. and Holzwarth,A.R., (1989). Biophys. J. submitted:
(18) Löfroth,J.-E., (1986). J. Phys. Chem. 90: 1160–1168.
(19) Lee,C.-H., Roelofs,T.A., and Holzwarth,A.R., (1989). this volume.
(20) Melis,A., (1984). J. Cell. Biol. 24: 271–285.

SELECTIVE CLEAVAGE OF THE LHCP PRECURSOR MAY DETERMINE
THE RELATIVE ABUNDANCE OF THE TWO MATURE FORMS
(~26 AND 25 kD) FOUND IN VIVO.

Gayle K. Lamppa, Steven E. Clark, and Mark S. Abad
Dept. of Molecular Genetics and Cell Biology, University of Chicago, 920 E.
58th St., Chicago, IL 60637 USA

1.   INTRODUCTION
      The import of proteins into the chloroplast is a complex process, including
1) targeting of the precursor protein to the organelle, 2) binding to the envelope via
a "receptor", 3) translocation across the envelope, 4) intraorganellar localization to
the correct compartment and 5) proteolytic processing to remove the transit
peptide. Although this basic outline is known, the mechanism underlying these
steps is not understood, nor is the temporal relationship between the last three
clearly defined. We are investigating the import of the major light-harvesting
chlorophyll a/b binding protein (LHCP) associated with PSII, which is
synthesized with a ~34 amino acid transit peptide. Specifically, we have
investigated the determinants that reside in the structure of pLHCP itself that are
essential for import, localization to the thylakoids and processing. In vivo LHCII
is composed of two major polypeptides of ~26 and 25 kD. The origin of these
forms has not been previously resolved, although we have recently presented
evidence that pLHCP generated from a single wheat gene can give rise to these
two forms during in vitro import into chloroplasts (1). Multiple forms of mature
protein have also been obtained whether the pLHCP gene originates from pea (2),
tomato (3), corn (4) or Lemna (5). On the other hand, we find that in an
organelle-free reaction optimized for pLHCP cleavage only the 25 kD peptide is
released (1, 6). Here we summarize our recent results which show that mature
LHCP contains the information necessary for its localization to the thylakoids (7),
that processing is not coupled to translocation into the organelle, and finally, that a
single LHCP precursor substrate can be genetically modified so that either the 25
kD or 26 kD form becomes the sole product of an import reaction, and cleavage in
the organelle-free assay is inhibited (8).

2.   PROCEDURE
2.1   Materials and Methods
              2.1.1. Transcription, translation, and import reactions. The
              procedures used have been previously described (1). A wheat gene
              (9) was inserted 3' to the SP6 promoter and the transcripts produced
              using SP6 polymerase were translated in either a wheat germ or
              reticulocyte lysate. After import reactions, the pea chloroplasts were
              either left untreated and hypotonically lysed, or treated with
              thermolysin to remove proteins on the exterior. Membrane and
              soluble fractions were separated by centrifugation and analyzed by
              SDS-PAGE.

M. Baltscheffsky (ed.), Current Research in Photosynthesis, Vol. II, 231–236.
© 1990 *Kluwer Academic Publishers. Printed in the Netherlands.*

2.1.2 <u>Organelle-free processing.</u> A soluble chloroplast extract was prepared as described and the reactions carried out as optimized (6).

3.   RESULTS AND DISCUSSION
3.1   <u>Mature LHCP contains the signal for thylakoid insertion.</u>
        Radiolabeled pLHCP was synthesized in vitro from a wheat gene. We have previously addressed the point that although there are also two minor forms of the precursor synthesized, the 31 kD polypeptide is the most abundant, cross-reacts with LHCP-specific antibody, and alone yields the two mature forms (1). The in vitro approach allows us to mutagenize the pLHCP gene and subsequently produce modified forms of the precursor that can be used in import assays with isolated chloroplasts. Thus, we can determine how structural changes in pLHCP affect different steps of the import pathway.

3.2   To determine if the cognate transit peptide of pLHCP was essential for transport into the chloroplast, as well as for localization and insertion of the mature protein into the thylakoids, it was replaced with the transit peptide of the precursor of the small subunit (pS) of Rubisco. The hybrid protein contains the 47 amino acid transit peptide of pS and the first four amino acids of mature S linked to mature LHCP. Thus, it contains the cleavage site of pS and the putative cleavage of LHCP identified previously (10) at methionine 34 (met34). When this hybrid protein was used in an import reaction, it was successfully imported, processed and localized to the membrane fraction. To demonstrate that it was indeed associated with the thylakoids, the envelopes were separated using sucrose step gradients. Although the pLHCP was found in the envelope fraction, only the thylakoids contained the mature LHCP (7). Evidence was also presented that the protein was resistant to extraction by 0.1 N NaOH, indicating that the protein was not peripherally associated with the thylakoids. To refine that analysis, we have also examined the orientation of the protein in the thylakoids using trypsin, which has been found to remove only the N-terminus of LHCP yielding a ~24 kD resistant product if it is correctly inserted (10). Figure 1 shows the results of digesting the thylakoid membranes with trypsin after an import reaction using either the wild type precursor or the hybrid protein. Both of these substrates produce the same size resistant product. Taken together, these results demonstrate that LHCP can be transported into the chloroplast by the transit peptide of S, and most importantly, upon import it is processed and correctly integrated into the thylakoids. Thus, it is not the transit peptide that contains the essential information for this latter step, but mature LHCP itself contains the signal for intraorganellar routing.

3.3   <u>Separation of two processing events by mutagenesis at the transit peptide-mature protein junction.</u>
        The determinants of processing that reside within the structure of pLHCP were investigated by making mutations at the junction of the transit peptide and mature protein (8). Our goal was to determine the relationship between the two mature forms (~25 and 26 kD) of LHCP found upon import. We first deleted the putative cleavage at methionine 34, including the residues asn33-met34-arg35, producing the mutant pΔ3. When this modified precursor

was used in an import reaction, it was translocated into the organelle and radiolabeled protein was localized to the thylakoids. However, pΔ3 was processed to only one form that co-migrated with the 25 kD peptide found upon import of the pLHCP. Using a chloroplast soluble extract in the organelle-free assay optimized for pLHCP, the mutant pΔ3 also gave rise to only a 25 kD peptide. We conclude that deletion of the cleavage site at met34, which we refer to as the primary cleavage site, does not affect processing at a downstream, secondary site in pLHCP.

3.4   Two additional mutants with changes in the transit peptide-mature protein junction domain were created. In the mutant p+4 four amino acids were inserted immediately at the N-terminus of the mature protein, and arg35 was converted to proline. These changes disrupted an alpha-helix that is predicted to extend through this domain based on the method of Garnier-Osguthorpe-Robson (11), and a cluster of basic residues surrounding met34. In the insertion mutant p+4alpha, the predicted alpha-helix was retained, but the distribution of the basic residues was still altered. Our results have shown that p+4 is imported into the chloroplast at the same efficiency as the wild type pLHCP. This mutant, however, is poorly processed, although both the primary and secondary cleavage sites were utilized. At least 60% of the thermolysin-resistant radiolabeled protein was the unprocessed precursor. Thus, transport across the chloroplast envelope can occur without processing of pLHCP, an observation also made recently for pS (12), establishing for two different precursors that processing and translocation are not obligatorily coupled. Furthermore, p+4 was inserted into the thylakoids as assessed by trypsin resistance. Nevertheless, p+4 was also a poor substrate in the organelle-free reaction, where only 5% was cleaved giving rise to the 25 kD peptide. After incubating p+4alpha with isolated chloroplasts, only one thermolysin-resistant peptide was found in the membrane fraction. In contrast to products of pΔ3 import, p+4alpha yielded only the larger processed form obtained upon import of the wild type precursor, i.e. the 26 kD peptide. An example of this reaction is shown in Figure 2. When used in an organelle-free reaction, p+4alpha was not a cleavable substrate. Thus, recognition of the secondary site was disrupted in this mutant although the alpha-helix has been maintained. The two mutants pΔ3 and p+4alpha definitively show that a single precursor substrate gives rise to two processed forms of LHCP during import into the chloroplast. Details of this analysis have been described (8).

3.5   The correlation between a mutation that affects cleavage at the secondary site during import and a loss of processing in the organelle-free reaction emphasizes that the conditions of this reaction are specific for cleavage at the secondary site of pLHCP only. However, pS is cleaved under identical conditions (6), and the processing enzyme has properties that are very similar to the enzyme that cleaves the precursors of both S and plastocyanin described earlier (13), indicating that it is a bona fide transit peptidase. Although a number of conditions have been varied, production of the 26 kD peptide from pLHCP has not been observed. Significantly, there is not an accumulation of the 26 kD peptide when cleavage at the secondary site is impaired, and thus we conclude it is not an intermediate that normally gives rise to the 25 kD peptide.

In other words, there are two separately mutable cleavage sites in pLHCP that may be used independently to give rise to the 25 and 26 kD peptides, as indicated schematically in Figure 3.

3.6   We propose as a working hypothesis that selective cleavage of pLHCP at the primary or secondary site produces the two major subpopulations of LHCII found in vivo. Utilization of the primary cleavage site results in the simple removal of the 34 amino acid transit peptide. Cleavage at the secondary site would remove both the transit peptide and a cluster of basic amino acids at the N-terminus of LHCP that has been implicated in thylakoid stacking (10). Anderson and Andersson (14) have presented a model for the organization of LHCII describing both an inner and peripheral pool of LHCP. Whereas the inner pool is composed of only the ~26 kD peptide, the peripheral pool, which shows the most significant changes in response to the light environment and during development (15, 16), contains both the ~26 kD and 25 kD peptides. Interestingly, cleavage at the secondary site, resulting in the loss of the basic N-terminus of LHCP, would make the 25 kD peptide more susceptible to the charge repulsion effect that has been proposed to accompany its preferential phosphorylation (17). From our results one prediction is that selective cleavage at either the primary or secondary site of the precursor would determine the relative abundance of the two major forms of LHCP. Thus, depending on physiological conditions, the chloroplast could regulate the size and composition of the peripheral component of LHCII. This hypothesis can be readily tested by performing in vitro import reactions using chloroplasts that have been isolated from plants grown under different light regimes, and from different stages of development.

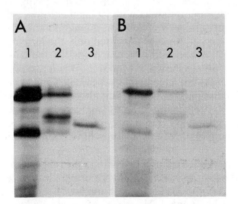

FIGURE 1. Insertion of LHCP into the thylakoids in the correct orientation following transport into the chloroplast by the transit peptide pS. RNA was transcribed from genes coding for pLHCP and the hybrid protein was translated in a wheat germ lysate, and the products (lanes 1, panel A, pLHCP; panel B, hybrid) were incubated with chloroplasts in an import reaction. The total membrane-associated proteins are shown before (lanes 2) and after (lanes 3) trypsin treatment.

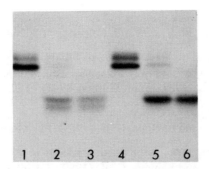

FIGURE 2. Import and processing of the precursor mutant p+4alpha produces only the ~26kD peptide. The wild type precursor (lane 1) and the mutant (lane 4), generated from a restructure gene (see Clark et al., 1989) were incubated with chloroplasts and the total membranes were analyzed from the pLHCP (lane 2) or the mutant (lane 4) reaction. Lanes 3 and 6 show the respective membrane-associated protein from thermolysin-treated chloroplasts.

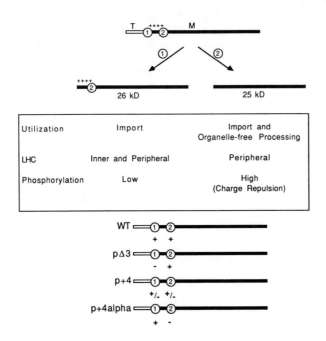

FIGURE 3. Predicted maturation of pLHCP upon import into chloroplasts. Utilization of the primary site produces the ~26 kD peptide, and the secondary cleavage site yields a 25 kD peptide lacking the basic N-terminus of LHCP. See Discussion for the possible role of these peptides in LHC (after 14) and upon phosphorylation (after 14, 17).

REFERENCES
1 Lamppa, G. K. and Abad, M. S. (1987) J. Cell Biol. 105, 2641-2648.
2 Cline, K. (1988) Plant Physiol. 86, 1120-1126.
3 Pichersky, E., Hoffman, N. E., Malik, V. S., Bernatzsky, R., Tanksley, S., Szabo, L., and Cashmore, A. J. (1987) Plant Mol. Boil. 9, 109-120.
4 Dietz, K. and Bogorad, L. (1987) Plant Physiol. 85, 816-822.
5 Kohorn, B. D., Harel, E., Chitnis, P. R., Thornber, J. P. and Tobin, E. (1986) J. Cell Biol. 102, 972-981.
6 Abad, M. S., Clark, S. E. and Lamppa, G. K. (1989) Plant Physiol. 90, 117-124.
7 Lamppa, G. (1988) J. Biol. Chem. 263,14996-14999.
8 Clark, S. E., Abad, M. E. and Lamppa, G. K. (1989) J. Biol. Chem, in press.
9 Lamppa, G., Morelli, G. and Chua, N.-H. (1985) Molec. Cell Biol. 5, 1370-1378.
10 Mullet, J. (1983) J. Biol Chem. 258, 3900-3908.
11 Garnier, J., Osguthorpe, D.J. and Robson, B. (1978) J. Mol. Biol. 120, 97-120.
12 Reiss, B., Wasmann, C., Schell, J. and Bohnert, H.J. (1989) Proc. Natl. Acad. Sci. USA 86, 886-890.
13 Robinson, C. and Ellis, J. (1984) Eur. J. Biochem. 142, 337-342.
14 Anderson, J. A. and Andersson, B. (1988) TIBS 13, 351-355.
15 Larsson, , U. K., Sunby, C. and Andersson, B. (1987a) Biochim Biophys. Acta 894, 59-68.
16 Larsson, U. K., Anderson, J. M. and Andersson, B. (1987b) Biochim. Biophys. Acta 894, 69-75.
17 Bennet, J. (1983) Biochem. J. 212, 1-13.

THE EXTRACTION AND ASSAY OF REFRACTORY CHLOROPHYLLS AND A SIMPLE
METHOD TO CORRECT DATA FROM ARNON'S EQUATIONS

ROBERT J. PORRA
Division of Plant Industry, Commonwealth
Scientific and Industrial Research
Organization, GPO Box 1600, Canberra, ACT 2601,
Australia

1. CORRECTION OF DATA FROM ARNON'S EQUATIONS

In 1941, Mackinney (1) published specific extinction coefficients
(α; $g/l^{-1}/cm^{-1}$) for chlorophylls (Chls) a and b dissolved in 80%
aqueous acetone. Also in 1941, Arnon (2) used these coefficients to
derive his now-famous simultaneous equations for solving Chl a and b
concentrations in the same solvent. Many workers (3-6) have since
shown that Mackinney's coefficients were low, especially those of Chl
b, and published more accurate equations but there has been a
reluctance to use them probably because no conversion factors were
provided to correct older data: researchers seemed reluctant to
change if unable to compare new data with older results.

Mackinney's low coefficients may reflect use of impure Chls a and
b or oxidation of the Chls during weighing procedures. To avoid such
problems, Porra et $al.$ (6) prepared pure diethylether solutions of
Chls a and b and used the extinction coefficients of Smith and Benitez
(7) to calculate Chl concentrations before evaporating off the
diethylether and replacing it with buffered 80% aqueous acetone: the
coefficients in Ref. 7 were verified to within an error of less than
1% by magnesium determination using atomic absorption
spectrophotometry (6). The new specific coefficents (α) in 80%
acetone are given below with the new simultaneous equations (1) and
(2) derived from them for solving Chl a and b concentrations. For
comparison Mackinney's old coefficients appear in brackets.

Chl a: $\alpha^{663.6} = 85.95 \ (82.04); \quad \alpha^{646.6} = 20.79 \ (16.75)$

Chl b: $\alpha^{663.6} = 10.78 \ (9.27); \quad \alpha^{646.6} = 51.84 \ (45.60)$

Chl a ($\mu g/ml$) $= 12.25 \ A^{663.6} - 2.55 \ A^{646.6}$ ....[1]

Chl b ($\mu g/ml$) $= 20.31 \ A^{646.6} - 4.91 \ A^{663.6}$ ....[2]

M. Baltscheffsky (ed.), Current Research in Photosynthesis, Vol. II, 237–240.
© 1990 Kluwer Academic Publishers. Printed in the Netherlands.

New specific (α) and millimolar (ϵ_{mM}; $mmol/l^{-1}/cm^{-1}$) extinction coefficients for Chls *a* and *b* in buffered 80% aqueous acetone, methanol and N,N-dimethylformamide, and the simultaneous equations derived from them giving Chl concentrations in both in $\mu g/ml$ and nmol/ml, have now been published by Porra *et al.* (6): the equations give consistent Chl concentrations in all three solvent systems.

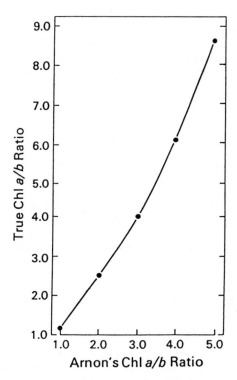

Fig. 1. True Chl a/b ratios plotted against Arnon's Chl a/b ratios.

To convert data from Arnon's equations to be consistent with equations [1] and [2] (above), correction factors were obtained empirically by a method which could be of more universal application. Using Mackinney's coefficients (in brackets above), the absorbance of 80% aqueous acetone solutions of Chl mixtures, with Arnon Chl *a/b* ratios, (Chl *a/b*)^A, of 1.0, 2.0, 3.0, 4.0 and 5.0, were calculated at 663.6 and 646.6nm. When these absorbances were inserted into equations [1] and [2] true ratios, (Chl *a/b*)^T, were calculated and plotted against (Chl *a/b*)^A (Fig. 1): an error of over 1.5-fold is observed at an Arnon ratio of 4.0.

These calculations showed that total Chl from Arnon's equations, $(Chl\ a + b)^A$, was consistently over-estimated (see equation [3] below). Having thus obtained $(Chl\ a/b)^T$, the true Chl a and b concentrations can be derived using equations [4] and [5].

$$(Chl\ a + b)^T\ =\ 0.895(Chl\ a + b)^A \ldots\ldots\ldots [3]$$

$$(Chl\ b)^T\ =\ (Chl\ a + b)^T/[(Chl\ a/b)^T + 1] \ldots\ldots [4]$$

$$(Chl\ a)^T\ =\ (Chl\ a + b)^T.(Chl\ a/b)^T/[(Chl\ a/b)^T + 1] \ldots [5]$$

2. EXTRACTION AND ASSAY OF REFRACTORY CHLOROPHYLLS

The difficulty of extracting Chls from many marine and freshwater algae using the extractants normally employed with higher-plants has been known for decades (cf. 6). Possibly the Chls are "refractory" to extraction because of their bonding in the membrane-spanning proteins or because of their immediate molecular environment. Alternatively, the cell wall of the "recalcitrant" cells may be impervious to these extractants.

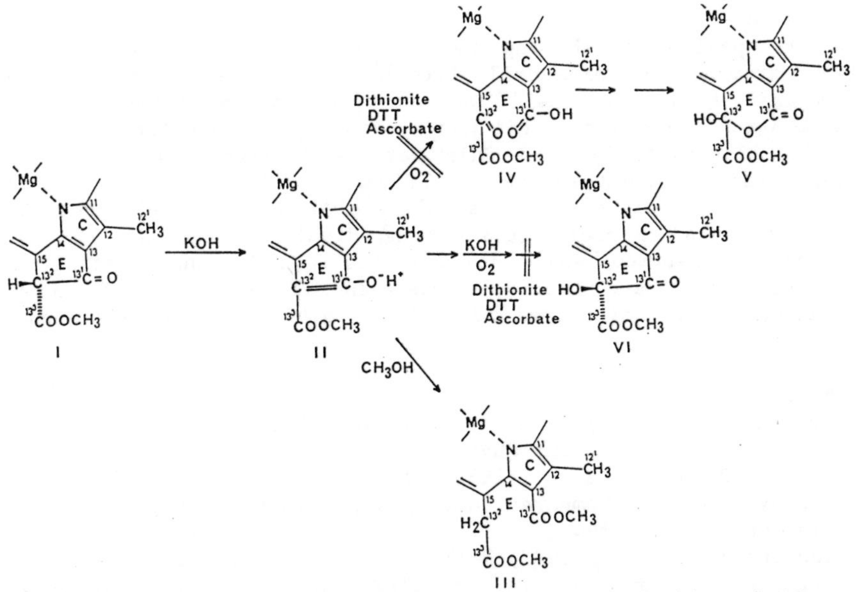

Fig. 2. Oxidation and methanolysis reactions of chlorophylls

In 1974, Porra and Grimme (8) extracted Chls aerobically from "recalcitrant" *Chlorella fusca* cells, with 2.1M pyridine in 0.35M NaOH. The Chls were oxidized to and measured as their allomerization products, Mg-cyclic hydroxylactones a and b (Fig. 2; V). Recently, a less pungent assay was developed by extracting at 60°C with aqueous methanol containing 15% H_2O and 2% KOH whereby the Chls are converted to and assayed as their more stable methanolysis products, Mg-rhodochlorins (Mg-Rchlns) (Fig. 2; III). Mg-Rchlns a and b have peaks at approximately 640 and 623nm, respectively, depending on the H_2O content. Extraction with aqueous alkaline methanol totally removed Chls a and b from the notoriously recalcitrant green alga, *Nanochloris atomus*, but the addition of 1.5mM dithionite was needed to ensure inhibition of competing allomerization reactions producing Mg-cyclic hydroxylactones (Fig. 2; V) or 13^2 hydroxy- (or methoxy-) Chls (Fig. 2; VI). The millimolar extinction coefficients (ϵ_{mM}) for Mg-Rchlns a and b in this aqueous alkaline methanol are given below as well as simultaneous equations (6) and (7) derived from them for solving the concentrations of Chls a and b (as Mg-Rchlns a and b):

$$\text{Chl } a \; : \; \epsilon_{mM}^{640} = 47.93; \quad \epsilon_{mM}^{623} = 17.32$$

$$\text{Chl } b \; : \; \epsilon_{mM}^{640} = 7.18; \quad \epsilon_{mM}^{623} = 17.69$$

$$\text{Chl } a \text{ (nmol/ml)} = 24.45A^{640} - 9.93A^{623} \dots\dots[6]$$

$$\text{Chl } b \text{ (nmol/ml)} = 66.25A^{623} - 23.94A^{640} \dots\dots[7]$$

Early experiments, showing successful extraction of Chls by pure methanol from *Nannochloris* cells broken in a Chlorella press, suggest that alkali hydrolyzes cell wall components to render the Chls accessible to extractant: this hydrolysis may explain the need to add 15% H_2O. Surprisingly, the Chls were also extracted with aqueous methanol containing dithionite or DTT but no KOH: this suggests that the component hydrolyzed, when alkaline methanol is used, is a cell-wall structural protein (possessing disulphide bonds (9)) which maintains an impervious wall only when its peptide (and especially its disulphide bonds) are intact. The general applicability of this explanation of refractory chlorophylls to other recalcitrant algae is being examined.

REFERENCES

1. Mackinney, G. (1941) J. Biol. Chem. 140, 315-322.
2. Arnon, D.I. (1941) Plant Physiol. 24, 1-15.
3. Ziegler, R. and Egle, K. (1965) Beitr. Biol. Pflanzen 41, 11-37.
4. Jeffrey, S.W. and Humphrey, G.F. (1975) Biochem. Physiol. Pflanzen 167, 191-194.
5. Lichtenthaler, H.K. (1987) Methods Enzymol. 148, 350-382.
6. Porra, R.J., Thompson, W.A. and Kriedemann, P.E. (1989) Biochim. Biophys. Acta, 975, 384-394.
7. Smith, J.H.C. and Benitez, A. (1955) in Modern Methods of Plant Analysis (Paech, K. and Tracey, M.V., eds.), Vol. 4, pp.143-196, Springer-Verlag, Berlin.
8. Porra, R.J. and Grimme, L.H. (1974) Analyt. Biochem. 57, 255-267.
9. Thompson, E.W. and Preston, R.D. (1968) J. Exp. Bot. 19, 690-697.

FORMATION OF CHLOROPHYLL a-PROTEIN COMPLEXES ABSORBING AT 685 NM
IN THE PRESENCE OF TETRAHYDROFURAN

KAKU UEHARA[1], YUKO HIOKI[1] and MAMORU MIMURO[2], Department of Applied
Chemistry, University of Osaka Prefecture[1],Sakai, Osaka 591; National
Institute for Basic Biology[2], Okazaki, Aichi 444, Japan.

1. INTRODUCTION

Chlorophyll a (chl a) in thylakoid membrane takes several forms
with different absorption maxima (chl forms) and act as a light-
harvesting antenna or a primary electron donor in the photochemical
reaction center. We have reported (1a,b) the chl a forms specifically
formed in the solution of poly(vinyl alcohol), poly(vinyl pyrrolidone),
and bovine serum albumin (BSA). A new type of chl form was also
suggested in the case of dimethyl sulfoxide (DMSO) (1c,d). Now we
succeeded in preparing a novel chl a form (A-685) in aqueous
tetrahydrofuran (THF) only in a narrow range of its concentration.
Present study aimed to analyze detailed patterns of absorption and
resonance Raman spectra of the chl a species and incorporate them into
BSA or apocatalase (AC) as a model of the chl a-protein complex.

2. MATERIALS AND METHODS

Chl a was isolated from fresh spinach leaves and purified
according to the method of Iriyama et al. (2). BSA (crystallized and
lyophilized) was obtained from Sigma Chemical Co. AC was prepared from
catalase (Sigma) according to Teale's method (3). Tetrahydrofuran
(THF), dioxane and acetone were commercial GR grade reagents and were
redistilled before use. Chl a dissolved in THF (or other organic
solvents) was added to the solution containing 0.1 w/v % BSA, 1 mM
phosphate buffer (pH 6.98), and mixed with stirrer until a homogeneous
dispersion was obtained. Final concentration of chl a was 1.5×10^{-5} M.
Absorption spectra of chl a solution were resolved to Gaussian
component bands by curve-fitting. Computer algorithm was based on the
least-square method (4, also see 1b). Resonance Raman spectra of the
chl a agregates were measured under the pre-resonant conditions with
Soret absorption band by using 457.9 nm line (<50 mW) of Ar^+ laser (NEC
GLG-2023) and a Jasco NR-1000 Raman spectrometer (1d).

3. RESULTS AND DISCUSSION
3.1 Formation of A-685

Figure 1 shows a typical example of the absorption spectra of 6
v/v % THF aqueous solution of chl a in the presence of 0.1 w/v % BSA.
Increase in the absorbance at 685 nm occurred with the decrease in that

M. Baltscheffsky (ed.), Current Research in Photosynthesis, Vol. II, 241–244.
© 1990 *Kluwer Academic Publishers. Printed in the Netherlands.*

at 672 nm. Such a marked spectral change in the red region (α-band)
may be due to the transformation from chl a micelles dispersed in water
(A-672) (5) to a chl a-THF aggregate (A-685). There were substantial
hyperchromism in the red band and hypochromism in the blue band induced
upon formation of the aggregated species. The 685 nm band is very
sharp and the peak height of the α band is higher than that of 438
nm Soret band (α/Soret=1.19). On the other hand, chl a in 100 % of THF
showed absorption maximum of α and Soret bands at 664 and 435 nm,
respectively with the absorption ratio of α/Soret of 0.752.

The A-685 was formed only in a narrow range of THF concentration
between 2 and 12 %. The maximum rate for the formation was observed in
6 % of THF. When its concentration exceeds 12 %, only the 664 nm
monomeric form was detected. Formation of A-685 seems to be closely
correlated with the decrease in water activity in THF (6); it is
reported to be 0.990 (2 v/v %) and 0.793 (12 v/v %). Over 12 % of THF,
the water activity increases again. Formation of A-685, thus might be
induced by a special structure of the THF-water solution under a lower
water activity.

After the transformation from A-672 to A-685 was equilibrated, the
peak intensity of 685 nm gradually decreased with a lapse of time.
This was due to a formation of micro-crystalline (data not shown). BSA
supressed the formation of micro-crystalline, thus the A-685 was
conserved for a long time (see Fig. 1).

3.2 Gaussian deconvolution of Absorption spectra

In order to clarify the characteristic aggregation of chl a in
THF-water mixture, curve-fitting analysis was carried out on the
absorption spectra in the equilibrated state in the wavelength region
from 600 to 800 nm (Fig. 2). Figure 2a shows a Gaussian resolution of
the absorption spectrum of the chl a species absorbing at 685 nm
obtained in a 6 v/v % THF solution in the presence of BSA. The best
fit was obtained from the components locating at 628.1, 666.8, 674.1,
686.2 and 707.2 nm with bandwidths of 16.8-51.4 nm. It is interesting
to note an exclusive formation of a major band at 686.2 nm. However,
this kind of selective formation was not detected when other organic
solvents were used (Fig. 2b and 2c). In the case of dioxane, two
additional components were found at 690.8 and 697.3 nm, and there were
several components in the acetone-BSA system.

3.3 Raman spectra

Figure 3 shows a Raman spectrum of chl a in the presence of 6 v/v
% THF and 0.1 w/v % BSA. Presence of the carbonyl stretching line at
1697 cm^{-1} clearly indicates that keto group is free from both of
coordination to Mg atom and hydrogen bonding to a water molecule.
Central Mg atom is 5-coordinated as shown by three lines at 1610, 1550
and 1526 cm^{-1} (7). On the C-N pyrrolic bond, marked changes occurred;
original four bands (1214 m, sh; 1189 vs; 1160 m; 1149 m) reported by
Lutz (8) were observed as a triad lines in 1208, 1183 and 1156 cm^{-1}
with the lowest component being missing. This indicates that the
pyrrolic N might interact with a hydrogen atom attached to 2-position
carbon of the coordinated THF bridged to another THF by a water
molecule ($C_4H_8O\cdots H-O-H\cdots OC_4H_8$). Such a interaction of pyrrolic

nitrogen of chl a with addenda has been proposed by Gurinovich and
Strelkova (9). These results indicate that A-685 is a new chl a form
attained by a stacking of chl a macrocycles on the surface of polypeptides. The THF-water hydrogen bonding adduct (THF·H₂O·THF) might be
present in 2-12 % THF and might act as a mold to form A-685 (Fig. 4).

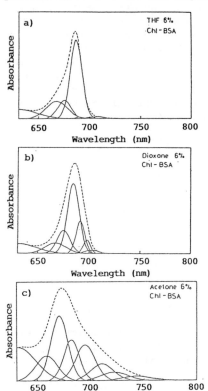

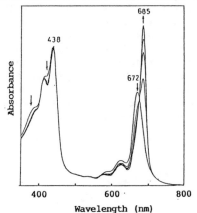

FIGURE 1. Absorption spectra of chl
a-aqueous THF(6 v/v%)-BSA system.
(Time=0, 15, 30, 60 min, 4, 24 hr(
superimposed on 4 hr) after mixing)

FIGURE 2. Gaussian deconvolution
of absorption spectra for
1.5×10⁻⁵ M chl a in 6 v/v % THF
aqueous solution (a), in 6 v/v %
dioxane aqueous solution (b) and
in 6 v/v % acetone aqueous
solution (c).

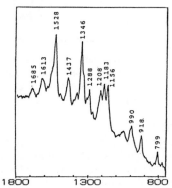

FIGURE 3. Resonance Raman spectra
of chl a in 6 v/v % THF and 0.1
w/v % BSA.

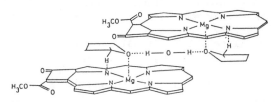

FIGURE 4. A possible model of A-685.

3.4 Difference in binding behavior between BSA and apocatalase
    Formation of the A-685 was affected by the properties of the
polypeptides. When the chl a was incorporated to BSA with THF, a
predominant formation of A-685 was observed (Fig. 2a). The proportion
of this form was kept almost constant, irrespective of the
concentration of BSA up to 0.3 % (Fig. 5b). On the other hand, when
apocatalase was used, a gradual decrease in the proportion of the A-685
was clearly observed (Fig. 5a) with increase in the apocatalase
concentration. Apocatalase is known to form tetramer with binding
sites for 4 heme molecules in the inner hydrophobic domain. Difference
in the properties of polypeptides leads to the idea that chl a in the
inner domain is kept as a monomeric form due to absence of the
THF·H$_2$O·THF species and/or due to an interaction with histidine
residue(s), which suppresses the formation of the A-685.

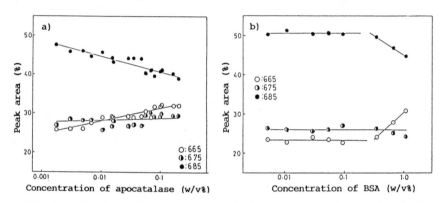

FIGURE 5.   Relationship between protein concentration and relative peak
            area of each Gaussian component of chl a forms formed in
            aqueous THF(6 v/v %)-protein system: (a), apocatalase (AC);
            (b), bovine serum albumin (BSA).

REFERENCES
1 a) Uehara, K., Nakajima, Y., Yonezawa, M. and Tanaka, M. (1981) Chem.
   Lett., 1643-1646. b) Uehara, K., Mimuro, M., Fujita, Y. and Tanaka,
   M. (1988) Photochem. Photobiol., 48, 725-732. c) Uehara, K.,
   Shibata, K., Nakamura, H. and Tanaka, M. (1982) Chem. Lett., 1445-
   1448. d) Uehara, K., Suzuki, H., Hioki, Y., Yamada, H. and Tanaka,
   M. (1988) Chem. Express, 3, 427-430.
2 Iriyama, K., Shiraki, M. and Yoshiura, M. (1977) Chem. Lett., 787-788.
3 Teale, F.W.J. (1959) Biochim. Biophys. Acta, 35, 543 (1959).
4 Mimuro, M., Murakami, A. and Fujita, Y. (1982) Arch. Biochem.
   Biophys., 215, 266-273.
5 Love, B.B. and Bannister, T.T. (1963) Biophys. J., 3, 99-113.
6 Pinder, K.L. (1973) J. Chem. Eng. Data, 18, 275-277.
7 Fujiwara, M. and Tasumi, M. (1986) J. Phys. Chem., 90, 250-255.
8 Lutz, M.(1984) in Advances in Infrared and Raman Spectroscopy (Clark,
   R.J.H and Hester, R.E., ed.), Vol. 11, pp.211-300, Wiley,Heyden.
9 Gurinovich, G. P. and Strelkova, T. I. (1968) Biofizica, 13, 782-792.

PHOTOOXIDATION AND PHEOPHYTIN FORMATION OF CHLOROPHYLL IN THE LIGHT-
HARVESTING CHL-a/b-PROTEIN COMPLEX EXPOSED TO FATTY ACIDS:
PROTECTIVE ROLE OF THE INTACT APOPROTEIN

DOROTHEA SIEFERMANN-HARMS, Kernforschungszentrum Karlsruhe,
Institut für Genetik und Toxikologie, Postfach 3640,
D-7500 KARLSRUHE 1, FRG

1. INTRODUCTION

   Pure chlorophylls (Chl) in organic solution are readily bleached in
the light or converted to pheophytin at low pH. When organized in the
light-harvesting Chl-a/b-protein complex of Photosystem II (LHC), however, they are stable under light (1) and under strongly acidic conditions (2). Photo- and acid stability of the LHC-bound pigments are destroyed in presence of the amphiphilic detergent Triton X-100 and
of the lipophilic terpene limonene (1). Photodestruction of the pigments in Triton- or limonene-treated LHC requires O_2 and is prevented
under anaerobic conditions. These observations suggest that the LHC
apoprotein plays an important role in protecting the Chls from the
destructive action of O_2 and H^+ (1). In the present study the LHC is
exposed to fatty acids of increasing hydrocarbon chain length. It is
asked whether fatty acids destabilize the LHC and whether destabilization requires a minimal length of the lipophilic hydrocarbon chain.

2. MATERIALS AND METHODS

   LHC was prepared from spinach thylakoids according to (3). The procedure included short-term solubilization of the membranes with Triton
X-100 (Chl/Tr=1/30; w/w) and isoelectric focusing of the Chl-protein
complexes on digitonin-containing polyacrylamide gel plates. During
electrophoresis, the Triton associated with LHC is replaced with digitonin. Photostability was assayed as in (1), and the average photon
flux density of white actinic light was measured in the middle of the
cuvette using a Li-185B quantum radiometer (WALZ). Acid stability was
monitored as absorbance decrease at 675 nm with a DW-2000 spectrophotometer (SLM INSTRUMENTS) using the absorbance of the sample at 725 nm
as reference. Fluorescence excitation and emission spectra were measured with a Model LS-5 fluorescence spectrophotometer (PERKIN ELMER)
using 10-nm slid widths. The excitation spectra were corrected for
equal quantum number. Saturated fatty acids (6:0 to 18:0; even-carbon,
straight chain) were from SERVA (No. 39044), oleic acid (18:1) and linoleic acid (18:2) were from ROTH (No. 7213.1 and 7216.1). All fatty
acids were added as ethanolic solutions.

M. Baltscheffsky (ed.), Current Research in Photosynthesis, Vol. II, 245–248.
© 1990 *Kluwer Academic Publishers. Printed in the Netherlands.*

3. RESULTS

As shown in Fig. 1, photooxidation of LHC-bound Chl-a at pH 7.8 and pheophytin formation of LHC-bound Chl-a at pH 1.3 are hardly enhanced by fatty acids of 6 to 12 carbon atoms, whereas fatty acids of 14 to 18 carbons accelerate these reactions significantly. Within the C_{18} fatty acids tested, desaturation improves the ability of the acids to destroy photo- and acid stability of the LHC. These results do not appear to be explained simply by differences in the partitioning of the different fatty acids between lipophilic LHC and aqueous solvent. Namely, while the molar solubility of saturated fatty acids in both, lipophilic cyclohexane and water decreases by a factor of 20 for acids from 12 to 18 carbons, the solubility ratio for either fatty acid in these solvents changes only slightly (calculated from Ref. 4).

The fatty acids tested here cause little change of the fluorescence excitation spectrum of LHC for Chl-a emission at 680 nm and of the emission spectra of the LHC for Chl-b excitation at 470 nm or predominant carotenoid excitation at 455 nm. This is in contrast to the effect of Triton X-100 at 250 μM, i.e. a concentration enhancing photooxidation and pheophytin formation of Chl-a at a degree similar to 30 μM linoleic acid (Fig. 1). The results show that the efficient energy transfer from carotenoids and Chl-b to Chl-a taking place between the highly ordered pigments of intact LHC (2) is maintained in the presence of fatty acids.

FIGURE 1: Effect of fatty acids on the photostability (top), acid stability (middle) and fluorescence behavior (bottom) of LHC II -- comparison with Triton X-100.

Assays contained LHC equivalent 2.05 μg Chl a+b/ml in 45 mM Tricine-Na buffer pH 7.8, 1 % ethanol (control), 1 % ethanol + 30 μM fatty acid (as indicated), or 250 μM Triton X-100 (Triton). Seven saturated even-chain fatty acids (6:0 to 18:0) and two unsaturated fatty acids (18:1; 18:2) were examined. All assays were run at room temperature.

Top: Photooxidation of LHC-bound Chl-a induced by three 10-min periods of white light at average photon flux density of 2800 μE $m^{-2}s^{-1}$ was examined. Between the light periods, absorbance spectra were monitored and Chl-a destruction was determined from the absorbance decrease in the 'red' maximum of LHC (676 nm for LHC ± fatty acid; 674 nm for LHC + Triton). Under anaerobic conditions (50 mM glucose + 0.3 mg/ml glucose oxidase) no photodestruction of the LHC-bound pigments was observed at either condition (not shown).

Middle: Pheophytin formation was monitored as absorbance decrease at 675 nm after lowering the pH to pH 1.3 with concentrated HCl. The rate of pheophytin formation after 3 min at pH 1.3 is presented.

Bottom: Fluorescence ratios F650ex470/F680ex470 and F680ex455/F680ex435 are presented as white and black columns, respectively. The former ratio increases under conditions of reduced energy transfer from Chl-b to Chl-a, the latter ratio decreases under conditions of reduced energy transfer from carotenoids to Chl-a.

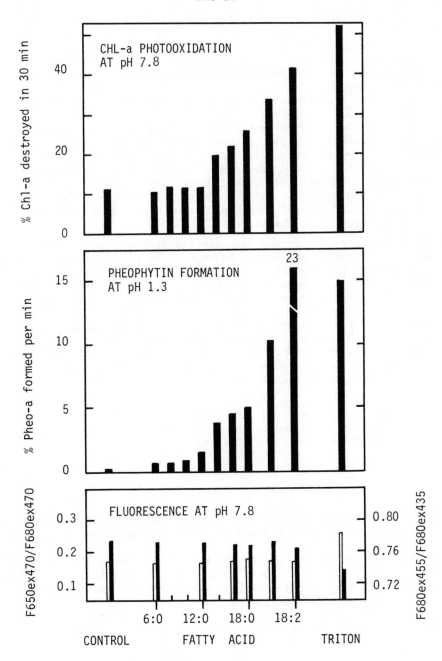

LHC II

4. DISCUSSION

The ability of fatty acids to destabilize LHC depends on the length of their hydrocarbon chain. Little destabilizing effect was observed for fatty acids with 12 or less carbon atoms (length of the expanded molecule up to 15 Å; Ref.5) whereas fatty acids with 14 to 18 carbon atoms (17.6 to 22 Å) caused significant destabilization. Two properties of the intact LHC have been used to assay destabilization:
- photostability, i.e. the ability of LHC apoprotein to protect its excited Chl from O_2 attack,
- acid stability, i.e. the ability of LHC apoprotein to protect its Chl from H^+ attack.

These two tests characterize properties of the apoprotein, whereas fluorescence properties of the LHC provide information on the organization of LHC-bound pigments (2). The fatty acids tested here did not alter the fluorescence properties, which is in contrast to Triton X-100 that strongly affects both, the fluorescence excitation and emission spectrum. Consequently, fatty acids at molecular lengths of 17 to 22 Å render the LHC apoprotein permeable for O_2 and H^+ but do not change the arrangement of the pigments.

Based on electron microscopy and electron diffraction of three-dimensional LHC cristals, Kühlbrandt (6) suggested the LHC to be a trimer composed of three protein monomers surrounding a lipophilic cavern that harbours the Chl. The protein monomers consist of several lipophilic α-helices arranged in parallel with a center-to-center distance of 12 to 15 Å. In view of this model the presented data suggest, first, that the α-helices of the intact LHC form a barrier protecting the Chls from O_2 and H^+ attack and, second, that fatty acids at a minimal length of 17.6 Å (14:0) destroy the barrier function of the α-helices without affecting the arrangement of the pigments. The mode of fatty acid action remains to be established.

ACKNOWLEDGEMENTS. I thank Karin Lisiecki for expert technical assistance. This work was supported by the Projekt Europäisches Forschungszentrum für Maßnahmen zur Luftreinhaltung.

REFERENCES
1 Siefermann-Harms, D. (1989) J. Photochem. Photobiol. 4(2), in press.
2 Siefermann-Harms, D. and Ninnemann, H. (1982) Photochem. Photobiol. 35, 719-731.
3 Siefermann-Harms, D. and Ninnemann, H. (1979) FEBS Lett. 104, 71-77.
4 Singleton, W.S. (1960) in Fatty Acids - Their Chemistry, Properties, Production, and Uses (Markley, K.S. ed.), 2nd Ed., Part 1, pp. 609-678, Interscience Publishers, Inc., New York.
5 O'Connor, R.T. (1960) in Fatty Acids - Their Chemistry, Properties, Production, and Uses (Markley, K.S. ed.), 2nd Ed., Part 1, pp. 285-378, Interscience Publishers, Inc., New York.
6 Kühlbrandt, W. (1988) J. Mol. Biol. 202, 849-864.

PROPERTIES OF THE MINOR CHLOROPHYLL A/B PROTEINS CP29, CP26 AND CP24 FROM *Zea mays* PHOTOSYSTEM II MEMBRANES.

P. Dainese, M.L. Di Paolo, M. Silvestri and R. Bassi.
Dipartimento di Biologia, Università di Padova, via Trieste   75 I–35121 Padova – Italy.

1.INTRODUCTION.
The light–harvesting apparatus of higher plants is composed of several chlorophyll binding proteins. Recently, beside the light harvesting complex II (LHC II), others chlorophyll a/b proteins have been described from Photosystem (PS) II membranes, namely CP29, CP26 and CP24 (1–3). They are present in small amounts in the thylakoid membrane, have lower chlorophyll contentent b with respect to LHCII and their physiological role is still unclear. In this work we have purified these complexes by non–denaturing isoelectrofocusing (IEF), this technique allowing the isolation of pure complexes in native state. The proteins have been characterized by immunological and spectroscopic techniques. Their properties are compared to those of the major antenna complex (LHCII) and of the chlorophyll a/b proteins of PSI (LHCI).

2. PROCEDURE.
Membranes: thylakoid and PSII membranes were obtained from 2–3 weeks old *Zea mays* (*L.*) seedlings as previously   reported (2). Chlorophyll protein complexes: PSI–200 LHCI–730 and   LHCI–680 were purified as in ref. 5. CP29, CP26 and CP24 as well as LHCII were isolated by non–denaturing IEF (4) and further purified by ultracentrifugation in 0.1–1 M sucrose gradient including 0.06% dodecylmaltoside (DM). Electrophoresis: analytical SDS–urea PAGE and non–denaturing SDS–glycerol PAGE were as in ref. 2. Immunological techniques: Polypeptides were separed by SDS–urea PAGE and transferred to nitrocellulose according to standard methods. Filters were assayed with polyclonal antibodies and the binding revealed with alkaline phosphatase coupled anti–rabbit IgG. The preparation of polyclonanal antibodies against chl a/b proteins has been described in ref. 6. Spectroscopy: steady–state absorption spectra were obtained at room temperature using a Perkin–Elmer Lambda 5 spectrophotometer. Circular dichroism measurements were made at 4° C in a Jasco DP 501 N spectropolarimeter equipped with data processor.

3 RESULTS AND DISCUSSION.
3.1 *Isolation of chl a/b proteins.* When PSII membranes were solubilized with 1% (w/v) dodecylmaltoside and fractionated by non–denaturing IEF in granulated gel (fig.1), eleven green bands were obtained. The first four ones, starting from the anode, contain different LHCII populations; CP26 was in fraction 5, CP24 in fraction 6 and CP29 in fractions 7–9. Since an LHCII population comigrated with CP26 and the PSII RC complex with CP29, fractions from IEF were subjected to sucrose gradient ultracentrifugation, since

the complexes have different sedimentation rate (fig. 2). After ultracentrifugation PSII RC was pelleted (tube 7–11) while chl a/b proteins migrated into two bands. The upper band contained the minor chl a/b proteins, the lower one LHCII. An exception to this pattern was IEF 1 band that migrated at the lower density although containing LHCII.

3.2 *Immunological characterization.* The results of assaying purified chl a/b proteins with polyclonal antibodies are shown in fig. 4. Many of the apoproteins share epitops thus suggesting conserved aminoacid sequences. However strong cross–reactions only are obtained between complexes that have common characteristic in their optical spectra (see section 3.3). Thus the polypeptides belonging to LHCII are very similar to each other and exhibit extensive cross–reactions. CP26 and CP29 also show strong cross–reaction as well as CP24 and LHCI–680. It is interesting to notice that CP24 is recognized by the antibody raised against CP26 but not by the one raised against CP29. A 25 kDa polypeptide belonging to LHCI out of four closely migrating ones in the 25.5–21 kDa range is recognized by several antibodies raised against PSII chl a/b proteins thus suggesting that the other LHCI polypeptides are more divergent.

3.3 *Spectroscopy.* The absorption spectra of the chl a/b proteins are shown in figure 3. This can be classed into two groups according to the chl a absorption maxima values: CP26, CP29 and LHCI–730 have a 677 nm peack while LHCII,

Fig.1 Schematic drawing of the fractionation of PSII membranes by IEF in 0.06% DM : distance versus pH.   Fig.2 Sucrose gradient ultracentrifugation of the IEF fractions. The gradient was run in a TST 60.4 Kontron rotor, at 58000 rpm for 12 hrs.   Fig.3 Absorption spectra of the chl a/b proteins of PSII in 0.06% DM, 10 mM Hepes pH 7.5.

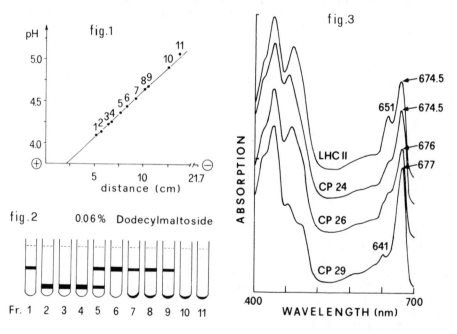

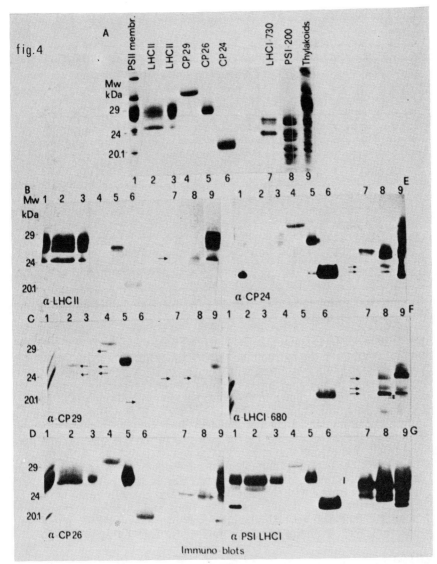

Fig.4 Cross–reactivity pattern of purified chl a/b proteins. A) Coomassie stained gel; B–G) filters assayed with polyclonal antibodies to individual chl a/b proteins.

CP24 and LHCI–680 absorb at about 674 nm. Appreciable differences are also observed in the chl b shoulder. This is at 641 nm in CP29 while at 651 nm in LHCII and CP24. CP26 exhibits both chl b absorption forms. Chl b in LHCI–680 and 730 absorbs with a small peak at 645 nm (5).Circular dichroism spectra are shown in fig. 5. They were obtained from samples dissolved in 0.06% DM. In the LHCII spectrum all the excitonic features previously

fig.5

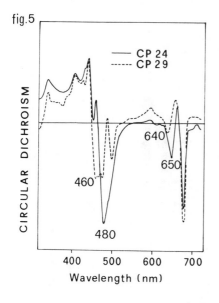
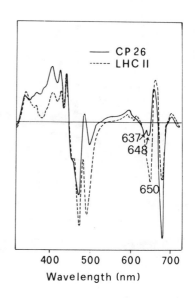

Fig.5 Circular dichroism spectra of the chl a/b proteins of PSII in 0.06% DM, 10 mM Hepes pH 7.5, at 4 C.

described with octylglucoside as a detergent (7,8) were observed.
In the minor complexes the extrema of chl b/b and chl a/b excitonic splitting signals in the Soret band are shifted with respect to the values found in LHCII samples, according to the absorption maxima of the interacting pigments. In the Q band differences are shown in the chl b negative signals that is at 650 nm in LHCII and CP24, while points at 640 nm in CP29; CP26 exibits two minima at 637 nm and 648 nm. In LHCI–730 and 680 chl b negative signals points at 655 nm. Similar excitonic patterns can be revealed in the CD spectra of CP26, CP29 and LHCI–730 (5), as well as in CP24 and LHCI–680.
CONCLUSIONS: the data of immunological relatedness are in good agreement with data from absorption and CD spectra; they indicate that: a) LHCII presents specific features with respect to the other chl a/b proteins in the sedimentation rate, immunological cross–reactions and pigment organization; b) CP26 and CP29 are very similar to each other as well as CP24 and LHCI–680; c) CP26 resumes some characteristics of both CP24 and CP29.

REFERENCES:
1) Machold, O. and Meister, A. (1979) Biochim.Biophys. Acta 546, 472–480.
2) Bassi, R., Hoyer–Hansen, G., Barbato, R., Giacometti, G.M. and Simpson, D.J. (1987) J.Biol.Chem. 262, 13333–13341.
3) Dunahay, T.G. and Staehelin, L.A. (1986) Plant Physiol. 80, 429–434.
4) Dainese, P., Hoyer–Hansen, G. and Bassi, R. (1989), submitted.
5) Bassi, R. and Simpson, D.J. (1987) Eur.J.Biochem. 163, 221–230.
6) Di Paolo, M.L., dal Belin Peruffo, A. and Bassi, R. (1989) submitted.
7) Ide, J.P., Klug, D.R., Kuhlbrandt, W., Giorgi, L.B. and Porter, G. (1987) Bichim.Biophys.Acta 893, 349–364. 8) Bassi, R., Silvestri, M., Dainese, P., Giacometti, G.M. and Moya, I. (1989) submitted.

THE 20 kDA APO-POLYPEPTIDE OF THE CHLOROPHYLL a/b PROTEIN COMPLEX CP24 - CHARACTERIZATION AND COMPLETE PRIMARY AMINO ACID SEQUENCE

MICHAEL SPANGFORT[1], ULLA K. LARSSON[1], ULF LJUNGBERG[1,4],
MARGARETA RYBERG[2] AND BERTIL ANDERSSON[3]
DEPARTMENTS OF BIOCHEMISTRY, UNIVERSITY OF LUND[1], AND UNIVERSITY OF
STOCKHOLM[3], DEPARTMENT OF PLANT PHYSIOLOGY, UNIVERSITY OF GÖTEBORG[2]
(SWEDEN)
DIETER BARTLING[4], NORBERT WEDEL[4] AND REINHOLD G. HERRMANN[4]
BOTANISCHES INSTITUT DER LUDWIG-MAXIMILIAN UNIVERSITÄT[4], MÜNCHEN (FRG)

1. INTRODUCTION

The light harvesting apparatus of higher plant photosystem II
(PSII) is a highly complex and heterogenous structure consisting of
several chlorophyll-binding proteins including the minor chlorophyll
a/b complexes, CP29, CP27 and CP24. CP24 was first identified by
Dunahay and Staehlin (1) and is estimated to contain only about 5% of
the PSII chlorophyll. It is proposed to contain one (2) or several
polypeptides in the range of 20-24 kDa (1). CP24 has been suggested
to act as a linker protein between the light-harvesting antenna and
the core of PSII (1). Others have suggested it to be associated with
the light-harvesting apparatus of PSII (3,4).

In this study we have characterized a 20 kDa polypeptide by a
combination of biochemical and molecular genetical approaches and demonstrated that it is the chlorophyll binding apo-polypeptide of
CP24. In addition we have isolated cDNA clones for the entire precursor protein which has allowed a detailed molecular characterization
of the chlorophyll-protein and its biogenesis.

2. MATERIALS AND METHODS

Extrinsic and loosely bound hydrophobic proteins were removed
from isolated spinach PSII membranes by treatment with 3 M NaSCN,
0.01% Triton X-100, 50 mM $CaCl_2$, 10 mM MES pH 6.5 (5). Partly denaturing electrophoresis was run as in (1) using n-octyl β-D-glycanopyra-
noside and small amounts of SDS to solubilize PSII membranes in the
presence of 40% glycerol. For polypeptide analysis of the resolved
chlorophyll-protein complexes, the chlorophyll containing bands were
excised and re-electrophoresed under denaturing conditions using
12-23% polyacrylamide gels with 4 M urea. For N-terminal sequencing,
the 20 kDa apo-protein was electrophoretically transferred from the
gel to a PVDF membrane, cut out and sequenced on an Applied Biosystem
model 470 sequenator. Polyclonal antibodies against the 20 kDa polypeptide were obtained by elution from preparative denaturing SDS-

polyacrylamide gels and injection into rabbit. Isolation and sequencing of cDNA clones from spinach λgt11 expression libraries were performed as in (6). In vitro transcription, translation and organelle uptake were performed as in (6). Hydropathy plotting was performed according to (7) with an 11-point moving average.

3. RESULTS AND DISCUSSION

CP24 resolved from NaSCN treated PSII membranes by mild electrophoresis, was found to consist of only one polypeptide with the apparent molecular weight of 20 kDa (Fig. 1, lane D). When CP24 was isolated from untreated PSII membranes, it showed a multipolypeptide composition and thus the identity of the pigment binding polypeptide(s) could not be firmly established. This problem was overcome by the NaSCN treatment which removes several extrinsic polypeptides contaminating the CP24.

Immunoblotting using polyclonal antibodies raised against the 20 kDa apo-protein showed that CP24 is heavily enriched in PSII preparations derived from the appressed thylakoid regions. In contrast, the 20 kDa apo-protein of CP24 could not be found in PSI preparations. The connection of CP24 to PSII was further substantiated by electron-microscopy of immunogold decorated thin sections of spinach leaves, where the majority of the labelling was found in the appressed grana regions.

By antibody screening of a λgt11 cDNA expression library prepared from spinach poly (A+)-RNA cDNA clones encoding the entire precursor protein of CP24 were isolated. N-terminal amino acid sequence of the 20 kDa polypeptide of CP24 matched the corresponding sequence deduced from the nucleotide sequence. The nuclear encoded precursor protein is composed of 261 amino acids while the mature protein contains 210 amino acids (Table 1). When the isolated cDNA was translated in vitro the product was imported into chloroplasts at high efficiency and processed correctly to its mature size (Fig. 1).

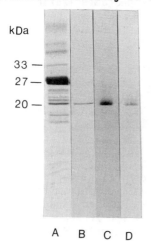

kDa

33 —
27 —
20 —

A B C D

Figure 1. Import of in vitro synthesized ^{35}S-methionine labelled CP24 precursors into intact spinach chloroplasts. A: SDS-PAGE of thylakoid membranes used in in vitro translation and uptake experiment. B: ^{35}S-autoradiogram of SDS-PAGE gel used in lane A. C: ^{35}S-autoradiogram of CP24 isolated from thylakoid membranes used in lane A. D: Commassie stained SDS-PAGE of CP24 isolated from NaSCN treated photosystem II membranes.

The hydropathy plot of the 20 kDa protein predicts that it possess two membrane spanning regions (Fig. 2). Each of these membrane spans contain a histidine residue which is part of an consensus amino acid sequence (Ala-X-X-X-His) believed to be involved in the coordination of chlorophyll in photosynthetic bacteria (8).

The overall homology between the chlorophyll binding 20 kDa polypeptide and LHCII and LHCI is only about 40%. However, there are clearly conserved domains (60-80%) which are predominantly located within the two predicted transmembrane segments and their flanking regions. Interestingly, the two predicted spanning regions of the 20 kDa polypeptide can only be aligned with the first and third membrane span of LCHII proposed by (9). If correct, the consequence would be that almost identical helices might be arranged either antiparallell as in CP24, or parallell as in LHCII. Alternatively, our data give support for models of LCHII with two or four membrane spans. In the latter case span 1 and 4 of LHCII (10) would correspond to the transmembrane helices predicted for CP24.

The transit sequence of the 20 kDa polypeptide is relatively long, 51 amino acids. It has a positive overall charge and shows a hydrophobic domain which preceeds the terminal cleavage site. Strikingly, the transit sequence do not show the same secondary profile as normally seen for the LCHII precursor proteins but shows a

Table 1. Amino acid sequence of the 20 kDa apo-protein of CP24 deduced from isolated cDNA. Arrow indicates cleavage site for transit peptide. Boxed areas indicate areas of homology with LHCII and LHCI. Underlined stretches indicate putative membrane spanning regions.

```
Met Ala Ala Ala Thr Ser Ala Thr Ala Ile Val Asn Gly Phe Thr Ser Pro
                              10

Phe Leu Ser Gly Gly Lys Lys Ser Ser Gln Ser Leu Leu Phe Val Asn Ser
            20                          30

Lys Val Gly Ala Gly Val Ser Thr Thr Ser Arg Lys Leu Val Val Val Ala
 ▼                      40                              50

Ala Ala Ala Ala Pro Lys Lys Ser Trp Ile Pro Ala|Val Lys Gly Gly Gly
                              60

Asn Phe Leu Asp Pro Glu Trp Leu Asp Gly Ser Leu Pro Gly Asp Phe Gly
    70                              80

Phe Asp Pro Leu Gly Leu Gly Lys Asp Pro Ala Phe Leu Lys Trp Tyr Arg
                90                          100

Glu Ala Glu Leu Ile His Gly Arg Trp Ala Met Leu Ala Val Leu Gly Ile
                        110

Phe Val Gly Gln Ala Trp Thr Gly Ile Pro Trp Phe Glu Ala|Gly Ala Asp
-120                             130

Pro Gly Ala Val Ala Pro Phe Ser Phe Gly Thr Leu Leu Gly Thr Gln Leu
                140                         150

Leu Leu Met Gly Trp Val Glu Ser Lys Arg Trp Val Asp Phe Phe Asp Pro
                160                         170

Asp Ser Gln Ser Val Glu Trp Ala Thr Pro Trp Ser Arg Thr Ala Glu Asn
                180

Phe Ser Asn Ser Thr Gly Glu Gln Gly|Tyr Pro Gly Gly Lys Phe Phe Asp
    190                         200

Pro Leu Ser Glu Leu Ala|Gly Thr Ile Ser Asn Gly Val Tyr Asn Pro Asp Thr
                210                         220

Asp Lys Leu Gly Arg Leu Lys Leu Ala Glu Ile Lys His Ala Arg Leu Ala
                        230

Met Leu Ala Met Leu Ile Phe Tyr Phe Glu Ala Gly Gln Gly Lys Thr Pro
    240                         250

Leu Gly Ala Leu|Gly LeuX
            260
```

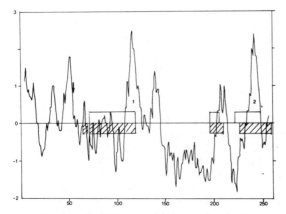

Figure 2. Hydropathy plot of the precursor 20 kDa apo-protein of CP24. Arrow indicates cleavage site for transit peptide. Boxed ares indicate regions of homology with LHCII (open) and LHCI (striped). Arabic numbers indicate putative membrane spanning regions.

more close resemblance to the transit sequences of the lumenal extrinsic proteins of the water-splitting complex (11). This may indicate that CP24 is inserted into the thylakoid membrane following a different mechanism than LHCII. Possibly, the insertion of CP24 leads to an exposure of the N-terminus at the lumenal side of the membrane. Another speculation is that CP24 is imported into the lumen and subsequently inserted from the inner side of the membrane in analogy with several mitochondrial inner membrane proteins (12).

REFERENCES

1   Dunahay, T.G. and Staehelin, L.A. (1986) Plant Physiol. 80, 429-434
2   Chitnis, P.R. and Thornber, J.P. (1988) Photosyn. Res. 16, 41-63
3   Bassi, R., Höjer-Hansen, G., Barbato, R., Giacometti, G.M. and Simpson, D.J. (1987) J. Biol. Chem. 262, 13333-13341
4   Stayton, M.M., Brosio, P. and Dunsmuir, P. (1987) Plant Mol. Biol. 10, 127-137
5   Ljungberg, U., Åkerlund, H.-E. and Andersson, B. (1986) Eur. J. Biochem. 158, 477-482
6   Lautner, A., Klein, R., Ljungberg, U., Reiländer, H., Bartling, D., Andersson, B., Reinke, H., Beyreuther, K. and Herrmann, R.G. (1988) J. Biol. Chem. 262, 10077-10081
7   Kyte, J. and Doolittle, R.F. (1982) J. Mol. Biol. 157, 105-132
8   Zuber, H., Sidler, W., Fuglistaller, P., Brunisholz, R. and Theiler, R. (1985) in Molecular Biology of the Photosynthetic Apparatus (Steinbach, K.E., Bonitz, S., Arntzen, C.J. and Bogorad, L., eds.) pp. 183-195, Cold Spring Harbour Laboratory
9   Karlin-Neumann, G.A., Kohorn, B.D., Thornber, J.P. and Tobin, E.M. (1985) J. Mol. Appl. Genet. 3, 45-61
10 Anderson, J.M. and Goodchild, D.J. (1987) FEBS Lett. 213, 29-33
11 Andersson, B. and Herrmann, R.G. (1988) in Plant Membranes - Structure, Assembly and Function (Harwood, J.L. and Walton, T.J., eds.) pp. 33-45, Biochemical Society, London
12 Hartl, F.-U., Pfanner, N., Nicholson, D.W. and Neupert, W. (1989) Biochim. Biophys. Acta 988, 1-45

PHOSPHORYLATION OF THE LHC II-APOPROTEINS OF CHLAMYDOMONAS REINHARDII

SIGRIST M. and BOSCHETTI A., University of Berne, Institut fuer Biochemie, Freiestrasse 3, 3012 BERN, SWITZERLAND

1. INTRODUCTION

The reversible phosphorylation of the apoproteins of the light-harvesting complex associated with photosystem II ("LHC II-apoproteins") is essential for the regulation of energy distribution between the two photosystems and thylakoid stacking (1,2). In the last years, the phosphorylation of the LHC II-apoproteins of various plant species has been thoroughly investigated. Generally, the phosphorylation site is assumed to be located at a threonine near the N-terminus of the proteins (2, 3).

In the green alga Chlamydomonas reinhardii, we can distinguish three LHC II-apoproteins with apparent molecular weights of 24, 25 and 29 kD (4). We can isolate a mixture of these three proteins on a preparative scale by extraction of thylakoid membranes with organic solvents and gel filtration (5). When subjected to isoelectric focusing, this mixture separates into more than 10 bands (6).

The localization of the phosphorylation sites of the LHC-proteins of Chlamydomonas has not been determined so far. Also the molecular differences between the various protein bands produced by isoelectric focusing of the LHC II-apoproteins are not clear. With our experiments, we try to answer the question, if the high amount of bands produced by isoelectric focusing represents proteins with different degrees of phosphorylation.

2. MATERIALS AND METHODS

Labelling of cells of Chlamydomonas with [^{32}P]phosphate in vivo was performed according to Michel et al. (7).

Proteolytic fingerprints of proteins were described earlier (5).

The limited chymotryptic digestion of the LHC II-apoproteins was done with electroeluates of gel pieces from SDS-PAGE, containing about 0.1% SDS.

For the isoelectric focusing, we used a flatbed gel-system containing 4 M urea, 0.5% digitonine and 1% Nonindet NP 40 and focused overnight at 200 V. In order to determine which of the three possible amino acids are phosphorylated, we separated the three [^{32}P]-labelled LHC II-apoproteins

M. Baltscheffsky (ed.), Current Research in Photosynthesis, Vol. II, 257–260.

by SDS-PAGE. After electroelution, they were hydrolized in HCl-vapour (22 h, 110°C). The resulting mixture of amino acids was derivatized with phenyl-isothiocyanate and separated with reversed phase HPLC. The radioactivity in the HPLC-fractions corresponding to phospho-serine, phospho-threonine and phospho-tyrosine was measured.

3. RESULTS AND DISCUSSION

3.1. In Chlamydomonas reinhardii, three LHC II-apoproteins with apparent molecular weights of 24, 25 and 29 kD can be distinguished by SDS-PAGE. At least two of the three LHC II-apoproteins of Chlamydomonas can be phos-phorylated (Fig. 1). When digested with S. aureus V8 protease, the three polypeptides show different frag-mentation patterns. Autoradiographs reveal phosphory-lated and non-phosphorylated fragments (Fig. 2). The 25 kD-protein seems not to be phosphorylated. This assumption is based on the proteolytic fragmentation patterns of the three LHC-proteins (Fig. 2 and 3), and on the isoelectric focusing of them (Fig. 4). With one exception, all slightly labelled bands of the 25 kD-protein in Fig. 2 to 4 can be explained by contamina-tions of the 25 kD-protein with the 24 kD-protein, which are located very closely to each other on SDS-PAGE.

3.2. Isoelectric focusing separates each of the LHC II-apo-proteins into several polypeptide bands (Fig. 4). One band of the 24 kD-protein and two or three of the 29 kD-protein are phosphorylated. The origin of the more than 8 unlabelled bands of the 25 kD-protein separated by isoelectric focusing is still not clear. It may be due to different species with different amino acid

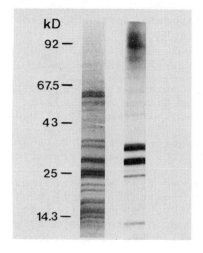

kD
92 —

67.5 —

43 —

25 —

14.3 —

FIGURE 1:
Separation on SDS-PAGE (7.5-15% acrylamide) of thylakoid membranes from Chlamydomonas reinhardii, labelled with [^{32}P]phosphate in vivo. Shown are the Coomassie-stai-ned gel (on the left side) and the corresponding auto-radiograph (right side).

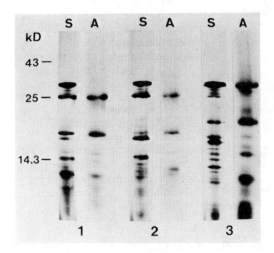

FIGURE 2:
Limited proteolysis of
the LHC II-apoproteins
from [^{32}P]phosphate
labelled cells with <u>S.
aureus V8</u> protease.
Separation of the diges-
ted products in a 15 %
polyacrylamide gel.
S: Fragmentation patterns
   revealed by silver-
   staining.
A: Autoradiograph of the
   same gel.
1: 24 kD-protein
2: 25 kD-protein
3: 29 kD-protein

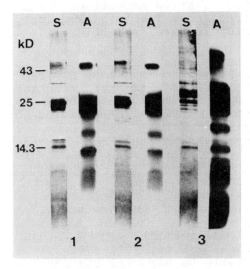

FIGURE 3:
Limited proteolysis of
the polypeptides of 24,
25 and 29 kD from [^{32}P]-
phosphate labelled cells
with chymotrypsin.
Separation of the digested
products in a 15 % poly-
acrylamide gel.
S: Fragmentation patterns
   revealed by silver-
   staining.
A: Autoradiograph of the
   same gel.
1: 24 kD-protein
2: 25 kD-protein
3: 29 kD-protein

sequences, or due to unknown secondary modifications.

3.3. The prefered phosphorylation site of the two LHC II-
apoproteins of 24 and 29 kD must be at a threonine
(Table 1). This is in good agreement with results of
LHC II-apoproteins of other species (e.g. pea (3)),
where the phosphorylation site is localized at a
threonine near the N-terminus.

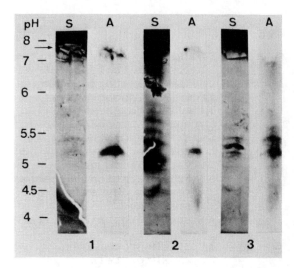

FIGURE 4:
Isoelectric focusing of
the LHC II-apoproteins
from [^{32}P]phosphoryla-
ted cells.
S: Silver-staining of
   the gel after iso-
   electric focusing.
A: Autoradiograph of
   the same gel.
1: 24 kD-protein
2: 25 kD-protein
3: 29 kD-protein
The arrow indicates the
starting point of the
isoelectric focusing.

TABLE 1: Radioactivity in the HPLC-fractions of the phospho-
aminoacids, coming from the three LHC II-apoproteins. Indicated are the relative amounts of ^{32}P in
the separated HPLC-fractions. The total P-amino-
acids in the 29 kD-protein were set arbitrarily to
100.

24 kD-protein		25 kD-protein		29 kD-protein	
P-serine	15.1	P-serine	1.8	P-serine	21
P-threonine	32.9	P-threonine	15.2	P-threonine	59
P-tyrosine	5.9	P-tyrosine	2.0	P-tyrosine	20
Total:	54		19		100

REFERENCES
1 Allen J.F., Bennett J., Steinback K.L. and Arntzen C.J.
  (1981) Nature 291, 25-29
2 Bennett J. (1983) Biochem. J. 212, 1-13
3 Mullet J. (1983) J. Biol. Chem. 258/16, 9941-9948
4 Michel H.P., Schneider E., Tellenbach M. and Boschetti A.
  (1981) Photosynth. Res. 2, 203-212
5 Sigrist M., Zwillenberg C., Giroud Ch., Eichenberger W.
  and Boschetti A. (1988) Plant Science 58, 15-23
6 Sigrist M., Zwillenberg-Fridman C., Giroud Ch., Eichenberger W. and Boschetti A. (1989) in Techniques and New
  Developments in Photosynthesis Research (Barber J. and
  Malkin R., eds), pp. 149-152
7 Michel H.P., Tellenbach M. and Boschetti A. (1983)
  Photosynth. Res. 2, 203-212

THE MAJOR LIGHT-HARVESTING CHLOROPHYLL a/b PROTEIN (LHC IIb): THE SMALLEST SUBUNIT IS A NOVEL CAB GENE PRODUCT

DARYL T. MORISHIGE and J. PHILIP THORNBER
Dept. of Biology, University of California, Los Angeles,
California 90024-1606, USA

1. INTRODUCTION

Conversion of light into chemical energy in oxygenic photosynthesis is essentially driven by two pigmented multiprotein photosystem complexes acting in series. Each photosystem consists of a core complex involved in primary charge separation and a light-harvesting antenna complex (LHC), which increases the light capturing ability of the photosystem.

The light-harvesting complex (LHC II) of photosystem II (PS II) contains at least four chlorophyll-proteins with apparent sizes ranging from 31 to 21kDa in barley (1). The major subunit, LHC IIb, binds approximately equal amounts of chlorophyll a and b, representing about 45% of the total chlorophyll. Along with its major role as a light-harvesting antenna, LHC IIb has also been implicated in cation-mediated stacking of grana membranes and in regulation of energy distribution to the two photosystems. This pigment-protein complex can be isolated as an oligomer, probably a trimer, from non-denaturing PAGE. The trimer is thought to reflect the state of association of LHC IIb in the thylakoid membrane in vivo (2).

The LHC IIb complex contains three apoproteins of 28, 27 and 25kDa in most higher plants, which are predicted to be coded by a small nuclear gene family of 3 to 16 members, depending on species. Gene sequences coding for the apoproteins can so far be divided into two groups: Type I sequences containing no introns and Type II sequences containing an intron. The deduced amino acid sequences derived from both Type I and II gene sequences indicate high degrees of homology between them, although distinct and conserved differences are also readily apparent (3).

At present it is unclear exactly which gene family members are expressed and give rise to each of the three LHC IIb apoproteins found in vivo. All reported attempts to sequence these apoproteins have indicated so far that their N-terminal residue is blocked. Notwithstanding, we have obtained a partial amino-terminal sequence of the smallest LHC IIb apoprotein, which has a size of 25kDa in barley. Although this sequence displays an obvious homology to the other known LHC IIb sequences, it lacks about 10 residues at the N-terminus. Furthermore, some portions of this sequence are characteristic of both Type I and II sequences, while other portions are specific to it, thus indicating that this polypeptide is probably a wholly different type of LHC IIb component.

2. PROCEDURE

2.1 Materials and methods

Barley seedlings (Hordeum vulgare cv. Prato) were grown for 7 days under natural light conditions in a greenhouse. PS II enriched membrane fractions were obtained (4) but with an additional wash with 1M $CaCl_2$ to remove the oxygen-evolving complex. The PS II preparation was solubilized (5) and fractionated into individual chlorophyll-protein complexes on non-denaturing PAGE (6). Oligomeric LHCIIb was excised from the gels and stored in distilled water at -20° C prior to further processing. For isolation of LHC IIb apoproteins, polyacrylamide strips containing oligomeric LHC IIb were soaked in denaturing buffer containing SDS and beta-mercaptoethanol and the proteins were separated by SDS-PAGE, using the buffer system of Laemmli (7) to which 4M urea was added to the separating gel and 1mM sodium thioglycolate to the electrode buffer. Protein bands were stained, excised (8) and sequenced on an Applied Biosystems Model 470A gas phase sequenator. Western blots were performed as described previously (9).

3. RESULTS AND DISCUSSION
3.1. Isolation of LHCIIb Apoproteins
SDS-PAGE analysis of PS II enriched membrane fractions showed them to be generally lacking in proteins other than those typically found associated with PS II (Fig. 1a). LHC IIb was initially isolated in its oligomeric form by separation of PSII components on non-denaturing PAGE. The apoprotein for protein micro-sequencing was purified from the isolated LHC IIb by SDS-PAGE in the presence of 4M urea (Fig. 1a). Confirmation that the 25kDa LHCIIb apoprotein was an LHC IIb component was obtained by Western blot analysis using the monoclonal antibody MLH10 (a gift of Dr. Silvia Darr), which reacts with each of the LHC IIb apoproteins (10) (Fig. 1b). Further characterization indicated that the 25kDa protein, as expected, did not react with the MLH1 antibody, which reacts specifically with the 28kDa LHC IIb species (Fig. 1b).

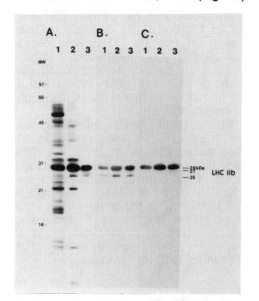

Fig. 1. Analysis of LHC IIb polypeptides. (A) SDS-PAGE of PS II fractions. (B and C) Western blot analysis of LHC IIb apoproteins using (B) MLH9 and (C) MLH1 antibodies (kindly provided by Dr. S. Darr). Fractions in each lane are: (1) whole thylakoids; (2) PS II enriched membrane preparation; (3) isolated LHC IIb oligomer.

3.2. Amino Acid Sequence of LHCIIb

The sequence of the first 59 residues of the protein was obtained and aligned with those of Type I and II polypeptides (Fig. 2). Overall, the 25kDa LHC IIb entity is 12 and 9 amino acids shorter at the amino terminus than either Type I or Type II LHC IIb sequences, respectively. Its sequence homology ranges from 73 to 78%. The observed truncation of the apoprotein most likely explains its smaller size and also why this polypeptide is not phosphorylated *in vitro* (1,11,12), since the site of phosphorylation has been shown to be present at the amino-terminus of the LHC IIb polypeptide, probably at a threonine residue (#3) (11). Additionally, a trypsin-removable amino terminal fragment of 1-3kDa has been implicated in cation-mediated stacking of grana thylakoids (13,14). The absence of this fragment in the 25kDa polypeptide indicates that this protein is probably not involved in stacking as the other LHC IIb components.

```
                                    10        20        30        40        50
25kDa LHC IIb APOPROTEIN         GNDPWYGPDI VKYLGPFSAQ TPKYLNGEFP GDYGWDTAGL SADIEHFARN RALIVIKGR
                                 ||| | | |  || | | |   || | | |              || | | |    | | | ||
TYPE I LHC IIb    MRKTAATKKVG----S*  * R  * *    GE  S S  †               P T  K    E E  H*
TYPE II LHC IIb   MRRTV-KAVP----QSI  E R  P F    E*  * S  T               P T  *    E E  HC
                                    1              2                                 3
```

Fig 2. Sequence of the first 59 amino-terminal residues of the 25kDa LHC IIb apoprotein and comparison with typical Type I (barley cab2 (15)) and Type II (Lemna ab19 (16)) LHC IIb sequences. Residues in the two lower sequences are left blank if they are identical to the corresponding 25kDa residue. 1, 2 and 3 on the diagram indicate regions of divergence (see text).

Within the first 59 residues of the 25kDa subunit there are three regions of divergence with only 37.5 to 60% homology to the other two types (Fig. 2). Within each of these blocks some amino acids can be matched to either the Type I or the Type II LHC IIb sequences (Fig. 2). The first divergent region, closest to the amino-terminus, contains several residues characteristic of Type I LHC IIb sequences; for example Pro (at residues #4 and #8), Val (#11) and Tyr (#13). Other residue changes are also apparent, which do not correspond to either Type I or II sequences. The amino acid sequence 'EQT' (Glu-Gln-Thr) is present in all Type II sequences observed so far (15). The 'QT' portion of this motif is also present at residues #20 and 21 within the second region of divergence in the 25kDa LHC IIb sequence. In the third such region (from residues #44 to 59) Type I or Type II residues are found only at one position each, residue #58 and #49, respectively. Other differences within the first and third domains generally yield more hydrophobic domains, while in the central divergent domain a slightly more polar environment is apparent. No other LHC IIb protein or gene sequence examined so far in any plant species has exhibited such chimeric characteristics, containing both Type I and II-like regions. Moreover, some portions of this sequence are novel. The LHC IIb fragment sequenced also appears to be more hydrophobic than the other LHC IIb proteins within this region. These differences could reflect functional differences between various LHC IIb subunits or differences in spatial arrangement of the LHC IIb components around the reaction center, which may have relevance to the observation that different LHC IIb components have different affinities of binding to the PSII core complex (1).

The data presented here indicate that the sequence of the first 59 residues of the 25kDa LHC IIb component is very different from previously determined LHC IIb sequences and thus the sequence should be regarded as a Type III sequence. These differences could indicate a different three-dimensional structure of this polypeptide in the thylakoid membrane, as well as a fuctional difference among the LHC IIb complexes. Gene sequences coding for this protein are now being isolated in order to better understand the structure of the full-length sequence and the function of this chlorophyll-binding polypeptide in light-harvesting and energy transduction.

ACKNOWLEDGEMENTS We wish to thank Dr. Audree Fowler and Ms. Janice Bleibaum for carrying out the protein sequencing. This research was supported by NSF Grant DMB 87-16230. D.T.M. was supported by a McKnight Fellowship.

REFERENCES
1. Peter, G.F. and Thornber, J.P. (1989) J. Biol. Chem. submitted.
2. Kuhlbrandt, W. (1984) Nature(London) 307: 478-480.
3. Stayton, M.M., Black, M., Bedbrook, J. and Dunsmuir, P. (1986) Nucl. Acids Res. 14: 9781-9796.
4. Berthold, D.A, Babcock, G.T. and Yocum, C.F. (1981) FEBS Lett. 133:265-268.
5. Dunahay, T.G. and Staehelin, L.A. (1986) Plant Physiol. 80: 429-434.
6. Kirchansky, J.J and Park, R.B. (1976) Plant Physiol. 58: 345-349.
7. Laemmli, U.K. (1970) Nature(London) 227: 680-685.
8. Hunkapiller, M.W., Lujan, E., Ostrander, F. and Hood, L. (1983) Meth. Enz. 91: 227-236.
9. Towbin, H., Staehelin, T. and Gordon, J. (1979) Proc. Natl. Acad. Sci. USA 76(9): 4350-4354.
10. Darr, S.C., Somerville, S.C. and Arntzen, C.J. (1986) J. Cell Biol. 103: 733-740.
11. Mullet, J.E. (1983) J. Biol. Chem. 258: 9941-9948.
12. Bassi, R., Hoyer-Hansen, G., Barbato, R., Giacometti, G.M. and Simpson, D.J. (1987) J. Biol. Chem. 262: 13333-13341.
13. Steinback, K.E., Burke, J.J. and Arntzen, C.J. (1979) Arch. Biochem. Biophys. 195: 546-557.
14. Mullet, J.E. and Arntzen, C.J. (1980) Biochim. Biophys. Acta 589: 100-117.
15. Chitnis, P.R. and Thornber, J.P. (1988) Photosyn. Res. 16: 41-63.
16. Karlin-Neumann, G., Kohorn, B., Thornber, J.P. and Tobin, E.M. (1985) J. Mol. Applied Genet. 3: 45-61.

CHARACTERIZATION OF ISOLATED INNER AND OUTER SPINACH LHCII

BERTIL ANDERSSON[1] AND MICHAEL SPANGFORT[2]

DEPARTMENTS OF BIOCHEMISTRY, [1]ARRHENIUS LABORATORIES, UNIVERSITY OF STOCKHOLM AND [2]UNIVERSITY OF LUND, SWEDEN

1. INTRODUCTION

The LHCII is both the most abundant and heterogenous component of plant thylakoids (1). The heterogeneity relates to number of polypeptides, multiple genes, protein-phosphorylation pattern and association to the PSII core. Based upon several studies on phosphorylated or heated thylakoid membranes it has been shown that LHCII consists of two functionally different subpopulations (for review see 2). One of the LHCII subpopulations is in close association with the PSII core and is dominated by a 27 kDa polypeptide. The other subpopulation, containing a 27 and 25 kDa polypeptide in a ratio about 1.5:1, is located more peripherally with respect to PSII from which it can be reversible disconnected as a result of protein phosphorylation. This "outer" LHCII has therefore been suggested to be responsible for the short term acclimation of the PSII light-harvesting apparatus. Studies on LHCII isolated from leaves grown at different light intensities show that this outer pool is also responsible for the long term acclimation of the PSII antenna (3, Mäenpää and Andersson, these proceedings). In this communication we report an isolation procedure and a partial biochemical characterization of the two LHCII populations.

2. MATERIALS AND METHODS

2.1. Isolation procedure

Isolation of the bulk LHCII was performed mainly according to (4) followed by 300 mM KCl induced aggregation of the complex. The pellet washed in destilled water was solubilized by the addition of 1% Triton X-100, 0.5% β-octylglucoside. 0.5% glycine, 1.5% ampholine (pH 5.0-3.5), 0.5% ampholine (pH 4.5-2.5). The final concentration of LHCII was 1 mg chl/ml. After stirring for 5 min in ice, sucrose was added to a final concentration of 54.0% and the sample was loaded on to a LKB 8100 ampholine electrofocusing column. The sample was overlayed with a 50%-5% sucrose gradient containing 0.5% Triton X-100, 0.3% octyl β-glucoside, 0.5% glycine, 1.5% ampholine (pH 5.0-3.5) and 0.5% ampholine (pH 4.5-2.5). The electrofocusing was run in the dark for 72 h at 5W constant power. The anode solution was 0.25 M H_3PO_4 and the cathode solution was 0.25 M NaOH in 60% sucrose.

M. Baltscheffsky (ed.), Current Research in Photosynthesis, Vol. II, 265–268.
© 1990 *Kluwer Academic Publishers. Printed in the Netherlands.*

The chlorophyll containing fractions obtained were collected and
dialysed against 0.2 M NaCl, 20 mM Tricine, pH 7.5 for 2x1 hour and
against 5 mM NaCl, 5 mM Tricine, pH 7.5 over night in the dark. The
samples were then treated with BioBeads for 2 h. KCl was added to a
final concentration of 300 mM pH 7.2. After incubation at room temperature for 5 min and stirring, the samples were collected by centrifugation at 40 000 xg for 15 min.

2.2. Analysis

Denaturing one-dimensional SDS-PAGE was performed according to
Laemmli (5) and "green" SDS-PAGE according to (6). Two-dimensional
isoelectric focusing/SDS-PAGE was run as in (7). Absorption and
fluorescence spectra were recorded by standard methods. Aggregation
was monitored by 180° light scattering.

3. RESULTS

After termination of the column isoelectric focusing three
green bands were obtained (Fig. 1). Two of these, focusing at pH
4.30 and 4.45 respectively, belong to LCHII while a third minor band
focusing at pH 4.65 belong to the CP29 chl a/b protein. The LHC II
fraction focusing at pH 4.30 contained both the 27 and 25 kDa polypeptide in a proportion of about 1.5. The fraction focusing at pH
4.45 consisted only of the 27 kDa polypeptide. This shows that the
two fractions represent the outer and inner LHCII pools respectively.
The distribution of chlorophyll between the two fractions were une-
ven. The alkaline fraction contained 42% of the chlorophyll whereas
the acidic fraction contained 58% (Fig. 1). The chlorophyll proportion between the two subpolulations is dependent on the light regime
under which the plant was grown (3). The obtained ratios between the
two LCHII pools correspond to estimations made for spinach grown at
high light intensities (Mäenpää and Andersson, these proceedings).

Using "green" SDS-PAGE it was found that both LHCII subpopulations have the same tendency to form oligomers. Thus for both fractions a ratio between the oligomeric and monomeric forms of 3.75 was
found. This suggests that the formation of oligomers is not dependent
on the relative amount of two polypeptides or their isoforms. The inner LHC II pool showed a very prompt aggregation in response to the

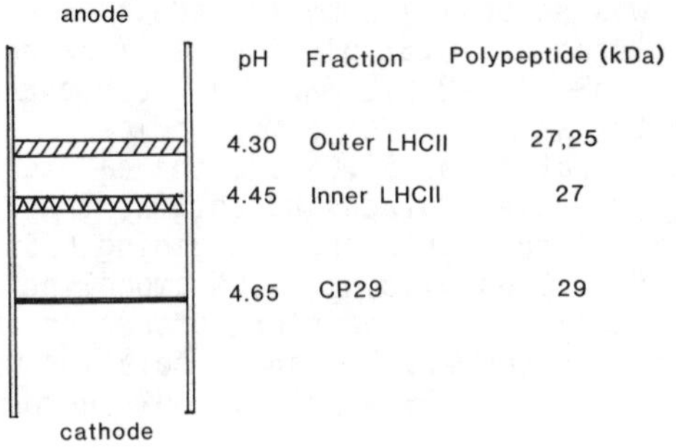

FIGURE 1. Chlorophyll
bands obtained by iso-
electric focusing of
purified spinach LHCII.

Table 1. Summary of the pigment and polypeptide composition and aggregation behaviour of the outer and inner LHC II pool collected after non-denturing isoelectric focusing of isolated bulk LHC II.

Fraction collected from non-denaturing IEF	Outer LHC II	Inner LHC II
Isoelectric point	4.30	4.45
Relative amount chlorophyll (%)	58	42
Chl a/b ratio	1.0	1.0
Absorbtion maximum (500-720 nm)	673, 652	673, 652
Fluorescence maximum (77 K, nm)	679	679
Chl/protein (mol:mol)	8	8
Apo-protein (SDS-PAGE, kDa)	27, 25	27
Apo-protein (IEF, pH)	4.70, 4.63, 4.57, 4.52, 4.60, 4.56	4.70, 4.63, 4.57, 4.52
Aggregation behaviour (Mg^{2+})	+	++++

added Mg^{2+}-ions in contrast to the outer LHCII pool. At 10 mM Mg^{2+} the relative scattering of the inner LHCII pool was four times higher than the outer pool. The presence of the 25 kDa polypeptide therefore seems to reduce the Mg^{2+}-induced aggregation, which may be due to a higher degree of exposed negative charges.

Strikingly, the chlorophyll composition and organization of the two LHCII subpopulations are the same (Table I). Both contain 8 chlorophyll molecules per polypeptide. Bulk LHCII contains 10 chlorophylls per polypeptide so there is some loss of chlorophyll during the isolation procedure. Both LHC II fractions have the same chlorophyll a/b ratio of 1.0. In addition the absorption spectra of the two fractions are the same showing two main absorption peaks at 673 nm and 652 nm. Both fractions showed identical fluorescence emission

spectra with an emission peak at 679 nm. The 77 K fluorescence excitation spectra in the range of 400-500 nm measured at the emission peak wavelength were the same with peaks at 440 nm and 470 nm.

As mentioned above the polypeptide composition is different. However, both subpopulations contain a 27 kDa polypeptide. It was therefore of interest to investigate whether the 27 kDa species of the outer and inner LHCII are the same. This was done by two-dimensional electrophoresis. The 27 kDa polypeptide of both subpopulations were resolved into four subspecies in the pH range of 4.40-4.70 (27a - 27d, Fig. 3). The relative abundance of the two most acidic forms are the same in both subpolulations while the two most basic differ. In the outer LHCII population the 27c/27d polypeptide ratio is 1.8 while it is close to unity in the inner pool. The 25 kDa polypeptide of the outer pool was resolved into two bands which focused at pH values close to the 27b and 27c polypeptides.

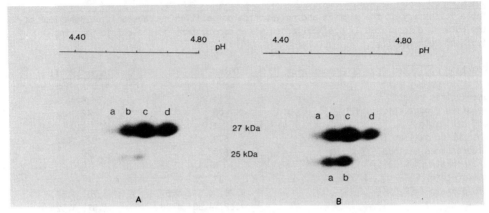

FIGURE 2. Polypeptide composition of inner (A) and outer (B) LHCII sub-populations as revealed by isoelectric focusing followed by SDS-PAGE.

4. DISCUSSION

Our result give strong support for the existence of two LHCII pools with identical pigment composition but with different polypeptide composition. We believe that this provides a molecular mechanism to connect short and long term acclimation of the PSII antenna. Under low light conditions the PSII antenna becomes larger due to a specific increase of the outer LHCII which is rich in the 25 kDa polypeptide (3). This polypeptide has the potential of undergoing a rapid phosphorylation when PSII receives to much light (8,9). Thus, in response to a sudden increase in light intensity after a period of low light the excess portion of the antenna can rapidly be disconnected from PSII through protein phosphorylation. The presence of polypeptides with the same light-harvesting properties but with distinct regulatory roles probably is one reason for the heterogenous gene family of LHCII.

REFERENCES

1 Green, B.R. (1988) Photosyn. Res. 15, 3-32
2 Anderson, J.M. and Andersson, B. (1988) Trends Biochem. Sci. 13, 351-355
3 Larsson, U.K., Anderson, J.M. and Andersson, B. (1987) Biochim. Biophys. Acta 894, 69-75
4 Burke, J.J., Ditto, C.L. and Arntzen, C.J. (1978) Arch. Biochem. Biophys. 187, 252-263
5 Laemmli, U.K. (1970) Nature 227, 680-685
6 Andersson, B. and Anderson, J.M. (1980) Biochim. Biophys. Acta 593, 427-440
7 Remy, R., Ambard-Bretteville, F. and Dubertret, G. (1985) FEBS Lett. 188, 43-47
8 Larsson, U.K., Sundby, C. and Andersson, B. (1987) Biochim. Biophys. Acta 894, 59-68
9 Islam, K. (1987) Biochim. Biophys. Acta 893, 333-341

RESOLUTION OF UP TO EIGHTEEN CHLOROPHYLL-PROTEIN COMPLEXES FROM VASCULAR PLANT THYLAKOIDS USING A NEW GREEN GEL SYSTEM.

Keith D. Allen, Tanya G. Falbel, Sidney L. Shaw, Anita Bennett, and L. Andrew Staehelin,. MCD Biology, Univ. of Colorado, Boulder, Colorado 80309-0347 USA.

Introduction. The complexity of the thylakoid membrane frequently necessitates its separation into component parts before meaningful analysis may be carried out. Thylakoid fractionation, typically via disruption of the bilayer with detergents, and subsequent manipulations required for various analytical techniques, always raises the question of the extent to which the solubilized experimental material is representative of the *in vivo* state. We report here on the application of a new native green gel system to five higher plant species. This system resolves as many as eighteen chlorophyll-protein complexes with very little release of free pigment and with a degree of preservation of subunit-subunit interactions that has not been obtainable with previous systems, suggesting that this system yields a more accurate picture of the native condition of the membrane. The system was originallydeveloped for use with *Chlamydomonas* thylakoids, from which up to twenty chlorophyll-protein complexes may be resolved (Allen and Staehelin, these Proceedings).

Materials and Methods. Fresh spinach was obtained at a local farmer's market. Barley, pea, cucumber and *Arabidopsis thaliana* were grown under fluorescent bulbs at an illumination of about 300 μE/m² sec. Thylakoid membranes were prepared from all species essentially as described by Camm and Green (1980). Fractionation ofstacked and unstacked thylakoids was carried out using a protocol based on the Digitonin system described by Leto et al. (1985) modified to eliminate the use of Triton X-100. Details of the green gel system will be dealt with in an upcoming paper (Allen and Staehelin, manuscript in preparation).

Results and Discussion. Figure 1 shows an example of separation of chlorophyll-protein complexes from barley, pea, spinach, cucumber and *Arabidopsis*. As is the case with *Chlamydomonas*, the green band pattern may be divided into four zones of increasing electrophoretic mobility: PSI-LHCI complexes, PSII-LHCII complexes, oligomeric light harvesting antenna of PSII (LHCII*), and various monomeric antenna complexes (i.e. CP29, CP24, etc.). While this degree of similarity exists between all species examined to date, the degree of interspecies variability revealed by our new gel system, as evident in Figure 1 and discussed further below, precludes an across-the-board, exact assignment of green bands to every species. An advantage of this non-uniformity

M. Baltscheffsky (ed.), Current Research in Photosynthesis, Vol. II, 269–272.
© 1990 *Kluwer Academic Publishers. Printed in the Netherlands.*

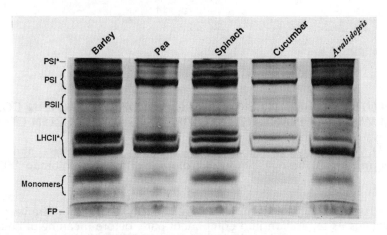

PSI*—
PSI {
PSII {
LHCII* {
Monomers {
FP —

Figure 1. Chlorophyll-Proteins from five higher plant species

is that it opens up a new avenue for the investigation of interspecies variation in chlorophyll-protein complex composition. The disadvantage is that for each new species, specific green bands cannot a priori be assigned specific identities.

LHCII* Complexes. There are a variety of specific differences between the species shown in Figure 1, one of the most striking is the number and position of the LHCII* bands. Pea, for example, on the most favorable gels, shows just two main LHCII* bands plus a faint upper band which is not well resolved here, whereas *Arabidopsis*, on very good gels shows as many as five LHCII* bands (just visible in the fluorescence photograph). The multiplicity of LHCII* bands resolved in cucumber and *Arabidopsis* is particularly interesting in light of the simplicity of the cab gene family in each of these species (Greenland, *et al.*, 1987, Leutwiler, *et al.*, 1986). While we have demonstrated the presence of multiple LHCII apoproteins in *Arabidopsis* (Shaw, Allen and Staehelin, manuscript in preparation), this diversity of LHCII* bands underscores the point that the multiplicity of LHCII* complexes resolved by this gel system cannot be explained solely on the basis of differential trimer assembly from a heterogeneous LHCII apoprotein pool. Preliminary evidence indicates that the binding of various polypeptides, such as CP29, to LHCII* trimers is probably responsible for the multiple forms of this complex resolved here..

2D Gel Analysis. Interspecies variablity can be visualized in much greater detail when a vertical strip is cut out from a green gel, solubilized in Laemmli solubilization buffer, and run out in a second dimension on a fully denaturing gel. Silver stained 2D gels of this sort are shown for spinach (Figure 2a) and *Arabidopsis* (Figure 2b). These gels were run using strips taken from the same green gel shown in Figure 1. While the four zones of the green gel (PSI-LHCI, PSII-LHCII, LHCII*, monomers) may be delineated on these 2D gels, there is substantial variation in the degree of overlap between the PSI-LHCI and PSII-LHCII regions. In spinach, there is a clear boundary between these two zones, with the PSI-LHCI region, easily recognized by the presence of the P700 apoproteins at about 65kDa, having a lower electrophoretic mobility than the PSII-LHCII region, most easily recognized by the presence of the apoproteins of CP47 and CP43 at about 45kDa. In contrast, with the acrylamide mixture used

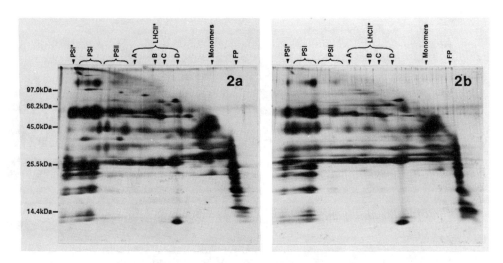

Figure 2. 2D SDS-PAGE analysis of Spinach (2a) and *Arabidopsis* (2b) thylakoids.

here, these two regions overlap substantially in *Arabidopsis*. This emphasizes the fact that with each new species the particular acrylamide matrix used for routine analysis will have to be optimized to yield the maximum separation between the four regions resolved by this gel system.

Stacked/Unstacked Fractionation. One of the questions arising from the resolution of multiple LHCII* bands, particularly since similar, though never identical patterns are obtained from such a variety of species (eight species to date), is what are the functional differences between these LHCII* subpopulations. One approach we are taking toward this question is to examine the presence of these complexes in grana versus stroma-exposed thylakoids, and in particular to look for changes in this distribution during the state 1-state 2 transition. This work, currently in progress, will be dealt with in a future publication. As an example of the first phase of this project, figure 3 shows separation of chlorophyll-proteins from whole spinach thylakoids, from a grana-enriched fraction, and from a stroma lamella fraction. 2D analysis of this green gel shows that the low electrophoretic mobility bands in the grana fraction are almost exclusively PSII-LHCII complexes, while the bands of similar electrophoretic mobility in the stroma lamella fraction are almost exclusively PSI-LHCI complexes (not shown). More importantly, we find that two LHCII* bands, designated LHCII* B & C, are enriched in the unstacked fraction, whereas the main LHCII* band, LHCII* D, is enriched in the grana. Analysis of 2D gels shows that the complexes enriched in the stromal lamellae are in fact LHCII* and not dissociated LHCI. This indicates that our new gel system resolves stroma-enriched from grana-enriched LHCII* populations, and lends support to the notion that the multiple LHCII* bands do in fact represent distinct complexes in the membrane. We have obtained similar results with cucumber and pea. We

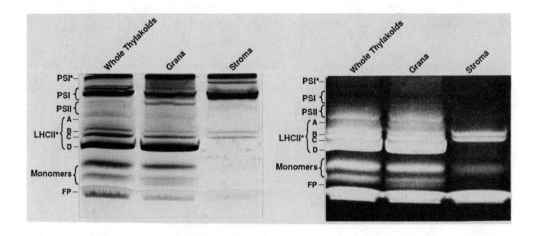

Figure 3. Separation of chlorophyll-protein complexes from grana- and stroma-enriched thylakoid fractions.

complexes during the state 1-state 2 transition.We would like to thank Janet Meehl for superb technical assistance. Tanya Falbel is a Howard Hughes Medical Institute graduate fellow. Supported by NIH grant GM22912 to LAS.

References.

Camm, E.L., and B.R. Green (1980) Plant Physiol. **66**:428-432.
Greenland, A.J., M.V. Thomas, and R.M. Walden (1987) Planta **170**:99-110.
Leto, K.J., E. Bell, L. McIntosh (1985) EMBO J. **4**:1645-1653.
Leutwiler, L.S., E.M. Meyerowitz, and E.M. Tobin (1986) Nuc. Acids Res. **14**:4051-4064.

HETEROGENEITIES OF THE LONG-TERM ACCLIMATION OF LIGHT-HARVESTING IN PHOTOSYSTEM II

Pirkko Mäenpää[*] and Bertil Andersson
Dept. of Biochemistry, Arrhenius Laboratories, University of Stockholm, S-106 91 Stockholm, Sweden, [*]Dept. of Biology, University of Turku, SF-20500 Turku, Finland

Introduction

To optimize photosynthesis and minimize damage the chloroplast thylakoid is able to react sensitively to environmental changes in particular to light. This involves both short- and long-term acclimations. Short-term acclimations take place within minutes while long-term acclimations take place within hours or annual seasons (1). According to the current knowledge PS II proteins seem to play the key role in the acclimation of the thylakoid functions (2).

The complex, highly organized light-harvesting apparatus of PS II consists of several polypeptides carrying chlorophyll (3). The major component is the chlorophyll a/b protein complex LHC II which binds half of total chlorophyll. Several kinds of experimental studies have revealed that LHC II is heterogenous consisting of two subpopulations desigrated LHC II inner and outer (for review see 1). The inner pool is more tightly bound to the PS II core. The outer pool is more loosely or peripherally bound to PS II from which it can be disconnected by protein phosphorylation which i.e. mediates short-term light acclimations of the PS II antenna. Moreover, LHC II outer also seems to play a role in the long-term acclimation of the plant to different light intensities (4). The two pools of LHC II have the same pigment composition of chlorophyll but differ in their polypeptide composition (5, Andersson and Spangfort, these proceedings). The inner pool consists only of a 27 kDa polypeptide while the outer pool has both a 27 and a 25 kDa polypeptide in a ratio of approximately 1.5.

In this study, we have analyzed long-term light acclimation of PS II_α and PS II_β with respect to the heterogeneity of LHC II.

Material and methods

Spinach was grown at 25-30°C in a 10 h light/14h dark cycle. The photosynthetic photon flux density was 475 (high light) and 185 (low

M. Baltscheffsky (ed.), Current Research in Photosynthesis, Vol. II, 273–276.

light) µmol photons m^{-2}s^{-1}. The leaves were used at the age of 5 weeks. Stacked chloroplast thylakoids were isolated by standard procedures. Vesicles derived from the stroma exposed thylakoids were isolated by Yeda press fragmentation and differential centrifugation (6). Chlorophyll protein complexes were resolved by a mild SDS-PAGE using an acrylamide gradient of 8-12%. The electrophoresis was run for 1-1.5 h at a constant current of 15 mA/gel.

The two-dimensional electrophoresis was run according to (7) in order to quantify the relative amounts of the 27 and 25 kDa LHC II apopolypeptides.

Results and Discussion

Long-term acclimation and LHC II heterogeneity

In whole thylakoids, we obserwed the typical long-term acclimation of the PS II antenna in response to different light intensities (Table I): LHC II/CPa had increased from 4.0 (high light) to 5.5 (low light) and this was accompanied by a decrease in the chlorophyll a/b ratio from 2.9 to 2.6. The analysis of the polypeptide composition of LHC II showed a decrease of the 27/25 kDa polypeptide ratio from 3.3 in high light to 2.6 in low light (Table II). This change suggest a relative increase in the proportion of the outer LHC II. Knowledge of the 27/25 ratios of the isolated peripheral and inner LHC II populations (5) enabled us to calculate the relative amounts of these two LHC II populations in thylakoids grown at the different light intensities. In high light, the thylakoids had 42% of the inner and 58% of the outer LHC II, compared with 30 and 70% for low light thylakoids (Table II). The new LHC II units synthesized in low light in order to improve the light-harvesting capacity, can be calculated to have a 27/25 ratio of 1.52. This is exactly the ratio found for the isolated peripheral LHC II pool (Spangfort et al. 1987), which shows that only this pool takes part in the long-term light acclimation of PS II (Fig. 1).

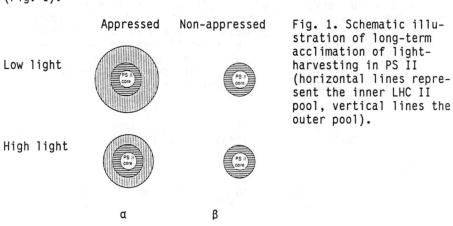

Appressed   Non-appressed

Low light

High light

α   β

Fig. 1. Schematic illustration of long-term acclimation of light-harvesting in PS II (horizontal lines represent the inner LHC II pool, vertical lines the outer pool).

Table I. Long-term light acclimation in the antenna of PS II. Thylakoids were isolated from spinach grown at different light intensities and subfractionated to yield stroma lamellae vesicles. Chlorophyll proteins were resolved by mild SDS-PAGE.

	HIGH LIGHT		LOW LIGHT	
	Thylakoids	Stroma lamellae	Thylakoids	Stroma lamellae
LHCII/CPa	4.0	2.5	5.5	2.6
PS I/PS II	0.43	2.1	0.45	2.9
chl a/b	2.9	6.1	2.6	6.1

Table II. Changes in the 27/25 apopolypeptide ratio of LHC II and in the relative proportion the inner and outer LHC II pools as a function of light intensity. The 27/25 ratio is quantified after a two-dimensional gel electrophoresis. Knowledge of the 27/25 ratios of the isolated inner and outer LHC II pools (5) allowed the calculation of the relative proportions of the pools.

	HIGH LIGHT		LOW LIGHT	
	Thylakoids	Stroma lamellae	Thylakoids	Stroma lamellae
27/25	3.3	4.5	2.6	4.7
% LHC II				
-inner	42	55	30	56
-outer	58	45	70	44

PS II β and long term acclimation

The LHC II/CPa ratio in non-appressed thylakoids is low, only 2.5-2.7 (Table I), compared to unfractionate thylakoids. However, a high relative amount of inner LHC II (56%) can be calculated from the high value (4.6) of the 27/25 ratio (Table II).

In contrast to unfractionated thylakoids, in the stroma thylakoids none of the ratios examined, LHC II/CPa, chlorophyll a/b ratio or the 27/25 kDa polypeptide ratio, changes in response to varying light intensity during growth (Tables I and II). This shows that the changes of the LHC II antenna take place in the appressions and concern PS II α and that PS II β does not undergo long-term light acclimation of its antenna.

Although we did not see a change in the antenna size of PS II in response to varying light there was a change in the number of PS II units in the stroma thylakoids. The PS I/PS II ratio CPI/(CPa + LHC II)) in high light is 2.1 and in low light 3.0 (Table I). Notably this ratio was constant in the unfractionated thylakoids. Since all PS I are located in the non-appressed region (8) and the proportion of chlorophyll connected with PS I does not change during light acclimation (2), the variations in the PS I/PS II ratio in stroma thylakoids can be ascribed to PS II β. The physiological significance of this variation is not obvious. However, it can be speculated that in high light there could be a requirement for a high number of PS II β centers. At increased light intensities there is a high turnover of PS II centers due to D_1-protein degradation. The PS II β centres, which are resistant to photoinhibition (9) could act as a reserve pool ready to compensate for photodamaged PS II α. Alternatively the increased proportion of CPa in high light originates from photodamaged PS II α. It has recently been shown that the D_1 protein degradation is accompanied by movement of free CPa from the appressed to the non-appressed thylakoid regions (Virgin et al. these proceedings).

Acknowledgements. This work was supported by the Swedish Natural Research Council and the Academy of Finland.

References

1. Anderson, J.M. and Andersson, B. (1988) Trend. Biochem. Sci. 13, 351-355.
2. Chow, W.S., Anderson, J.M. and Hope, A.B. (1988) Photosynth. Res. 17, 277-281.
3. Peter, F.G., Machold, O. and Thornber, J.P. (1988) in: Plant Membranes: Structure, Assembly and Function (Harwood, J. and Walton, T.J., eds.), pp. 17-31, The Biochemical Society, London.
4. Larsson, U.K., Anderson, J.M. and Andersson, B. (1987) Biochim. Biophys. Acta 894, 69-75.
5. Spangfort, M., Larsson, U.K., Anderson, J.M. and Andersson, B. (1987) FEBS Lett. 224, 343-347.
6. Andersson, B., Åkerlund, H.-E. and Albertsson, P.-Å. (1976) Biochim. Biophys. Acta 593, 427-440.
7. Larsson, U.K. and Andersson, B. (1985) Biochim. Biophys. Acta 809, 396-442.
8. Andersson, B. and Anderson, J.M. (1980) Biochim. Biophys. Acta 593, 427-440.
9. Mäenpää, P., Andersson, B. and Sundby, C. (1987) FEBS Lett. 215, 31-36.

RESTORATION OF AN OLIGOMERIC FORM OF THE LIGHT-HARVESTING ANTENNA CP II
AND OF A FLUORESCENCE STATE II-STATE I TRANSITION BY Δ3-TRANS-HEXADECE-
NOIC ACID-CONTAINING PHOSPHATIDYLGLYCEROL, IN A MUTANT OF CHLAMYDOMONAS

JACQUES GARNIER, BENRUI WU, JEANNINE MAROC, DENISE GUYON and
ANTOINE TREMOLIERES

Laboratoire de Biochimie Fonctionnelle des Membranes
Végétales, C.N.R.S., Bâtiment 9, F-91198 Gif-sur-Yvette
Cedex, France.

1. INTRODUCTION

Phosphatidylglycerol (PG) containing Δ3-trans-hexadecenoic acid
($C16:1$-trans) is a phospholipid characteristic of the photosynthetic
membranes. Several works concerning higher plants (1-4) or the unicellular green alga Chlamydomonas reinhardtii (5,6) have suggested that
$C16:1$-trans could be involved in the formation and the stability of an
oligomeric form of the main light-harvesting Chl a + b antenna (LHCP or
CP II) and, consequently, in the efficiency of the light energy capture
and transfer. However, other observations have not agreed with such a
suggestion (7,8). We report here a restoration experiment using two
mutants of C. reinhartdii: mf 2, a PS II-lacking but low-fluorescent
mutant which is unable to synthesize $C16:1$-trans, does not show any
oligomeric form of CP II and shows anomalies affecting the regulation
of the excitation energy distribution; Fl 39, a classical PS II-lacking
high-fluorescent mutant, used as a control.

2. MATERIAL AND METHODS

The wild type of C. reinhardtii and the mutants Fl 39 and mf 2 have
been previously described (5,9). Algae were grown in the light in Tris-
acetate-phosphate medium, lipids and chlorophyll-protein complexes (CP)
were analyzed and low-temperature fluorescence emission spectra of
whole cells were measured as in refs. 5,9,10. State I conditions (oxidized plastoquinone (PQ) pool) were obtained by aeration of the cell
suspensions with mild shaking (in the presence of 10 μM DCMU in the
case of the wild type) for 25 min. State II conditions (reduced PQ
pool) were obtained by incubating the cells in the presence of 5 mM
NaN_3 for 25 min in the dark.

Liposomes of $C16:1$-trans-containing PG (PG-$C16:1$-trans) were prepared from spinach leaves. They were added to the algae suspensions
(0.10 mg ml^{-1}) which were then allowed to incubate at 25°C in the light
with mild shaking, for 39 h before analyses and fluorescence measurements.

M. Baltscheffsky (ed.), Current Research in Photosynthesis, Vol. II, 277–280.

3. RESULTS

The wild type and the mutant Fl 39 contained C16:1-trans in their PGs but no C16:1-trans was detected in the PG of the mutant mf 2, as shown by the capillary-gas-liquid chromatogram on Fig. 1. However, after incubation of cells of mf 2 in the presence of liposomes of PG-C16:1-trans for 39 h, a peak of C16:1-trans was clearly seen for the PG of this mutant (mf 2 + PG-C16:1-trans).

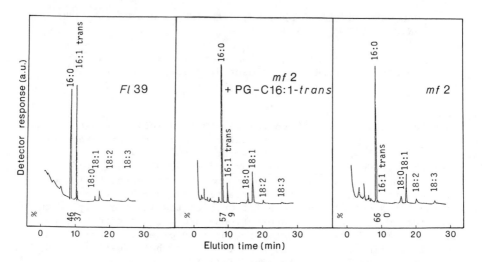

FIG 1. Fatty acid composition of phosphatidylglycerol in the mutants Fl 39 and mf 2.
(%: relative importance of the areas of the different peaks).

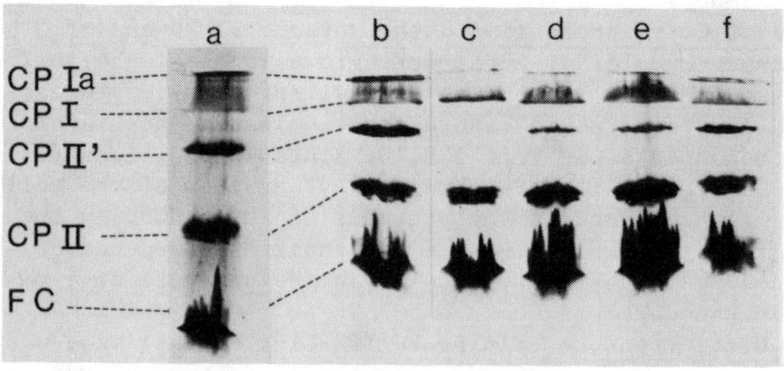

FIG 2. Chlorophyll-protein complexes of the wild type (a) and of the mutants Fl 39 (b,f) and mf 2 (c-e), without (a-c) and after (d-f) incubation of the cells in the presence of liposomes of PG-C16:1-trans.

Fig. 2 shows lithium dodecylsulfate/polyacrylamide gel-electrophore-
tograms of CPs for the different strains. CP II', the oligomeric form
of CP II, was present for the wild type and the mutant Fl 39 (lanes a,
b,f), but no band of CP II' was seen for the mutant mf 2 (lane c).
However, bands of this CP II' clearly appeared after incubation of
mf 2 cells in the presence of PG-C16:1-trans liposomes (lanes d,e).

Fluorescence emission spectra at 77 K (Fig. 3) indicated important
state II-state I transitions in the case of the wild type and of the
mutant Fl 39. For the wild type, in state II, the emission of PS II at
686 nm (F686) was only slightly more important than that of PS I in
the 714 nm region (F714). This PS II emission was clearly higher in
state I, the ratios F686/F714 being 1.12 (state II) and 1.95 (state I).
For the PS II-lacking mutant Fl 39, in state II, the emission of the
antenna CP II at 682 nm (F682) was clearly lower than that of PS I in
the 712-714 nm region (F712), F682/F712 being 0.31. Both these emissions were nearly equivalent in state I (F682/F712 = 0.97).

On the other hand, in the case of the mutant mf 2, even if a weak
state II-state I transition occurred, the ratios F682/F712 were very

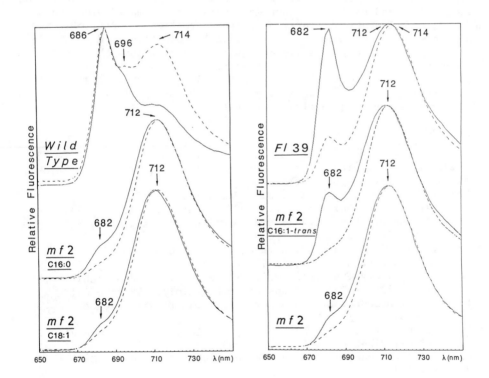

FIG 3. Low-temperature fluorescence emission spectra of cells of the
wild type and of the mutants Fl 39 and mf 2, in state I (solid line)
and in state II (dashed line).

low both in state II (0.12) and in state I (0.20). This indicates a highly predominant energy transfer towards PS I, whatever the oxido-reduction level of the PQ pool. But, when mf 2 cells had been incubated in the presence of PG–C16:1-trans liposomes (mf 2 C16:1-trans), F682/F712 in state I (0.46) was more than twofold increased and so became 3.8 times higher than in state II (0.12), indicating the restoration of an appreciable state II–state I transition. The occurrence of such a restoration was constantly observed during seven other independent experiments using various concentrations of PG–C16:1-trans liposomes. On the other hand, no restoration of an appreciable state II–state I transition occurred when mf 2 cells had been incubated in the presence of liposomes of PG-di-palmitate (mf 2 C16:0, F682/F712 = 0.12 and 0.23) or of phosphatidylcholine-di-oleate (mf 2 C18:1, F682/F712 = 0.13 and 0.17).

4. CONCLUSION

These results pointed out a strong correlation between the presence of C16:1-trans into PG, the formation of an oligomeric form of CP II and the occurrence of a state II–state I transition in the regulation of the excitation energy distribution between the main light-harvesting antenna CP II and PS I. This correlation is not a simple coincidence, as shown by the double restoration of the formation of CP II oligomer and of the occurrence of a state II–state I transition when PG–C16:1-trans, and exclusively this lipid, was incorporated into the thylakoid membrane. Taking into account the results from other authors, we propose, as a working hypothesis, that C16:1-trans could play a role in stabilizing the light-harvesting Chl a + b antenna in its oligomeric form necessary for an efficient state II–state I transition.

REFERENCES

1 Dubacq, J.-P. and Trémolières, A. (1983) Physiol. Vég. 21, 293–312
2 Rémy, R., Trémolières, A. and Ambard-Bretteville, F. (1984) Photobiochem. Photobiophys. 7, 267–276.
3 Huner, N.P.A., Krol, M., Williams, J.P., Maissan, E., Low, P.S., Roberts, D. and Thompson, J.E. (1987) Plant Physiol. 84, 12–18
4 Krol, M., Huner, N.P.A., Williams, J.P. and Maissan, E. (1988) Photosynth. Res. 15, 115–132
5 Maroc, J., Trémolières, A., Garnier, J. and Guyon, D. (1987) Biochim. Biophys. Acta 893, 91–99
6 Manuil'skaya, S.V., Ladygin, V.G., Mikhono, A.I. and Shirshikova, G.N. (1987) Biochemistry (transl. from Biokhimiya) 52, 626–631
7 Browse, J., McCourt, P. and Somerville, C.R. (1985) Science 227, 763–765
8 McCourt, P., Browse, J., Watson, J., Arntzen, C.J. and Somerville, C.R., (1985) Plant Physiol. 78, 853–858.
9 Garnier, J., Maroc, J. and Guyon, D. (1987) Plant Cell Physiol. 28, 1117–1131
10 Garnier, J., Maroc, J. and Guyon, D. (1986) Biochim. Biophys. Acta 851, 395–406

CIRCULAR DICHROISM OF PIGMENT-PROTEIN COMPLEXES OF HIGHER
PLANTS

CHONG CI LI,BEIJING AGRICULTURAL UNIVERSITY, BEIJING,CHINA
XU CHUN-HUI, DAI YUN-LING, ZHOU FU-HONG, WANG KE-BIN, ZHANG
GUO ZHENG,   INSTITUTE OF BOTANY, ACADEMIA SINICA, BEIJING,
CHINA

1. INTRODUCTION
    Circular dichroism measurement is a convenient method
to detect the conformation of molecules,especially protein
molecules [1,2] . We used this method to pigment-protein
complexes,PSII particles and chloroplasts of higher plants.
The helix, β-pleated sheet,β-twist,and unordered coil forms
of proteins each has a characteristic circular dichroism
(CD) spectrum, the CD spectrum of a protein molecule is
the sum of contributions of these forms. We can determine
the fractions of each form in a protein molecule from the
CD spectrum of the protein.
    Light illuminating may cause conformational change in
pigment-protein complexes and CD is perhaps the most
convenient probe to detect conformational change, so we try
to use CD to detect light induced conformational change in
photosynthetic pigment-protein complexes and we observed
these changes.
2. MATERIAL AND METHOD
    Spinach (Spinacia oleracea L.) plants were bought from
the market.
    Chloroplasts were isolated according to Xu et al. [4] ,
and photosystem II preparation was prepared as discribed by
Tang et al. [5].
    Chlorophyll-protein complexes were resolved at 4°C by
using SDS-PAGE according to Xu et al.[4]. After electrophoresis ,CPI- and LHCII - containing gels were then cut off
from the gel column and extracted with 0.3 M Tris (pH 8.8)
seperately, the extracts were used as samples.
    A JASCO J-500 type spectropolarimeter with a DP 500N
data processor was used to obtain CD spectra.The sample was
filled in a cuvette of 1 mm. optical path. We put this
cuvette in a dark box 5 minutes to get "dark adapton", and
then put it into the spectropolarimeter to do   CD
measurement, and the spectrum thus obtained is " dark

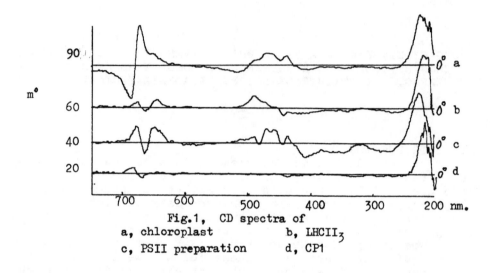

Fig.1, CD spectra of
a, chloroplast   b, LHCII₃
c, PSII preparation   d, CP1

spectrum". After these, the cuvette was taken out and put in a strong light beam to be illuminated for 30 seconds, this light beam (actinic light) came from an incandescent lamp and with an intensity of 125 mW/cm^2, the cuvette was put into the spectropolarimeter again, 3 seconds after the cuvette was taken out from the actinic light beam the spectropolarimeter began to take CD spectrum . this spectrum is " light induced spectrum". Data from these spectra were used to calculate the fractions of helix (HX), β-pleated sheet (BS), β-twist (BT) and unordered (RS) forms by Chang and Yang's method [1,2,3].

3. RESULT AND DISCUSSION

3.1 Fig.1 shows dark CD spectrum of some photosynthetic material. Using data from these spectra we obtained the following result:

For CP1   HX: 13.0% , BS: 2.8% , BT: 45.1% , RS: 39.1%
For LHCII HX: 25.3% , BS: 34.5% , BT: 33.6% , RS: 6.7%

3.2   Fig.2 shows the difference of dark and light induced spectrum of CP1, the upper curve is dark spectrum and the lower one is light induced . The difference is clear and the effect of actinic light was fading with time. Though this spectra show conformational change induced by actinic light clearly, it cannot be used to calculate the fractions of the forms, the light induced spectrum shows that CD changed with both wavelength and time. In order to

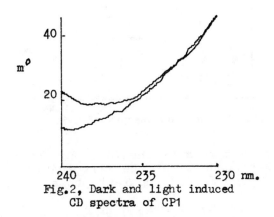

Fig.2, Dark and light induced
CD spectra of CP1

solve this problem, instead of using wavelength scanning
spectrum, we measured CD value and recorded its change with
time while measuring wavelength was fixed (time scan).
Fig.3 is the result of these measurement, in this fig.
there are 11 pairs of segments of curve, every this segment
represents the CD value of the sample measured under a
fixed wavelength, the horizontal axis is time axis, every
segment shows the CD change in a duration of 5 sec. A pair
of segments represent the CD value of same wavelength the
upper segment represents "dark adapted" value and the lower
segment gives the light induced. Different pair corresponds
to different wavelength, the wavelength difference is 1 nm.
to the next pair, from 240 nm. to 230 nm. there are 11
pairs. The start point of the lower segment corresponds to
3 second after the end of sample illuminating, so if we
connect all the start point of the lower segment ,we will
obtain a "3 second after illumination" CD spectrum of the
sample. From this spectrum we can calculate the fractions
of the "forms" of CP1, 3 second after illumination :
  HX: 3.98% , BS: 54.62% , BT: 2.32% , RS: 39.1%
Compare this value with those we obtained from the dark
spectrum of CP1,we found the conformation largely changed,
helix released, β-pleated sheet increased, the decreasing
of helix may be important in chemical reaction and energy
transfer.
    3.3 We did not find light induced CD changed in
pigment part which is represented by 680 nm. band and
480 nm. band, nor any light induced CD change in LHCII, but
this does not mean there were no CD change in LHCII, in our

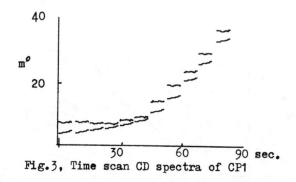

Fig.3, Time scan CD spectra of CP1

experiment we did not measure the fast CD change, our measuring started 3 seconds after the illumination. This is rather too slow, so even in CP1 the fast phase of CD change was unobserved.

Reference
1 Chen,Y.H. and Yang,J.T. (1974) Biochem. 13, 3350-3359
2 Chen,Y.H. and Yang,J.T. (1972) Biochem. 11, 4120-4131
3 Chang,C.T. and Yang,J.T. (1978) Anal Biochem 13,91
4 Xu,C.H. et.al. (1981) Acta Botanica Sinica 23, 40-46
5 Tang,P.S.,Dai,Y.L. et.al. (1984) in Advance in Photosynthesis Research (Sybesma,C., ed.),Vol I,pp.359-362
6 Shepanski,J.F. and Knox,R.S. (1981) Israel Journal of
  Chemistry 21,325-331
7 Brecht,E., Demeter,S. and Faludi-Daniel,A. (1981) Photo-
  biochemistry and Photobiophysics 3, 153-157
8 Frackowiak,D. Bauman,D. and Stillman,M.J. (1982)
  Biochimica et Biophysica Acta 681, 273-285

ISOLATION OF THE LHC I COMPLEX OF BARLEY CONTAINING MULTIPLE PIGMENT-PROTEINS

SHIVANTHI ANANDAN and J. PHILIP THORNBER
Dept. of Biology, University of California,
Los Angeles, California 90024-1606, USA

1. INTRODUCTION

Photosystem I (PS I) in higher plants can be conceived to be composed of two pigmented parts:
--The reaction center-containing core complex (CC I);
--The bulk of the antenna of PS I (LHC I).
Whereas CC I has been obtained as a multi-protein complex (1-3) free of the LHC I light-harvesting pigment-proteins, LHC I itself has been obtained from higher plants only as a series of individual pigment-proteins, LHC Ia, b, c and d (4-9, see ref. 10 for review). In the green alga *Chlamydomonas reinhardtii*, however, a single, green complex (CP0) that is essentially that alga's LHC I complex, has been isolated (11). CP0 is of a higher apparent molecular weight than CC I and has some five polypeptide subunits that are distinct from those of CC I (11,12).

We report here that it is possible to isolate from higher plant thylakoids a multi-protein and pigmented LHC I particle that is free of CC I components and which is equivalent to CP0 of *C. reinhardtii*. The higher plant multimeric LHC I contains four subunits of 24, 21, 17 and 10kD, each of which almost certainly is an apoprotein of the four pigment-proteins in LHC I (LHC Ia, b, c and d) (10); however, its size on non-denaturing polyacrylamide gel electrophoresis (PAGE) is less than that of CC I and hence it is considerably smaller than the CP0 of *C. reinhardtii*; however, note that the subunits are approx 5kDa smaller in higher plants.

2. PROCEDURE

2.1 Materials and Methods

Barley (*Hordeum vulgare* var. Prato) seedlings were grown in a greenhouse under normal growth conditions.

2.1.1. Isolation of PS I:

The preparation of barley thylakoid membranes and PS I vesicles was essentially the same as described for *C. reinhardtii* (13), with the following important modifications: After removal of the proton-ATPase complexes by octyl glucoside/sodium cholate solubilization and high speed centrifugation (14), the thylakoid membranes were resuspended in 25mM Tricine, pH 8.0 buffer but, unlike previous procedures (7,13), Triton-X100 was not added for membrane solubilization since it disrupted the integrity of the LHC I complex. Rather, the membrane suspension was loaded onto a DEAE-cellulose column, which was washed with 0.1% (w/v) dodecyl maltoside.
A PS I-enriched fraction was subsequently eluted from the column with a

M. Baltscheffsky (ed.), Current Research in Photosynthesis, Vol. II, 285–288.
© 1990 *Kluwer Academic Publishers. Printed in the Netherlands.*

buffered 0-0.3M NaCl gradient containing 0.1% dodecyl maltoside. The eluted material was loaded on to the top of a 5%-25% (w/v) sucrose density gradient and centrifuged at 80,000xg for approx. 24hrs. The heaviest pigmented band proved to be the PS I complex.

2.1.2. Polyacrylamide Gel Electrophoresis:
    Non-denaturing PAGE was carried out as described by Peter et al. (8). Purified PS I isolated from sucrose gradients was incubated at 37 C for 20 mins. and electrophoresed on a Deriphat non-denaturing gel. Denaturing SDS-PAGE was by a modification of the method of Laemmli (8), in which 4M urea was contained in the separating gel.
    All reagents and chemicals were obtained from Sigma Chemical Company. DEAE-cellulose for column chromatography was purchased from Whatman.

3. RESULTS AND DISCUSSION

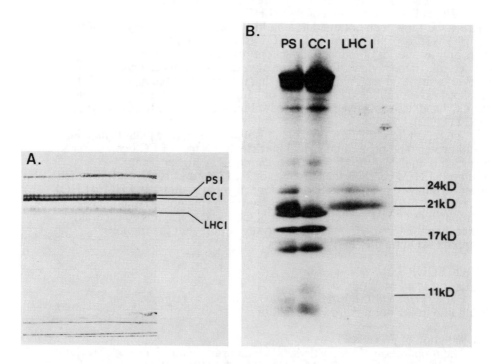

Figure 1. A: Non-denaturing Deriphat 160-PAGE of isolated PS I after treatment at 40^{0}; note that some of the original PS I contibutes the uppermost band. B: SDS-PAGE of each of the green bands from part A.

    Non-denaturing PAGE of the purified PS I complex yielded three pigment-protein bands (Fig.1). These pigment-protein complexes were subsequently identified as PS I, CC I and LHC I in order of decreasing size. CC I is blue-green, typical of other chl *a* and beta-carotene containing

material, whereas the other two fractions are yellow-green and contain chls
and b, and xanthophylls.

The pigment-protein complexes were identified further by:-
(a) <u>Polypeptide subunit composition</u> (Fig. 1b).

The polypeptide compositions of the PS I and CC I pigment-protein bands
is similar to those obtained previously for other organisms (1,3,7,13): Note,
however, that PS I does not contain any LHC IIb subunits, a frequent
contaminant of PS I preparations, which we ascribe to our not using
Triton-X100 for the purification of PS I. The polypeptide composition of the
LHC I pigmented band represents those PS I protein subunits that are not
contained in CC I. This then indicates that the LHC I pigment-protein complex
indeed contains components of the PS I antenna. The 21kD polypeptide, the LHC
Ib apoprotein, is often seen as a doublet.

(b) <u>Spectroscopy.</u>

TABLE I.   Some spectral characteristics of the three pigmented protein bands
in Fig Ib.

Fraction	Absorption λ max.	77K emission λmax.
PS I	676nm	720nm
CC I	678nm	690nm
LHC I	673.5nm	730nm

The spectroscopic data indicate that both the PS I and LHC I fractions
show long wavelength fluorescence at 77K characteristic of the higher plant
PS I antenna; however, we might have expected the emission maximum of PS I
to be at 730nm and that of CC I to be at about 720nm, the more commonly
observed values. The shorter wavelengths might have been obtained because
the surfactant surrounding the pigment-protein had shifted the emission
maximum quite substantially, as demonstrated by Nechushtai et al (15).

It has been previously suggested that there are four pigment-proteins in
LHC I with apoprotein sizes of 24, 21, 17 and 11 kDa. Lam (4,5) and others(6)
showed that the 21kD subunit was a chlorophyll-protein (LHCP 1b) with a 730nm
fluorescence at 77 K and that a second pigment-protein was probably present.
Subsequently, Vainstein et al (9) demonstrated in maize that there are at
least three LHC I pigment-proteins (LHC Ia, b and c) with apoprotein sizes of
24, 21 and 17kDa, respectively. Peter et al. (8) showed the presence of four
pigment-proteins in LHC I, the fourth having an apoprotein of 11kDa. We
therefore conclude from our studies that these four polypeptides of LHC I in
barley (Fig.1b) occur as a separate and distinct multi-protein complex from
that of CC I, and that the two together constitute the bulk and perhaps all
of PS I. There may, of course, be smaller molecular weight polypeptides
(<10kDa) in PS I, similar to those in PS II, that have yet to be identified.
While our data were obtained using barley, similar work on other plants
indicates that multiprotein complexes of the LHC I pigment-proteins is
perhaps a general phenomenon in higher plants (cf.9).

Biochemical descriptions of the four pigment-proteins of LHC I are not yet well advanced, and, in particular, one of their most desired characteristics, their primary structures, has not been unequivocally determined. From our data on amino acid sequencing of the N-terminus of these polypeptides (S. Anandan, A. Vainstein and J.P. Thornber, FEBS Lett., submitted) we conclude that the putative LHC I clone of Hoffman et al. (16) is that of the LHC Ia apoprotein, that one of the 21kDa subunits is blocked, that no clone exists so far for the other LHC Ib subunit, and that the primary sequence of the 17 kDa component (LHC Ic) is known. While the sequence of the LHC Ia apoprotein shows considerable homology to that of LHC IIb, that of LHC Ic shows virtually no homolgy other than that it probably has the same number of membrane-spanning segments (cf. 17).

4. ACKNOWLEDGEMENTS
The research was supported by grants from the National Science Foundation (DMB 87-16230) and the United States Department of Agriculture (88-37262-3557). S.A. was supported by a McKnight fellowship.

REFERENCES

1   Mullet, J.E., and Arntzen, C.J. (1980) Plant Physiol. 65, 814.
2. Bengis, C., and Nelson, N. (1977) J. Biol. Chem. 252, 4564.
3. Nechushtai, R., and Nelson, N. (1981) J. Biol. Chem. 256, 11624.
4. Lam, E., Ortiz, W., Mayfield, S., and Malkin,R. (1984) Plant Physiol. 74, 650.
5. Lam, E., Ortiz, W., and Malkin, R. (1984) FEBS Lett. 168, 10.
6. Bassi, R., Machold, O., and Simpson, D. (1985) Carlsberg R. 50,145.
7. Nechushtai, R., Peterson, C.C., Peter, G.F., and Thornber,J.P. (1987) Eur. J. Biochem. 164, 345.
8. Peter, G.F., Machold, O., and Thornber, J.P. (1988) in PLANT MEMBRANES: STRUCTURE, ASSEMBLY AND FUNCTION, Harwood, J.L. and Walton, T.L. eds. The Biochemical Society, London. p.17.
9. Vainstein, A., Peterson, C.C., and Thornber, J.P. (1989) J. Biol. Chem. 256, 4058.
10. Thornber, J.P., Morishige, D.T., Anandan, S., and Peter, G.F. (1989) In THE CHLOROPHYLLS, H. Scheer, ed. CRC UniScience Series CRC Press. Boca Raton, Florida in press.
11. Wollman, F.A., and Bennoun, P. (1982) Biochim. Biophys. Acta 680,352.
12. Ish-Shalom, D., and Ohad, I. (1983) Biochim. Biophys. Acta 722, 498
13. Schuster, G., Nechushtai, R., Ferriera P.G., Thornber, J.P., and Ohad, I. (1988) Eur. J. Biochem. 177,411.
14. Nechushtai, R., Nelson, N., Mattoo, A., and Edelmann, M. (1981) FEBS Lett. 125, 115.
15. Nechushtai, R., Nourizadeh, S.D., and Thornber, J.P. (1986) Biochim. Biophys. Acta 848,193.
16. Hoffman, N.E., Pichersky, E., Malik, V.S., Castresana, C., Ko, K., Darr S.C., and Cashmore, A.R. (1987) Proc. Natl. Acad. Sci. USA. 84, 8844.
17. Karlin-Neumann, G.A., Kohorn, B.D., Thornber, J.P., and Tobin, E.M. (1985) J. Mol. Appl. Genet. 3, 45.

FEMTOSECOND DYNAMICS OF CAROTENOID TO CHLOROPHYLL ENERGY TRANSFER IN THYLAKOID MEMBRANE PREPARATIONS FROM *Phaeodactylum tricornutum* AND *Nannochloropsis* sp.

J. K. Trautman*, A. P. Shreve*, T. G. Owens[†], and A. C. Albrecht*
Department of Chemistry* and Section of Plant Biology[†],
Cornell University, Ithaca, NY 14853 USA

INTRODUCTION

Carotenoids serve as light-harvesting pigments in nearly all photosynthetic organisms. Despite the ubiquity and importance of carotenoid-to-chlorophyll (chl) energy transfer, a thorough description of the process is lacking. Studies on photosynthetic bacteria have shown that both the quantum efficiency and the dynamics of carotenoid-to-bacteriochlorophyll singlet energy transfer vary considerably among species. Transfer efficiencies from ~20% to ~100% have been reported [1], while transfer times from ~0.2 [2] to ~5 ps [3, 4] have been measured. The reasons for the variability are not certain. Here we report time-resolved measurements of carotenoid-to-chl a singlet energy transfer in thylakoid membrane preparations from the diatom *Phaeodactylum tricornutum* and the eustigmatophyte *Nannochloropsis* sp. (clone GSB Sticho) and discuss the implications of our results for the description of carotenoid-chl coupling.

EXPERIMENTAL

Our femtosecond laser system is similar to that described in [5]. It consists of a colliding-pulse-modelocked (cpm) laser, a four-stage dye amplifier, continuum generation and a single-stage continuum amplifier. In the present work, the pump pulse is an amplified continuum pulse with ~10 nm bandwidth whose central wavelength is varied between 480 and 540 nm; the pump energy is about 5 μJ per pulse. The probe pulse is an unamplified continuum pulse. The probe wavelength of 670 nm is selected by a monochromator positioned after the sample cell. Pump-probe cross-correlations are typically 240 fs. Both the pump and probe beams are linearly polarized. The relative polarization of pump and probe is controlled with a $\lambda/2$ plate in the pump beam. Samples are circulated through a flow system; the sample reservoir is maintained at a temperature of ~ 10° C by an ice bath. The concentration of the solutions is adjusted to obtain an optical density of approximately 0.3 for a 2 mm path length at the excitation wavelength. Thylakoid membranes are prepared in 100 mM Tris-borate buffer as described in [6]. The data are fit with a non-linear least squares routine to the convolution of the cross-correlation with a function representing a kinetic model.

M. Baltscheffsky (ed.), Current Research in Photosynthesis, Vol. II, 289–292.
© 1990 *Kluwer Academic Publishers. Printed in the Netherlands.*

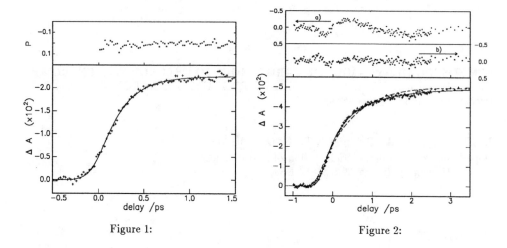

Figure 1:   Figure 2:

Figure 1: Induced transmission and its polarization at 670 nm following excitation at 520 nm in GSB thylakoids. The transfer time is 0.24±.04 ps.

Figure 2: Bleach at 670 nm following 520 nm excitation in *P. tricornutum* thylakoids. Fits from both one (– –) and two (—) channel models are overlaid. The transfer time from the one channel model is 0.9±.1 ps; the times from the two channel model are 0.5±.1 and 2.0±.5 ps with relative amplitudes of 1.7 ± .7 : 1. The residuals for the one channel fit are shown in curve a); those for the two channel fit are shown in curve b).

RESULTS AND DISCUSSION

The carotenoid-to-chl a energy transfer rate is determined by pumping the carotenoid then probing the chl a $S_0 \rightarrow S_1$ transition at various times after the excitation pulse. In the 480 – 540 nm spectral region, about 95% of the thylakoid absorbance is due to carotenoids in the light-harvesting-complexes (lhcs), so, the energy transfer times determined in this study are those appropriate to the lhc. Fig. 1 shows the rise of the chl a bleach at 670 nm following carotenoid excitation at 520 nm in GSB thylakoids. The polarization [7] of the transient absorption is shown in the top part of the figure. Fig. 2 shows the induced transmission at 670 nm following excitation at 520 nm in *P. tricornutum* thylakoids and the residuals from both one and two channel fits. The uncertainties in the reported values are from the dispersion in the best fit parameters to multiple data sets taken over a few days. There is no significant change in any of fit parameters with excitation wavelength between 480 and 540 nm, though better signal-to-noise may reveal such a dependence.

For each of these species, the carotenoid-to-chl a energy transfer times are at least 30 times shorter than the carotenoid *in vitro* S_1 lifetimes (for a discussion of carotenoid electronic states see [8]). The primary carotenoid in the GSB lhc is violaxanthin; we have measured a ground state recovery time for violaxanthin in ethanol of ~13 ps. Fucoxanthin is the primary carotenoid in the lhcs of *P. tricornutum*; its *in vitro* ground state recovery time is ~30 ps. Assuming that the S_1 lifetime is not shorter *in vivo* than *in vitro* (which is a reasonable assumption), then these short transfer times mean that energy transfer efficiencies less than ∼95% imply the existence of a subpopulation of uncoupled carotenoids. In lhcs isolated from *P. tricornutum*, the efficiency varies from $90 \pm 10\%$ at 540 nm to $50 \pm 10\%$ at 490 nm [8]. The wavelength dependence of the energy transfer efficiency and the wavelength independence of the transfer times in *P. tricornutum* suggest that there is an inhomogenous distribution of carotenoid $S_0 \rightarrow S_2$ transition energies and that the red-shifted carotenoids are more strongly, perhaps exclusively, coupled to chl *a*. However, this does not mean that the red-shift is essential to efficient transfer. Rather, it is likely that in *P. tricornutum* lhcs, the 'coupled' carotenoid binding site incidently induces a red-shift of the $S_0 \rightarrow S_2$ transition.

The absence of any polarization, in GSB thylakoids, is a very interesting result. Interpretation of the polarization is not as straightforward in transient absorption experiments as in fluorescence studies. For example, in the present work, the signal at 670 nm has a component due to chl *a* ground state depletion and a component due to chl *a* $S_1 \rightarrow S_n$ absorption. The transition dipole of the transient response will be a vector sum of the $S_0 \rightarrow S_1$ and $S_1 \rightarrow S_n$ transition dipoles. The observed response at 670 nm is a bleach, so, at this wavelength, the *in vivo* $S_0 \rightarrow S_1$ cross-section is clearly larger than the $S_1 \rightarrow S_n$ cross-section (for *in vitro* measurements see [9]). The direction of the excited state transition dipole is not known. Nevertheless, the polarization yields information on the relative orientations of the carotenoid $S_0 \rightarrow S_2$ transition dipole and the well-defined, if unknown, chl *a* 670 nm transient bleach transition dipole. The expression for the polarization, P, as a function of the angle, θ, between the (non-degenerate) absorption and probe transition dipoles is

$$P = \frac{2cos\theta - sin\theta}{4cos\theta + 3sin\theta}.$$

Assuming a single relative orientation of carotenoid and chl *a* in GSB lhcs, θ is $63 \pm 8°$. There is no independent evidence for this assumption. But, given that there is a single transfer time, then if there are multiple relative orientations, the transfer time cannot depend on the relative orientation and the average relative orientation is such that zero polarization is observed.

The carotenoid-to-chl *a* energy transfer in *P. ticorutum* thylakoids is best fit by a two channel model as demonstrated in Fig. 2. The polarization measured for a excitation wavelength of 520 nm, has a small, but nonzero, value of ∼ 0.08 which decays to zero with an approx. 20 ps time constant. For a single carotenoid-chl *a* relative orientation, θ is ∼ 53°. The two transfer times could be a result of two binding sites, in which case, a single relative orientation may be incorrect. If there are two orientations giving rise to two transfer times, one can, in principle, extract the two angles from the evolution of $P(t)$ in the first few picoseconds. In the present experiments, the signal-to-noise is sufficient only to give a rough estimation of the angles. Both $P(t)$ and the polarization independence of the amplitude ratio of the two channels imply that, if there are two angles, they are in the range $25° \leq \theta_1, \theta_2 \leq 65°$.

Finally, we turn to the question of coupling. The recognition that naturally occuring carotenoids have a dipole forbidden S_1 state lying below the dipole allowed S_2 state, as do long, all-trans C_{2h} polyenes, has led to the general acceptance of intermolecular exchange interaction as the carotenoid-chl coupling mechanism [1]. However, we believe that the carotenoid-chl coupling warrents further investigation. Irrespective of the origin of the coupling, the magnitude of the coupling integral, which includes both Coulomb and exchange terms, can be calculated from the general 'golden rule' expression for the energy transfer rate by using the experimentally determined transfer rate and the chl absorption and carotenoid emission spectra. Carotenoid S_1 emission has never been observed, but we have recently determined the two-photon absorption spectrum of the coupled carotenoids in *P. tricornutum* thylakoids [8]. By reflecting this spectrum about the '0-0', an estimation of the spectral overlap integral has been obtained. The magnitude of this integral is not very sensitive to the position of the S_1 origin, so shifts up to 1000 cm^{-1} do not make a significant difference in the transfer efficiency. This insensitivity and the fact that polyene A-states are generally less susceptible to environmentally induced shifts than are B-states [10] are the reasons we believe the red-shift of the $S_0 \rightarrow S_2$ transition is incidental to the increased coupling efficiency of the red-shifted carotenoids. Using the estimated spectral overlap integral, coupling energies on the order of 60 and 120 cm^{-1} are calculated for transfer times of 0.25 and 1 ps, respectively. Extensive calculations of Coulomb and exchange integrals for aromatic molecular crystals have been preformed by Jortner, Rice and co-workers [11]. An order of magnitude estimate of coupling integrals between π-electron systems can be obtained from their work. The 'distance' between the carotenoid and chl a must be 5–10 Å for the exchange integral to be $\sim$100 cm^{-1}. But, for separations < 10 Å, the Coulomb integral may well be $\sim$100 cm^{-1} also, even though the carotenoid $S_1 \rightarrow S_0$ transition has a vanishing dipole moment. We are currently investigating the various contributions to the carotenoid-chl coupling integrals. Of particular interest is the angular dependence of the coupling given that there appears to be a single relative orientation of carotenoid and chl a. In conclusion, we note that we have found no correlation between between carotenoid-to-chl energy transfer efficiencies and transfer rates in either of the algal thylakoids studied here or in the B800-850 lhcs studied previously [2]. Thus, the suggestion that the transfer efficiency is determined by the relative rates of energy transfer and carotenoid $S_1 \rightarrow S_0$ internal conversion, though reasonable, is not generally correct.

ACKNOWLEDGEMENTS

ACA thanks the NSF, Grant CHE–8617960, the NIH, Grant GM–10865 and the Cornell Material Science Center; TGO thanks the NSF, Grant DMB–8803626.

REFERENCES

1. Cogdell, R.J. and Frank, H.A. (1987) *Biochim. Biophys. Acta* **895**, 63–79.
2. Trautman, J.K., Shreve, A.P., Violette, C.A., Frank, H.A., Owens, T.G. and Albrecht, A.C. (submitted to *PNAS*).
3. Wasielewski, M.R., Tiede, D.M. and Frank, H.A. (1986) *Ultrafast Phenomena V. Springer Series in Chemical Physics*, (G.R. Fleming and A.E. Siegman eds.), Vol. 46, 388–392.
4. Gillbro, T., Cogdell, R.J. and Sundstrom, V. (1988) *FEBS Letters* **235**, 169–172.
5. Gauduel, Y., Migus, A., Martin, J.L., Lecarpentier, Y. and Antonetti, A. (1985) *Ber. Bunsenges. Phys. Chem.* **89**, 218–222.
6. Owens, T.G. and Wold, E.R. (1986) *Plant Physiol.* **80**, 732–738.
7. Albrecht, A.C. (1961) *J. Mol. Spec.* **6**, 84–108.
8. Shreve, A.P., Trautman, J.K., Owens, T.G. and Albrecht, A.C. (1989) *these proceedings*.
9. Shepanski, J.F. and Anderson, R.W. (1981) *Chem. Phys. Lett.* **78**, 165–173.
10. Birge, R.R. and Pierce, B.M. (1979) *J. Chem. Phys.* **70**, 165–178.
11. Rice, S.A. and Jortner, J. (1965) in *Physics of Solids at High Pressures* (Tomizuka, C.T. and Emrick, R.M. eds.), Academic Press, 63–168.

CAROTENOID TO CHLOROPHYLL *a* SINGLET ENERGY TRANSFER:
DIRECT EVIDENCE FOR INVOLVEMENT OF THE CAROTENOID 'A' STATE
IN AN ALGAL LIGHT-HARVESTING SYSTEM

A.P. Shreve[†], J.K. Trautman[†], T.G. Owens[‡] and A.C. Albrecht[†]
[†]Department of Chemistry and [‡]Section of Plant Biology
Cornell University, Ithaca, NY 14853

INTRODUCTION

Carotenoids are an important component of the light-harvesting antenna in photosynthetic systems [1]. Their intense blue-green absorptions, together with carotenoid to chlorophyll energy transfer, allow photosynthetic systems to utilize incident radiation that would otherwise be wasted. Measurement of carotenoid to chlorophyll energy transfer efficiency and energy transfer rates provides important information about the details of the function of carotenoids in light harvesting. In this work we report a measurement of carotenoid to chlorophyll *a* singlet energy transfer efficiency in thylakoid membranes of the algal diatom *P. tricornutum*. We also present a two-photon excitation spectrum that directly verifies the *in vivo* existence and energy transfer capability of an energetically low-lying carotenoid electronic state (A state) not seen in the absorption spectrum. Mechanistic considerations arising from these results and from time-resolved measurements of carotenoid to chlorophyll *a* energy transfer [2] are discussed.

The electronic state structure of carotenoids is closely related to that of extensively studied polyenes [3]. A comparison of ground state recovery times and emission yields [4, 5, 6] and a preresonance Raman excitation profile study [7] have indicated that *in vitro* the lowest energy excited singlet electronic state in carotenoids is not the electronic state appearing in the absorption spectrum. Rather, a state analogous to the one-photon forbidden, two-photon allowed 2^1A_g electronic state of C_{2h} symmetry polyenes appears to be the lowest excited electronic state, while a state analogous to the strongly (one-photon) absorbing 1^1B_u electronic state of C_{2h} symmetry polyenes is seen in the absorption spectrum. We shall refer to these states as the A and B states, respectively. Only the excitation profile experiment has provided information about the energy gap between the A and B states; for *in vitro* β-carotene the A state is ~ 3500 cm^{-1} lower in energy than the B state [7].

There has been much speculation that the A state is important in carotenoid to chlorophyll energy transfer. Depending upon the size of the A–B state energy gap and the relative widths of the A and B state emissions, energy transfer to chlorophyll from the energetically lower carotenoid A state might have more favorable donor-acceptor spectral overlap than transfer from the carotenoid B state. Also, since B to A internal conversion occurs within ~ 100 fs following initial population of the optically accessible B state [4, 5, 6], transfer solely from the B state would have to be extremely rapid. There has, however, never been direct evidence of the involvement of a carotenoid A state in carotenoid to chlorophyll

M. Baltscheffsky (ed.), Current Research in Photosynthesis, Vol. II, 293–296.
© 1990 *Kluwer Academic Publishers. Printed in the Netherlands.*

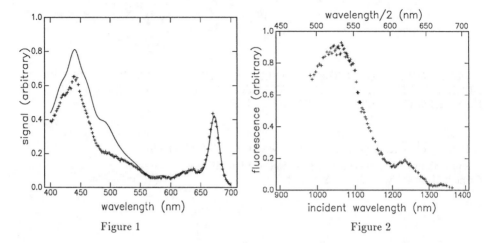

Figure 1

Figure 2

Figure 1: Fluorescence excitation spectrum (symbols) for chlorophyll a emission (λ=720 nm). Also shown is the spectrum of fraction of incident light absorbed (line). The curves are scaled to match across the chlorophyll a Q_y absorption.

Figure 2: Two-photon fluorescence excitation spectrum for chlorophyll a emission. The incident wavelength is shown on the bottom axis, the one-photon wavelength with the same energy as two incident photons is shown on the top axis.

energy transfer, nor of the *in vivo* existence of a carotenoid low energy A state. In addition to providing such evidence, the present work determines the *in vivo* A–B state energy gap, although interpretation of this result is complicated by several factors in *P. tricornutum*.

EXPERIMENTAL

Both one- and two-photon excitation profiles for chlorophyll a fluorescence are presented. The one-photon spectrum was obtained using a photon corrected commercial fluorimeter, the two-photon spectrum was obtained using tunable near-ir radiation obtained by Raman shifting the output of a high power pulsed visible dye laser. The two-photon response varied quadratically with incident laser power and was corrected for variations in incident power by use of a reference signal from second harmonic generation in KDP powder [8]. Thylakoid membrane samples were prepared by disruption of cells in a French pressure cell followed by centrifugation. The samples were dissolved in a buffered solution (50mM Tris borate, pH 8.0) of water (one-photon experiments) or D_2O (two-photon experiments). During experiments the sample temperature was maintained at $\sim$10° C.

RESULTS AND DISCUSSION

The one-photon excitation spectrum and fraction absorbed spectrum (Figure 1) allow us to determine the overall carotenoid to chlorophyll a energy transfer efficiency. The data shown are for isolated light-harvesting complexes from *P. tricornutum*. We find a wavelength dependent transfer efficiency whose value changes from nearly 100% for wavelengths to the red of 540 nm to a minimum of about 50% near 490 nm and rises to about

80% through the chlorophyll a/chlorophyll c Soret regions. As discussed elsewhere [2], because of the rapidity and the wavelength independence of the kinetics of carotenoid to chlorophyll a energy transfer we believe the wavelength dependence of the energy transfer efficiency is a result of the absorption of a pool of carotenoids unable to transfer to chlorophyll. We also see less than unit carotenoid to chlorophyll a energy transfer efficiency in thylakoid membrane preparations of the Eustigmatophyte *Nannochloropsis* sp. Similarly, given the extremely rapid carotenoid to chlorophyll a energy transfer time (~ 0.2 ps) in this system, we believe that the transfer efficiency implies that a fraction of carotenoids simply do not transfer their energy to chlorophyll.

The two-photon excitation spectrum (Figure 2) provides direct evidence that an electronic state with strong two-photon absorption strength exists in the carotenoid spectral region. Further, the state must be capable of transferring its energy to chlorophyll a in order for us to see chlorophyll a fluorescence. We have also obtained *in vitro* two-photon fluorescence excitation spectra of both chlorophyll a and chlorophyll c (not shown); neither demonstrates any feature resembling the large peak seen in Figure 2. Thus, we assign the feature peaking at an incident wavelength of 1060 nm to two-photon absorption of a carotenoid A state with subsequent carotenoid to chlorophyll a energy transfer.

The determination of an A to B state energy gap from our results is complicated by several factors. First, there are several different carotenoids in *P. tricornutum*, the predominant one ($\sim 60\%$ of total) being fucoxanthin. Each carotenoid could well have different A and/or B state energies. Second, the one-photon absorption and fluorescence excitation spectra (Figure 1) have an unusually extended red-wavelength tail in the carotenoid region. This feature is not seen for *in vitro* carotenoid absorption spectra and is not well understood. The two-photon spectrum (Figure 2) has a similarly shaped red-wavelength tail; the possibility exists that the one- and two-photon spectra are probing a distribution of excited B and A state energies, respectively, resulting from different carotenoids and/or different binding environments. Also, the interpretation of the red-wavelength tail of the carotenoid region in the two-photon spectrum is complicated by the contribution of chlorophyll a states. It appears that the *in vivo* two-photon intensity distribution among the chlorophyll a Q_x and Q_y (0,0) and (0,1) states is different from that seen in the *in vitro* two-photon spectrum we have obtained [unpublished result]. Notwithstanding the above complications, by comparing the one- and two-photon excitation spectra we estimate an energy gap of at most a few hundred cm^{-1} between the A and B states. Precise determination of A to B energy gaps for particular carotenoids awaits further experiments in systems with more precisely determined carotenoid composition and spectral characterization.

There are important mechanistic implications resulting from the occurrence of energy transfer to chlorophyll from the carotenoid A state. In the point group C_{2h} the transition dipole between the polyene 2^1A_g first excited state and the 1^1A_g ground state is zero by symmetry; thus, energy transfer from the 2^1A_g state via transition dipole-transition dipole coupling is not possible. To the extent that the A state is not seen in the absorption spectrum of carotenoids, and it has never been unambiguously observed, this conclusion remains valid for carotenoids whose first excited state is perturbed from A_g symmetry as a result of either non-C_{2h} molecular symmetry, environmental perturbations or vibronic coupling effects. The remaining possibilities for energy transfer mechanisms are higher order Coulombic interactions, i.e., quadrupole and higher order terms in the multipole expansion of the coupling Hamiltonian, and exchange coupling. The latter mechanism has received much more attention than the former, perhaps because exchange coupling is the mechanism of triplet energy transfer. Exchange coupling requires significant orbital overlap between the donor and acceptor molecules and is therefore effective only for a separation distance of a few Ångstroms. The former type of interaction, which becomes increasingly important with decreasing intermolecular distances, has been examined for some molecular systems [9, 10] but is generally not discussed. For intermolecular distances on the order of molecular sizes, truncation of the multipole expansion at the level of dipole-dipole interaction fails badly [10]. The errors arising from such a truncation can be as large as or larger than the contribution of exchange terms to the intermolecular interaction energy. Using measured carotenoid to chlorophyll a energy transfer rates [2] and estimated carotenoid emission/chlorophyll a absorption spectral overlap integrals, we find an intermolecular interaction of ~ 100 cm^{-1}. An analysis of anthracene crystals has found intermolecular coupling contributions of this size from higher order multipole interactions [9]. We plan to carry out a detailed theoretical investigation of carotenoid/chlorophyll Coulombic coupling in an effort to determine whether such interactions might contribute to energy transfer even though the carotenoid A state transition dipole is quite small, or whether exchange coupling is, in fact, the dominant energy transfer mechanism.

To summarize, we have used two-photon spectroscopy to excite the carotenoid A state in an algal thylakoid membrane and have directly demonstrated the role of this state in carotenoid to chlorophyll singlet energy transfer. Two possible energy transfer mechanisms have been discussed; although exchange coupling is known to be the mechanism of triplet energy transfer and may well be the dominant mechanism of carotenoid to chlorophyll singlet energy transfer, we have not yet been able to rule out the possibility of short range Coulomb interactions contributing to the intermolecular coupling. The technique of two-photon excitation spectroscopy applied to other photosynthetic light-harvesting systems will allow the precise *in vivo* determination of heretofore unknown carotenoid A–B state energy gaps.

ACKNOWLEDGEMENTS

Support for this work is gratefully acknowledged: ACA thanks the NSF, Grant CHE–8617960, the NIH, Grant GM–10865 and the Cornell University Materials Science Center; TGO thanks the NSF, Grant DMB–8803626. We also thank Jim Slattery and Nathalie Miller for technical assistance.

REFERENCES

[1] Cogdell, R.J. and Frank, H.A., (1987) *Biochim. Biophys. Acta*, **895** 63–79.

[2] Trautman, J.K., Shreve, A.P., Owens, T.G. and Albrecht, A.C., these proceedings.

[3] Hudson, B.S., Kohler, B.E. and Schulten, K., (1982) *Excited States*, **5** 1–95.

[4] Wasielewski, M.R. and Kispert, L.D., (1986) *Chem. Phys. Lett.*, **128** 238–243.

[5] Bondarev, S.L., Dvornikov, S.S. and Bachilo, S.M., (1988) *Opt. Spectrosc. (USSR)*, **64** 268–270.

[6] Gillbro, T. and Cogdell, R.J., (1989) *Chem. Phys. Lett.*, **158** 312–316.

[7] Thrash, R.J., Fang, H.L.B. and Leroi, G.E., (1977) *J. Chem. Phys.*, **67** 5930–5933.

[8] Jones, R.D. and Callis, P.R., (1988) *J. Appl. Phys.*, **64** 4301–4305.

[9] Rice, S.A. and Jortner, J., (1965) in *Physics of Solids at High Pressures* (Tomizuka, C.T. and Emrick, R.M., eds.), Academic Press, 63–168.

[10] Chang, J.C., (1977) *J. Chem. Phys.*, **67** 3901–3909.

PICOSECOND CHLOROPHYLL FLUORESCENCE FROM HIGHER PLANTS

STEVEN W. MCCAULEY,[*] EDITH BITTERSMANN, MARC MUELLER and
ALFRED R. HOLZWARTH   Max Planck Institut fuer Strahlenchemie,
Stiftstrasse 34-36, D4330 Muelheim a.d. Ruhr, F.R. Germany

1. INTRODUCTION
    Light energy absorbed by a Chl molecule creates an exciton which
can produce photochemistry, heat or fluorescence. Fluorescence
lifetime measurements have demonstrated that the observed fluorescence
is a sum of several lifetime components. We present evidence that:
1) The fluorescence lifetimes are trap-limited in both PSI and PSII
2) PSII fluorescence decays with biexponential kinetics
3) Separate fluorescence lifetime components can be observed from
   PSII-alpha and PSII-beta
    These results are in agreement with previous results from this
laboratory described in (1,2,3,4).

2. MATERIALS AND METHODS
    Picosecond fluorescence decays were measured using a single photon
timing apparatus previously described (1). The sample was excited with
laser pulses at either 630 nm or 692 nm and fluorescence emission was
measured at wavelengths from 670 to 740 nm. Data analysis was
performed using a global deconvolution procedure in which the decays at
all emission wavelengths are analysed simultaneously in order to
minimize the number of free parameters in the fit. The data have from
10,000 to 65,000 counts in the peak channel depending on the experiment.
Chloroplasts were prepared from peas and barley as described in (5,6).
Aliquots of the sample were routinely withdrawn and examined during the
fluorescence measurements to ensure that the chloroplasts were not
damaged by the flow cell.

3. RESULTS AND DISCUSSION
    After being absorbed, a photon creates an exciton which will have
some finite equilibration time in the antenna Chl. This equilibration
time reflects both thermal equilibration with the protein matrix and
spatial equilibration over the entire ensemble of antenna Chls. If
this equilibration time is rapid compared to the fluorescence lifetime
(trap-limited) then the fluorescence emission spectrum should be always

* Permanent Address: Calif. State Polytechnic Univ. Pomona, CA 91768 USA

M. Baltscheffsky (ed.), Current Research in Photosynthesis, Vol. II, 297–300.
© 1990 *Kluwer Academic Publishers. Printed in the Netherlands.*

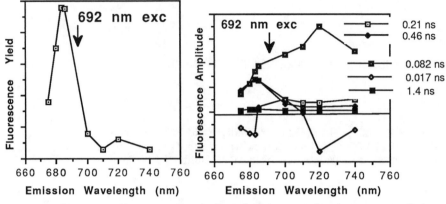

Fig 1 Steady-state fluorescence from pea chloroplasts in the Fo state. Most of the emission is blue-shifted relative to the excitation light.

Fig 2 Time-resolved spectra of data from Fig 1. The 17 ps component has both positive and negative amplitudes indicating energy transfer between pigments.

the same regardless of the excitation wavelength. In contrast, if the equilibration time is comparable to the overall fluorescence lifetime (diffusion-limited) then excitation at far-red wavelengths should dramatically shorten the fluorescence lifetimes since molecules near the reaction center will be preferentially excited. We measured both the red-shifted (stokes-shifted) and blue-shifted (antistokes-shifted) fluorescence upon excitation at 630 nm and 692 nm. Fig 1 shows the steady state fluorescence emission observed with 692 nm excitation. The fluorescence emission peak is near 680 nm for either 630 nm or 692 nm excitation. A time resolved Decay Associated Spectrum (DAS) of the data in Fig 1 is shown in Fig 2. The three signals with large positive amplitudes have lifetimes very close to those observed with 630 nm excitation [ref (2) and Fig 3a] confirming the trap-limited model. In addition there is a very fast component with a 17 ps lifetime with both positive and negative amplitudes indicating that it is associated with the energy transfer processes between the pigments (1,4).

There is a difference in the shape of the fast (80 - 100 ps) lifetime component of the DAS shown in Fig 2 compared with that obtained with 630 nm excitation[(2), Fig3a]. With 692 nm excitation the emission peak at 680 nm is significantly reduced relative to the shoulder at 720 nm for the fast lifetime component. The change in shape suggests that the fast lifetime component is a composite of an emission centered at 680 nm produced by PSII and an emission with a broad peak near 720 nm produced by PSI. A model was previously developed in this laboratory to describe biexponential fluorescence decays observed from isolated, homogeneous reaction center preparations from Synechococcus (3). Roughly speaking, at Fo conditions one lifetime is expected to reflect the pheophytin re-oxidation kinetics of several hundred ps. The second lifetime is predicted to be proportional to the number of pigment molecules in the PSII antenna. Thus at Fo conditions the PSII-beta

centers with an antenna size of 100 Chl molecules should have a
lifetime slightly longer than the 80 ps lifetime observed in the 80 Chl
Syn particles. The 250 Chl in the PSII-alpha antenna should produce a
lifetime about three times longer than the 80 ps lifetime of the Syn
particles. In addition, both PSII-alpha and PSII-beta should produce a
component with a lifetime of about 500 ps due to reaction center
primary photochemistry. Thus the predicted lifetimes are: fast, about
100 ps (PSII-beta); middle, about 250 ps (PSII-alpha); and slow, about
500 ps (PSII alpha and PSII-beta). Such an assignment is also
consistent with excitation spectra which show that the 250 ps component
is enriched in Chl b.

In order to verify that the PSII-beta is specifically responsible
for the 100 ps PSII lifetime component observed at Fo conditions, we
performed experiments to close PSII-beta but leave PSII-alpha open. It
has been shown that PSII-beta is only weakly coupled to the plastoquinone pool so that in the absence of DCMU it is possible to create a
state, Fpl, in which the PSII-alpha centers are predominantly open but
most PSII-beta centers are closed (7). If the fast, 100 ps, signal at
Fo is really a composite of PSI and open PSII-beta centers then the
amplitude of this signal should diminish during the Fo - Fpl transition
but be constant afterwards. Fig 3a,b,c shows that such behavior is
observed during the Fo - Fpl - Fm transition.

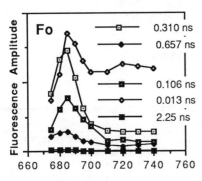

Fig 3 a,b,c   Fo, Fpl, and Fm signals
from pea chloroplasts taken during one
day from the same batch of plants.   To
minimize sample degradation in the flow
cell, a separate liter of chloroplast
suspension was used at each emission
wavelength for the Fpl measurements. The
sample was more stable during the Fo and
Fm measurements.   The amplitude of the
very fast (13 - 17 ps) component was
very high in these samples and has been
reduced by a factor of 2 to fit on the
same scale as the other components.

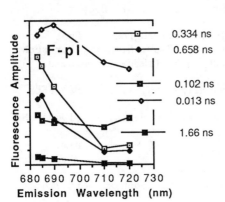

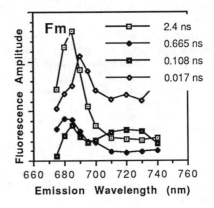

The samples used for the experiments shown in Fig 3 were grown under yellow light in order to enhance the PSI signals. The very fast 13 ps component was always more pronounced in peas grown under yellow light and suppressed in the samples grown under red light suggesting that it is primarily associated with PSI. The amplitudes of the other signals from the plants grown under the different light regimes behaved as expected from the assignment given in the table below.

A final test of the model of biexponential PSII fluorescence decay was performed using the chlorina Chl b- barley mutant. This mutant does not display the PSII-alpha/beta antenna size heterogeneity but rather has a uniform population of unconnected antennae with 50 Chl a associated with each PSII (6). In agreement with the model, at Fo we observed lifetimes of about 60 and 300 ps due to PSII and a lifetime of about 95 ps associated with PSI (data not shown). As the PSII reaction centers are closed, the amplitude of the 60 ps component decreases while the amplitude of a component with a lifetime of about 1 ns increases in a complementary fashion. All aspects of this work will be discussed more fully elsewhere.

Source	Total Chl [from ref (8)]	Chl a	Chl b	Approximate Fo Lifetimes (ps)
PSII-alpha	250	180	70	250, 500
PSII-beta	100	80	20	100, 500
PSII b- barley	50	50	0	60, 300
PSI	200	170	30	90
Uncoupled Chl				1500 - 2500
Exciton Equilibration				15

ACKNOWLEDGEMENTS: We thank Prof. K. Schaffner for continuing support of this work. S. McCauley was supported by a NATO fellowship.

REFERENCES
1 Holzwarth, A.R., Wendler, J. and Suter, G.W. (1987) Biophys. J. 51, 1-12
2 Schatz, G.H. and Holzwarth, A.R. (1987) in: Progress in Photosynthesis Research (Biggins, J. ed.) vol I, 67-69, Nijhoff, Dordrecht
3 Schatz, G.H., Brock, H. and Holzwarth, A.R. (1988) Biophys. J. 54, 397-405
4 McCauley, S. W., Bittersmann, E. and Holzwarth, A.R. (1989) FEBS Lett 249, 285-288
5 Glick, R.E., McCauley, S.W., Gruissem, W. and Melis, A. (1986) PNAS USA 83, 4287-4291
6 Ghirardi, M.L., McCauley, S.W. and Melis, A. (1986) Biochim. Biophys. Acta 851, 331-339
7 Melis, A. (1985) Biochim. Biophys. Acta 808, 334-342
8 Melis, A. and Anderson, J.M. (1983) Biochim. Biophys. Acta 724, 473-484

INTERACTION BETWEEN LHC-II ANTENNA AND PS 2 CORE IN THYLAKOID
VESICLES.

Lars Olof Pålsson,[a] Tomas Gillbro,[a] Per Svensson[b] and
Per Åke Albertsson.[b]

a) Department of Physical Chemistry, University of Umeå,
S-901 87 Umeå, Sweden

b) Department of Biochemistry, University of Lund,
S-211 00 Lund, Sweden

1. Introduction:
Photosystems 1 and 2 in the thylakoids of green plants are mainly
concentrated in the stroma and grana regions, respectively. This
natural partition has been utilized by Svensson and Albertsson to
prepare vesicles enriched in PS 2, so called BS particles. One
advantage of this method compared to other PS 2 enriched
preparations, like for instance BBY particles, is that no
detergents have been used. The purpose of our work has been to
study the interaction between the light-harvesting chlorophyll
a/b complex (LHC-II) and the PS 2 core particle and how this
interaction is influenced by the addition of detergents. For this
purpose we have studied the energy transfer between LHC-II and
the PS 2 core particle with picosecond and fluorescence
spectroscopy.

2. Materials and methods:
The BS particles were prepared from inside out vesicles from
spinage thylakoids that had been broken by a mechanical press
treatment. These vesicles were separated further by partition
with an aqueous polymer two-phase system (1). The vesicles thus
obtained have a diameter of about 0.2 μm and contain only trace
amounts of PS 1 (P700).
A synchronously pumped DCM dye laser was used as the picosecond
light source in the pump-probe experiments. A Soleil-Babinet
compensator in the excitation beam was set so that the
polarization of the excitation and probe beams were parallel or
perpendicular. Fluorescence anisotropies were measured with a
Spex fluorolog spectrometer. The time resolved fluorescence was
measured by single photon counting.

M. Baltscheffsky (ed.), Current Research in Photosynthesis, Vol. II, 301–304.
© 1990 *Kluwer Academic Publishers. Printed in the Netherlands.*

3. Result and discussion:

3.1. Time-resolved anisotropy:
The time-resolved anisotropy was calculated from two different
absorption recovery kinetics; i.e. with the analyzing light
perpendicular or parallel to the excitation light. The magnitude
of the amplitude of each decay curve at a certain time gave the
anisotropy through the well known formula. The excitation and
analyzing wavelength was 670 nm. This value of the wavelength
was chosen in such a way that mainly the LHC-II was excited. The
result reveals a very rapid decay of the anisotropy in LHC-II
with a lifetime of 8 ps. This is shown in fig. 1. The conclusion
to be drawn from this result is that the energy migrates very
rapidly from LHC-II to the PS 2 core particle.

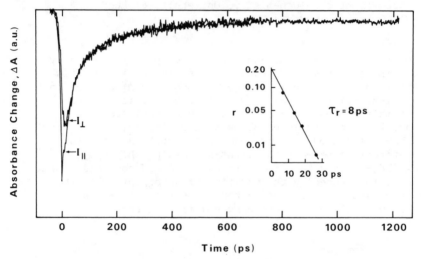

Fig.1. The time resolved anisotropy.

3.2. Fluorescence yield and anisotropy:
The steady state fluorescence measurements were performed at
665 nm. The emission from our sample was then scanned from 670 to
750 nm. This resulted in an emission spectrum with a maximum
around 684 nm. If one takes the small Stokes shift into account,
clearly this must be the emission from the PS 2 core
chlorophylls. It is thus reasonable to assume that we have indeed
achieved an effective energy transfer from the LHC-II to the PS 2
core, i.e. the system seems to be intact. The experiment was then
continued by adding small amounts of Triton X-100. As a result of
this titration we could see a spectral shift of the emission
maximum towards shorter wavelengths. The total fluorescence
yield seemed to increase dramatically compared to the yield
measured before the addition of Triton X-100. Furthermore, the
fluorescence anisotropy increased from a value of below 0.1 to

around 0.3. These changes seem to occur when the amount of
Triton X-100 added to the sample reaches 0.010-0.020%.
These results clearly indicate a disturbed energy transfer from
the LHC-II to the PS 2 core particle. The spectral shift of the
emission maximum towards shorter wavelengths implies that the
emission no longer has its origin in the PS 2 core, but rather in
the LHC:s of PS 2. The dramatic increase of the yield also
supports this assumption. The increase in the anisotropy seems to
strengthen our hypothesis of an interrupted energy transfer from
the LHC:s to the PS 2 core particle. This indicate a disturbed
interaction between LHC-II and the the PS 2 core particle.

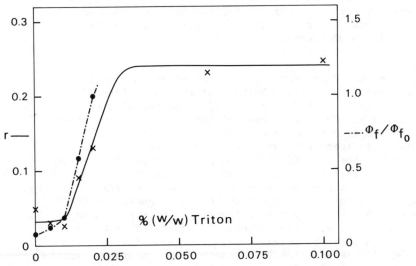

Fig.2. The steady state anisotropy and relative increase in
the quantum yield as a function of Triton concentration.

3.3. Fluorescence kinetics:

We have also studied the fluorescence kinetics of BS particles
by single photon counting. We operated at an excitation
wavelength of 648 nm and the kinetics were studied at 685 nm.
It was suitable to fit the resulting fluorescence decay curve
to a three exponential kinetic model. This also resulted in a
good fit with three well resolved components. The two fastest
components dominated over the third slowest one; the amplitude of
this component was less than 1% of the total decay. The two
fastest components, with the lifetimes of $\approx$ 120 ps and $\approx$ 300 ps,
originates from the PS 2 core, i.e. energy trapping and charge
separation processes. The third component, with a lifetime of $1\approx$
ns, represents fluorescence originating from the LHC-II complex
or free chlorophyll a (2). The same procedure as in the steady
state experiments was then performed; small amounts of Triton
X-100 was added to the BS vesicles. The result of this treatment

was a remarkable increase, both in lifetime and amplitude of the third component. The fastest component remained relatively unchanged, allthough one could see a tendency of an increase in lifetime. This could be interpreted as a slightly less efficient energy trapping reaction in the reaction center of PS 2.
The increase, both in lifetime and in amplitude of the slow component, reveals an increase in the chlorophyll fluorescence. The lifetime increased to $\simeq$ 4 ns. This indicate a less efficient energy transfer from LHC-II to the PS 2 core-particle. We also calculated the yield by integrating each kinetic trace. The yield given by the measurement with the highest concentration of Triton X-100 served as a reference. We then calculated the relative yield and plotted this number against the added amount Triton X-100. This plot showed that the critical amount of Triton X-100 is about 0.015%.

3.4. Summary:
As a summary of our experiments it is reasonable to draw the general conclusion that Triton X-100 disturbs the interaction between LHC-II and the PS 2 core particle. The validity of this conclusion is based upon observations made in steady state fluorescence and time resolved picosecond fluorescence experiments. Both these methods reveal a disturbed energy transfer from the LHC-II to the PS 2 core particle. Based upon the results obtained in the steady state experiments and the absorption of the sample, we estimated the number of Triton X-100 molecules, sufficient to interrupt the energy transfer to be 46 molecules per 250 chlorophyll a. Integral proteins are known to interact extensively with the hydrocarbon chains of membrane lipids and so they can be released only by agents that compete for this nonpolar interaction.(4). Anderson and Andersson reports of a picture of PS 2 with the core particle surrounded by LHC-II protein complexes.(3). According to this picture the LHC-II is divided into two sub populations; an inner LHC-II pool which is tightly bound to the PS 2 core particle and an peripheral pool which surrounds the inner pool and the PS 2 core. Within this model the interpretation must be that Triton X-100 affects the interaction between the inner LHC-II pool. It is reasonable to draw this conclusion since we observed only a single rise in the quantum yield. If the peripheral LHC-II pool should have been disconnected first and then the inner LHC-II pool, we would have expected to observe an increase of the fluorescence quantum yield in two steps.

References:
1. Svensson P. and Albertsson P.Å. (1989) Photosynthetic Research 20,249-259
2. McCauley S.W., Bitterman E. and Holzwarth A.R.(1989) FEBS, 249, 285-288
3. Anderson J.M. and Andersson B. (1988) TIBS 351-355
4. Streyer L. (1981) Biochemistry Freeman & Company

Competition between trapping and annihilation in PS II

W. Leibl, J. Breton[*], J. Deprez[*] and H.-W. Trissl

Abt. Biophysik, Univ. Osnabrück, D–4500 Osnabrück, F.R.G.

[*]Dept. Biologie, Centre d'Etudes Nucléaires de Saclay, F–91191 Gif–Sur–Yvette, France

Introduction

To study the exciton transfer and primary charge separation in photosystem II we used picosecond flashes of varying energies. If a significant fraction of the reaction centers (RCs) is closed by a flash, the excitation density is so high that two or more excitons are created simultaneously in the pool of antenna pigments and their interaction has to be taken into account. Excitons may be lost by singlet–singlet annihilation before they are trapped by the photochemistry in the RC. Annihilation leads to an apparent acceleration of all other reactions connected with the exciton dynamics. The quantitative treatment of this competitive deactivation path allows the bimolecular rate constant of exciton–exciton interaction to be determined that characterizes a given antenna bed. Furthermore, the knowledge of this constant is needed for the analysis of kinetic data obtained under annihilation conditions.

In the present work the exciton dynamics and trapping (reversible) in photosystem II is studied by measuring the photochemical path into the RC with a photoelectric technique based on the orientation of membrane fragments. In this technique the electrogenicity of the primary charge separation and charge stabilization gives rise to a photovoltage. The change in the photovoltage amplitude evoked by long and short flashes, as well as the energy dependence of both, amplitudes and kinetics were analyzed by a reversible reaction scheme. This analysis gives values for the molecular rate constants, that describe exciton–exciton interaction, reversible trapping, and charge stabilization in PS II.

Materials and Methods

PS II–membranes were prepared from pea leaves (*Pisum sativum*) according to Berthold et al. [1] with the modification described in ref. [2]. The membranes were separated by a mild trypsin treatment. For this the membranes were diluted in low salt resuspension medium to a chlorophyll concentration of 100 μg/ml and incubated at room temperature with 2 μg/ml trypsin from bovine pancreas. After 5 min. trypsination was stopped by addition of a 20–fold excess of trypsin inhibitor and the preparation was concentrated by centrifugation. For the measurements the chlorophyll concentration of the sample was adjusted to 2 mg/ml yielding an optical density at 532 nm of 0.1. Photovoltage measurements were carried out in a capacitive microcoaxial cell of 3x0.1 mm dimensions [3]. The excitation source was a frequency doubled Nd–YAG laser delivering flashes at 532 nm of either 12 ns or 30 ps duration. Orientation by an

M. Baltscheffsky (ed.), Current Research in Photosynthesis, Vol. II, 305–308.
© 1990 *Kluwer Academic Publishers. Printed in the Netherlands.*

electric field was done in the measuring cell, applying short DC–pulses (120 V/cm, 30 ms) through a bias–DC–T block (Picosecond Pulse Labs) before the flash. After amplification the signals were recorded on a 7–GHz digitizing oscilloscope (Tektronix 7250). Single traces were averaged and analyzed on a personal computer by iterative convolution of a trial function with the time response of the apparatus varying a minimum number of parameters. The time response of the setup was determined by the analysis of the photovoltage from oriented purple membranes [4].

For comparative measurements of the photovoltage induced by long and short flashes the RC–discharge time of the cell capacitance into the input impedance of the amplifier was slowed down by the use of a high–impedance converter. In these measurements a 1–GHz oscilloscope (Tektronix 7104) equipped with a digitizing camera (Thomson CSF, TSN 1150) was used.

Results and Discussion

The PS II–photovoltage shows in the case of oxidized Q_A two rising phases with similar electrogenicity whereas with reduced Q_A the amplitude is strongly diminished, the slow rise is missing and the faster decay indicates a backreaction (Fig. 1). We interpret the fast rise in open and closed RCs as the appearance of the first charge separated state in the RC and define this process as 'trapping'. This radical–pair formation is followed by electrogenic charge stabilization in open and a back reaction in closed RCs [5].

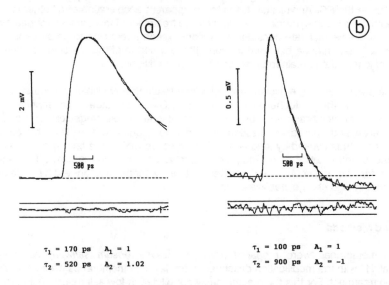

$\tau_1 = 170$ ps	$A_1 = 1$	$\tau_1 = 100$ ps	$A_1 = 1$
$\tau_2 = 520$ ps	$A_2 = 1.02$	$\tau_2 = 900$ ps	$A_2 = -1$

Fig. 1: Typical time courses of the photovoltage obtained from oriented PS II–membranes with oxidized (a) or reduced (b) Q_A. In (b) the RCs were closed by the addition of 100 μM DCMU and preillumination. The amplitudes are normalized (see scaling). Solid lines show the best fit that was obtained by the convolution of a biexponential displacement current (parameters stated below the graphs) with the response function of the apparatus. The residual plots with lines indicating ±5% deviation are also shown.

We measured the energy dependence of the kinetic parameters as well as the dependence of the photovoltage amplitude on the flash duration in open RCs (Fig. 2). We found the trapping kinetics, that was 300 ps in the low energy limit, to be considerably accelerated with increasing excitation energy. The comparision of the photovoltage amplitude under non-annihilating (12–ns flashes) and annihilating conditions (30–ps flashes) shows, that there are significant losses due to annihilation at energies higher than about 10 $\mu J/cm^2$ reaching a factor of 2 when in the average more than one exciton is created simultaneously per RC ($E>100\ \mu J/cm^2$).

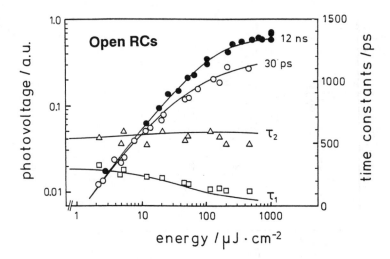

Fig. 2: Energy dependence of the fit parameters of the PS II photovoltage (apparent kinetics and amplitude) in the case of open RCs. Solid lines represent the best fit according to the theoretical model for reversible trapping to all data with the parameters given below.
Squares: time constant of fast rise; triangles: time constant of second phase; open circles: amplitude with 30–ps excitation; closed circles: amplitude with 12–ns excitation.

For a theoretical treatment we define a bimolecular annihilation rate constant γ [6] and include it in a reaction scheme that accounts for a reversibility of trapping with k_1 and k_{-1} as the rate constants of trapping and detrapping, respectively [5]. The global analysis of all dependences with one set of parameters (solid lines in Fig. 2) on this basis gives the following values:

	γ	k_1	k_{-1}
open RCs	$(74\ ps)^{-1}$	$(500\ ps)^{-1}$	$(2500\ ps)^{-1}$
closed RCs	$(74\ ps)^{-1}$	$(1500\ ps)^{-1}$	$(330\ ps)^{-1}$

The annihilation rate constant γ in PS II is much the same as in PS I, as found by analogous measurements but with an irreversible reaction scheme. This correlates with the similar structure and pigment composition of the two antenna systems of higher plants and shows that this functional parameter is rather independent of the mechanism (irreversible/reversible) and the rate of trapping. If in analogy to the theory of exciton dynamics for irreversible trapping [6] a parameter $\alpha = \gamma / 2k_1$ is defined, which describes the competition between trapping and annihilation, a value of $\alpha \approx 3.5$ can be calculated. In comparision to PS I ($\alpha = 0.6$) this higher value indicates a much stronger effect of annihilation in PS II, which is a consequence of the slower trapping time in PS II than in PS I (90 ps). Thus the bimolecular process of annihilation leads to an acceleration of the apparent trapping time already at excitation energies one order of magnitude lower than the energy at which bimolecular interaction between excitons and the trap (saturation) becomes important. This is seen by the simulation of the energy dependence of the kinetics with and without annihilation (Fig. 3).

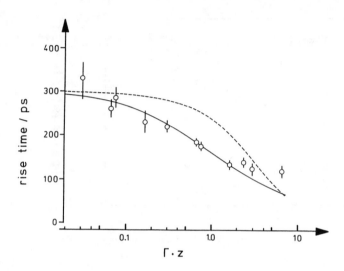

Fig. 3: Simulation of the energy dependence of the trapping kinetics in PS II as measured by the fast photovoltage rise. Solid line: Fit with annihilation; dashed line: same parameters, but without annihilation. The excitation energy is expressed in effective hits per trap, $\Gamma \cdot z$, where Γ is the photosynthetic quantum yield.

References:

[1] Berthold,D.A., Babcock,G.T. and Yocum,Ch.F. (1981) FEBS Lett. 134, 231–234
[2] Ono,T.–A. and Inoue,Y. (1985) Biochim. Biophys. Acta 806, 331–340
[3] Trissl,H.–W., Leibl,W., Deprez,J., Dobek,A. and Breton,J. (1987) Biochim. Biophys. Acta 893, 320–332
[4] Trissl,H.–W., Gärtner,W. and Leibl,W. (1989) Chem. Phys. Lett. 158, 515–518
[5] Leibl,W., Breton,J., Deprez,J. and Trissl,H.–W. (1989) Photosynth. Res. in press
[6] Deprez,J., Paillotin,G., Dobek,A., Leibl,W., Trissl,H.–W. and Breton,J. Biochim. Biophys. Acta, submitted

EXCITATION ENERGY FLOW IN THE MARINE DINOFLAGELLATE
Protogonyalux tamarensis.

Mamoru Mimuro[1], Naoto Tamai[2,4], Takashi Ishimaru[3,5] and Iwao Yamazaki[2,4]
[1]National Institute for Basic Biology, [2]Institute for Molecular Science, Myodaiji, Okazaki, Aichi 444 and [3]Ocean Research Institute, University of Tokyo, Nakano, Tokyo 164, (Japan).
Present address: [4]Department of Chemical Process Engineering, Facluty of Engineering, Hokkaido University, Sapporo 060 and [5]Department of Aquatic Biosciences, Faculty of Fisheries, Tokyo University of Fisheries, Minato, Tokyo 108 (Japan).
Abbreviations used: DCMU, 3-(3,4-dichlorophenyl)-1,1-dimethylurea.

Introduction

Carotenoid is the main light harvesting antenna pigment of RC II in some algal phyla [1]. Energy transfer process from carotenoid to chl is less characterized, compared with the situation of chl or phycobiliproteins. The electron exchange mechanism [2] is proposed for this process, contrary to the case of Förster mechanism [3] for chl or phycobiliproteins.

Peridinin, the main light harvesting pigment in dinoflagellates [1], are associated with two kinds of pigment protein complexes; water-soluble and membrane-bound complexes [1]. Both of them are functional in photosynthesis. Energy transfer mechanism in this complex, however, has not yet been elucidated. This is mainly due to the lack of information on the time-dependent behaviour of component(s) and fluorescence properties of carotenoid, which are critical for the analysis, as shown for the case of chl or phycobiliproteins [4,6].

In this study, we adopted two kinds of fluorescence spectroscopy, steady-state and the time-resolved spectroscopy in the picosecond time range, for the analysis of energy flow in whole cells of the marine dinoflagellate *Protogonyalux tamarensis* under the excitation condition of peridinin. Results show unique fluorescence components in this species and characteristic energy flow among them.

Materials and methods

Algal culture: Protogonyalux tamarensis was cultured in the enriched seawater medium [5] at 15°C. Light condition was 12 h light $(75\mu E/m^2/sec)$ and 12 h dark. Cells at the stationary growth phase were used for measurements.

Steady-state and time-resolved fluorescence spectroscopy: Absorption and fluorescence spectra were measured with a Hitachi 557 spectrophotometer and a Hitachi 850 spectrofluorometer, respectively. The time-resolved fluorescence spectra were measured with the apparatus reported previously [4,6]; in principle, the time-correlated single photon counting system under a low excitation condition. The pulse intensity (540 nm, 6 ps (fwhm)) was in a range of 10^8 to 10^9 photons/cm^2. The time resolution of our optical set-up was 6 ps. Correction of spectral sensitivity and data treatment were carried out as reported previously [4,6].

M. Baltscheffsky (ed.), Current Research in Photosynthesis, Vol. II, 309–312.
© 1990 *Kluwer Academic Publishers. Printed in the Netherlands.*

Results and Discussion

Steady-state fluorescence spectra: Fig. 1A shows the fluorescence spectra of the dinoflagellate *P. tamarensis* at 15°C under the excitation of peridinin. The main emission was located at 684 nm (F684), with a small bump around 673 nm (F673), as revealed by the second derivative spectrum. The F683 was DCMU-sensitive; the difference spectrum was essentially the same as the spectrum without DCMU. The DCMU-sensitive increase in the fluorescence yield agrees to the observation in higher plants or algae [7].

The fluorescence spectrum at –196°C drastically changed (Fig. 1B); the main emission was located at 689 nm (F689) with a small band at 670 nm (F670). The second derivative spectrum indicates the presence of two additional bands at 683 (F683) and 698 nm (F698). F670 and F683 at –196°C most probably correspond to F673 and F684 detected at 15°C. In the wavelength region longer than 700 nm, the fluorescence intensity is very low, where photosystem (PS) I emission is expectable. A small bump can be observed around 725 nm, though it was not well resolved by the derivative spectrum.

At –196°C, three typical fluorescence bands are known in higher plants and algae [7]; F685, F695 and F735. The former two originate from PS II and the last one, PS I [7]. In *P. tamarensis*, however, F695 and F735 are apparently missing; instead F689 and F725 can be assigned to be comparable components. This difference suggests the difference in the constitution of polypeptides; CP-47 and/or LHCI.

Time-resolved fluorescence spectrum: Fig. 2A show the time-resolved fluorescence spectra at –196°C under the preferential excitation of peridinin. Just after the excitation, a clear band was detected around 649 nm, originating from chl *c*, however it decayed very fast (within 50 ps). Other components located at 670 and 683 nm became evident with time. The 683 nm maximum, observed at 10 ps gradually shifted to 689 nm. A significant intensity was observed around 670 nm even at 400 ps, indicating the presence of a long-lived component. The spectra after 400 ps were invariant up to 1 ns. In the wavelength region longer than 700 nm, there was no clear emission maximum. However, one should notice that the relative intensity around 700 nm was high even in a later time, suggesting presence of PS I component band(s).

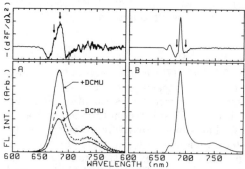

Fig. 1. Fluorescence spectra of *P. tamarensis* at 15°C (A) and at –196°C (B) with respective second derivative spectra. Arrows indicate the locations of component bands. In (A), broken line shows DCMU-sensitive fluorescence.

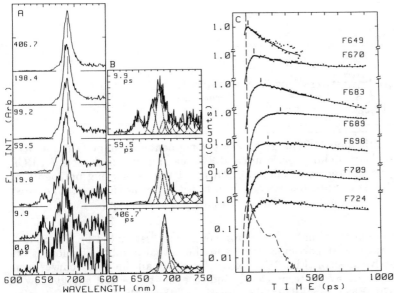

Fig. 2. Time-resolved fluorescence spectra of *P. tamarensis* at −196°C (A), their deconvoluted patterns (B) and rise and decay curves of individual fluorescence components (C). In (A), each time-resolved spectrum was shown after normalization to the maximum intensity. In (C), vertical line shows the time zero and broken lines, pulse profile. Small bars over the decay curves indicate the time when the maximum intensity was observed.

Analysis of energy flow by rise and decay kinetics: Energy flow among fluorescence components was resolved by kinetics analysis. For this purpose, we obtained the rise and decay curves of individual fluorescence components and estimated their lifetimes. In this sense, our method is critically different from the analysis of "decay component". First, the time-resolved spectra were resolved into components by deconvolution with the assumption of Gaussian band shape [5,7]. Nine components were necessary for the best fit; four are evident in the time-resolved spectra (F649, F670, F683 and F689) and the two, found in the steady-state spectrum (F698 and F724) (Fig. 1). Additional three components were further introduced (F709, F735 and F755). For the best fit, the intensity was preferentially changed, with the locations and bandwidths being kept almost constant (Fig. 2B).

Table 1. Lifetimes of fluorescence components in *P. tamarensis* at −196°C.

Components	Rise term	Decay term			
	τ (ps)	τ_1 (ps)	A_1	τ_2 (ps)	A_2
F649		40	0.85	235	0.15
F670	18	55	0.79	1250	0.21
F683	55	75	0.85	350	0.15
F689	250	350	0.90	1250	0.10
F698	91	115	0.83	1110	0.17

τ; lifetimes and A; amplitudes.

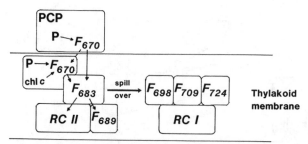

Fig. 3. Schematic model of energy flow in the pigment system of *P. tamarensis*. PCP, peridinin-chl *a*-protein; P, peridinin and RC, reaction center. Except for PCP, individual components represent spectral forms, not the associating polypeptides. Broken line indicates the possible energy flow, but it is not defined yet. The direct energy donor to RC I is not clear. For details, see the Discussion.

Rise and decay curves of individual components were estimated by the relative intensity in the spectra at particular time and the actual number of photons observed for respective spectra (Fig. 2C). Except for F670, all the decay curves seem exponential. These decay patterns clearly indicate the sequential energy flow in the order of F670, F683 and F689. The kinetics of three PS I components were similar to each other and their decay was faster than that of the F689. This clearly indicates that the energy transfer to PS I components does not occur through F689; F683 is most probably an energy distributor to the PS I components (spill over).

Lifetimes of individual components were estimated by convolution calculation with the assumption of exponential decay kinetics (Table 1). The decay of F670 agrees to the rise of F683. Similarly, the decay of the F683 (75 ps) well corresponds to the rise of the F689 and F698 when we assume parallel transfer from F683 ($1/250 + 1/91 = 1/67$). On the contrary, the decay of chl c is not consistent with the rise of F670, indicating that chl c is not the intermediate of the energy transfer from peridinin to chl a. The 18 ps rise term of F670 is, thus, most probably the transfer time from peridinin to chl a at $-196°C$. At physiological temperature, this transfer time is expected to be shorter, as similar to the case of energy flow among chlorophyll molecules.

References
1. Siefermann-Harms, D. (1985) Biochim. Biophys. Acta, 811, 325–355.
2. Dexter, D.L. (1953) J. Chem. Phys., 21, 836–850.
3. Förster, T. (1948) Ann. Phys. Leipzig., 2, 55–75.
4. Mimuro, M., Yamazaki, I., Tamai, N. and Katoh, T. (1989) Biochim. Biophys. Acta, 973, 153–162.
5. Ogata, T., Ishimaru, T. and Kodama, M. (1987) Marine Biology, 95, 217–220.
6. Shimada, K., Mimuro, M., Tamai, N. and Yamazaki, I. (1989) Biochim. Biophys. Acta, 975, 72–79.
7. Murata, N. and Satoh, K. (1986) In Light Emission by Plants and Bacteria, (Govindjee, Amesz, J. and Fork, D.C. eds.), pp. 137–159, Academic Press, New York.

CHLOROPHYLL SPECTRAL HETEROGENEITY AND ENERGY TRANSFER TO PSII   REACTION
CENTRES.

Flavio M.Garlaschi, Giuseppe Zucchelli and Robert C. Jennings
Centro CNR Biologia Cellulare e Molecolare delle Piante,
Dip. di Biologia, Univ. di Milano, Via Celoria 26, 20133 Milano, Italy.

1. INTRODUCTION
    The absorption of light by the photosystems (PS) of green plants is
achieved by a large array of pigment molecules, bound to chl-protein
complexes (1-3), which transfer the excitation energy to reaction centres (RCs) where primary charge separation occurs. The antenna matrix
system is formed by two chlorophyll (chl) species, chla and chlb, with
chlb constituting about 35% of the PSII antenna system. Chla is present
as at least five different spectral forms (4,5), which can be arranged,
with respect to wavelength, in a series in which the absorption maxima
differ by 7nm-11nm. Several authors have suggested that energy may be
transfered from peripheral antenna towards RCs along a "downhill" energy
gradient in which the long wavelength chl spectral forms are preferentially located in the inner antenna, close to RCs (6-8). Experimental
evidence in favour of this concept has been presented for photosynthetic
bacteria (9) but not for higher plant PS. In this communication we
address this problem by analysing energy transfer efficiency to RCs
both within and between PSII units as a function of the chl spectral
forms.

2. MATERIALS AND METHODS
    Spinach BBY-grana and LHCII were prepared and their room temperature
absorption spectra were deconvoluted in asymmetric gaussian components
as described in (10).
    The Fo and Fm fluorescence values were measured as in (11), with
DCMU and hydroxylamine addition after Fo determination. The appropriate
excitation wavelengths (between 645-701 nm) were obtained with combinations of interference filters; emission was measured at 745nm. The stray
light to signal ratio was considerably less than 0.05.
    Energy transfer between PSII units was determined by analysing the
normalised variable fluorescence as a function of the area growth above
the fluorescence induction curve (12), measured in the presence of DCMU
and hydroxylamine.

3. RESULTS AND DISCUSSION.
    Relative energy transfer efficiency to RCs was determined by meas-
uring the fluorescence quenching of open RCs as the Fv/Fo ratio
(12,14)(Fv/Fo-trapping efficiency) for different absorption wavelengths.

M. Baltscheffsky (ed.), Current Research in Photosynthesis, Vol. II, 313–316.
© 1990 Kluwer Academic Publishers. Printed in the Netherlands.

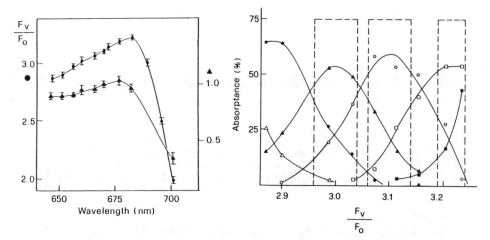

FIGURE 1. Fv/Fo-trapping efficiency of PSII RCs as a function of absorption wavelength. ● BBY-grana; ▲ chlorina barley mutant thylakoids.
FIGURE 2. Fv/Fo-trapping efficiency of PSII RCs as a function of the fractional absorptance of the major spectroscopic chl forms. Fv/Fo data of BBY-grana from fig.1. △638nm, ●650nm, ▲661nm, ○670nm, □677nm, ■684nm.

The data in fig.1 (●) indicate that transfer to PSII RCs is a function of the absorption wavelength, with maximal transfer occurring from antenna absorbing around 683nm. To analyse energy transfer to RCs in terms of the spectroscopic chlorophyll species, the Fv/Fo values have been related to the fractional absorptance of each chl form (fig.2). By appropriate selection of Fv/Fo intervals (the three areas indicated by the broken lines), it is possible to establish the following indipendent sequences of energy transfer efficiency to RCs:
(1)   684nm > 670nm > 650nm;   (2)   677nm > 661nm.
The following considerations can be made: a) the non fluorescing chlb 650nm band represents here the chla form(s) preferentially accepting excitation from chlb, i.e. (from the above sequences) either the 661nm or the 677nm species or both; b) the absolute values of the slopes of the curves of fig.2 in the selected areas are rather similar, thus suggesting that the differences in transfer efficiency between the various spectral components in the above transfer sequences are similar. We therefore conclude that sequence 2 lies somewhere to the right of the 684nm species in sequence 1, indicating this species as the most efficient at transfering energy to PSII RCs.
    To establish whether these relative transfer efficiencies represent transfer to RCs within or between PSs (15,16), we have measured excitation transfer between PSII units as a function of the absorption wavelength and calculated Ψ_{22}, the PSII connection parameter of Butler (16, equation 10) for the various excitation wavelengths (Table 1). The data show that PSII-PSII energy transfer from the shorter wavelength spectral forms is greater than from the longer wavelength absorbing forms, an opposite situation to that observed for Fv/Fo transfer efficiency, which therefore seems to be determined by transfer to RCs within PSII units.

Table 1. Wavelength dependence of energy transfer between PSII units.

Absorption (nm)	683	678	673	666	662	651
Fv(t)	.357	.352	.347	.338	.337	.341
	(.005)	(.007)	(.007)	(.007)	(.006)	(.010)
ψ_{22}	.32	.33	.36	.39	.40	.40

Fv(t): the normalised variable fluorescence at 50% area growth; in parentheses the interval estimates of the mean at 95% confidence level.

As the bulk of PSII antenna is made up of LHCPII which contains all the spectral bands (2,10), it is reasonable to ask if these Fv/Fo transfer efficiencies are associated with the spectral bands or with the location of the spectral species in the antenna. We have measured Fv/Fo as a function of wavelength in thylakoids of the chlorina barley mutant containing only the core antenna of PSII. The data, (▲) of fig.1, are qualitatively similar to those for BBY-grana, with energy transfer to RCs decreasing significantly at absorption wavelengths lower than 677nm, thus indicating that the observed efficiencies are associated with the bands rather than with their location in the outer or inner antenna.

Two antenna models may be considered to explain the present observations. 1) The long wavelength spectral forms, particularly the 684nm, have a closer topological relationship with RCs than the short wavelength species. This model, theoretically analysed by several authors (6-8), constitutes the basis of the so called "funnel" concept of antenna organisation. 2) There is no particular macroscopic topological distribution of the spectral forms with respect to RCs. In this case transfer to RCs would be determined essentially by the transfer microparameters of the donor-acceptor antenna chlorophylls. The short wavelength spectral forms are expected to be able to transfer energy to a greater variety of antenna chlorophylls than the longer wavelength forms. In this context the shorter wavelength forms will limit the number of transfer possibilities available to the longer wavelength foms, thus bringing about a situation in which the number of transfer steps to reach RCs is smaller for the longer wavelength forms. This suggestion is similar to the "antitrap" model suggested by Knox (17).

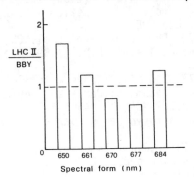

Fig.3 The ratio of the relative amounts of the spectral forms in LHCII and BBY-grana.

To distinguish between these models we examined the ratio of the relative amounts of the different spectral forms in LHCII and BBY-grana. Fig.3 shows that the 684nm form is present at high levels in LHCII (15%-20% of Qy absorption (10)). This suggests that the 684nm component is not enriched in the core antenna complexes, in agreement with the absence of the 684nm component in the CP47 core complex (18). Thus it is difficult to explain the high Fv/Fo efficiency of this spectral form in terms of the "funnel" model. We suggest that "antitrap" considerations best account for the high Fv/Fo transfer efficiency of the 684nm spectral form. The data of fig.3 concerning the remaining chl species are in agreement with the "funnel" model. We therefore feel that while the "antitrap" concept best explains the 684nm data, energy transfer from LHCII to the core complexes may well have a "funnel" componenent.

In the context of the "antitrap" model it is interesting to note that chlb in PSII antenna displays a Qy transition dipole strength weaker than that of chla (10), in analogy with the situation in organic solvents (19). This low Qy absorption "efficiency", difficult to understand in terms of the light harvesting economy, can be rationalised by the "antitrap" hypothesis. In this case the low chlb Qy transition dipole strength would considerably enhance the "antitrap" properties of this chlorophyll species.

REFERENCES

1 Anderson, J.M. (1986) FEBS Letters 117, 327-331.
2 Thornber,J.B. (1986) Enc. Plant Physiol. N.S. 19, 98-142.
3 Anderson,J.M. (1986) Ann. Rev. Plant Physiol. 37, 93-136.
4 French,C.S., Brown,J.S., and Lawrence,M.C. (1972) Plant.Physiol. 49, 421-429.
5 Van Ginkel,G. and Kleinen Hammans,J.W. (1980) Photochem. Photobiol. 31, 385-395.
6 Seely,G.R. (1973) J. Theor. Biol. 40, 173-187.
7 Shipman,L.L. and Housman,D.L.(1979) Photochem.Photobiol. 29, 1163-1167.
8 Fetisova,Z.G., Borisov,A.Yu. and Fok,M.V. (1985) J.Theor.Biol. 112, 41-75.
9 Freiberg,A., Godik,V.I., Pullerits,T. and Timpman,K. (1989) Biochim. Biophys. Acta, 973, 93-104.
10 Zucchelli,G., Jennings,R.C. and Garlaschi,F.M. (1989) these proceed.
11 Jennings,R.C., Garlaschi,F.M., Gerola,P.D., Etzion - Katz,R. and Forti,G. (1981) Biochim.Biophys.Acta 638 , 100-107.
12 Melis,A. and Duysens,L.N.M. (1979) Photochem. Photobiol. 29, 373-382.
13 Jennings, R.C., Zucchelli, G. and Garlaschi, F.M. (1989) Biochim.Biophys.Acta 975, 29-33.
14 Kitajima,M. and Butler,W.L. (1975) Biochim.Biophys.Acta 376, 105-115.
15 Joliot,A. and Joliot,P. (1984) C.R. Acad.Sci.Paris 258, 4622-4625.
16 Butler,W.L. (1980) Proc.Natl.Acad.Sci.USA, 77, 4697-4701.
17 Knox, R.S. (1977) in Topics in Photosynthesis (Barber, J. ed.) vol. 2, pp 55-97, Elsevier, Amsterdam.
18 Van Dorssen,R.J., Breton,J., Plijter,J.J., Satoh,K., van Gorkom,H.J. and Amesz,J. (1987) Biochim.Biophys.Acta 893, 267-274.
19 Goedheer,J.C. (1966) in The Chlorophylls. (Vernon,L.P. and Seely,G.R.,eds.), pp 147-184, Academic Press, N.Y. and London.

DOES LHCPII HAVE A LONG WAVELENGTH CHLOROPHYLL A SPECTRAL FORMS?

Giuseppe Zucchelli, Robert C. Jennings and Flavio M. Garlaschi
Centro C.N.R. Biologia Cellulare e Molecolare delle Piante, Dipartimento di Biologia, Universita'di Milano, via Celoria 26, 20133 Milano (Italy).

1. INTRODUCTION

The absorption spectra of photosynthetic membranes show a complexity that can be interpreted as being due to the presence of different spectral forms of chlorophyll a (chla) (1), having the same chemical structure but with their spectral properties modified by local effects (2). The wavelength spacing between neighbour spectral species of chl is in the range 7-11nm, an energy difference that, due to a similar Stokes shift, determines a maximum Forster overlap integral between "sequential" forms of chls (3). The transfer of excitation energy from the peripheral antenna towards the RCs is usually described in terms of the dipole-dipole R^{-6} theory of Forster (4). It is therefore necessary to understand the absorbance of the chls in the native state in order to appreciate their role in the photosynthetic apparatus. To this end the decomposition of the absorption spectra of photosynthetic membranes or chl-protein complex preparations in a linear combination of gaussians, has become a technique to interpret the complexity of the membrane absorption spectra in terms of different spectral species of chla (5-8). These studies indicate that the LHCPII does not seem to contain chl forms with absorption maxima above 677-678 nm and that the spectral species with absorption maxima at longer wavelength are almost exclusively associated with the antenna-chlorophyll proteins tightly bound to PSII or PSI(5,7).

We present an analysis of the room temperature (RT) spectra of various thylakoids and chl-protein complexes preparations by spectral decomposition in. terms of asymmetric gaussian functions, with the aim of obtaining more information about the spectral composition of LHCPII.

2. MATERIALS AND METHODS

LHCPII was prepared either from spinach or pea leaves according to Ryrie et al.(9). Final resuspension was in sucrose 0.05M, Tricine 5mM (pH8). Chla/chlb was 1.1 for spinach-LHCPII and 1.2 for pea-LHCPII preparations.

BBY-grana from spinach leaves were prepared as described by van Dorssen et al. (7). This preparation contains both LHCPII and PSII core protein complexes.

Thylakoids from chlorina barley mutant and its wild type were prepared as previously described (10) and resuspended in Tricine 30mM (pH 8), NaCl 10mM, MgCl 5mM, sucrose 0.2M.

M. Baltscheffsky (ed.), Current Research in Photosynthesis, Vol. II, 317–320.
© 1990 *Kluwer Academic Publishers. Printed in the Netherlands.*

Pea plants were grown both in continuous light as well as in an intermittent light regime (Iml) according to Armond et al.(11). Thylakoids were isolated as described above for barley.

The decomposition of the smoothed absorption spectra in gaussian components was performed as previously described (12) but with four free parameters for each: the wavelength of the maximum, the height of the band and the two independent half widths. The program runs on a Vax 8650 computer (Digital). The graph of the residuals and the χ^2 are used to judge the goodness of the fit (13).

3.   RESULTS and DISCUSSION

The RT absorption spectra of spinach-LHCPII and spinach-BBY-grana and the relative gaussian analyses are shown in fig.1A and fig.1B respectively. All the major chl species are present in both spectra. Of particular interest is the presence of the bands with maxima at 684nm and 694nm in LHCPII. As chlb is associated only with LHCPII in PSII preparations, normalising the two spectra to the area of the 650nm band (the band normally associated with chlb) we estimate that about 70%-80% of the 683nm species found in the BBY-grana spectrum may be LHCPII in origin. This is in contrast with other reports (5,7) that indicate the absence of chl forms with absorption maxima at wavelengths longer than 677-678 nm in LHCPII protein-complex. However, spectroscopic analysis of the CP47 PSII complex does not support an enrichment in the long wavelength antenna species near the RCs (14).

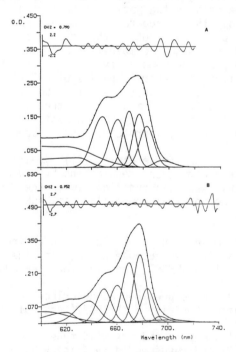

Figure 1
Room temperature absorption spectra of spinach-LHCPII (A) and spinach-BBY-grana (B) suspensions.
The experimental data range over the 600-740nm wavelength interval and are the dotted curves while the full lines are the sum of the gaussian components. Plots of the residuals are also shown with the values.

Table 1
Gaussian parameters for the decomposition of the room temperature absorption spectra of chlorina barley mutant and its wild type, Iml grown peas and continuous light grown peas.

Band no	barley w.t.	barley mut.	Iml	green peas
x^2	0.6	0.9	1.1	0.9
1 λ max (nm)	649	649	649	648
FWHM	8.53 7.68	12.66 10.19	10.50 9.50	7.41 6.69
area	0.15	0.07	0.05	0.16
2 λ max	661	661	662	659
FWHM	8.38 6.40	9.80 7.94	11.99 6.48	7.16 6.38
area	0.18	0.17	0.16	0.18
3 λ max	670	669	669	668
FWHM	7.14 5.83	7.70 6.47	8.02 6.11	6.36 6.21
area	0.24	0.24	0.24	0.23
4 λ max	678	678	677	677
FWHM	6.95 6.14	7.52 7.53	7.31 7.17	6.41 6.17
area	0.24	0.27	0.27	0.25
5 λ max	683	683	682	684
FWHM	7.69 7.18	8.27 8.02	8.49 7.84	7.29 6.61
area	0.24	0.24	0.22	0.23
6 λ max	693	695	692	694
FWHM	9.41 7.64	10.05 9.84	11.00 9.34	8.63 8.41
area	0.08	0.08	0.10	0.09
7 λ max	709	714	709	707
FWHM	6.65 5.23	3.60 3.29	2.62 4.57	2.21 10.50
area	0.02	0.004	0.006	0.01

The percentage of each component was calculated from the sum of the area under the chla bands (λ >661). The Full Width at Half Maximum (FWHM) is given as left and right value. The FWHM of each band is the sum of the two values. All the parameters were left free in these fitting.

The possibility that the longer wavelength bands might be not necessary to obtain a good numerical fit was rejected after several analyses of the spinach LHCPII absorption spectrum. The omission, or a strong reduction of the fractional contribution of the long wavelength bands (λ >678nm) (data not shown), yields overall fits less than satisfactory, with strong asymmetry of the bands on the long wawelength side (in

particular for the 669nm band). This asymmetry, not found in preparations where the 683nm band is accepted to be present (e.g. BBY specrum),
is inconsistent with the expected asymmetry towards higher energy of the
chl bands (1). We also find substantial changes in the peak positions
of some of the bands with respect to the analysis of fig.1 and
previously published data (5).

Our conclusion about the presence of the 683nm band in LHCPII is
also supported by analysis of thylakoids of the chlorina barley mutant
and Iml grown peas, both lacking LHCPII (Table 1). The absence of the
683nm band in LHCPII would imply a larger fractional contribution of
this band in the LHCPII-less thylakoids with respect to the normal ones,
due to a "dilution" of the 683nm component when LHCPII is present. The
data in Table 1 show a similar fractional contribution of all the chla
spectral species to the total chla area, including the long wavelength
bands at 684nm and 694nm, thus indicating their presence in LHCPII.

Our conclusions do not seem in close agreement with the idea of an
isotropic distribution of the chls spectral species, with the long
wavelength absorbing forms being present at higher levels in the inner
antenna, close to the RCs.

REFERENCES
1 French,C.S., Brown,J.S. and Lawrence,M.C. (1972) Plant Physiol. 49,
  421-429
2 Lutz,M. (1977) Biochim.Biophys.Acta 460, 408-430
3 Shipman,L.L. and Housman,D.L. (1979) Photochem.Photobiol. 29, 1163-
  1167
4 Knox,R.S. (1975) in Bioenergetics of Photosynthesis (Govindjee ed.)
  pp.183-221, Academic Press, New York
5 Brown,J.S. and Schoch,S. (1981) Biochem.Biophys.Acta 636, 201-209
6 Brown,J.S., Anderson,J.M. and Grimme,L. (1982) Photosynthesis Res. 3,
  279-291
7 van Dorssen,R.J., Plijter,J.J., Dekker,J.P., den Ouden,A., Amesz,J.
  and van Gorkom,H.J. (1987) Biochim.Biophys.Acta 890, 134-143
8 Brown,J.S. and Schoch,S. (1982) Photosynthesis Res. 3, 19-30
9 Ryrie,I.J., Anderson,J.M. and Goodchild,D.J. (1980) Eur.J.Biochem.
  107, 345-354
10 Zucchelli,G., Garlaschi,F.M. and Jennings,R.C. (1988) Biochim.
   Biophys.Acta 934, 144-150
11 Armond, P.A., Arntzen,C.J., Briantais,J.M. and Vernotte,C. (1976)
   Arch.Biochem.Biophys. 175, 54-63
12 Zucchelli,G., Garlaschi,F.M. and Jennings,R.C. (1988) J.Photochem.
   Photobiol., B:Biology 2 483-490
13 Bevington,P.R. (1969) Data Reduction and Error Analysis for the
   Physical Sciences., Mc.Graw-Hill, New York
14 van Dorssen,R.J., Breton,J., Plijter,J.J., Satoh,K., van Gorkom,H.J.
   and Amesz,J. (1987) Biochim.Biophys.Acta 893, 267-274

A SPECTROSCOPIC STUDY OF A PHOTOSYSTEM I ANTENNA COMPLEX

ISHITA MUKERJI AND KENNETH SAUER, DEPARTMENT OF CHEMISTRY AND
CHEMICAL BIODYNAMICS DIVISION, LAWRENCE BERKELEY LABORATORY,
UNIVERSITY OF CALIFORNIA, BERKELEY, CA 94720 USA

1. INTRODUCTION

The unusual long wavelength fluorescent behavior of Photosystem I (PSI) has been well documented.(1) This study investigates the origin and temperature dependence of this emission using an intact peripheral antenna preparation isolated from a PSI complex originally extracted from spinach. This antenna complex (LHCP-I) contains polypeptides in the 19-24 kDa range and exhibits a red shift in emission maximum from 685nm (F685) to 735nm (F735) as the temperature is lowered. Fluorescence excitation spectra demonstrate that chlorophyll b (chl b) preferentially stimulates the long wavelength emission at both room temperature and 77K and also indicate the presence of a long wavelength absorber in the 703-708nm range. Excitation polarization scans show a rising polarization value reaching a maximum of 0.3 from 705nm to 725nm, confirming the presence of a long wavelength pigment or pigments which are primarily responsible for emission at 735nm (F735). Absorption spectra demonstrate that this species comprises a small percentage of the total pigment population in the light harvesting antenna. The overall fluorescence yield of the complex increases as the temperature is lowered suggesting the presence of a quenching mechanism which does not involve the reaction center, P700.

2. MATERIALS AND METHODS

PSI-200 particles were isolated as described.(2) LHCP-I particles were prepared following the method of Haworth et. al. (3) with one modification. Linear sucrose density gradients were prepared with .05% lauryl maltoside instead of 1.0%. Purity of the material was determined by SDS-PAGE. The Bio-Rad silver stain procedure was used to detect the protein bands. Steady state fluorescence measurements were performed as described.(2) Samples were diluted to <0.1 absorbance at 675nm. Polarization measurements were done with Glan Thompson polarizers for both excitation and emission. These measurements were done at 278K with samples diluted to .01 mg/ml chl in 60% glycerol, 40% 0.05M Tricine, pH=7.8. Sample temperature was changed and controlled by a temperature regulating recirculating bath. (Neslab RTE-5B)

3. RESULTS AND DISCUSSION

Four polypepetides in the 19-24 kD range, which contain approximately 100 chl a and chl b molecules, comprise the antenna complex.(4,5) Although the exact distribution of pigment is uncertain, recent biochemical studies show the majority of the chl b is located on one protein. (6,7) In this study the LHCP-I complex used at room temperature has an emission maximum at 685nm (F685) with a broad shoulder ranging from 710-740nm. At 77K a dramatic shift in wavelength maximum from 685nm to 733nm is observed (Fig.1) The position of the emission peaks are located at higher energy than what has previously been reported for a reaction center complex containing the light harvesting antenna with 200 chl/P700 (PSI-200).(2) Components in the reaction center antenna contribute to the long wavelength fluorescence in the holocomplex, causing the

M. Baltscheffsky (ed.), Current Research in Photosynthesis, Vol. II, 321–324.

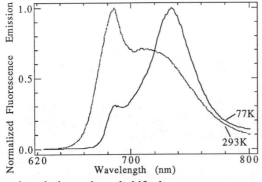

Figure 1: Steady state fluorescence emission of LHCP-I at 293K and 77K.Excitation done at 435nm. Sample originally in 0.1-0.2 M sucrose diluted 5 fold. 293K: Sample dilution done with 50.0mM Tricine, pH=7.8. 77K: Sample dilution done with 40% 50.0mM Tricine, pH=7.8, 60% glycerol.

peak emission to be red-shifted.

Excitation spectra of LHCP-I were taken at 77K. (Fig.2) Peaks at 468nm and 650nm, the absorption maxima of chl b, are noticeably enhanced for F735 in comparison with that for F685. Our data correlate well with biochemical evidence, which indicates that chl b is intimately connected with fluorescence at longer wavelengths.(3,5,6) An additional feature of the excitation spectra is a small shoulder observed between 703-708nm. This shoulder confirms the presence of a long wavelength absorber originally proposed by Butler to be responsible for emission at 720nm in whole leaves.(8) We assign this component to C705. Both chl b and C705 enhance F735 in LHCP-I.

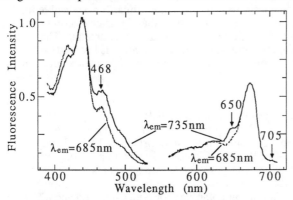

Figure 2: Steady state excitation spectra of LHCP-I. Spectra taken at 77K with emission at 685nm or 735nm. Samples frozen to a cracked glass in 40% 50.0mM Tricine, pH=7.8, 60% glycerol.

Excitation polarization studies have also been done on the LHCP-I complex. (Fig. 3) For 735nm emission a polarization value of approximately zero is observed using excitation wavelengths from 600nm to 675nm. This value rises over the wavelength range 675nm to 705nm reaching a maximum near 0.3 and then levels off from 705nm to 725nm. In general, polarization values of 0.3 or more indicate that the relative angle between absorption and emission dipoles is small. For 690nm emission the polarization values obtained are similar to those observed when λ_{em}=735nm. Polarization values of approximately zero are suggestive of depolarized emission. In this instance the depolarization undoubtedly results from energy transfer processes occuring within the antenna complex. The polarized fluorescence observed from excitation wavelengths greater than 705nm is indicative of emission arising from a pigment or pigments, lying at lower energy than the majority of the LHCP-I chl and probably lower than the reaction center of PSI.

The temperature dependence of LHCP-I fluorescence has also been investigated.

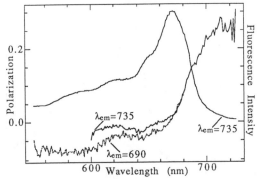

Figure 3: Excitation polarization of LHCP-I. Emission wavelengths at either 690nm or 735nm. Steady state excitation spectrum with λ_{em}=735nm. T=278K. Sample in 40% 50.0mM Tricine, pH=7.8, 60% glycerol.

Figure 4a depicts the emission of the antenna complex as a function of temperature. It can be seen that the fluorescence yield of the complex increases as the temperature decreases. There is no concomitant increase in absorption cross-section as the temperature is lowered (data not shown). In Figure 4b the same data are depicted normalized to emission maximum, demonstrating that the yield of F735 increases at a greater rate than the fluorescence yield of F685. This behavior contrasts markedly with what is observed for PSI-200. For the reaction center containing complex the fluorescence yield of the shorter wavelength component (F690) remains relatively temperature independent, while the yield of the long wavelength component increases dramatically.(2) The increase in fluorescence intensity as the temperature is decreased implicates a high temperature quenching mechanism for the excited state. This process must operate independently of the reaction center and its chemical state, because reaction centers are not present in this preparation. Additionally, the quenching efficiency of this process decreases with decreasing temperature. The increase of F735 relative to F685 as the quenching efficiency lessens can be attributed to more of the excitation reaching the long wavelength "sink" C705. Changes in excitation transfer pathway as a function of temperature can be addressed by time-resolved fluorescence measurements, which are in progress in our laboratory. The overall fluorescence yield of the antenna complex exhibits Arrhenius behavior. An average activation energy of 1550 cm^{-1} +/- 150 cm^{-1} is obtained, assuming that the integrated area under the curve is proportional to the fluorescence rate constant. This energy corresponds to a composite of processes, which are temperature dependent. Preliminary deconvolution of the spectral components indicates depopulation of the excited state is rate-limiting. Further analysis is necessary in order to elucidate the mechanisms which are occuring in LHCP-I.

     In summary our spectroscopic study of the peripheral light harvesting complex of PSI indicates that chl b is intimately connected with the origin of the long wavelength fluorescence. Excitation spectra also demonstrate the presence of a component lying at lower energy than the reaction center, which stimulates fluorescence emission at 735nm. The interaction between chl b and this component is unclear; CD spectra do not indicate the presence of excitonic coupling.(5) High polarization values upon excitation in the 705-725nm range imply that the F735 emission arises predominantly from a long wavelength absorber, C705. Thus the polarization spectra correlate well with the excitation spectra in associating C705 with the light harvesting antenna of PSI as well as identifying it as the origin of F735. Recent studies on the light harvesting antenna of Rb. sphaeroides demonstrate that a long wavelength species is an integral part of the antenna. (9) The nature and function of such species, which lie at lower energy than their associated reaction center remains a perplexing question. It is possible that these pigments facilitate energy transfer to the reaction center or conversely, operate as photoprotection

II.5.**324**

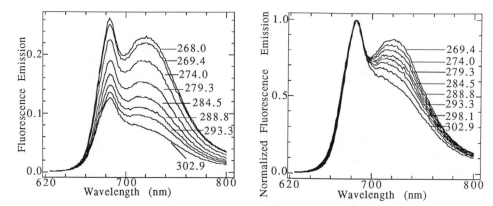

Figure 4: Temperature dependence of LHCP-I. All spectra taken on the same sample at indicated temperatures (K). a) Sample diluted approximately 5 fold in 40% 50.0mM Tricine, pH=7.8, 60% glycerol. b) Normalized steady state fluorescence emission. Sample preparation as in Fig. 4a.

devices for the reaction center. The temperature dependent behavior of LHCP-I, however, intimates a quenching mechanism, which is independent of the reaction center. Alternately, as Schuster et. al.(10) suggest, some of the light harvesting apoproteins may serve as control elements in energy transfer to the reaction center but do not contain pigment. In this case temperature dependent changes in protein conformation could be giving rise to the behavior observed. Experiments are in progress to further elucidate the nature of the quenching mechanism acting in LHCP-I and also to determine the relation between chl b and C705.

ACKNOWLEDGEMENTS

We would like to thank M.F.J. Talbot for considerable help in isolating LHCP-I and data collection. This research was supported by the Director, Office of Basic Energy Sciences, Division of Biological Energy Research of the Department of Energy under contract DE-AC03-76SF00098.

REFERENCES
[1]Butler, W.L., Tredwell, C.J., Malkin, R. and Barber, J. (1979) Biochim. Biophys. Acta 545, 309-315.
[2]Mukerji, I. and Sauer, K. (1989) in Photosynthesis (Briggs, W.H., ed.) A.R. Liss, New York in press.
[3]Haworth, P., Watson, J.L. and Arntzen, C.J. (1983) Biochim. Biophys. Acta 724, 151-158.
[4]Lam, E., Ortiz, W., Mayfield, S. and Malkin, R. (1984) Plant Physiol. 74, 650-655.
[5]Lam, E., Ortiz, W. and Malkin, R. (1984) FEBS Lett. 168, 10-14.
[6]Vainstein, A., Peterson, C.C. and Thornber, J.P. (1989) J. Biol. Chem. 264, 4058-4063.
[7]Nechushtai, R., Peterson, C.C., Peter, G.F. and Thornber, J.P. (1987) Eur. J. Biochem. 164, 345-350.
[8]Butler, W.L. (1961) Arch. Biochem. Biophys. 93, 413-422.
[9]Hunter, C.N., van Grondelle, R. and van Dorssen, R.J. (1989) Biochim. Biophys. Acta 973, 383-389.
[10]Schuster, G., Nechushtai, R., Ferreira, P.C.G., Thornber, J.P. and Ohad, I. (1988) Eur. J. Biochem. 177, 411-416.

POLARIZED PUMP-PROBE SPECTROSCOPY OF PHOTOSYSTEM I ANTENNA EXCITATION
TRANSPORT

TIMOTHY P. CAUSGROVE, SHUMEI YANG, and WALTER S. STRUVE, DEPARTMENT
OF CHEMISTRY and AMES LABORATORY-USDOE, IOWA STATE UNIVERSITY, AMES,
IOWA 50011, U.S.A.

I. INTRODUCTION
    Electronic excitation transport (EET) is currently being widely
studied in photosystem I light-harvesting and core antennae of green
plants. In this work, we have extended our earlier ultrafast pump-
probe experiments on PSI-60 particles [1] to PSI-200 particles
(Chl/P700 ~ 200) from spinach chloroplasts. Our magic-angle Chl a Q_y
photobleaching decays parallel the multiexponential fluorescence
decays reported elsewhere for particles of similar size [2-4]. The
depolarization lifetimes in the corresponding anisotropic decays show
marked wavelength dependence between 660 and 681 nm.

2. EXPERIMENTAL
    Native PS I particles (Chl/P700 ratio ~ 200) were isolated from
spinach chloroplasts following the procedure of Mullet et. al. [5,6].
    The pump-probe apparatus was identical to one described
previously [1]. A Coherent Antares 76-s Nd:YAG laser generated 70 ps
532 nm pulses with ~ 2W average power at 76 MHz repetition rate. A
hybrid mode-locked dye laser (DCM lasing dye, DDCI saturable dye)
equipped with a Coherent 7210 cavity dumper yielded ~ 1.5 ps pulses
between 645 and 681 nm.

3. ISOTROPIC PHOTOBLEACHING DECAY
    At least three lifetime components are required to describe the
magic-angle photobleaching decays in the Chl a Q_y absorption region,
660-681 nm: 1-2 ps, 25-40 ps, and 200-250 ps. The second component
resembles the "fast" PS I antenna fluorescence components observed by
Owens et. al. [2] and by Mukerji and Sauer [4]. The third component
is similar to the "intermediate" fluorescence components observed in
PS I preparations with Chl/P700 greater than 65 [2,4]; it was not
observed in our PSI-60 work [1]. These isotropic profiles exhibit
little wavelength dependence between 660 and 681 nm.
    The 200-250 ps long component is absent at the three shortest
wavelengths studied (645, 650, and 655 nm), where strong Chl b
absorption occurs. This decay accelerates toward shorter wavelengths, reaching ~ 2 ps lifetime at 645 nm. Since Mukerji and Sauer

M. Baltscheffsky (ed.), Current Research in Photosynthesis, Vol. II, 325–328.

have shown that Chl b excitation efficiently sensitizes F735
fluorescence from long-wavelength Chl a pigments in the peripheral
antenna [4], this lifetime may reflect EET between Chl b and F735.

4. ANISOTROPIC PHOTOBLEACHING DECAY

Representative Chl a Q_y anisotropic photobleaching profiles,
obtained using parallel and perpendicular polarizations (upper and
lower profiles respectively) are shown for 665 and 675 nm in
Fig. 1. The simplest functions capable of modeling these and other
polarized profiles for 660 through 681 nm have the form

$$A_{\parallel}(t) = P(t)\{1 + 0.8[(1-a)r(t) + a]\}$$
$$A_{\perp}(t) = P(t)\{1 - 0.4[(1-a)r(t) + a]\} \qquad (1)$$

Here $P(t)$ is the isotropic decay, measured with pump and probe
polarizations separated by $54.7°$; $r(t)$ is an anisotropy decay
function which approaches zero at long times.

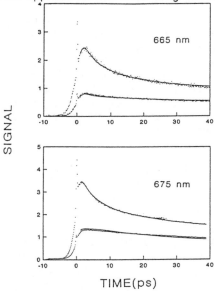

TIME(ps)

FIGURE 1. Anisotropic photobleaching transients for PSI-200
particles at 665 and 675 nm. Continuous curves are
optimized convolutions of Eqs. 1 with the laser pulse
autocorrelation functions.

The anisotropy function $r(t)$ was modeled as single-exponential in
profile fits in which the triexponential parameters in the isotropic
decay function $P(t)$ were frozen at the values found in magic-angle
profile analyses. Final depolarization lifetimes τ (based on $r(t) =$
$\exp(-t/\tau)$) and residual anisotropy parameters a are shown in Table I.

TABLE I. Average fitting parameters for anisotropic profiles

Wavelength, nm	τ, ps	a
660	12.2	0.53
665	9.6	0.47
670	5.9	0.32
675	5.0	0.44
681	6.3	0.52

The average depolarization lifetimes τ, plotted as open circles versus pump-probe wavelength in Fig. 2, increase from 5 to 12 ps as the wavelength is tuned to the blue from 675 to 660 nm. We have simulated this dependence by modeling the PS I core antenna absorption spectrum with Gaussian curve analysis of the Chl a Q_y absorption spectrum of highly enriched PS I particles [7]. According to Förster theory, EET from Chl a spectral component i to spectral component j in the core antenna will occur with rate proportional to

$$W_{ij} = \int f_i(\omega)\varepsilon_j(\omega)d\omega/g_i g_j\omega^4 \qquad (2)$$

where $f_i(\omega)$ and $\varepsilon_j(\omega)$ are the donor fluorescence and acceptor absorption spectra respectively. If the spectral forms arise from exciton splittings, all of the g_i are unity; otherwise, the g_i are proportional to the number of chromophores sharing the same component spectrum. Excitation will then migrate from an initially pumped

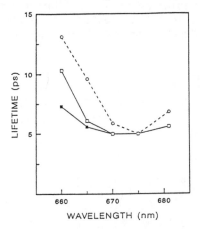

FIGURE 2. Wavelength variation of depolarization lifetimes τ. Open circles are average experimental lifetimes. Open squares are theoretical lifetimes computed assuming delocalized exciton states ($g_i = 1$) and normalized to 5 ps at 675 nm; solid squares are lifetimes calculated assuming excitations are localized on single chromophores.

spectral component i to other components j according to the decay law

$$P_i(t) = \exp\left(-t \sum_j W_{ij} g_j\right) \tag{3}$$

if the (unknown) distance and orientational factors are not considered. The overall migration rate observed at pump-probe wavelength $\lambda = 1/\omega$ the assumes the multiexponential form

$$P(\omega,t) = \sum_i \varepsilon_i(\omega) P_i(t) \tag{4}$$

The calculated depolarization lifetimes are compared with the experimental lifetimes in Fig. 2.

5. CONCLUSIONS

5.1 At least three exponential decay components are required to describe the Chl a isotropic photobleaching signal between 660 and 681 nm: < 5 ps, 25-40 ps, and 200-250 ps.

5.2 The isotropic decay becomes far more rapid at 645-655 nm, and may reflect on EET from Chl b to F735 in the peripheral antenna.

5.3 Since the Chl a isotropic decay shows no discernible wavelength dependence from 665 to 681 nm, we find no evidence of sequential downhill EET from higher- to lower-energy spectral forms.

5.4 The 5-12 ps depolarization lifetimes indicate that while subpicosecond equilibration of excitation may occur among Chl a spectral forms [2], such rapid equilibration does not extend over the entire antenna. In a possible scenario consistent with our data and the finding of Shubin et. al. [8] that the PS I core antenna contains several similar clusters of 6 to 8 Chl a pigments each, the rapid spectral equilibration may occur between chromophores inside a cluster, while the slower EET (manifested in the depolarization lifetimes) may occur between clusters.

6. ACKNOWLEDGEMENTS

We thank John Golbeck for isolating the PSI-200 preparations, and we are indebted to Gerald Small, Kenneth Sauer, John Golbeck, and Graham Fleming for valuable discussions.

REFERENCES
1 Causgrove, T. P., Yang, S., Struve, W. S. (1988), J. Phys. Chem. 92, 6121
2 Owens, T. G., Webb, S. P., Alberte, R. S., Mets, L., Fleming, G. R. (1988), Biophys. J. 53, 733
3 Wittmershaus, B. (1987), in Progress in Photosynthesis Research (Biggins, J., ed.), Vol. 1, pp. 75-82, Martinus Nijhoff, The Hague
4 Mukerji, I., Sauer, K. (1988), in Proc. C. S. French Symposium on Photosynthesis, Alan R. Liss Publishers, New York
5 Mullet, J. E., Burke, J. J. Arntzen, C. J. (1980), Plant Physiol. (Bethesda) 65, 814
6 Golbeck, J. H. (1987), J. Membrane Sci. 33, 151
7 Ikegami, I., Itoh, S. (1988), Biochim. Biophys. Acta 934, 39
8 Shubin, V. V., Karapetyan, N. V., Krasnovsky, A. A. (1986), Photosynth. Res. 9, 3

Competition between trapping and annihilation in photosystem I

H.-W. Trissl, J. Breton[*], J. Deprez[*], A. Dobek[%], G. Paillotin and W. Leibl

Abt. Biophysik, FB Biologie/Chemie, University, D-4500 Osnabrück, F.R.G.

[*]Dept. Biologie, Centre d'Etudes Nucléaires de Saclay, F-91191 Gif-Sur-Yvette, France

[%]Institute of Physics, A. Mickiewicz University, 60-780 Poznan, Poland

INTRODUCTION

The study of exciton transfer and primary charge separation in photosynthesis requires excitation by picosecond flashes. If a significant fraction of the reaction centers (RCs) shall be closed by a flash, the excitation density must be chosen such high that more than one exciton resides at the same time in the pool of antenna pigments. Then excitons can be lost by singlet-singlet annihilation before they are trapped by the photochemistry in the RC. Annihilation leads to an apparent acceleration of all other reactions connected with the exciton dynamics. The quantitative treatment of this competitive deactivation path allows the bimolecular rate constant of exciton-exciton annihilation to be determined that characterizes a given antenna bed.

We have studied exciton annihilation and trapping in photosystem I by probing the photochemical path into the RC with a photoelectric technique based on the light-gradient effect [1,2]. The comparison of the photovoltage evoked by long and short flashes (i.e. without and with annihilation) and time-resolved measurements together with a theory on exciton dynamics allowed us to determine (i) the bimolecular rate constant for annihilation, (ii) a parameter that describes the competition between trapping and annihilation, and (iii) the rate constant of trapping in the low energy limit.

MATERIALS AND METHODS

Chloroplasts with stacked membranes were prepared from pea leaves (*Pisum sativum*) following the procedure described in ref. [3]. The chlorophyll concentration used was 3.5 mM. Photovoltage measurements were carried out in a capacitative microcoaxial cell of 3 x 0.1 mm dimensions [4]. After amplification the signals were recorded on a 7-GHz digitizing oscilloscope (Tektronix 7250). Single traces were averaged and analyzed on a personal computer.

M. Baltscheffsky (ed.), Current Research in Photosynthesis, Vol. II, 329–332.
© 1990 *Kluwer Academic Publishers. Printed in the Netherlands.*

The excitation source was a frequeny-doubled Nd-YAG laser delivering flashes at 532 nm of either 12 ns or 30 ps duration. The response function of the microcoaxial cell was determined by analysis of the photovoltage of oriented purple membranes [5].

RESULTS

To eliminate electrogenic contributions of photosystem II the chloroplasts were incubated with DCMU (100 μM) and preilluminated. Photosystem I activity was held constant by addition of 10 mM ascorbate. Fig. 1a shows the time resolved deconvoluted photovoltage evoked by 12-ns flashes at different energies as indicated. The time courses can be ascribed to the light-gradient effect and quantitatively accounted for by an appropriate theory [6].

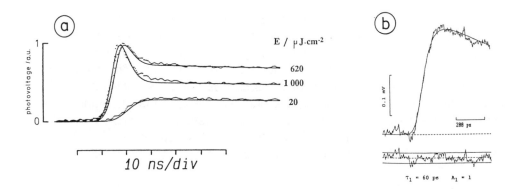

Fig. 1: a) Photovoltage evoked by 12-ns flashes of different energies recorded at 1 GHz. The traces are deconvoluted by the discharge time of the measuring cell. b) Photovoltage evoked by 30-ps flashes recorded at 7 GHz. The solid line represents the best fit of an exponential function with the response function of the apparatus. The lower traces are the residuals with lines indicating $\pm$ 5 % deviations.

Excitation by 30-ps flashes of 90 μJ/cm^2 and detection by 7-GHz electronics evoked a photovoltage whose kinetics can be analyzed by a displacement current with an exponential time constant of τ_1 = 60 ps and its convolution with the response function of the measuring cell (Fig. 1b). At higher energies the photovoltage rose faster and at lower energies slower. The dependence of the time constant of the displacement current on the excitation energy is shown in Fig. 2a. Furthermore, the 30-ps excitation led to smaller amplitudes than the 12 ns excitation as seen in Fig. 2b.

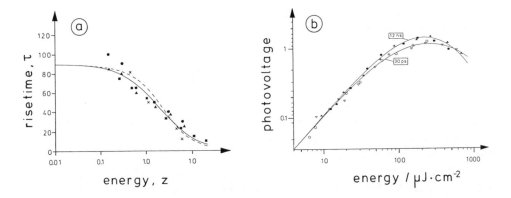

Fig. 2: a) Energy dependence of the deconvoluted rising phase of the photo-voltage (data from different preparations). The solid line is the best fit of eq. 1. b) Double logarithmic plot of the energy dependence of photo-voltage amplitudes remaining after the flash. Flash duration under non-annihilating conditions 12 ns and annihilating conditions 30 ps.

THEORY

The exciton interactions are described by an overall bimolecular annihilation rate constant $\gamma = \gamma_1 + 2\gamma_2$ which accounts for the two singlet-singlet reactions:

$$S_1 + S_1 \xrightarrow{\gamma_1} S_1 + S_o$$

$$S_1 + S_1 \xrightarrow{\gamma_2} S_o + S_o$$

With the assumption of a fast equilibration of the excitation energy between neighbouring photosynthetic units and the same quenching power of reaction centers in the states P-700 and P-700$^+$ (open and closed, respectively) the time-dependent exciton density, $n(t)$, and the fraction of open reaction centers, $q_o(t)$, can be written:

$$dn(t)/dt = -(k_t + k_l)\, n(t) - 1/2\, \gamma\, n(t)^2$$

$$dq_o(t)/dt = -k_t\, n(t)\, q_o(t)$$

where k_t is the trapping rate constant and k_l the sum of the rate constants of all monomolecular loss processes like fluorescence and non-photochemical quenching. The photosynthetic quantum yield Γ is given by $\Gamma = k_t/k$, where k is the overall quenching rate constant $k = k_t + k_l$ ($1/k$ = apparent trapping time).

The two-state description of the RC is sufficient, because there is no hint for a second electrogenic reaction in the time range between 50 ps and 50 ns.
From the solution

$$q_o(t) = (1 + \Gamma z \alpha (1 - \exp(-k\, t))^{-1/\alpha} \qquad (1)$$

the fraction of closed RCs, $q_c(t) = 1 - q_o(t)$, and from this the photovoltage, $V(t,z)$, can be calculated. In eq. 1 α is a parameter that describes the competition between trapping and annihilation, $\alpha = \gamma/(2k_t) = \gamma/2\Gamma k$, and z is the excitation energy expressed in hits/trap.
This equation was used to fit simultaneously (solid lines in the figures) the energy dependence of both, the kinetics and the amplitude of the photovoltage, thereby taking into account the specific lightgradient effects [6]. This analysis yields a trapping rate constant of $k_t = (90\ \mathrm{ps})^{-1}$, an annihilation rate constant of $\gamma = (75\ \mathrm{ps})^{-1}$, and a competition parameter of $\alpha = 0.6$. The photosynthetic quantum yield was assumed to be high ($\Gamma \approx 1; k_l \ll k_t$).
The annihilation rate constant is much the same as in photosystem II, which correlates with the similar structure and pigment composition of the two antenna systems present in higher plants. The competition parameter however is significantly smaller than in photosystem II, which is explained the faster trapping time in photosystem I (90 ps) than in photosystem II (300 ps) [7].

REFERENCES

1. Fowler,C.F. and Kok,B. (1972) in "6. Intern. Congr. Photobiol.", Bochum. Abstr. Nr. 417
2. Witt,H.T. and Zickler (1973) FEBS Lett. 37, 307-310
3. Steinback,K.E., Burke,J.J. and Arntzen,C.J. (1979) Arch. Biochem. Biophs. 195, 546-557
4. Trissl,H.-W., Leibl,W., Deprez,J., Dobek,A. and Breton,J. (1987) Biochim. Biophys. Acta 893, 320-332
5. Trissl,H.-W., Gärtner,W. and Leibl,W. (1989) Chem. Phys. Lett. 158, 515-518
6. Leibl,W. and Trissl,H.-W. Biochim. Biophys. Acta, submitted
7. Leibl,W., Breton,J., Deprez,J. and Trissl,H.-W. (1989) Photosynth. Res., in press

CORD-LIKE PHYCOBILISOMES OF *RHODOSORUS MARINUS* GEITLER: FINE STRUCTURE AND ITS FUNCTIONAL IMPLICATIONS.

Teresa Dibbayawan[1], Maret Vesk[2] and A.W.D. Larkum[1], School of Biological Sciences[1]; Electron Microscope Unit[2], University of Sydney, NSW 2006, Australia.

Introduction

Rhodosorus marinus is a unicellular, marine, red alga common in tropical and subtropical waters. We recently isolated it for the first time in Australia, and in the course of a routine ultrastructural investigation found that it had phycobilisomes of most unusual structure and arrangement.

Materials and Methods

Rhodosorus marinus was cultured in Provasoli's enriched seawater medium under continuous low light ($20\mu Em^{-2}s^{-1}$) at 20°C. Cells in late exponential phase were used. For phycobilisome isolation harvested cells were resuspended in SPC medium (0.5M sucrose, 0.5M potassium phosphate, 0.3M potassium citrate, pH 7.2) and passed through a French pressure cell at 69 000 kPa. Triton X-100 was then added to a final concentration of 1% v/v. The mixture was stirred in the dark for 30 min at 5°C then centrifuged for 30 min at 25 000g. The supernatant was layered on to continuous gradients of 10-40% sucrose in 0.5M potassium phosphate and 0.3M potassium citrate (pH7.2) containing 0.1% v/v Triton. They were centrifuged for 16h at 36 000 rpm in a Beckman SW40 rotor. A quick isolation was also carried out by freezing the cells in liquid nitrogen and fracturing them in a LN_2-cooled pestle and mortar. The fractured cells were then thawed and centrifuged in a Beckman Microfuge B for 2 min. The supernatant consisted of phycobilisomes both free and attached to small thylakoid fragments.

Absorption spectra were obtained on a Pye-Unicam SP8800 spectrophotometer while fluorescence measurements were made on a Perkin-Elmer MDF44B spectrofluorometer at -196°C.

For thin section electron microscopy cells were frozen in LN_2-cooled Freon 22 then substituted at -80°C in 2% glutaraldehyde in anhydrous acetone for 3 days then in 1% OsO_4 in acetone for 2 days. Cells were then brought up to room temperature and embedded in Spurr's resin. Sections were stained with uranyl acetate and lead citrate.

Isolated phycobilisomes and thylakoid fragments were negatively stained, after fixation with 1% glutaraldehyde in SPC, with 1% phosphotungstate, pH 7.0, or 1% ammonium molybdate pH 7.0. Freeze-fracturing/etching of cells frozen as above was carried out in a Balzers BAF300 freeze etching apparatus. All specimens were examined in a Philips EM400 electron microscope at 100kV.

M. Baltscheffsky (ed.), Current Research in Photosynthesis, Vol. II, 333–336.
© 1990 *Kluwer Academic Publishers. Printed in the Netherlands.*

Results and Discussion

Fig. 1 shows a typical thin-section view of a *Rhodosorus* cell. Phycobilisomes can be seen in their various aspects. They appear trapezoidal in face views (inset) with average dimensions of 37nm at the base, 27nm at the top and 27nm high. Each phycobilisome can be seen to have a plug-like structure at its base, embedded in the thylakoid. Ueda and Chida[1] also observed similar structures in *Cyanidium caldarium*. These plugs possibly represent the 95kDa polypeptides isolated by Redlinger and Gantt[2] and Hiller et al.[3]. Other planes of section show the phycobilisome to have quite a complex structure. The best interpretation of the confusing pattern seems to be that the phycobilisomes are actually continuous cords of various lengths. Freeze-etch replicas (Fig. 2) confirm this interpretation. The cords appear to be randomly arranged and vary a great deal in length. Micrographs of negatively-stained thylakoid fragments and free phycobilisomes also support this cord-like structure (Figs 3,4,5). However, Triton-isolated phycobilisomes did not stay intact as negative staining showed them to have dissociated into rods (Fig. 6).

Freeze-fracture replicas revealed the presence of parallel rows of particles on the EF face (Figs 7,8) of the thylakoids. These rows of EF particles are observed in several species of red and blue-green algae; the particles are believed to be part of PSII[4]. Regular arrays of particles were also seen on the PF face of the thylakoid (Fig. 8). These particles were more numerous and slightly smaller than the EF particles.

The absorption and fluorescence spectra of the isolated phycobilisomes (Figs 9,10) indicated the loss of some allophycocyanin during isolation. The 650nm shoulder on the absorbance spectrum was greatly reduced while fluorescence emission had the greatest peak at 645nm (from phycocyanin) and only a small peak at 680nm (allophycocyanin). This uncoupling of phycobilisome was also shown by the negatively stained sample of isolated phycobilisomes (Fig. 6) and is in agreement with the finding of Gantt et al.[5] that isolation at low temperature results in poor integrity of phycobilisomes.

It is clear that the ultrastructure of the phycobilisomes of *Rhodosorus* is markedly different to any previously described. They seem also to have a close relationship with the particle arrangement on both PF and EF faces of the thylakoid membrane.

We thank Drs Guy Cox and Jane Chrystal for assistance and advice.

References
1. Ueda, K., and Chida, Y. 1987. Br. Phycol. J. 22: 61-65
2. Redlinger, T. and Gantt, E. 1983. Plant Physiol. 73: 36-40
3. Hiller, R.G., Post, A. and Stewart, A.C. 1983. FEBS Lett. 156: 180-184
4. MacColl, R. and Gerard-Friar, D. *in* Phycobiliproteins. CRC Press, Florida, pp 163-169
5. Gantt, E., Lipschultz, C.A, Gabrowski, J. and Zimmerman, K. 1979. Plant Physiol. 63: 615-620

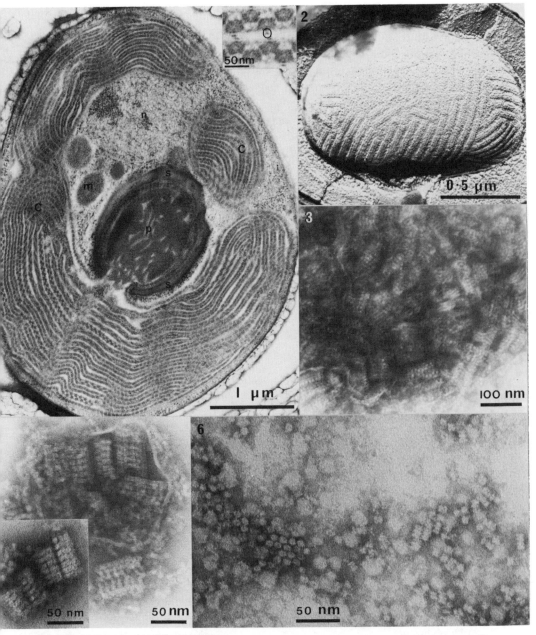

Fig. 1. Thin section of a *Rhodosorus* cell, showing the chloroplast and other organelles.
Various views of the phycobilisomes can be seen due to the angles at which different
thylakoids have been sectioned. Plug-like structures are visible in the inset (circle).
c = chloroplast; m = mitochondrion; n = nucleus; p = pyrenoid; s = starch grain.

Fig. 2. Freeze-etch replica of a thylakoid membrane showing the cord-like phycobilisomes.
Note the variability in length and orientation of the phycobilisomes.

Figs 3, 4 & 5. Negatively stained thylakoid fragments with the attached phycobilisomes
(3 & 4), and free phycobilisomes (5), from cells fractured at -196°C.

Fig. 6. Negatively stained phycobilisomes prepared with Triton X-100. Note the presence
of phycobiliprotein rods and the absence of intact phycobilisomes.

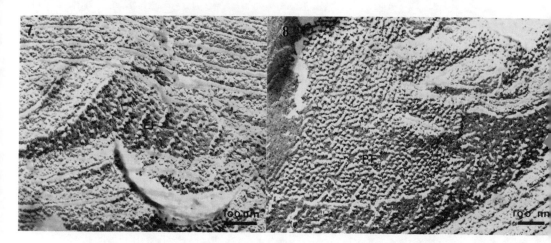

Figs 7&8. Freeze-fracture replicas of the thylakoid membranes. Fig. 7 shows the parallel rows of particles on the EF face while Fig. 8 shows regular arrays of particles on the PF face as well as the rows of EF particles.

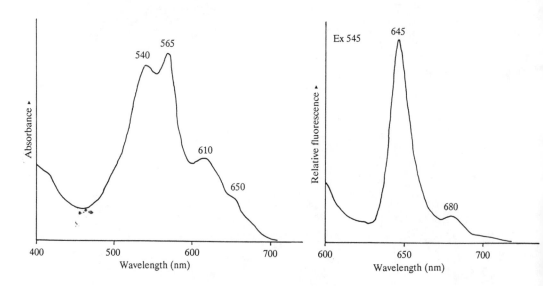

Fig. 9. Absorption spectrum of isolated phycobilisomes.

Fig. 10. Fluorescence emission spectra of isolated phycobilisomes at -196°C. Excitation was at 545nm.

SPECTROSCOPIC AND ORIENTATIONAL PROPERTIES OF
CHLOROPHYLLS a AND b IN LIPID MEMBRANES

MARNIX VAN GURP, GIJS VAN GINKEL AND YEHUDI K. LEVINE
Department of Molecular Biophysics, Buys Ballot Laboratory, University
of Utrecht, Princetonplein 5, Utrecht 3584 CC, The Netherlands.

1. INTRODUCTION
The efficiency of energy transfer in photosynthesis depends on the
relative orientations of the emission and absorption transition moments
respectively of the donor and acceptor chlorophyll molecules. This is
determined by the mutual orientation of the chromophores within the
structure of the photosynthetic membranes. In order to gain a better
insight into the molecular mechanism of energy transfer, it is
necessary to characterize the directions of the transition moments in
the frame of the chromophores. This can be achieved by combining the
results of angle-resolved linear dichroism and fluorescence
depolarisation measurements on macroscopically oriented lipid membranes
with the results of emission-resolved fluorescence anisotropy data from
isotropic systems (vesicles) (1).

2. EXPERIMENTAL APPROACH
The measuring techniques and their information contents are described
extensively in ref. (1) and will only be summarized below.
2.1. Angle-resolved linear dichroism (LD) measurements across the
     absorption spectrum of chlorophyll yield the order parameter S_μ
     of the <u>effective</u> transition moment.

$$S_\mu = \frac{A_V - A_H}{A_V + (3\sin^2\omega - 1)A_H} = \tfrac{1}{2} <3\cos^2\beta_\mu - 1>$$

A_H, A_V = horizontal and vertical absorption respectively
ω = the angle within the sample, see fig. 1
β_μ = the polar angle of the absorption moment with
            respect to the the normal to the bilayer plane

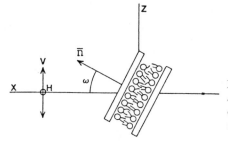

Figure 1. Experimental geometry of
a linear dichroism experiment on
ordered membranes in a slab-shaped
sample.

2.2. Excitation fluorescence anisotropy (FA) measurements using narrow-band detection at the two emission maxima of chlorophyll yield the FA (r_1 and r_2) for the two _effective_ emission transitions, see figure 2.

$$FA = r = \frac{I\| - I_\perp}{I\| + 2I_\perp} = 0.4\; P_2(\cos\epsilon)$$

P_2 = second order Legendre polynomial
$\epsilon = \beta_\mu - \beta_\nu$ = the angle between absorption and emission moment
β_μ, β_ν = the polar angle of the absorption and emission moment respectively

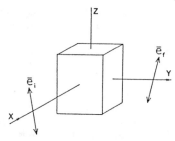

Figure 2. Experimental geometry of a 90° fluorescence anisotropy experiment. Excitation is along the X-axis, fluorescence is detected along the Y-axis.

2.3. Angle-resolved fluorescence depolarization (AFD) measurements using detection at the two emission maxima of chlorophyll yield the order parameters $S_{\nu 1}$ ands $S_{\nu 2}$ of the two _effective_ transition moments as well as S_μ (1). Note that these values are not affected by energy transfer processes. The experimental geometry of AFD measurements is shown in figure 3.
The exciting light is horizontally polarized and is incident on the sample at an angle θ. The intensities of the horizontally (I_H) and vertically (I_V) polarized emission are measured at an angle φ to the normal of the sample plane.
AFD yields:

$$R_e = \frac{I_H}{I_V} = f(\theta, \varphi)$$

From these data one can extract (S_μ, S_ν, G_0, G_1, G_2) in which G_0, G_1, G_2 are the correlation functions describing the molecular dynamics. These are irrelevant for the purpose of this study.
The order parameters S_μ and S_ν can be written in terms of order parameters describing the average orientation of the chromophore frame in the sample frame and the angle of the transition moments in the chromophore frame using Wigner rotation matrices elements (1,2).

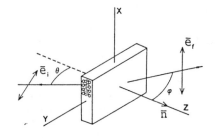

Figure 3. Experimental geometry of an angle-resolved fluorescence depolarization experiment. Excitation is at an angle θ to the membrane director $\bar{n}$, emission at an angle φ to the membrane director (= Z-axis). Both are in the XZ-plane. $\bar{e}_i$ and $\bar{e}_f$ define the polarization directions of the light.

3. RESULTS

In figure 4 the order parameters S_μ of chlorophyll a in planar digalactosyldiglyceride (DGDG) membranes are plotted as a function of the wavelength of excitation. This curve was obtained with angle-resolved linear dichroism measurements. A similar curve was obtained for chlorophyll b (data not shown).

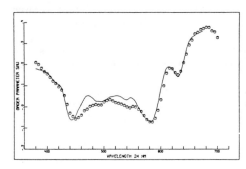

Figure 4. Order parameters S_μ of chlorophyll a in DGDG membranes (1:250) as a function of the wavelength of excitation, as found from linear dichroism experiments. The continuous line is a theoretical fit based on fluorescence anisotropy measurements in castor oil. The errors are ± 0.02 at wavelengths of high absorption and ± 0.08 at wavelengths of low absorption.

As can be seen from table 1, the order parameters S_μ can be equally well obtained from LD as from AFD measurements. The table also gives the calculated value of S_μ obtained from a fit to the values of r_1 and r_2, the fluorescence anisotropy measured at the two respective emission wavelengths of chlorophyll a (3).

TABLE 1

Order parameters S_μ, $S_{\nu 1}$ and $S_{\nu 2}$ of chlorophyll a in planar bilayers of DGDG. Also plotted are the values of the fluorescence anisotropy of chlorophyll a in castor oil at the two emission wavelengths of chlorophyll a (r_1 at 680 nm, r_2 at 750 nm), see ref.3.

λ(nm)	S_μ (LD)	S_ν (AFD)	S_ν (calc)	r_1	r_2
380	.136±.013		.121	.208	.160
405	.083±.006	.078±.007	.085	.174	.137
415	.061±.007		.057	.148	.107
450	-.110±.016		-.106	-.008	.008
615	.118±.014	.123±.009	.134	.221	.161
670	.282±.009	.275±.006	.283	.261	.298

$S_{\nu 1}(680) = .306 \pm .002$
$S_{\nu 2}(750) = .280 \pm .002$

The directions of the emission moments $\bar{\nu}_1$ and $\bar{\nu}_2$ and the Q_y absorption moments of chlorophyll a and b in the molecular frame can now be obtained from the measured order parameters S_μ and the fluorescence anisotropies r_1 and r_2 (table 1) on assuming the transitions to be pure. We now find:

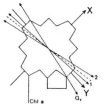 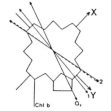

	Chl a	Chl b
$\beta_{\nu 1}$	5°	16°
$\beta_{\nu 2}$	-5°	-1°
$\beta_\mu(Q_y)$	19°	28°

4. CONCLUSIONS

The combination of the results of all three types of experiments allows us to disentangle the information about the directions of the transition moments in the chromophore plane from the order parameters describing the orientation of the chromophores in the bilayers. We find from our experimental data:

1) To a good approximation the Q_y-absorption and the two emission transition moments can each be characterized in terms of a pure dipole moment.

2) A reconstruction of the orientation distribution function using the Maximum Entropy Formalism (4) reveals that the chlorophyll chromophores are most likely to be oriented with their planes perpendicular to the bilayer plane, see fig.6.

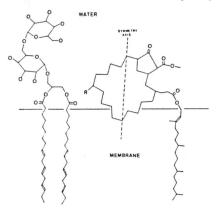

FIGURE 6. Orientation of a chlorophyll molecule in the DGDG membrane. The polar groups in DGDG (left) and chlorophyll (right) are indicated. The chlorophyll symmetry axis is mainly perpendicular to the membrane plane, but the porphyrin ring also has a small probability to lie flat on the membrane plane. The R-group is $-CH_2$ in chlorophyll-a and $-CHO$ in chlorophyll-b.

REFERENCES
1. Van Gurp, M., van Ginkel, G. and Levine, Y.K. (1988), J. Theor. Biol. 333-349.
2. Van Gurp, M. and Levine, Y.K. (1989) J. Chem Phys. 90, 4095-4102.
3. Van Gurp, M., van Ginkel, G. and Levine Y.K. (1989) Biochim Biophys. Acta 973, 405-413.
4. Levine, R.D. and Tribus, M. (1979) The Maximum Entropy Formalism, MIT Press, Cambridge.

RECONSTITUTION OF LIGHT HARVESTING COMPLEXES: A SINGLE APOPROTEIN BINDS CHLa, CHLb, AND XANTHOPHYLLS

KIRK CAMMARATA, F. GERALD PLUMLEY, AND GREGORY W. SCHMIDT, Botany Dept., Univ. of Georgia, Athens GA 30602, USA and Institute of Marine Science, Univ. of Alaska, Fairbanks AK 99775, USA (F.G.P.)

INTRODUCTION

Although it is the major antenna for photosynthesis, little structural information exists on the light harvesting chlorophyll-protein complex (LHCPII) of higher plants/algae. The functional unit of LHCPII is probably a trimer of monomeric apoproteins non-covalently associated with 6-7 Chl a, 5-6 Chl b, and 3 xanthophylls (see 1-2 for reviews). Several 24-30 kD apoproteins are distinguishable by SDS-PAGE for most species. However, it has not been possible to assign functions in light harvesting/energy transfer processes to the individual apoproteins. They are encoded by large multigene families whose products show a high degree of similarity at the amino acid sequence level and are post-translationally modified. Since LHCPII apoproteins contain only 3-4 histidyl residues, most of the chlorophyll is ligated differently than that of the bacterial photosynthetic reaction centers (3).

Plumley and Schmidt (4) demonstrated that LHCPII apoproteins could be reconstituted *in vitro* to yield CPII pigment-protein complexes with spectral characteristics nearly identical to those of the "native" CPII complex isolated by LDS-PAGE at 4°C. Reconstitution exhibited an absolute requirement for all components (apoproteins, Chls a and b, lutein, violaxanthin, and neoxanthin). Here, we show reconstitution of a single LHCPII gene product expressed *in vivo* by E. coli, and characterize the resultant CPII.

METHODS

Reconstitution of LHCPII from apoproteins and thylakoid pigments extracted by 80% acetone was described by Plumley and Schmidt (4). Aliquots of pigments in ether/ethanol were transferred directly to the apoproteins solubilized in 2% LDS and then subjected to 3 cycles of freeze/thaw prior to electrophoresis at 4°C. Reconstitution controls consisted of reconstituted samples heated (100°C, 1 min) just prior to electrophoresis. Subsequent analyses of reconstituted vs "native" CPII pigment-protein complexes were performed directly on excised polyacrylamide gel slices or following extraction into 2 mM Tris-Cl, pH

M. Baltscheffsky (ed.), Current Research in Photosynthesis, Vol. II, 341–344.
© 1990 *Kluwer Academic Publishers. Printed in the Netherlands.*

8.0. Triton X-100/sucrose density gradient derived light harvesting complexes (LHCII) were prepared according to (5).

pAB96, a cDNA clone for a pea LHCPII gene encoding most of the mature apoprotein (6) was a gift from A. Cashmore. *In vitro* and *in vivo* expression of AB96 was directed by the pDS12/RBSII-1 vector, a modified version of the pDS5 vector described by Bujard et al. (7). The fusion protein product contains eight additional amino acids at the amino terminus of AB96. For *in vivo* expression, late-log phase cells of *E. coli* harboring the pDS12/RBSII-1 expression vector containing AB96 were lysed by resuspension in 2% LDS and sonication. Measurement of corrected fluorescence and CD spectra was described previously (4).

RESULTS AND DISCUSSION

Figure 1 shows a typical unstained "green gel" (LDS-PAGE, 4°C) of heated (H, 100°C) and non-heated (NH, 0°C) 2% LDS solubilized pea LHCII, and control (C) and reconstituted (R) samples of light harvesting apoproteins. The CPII pigment-protein complex from NH LHCII is referred to as "native" CPII. Heat treatment (control) demonstrates that pigments do not bind non-specifically during electrophoresis. CPII pigment-protein complexes can be reconstituted from both total pea LHCII

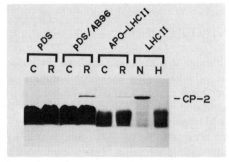

Figure 1

apoproteins and from a single species of light harvesting apoprotein from whole cell lysates of *E. coli* expressing the AB96 gene. No CPII complexes were observed in subsequently heated samples nor in lysates of *E. coli* harboring only the non-recombinant vector(pDS). These results show that a single species of light harvesting apoprotein can be reassembled with pigments to form a CPII complex.

We have examined the biochemical composition of "native" CPII and reconstituted CPII following LDS-PAGE at 4°C (data not shown). Pigment analyses of "native" CPII showed a Chl a/b ratio =1, the presence of lutein and neoxanthin as major xanthophyll pigments, and only trace amounts of violaxanthin. In contrast, Triton X-100 derived light harvesting complexes (LHCII) differ by having a Chl a/b ratio =1.4 and more violaxanthin and lutein. Since violaxanthin is essential for reconstitution of LHCPII (4), the depletion of this xanthophyll (as well as some Chl a) during electrophoresis illustrates the stringency of LDS-PAGE (4°C) as a criterion for reconstitution of LHCPII. The pigment and protein composition of reconstituted CPII is similar to that of "native" CPII (including xanthophyll/Chl b ratios) except for a slightly diminished Chl a/b ratio. Moreover, rocket immunoelectrophoresis indicates approximately similar stoichiometry of pigments and proteins.

The spectral properties and pigment organization of reconstituted AB96 gene product were compared to those observed for "native" CPII and CPII reconstituted from total LHCII apoproteins. Qualitatively similar absorption spectra were observed (data not shown) following recovery from LDS-PAGE. The relative amounts of Chl a and Chl b varied, but this was previously observed for "native" LHCPII (8) and reconstituted LHCPII (4). Chl a/b ratios from pigments solubilized in 80% acetone ranged from 0.72 to 1.1. It is apparent that stability and/or degradation during electrophoresis are important determinants of the apparent pigment composition.

Fluorescence spectroscopy of reconstituted AB96 gene product shows intra-molecular energy transfer properties qualitatively similar to those of native CPII (Fig. 2). A high proportion of the 470 nm excitation energy absorbed by Chl-b (and all of the 438 nm light absorbed by Chl-a) is transferred to a form of Chl-a which fluoresces at 681 nm (Fig. 2,

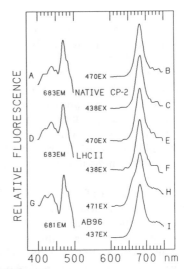

Figure 2

traces H,I). However, complete energy transfer from Chl-b to Chl-a (and from Chl-a to Chl-a) is observed for "native" CPII or CPII reconstituted from total LHCII apoproteins (Fig. 2, traces B,C,E, and F; 4; 9; 10). For reconstituted AB96, the 665 nm Chl-b fluorescence emission shoulder indicates that a small proportion of the Chl is excitationally uncoupled and, therefore, improperly oriented. Excitation spectra (Fig. 2, traces A, D, and G) confirm that Chl-a, Chl-b, and xanthophylls (shoulders at 485 nm and 492 nm) contribute to the observed 683 nm Chl-a fluorescence. In no case was the 683 nm emission peak blue-shifted by more than 1-2 nm.

The organization of pigments incorporated into reconstituted LHCII apoproteins was assessed by the absorption of left- vs right- circularly polarized light (Fig. 3). CD spectra of reconstituted total LHCII apoproteins (Fig. 3, trace B) were essentially identical to those of native CPII (Fig. 3, trace A). The transition from the 670 nm (+) signal to the 650 nm (-) signal is characteristic of a specific organization permitting exciton splitting between Chl-b molecules (10). The signal at 683 nm (-) in reconstituted total apoproteins demonstrates reassembly of a specific pigment orientation, perhaps a specialized Chl-a of LHCPII (10). The

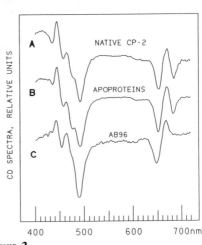

Figure 3

reconstituted AB96 gene product (Fig. 3, trace C) possesses the pigment-protein and pigment-pigment interactions responsible for exciton splitting between Chl-b molecules. However, the reconstituted AB96 gene product differed qualitatively from native CPII by a complete absence of the 683 nm (-) signal and quantitatively by reduced signal at 477 nm. Thus, there is at least one specific pigment orientation that is either not reconstituted *in vitro* or unstable and lost during the PAGE/recovery steps. Alternatively, this result may be due to an intrinsic property of the AB96 pigment-protein complex providing there are no serious artifacts resulting from *E. coli* expression of the AB96 fusion protein product. Clearly, however, *in vitro* reconstitution of a single species of LHCII apoprotein synthesized by *E. coli* preserves the integrity of most of the pigment-protein and pigment-pigment interactions found in "native" CPII.

The reconstitution of single LHCPII gene products, whose expression can be directed *in vivo* or *in vitro*, provides a unique system to directly analyze pigment-protein associations in both genetically and chemically altered apoproteins and pigments. Our initial work (data not shown) indicates that reconstitution is unsuccessful following deletion of the 28 C-terminal amino acids of AB96. However, LHCPII precursor polypeptides, apoproteins from trypsinized thylakoids, and phosphorylated LHCPII can be reconstituted.

REFERENCES

1. Green, B.R. (1988) Photosyn. Res. 15: 3-32.
2. Chitnis, P.R. and J.P. Thornber. (1988) Photosyn. Res. 16: 41-63.
3. Deisenhofer, J., O. Epp, K. Miki, R. Huber and H. Michel. (1986) Nature, 318:618-24.
4. Plumley, F. G. and G. W. Schmidt.(1987) Proc. Natl. Acad. Sci. 84:146-150.
5. Burke, J.J., C.L. Ditto,and C.J. Arntzen. (1978) Arch. Biochem. Biophys. 187:252-263.
6. Coruzzi, G., R. Broglie, A. Cashmore and N.-H. Chua. (1983) J. Biol. Chem. 258: 1399-1402.
7. Bujard, H., R. Gentz, M. Lanzer, D. Stueber, M. Mueller, I. Ibrahimi, M.-T. Haeuptle and B. Dobberstein. (1987) Methods Enzymol. 155: 416-433.
8. Green, B.R., and E.L. Camm. (1982) Biochim. Biophys. Acta. 681:256-262.
9. Shepanski, J.F., D.J. Williams and Y. Kalisky. (1987) Biochim. Biophys. Acta 766:116-25.
10. Van Metter, R.L. (1977) Biochim. Biophys. Acta 462:642-658.

SPECTRAL RESOLUTION OF THE ABSORPTION AND EMISSION TRANSITIONS OF CHLOROPHYLLS.

MARNIX VAN GURP, GIJS VAN GINKEL AND YEHUDI K. LEVINE
Department of Molecular Biophysics, Buys Ballot Laboratory,
University of Utrecht, Princetonplein 5, Utrecht 3584 CC, The
Netherlands.

INTRODUCTION
Chlorophyll molecules are the major pigments of the photosynthesis process. The efficiency of intermolecular energy transfer of this process is determined by the spectral overlap of the absorption and emission bands as well as by the relative orientations of the respective transition moments.
In order to characterize these orientations both within chlorophyll-protein complexes and in the photosynthetic membranes it is necessary to determine the directions of the transition moments in the chromophore frame. The first step in this study is the spectral resolution of the transition moments contributing to the absorption and emission bands. Such a study is impeded by the following problems:
1)   Chlorophyll molecules have a low symmetry which hampers the calculation of transition moment directions on the basis of symmetry considerations,
2)   The transition bands of chlorophyll overlap across the entire absorption wavelength region,
3)   Chlorophyll molecules have a high mutual affinity leading to the formation of dimers and aggregates.

EXPERIMENTAL APPROACH
One of the easiest and most commonly used techniques to study the anisotropic optical properties of dye molecules is fluorescence anisotropy (FA). A dilute solution of the dye is excited with vertically polarized light and the fluorescence emission polarized parallel ($I_\parallel$) and perpendicular ($I_\perp$) to the electric field vector of the exciting beam are detected with a 90°-scattering geometry, see figure 1. The FA is defined as:

$$FA = r = \frac{I_\parallel - I_\perp}{I_\parallel + 2I_\perp}$$

In the case of well-separated transition moments, the FA is a direct measure for the angle ϵ between the absorption and emission moment in

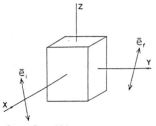

Figure 1: Experimental geometry of a 90° fluorescence anisotropy experiment. Excitation is along the X-axis, the fluorescence is detected along the Y-axis.

the dye molecule (1)

$$r = 0.2 \ (\ 3\cos^2 \epsilon - 1)$$

$\epsilon = (\ \beta_\mu - \beta_\nu \ ) = $ the angle between the absorption and emission transition moments.

$\beta_\mu, \ \beta_\nu = $ the polar angles of the absorption and emission moment respectively in the plane of the chromophore.

In the case of mixed transitions, we have the weighted sum of the anisotropies belonging to the different "overlapping" transitions (2)

$$r = \underset{i,j}{\Sigma} f_{ij} \cdot r_{ij} = 0.2 \ (\ 3\underset{i,j}{\Sigma} f_{ij} \cos^2 \epsilon_{ij} - 1 \ )$$

$\epsilon_{ij} = $ the angle between the absorption moment i and the emission moment j in a specific molecule.

The fluorescence anisotropy was determined in two ways:
1) The *emission anisotropy*: excite in the Q_y-absorption band around 650 nm, see figure 2, and scan across the emission band.
2) The *excitation anisotropy*: scan the absorption band and detect separately at wavelengths corresponding to the two emission maxima, see figure 2.

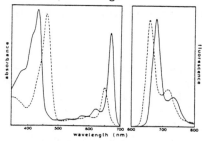

Figure 2: Absorption (left) and fluorescence (right) spectra of chlorophyll a (——) and chlorophyll b (- - -) in castor oil.

RESULTS

The emission anisotropy is found to vary across the emission band, see figure 3. This indicates the presence of at least two overlapping transitions.

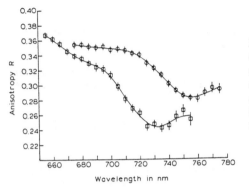

Figure 3: Emission wavelength dependence of the fluorescence anisotropy of chlorophyll a (o) and chlorophyll b (□) in castor oil at 4°C. Wavelength of excitation is 668 nm for chlorophyll a and 649 nm for chlorophyll b.

The excitation anisotropy spectra of chlorophyll a recorded at two different emission wavelengths are distinct and exhibit several cross-over points, see figure 4. Similar results were found for chlorophyll b (data not shown). This indicates that at the corresponding wavelengths more than one transition moment is excited.

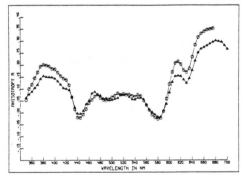

Figure 4: Excitation wavelength dependence of the fluorescence anisotropy of chlorophyll a in castor oil at 4°C. Wavelengths of emission are 680 nm (o) and 750 nm (△).

CONCLUSIONS

A good measure for the overlap of the excitation transitions appears to be the difference, P, of the two effective angles calculated from the two anisotropies at every excitation wavelength. This "pureness" parameter is calculated as

$$ P = \mid \cos^{-1} [\{(5r_1+1)/3\}^{1/2}] - \cos^{-1} [\{(5r_2+1)/3\}^{1/2}] \mid $$

where r_1 and r_2 are the two anisotropies shown in figure 4. The spectrum of "pureness", figure 5, shows that the absorption bands of chlorophyll a consist of two overlapping transitions, with the sole exception of the Q_y-band. In addition, the fact that the FA values at the cross-over points deviate from 0.1 indicates that the absorption transition moments are not orthogonal. Similar results were obtained for chlorophyll b (data not shown).

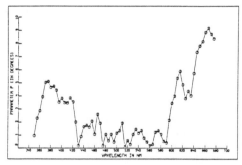

Figure 5: Pureness P (in degrees) of the absorption transitions of chlorophyll a in castor oil. In the case of pure transitions P reaches the same maximal value at each wavelength.

We conclude that the values of the fluorescence anisotropy cannot thus be interpreted in terms of a single angle between the absorption and emission moments.

REFERENCES
1) van Gurp, M., van Ginkel, G. and Levine, Y.K. (1988)
    J. Theoret. Biol., 131, 333-349.
2) van Gurp, M., van Ginkel, G. and Levine, Y.K. (1989)
    Biochim. Biophys. Acta, 973, 405-413.

ON THE MECHANISMS FOR THE PHOTOINHIBITION OF THE ELECTRON TRANSFER AND THE LIGHT INDUCED DEGRADATION OF THE D1 PROTEIN IN PHOTOSYSTEM II

STENBJÖRN STYRING[1], CAROLINE JEGERSCHÖLD[1], IVAR VIRGIN[1], ANDERS EHRENBERG[2] and BERTIL ANDERSSON[1]. Department for Biochemistry[1] and Department for Biophysics[2], Arrhenius Laboratories for Natural Sciences, University of Stockholm, Stockholm, Sweden.

Introduction

Photoinhibition (1) occurs when oxygenic photosynthetic organisms or isolated photo- synthetic membranes are exposed to strong illumination. It results in impaired electron tran- sport and decreased CO_2 assimilation and is caused by inhibition of reactions in photosystem II.

PS II catalyzes the light driven electron transport from water to plastoquinone. It is an enzyme complex containing a series of redox components and is thought to be constructed in analogy to the photosynthetic reaction center from purple bacteria. Thus, the reaction center is composed of a dimer of two hydrophobic proteins which are denoted D1 and D2. These contain the redox components needed to transfer an electron from the primary donor, P_{680} via the intermediary electron acceptor, a pheophytin molecule, to the first and second quinone electron acceptors, Q_A and Q_B (2). The D1/D2 protein dimer also carries tyrosine$_z$ the immediate electron donor to P_{680} and ,at least partly, the manganese cluster involved in the water splitting reaction (3). In addition to the D1 and D2 proteins PSII contains a large number of subunits (4) which bind antenna chlorophylls and catalytic ligands like Ca^{2+} and Cl^-. In addition PSII contains cytochrome b_{559} which is present also in purified preparations.

The observation that electron transport reactions in PSII are inhibited during photoinhibition was followed by the discovery that the so called Q_B-binding protein was turned over rapidly during illumination (5). It was therefore suggested that photoinhibition was the result from modifications of the Q_B-site caused by the strong illumination and that turnover of the Q_B-binding protein was the reason for photoinhibition (5). However, the identification of the Q_B-site as the locus for the photoinhibition of the electron transport is not unchallenged and several different photoinduced lesions between tyrosine$_z$ and Q_A have been proposed (6-10). Today it is known that the Q_B-binding protein is identical to the D1 reaction center protein which makes it possible to reconcile the inhibition of electron transfer at the level of other redox components than Q_B with the degradation of the D1 protein. However, these processes are not necessarily tightly coupled. We have shown that inhibition of electron transport (at the acceptor side; see below) preceeded the degradation of the D1 protein in isolated thylakoid membranes (3). Moreover, an enhanced turnover of both the D1 and D2 proteins was shown to occur in NH_2OH washed leaves and thylakoids

M. Baltscheffsky (ed.), Current Research in Photosynthesis, Vol. II, 349–356.

(9). In such preparations the electron transfer inhibition is located to the donor side of PSII (9,10) and thus distinct from the inhibition caused by strong illumination of intact thylakoid membranes.

In this communication we have used EPR spectroscopy to analyse the photoinhibition of the electron transfer in vitro in thylakoid and PSII enriched membranes. The mechanism for the photodamage of the D1 protein has also been addressed in experiments with Cl-depleted thylakoid membranes (see also 11). In an accompanying paper (12) we describe the structural changes in PSII and the lateral distribution of PSII proteins after the degradation of the D1 protein.

Materials and methods

Thylakoid membranes and PSII enriched membranes were prepared from spinach leaves. Cl-depletion of thylakoid membranes was performed as described in (11). The degree of Cl-depletion of the thylakoid membranes was 60-70%. Photoinhibition of thylakoid membranes at pH 7.4 or PSII enriched membranes at pH 6.3 was performed aerobically at 20°C using heat-filtered white light. The light intensity was varied with neutral density filters. The experiments described in figures 1-3 were performed with a light intensity of $5000\mu E/m^2sec$ at a chlorophyll concentration of $100\mu g/ml$.After the illumination the samples were concentrated by centrifugation and used for EPR measurements, protein analysis and oxygen evolution measurements. The oxygen evolution was measured with phenyl-p-benzoquinone as exogenous electron acceptor. Quantitative immunoblotting of the D1 protein was performed as described in (3). Low temperature EPR spectroscopy was carried out with a Bruker ESP 300 spectrometer equip- ped with an Oxford Instruments cryostat and temperature controller. Incubation with formate (25mM) and dithionite (50mM) was performed at 20°C in the dark for 10min. Illumination of EPR samples was done in an unsilvered dewar using a 1000W projector lamp. In order to perform a single charge separa- tion, illumination of unreduced samples was done at 198K for 4 min. In experiments intended to phototrap reduced pheophytin, illumination of dithionite reduced samples was performed for 25min at 20°C.

Results and discussion

EPR characterization of the photoinhibition of the electron transport through PSII.

Figure 1A shows that photoinhibition decreases the formation of the S_2 -state multiline signal. This correlated with the inhibition of the oxygen evolution both in PSII enriched membranes (figure 1B) and in thylakoid membranes (3). In the experiments the S_2-state multiline EPR signal was induced by illumination at 198K of the EPR samples prepared from the photoinhibited samples. At this temperature, only one electron is taken from the donor side of PSII. Normally the S_1 to S_2 transition dominates but in centers where this transition cannot occur electron donation from either $cytb_{559}$ or a chlorophyll molecule can be observed (13). We have measured these putative donors and the results show that photoinhibition leads to a gradual decrease of the low temperature electron donation to P_{680}^+ from all of the known electron donors in PSII, i.e. the Mn-cluster, $cytb_{559}$ or a chlorphyll molecule (14). The decrease in electron donation closely follows the inhibition of steady state electron transfer from water to an electron acceptor acting in the Q_B-site. This suggests that the damage induced by the the photo- inhibition should be sought in the electron transport chain prior to Q_B since the electron never reaches Q_B during illumination at 198K (the transfer between Q_A and Q_B is blocked at 198K). Furthermore, the oxidation of the other known low temperature donors was inhibited with similar kinetics as the oxygen evolution. Under normal circumstances, P_{680}^+ is reduced from

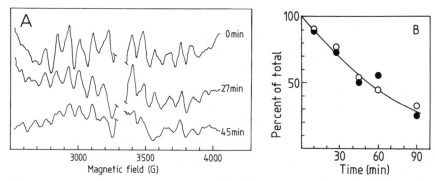

Figure 1. A. Decrease of the S_2-state multiline EPR signal as a consequence of photoinhibition of PSII enriched membranes. The EPR spectra show the signals induced by illumination at 198K. EPR conditions: 10K; mod.ampl. 22G; freq. 9.239GHz; power 20mW. B. Time course for the photoinhibition of the oxygen evolution (open) and the formation of the S_2-state multiline EPR signal (closed).

the donor side of PSII only when the electron has been transferred from pheophytin⁻ to Q_A after the charge separation. Otherwise the primary radical pair rapidly recombines and no electron will be taken from the donor side. Therefore, the decreased electron donation to P_{680}^+ in the photoinhibited samples suggests that the primary result of photoinhibition is an impairment of the photochemical reduction of Q_A.

There are two likely possibilities for such an inhibition on the acceptor side of photosystem II. Either the primary charge separation reaction is blocked or the function of Q_A to stabilize the negative charge is lost. These possibilities were tested

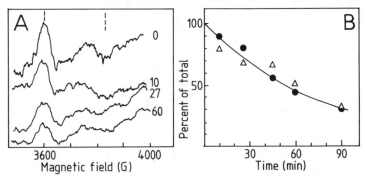

Figure 2. A. The effect of photoinhibition on the formation of the EPR spectrum from the Q_A^--Fe^{2+} signal. The bars indicate the spectral features that belong to the signal. Q_A was reduced chemically with dithionite and the spectra are recorded in the presence of formate to enhance the signal size. EPR conditions: 4K; mod. ampl. 32G; freq. 9.239GHz; power 32mW. B. The effects of photoinhibition of PSII enriched membranes on the oxygen evolution (circles) and the formation of the Q_A^--Fe^{2+} signal. The amplitude at g=1.82 was used as a measure of the size of the EPR signal.

by measurements of the EPR signals from Q_A^- and pheophytin$^-$ in photoinhibited samples. The observed EPR spectrum from the reduced quinone acceptor, Q_A^-, depends on magnetic interactions between the reduced quinone and the nearby situated ferrous iron. The size of the signal can be enhanced more than tenfold by the addition of formate. This technique was applied in an experiment in which PSII enriched membranes were photoinhibited for various times. In the prepared EPR samples Q_A was reduced, in the presence of formate, either photochemically at 198K or chemically by reduction with dithionite. Figure 2A shows the EPR spectra from chemically reduced samples and it is seen that the signal size is progressively diminished during photoinhibition. The decrease correlates with the inhibition of oxygen evolution (figure 2B) both in the chemically reduced samples (figure 2) and in the photochemically reduced samples (not shown).

Also the total amount of photochemically reducible pheophytin can be measured by EPR spectroscopy. In this case quantitative photoreduction of pheophytin is achieved using extensive illumination under reducing conditions at room temperature. With this technique pheophytin is trapped in the reduced form giving rise to a free radical EPR signal with a high g-value (g=2.0037) and large line width (13-14G). In the experiment samples photoinhibited for various times were reduced by dithionite and then illuminated at 20°C for 25min. Figure 3A shows the radical region of the EPR spectrum recorded after this treatment and the signal has the correct EPR parameters to be assigned to reduced pheophytin. The size of the signal in the control sample amounted to 1.0-1.1 radical per PSII reaction center as compared to Signal II$_{slow}$. The amplitude of the signal decreased as a result of the photoinhibitory treatment but the decrease was much slower than the inhibition of the oxygen evolution (figure 3B). This shows that the primary charge separation reaction was still operational in the photoinhibited centers although the capacity to transfer the electron to Q_A was lost.

The main conclusion from the EPR measurements is that the strong photoinhibitory illumination impairs the function of Q_A leaving the primary charge separation reaction intact. We conclude that this inhibition is the primary lesion in the photosynthetic electron transport

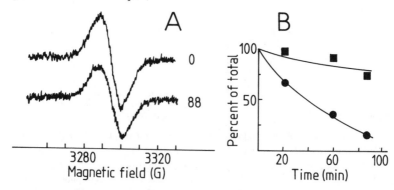

Figure 3. A. Effects of photoinhibition for various times on the formation of the free radical signal from pheophytin$^-$ induced in photoinhibited samples by extensive illumination for 25min at 20°C in the presence of dithionite. EPR conditions: 15K; mod. ampl. 2.5G; freq. 9.239GHz; power 63nW. B. Timecourse for the photoinhibition of the oxygen evolution (circles) and the formation of the free radical signal from pheophytin$^-$ (squares).

from water to exogenous electron acceptors induced by strong illumination. This result is at variance with the, until recently predominating, hypothesis that the origin for photoinhibition is the impairment of the function of Q_B (5,15). However, our results are in agreement with optical measurements and with recent thermoluminescence measurements (6,7).

The question then arises - what is the fate of Q_A following photoinhibition? One possibility is that intense illumination leads to double reduction of Q_A in a low quantum-yield reaction. Under strong continuous illumination the plastoquinone pool is rapidly reduced and Q_A^- will be the dominating species in the acceptor side complex. The illumination continuously induces charge separation reactions. In the presence of Q_A^- the formed radical pair normally recombines fast but the electron donation from tyrosine$_Z$ to P_{680}^+ is very fast and it is likely that P_{680}^+ can be reduced from tyrosine$_Z$ (and ultimately from water) in a fraction of the centers. In those centers the electron becomes trapped on pheophytin. Pheophytin$^-$ is a fairly strong reductant ($E_m \approx$ -610mV) and it is likely that it can reduce Q_A a second time. This reaction is known to occur in photosynthetic purple bacteria during illumination under reducing conditions. Similar reactions have also been proposed to occur in PSII (16). The fate of Q_A^{2-} (or QH_2) is unknown but it is possible that it can leave the Q_A-site in a reaction which most likely would constitute the first irreversible step in photoinhibition.

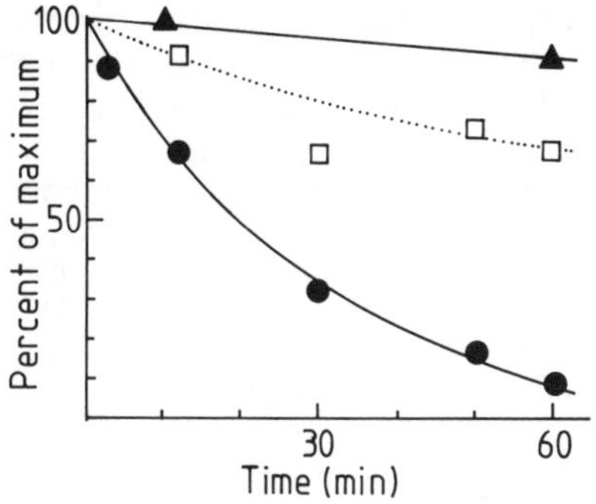

Figure 4. Timecourse for the inhibition of the oxygen evolution (circles) and the degradation of the D1 protein (triangles) induced by low light photoinhibition ($\approx$700µE/m^{2}sec) of Cl-depleted thylakoid membranes (100µg chl/ml). The dotted line (squares) shows the inhibition of oxygen evolution when the photoinhibition was performed in the presence of 30mM Cl$^-$.

Light dependant degradation of the D1 protein in Cl-depleted thylakoid membranes.

It was earlier reported that photoinhibition in intact thylakoid membranes is a multistep event and that inhibition of electron transport is followed by a slow degradation of the reaction center proteins D1 and D2 (3). From the spectroscopic data presented above we conclude that the primary damage to the reaction center proteins is caused by the primary charge separation or donor side reactions in centers were the function of Q_A has been impaired. To further test the hypothesis that the protein degradation is initiated by reactions on the oxidizing side of PSII, we have compared the light-dependent degradation of the D1 protein in intact and in Cl-depleted thylakoid membranes. Cl-depletion is known to block the S_2 to S_3 transition (17) leading to slower electron donation to P_{680}^+ after multiple turnovers of the system (18). Figure 4 shows the effect of low-intensity continuous illumination ($700\mu E/m^2 \cdot sec$) of Cl-depleted thylakoid membranes. It is seen that the oxygen evolution is inhibited with a half time of approximately 18min. This should be compared to the photoinhibition of non-depleted thylakoid membranes in which the oxygen evolution was inhibited with a halftime of about 25 min at 10 times higher light intensity (3,11). Thus, the oxygen evolution in Cl-depleted thylakoid membranes is 15 times more sensitive to illumination than in normal thylakoid membranes. The same observation was made for the degradation of the D1 protein. In the Cl-depleted thylakoid membranes 60 min illumination at $700\mu E/m^2sec$ resulted in about 10% degradation of the D1 protein (figure 4) while no degradation could be observed at this light intensity in intact thylakoid membranes.

The degradation of the D1 protein was further characterized in an experiment in which the Cl-depleted thylakoids were illuminated for 10min at different light intensities (figure 5).The oxygen evolution is very sensitive to illumination and with a light intensity of $3000\mu E/m^2sec$ it is completely inhibited after 10 min illumination. The D1 protein is degraded in a slower reaction but with a light intensity of $7800\mu E/m^2sec$ almost 85% of the D1 protein was degraded within 10min. In non-depleted thylakoids a similar illumination protocol resulted in only 5-10% degradation of the D1 protein (3). From this experiment approximate half times for the degradation of the D1 protein at different light intensities was calculated and at $2000\mu E/m^2sec$ the half time for the reaction was 12-15 min. Also shown in figure 5 is that the presence of DCMU during the photoinhibition experiment protected the Cl-depleted thylakoids against photodamage. Both the oxygen evolution (measured after the removal of the DCMU by centri- fugation and resuspension of the samples) and the D1 protein were much less susceptible to the illumination than in its absence (figure 5). This is in contrast to the result in non-depleted thylakoid membranes were DCMU did not protect against photoinhibition or degradation of the D1 protein (11). In addition, the presence of Cl$^-$ during the illumination protected PSII against photodamage (figure 4).

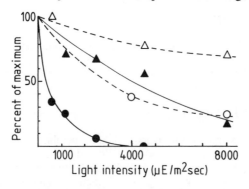

Figure 5. Photoinhibition of Cl-depleted thylakoid membranes in the absence (filled symbols) and the presence (open symbols) of 10μM DCMU. Cl-depleted thylakoid membranes (100μg chl/ml) were illuminated for 10min with light of varying intensity. The oxygen evolution (circles) and the degradation of the D1 protein (triangles) were followed.

In these experiments we have studied the degradation of the D1 protein in Cl-depleted thylakoid membranes as a model for the situation in non-depleted thylakoid membranes. We have chosen this material since our spectroscopic experiments suggests that the degradation of the D1 protein is triggered from reactions on the oxidizing side of PSII despite the fact that the inhibition of the electron tranfer is at the level of the function of Q_A. The inhibition pattern in Cl-depleted thylakoid membranes is well established and is known to result from a block in the S-cycle between the S_2 and the S_3 state. Furthermore, the inhibition induced by Cl-depletion is reversible which shows that this material is less modified than for example NH_2OH- or TRIS-washed thylakoids which also are known to be inhibited on the donor side of PSII.

The main conclusion from our experiments is that Cl-depletion renders PSII very sensitive to photodamage even at light intensities were no or very little photoinhibition is observed in normal thylakoids. The most likely explanation for this increased sensitivity is that the continuous illumination leads to the formation of long lived highly oxidizing radicals on the donor side of PSII. In Cl-depleted thylakoid membranes the S_2 to S_3 transition is blocked. Thus, one electron can be taken from the Mn-cluster and probably one more from tyrosine$_Z$ (18). Therefore, only one or two normal reductions of P_{680}^+ can take place. Then the next charge separation leads to the formation of the radical pair $P_{680}^+ Q_A^-$ (there is no inhibition at the acceptor side at this early stage of the illumination). However, there is no fast donor to P_{680}^+ present anymore. This increases the lifetime of P_{680}^+ which is a highly oxidizing species ($E_m \approx 1.1V$). In most centers the recombination between Q_A^- and P_{680}^+ will take place but we hypothesize that in a small fraction of the centers P_{680}^+ oxidizes nearby redox- or protein components leading to irreversible damage of the D1 protein. This would then be the origin for the fast destruction of the D1 protein since also low illumination results in the accumulation of oxidizing species in Cl-depleted membranes. Furthermore, with this model it is easy to understand the protective function of DCMU in Cl-depleted membranes. In the presence of DCMU only one electron is transferred to the acceptor side of PSII. This electron ends up at Q_A and further stable charge separations are prevented (at high illumination double reduction of Q_A can occur as described above but this is a slow event compared to the photoinhibition discussed here). The electron is taken from the Mn-cluster which is oxidized to the S_2-state. In Cl-depleted membranes this oxidation is allowed and the result is that P_{680}^+ is reduced rapidly. Since no further stable charge separation reactions will occur, no strongly oxidizing components on the donor side of PSII will be accumulated.

Whether P_{680}^+ alone is the cause for the oxidative damage or if also tyrosine$_Z^+$ or abnormal oxidation states of the Mn-cluster participate in the oxidizing reactions cannot be deduced from these experiments alone. However, we have observed that the electron transfer from the Mn-cluster to tyrosine$_Z$ is inhibited before the electron transfer between tyrosine$_Z$ and an exogenous acceptor (11) while the kinetics for the latter inhibition are similar to those of the degradation of the D1 protein. This suggests that the primary damage during photoinhibition in Cl-depleted thylakoids is between the oxygen evolving complex and tyrosine$_Z$ but that it is the inhibition of the electron transfer between tyrosine$_Z$ and the acceptor side that is coupled to the photodamage and degradation of the D1 protein.

Concluding remarks.

In this communication we have shown that photoinhibition of the electron transfer through PSII in thylakoid membranes and PSII enriched preparations is due to impairment of the function of the first quinone acceptor Q_A which probably becomes double reduced during strong illumination. Under these circumstances the D1 protein is degraded in a much slower reaction which is suggested to be triggered by the charge separation reaction or donor side reactions in perturbed centers (14). In Cl-depleted thylakoids the electron transfer reactions and the D1 protein are much more sensitive to illumination and we have shown (11, see also 9,10) that the primary inhibition is the electron transfer between the Mn-cluster and tyrosine$_Z$. In a slower reaction the electron transfer between tyrosine$_Z$ and electron acceptors is inhibited with kinetics which are quite similar to those of the degradation of the D1 protein (11). The protective effect of DCMU on the fast degradation of the D1 protein in Cl-depleted thylakoids seems to exclude the involvement of acceptor side components in the reactions that trigger the protein damage. From these studies we propose that photoinhibition of the electron transport through PSII have different origin under different conditions. However, both when the photoinhibition is caused by acceptor side lesions or donor side inhibitions the degradation of the D1 protein is proposed to be due to the formation of long-lived oxidizing components on the oxidizing side of PSII. Thus, although both processes are light dependent they are not necessarily coupled to each other. Instead it is quite likely that the D1 protein is damaged, in a small fraction of the centers, continuously during illumination due to the strongly oxidizing species that are formed during the light reactions. In this model the degradation of the D1 protein is merely a consequence of the complicated chemistry involved in abstracting electrons from water. This would also explain why the light dependant degradation of the reaction center proteins seems to be restricted to PSII which is the only photosystem working at these high potentials.

Acknowledgements.

This work was financed by the Knut and Alice Wallenbergs foundation and The Swedish Natural Science Research Council.

References

1. Powles, S.B. (1984) Annu. Rev. Plant Physiol. 35, 15-44
2. Michel, H. and Deisenhofer, J. (1988) Biochemistry 27, 1-7
3. Virgin, I., Styring, S. and Andersson, B. (1988) FEBS Lett 233, 408-412
4. Andersson, B. and Åkerlund, H.-E. (1987) in: The light reactions (Barber, J. ed) 379-420, Elsevier
5. Kyle, D.J., Ohad, I. and Arntzen, C. (1984) Proc. Natl. Acad. Sci. USA, 81, 4070-4074
6. Allakhverdiev, S.I., Setlikova, E., Klimov, V. and Setlik, I. (1987) FEBS Lett 226, 186-190
7. Vass, I. , Mohanty, N. and Demeter, S. (1988) Z. Naturforsch. 43C, 871-876
8. Demeter, S. , Neale, P.J. and Melis, A. (1987) FEBS Lett 214, 370-374
9. Callahan, F.E., Becker, D.W. and Cheniae, G.M. (1986) Plant Physiol. 82, 261-269
10. Theg, S., Filar, L.J. and Dilley, R.A. (1986) Biochim. Biophys. Acta 849, 104-11
11. Jegerschöld, C. and Styring, S. (1989) in these proceedings
12. Virgin, I., Hundal, T., Styring, S. and Andersson, B. (1989) in these proceedings
13. De Paula, J., Innes, J.B. and Brudvig, G.W. (1985) Biochemistry 24, 8114-8120
14. Styring, S., Virgin, I., Ehrenberg, A. and Andersson, B. (1989) Biochim. Biophys. Acta submitted
15. Ohad, I., Koike, H., Shochat, S. and Inoue, Y. (1988) Biochim. Biophys. Acta 993, 288-298
16. Van Mieghem,F., Nitschke,W., Mathis,P. and Rutherford,A.W. (1989) Biochim. Biophys. Acta in press
17. Ono,T., Zimmermann J.L., Inoue,Y. and Rutherford,A.W. (1986) Biochim.Biophys.Acta 851, 193-201
18. Ono, T., Conjeaud, H., Gleiter, H., Inoue, Y. and Mathis, P. (1986) FEBS Lett 203, 215-219

ZEAXANTHIN-ASSOCIATED ENERGY DISSIPATION AND THE SUSCEPTIBILITY OF VARIOUS ORGANISMS TO LIGHT STRESS

BARBARA DEMMIG-ADAMS
Department of EPO Biology, Campus Box 334,
University of Colorado, Boulder, CO   80309, USA

1.   INTRODUCTION

Sunlight which is harvested by the photosynthetic apparatus has the potential to destroy this apparatus; if excitation energy was allowed to accumulate, the combination of a photosensitive pigment (chlorophyll), light, and oxygen could result in photooxidative processes (1). Several lines of evidence have suggested that one (or several) regulated process(es) can harmlessly dissipate an excess of excitation energy directly within the photochemical apparatus (e.g. 2-5). We have presented evidence (2) that one dissipation process occurs in the antenna chlorophyll (6) and have suggested that it is mediated by the carotenoid zeaxanthin (7). Upon exposure to an excess of light, zeaxanthin (an epoxide-free xanthophyll) is formed rapidly in the thylakoid membranes from violaxanthin (a di-epoxide), as part of the xanthophyll cycle (e.g. 8). The role of zeaxanthin in energy dissipation was suggested by a close correlation between the zeaxanthin content of leaves and the rate constant for radiationless energy dissipation in the antenna chlorophyll, as calculated from the quenching of chlorophyll fluorescence (9-11). Such a correlation was initially reported to exist after some dark incubation time for a rather slowly relaxing type of fluorescence quenching (7,9). A similar correlation also exists during illumination of leaves with (excessive) actinic light for a kind of fluorescence quenching which relaxes very rapidly upon return to darkness (10,11). This kind of fluorescence quenching with rapid induction and relaxation kinetics is commonly termed "energy-dependent", "pH-dependent", or "high-energy-state" quenching.

M. Baltscheffsky (ed.), Current Research in Photosynthesis, Vol. II, 357–364.
© 1990 Kluwer Academic Publishers. Printed in the Netherlands.

In the following, evidence for a causal relationship between zeaxanthin and fluorescence quenching is discussed, as well as the relationship between zeaxanthin and photoprotection.

2. PROCEDURES

Measurements of chlorophyll a fluorescence with a modulation fluorometer (Walz, Effeltrich, FRG) and pigment analyses with TLC are described elsewhere (7). The calculations of parameters derived from chlorophyll fluorescence are described in 10 (cf. also 6). Plant material and treatments are described in the legends.

3. RESULTS AND DISCUSSION

3.1. <u>Evidence for a causal relationship between zeaxanthin and radiationless energy dissipation</u>. Figure 1 shows a typical time course of nonphotochemical fluorescence quenching which develops in leaves upon exposure to an excess of light. Such quenching was accompanied by a quenching of initial fluorescence (F_O) and relaxed rather rapidly upon return to darkness (Figure 1A; cf. 10). This kind of quenching was not observed in leaves

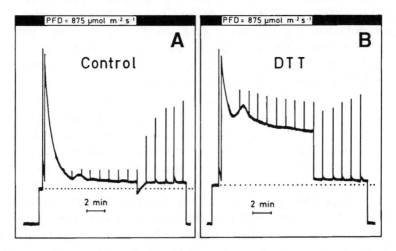

FIGURE 1. Original traces of chlorophyll fluorescence from spinach leaves exposed to a PFD of 875 μmol m^{-2} s^{-1} (red light) in 5% CO_2 at 25°C for 10 min. Leaves were harvested, their petioles rapidly placed in distilled water (control) or in a solution of 3 mM DTT, and the leaves maintained under 40 μmol photons m^{-2} s^{-1} at 25°C for 90 min prior to obtaining the above traces. Light- and CO_2-saturated rate of O_2 evolution = 300 μmol mg^{-1} Chl h^{-1} for both control and DTT-treated leaves under these conditions. Data from 13.

treated with dithiothreitol (DTT; Fig. 2B) which is an inhibitor of the violaxanthin de-epoxidase (12) and completely prevents zeaxanthin formation (13). Figure 2 shows this component of fluorescence quenching, expressed as the difference in k_D, the rate constant of radiationless energy dissipation in the antenna chlorophyll (2,6,10), between untreated and DTT-treated leaves. This DTT-sensitive component exhibited a very close correlation with the zeaxanthin content and the quenching of F_O in the (untreated) leaves.

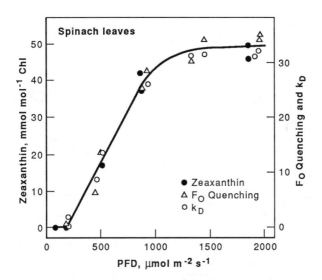

FIGURE 2. Zeaxanthin content of control spinach leaves exposed to various PFDs for 10 min and the DTT-sensitive portions of k_D and of F_O quenching. The DTT-sensitive portions, k_D (control) - k_D (DTT) and ΔF_O (control) - ΔF_O (DTT), were obtained by subtracting the values of k_D or the % changes in F_O, respectively, after 10 min exposure to various PFDs in DTT-treated leaves from the corresponding values obtained from the untreated controls. See legend of Figure 1 for further details. Data from 13.

In a second set of experiments, chlorophyll fluorescence characteristics were compared between lichen thalli with green or blue-green algal phycobionts. Green algae are known to possess the xanthophyll cycle, whereas blue-green algae lack the xanthophyll cycle, i.e. they lack the epoxide forms violaxanthin (di-epoxide) and antheraxanthin (mono-epoxide) which are the precursors of zeaxanthin within the cycle (8). Lichen thalli with green algae responded very much like the untreated leaves, whereas the response of those with blue-green algae (zeaxanthin-free) was similar to that of DTT-treated leaves (Fig. 3; cf. 14). Figure 3 shows the relationship between nonphotochemical fluorescence quenching, q_{NP}, part of which is indicative of radiationless energy dissipation, and photochemical quenching which

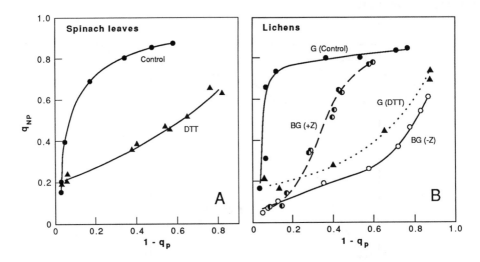

FIGURE 3. Relationship between nonphotochemical (q_{NP}) and photochemical (q_P) fluorescence quenching in control and DTT-treated leaves (A) and lichen thalli (B) exposed to various PFDs for 10 min. The parameter $1-q_P$ is an approximate measure of the reduction state of PS II centers. (A) See legend of Figure 1 for further details. Data from 13. (B) Included are, firstly, the two partners of a *Pseudocyphellaria* phycosymbiodeme, in which lobes with green algae and those with blue-green algal phycobionts grow together in one organism. *Pseudocyphellaria rufovirescens* (Church. Bab.) D. Galloway, with a green (G) algal phycobiont, contained 42.9 mmol zeaxanthin mol^{-1} chlorophyll following exposure to light when untreated (control; filled circles), and no zeaxanthin when treated with DTT (filled triangles). Thalli were pretreated with 3 mM DTT under 2 μmol photons m^{-2} s^{-1} at 15°C for a minimum of 1 h. The blue-green (BG) algal partner, *P. murrayi* D. Galloway (open circles), contained no zeaxanthin (-Z). Prior to the treatment, *P. rufovirescens* and *P. murrayi* had been maintained for 1 week at 10 μmol m^{-2} s^{-1} and 15°C. Secondly, the response of another blue-green algal lichen *Peltigera polydactyla* (Neck.) Hoffm. (half-filled circles) is depicted, which was harvested directly from the field after a number of sunny days and contained 18.5 mmol zeaxanthin mol^{-1} chlorophyll (+Z). Data from 14.

is an approximate measure of the reduction state of the photosystem II (PS II) centers. It is thought that the reduction state of PS II centers is maintained low, i.e. overexcitation of these centers avoided, by virtue of radiationless dissipation of excess excitation energy within the photochemical system (e.g. 5). The response of the (untreated) green algal lichens could be manipulated to become very similar to the response of the zeaxanthin-free blue-green algal lichens by pretreatment with DTT. Conversely, the response of another blue-green algal lichen, *Peltigera polydactyla* (which was collected directly from the field and was found to contain some zeaxanthin), was intermediate between the green and the zeaxanthin-free blue-green algal lichens. During long-term exposure to excessive light (days to weeks), *P. polydactyla* accumulated zeaxanthin, presumably from β-carotene (14).

We conclude that zeaxanthin does indeed mediate the radiationless dissipation of excitation energy in the antenna chlorophyll, which is responsible for the kind of fluorescence quenching associated with F_O quenching. Since this kind of fluorescence quenching is very rapidly reversible in spinach leaves (Fig. 1) we also conclude that there probably is an additional regulatory mechanism which controls the activity of zeaxanthin through the "high-energy state" of the thylakoid membrane. Further results are discussed elsewhere (13,15) which show that an additional, DTT-insensitive type of nonphotochemical fluorescence quenching, which also relaxes rapidly but is not associated with zeaxanthin nor F_O quenching, develops in isolated chloroplasts and, under certain circumstances, also in leaves.

3.2. Zeaxanthin and Photoprotection. Overexcitation of PS II centers is thought to lead to "photoinhibitory damage" involving inactivation and/or destruction of components of the photochemical apparatus. Figure 4A shows that, at a given PFD, the reduction state of PS II centers was higher by 20-30% (difference in $1-q_P$ = 0.2-0.3) in the zeaxanthin-free versus the zeaxanthin-forming organisms, i.e. DTT-treated leaves versus untreated leaves and blue-green algal lichens versus green algal lichens.

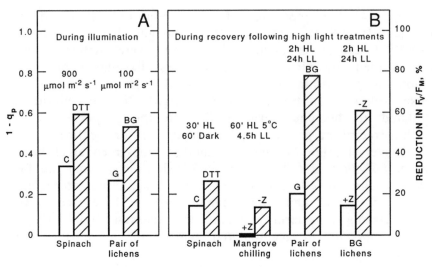

FIGURE 4.   (A) Approximate reduction state of PS II centers in untreated and DTT-treated spinach leaves as well as in the two partners of the *Pseudocyphellaria* phycosymbiodeme (G = green, and BG = blue-green algal partner) after exposure to the PFD indicated above the columns for 10 min. (B)   Inhibition of PS II photochemical efficiency, F_V/F_M, after a period of recovery from high light treatments in various organisms.   The duration of the exposure to high light (HL) is indicated above the columns in min (') or h as well as the duration of the recovery process in darkness or low light (LL).   Control values (prior to high light exposure) of F_V/F_M were equal to 0.84 (C = control) and 0.83 (DTT = DTT-treated) in the spinach leaves (data from 13); 0.83 (+Z = with zeaxanthin) and 0.83 (-Z = without zeaxanthin) in the mangrove (*Rhizophora mangle* L.) leaves (data from 18); 0.70 (G = green algal lichen *Pseudocyphellaria rufovirescens*) and 0.67 (BG = blue-green algal lichen *P. murrayi*) (data from 16); and 0.62 (+Z = with zeaxanthin) and 0.59 (-Z = without zeaxanthin) in thalli of the blue-green (BG) algal lichen *Peltigera polydactyla* taken directly from the field (+Z) and after cultivation at low PFD (10 μmol m^{-2} s^{-1}) for 2 weeks (-Z), respectively.   Data from 17.   During the recovery period thalli were continuously maintained under 10 μmol photons m^{-2} s^{-1} at 15°C, and all determinations of fluorescence were preceded by a 5 min period of darkness.

Figure 4B depicts the effects of a 2h exposure to high PFD on the efficiency of photochemical energy conversion subsequent to this exposure in leaves and lichen thalli.   In leaves we found it difficult to induce a strong and sustained depression of the photochemical efficiency of PS II (F_V/F_M) in either untreated or DTT-treated leaves.   However, we did observe small but reproducible differences between the two groups with DTT-treated leaves showing a greater component of "irreversible" reductions in F_V/F_M. In contrast, there were very pronounced differences between zeaxanthin-containing and zeaxanthin-free lichen thalli (Fig. 4B). In thalli of the lichen pair *Pseudocyphellaria rufovirescens* and *P. murrayi* the exposure to high PFD caused a very pronounced depression in F_V/F_M to zero in both green and blue-green algal lichens which was followed by a relatively rapid and complete recovery within a day in the green algal lichen, and by a very slow and incomplete recovery of F_V/F_M in the blue-green algal lichen (16,17). These changes in F_V/F_M were quantitatively similar to changes in the photon yield of photosynthesis in both the green and the blue-green algal lichen (16,17). Zeaxanthin-free and zeaxanthin-containing thalli of *Peltigera polydactyla* were also compared with respect to their response to a similar 2h high light treatment (Fig. 4); the zeaxanthin-free thalli exhibited a similarly slow recovery to that of the zeaxanthin-free blue-green portion of the *Pseudo-cyphellaria* phycosymbiodeme. In contrast, the zeaxanthin-containing thalli of *Peltigera polydactyla* showed a similarly rapid recovery to that of the green algal partner of the phycosymbiodeme (14,16,17).

The depression in F_V/F_M in the green algal lichen following exposure to high light was due mainly to a strong and reversible decrease in F_M, whereas that in the blue-green algal lichen was due primarily to a strong and fairly sustained increase in F_O (16). These fluorescence characteristics are those which were previously suggested to be indicative (decrease in F_M) of increased radiationless energy dissipation and (increase in F_O) of a decreased rate of photochemistry or excitation transfer into PS II centers (2,6).

We conclude that the changes in F_O, F_M, and F_V/F_M in the zeaxanthin-containing versus zeaxanthin-free lichens support the suggested function of zeaxanthin in photoprotection in that zeaxanthin-associated energy dissipation in the antennae prevents the sustained reductions in photochemical efficiency which are observed in zeaxanthin-free systems.

ACKNOWLEDGEMENTS

I wish to thank Profs. O. L. Lange, K. Winter, and F.-C. Czygan for the opportunity to carry out these studies in Würzburg. This work was supported by the Deutsche Forschungsgemeinschaft (Forschergruppe Ökophysiologie and Sonderforschungsbereich 251 of the University of Würzburg) and the Fonds der Chemischen Industrie. I am grateful to O. Björkman and W. Bilger for making their unpublished data on the DTT effect available to me. I also thank my husband, W. Adams, who was involved in all of the fundamental aspects of the studies reported here.

REFERENCES

1   Krinsky, N.I. (1979) Pure Appl. Chem. 51, 649-660
2   Demmig, B. and Björkman, O. (1987) Planta 171, 171-184
3   Horton, P. and Hague, A. (1988) Biochim. Biophys. Acta 932, 107-115
4   Krause, G.H. and Behrend, U. (1986) FEBS Lett. 200, 298-302
5   Weis, E. and Berry, J.A. (1987) Biochim. Biophys. Acta 894, 198-208
6   Kitajima, M. and Butler, W.L. (1975) Biochim. Biophys. Acta 376, 105-115
7   Demmig, B., Winter, K., Krüger, A. and Czygan, F.-C. (1987) Plant Physiol. 84, 218-224
8   Hager, A. (1980) in Pigments in Plants (Czygan, F.-C., ed), pp. 57-79, Fischer, Stuttgart
9   Demmig, B., Winter, K., Krüger, A. and Czygan, F.-C. (1988) Plant Physiol. 87, 17-24
10 Demmig-Adams, B., Winter, K., Krüger, A. and Czygan, F.-C. (1989) Plant Physiol. 90, 881-886
11 Demmig-Adams, B., Winter, K., Krüger, A. and Czygan, F.-C. (1989) Plant Physiol. 90, 887-893
12 Yamamoto, H.Y. and Kamite, L. (1972) Biochim. Biophys. Acta 267, 538-543
13 Demmig-Adams, B., Adams, W.W. III, Heber, U., Neimanis, S., Winter, K., Krüger, A., Czygan, F.-C., Bilger, W. and Björkman, O. (1990) Plant Physiol., submitted
14 Demmig-Adams, B., Adams, W.W. III, Czygan, F.-C., Schreiber, U. and Lange, O.L. (1990) Planta, accepted
15 Adams, W.W. III, Demmig-Adams, B., and Winter, K. (1990) Plant Physiol., submitted
16 Demmig-Adams, B., Adams, W.W. III, Green, T.G.A., Czygan, F.-C. and Lange, O.L. (1990) in preparation
17 Demmig-Adams, B., Máguas, C., Adams, W.W. III, Meyer, A., Kilian, E. and Lange, O.L. (1990) Planta, accepted
18 Demmig-Adams, B., Winter, K., Krüger, A. and Czygan, F.-C. (1989) Plant Physiol. 90, 894-898

EFFECT OF TEMPERATURE AND PFD ON THE SUSCEPTIBILITY OF LEAVES TO PHOTOINHIBITION AND RECOVERY.

Dennis H. Greer and W.A. Laing, Plant Physiology Division, DSIR,   Private Bag, Palmerston North, New Zealand

INTRODUCTION

Leaves of many plants are susceptible to photoinhibition of photosynthesis. This results from exposure to photon flux densities (PFD) in excess of that normally experienced during growth and is manifest as a reduction in photosynthetic activity (1). However, photoinhibition can also occur when leaves are unable to utilise the available excitation energy through the effects of plant stress on photosynthesis, (2,3,4,5). The impact of this stress-induced photoinhibition on photosynthetic activity and consequent growth of plants is, however, largely unknown. However, willow leaves experienced about 10-20% photoinhibition under natural conditions throughout much of the growing season (6) and tropical fruit tree species become photoinhibited in cool winter conditions (7). By contrast, tropical grasses showed no evidence of photoinhibition in midsummer conditions (8). Therefore, little attention has been paid to defining conditions that make plants susceptible to photoinhibition. In this paper, the prevailing leaf environment and also the growth conditions that cause plants, but in particular *Actinidia deliciosa* (kiwifruit), to become susceptible to photoinhibition and those that influence the subsequent recovery, are addressed.

DEFINITION OF PHOTOINHIBITION

During exposures to excess light, photosynthetic activity declines. Notably, the photon yield is reduced but also the light-saturated maximum net photosynthesis declines to a lessor degree (9). Concomitant changes in chlorophyll fluorescence at 692 nm and 77K also occur (10). The maximum fluoresence (F_m) is markedly quenched whereas the instantaneous fluorescence (F_o) can rise or fall depending on whether primary photochemistry of PSII is being inactivated or changes occur in long-term radiationless excitation energy dissipation from the PSII antennae (11). In this paper, photoinhibition is recognised from increases in F_o and is measured by decreases in the variable fluorescence (F_v). In kiwifruit leaves, there is a linear relationship between F_v and the photon yield (ϕ_i) and a curvilinear relationship between F_v/F_m and ϕ_i (9,12). Similar relationships were observed by Björkman (11) in cotton exposed to conditions causing a rise in F_o. Photoinhibition is initially rapid when leaves are first exposed to high light and it follows exponential kinetics to reach a steady-state change in F_v, F_v/F_m, ϕ_i and net photosynthesis in about 400-500 min (9,13).

M. Baltscheffsky (ed.), Current Research in Photosynthesis, Vol. II, 365–372.

INTERACTIVE EFFECTS OF THE CURRENT TEMPERATURE AND PFD

The susceptibility of plants to photoinhibition increases directly with increases in PFD (13,14,15). Similarly, photoinhibition declines with increasing temperature (2,12,16). However, leaf temperatures and PFD interactively affect the susceptibility of plants to photoinhibition. For kiwifruit leaves, photoinhibition at low temperatures is barely dependent on the PFD (Fig. 1) but photoinhibition is very severe even at moderate PFDs.

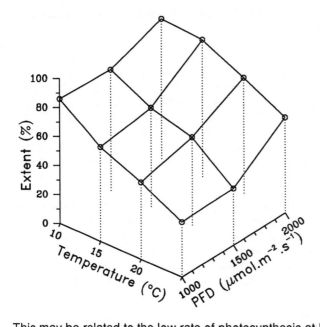

Figure 1. Interactive effects of temperature and PFD on the extent of photoinhibition in kiwifruit leaves.

This may be related to the low rate of photosynthesis at low temperatures since the susceptibility to photoinhibition is directly increased when photosynthesis is reduced (Fig. 2) by manipulating the CO_2 concentration (17). Thus, a major cause of photoinhibition at low temperature is most likely the low temperature-induced

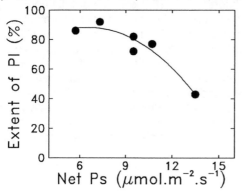

Figure 2. The effect of net photosynthesis (Ps) on the susceptibility of kiwifruit leaves to photoinhibition after a 440 min exposure to high light.

decrease in net photosynthesis (18), by exacerbating the difference between available excitation energy and its productive utilisation. Combinations of both high PFD and low temperatures cause such severe photoinhibition that irreversible damage results and loss of chlorophyll and early leaf senescence occurs (12,16).

At higher leaf temperatures (Fig. 1), photoinhibition is more markedly dependent on the PFD, with minor damage at low PFDs and increasing damage at high PFDs (see also 15). However, decreasing temperature has a greater effect in increasing photoinhibition than increasing PFD. This is possibly related to leaf temperature having a continuous effect over a wide range on the photosynthetic demand for energy whereas those PFDs in excess only occur above the PFD for light-saturation of photosynthesis.

EFFECT OF GROWTH CONDITIONS ON PHOTOINHIBITION

Shade-grown plants have been well documented to be more susceptible to photoinhibition than sun plants (14,19). This might be accounted for by morphological changes within the chloroplast, notably increased granal stacking for improved light-harvesting and a lower photosynthetic capacity in the shade leaf (20). Exposure of such leaves to high-light combines a large capacity to absorb radiation with little capacity to utilise it, and typical photoinhibition of photosynthesis results. Kiwifruit leaves grown at high PFD of 1300 $\mu mol.m^{-2}.s^{-1}$ take longer to become photoinhibited irrespective of the PFD (Fig. 3) compared with plants grown at 700 $\mu mol.m^{-2}.s^{-1}$. However, there is little difference in their relative capacity to cope with increasing PFD.

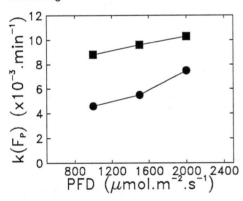

Figure 3.The effect of PFD on the rate constant for photoinhibition, $k(F_p)$ in kiwifruit leaves grown at 700 ($\blacksquare$) and 1300 $\mu mol.m^{-2}.s^{-1}$ ($\bullet$).

In the longer term, however, the extent of photoinhibition is little influenced by the growth PFD, unless the plants are grown in shade (Fig. 4a). Similar results were obtained by Powles and Critchley (14) who showed susceptibility to photoinhibition in *Phaseolus vulgaris* only increased significantly when grown in 6% of full sunlight. That is, plants grown at moderate to high PFDs are about equally susceptible to photoinhibition but shade-grown plants are significantly more susceptible. Photoinhibition in shade-grown kiwifruit leaves is less temperature-dependent than in leaves grown at higher PFD (Fig. 4b) but differences in susceptibility are not evident at low temperatures.

The growth of kiwifruit plants at moderate PFDs and progressively lower temperatures induces a distinctive semi-permanent inability to fully utilize the available light energy as apparent from a sustained quenching of fluorescence and photon yield, and thus chronic photoinhibition results (Fig. 5). Kiwifruit plants grown at 15/10°C and 700 $\mu mol.m^{-2}.s^{-1}$ were severely inhibited in comparison with comparable plants grown at 30/25°C. This chronic photoinhibition probably arises from decreased energy demand as a consequence of the low-temperature induced decline in photosynthesis but probably also from increased dissipation of energy by non-radiative means (9). At intermediate temperatures there is a gradient of effect

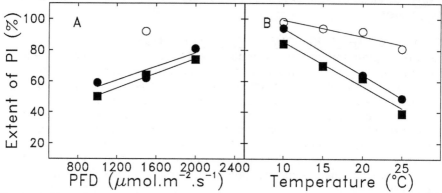

Figure 4. The effect of PFD (A) and temperature (B) on the extent of photoinhibition in kiwifruit leaves exposed to a high PFD from plants grown at 300 (o), 700 (•) and 1300 $\mu mol.m^{-2}.s^{-1}$ (■)

on F_v, consistent with rising photosynthetic activity with increasing temperature. Chronic photoinhibition takes up to 20 days to recover (9) and thus probably requires significant synthesis of the chloroplast (2,21). Similar temperature-induced chronic photoinhibition has been observed in spinach (22) and in maize (16).

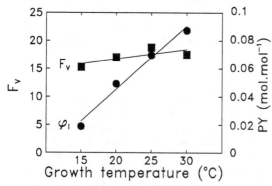

Figure 5. Predawn changes in F_v and photon yield (PY) in kiwifruit leaves from plants grown at a range of temperatures and a PFD of 700 $\mu mol.m^{-2}s^{-1}$.

In spite of low-temperature-grown plants being chronically photoinhibited, these plants were more resistant to induced photoinhibition, i.e. F_v was quenched about 5-15% less than in high-temperature-grown plants (Fig. 6), over a range of leaf temperatures. (see also 22). In part, this might be attributed to an increased capacity to dissipate energy non-radiatively in plants acclimated to low compared with high temperatures particularly during exposures at temperatures above the growth temperature (9). Plants grown at high temperatures have an apparently lower capacity to divert excitation energy to non-radiative pathways and are therefore more susceptible to photoinhibition at low temperatures than their low-temperature grown counterparts.

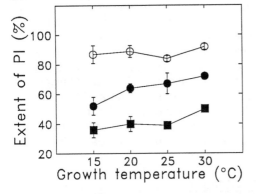

Figure 6. The extent of photoinhibition in kiwifruit leaves from plants grown at a range of temperatures after exposure to a high PFD and at leaf temperatures of 10 (o), 20 (•) and 25°C (■).

RECOVERY FOLLOWING PHOTOINHIBITION

Although recovery is thought to occur concomitantly with photoinhibition, it is most clearly seen when the incident PFD is markedly reduced. There is no discernable lag and recovery of F_v follows pseudo exponential kinetics to reach completion in about 300 min at optimal conditions. Studies with protein synthesis inhibitors, which block recovery, suggest one or more chloroplast-encoded proteins need to be synthesised *de novo* for recovery to proceed (2,21). Nuclear-encoded protein synthesis, on the other hand, does not appear to be a prerequisite for recovery to occur in higher plants (2).

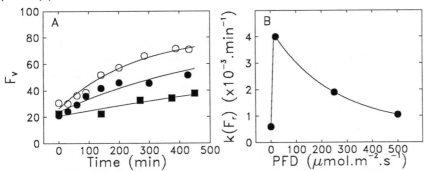

Figure 7. (A) The time-course of recovery from photoinhibition in kiwifruit leaves at 0 (■), 20 (o) and 250 μmol.m^{-2}.s^{-1} (•) and (B) the rate constant for recovery, k(F$_r$) as a function of PFD.

Recovery is linearly dependent on the extent of photoinhibition, with slower rates of recovery with increased extents of photoinhibition (15,23,24). Severe photoinhibition is irreversible and photo-oxidation of chlorophyll ensues (1,12,16). The recovery process is apparently destroyed under these circumstances since leaves cannot recover even if replaced in favourable conditions. Recovery, involving biosynthesis, is also highly temperature-dependent and increases from negligible rates at low temperatures around 10°C to maximum rates at around 30-35°C. Similar results have been observed with *Phaseolus vulgaris* (2) and maize (16). Where recovery is slow, however, it can proceed to completion given sufficient time, suggesting the effect of temperature is only through its effect on the rate of recovery (24). However, there is interspecific varation in the ability of leaves to recover at low temperatures (16). Light is also required for recovery to proceed at maximum rates (2,25), although recovery can occur in the dark at very slow rates (Fig. 7a). With low levels of light (10-20 $\mu mol.m^{-2}.s^{-1}$), there is a dramatic rise in the rate of recovery (2,23), for kiwifruit leaves up to 7-fold higher than the dark rate (Fig. 7b). At higher PFDs, however, there is a decline in the rate of recovery such that a PFD of 500 $\mu mol.m^{-2}.s^{-1}$, the rate of recovery approaches the slow dark rate. A similar effect was evident in *Phaseolus vulgaris* (2). This suggests the role of light is not to provide immediate energy for recovery to proceed, as previously proposed (25) but rather is more likely required to induce protein synthesis.

EFFECT OF GROWTH CONDITIONS ON RECOVERY

The rate of recovery in kiwifruit plants grown in shade is similar to that for plants grown in high-light (13). Thus growth light has little effect on the capacity of higher plants to recover. This is consistent with the view that recovery is a biosynthetic process unrelated to the changes that PFD induce in leaves, particularly those related to light harvest. However, in cyanobacteria and red algae, high-growth light favours high recovery rates compared to low growth light (24,26).

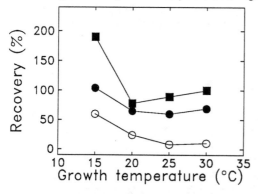

Figure 8. The extent of recovery from photoinhibition at leaf temperatures of 10 (o), 20 (●) and 25°C (■) in kiwifruit plants grown at a range of temperatures .

In contrast, growth temperature induces significant changes in the recovery process. Most notable is an increased capacity for recovery at low temperatures for plants grown at those temperatures. Whereas there is negligible recovery at 10°C in kiwifruit plants grown at high temperatures, plants grown at 20/15°C recovered by 24% and those grown at 15/10°C by 60% in 450 min (Fig. 8). However, acclimation to low temperatures does not affect the capacity for recovery at high temperatures though growth at high temperatures improves the capacity for recovery at those temperatures. An increased capacity for recovery also occurs in spinach acclimated to low temperature (22). Of all factors that influence the recovery process, however, the current temperature has the dominating influence.

RECOVERY DURING PHOTOINHIBITION

Photoinhibition follows exponential kinetics and reaches a steady-state within about 300-400 min of exposure to high-light in spite of the photoinhibitory stress persisting (12). Inactivated reaction centres become fluorescence quenchers in these circumstances and act as traps to convert excitation energy to heat whereas the remaining reaction centres continue normal photochemistry (22). Because photoinhibition comes to a temperature-dependent steady-state, it is evident that some process is restricting the degree of inactivation and that this process depends on temperature. There is evidence indicating recovery is occurring concomitantly with photoinhibition and that the observed photoinhibition is the net difference between the rate of damage and the rate of repair (2,21). However, from the effect of PFD on post-photoinhibition recovery, i.e. increasing inhibition, then extrapolating to those PFDs where photoinhibition occurs, suggests little or no recovery could occur during photoinhibition.

Alternatively, like photoinhibition being the net difference between damage and repair, the observed recovery is also the net difference beween further damage and repair. In the presence of high-light the rate of damage dominates over the rate of repair and photoinhibition results while the reverse occurs in weak light and recovery is observed. Recovery would therefore be inhibited by increasing PFD because the underlying rate of damage increases concomitantly with increases in PFD, even at PFDs when photodamage would not usually occur in healthy leaves. In all circumstances, the rate of repair should only depend on temperature, providing sufficient light is available for the initial induction of protein synthesis. Thus the net rate of recovery declines as the PFD increases.

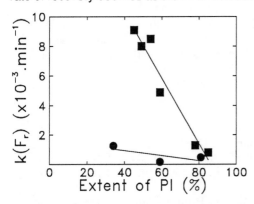

Figure 9.The rate constant for recovery, $k(F_r)$ in kiwifruit leaves as a function of the extent of photoinhibition at a PFD of 20 (■) and 700 μmol.m^{-2}.s^{-1} (●).

However, it remains unclear why a PFD below that during growth should have an inhibitory effect, once the plant has become photoinhibited. One possibility is that after a steady-state of photoinhibition has occurred, the photochemical apparatus becomes increasingly sensitive to excess light. Moderate PFDs should, therefore, have much less influence on the net rate of recovery if the initial level of photoinhibition is only slight to moderate. However, even though recovery at 700

μmol.m^{-2}.s^{-1} does show some dependency on the extent of photoinhibition (Fig. 9), it is much less so than recovery at 20 μmol.m^{-2}.s^{-1} and recovery remains severely depressed even after slight photoinhibition. This substantiates that the recovery process has become increasingly sensitive to PFD. The rate of recovery at 20 μmol.m^{-2}.s^{-1} at least, therefore, represents the true rate of recovery since this PFD is unlikely to cause photodamage.

REFERENCES
1 Powles, S.B. (1984) Ann. Rev. Plant Physiol. 35, 15-44
2 Greer, D.H. Berry, J.A. and Björkman, O. (1986) Planta 168, 253-250
3 Strand, M. and Öquist, G. (1985) Physiol. Plant. 64, 425-430
4 Björkman O. and Powles, S.B. (1984) Planta 161, 490-504
5 Ferrar, P.J. and Osmond, C.B. (1986) Planta 168, 563-570
6 Ogren, E. (1988) Planta 175, 229-236
7 Smillie, R.M., Hetherington, S.E., He, J. and Nott, R. (1988) Aust. J. Plant Physiol. 15, 207-222
8 Ludlow, M.M., Samarakoon, S.P. and Wilson, J.R. (1988) Aust. J. Plant Physiol. 15, 669-676
9 Greer, D.H. and Laing, W.A. (1989) Planta (in press)
10 Powles, S.B. and Björkman, O. (1982) Planta 156, 97-107
11 Björkman, O. (1987) in Photoinhibition (Kyle, D.J., Osmond, C.B. and Arntzen, C.J. eds.), Vol. 9, pp 123-144, Elsevier, Amsterdam
12 Greer, D.H., Laing, W.A. and Kipnis, T. (1988) Planta 174, 152-158
13 Greer, D.H. and Laing, W.A. (1988) Planta 175, 355-363
14 Powles, S.B. and Critchley, C. (1980) Plant Physiol. 65, 1181-1187
15 Demmig, B. and Björkman, O. (1987) Planta 171, 171-184
16 Greer, D.H. and Hardacre, A.K. (1989) Aust. J. Plant Physiol. 16 (in press)
17 Björkman, O. and Demmig, B. (1987) Planta 170, 489-504
18 Öquist, G., Greer, D.H. and Ogren, E. (1987) in Photoinhibition (Kyle, D.J., Osmond, C.B. and Arntzen, C.J. eds.), Vol. 9, pp 67-87, Elsevier, Amsterdam
19 Anderson, J.M. and Osmond, C.B. (1987) in Photoinhibition (Kyle, D.J., Osmond, C.B. and Arntzen, C.J. eds.), Vol. 9, pp 1-38, Elsevier, Amsterdam
20 Anderson J.M., Chow, W.S. and Goodchild, D.J. (1988) Aust. J. Plant Physiol. 15, 11-25
21 Ohad, I., Kyle, D.J. and Arntzen, C.J. (1984) J. Cell Biol. 99, 481-485
22 Krause, G.H. (1988) Physiol. Plant. 74, 566-574
23 Greer, D.H. and Laing, W.A. (1988) Planta 174, 159-165
24 Bose, S., Herbert, S.K. and Fork, D.C. (1988) Plant Physiol. 86, 946-950
25 Skogen, D., Chaturvedi, R., Weidemann, F. and Nilsen, S. (1986) J. Plant Physiol. 125, 195-205
26 Samuelsson, G., Lönneberg, A., Gustafsson, P. and Öquist, G. (1987) Plant Physiol. 83, 438-441

EFFECTS OF PHOTOINHIBITION ON THE TURNOVER OF P680 IN OXYGEN EVOLVING AND TRIS-TREATED PS-II-MEMBRANE FRAGMENTS FROM SPINACH

B. Geiken[a], H.-J. Eckert[a], J. Bernarding[b], Napiwotzki[b], and G.Renger[a], [a]Max-Volmer-Institut für Biophysikalische und Physikalische Chemie und [b]Optisches Institut, Technische Universität Berlin, Straße des 17. Juni 135, 1 Berlin 12, Germany

1. INTRODUCTION

Prolonged illumination of higher plants with intense visible light leads to photoinhibition as observed by diminution of O_2 evolution and electron transport rate through photosystem II (PS II) and by a decrease of variable fluorescence yield (for review see Ref. 1 and 2). The molecular mechanism of photoinhibition is not yet clear and there is still some discussion about the exact site(s) of the primary events. Most authors localized inhibition within the PS II reaction center or at the Q_B-binding site. In addition for chloroplats with already inhibited oxygen evolution capacity, the involvement of PS II donor side components has been reported.

In this study comparative measurements are presented of O_2 evolution and flash induced absorption changes at 830 nm (ΔA_{830}), reflecting the turnover of P680 in O_2-evolving and of DCIP-reduction (DPC$\rightarrow$DCIP) and ΔA_{830} in Tris-treated PS II membrane fragments at different degrees of photoinhibition.

2. MATERIALS AND METHODS

PSII membrane fragments were prepared from spinach as described in Ref. 3 with the modifications as in Ref. 4. These preparations evolved oxygen at a typical rate of 200 μmol O_2/(mg Chl h). For the experiments of Fig.3 and Fig. 4 standard Tris-treatment was used to inhibit oxygen evolution.

Photoinhibition treatment was carried out in the following way: 22ml of the sample (100 μM Chl., 20 mM Mes (pH 6.5), 1 mM NaCl) was kept on ice in a 4 cm wide Petri dish and exposed to white light from a slide projector at an incident intensity of 850 W/m^2. To achieve uniform illumination the sample was constantly stirred. After the time-intervals indicated in the figures, 2 ml of the sample was removed to perform the different measurements.

Oxygen evolution was measured in the presence of $K_3Fe(CN)_6$ (2 mM) and phenyl-p-benzoquinone (Ph-p-BQ, 200 μM) at a Chl-concentration of 25 μg/ml using a Clark type electrode. The rate of DCIP photoreduction with diphenylcarbazide (DPC) as a donor was spectrophotometrically monitored at 590 nm. The reaction mixture contained 5 μM Chl, 40 μM DCIP and 600 μM DPC.

830 nm absorption changes were measured with a single beam flash photometer as described in Ref. 5 at a Chl.-concentration of 50 μg/ml using 1 mM $K_3 Fe(CN)_6$ and 100 μM PH-p-BQ as electron acceptors. Optical pathlength: 4 cm; time between the actinic laser flashes (λ = 532 nm, FWHM: 3 ns): 1 s.

3. RESULTS AND DISCUSSION

In oxygen evolving PS II membrane fragments the reduction of P680$^+$ is known to occur predominantly in the ns time scale. Elimination of O_2 evolution by Tris-treat –

M. Baltscheffsky (ed.), Current Research in Photosynthesis, Vol. II, 373–376.
© 1990 *Kluwer Academic Publishers. Printed in the Netherlands.*

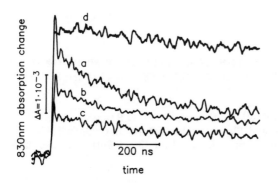

FIGURE 1
Absorption changes at 830 nm induced by repetitive laser flashes in oxygen evolving PS II membrane fragments after different time intervals of illumination with white light (850 W/m^2). a, control; b, 30 min.; c, 60 min. For comparison the effect of NH$_2$OH on the control sample is also shown (trace d). Experimental conditions as described in Materials and Methods.

ment or incubation with NH$_2$OH leads to retardation of the P680$^+$ reduction kinetics as is shown in Fig. 1 by drastic slowing of the ΔA_{830} relaxation upon addition of NH$_2$OH to the control sample. In contrast to this phenomenon the most obvious effect of the photoinhibition of oxygen evolving PS II membrane fragments is a decrease of the total initial amplitude of ΔA_{830} rather than a retardation of the relaxation kinetics. This is demonstrated more clearly in Fig. 2, which depicts the total initial amplitude of 830 nm absorption changes, ΔA_{830}^{total}, the extent of ns kinetics $\Delta A^{ns} = \Delta A_{830}(t=0) - \Delta A_{830}(t=900ns)$, and the rate of oxygen evolution as a function of preillumination time. In a control experiment carried out in the dark under otherwise identical conditions we did not find a measurable decrease of O_2 evolution within 60 min. At the time resolution used here (ca. 15 ns) ΔA_{830}^{total} reflects the number of PS II reaction centers capable of performing a "stable" charge separation from P680 to Q_A. Fig. 2 shows that within the scattering of the data ΔA_{830}^{ns}, ΔA_{830}^{total}, and O_2 exhibit the same decline with progressing photoinhibition. This indicates that photoinhibition of oxygen evolving PS II membrane fragments is mainly due to a loss of stable charge separation within the reaction center (as indicated by the decrease of ΔA_{830}^{total}) and that donor side effects are negligible or at most of minor relevance.

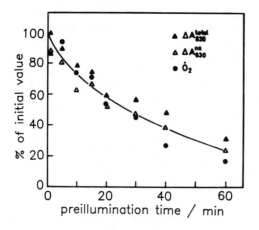

FIGURE 2
Extent of the total signal amplitude (ΔA_{830}^{total}) and of the nanosecond decay components (ΔA_{830}^{ns}) of 830 nm absorption changes and oxygen evolution rate (O_2) in oxygen evolving PS II membrane fragments as a function of illumination time. Experimental details as described in Materials and Methods. Light intensity: 850 W/m^2.

In order to exclude any effect due to kinetic limitations of Q_A^- reoxidation between the actinic flashes we measured ΔA_{830} induced by a single flash in dark adapted samples. To achieve a reasonable signal to noise ratio these measurements had to be carried out at a reduced time resolution that does not permit the detection of decay components in the ns time domain. Therefore the $P680^+$ reduction was slowed down by addition of NH_2OH (see Fig. 1). Even under this conditions practically the same decrease of ΔA_{830}^{total} was found (data not shown) as under repetitive flash excitation as shown in Fig. 2. This indicates that the observed loss of stable charge separation is not due to a limited reoxidation of Q_A^- but to an inhibition either of the primary radical pair ($P680^+Pheo^-$) formation or of the reoxidation of $Pheo^-$ by Q_A.

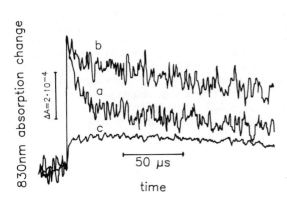

FIGURE 3
Absorption changes at 830 nm induced by a single laser flash in dark adapted (> 20 min. on ice) Tris-treated PS II membrane fragments (a, control; b, 1 min. illumination). For the measurement of the sample illuminated for 40 min. (trace c) 16 signals were averaged at a repetition rate of 1 Hz. Electron acceptors: 1 mM $K_3Fe(CN)_6$ and 100 μM Ph-p-BQ. 2 mM NH_2OH was added as electron donor. Optical pathlength: 1 cm; electrical bandwidth of the detection system: 1 MHz.

Fig. 3 shows the time course of ΔA_{830} in Tris-treated PS II membrane fragments completely deprived of oxygen evolution capacity in the presence of NH_2OH as electron donor. Before illumination the relaxation of ΔA_{830} is dominated by a component with a half-life time of about 10 μs (Fig. 3, trace a). These kinetics

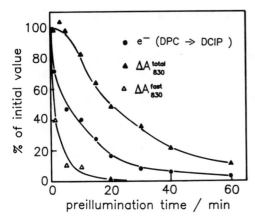

FIGURE 4
Extent of the total signal amplitude (ΔA_{830}^{total}) and of the fast μs decay component (i.e. $\Delta A_{830}^{fast} = \Delta A_{830}$ (t = 0) $- \Delta A_{830}$(t = 40 μs) and rate of DCIP reduction in Tris treated PS II membrane fragments as a function of preillumination time. 40 μM DCIP and 600 μM DPC were added as electron acceptor and donor, respectively, about 1 min. before all measurements. Electrical bandwidth.: 1 MHz.

reflect the reduction of $P680^+$ by Y_z (6). After short photoinhibition (1 min) the ΔA_{830} relaxation kinetics become highly retarded giving rise to a slow component with half-life times of about 260 μs (deduced from measurements in a longer time scale, not shown). This kinetics can be attributed to a backreaction between Q_A^- and $P680^+$ in reaction centers with blocked electron transfer between Y_z and $P680^+$ (6, 7). A more detailed analysis (see Fig. 4) shows that the extent of the fast component, ΔA_{830}^{fast}(Tris), as well as the rate of DCIP reduction (with DPC as donor) decline much faster than ΔA_{830}^{total} thereby indicating an inhibition of the electron transfer from Y_z to $P680^+$.

4. CONCLUSIONS

The above findings show that Tris-treatment leads to a much higher susceptibility of the $P680$-Y_z segment to photoinhibition. As previously suggested (8, 9) this might be a result of detrimental effects of $P680^+$ and/or Y_z^{ox} which have a much longer life time in Tris-treated than in control samples. However, the data do not support the idea that $P680^+$ is also responsible for the loss of the capability to stable charge separation within the reaction center because the susceptibility of this site to photoinhibition is only slightly affected by Tris-treatment (compare the decline of ΔA_{830}^{total} in Fig.2 and Fig. 4). The loss of $P680^+Q_A^-$ formation might be due to a double reduction and subsequent protonation of Q_A (forming Q_AH_2) as suggested in Ref. 9. This idea is supported by our previous results which showed a light induced retardation of radical pair recombination ($P680^+Pheo^- \longrightarrow P680\ Pheo$) upon preillumination of PS II membrane fragments in the presence of dithionite (11).

ACKNOWLEDGEMENTS

Financial support from ERP Sondervermögen (J.B.,ERP 2603) and from Deutsche Forschungsgemeinschaft (SfB 312) is gratefully acknowledged.

4. REFERENCES

1 Powles, S.B. (1984) Annu. Rev. Plant Physiol. 35, 15

2 Critchley, C. (1988) Aust. J. Plant. Physiol. 15, 27-41

3 Berthold, O.A., Babcock, G.T., and yocum, C.F. (1981) FEBS Lett. 134, 231-234

4 Völker, M., Ono, T., Inoue, Y. and Renger, G. (1985) Biochim. Biophys. Acta 806, 25 - 34

5 Eckert, H.-J., Wydrzynski, T. and Renger, G. (1988) Biochim. Biophys. Acta 932, 240 - 249

6 Weiss, W. and Renger, G. (1986) Biochim. Biophys. Acta 850, 173-183

7 Ford, R.C. and Evans, M.C.W. (1985) Biochim. Biophys. Acta 807, 1 - 9

8 Theg, S. M., Filar, L.J. and Dilley, R.A. (1986) Biochim. Biophys. Acta 859, 104 - 111

9 Callahan, F.E., Becker, D.W. and Cheniae, G.M. (1986) Plant Physiol. 82, 261 - 269

10 Van Mieghem, F., Nitschke, W., Mathis, P. and Rutherford, A. W. (1989) Biochim. Biophys. Acta (in press)

11 Eckert, H.-J., Renger, G., Bernarding, J., Faust, P.,Eichler, H.-J. and Salk, J. (1987) Biochim.Biophys. Acta 893, 208 - 218

THE MECHANISM OF PHOTOINHIBITION OF SPINACH THYLAKOIDS

ALOYSIUS WILD, MICHAEL RICHTER, AND WOLFGANG RÜHLE
INSTITUT FÜR ALLGEMEINE BOTANIK DER JOHANNES GUTENBERG-
UNIVERSITÄT, SAARSTR. 21, D-6500 MAINZ, FRG

INTRODUCTION
There is conflicting evidence as to wether D1-protein is the primary
target of photoinhibition [1] or P$_{680}$, the reaction centre of photosystem II [2]. The present paper desribes photoinhibition within a two
step process consisting of an oxygen radical induced inactivation at the
Q$_B$-site followed by damage to reaction centre II through the degradation
of the D1-protein.

MATERIALS AND METHODS
All experiments were carried out with isolated spinach thylakoids. The
isolation procedure and the photoinhibitory treatment have been previously described [3]. The D1-protein content of thylakoids was determined through the binding of ^{14}C-atrazine. The reaction centre II was
characterized by the capacity for Q$_B$-independent reduction of SiMo and
the measurement of variable fluorescence (F$_v$/F$_m$). Whole chain electron
transport was measured polarographically through ferricyanide or methylviologen mediated Hill-reactions. The Q$_A$-Q$_B$-electron transfer was further examined by means of fluorescence relaxation kinetics. The possible
involvement of oxygen radicals in the mechanism of photoinhibition was
investigated through radical scavenging experiments, in which thylakoids
were exposed to high intensity light in the presence of saturating
amounts of either glutathione and ascorbate or SOD and catalase. To get
further information about the possible role of the particular reactive
hydroxyl radical thylakoids were treated with a Fenton-reaction mixture
in the dark. For studying the influence of lowered oxygen concentration
on photoinhibition thylakoids were exposed to high light conditions in an
oxygen free medium under a nitrogen atmosphere. Further details are
given in [3,4].

RESULTS AND DISCUSSION
Photoinhibition at 20°C caused a significant loss of atrazine binding
sites. This degradation of D1-protein was strongly inhibited at 0°C compared to 20°C (Fig.1), probably due to the inhibition of a membrane
bound protease activity through lowering the temperature. The functional
properties of reaction centre II, i.e. PSII-photochemistry (H$_2$O $-->$ SiMo)

M. Baltscheffsky (ed.), Current Research in Photosynthesis, Vol. II, 377–380.
© 1990 *Kluwer Academic Publishers. Printed in the Netherlands.*

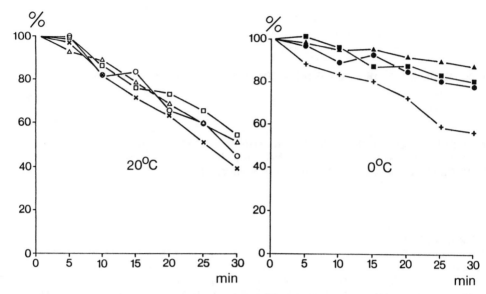

FIGURE 1. The time course of photoinhibition at 20°C and 0°C. Symbols represent: (□,■) atrazine binding sites, (○,●) PSII—electron transport (H₂O -> SiMo), (△,▲) Fᵥ/Fₘ, (✗,+) whole chain electron transport (H₂O -> MV).

and variable fluorescence (F_v/F_m), were controlled by D1—degradation as revealed by the parallel decline at 20°C and the similar degree of protection at 0°C of atrazine binding sites, variable fluorescence and PSII—electron transport. This is consistent with the D1—protein being a constituent of reaction centre II [5]. The whole chain electron flow (H_2O --> MV) however declined in a temperature independent way (Fig.1).
This inactivation could neither be localized at the water splitting enzyme nor at photosystem I which both did not contribute to the observed inactivation as tested by DPC to MV and DAD to MV Hill—reactions. Fluorescence relaxation studies confirmed that photoinhibition at 0°C led to an impairment of the Q_A^-—reoxidation as can be concluded from the slower decline of fluorescence following saturating single turnover flashes (Fig.2) [3]. This implies a partial inhibition of the electron transfer through the Q_B—binding site.
Exposure of thylakoids to high intensity light in the presence of the antioxidants glutathione and ascorbate or the enzymes SOD and catalase resulted in comparable though not total protection of atrazine binding sites and photochemistry (H_2O --> Fecy). Photoinhibition was nearly completely suppressed upon combination of the antioxidant with the enzymatic radical protective system though both had been applied at saturating amounts (Fig.3). This implies a major contribution of oxygen activation to the mechanism of the observed photoinhibition.

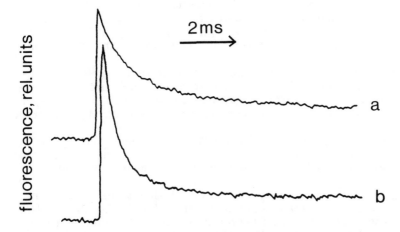

FIGURE 2. Fluorescence relaxation kinetics following saturating single
turnover flashes of thylakoids photoinhibited at 0°C (a) and measured at
20°C compared to a dark control (b).

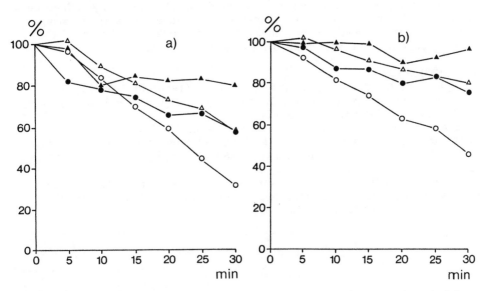

FIGURE 3. The decline of electron transport capacity ($H_2O \rightarrow$ Fecy) (a)
and atrazine binding sites (b) in the presence of i) SOD/catalase (●),
ii) glutathione and ascorbate (△) or a combination of i) and ii) (▲); (○)
represents controls without additions.

The fact that the antioxidant and the enzymatic protective system complement one another in radical detoxification possibly indicates some repair properties of the antioxidants towards oxidized amino acids [6] or results from the recycling of oxidized α-tocopherol by the glutathione-ascorbate-system [7].

Similar phenomena as observed during photoinhibition, i.e. loss of D1-protein, photochemistry and variable fluorescence, were induced by treatment of thylakoids with hydroxyl radicals generated within the suspensions through a Fenton-reaction superimposed by a weak light illumination [4].

Photoinhibition in the presence of low oxygen concentration (11 μM) was not pronounced but could largely be prevented by the enzymes SOD and catalase as was observed during photoinhibition under normal air conditions [4].

Summarizing our results, we propose photoinhibition to be a two step process consisting of a radical induced inactivation of the Q_B-function followed by the degradation of D1-protein turning the reaction centre II non functional. The radical modification of the protein has been made distinguishable from the degradation by lowering the temperature during photoinhibition.

We suppose D1-degradation to be part of the defense mechanism against strong photooxidative damage to the entire photosynthetic apparatus. The protein could perhaps function in thylakoids in the same way a fuse does in an electric curcuit. In case of energy overload a widespread damage being difficult to repair is prevented through quick destruction of the fuse component, thus switching off the system function.

REFERENCES

[1] Kyle D.J., Ohad I., Guy R. and Arntzen C. (1984) in Adv. in Photosynth. Res. (Sybesma, C., ed.), pp. 167–170, Martinus Nijhoff/Dr. W. Junk Publishers, The Hague
[2] Cleland R.E. (1988) Austr. J. Plant Physiol. 15, 135–150
[3] Richter M., Rühle W. and Wild A. (1989 a) Photosynth. Res., in press
[4] Richter M., Rühle W. and Wild A. (1989 b) Photosynth. Res., in press
[5] Barber J. (1987) TIBS 12, 321–326
[6] Hoey B. and Butler J. (1984) Biochim. Biophys. Acta 791, 212–218
[7] Scarpa M., Rigo A., Maiorino M., Ursini F. and Gregolin C. (1984) Biochim. Biophys. Acta 801, 215–219

UV-PHOTOINHIBITION : STUDIES *IN VITRO* AND IN INTACT PLANTS

C.T. YERKES, D.M. KRAMER, J.M. FENTON and A.R. CROFTS, Biophysics Division, U. of Illinois, 607 S. Mathews, Urbana IL 61801, U.S.A.

1. INTRODUCTION

Plants exposed to intense illumination undergo an inhibition of photosynthesis in a process called photoinhibition. Early studies of photoinhibition, using chloroplasts and monochromatic light, identified two spectral ranges of photoinhibitory light, which gave rise to somewhat different effects (1-4). The action spectrum showed a UV light effect, mainly in the UV-B range, and a visible light effect. The quantum yield in the UV range was about a hundredfold greater than that in the visible range, which had the action spectrum of photosynthetic pigments. The UV-photoinhibition was specifically related to PS II. Some controversy exists as to whether the locus of UV-photoinhibition lies on the donor (1-9) or acceptor (10-12) side of PS II. It has also been suggested that in plants, the action spectrum of UV photoinhibition may reflect DNA damage (13). This work represents an attempt to further clarify the mechanism of UV-photoinhibiton of PS II in isolated PS II preparations, chloroplasts and intact plants.

2. PROCEDURE

2.1 EPR spectra were taken on a Bruker ER220D-SRC spectrometer, with a Bruker ER4103TM cavity and a Wilmad TM flat cell or tissue cell. The PSII preparation was a modification of the procedure of Kuwabara and Murata (14).
2.2 Fluorescence studies of plants were conducted on instruments developed in the lab, a fluorescence video imaging photometer (15) or a field flash kinetic fluorimeter (16).
2.3 Absorption studies of leaves were conducted on a field flash spectrophotometer (17).
All experimental conditions are noted in the figure legends.

3. RESULTS AND DISCUSSION

3.1 EPR studies of the effects of UV-damage.
We have made a preliminary study of the effects of UV-treatment on the signals of EPR detectable species in PS II preparations, isolated chloroplasts and leaf segments.

Fig. 1

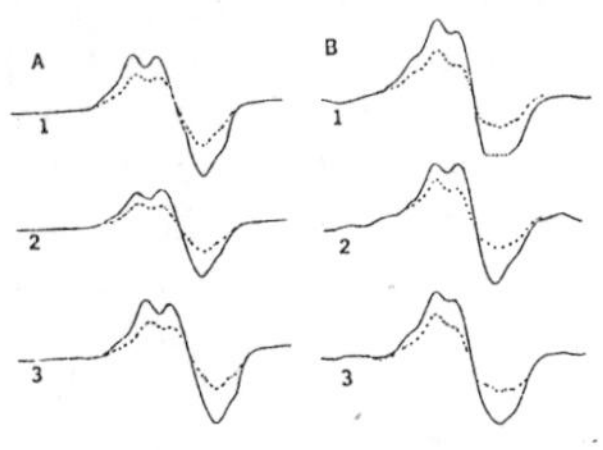

In contrast to the results of Kyle et al. (11), we have found marked effects on the amplitude of Signals IIs (Y_D^+) and IIf (Y_Z^+) in Tris-washed chloroplasts and PS II preparations. Fig. 1 shows EPR spectra of (A) PS II preparations and (B) chloroplasts before (1) and after (2) UV-irradiation, and (3) following illumination filtered by plexiglass to remove the UV-component. UV-treatment leads to a loss of Signal IIf (Y_Z^+) and a smaller loss of Signal IIs. No signal amplitude is lost upon filtered irradiation. In the Tris-washed chloroplasts, UV-irradiation also led to a relative increase in the amplitude of Signal I ($P700^+$) during illumination (Fig. 1B, solid line), indicating an inhibition of

M. Baltscheffsky (ed.), Current Research in Photosynthesis, Vol. II, 381–384.

electron transfer to PS I. In leaf fragments we also observed a relative increase in Signal I amplitude ($P700^+$) following UV-irradiation. These 100 G traces are centered at 3475 G, with a modulation amplitude of 8 G_{pp}, 20 mW power.

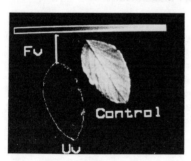

In confirmation of the results of Renger et al.(18), we also measured the release of Mn from O_2 evolving systems following UV treatment. Fig. 2 shows EPR spectra of (A) PS II preparations and (B) and leaf fragments 1) before and 2)after UV-illumination, with 3) a control of UV-filterd illumination. After 60 min. UV-irradiation, 40% of the functional manganese in the PS II preparations 4) had been released from the membranes. The kinetics of Mn release correlate well with the rate of Signal IIf loss in Tris-washed PS II

Fig. 2

preparations. It is difficult to quantify the manganese release in leaf fragments because of the high initial concentration of $Mn^{2+}:6H_2O$. Illumination with visible light, following UV-irradiation, results in an additional 50% increase (broken line) in the hexaquo manganese signal in leaf fragments. A similar light induced increase is not seen in non-UV treated or control leaves. Experimental conditions as above except, 100 O scan width. Observation of specific PS II effects of UV-irradiation in leaves as well as PS II preparations demonstrates that the the earliest locus of UV-damage in plants is most likely PS II and not the plant DNA.

3.2 Fluorescence studies of intact plants.

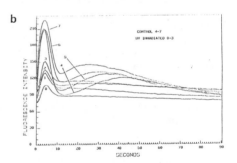

Fig. 3A shows photographs of the false-color enhanced video images of fluorescence from leaves of the same plant, one exposed to UV, and the other exposed to the same light, but screened by a plexiglass filter. Fig. 3B shows the induction curve for fluorescence measured at different points on the two leaves. The effects of UV treatment are reflected in a lower level of variable fluorescence and in modifications to the pattern of the induction curves. The initial fluorescence was not affected. These results are similar to those previously reported in experiments measuring induction curves from treated chloroplasts and leaves (5,19). As others have pointed out previously (5,19), the lowering of the variable fluorescence yield is most easily interpreted as due to the presence of a quencher in the reaction center, generated on illumination of the UV-damaged centers. As a preliminary hypothesis, it seems reasonable to conclude that $P680^+$ is the quencher and that its production reflects an inhibition of the pathway by which the primary donor is reduced.

Figures 4 A and B show Q_A^- oxidation, measured by decline of fluorescence yield.

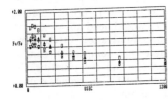

Traces show kinetics following A), the first actinic flash and B), a second actinic flash, in pea leaves UV-irradiated for 0-60 min. A progressive loss in fluorescence amplitude is seen with UV-exposure time. The half-time of the residual fluorescence decay remains unaffected (200 us $\pm$ 40 us). Controls with filtered UV light show no such loss in fluorescence amplitude and no change in decay kinetics.

Fig. 4 A(top), B(bottom)

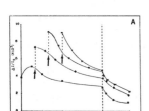

3.3 Spectrophotometric assay of the site of inhibition
We have measured the 515 nm electrochromic changes in UV-inhibited (5-B) and control (5-A) Amaranthus Hybridis leaves (Fig. 5). The electrochromic change reflects the generation of a membrane potential (20). Following a single flash, a fast phase (phase a, <1 us rise), is followed by a slow phase (phase b) with a rise time of 4-10 ms, and then by a decay. Phase a is associated with the electrogenic electron transfer through PS I and PS II, which contribute nearly equal components. Phase b reflects the electrogenic turn over of the cyt b_6/f complex and, in uninhibited centers, has a magnitude of about 0.5 that of phase a. The decay reflects the turnover of the ATP-synthase and leakage across the thylakoid membrane. The relative magnitudes of phases a and b following a single flash or a train of flashes provide information on the fractional turnover of the different electrogenic reactions leading to the charging of the membrane.

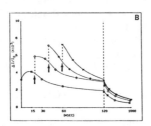

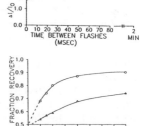

Fig. 5

As shown in Fig. 5, the UV-treated leaves show a reduced amplitude of phase a on the first flash and a reduced ratio of the fast phase on the first and second flash, when flashes were spaced 20 ms apart. These changes are consistent with an inhibition close to one or both of the reaction centers, which prevents a reopening during the 20 ms between flashes. The time course for re-opening (= control, = UV) was markedly modified; the component of phase a recovering rapidly (< 5 ms) was diminished and the remainder recovered much more slowly in UV-treated leaves. As far as we are aware, these experiments are the first direct demonstration of inhibition in the electron transfer chain in UV-treated intact plants.

3.4 Discussion

The main conclusions that can be drawn from these results are:

i) UV-photoinhibition leads to a loss of activity in an increasing fraction of PS II centers. Inhibited centers show no activity. Remaining centers show a normal acceptor activity.

ii) Inactivated centers lose manganese, and the rate of loss of Mn correlates with the rate of loss of EPR signals IIf and IIs, and an increase in the amplitude of EPR signal I, when PS I is present.

iii) Inactivation is associated with a loss of variable fluorescence, presumably because of the presence of a quencher for fluorescence in damaged centers.

These features can be explained by any effect on PS II which leads to loss of function, loss of assembly, and creation of a fluorescence quenching state in inactivated centers. The most economical explanation is direct UV damage to the tyrosine residues, Y_D and Y_Z, associated with EPR signals IIs and IIf. This would lead to all of the above effects, with P680$^+$ formed, but not re-reduced upon illumination in damaged centers, providing the quenching for fluorescence. An interesting comparison can be made between Kok's action spectrum of UV-photoinhibition (3) and the putative absorption spectrum of Y_Z^+ (21), which show similar features in the UV-B range, a peak between 250 and 260 nm and a pronounced shoulder at about 270 nm

REFERENCES

1 Kok, B. (1956) Biochim. Biophys. Acta 21, 234.

2 Kok, B., Gassner, E.B. and Rurainski, H.J. (1965) Photochem. Photobiol. 4, 215-227.

3 Jones, L.W. and Kok, B. (1966) Plant Physiol. 41, 1037-1043.

4 Jones, L.W. and Kok, B. (1966) Plant Physiol. 41, 1044-1049.

5 Yamashita T. and Butler, W.L. (1969) Plant Physiol. 44, 1342-1346.

6 Iwanzik, W., Trevini, M., Dohnt, G., Voss, W., Weiss, P. and Renger, G. (1983) Plant Cell Physiol. 29, 721-726.

7 Noorudeen, M. and Kulandaivelu, G. (1982) Physiol. Planta 55, 161-166.

8 Theg, S.M., Filar, L.J. and Dilley, R.A. (1986) Biochim. Biophys. Acta 849, 104-111.

9 Miyao, M. and Murata, N. (1986) Photosynth. Res. 10, 489-496.

10 Kyle, D.J. (1987) in Photoinhibition (Kyle, D.T., Osmond, C.B. and Arntzen, C.J., eds.) Elsevier Science Publ., Amsterdam, pp. 197-226.

11 Kyle, D.J., Ohad, I. and Arntzen, C.J. (1984) Proc. Natl. Acad. Sci. U.S.A. 81, 4070-4075.

12 Vonshak, A., Guy, R., Poplawsky, R. and Ohad, I. (1988) Plant Cell Physiol. 29, 721-726.

13 Caldwell, M.M. (1981) in Encyclopedia of Plant Physiology, new series, Phyiol. Plant Ecol. I (Lange, O.L., Nobel, P.S., Osmond, C.B. and Ziegler, H., eds.) vol. 12A, Springer-Verlag, Berlin, p 169.

14 Kuwabara, T. and Murata, N. (1982) Plant Cell Physiol. 23, 533-539.

15 Fenton, J.M. (1989) Biotechnology, submitted.

16 Kramer, D.M. and Crofts, A.R. in preparation

17 Kramer, D.M. and Crofts, A.R. (1989) Photosynth. Res., in press

18 Renger, G., Volker, M., Eckert, H.J., Fromme, R., Hohm-Veit, S. and Graber, P. (1989) Photochem. Photobiol. 49, 97-105.

19 Bjorn, L.O., Bornman, J.F. and Olsson, E. (1983) in Stratospheric Ozone Reduction, Solar Ultraviolet Radiation and Plant Life (Worrest, R.C. and Caldwell, M.M., eds.) Springer-Verlag, Berlin, pp.d 185-198.

20 Witt, H.T. (1975) Biochim. Biophys. Acta 505, 355-427.

21 Diner, B.A. and de Vitry, C. (1984) Adv. Photosynth. Res. (Sybesma, C., ed.) Vol. I, Martinus Nijhoff/Dr. W. Junk, Publ., The Hague, pp. 407-411.

THE EFFECT OF UV-B RADIATION ON PHOTOSYNTHESIS AND PHOTOSYSTEM II OF PHYTOPLANKTONIC AND BENTHIC ALGAE AND SEAGRASSES

A.W.D. LARKUM AND W.F.WOOD

School of Biological Sciences, University of Sydney, NSW 2006, AUSTRALIA.

1. INTRODUCTION

With the development of the Ozone Hole over Antarctica, and probably thinning over the Arctic as well, concern over the action of harmful UV radiation (mainly UV-B, 280-320 nm) has increased. Even under present levels of UV-B radiation, it is now well documented that UV-B (and UV-C radiation) has a strong inhibitory effect on photosynthesis[1,2]. The effect has been proposed to be on photosystem II and more specifically on the reaction centre of photosystem II[3], although the specific lesion and any ancillary damage still need to be worked out. Although it was earlier thought that UV-B radiation does not penetrate ocean waters in significant amounts, it is now generally agreed that harmful doses may occur to depths of 10 m. Wood[4] showed an effect on growth of the kelp *Ecklonia radiata* and predicted effects as deep as 10 m in oceanic waters off W. Australia. However algae, like other plants may possess adaptative mechanisms to lessen the effects of UV-B radiation. However apart from a few indications[5,6] little is known of the action of UV-B on algae or of the protective strategies which algae may exhibit.

2. METHODS

Benthic algae and seagrasses were collected locally. Unicellular algae were cultured as previously described[7]. A Clark-type electrode (Rank Bros., Bottisham) was used to measure photosynthesis (under saturating white light- 400 $\mu E.m^{-2}.s^{-1}$) and respiration. Fluorescence kinetics were measured using a specially-constructed fluorimeter utilising an EMI 9558B PM and a storage oscilloscope (Tektronix 5103N). Exciting light was at 400-500 nm (Corning 5-56 blue glass filter) onto discs of plant material. Fluorescence was measured at 685 nm using a interference filter. All fluorescence measurements were done after a dark period of 20 min.

A xenon arc (ORC 1000W lamp) was used from which infrared and UV-C radiation were filtered out. To remove UV radiation (0.035 mW cm^{-2}) a polycarbonate screen was placed in the light path leaving only photosynthetically active radiation (PAR)(160 μE m^{-2} s^{-1}).

3. RESULTS.

Photosynthesis (oxygen evolution) and respiration were measured in a number of marine benthic algae after a given period of irradiation of PAR±UVB. There was no effect on respiration. For PAR+UVB there was a variable effect (Table 1), with littoral algae showing less effect than sublittoral algae. The effect of PAR+UVB on fluorescence rise kinetics was also examined. This has been done on marine benthic algae and seagrasses(Table 2) and on marine phytoplanktonic algae (Table 3).

All material tested showed a depression in variable fluorescence relative to the control material which received only visible light, with the exception of *Homeostrichus sinclairii* which showed strong photoinhibition and inhibition of variable fluorescence in

M. Baltscheffsky (ed.), Current Research in Photosynthesis, Vol. II, 385–388.

Table 1. The effect of irradiation in PAR+UVB for 15 or 30 min. on gross photosynthesis (oxygen evolution) of several benthic marine algae from New South Wales. The rate of photosynthesis is expressed as a percentage of the rate for algae irradiated only with PAR for the given period.

Species	Algal type	Habit	15' UVB %	30'UVB %
Enteromorpha intestinalis	Green	Littoral	95	90
Microdictyon umbilicatum	Green	Sublitt.	90	75
Ecklonia radiata	Brown	Sublitt.	85	50
Colpomenia sinuosa	Brown	Sublitt.	88	61
Porphyra sp.	Red	Littoral	100	94
Griffithsia pacifica	Red	Sublitt.	85	68
Kallymenia cribrosa	Red	Sublitt.	75	45

Table 2. Fluorescence yield of macroalgae and seagrasses. Treatment time is indicated time. %, indicates percent of control F_v. t, indicates time (s) to max fluorescence.

Macroalgae

Alga	Type	±UV-B	Treatment (min)	Fo	Fm	Fv	%	t
Ecklonia radiata	brown	-UV	30+30	50	84	34	100	6.5
		+UV	30+30	50	65.5	25.5	41	2
Padina australis	brown	-UV	30+30	50	71	21	100	5.5
		+UV	2+30	50	67	17	83	4.5
		+UV	30+30	50	60	10	48	5.5
Enteromorpha intestinalis	green	-UV	30+30	50	187	137	100	9.5
		+UV	30+30	50	83	33	24	6
Kallymenia cribrosa	red	-UV	2+30	50	60	10	100	
		-UV	30+30	50	46.7	6.7	67	
		+UV	2+30	50	57	7	73	
		+UV	30+30	50	56	6	64	

Seagrasses

Alga	Type	±UV-B	Treatment (min)	Fo	Fm	Fv	%	t
Halophila ovalis		-UV	30+30	50	69	19	100	6
		+UV	30+30	50	65	15	79	2
Posidonia australis		-UV	30+30	50	68	18	100	10
		+UV	30+30	50	54	4	22	2

visible light (Table 2). A typical trace with and without UVB is shown in Fig. 1 for. *Kallymenia cribrosa.*
Like the oxygen evolution results, the greatest effects on variable fluorescence were seen in sublittoral, shade algae such as *Kallymenia cribrosa, Homeostrichus sinclairii*

and *Ecklonia radiata*. Similarly the seagrass *Halophila ovalis* which grows in shallow water in full sunlight was less affected than the deeper-growing, more shaded *Posidonia australis* (Table 2). Planktonic algae also showed inhibition, both following visible light and in the presence of UV (Table 3). Inhibition by PAR+UV was always greater than with PAR alone and in several cases approached 100% (Table 3).

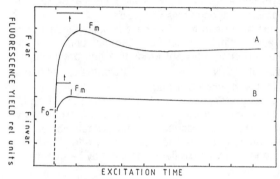

Fig. 1.The fluorescence rise curves for discs of *Kallymenia cribrosa* irradiated with PAR or PAR+UVB for 20 min prior to measurement of fluorescence rise. F_o, invariable fluorescence; F_m, maximum fluorescence; F_v, variable fluorescence (F_m-F_o); t, time to max fluorescence.

Table 3. Fluorescence yield of planktonic microalgae.

Alga	Type	±UV-B	Treatment	Fo	Fm	Fv	%	t
Chlorella	green	-UV	0+30	50	85	35	100	11.5
pyrenoidosa		-UV	30+30	50	78.4	28.4	81	10.5
		-UV	60+30	50	70.3	20.3	58	13
		+UV	30+30	50	55.6	5.6	16	2.5
		+UV	60+30	50	52.1	2.1	6	2.3
Pheodactylum	diatom	-UV	0+30	50	78	38	100	6
tricornutum		-UV	30+30	50	64.4	14.4	38	8
		-UV	60+30	50	67.5	17.5	46	7
		+UV	30+30	50	51.1	1.1	3	2
		+UV	60+30	50	51.1	1.1	3	2
Amphidinium	dino-	-UV	0+30	50	55.1	5.1	100	4
carterae	flagellate	-UV	30+30	50	54	4	80	4
		+UV	30+30	50	51	1.0	20	1
		+UV	60+30	50	50	0	0	0
Pavlova	Prymnesio-	-UV	30+30	50	63	13	100	6
lutherii	phyte	+UV	30+30	50	51	1	8	1

4. DISCUSSION

Although it has been shown that ambient levels of UV in the first 5-10 m of ocean waters may inhibit photosynthesis and growth of subtidal marine algae[5,9,10] and cause

II.6.388

destruction of photopigments, the site and time course of this inhibition has not been known.

This study has shown that treatment of algae for short periods with simulated sunlight containing UV (equivalent to bright spring day-time levels at the surface of the sea off Sydney [Latitude 34° S]) will depress the rate of photosynthesis as measured by oxygen evolution. This effect is stronger than the effect of photoinhibition but both are manifested to the greatest degree in deepwater shade algae. This suggests that algae living in high-light habitats develop protective mechanisms cf. Wood[5].

Inhibition of variable fluorescence has also been found to be a sensitive indicator of UV irradiation but once again there is also a similar effect from photoinhibition (but to a lesser degree). The loss of variable fluorescence after UV irradiation has previously been observed in chloroplasts and leaves of higher plants[3,11] and indicates a lesion in photosystem II. Our results are consistent with those of Renger et al.[3] indicating a lesion on the oxidizing side of P680, possibly at Y. This would explain the inhibition of variable fluorescence, since Q would not become reduced. However such an explanation is not consistent with the inhibition of variable fluorescence during photoinhibition. The primary effect of photoinhibition is generally thought to be a lesion after P680 (between phaeophytin and Q_B). Thus the loss of variable fluorescence may be due to some other effect, such as quenching by P680+.

The present results show that all marine plants, which may broadly be classified as shade plants[12], are sensitive to UV irradiation. The most sensitive organisms were found to be phytoplanktonic microalgae. Significantly it is the phytoplankton which may be most at risk should a significant ozone depletion event occur over the productive waters of the the Southern Ocean.

ACKNPWLEDGEMENTS

We wish to thank R.G. Hiller for the supply of phytoplanktonic algae. This work was supported by a grant from the Australian Research Council

REFERENCES.
1. Caldwell, M.M. (1981) Plant response to solar ultraviolet radiation In "Encyclopedia of Plant Physiology" NS 12A (Eds. O.L.Lange). Springer Verlag, Berlin.
2. Worrest, R.C. and Caldwell, M.M. (Eds.) (1986) Stratospheric Ozone Reduction, Solar Ultraviolet Radiation and Plant Life. Springer Verlag, Berlin.374 pp.
3. Renger,G., Volker,M., Eckert, H.J., Fromme, R. Homm-Veit, S. & Graber, P. 1989. Photochem. Photobiol. 49, 97-105
4. Wood, W.F. 1987. Mar. Biol. 96, 143-150
5. Wood, W.F. 1989a. Aquatic Biol. 33, 41-51
6. Carreto, J.I. et al. 1989. Biological Environmental Science & Toxicology, (Eds. Okaichi, Anderson &Nemoto) pp. 333-336, Elsevier, Amsterdam
7. Chrystal, J. and Larkum, A.W.D. 1988. Biochim. Biophys. Acta 932, 189-194
9. Lorentzen, C.J. 1979. Limnol. Oceanogr. 24, 1117-1120
10. Wood, W.F. 1989b. Trans, Menzies Foundation (Melbourne) 15, in press;
11. Björn, L.O., Bornman, J.F. and Olsson, E. (1986) Stratospheric Ozone Reduction, Solar Ultraviolet Radiation and Plant Life. R.C.Worrest and M.M.Caldwell (eds.), pp185-197, Springer Verlag, Berlin.374 pp.
12. Bowes, G. (1985) In: W.J.Lucas and J.A. Berry (eds), Inorganic Carbon Uptake by Aquatic Photosynthetic Organisms. pp.187-210, American Society of Plant Physiologists, Rockville, Md

AMBIGUOUS ROLE OF OXYGEN IN THE PHOTOINACTIVATION OF PSII PARTICLES.

J. Masojídek[x], L.Nedbal, J.Komenda, O.Prášil and I.Šetlík
Inst.Microbiology, 379 81 Třeboň, Czechoslovakia
[x]present address: King's College, London W8 7AH, England

1. INTRODUCTION

The PSII photoinactivation <u>in vitro</u> can be accelerated by anaerobic conditions (1-5). The protecting role of oxygen is probably due to its capacity to accept electrons delivered by PSII. On the other hand, the active species created by the oxygen reduction are probably responsible for the second, antagonistic role of oxygen in PSII photoinactivation that is expressed when the aerobic photoinactivation is slowed down by lowering the partial pressure of oxygen or by adding scavengers of oxygen radicals (3,6).

In this paper, we show that the PSII photoinactivation is a complex sequence of events with different sensitivity to protecting and damaging roles of oxygen.

2. MATERIALS AND METHODS

Oxygen evolving PSII particles were isolated from pea chloroplasts and resuspended to final chlorophyll concentration 15 μg/ml in the medium of the following composition: 300 mM sucrose, 35 mM NaCl, 5 mM $MgCl_2$ and 50 mM MES (pH 6.5). Four sets of conditions were applied during photoinactivation treatment: (1) O-conditions with medium saturated with air; (2) LO-conditions with medium flushed with argon; (3) A-conditions with medium flushed with argon and with last traces of oxygen scavenged by the glucose/glucose-oxidase treatment; (4) R-conditions with added dithionite which removed oxygen and reduced the medium redox potential below -300 mV. The particles were exposed to 100 W/m^2 white light at 20°C for up to 10 hours. The electron transport through PSII was assessed by DCPIP photoreduction. The Fo and Fv components of Chla-fluorescence were measured using laboratory-build phosphoroscoppe. The pheophytin photoreduction was determined in samples with added dithionite as light induced change in absorption at 685 nm. The spectrum of the change was identical with the reduced-oxidized difference spectrum of pheophytin. The electrophoretic analysis of pigment-proteins was performed after solubilization of particles by n-octyl-glucoside. The D1-polypeptide was detected by Western blotting.

M. Baltscheffsky (ed.), Current Research in Photosynthesis, Vol. II, 389–392.
© 1990 *Kluwer Academic Publishers. Printed in the Netherlands.*

3. RESULTS AND DISCUSSION

The decay processes occuring during photoinactivation of PSII
particles (Fig.1) can be associated according to their halftimes into
three groups: (1) the fast photoinactivation including the rapid
reduction of Hill reaction activity (HRA) and antiparallel rise of Fo;
(2) the slow photoinactivation reflected in this figure by decline of
Fm and (3) the very slow photoinactivation of the pheophytin
photoreduction (Pheo). These processes affect the prostetic groups of
the PSII reaction center while substantial destruction of its proteins
occurs during first 10 hours of light treatment only under
O-conditions.

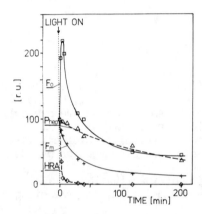

FIGURE 1. The changes in fluorescence (Fo,Fm), in Hill reaction
activity (HRA) and in pheophytin
photoreduction (Pheo) during
photoinactivation under
R-conditions.

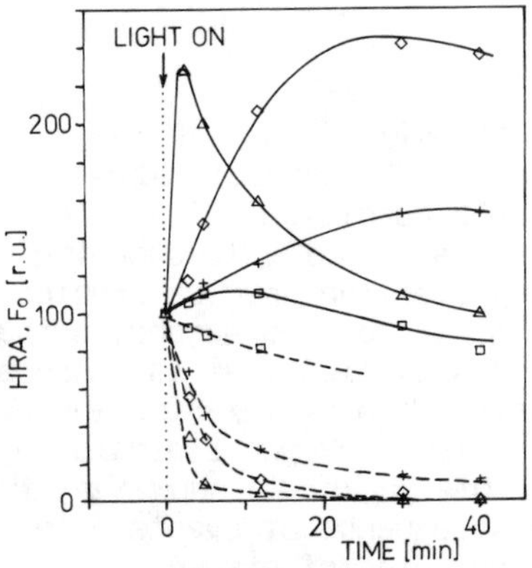

FIGURE 2. Fast photoinactivation of
HRA (dashed line) accompanied with
rise of Fo (full line) under LO-(+)
A-(◊) and R-conditions (△). The
fast photoinactivation does
not occur under O-conditions (□).

The extent and the rate of the Fo rise during <u>fast
photoinactivation</u> are maximal under R-conditions and are declining with
increasing oxygen concentration from A- to LO- and O-conditions
(Fig.2). Similar relation holds for the rate of the decline of Hill
reaction activity. The oxygen protects against the fast
photoinactivation by accepting electrons from PSII and it can be
replaced in this role by ferricyanide (6). Under R-conditions, the lack
of electron acceptors is combined with electron donation from
dithionite which further accelerates the process. We have suggested (6)
that during the fast photoinactivation an anomalous stable state
$(Q_A^-)_{STAB}$ is created which keeps the reaction centers closed and highly
fluorescent.

The decline of Hill reaction activity under O-conditions (Fig.3)
is much slower than that observed in anaerobiosis during fast
photoinactivation (Fig.2). It is called <u>slow photoinactivation</u>, here,

and it is characteristic by decline of Fm. Since the Fm decline is observed also under R-,A- and LO-conditions (Fig.3), it is likely that the process which results in slow photoinactivation under O-conditions occurs also in absence of oxygen. We have tentatively suggested (6) that it is due to formation of neutral non-functional state labeled arbitrarily $(Q_AH)_{STAB}$. In this state, the electron transfer in Hill reaction is inhibited and the fluorescence emission is low as if the reaction centers were opened. The rate of the slow photoinactivation declines with lowering of oxygen concentration and increases again when the anaerobiosis is combined with electron donation from dithionite under R-conditions. It is likely that the difference between the rates under O- (□) and A-conditions (◊) is rather due to an effect of oxygen radicals (3,6) instead of direct effect of oxygen on the slow photoinactivation. Mechanism of the acceleration caused by dithionite is not clear.

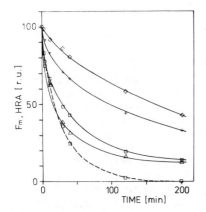

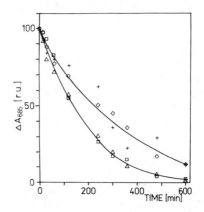

FIGURE 3. Slow photoinactivation of HRA (dashed line-□) accompanied with decline of Fm (full line-□) under O-conditions. The decline of Fm under LO- (+), A- (◊) and R-conditions (△) is also shown.

FIGURE 4. Very slow photoinactivation of pheophytin photoreduction under O- (□), LO- (+), A- (◊) and R-conditions (△).

Very slow photoinactivation of the light induced photoreduction of pheophytin measured in presence of dithionite (Fig.4) is much slower than the loss of the Hill reaction activity. It indicates that neither fast nor slow photoinactivation result in a complete disruption of the reaction centers. More likely their mechanisms are based on modifications concerning Q_A, as suggested above, because they preserve the primary donor and acceptor intact making the pheophytin photoreduction possible. The very slow photoinactivation, similarly to the slow process, can be slowed down by removing oxygen and accelerated again by electron donation from dithionite (cf.Fig.4).

Very slow changes occur also in the structure of particles photoinactivated under O-conditions. During 8 hours of light exposure, the chlorophyll absorption declines to about 25% of its initial value while the ratio Chla/Chlb decreases from 1.9 to 1.4. Also the emission spectra change significantly (7). Comparison of the pigment-protein pattern of active particles (Fig5a) and particles irradiated for two (Fig.5b) or six hours (Fig.5c) under O-conditions shows extensive degradation. Corresponding changes during light treatment under R-conditions (Fig.5a,d,e) as well as under A-conditions (not shown) are negligible.

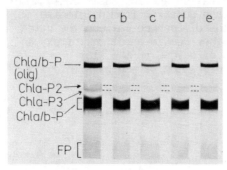 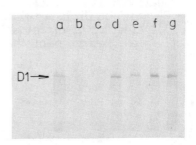

FIGURE 5. Changes in pigment-protein composition under O-(b,c) and R-conditions (d,e). Time of irradiance: a -dark control; b,d - 2 hours; c,e, - 6 hours.

FIGURE 6. Changes in the amount of Dl-protein under O-(b,c) R-(d,e) and A-conditions (f,g). Time of irradiance: a - dark control; b,d,f - 2 hours; c,e,g - 6 hours.

It was suggested (reviewed in 8) that a dominant role in PSII photoinactivation is played by Dl-protein. Its amount detected by Western blotting really declines during light treatment under O-conditions (Fig.6). In contrast to that there are only negligible variations in the amount of the protein under R- and A-conditions. Thus, the Dl-protein degradation is a secondary process occuring only under O-conditions.

REFERENCES
1. Trebst, A. (1962) Z. Naturforsch. 17b, 660-663
2. Krause, G.H., Köster, S. and Wong, S.C. (1985) Planta 165, 430-438
3. Barényi, B. and Krause, G.H. (1985) Planta 163, 218-226
4. Krause, G.H. and Laasch, H. (1987) in Progress in Photosynth.Research (Biggins, J.ed.) Vol. 4, pp. 19-26, Martinus Nijhoff, Dordrecht
5. Krause, G.H. and Cornic, G. (1987) in Photoinhibition (Kyle, D.J., Osmond, C.B., Arntzen, C.J. eds.), pp. 169-196
6. Šetlík, I., Allakhverdiev, S.I., Nedbal,L., Šetlíková, E., and Klimov, V.V. (1989) Photosynth. Res., in press
7. Nedbal, L., Masojídek, J., Komenda, J. Prášil, O. and Šetlík, I., submitted to Photosynth. Res.
8. Kyle, D.J. (1985) Photochem. Photobiol. 41, 107-116

PHOTOINACTIVATION OF PHOTOSYNTHETIC ELECTRON TRANSPORT UNDER ANAEROBIC AND AEROBIC CONDITIONS IN ISOLATED THYLAKOIDS OF SPINACH

REKHA CHATURVEDI, M. SINGH AND P. V. SANE
BIOCHEMISTRY AND PLANT PHYSIOLOGY LABORATORY,
NATIONAL BOTANICAL RESEARCH INSTITUTE, LUCKNOW 226001, INDIA

INTRODUCTION

The photosynthetic organisms and isolated chloroplasts are susceptible to photoinactivation of photosynthesis on exposure to high light intensities (1, 2, 3). The damage due to photoinactivation appears to be located mainly on PS II (1). The Q_B or D_1 protein which is also considered to comprise the reaction center of PS II (4) is implicated in photoinactivation. The inhibition of electron flow on oxidising side of PS II accelerates the photoinhibitory damage (5). Inactivation LHC II kinase, during photoinactivation reflects an inhibitory effect on state 1 and 2 transitions (6). Presence of Oxygen promotes photoinactivation (7), however, anaerobic conditions promote photodamage (8, 10).

The role of oxygen products in photodamage is unclear. There is also no agreement on the sites of photoinactivation in the presence or absence of oxygen. In order to investigate these points, photoinactivation of uncoupled chloroplasts under various conditions was studied.

MATERIALS AND METHODS

The broken chloroplasts were prepared from market spinach according to the method of Kuwabara and Murata (11). Photosynthetic electron transport reactions were monitored polarographically or spectrophotometrically with the appropriate artificial electron acceptor-donor systems at 30°C and pH 7.0. The photoinhibitory treatments to the chloroplast suspension (150 ug.ml^{-1}), were performed in the temperature regulated chamber of the oxygen electrode, at a PFD of 2500 umol m^{-2}s^{-1}. For the aerobic conditions, pre air bubbled suspension buffer was taken while anaerobic conditions were created with use of glucose/glucose oxidase system in the suspension buffer prebubbled with nitrogen. The chloride free thylakoids were prepared in absence of chloride salts. Trypsinization of thylakoids was done according to Arntz and Trebst (12). The inhibitor DCMU after the treatment, was removed by 10 min. The membranes after the photoinhibitory treatments were centrifuged and resuspended. The chlorophyll concentration was estimated according to Arnon (13).

RESULTS AND DISCUSSION

Fig. 1 shows that photoinactivation of whole chain electron transport increases with the increase in PFD (Photo fluence density) and time of incubation. The photoinactivation of PS II was greater under anaerobic conditions and reached 100% in 20 min at an intensity of 2500 umol m^{-2}s^{-1} (Fig. 2).

M. Baltscheffsky (ed.), Current Research in Photosynthesis, Vol. II, 393–396.
© 1990 Kluwer Academic Publishers. Printed in the Netherlands.

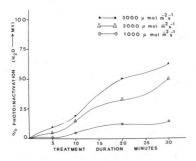

Fig. 1. The time course of photoinactivation of whole chain electron transport $(H_2O -- MV)$ on preillumination.

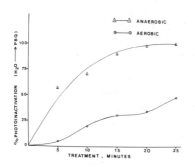

Fig. 2. Time course of photoinactivation of PS II activity $(H_2O -- PBQ)$ on preillumination with white light (25000 umol $m^{-2}s^{-1}$) under aerobic and anaerobic conditions.

Under aerobic conditions this damage was only 40% in 20 min. Apparently presence of oxygen provides proreaction against photodamage. A study of different electron transport reactions following exposure of chloroplasts for 10 min at 2500 u mol $m^{-2}s^{-1}$, showed that absence of oxygen increased photodamage (Fig. 3). The least affected activity was reduced by about 20% whereas under aerobic conditions there was little, if any, inhibition. PS I has been reported to be photoinhibited in isolated intact chloroplasts under anaerobic conditions by Satoh and Fork (9, 10). This was shown to be due to photodestruction of its reaction centre. Under aerobic conditions, inhibition of PS I has been reported (8, 14). In general, PS I is considered to be insensitive to many adverse/stress conditions.

The susceptibility of PS II to photodamage particularly under anaerobic conditions, is brought by the data in Fig. 3. Those reactions that involve water oxidation, i.e., H_2O to MV, H_2O PBQ and H_2O DCPIP were strongly affected under anaerobic conditions. As against this DPC -- MV, which does not require water oxidation was relatively less affected. A comparison of H_2O -- MV and DPC -- MV, clearly brings out that one of the sites of photoinactivation is water oxidation whereas the other sites could be either the reaction centre itself or Q_B. Inactivation of PS II, involving all the three sites mentioned above has been reported (3, 15). The data in Fig. 3 also suggests that the mechanism of photoinactivation under aerobic and anaerobic conditions is different. The oxygen protection against photoinactivation may be due to its ability to accept electrons.

The role of Q_B protein in photoactivation was investigated using trypsinized membranes and 1 uM DCMU. In the absence of DCMU the whole chain electron transport as also PS II was equally affected in trypsinized chloroplasts. 1 uM DCMU protected PS II and whole chain activities from photoinactivation only in the trypsinized membranes. As DCMU binds with Q_B protein and trypsin selectively degraded this protein, DCMU protection against photoinactivation to Q_B could not be seen, as DCMU had little or no Q_B to bind with. The DCMU protection against photoinactivation could be interpreted

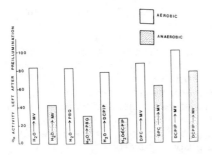 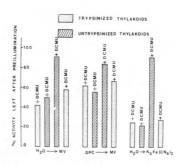

Fig. 3. Photoinactivation of various electron transport reactions on preillumination for   0 min with strong white light (2500 umol m^{-2}s^{-1}) under
aerobic and anaerobic conditions.

Fig. 4. The effect of trypsinization (2 min) on photoinactivation of the partial
electron transport reactions, on preillumination for 10 min with strong
white light under anaerobic conditions in   absence   or absence of
1 uM DCMU.

Table 1. The photoinactivation (PI) of the partial electron flow activities on
preillumination for 10 min of (a) Cl$^-$ sufficient thylakoids at 40°C,
(b) chloride free and chloride added thylakoids, and, (c) Tris, pH 8.0
incubated thylakoids at 25°C.

Temperature and duration of treatment	H$_2$O--PBQ	PI %	H$_2$O--MV	PI %	DPC--MV	PI %	DCPIP	PI %
(a) 40°C, 10 min	D 140±9	59	103±11	48	110±7	30	350±15	15
	L 57±7		54±7		74±8		297±12	
(b) Cl free	D 71±5	52	80±6	50	105±5	12	277±12	12
25°C, 10 min	L 34±4		40±5		92±7		244±10	
50 mM Cl added	D 116±9	14	115±10	20	118±11	18	285±15	Zero
25°C, 10 min	L 99±7		92±8		97±8		285±15	
(c) Tris, pH 8.0 incubated	D 20±5	100	27±6	37	106±8	55	330±10	Zero
25°C, 10 min	L 0		17±5		48±7		330±12	

PI= photoinactivation; D= dark treated;   L= light treated

in terms of stability of S$_2$ state which is the only state generated in DCMU
treated chloroplasts. The inability of DCMU in trypsin treated chloroplasts
can be easily interpreted on this basis.

Table 1 shows the preincubation at 40°C in light inactivates water oxidation to the extent of 50 to 60%. The situation is more or less similar in Cl^{-1}

free chloroplasts. This DPC--MV reaction is much less inhibited, it is suggested that the primary site of photoinactivation under the conditions used must be water oxidation complex. An interesting result seen in Table 1 is that Tris treated chloroplasts show considerable photoinactivation of DPC--MV reaction. Since PS I is unaffected, it is apparent that Tris treatment renders PS II photoinactivation sites even more susceptible.

Following conclusions are drawn from the present study:

1) Photoinactivation of isolated chloroplast activities is more pronounced under anaerobic treatment.
2) The PS II electron flow is the susceptible activity and the inactivation could occur at the water oxidation, reaction centre or Q_B site.
3) DCMU protection against photoinactivation may be due to the stability of S_2 state against damage.
4. Oxygen, despite its toxic effects, offers protection against photo-inactivation.

REFERENCES

1. Powles, S.B. (1984) Ann. Rev. Plant Physiol., 35, 15-44.
2. Cornic, G. and Miginiac-Maslow, M. (1985) Plant Physiol., 78, 724-727.
3. Barneyi, B. and Kranse, G.H. (1985) Planta, 163, 218-226.
4. Trebst, A. and Depka, B. (1985) in Current Physics Series (Michel-Beycerle, M.E., ed.), pp 215-223, Springer-Heidelberg.
5. Cleland, R. and Melis, A. (1987) Plant Cell and Environ., 10, 747-752.
6. Canani, O., Schuster, G. and Ohad, I. (1989) Photosynthesis Res, 20, 129-146.
7. Krause, G.H., Kirk, M., Heber, U. and Osmond, C.B. (1978) Planta, 142, 229-233.
8. Powles, S.B. and Bjorkman, O. (1982) Planta, 156, 97-107.
9. Satoh, K. and Fork, D.C. (1982a) Plant Physiol., 70, 1000-1008.
10. Satoh, K. and Fork, D.C. (1982b) Photobiochem. Photobiophys, 4, 153-163.
11. Kuwabara, T. and Murata, N. (1982) Plant Cell Physiol., 23, 533-539.
12. Arntz, C. and Trebst, A. (1986) FEBS LETT, 194, 43-49.
13. Arnon, D.I. (1949) Plant Physiol., 24, 1-15.
14. Satoh, K. (1970) Plant and Cell Physiol., 11, 15-27.
15. Critchley, C. (1981) in Photosynthesis VI: Photosynthesis and productivity and Environment (Akoyunoglou, G, ed.) pp 297-305, Balaban International Science Services, Philadelphia.

PHOTOINHIBITION OF PHOTOSYNTHESIS AND TURNOVER OF THE 32 KD CHLOROPLAST
PROTEIN IN VARIOUS ATMOSPHERES

HUASHI GONG AND STEIN NILSEN, DEPARTMENT OF BIOLOGY, THE PHYTOTRON,
UNIVERSITY OF OSLO, P.O. BOX 1066 BLINDERN, 0316 OSLO 3, NORWAY

INTRODUCTION
    Photoinhibition of photosynthesis is strongly affected by environ-
mental factors such as atmospheric CO_2 and O_2 (1) and is greatly
increased in a CO_2- and O_2-free atmosphere (1,2). The increased
photoinhibition was interpreted as the result of damage to PSII (2)
under conditions where the terminal electron acceptors were lacking,
rendering the photosynthetic membrane susceptible to photodamage (3).
    During photoinhibition, the 32 kD protein of the Q_B acceptor in
PSII is primarily damaged by high irradiation and a high rate of
turnover of this protein occurs (4,5). The proposed mechanisms for
damage to the 32 kD protein are by the quinone anion radical ($Q_B^-\cdot$)
generated by high light or by the oxygen radical generated by the
interaction of molecular oxygen with quinone anion (6).
    The purpose of this study is to clarify: effect of O_2 interacted
with CO_2 on photoinhibition; relationship between the increased
photoinhibition reported in a CO_2- and O_2-free atmosphere and damage to
the 32 kD protein; role of oxygen on the damage to the 32 kD protein.

MATERIALS AND METHODS
    Axenic cultures of Lemna gibba L, G_3 were cultivated for the
experiments (7,8).
    Photosynthetic measurements were carried out at 20°C in a closed
gas exchange system (2). Photoinhibition was calculated as the difference in net CO_2 uptake before and after photoinhibition.
    Pulse-chase experiments were performed in the gas exchange cuvette.
During pulse period, 20 plants were incubated in 4 ml cultivating
medium containing 143 µCi (^{35}S)methionine (>1000 Ci/mmol, Amersham)
under a PFD of 250 µmol m^{-2} s^{-1} at 20°C for 20 min. At the end of the
pulse, 10 plants were removed for thylakoid preparation. The other 10
plants were rinsed and incubated for 60 min in 6 ml cultivating medium
containing 1 mmol methionine. Two different light intensities and
various atmospheres were used during the chasing period.
    Thylakoid membrane extracts were prepared after the pulse or chase
(8,9).
    LDS electrophoretic separation of the membrane polypeptides,
autoradiography, and densitometric analysis were performed as previously reported (8).

RESULTS
    When intact plants were photoinhibited for 90 min, photoinhibition
of photosynthesis was much higher in N_2 than in air and increased

M. Baltscheffsky (ed.), Current Research in Photosynthesis, Vol. II, 397–400.

linearly with increasing PFDs in air and up to 1750 μmol m^{-2} s^{-1} in N$_2$ (Fig.1). Under high PFDs, degree of photoinhibition was higher in the atmospheres lacking CO$_2$ than those containing CO$_2$ (Table 1). O$_2$ decreased the degree of photoinhibition when CO$_2$ is absent but not when CO$_2$ is present in the atmospheres. Under a PFD of 2800 μmol m^{-2} s^{-1} in presence of CO$_2$, O$_2$ increased the degree of photoinhibition. Visible injure on surface of the fronds from 16% of the photoinhibited (2800 μmol m^{-2} s^{-1} in air) plants was observed (Figure not shown), indicating a degree of photooxyditive damage.

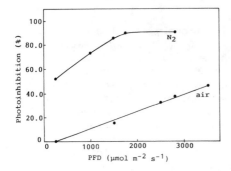

Fig.1. Effect of PFD on photoin-hibition of photosynthesis. Photosynthetic measurement was carried out at a PFD of 250 μmol m^{-2} s^{-1} in air before and after a 90 min photoinhibitory treatment. Each point was the mean of 3-7 replicates.

Table 1. Photoinhibition of photosynthesis at various PFDs and atmospheres. Photosynthetic measurement was carried out at the same condition as Fig.1. Each value is the mean ± SD of: 1) 3 replicates; 2) 5-7 replicates. T test showed a highly significant difference (P<0.01) between 2c and 2d, but no significant difference between 2a and 2b.

PFD (μmol m^{-2} s^{-1}), atmosphere	Photoinhibition (%) ± SD
250, air	1) 0
250, air minus O$_2$	1) 0
1500, air	2a) 15.4 ± 7.6
1500, air minus O$_2$	2b) 16.1 ± 5.2
1500, N$_2$	1) 85.9 ± 0.6
1500, air minus CO$_2$	1) 47.3 ± 1.7
2800, air	2c) 37.4 ± 2.9
2800, air minus O$_2$	2d) 27.6 ± 2.2
2800, N$_2$	1) 90.7 ± 2.1
2800, air minus CO$_2$	1) 74.7 ± 2.5

Intact plants were pulse-labeled with (^{35}S)methionine, and then the synthesized chloroplast proteins were chased during photoinhibitory treatments at various combinations of PFDs and atmospheres. Fig.2 and 3 showed that degradation of 32 kD protein was light-dependent both in the presence and absence of O$_2$, but more light-dependent in the presence of O$_2$. At PFD of 1500 μmol m^{-2} s^{-1}, the presence of O$_2$ increased degradation of the 32 kD protein, regardless of whether CO$_2$ was present in the atmosphere, but had little influence on degradation of other chloroplast proteins (Fig.2). In N$_2$, comparatively low

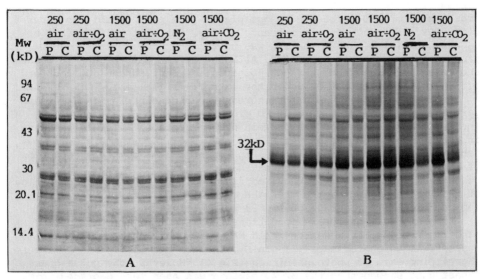

Fig.2. Electropherogram (A) and autoradiograph (B) of thylakoid membrane proteins. For the (^{35}S)methionine-labeled samples, intact plants were pulse-labeled for 20 min in PFD of 250 μmol m^{-2} s^{-1} in air (P), then the radioactivity was chased (C) under a PFD of 250 μmol m^{-2} s^{-1} in air or air minus O_2, or PFD of 1500 μmol m^{-2} s^{-1} in air, air minus O_2, N_2, or air minus CO_2.

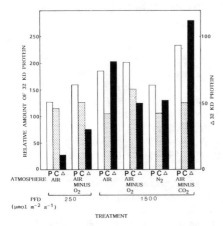

Fig.3. Relative amount of 32 kD protein calculated from densitometric scanning graph of Fig.2B. P=relative amount of 32 kD protein after pulse; C=amount after chase under various photoinhibitory conditions; Δ=degradation of 32 kD protein during photoinhibition=P-C

degradation of the 32 kD protein occurred, although from table 1, the highest degree of photoinhibition was observed.

DISCUSSION

O_2 has two opposing effects on photoinhibition. It can reduce the photoinhibition by photorespiration through which the excess energy is partly dissipated (10); it can also increase the photoinhibition as a toxic element which damages the photosynthetic apparatus (1). In a CO_2-

free atmosphere, O_2 protected <u>Lemna</u> plants from photoinhibition under high PFDs (Table 1). In the presence of CO_2, the protective effect of O_2 was not visible. When the PFD was up to 2800 µmol m^{-2} s^{-1}, O_2 damaged photosynthetic apparatus. Although O_2 can help plants to reduce the damage of high light through photorespiration, it can not counteract the toxic effect of O_2 under the extremly high light.

Another possible reason for increased photoinhibition in O_2 under very high light is that more 32 kD protein is damaged, although increased degradation of the protein did not cause a visible increase in inhibition of CO_2 uptake at PFD of 1500 µmol m^{-2} s^{-1} (Fig.2, 3 and table 1). During photoinhibition, high light causes complete reduction of the plastoquinone pool which may damage the 32 kD protein (4,5). Our results showed that O_2 was required for the light-dependent degradation of this protein, indicating that the oxygen radical was involved during the photoinhibitory damage of the 32 kD protein.

As proposed, any stress conditions leading to restriction of the electronic transport acceptor would make the photosynthetic membrane susceptible to photodamage (3). In N_2, the absence of CO_2 and O_2 led to a great increase of photoinhibition (Fig.1). However, the pulse-chase experiments showed that the 32 kD protein was even less degraded in N_2 than in air (Fig.2 and 3). This indicated a different mechanism of photoinhibition in the absence of CO_2 and O_2, supported by earlier experiments showing the same degree of photoinhibition in N_2 as in air (at low temperature) but sharply different recovery patterns (8). The N_2 increased photoinhibition may be caused by some additional effects, such as inhibition of the light regulated enzymes (e.g. Rubisco) (1) or impairment of PSI under extremely reducing conditions (11), as well as the damage of PSII.

REFERENCES
1 Krause, G.H. and Cornic, G. (1987) in Topics in Photosynthesis (Barber, J. ed.), Vol.9, pp.169-196, Elsevier, Amsterdam
2 Nilsen, S. and Dannielsen, S. (1984) J. Plant Physiol. 115, 39-48
3 Kyle, D.J. (1987) in Topics in Photosynthesis (Barber, J. ed.), Vol.9, pp.197-226, elsevier, Amsterdam
4 Kyle, D.J., Ohad, I. and Arntzen, C.J. (1984) Proc. Natl. Acad. Sci.
5 Ohad, I., Kyle, D.J. and Arntzen, C.J. (1984) J. Cell Biol. 99, 481-485   U.S.A. 81,4070-4074
6 Kyle, D.J. and Ohad, I. (1986) in Encyclopedia of Plant Physiology, New Series (Pirson, A. and Zimmermann, M.H. ed.), Vol.19, pp.468-475, Springer-verlag, Berlin
7 Chaturvedi, R., Haugstad, M.K. and Nilsen, S. (1982) Physiol. Plant. 56, 23-27
8 Gong, H. and Nilsen, S. (1989) J. Plant Physiol. (in press)
9 Mills, W.R. and Joy, K.W. (1980) Planta 148,75-83
10 Powles, S.B. and Osmond, C.B. (1978) Aust.J. Plant Physiol. 5,619-629
11 Inoue, K., Fujii, T., Yokoyama, E. Matsuura, K., Hiyama, T. and Sakurai, H. (1989) Plant Cell Physiol. 30, 65-71

PHOTOINHIBITION IN CYANOBACTERIA: SENSITIVITY TO CALCIUM OR SODIUM

JERRY J. BRAND[1], JINDONG ZHAO[1], GABRIELE WÜNSCHMANN[1]
AND JOHN H. GOLBECK[2]
[1]Dept. of botany, Univ. of Texas, Austin, TX 7713 USA; and
[2]Dept. of Chemistry, Portland State University, Portland, OR 97207 USA

1. INTRODUCTION

Cyanobacterial cultures soon cease growing when placed under otherwise normal growth conditions, except in medium devoid of Ca^{2+} and Na^+. The nature of the ion requirement has been studied in *Synechococcus* 6301 and related strains, which resume growth within a few h when either a Ca^{2+} or a Na^+ salt is added to the deficient medium [1]. Inhibition of growth correlated with inactivation of photosynthesis, and the site of inhibition was at or near Reaction Center II (RCII) [2,3]. Inhibition of RCII required illumination in the ion-deficient medium and the rate of inactivation increased with increasing photon flux density, indicating a kind of high quantum yield photoinhibition, sensitisitized at low light intensity under Ca^{2+} and Na^+ stress. Those observations did not prove a site of ion function since the photoinhibition could have been a secondary event sensitized by ion stress, but did indicate that Na^+ and Ca^{2+} might be interchangeable in some required cyanobacterial function. Apparently all cyanobacteria demonstrate the ion requirement, although some are specific for Ca^{2+} while others can utilize Na^+ as well [4]. *Synechocystis* 6714 was unique among the cyanobacteria examined in that only Na^+ satisfied the ion requirement. Sequential inhibitory events could be resolved in *Synechocystis* during the low-light-intensity photoinhibition [5]. Initially O_2-evolution was inactivated; continued illumination resulted in inhibition of RCII. The addition of millimolar Na^+ to the culture medium of cells in the early state of impaired O_2 evolution fully restored photosynthetic electron transport activity within 10 min. In contrast, the addition of Na^+ to cultures at the secondary state of inhibition (with impaired RCII activity) restored electron transport activity only slowly, in a process which required new protein synthesis [6].

2. MATERIALS AND METHODS

Liquid cultures of *Synechocystis* PCC 6714 and *Synechococcus* PCC 6301 were maintained under log growth in continuous culture turbidostats, then transferred at a chlorophyll (Chl) concentration of 5 µg/ml to glass test tubes of 25 mm diameter in standard growth medium for experimental treatments (details in [2]). Cells were photoinhibited by illumination at a photon flux density of 1220 $\mu E \cdot m^{-2} \cdot s^{-1}$ at the cell surface. For Ca^{2+} or Na^+ depletion experiments the cells were suspended in otherwise

M. Baltscheffsky (ed.), Current Research in Photosynthesis, Vol. II, 401–404.
© 1990 *Kluwer Academic Publishers. Printed in the Netherlands.*

normal medium except without the respective ion (residual Na^+ and Ca^{2+} concentrations were $<10^{-7}$ M), then illuminated under normal growth light. Photosynthetic O_2 evolution was measured with a Clark-type electrode [6]. The dark rate of O_2 uptake prior to illumination was subtracted from each measured rate of O_2 evolution. Red (narrow-band 682 nm), or yellow (Corning CS 3-70) measuring light was used.

Fluorescence induction kinetics were measured at room temperature following 5 min of dark adaptation [6]. Orange or blue-green excitation illumination was provided by passing the light through a 620 nm interference filter at a light intensity of 80 $\mu E \cdot m^{-2} \cdot s^{-1}$, or through a Corning CS 4-96 filter at 100 $\mu E \cdot m^{-2} \cdot s^{-1}$, respectively. Fluorescence emission was measured at the excitation surface at 180° with respect to the direction of excitation. Emission at 688 nm was detected with a Hamamatsu R-928 photomultiplier, processed with a Hamamatsu 1240 photon counter and recorded either immediately on a recorder or after storage of the digitized signal on a computer.

Flash-induced P_{680} absorption changes were measured at 820 nm with a flash-kinetic spectrometer similar to that described previously [7]. The signal was amplified with a Model 115 preamplifier (EG&G), captured on an 8-bit transient digitizer (Biomation 8100 and Model 4880 IEEE Interface), then stored and averaged. Membrane preparations which retained photosynthetic O_2 evolution activity were diluted to a concentration of 10 μg $Chl \cdot ml^{-1}$ in 3.0 ml of 0.1 M succinate buffer, pH 5.0, and incubated at 55° C for 5 min. The heat treatment, which fully inactivates O_2 evolution in cyanobacterial membranes, also eliminates the 30 ns optical transient, leading to P_{680}^+ re-reduction on a μs timescale. The sample was placed in a rectangular cuvette 10 mm on a side, and potassium ferricyanide was added to a final concentration of 5 mM. The cuvette was maintained at 20° C in the flash kinetic spectrometer. Repetitive actinic flashes were applied with a Phase-R DL-1200 flashlamp-pumped dye laser (50 mJ pulse energy for 400 ns FWHM at 660 nm) or a PTI PL-2300 nitrogen laser (1.4 mJ pulse energy for 800 ps FWHM at 337 nm); there was no difference in the amplitude or kinetics of the P_{680} response to either excitation wavelength. Typically, four sets of 1024 flashes were given at a 1 Hz repetition rate, and the transient absorption change was averaged during each set. The four individual accumulated data sets were examined for changes in the signal before averaging them together; no deterioration of P_{680} photooxidation was detected during the 1 hour required to complete the 4,096 flashes. After completing this measurement, a fresh sample was prepared and treated identically, except that 40 μM tetraphenylboron was added immediately before measurement [8]. This eliminated nearly all of the 820 nm absorption transient by causing reduction of P_{680}^+ within the timescale of the recorded measurement. The transient in the presence of tetraphenylboron was then subtracted from the transient in its absence, and the difference was recorded as the absorption change due to light-induced P_{680}^+ turnover.

3. RESULTS AND DISCUSSION

The quantum yield of photosynthetic O_2 evolution and the variable fluorescence yield decreased exponentially and in parallel when *Synechococcus* cultures were illuminated at high light intensity to afford photoinhibition in complete growth medium. Membranes were prepared from cell cultures at various stages of photoinhibition, and their flash-induced reversible P_{680} photo-oxidation was measured as described in Materials and Methods. In control (non-inhibited) cells most of the 820 nm transient signal decayed as a single exponential with a half-time of approximately 30 μs. The amplitude of the P_{680}^+

transient was diminished in membranes from cells which were photoinhibited, and the decrease was proportional to the decrease in variable fluorescence and in quantum yield of O_2 evolution. We detected no change in the re-reduction kinetics of P_{680}^+ in partially photoinhibited membranes, although the instrumentation would not have detected an absorption transient of < 2 μs. Thus, photoinhibition may result in the loss of charge separation in PSII, although a very fast re-reduction of P_{680}^+, as might occur if I^- or Q_A^- oxidation were inhibited, could not be excluded. *Synechococcus* cells were prepared in medium devoid of Na^+ and Ca^{2+}, then illuminated in normal growth light to inhibit photosynthetic electron transport and variable fluorescence. Membranes isolated from these cells showed diminished amplitude, but not altered kinetics, of the P_{680}^+ transient. By this and any other criterion we examined (loss of variable fluorescence, loss of all PSII partial electron transport activities, destabilization of the membranes to detergent preparations of PSII particles, restoration of photosynthetic competence only after new protein synthesis) the weak light-photoinhibition in ion-deficient medium appeared identical to photoinhibition seen at high light intensity in complete medium.

Synechocystis cells were illuminated at normal growth intensity in medium devoid of Na^+ to afford inhibition of photosynthetic activity. After 1 hour the cells had lost nearly all variable fluorescence and the ability to evolve O_2, although RCII was fully functional. After an additional 5 hours of illumination RCII activity was inhibited as well. Addition of Na^+ to the growth medium fully restored photosynthetic activity in cells at either stage of inhibition, but the nature of the restoration was very different, depending on the stage of inhibition from which restoration was begun. When Na^+ was added after only 1 hour of inhibition time, then the quantum efficiency of photosynthetic electron transport activity, as measured in white light, was fully restored within 10 min, even in darkness or in the presence of protein-synthesis inhibitors. Variable fluorescence was restored in parallel. However, when photosynthetic activity or variable fluorescence were measured in light not absorbed by phycobiliproteins (<450 nm or >685 nm), then the quantum efficiencies of these activities were observed to restore much more slowly, and required new protein synthesis. Photosynthetic O_2 evolution and variable fluorescence were also measured at various wavelengths during the inhibition process. The quantum yields declined at the same rate regardless of the excitation wavelength employed for measurements. These results lead to the conclusion that weak-light photoinhibition of *Synechocystis* in Na^+-deficient medium inactivates O_2 evolution, and at the same time or immediately thereafter disconnects PSII core chlorophyll from RCII. The phycobilisome remains functionally attached to the reaction center. Sodium added to the medium is rapidly taken up by the cells and restores O_2 evolution activity without immediate re-attachment of the chlorophyll-binding proteins. Re-attachment only occurs gradually in a process which requires new protein synthesis, although radiolabelling experiments show that very little new protein in the 40-50 kD range is synthesized during the time of re-association.

When Na^+ is added to the inhibited culture after 5-6 hours of illumination in Na^+-deficient medium to inhibit RCII activity, then variable fluorescence and the quantum yield of photosynthetic electron transport is restored at the same rate, regardless of the excitation wavelength. Restoration is slow and requires new protein synthesis. Thus, restoration from this second stage of inhibition produces active PSII units with fully functional accessory pigments.

The sequence of events which occurs upon illumination in Na^+-deficient medium is illustrated in the model shown below. The rates of both the primary and the secondary processes increase with increasing light intensity, but the rate of the second process (inactivation of RCII) is a steeper function of light intensity. Thus, at high light intensities no intermediate state of inactive O_2 evolution and disconnected core chlorophyll is observed. It may be that this sequence of events (inactivation of O_2 evolution, disconnection of core chlorophyll, then inactivation of RCII) may occur during normal photoinhibition at high photon flux densities, but the intermediate stages would not be seen at these high light intensities.

MODEL SHOWING SEQUENTIAL EVENTS WHICH OCCUR DURING PHOTOINHIBITION AT LOW LIGHT INTENSITY IN Na⁺-DEFICIENT MEDIUM

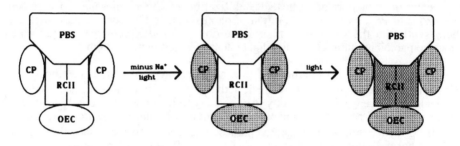

Shown in this model are phycobilisome (PBS), reaction center of PSII (RCII), PSII core chlorophyll-binding proteins (CP), and oxygen-evolving complex (OEC). Darkened structures indicate components in a nonfunctional form.

4. ACKNOWLEDGEMENT

This work was supported by R. A. Welch Grant F-867.

REFERENCES

1 Becker, D.W. and Brand, J.J. (1982) Biochem. Biophys. Res. Commun. 109, 1134-1139
2 Becker, D.W. and Brand, J.J. (1985) Plant Physiol. 79, 552-558
3 Brand, J.J., Mohanty, P. and Fork, D.C. (1983) FEBS Lett. 155: 120-124
4 Brand, J.J. And Becker, D.W. (1988) *in* Methods in Enzymol. Vol. 167 (Packer, L. and Glazer, A.N, eds) pp. 280-285, Academic Press, New York
5 Zhao, J. and Brand, J.J. (1988) Arch. Biochem. Biophys. 264, 657-664
6 Zhao, J. and Brand, J.J. (1989) Plant Physiol. 90, (in press)
7 Golbeck, J.H. and Warden, J.T. (1985) Biochim. Biophys. Acta 806, 116-123
8 Velthuys, B.R. (1981) FEBS Lett. 126, 272-276

STUDIES OF THE MECHANISM FOR PHOTOINHIBITION OF THE ELECTRON TRANSPORT THROUGH PHOTOSYSTEM II.

CAROLINE JEGERSCHÖLD and STENBJÖRN STYRING, Department of Biochemistry, Arrhenius laboratories for Natural Sciences, University of Stockholm, S-10691 Stockholm, Sweden

Introduction

The reaction center of photosystem II (PSII) is composed of two hydrophobic proteins, D1 and D2, which carry the redox components necessary for photochemical charge separation between tyr_Z on the donor side and the secondary quinone acceptor, Q_B. In addition it is likely that also the Mn-cluster involved in the oxidation of water is bound to the D1/D2 heterodimer.

Strong illumination of photosynthetic organisms and preparations inhibits the electron transport through PSII (1). In subsequent reactions the illumination also results in degradation of the reaction center proteins D1 and D2 (2). We have shown (3,4) that strong illumination impairs the function of the primary quinone acceptor Q_A, probably by double reduction. In the inhibited centers the primary charge separation reaction is still operational and it was proposed that this reaction or donor side reactions in perturbed centers lead to the degradation of the reaction center proteins D1 and D2 (3,4). This was corroborated in a study (3) of the photoinhibition in Cl^--depleted thylakoids in which the water oxidation is reversibly inhibited (5). In such thylakoids the light dependant degradation of the D1 protein is ≈ 15 times faster than in intact thylakoids (3). Treatments that decrease the formation of strongly oxidizing species on the donor side of PSII in Cl^--depleted thylakoids protected the D1 protein against photodamage. This supported the hypothesis that donor side reactions are responsible for the degradation of the reaction center proteins (3). The electron transport in Cl^--depleted thylakoids is very sensitive to photoinhibition, possibly due to a block of the electron transfer between tyr_Z and P_{680} (6), and it was suggested that this mechanism was similar to the mechanism for the photoinhibition occurring in vivo.

Here we present the results from experiments carried out in intact or Cl^--depleted thylakoid membranes in order to compare the mechanism for the photoinhibition of the electron transport in such membranes.

Materials and Methods

Cl^- depletion of thylakoids was done by washing the membranes twice in 200mM Hepes-NaOH (pH7.5) and then subjecting them to 200mM Hepes-NaOH (pH 8.0) (2mL/g leaves) with gramicidin (6mg/mL) for 30 min in the dark at 20°C. The procedure resulted in 60-70% Cl^--depletion of the membranes. The depleted membranes were centrifuged and resuspended in 20mM Hepes-NaOH (pH 7.5), 0.2M sucrose and 5mM $MgSO_4$. Photoinhibition was performed at 20°C in 10mM NaP_i (pH 7.4), 100mM sucrose and 5mM either $MgSO_4$ or $MgCl_2$ with the indicated additions. Replenishment with Cl^- was done by the addition of 40mM NaCl for Tris-HCl pH 8.2. Oxygen evolution was measured with 0.5mM PPBQ as

M. Baltscheffsky (ed.), Current Research in Photosynthesis, Vol. II, 405–408.

acceptor (2). Electron transport from diphenyl carbazide (DPC) to 2,6-dichlorophenol-indophenol (DCPIP) was measured at 590-540nm in a spectrophotometer equipped for side-ways illumination. The assay was performed in the photoinhibition buffer in the presence of 40mM NaCl, 35μM DCPIP and 1mM DPC. Photoinhibition was performed using white light filtered through heatfilters and neutral density filters. The D1 protein was quantified by Western blotting (2).

Results and Discussion.
Photoinhibition in thylakoid membranes. The effect of DCMU.

Figure 1 shows the results from an experiment in which thylakoid membranes were illuminated for various times with or without DCMU. In both cases the oxygen evolution was inhibited with similar kinetics. Also the degradation of the D1 protein was similar but approximately 4 times slower than the inhibition of the oxygen evolution (2). This experiment shows that DCMU neither protects the electron transport through PSII nor the D1 protein against photoinhibitory damage when isolated thylakoids are illuminated with strong light. We have shown (3,4) that photoinhibition of the electron transfer probably is due to double reduction of the first quinone acceptor, Q_A. In light of these data it is easy to reconcile the lack of effect of DCMU on the photoinhibition under these circumstances. DCMU binds in the Q_B site and prevents electron transfer to the plastoquinone pool. In the strong light, in the presence of DCMU, Q_A^- dominates in the acceptor complex. However, the charge separation reaction and the water splitting complex are still operational and it is likely that the strong illumination will lead to accumulation of reduced pheophytin which eventually reduces Q_A a second time. The reactions are similar to those proposed to take place during strong illumination in the absence on DCMU (3,4).The the charge separation or donor side reactions which are not affected by the presence of DCMU lead to the degradation of the D1 protein .

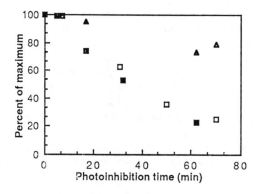

Figure 1. Time course for the photoinhibition of the oxygen evolution (squares) and the degradation of the D1 protein (triangles) in the absence (open symbols) and the presence of 10μM DCMU (closed symbols). Thylakoid membranes were photoinhibited with strong light ($6000\mu E/m^2sec$) for various times. Before the measurements of the oxygen evolution the DCMU was removed by repeated centrifugation and resuspension of the membranes.

Photoinhibition of Cl-depleted thylakoid membranes.

Figure 2 shows the time course for the photoinhibition of Cl-depleted thylakoid
membranes under various conditions. The oxygen evolution was inhibited faster than in
figure 1 although only 30% of the light was used. In fact the Cl-depleted material was
≈20 times more sensitive to photoinhibition than the intact material. Figure 2A shows that
the presence of 2mM ferricyanide during the photoinhibition did not alter the kinetics for
the inhibition of the oxygen evolution.
This suggests that it was not acceptor side modifications that inhibited the electron
transfer since ferricyanide would have kept Q_A oxidized for a prolonged period of time
during the photoinhibition. In intact material however, such protective effects of
ferricyanide against photoinhibition have been observed (7).

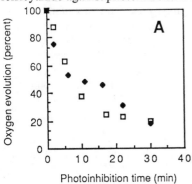 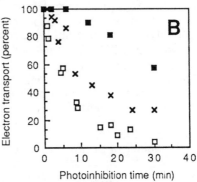

Figure 2. Photoinhibition (1900µE/m^{2}sec) of Cl$^-$-depleted thylakoid membranes (≈60-70% depletion).
A. Inhibition of the oxygen evolution in the presence (diamonds) and absence (squares) of 2mM
ferricyanide during the photoinhibition. **B.** Inhibition of the oxygen evolution (open squares); inhibition
of the electron transport from DPC to DCPIP (crosses); inhibition of the oxygen evolution after
replenishment with Cl$^-$ before the photoinhibition experiment (closed squares).

Figure 2B shows the effect of photoinhibition on different partial reactions. In analogy to
what has been found earlier (5,6) we observe reversibility in the Cl-depletion. When the
depleted thylakoids were replenished with Cl$^-$ the oxygen evolution was 6-8 times more
stable against photoinhibition. In addition the effect of photoinhibition on the oxygen
evolution and the electron transport between tyr$_Z$ and the Q_B-site was compared. In the
experiment the photoinhibited Cl$^-$-depleted thylakoids were assayed either for the oxygen
evolution in the presence of Cl$^-$ or for the electron transport between DPC and DCPIP. In
the latter case the thylakoids were tris-washed before the assay to facilitate the donation
from DPC to tyr$_Z$. It is seen that the electron transfer from DPC to DCPIP was about
three times less sensitive to photoinhibition than the electron transport between water and
PPBQ .

The results in figure 2B suggests that photoinhibition in Cl$^-$-depleted thylakoids is a
sequential event. Initially the illumination inhibits the electron transfer from the Mn-
cluster to tyr$_Z$. This shows up as an inhibition of the oxygen evolution which is not
reversible by the readdition

of Cl^-. The origin of this inhibition is not clear but it is probably due to changes in the Mn-cluster induced by the illumination in the absence of Cl^-. It is known that Cl^--depletion induces conformational changes in the Mn-cluster since lack of Cl^- prevents the formation of the multiline EPR signal originating from the S_2-state (5). The inhibited centers are still capable of electron transfer from tyr_Z to Q_B which shows that the photodamage of the D1 protein has not started at this stage of the photoinhibition. However, the electron transfer from tyr_Z to Q_B is also inhibited by light ($t_{1/2}$ for the inhibition ≈ 15min). It is very interesting that this inhibition occurs approximately three times slower than the inhibition of the oxygen evolution since a similar difference was observed between the inhibition of the oxygen evolution and the degradation of the D1 protein in Cl^--depleted thylakoids (3). This correlation then suggests that the electron transfer between tyr_Z and Q_B is not inhibited until, or possibly just before, the photodamage of the D1 protein occurs. We suggest that the continued illumination results in the accumulation of strongly oxidizing components on the donor side of PSII (tyr_Z^+ and/or P_{680}^+) that are more longlived than normally since no electrons from water are available. When longlived, these species are likely to inhibit the photochemistry and may initiate the degradation of the reaction center proteins by direct cleavage of nearby aminoacids in the D1 or D2 proteins or by oxidation of a protein bound chromophore (8).

Concluding remarks.

The photoinhibition of electron transport in thylakoids (and probably in vivo) is due to acceptor side limitations in PSII. The direct origin for the inhibition is probably the double reduction of Q_A. In Cl^--depleted thylakoids the photoinhibition of the electron transport is a multistep reaction on the donor side of PSII. The primary lesion is between the Mn-cluster and tyr_Z and in a slower reaction the electron transfer between tyr_Z and Q_B is blocked. The degradation of the D1 protein is initiated by donor side reactions or the primary photochemistry in intact and Cl^--depleted thylakoids and we suggest that the degradation is caused by the same reactions in both cases. It is likely that the photodamage of the D1 protein is induced by strongly oxidizing components on the donor side of PSII in situations when these become more longlived than what is normal. In vivo several such cases can be imagined and in our experiments we have applied Cl^--depletion to induce this situation.

This work was supported by the Swedish Natural Science Research Council. S. S. was supported by a long term grant for biotechnological basic research financed by the Knut and Alice Wallenbergs foundation. We thank Ivar Virgin for help with the analysis of the D1 protein.

References.

1. Powles, S.B. (1984) Annu.Rev. Plant Physiol. 35, 15-44
2. Virgin, I., Styring, S. and Andersson, B. (1988) FEBS Lett. 233, 408-412
3. Styring, S., Virgin, I., Jegerschöld, C. and Andersson, B. (1989) these proceedings
4. Styring, S., Virgin, I., Ehrenberg, A. and Andersson, B. (1989) Biochim. Biophys. Acta submitted
5. Ono,T.,Zimmermann,J.L.,Rutherford,A.W., Inoue,Y. (1986) Biochim.Biophys.Acta 851,193-203
6. Theg, S.M., Filar, L.J. and Dilley, R.A. (1986) Biochim. Biophys. Acta 849, 104-111
7. Ohad, I., Kyle, D.J. and Hirschberg, J. (1985) Embo J. 4, 1655-1659
8. Thompson, L.M. and Brudwig, G.W. (1988) Biochemistry 27, 6653-6658

MECHANISM OF THE LIGHT DEPENDENT TURNOVER OF THE D1 PROTEIN

Noam Adir, Susana Shochat, Yorinao Inoue* and Itzhak Ohad,
Department of Biological Chemistry, The Hebrew University of Jerusalem, Jerusalem, Israel and
*Solar Energy Research Group, The Institute of Physical and Chemical Research, (Riken),
Wako-Shi, Saitama, Japan

1. INTRODUCTION

The D1 protein is one of the major components of reaction center II (RCII) and contains within one of its membrane intrinsic loops the binding site of Q_B (1). In light exposed chloroplasts *in vivo*, the protein is specifically and continuously degraded and resynthesized (turnover, (2)). The synthesis of D1 appears to be subject to translation control (3). The rate of D1 turnover is light intensity dependent (4), and it has been proposed that the phenomenon of photoinhibition and its recovery are related to the light induced turnover of D1 (5). Thermoluminescence measurements (6) have indicated that the primary light induced damage to RCII is localized at the level of the D1 protein and affects the redox potential of Q_B^- (7). This phenomenon correlated in time with the light accelerated synthesis of the D1 protein. The D1 protein encoded by the chloroplast psbA gene, is synthesized as a precursor (pD1) by thylakoid bound ribosomes located on the stroma lamellae (8) and appears as a mature protein in grana localized RCII (2). The degradation of D1 can occur in absence of simultaneous pD1 synthesis (9). Experimental results, part of which are presented here, demonstrate that the turnover (7,10) of D1 is a direct result of a light induced conformational change of RCII leading to an irreversible modification of D1 which triggers its degradation. The modified RCII, impaired in its electron flow activity, translocates to the nonappressed stroma domains where it serves as an acceptor for pD1.This shuttle process regulates the synthesis of D1 and accounts for the maintenance of a constant population of functional RCII in light exposed chloroplasts.

2. RESULTS AND DISCUSSION

2.1) Light induced reversible change of RCII

The light induced change in RCII of *Chlamydomonas reinhardtii* cells is detected as a shift in the temperature peak of the thermoluminescence glow curve resulting from $S_{2,3}Q_B^-$ charge recombination, by 20-25 °C (7).This reduction in the activation energy indicates a destabilization of the semiquinone Q_B^-. Light fluency close to or above saturation of photosynthesis is sufficient to induce this change in the entire population of RCII present in the sample within 20-40 min. (7,11). At this stage the process is reversible within 15-20 min. if the cells are transferred to low light intensity (*Fig.1*) and recovery does not require *de novo* chloroplast translation activity (7). The light induced change in RCII is stable in thylakoids isolated from light exposed cells (*Fig. 2*). These results are interpreted as evidence for a light induced, reversible conformational change of RCII affecting the Q_B binding site located within the D1 protein. The lowering of the redox potential of Q_B^- may alow equilibration of the charge with Q_A. Hence the rise in the intrinsic fluorescence observed in cells or thylakoids obtained from cells exposed to high light intensities (7,10). The conformational change of RCII does not alter the primary photochemistry of charge separation as indicated by the extent of p_{680}^+ formation measured by absorbtion changes at 832 nm and $S_{2,3}Q_B^-$ as measured by charge recombination.

M. Baltscheffsky (ed.), Current Research in Photosynthesis, Vol. II, 409–413.
© 1990 *Kluwer Academic Publishers. Printed in the Netherlands.*

The slow phase of p_{680}^+ reduction accounting for about 20% of the total extent shows a $t_{1/2}$ of about 1-3 msec. in RCII from light treated cells as opposed to 300-400 usec in the control cells. The persisting p_{680}^+ could act as a fluorescence quencher (12) and thus explain the lowering of the maximal fluorescence, Fm, observed in photoinhibited cells (7,10). Thus the loss of Fv, (variable fluorescence, (Fm-Fo)/Fo), can be explained by the Q_B^- destabilization and reduction of p_{680}^+. EPR measurements showed only a small reduction in signal II indicating changes in the oxidizing side of RCII which could explain the slower reduction rate of p_{680}^+ by Z, identified as tyrosine 161 of the D1 protein (13).

These changes in RCII account for the partial loss of RCII electron flow (photoinhibition), detected in high light treated cells (7,11). The aformentioned changes in RCII properties correlate with the change in the peak temperature of the glow curve arising from $S_{2.3}Q_B^-$ charge recombination ("B" band, (7)). Unoccupancy of the Q_B site by plastoquinone protects RCII against this light induced change. Such a situation can be generated by addition of DCMU which occupy the site and by DBMIB, (11), or by mutation to a cytochrome b_6/f less condition (14), both promoting accumulation of plastoquinol. Hence electron flow via the Q_B site is involved in this process.

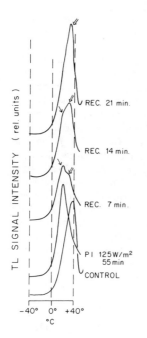

2.2) Light induced irreversible change of D1 protein

The measured changes in RCII properties represent an average of the RCII population present in the tested sample. When the peak temperature of the glow curve is completely shifted to the minimal temperature equivalent to that of the $S_{2.3}Q_B^-$ emission, all the reaction centers have been modified with respect to this parameter. Thus in any given RCII the same alteration of the Q_B binding site has occured. In a similar way, at this stage, the p_{680} can be oxydized

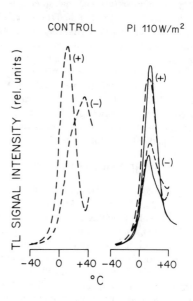

Figure 1. Thermoluminescence measurements showing peak temperature shift of the glow curve obtained from $S_{2.3}Q_B^-$ charge recombination in photoinhibited and recovering cells.
Photoinhibition (PI), was at 125 W.m^{-2} for 55 min; recovery was at 5 W.m^{-2}; single and double arrows, B and "B" emission bands respectively (7)

Figure 2. Persistence of the light induced modification of RCII in thylakoids (broken lines) isolated from light treated cells (continuous line).(-),(+),charge recombination of $S_{2.3}Q_B^-$ and $S_{2.3}Q_A^-$ recorded in absence or presence of DCMU respectively; PI, photoinhibition for 45 min.

and Q_A can be reduced in all RCII much the same way, the rise in F_0 level which almost doubles, reaches a plateau (*Fig.3*). However this is not the case with the changes observed in the rate of p_{680}^+ reduction, formation of the cation radical Z^+ detected by EPR signal II, and the reduction of Fm. Since these changes are not complete while the former ones have reached a plateau, one can conclude that they affect only a fraction of the RCII population. As such they represent a more advanced state of light induced damage to the the RCII which have already been altered with respect to the former properties. The fraction of RCII exhibiting this more advanced state of damage under the experimental conditions used, can be estimated to 10-20% of the total. One should note that both the primary change, related to the Q_B binding site and the secondary one related to Z^+, are both localized within the D1 protein presumably in the transmembrane helices III and V adjacent to the p_{680} binding site shared by both the D1

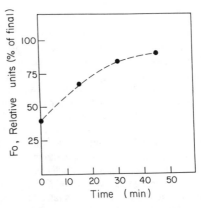

Figure 3. Rise in the Fo level of cells as a function of photoinhibition time. Cells (45 ugchl./ml) were exposed to 150 W.m^{-2} and fluorescence rise kinetics was recorded as in (7).

loop IV and D2 loop IV (1,15). The experimental results so far described indicate a sequential efect on the segments of D1 containing both, the secondary electron donor and acceptor radicals of RCII without damage to the D1 segment binding the ligands involved in the primary charge separation shared by the D2 protein as well (1,15). It is thus possible that occurence of both these alteration may affect specifically the D1 protein in an irreversible way which promotes its removal (degradation) and replacement. The experimental results presented in Fig.4 demonstrate that indeed an ireversible change can be identified in D1 protein isolated from light exposed cells and affecting about 8-10% of the total D1. This change is detected by the presence of a fragment of about 16kDa resistent to exhaustive trypsin digestion of isolated denatured D1 which could have arisen only if an internal cross link had occurred between loops II and III of the D1 protein which otherwise considering the trypsin cleavable sites (1), should generate trypsin fragments considerably shorter. The amount of D1 exhibiting this behaviour increases in the high light treated cells as compared with cells exposed to low, growth light intensities.

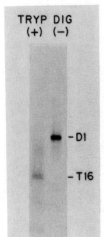

TRYP DIG
(+) (−)

- D1

- T16

2.3) Replacement of irreversibly altered D1

Exposure of cells to light should result in a steady state condition which a certain fraction of the RCII population contains irreversibly altered D1 molecules destined to degradation. The fraction of this population should increase with the light intensity. If this were the case one would expect that the degradation of the damaged D1 will continue irespective of the light intensity. To test this hypothesis cell suspensions were exposed to high or low light and then each suspension was further incubated in the dark, low or high light respectively and the residual amount of D1 was detected by immunoblotting. The results of such an experiment (*Fig.5*), show that indeed more D1 is lost at low light intensity or in the dark, in cells preilluminated with high light, as compared to cells preilluminated at low light intensity. These results are in agreement with previously published data demonstrating persistence of accelerated D1 synthesis in low light, proportional to the light intensity at which cells have been pretreated (7).

Figure 4. Presence of a 16 kDa fragment obtained by exhaustive Trypsin digestion of D1 isolated from light treated cells .
D1 was isolated from cells exposed to 200 W.$^{-2}$m for 60 min. as described by Adir and Ohad (11); digestion was carried out at a trypsin concentration of 50ug/ml for 30 min at 25 °C.

2.4) Role of RCII in the light-controled synthesis of D1.

The changes in RCII and the D1 protein occur in the grana domains whereas the synthesis of pD1 is confined to the nonapressed stroma domains of the thylakoid membranes (8). Both processes are simultaneous and are regulated by the same effector, light. However their interconnection is not yet clear. The modified RCII could serve as an acceptor of pD1, thus regulating its synthesis at the translation level or protecting it from proteolysis. This could establish an operational connection between the light controled degradation and the synthesis of D1 protein which could respond to light intensity changes as well. Experiments devised to test this possibility indeed demonstrated that ^{35}S labeled pD1 is integrated in reaction centers located in the nonapressed membrane domains and appears as a mature D1 protein in RCII located in the grana thylakoids (*Fig.6*). Exposure of cells to high light intensity increases the amount of RCII translocation to the nonapressed membrane regions (data not shown).

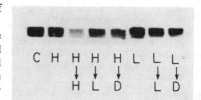

Figure 5. Enhanced D1 degradation induced by high light continues following transfer of cells to low light or dark for 1 hour. The cells were then incubated in H or L light or dark (D) as indicated for 3 hours. All incubations were carried out in the presence of 200ug/ml chloramphenicol. Residual D1 was quantitated by western blotting; C. control untreated cells.

3. CONCLUSIONS

The light-induced inactivation of RCII, its recovery and the turnover of the D1 protein can be described as resulting from a sequence of events affecting RCII (scheme 1), as follows: i), a reversible conformational change of D1 causing a destabilisation of Q_B^-;ii), a modification of the D1 protein resulting in the inactivation of Z the reductant of p_{680}^+ and leading to an irreversible modification of D1; this may act as a recognition signal for the proteolysis of the modified D1 possibly via exposure of the PEST sequence (16); iii), migration of the modified RCII from the grana to the nonapressed thylakoid domains where pD1 is synthesized and integrated in RCII; iiii), translocation to the grana as a functional RCII. Stage (i), accounts for rise in Fo, and partial loss of electron flow; its reversion does not require de novo synthesis of D1. Stage (ii), accounts for decrease in Fm, further loss of electron flow activity and targeting of D1 for degradation; this stage can not be reversed in absence of D1 synthesis.

Stages (i,ii), are mediated by light dependent electron flow via the Q_B site and account for the light intensity dependence of photoinhibition and D1 degradation. Protection against (i,ii) by conditions which reduce the occupancy of Q_B site by plastoquinone (11,14), are in agreement with this conclusion. Stages (iii, iiii), account for the light dependent regulation of D1 synthesis possibly via a translational control mechanism in which RCII serves as an acceptor of pD1.

The above scheme represents a general hypothesis accounting for the major phenomena related to the light dependent D1 turnover and photoinhibition. The difference between the turnover detected at low light intensities, and photoinhibition detected at high light fluency is only a matter of degree, or detection threshold rather than a qualitative difference in the mechanism of these phenomena which are different aspects of the same process.

Figure 6. The D1 precursor (pD1) is directly integrated in RCII. Thylakoids from cells pulse labeled for 5 min with ^{35}S-L methionine were resolved into chlorophyll-protein complexes by nondenaturing PAGE (17), (horizontal gel strip); the polypeptide composition of the complexes was resolved by denaturing SDS-PAGE in the second dimension (stained gel, CBB); RCII components are encircled; pD1, (arrow), detected by autoradiography, (A), corresponds to the lane identified as RCII.

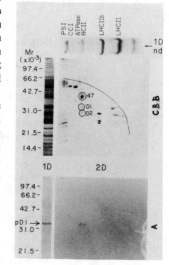

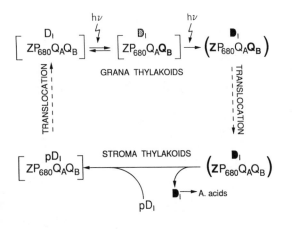

Scheme 1. Sequential events in the process of D1 turnover. The reversibe conformational change of D1 is labeled as D₁ ;modification of Qв site and Z are indicated by heavy lines; ●₁ , irreversibly modified D1 targeted for degradation; rectangular brackets, functional RCII; curved brackets, photoinhibited RCII; pD1, precursor D1 protein synthesized by polyribosomes bound to nonappressed membrane domains; The exact sites of D1 degradation and palmitoylation are not known.

ACKNOWLEDGMENTS

This work was supported by reserch grants awarded to I.O by the Israeli Academy of Science, and in cooperation with K.Kloppstech, University of Hanover, F.R.G. by the National Council of R.and D., joint German-Israel program in biotechnology and the Deutsche Forschungsgemeinschaft.

REFERENCES

1   Trebst, A. (1987) Z. Naturforsch. 42c, 742-750
2   Mattoo, A. K., Hoffman-Falk, H., Marder, J. and Edelman, M. (1984) Proc. Natl. Acad. Sci. U.S.A. 81, 1380-1384
3   Jensen, K., Herrin, D. J., Plumely, F. G. and Schmidt, G. W. (1986) J. Cell Biol. 103, 1315-1325
4   Fromm, H., Devic, M., Fluhr, R. and Edelman, M. (1985) Embo J. 4, 91-295
5   Kyle, D. J., Ohad, I. and Arntzen, C.J. (1984) Proc.Natl. Acad. Sci. U.S.A. 81, 4070-4074
6   Rutherford, A. W., Renger, G., Koike, H. and Inoue, Y. (1984) Biochim. Biophys. Acta 767, 548-556
7   Ohad, I. Koike, H., Shochat, S. and Inoue, Y. (1988) Biochim. Biophys. Acta 933, 288-298
8   Herrin,D., Michaels, A. and Hikey,E. (1981) Biochim. Biophys. Acta 655, 136-145
9   Schuster, G., Timber, R. and Ohad, I. (1988) Eur. J. biochem. 177, 403-410
10 Kyle, D. J. (1987) in Photoinhibition (Kyle,D. J., Osmond, C.B. and Arntzen, C. J. eds) pp.197-226, Elsevier, Amsterdam
11 Ohad, I. Adir, N., Kyle, D. J. and Inoue, Y. (1989) submitted
12 Itoh, S., Yerkes, C. T., Koike, H. Robinson, H. H. and Crofts A. R. (1984) Biophys. Acta 766, 612-622
13 Debus, R. J., Barry, A., Sithole, I., Babcock, G. T. and McIntosh, L. (1988) Biochemistry, 27, 9071-9074
14 Ohad, I., Shochat, S., Adir, N., Mets, L. amd Inoue, Y. (1989) submitted
15 Michel, M. and Deisenhofer, J. (1988) Biochemistry 27, 1-6
16 Greenberg, B. M., Gaba, V., Matoo, A. and Edelman, M. Embo J. (1987) 6, 2865-2869
17 Nechustai, R., Schuster, G., Nelson, N. and Ohad, I. Eur. J. Biochem. (1986) 159, 157-161

THE ROLE OF PHOTOSYSTEM II D1 APOPROTEIN METABOLISM IN THE PHYSIOLOGY OF PHOTOINHIBITION

C.A. SHIPTON, J.B. MARDER, AND J. BARBER AFRC
Photosynthesis Research Group, Imperial College, London SW7 2AY U.K.

INTRODUCTION

The reaction centre of photosystem II (PSII) contains several proteins including D2,D1, cytochrome $b559$ and the psbI gene product, and is closely associated with many others (proteins of the oxygen evolving complex, the 9kDa phosphoprotein, chlorophyll binding proteins and LHCII). Apart from the haem of cytochrome $b559$, D1 and D2 bind all the reaction centre pigments and also provide the quinone binding sites. Interestingly, only D1 consistently shows rapid light-driven turnover which may reflect a physiological need to replace photodamaged molecules of this polypeptide.

Various mechanisms have been proposed for the photodamage to this protein including attack of D1 by toxic oxygen species produced during the electron transport function of PSII (1), and simple 'wear and tear' effects caused by interaction with highly reactive quinone radicals (2). Little is known about the mechanism of D1 breakdown. A membrane-bound 23.5 kDa breakdown product has been identified and the in vivo cleavage site located to a functionally active region (3). Removal of non-functional D1 from the PSII reaction centre is suggested to be carried out by a highly efficient membrane-bound protease. The turnover of the D1 protein obviously plays a very important role in the maintenance of fully functional PSII reaction centres. It is hoped that more precise resolution of the cleavage site and isolation of the D1 protease may help to elucidate the processes involved in damage and replacement of this protein occuring under 'normal' and photoinhibitory light intensities.

MATERIALS AND METHODS

Lemna minor was grown autotrophically in axenic culture in flasks containing half-strength Hutners medium (4), at room temperature under a 15h photoperiod of $70\mu E/m^2/sec$ quantum flux. Peas and wheat were grown in vermiculite in a glasshouse maintained at 20-25°C. Labelling of D1 with $[^{35}S]$ - methionine was carried out as described in (5). Photoinhibitory treatment was carried out under a tungsten-halogen lamp screened with a water bath to remove excess infra-red radiation.

Two methods were used for homogenization of leaf samples, utilizing a motor-driven ground glass tissue grinder : (1) wheat and Lemna samples were homogenized in 5 ml/g fresh weight homogenization buffer (0.4 M sucrose 10 mM NaCl, 10 mM Na-tricine, pH 8.0), just after the addition of a small amount of sodium isoascorbate; pea leaf samples were homogenized in a small volume of acetone, centrifuged at 25 000 xg and air dried after removal of the supernatent. Isolation of the total membrane fraction from wheat and Lemna homogenates and enzyme digestions were performed as stated in (6) using Lys-C (Boehinger) at 100 $\mu g/ml$ and/or V8 protease (Sigma) at 30 or 100 $\mu g/ml$. Solubilisation, SDS-polyacrylamide gel electrophoresis, transfer to nitrocellulose membrane and immunodetection using rabbit antisera raised against the psbA gene product (7) were also carried out according to (6).

M. Baltscheffsky (ed.), Current Research in Photosynthesis, Vol. II, 415–418.
© 1990 *Kluwer Academic Publishers. Printed in the Netherlands.*

RESULTS AND DISCUSSION

The accumulation of the 23.5 kDa in vivo breakdown fragment has been immunologically followed by Greenberg et al (3), but no other smaller fragments have been recognised by this method.   Schuster et al (8) have however identified other membrane bound polypeptides in maize and Solanum nigrum in the size range 8-14 kDa (unpublished) which may be further breakdown products of the major D1 fragment.

The location of the cleavage site during D1 turnover was obtained by comparing the 23.5 kDa in vivo generated polypeptide with a known fragment of wheat D1 (NH$_2$ → Lys 238) (Fig.1).   By calculating the molecular weights of these fragment from several gels, it was found that the size difference was 0.7-0.9 kDa placing the site for in vivo cleavage in the sequence Glu-Glu-Glu (residue 243-245).   It can also be seen from this figure that the same '23.5 kDa' fragment is produced in small amounts during light-incubation and in larger concentration by photoinhibition suggesting that D1 cleavage occurs at the same position under physiological and photoinhibitory light levels.   According to currently accepted models of D1 organization (9,10,11), the in vivo cleavage site is located in the stromally-exposed connection between transmembrane helices IV and V.   This phylogenetically - conserved region (12) also contains a PEST- like sequence rich in glutamic acid (E), serine (S) and threonine (T) (residues 225 → 238), which may be responsible for the destabilization of the α-helical structure prior to degradation (3). Rogers et al (13) have claimed that all rapidly degraded eukaryotic proteins of known sequence contain one or more PEST sequences.   However, as these amino acid arrangements are also noted in relatively stable proteins, rapid degradation cannot be controlled uniquely by their presence and must also rely on other factors.   The dual nature of these PEST sequences have been examined by Ghoda et al (14) in a study of ornithine decarboxylase degradation.   Truncated versions of this enzyme, minus a PEST sequence, show greatly enhanced stability whilst another PEST sequence remaining in the non-deleted portion presumably has no effect on turnover rates.   Light-induced damage could be a factor involved in the activation of the 'PEST' sequence leading to removal of D1 from the reaction centre.

D1 is thought to be homolgous to the L-subunit of bacterial reaction centres.   The L-subunit does not exhibit rapid turnover rates and does not contain either a PEST-like sequence or the 'cleavage sequence' QEEE, the hydrophilic loop being much reduced in this protein.   The PSII reaction centre protein D2 contains a similar sequence (QAEE) to the 'cleavage sequence' of D1, but shows negligable rates of turnover under physiogical light intensities (15) and does not contain a PEST-like sequence either.

As D1 was thought to be cleaved around the 3 consecutive glutamate residues (Glu 243 → Glu 245), a glutamate specific protease (S. aureus V8) was employed to try to generate a fragment comparable to the 23.5 kDa fragment.   When wheat D1 is digested with different concentrations of V8 several sets of fragments are produced (Fig. 2), indicating that cleavage occurs preferentially at one particular site resulting in fragments of 21 and 8 kDa but also occurs to a lesser extent further towards the carboxy terminal producing a polypeptide of greater than 23 kDa.   Greenberg et al (3) have demonstrated that large fragments produced on V8 digestion (designated Sa22 and Sa21) are the amino terminal portion of D1.   The fragment produced in low found concentration in these experiments with a molecular weight greater than 23 kDa is thought to be larger than Sa22 and Sa21 as mentioned by other authors (3,16,17).   Figures 3a and 3b show the antigenicity of the fragments shown in Fig. 2.   If D1 is cleaved by V8 at site (A), the minor fragment remains antigenic whilst the major fragment is not antibody - reactive.   If V8 cleavage occurs at site (B), the converse is found, suggesting that the antigenic site is located between the V8 digestion sites.   Previous work has located site (A) to between residues 225-238 and site (B) to near residue 238 (17).   If the D1 protein is digested with Lys-C prior to cleavage with V8, neither band retains its antigenicity implying destruction of the antigenic site (not shown).   This loss of antigenicity after Lys-C and V8 digestion

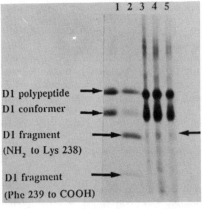

Fig. 1. Mapping the cleavage site of D1 by comparison of radiolabelled in vivo generated 23.5 kDa fragment (unlabelled arrow) with a known wheat D1 fragement. (1) undigested wheat thylakoids; (2) Lys-C digested wheat thylakoids; (3) Lemna thylakoids from light-incubated [70 μE/m^2/sec] plants; (4) Lemna thylakoids from photoinhibited [800 μE/m^2/sec] plants; (5) as for (3) digested with Lys-C.

D1 polypeptide →
D1 conformer →

D1 fragment
(NH$_2$ to Lys 238) →   ←

D1 fragment
(Phe 239 to COOH) →

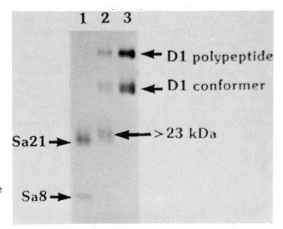

Fig. 2. [^{35}S]-labelled fragments produced during digestion of wheat thylakoids with V8 protease at concentration of 100 μg/ml (lane 1) and 30 μg/ml (lane 2); lane 3 shows undigested control.

← D1 polypeptide
← D1 conformer
Sa21 → ←→ 23 kDa
Sa8 →

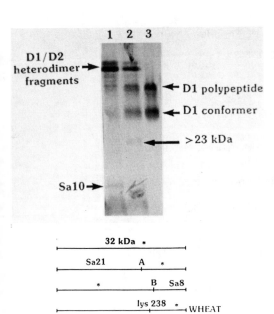

D1/D2
heterodimer
fragments →
← D1 polypeptide
← D1 conformer
→ >23 kDa
Sa10 →

32 kDa *
Sa21   A   *
*   B   Sa8
lys 238   * ⊣ WHEAT

Fig. 3. (a) Western blot showing the antigencity of wheat D1 breakdown products after digestion with V8 protease at concentrations of 100 μg/ml (lane 1) and 30 μg/ml (lane 2); lane 3 shows undigested control. Sa10 is a fragment previously reported by Marder et al (17).

(b) Map of the D1 digestion fragments and suggested V8 cleavage sites. Antigenic fragments are marked *. Sa21 and Sa8 are fragments found also by Marder et al (17).

is probably due to removal of all or part of the sequence which confers antigenicity. However, digestion with Lys-C alone results in the immunological detection of only the smaller fragment, giving even more accurate location of the antigenic site to between Lys

It may be seen from these data that V8 digestion at low enzyme concentrations produces a fragment comparable in size and antigenic properties to the in vivo generated '23.5 kDa' breakdown product of D1. V8 digestion of D2 also produces a polypeptide of around this size (not shown) suggesting cleavage at the QAEE motif. QEEE is predicted to be a strong antigenic determinant contributing both to hydrophilicity (18) and chain flexibility (19).

Interestingly the sequence QEEE is found in many other proteins and may play some role in their catabolism; these include cytochrome P450, many adenovirus DNA-binding proteins, ferredoxin, seed storage proteins including glycinin and legumin, as well as all known protein sequences for HIV-1 negative factor.

There are numerous examples of new proteins replacing old in response to an endogenous or environmental cue (20) and many models have been produced for predicting mechanisms for protein turnover. The one protein-one protease concept is not considered likely to be of widespread occurrence in cells (21) but is thought to be the major mechanism controlling D1 turnover. Hilditch et al (22) have proposed two separate mechanisms for D1 turnover in senescing Festuca leaves, one being rapid and light-dependent, the other slower and light-independent. The former mechanism is thought to be controlled by a D1 specific protease which has yet to be identified, but is suggested to be a membrane-bound thiolendoprotease (23). Further work in this project is to isolate and characterise the protease responsible for turnover of this essential PSII protein.

REFERENCES

1. Kyle, D. (1985) Photochem. Photobiol. 41(1): 107-116.
2. Arntzen, C.J. et al (1984) In: Biosyn. Photosyn. App., UCLA Symp. Series no. 14 pp 313-324.
3. Greenberg, B.M. et al (1987) EMBO J. 6: 2865-2869.
4. c.f. Posner, H.B. (1967) In: Meth. Dev. Bio. (eds. Witt, F.A. and Wessels, N.K.) Crowell, N.Y., pp 301-317.
5. Marder, J.B. et al (1986) Methods Enzymol. 118: 384-396.
6. Marder, J.B. et al (1987) Plant Mol. Biol. 9: 325-333.
7. Nixon, P.J. et al (1987) FEBS Lett. 209: 83-86.
8. Schuster, G. et al (1988) EMBO J. 7: 1-6.
9. Trebst, A. (1986) Z. Naturforsch 41c: 240-245.
10. Barber, J. and Marder, J.M. (1986) Biotech. Genet. Eng. Revs. Vol. 4, Intercept, Newcastle-upon-Tyne, U.K. pp 355-404.
11. Sayre, R.T. et al (1986) Cell 47: 601-608.
12. Curtis, S.E. and Haselkorn, R. (1984) Plant Mol. Biol. 3: 249-258.
13. Rogers, S. et al (1986) Science 234: 364-368.
14. Ghoda, L. et al (1989) Science 243: 1493-1495.
15. Gounaris, K. et al (1987) FEBS Lett. 211: 94-98.
16. Reisfeld, A. et al (1982) Eur. J. Biochem. 124: 125-129.
17. Marder, J.B. et al (1984) J. Biol. Chem. 259: 3900-3908.
18. Hopp, T.P. and Woods, K.R. (1981) Proc. Natl. Acad. Sci. USA 78: 3824-828.
19. van Regenmortel, M.H.V. (1986) TIBS 11: 36-39.
20. Davies, D.D. (1982) In: Encylopedia of Plant Phys. New Series Vol. 14A, D. Boulter and B. Parthier (eds.) (Springer-Verlag, Berlin) pp 189-228.
21. Ferreira, R.B. and Davies, D.D. (1986) Planta 169: 278-288.
22. Hilditch, P. et al (1989) Biosystems 22: 241-248.
23. Wettern, M. and Galling, G. (1985) Plant 166: 474-482.

PS2 PROTEINS INVOLVED IN PHOTOINHIBITION

M.T. Giardi*, R. Barbato, P. Dainese, F. Rigoni and G.M. Giacometti,
* IREV–CNR, via Salaria Km 29.3 00016 Monterotondo Scalo; Rome. Italy.
Dipartimento di biologia, Universita' degli studi di Padova, via Trieste 35121
Padova Italy

1. INTRODUCTION

There is general agreement that photoinhibition is based primarily on an inactivation of the electron transport system and the dominant effect seems to be an alteration of the PS2.

It has been suggested that the primary damage occurs at the Q_B site via reactions of oxygen radicals. This is based on evidence that photoinhibition in isolated thylakoids from cells of *Chlamydomonas reinhardtii* decreases the binding of atrazine to the Q_B site. Depletion of D_1 protein was observed in photoinhibited cells with formation of two breakdown products. Depletion of D_1 protein was also reported in illuminated spinach thylakoids but no degradation products were observed (1–2). However D_1 disappearance is observed with a delay (whitin hour/s) compared to inhibition of electron transport activity (whitin minutes). An alternative view is that photoinhibition involves primarily P680. In fact susceptibility to light has also been correlated with conditions that prolong the lifetimes of $P680^+$. However, since these components are located in the heterodimer D_1/D_2 a close interrelation between structural changes and alteration of the activity at various sites can be expected. (3)

The main purpose of our work is to obtain more information on photoinhibition mechanism focusing on the effects observed immediately after irradiation and following the behaviour of PS2 proteins in longer–term experiments.

2. MATERIALS AND METHODS

2.1. Photoinhibition of thylakoids – Isolated spinach thylakoids or enriched PS2 particles (BBY), were resuspended in 0.3 M sucrose, 50 mM Tricine, 15 mM NaCl and 5 mM $MgCl_2$ buffer in a flat cuvette (160x140x1.5 mm). The cuvette was kept in a glass water bath at 20°C and illuminated by a tungsten–halogen lamp providing 200 W/m^2 at the surface of the thylakoids suspension. Control samples were obtained by maintaining the suspension at 20° in the dark.

2.2. Photosynthetic activity was assayed with the $H_2O->DCIP$ and $DPC->DCIP$ systems and with variable fluorescence.

2.3. Gel electrophoresis and immunological assays – Aliquots of membranes were pelletted, solubilized, and then loaded (8 μg chlorophyll) onto a 12–18 %

M. Baltscheffsky (ed.), Current Research in Photosynthesis, Vol. II, 419–422.
© 1990 *Kluwer Academic Publishers. Printed in the Netherlands.*

acrylamide gradient gel containing 6 M urea. The proteins were blotted onto a nitrocellulose filter. Blots were incubated with antibodies (against D_1, 18 KD of the oxygen–evolving complex and the minor antennas CP29 and CP26) and then with anti rabbit IgG–alkaline phosphatase conjugate.

2.3. Herbicide binding – The amount of radiolabelled herbicide bound to membranes was followed at different illumination times and the activity expressed as per cent of initial value.

3. RESULTS AND DISCUSSION

3.1. Short–term effect of illumination. – Fig 1 shows the time–course of photoinhibition assayed as $H_2O \rightarrow DCIP$ electron transport activity. After 20 min illumination, 50% of initial activity was lost when chlorophyll concentration was 500 $\mu g/ml$. We confirmed that the rate of DCIP reduction by PS2 cannot be enhanced by addition of diphenylcarbazide or Ca^{++}.

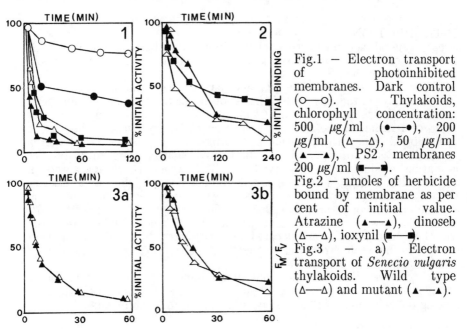

Fig.1 – Electron transport of photoinhibited membranes. Dark control (o—o). Thylakoids, chlorophyll concentration: 500 $\mu g/ml$ (•—•), 200 $\mu g/ml$ ($\triangle$—$\triangle$), 50 $\mu g/ml$ (▲—▲), PS2 membranes 200 $\mu g/ml$ (■—■).

Fig.2 – nmoles of herbicide bound by membrane as per cent of initial value. Atrazine (▲—▲), dinoseb ($\triangle$—$\triangle$), ioxynil (■—■).

Fig.3 – a) Electron transport of *Senecio vulgaris* thylakoids. Wild type ($\triangle$—$\triangle$) and mutant (▲—▲).

As expected the sensitivity of thylakoids to photoinhibitory damage is dependent on chlorophyll concentration. Low chlorophyll concentrations lead to more rapid inhibition of electron transport probably as a consequence of a higher exposition of membranes to light.

PS2 enriched particles (BBY) show a behaviour similar to thylakoids.

Atrazine, Ioxynil and Dinoseb were used to check the herbicide binding integrity. These herbicides are known to prevent the electron transfer from the primary to the secondary quinone electron carriers (Q_A and Q_B) of PS2 and they have been shown able to bind the isolated reaction centre in a defined stoichiometric ratio (4). The nmoles of bound herbicide were determined in thylakoids at different times of illumination (500 $\mu g/ml$ chlorophyll concentration). Through the first 30 min of illumination the loss of PS 2 activity correlates well with the loss of binding activity, particularly for Ioxynil (fig 2). Nevertheless, the atrazine–resistant mutant *Senecio vulgaris* shows the same inhibition of electron transport as the wild type (fig.3a–b), suggesting P680$^+$ rather than Q_B site as the primary photoinhibition target.

3.2. Long–term effect of illumination – The photoinhibition process was followed through a period in which chlorophyll or carotenoids decrease was under 10%. Thus bleaching of chlorophyll is a subsequent event compared to the process observed in our experiments.

The protein content was detected by SDS–PAGE and immunoblotting. The depletion of some PS2 proteins was observed to start just after the inhibition of electron transport i.e. within 10 to 60 min depending on chlorophyll concentration; the reaction centre component D_1, the 18 KD protein of the oxygen–evolving complex, the apoproteins of the two minor complexes CP26 and CP29 seem to be particularly affected by light (fig 4).

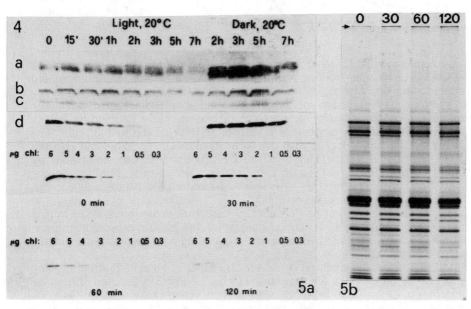

Fig.4 – Immonoblot of PS2 proteins: a) D1, b) CP26, c) CP29. d) 18 KD protein.
Fig.5 – a) Gel electrophoresis and b) immunoblot of 18 KD protein of photoinhibited thylakoids (200 μg chl/ml).

In order to compare the kinetics of disappearance of these proteins, samples were illuminated for 0, 30, 60 and 120 min. at a chlorophyll concentration of 200 $\mu g/ml$. Each sample was assayed with antibodies using eight different amounts of chlorophyll ranging from 6 to 0.3 $\mu g/ml$. The level of protein depletion is measured by the decrease of antigenic reaction. In fig 5a is reported the immunoblot pattern of the experiment testing the 18 KD protein. For each protein we compared the lowest chlorophyll amount at which antigenic reaction was still detectable.

In fig. 5b the results are shown as time–course for the protein depletion.

The kinetics appear to be similar for D_1, CP26 and CP29 while the 18 KD protein of the oxygen–evolving complex is depleted at a slower rate.

Together with the depletion of these proteins a formation of aggregated products on the top of stained gel was observed (fig.4a).

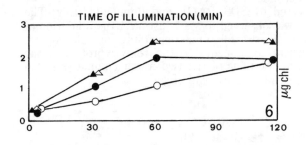

Fig.6 – Kinetics of proteins disap–pearance of CP29 (▲—▲), CP26 (△—△). D1 (●—●) and 18 KD protein (○—○).

In photoinhibited PS2 particles we observed the release of the extrinsic proteins of the oxygen evolving complex as well as the formation of aggregated products (data not shown).

Our results on inhibition of herbicide binding activity agree with the involvement of the Q_B site in photoinhibition. In fact the binding curves correlates with the loss of electron transport activity in the first 30 min. The best correlation was observed with the herbicide Ioxynil. Atrazine and Dinoseb showed a residual binding even when D_1 protein was not detectable by immunoblotting (data not shown) indicating non–specific binding or the involvement of other proteins in their association with thylakoids. This is in accordance with previous observations (3).

The appearance of aggregation products suggests that depletion of PS2 proteins could be a consequence of a general damage of the photosynthetic membrane triggered by a specific event (possibly on D_1) leading to a destabilization of the entire PS2 structure.

The formation of aggregated products is usually observed after heating thylakoids at 50° C for a few minutes. During photoinhibition, an increasing proportion of centres can be thought to convert the excitation energy to heat. Thus the possibility must be considered that proteins aggregation was a consequence of local internal heating.

REFERENCES
1) D.J. Kyle, I. Ohad and C.J. Arntzen. 1984. Proc. Natl. Acad. Sci. USA, 81, 4070–4074.
2) I. Ohad, D.J. Kyle and J. Hirschberg. 1985. The EMBO J., 4(7), 1655–1659
3) G.H. Krause. 1988. Physiologia Plantarum 74, 566–574
4) M.T. Giardi, J. Marder and J. Barber. 1988. Biochim. Biophys. Acta 934, 64–71

CONSEQUENCES OF LIGHT INDUCED D1-PROTEIN DEGRADATION ON THYLAKOID MEMBRANE ORGANIZATION

I. Virgin, T. Hundal, S. Styring and B. Andersson
Department of Biochemistry, Arrhenius Laboratories,
University of Stockholm, S-106 91 Stockholm, Sweden

1. INTRODUCTION

Photosystem II (PS II) of higher plant possess unique properties with respect to function, organization and protein turnover. It is a multisubunit protein complex which is composed of at least 20 different polypeptides (1). The two reaction center polypeptides, designated D1 and D2, appear to carry all the redox components necessary for the primary photochemistry of PS II (2) and possibly also the Mn (3). The great majority of the PS II units is located in the appressed thylakoid regions in association with its chlorophyll a/b antenna (4). PS II has a central catalytic role, but it also plays a central role in the long and short term acclimation of the photosynthetic apparatus. It is also the target for the photoinhibition process which leads to impaired electron transport capacity and the subsequent breakdown of the two reaction center subunits, in particular the D1-protein.

The loss of the D1-protein raises several questions concerning the organization of PS II under photoinhibited conditions. These relate to ligation of cofactors, assembly of intrinsic and extrinsic proteins, site and mechanism of repair. Here we have used different techniques i.e. Mn analysis, immunoblotting and thylakoid membrane subfractionation to study in vitro the consequences of D1-protein degradation on the organization of the PS II complex.

2. RESULTS AND DISCUSSION

In a previous study we showed that D1-protein degradation in response to strong light can occur in vitro and that it is a subsequent event to the photoinhibition of electron transport (3). Furthermore, the degradation rate of the D1-protein showed a very close correlation to the release of Mn from the membrane. Apart from the D1-protein, and to a lesser extent the D2-protein degradation, no changes in the level of other PS II polypeptides could be detected.

M. Baltscheffsky (ed.), Current Research in Photosynthesis, Vol. II, 423–426.

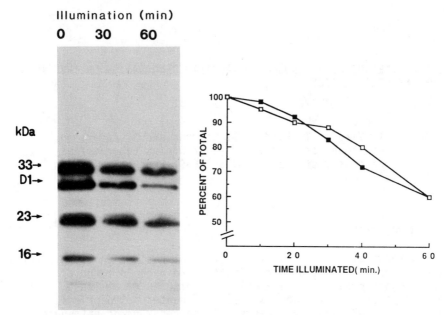

Figure 1 Immunoblotting of inside-out thylakoids isolated from
         photoinhibited intact thylakoids showing a loss of the
         extrinsic proteins and degradation of the D1-protein.

Figure 2 Levels of D1-protein (■) and 33 KDa (□) extrinsic
         protein in illuminated inside-out thylakoid vesicles.

Several studies have suggested a close association between the
33, 23 and 16 kDa extrinsic proteins and the D1-protein (1). It was
therefore of interest to investigate whether the three proteins
still were bound to the inner thylakoid surface and associated with
PS II after degradation of the D1-protein. This was done by isolation of inside-out vesicles from control and photoinhibited spinach
thylakoids using phase partition technique (4). As revealed by immunoblotting, inside-out vesicles isolated from photoinhibited thylakoids showed a marked reduction of all three proteins as compared to
inside-out vesicles isolated from dark control thylakoids (Fig.1).
In another experiment, inside-out vesicles were first isolated and
then exposed to strong light. The result revealed a concomitant release of the 33, 23 and 16 kDa proteins from the exposed inner surface of the everted thylakoid vesicles which correlated closely with
the D1-protein degradation (Fig.2). These results show that the
extrinsic proteins are released into the thylakoid lumen following
photoinhibition and that there is an association between the
D1-protein and the 33, 23 and 16 kDa proteins. Moreover, the observec
D1-protein disappearance in inside-out vesicles shows that the degradation system is present in the appressed thylakoid region.

The question then arises whether the Mn is lost from the thylakoid membrane due to D1-protein degradation or as a consequence of
the release of the 33 kDa protein. To answer this question, inside-
out thylakoids were treated with 2 M CaCl$_2$, prior to photoinhibition.
This treatment removes the three extrinsic proteins but leaves the
Mn membrane bound (6). When these polypeptide depleted inside-out
vesicles were exposed to strong light there still existed a close
correlation between the D1-protein degradation and the Mn release.
This suggests a close association between the Mn and the D1-protein
although a release of Mn ions due to a general disassembly of PS II
can not be excluded at present.

For the survival of the plant after photoinhibition a rapid repair of PS II is necessary. A crucial step is the synthesis of the
new D1-protein and its reassembly into PS II. It remains to be
established if the PS II subunits, after D1-protein degradation,
remain in the appressed thylakoid regions or migrate to the non-
appressed thylakoids which is the site for the insertion of the
newly synthesized D1-protein (7). In an effort to study the effect
of D1-protein degradation on the lateral location of the PS II polypeptides, thylakoids were subjected to strong light followed by
Yeda-press fragmentation and isolation of stroma lamellae vesicles.
The isolated vesicles were analyzed for changes in the level of PS
II proteins by mild SDS-PAGE or immunoblotting. In the latter case,
antibodies against each of the D1- and D2- proteins, cytochrome
b-559, 33, 22, and 10 kDa proteins were used. The increase of the
various PS II proteins was quantified (Table 1) after normalization
to the relative amount of the CFo subunit II, which is not affected
by photoinhibition.

TABLE 1

Increase/decrease of PS II polypeptides in stroma lamellae vesicles after photoinhibition of thylakoid membranes. The total reduction in the D1-protein level in the thylakoids during the illumination was 20%.

Protein	Increase/decrease
D1-protein	-10
D2-protein	+20
Cyt b-559	+50
33 kDa protein	+60
22 kDa protein	-20
10 kDa protein	+20
CPa(CP47 + CP43)	+180

The most pronounced increase in the stroma lamellae vesicles is
found for the two chlorophyll proteins CP 47 and CP 43. The resolution of the mild SDS-PAGE did not allow an accurate quantification
of each of the two chlorophyll a proteins. However the shape of the

partially resolved chlorophyll a peaks after scanning the gel suggested an equally high migration of both complexes. The increase of CP
47 and CP 43 in the non-appressed regions was 180% which suggests a
quantitative disassociation and migration of these two subunits from
all the D1-protein depleted PS II centers. For the cytochrome b-559,
D2-protein, 10 kDa protein and extrinsic 33 kDa protein there is an
increase in the region of 20-60% suggesting a partial migration into
the stroma exposed regions from PS II complexes depleted in D1-pro-
tein. For the D1-protein and the 22 kDa protein there is an decrease
in the order of 10-20% in the stroma lamellae vesicles. Since there
is no photo-inhibition and presumably no D1-protein degradation in
stroma lamellae vesicles (8) and the total amount of the 22 kDa protein is not affected by photoinhibition this suggests a migration of
both proteins from the non-appressed regions to the appressed regions. The molecular mechanism and physiological significance for
such a migration are under current investigation. A slight decrease
in the chlorophyll a/b ratio from 6.8 to 6.4 was observed but there
was no increase of LHC II in the stroma thylakoids following photoinhibition. The yield of stroma lamellae vesicles from control and
photoinhibited thylakoids was virtually the same, indicating that
there was no significant destacking induced by photoinhibition.

As seen in Table 1 the extent of migration is different for the
various PS II subunits indicating that a damaged photosystem does
not leave the appressed thylakoid region as one entity. The individual migration of polypeptides suggests a partial disassembly of the
PS II core. It remains to be shown to what extent the lateral migration of photosystem II subunits from the appressed regions to the
nonappressed regions is part of a repair cycle following photoinhibition.

In conclusion, our present study shows that repair of photosystem II after strong illumination and photoinhibition does not only
involve biosynthesis and insertion of D1-protein. It also involves
religation of manganese, assembly of several integral and extrinsic
photosystem II subunits, and lateral migration between the two thylakoid regions.

REFERENCES
1. Andersson, B. and Åkerlund, H.-E. (1987) in: The Light Reactions
   (Barber, J.ed.) pp. 379-420, Elsevier, Amsterdam.
2. Nanba, O. and Satoh, K. (1987) Proc.Natl.Acad.Sci. USA 84,
   109-112.
3. Virgin, I., Styring, S. and Andersson, B. (1988) FEBS Lett. 233,
   408-412.
4. Andersson, B. and Åkerlund, H.-E. (1978) Biochim. Biophys. Acta
   503, 462-472.
5. Anderson, J.M. and Andersson, B. (1988) Trends Biochem. Sci. 13,
   351-355.
6. Ono, T. and Inoue, Y. (1984) FEBS Lett. 168, 281-286.
7. Mattoo, A.K. and Edelman, M. (1987) Proc. Natl. Acad. Sci. USA,
   84, 1497-1501.
8. Mäenpää, P., Andersson, B. and Sundby, C. (1987) FEBS Lett. 215,
   31-36.

MUTATIONS IN D_1 PROTEIN RESPONSIBLE FOR A FASTER PHOTOINHIBITION PROCESS

D. KIRILOVSKY, G. AJLANI, M. PICAUD, A.-L. ETIENNE
UPR 407, Laboratoire de Photosynthèse, 91198 GIF SUR YVETTE, FRANCE

1. INTRODUCTION
   Photoinhibition is the decrease of photosynthetic activity induced by high light intensity (1,2). The site of photodamage is localized at the reaction center of photosystem II (PSII) which contains a hetero-dimer of D_1 and D_2. Photoinhibition leads to degradation of D_1 (3,4,5). The process involves a reversible damage, followed by an irreversible inhibition of PSII activity (6). We have found a herbicide-resistant mutant of the cyanobacteria *Synechocystis* 6714, AzV, which has an increased light sensitivity leading to a faster loss in the ability to recover PSII activity (6). The D_1 protein binds the secondary quinone Q_B and PSII-directed herbicides in the same niche formed by an hydrophylic loop (the "Q_B pocket"). In this work we show that the special behavior of the mutant AzV, is due to a particular modification of the Q_B pocket of the D_1 protein.

2. MATERIALS AND METHODS
2.1. Growth conditions: Wild type and mutant cells of *Synechocystis* 6714 and 6803 were grown under the conditions previously described (6).
2.2. Sequencing of the *psb*A gene: The sequencing of the *psb*A gene coding for D_1 protein was done as described in (7,8).
2.3. Transformation of *Synechocystis* 6803: *Synechocystis* 6803 was plated on top agar plates. 10 µl of 2 kb DNA fragments containing the *psb*A gene of the mutant were spotted directly onto the surface of the plate. After 16 hours incubation in light, 10^{-3} M atrazine was added and the transformants were the only colonies to survive.
2.4. Photoinhibition experiments: It was carried out at 27°C at a cell concentration of 30 µg chl/ml. The light intensity was about 2000 W/m^2. For the recovery, the cells were transferred into fresh medium and incubated in standard conditions (shaking, 34°C and light intensity: 20 W/cm^2).
2.5. Fluorescence measurements: The kinetics of photoinhibition and recovery were followed by variable fluorescence measurements as previously described (8).
2.6. Degradation of D_1 protein: Incubation for 1 hour in the presence of $^{35}SO_4{}^{2-}$ was followed by addition of non radioactive sulfate. Thylakoids were isolated, photoinhibited for 90 min under high light intensity (500 W/m^2). Samples were taken at different times. The SDS polyacrylamide gel of the thylakoids protein was done in

M. Baltscheffsky (ed.), Current Research in Photosynthesis, Vol. II, 427–430.
© 1990 *Kluwer Academic Publishers. Printed in the Netherlands.*

the presence of 4 M Urea and autoradiographed.

3. RESULTS

3.1. Transformation with the *psb*A gene of AzV: A 2 kb DNA fragment containing one copy of the *psb*A gene was used to transform wild type
cells. *Synechocystis* 6803 was utilized as the recipient strain
since *Synechocystis* 6714 is poorly transformable. The transformed
cells (AzV$_{6803}$) presented the same herbicide resistance as the
original mutant (AzV$_{6714}$) (Table 1).

TABLE 1. I_{50} concentrations of different herbicides in wild type
(WT$_{6714}$ and WT$_{6803}$); AzV$_{6714}$ and transformed cell (AzV$_{6803}$)[a]

	I_{50} atrazine (M)	I_{50} DCMU (M)	I_{50} metribuzin (M)
WT$_{6714}$	3×10^{-6}	2×10^{-7}	10^{-6}
AzV$_{6714}$	2×10^{-4}	5×10^{-7}	4×10^{-4}
WT$_{6803}$	3×10^{-6}	2.5×10^{-7}	10^{-6}
AzV$_{6803}$	2×10^{-4}	5×10^{-7}	4×10^{-4}

(a): I_{50}: concentration of the herbicide needed to block half of the
maximal variable fluorescence.

3.2. Photoinhibition and recovery of the transformed cells: Cells photoinhibited for 60 or 90 min were resuspended in fresh medium and
incubated at low light for up to four hours. The time-courses of
recovery for WT$_{6803}$, AzV$_{6803}$ are shown in Fig. 1.

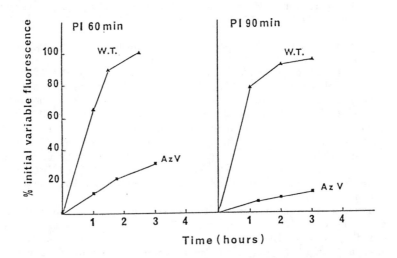

FIGURE 1. Recovery of variable fluorescence of *Synechocystis* 6803
(wild type) (▲--▲) and of transformed cells AzV$_{6803}$ (■--■)
photoinhibited for 60 and 90 min.

For the wild type 6803 photoinhibition was still reversible after 90 min of cell exposure to high light. On the other hand AzV_{6803} cells were unable to recover any activity when photoinhibited for 90 min and only partially when photoinhibited for 60 min. Thus in AzV_{6803} the reversible step was reached faster than in wild type, as was the case in AzV_{6714}.

These results demonstrate that the mutations present in the AzV psbA gene is sufficient to confer the increased sensitivity to high light and that no other gene is involved.

3.3. Comparison of the psbA sequence of wild-type and AzV: The analysis of the psbA gene sequence showed two nucleotide changes in AzV with respect to the wild type. These changes result in a modification of Phe 211 to Ser and of Ala 251 to Val in the AzV D_1 protein (Fig. 2). Both modifications are localized in the Q_B pocket.

```
              211                          231
    W T    ---LFSAMHGSLVTSSLVRETTEVESQNYGYKFGQ


    AzV    ----S--------------------------------------------------------


              251                          271
    W T    EEETYNIVAAHGYFGRLIFQYASFNNSRSLH-------


    AzV    ------------------V--------------------------------------
```

FIGURE 2. Comparison of the aminoacid sequence of the Q_B niche from *Synechocystis* 6714 wild type (WT) with AzV mutant. For the mutant only the differences are given. The possible position of the PEST Signal is overlined.

4. DISCUSSION

4.1. The two mutations (Phe 211 to Ser, Ala 251 to Val) of D_1 in AzV are sufficient to account not only for atrazine resistance but also for the increased sensitivity of AzV to photoinhibition. AzV was derived from an other atrazine resistant mutant AzI which has an unmodified behavior in high light and a single mutation (Phe 211 to Ser)(8). The mutated Ala 251 is near a region rich in glutamate (E) Serine (S), threonine (T) (PEST Signal) which could be the primary determinant for the rapid degradation of high-turn over proteins (9,10). *In vitro* experiments of photoinhibition with thylakoids indicate that the rate of proteolysis of D_1 is slower in AzV than in the wild type (Fig. 3). Whether this difference is associated to the faster inactivation of PSII remains to be elucidated.

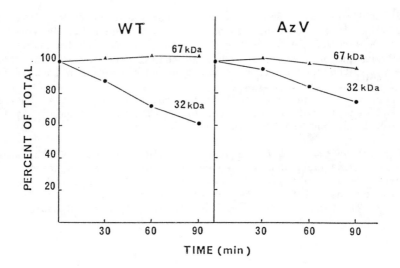

FIGURE 3. Degradation of the D_1 protein during photoinhibition of
thylakoids isolated from *Synechocystis* 6714 wild type and
AzV mutant cells. The radioactivity of the bands were calculated as a percentage of the total radioactivity.

REFERENCES
1 Kyle, D.J. (1987) in Photoinhibition (Kyle, D.J., Osmond, C.B.,
  Arntzen, C.J., eds.), Chapter 9, pp. 197-226, Elsevier Publishers BV
2 Cleland, R.E. (1988) Aust. J. Plant Physiol. 15, 135-150
3 Kyle, D.J., Ohad, I. and Arntzen, C.J. (1984) Proc. Natl Acad. Sci.
  USA, 81, 4070-4074
4 Lönneborg, A., Kalla, S.R., Samuelsson, G., Gustafsson, P. and
  Oquist, G. (1988) FEBS Lett. 240, 110-114
5 Schuster, G., Timberg, R. and Ohad, I. (1988) Eur. J. Biochem. 177,
  403-410
6 Kirilovsky, D., Vernotte, C., Astier, C. and Etienne, A.-L. (1988)
  Biochim. Biophys. Acta 933, 124-131
7 Ajlani, G., Kirilovsky, D., Picaud, M. and Astier, C. (1989) Plant
  Mol. Biol. (in press)
8 Kirilovsky, D., Ajlani, G., Picaud, M. and Etienne, A.-L. (1989)
  Plant Mol. Biol. (in press)
9 Rogers, S., Wells, R. and Rechsteiner, M. (1986) Science 234, 364-
  368
10 Greenberg, B.M., Gaba, V., Mattoo, A.K. and Edelman, M. (1987) EMBO
  J. 6, 2865-2869

SUSCEPTIBILITY OF PHOTOSYNTHESIS TO PHOTOINHIBITION OF psbA GENE-INACTIVATED STRAINS OF ANACYSTIS NIDULANS

ZBIGNIEW KRUPA, GUNNAR ÖQUIST, PETTER GUSTAFSSON AND SUSAN S. GOLDEN

Dept. Plant Physiology, M.Curie-Skłodowska Univ., 20-033 Lublin, Poland - CPBP 05.02 (Z.K.); Dept. Plant Physiol., Univ. of Umeå, S-901 87 Umeå, Sweden (G.Ö., P.G.) and Dept. Biol., Texas A and M Univ., College Station, TX 77843, USA (S.S.G.)

1. INTRODUCTION

Under high light conditions photoinhibition of photosynthesis may occur (1,2). The primary site of photoinhibition has been suggested to be located within the D1 protein (also called Q_B- or herbicide-binding protein) to which the PSII reaction centre is bound (3,4). Photosynthetic organisms are able to recover from photoinhibition because of a repair process which occurs when plants are placed again under favourable growth conditions (5,6). Most convenient in studies of photoinhibition and recovery are cyanobacteria of which Anacystis nidulans has been extensively investigated in our laboratory (5-8). We have previously shown that the rate of photoinhibition and the rate of recovery of photosynthesis in A.nidulans were dependent on the growth light conditions (7,8). It has been also found that the rate of the synthesis of the D1 protein plays a major role both in the susceptibility of photosynthesis to photoinhibition and during the recovery process (3,6). It is established that the genome of A.nidulans contains three psbA genes (9). These genes can be inactivated in the Anacystis chromosome, singly or in pairs, and it was shown that each gene alone provides sufficient protein product to support normal photosynthesis (9). Wild type strain R2 has been described by these authors as having all three psbA genes active, although the psbAI provides about 94% of the psbA genes transcripts. In mutant R2S2C3 the only active gene is psbAI, highly expressed under low and normal light conditions and producing the D1:I protein. Mutant R2K1 has the psbAI gene inactivated and possess psbaII and psbAIII genes highly expressed under very high light and producing identical D1:II and D1:III proteins.
In the present work we have characterized the susceptibility of photosynthesis to photoinhibition in A.nidulans strain R2 and its psbA gene mutants R2S2C3 and R2K1. Since repair of photodamage provides a mean to avoid net photoinhibition (8) we have also investigated the recovery kinetics after photoinhibition.

2. MATERIALS AND METHODS

Anacystis nidulans strain R2 and its two psbA gene mutants (R2S2C3 and R2K1) described by Golden et al. (9) were grown in an inorganic medium (10) at 38°C exposed to continuous PAR of 50µmolm^{-2}s^{-1}.

M. Baltscheffsky (ed.), Current Research in Photosynthesis, Vol. II, 431–434.

5% CO_2 in air was flushed over the culture to avoid changes in antenna size due to low inorganic carbon content in the medium. The cultures used for photoinhibitory treatments were always in the logarithmic phase of growth.

Cell densities were determined from absorbance measurements at 750 nm and cell number was estimated as in Lönneborg et al. (5). The amounts of phycocyanin and chlorophyll a were calculated from the corrected values of absorbances at 625 nm and 678 nm as described by Myers et al. (11).

For the photoinhibitory treatments the cells were prepared as in Samuelsson et al. (7). The incident PAR was varied by placing the halogen lamp at different distances from the algal samples. The controls were incubated in dim light of about 5 $\mu mol\ m^{-2} s^{-1}$. Where indicated, the translation inhibitor streptomycin was used before or immediately after the light treatment to a final concentration of 250 µg/ml. Reactivation of photosynthesis after photoinhibition was done in dim light of PAR of 20 $\mu mol\ m^{-2} s^{-1}$. All operations were performed at 38°C.

Photosynthesis was measured with a Clark-type O_2 electrode at a non-saturating PAR of 55 $\mu mol\ m^{-2} s^{-1}$ and at 38°C. Prior to the measurements, 20 µl of 1 M $NaHCO_3$ solution was added to certify saturating CO_2 conditions.

Fluorescence kinetics were measured at 77K using the trifurcated fiberglass centered fluorescence spectrometer described earlier (12). F_v and F_m values were calculated from the chartpen recordings.

3. RESULTS AND DISCUSSION

The cyanobacterium Anacystis nidulans shows similar responses in photosynthesis to excessive light as green algae and higher plants (4). The susceptibility to photoinhibition was monitored in the wild type R2 and the two mutants R2S2C3 and R2K1. Immediately after termination of photoinhibition the translation inhibitor streptomycin was added to prevent recovery prior to photosynthesis or fluorescence measurements. The results show that all three strains had a similar response with respect of susceptibility to photoinhibition (Table 1). In the PPFD range of 0-500 $\mu mol\ m^{-2} s^{-1}$ the R2K1 mutant appears to be somewhat less sensitive to photoinhibition than do the other mutant R2S2C3 and the wild type R2 (Table 1). This is shown both by the 77K fluorescence induction kinetics data (F_v/F_m ratios) as well as by the O_2 evolution measured as $\mu mol\ O_2$ evolved*mg $Chl^{-1} h^{-1}$.

To investigate whether there was any molecular modification of the PSII reaction centre of the R2K1 mutant that made it more resistant intrinsically to photoinhibition we performed photoinhibition experiments in the presence of streptomycin to inhibit all recovery from photoinhibition. The increase of susceptibility to photoinhibition was observed and all three strains showed similar sensitivities (data not shown).

Table 2 shows the recovery of Anacystis wild type and its mutants from the photodamage. Fluorescence and O_2 evolution measurements clearly show that after photoinhibition the R2K1 mutant recovers approximately 3 times faster than do the other mutant and the wild

TABLE 1. Photoinhibition of photosynthesis in A.nidulans strain R2 and its psbA genes mutants R2S2C3 and R2K1

PPFD µmol m^{-2}s^{-1}	% of inhibition *					
	F_v/F_m			O_2 evolution		
	R2	R2S2C3	R2K1	R2	R2S2C3	R2K1
0	0	0	0	0	0	0
250	26.5	34.8	10.6	47.7	53.5	33.0
500	33.8	43.9	30.1	65.7	65.0	57.7
1000	50.5	52.2	43.1	75.4	74.9	66.2
2000	67.3	61.0	54.2	78.4	76.7	65.8

* $1.3 < SD < 12.2$

TABLE 2. Recovery of photosynthesis after partial photoinhibition (about 40%) of A.nidulans strain R2 and its psbA genes mutants R2S2C3 and R2K1

Recovery time, min	Δ recovery, %					
	F_v/F_m			O_2 evolution		
	R2	R2S2C3	R2K1	R2	R2S2C3	R2K1
10	7.6	4.6	22.0	9.2	7.8	27.4
20	10.3	13.2	26.8	13.8	13.1	37.2
30	12.6	15.9	29.2	20.3	12.1	45.6
40	17.6	20.6	34.4	22.8	19.0	47.4
50	23.0	25.3	35.3	24.7	19.3	50.9
60	30.6	29.7	38.0	35.6	29.2	54.3
Final values after 90 min, % of control	97.1	95.0	107.0	95.4	96.3	113.3

* $1.9 < SD < 12.8$

type. The similar phenomenon has been observed previously (6) for A.nidulans grown in low and high light conditions. The capacity to recover after about 40% photoinhibition was approximately 3 times higher in high light grown cells than in low light grown cells.

It can be concluded from the data presented here that the intrinsic susceptibility of the PSII complex to excessive light is similar for

for the wild type R2 and both mutants (R2S2C3 and R2K1) of <u>Anacystis</u> <u>nidulans</u>. The major difference observed between these strains is the very high ability of the R2K1 mutant to recover from photodamage, most likely due to very fast re-synthesis of the D1 protein. Since its <u>psbAII</u> and <u>psbAIII</u> genes are highly expressed under very high light conditions our future work will be focused on the molecular mechanisms regulating the response of the repairing machinery to the photoinhibitory environmental conditions.

REFERENCES

1 Powles, S.B. (1984) Annu. Rev. Plant Physiol. 35, 15-44
2 Öquist, G. (1988) in Light in Biology and Medicine (Douglas H.R., Moan, J., Dall'Acqua, F., eds.), Vol. 1, pp. 433-440, Plenum Publishing Co.
3 Ohad, I., Kyle, D.J. and Arntzen, C.J. (1984) J. Cell Biol. 99, 481-485
4 Deisenhofer, J., Epp, O., Miki, K., Huber, P. and Michel, H. (1985) Nature 318, 618-624
5 Lönneborg, A., Lind, L.K., Kalla, R., Gustafsson, P. and Öquist, G. (1985) Plant Physiol. 78, 110-114
6 Lönneborg, A., Kalla, R., Samuelsson, G., Gustafsson, P. and Öquist, G. (1988) FEBS Lett. 240, 110-114
7 Samuelsson, G., Lönneborg, A., Rosenqvist, E., Gustafsson, P. and Öquist, G. (1985) Plant Physiol. 79, 992-995
8 Samuelsson, G., Lönneborg, A., Gustafsson, P. and Öquist, G. (1987) Plant Physiol. 83, 438-441
9 Golden, S.S., Brusslan, J. and Haselkorn, R. (1986) EMBO J. 5, 2789-2798
10 Siva, B., Rao, K., Brand, J.J. and Myers J. (1977) Plant Physiol. 59, 965-969
11 Myers, J., Graham, J.R. and Wang, R.T. (1978) J. Phycol. 14, 513-518
12 Ögren, E. and Öquist, G. (1984) Physiol. Plant. 62, 193-200

ACTIVATION OF A RESERVE POOL OF PHOTOSYSTEM II IN CHLAMYDOMONAS
REINHARDTII COUNTERACTS PHOTOINHIBITION

PATRICK J. NEALE AND ANASTASIOS MELIS, PLANT BIOLOGY, UNIVERSITY OF
CALIFORNIA AT BERKELEY, BERKELEY CA 94720 USA

1. INTRODUCTION
    Photoinhibition is a phenomenon of damage to the photosystem II
(PSII) reaction center that occurs during exposure of plants (1) or
algae (2) to very high irradiances. Measurements of the photoreduction
of the primary acceptor pheophytin (Pheo) in PSII have shown that
photoinhibition coincides with a loss of the activity of the PSII
primary charge separation (3). PSII exists in several forms and the so-
called PSII heterogeneity has been described both in terms of functional
size (4) and ability to reduce plastoquinone (5). The large and small
size antenna centers have been termed PSIIα and PSIIβ, respectively.
Under normal growth conditions in spinach, the PSIIα centers perform
electron-transport (Q_B-reducing) whereas the PSIIβ are unable to
transfer electrons to plastoquinone (Q_B-nonreducing) even though they
can perform a normal charge separation and electron-transfer to Q_A (5).
Here we show that a strong-irradiance treatment causes PSIIβ to become
active in electron transport. This phenomenon appears to be a mechanism
to compensate for photoinhibition damage to the PSIIα.

2. MATERIALS AND METHODS
    Chlamydomonas reinhardtii was grown at a low light (LL) intensity
of 15 μmol m^{-2} s^{-1} as previously described (6). Growth rate was 0.5 d^{-1}
. Cells were used in exponential phase. Previously described
procedures were used to measure the concentration of Pheo (3), analyse
the PSII antenna size heterogeneity based on the area growth over the
fluorescence curve measured in the presence of DCMU (4) and measure the
initial fluorescence yield increase in the absence of DCMU, an indicator
of the pool size of PSII-Q_B-nonreducing (5). Rates of oxygen evolution
were measured as described (6), except that initial O_2 concentration was
lowered to 20% saturation by bubbling with N_2. Strong-irradiance
treatments were administered using a halogen light source with a 15 cm
thick water filter at an intensity of 2000 μmol m^{-2} s^{-1} and temperature
of 25°C. Each measurement was replicated with 3 cultures.

3. RESULTS AND DISCUSSION
Control LL grown cells have a ratio of Chl:Pheo of 500 indicating 2.0
mmol of photochemically competent PSII (i.e. PSII able to generate a
stable charge separation). These cells are quite sensitive to
photoinhibition (Table 1). After 60 min of strong irradiance exposure
less than half of the PSII centers were able to form a stable charge
separation to Pheo. The kinetics of PSII photochemistry defined from the
fluorescence induction curve of isolated thylakoid membranes in the

M. Baltscheffsky (ed.), Current Research in Photosynthesis, Vol. II, 435–438.

TABLE 1   CONCENTRATION OF PHOTOSYSTEM II REACTION CENTER IN CONTROL AND
STRONG-IRRADIANCE TREATED C. REINHARDTII.   Units are mmol of PSII per
mol of Chl a+b or percentage of total PSII.

Exposure duration (min)	Total PSII mmol	PSIIα mmol	%	PSIIβ mmol	%
0	2.0	1.4	70	0.60	30
15	1.5	0.64	43	0.76	51
30	1.2	0.44	37	0.74	62
60	1.3	0.38	29	0.87	67

presence of DCMU indicated two distinct antenna size configurations.
The larger (PSIIα) has about three times larger functional antenna than
the smaller (PSIIβ) (result not shown, cf. (6)).   In control LL cells
they are present in the relative proportion of 70% PSIIα and 30% PSIIβ
(Table 1).   Strong-irradiance treatment significantly increased the
proportion of PSIIβ, so that they accounted for the majority of reaction
centers (Table 1).   However, note that there is little change in the
absolute concentration of PSIIβ (i.e. % PSIIβ x Total PSII
concentration) at about 0.76 mmol per mol Chl a+b.   Strong-irradiance
exposure rapidly photoinhibited the PSIIα, with only 25% of PSIIα
activity remaining after 60 min exposure.   These results are consistent
with previous measurements of strong-irradiance treated thylakoids
(3,8), and show that photoinhibition mainly damages PSIIα.

The fluorescence induction curve in the absence of DCMU has two
phases of increase.   Starting from a non-variable yield (F_o)
fluorescence increases to an initial plateau (F_{pl}), followed by a second
increase to a peak (F_p) (5).   The increase from F_o to F_{pl} is interpreted
to arise from PSII reaction centers which are photochemically competent
but unable to transfer electrons efficiently from Q_A^- to Q_B (5).   This
fluorescence rise accounts for about 15% of total variable fluorescence
and has been shown to emanate from the PSIIβ-Q_B-nonreducing (5).

The amplitude of the exponential fluorescence increase from F_o to
F_{pl} is lowered upon strong-irradiance treatment, suggesting that the
relative concentration of Q_B-nonreducing centers is lowered (Fig. 1).
The lowering occurs rapidly, only 20 % of the exponential amplitude
remains after 15 min of strong-irradiance exposure.   As was noted above
(Table 1), such a lowering in the amplitude of the initial fluorescence
yield increase should not be attributed to photoinhibition of PSIIβ,
which is resistant to damage (7,8).   Instead, such lowering may be a
manifestation of the conversion of Q_B-nonreducing centers into a Q_B-
reducing state (see also below).   Similar lowering of the F_o to F_{pl}
amplitude has been observed in other species of algae and higher plants
upon strong-irradiance exposure, but has not been attributed to changes
in the functional state of PSII Q_B-nonreducing (9,10).

Only Q_B-reducing centers participate in steady-state photosynthetic
electron-transport (oxygen evolution), whereas the Pheo assay measures

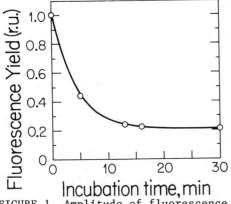

FIGURE 1. Amplitude of fluorescence yield increase from F_o to F_{pl} (pool size of PSII Q_B-nonreducing) in as a relation to period of strong-irradiance exposure.

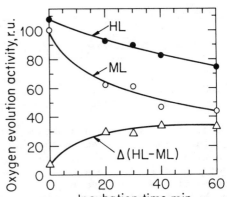

FIGURE 2. Rates of photosynthetic activity (O_2 evolution) as a function of strong-irradiance treatment. Control (100%) rate was 675 fmol O_2 cell^{-1} h^{-1}.

total PSII content (both Q_B-reducing and Q_B-nonreducing). Thus, any change in the contribution of PSII β (Q_B-nonreducing) to electron transport should be manifested as additional oxygen evolution. Oxygen evolution was measured both at the normally saturating (for LL cells) irradiance of 230 μmol m^{-2} s^{-1} (ML) as well as the much higher intensity of 1500 μmol m^{-2} s^{-1} (HL), in order to detect the activity of the PSIIβ. A period of 3 min exposure to each intensity was sufficient to accurately measure the rates. It was established that prior to strong-irradiance treatment, the rate of photosynthesis (oxygen evolution) under HL exceeded that under ML by less than 10% (Fig. 2). Following a strong-irradiance treatment there is a loss in oxygen evolution capacity due to photoinhibition (Fig. 2). After 60 min only 45% of the initial activity (as measured by ML) remained. However, there is less relative change in O_2 evolution than in PSIIβ centers, which decreased to 25% of initial concentration (Table 1). Moreover, the rate of photosynthesis by strong-irradiance treated cells in HL was substantially greater than that measured under ML (Fig 2). After 60 min strong-irradiance exposure, HL activity decreased from 107% to 70% relative to the ML control. Since HL should saturate the rate of photosynthesis in both PSIIα and PSIIβ, it may be concluded that net loss of PSIIα activity due to photoinhibition was partially compensated through a conversion of a portion of the PSIIβ pool from Q_B-nonreducing to Q_B-reducing status.

Thus, it appears that as a result of strong-irradiance treatment, and in spite of substantial activity loss by PSIIα (photoinhibition), a new set of PSII centers is now engaged in O_2 evolution. The exact nature of the mechanism and the regulation of the conversion of PSIIβ-Q_B-nonreducing to PSIIβ-Q_B-reducing is unknown and more work is required. The present results suggest that PSIIβ is a reserve pool of PSII, readily available to the chloroplast in case of catastrophic photoinhibition. This activation should be viewed in the context of a cycle in which PSII become damaged and repaired as hypothesized (11) to

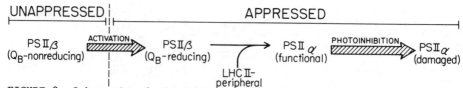

FIGURE 3. Schematic of the PSII repair cycle adapted from 11. Wide arrows indicate steps emphasized during strong-irradiance exposure.

occur in the thylakoid membrane (Fig. 3). The PSIIβ are known to be preferentially located in the unappressed stroma-exposed thylakoids, whereas the PSIIα, which have a full complement of LHCII-peripheral polypeptides, are localized in the appressed membranes (4). The activation may involve inclusion of the PSIIβ into the appressed membrane region and processing of a reaction center polypeptide to enable the reduction of plastoquinone. It has been shown that de novo synthesis of the 32-KD, or "D1", reaction center polypeptide involves initial association with the stroma followed by translocation to the grana after covalent modification (12). Once damaged, the PSII core-complexes are hypothesized to separate from the LHCII-peripheral and return to the unappressed membranes (11). Here repair would take place, including the removal of the D1 protein. After repair, the center would rejoin the PSIIβ reserve pool. This cycle has been hypothesized to take place even under normal irradiance conditions (11). If so the activation process suggested here may represent a temporary acceleration of one phase of the cycle. It is notable that after conversion to a Q_B-reducing form, the PSIIβ retain their small antenna size and do not associate with the peripheral LHC in the appressed membranes. This would be advantageous as a protection against further damage to PSII as long as strong-irradiance exposure continues. This light-activated "reserve" pool of PSII may play an important role in sustaining plant growth and productivity under adverse light-conditions in the natural environment.

REFERENCES
1 Powles, S.B. (1984) Ann. Rev. Plant. Physiol. 35, 15–44
2 Neale, P. J. (1987) in Photoinhibition (Kyle, D., Arntzen, C. J. and Osmond, B., eds.), pp. 39–65, Elsevier, Amsterdam
3 Demeter, S., Neale, P.J. and Melis, A. (1987) FEBS Lett.214, 370–374
4 Anderson, J. A. and Melis, A. (1983) Proc. Natl. Acad. Sci.,USA 80, 745–749
5 Melis, A. (1985) Biochim. Biophys. Acta 808, 334–342
6 Neale, P. J. and Melis, A. (1986) J. Phycol. 22, 531–538
7 Cleland, R.E., Melis, A. and Neale, P.J. (1986) Photosynth. Res. 9, 79–88
8 Maenpaa, P., Andersson, B. and Sundby, C. (1987) FEBS Lett. 215,31–36
9 Critchley, C. and Smillie, R.M. (1981) Austr. J. Pl. Phys. 8, 133–141
10 Whitelam, G.C. and Codd, G.A. (1984) Plant Cell Physiol. 25, 465–471
11 Guenther, J. and Melis, A (1989) Photosynth. Res., in the press
12 Matoo, A.K. and Edelman, M. (1987) Proc. Natl. Acad. Sci., USA 84, 1497–1501

EFFECTS OF LIGHT AND TEMPERATURE ON PSII HETEROGENEITY

E.-M. Aro[1], E. Tyystjärvi[1] and A. Nurmi[2], [1]Dept of Botany, Univ. of Turku, SF-20500 Turku and [2]Dept of General Botany, Univ. of Helsinki, Viikki, SF-00710 Helsinki, Finland

1. INTRODUCTION

It is generally accepted that nearly 30% of PSII (PSIIß) is located in non-appressed thylakoid regions where it is associated with smaller light-harvesting chl a/b antenna (LHCII) than the bulk of PSII (PSIIα) in grana partitions (1). In addition to this antenna size heterogeneity there are PSII populations differing from each others in the properties of the reducing side. PSII-Q_B-reducing centers are connected to the plastoquinone pool functioning in vivo in electron transfer from water to NADP. PSII-Q_B-nonreducing centers are inefficient in this respect due to impaired electron transfer from Q_A to Q_B. It has been suggested that in mature spinach leaves the PSIIß and PSII-Q_B-nonreducing constitute one and the same pool of PSII centers but under light of present knowledge, however, this generalization is not always valid (1).

It has been suggested that PSIIß centers are not susceptible to photoinhibition (2) while PSIIα centers were the primary target for inhibition under high light conditions. Phosphorylation of LHCII which increases the proportion of PSIIß centers has been suggested to protect from photoinhibition (3). However, dephosphorylation of mobile LHCII pool (4,5,6) has been reported during photoinhibitory conditions in vivo.

The aim of the present study was to monitor the changes in PSII heterogeneity during exposure of attached leaves to high light at different temperatures and secondly to elucidate the sensitivity of different PSII populations to photoinhibition in vivo.

2. MATERIAL AND METHODS

Pumpkin plants were grown in the greenhouse at a PFD of 150 µmol m^{-2}s^{-1} and transferred to PFD of 15 µmol m^{-2}s^{-1} for one day before the experiments. High light treatments (750, 1500 and 2500 µmol photons m^{-2}s^{-1}) were given to attached leaves at room temperature (RT) and at 1°C.

To study the PSII antenna heterogeneity the fluorescence induction kinetics of isolated thylakoids was monitored in the presence of 20 µM DCMU. ßmax value representing the percentage of PSIIß centers was calculated from biphasic

M. Baltscheffsky (ed.), Current Research in Photosynthesis, Vol. II, 439–442.

increase in the area above the DCMU curve by extrapolating
the exponential ß phase to zero time. Relative changes in
the concentration of Q_B-nonreducing PSII centers were
monitored from variable fluorescence yield in the presence
of 1 mM ferricyanide (FeCN) where the area growth displayed
exponential kinetics. All curves were computer stored and
processed.

For freeze fracturing, glycerol was added to the chloroplast suspension to a final concentration of 30% (v/v).
Collected pellets were frozen in the liquid phase of partially solified freon 22 cooled by liquid nitrogen.
Replicas were prepared according to standard procedures.

3. RESULTS AND DISCUSSION

Attached pumpkin leaves were photoinhibited upon
exposure to high light both at RT and at 1°C (7). Only at
the lowest PFD of 750 µmol m^{-2}s^{-1} at RT no signs of PSII
photoinhibition were recorded. Also an increase in the
proportion of PSIIß centers (β_{max} value) occurred at all
light treatments. The magnitude and kinetics of the
increase were dependent on the brightness of light and on
the temperature (Fig. 1A).

It can be argued that the increase in the proportion of
isolated PSIIß centers is just a result from the inhibition
of PSIIα centers or was the PSIIα/ß interconversion also
involved? Resolving the area components above the DCMU
trace showed, as expected, that the increase in β_{max} value
was always connected with a loss of PSIIα centers (Fig. 2).
At room temperature, however, the initial loss was
compensated with a corresponding increase in PSIIß centers
(Fig. 2A) provided the light treatment was not too severe.
At PFD of 2500 µmol m^{-2}s^{-1} this interconversion was no more
perfect (Fig.2B). The view that the new PSIIß centers were

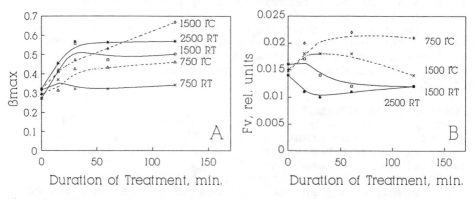

Fig. 1. Changes in β_{max} value (**A**) and variable fluorescence
with FeCN (**B**) measured from thylakoids isolated from pumpkin leaves treated in high light either at RT or at 1°C.

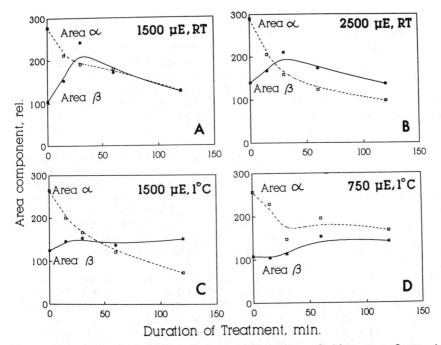

Fig. 2. Changes in α and ß components of the complementary area above the fluorescence trace of DCMU poisoned thylakoids. Thylakoids were isolated from pumpkin leaves exposed to high light at RT (**A,B**) or at 1°C (**C,D**).

Q_B-reducing was supported by measuring variable fluorescence in the presence of FeCN: the yield rather decreased upon exposure of leaves to high light at RT (Fig.1B). Further, the stable particle density on EFs fracture face of the thylakoid membranes indicated that no migration of PSII core particles from grana partitions took place (Table 1).

The best known mechanism for the formation of PSIIß-Q_B-reducing centers in grana at high light is the phosphorylation of peripheral LHCII (1). We have no data of phosphorylation but enormous drop in the density of the particles on the PFs fracture face, where the mobile LHCII is thought to cleave, supports strong modifications in the peripheral antenna of PSII.

Table I. Particle densities (particles/μm^2) on different freeze fracture faces of thylakoids isolated from leaves exposed to high light (1500 $\mu mol\ m^{-2}s^{-1}$) for 60 min.

	PFu	PFs	EFs	EFu
Control	5640	4385	2213	537
High light, RT	4972	3178	2274	398
High light, 1°C	5377	5067	1842	729

After initial increase (within 30 min) in the PSIIß
centers there occurred a parallel loss of both PSIIα and
PSIIß centers when photoinhibition advanced further at RT
(Fig.2A,B). Accordingly the newly formed PSIIß centers did
not provide any long-term protection against photoinhibition but the possible effect was only transient. As
dephosphorylation of LHCII (4,5,6) has lately been reported
during photoinhibition the newly formed PSIIß centers were
possibly converted back to PSIIα centers and subsequently
photoinhibited.

Decrease in variable fluorescence in the presence of
FeCN indicates a net loss of PSII-Q_B-nonreducing centers at
RT during high light exposure of the leaves. Concomitantly
there occurred a decrease in the density of EFu particles
in freeze fracture replicas of the thylakoids. These
observations are consistent with the hypothesis that
PSIIß-Q_B-nonreducing centers from stroma thylakoid
membranes are used to replace the photoinhibited PSII
centers in grana partitions (1).

The transient increase in PSIIß centers upon onset of
high light exposure at RT probably protects leaves from extensive photoinhibition upon sudden exposure to high light
when the repair mechanisms are not yet fully activated.

At $1^{o}C$ there was likewise a decrease in PSIIα centers
from the beginning of the high light treatment but contrary
to RT this was not compensated by an increase in PSIIß centers. This is probably due to restricted movement of mobile
LHCII at low temperature as can be interpreted from the
stability of the PFs fracture face, too (Table 1). Fv in
the presence of FeCN showed no decline within one hour con-
vincing that the PSIIß-Q_B-nonreducing centers are insensitive to photoinhibition so strongly supporting the in
vitro experiments with isolated stroma thylakoid vesicles
(2). On the other hand it is also evident that at low
temperature these PSII centers were not readily accessible
to replace the damaged α centers in grana patritions.

REFERENCES
1 Melis, A., Guenther, G., Morrissey, B. and Ghirard, M.
   (1988) In Applications of Chlorophyll Fluorescence
   (Lichtenthaler, H., ed.), pp. 33-43. Kluwer, London.
2 Mäenpää, P., Andersson, B. and Sundby, C. (1987) FEBS
   Lett. 215, 31-36.
3 Horton, R. and Lee, P. (1985) Planta 165, 37-42.
4 Schuster, G., Dewit, M., Staehelin, L.A. and Ohad, I.
   (1986) J. Cell Biol. 103, 71-80.
5 Demmig, B., Cleland, R.E. and Björkman, O. (1987) Planta
   172, 378-385.
6 Canaani, O., Schuster, G. and Ohad, I. (1989) Photosynthesis Res. 20, 129-146.
7 Tyystjärvi, E. and Aro, E.-M. These Proceedings.

PHOTOINHIBITION IN THE C_4 GRASS *Zea mays*.

Ripley, B.S., A.M. Amory, N.W. Pammenter and C.F. Cresswell. FRD/UN
Photosynthetic Nitrogen Metabolism Research Unit, Department of Biology, University of Natal, Durban, South Africa.

1. INTRODUCTION

Photoinhibition occurs under conditions of excess reductant production (1). Under normal conditions the carbon reduction processes utilize reductant, which are influenced by ambient CO_2 concentrations (2). Several processes including photorespiration and the anti-oxidant system, may utilize reductant even in the absence of CO_2 and are considered to have a protective function during photoinhibition (3), both are influenced by ambient O_2 concentrations (4,5). This study investigated the role of the carbon reduction processes, the anti-oxidant system and photorespiration in utilizing reductant by varying the O_2 and CO_2 concentrations during photoinhibition. In addition, CO_2 response curves were used to monitor the efficiency of the carboxylation processes as well as the level of carbon reduction cycling during the recovery from photoinhibition.

2. PROCEDURE

Seeds were planted in a high light constant temperature growth chamber and on shoot emergence were grown for a further 9 days before use. Using sdtandard techniques rates of water vapour and CO_2 exchange were measured before and following inhibitory treatments.

O_2 & CO_2 EFFECT: Plants were photoinhibited with high light intensity (2000 μmol m^{-2} s^{-1}) in the prescence of various O_2 or CO_2 concentrations and permitted to recover at low light intensity (550 μmol m^{-2} s^{-1}) and ambient O_2 and CO_2 concentrations. Each treatment was replicated at least four times.

CO_2 RESPONSE CURVES: Following a photoinhibitory treatment (high light and 0% O_2 and CO_2) each plant was permitted to recover at a particular CO_2 concentration. This was repeated in triplicate for the concentrations 20, 60, 120, 345 and 600 μmol mol^{-1}. This data was normalized and regressions were fitted from which CO_2 response curves were interpolated.

M. Baltscheffsky (ed.), Current Research in Photosynthesis, Vol. II, 443–446.
© 1990 *Kluwer Academic Publishers. Printed in the Netherlands.*

3. RESULTS

CO_2 assimilation was inhibited by 30 minutes of high light in the abscence of both O_2 and CO_2. On returning the plant to normal CO_2, O_2 and low light, assimilation rate recovered and was saturated by 60 minutes. Recovery was, however, incomplete (Fig. 1). Changes in stomatal conductance paralleled the recovery of assimilation rate following inhibition.

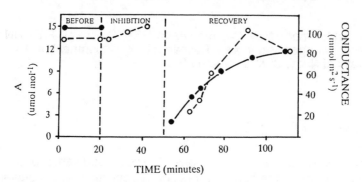

Figure 1. Typical CO_2 assimilation (——) and stomatal conductance (–––) before, during and following a photoinhibitory treatment (light intensity of 2000 μmol m^{-2} s^{-1}, 0% CO_2 and O_2).

Marked photoinhibition was found when plants were inhibited without CO_2, or at CO_2 concentrations less than 35 umol mol^{-1}. If CO_2 concentrations were increased to 35 μmol mol^{-1} or more less inhibition was obtained. The saturated recovery was little effected by CO_2 concentration, although recovery was slightly higher at concentrations in excess of 35 μmol mol^{-1} (Fig. 2).

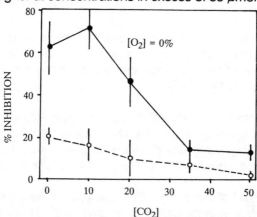

Figure 2. Percent inhibition obtained immediately following (——) and after 80 minutes of recovery (–––), when plants were photoinhibited in the presence of various CO_2 concentrations.

If O_2 was supplied at concentrations between 2 and 21% during photoinhibitory treatments there was less inhibition that if no O_2 or high O_2 concentrations were present. This effect was most prominant immediately following inhibition, but remained even after 80 minutes of recovery.

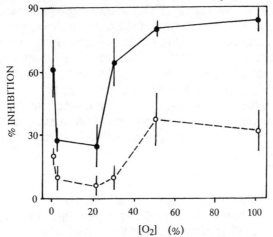

Figure 3. Percent inhibition obtained immediately following (——) and after 80 minutes of recovery (–▼–), when plants were photoinhibited in the presence of various O_2 concentrations.

Both the carboxylation efficiency and the saturation levels were decreased by photoinhibition and recovered with time, as indicated by the increase in both the initial slopes and the saturation levels of the CO_2 response curves (Fig 4). CO_2 concentration at which assimilation became CO_2 saturated was unaltered by recovery time.

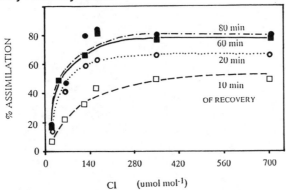

Figure 4. CO_2 response curves constructed at various time intervals during the recovery from photoinhibitory treatments (light intensity 2000 μmol m^2 s$_{-1}$, 0% O_2 and CO_2

4. DISCUSSION

At low CO_2 or O_2 it appears that reductant was utilized during the treatment and that thisprotected these C_4 plants from photoinhibition. This suggests the involvement of the carbon reduction processes, photorespiration and the anti-oxidant system. Low O_2 (2 - 21%) allowed greatest recovery once plants were returned to normal conditions. O_2 concentrations greater than 30% enhanced inhibition and decreased recovery suggesting an enhanced production of O_2^- radicals at these concentration. Recovery was greatest for the plants supplied with the higher CO_2 concentrations between the range 0 to 50 mol mol^{-1}.

The recovery of assimilation rate included both an increase in the efficiency of the carboxylation processes and the level of carbon reduction cycling. This was probably due to increasing reductant production as the light reactions recovered, which would both induce carboxylation enzymes and allow greater levels of carbon cycling.

REFERENCES
1 Powles S.B. (1984) Ann. Rev. Plant Physiol. 35, 15-44
2 Farquar G.D. and Sharkey T.D. (1982) Ann. Rev. Plant Physiol. 33, 317-345
3 Krause G.H. (1988) Physiologia Plantarum 74, 566-574
4 Ogren W.L. (1984) Ann. Rev. Plant Physiol. 35, 443-478
5 Elstner E.F. (1982) Ann. Rev. Plant Physiol. 33, 73-96

PHOTOINHIBITION OF PHOTOSYNTHESIS AND ITS RECOVERY IN LOW AND HIGH LIGHT ACCLIMATIZED BLUE-GREEN ALGA (CYANOBACTERIUM) SPIRULINA PLATENSIS

RADHEY SHYAM AND P.V. SANE, PLANT PHYSIOLOGY AND BIOCHEMISTRY NATIONAL BOTANICAL RESEARCH INSTITUTE, LUCKNOW 226001, INDIA

INTRODUCTION

The susceptibility to photoinhibition in sun and shade plants is governed by their ability to recover from photoinhibition (1). It has recently been proposed that a repairing mechanism is operational during photoinhibitory process and photoinhibition occurs when the rate of damage exceeds the rate of repairing system. The present study on the low and high light acclimatized S. platensis was undertaken to investigate if photoinhibition is the net result of a balance between the rate of damage and its repair by de novo protein synthesis.

MATERIAL AND METHODS

S. platensis was grown in an inorganic medium (2) at $28\pm1°C$ under continuous PFD of 20 μmol $m^{-2}s^{-1}$ for low light grown alga (LLG) and 125 μmol $m^{-2}s^{-1}$ for high light grown alga (HLG) provided by fluorescent tubes. Dry weight, pigment content and photosynthetic O_2 evolution were measured by routine procedures. Photoinhibitory treatment was given using projector lamp and recovery from photoinhibition was carried out in low PFD of 10 μmol $m^{-2}s^{-1}$. The preparation of spheroplasts and measurement of photochemical activity were accomplished as per method used by Laczko (3).

RESULTS AND DISCUSSION

Tables 1 and 2 show the pigment composition and photochemical activity of LLG and HLG S. platensis. The adaptation of the algal cells is reflected in the pigment composition as observed in other blue green algae. The requirement of high PFD for light saturated O_2 evolution (Fig. 1) and high PS II photochemical activity in HLG in the present study may be attributed to high aggregation state of pigment-protein complexes of phycobilisome resulting in increased energy transfer to photosystem II (3,4). The present study, shows that LLG and HLG S. platensis differ in the degree of susceptibility of photosynthesis to photoinhibition (Figs. 2 and 3). The HLG required substantially higher PFD (median inhibitory PFD about 800 μmol $m^{-2}s^{-1}$ as compared to 500 μmol $m^{-2}s^{-1}$ for LLG) or longer exposure time at lower PFD. At an exposure of 1000 umol $m^{-2}s^{-1}$ the time required for about 50% inhibition for HLG was about 30 min in excess to that required for LLG. This finding is consistent with the earlier studies of photoinhibition of photosynthesis in algae and vascular plants growing in low and high light intensity (5). The loss of photosynthetic O_2 evolution due to photoinhibitory damage in both LLG and HLG S. platensis is manifested at thylakoid membrane level in the spheroplasts by inhibition of rate of PS II electron transport (Table 2). The specific site

M. Baltscheffsky (ed.), Current Research in Photosynthesis, Vol. II, 447–450.

Table 1. Pigment composition of LLG and HLG Spirulina platensis

	% Dry wt of cells			Pigment ratios		
	Chla	Phycocyanin	Carotenoid	Chl a	Phycocyanin	Carotenoid
LLG	1.36	14.29	0.286	1	10.5	0.2
HLG	0.87	8.09	0.423	1	9.3	0.5

of damage, however, could not be worked out in the present study. There is now sufficient evidence to suggest that during photoinhibition Q_B protein is degraded and removed from the membrane (6) and recovery from photoinhibition, required chloroplast directed protein synthesis.(1,6). Thus the degradation and resynthesis of the D_1 protein may be correlated with the photoinhibition of photosynthesis and its recovery. Lack of recovery of photosynthesis from photoinhibition in the presence of translation inhibitor streptomycin in S. platensis in the present study (Fig. 5) is similar to that reported for Anacystis nidulans (7), Chlamydomonas (8) and vacuolated and non-vacuolated strains of Spirulina (9) and substantiate the finding that protein synthesis is required for recovery of photoinhibited cells.

Table 2. Light saturated electron transport rates of spheroplasts isolated from LLG and HLG S. platensis before and after photoinhibitory treatment

Treatment	PS II (H_2O -- FeCN+DBMIB) nmol O_2 evolved (mg dry wt)$^{-1}$ h^{-1}	PS I (Asc/DCIP -- MV; DCMU) nmol O_2 consumed (mg dry wt)$^{-1}$ h^{-1}
Control LLG 1000 µmol m^{-2}s^{-1} 28°C, 2 h	1200 ± 85 380 ± 52	1400 ± 40 1360 ± 32
Control HLG 1000 µmol m^{-2}s^{-1} 28°C, 2 h	2300 ± 58 950 ± 35	2000 ± 38 1920 ± 30

The level of carotenoid in two types of cultures may also play a decisive role in susceptibility to photoinhibition. The higher carotenoid content might provide some protection against photoinhibition in HLG S. platensis (10). However, the faster rate of recovery under reactivating condition (Fig. 4) and requirement of high PFD (Figs. 2,3) for photoinhibition of HLG as compared to LLG S. platensis suggest that susceptibility of photosynthesis to photoinhibition depends on the ability to recover. That the repairing mechanism is operational during photoinhibitory process is indicated by the fact that the recovery in S. platensis like A. nidulans (11) lacks a lag phase and starts immediately after transferring to reactivating condition (Fig. 4). This is further substantiated from the faster rate of photoinhibition when streptomycin is included during photoinhibitory treatment (Fig. 6). The HLG alga having higher capacity of recovery gets photoinhibited faster as compared to LLG alga which has low recovery capacity. From the above results and

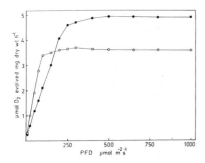

Fig. 1. Light response curve of photo-synthetic O_2 evolution by S. platensis acclimatized to grow under low (20 µmol $m^{-2}s^{-1}$) and high (125 µmol $m^{-2}s^{-1}$) PFD, low light grown (0); high light grown (●).

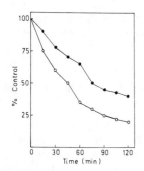

Fig. 2. Photosynthetic O_2 evolution (% of control) as a function of exposure time of photoinhibitory treatment of PFD of 1,000 µmol $m^{-2}s^{-1}$ in S. platensis, low light grown (0); high light grown (●).

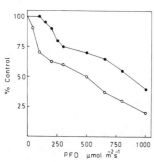

Fig. 3. Photosynthetic O_2 evolution (% of control) as a function of exposure to different PFDs for 90 min in low light (0) and high light (●) grown S. platensis.

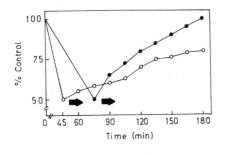

Fig. 4. Reactivation of photosynthetic O_2 evolution (% of control) as a function of time in 50% photo-inhibited low light (0) and high light (●) grown S. platensis. The arrows indicate transfer to reactivating conditions.

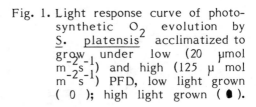

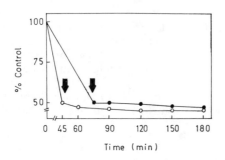 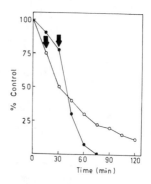

Fig. 5. Effect of streptomycin on reactivation of photosynthetic O_2 evolution (% of control) as a function of time in 50% photoinhibited low light (0) and high light (●) grown S. platensis. The arrows indicate transfer to reactivating conditions with streptomycin (250 μg ml^{-1}).

Fig. 6. Effect of streptomycin on the time dependence of photoinhibition of photosynthetic O_2 evolution in low light (0) and high light (●$_1$) grown S. platensis. Arrows- addition of streptomycin (250 μg ml^{-1}) during photoinhibitory treatment.

data obtained from other studies, susceptibility of photosynthesis to photoinhibition may be attributed to turnover rate of D_1 protein of PS II reaction center. The present study also strengthens the hypothesis that the photoinhibition is the net result of a balance between the rate of damage and its repair by de novo protein synthesis.

REFERENCES
1. Oquist, G. (1987) in Progress in Photosynthetic Research (Biggins, J., ed.), Vol. 4, pp. 1-10, Martinus Nijhoff Publ., Dordrecht
2. Zarouk, C. (1966) Ph.D. Thesis, Univ. of Paris, Paris
3. Laczko, I. (1985) Arch. Microbiol. 141, 112-115
4. Laczko, I. and Kaiseva, E. (1987) Photochem. Photobiol. 46, 421-425
5. Powles, S.B. (1984) Annu. Rev. Plant Physiol. 35, 15-44
6. Kyle, D.J. and Ohad, I. (1986) in Encyclopedia of Plant Physiology, N.S. (Staehelin, L.A. and Arntzen, C.J., ed.) Vol. 49, pp. 468-475, Springer-Verlag, Berlin
7. Samuelsson, G., Lonneborg, A., Rosenquist, E., Gustafsson, P. and Oquist, G. (1985) Plant Physiol. 79, 992-995
8. Lidholm, J., Gustafsson, P. and Oquist, G. (1987) Plant Cell Physiol. 28, 1133-1140
9. Vonshak, A., Guy, R., Oplawsky, R. and Ohad, I. (1988) Plant Cell Physiol. 29, 381-392
10. Krinsky, N.I. (1966) in Biochemistry of chloroplast (Goodwin, I.W. ed.) Vol. 1, pp. 423-430, Academic Press, New York.
11. Samuelsson, G., Lonneborg, A., Gustafsson, P. and Oquist, G. (1987) Plant Physiol. 83, 438-441

PHOTOINHIBITION IN THYLAKOIDS AND INTACT CHLOROPLASTS OF
CODIUM FRAGILE (SURINGAR) HARIOT.

ANDREW H COBB[1], RACHEL M HOPKINS[2], MICHAEL L WILLIAMS[3] AND
ROBERT V SEALEY[1]

[1]Department of Life Sciences, Faculty of Science, Nottingham
Polytechnic, Nottingham, NG11 8NS, UK; [2]Division of Biosphere
Sciences, King's College, University of London, UK; [3]School of Plant
Biology, UCNW, Bangor, UK.

1.   INTRODUCTION

There is a general acceptance in the literature that photosystem
II (PSII) is the primary site of photoinhibition and that
prolonged exposure to excessive photosynthetic photon flux
density (PPFD) results in pigment loss and lipid breakdown due
to photooxidation (as reviewed in 1). However, growth of the
marine alga C. fragile is adapted to low PPFD (2,3,4) even
though its intertidal habitat is regularly exposed to wide
extremes of PPFD on both a seasonal and daily basis. Therefore,
this alga is especially at risk of photoinhibition and
photooxidation at the higher PPFD's occurring at low tide.
Experiments described in this paper illustrate that chloroplasts
and thylakoids isolated from this alga photoinhibit at
irradiances supra-optimal for photosynthesis (PS). As with
other photosynthetic organisms, the primary lesion appears to be
associated with PSII and photooxidative damage occurs with
prolonged exposure to light.

2.   MATERIALS AND METHODS

Vegetative and reproductive algal fronds were sampled from
intertidal rockpools at Bembridge, Isle of Wight (UK) and
maintained as previously described (5). Due to the notoriously
robust nature of C. fragile chloroplasts in vitro (6), thylakoid
isolation was only achieved after freezing isolated chloroplasts
for 100 min. Oxygen exchange by isolated chloroplasts (7) was
measured at 0 to 1000 μmol m^{-2} s^{-1} (PPFD) at 10°C (8) using a
DW1 oxygen electrode (Hansatech Ltd, UK). Chloroplast density
within the electrode vessel was varied from 25 to 200 μg
chlorophyll cm^{-3}. Time course studies followed oxygen exchange
over a 10 min dark, 20 min light, 10 min dark incubation regime
with illumination provided by a 250 w tungsten-halogen, Halight
24/250 projector.

Stirred thylakoid suspensions (3 to 4 cm^{3}) were illuminated at

M. Baltscheffsky (ed.), Current Research in Photosynthesis, Vol. II, 451–454.

100 and 1000 μmol m^{-2} s^{-1} (PPFD) for up to 100 min with 200 mm^3 samples being removed for oxygen exchange studies. The following photosystem activities were determined in 1 cm^3 reaction volumes at 11 to 16°C; PSI and PSII combined, measured by electron transport from water to 7.5 mol m^{-3} ferricyanide; PSII, measured by electron transport from water to 5 mol m^{-3} dimethylbenzoquinone (DMBQ); PSI, measured by electron transport from the reducing couple 5 mol m^{-3} dichlorophenolindophenol (DCPIPH$_2$) /5 mol m^{-3} ascorbate to 0.2 mol m^{-3} methyl violgen (MV), in the presence of 0.05 mol m^{-3} 1-(3,4-dichlorophenyl)-1, 1-dimethyl urea (DCMU) (9). Photooxidation in isolated thylakoids incubated for 3h at 50 to 1000 μmol m^{-2} s^{-1} (PPFD) was assessed by the spectrophotometric determination of fatty acid peroxidation as malondialdehyde production (10).

3.   RESULTS AND DISCUSSION

Chloroplasts isolated from both vegetative and reproductive fronds exhibited similar trends in PS to varying PPFD and chlorophyll content within the electrode vessel. Typical light saturation curves are illustrated in Figure 1. Maximum net PS occurred at 60 μmol m^{-2} s^{-1} (PPFD) for a chlorophyll content of 25 μg cm^{-3} as opposed to 250 μmol m^{-2} s^{-1} (PPFD) for a chlorophyll content of 200 μg cm^{-3}. This illustrates considerable light harvesting efficiency and excitation energy transfer at low PPFD and supports previously published data on the dynamics of PS within this alga (2,3,4,5 and 12). However, no significant saturation plateau was observed at the lower chlorophyll concentration. Indeed, a marked decline in net PS indicative of photoinhibition occurred once the optimum PPFD was surpassed. In general, the higher the chlorophyll concentration within the electrode vessel, the higher the PPFD required to produce maximum PS and the less dramatic the reduction in net PS once irradiance was increased beyond the optimum.

Further studies examined photosystem activity of isolated thylakoids at varying PPFD (Figures 2A and 2B). At both 100 and 1000 μmol m^{-2} s^{-1} the decline in PSII activity was rapid and reached a maximum of 60% after approx. 40 and 5 min respectively. As the chlorophyll content within the electrode vessel was maintained at 20 μg, these results suggest a constant potential for PSII activity and inhibition within the experimental system. It is clear from the results obtained that PSII is the primary site of lesion within the photosynthetic electron transport chain of C. fragile chloroplasts when incubated under conditions favouring photoinhibition. Furthermore, prolonged thylakoid exposure to such conditions produced clear evidence of photooxidation as measured by the production of malondialdehyde (MDA) (Figure 3) and chlorophyll degradation (Figure 4). These data illustrate the

susceptibility of isolated choroplasts and thylakoids of
C. fragile to these photodestructive processes even at the
relatively low PPFD of 100 µmol m^{-2} s^{-1}. This raises the
question of how this alga is adapted to survive in the
intertidal habitat at varying PPFD. The intact frond must
presumably possess some photoprotective features that are absent
in the isolated chloroplasts or thylakoids, and these are
discussed in the following paper (13).

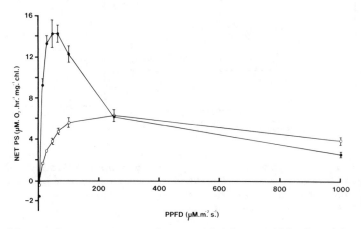

FIG 1: Effect of PPFD on net photosynthesis at 10°C by chloroplast
suspensions equivalent to 25 µg cm^{-3} (●) and 200 µg cm^{-3} (○). Each
point = x̄ ± S.E, where n = 5-7.

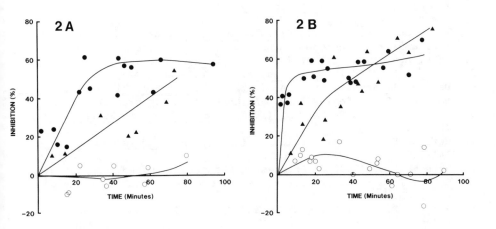

FIG 2: Time-course of inhibition of electron transport in isolated
thylakoids (equivalent to 20 µg cm^{-3} chlorophyll) at (A) 100, and
(B) 1000 µmol m^{-2} s^{-1} PPFD. PSI (○); PSII (●); PSI and PSII (▲).
Each point is a single observation.

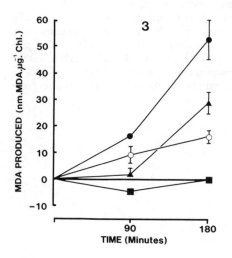
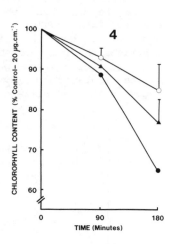

FIGS 3 and 4: Time-course of MDA production from (3), and chlorophyll content of (4), isolated thylakoids exposed to 50 (■), 100 (O), 500 (▲) and 1000 (●) µmol m^{-2} s^{-1} PPFD. Each point = $\bar{x}$ ± S.E, where n = 5.

REFERENCES

1. Kyle, D.J., Osmond, C.B. and Arntzen, C.J. (1987). Topics in Photosynthesis. Vol.9. Photoinhibition. Elsevier.
2. Ramus, J. (1978). J. Phycol. 14, 352-362.
3. Benson, E.E. and Cobb, A.H. (1983). New Phytol. 95, 581-594.
4. Anderson, J.M. (1985). Biochim. Biophys. Acta. 806, 145-153.
5. Williams, M.L. and Cobb, A.H. (1985). New Phytol. 101, 79-88.
6. Cobb, A.H. and Rott, J. (1978). New Phytol. 81, 527-541.
7. Cobb, A.H. (1977). Protoplasma. 92, 137-146.
8. Delieu, T. and Walker, D.A. (1972). New Phytol. 71, 201-225.
9. Hopkins, R.M., Sealey, R.V. and Cobb, A.H. In preparation.
10. Heath, R.L. and Packer, L. (1968). Arch. Biochem. Biophys. 125, 189-198.
11. Herron, H.A. and Mauzerall, D. (1972). Plant Physiol. 50, 141-148
12. Benson, E.E. (1983). Studies on the structure and function of Codium fragile chloroplasts. Ph.D. Thesis, Trent Polytechnic Nottingham.
13. Sealey, R.V., Williams, M.L. and Cobb, A.H. (1989). (This volume).

ACKNOWLEDGEMENTS

We thank the Science and Engineering Research Council of the UK for financial support.

ADAPTATIONS OF <u>CODIUM FRAGILE</u> (SURINGAR) HARIOT FRONDS TO PHOTOSYNTHESIS AT VARYING FLUX DENSITY

ROBERT V SEALEY[1], MICHAEL L WILLIAMS[2] AND ANDREW H COBB[1]

[1]Department of Life Sciences, Faculty of Science, Nottingham Polytechnic, Nottingham, NG11 8NS, UK; [2]School of Plant Biology, UCNW, Bangor, UK.

1.   INTRODUCTION

The intertidal alga <u>Codium fragile</u> exhibits shade adaptations enabling efficient photosynthesis (PS) at the low photosynthetic photon flux densities (PPFD) experienced at high tide. Thus, chloroplasts contain high levels of siphonoxanthin, siphonein and chlorophyll b (1,2,3), reveal both low chlorophyll a:b and high photosystem II: photosystem I ratios (1,4,5) and possess 75% of the total pigment content within the light harvesting complexes (1). However, the intertidal habitat is subjected to regular extremes of PPFD on a daily and a seasonal basis so that this alga is at great risk of photoinhibition and subsequent photooxidation at the higher PPFD's encountered at low tide. Indeed, isolated chloroplasts and thylakoids are particularly vulnerable to these photodestructive processes (6). In contrast, this paper provides evidence that intact fronds of <u>C. fragile</u> are able to avoid or tolerate photoinhibition and hence photooxidative damage and possess the ability to re-distribute excitation energy between the photosystems (4,5).

2.   MATERIALS AND METHODS

Vegetative and reproductive fronds were sampled from intertidal rockpools at Bembridge, Isle of Wight (UK) and maintained as described previously (7). Oxygen exchange by frond tips was measured polarographically at 0 to 20°C using a gaseous phase, LD2 oxygen electrode (Hansatech Ltd, UK) (8). Incident light was varied from 0 to 1109 μmol m^{-2} s^{-1} (PPFD) using an LS2, tungsten-halogen light source in conjunction with a series of neutral density filters.

Photosystem II (PSII) fluorescence was continually monitored at 678 nm over a series of light treatments using a Perkin Elmer LS-5 Luminescence Spectrometer. Frond tips (3 cm) of vegetative tissue were preincubated (dry) with light of 709 nm (photosystem I (PSI) light) for 10 min then excited with light of 435 nm (PSII light) only. After approx. 15 min the frond tips were illuminated with both PSI and PSII light combined and then PSII

M. Baltscheffsky (ed.), Current Research in Photosynthesis, Vol. II, 455–458.

light only. Excitation and emission optima were taken from Anderson (1983; 1985).

3. RESULTS AND DISCUSSION

Both vegetative and reproductive algal frond tips exhibited a similar photosynthetic response over the temperature and light ranges studied (Figure 1). Net rates increased rapidly as PPFD increased from 0 to 80 μmol m^{-2} s^{-1} with saturation of PS occurring at 200 μmol m^{-2} s^{-1}. Saturation of PS at such low PPFD's suggests considerable light harvesting efficiency and excitation energy transfer (9) and is typical of C. fragile (1,2,3,10). Furthermore, increased PPFD up to 1,200 μmol m^{-2} s^{-1} did not result in a decline in PS. Such an extended PS saturation plateau indicates that C. fragile fronds, unlike isolated chloroplasts and thylakoids (6), are able to avoid photoinhibition under conditions of prolonged exposure to light. Maintenance of a suitable ratio of activities of the two photosystems may be seen as important in preventing the onset of photoinhibition, especially considering the high PSII: PSI ratios present within C. fragile chloroplasts (2,3,11,12). Figure 2 clearly illustrates the ability of chloroplasts within the algal frond to re-distribute excitation energy over a range of light treatments. When light exciting PSII only is provided to frond tips previously adapted to PSI light, PSII fluorescence increases to a maximum, then falls over a period of 10 min to a lower constant value which is relatively unaffected by re-provision of PSI light. This is indicative of a re-distribution of excitation energy from PSII to PSI (4,5,11,12) or an alleviation of the over excitation of PSII. Such "state transitions" could not be induced in isolated chloroplast preparations.

It is apparent that whilst isolated chloroplasts and thylakoids of C. fragile are most susceptible to photoinhibition and photooxidative damage, intact fronds are surprisingly tolerant. Photoprotective mechanisms must therefore exist in situ that are absent in organello. We believe that the answer involves the arrangement of the chloroplasts within the algal frond.
C. fragile possesses a compact, dichotomous thallus consisting of closely interwoven coenocytic siphons or filaments (13, 14). The outer layer of the thallus is constructed of the dilated tips (utricles) of the siphons and it is in these structures only that the chloroplasts are situated (Figure 3). The chloroplasts are arranged peripherally, in stacks, around a large central vacuole in such numbers as to confer an optically dense nature to the thallus. It has been suggested (15) that the presence of the large vacuole serves to reflect incident light around the thin column of cytoplasm thus increasing the chance of chloroplast interaction. As considerable light

attenuation would operate within the utricle a degree of
'self-shading' of chloroplasts would presumably occur. Hence,
it would seem that the number and arrangement of chloroplasts
within the frond confers a vital mechanism in the avoidance of
photoinhibition by this alga.

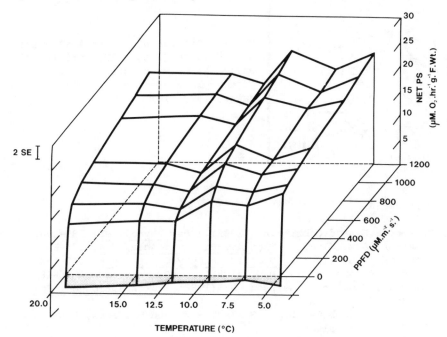

FIG 1: Relationship between light intensity, temperature and net
photosynthesis by frond tips. Each point = mean of 10 observations ±
overall S.E of the 48 observations.

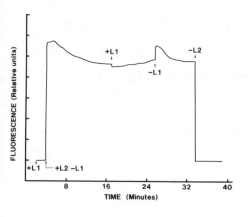

FIG 2: Time-course of PSII
fluorescence emission at 687 nm
from frond tips pre-incubated
for 10 min at 10°C in PSI light
(709 nm - L1) and then subjected to a regime of PSI and/or
PSII (435 nm - L2) light as
indicated.

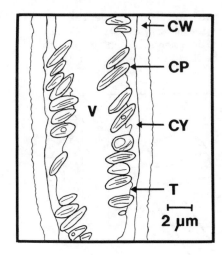

FIG 3: Diagram of internal structure of a utricle (T.S.). CW, utricle cell wall; CP, chloroplasts; CY, cytoplasm T, tonoplast; V, vacuole. After Hawes, 1979 (16).

REFERENCES

1. Benson, E.E. and Cobb, A.H. (1983). New Phytol. 95, 581-594.
2. Anderson, J.M. (1983). Biochim. Biophys. Acta. 724, 370-380.
3. Anderson, J.M. (1985). Biochim. Biophys. Acta. 806, 145-153.
4. Allen, J.F. and Holmes, N.G. (1986). FEBS Lett. 202, 175-181.
5. Anderson, J.M. and Andersson, B. (1988). Trends Biochem. Sci. 13, 351-355.
6. Cobb, A.H., Hopkins, R.M., Sealey, R.V. and Williams, M.L. (1989). (This volume).
7. Williams, M.L. and Cobb, A.H. (1985). New Phytol. 101, 79-88.
8. Delieu, T. and Walker, D.A. (1981). New Phytol. 89, 165-178.
9. Herron, H.A. and Mauzerall, D. (1972). Plant Physiol. 50, 141-148.
10. Arnold, K.E. and Murray, S.N. (1980). J. Exp. Mar. Biol. Ecol. 43, 183-192.
11. Fork, D.C. and Satoh, K. (1986). Ann. Rev. Plant Physiol. 37, 335-361
12. Allen, J.F. and Melis, A. (1988). Biochim. Biophys. Acta. 933, 95-106.
13. Lee, R.E. (1980). Phycology. Cambridge University Press.
14. Bold, H.C. and Wynne, M.J. (1985). Introduction to the Algae. Prentice Hall International, Inc, London.
15. Ramus, J. (1978). J. Phycol. 14, 352-362.
16. Hawes, C.R. (1979). New Phytol. 83, 445-450.

ACKNOWLEDGEMENTS

We thank the Science and Engineering Research Council of the UK for financial support and Paul Allison for help with the fluorescence studies.

TEMPERATURE DEPENDENCY OF PHOTOINHIBITION IN PUMPKIN

Esa Tyystjärvi and Eva-Mari Aro
Dept. of Biology, Univ. of Turku, SF-20500 Turku, Finland

1. INTRODUCTION

   Photoinhibition of photosynthesis proceeds faster in lower
temperature. Both decrease in dissipation of excitation energy by
photosynthesis and inhibition of the repair process have been suggested
to cause the acceleration of photoinhibition in chilling temperatures.
The estimated degree of temperature dependency may, however, depend on
which symptoms of photoinhibition are measured.

   PSII exists in at least two subpopulations, of which only B-PSII
takes part in the whole-chain electron transfer. Non-B-PSII cannot
reduce plastoquinone but can donate electrons to certain quinone
acceptors (1). In fact, PPBQ, a common quinone acceptor, is often used
to measure the PSII activity of isolated stroma thylakoid vesicles
which are known to contain only non-B-PSII. Non-B-PSII is insensitive
to photoinhibition in vitro (2), and it has been suggested that non-B-
PSII is used to replace damaged PSII-centers (3). These properties of
non-B-PSII can lead to severe under- or overestimations of photoinhibition in vivo, if electron transfer to quinone acceptors is used as a
criterion. The same is true for fluorescence: due to their capability
to primary photochemistry, the non-B-PSII's probably have high F_V/F_m.

   In this study, attached leaves of chilling-sensitive pumpkin were
treated in high light at room temperature or at 1°C, where diffusion-
and enzyme-dependent repair processes are at a minimum.

2. MATERIALS AND METHODS
   Attached leaves of pumpkin (Cucurbita pepo L.) were photoinhibited
at 750, 1500 or 2500 umol PAR $m^{-2}s^{-1}$ either at room temperature (RT) or
at 1°C, in saturated humidity. After the treatment, different photosynthetic parameters were measured either from leaf discs (fluorescence
induction at 77 K, apparent quantum yield of oxygen evolution), or from
thylakoids isolated from treated leaves (electron transfer activities,
fluorescence induction in the presence of DCMU or FeCN, atrazine
binding).

3. RESULTS AND DISCUSSION
   Fig. 1.a. shows a fast drop of $\emptyset_{app}$ at 1°C in the light, accompanied
by a much smaller decrease in 77 K F_V/F_{max} of leaf discs. F_V/F_{max}
measured from DCMU-poisoned thylakoids decreased in the same way as the
77 K fluorescence of leaf discs (Fig. 1.b.). It is evident that the
severity of the inhibition at 1°C is underestimated by F_V/F_{max}.

M. Baltscheffsky (ed.), Current Research in Photosynthesis, Vol. II, 459–462.
© 1990 Kluwer Academic Publishers. Printed in the Netherlands.

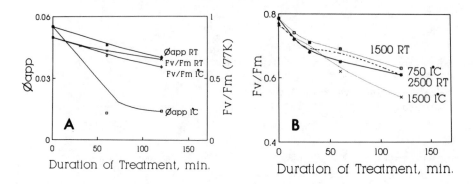

Fig. 1. (a) The effects of light treatments (1500 umol PAR $m^{-2}s^{-1}$) at RT or at $1^{\circ}C$ on 77 K F_V/F_{max} and $\emptyset_{app}$ of pumpkin leaves. (b) The effects of light treatments (750 to 2500 umol PAR $m^{-2}s^{-1}$) on F_V/F_{max} measured from DCMU-poisoned thylakoids isolated after the treatment.

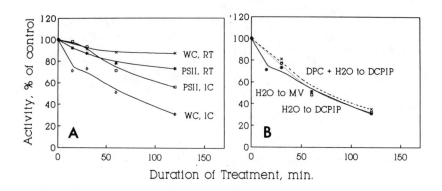

Fig. 2. (a) The effect of light treatments (1500 umol PAR $m^{-2}s^{-1}$) at RT or at $1^{\circ}C$ on PSII (H_2O to PPBQ) and whole-chain (H_2O to MV) electron transfer. (b) The effect of light treatments (1500 umol $m^{-2}s^{-1}$, $1^{\circ}C$) on PSII activity (H_2O to DCPIP, dotted line, H_2O + DPC to DCPIP, hatched line). The whole-chain activity (solid line) is included for comparison.

The low-temperature inhibition was further characterized by an extensive study of thylakoid functions. When the light treatment was given at $1^{\circ}C$, the whole-chain (WC) activity was inhibited much more than PSII electron transfer to PPBQ (Fig. 2.a.). At RT, PPBQ-dependent oxygen evolution was slightly more inhibited than WC-activity (Fig. 2. a.). After 2-h treatments at 1500 umol PAR $m^{-2}s^{-1}$, the number of atrazine-binding sites had decreased from 4.5 nmol atrazine bound per mg chl to 4.4 at room temperature and to 3.8 at $1^{\circ}C$. Thus, much faster loss of the D1 protein cannot be the reason to the reduction of the whole-chain activity and quantum yield at 1°C.

Photosystem I or cytochrome b_6f-complex were not affected at 1°C, as judged from lack of inhibition of electron transfer activity from ascorbate-DCPIP to MV or from duroquinol to MV (not shown). Measurements of PSII activity using DCPIP as electron acceptor finally proved that the loss of WC activity indeed was a result of impairment or PSII activity (Fig. 2.b.). Fig. 2.b. also shows that the oxidizing side of PSII remained undamaged in the treatment at 1°C.

Variable fluorescence measured in the presence of FeCN reflects the closure of the non-B-PSII centers (4). Measurements of F_V(FeCN) (5, Fig. 1.b.) showed that when the leaves had been treated at 1°C, F_V(FeCN) remained constant for the first hour, while room-temperature treatments led to a decrease. This can be understood, if the non-B-PSII-pool is used to replace $PSII_\alpha$ after photoinhibition at RT, but not at 1°C.

The differences in the inhibition of PSII and WC electron transfer activities (H_2O to PPBQ and H_2O to MV, respectively) support the view that only B-PSII ($PSII_\alpha$) is photoinhibited. The results also support the hypothesis (3), that a repair process replaces photoinhibited $PSII_\alpha$ centers by non-B-PSII and synthetizes new non-B-PSII. In the chilling sensitive pumpkin, this process seems to function at RT but not at 1°C. The difference between photoinhibition occurring simultaneously with an active repair process and inhibition without repair is best illustrated by plotting the ratio of WC activity to PPBQ reduction as a function of WC activity. Fig. 3. compares experimantal results with theoretical curves, obtained by simulating competition between photoinhibition and repair. The repair process was assumed to include both replacement of photoinhibited α-centers by non-B-PSII and synthesis of new non-B-PSII (cf. Fig. 3. for details). The upper curve is only schematic, because actual rates of replacement and synthesis in the different PPFD's are unknown. Anyway, inhibition of WC-activity is expected to be slower than inhibition of PPBQ-activity always, when the rates of replacement and synthesis are comparable to the rate of photoinhibition, and when the inhibition is not very severe. The exact shape of the lower curve (without repair) depends only on the proportion of non-B-PSII.

Although experimental points do not completely fit the rough simulation, it is clear that the rates of the repair process form the basis of the observed differences in photoinhibition of PSII at RT and at 1°C in the chilling sensitive pumpkin.

Generally, when the repair processes are functioning, measurements of PSII electron transfer to quinone acceptors usually overestimate actual photoinhibition (loss of whole-chain activity). On the contrary, when the repair process is completely inhibited, severe underestimations are likely to occur. The same is in principle true for simple F_V/F_{max} measurements.

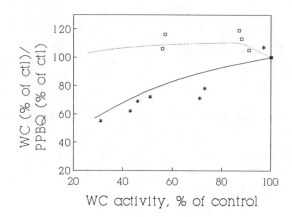

Fig. 3. The ratio of normalized whole-chain (H_2O to MV) and PSII (H_2O to PPBQ) electron transfer activities in thylakoids isolated after photoinhibition treatments (750 to 2500 umol PAR $m^{-2}s^{-1}$ for 30 to 240 min.) at RT (□) or at 1°C (*), plotted against normalized WC activity. Each experimental point represents the mean of 3-7 treatments of attached leaves. The upper simulated curve was drawn assuming that the rate of replacement of inhibited centers is 60 %, and the rate of synthesis of non-B-PSII 50 % of the rate of photoinhibition. In the lower curve, no repair processes are assumed. 30 % of all PSII centers were assumed to be initially of non-B-type.

The inhibition of $\emptyset_{app}$ at 1°C in the light is probably a result of several factors. In addition to inhibition of PSII, the reactions of the carbon reduction cycle may be inhibited at low temperature in the light (6).

REFERENCES
1   Graan, t. and Ort, D.R. (1986) Biochim. Biophys. Acta 852, 320-330.
2   Mäenpää, P., Andersson, B. and Sundby, C. (1987) Febs lett. 215, 31-36.
3   Melis, A. (1988) in Applications of Chlorophyll Fluorescence (H.K. Lichtenthaler, ed.), pp. 33-43, Kluwer Academic Publishers, Dordrecht.
4   Melis, A. (1985) Biochim. Biophys. Acta 808, 334-342.
5   Aro, E.-M., Tyystjärvi, E. and Nurmi, A. (1989), this volume
6   Sassenrath, G.F., Ort, D.R. and Portis, Jr. A.R. (1987) in Prog. in Photos. Res. 4 (Biggins, J. ed.), pp. 103-106, Martinus Nijhoff, Dordrecht.

PHOTOINHIBITION OF PHOTOSYNTHESIS IN A WINTER WHEAT CROP

Q.J. GROOM, S.P. LONG and N.R. BAKER, Dept. of Biology, University of Essex, Colchester, CO4 3SQ, UK.

1. INTRODUCTION

It is well established that exposure of many plants to low temperatures and high light can cause photoinhibition of photosynthesis (1), and recently this phenomenon has been demonstrated for maize leaves in the field (2). Maize is a chilling sensitive species and would be expected to experience photoinhibition at low temperatures in high light. However, it has not been ascertained whether chill-induced photoinhibition occurs in cold tolerant crops in the field. Photoinhibition of photosynthesis has been shown to result in a decrease in quantum yield of oxygen evolution (3) and a quenching of chlorophyll fluorescence (4), consequently these parameters can be used as useful probes of photoinhibition in leaf tissue. In this study measurements of the quantum yield of oxygen evolution and chlorophyll fluorescence were made on leaves of a wheat crop during the winter to evaluate whether photoinhibitory damage to photosynthesis occurred under field climatic conditions.

2. MATERIALS AND METHODS

Seeds of _Triticum aestivum_ cv. Bezostaya a winter wheat, were sown in a field plot at the University of Essex (N51°52', E0°57') on 26/9/1988. The youngest fully expanded leaves were selected at random and used for all measurements. Some plants were shaded from direct sunlight using plastic screens. Air and soil temperatures and photosynthetic photon flux density (PPFD 400-700nm) were monitored at 10 minute intervals using a Delta-T weather station located next to the plot.

The apparent quantum yield of oxygen evolution (ϕ) for leaves was measured using a computer controlled leaf disc oxygen electrode, over a PPFD range 0-150 $\mu mol.m^{-2}.s^{-1}$ and in saturating CO_2 (5).

The ratio of variable (Fv) to maximal (Fm) fluorescence, Fv/Fm, was measured using a modulated fluorimeter (6). Leaves were dark adapted for 10 to 15 minutes prior to measuring minimal fluorescence (Fo) using a weak modulated yellow light (1 $\mu mol.m^{-2}.s^{-1}$). Fm was determined by exposing the leaf to white actinic light with a PPFD of 1600 $\mu mol.m^{-2}.s^{-1}$.

3. RESULTS AND DISCUSSION

The winter of 1988/89 in N.E.Essex was unusually mild. The winter wheat crop had adequate water throughout the winter but was never water-logged. The soil surface did freeze at night on occasions, however, the mean soil temperature at a depth of 10cm was always above

M. Baltscheffsky (ed.), Current Research in Photosynthesis, Vol. II, 463–466.
© 1990 _Kluwer Academic Publishers. Printed in the Netherlands._

0°C. Consequently it can be assumed that the plants were not exposed to
water stress induced by either drought or freezing of the soil water.
     The changes in Fv/Fm during the day are shown in Fig.1 for leaves
on four selected days with rather different climatic conditions. The
air temperature and PPFD above the wheat canopy throughout these days
are shown in Fig.2. On the two cold days (29/1/1989 and 23/2/1989)
Fv/Fm decreased throughout the morning and then recovered in the
afternoon.

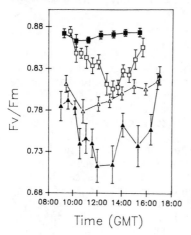

Figure 1. Changes in Fv/m between 8.00
and 18 h on 29/1/1989 (□ , a cold,
sunny day), 5/2/1989 (■ , a warm,
cloudy day), 23/2/1989 (▲ , a cold,
sunny day) and 30/3/1989 (△ ,a warm,
sunny day).

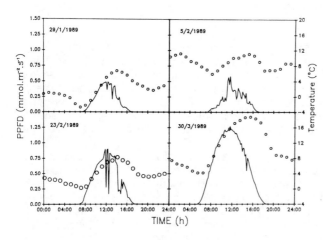

Figure 2. Changes in
temperature (°C) and
photosynthetically-
active photon flux
density (PPFD) during
the day on 29/1/1989,
5/2/1989, 23/2/1989
and 30/3/1989, i.e.
the days on which the
Fv/Fm data shown in
Fig.1 was collected.

Although the decrease in Fv/Fm was only ca. 7% on these days, it should
be emphasised that this was significant. During the morning of the
30/3/1989, which was a relatively warm and sunny day, a small decrease
in Fv/Fm was observed that was reversed during the afternoon. However
on the 5/2/1989, a warm cloudy day, Fv/Fm did not change significantly.
These data clearly demonstrate that Fv/Fm was depressed on the mornings

during which temperatures were below 4°C. Multiple regression analysis on data collected over the winter demonstrated that the reductions in Fv/Fm at midday were correlated significantly with low temperature and high light (data not shown).

The apparent quantum yield of oxygen evolution (ϕ) was measured daily at times between 08.00 and 16.00 hrs. Data were collated into four groups based on climatic conditions of light and temperature (Table 1). Values of ϕ proved to be more variable than Fv/Fm values and no significant differences were found between ϕ on days with different temperatures and light levels. When ϕ was measured on plants that had been shaded artificially in the field, no significant differences were observed between shaded and non shaded leaves in the separate climatic groups. However, as a whole shaded leaves did have a higher, although not significantly different, ϕ than unshaded leaves (data not shown). Consequently, measurements of ϕ provide no evidence that photoinhibition is occurring in the winter wheat crop in the field. It may well be that quantum yield measurements in the oxygen electrode are not sufficiently accurate to detect small decreases in ϕ due to photoinhibition. However, the fluorescence measurements suggest that decreases in the photochemical efficiency of PS2 of ca. 18% were occurring in leaves during the winter, and it would be surprising if such changes were reflected directly in ϕ that they would not be observed as significant differences by measurement of ϕ in the oxygen electrode.

It is tempting to interpret the decrease in Fv/Fm during the mornings when temperatures are low and the light high as being indicative of the classical photoinhibitory damage to the D_1 reaction centre protein of PS2. Most certainly decreases in Fv/Fm have been shown to occur in parallel with damage to the D_1 protein (7). However, recently it has been shown that Fv/Fm measured at steady state photosynthesis decreases when the light intensity is increased from zero to a level close to saturation for photosynthesis (8,9). It is unlikely under such physiological conditions that damage to the D_1 protein is occurring. Such light-induced decreases in Fv/Fm are likely to the result of the development of a quenching of excitation energy in the PS2 antennae (8,9), which has been speculated to be a control mechanism for regulating the rate of excitation of PS2 reaction centres (10,11). It can be speculated that the decline in Fv/Fm in the winter wheat leaves on cold, sunny mornings is a manifestation of such a regulation of excitation energy distribution rather than damage to PS2 reaction centres. The rapid recovery of Fv/Fm during the afternoon would support this suggestion. It should be emphasised that any decrease in Fv/Fm, irrespective of the mechanism producing it, would be expected to result in a decrease in the quantum efficiency of non-cyclic electron transport and most probably the quantum yield of carbon assimilation. Consequently, a light-induced regulatory mechanism for the control of excitation distribution which decreases Fv/Fm can be considered a form of photoinhibition of photosynthesis, although it is not what might be considered as 'classical' photoinhibition mediated via damage to PS2 reaction centre D_1 proteins. It is to be hoped that sufficiently sensitive and rapid measurements of the quantum yield of

O_2 or CO_2 assimilation can be developed to study this phenomenon in more detail.

Table 1. Apparent quantum yields of oxygen evolution (ϕ) of wheat leaves in different climatic conditions during the winter. The mean intergrated PPFD and mean air temperature for days in each climatic group are given. n is the number of leaves measured.

Parameter	Climatic Conditions			
	Low light Low temp.	Low light High temp.	High light Low temp.	High light High temp.
Intergrated PPFD $(mol.m^{-2})$	2.70	2.63	7.77	6.75
Air temp. (°C)	3.82	7.79	2.56	8.29
ϕ (Standard deviation)	0.081 (0.008)	0.086 (0.010)	0.080 (0.009)	0.078 (0.014)
n	36	55	67	32

ACKNOWLEDGEMENTS

This work was supported by the AFRC (AG84/4). QJG was the recipient of a NERC studentship.

REFERENCES

1. Powles, S.B. (1984) Ann.Rev.Plant Physiol. 35, 15-44.
2. Baker, N.R., Bradbury, M. and Farage, P.K., Ireland, C.R. and Long, S.P. (1989) Phil. Trans. Roy. Soc. Lond. B. 323, 295-308.
3. Demming, B. and Bjorkman, O. (1987) Planta, 170, 171-184.
4. Baker, N.R. and Horton, P. (1987) in Photoinhibition (Kyle, D., Arntzen, C.J. and Osmond, C.B., eds.) pp. 145-168, Elsevier, Amsterdam.
5. Walker, D.A. (1987) The use of the oxygen electrode and fluorescence probes in simple measurements of photosynthesis. Oxygraphics Ltd, Sheffield
6. Ogren, E. and Baker, N.R. (1985) Plant Cell Environ. 8, 539-547.
7. Bradbury, M. and Baker, N.R. (1986) Plant Cell Environ. 9, 289-297.
8. Harbinson, J., Genty, B. and Baker, N.R. (1989) Plant Physiol., in press.
9. Genty, B., Harbinson, J. and Baker, N.R. (1990) Plant Physiol. Biochem., in press
10. Weis, E. and Berry, J.A. (1987) Biochim. Biophys. Acta 894, 198-208.
11. Krause, G.H. and Laasch, H. (1987) in Progress in Photosynthesis Research (Biggins, J., ed.), Vol IV, pp. 19-25, Martinus Nijhoff, Dordrecht.

SPRING AND WINTER WHEATS EXHIBIT DIFFERENTIAL SUSCEPTIBILITY TO LOW
TEMPERATURE INHIBITION OF PHOTOSYNTHESIS.

V.M. HURRY AND N.P.A. HUNER. Department of Plant Sciences. University of
Western Ontario. London. CANADA. N6A 5B7.

1. INTRODUCTION

Acclimation of cereals to low temperatures and the development of maximum
freezing tolerance requires growth and development during prolonged exposure to low,
non-freezing temperatures (0-5°C)[1]. For winter cereals the exposure to cold-hardening
temperatures coincides with the early growth and development of the seedling in
autumn. The development of a crown capable of overwintering is therefore dependent
on the capacity of these seedlings to photosynthesise and develop under a cold-
hardening regime. The effects of short-term chilling on photosynthetic competence of
leaves grown under warm temperature regimes are well documented. However,
experiments carried out with plants acclimated to cold-hardening conditions are scarce
and report variable responses. For example, cold hardened *Spinacea oleracea*[2] and
Secale cereale[3] showed increased resistance to photoinhibition when acclimated to low
temperatures. However, frost hardened and non-hardened needles of *Pinus sylvestris*[3,4]
and *Pinus contorta*[4] and seedlings of spring barley (*Hordeum vulgare*)[3] were reported
to be equally susceptible to photoinhibition when exposed to short term
photoinhibitory conditions.

This differential avoidance of photoinhibition, particularly in the winter and
spring cereals, suggests that photoinhibition may be an important factor limiting cold
tolerance in cereals. In the present study we have examined the photosynthetic
characteristics of six cultivars of wheat which exhibit different levels of cold tolerance.
Spring and winter wheats were grown at hardening and non-hardening temperatures
to determine if the two groups show any differential photosynthetic response to
growth at low, cold-hardening temperature.

2. MATERIALS AND METHODS

Three winter (cv. Monopol, cv. Kharkov, cv. Augusta) and 3 spring (cv.
Glenlea, cv. Katepwa, cv. Marquis) cultivars of wheat (*Triticum aestivum* L.) were

M. Baltscheffsky (ed.), Current Research in Photosynthesis, Vol. II, 467–470.
© 1990 *Kluwer Academic Publishers. Printed in the Netherlands.*

germinated under controlled environment conditions with a day/night temperature regime of 20/16°C, at a PPFD of 250 μmol m^{-2} s^{-1} and a 16-h photoperiod. After 7 days, both winter and spring seedlings were hardened by transfer to a temperature regime of 5/5°C. Control plants remained under the 20/16°C regime.

Measurement of CO_2 gas exchange rates were conducted on the attached fully expanded 3rd or 4th leaves of hardened and non-hardened plants at 25 and 77 days of age respectively. At these ages both leaves were fully expanded and the plants were considered to be of the same physiological age based on comparative growth kinetics at 5°C and 20°C. Measurements were made at 20 and 5°C air temperature in a controlled environment growth chamber such that the temperature of the measured leaf and the remainder of the plant were comparable. Plants that experienced a shift in temperature prior to measurement of gas exchange were allowed to equilibrate for 8 hours in the dark at the measurement temperature. Plants were allowed to equilibrate for 1 hour to changes in light intensity. All measurements of CO_2 concentration were made in a closed gas exchange system using a LI-COR 6200 portable infra-red gas analyzer. Light intensity was monitored at leaf height with a quantum sensor (Model LI-190S-1, LI-COR Inc., Lincoln, Neb.). Three separate leaves in 4 pots were sampled at each of 10 light intensities and the values within each pot were pooled to give 4 replicate measurements per cultivar at each light intensity. Apparent quantum efficiencies were calculated from this data. The data were subjected to analysis of variance.

In addition to the gas exchange data, hardened spring (Glenlea) and winter (Monopol) seedlings were exposed to 1000 μmol m^{-2} s^{-1} PPFD for 0,1,3 and 6 hours at 5°C. The 77K fluorescence emission spectra of isolated thylakoids were then measured using a LS-1 steady state spectrophotometer (Photon Tech. Intl.) to examine relative changes in energy distribution.

3. RESULTS AND DISCUSSION

Acclimation of spring and winter cultivars of wheat to cold hardening temperatures results in differential expression of photoinhibition of photosynthesis, measured as a decrease in optimal photon yield of CO_2 assimilation. Winter cultivars grown at 5°C, 250 μmol m^{-2} s^{-1} PPFD and a 16-h photoperiod showed no evidence of photoinhibition, however all three spring cultivars showed losses of apparent quantum efficiency in excess of 30% compared to 20°C grown controls (Table 1). In addition, it was shown that the spring cultivar Glenlea was equally photoinhibited when grown under either short or long days at 5°C. Again the winter cultivar Monopol yielded similar quantum efficiencies under all three growth regimes and at both measurement temperatures (Table 2). Recovery was seen with Glenlea following incubation of the cold hardened seedlings at 20°C in the dark for 8 hours (Table 2), although in the first experiment the degree of photoinhibition in the three spring cultivars was greater and only partial recovery was seen overnight (Table 1). Further evidence of the differential ability of spring and winter cultivars to develop resistance to low temperature photoinhibition is presented in Figure 1. Following exposure of both cultivars to high light at 5°C, preferential quenching of the 685nm and 695nm fluorescence peaks was observed in the spring cultivar and this decline in fluorescence yield increased with increased time of exposure. The overall characteristics of the spectra remained the same however, suggesting that the normal light harvesting apparatus connected to the reaction centres was maintained. No such decline in fluorescence yield was seen in the thylakoids isolated from the winter cultivar Monopol, even after 6 hours exposure.

Table 1. Effect of growth and measurement temperature on apparent quantum yield (μmol CO_2 . μmol 400-700nm photons) of winter and spring wheat cultivars.

		Non-hardened		Hardened	
		Meas. temp.		Meas. temp.	
		20°C	5°C	20°C	5°C
	Monopol	0.041	0.047	0.042	0.042
WINTER	Kharkov	0.040	0.040	0.045	0.045
	Augusta	0.042	0.045	0.044	0.040
	Glenlea	0.040	0.046	0.034	0.024
SPRING	Katepwa	0.048	0.047	0.027	0.026
	Marquis	0.046	0.045	0.035	0.029

Table 2. Apparent quantum yield measured at both 5 and 20°C for the winter and spring wheat cultivars Monopol and Glenlea.

		CULTIVAR	
Measurement Temperature	Growth Regime	MONOPOL	GLENLEA
5°C	20°C/16hr	0.051	0.052
	5°C/16hr	0.050	0.042
	5°C/10hr	0.055	0.042
20°C	20°C/16hr	0.053	0.053
	5°C/16hr	0.055	0.050
	5°C/10hr	0.055	0.052

It appears therefore that the winter cultivars have mechanisms in place that enable them to resist photoinhibition at cold hardening temperatures and moderate PPFD's while the spring cultivars do not, and that these mechanisms operate independent of the influence of day length. Similar results have been reported for changes in *in vivo* fluorescence kinetics[4]. No significant ability to develop a resistance to low temperature photoinhibition of photosynthesis was found in spring cereals while winter rye developed a high resistance in those leaves that developed at low temperature. Furthermore Oquist and Huner[3] showed that photoinhibition could be detected at light intensities as low as 50 μmol m^{-2} s^{-1}. The results reported in this paper and those of Oquist and Huner[3] suggest that spring cereals both in the field in the fall and winter and those routinely grown in growth chambers at low temperatures experience conditions photoinhibitory to photosynthesis.

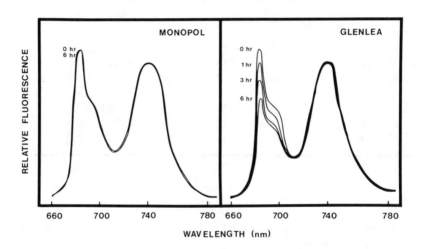

Figure 1. The Chl *a* fluorescence emission spectra at 77K of thylakoids (5 μg Chl ml^{-1}) isolated in the presence of cations from hardened winter (Monopol) and spring (Glenlea) wheat seedlings preilluminated at 1000 μmol m^{-2}s^{-1} for 0,1,3 and 6 hours at 5°C. The excitation wavelength was 440 nm and the spectra were nomalised to the 735 nm peak.

4. REFERENCES

1. Krol, M., Griffith, M., Huner, N.P.A. (1984) Can. J. Bot. 62, 1062-1068
2. Somersalo, S. and Krause, G.H. (1989) Planta 177, 409-416
3. Oquist, G. and Huner, N.P.A. (1989) Planta, in press.
4. Oquist, G. and Malmberg, G. (1989) Photosynth. Res. 20, 261-277

EFFECTS OF COLD ACCLIMATION ON THE SUSCEPTIBILITY OF PHOTOSYNTHESIS TO PHOTOINHIBITION

GUNNAR ÖQUIST and NORMAN P.A. HUNER*, Dept. of Plant Physiology, Univ. of Umeå, S-901 87 Umeå, Sweden; Dept. of Plant Science*, Univ. of Western Ontario, London, Ontario N6A 5B7, Canada

INTRODUCTION

At low temperatures plants become very sensitive to photoinhibition of photosynthesis. This has been ascribed to low temperatures inhibiting 1) photosynthesis, 2) de novo protein synthesis necessary for repair of photodamage and 3) alternative ways of dissipating excessive excitation (1). In this communication we have studied whether cold acclimation of freezing tolerant species like Scots pine and winter rye induces increased resistance to photoinhibition, which acclimation might be beneficial for the survival of hardy plants in the field during autumn and winter. Comparisons have been made with spring barley with low freezing tolerance.

MATERIALS AND METHODS

Seeds of Scots pine (Pinus sylvestris L.; open pollinated, grafted clone AC 1022, N65°17' E16°43', altitude 500 m, collected in the orchard Öst-Teg, Umeå) were germinated, grown and cold acclimated in climate chambers according to (2). This seedlings only contained primary needles. Seedlings with secondary needles were obtained from the Forest Tree Nurcery of Piparböle, Umeå. They were grown in a glass house and cold acclimated according to the procedure described in (2). The cereals winter rye cv. Muskateer (Secale cereale L.) and spring barley cv. Gunilla (Hordeum vulgare L.) were grown and cold acclimated basically according to (3). Muskateer was obtained from Agriculture Canada, Swift Current, Saskatchewan, Canada, and Gunilla from Svalöf AB, Röbäcksdalen, Umeå, Sweden.

To induce photoinhibition of photosynthesis non hardened and cold hardened plants were, unless otherwise specified, exposed to a continuous photosynthetic photon flux density (PPFD) of 400 umol $m^{-2}s^{-1}$ (metal halogen lamps Osram HQI-T 400W/DH) at 5 °C. Since vertically oriented cereal leaves were not very much affected by photoinhibitory light coming from above, we positioned the leaves horizontally during photoinhibition.

Chlorophyll fluorescence kinetics of leaves (adaxial side) and needles (upper surface) were measured at room temperature by a Plant Stress Meter (BioMonitor AB S.C.I., Umeå, Sweden). The ratio Fv/Fm was used as a measure of the photochemical efficiency of photosystem II. The plants were dark adapted for at least 45 min prior to fluorescence measurements.

M. Baltscheffsky (ed.), Current Research in Photosynthesis, Vol. II, 471–474.
© 1990 Kluwer Academic Publishers. Printed in the Netherlands.

RESULTS AND DISCUSSION

To induce photoinhibition of photosynthesis cold hardened and non hardened winter rye, spring barley and Scots pine were exposed to a stepwise increase of the PPFD at 5 °C (Figure 1A-D). Fully expanded, secondary leaves of rye and barley developed under the two growth regimes were used. For pine both primary and secondary needles were considered. It appears that leaves of winter rye developed at 5 °C had acquired an increased resistance to photoinhibition, whereas neither spring barley nor Scots pine did show any significant increase in resistance to photoinhibition upon cold acclimation.

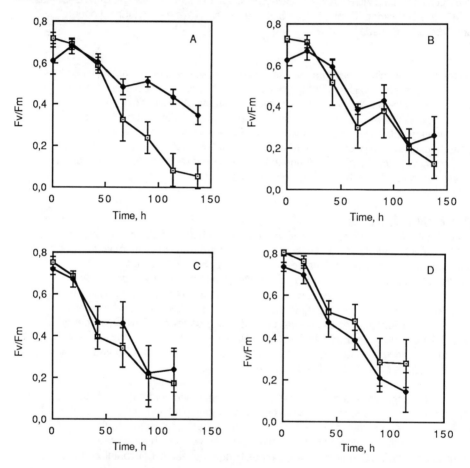

Figure 1. Time dependent photoinhibition of photosynthesis measured as the decrease of the chlorophyll fluorescence Fv/Fm ratio in non hardened (□) and cold hardened (♦) (A) winter rye, (B) spring barley, seedlings of Scots pine with (C) primary and (D) secondary needles. The PPFD of the photoinhibitory light was: 0 - 18 h, 100 umol m^{-2}s^{-1}, 18 - 42 h, 230 umol m^{-2}s^{-1} and after 48 h 400 umol m^{-2}s^{-1}. Temperature during photoinhibition was 5 °C. Standard deviations are given for n = 10.

Primary winter rye leaves developed at a day/night temperature regime of 25/15 $^{\circ}$C and then transferred to the low temperature of 5 $^{\circ}$C for cold acclimation did not increase their resistance to photoinhibition (data not shown). In fact longer periods (more than one week) of cold acclimation of such leaves induced chlorosis demonstrating the limited ability of rye leaves to acclimate to low temperature when developed at high temperatures.

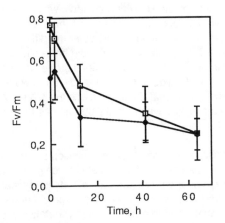

Figure 2. Time dependent photoinhibition of photosynthesis measured as the decrease of the chlorophyll fluorescence Fv/Fm ratio in non hardened (▫) and cold hardened (♦) seedlings of Scots pine grown and cold hardened under a photoperiod of 17 h and a PPFD of 50 umol m^{-2}s^{-1}. PPFD and temperature of phoitoinhibitory conditions were 400 umol m^{-2} s^{-1} and 5 $^{\circ}$C, respectively. Standard deviations are given for n = 10.

The standard cold acclimation program used for pine consisted of both a decrease in photoperiod from 17 to 8 h to induce bud formation and a decrease of the PPFD from 250 to 50 umol m^{-2}s^{-1} when the seedlings were transferred to the cold hardening temperature regime of 4 $^{\circ}$C (2). To address the question of whether cold acclimated pine acquired a shade acclimation that cancelled out a cold hardening induced decrease of the sensitivity to photoinhibition we grew and cold acclimated seedlings of Scots pine under similar light conditions (50 umol m^{-2}s^{-1}; photoperiode 17 h) but with the same temperature program as used in the standard procedure for cold hardening of pine (2). Figure 2 shows that even when treated under an identical light regime during growth and cold acclimation non hardened and cold hardened Scots pine reached the same level of photoinhibition when exposed to 400 umol m^{-2}s^{-1} at 5 $^{\circ}$C. The finding that pine at the onset of photoinhibition had a relatively low Fv/Fm ratio (Figure 2) is explained by these seedlings becoming partly photoinhibited under long day conditions at 5 $^{\circ}$C even at such a low PPFD as 50 umol m^{-2}s^{-1}.

We conclude that cold acclimation of winter rye increases its resistance to photoinhibition, whereas spring barley and Scots pine have the same susceptibilities to photinhibition in non hardened and cold hardened states. From this follows that an increased resistance to photoinhibition upon cold acclimation is not related to freezing resistance since both winter rye and Scots pine become very freezing tolerant (frost killing temperatures around -30 $^{\circ}$C) under the cold hardening conditions used in this work.

Furthermore, leaves of winter rye have to develop at low temperatures in order to acquire increased resistance to photoinhibition. However, spinach, which has a very much lower frost tolerance than winter rye, is reported to acquire increased resistance to photoinhibition during cold acclimation (4). Whether the different results obtained with winter rye and spinach, with respect of cold hardening induced resistance to photoinhibition, depend on different developmental strategies of the two species can not be said at present. In *Chlamydomonas reinhardtii* (5), however, an increased resistance to photoinhibition upon cold acclimation occurred in a culture of dividing and growing cells, which is a similar developmental strategy as that of winter rye.

We tentatively believe that an increased resistance to photoinhibition during cold acclimation of pine would probably not be of any selective value since growth is largely terminated in the autumn. In winter rye on the other hand an increased resistance to photoinhibition would be beneficial for the maintainence of active growth and development at low temperatures in that it has to establish itself vegetatively for full development the following summer. Since pine unlike winter rye enters a dormant state during the fall, photoinhibition of photosynthesis in pine may even be of significant importance as a mechanism for controlled dissipation of excessive excitation. Photoinhibition of photosynthesis is a significant component of the winter stress effects that Scots pine encounters during the winter (6). Without such a down-regulation of photosystem II in dormant pine exposed to prevailing low, freezing temperatures the needles might be endangered by photodynamic damages. With this view photoinhibition of photosynthesis of pine at low temperatures is a naturally occurring phenomenon of physiological and ecological significance for the successful establishment of evergreens in cold, temperate climates.

ACKNOWLEDGEMENT
The work was supported by the Swedish Natural Science Research Council.

REFERENCES
1 Öquist, G. (1987) in Progress in Photosynthesis Research (Biggins, J., ed.), Vol. IV, pp. 1 - 10, Martinus Nijhoff Publishers, Dordrecht
2 Strand, M. and Öquist, G. (1985) Physiol. Plant. 64, 425 - 430
3 Huner, N. P. A. (1985) Can. J. Bot. 63, 506 - 511
4 Somersalo, S. and Krause, G. H. (1989) in Applications of chlorophyll fluorescence (Lichtenthaler, H., ed.), pp. 157 - 164, Kluwer Academic Publishers, Dordrecht
5 Falk, S., Samuelsson, G. and Öquist, G. (1989) Physiol. Plant. Submitted.
6 Öquist, G. and Ögren, E. (1985) Photosynth. Res. 7, 19 - 30.

INTRASPECIFIC VARIATION IN SUSCEPTIBILITY TO PHOTOINHIBITION DURING CHILLING OF CYPERUS LONGUS L POPULATIONS FROM EUROPE.

Anne. E Gravett and S.P Long , Dept. of Biology, University of Essex, Colchester, U.K.

1. INTRODUCTION

Cyperus longus L.(Cyperaceae) is a C4 sedge which is common throughout southern Europe, but also occurs as far north as the British Isles. Other C4 species such as Zea mays are well known to be susceptible to photoinhibition during the chilling conditions typical of spring and early summer in cool temperate climates.
Ecotypic variation has been reported within the species with regard to climate, (1) ; southern populations are predominantly ssp.badius (Desf.) Murb. and northern populations predominantly ssp.longus. This study investigated the hypothesis that more northerly populations of this C4 species are genetically less susceptible to photoinhibition during chilling, by monitoring changes in the ratio of variable to maximum chlorophyll fluorescence (Fv/Fm) before and after chilling in high light.

2. MATERIALS AND METHODS

2.1. Plant Material

Seed of six ecotypes of C.longus were collected from 5 locations around Europe (shown in Table 1). Three of the six ecotypes belonged to the ssp. badius and the remaining three to the ssp.longus (see table 1).
The seed was germinated in light and then transferred to pots. The plants were kept under greenhouse conditions with average temperatures of 24/18°C (day/night) and supplemented light, which was set at a daylength of 16 hours. The plants were watered daily and fed weekly with full strength Long Ashton nutrient solution.
When the plants were 2 months old, dark and light chilling experiemnts were carried out.

M. Baltscheffsky (ed.), Current Research in Photosynthesis, Vol. II, 475–478.

Table 1 Places of origin of the six C.longus ecotypes,
    and the subspecies of each.

Collection No.   Origin   subspecies

1	Trieste,(Italy)	badius
2	Siena ,(Italy)	badius
3	Coimbra,(Portugal)	badius
4	Cornwall,(Britain)	longus
5	Paris, (France)	longus
6	Siena, (Italy)	longus

2.2. Chilling Treatments

1. The plants were chilled at 4°C for 15 hours in the dark and then at addition of 6hours at a PPFD of $1000\,\mu mol\,m^{-2}s^{-1}$. After chilling the plants were recovered for 5 hours at 25°C with a PPFD $50\,\mu mol\,m^{-2}s^{-1}$
2. Plants were chilled for 15 hours at 4°C with a PPFD of $1000\,\mu mol\,m^{-2}s^{-1}$. Plants were recovered at 25°C with a PPFD of $50\,\mu mol\,m^{-2}s^{-1}$, for 24 hours.
The treatments used the most recently expanded leaves.

2.3. Chlorophyll fluorescence measurements

The ratio of variable (Fv) to maximal (Fm) fluorescence was measured using a modulated fluorimeter (M.F.M.S. Hansatech, UK) as described by Ogren and Baker in 1985(2). Measurements were carried out on the leaf before and after chilling, and the Fv/Fm ratio monitored over the recovery period, making sure that the same location was used on the leaf for each measurement. Damage was assessed by determining the percentage reduction in the Fv/Fm ratio. This was calculated using the percentage decrease from the pre-chilled value. In addition, percentages were then plotted to show their increase with time of recovery and the area above the curve of these plots was used . The decrease, integrated with respect to time, represents the combined effects of loss of potential for CO_2 assimilation due to both photoinhibition and capacity for recovery.These units are referred to here as integrated units.

3. RESULTS

No significant difference, (t,p >0.05) in chilling sensitivity between the two subspecies, following treatment 1. (see Fig.1.a. and Fig.1.b.)which would simulate the cold nights and cold bright mornings that might be encountered in temperate climates. However, some ecotypic variation ,based on region of origin, was found. To examine the possibility of a subspecies difference under more severe chilling, treatment 2. was employed.

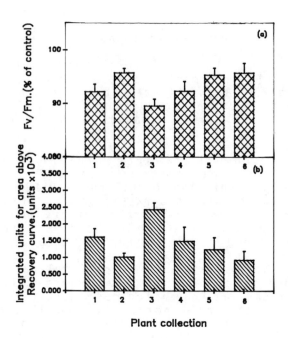

Fig.1.
Graph showing
treatment 1.
a) Integrated
units for area
above recovery
curve
b) Initial
Fv/Fm after
chilling.
(Bars above the
columns are
s.e., d.f.=30)

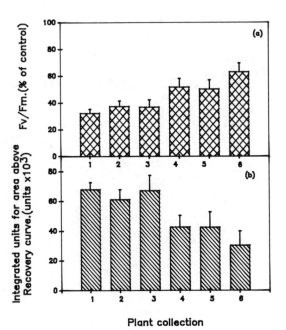

Fig.2.
Graph showing
treatment 2.
a) Integrated
units above
recovery curve.
b) Initial
Fv/Fm after
chilling.
(bars above the
columns are
s.e., d.f.=30)

More severe damage was observed when the plants were chilled for 15 hours in high light. Ssp. badius was significantly more photoinhibited than ssp.longus (t, p <0.01) (see Fig.2.a. and Fig.2.b.). The coll.6. ssp.longus from Siena showed a significantly greater tolerance to the cold treatment than the other ecotypes (t,p <0.01). Fig 2.b. shows treatment 2 using the area above the curve for ecotype comparisons. Ssp.longus is shown to be significantly less damaged by the treatment than the ssp.badius. (t, p <0.05).

4. DISCUSSION

These results show infra-specific and infra-subspecific variation in susceptibility to photoinhibition during chilling in C.longus. Differences are largely commensurate with geographic origin, northern collections generally being the more tolerant. However, the Siena collections are an exception to this pattern, which might be explained by the higher altitude of this site.

Previously Potvin has examined C4 cold tolerance of ecotypes ofEchinochloa crus-galli , cotrasting climates and shown biochemical and physiological adaptations to low temperature in the more northerly populations, (3,4,5). However, this work did not consider photoinhibition. This present study shows that greater tolerance to photoinhibition exists in some ecotypes and may be a further factor involved in allowing improved cold tolerance.

References

1 Collins, R.P., McNally, S.F., Simpson, D.A. & Jones, M.B. (1988). New Phytol., **110**,279-289
2 Ogren, E. and Baker, N.R. (1985) Pl. Cell. Environ.**8**,539-547.
3 Potvin, C. (1986a) J.Ecol.**74**,915-923
4 Potvin, C. (1986b) Physiol. Plant. **69**,659-664.
5 Potvin, C., Simon, J. and Strain, B.R. (1986) Oecologia. (Berl.) **69**,499-506

PHOTOINHIBITION IN SPINACH LEAVES AT LOW TEMPERATURE IN THE FIELD

SUSANNE SOMERSALO[1] and G. HEINRICH KRAUSE

Institute for Biochemistry of Plants, Heinrich Heine University,
D-4000 Düsseldorf 1, FRG. [1]Permanent address: Department of Biology,
University of Turku, SF-20500 Turku, Finland

1.   INTRODUCTION
High light under field conditions has been shown to induce inhibition
of photosynthesis. This may occur in plants not suffering from any
other stress factors (1), but is promoted by unfavorable environmental
conditions. Photoinhibition in the nature has been well documented in
conifers at freezing temperatures during winter (2,3). For herbaceous
plants of moderate climate zones, high light at chilling temperatures
is a common condition during the winter season. Night frosts, preceding
bright days, may impose additional stress upon the plants. On the other
hand, cold acclimation has been shown to decrease the susceptibility of
the plants to photoinhibition (4). To assess the role of photoinhibition in cold acclimated herbaceous plants in their natural environment,
we studied the effects of night frost and of high solar irradiation on
cool days on photosynthesis of spinach (Spinacia oleracea L.) growing
in the field during winter. Fluorescence emission (at 20°C and 77 K)
was used to characterize stress effects.

2.   PROCEDURE
2.1.   Material: Spinach plants were grown in the field under natural
light and temperature conditions. The plants were used in the cold-
acclimated state between December and March. The frost-killing point of
the leaves, T_{50}, was between -10.8°C and -12.5°C. All the measurements
were carried out under laboratory conditions.

2.2.   Room temperature fluorescence of leaf discs was measured with a
Hansatech fluorometer (Hansatech, Kings Lynn, Norfolk, U.K.) as described before (4).

2.3. O_2 evolution of the leaf discs was determined with a Hansatech
leaf disc electrode at limiting red light (200 µmol photons m^{-2} s^{-1})
similar to ref. 4.

2.4.   77 K fluorescence of the leaf discs was measured at two wavelengths, 694 nm for photosystem (PS) II and 735 nm for PS I, as
described earlier (4).

M. Baltscheffsky (ed.), Current Research in Photosynthesis, Vol. II, 479–482.
© 1990 Kluwer Academic Publishers. Printed in the Netherlands.

3. RESULTS AND DISCUSSION

3.1. Freezing stress: After frost nights (minimum temperatures between
-1.5°C and -4.1°C), the yield of variable fluorescence (F_V) of PS II
measured at 20°C (Fig. 1, columns C) and at 77 K (not shown) was decreased and the F_V/F_M ratio lowered. This decline resulted partly from
a slight decrease in maximal fluorescence and partly from an increase in
initial fluorescence (F_0). The pronounced increase of F_0 points to less
efficient energy trapping by PS II reaction centers or to an impaired
connection between the antenna and the reaction center. The changes in
fluorescence characteristics induced by night frost required several
frostless days and nights (minimum temperature around +1°C) to recover
(data not shown).

Slight frost (minimum temperatures between 0°C and -1.5°C) did not have
any effect on the light-limited O_2 evolution of the leaves (Fig. 2a).
Lower night temperature (minimum -7.1°C, which still was considerably
above the killing point) caused a decrease of O_2 evolution by about 50%
(Fig. 2a).

3.2. High light stress: High solar irradiation during cool days after
frostless nights caused a significant quenching of variable fluorescence,
leading to a lowered F_V/F_M ratio (Fig. 1, columns B). No change in initial fluorescence was found. Interestingly, there was no synergism between
high light and preceding moderate freezing stress (compare columns B and
D, Fig. 1). A possible explanation of the relatively small light effect
in frost-stressed leaves could be a freezing-induced impairment of PS II
energy trapping, which would diminish over-excitation of the reaction
center in high light after frost.

The quenching of variable fluorescence was presumably due to thermal
deactivation. Neither night frosts alone, nor night frosts and following bright days caused a significant change in the slope of the plot of
PS I versus PS II fluorescence induction at 77 K (data not shown).
(An increase in this slope may indicate increased transfer of excitation
energy from PS II to PS I; see refs. 4,5).

Significant effects of high solar radiation on rates of O_2 evolution
could neither be detected after frostless nights (not shown) nor after
frost nights (Fig. 2b). This can be explained by very fast recovery from
photoinhibition taking place at the measuring temperature (20°C). The
fluorescence changes caused by high light stress were fully reversible
in about 1 hour in dim light at +4°C, independently of the preceding
night temperature (Fig. 3a,b). It should be noted that during this time
only the high-light effect was reversed, however not the effect of preceding frost.

On the basis of the fluorescence changes and the fast and complete recovery, the photoinhibition observed here can be regarded as an protective system of thermal dissipation of excess light energy. Intermediate
light flux densities, however, inhibited the recovery (Table 1). This is
in agreement with other studies (6,7), showing that recovery is optimal
in very low light. On the other hand, impaired recovery in intermediate
light does not support the hypothesis of "simultaneous damage and repair"

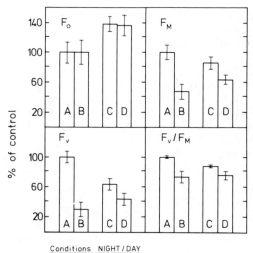

Conditions NIGHT / DAY

A. no frost / low light (= controls)

B. no frost / high light (900 μmol m^{-2} s^{-1})

C. frost (-1.5° to -4.1°C) / low light

D. frost (-1.5° to -4.1°C) / high light

FIGURE 1. Characteristics of room temperature fluorescence of spinach leaves exposed to freezing and/or light stress in the field. A, leaves collected in the morning when solar irradiation was low (100-150 μmol photons m^{-2}s^{-1}) after frostless nights (minimum temperature between +2 and +5°C). B, leaves collected at noon time from bright sunshine after frostless nights. C, leaves collected in mornings after night frost. D, leaves collected at noon time from bright sunshine after night frost. All the values are expressed as % of those of non-stressed control leaves (A). Mean control value of F_V/F_M was 0.84. Standard deviations (SD) are shown, n = 7 to 13.

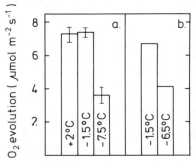

FIGURE 2. Effect of freezing and light stress on photosynthesis (O_2 evolution) of spinach leaves grown in the field. Minimum night temperatures are given in the graph. a) Effect of night frost. Leaves were collected in the morning; SD indicated, n = 3. b) Effect of night frost and bright sunshine on the following day (about 900 μmol photons m^{-2}s^{-1}). Leaves were collected around noontime. The columns represent means of two different leaves.

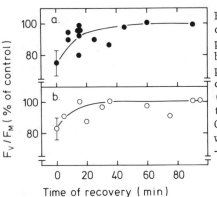

Time of recovery (min)

FIGURE 3. Recovery of the F_V/F_M ratio of spinach leaves at +4°C and 5 μmol photons m^{-2}s^{-1} after photoinhibition by high solar irradiation (900 μmol photons m^{-2}s^{-1}) for several hours on days (a) after frostless nights and (b) after frost nights. The mean control value after frostless nights was 0.84 ± 0.02 and after frost nights with minimum temperatures of -1.5 to -4.1°C, 0.75 ± 0.04 (n = 11 to 13).

suggested by several authors (see refs. 2,6). If photoinhibition is a protective mechanism against excessive excitation, recovery taking place in relatively high light would not be of benefit.

TABLE 1. Partial recovery of the F_V/F_M ratio of spinach leaves in the field during cloudy weather (about 300 to 400 µmol photons $m^{-2}s^{-1}$) after bright sunshine (about 900 µmol photons $m^{-2}s^{-1}$) of several hours on days after frostless nights (minimum temperatures between +2°C and +5°C). SD indicated when $n \geq 4$, in other cases values of single leaves are given.

	control	inhibited	recovered		
			1 h	3 h	over night
F_V/F_M	0.836 ± 0.014 (n = 11)	0.626 ± 0.068 (n = 14)	0.747 0.775	0.702 0.757	0.821 ± 0.004 (n = 4)

4.   ADDENDUM

The authors thank the Deutsche Forschungsgemeinschaft (SFB 189) and the Academy of Finland for support.

REFERENCES
1 Ögren, E. (1988) Planta 175, 229-236
2 Öquist, G., Greer, D.H. and Ögren, E. (1987) in Photoinhibition, Topics of Photosynthesis (Kyle, D.J., Osmond, C.B., Arntzen, C.J., eds.) Vol. 9, pp. 67-87, Elsevier, Amsterdam
3 Bolhár-Nordenkampf, H.R. and Lechner, E.G. (1988) Photosynth. Research 18, 287-298
4 Somersalo, S. and Krause, G.H. (1989) Planta 177, 409-416
5 Ögren, E. and Öquist, G. (1984) Physiol. Plant. 62, 193-200
6 Greer, D.H., Berry, J.A. and Björkman, O. (1986) Planta 168, 253-260
7 Samuelsson, G., Lönneburg, A., Gustafsson, P. and Öquist, G. (1987) Plant Physiol. 83, 438-441

INCREASE IN ACTIVITIES OF SCAVENGERS FOR ACTIVE OXYGEN IN SPINACH
RELATED TO COLD ACCLIMATION IN EXCESS LIGHT

SUSANNE SCHÖNER[1], CHRISTINE FOYER[2], MAUD LELANDAIS[2] and
G. HEINRICH KRAUSE[1]

[1]Institute for Biochemistry of Plants, Heinrich Heine University,
D-4000 Düsseldorf 1, FRG and [2]Laboratoire du Métabolisme et de
la Nutrition des Plantes, INRA, F-78026 Versailles cedex, France

1. INTRODUCTION
    Chloroplasts are capable of generating potentially destructive oxy-
gen species such as superoxide anion radicals ($O_2{}^{\cdot-}$), hydrogen peroxide (H_2O_2) and $\cdot OH$ radicals (see ref. 1). Illumination of leaves at
chilling temperatures close to $0^\circ C$ restricts photosynthetic energy
turnover and appears to enhance the activation of dioxygen. Light-
dependent chilling damage by active oxygen species has been reported
(2). Photoinhibition of photosynthesis is known to be promoted by chilling temperatures (see refs. 3-5). For spinach plants it was shown that
long-term cold acclimation under moderate light stress substantially decreased the susceptibility to photoinhibition at $+4^\circ C$ (5). In the present study, we tested whether such cold acclimation is related to increased activities of protective systems against active oxygen. Several
enzymes scavenging $O_2{}^{\cdot-}$ and H_2O_2 were assayed. Ascorbate contents and
pigment composition were determined.

2. PROCEDURE
2.1. Plant material: Spinach (Spinacia oleracea L.) plants were acclimated to $1^\circ C$ (cold-hardened material) or maintained at $18^\circ C$ under the
same light regime (unhardened controls). For details see ref. 5.
2.2. Enzyme assays: Intact chloroplasts were isolated and then osmotically shocked. The lysates were used for determination of the stromal
activities of ascorbate peroxidase (6), monodehydroascorbate reductase
(7) and dehydroascorbate reductase (6). Superoxide dismutase (SOD) was
assayed (8) in a protein extract derived from chloroplasts solubilized
in the presence of 2.5% Triton-X-100. Catalase activity was determined
(9) in leaf homogenates.
2.3. Electrophoretic analyses: Spinach leaves were powdered in liquid
N_2, and the proteins were extracted. Samples corresponding to 7 µg
chlorophyll were separated by isoelectric focusing and stained for SOD
activity via the nitroblue tetrazolium (NTB) colour reaction (10).
2.4. Determination of ascorbate: Ascorbate was extracted from leaf
tissue with 2% metaphosphoric acid and determined according to ref.11.
2.4. Pigments: Fresh leaf material was homogenized in pure acetone. The

M. Baltscheffsky (ed.), Current Research in Photosynthesis, Vol. II, 483–486.
© 1990 Kluwer Academic Publishers. Printed in the Netherlands.

pigments were separated by thin layer chromatography and photometrically quantified (12).

3. RESULTS AND DISCUSSION

As the chlorophyll a+b content of leaves gives a measure of potential absorption of excess light energy, the activities of scavenger enzymes are referred to chlorophyll. Fig. 1 shows a comparison of superoxide dismutase (SOD) activities in chloroplasts isolated from unhardened and hardened spinach leaves. A strongly increased activity is seen in the hardened spinach. Fig. 2 demonstrates that this increase is based on the synthesis of an SOD isoenzyme, which cannot be detected in the unhardened leaves. According to its sensitivity to KCN after polyacrylamide gel electrophoresis (not shown), the isoenzyme formed during cold hardening is a Cu,Zn-SOD.

The action of SOD leads to formation of H_2O_2 in the chloroplasts. H_2O_2 may inactivate enzymes of the carbon reduction cycle and together with $O_2 \cdot^-$ may form the very reactive $\cdot OH$ radicals (see ref. 1). Scavenging of H_2O_2 seems to be achieved predominantly by ascorbate peroxidase and monodehydroascorbate reductase (1). Table 1 shows that the activities of these enzymes are increased due to cold hardening. Furthermore, the concentration of ascorbate, the reactant for H_2O_2 scavenging, is much higher (about 100%) in hardened than in unhardened leaves (data not shown). In contrast, the activity of the dehydroascorbate reductase did not change in relation to cold hardening (Table 1). It has been proposed before (1) that this enzyme plays a less important role in the H_2O_2 scavenging system and may not be rate-limiting. The activity of the peroxisomal enzyme catalase was decreased in hardened leaves (Table 1). The main function of catalase is the decomposition of H_2O_2 formed in the peroxisomes in the photorespiratory cycle (see ref. 1). The decrease in catalase activity might be related to diminished carbon turnover in photorespiration at chilling temperatures. Inactivation of catalase induced by high light has been described (13).

Cold acclimation caused significant changes in the leaf pigment composition, as seen from the carotenoid/chlorophyll ratios given in Fig. 3. Apparently, the contents of carotenoids that participate in the xanthophyll cycle, zeaxanthin (which was not separated from lutein) and violaxanthin, increased relative to chlorophyll content. The levels of neoxanthin and β-carotene remained constant. The xanthophyll cycle has been suggested to play a protective role against effects of excess light (14). The increased carotenoid/chlorophyll ratio shown in Fig. 3 may, however, also reflect the general role of carotenoids to deactivate triplet chlorophyll and singlet oxygen (see ref. 1). Those species might be formed at an increased rate under chilling and excess light conditions.

In conclusion, long-term acclimation under conditions of slightly excessive light absorption leads to increase in the activity of scavenger systems for potentially damaging active oxygen species. These adaptive changes might contribute to the lowered susceptibility of hardened plants to photoinhibition.

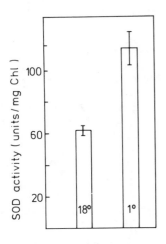
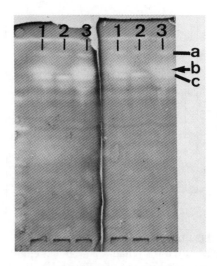

FIGURE 1. Superoxide dismutase activity in chloroplasts of hardened
spinach leaves (1°) and unhardened controls (18°). Mean values ± SD
are given (n = 6 for the hardened plants, and n = 5 for the controls).

FIGURE 2. Separation of superoxide dismutase isoenzymes by isoelectric
focusing. For SOD activity staining, the NTB method was used.
Lanes: 1, hardened spinach (about 2 weeks of cold acclimation);
2, unhardened control plants; 3, hardened spinach (about 2 months of
cold acclimation). Protein bands: a,c, major bands with SOD activity of
unhardened leaves; b, new band with SOD activity observed after cold
acclimation.

TABLE 1. Activities of enzymes scavenging H_2O_2 in leaves of unhardened
and cold-hardened spinach plants. Mean values ± SD are given
(number of experiments in parentheses). The chloroplast data
(see Procedure) were corrected for 100% envelope integrity.

	Activity (μmol mg^{-1} chlorophyll h^{-1})	
	unhardened plants	hardened plants
Ascorbate peroxidase	267 ± 26 (4)	349 ± 49 (4)
Monodehydroascorbate reductase	84 ± 10 (5)	114 ± 12 (5)
Dehydroascorbate reductase	150 ± 13 (3)	148 ± 12 (5)
Catalase	67500 ± 7800 (6)	49900 ± 1700 (6)

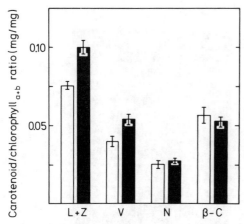

FIGURE 3. Changes in carotenoid/
chlorophyll a+b ratios induced by
cold acclimation of spinach.
White bars, leaves of control
plants (18°C); black bars, leaves
of hardened plants (1°C). Mean
values ± SD of 4 separate preparations are shown.
Abbreviations: L+Z = lutein + zeaxanthin, V = violaxanthin, N =
neoxanthin, β-C = β-carotene.

4. ADDENDUM

The authors thank the Deutsche Forschungsgemeinschaft (SFB 189) and
the OECD (Co-operative Research Project on Food Production and Preservation: Photosynthesis, Growth and Environment) for financial support.

REFERENCES
1 Asada, K. and Takahashi, M. (1987) in Topics in Photosynthesis Vol.9,
   Photoinhibition (Kyle, D.J., Osmond, C.B. and Arntzen, C.J., eds.)
   pp. 227-287, Elsevier, Amsterdam
2 Wise, R.R. and Naylor, A.W. (1987) Plant Physiol. 83, 278-282
3 Öquist, G., Greer, D.H. and Ögren, E. (1987) in Topics in Photosynthesis, Vol. 9, Photoinhibition (Kyle, D.J., Osmond, C.B. and
   Arntzen, C.J., eds.) pp. 67-87, Elsevier, Amsterdam
4 Smillie, R.M., Hetherington, S.E., Hie, J. and Nott, R. (1988) Aust.
   J. Plant Physiol. 15, 207-222
5 Somersalo, S. and Krause, G.H. (1989) Planta 177, 409-416
6 Nakano, Y. and Asada, K. (1981) Plant Cell Physiol. 22, 867-880
7 Hossain, M.A., Nakano, Y. and Asada, K. (1984) Plant Cell Physiol.
   25, 385-395
8 Asada, K., Takahashi, M. and Nagate, M. (1974) Agr. Biol. Chem. 38,
   471-473
9 Aebi, H.E. (1983) in Methods of Enzymatic Analysis (Bergmeyer, H.U.,
   Bergmeyer, J. and Grassl, M., eds.) pp. 273-286, Verlag Chemie,
   Weinheim
10 Beauchamp, C. and Fridovich, I. (1971) Anal. Biochem. 44, 276-287
11 Hughes, R.E. (1956) Biochem. J. 64, 203-208
12 Hager, A. and Meyer-Bertenrath, T. (1966) Planta 69, 198-217
13 Feierabend, J. and Engel, S. (1986) Arch. Biochem. Biophys. 251,
   567-576
14 Demmig, B., Winter, K., Krüger, A. and Czygan, F.C. (1987) Plant
   Physiol. 84, 218-224

THE EFFECT OF PHOTOINHIBITION, SALT STRESS AND THEIR INTERACTION ON PHOTOSYNTHESIS IN SORGHUM.

PRABHAT K. SHARMA and DAVID O. HALL,
DIVISION OF BIOSPHERE SCIENCES, KING'S COLLEGE LONDON, CAMPDEN HILL ROAD, LONDON W8 7AH, UK.

INTRODUCTION:

When photosynthetic organisms are exposed to light levels in excess to those which can be dissipated by the normal photochemical processes, their photosynthetic capacity is reduced (1). Environmental stresses such as low temperature, high temperature, salinity and drought often amplify the photoinhibition.

Sorghum is a chilling-sensitive crop which is widely grown in arid-zones and is very often exposed to stresses such as light, temperature, salinity and drought. However, few studies have been done to understand the physiological and biochemical processes operating under stress conditions in sorghum. This study examines how sorghum protects itself against conditions inducing photoinhibition of photosynthesis, characterizes this damage at the leaf level and attempts to understand the role of xanthophyll cycle pigments and ß-carotene during photoinhibition. It also analyses the short term effect of salt stress and interaction of salt stress with photoinhibition on CO_2 assimilation, chlorophyll fluorescence and carotenoid composition in sorghum.

MATERIALS AND METHODS:

Growth conditions, photoinhibition conditions, CO_2 exchange measurements and fluorescence measurements from leaves are described in (2). Pigment analysis was carried out according to Neill et al (3).

RESULTS AND DISCUSSION:

The CO_2 assimilation rate (Ar) of salt-grown (no photoinhibition) plants showed a decrease of up to 22% in Ar. However, interaction of salt and photoinhibition resulted in an increased inhibition of Ar with 83-86% inhibition at 5°C and 35-55% at 20°C (Fig. 1). Stomatal conductance (gs) was more affected during interaction of salt and photoinhibition than the CO_2 assimilation rate. Plants photoinhibited at 5°C and 1600 PPFD showed a decrease of 70% in gs compared to 5% at 20°C. Salt stress plants showed between 13-33% inhibition in gs, this was increased by the interaction with photoinhibition (Fig. 2). This decrease in the CO_2 assimilation rate was not due to decrease in the stomatal conductance as internal CO_2 concentration in stressed plants remain as high as was observed in the control plants (data not shown).

Munns and Termmat (4) showed in a number of spp. including barley

M. Baltscheffsky (ed.), Current Research in Photosynthesis, Vol. II, 487–490.
© 1990 *Kluwer Academic Publishers. Printed in the Netherlands.*

and wheat that an osmotic potential causing a water deficit was not the limiting factor in growth and CO_2 assimilation. They also tested the effect of Na^+ and Cl^- ions in these two spp. causing excessive accumulation of these ions and came to conclusion that in the case of short term (10-12 day) salt stress, it is unlikely to effect photosynthesis.

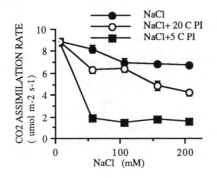 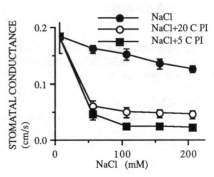

Fig.1 The effect of salt stress and interaction with photoinhibition on CO_2 assimilation rate in leaves. PI alone at $5^{\circ}C$= 3.28 umol m^{-2} s^{-1} (not shown), PI alone at $20^{\circ}C$= 7.04 umol m^{-2} s^{-1} (not shown).

Fig. 2 The effect of salt stress and interaction with photoinhibition on stomatal conductance. PI alone at $5^{\circ}C$ = 0.04 cm/s (not shown), PI alone at $20^{\circ}C$= 0.17 cm/s (not shown).

680 nm chlorophyll fluorescence (F680) of sorghum leaves at $20^{\circ}C$ (without DCMU) followed the typical pattern. Upon illumination fluorescence rose rapidly from an initial level (Fo) to a peak Fm which was follwed by a level (S) then to a second maximum M (terminology after 5). Thereafter fluorescence gradually declines to a steady state level of emission (T), which was achieved within 2 min. in control plants. However, photoinhibited plants showed a decrease in the level of variable fluorescence (Fv), and a lower steady state (T) which was achieved within 45 sec. of illumination. The changes in fluorescence yield at Fm were mainly attributed to changes in variable fluorescence, Fv, (Fv=Fm-Fo), because the initial level of fluorescence (Fo) remain largely unchanged during the study.

Fm (with DCMU) examined under irradinace of 1600 umol m-2 s-1 showed a decrease of 63% after 6 hours at $5^{\circ}C$; photoinhibition at $20^{\circ}C$ resulted in a 26% decrease in the Fm. At other irradiances decreases in Fm were also observed (Fig 3). Plants grown at low salt concentrations did not show any significant changes in Fm; however, at 200 mM NaCl level there was a significant decrease (33%). An interaction of salt stress with photoinhibition enhanced the decline in Fm level. This interaction proved more damaging at $5^{\circ}C$ (53-64% decrease) compared to at $20^{\circ}C$ (32-47%) (Fig. 4). Differences in fluorescence characteristics may be attributed to different degrees of photoinhibitory damage to PS II. A decrease in the extent of the rise in Fv indicates an altered redox state of QA. This may result from photoinhibitory damage to the oxidising side of the PS II reaction centre or damage to the reaction centre itself leading to a lower reducing capability. A decrease in the Fv can also be due to nonphotochemical quenching (6).

Changes in the pigment composition of sorghum leaves upon photoinhibition and salt stress and interaction of salt stress with photoinhibition are shown in (Table 1). This indicate that the carotenoid composition of sorghum leaves upon photoinhibition altered with a specific increase in zeaxanthin (Z) and a decrease in violaxanthin (V). Most of the V is converted to Z during photoinhibition.

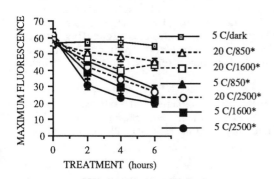

Fig. 3 The effect of photoinhibition
on maximum chlorophyll fluorescence
level (Fm). *= umol m^{-2} s^{-1} PPFD.

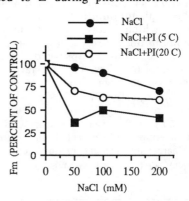

Fig. 4 The effect of salt stress and
interaction with photoinhibition
on maximum fluorescence level.

This conversion of V into Z was relatively higher when photoinhibited at 5 °C than at 20° C. The ß-carotene content also decreased after photoinhibition. This decrease in ß-carotene was coupled with the increased formation of 5,6- epoxide ß-carotene which also confirms the degradation of ß-carotene, probably to Z. The pigment composition of salt stress plants was different to that observed in photoinhibited plants. V decreased in comparison to control. Z formation showed a linear increase with increasing salt stress. In salt stress plants neoxanthin (N) contents decreased in comparison to control and photoinhibited plants. Photoinhibition of salt stressed plants resulted in carotenoid changes qualitatively similar to those observed in photoinhibited plants with no salt stress. However, quantitatively Z formation was much greater in plants grown under conditions of salt stress and then photoinhibited compared to plants which were salt stressed only. Neoxanthin contents were also decreased. A decreases in ß-carotene were also observed in plants photoinhibited in the presence of salt. No significant changes in lutein and chlorophyll contents were observed in any case (Tab. 1).

Our results indicate a protective function of carotenoids, especially those in the xanthophyll cycle (V and Z) against photoinhibition as also observed by (7,8) and upto lesser extent to salt stress. Such damage appears to occur when the photosynthesizing system can not increase the content of protective compound, Z; thus we observed more damage at 5°C than at 20°C. This suggest that changes in the xanthophyll cycle are temperature dependent. Under chilling conditions dissipation of excessive radiant energy by carotenoids is less than at $20^{\circ}C$ since at $5^{\circ}C$ there is less conversion of V to Z. Thus at $20^{\circ}C$ there is greater protective effect from the light due the higher Z content. This suggest that chilling alone may not result in a direct inhibition of photosynthesis but has a greater effect on the alternative pathways of energy dissipation such as carotenoids metabolism and photorespiration. The degradation of ß-carotene (7) and the formation of 5,6-epoxide ß-carotene may also play some role in protection against photoinhibition . N contents decreased significantly under salt stress which may be significant. Interaction of salt stress and photoinhibition also caused changes in the xanthophyll cycle components similar to those observed in photoinhibition alone. suggesting that photoinhibition has the primary influence on carotenoid pigment although salinity on its own also results in carotenoid changes (eg. N, V and Z) which may be significant.

Table 1- The effect of salt stress and interaction of salt stress with photoinhibition on carotenoid and chlorophyll composition. Data shown as percent of total carotenoid content or total chlorophyll content (Chl "a"+"b"). PI=Photoinhibition at 1600 umol m^{-2} s^{-1} for 4 hours.

CAROTENOD & CHLOROPHYLL	CONTROL	PI (5 C) 1600*	PI (20 C) 1600*	50 mM NaCl	100 mM NaCl	200 mM NaCl	PI (5 C) +50mM NaCl	PI (5 C) +100mM NaCl	PI (5 C) +200mM NaCl	PI (20 C) +50mM NaCl	PI (20 C) +100mM NaCl	PI (20 C) +200mM NaCl
NEOXANTHIN	11.5	10.3	9.6	7.9	6.9	7.6	8.0	7.7	7.7	6.1	6.9	7.9
VIOLAXANTHIN (V)	6.3	1.9	3.0	1.6	2.2	1.9	0.7	2.4	1.8	0.8	1.5	2.2
5,6-EPOXIDE LUTEIN	0.0	0.0	1.6	0.4	0.6	2.8	1.2	0.4	1.7	1.5	1.6	2.2
ANTHERAXANTHIN (A)	0.3	0.3	0.7	0.7	0.6	1.2	0.0	0.8	1.8	0.7	0.6	2.4
LUTEIN	44.9	50.2	40.3	50.9	44.2	56.8	49.3	50.0	47.1	47.3	43.1	48.9
ZEAXANTHIN (Z)	0.0	10.3	10.7	0.5	1.5	3.6	10.3	9.3	8.8	12.2	9.9	8.0
V+A+Z	6.6	12.5	14.4	2.9	4.5	6.7	10.7	12.5	12.4	13.7	12.0	12.6
5,6-EPOXIDE-B-CAROTENE	0.0	1.6	0.8	0.0	0.0	0.5	0.9	0.9	1.1	0.7	0.5	1.7
B-CAROTENE	37.0	29.9	34.0	38.1	40.9	26.0	30.6	32.4	31.4	31.3	36.4	28.5
CHLOROPHYLL "a"	69.0	67.0	66.0	66.0	63.0	67.0	72.0	70.0	72.0	73.0	71.0	67.0
CHLOROPHYLL "b"	31.0	33.0	34.0	34.0	37.0	37.0	28.0	30.0	28.0	27.0	29.0	33.0
CAROTENE/CHLOROPHYLL	0.4	0.4	0.5	0.5	0.5	0.4	0.4	0.4	0.4	0.5	0.5	0.5

REFERENCES:
1. Powles, S.B. (1984) Annu. Rev.   Plant Physiol. 55: 15-31.
2. Sharma, P.K. and Hall, D.O. (1989) in Techniques and new developments in photosynthesis research (Barber, J and Malkin, R., eds.), pp. 571-577, Plenum Press, New York.
3. Neill, S.J., Horgan, R. and Parry, A.D. (1986) Planta 169: 87-96.
4. Munns, R, and Termaat, A (1984) Aust. J. Plant Physiol. 13: 143-160.
5. Krause, G.H. and Weis, E. (1984) Photosynthesis Res. 5: 139-154.
6. Krause, G.H. (1988) Physiol. Plant. 74: 566-574.
7.Demmig, B., Winter, K., Kruger, A. and Czygen, F.C. (1987) Plant Physiol. 84: 218-224.
8. Demmig, B., Winter, K., Kruger, A. and Czygen, F.C. (1988) Plant Physiol. 87: 17-24.

TURNOVER OF THE XANTHOPHYLL CYCLE DURING PHOTOINHIBITION AND
RECOVERY

Christine H. FOYER[1], Marie DUJARDYN[1] and Yves LEMOINE[2]

[1] Laboratoire du Métabolisme, INRA, 78026 Versailles, France
[2] Laboratoire de Cytophysiologie végétale, ENS, 75231 Paris cedex 05, France

1. INTRODUCTION
The biochemistry of the violaxanthin cycle is well-characterised (1)
but no clear function of this cycle, in relation to photosynthesis, has been
demonstrated. Demmig *et al.* (2, 3) have suggested that zeaxanthin formation
is related to a special function of this carotenoid under photoinhibitory
conditions that serves to prevent damage. The xanthophyll cycle thus may
play a crucial role in the protection of the photosynthetic apparatus
against photoinhibitory damage in times of stress. Increases in the
zeaxanthin content of water-stressed *Nerium oleander* leaves were shown to
be linearly related to changes in the rate constant of radiationless
dissipation of excitation energy as evidenced by a decrease in the Fv/Fm
ratio (3). Thus, zeaxanthin acting in a dissipative role is a quencher of
chlorophyll *a* fluorescence. A direct reaction with the singlet excited state
of chlorophyll is suggested possibly involving an electron transfer process
(3). Strong light is known to favour the enzymatic de-epoxidation of
violaxanthin to zeaxanthin. The depoxidase requires ascorbate and a low pH
(pH 5.0) for activity. The low pH optimum suggests that this reaction occurs
in the lumen of the thylakoid membrane. However, the presence of a
functional PS II (4, 5) is not required for zeaxanthin formation and the
operation of the xanthophyll cycle. The formation of violaxanthin from
zeaxanthin is light-independent and requires NADPH and molecular O_2 for
the epoxidation sequence which has an optimum of pH 7.5. In the present
study low-light grown barley leaves were subjected to irradiances far in
excess of that encountered during development in order to study the
relationship between turnover of the xanthophyll cycle and
photoinhibition and recovery.

2. MATERIALS AND METHODS
Hordeum vulgare L. var. Cytris was grown in pots in a growth
chamber at 22°C in a low light regime (280 μE m^{-2} s^{-1}) until the fourth leaf
was well-developed. The fourth leaf only was used in the following
experiments. CO_2 assimilation was measured using infra-red gas analysis.
Chlorophyll *a* fluorescence measurements were made at 77 K on leaf
samples taken at the times indicated and given a five minute dark treatment
prior to freezing. Carotenoid measurements were made on samples of whole
leaves, in which metabolism was stopped by pulverisation in liquid N_2.
Pigments were separated by non-aqueous reverse phase high pressure

M. Baltscheffsky (ed.), Current Research in Photosynthesis, Vol. II, 491–494.
© 1990 *Kluwer Academic Publishers. Printed in the Netherlands.*

liquid chromatography using a mixture of acetonitrile and methanol (70:30, v/v) on a Dupon Zorbax octodecyl silica column.

3. RESULTS AND DISCUSSION

Zeaxanthin was absent from the barley leaves in darkness or leaves exposed to 280 μE m^{-2} s^{-1}. However, conversion of violaxanthin to zeaxanthin was initiated upon exposure to irradiances above 300 μE m^{-2} s^{-1}, the zeaxanthin content of the leaves increasing with increasing irradiance (fig. 1). The zeaxanthin content of the leaves increased with increasing irradiance at the expense of violaxanthin alone (figs 1 and 2). The total sum of the leaf violaxanthin, antheraxanthin and zeaxanthin contents remained relatively constant and did not increase at the expense of β-carotene.

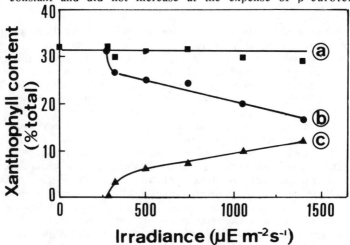

FIGURE 1. The effect of irradiance on zeaxanthin formation in barley leaves values are expressed as a percentage of the total leaf xanthophyll contents. Samples were taken after 1 h irradiance. Violaxanthin + Antheraxanthin + Zeaxanthin (a) ; Violaxanthin (b) ; Zeaxanthin + Antheraxanthin (c).

When barley leaves were exposed to a high irradiance (1400 μE m^{-2} s^{-1}) photoinhibition rapidly followed (fig. 2 a). The Fo level of chlorophyll a fluorescence (measured when all the PS II reaction centres were open) was unchanged by exposure to high light, however the maximum fluorescence yield, Fm (when all the PS II reaction centres are closed) decreased with the duration of high light treatment for up to 2 h and thereafter remained at the constant lower level throughout the duration of the high light treatment. Accordingly, the yield of variable fluorescence, Fv (Fv = Fm - Fo) decreased as a function of duration of high irradiance up to 2 h and was subsequently constant while the high light persisted. The ratio of Fv/Fm is a measure of the photochemical efficiency of PS II and the decrease in this ratio following exposure to high light reflects the loss of PS II efficiency that accompanied high irradiance (fig. 2 a).

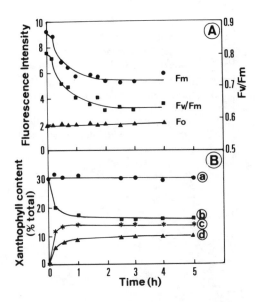

FIGURE 2.
The effect of high irradiance (1400 µE m^{-2} s^{-1}) on quenching of chlorophyll a fluorescence (A) and barley leaf xanthophyll contents (B). Violaxanthin + Antheraxanthin + Zeaxanthin (a) ; Violaxanthin (b) ; Zeaxanthin + Antheraxanthin (c) ; Zeaxanthin (d).

Zeaxanthin formation was rapid following exposure to high light (fig. 2 b) ; 70-80 % of the total zeaxanthin pool was formed after 10 minutes irradiance at 1400 µE m^{-2} s^{-1}. Thus, the kinetics of zeaxanthin formation (fig. 2 b) were very different from the kinetics of decrease of Fm or the Fv/Fm ratio that accompanied exposure to high light (fig. 2 a).

Changes in the capacity for carbon assimilation accompanied the loss of variable fluorescence. Following the transition to high irradiance carbon assimilation rapidly increased but as photoinhibition progressed the CO_2 assimilation rate decreased slowly throughout the period of high irradiance (fig. 3).The inhibition of carbon assimilation was much more severe when measured at low irradiance reflecting the decrease in quantum efficiency that accompanied photoinhibition. After 2 h 30 min at 1400 µE m^{-2} s^{-1} the irradiance was abruptly decreased to 280 µE m^{-2} s^{-1} (fig. 3). When the leaves were returned to low irradiance the capacity for CO_2 assimilation was much lower (by up to 30 %) than that measured prior to exposure to high light. The capacity for CO_2 assimilation recovered slowly to its original value over a 2 h period (fig. 3 a). Changes in the violaxanthin and zeaxanthin contents of the leaves accompanied the transition to low irradiance (fig. 3 b). The high level of zeaxanthin synthesised in response to high irradiance quickly decreased when the leaves were returned to low light (fig. 3 b). However, although the initial conversion of zeaxanthin to violaxanthin was rapid it soon slowed to a much lower rate such that zeaxanthin and antheraxanthin persisted in the leaves long after the time taken for the capacity for CO_2 fixation at low irradiance to recover (fig. 3 a and b).

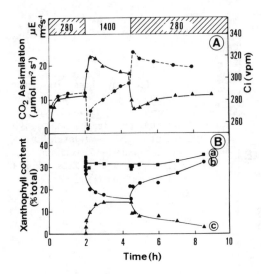

FIGURE 3.
Effect of varying irradiance on the rate of CO_2 assimilation and calculated internal CO_2, Ci (A) and the xanthophyll contents of the leaf (B). Conditions of irradiance are given at the top of the figure. Other details are as for figure 2.

The data presented here show that zeaxanthin formation alone does not result in a reduction in PS II efficiency. Zeaxanthin synthesis preceded the changes in fluorescence that characterised photoinhibition. Similarly, zeaxanthin was present in the leaves after recovery from photoinhibition was complete. Carotenoids are essential for protection against singlet oxygen and triplet chlorophyll radicals. They form excited triplets by energy migration which are then dissipated by radiationless decay. Zeaxanthin has been suggested to be involved in an additional quenching process (2, 3). In this study zeaxanthin formation preceded quenching of chlorophyll a fluorescence and thus further processes must be involved before quenching is facilitated.

REFERENCES
1 Yamamoto, H.Y. (1979) Pure and Appl. Chem. 51, 639-648
2 Demmig, B., Winter, K., Krüger, A. and Czygan, F.C. (1987) Plant Physiol. 84, 218-224
3 Demmig, B., Winter, K., Krüger, A. and Czygan, F.C. (1988) Plant Physiol. 87, 17-24
4 Ladygin, V.G. and Shirshikova, G.N. (1987) Soviet Plant Physiol. 34, 854-858
5 Pfündel, E. and Strasser, R.J. (1988) Photosynth. Res. 15, 67-73.

We thank Maud Lelandais and Gerald Zabulon for excellant technical assistance.

ZEAXANTHIN FORMATION IN q_E-INHIBITED CHLOROPLASTS

ADAM M. GILMORE AND HARRY Y. YAMAMOTO, Department of Plant Molecular Physiology, CTAHR, University of Hawaii at Manoa, Honolulu, HI, 96822, U.S.A.

1. INTRODUCTION

Nonphotochemical fluorescence quenching, q_E, appears to have several components (1). A slowly relaxing component has been correlated with zeaxanthin formation (2). Development of q_E and zeaxanthin formation are both dependent on formation of a trans-thylakoid ΔpH (3,4). Since antimycin inhibits q_E without inhibiting ΔpH (3), the relationship between q_E and zeaxanthin was investigated with antimycin. We show herein that ascorbate, which is required for zeaxanthin formation in isolated chloroplasts (4), stimulated induction of a q_E component possibly related to zeaxanthin formation. However, antimycin inhibited this q_E without inhibiting zeaxanthin formation.

2. MATERIALS AND METHODS

Osmotically shocked chloroplasts were isolated from *Pisum sativum* L. cv. Manoa seedlings according to Horton and Black (5) with minor modifications. Absorbance and room-temperature chlorophyll fluorescence induction were measured simultaneously with a DW-2000 UV-VIS spectro-photometer (SLM-Aminco) and a PAM 101 Chlorophyll Fluorometer (Heinz Walz, Effeltrich, FRG). Actinic light intensity was 350 μmol photon m^{-2} s^{-1} unless stated otherwise. And saturating flash intensity was approximately 1600 μmol photon m^{-2} s^{-1}; both actinic and saturating lights were passed through red Corning CS2-58 and infrared filters. Calculation of fluorescence values was according to Schreiber *et al.* (6). The 505-nm absorbance change was determined according to Yamamoto (7). Chloroplast concentration for all reactions was equivalent to 15μg total chlorophyll per ml unless otherwise stated. HPLC pigment analysis was according to Siefermann-Harms (8). Carotenoid concentrations were analyzed as area percent.

3. RESULTS AND DISCUSSION

3.1. Figure 1 shows typical (A) q_E induction and (B) 505-nm change under MV-mediated linear electron transport in the presence and absence of ascorbate. Ascorbate enhanced q_E above a large no-ascorbate 'basal' level and stimulated zeaxanthin formation as indicated by a large irreversible 505-nm absorbance change. The 505-nm change without ascorbate was small, reversible, and presumed to be from changes in light scattering and not de-epoxidation; pigment analysis confirmed that no de-epoxidation occurred under these conditions (data not shown). Figure 1 also shows that in the presence of ascorbate the kinetics of de-epoxidation and total q_E differed significantly.

Figure 2 shows the effects of ascorbate concentration on the final extent of q_E and xanthophyll composition after illumination under (A) linear and (B) cyclic electron-transport conditions. In the absence of ascorbate the basal q_E was about 0.30 but no de-epoxidation was evident under either electron-transport condition. In the presence of ascorbate, the extent of the additional ascorbate-stimulated q_E and de-epoxidation appeared to correlate under both conditions, although more closely under linear electron transport. Development of q_E and zeaxanthin leveled off at 5mM and 30mM ascorbate for linear and cyclic conditions, respectively.

3.2. Figure 3 shows that antimycin inhibited the development of ascorbate-enhanced q_E under linear (A) or cyclic (B) electron-transport conditions. Although the inhibition was strong, it was incomplete. In the presence of antimycin, a small amount of q_E developed slowly. Its slow kinetics

M. Baltscheffsky (ed.), Current Research in Photosynthesis, Vol. II, 495–498.
© 1990 *Kluwer Academic Publishers. Printed in the Netherlands.*

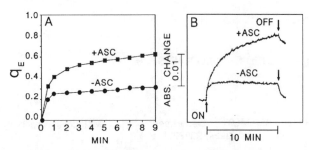

FIGURE 1. (A) q_E induction curves for osmotically-shocked pea chloroplasts in the absence (•) and presence (■) of ascorbate under linear electron transport. (B) 505-nm change kinetics acquired simultaneously with fluorescence induction curves in (A). Illumination was 350 μmol photons m^{-2}s^{-1}. Reagent concentrations were 30μg total chlorophyll, 60mM ascorbate when present, and 0.1mM MV.

and resistance to antimycin suggest that resistant q_E has a different origin than antimycin sensitive q_E. Addition of antimycin during illumination led to slight reversals of previously developed q_E for both the linear and cyclic systems. The nature of these reversals is unclear; they could be a direct effect of antimycin on the q_E-inhibiting target site.

Table 1 summarizes experiments on the relationship between q_E and zeaxanthin formation under various conditions. Experiment 1 shows that under MV-mediated linear electron transport, antimycin inhibited both basal and ascorbate-enhanced q_E but had no effect on ascorbate-induced de-epoxidation. Also, no zeaxanthin was present or formed in the absence of ascorbate so involvement of zeaxanthin in basal q_E can be excluded. The possibility that the antimycin-resistant q_E component is related to zeaxanthin formation is unlikely inasmuch as the levels observed were similar in the presence and absence of de-epoxidation. Experiment 2 shows that DBMIB inhibited both q_E and zeaxanthin formation. Adding PMS restored zeaxanthin formation completely and q_E to about the basal level under linear electron flow in Experiment 1. Experiment 3 shows that while antimycin inhibited q_E development under PMS-mediated cyclic electron transport, as was also shown in Figure 3-B, zeaxanthin formation was not inhibited. Since violaxanthin de-epoxidase requires an acidic lumen for activity (4), it can serve as an endogenous pH probe. Formation of zeaxanthin in the presence of antimycin in this experiment and in Exp. 1 indicates, in agreement with Oxborough and Horton (3), that antimycin does not inhibit ΔpH formation.

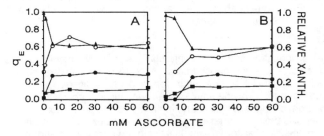

FIGURE 2. The effects of ascorbate concentration on extent of de-epoxidation and q_E development after 9 min. illumination under (A) linear and (B) cyclic electron-transport. Symbols are (o) q_E, (▲) violaxanthin, (•) zeaxanthin, and (■) antheraxanthin.

Overall, these experiments resolved q_E induction into three components, namely, (I) the basal component that is independent of ascorbate and zeaxanthin, (II) the ascorbate-induced component possibly related to zeaxanthin, and (III) a small component that is apparently resistant to antimycin. All three q_E components can be mediated by linear or cyclic electron transport. Since antimycin inhibits component (II) but not zeaxanthin formation, q_E development is not obligatory for zeaxanthin formation.

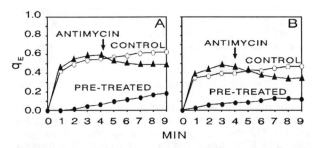

Since q_E develops under both MV-mediated and PMS-mediated electron transport, q_E appears to be a PSI activity which is expressed as PSII fluorescence quenching. Oxborough and Horton (3) have suggested the antimycin target site could be a cyclic electron-transport component that is independent of the linear electron-transport pathway. Cytochromes b_{563}, b_{559}, and a 'ferredoxin quinone reductase' (FQR) were considered as possibilities

FIGURE 3. The effects of 1μM antimycin on q_E when added prior to and during illumination under (A) linear and (B) cyclic electron transport conditions.

(3). Although these electron-transport components are not directly involved in the PMS-ascorbate mediated cyclic electron path, their involvement in redox control of q_E cannot be ruled out since their redox states may be indirectly affected under these conditions.

TABLE 1: Effects of ascorbate, antimycin A, DBMIB, and PMS on extent of de-epoxidation and q_E.

EXPT.	CONDITION	Anti-A	q_E	Relative Conc.		
				Viol	Anth	Zeax
1.	Control, No Light		----	0.96	0.04	0.00
	No Asc, MV	–	0.49	0.97	0.03	0.00
	No Asc, MV	+	0.15	0.96	0.04	0.00
	Asc, MV	–	0.75	0.69	0.14	0.17
	Asc, MV	+	0.21	0.66	0.13	0.20
2.	Control, No Light		----	0.97	0.03	0.00
	Asc, DBMIB	–	0.05	0.97	0.03	0.00
	Asc, DBMIB, PMS	–	0.44	0.70	0.13	0.17
3.	Control, No Light		----	0.96	0.04	0.00
	Asc, DBMIB, PMS	–	0.62	0.61	0.16	0.24
	Asc, DBMIB, PMS	+	0.14	0.63	0.15	0.22

Ascorbate concentration was 60mM in Expt. 1 and 2 and 30mM in Expt. 3. Illumination was for 9 minutes in Expt. 1 and 2 and 500 μmol photon m^{-2} s^{-1} for 5 minutes in Expt. 2. When present, final concentrations were 1μM Anti-A, 2μM DBMIB, 50μM MV, 1μM PMS.

3.3. The mechanism of the putative xanthophyll-mediated quenching is as yet unexplained. Perhaps the ascorbate-enhanced q_E develops as a consequence of zeaxanthin forming a pigment-pigment or pigment-protein complex which interacts with PSII. Accordingly, antimycin's inhibitory effect on ascorbate-enhanced q_E may be explained as a direct or indirect block on zeaxanthin complex formation. Zeaxanthin formation and q_E development could also be completely independent phenomena that coincidentally respond to the redox state of electron transport components. Indeed, the availability of violaxanthin for deepoxidation has been related to a redox component near plastoquinone (4)

The mechanisms of basal and ascorbate-enhanced q_E may be similar based on their mutual sensitivity to antimycin. If the ascorbate-enhanced component is due to zeaxanthin, perhaps basal q_E is mediated by another carotenoid in chloroplasts. While only zeaxanthin can as yet be excluded, lutein or β-carotene appear to be likely candidates for basal q_E from their molecular structure and location in the photosynthetic apparatus. Both lutein and β-carotene are associated with PSI and PSII reaction center complexes (9). However, β-carotene is the primary carotenoid in reaction center II (9,10) and has been suggested to be an alternative source of zeaxanthin aside from violaxanthin (11). Lutein is the α-carotene analog of zeaxanthin and differs structurally from zeaxanthin only in the position of one double-bond. It is the major xanthophyll in chloroplasts and primarily associated with the light-harvesting proteins, especially the Chl a/b-Lutein proteins (9). Thus q_E development could be a consequence of β-carotene or lutein acting sequentially and additively with zeaxanthin at PSII to increase rates of nonradiative dissipation of energy. This activity requires a ΔpH and possibly redox or conformational changes.

REFERENCES

1 Demmig, B. and Winter, K. (1988) Aust. J. Plant Physiol. 15, 163-177
2 Demmig-Adams, B., Björkman, O., Bilger, W., Adams, W.W. III., Thayer, S., and Shih, C. (1989) Physiol. Plant. in press
3 Oxborough, K. and Horton, P. (1986) Photosyn. Res. 12, 119-128
4 Yamamoto, H.Y. (1979) Pure and Appl. Chem. 51, 639-648
5 Horton, H. and Black, M.T. (1980) Biochim. Biophys. Acta. 635, 53-62
6 Schreiber, U., Schliwa, U., and Bilger, W. (1986) Photosyn. Res. 10, 51-62
7 Yamamoto, H.Y. (1985) Methods in Enzym. 110, 303-312
8 Siefermann-Harms, D. (1988) J. Chromat. 448, 411-416
9 Siefermann-Harms, D. (1985) Biochim. Biophys. Acta. 811, 325-355
10 Searle, G.F.W. and Wessels, J.S.C. (1978) Biochim. Biophys. Acta. 504, 84-99
11 Demmig, B., Winter, K., Krüger, A., and Czygan, F.C. (1988) Plant Physiol. 87, 17-24

Acknowledgements. We wish to thank Dr. Olle Björkman for the pre-print of reference 2. This research was supported in part by the U.S. Department of Agriculture under CSRS Special Grant No. 88-34135-3603, managed by the Pacific Basin Advisory Group (PBAG).

ZEAXANTHIN FORMATION IN ETIOLATED LEAVES

Luis Montañes, Luis Heras, Jesús Val and Emilio Monge, EE Aula Dei (C.S.I.C.), Aptdo 202, 50080 Zaragoza, Spain

1. INTRODUCTION

Carotenoids and chlorophylls are essential compounds in the chloroplasts thylakoid membranes, but some carotenoids, in particular violaxanthin, are also located in the chloroplast envelope (1). Plastids from plants germinated and grown in the dark (etioplasts) have no photosynthetic activity and their lipidic structure is arranged in prolamelar bodies which are surrounded by membrane-containing carotenoids called prothylakoids (2). Although several authors report a structural role for carotenoids in chloroplast biogenesis (2), the two major functions are: pigments for light harvesting and photoprotection of enzymes, lipids and chlorophyll (3).

Carotenoids with a conjugated system longer than seven bounds inhibit the photobleanching of chlorophyll. This would explain why zeaxanthin with eleven double bounds provides better photoprotection than violaxanthin which has only nine double bounds (4). This conversion between the two xanthophylls is known as the violaxanthin cycle. In green plants, the enzymatic de-epoxidation of violaxanthin via antheraxthin to zeaxanthin, induced by high light intensity, takes place in the inner part of the granal thylakoid membrane, while the epoxidation, which is independent of light, occurs in the outer membrane (5). It has also been demonstrated that the de-epoxidase activity occurs in the course of the flash induced greening of bean leaves (6) or by infiltration of whole bean leaves with ascorbate at pH 5 (7).

In this paper we studied the evolution of photosynthetic pigments, in particular those of the xanthophyll cycle, during the first seven hours of exposure to low and high light

2. MATERIAL AND METHODS

Photosynthetic pigments were obtained from barley plants (*Hordeum vulgare*) either germinated and developed in vermiculite in complete dark for 15 days (E-plants), or submitted to several periods of illumination under two photosynthetically active photon flux densities (PPFD) of 250 (LL-treatment) and 1000 μmol m^{-2}s^{-1} (HL-treatment). In all cases 0.5 g of fresh matter was sampled by excising the distal, yellow portion of the leaves. The tissues were chopped and homogenized in 100% acetone in presence of sodium ascorbate (8). Absorbance spectra from 550 nm to 750 nm were recorded in a Shimadzu spectrophotometer mod. UV-3000. The pigments were analysed and quantified by using a HPLC system (6). In order to

M. Baltscheffsky (ed.), Current Research in Photosynthesis, Vol. II, 499–502.
© 1990 *Kluwer Academic Publishers. Printed in the Netherlands.*

separate the isomers lutein and zeaxanthin, which in most of the methods have the same retention time, other conditions were used (9).

3. RESULTS AND DISCUSSION

Chlorophyll appearance was monitored by absorption spectroscopy of 100% acetone extracts of samples taken at different times of LL-treatment (Fig. 1). By this method we observed a shift in the absorption maxima from 624 nm (maximum of protochlorophyll) in E-plants to 662 nm (maximum of chlorophyll-a), in leaves submitted to LL-treatment.

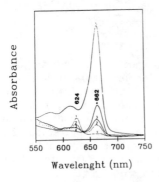

Fig. 1. Absorption spectra of 100% acetone extracts made from etiolated barley leaves (1); and after illumination under a PPFD of 250μmol m^{-2} s^{-1}: 10 minutes (2); 1 hour (3); 5 hours (4); and healthy green plants (5).

These changes were also followed by HPLC which showed that E-plants contained protochlorophyll but no traces of chlorophyll. After 10 minutes of the LL-treatment chlorophyll-a appeared together with one small peak corresponding to chlorophyll-b. Further illumination induced an increase in both chlorophylls within leaves (Fig. 2).

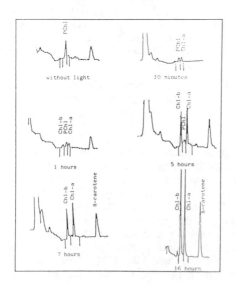

Fig. 2. Chromatograms showing the time course for the formation of chlorophyll-a, and chlorophyll-b, following illumination under a PPFD of 250 μmol m^{-2} s^{-1}. The scales were modified to enhance the peaks of the chlorophylls.

The accumulation of chlorophyll-a, chlorophyll-b, and protochlorophyll in leaves under LL-treatment is shown in Figure 3. During the 'lag phase', in this case the first four hours of illumination, the concentration of total chlorophyll in leaves remained virtually constant ($\approx$12 µg.g^{-1} of fresh matter)(Table 1). After this period a dramatic increase in chlorophyll-a but not in chlorophyll-b was observed (Fig. 3). Therefore, the ratio of chlorophyll-a/chlorophyll-b as well as the ratio of chlorophyll/carotenoids increased after the first four hours of LL-treatment (Table 1). The level of protochlorophyll in leaves remained unchanged and was independent of the periods of LL-treatment (Fig. 3), suggesting that this pigment is not the substrate for the formation of chlorophyll (10).

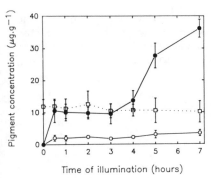

Fig. 3. Evolution of protochlorophyll (□), chlorophyll-a (●), and chlorophyll-b (○), following illumination of etiolated barley leaves under PPFD of 250 µmol m^{-2} s^{-1}

Table 1. Concentration (µg.g^{-1} of fresh matter) and relationships of photosynthetic pigments of the samples illuminated under two PPFDs: 250 (columns A) and 1000 µmol m^{-2} s^{-1} (columns B)

Time (hours)	Total Carotenoids A	B	Total Chl A	Chl a/b A	Chl/Carot A
Dark	73,92(8,12)	71,84(6,23)	0,00(0,00)	---	---
0,5	90,68(10,21)	96,48(9,23)	12,63(1,42)	5,13(0,21)	0,14(0,01)
1	89,85(9,23)	88,70(4,16)	12,02(2,38)	5,04(0,85)	0,13(0,01)
2	79,96(6,54)	82,18(5,23)	12,13(1,89)	4,96(0,23)	0,15(0,01)
3	86,97(9,18)	83,28(7,88)	11,27(0,98)	5,44(0,16)	0,13(0,02)
4	85,78(8,98)	93,82(8,22)	15,91(1,21)	6,13(0,32)	0,19(0,02)
5	87,60(7,51)	96,14(5,45)	30,79(4,26)	9,03(0,65)	0,35(0,01)
7	85,20(6,51)	102,60(15,83)	39,62(2,89)	10,45(0,52)	0,47(0,02)

Standard errors of the means of 9 replicates are given

Zeaxanthin did not appear in the samples taken in the dark, and similar levels (5±1.56 µmol.g^{-1}) were found in all the samples submitted to LL-treatments (Fig 4-A). After the lag phase (Fig. 3) in which PS1 seemed to be the only structure (9), the rapid synthesis of chlorophyll-a may indicate the higher rate of formation of reaction centres of PS1 and PS2 relative to other structures (11).

No synthesis of chlorophyll occurred in leaves under HL-treatment, probably due to photobleanching. Besides, after an initial increase, violaxanthin decreased coinciding with a dramatic increase of zeaxanthin (Fig. 4-B), while the level of anteraxanthin remained unchanged during the experimental period (results not shown).

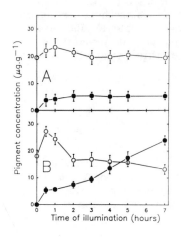

Fig. 4. Evolution of violaxanthin (O) and zeaxanthin (●) on illumination of etiolated barley leaves under PPFDs of 250 μmol m^{-2} s^{-1} (A) and 1000 μmol m^{-2} s^{-1} (B)

These results shown that the xanthophyll cycle is light dependent in etioplasts as it is in thylakoids. Therefore the de-epoxidation must take place in other stroma membranes like prothylakoids or plastid envelope which have no photosynthetic activity. This mechanism would be triggered in response to pH changes, suggesting the idea that the main role of the xanthophyll cycle may be the photoprotection of the chlorophyll by dissipating the energy that this pigment cannot process.

ACKNOWLEDGEMENTS

The authors wish to thank Mª Angeles Gracia for her excellent technical assistance.

REFERENCES
1 Jefrey, W., Douce, R. and Benson, A.A. (1974) Proc. Nat. Acad. Sci. USA 3,807–810.
2 Axelson, L., Dhalin, C. and Ryberg, H. (1982) Physiol. Plant. 55,111–116
3 Dahlin, C., Ryberg, H. and Axelson, L. (1983) Physiol. Plant. 59:562–566
4 Claos, H. (1961) Z. Natur. 168,445–449
5 Yamamoto, H-Y. (1979) Pure Appl. Chem. 51,639–648
6 Siefermann-Harms, D., Michel, J-M. and Collard, F. (1980) Biochim. Biophys. Acta 589:315–323
7 Pfündel, E. and Strasser, R.J. (1988) Photosyn. Res. 15,67–73
8 Val, J., Abadía, J. Heras, L. and Monge, E. (1986) J. Micronutr. Anal. 2:305–312
9 Rivas, J., Abadía, A. and Abadía, J. (1989) Plant Physiol. (in press)
10 Shioi, Y. and Sasa, T. (1983) Plant and Cell Physiol. 24,835–840
11 Chetverikov, A.G., Stanko, S.A., and Novikova, G.V. (1984) Biofizika 29,660–665

CHLOROPHYLL a FLUORESCENCE (77 K) AND ZEAXANTHIN FORMATION IN LEAF DISKS (*NICOTIANA TABACUM*) AND ISOLATED THYLAKOIDS (*LACTUCA SATIVA*)

Erhard Pfündel[1] and Reto J. Strasser[2], Inst. of Biology, Univ. of Stuttgart, Pfaffenwaldring 57, D-7000 Stuttgart 80, FRG[1]; Bioenergetics Laboratory, Univ. of Geneva, CH-1254 Lullier, Switzerland[2].

1. INTRODUCTION

In higher plants and in most of the eukaryotic algal classes light-dependent reversible interconversions of 5,6-epoxycarotenoids (xanthophyll cycles) were found (see [1,2,3] for a review). Two types of cycle are known. In higher plants as well as in Chlorophyceae and in Phaeophyceae the violaxanthin cycle is known to be present. It starts with the enzymatic de-epoxidation of violaxanthin (5,6,5',6'-diepoxyzeaxanthin) via antheraxanthin (5,6-monoepoxyzeaxanthin) to zeaxanthin induced by strong light; the back reaction occurring on a different pathway is light-independent. According to the transmembrane model of the violaxanthin cycle, the de-epoxidase which has its optimum at pH 5 and requires ascorbate for its activity *in vitro*, is located at the loculus side of the thylakoid membrane, while epoxidation takes place at the stroma side of the membrane (optimum at pH 7.5, cosubstrates: NADPH, O_2). The de-epoxidation system is present in both grana and stroma thylakoids [2]. The ability to de-epoxidate violaxanthin has been established in etiolated leaves [4].

In intact leaves of *Lemna gibba* zeaxanthin formation takes place during photosynthesis under light-saturating conditions [2]. Also processes causing inhibitory effects on photosynthesis are provoked under such conditions [5]. Bearing these observations in mind, investigations on a possible correlation between violaxanthin de-epoxidation and chlorophyll a fluorescence which undergoes characteristic changes during developing photoinhibition [5], were undertaken to obtain an approach to the function of the cycle.

2. MATERIALS AND METHODS

Nicotiana tabacum var. Samsun was grown in a glasshouse under natural daylight for 10 weeks (Aug.-Oct.). Prior to the experimental procedure plants were adapted to weak light for at least two hours (5 W/m², fluorescent tubes). For each series of experiments neighbouring leaf sections were cut out and subsequently illuminated for 20, 45 or 90 minutes, respectively (control: 0 min.). Illumination of the anatomical upper side was with strong red light (400 W/m²; radiation of a 150 W tungsten iodide lamp filtered through a 5 cm layer of water and a Corning 2403 glass filter). After light treatment disks were punched out of the leaf sections and subjected to fluorescence measurements followed by extraction for pigment analysis. Osmotically shocked chloroplasts were isolated as described in [6] from *Lactuca sativa* var. Grand Rapid cultivated outdoors or in a glasshouse for 3 to 6 weeks. Prior to isolation plants were kept in the dark for 10 hours.

M. Baltscheffsky (ed.), Current Research in Photosynthesis, Vol. II, 503–506.
© 1990 *Kluwer Academic Publishers. Printed in the Netherlands.*

Final chlorophyll concentration was 10 µg/ml. Light-driven de-epoxidation at pH 7.2 (300mM sorbitol, 50mM HEPES, 10mM NaCl, 16mM ascorbate) was induced by moderate red light (20 W/m^2; same light source as for *N. tabacum*, intensity reduction with neutral density filters). Aliquots were taken for fluorescence measurements. Light-independent de-epoxidation at pH 5 (300mM sorbitol, 50mM NaCitrate, 10mM NaCl, 1mM MgCl$_2$) was initiated by adding ascorbate (final concentration 16mM). Previous to fluorescence measurements and pigment extraction the thylakoids were washed in pH 7.2-buffer containing 1 mM MgCl$_2$. For high light treatments chloroplasts with different zeaxanthin content due to preincubation at pH 5 with or without 16 mM ascorbate were illuminated at pH 7.2 (300mM sorbitol, 50mM HEPES, 10 mM NaCl, 1mM MgCl$_2$, no ascorbate) with red light (520 W/m^2; RG 610 glass filter, Schott, Mainz).
Fluorescence measurements were carried out as described in [7]. Prior to freezing the samples were kept in the dark for 30 seconds. Excitation of the upper leaf side was at 633 nm (He-Ne laser). Fluorescence induction was measured at 695 nm (PS II emission) and 735 nm (PS I emission) simultaneously. Initial fluorescence ($F_{695}O$) and maximum fluorescence ($F_{695}M$) were derived from induction curves at 695 nm. Variable fluorescence was obtained from the expression $F_{695}V=F_{695}M-F_{695}O$, normalized variable fluorescence from $F_{695}V/F_{695}M$. In the case of leaf disks, the ratio of maximum fluorescence of PS II and PS I ($F_{695}M/F_{735}M$) was derived from induction curves, in thylakoid suspensions it was taken from fluorescence emission spectra.
Zeaxanthin formation was determined either by continuously recording the 505 nm absorbance change ($\Delta A 505$; λ(reference): 540 nm) [2,3] or by spectroscopic analysis of pigment extracts in 80% acetone. In the latter case difference spectra (treated minus non-treated) were calculated from absorbance spectra normalized to equal maximum absorbance in the red region. If zeaxanthin formation has occurred, then such difference spectra (ΔA_λ) in the blue-green part are very similar to the spectroscopic difference of equimolar ethanolic solutions of zeaxanthin minus violaxanthin ($\Delta\epsilon_\lambda$) with only negligible deviations from zero at longer wavelengths. Since no zeaxanthin could be detected in low light adapted *N. tabacum* as well as in dark adapted *L. sativa* (pigment analysis by thin-layer chromatography, data not shown) moles zeaxanthin per moles chlorophyll a were calculated as follows:

$$\frac{\text{mole zeaxanthin}}{100 \text{ mole chl. a}} = \frac{\Delta A_{491} \cdot MW_{chl.a}}{\Delta\epsilon_{489} \cdot d \cdot c_{chl.a}} \cdot 100$$

(ΔA_{491}: maximum absorbance difference of extracts (491 nm), $\Delta\epsilon_{489}$: corresponding maximum difference extinction coefficient (489 nm; 80mM^{-1}·cm^{-1}), $MW_{chl.a}$: molecular weight of chl. a, d: light path, $c_{chl.a}$: concentration of chl.a in mg/ℓ calculated from absorbance spectra according to [8]).

3. RESULTS

The zeaxanthin content in leaf disks of *N. tabacum* illuminated with strong red light reaches 90% of the steady state value after 20 minutes (Fig. 1A). In this period only a slight decrease of $F_{695}M$, $F_{695}V$ and $F_{695}M/F_{735}M$ is observed, while $F_{695}O$ and $F_{695}V/F_{695}M$ remain constant (Fig. 1B-1D). Changes in fluorescence characteristics observed within the first 20 minutes of illumination are continuously taking place during further illumination but with little zeaxanthin formation.
In the presence of ascorbate, maximum zeaxanthin content in isolated thylakoids is obtained after 10 minutes moderate red light at pH 7.2 (Fig. 2A, [2,3]) or 10 minutes at pH 5 in the dark [2,3]. During light-induced zeaxan-

thin formation fluorescence characteristics remain approximately constant (Fig. 2B-2D). At pH 5 this is also valid for $F_{695}V/F_{695}M$ and $F_{695}M/F_{735}M$, whereas $F_{695}O$, $F_{695}M$ and $F_{695}V$ decrease slightly (Fig. 3).
High light treatment of thylakoids lacking ascorbate thus not capable of zeaxanthin formation [1,2,3], leads to distinct drops in $F_{695}M$, $F_{695}V$, $F_{695}V/F_{695}M$ and $F_{695}M/F_{735}M$ (Tab. 1). These observations are valid for both preparations with high and low zeaxanthin content.

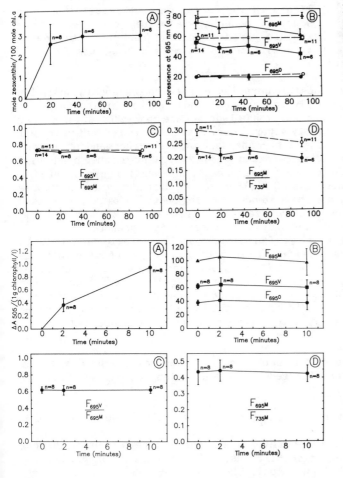

FIGURE 1: Relative zeaxanthin content and low temperature fluorescence of leaves of *N. tabacum*. Means of n measurements (±standard devtion) are shown. Filled symbols: Illumination with strong red light. Open symbols: Leaf sections kept in low light. Different initial values (t=0 min.) are due to a changed signal amplification.

FIGURE 2: Light-induced absorbance increase at 505 nm and low temperature fluorescence of isolated thylakoids of *L. sativa*
Means of 8 measurements (±standard dev.) are shown. Suspensions (+ascorbate) were illuminated with moderate red light. For Fig. 2B all series of measurements were normalized to the same $F_{695}M$ at t=0 minutes.

TABLE 1: Low temperature fluorescence of thylakoid suspensions with different zeaxanthin content, before (D) and after (L) high light treatment

mole zeax. 100 mole chl.a		$F_{695}O$	$F_{695}M$	$F_{695}V$	$\dfrac{F_{695}V}{F_{695}M}$	$\dfrac{F_{695}M}{F_{735}M}$
0	D	31	104	73	0.70	0.56
	L	30	57	27	0.47	0.39
7.8	D	27	98	71	0.72	0.56
	L	31	61	30	0.49	0.38

Each value represents the mean of 2 measurements. Suspensions were illuminated for 10 minutes with strong red light. No ascorbate was present.

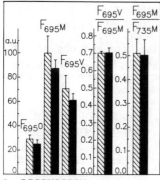

FIGURE 3: Low temperature fluorescence of thylakoid suspensions with different pH 5 -induced zeaxanthin content
Means of 4 measurements (±standard deviation) are shown. Thylakoids were preincubated for 10 minutes at pH 5 in the presence (filled bars) or in the absence of ascorbate (hatched bars). No zeaxanthin formation could be established in the latter case whereas in the presence of ascorbate a value of 6.9 mole zeaxanthin per 100 mol chlorophyll a (s. dev.: ±1.3 mole zeax./100 mole chl. a) was found.

4. DISCUSSION

This paper investigates a possible correlation between zeaxanthin formation and changes in chlorophyll a fluorescence related to photoinhibitory processes. Under our experimental conditions fluorescence characteristics either remain constant or are slightly altered during zeaxanthin formation in leaf disks (Fig.1) as well as during light-dependent and light-independent zeaxanthin formation in thylakoid suspensions (Figs.2+3). On the other hand, high light treatment of thylakoids lacking ascorbate, an essential cosubstrate for zeaxanthin formation, quenches PS II fluorescence distinctly and decreases $F_{695}V/F_{695}M$ (Tab. 1), as are known to occur during photoinhibitory processes [9]. We infer from our results that zeaxanthin increase and the strong fluorescence quenching of photoinhibition are uncorrelated phenomena.
On the contrary, Demmig at al [10] observed a linear relationship between fluorescence quenching and zeaxanthin formation during a stepwise increase of the light intensity or under a CO_2-depleted and O_2-reduced atmosphere. The authors suggest that zeaxanthin plays a protective role against excessive light. We conclude that more information on the conditions under which zeaxanthin formation is coupled or uncoupled to fluorescence quenching is required to establish a causality between these two phenomena.

5. ACKNOWLEDGEMENTS

This work was supported by the Deutsche Forschungsgemeinschaft and by a fellowship to E.P. by the Alfried Krupp von Bohlen und Halbach-Stiftung

6. REFERENCES

[1] Hager A. (1980) in Pigments in Plants (Czygan F.-C., ed.), pp.57-79, Fischer, Stuttgart
[2] Siefermann-Harms D. (1977) in Lipids and Lipid Polymers in Higher Plants (Tevini M. & Lichtenthaler H.K. eds.), Springer, Berlin, pp. 218-230
[3] Yamamoto H.Y. (1979) Pure Appl. Chem. 51, 639-648
[4] Pfündel E. and Strasser R.J. (1988) Photosynth. Res. 15, 67-73
[5] Krause G.H. (1988) Physiol. Plant. 74, 566-574
[6] Siefermann-Harms D. (1984) Photochem. Photobiol. 40, 507-512
[7] Graf J.A., Witzan K. & Strasser R.J. (1988) Z. Naturforsch. 43c, 431-437
[8] Ziegler R. and Egle K. (1965) Beitr. Biol. Pflanzen 41, 11-37
[9] Krause G.H. and Laasch (1987) Prog. in Photosynth. Res. 4, pp. 19-26, (Biggins J. ed.), Martinus Nijhoff, Dortrecht, The Netherlands
[10] Demmig B., Winter K., Krüger A. & Czygan F. (1987) Plant Physiol. 87, 218-224

PHOTOINHIBITION OF PHOTOSYNTHETIC BACTERIA

ROBYN E. CLELAND, DEBORAH REES, DAVID A. WALKER, PETER HORTON
Robert Hill Institute, University of Sheffield, Sheffield, S10 2TN, UK

INTRODUCTION

Photoinhibition of higher plants encompasses a range of phenomena, many of which stem from the requirement to harmlessly dissipate excess light energy. These responses to light stress are manifest as a decrease in the quantum yield of photosynthesis and a quenching of chl fluorescence and primarily affect PS II. In intact plants a number of processes have been suggested to protect the photosynthetic apparatus from the potentially harmful effects of excessive light when dissipation through photosynthesis itself is exceeded. These include ΔpH [1], phosphorylation [2] and the xanthophyll cycle [3]. When the capacity of these processes is exceeded direct damage to a component or components involved in the photochemistry of PS II takes place [4,5,6].

The crystallisation of the reaction centre of photosynthetic bacteria [7] has provided a detailed structural picture of the L and M protein subunits and their attached prosthetic groups. The PS II reaction centre appears to consist of a similar heterodimer of the D1 and D2 proteins and also cytochrome b_{559} [8]. The extent of homology between the two systems at the level of the prosthetic groups is still under investigation. Certainly the underlying sequence of electron transfer (reaction centre chl $\rightarrow$ pheophytin $\rightarrow$ primary quinone [1e$^-$] $\rightarrow$ secondary quinone [2e$^-$] $\rightarrow$ quinone pool) is the same, although the components involved are slightly different, e.g. Q_A is a plastoquinone molecule in plants and ubiquinone in *Rhodobacter capsulatus*. If there is significant homology between PS II and the bacterial reaction centre at the functional as well as the structural level [9] one would expect bacteria to also suffer photoinhibition. Here we report the results of a series of experiments designed to investigate whether photoinhibition can be induced in photosynthetic bacteria and if it is manifest in a similar way to higher plants, as damage to the reaction centre [4,5,10].

MATERIAL AND METHODS

Rhodobacter capsulatus was cultured photoheterotrophically and chromatophores prepared from French press extracts by ultracentrifugation. Photosynthetic activity was measured as the rate of oxidation of the reaction centre Bchl P_{870} at limiting light or as the steady state level of P_{870} oxidation at varying light intensities, by following the absorbance change 605–540 nm using an Aminco DW2000 dual wavelength spectrophotometer. Activity was assayed in the presence of 1 mM ferricyanide, 14 mM ferrocyanide which gave a redox potential of +385 mV and 2 μg.ml^{-1} valinomycin and 4 μM antimycin A which eliminated any contribution to the signal from the carotenoid bandshift.

Measurements of room temperature Bchl fluorescence were performed in the absence of the above agents using a Hansatech modulated fluorimeter with a photodiode capable of detecting wavelengths up to 900 nm. The instantaneous level of fluorescence, F_0, was excited with a measuring beam consisting of an array of

M. Baltscheffsky (ed.), Current Research in Photosynthesis, Vol. II, 507–510.

yellow modulated LEDs at an intensity of 0.5 μmol quanta.m^{-2}.s^{-1}. F_m, the maximum fluorescence yield, was determined using a saturating white light of 30000 μmol quanta.m^{-2}.s^{-1} provided by a heat filtered tungsten–halogen lamp (Volpi) with a variable power supply and defined by a 680 nm short pass filter. This lamp was used without the filter for high light treatments, which were carried out in a 1 cm cuvette at a Bchl concentration of 20 μM at room temperature. To obtain anaerobic conditions the sample was bubbled with nitrogen prior to the addition of glucose oxidase, glucose and catalase.

Redox titrations were performed with a micro–combination electrode using the following mediators: 40 μM TMPD, 40 μM DCIP, 20 μM each of 1,2–naphthoquinone, 1,4–naphthoquinone, 2,5–dihydroxy–p–benzoquinone, anthraquinone sulphonate and methyl viologen. Reductive titrations were performed with 1 mM dithionite, oxidative titrations with 150 mM ferricyanide.

RESULTS AND DISCUSSION

When chromatophores were exposed to 10000 μmol quanta.m^{-2}.s^{-1} in the presence of oxygen the rate of oxidation of the reaction centre P_{870} decreased as the time of illumination increased (Fig 1). The rate of reaction centre oxidation at limiting light provides a measurement of the quantum efficiency of photochemistry. Bchl fluorescence was also affected, both F_o and F_m declined resulting in a decrease in F_v/F_m which paralleled the loss of P_{870} oxidation (Fig 1). In contrast under anaerobic conditions the rate of P_{870} oxidation decreased more slowly than under aerobic conditions, F_v/F_m remained at normal levels as F_o and F_m were not significantly affected by the treatment (Fig 1). It seems likely that there are two separate mechanisms causing the inhibition of P_{870} oxidation in the presence and absence of oxygen.

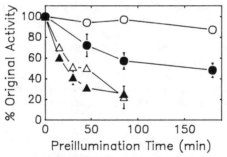

Fig 1. The response of chromatophores to high light in the presence (triangles) and absence (circles) of oxygen measured as the rate of P_{870} oxidation (closed symbols) and F_v/F_m (open symbols), n=3.

The capacity of the bacterial photosynthetic system can be assessed by measuring the extent of oxidation in continuous illumination. Exposure of chromatophores to high light for 30 min under aerobic conditions or 3 hr in the absence of oxygen produced a similar extent of inhibition of the light dependence curve for the steady state level of P_{870} oxidation (Fig 2). It can be seen that a greater degree of inhibition was observed at low light intensities than at saturating light levels. Under anaerobic conditions some inhibition of the steady state level of reaction centre oxidation was seen even at saturating light. These results suggest that at least under aerobic conditions the inhibition of the rate of P_{870} oxidation cannot be attributed to a reduction in the number of reaction centres.

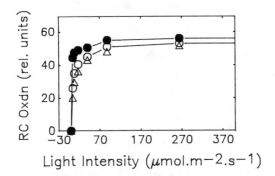

Fig 2. The light dependence of the steady state level of P_{870} oxidation before preillumination (●—●), after 30 min aerobic treatment (O—O) and 3 hr anaerobic treatment (△—△).

It was possible that the decline in P_{870} oxidation was brought about by an alteration in the redox potential of a reaction centre. Redox titrations of the rate of P_{870} oxidation showed that neither aerobic or anaerobic treatment significantly affected the optimum operating potential of the system (Fig 3). A number of molecules such as DBMIB are known to quench chl fluorescence by a nonphotochemical process [11]. When DBMIB was added to chromatophores both F_0 and F_m decreased. When plotted against each other the percentage change in these two parameters showed a negative deviation from linearity with increasing concentrations of DBMIB (Fig 4). After preillumination in the presence of oxygen a similar relationship between F_0 and F_m was observed. The equations of Butler [12] could also be used to produce a similar curve by increasing the rate constant for nonradiative decay in the antenna, k_D.

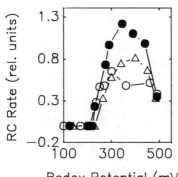

Fig 3. An oxidative redox titration of the rate of P_{870} oxidation before (●—●) preillumination, after 15 min aerobic treatment (O—O) and after 4 hr anaerobic treatment (△—△).

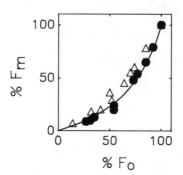

Fig 4. *The relationship between* F_o *and* F_m *in the presence of 0-40 μM DBMIB* (Δ—Δ) *and aerobic preillumination* (●—●). *The solid line represents the effect of increasing* k_D *according to [12].*

CONCLUSIONS

There are two possible explanations for the different behaviour of photosynthetic bacteria compared to higher plants under conditions of light stress. Firstly photosynthetic bacteria have the ability to rapidly dissipate excitation energy through cyclic electron flow and nonradiative dissipation in the antenna and therefore are not subject to the over-excitation which causes photoinhibition in higher plants. The second more likely explanation is that the lower redox potential of P_{870} in bacteria makes them resistant to the sort of oxidative destruction that may be involved in photoinhibitory damage in plants [10]. We suggest that the presence of oxygen activates a quenching mechanism in the antenna which results in a decline in the rate of P_{870} oxidation during exposure to high light. Under anaerobic conditions an unknown mechanism inhibits photochemistry, this may involve damage to a component of the photochemical apparatus. It is concluded that although PS II and the reaction centre of photosynthetic bacteria may be structurally similar they are not functionally analogous.

REFERENCES

[1] Krause, G.H. and Behrend, U. (1986) FEBS Lett. 200, 298-302.
[2] Horton, P. and Lee, P. (1985) Planta 165, 37-42.
[3] Demmig, B., Winter, K., Kruger, A. and Czygan, F.C. (1987) Plant Physiol. 84, 218-224.
[4] Cleland, R.E., Melis, A. and Neale, P.J. (1986) Photosynth. Res. 9, 79-88.
[5] Demeter, S., Neale, P.J. and Melis, A. (1987) FEBS Lett. 214, 370-374.
[6] Krause, G.H. (1988) Physiol. Plant. 74, 566-574.
[7] Deisenhofer, J., Epp, O., Miki, K., Huber, R. and Michel, H., (1984) J. Mol. Biol. 180, 385-398.
[8] Nanba, and Satoh, K (1987) Proc. Natl. Acad. Sci
[9] Michel, H. and Deisenhofer, J. (1988) Biochem. 27, 1-7.
[10] Cleland, R.E. and Melis, A. (1987) Plant Cell Environ. 10, 747-752.
[11] Kitajima, M. and Butler, W.L. (1975) Biochim. Biophys. Acta 376, 105-115.
[12] Butler, W.L. (1978) Ann. Rev. Plant Physiol. 29, 345-378.

PHOTOINHIBITION BY HIGH LIGHT IN A SHADE PLANT
ROLE OF O_2 CONCENTRATION

Marcel ANDRE[1], Michel DUCAMP[2] & Thomas BETSCHE[1]

[1]Dept. Biologie, Sce Radioagronomie, CEN Cadarache, F 13 108 St-Paul-lez-Durance, France - [2]CIRAD - IRCC - F 34032 Montpellier, France.

1. INTRODUCTION

It has been observed that high irradiance saturating the CO_2 uptake stimulated the O_2 uptake measured by $^{18}O_2$ (1 - 2). In those conditions, the O_2 uptake used more than 2/3 of the reducing equivalents produced by light. It is thus probable that, especially under these conditions, O_2 plays a protective role against photoinhibition in nature. In sun plants it is known that the presence of O_2 reduces or even prevents photoinhibition in C_3 plants induced by the absence of CO_2 (3 - 4). In shade plant photoinhibition was observed in presence of CO_2 after high light treatment (5 - 6). We investigated wether the sensitivity of coffee to phoinhibition depends upon the concentration of O_2 in the air.

2. MATERIALS and METHODS

Two years old plants of coffea arabica L. var. Caturra Rojo were obtained from <u>in vitro</u> culture by IRCC (Institut de Recherche du Café et du Cacao) in Montpellier (France).

2.1. Standard conditions for growth and experiments were :
120 μE m^{-2} s^{-1}; photoperiod 12/12 h; Thermoperiod 25/24°C the volume of nutrient solution (1 l/plant) was daily adjusted with water; totally renewed each two weeks. Automated growth chambers (700 l volume) were used to measure CO_2 uptake and respiration (7). $^{16/18}O_2$ exchange were determined in smaller chambers (14 l volume, 2 - 8).

2.2. Chlorophyll a fluorescence was measured in leaves sampled after 6 h in the light after a one hour period in the dark. The apparatus of Schreiber (9) was used.

3. RESULTS

3.1. Effect of light on CO_2 and O_2 uptakes.
The figure 1 shows that an increase of light by a factor of 3.8 resulted in a 1,8 fold increase of CO_2 uptake. In contrast the O_2 uptake which was of the same order as CO_2 uptake,

M. Baltscheffsky (ed.), Current Research in Photosynthesis, Vol. II, 511–514.
© 1990 Kluwer Academic Publishers. Printed in the Netherlands.

increased by a factor of 3.8. This corroborates results observed
in Hirschfeldia incana (1) and in two CAM plants (2) : O_2 uptake
uses almost twice as much reducing equivalents as the CO_2 uptake.
The photoinhibition was measured by the decrease of CO_2 uptake.
After returning to standard conditions, CO_2 uptake was 50%
of the value before high light treatment.

3.2. Effect of hypoxia during a light stress.
A similar treatment was imposed coffee plants put into twin
growth chambers of 700 l. During the high light treatment,
one chamber was maintained in hypoxia (1 to 4% O_2) by injections
of nitrogen slaved to the injections of CO_2. The gas exchange
pattern is shown figure 2 in hourly basis and figure 3 on a
daily basis. In standard atmosphere the results obtained in
small chamber were confirmed (figure 3a). The decrease during
light treatment was of 28% and the resulting photoinhibition
after returning in standard conditions was 50%. The hypoxia
stimulated photoinhibition with decreases of 44% and 76% during
and after the treatment (figure 3b).

TABLE 1. Test of fluorescence on detached leaves during the light
stress of fig. 3. Figures give the ratio F_v/F_m (variable/maximum
fluorescence). Before stress this ratio was 0.78 ± 0.01 and
0.76 ± 0.03 for shade and sun leaves respectively.

LEAVES	DAY 1		DAY 2	
Exposed	air	low O_2	air	low O_2
Base	-	0.223 ± 0.008	0. 621 ± 0.006	0.561 ± 0.004
Center I	0.727	0.392 ± 0.004	0.601 ± 0.005	0.559 ± 0.002
Center II	-	0.582 ± 0.009	0.660 ± 0.002	0.468 ± 0.002
tip	0.744	0.592 ± 0.004	0.679 ± 0.002	
Shaded				
Base	-	-	0.762 ± 0.001	0.711 ± 0.002
Center	0.791	0.791	0.764 ± 0.001	0.673 ± 0.002

FIGURE 1. Effect of the increase of irradiance from 124 to 460
$\mu E\ m^{-2}\ s^{-1}$ on photosynthetic CO_2 uptake (P) and on O_2 uptake (U).
Air temperature was maintained to 24.6 ± 0.2°C during the treatment
(↑).

FIGURE 2. Changes in profile of hourly CO_2 uptake during days of
stress (denoted 1, 2, 3) in comparison with the day before (0)
A) Experiment of fig.1;   B) Experiment of fig. 3A;   C) Experiment
of fig. 3B with hypoxia.

FIGURE 3. Effect of the increase of irradiance in CO_2 uptake
A) in standard atmosphere,   B) in low O_2 (1 - to 4%) during high
light treatment in sample of two plants. The irradiance was increased
(↑) from 230 ± 10 to 630 ± 10 $\mu E\ m^2\ s^{-1}$ during three days.

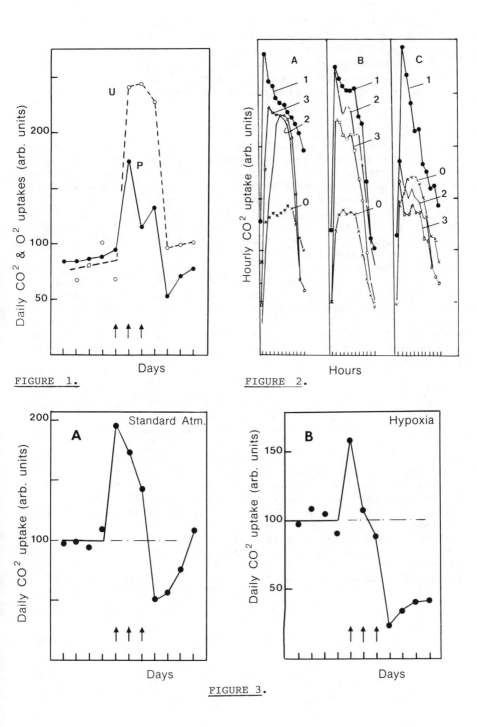

FIGURE 1.

FIGURE 2.

FIGURE 3.

Photoinhibition on the level of photosystem II was detected by the chlorophyll fluorescence measurements (Table 1). In both cases, but more with plants in hypoxia, sclerotic zones were observed on the second day, turning brown and black in successive days. Some young leaves turned dry. The fluorescence change was strongest at the base of leaves, the most exposed areas.

4. CONCLUSION

These and other results (1, 2) indicate that in high light, O_2 uptake uses the most part of reducing equivalents (fig.1). The decrease of light efficiency in high light (e.g. sun and shade plant behaviours) cannot be studied without reference to factors affecting this partitioning (temperature - internal CO_2 etc...).

The presence of such reactions is usefull, in our conditions, to protect plants against photoinhibition (fig. 3) even if CO_2 is present, contrarily to other results (3) where O_2 protect plants only if CO_2 level is very low.

Our long duration tests on whole plant seems better to simulate environmental constraints than classics short term test on leaves.

However, the observed protective effect do not exclude other effects of O_2 which can also be agressive (10) in other conditions.

ACKNOWLEDEGMENTS. We thank J. MASSIMINO, D. BIEYSSE, N. ROY and M. VIDAUD, and the staff of the Agrophysiology Laboratory for their help in experiments.

REFERENCES
1 Canvin, D.I. Berry, J.A., Badger, M.R., Fock, H., Osmond, C.B. (1980) Plant Physiol. 66, 302-307
2 Thomas, D.T., André, M. and Ganzin, A.M. (1987) Plant Physiol. Biochem. 25, 95-103
3 Cornic, G. (1976) C.R. Acad. Sci. Paris 282, 1955-1958
4. Powles, S.B. (1984) Ann. Rev. Plant Physiology, 35, 1-14
5. Powles, S.B. and Critchley C. (1980) Plant Physiol. 65, 1181-1187
6. Powles, S.B. and Thorne, S.W. (1981) Planta 152, 471-477
7. Du Cloux, H., André, M., Daguenet, A., Massimino, J. (1987) J. Exp. Bot. 38, 1421-1431
8. Gerbaud, A. and André, M. (1980) Plant Physiol. 66, 1032-1036
9. Schreiber, V., Schliwa, V., Bilger W. (1986) Photosynth. Res. 10, 51-62
10. Krause G.H., Köster, S., Wong, S.C. (1985) Planta 165, 430-438

PHOTOINHIBITION OF PHOTOSYSTEM TWO IS INCREASED BY FREEZING IN VIVO OR INHIBITION OF WATER OXIDATION IN VITRO

W.Q. Wang, D.J. Chapman and J. Barber
AFRC Photosynthesis Research Group, Department of Biochemistry, Imperial College, London SW7 2AY, UK

1. INTRODUCTION

Exposure of oxygenic organisms to light intensities higher than those used for growth causes reduction of photosynthetic capacities. It has been clearly shown that the primary sites of damage are the photosystems which drive the electron transfer reactions of photosynthesis and PS2 is particularly vulnerable (1). Chloroplasts, in which water oxidation has been inhibited by Cl^- depletion, Tris washing or hydroxylamine treatment, are particularly susceptible to photoinhibition (2,3). Inactivation of water oxidation can also be induced in vivo by freezing (4). We have therefore used this treatment to investigate this effect on susceptibility to photoinhibition. As a part of this study we have also determined what changes occur in the composition of PS2 as a result of freezing treatments and how the effects correlate with other treatments such as washing with 1 M NaCl and 1 M $CaCl_2$.

MATERIALS AND METHODS

Pea plants were grown in a controlled environment cabinet, Fisons Model 600G3/TTL, at 18°C, with a photoperiod of 16 hr light, 200 $\mu E/m^2/s$, and 8 hr dark. Spinach (Spinacea oleracea) was bought locally. Previously described methods (5) were used to prepare PS2 enriched membrane preparations from chloroplasts of Pisum sativum plants, to measure rates of oxygen evolution using a Clark type oxygen electrode with 0.5 mM phenylbenzoquinone (DBQ) as the artificial electron acceptor, to assay electron transfer by reduction of 0.04 mM 2,6-dichlorophenolindophenol (DCPIP) with or without 0.5 mM diphenylcarbazide (DPC) as an artificial electron donor and to determine the amounts of the extrinsic proteins with an enzyme-linked immunosorbent assay (ELISA). PS2 preparations were photoinhibited by treatment at 2000 $\mu E/m^2/s$, 10°C and 30 μg chlorophyll/ml in a buffer of 20 mM MES pH 6.0, containing 10% glycerol. The pH treatment was by resuspension of PS2 membrane pellets (centrifuged at 40,000 xg, 4°C, 20 min) in 20 mM MES or BTP buffer, 5 mM $MgCl_2$, 15 mM NaCl and 10% glycerol; high salt washes were by resuspension in either 1 M NaCl or 1 M $CaCl_2$ in MES buffer as above.

3. RESULTS AND DISCUSSION

PS2 enriched membrane preparations were isolated from pea plants grown in normal conditions or frozen at different temperatures overnight and assayed for photosynthetic electron transfer activity. Inhibition of electron transfer from

M. Baltscheffsky (ed.), Current Research in Photosynthesis, Vol. II, 515–518.

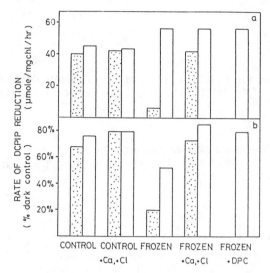

Fig. 1(a) Electron transport rates of PS2 enriched particles from control pea plants and those which have been frozen at -18°C overnight. **(b)** Photoinhibition (2000 $\mu E/m^2/s$, 30 μg Chl/ml, 10 min) of electron transfer in PS2 particles from control and frozen pea plants. $CaCl_2$ (10 mM), NaCl (20 mM) or DPC (0.5 mM) were added before light treatment to some samples as indicated. Electron transport to the artificial electron acceptor, DCPIP, assayed in the absence , or presence, of the artificial donor DPC (0.5 mM) (shaded and open areas respectively).

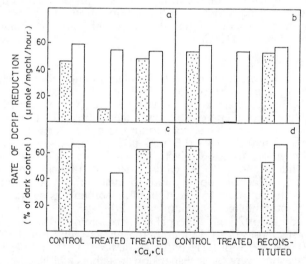

Fig.2 Comparison of rates of electron transport in PS2 particles before and after (a) 1 M NaCl and (b) 1 M $CaCl_2$ washes. Photoinhibition of PS2 particles washed with (c) 1 M NaCl and (d) 1 M $CaCl_2$. Salt additions in (a & c) were 10 mM $CaCl_2$ and 20 mM NaCl added to MES (20 mM) containing 30 μg Chl/ml before incubation at 10°C for 20 min in light. For reconstitution in (b & d) purified 33 kD extrinsic proteins were incubated on ice with the PS2 membranes before the light treatment. Electron transport to DCPIP was assayed in the absence or presence of DPC (0.5 mM) (shaded and open areas respectively).

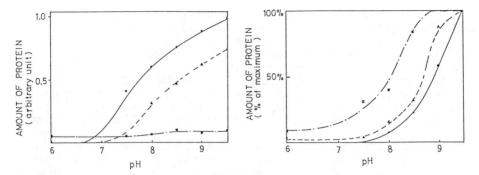

Fig.3 Effect of incubation at various pH values on the removal of the extrinsic 23 kD protein from PS2 membranes. PS2 enriched membrane preparations were isolated from pea plants (——), plants frozen at -3°C (– –) and at -18°C (– · –). The amount of 23 kD protein in the supernatant was assayed by ELISA.

Fig.4 Effect of incubation at different pH values on the removal of the extrinsic 33 kD protein from PS2 membranes. PS2 enriched membrane preparations were isolated from control pea plants (——), pea plants frozen at between -3°C (– –) and -18°C (– · –) overnight. The amount of the 33 kD protein in the supernatant was assayed by ELISA.

water to the artificial acceptor DCPIP after freezing of plants at -8°C (data not shown) or -18°C in the dark was observed. However, the electron transfer through the PS2 reaction centre was not inhibited in these samples, as indicated by the lack of affect on photoreduction of DCPIP in the presence of the artificial electron donor DPC (Fig.1a). This suggests that the lesion was on the oxidising side of PS2. PS2 membranes from both types of plant had reduced electron transfer rates from DPC to DCPIP after exposure to strong light, but the effect on PS2 from frozen plants was the most pronounced. This result suggests that PS2 from frozen peas is more susceptible to photoinhibition than those from controls. The ability of PS2 from frozen peas to oxidise water can be restored by addition of 10 mM $CaCl_2$, a treatment which does not bring about a significant change in PS2 membranes from control plants. The recovery of water oxidation by addition of calcium and chloride resulted in a greatly reduced effect of subsequent exposure to strong light. Addition of the artificial donor DPC prior to illumination also significantly reduced the rate of light induced loss of reaction centre activity (Fig.1b). Measurements of rates of reduction of DCPIP in the absence or presence of DPC demonstrated that treatment with 1 M NaCl (Fig.2a,c), 1 M $CaCl_2$ (Fig.2b,d), citrate buffer at pH 3.0 or BTP buffer at alkaline pH (data not shown) were all effective means of inhibiting water oxidation while maintaining full reaction centre activity. PS2 membranes treated by these methods showed a similar increased sensitivity of PS2 to light to those from frozen plants. These results corroborate the work of others in which chloride depletion, Tris washing or hydroxylamine treatment were shown to result in a similar enhancement of photoinhibition in chloroplasts. As a result of the inactivation of the water splitting reaction, without loss of reaction centre activity, highly oxidising chemical species such as $P680^+$ and Z^+ can be formed in the light but not readily reduced by the usual electron transfer process. In this state, destructive and uncontrolled oxidation of neighbouring molecules could arise and be the primary cause of the light induced damage to PS2. Indeed pea plants frozen in the dark were further damaged when transferred into normal conditions under weak growth light (data not shown).

Changes in molecular structure of the PS2 complex isolated from frozen plants are indicated by the results in Fig.3 and 4. No extrinsic 23 kDa protein could be detected using ELISA in supernatants obtained by treating PS2 membranes of frozen samples with buffers up to pH 9.5. Taking this result together with previous results from SDS-PAGE (6), we conclude that the extrinsic 23 kDa protein in the isolated PS2 membrane complex of plants after -18°C freezing is missing. Furthermore, the results from the ELISA, shown in Fig.4, indicate that the association of the extrinsic 33 kDa protein with PS2 membranes became more susceptible to removal by alkaline pH if the plants had been frozen at -18°C. The effect of freezing plants at -3°C was similar to -18°C although not so severe (Fig.3 & 4). The similarity between PS2 preparations from frozen plants and those washed by high salt concentrations suggests that a possible reason for the damage during freezing could be an increase in salt concentration near to the surface of the PS2 membrane caused by the water crystallization. Under some conditions, extrinsic proteins which have dissociated from the membrane could rebind to the membrane as we and others have demonstrated in vitro (5,7). This could possibly happen during the recovery process which follows freezing at -3°C.

ACKNOWLEDGEMENT

We thank Mr John De Felice for great help with techniques and the AFRC(UK) for financial support. WQW is grateful for his grant from the Chinese Academy of Sciences.

REFERENCES

1. Powles, S.B. (1984) Ann. Rev. Plant Physiol. 35, 15-44
2. Theg, S.M., Filar, L.J. and Dilley, R.A. (1986) Biochim. Biophys. Acta 849, 104-111
3. Callahan, F.E., Becker, D.W. and Cheniae, G.M. (1986) Plant Physiol. 82, 261-269
4. Marguliles, M.M. (1972) Biochim. Biophys. Acta 267, 96-103
5. Chapman, D.J., De Felice, J., Davis, K. and Barber, J. (1989) Biochem. J. 258, 357-362
6. Chapman, D.J., W.Q. Wang and J. Barber, (1988) In: Proceedings Plant Physiological Soc., New Delhi
7. Miyao, M. and Murata, N. (1987) In: Topics in Photosynthesis, Vol.9, Photoinhibition (ed. Kyle, D.J., Osmond, C.B. and Arntzen, C.J.) Pub. Elsevier Science Publ. Amsterdam, pp 289-307

OXYGEN QUENCHING OF TRIPLET STATES IN ISOLATED PHOTOSYSTEM 2
REACTION CENTRES: A MECHANISM FOR PHOTODAMAGE.

L.B. Giorgi, B. Crystall, P.J. Booth, J.R. Durrant, J.Barber*, D.R. Klug and G. Porter

Photochemistry Research Group and *AFRC Photosynthesis Research Group, Department of Pure and Applied Biology, Imperial College, London, U.K.

1) INTRODUCTION

Photosystem 2 (PS2) is involved in the oxidation of water which results in the liberation of oxygen, the mechanism of which is still poorly understood. Over the last few years, studies of PS2 have been greatly advanced by the isolation of the D1/D2/ cytochrome b-559 reaction centre complex (Nanba and Satoh, 1897; Barber et al., 1987). In particular, the lack of an antenna complex associated with this reaction centre has greatly simplified spectroscopic studies, although this reaction centre has been found to degrade rapidly under illumination, which hinders such investigations. In this paper we describe the stabilisation of the sample by the removal of oxygen and suggest a mechanism for photodamage which may be related to the rapid turnover of D1 *in vivo*.

The D1/D2/cytochrome b-559 complex contains 4 chlorophyll-a molecules, 2 pheophytin-a molecules, 1 cytochrome b-559 and some β-carotene; it contains no plastoquinone. In the absence of the secondary acceptors (quinone), electron transfer within this complex is limited to the formation of the primary radical pair $P680^+Pheophytin^-$. Absorption spectroscopy of this preparation has indicated the presence of a component decaying with a lifetime of 32-36 ns, corresponding to the lifetime of the primary radical pair (Danielius et al., 1987; Takahashi et al., 1988). More recently, time-resolved fluorescence studies (Mimuro et al., 1988; Seibert et al., 1988) have shown that this complex exhibits a lifetime of 25-35 nanoseconds; this has also been attributed to charge recombination of the primary radical pair, however, the fluorescence from this component was observed to be less than 2% of the total light emitted.

We have studied the microsecond and nanosecond kinetics of the D1/D2 reaction centre by time correlated single photon counting and transient absorption spectroscopy. Stabilisation of the reaction centre has been necessary to establish the kinetics correctly.

2) MATERIALS AND METHODS

Photosystem 2 reaction centre complexes were prepared from pea chloroplasts as described by Chapman et al., 1988 with the following variations. Exchange to 2 mM beta-lauryl maltoside was carried out after the first column purification in Triton X-100. Elution from the column was achieved using a NaCl gradient of 2 mMml⁻¹. The preparation was stored at -196°C. Samples were then resuspended in a buffer of 50 mM Tris-Cl (pH 7.2 or 8 at room temperature) containing 2mM maltoside to give a final chlorophyll concentration of 10μgml⁻¹. Anaerobic conditions were achieved by adding 5mM glucose, 0.1 mgml⁻¹ glucose oxidase and 0.05 mgml⁻¹ catalase.

The state of the reaction centres was monitored during all measurements by noting the Q_y-band absorption and fluorescence maxima. Steady state absorption measurements were made using a Perkin-Elmer 554 spectrophotometer and fluorescence measurements with a Perkin-Elmer MPF-4 fluorimeter. Samples were maintained at 4°C while all measurements were taken and during time-resolved fluorescence experiments, the samples were also

M. Baltscheffsky (ed.), Current Research in Photosynthesis, Vol. II, 519–522.
© 1990 *Kluwer Academic Publishers. Printed in the Netherlands.*

stirred.

Time resolved fluorescence measurements were carried out using a single photon counting apparatus. Transient absorption data were taken with a flash photolysis system as described by Durrant et al. 1989a.

3) RESULTS AND DISCUSSION
3.1) STABILISATION OF THE PS2 REACTION CENTRE

The yield of radical pair formation is a measure of the integrity of the PS2 reaction centre complex. Two of the possible processes that can be measured in order to give an indication of the yield of radical pair formation are (i) the long lived 37ns fluorescence component: this is attributed to charge recombination of the radical pair; and (ii) the P680 triplet state: this is primarily formed from the radical pair by a combination of nuclear induced singlet-triplet mixing and charge recombination (Durrant et al, 1989b). A decrease in the yield of the 37ns fluorescence component and a decrease in P680 triplet yield is indicative of a reduction in the yield of radical pair formation.

Another measure of the stability of the reaction centre complex is the position of its Q_y-band absorption and fluorescence maxima. The further to the red these maxima are, the more intact the complex (Seibert et al., 1988).

The instability of the reaction centre upon illumination under aerobic conditions can be clearly seen in the time resolved fluorescence data shown in figure 1 (Crystall et al., 1989a). The yield of the 37ns component is significantly reduced as the sample is subjected to dye laser excitation. The 6.5ns component has been assigned to chlorophyll which is energetically uncoupled from the process of charge separation (Crystall et al., 1989b and Booth et al., 1989). A shift in both the steady state absorption and fluorescence maxima to the blue occurs simultaneously with the loss of the 37ns component (see the insets in figure 1).

Instability of the particle is also evident from the P680 triplet yield data (the P680 triplet is identified by the spectrum in Durrant et al., 1989b). Figure 2a shows the loss of relative P680 triplet yield against total exposure to the 337nm excitation of the nitrogen laser under aerobic conditions. The loss of P680 triplet yield, and hence a reduction in the yield of radical pair formation, is accompanied by a blue shift in the absorption maxima (figure 2b) and a shortening of triplet lifetime from 34μs to a final value of 30μs (after 16,000 flashes).

Improved stability of the PS2 reaction centre can be achieved by the removal of oxygen. Under anaerobic conditions, the yield of the 37ns fluorescence component is only reduced by 8% after 10 minutes of illumination by a 20mW dye laser. The yield of this long lived fluorescence component is 44%, a twentyfold increase over previously observed yields. A typical fluorescence decay from PS2 reaction centres under anaerobic conditions is shown in figure 3. The position of the steady state absorption and fluorescence peaks also remain stable over this 10 minute period. This stabilising effect of anaerobic conditions is also seen in the P680 triplet yield.

Previous time resolved fluorescence studies have suggested only a 2% yield for the long lived component; the 44% yield observed here indicates a significant improvement in the stabilisation of the reaction centre.We have calculated that only 6% of the chlorophyll present in our samples is uncoupled from the process of charge separation.

3.2) MECHANISM OF OXYGEN CATALYSED PHOTODAMAGE

Figure 4 shows flash induced absorption transients observed at 740nm and 4°C in the PS2 reaction centre preparation which are assigned to the decay of the P680 triplet state. These have monoexponential lifetimes of (33 ± 3)μs under aerobic conditions, lengthening to (1.0 ± 0.1)ms when oxygen is removed from the sample. This change in lifetime of the P680

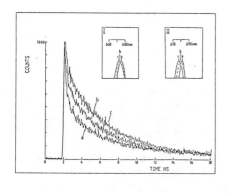

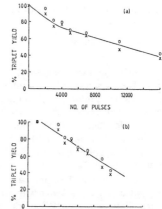

| Fig 1 | Fig 2 |

FIGURE 1: Fluorescence decays of the PS2 reaction centre preparation, under aerobic conditions, after a) zero, b) fifteen and c) thirty minutes of continuous laser excitation at 615nm, 20mW average power. Inset are I) the corresponding shifts in the absorption maximum; a) 675.6nm b) 674.3nm and c) 673.0nm II) the corresponding shifts in the fluorescence maximum; a) 682nm b) 680nm and c) 678nm. Note: only peak shifts are shown.

FIGURE 2: a) The relative reduction in triplet yield of P680, in PS2 reaction centres, is shown against exposure to laser illumination. The laser pulses had an energy of 0.5mJ at 337nm. (the total exposure being in terms of total number of 337nm pulses being absorbed by the sample) b) The correlation in reduction in relative triplet yield with shift in the Q-band absorption maximum.

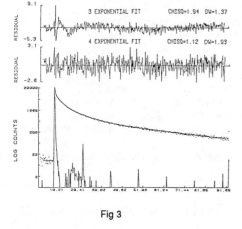

T_x	LIFETIME (ns).	TOTAL FLUORESCENCE EMITTED (%).
T_1	36.5 ± 2.5	44 ± 4
T_2	6.5 ± 1.0	40 ± 5
T_3	1.5 ± 0.5	11 ± 2
T_4	0.1 ± 0.1	5 ± 2

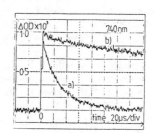

Fig 3

Fig4

FIGURE 3: A typical fluorescence decay of PS2 reaction centres under anaerobic conditions measured at 682nm with 20,000 counts in peak channel. Also shown are the residuals, chi-squared and Durbin-Watson parameters for a three and a four exponential fit to the data. The table in the inset gives the average of the result of analysing three such fluorescence decays to four exponentials. All parameters were free running during analyses. Note: the two shortest lifetimes are not necessarily physically significant. Full scale is 92ns.

FIGURE 4: Flash induced absorption changes observed in PS2 reaction centres at 740nm under a) aerobic and b) anaerobic conditions.

triplet state indicates that the following reaction is occurring under aerobic conditions:

$$^3P680 + ^3O_2 \rightarrow P680 + ^1O_2 \quad \dots\dots\dots\dots\dots\dots \quad (1)$$

Singlet oxygen is an extremely reactive species which is known to damage biological tissue (Asada and Takahashi, 1987). Therefore it seems likely that the inactivation of the isolated reaction centre by prolonged illumination under aerobic conditions is largely due to the formation of singlet oxygen. It is possible that this mechanism is the cause of the damage of PS2 *in vivo* which brings about photoinhibition and the necessity for the rapid turnover of the D1 polypeptide (Kyle et al., 1984).

The rates of oxygen quenching of both the P680 and carotenoid triplet states are approximately ten times less than those seen *in vitro* for chlorophyll-a and β-carotene (Durrant et al., 1989a). This indicates that either the local oxygen concentration, or the rate of oxygen diffusion, is lower within the reaction centre than in the aqueous medium.

The 1ms lifetime of the P680 triplet state is similar to the lifetime of chlorophyll-a in solution, which is 1.5-1.7ms. This indicates that the carotenoid present in this preparation is not quenching the P680 triplet state in the majority of reaction centres.

4) SUMMARY

The data presented:

a. confirms the correlation between sample activity and steady state absorption and fluorescence peaks;

b. confirms that the PS2 reaction centre has a increased susceptibility to photodamage in the presence of oxygen;

c. shows that the the fluorescence decay of the D1/D2 particle is dominated by a 37ns component which contributes 44% of the total fluorescence;

d. suggests that this increased susceptibility to photodamage is caused by oxygen quenching of the P680 triplet state, resulting in the formation of highly oxidising singlet oxygen.

REFERENCES

Asada, K. and Takahashi, M. (1987) in Topoics in Photosynthesis Vol. 9 (Kyle D.J., Osmond, C.B. and Arntzen, C.J. eds.) 227-288, Pub. Elsevier, Amsterdam.

Barber, J., Chapman, D.J. and Telfer, A. (1987) FEBS Lett. 220, 67-73.

Chapman, D.J., Gounaris, K. and Barber, J. (1988) Biochim. Biophys. Acta 933, 423-431

Crystall, B., Booth, P.J., Klug, D., Barber, J. and Porter, G. (1989a) FEBS Lett. 249, 75-78.

Crystall, B., Booth, P.J., Klug, D., Barber, J. and Porter, G. (1989b) Proceedings VIII International Congress on Photosynthesis.

Danielius, R.V., Satoh, K., Van Kan, P.J.M., Plijter, J.J., Nuijs, A.M. and Van Gorkom, H.J. (1987) FEBS Lett. 213, 241-244.

Durrant, J.R, Giorgi, L.B., Klug, D.R., Barber, J. and Porter, G. (1989a) Submitted FEBS Lett.

Durrant,J.R., Giorgi, L.B., Bell, M.A., Klug, D.R., Barber, J. and Porter, G. (1989b) Proceedings VIII International Congress on Photosynthesis.

Kyle, D.J., Ohad, I. and Arntzen, C.J. (1984), Proc. Nat. Acad. Sci. USA 81, 4070-4074.

Mimuro, M., Yamazaki, I., Itoh, S., Tamai, N. and Satoh, K. (1988) Biochim. Biophys. Acta 933, 478-486.

Nanba, N. and Satoh, K. (1987) Proc. Natl. Acad. Sci. USA 84, 109-112.

Seibert, M., Picorel, R., Rubin, A.B. and Connolly, J.S. (1988) Plant Physiol. 87, 303-306.

Takahashi, Y., Hansson, O., Mathis, P. and Satoh, K. (1988) Biochim. Biophys. Acta 893, 49-59.

CHLOROPLAST ENCODED PHOTOSYSTEM I POLYPEPTIDES OF BARLEY.

BIRGER LINDBERG MØLLER, HENRIK VIBE SCHELLER, JENS SIGURD OKKELS, BIRGIT KOCH, BIRGITTE ANDERSEN, HANNE LINDE NIELSEN, INGA OLSEN, BARBARA ANN HALKIER and PETER BORDIER HØJ, Department of Plant Physiology, Royal Veterinary & Agricultural University, 40 Thorvaldsensvej, DK-1871 Frederiksberg C, Denmark

1. INTRODUCTION.

In higher plants, photochemical transfer of electrons from plastocyanin to ferredoxin is catalyzed by photosystem I (PS I), a membrane-bound protein complex binding the reaction center (P700), the photoreducible electron acceptors (A$_0$, A$_1$, X, A and B) as well as antennae pigments (1). The core complex of PS I is defined as the simplest pigment-protein complex which is able to photoreduce NADP$^+$ in the presence of added plastocyanin, ferredoxin and ferredoxin-NADP$^+$ oxidoreductase. The core complex isolated from barley (*Hordeum vulgare L.*) photoreduces 80-340 µmol NADP$^+$/(h x mg chl) (2). The barley core complex is composed of polypeptides of apparent molecular masses of 82-, 18-, 16-, 14-, 9.5-, 9-, 4- and 1.5-kDa as determined from their electrophoretic mobility in SDS-polyacrylamide gels (3,4,5). The PS I core complex contains one copy of each of the two different 82-kDa polypeptides and one copy of the 18-, 16-, 9,5- and 9-kDa polypeptides per P700 (5). The stoichiometry of the remaining polypeptides of the core complex has not yet been determined. Variable amounts of a 15-kDa polypeptide have also been detected in barley but did not correlate with the activity of the preparation (2). The subunits of photosystem I are of dual genetic origin. Some are encoded by the chloroplast DNA whereas others are coded by nuclear DNA and synthesized as larger precursors and imported into the chloroplast by a processing mechanism. In this paper, the function of four chloroplast encoded polypeptides of the PS I core complex is discussed.

2. POLYPEPTIDE NOMENCLATURE.

Bengis and Nelson originally introduced a nomenclature system where the subunits of PS I were numbered according to their electrophoretic mobility in SDS-polyacrylamide gels (6). As the amino acid sequences of the various subunits of PS I are now being determined, the possibility of using these as a biochemical marker for each subunit has arisen. This should facilitate comparison of subunits from different plant species and eliminate erroneous assignments due to differences in the procedures used for analysis and isolation of the core complex. The genes for the PS I subunits have been denoted *psaA*, *psaB*, *psaC* etc. with the alphabetical ordering referring to the sequential order of their identification from a

M. Baltscheffsky (ed.), Current Research in Photosynthesis, Vol. II, 523–530.
© 1990 Kluwer Academic Publishers. Printed in the Netherlands.

number of different plants. In barley, the names for nuclear genes should begin with a capital letter in order to distinguish them from organellar genes. We suggest this nomenclature to be followed in other species. In agreement with the suggestions of Schantz and Bogorad (7), we denote the corresponding polypeptide subunits PSI-A, PSI-B, PSI-C etc. From the determined primary structure of the PS I subunits of barley, it is possible to relate most of these subunits to those identified in other species and to determine whether the subunits are nuclear or chloroplast encoded (Table I). One subunit, PSI-I, has yet only been reported in barley (27). No sequence information is available for the subunit migrating at 4 kDa in the SDS-polyacrylamide gels. A partial sequence available for the 14-kDa polypeptide is not homologous to any of the sequences reported in other species. Accordingly, no gene designation has been made for these two barley polypeptides in Table I.

Table 1: Nomenclature system for the PS I polypeptides of barley.
   The PS I polypeptides of barley have been named using the nomenclature of Schantz and Bogorad (7). Apparent molecular masses are based on electrophoretic mobilities in SDS-polyacrylamide gels (3,4,5). Calculated molecular masses are based on amino acid or nucleotide sequencing data and on plasma desorption mass spectrometry measurements (27,28). A capital P indicates the location of the gene in the nuclear genome.

Poly-peptide	Apparent molecular mass kDa	Calculated molecular mass kDa	Gene	Reference
PSI-A	82	nd	psaA	8-12
PSI-B	82	nd	psaB	8-13
PSI-C	9	8.8	psaC	4,7,11-12,14,15
PSI-D	18	nd	PsaD	16-22
PSI-E	16	10.8	PsaE	18-19,22-24
PSI-F	15	nd	PsaF	2,24,25
PSI-G	nd	nd	PsaG	19-25
PSI-H	9.5	10.2	PsaH	19,26
PSI-I	1.5	4.0	psaI	27
–	14	nd	–	4,5
–	4	nd	–	5

nd: not determined in barley

3. THE CHLOROPLAST ENCODED SUBUNITS
3.1. PSI-A and PSI-B.
   The PSI-A and PSI-B polypeptides with molecular masses around 82 kDa (3,4,5) are homologous as demonstrated from nucleotide sequencing of their chloroplast genes psaA and psaB in a number of plant species (8-13). A heterodimer of the polypeptides are thought to bind the reaction center P700, the primary acceptors A_0, A_1 and X, and about 60 chlorophyll a antennae molecules (4,5,6,29). This complex is often referred to as

P700-chlorophyll a-protein 1 or CP1. A hydropathy plot predicts that each of the polypeptides contains 11 membrane spanning helices (30). A similar prediction has been made for the membrane bound cytochrome P450 (31). Resolution of the crystal structure of soluble cytochrome P450$_{cam}$ (32) and protease treatments subsequently demonstrated that the membrane bound cytochrome P450 contains only two membrane spanning segments (31). It is possible that only a few membrane spanning helices serves to anchor the 82-kDa polypeptides to the thylakoid membrane whereas the remaining hydrophobic helices are buried within the protein.

The exact chemical nature of P700, A$_0$ and A$_1$ remains controversial (1) and the specific polypeptide segments of the heterodimer to which they are bound have not been identified. Center X has been identified as an Fe-S cluster by Mössbauer (33) and EPR spectroscopy (34) and is ligated to the polypeptide chain by 4 cysteinyl residues. The PSI-A/PSI-B heterodimer binds 4 iron atoms (3) and 4 acid labile sulfide atoms per P700 (4). In all species examined, the $psaA$ and $psaB$ genes both specify a conserved stretch of 12 amino acid residues: Phe-Pro-Cys-Asp-Gly-Pro-Gly-Arg-Gly-Gly-Thr-Cys. The cysteine residues in this conserved region are almost certainly the ligands of center X. The PSI-B polypeptide contains no additional cysteinyl residues and only one additional cysteinyl residues in the PSI-A polypeptide is conserved (4). Center X is therefore concluded to be a 4Fe-4S cluster bridged between the PSI-A and PSI-B polypeptides of the heterodimer (5). Shared ligation of an iron-sulfur cluster between two different polypeptide chains has also been reported in the Mg-ATP-binding Fe-protein of nitrogenase (35). The conserved 12 amino acid residue stretch containing the cysteines is located in a particularly conserved region of the PSI-A and PSI-B polypeptides and the hydropathy plot indicates that the cysteine containing segment is positioned in a loop connecting two hydrophobic α-helices. Since Center X donates electrons to the stromal side of the thylakoid this loop must be positioned on the stromal side of the thylakoid.

The heterodimer of PSI-A and PSI-B binds a number of chlorophyll a antennae molecules. A comparison of the sequence information from different species demonstrates that the PSI-A and PSI-B polypeptides contain 38 and 32 conserved histidine residues, respectively. The major part of these histidines (52 residues) are positioned in the hydrophobic α-helices. Histidine residues have been implicated in the coordination of chlorophyll in light-harvesting antennae complexes (36). The number of conserved histidines in the heterodimer corresponds well to the experimental value of 60 chlorophyll a/P700 in the barley core complex (4).

3.2. PSI-C

The PSI-C polypeptide has a molecular mass of 9 kDa and binds the iron-sulfur clusters A and B (4). The first proposal of the PSI-C polypeptide as being an iron-sulfur protein was based on its high cysteine content (37). The protein was isolated from PS I particles of barley and shown to carry zero-valence sulfur which is indicative for a denatured iron-sulfur center (4). The amount of zero-valence sulfur bound to the polypeptide corresponded to 8 acid-labile sulfides per molecule (4). The N-terminal amino acid sequence of the isolated protein permitted the identification of its corresponding chloroplast gene which

```
        1               10              20              30              40
Barley    S-H-S-V-K-I-Y-D-T│C│I-G│C│T-Q│C│V-R-A│C│P-T-D-V-L-E-M-I-P-W-D-G-C-K-A-K-Q-I-A-S-
Wheat     + + + + + + + + +│+│+ +│+│+ +│+│+ + +│+│+ + + + + + + + + + + + + + + + + + + + +
Maize     + + + + + + + + +│+│+ +│+│+ H│+│+ + +│+│+ + + + + + + + + + + + + + + + + + + + +
Spinach   + + + + + + + + +│+│+ +│+│+ +│+│+ + +│+│+ + + + + + + + + + + + + + + + + + + + +
Tobacco   + + + + + + + + +│+│+ +│+│+ +│+│+ + +│+│+ + + + + + + + + + + + + + + + + + + + +
Pea       + + + + + + + + +│+│+ +│+│+ +│+│+ + +│+│+ + + + + + + + + G + + + + + + + + +
Marcantia A + A + + + + + +│+│+ +│+│+ +│+│+ + +│+│+ + + + + + + + + + + + + + N + + + +

        50              60              70              80
Barley    A-P-R-T-E-D│C│V-G│C│K-R│C│E-S-A│C│P-T-D-F-L-S-V-R-V-Y-L-G-P-E-T-T-R-S-M-A-L-S-Y
Wheat     + + + + + +│+│+ +│+│+ +│+│+ + +│+│+ + + + + + + + + + + + + + + + + + + + + + +
Maize     + + + + + +│+│+ +│+│+ +│+│+ + +│+│+ + + + + + + + + + + + + + + + + + + + + + +
Spinach   + + + + + +│+│+ +│+│+ +│+│+ + +│+│+ + + + + + + + + + W H + + + + + + G + G +
Tobacco   + + + + + +│+│+ +│+│+ +│+│+ + +│+│+ + + + + + + + + + W H + + + + + + G + A +
Pea       + + + + + +│+│+ +│+│+ +│+│+ + +│+│+ + + + + + + + + + W H + + + + + + G + A +
Marcantia + + + + + +│+│+ +│+│+ +│+│+ + R│+│+ + + + + + + + + + N + + + + + + G + + +
```

FIGURE 1: Amino acid sequence of the PSI-C polypeptide from barley (38). The sequence from spinach (14) and the sequences deduced from the *psaC* gene in other species (7,11,12,15) are shown for comparison.

was designated *psaC* (4). The complete amino acid sequence of the PSI-C polypeptide has subsequently been determined in spinach (14) and barley (38) and has been deduced from sequencing of the *psaC* gene in a number of species (Fig. 1).

The amino acid sequence reveals the presence of two cysteine containing segments with a cysteine spacing identical to that known from the soluble 2[4Fe-4S] ferredoxins of bacteria. The PSI-C polypeptide is therefore concluded to be a 2[4Fe-4S] protein. The three dimensional structure for the soluble 2[4Fe-4S] ferredoxin from *Peptococcus aerogenes* has been determined by X-ray crystallography (39). Alignment analysis indicate an almost identical tertiary structure for the PSI-C polypeptide. The four cysteine residues anchoring one of the 4Fe-4S clusters are positioned in a more hydrophobic region of the protein compared to those anchoring the other center (4). Center B is known to be more sensitive to oxidative denaturation, mercurials and membrane impermeable probes than center A. The former cysteines have therefore been concluded to coordinate center A and the latter to coordinate center B (4).

Development of milder isolation procedures based on organic solvent extraction have permitted the isolation of the PSI-C polypeptide with more or less intact iron-sulfur clusters (14). Most remarkably, an iron-sulfur protein which was isolated in 1974 by Malkin et al. (40) has now proven to be the iron-sulfur protein carrying center A and B (41). The EPR spectra of the isolated partially native iron-sulfur proteins were somewhat different from those of center A and B (14,41). However, the original spectra of the iron-sulfur clusters as known from measurements using PSI particles were recovered when the isolated PSI-C iron-sulfur protein was combined with isolated CP1 (42). The bacterial ferredoxins are soluble. The fact that the phenylthiohydantoin derivatives of all the amino acid residues could be identified when the PSI-C polypeptide was sequenced (14,38), strongly indicates that the PSI-C polypeptide does not undergo a post-translational processing event which could provide a hydrophobic group to serve as a membrane anchor. Compared to the soluble 2[4Fe-4S] ferredoxins, the PSI-C polypeptide has a 10 residue loop positioned near the center of the polypeptide chain and 14 additional residues at the C-terminal end (38). The C-terminal is quite hydrophilic and the least conserved region of the polypeptide. The 10 amino acid residue loop is more hydrophobic and contains charged amino acid residues and is thus a more likely candidate as an anchor.

The homology between the protein from barley and the corresponding proteins from wheat, maize, tobacco, spinach, pea and *M. polymorpha* is 100, 99, 95, 95, 94, and 93%, respectively. The high degree of conservation of the primary structure of this protein is not solely imposed by its basic function of binding the two [4Fe-4S] clusters as apparent from the bacterial 2[4Fe-4S] ferredoxins which are much less homologous. The high homology between the PSI-C polypeptides of different plants (Fig. 1) could reflect restrictions imposed on the structure of these proteins in order to sustain membrane binding. However, slow evolution is a common characteristic of chloroplast genes.

The sulfur atoms of the iron-sulfur cluster of chloroplast ferredoxin are derived from cysteine and a soluble stromal enzyme system is involved in the cluster formation (43). No information is available on the mechanisms by which the [4Fe-4S] clusters are inserted into the PSI-C apoprotein.

3.3 PSI-I

Our recent studies have indicated the existence of PS I subunits with molecular masses below 5 kDa (5). A subunit migrating with an apparent molecular mass of 1.5 kDa has been isolated. The polypeptide is N-terminally blocked with a formyl-methionine residue. Partial amino acid sequences were obtained after removal of the blocking group and after isolation of fragments derived from enzymatical cleavage with pepsin (27). A comparison with the sequence of the chloroplast genome of tobacco and *M. polymorpha* identified the polypeptide as chloroplast encoded. We have designated the corresponding gene *psaI* and the polypeptide PSI-I. The PSI-I gene was identified on the chloroplast genome of barley and sequenced (Fig. 2) (27). The gene encodes a polypeptide containing 36 amino acid residues. The molecular mass of the polypeptide as deduced from the nucleotide sequence is 4008 Da in contrast to an apparent molecular mass of 1.5 kDa based on electrophoretic mobility. The molecular mass determination was verified by plasma desorption mass spectrometry of the isolated polypeptide (27). Large differences between apparent and actual molecular mass has also been reported for other thylakoid polypeptides like the 10.8-kDa PSI-E polypeptide of barley (23,28)

The PSI-I subunit is very hydrophobic (polarity index: 0.28) and tightly bound to CP1 at conditions otherwise used to dissociate the low molecular mass polypeptides from CP1. The hydropathy profile of the PSI-I polypeptide indicates the presence of a central hydrophobic region flanked by hydrophilic N- and C-terminals. The hydrophobic region is predicted to form an α-helix which may span the thylakoid membrane.

The PSI-I polypeptide is homologous to helix E of the D2 reaction center polypeptide of photosystem II (PS II) (Fig. 2) (27). The positional identity is 31% when compared with the sequence of D2 from barley (44). In PS II, a heterodimer of the homologous polypeptides D1 and D2 is

```
D2      /K-R-W-L-H-F-F-M-L-F-V-P-V-T-G-L-W-M-S-A-I-G-V-V-G-L-A-L-N-L-R-A-Y-D-F-V/
          .   | : :       : | | | : . | |  . : | | : : . : |  |   : :   . : |
PSI-I   M-T-D-L-N-L-P-S-I-F-V-P-L-V-G-L-V-F-P-A-I-A-M-T-S-L-F-L-Y-V-Q-K-K-I-V
        | . . |    .    : : | :  : | : : |  | |  .  .       | | :
ORF34   M-E-A-L-V-Y-T-F-L-L-V-S-T-L-G-I-I-F-F-A-I-F-F-R-E-P-P-K-V-P-T-K-K-N
```

FIGURE 2: The amino acid sequence of PSI-I from barley (27) compared with that of D2 of barley (44) and a putative polypeptide deduced from ORF 34 of tobacco (11)

known to bind the electron transfer components (45,46). Each of the proteins has five trans-membrane α-helices denoted A to E. Helices C and D are intimately involved in the binding of the reaction centre chlorophyll, the accessory chlorophylls and the pheophytins whereas the quinones Q_A and Q_B are bound to helix D and the loop connecting helices D and E. A histidine residue in helix E is involved in the binding of the non-heme iron of PS II specific iron-quinone complex (45). This histidine residue is not conserved in PSI-I. Apart from D2, the search for homologous proteins showed several ubiquinone-NADH oxidoreductases to be homologous to PSI-I (27). Unfortunately, the quinone-binding domain of the ubiquinone-NADH oxidoreductases has not been determined. If the PS I reaction center complex has a structure similar to that of PS II, an additional chloroplast encoded polypeptide homologous to PSI-I would be expected to be present in PS I. A search of the chloroplast genome of tobacco (11) revealed an open reading frame (ORF 34) which might encode such a hypothetical polypeptide (Fig.2). The observed homologies provide no direct clue to the specific function of PSI-I. Nevertheless, the observed homology between the PSI-I polypeptide and helix E of D2 and the strong association of PSI-I to CP1 makes it tempting to speculate that the hitherto overlooked PS I polypeptides with molecular masses below 5 kDa participate in the binding of P700, A_0 and A_1 of PS I in a manner similar to that of the membrane helices of D1 and D2 of PS II.

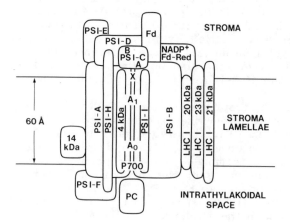

FIGURE 3: Proposed model for PS I.
The model is based on the available information on (1) the polypeptide composition of PS I, (2) the polypeptide stoichiometry, (3) the primary structure of the polypeptides, (4) nearest neighbour analysis by crosslinking and on (5) spectroscopical data.

4. CONCLUSION
A model indicating the possible organization of the PS I complex is shown in Fig. 3. Compared to the knowledge of PS II where high quality diffracting crystals have been obtained and analyzed (45), our understanding of PS I lacks behind. Nevertheless, a general picture of a symmetrical organization of the polypeptides within PS I and with chloroplast encoded polypeptides binding the reaction center as well as the primary electron acceptors are becomming apparent, thus bringing the similarities rather than the differences between the two photosystems in focus.

5. REFERENCES
1 Andréasson, L.-E. and Vänngård, T. (1988) Ann. Rev. Plant Physiol. Plant Mol. Biol. 39, 379-411
2 Scheller, H.V., Andersen, B., Okkels, S., Svendsen, I. and Møller, B.L. (1989) These prooceedings
3 Høj, P.B. and Møller, B.L. (1986) J. Biol. Chem. 261, 14292-14300
4 Høj, P.B., Svendsen, I., Scheller, H.V. and Møller, B.L. (1987) J. Biol. Chem. 262, 12676-12684
5 Scheller, H.V., Svendsen, I. and Møller, B.L. (1989) J. Biol. Chem. 264, 6929-6934
6 Bengis, C. and Nelson, N. (1977) J. Biol. Chem. 252, 4564-4569
7 Schantz, R. and Bogorad, L. (1988) Plant Mol. Biol. 11, 239-247
8 Fish, L.E., Kück, U. and Bogorad, L. (1985) J. Biol. Chem. 260, 1413-1421
9 Kirsch, W., Seyer, P. and Herrmann, R.G. (1986) Curr. Genet. 10, 843-855
10 Lehmbeck, J., Rasmussen, O.F., Bookjans, G.B., Jepsen, B.R., Stummann, B.M. and Henningsen (1986) Plant Mol. Biol. 7, 3-10
11 Shinozaki, K., Ohme, M., Tanaka, M., Wakasugi, T., Hayashida, N., Matsubayashi, T., Zaita, N., Chunwongse, J., Obokata, J., Yamagushi-Shinozaki, K., Ohto, C., Torazawa, K., Meng, B.Y., Sugita, M., Deno, H., Kamogashira, T., Yamada, K., Kusuda, J., Takaiwa, F., Kato, A., Tohdoh, N., Shimada, H. and Sugiura, M. (1986) EMBO J. 5, 2043-2049
12 Ohyama, K., Fukuzawa, H., Kohchi, T., Shirai, H., Sano, T., Sano, S., Umesono, K., Shiki, Y., Takeuchi, M., Chang, Z., Aota, S.-i, Inokuchi, H. and Ozeki H. (1986) Nature 322, 572-574
13 Cushman, J.C., Hallick, R.B. and Prince, C.A. (1987) In Progress in Photosynthesis Research (J. Biggins, ed.) IV, 667-670, Martinus Nijhoff, Dordrecht, The Netherlands
14 Oh-oka, H., Takahashi, Y., Kuriyama, K., Saeki, K. and Matsubara (1988) J. Biochem. 103, 962-968
15 Dunn, P.P. and Gray, J.C. (1988) Plant Mol. Biol. 11, 311-319
16 Scheller, H.V., Høj, P.B., Svendsen, I. and Møller, B.L. (1988) Biochim. Biophys. Acta 933, 501-505
17 Lagoutte, B. (1988) FEBS Lett. 232, 275-280
18 Münch, S., Ljungberg, U., Steppuhn, J., Schneiderbauer, A., Nechushtai, R., Beyreuter, K. and Herrmann, R.G. (1988) Curr. Genet 14, 511-518
19 Dunn, P.P., Packman, L.C., Pappin, D. and Gray, J.C. (1988) FEBS

Lett. 228, 157-161

20   Hoffman, N.E., Pichersky, E., Malik, V.S., Ko, K. and Cashmore, A. (1988) Plant Mol. Biol. 10, 435-445

21   Rhiel, E. and Bryant, D.A (1988) *In* Light-energy Transduction in Photosynthesis: Higher Plants and Bacterial Models (D.A. Bryant and S.E. Stevens, Jr., eds), Waverly Press

22   Alhadeff, M., Lundell, D.J. and Glazer, A.N. (1988) Arch. Microbiol. 150, 482-488

23   Okkels, J.S., Jepsen, L.B., Hønberg, L.S., Lehmbeck, J., Scheller, H.V., Brandt, P., Høyer-Hansen, G., Stummann, B. Henningsen, K.W., von Wettstein, D. and Møller, B.L. (1988) FEBS Lett. 237, 108-112

24   Franzén, L.-G., Frank, G., Zuber, H. and Rochaix, J.-D.(1989) Plant Mol. Biol. 12, 463-474

25   Steppuhn, J., Hermans, J., Nechushtai, R., Ljungberg, U., Thümmler, F., Lottspeich, F. and Herrmann, R.G. (1988) FEBS Lett. 237, 218-224

26   Okkels, J.S., Scheller, H.V., Jepsen, L.B. and Møller, B.L. (1989) FEBS Lett. 250, 575-579

27   Scheller, H.V., Okkels, J.S., Høj, P.B., Svendsen, I., Roepstorff, P. and Møller, B.L. (1989) J. Biol. Chem. submitted

28   Scheller, H.V., Okkels, J.S., Roepstorff, P., Jepsen, L.B. and Møller, B.L. (1989) These Proceedings

29   Warden,J. and Golbeck,J.H. (1986) Biochim. Biophys. Acta 849,30-33

30   Fish, L.E., Kück, U. and Bogorad, L. (1985) *In* Molecular Biology of the Photosynthetic Apparatus (Steinbeck, K.E. et al., eds), pp. 111-120, Cold Spring Harbor Laboratory, Cold Spring Harbor, NY

31   Nelson, D.R. and Strobel, H.W. (1988) J. Biol. Chem. 263, 6038-6050

32   Poulos, T.L., Finzel, B.C., Gunsalus, I.C., Wagner, G.C. and Kraut, J. (1985) J. Biol. Chem. 260, 16122-16130

33   Evans, E.H., Dickson, D.P.E., Johnson, C.E., Rush, R.D. and Evans, M.C.W. (1981) Eur. J. Biochem. 118, 81-84

34   Evans, M.C.W., Sihra, C.K., Bolton, J.R. and Cammack, R. (1975) Nature 256, 668-670

35   Hausinger, R.P. and Howard, J.B. (1983) J. Biol. Chem. 258, 13486-13492

36   Zuber, H. (1986) Trends Biochem. Sci. 11, 414-419

37   Lagoutte, B., Setif, P. and Duranton, J (1984) FEBS Lett. 174,24-29

38   Scheller, H.V., Svendsen, I. and Møller, B.L. (1989) Carlsberg Res. Commun. 54, 11-15

39   Adman, E.T., Sieker, L.C. and Jensen, L.H. (1973) J. Biol. Chem. 248, 3987-3996

40   Malkin, R., Aparicio, P.J. and Arnon, D.I. (1974) Proc. Natl. Acad. Sci. USA 71, 2362-2366

41   Wynn, R.M. and Malkin, R. (1988) FEBS Lett. 229, 293-297

42   Golbeck, J.H., Mehari, T., Parret, K. and Ikegami, I. (1988) FEBS Lett. 240, 9-14

43   Takahashi, Y., Mitsui, A., Hase, T. and Matsubara, H. (1986) Proc. Natl. Acad. Sci. USA 83, 2434-2437

44   Neumann, E.M. (1988) Carlsberg Res. Commun. 53, 259-275

45   Deisenhofer,J., Epp, O., Miki, R., Huber, R. and Michel, H. (1985) Nature 318, 618-624

46   Trebst, A. (1985) Z. Naturforsch. 41c, 240-245

RESOLUTION AND RECONSTITUTION OF THE PHOTOSYSTEM I REACTION CENTER COMPLEX IN GREEN PLANTS AND CYANOBACTERIA

JOHN H. GOLBECK
Department of Chemistry, Portland State University, Portland OR 97207

1. INTRODUCTION

The Photosystem I reaction center in green plants and cyanobacteria is a thylakoid-embedded, multi-protein complex containing antenna chlorophyll a (and $b)$ molecules, a chlorophyll electron donor, P700, a chlorophyll electron acceptor, A_0, a quinone intermediate electron acceptor, A_1, and three iron-sulfur clusters, F_X, F_B, and F_A [see ref. 1 for review]. The function of the acceptor molecules is to stabilize the transient charge separation between the primary reactants, P700 and A_0, by permitting rapid forward electron transfer to outcompete the inherent backreaction between the initial primary reactants. The iron-sulfur clusters, F_X, F_B and F_A, are clearly essential in stabilizing the early events of charge separation in Photosystem I.

The electron acceptors A_1 and F_X are now known to be associated with the P700- and A_0-containing reaction center polypeptides [2,3,4], while F_A and F_B are located on a separate 8.9-kDa polypeptide [5,6]. Our laboratory has recently developed a method for removing the low molecular mass proteins, including the F_A/F_B polypeptide from the Photosystem I core protein [7,8]. The latter, which consists of only the 82- and 83-kDa reaction center proteins, is fully functional in electron flow from P700 to F_X. Based on the apparent requirement of four cysteine residues for ligating low-potential iron-sulfur clusters, and the number of conserved cysteine residues on the $psaA$ and $psaB$ polypeptides (3 on the former and 2 on the latter), it is most likely that F_X is a bridged iron-sulfur cluster ligated by a pair of homologous cysteine residues from each reaction center polypeptide [1,2]. It is uncertain, however, if F_X is a [2Fe-2S] or a [4Fe-4S] cluster.

The isolation of the intact Photosystem I core protein has allowed us to determine the EXAFS and Mössbauer spectrum of F_X in the absence of F_A and F_B. In addition, the isolation procedure is gentle enough to allow reconstitution of the Photosystem I complex from the P700 & F_X-containing Photosystem I core protein and the isolated F_A/F_B polypeptide [9]. Here, we use the newly-developed Photosystem I core protein to show:

• EXAFS and Mössbauer results which indicate that F_X is a [4Fe-4S] cluster,
• F_X, F_B and F_A can be oxidatively denatured and reconstituted from $FeCl_3$ and Na_2S,
• The Photosystem I complex can be rebuilt from the reconstituted P700 & F_X-containing Photosystem I core protein and the reconstituted spinach F_A/F_B protein.

M. Baltscheffsky (ed.), Current Research in Photosynthesis, Vol. II, 531–538.
© 1990 *Kluwer Academic Publishers. Printed in the Netherlands.*

2. RESULTS

2.1. *Spectroscopic Identification of Iron-sulfur Center F_X as a [4Fe-4S] Cluster*

2.1.1. *EXAFS Spectroscopy*
with Ann McDermott, Vittal Yachandra, Ronald Guiles, Kenneth Sauer, Mel Klein and Kevin Parrett [ref. 10]

     Extended X-ray absorption fine structure has the ability to distinguish between [2Fe-2S] clusters, [4Fe-4S] clusters and six-coordinate iron (which is characteristic, for example, of the oxygen- and nitrogen-ligated non-heme iron in Photosystem II). In the case of [2Fe-2S] and [4Fe-4S] clusters, each iron has four sulfur neighbors at about 2.25 Å, and each iron has an iron neighbor at about 2.74 Å. However, [4Fe-4S] clusters are distinguishable from [2Fe-2S] clusters because the former have three iron neighbors whereas the latter clusters have only one iron neighbor. The amplitude of the backscattering is sensitive to the ratio of iron and sulfur backscattering in the beat region at $k = 7.5$ Å (where the dimer and tetramer oscillations are far out of phase) in the Fourier filtered k^3-weighted spectrum.

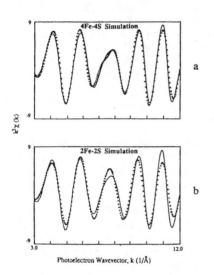

Fig. 1. Simulations of the k^3-weighted k-space Fe EXAFS data from the Photosystem I core protein containing F_X (solid line - experimental; dotted line - simulation). After background removal and weighting by k^3, data from k=3 to k=12 A^{-1} were Fourier filtered with window limits at R'=0.5 and R'=3.3 Å. The similation shown was performed by the method of Teo and Lee using two shells. The parameters for simulation (a) minic a [4Fe-4S] center and employ 4 S atoms at 2.27 Å with a Debye-Waller disorder parameter of 0.075 Å and 3 Fe neighbors at 2.7 Å with a disorder parameter of 0.1 Å. The parameters for simulation (b) mimic a [2Fe-2S] center and employ 4 S atoms at 2.26 Å with a Debye-Waller disorder parameter of 0.08 Å and 1 Fe neighbor at 2.7 Å with a disorder parameter of 0.07 A.

     The major difficulty with assigning a cluster identity for F_X is that the F_A and F_B clusters, which constitute 8 out of the 12 iron atoms in the Photosystem I core complex, contribute most of the backscattering to the EXAFS spectrum. This problem can be circumvented by using the newly isolated Photosystem I core protein incorporating the components P700, A_0, (A_1 by inference) and F_X, but devoid of F_A and F_B. In this preparation, the X-ray K-edge spectrum was found to be similar to that of four-coordinate [4Fe-4S] clusters and unlike six-coordinate iron complexes that are present in heat-denatured Photosystem I or oxidatively denatured ferredoxin. This indicates that the 4 iron atoms in the Photosystem I core protein are most certainly in the form of an intact iron-sulfur complex. The k-space spectrum of F_X (Fig. 1) can be simulated by assuming

4 sulfur neighbors at 2.27 Å and 2 to 3 iron neighbors at 2.7 Å, which is characteristic of [4Fe-4S] clusters (or a similar type of cluster with 2 to 3 iron neighbors for each iron) but not [2Fe-2S] clusters. The simulations suggest an average iron-iron bond distance of 2.69 to 2.70 Å in F_X, which is in contrast to the simulations on the Photosystem I core complex, with an average iron-iron bond length of 2.76-2.78 Å. In summary, the EXAFS data can be considered unambiguous in the assignment of a [4Fe-4S] cluster.

2.1.2. Mössbauer Spectroscopy
with Vasili Petrouleas, Jerry Brand, and Kevin Parrett [ref. 11]

The conclusion that F_X is a [4Fe-4S] cluster is also supported by a recent Mössbauer study of the P700 and F_X-containing Photosystem I core protein. Mössbauer spectroscopy is one of the best methods for determining the identity of an iron-sulfur cluster, and offers the added advantage that the degree of delocalization of the electron over the iron-sulfur cluster can be determined.

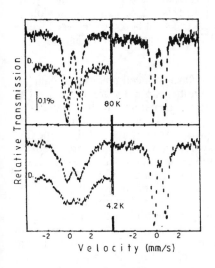

Fig. 2. Mössbauer spectra of the F_X cluster in the Photosystem I core protein. Left panels: Spectra following F_X reduction by illumination under simultaneous freezing of the sample in the presence of 1 mM DCPIP and 10 mM sodium ascorbate. Right panels: Spectra with F_X in the oxidized state obtained after subsequent dark adaptation at -8° C for 10 min. Spectra labaeled D are those left after subtraction of 15% of the spectra on the right. Spectra on the bottom panels were obtained in the presence of a 1 kG magnetic field applied perpendicular to the gamma rays.

The conclusions drawn from the following set of data (Fig. 2) show unambiguously that F_X is a [4Fe-4S] cluster: (1) In the oxidized state at 80 K, the isomer shift (midposition of the two absorption lines relative to metallic iron) of [2Fe-2S] proteins (Fe^{3+}-Fe^{3+}) is 0.26 mm/s in comparison with 0.43 for [4Fe-4S] proteins ($2Fe^{3+}$-$2Fe^{2+}$). In the F_X-containing Photosystem I core protein, the isomer shift is 0.42, in very good agreement with [4Fe-4S] proteins. (2) In the reduced state at 80 K, the extra electron is well localized on one of the two iron atoms of [2Fe-2S] proteins (Fe^{3+}-Fe^{2+}) and as a result the spectrum is composed of two well-separated (Fe^{3+} and Fe^{2+}) subspectra with corresponding isomer shifts of 0.26 and 0.60 mm/s. In the case of [4Fe-4S] proteins ($1Fe^{3+}$-$3Fe^{2+}$) the electron is delocalized and two closely spaced doublets with isomer shifsts of 0.50 and 0.60 mm/s are observed in *B. stearothermophilis*, or an average of 0.54 in *Chromatium* ferredoxin. In the F_X-containing Photosystem I core protein, the spectrum of the reduced cluster is asymmetrically broadened at 80 K, indicating the presence of two very closely spaced doublets with an average isomer shift of 0.55 mm/s. Again, this spectrum is compatible with a [4Fe-4S] cluster. (3) The spectra at 4.2 K in the reduced state of the [2Fe-2S] clusters is extended over a broad velocity range, while the splitting in the [4Fe-4S] cluster is much smaller. In the F_X-containing Photosystem I core protein, the splitting is even smaller. This observation is also compatible with a [4Fe-4S] cluster.

2.2. Reconstitution of the F_X Iron-sulfur Cluster in the Photosystem I Core Protein with Kevin Parrett [ref. 12]

Our current work with the Photosystem I core protein reconfirms that the F_X iron-sulfur cluster can be oxidatively converted to zero-valence sulfur by treatment with 3 M urea and 5 mM potassium ferricyanide [13,14]. Under these conditions, the P700 flash-induced optical transient has a lifetime of 5 μs due to the relaxation of the P700 triplet state, indicating that the P700 A_0 primary charge separation and recombination process has remained intact (Fig. 3a,b). We have now found that the F_X iron-sulfur cluster can be reconstituted by addition of ferrous iron, sodium sulfide, and ß-mercaptoethanol to the oxidatively-denatured Photosystem I core protein [see refs. 15 & 16 for methodology employed]. After incubation for 24 hr, the 5 μs optical transient becomes replaced with a 1.2-ms optical transient that is characteristic of the P700$^+$-F_X^- backreaction (Fig. 3c).

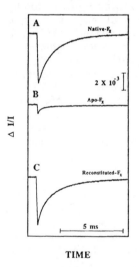

Fig. 3. Flash-induced absorption changes in the Photosystem I core protein. (A) Absorption transient in the native-F_X Photosystem I core protein. (B) Absorption transient in the apo-F_X Photosystem core protein prepared by oxidative denaturation with 3 M urea and 5 mM potassium ferricyanide. Studies at a faster digitizing rate showed that the P700 absorption transient had approximately the same magnitude with a half-time of 5 μs (not shown). (C) Absorption transient in the reconstituted-F_X Photosystem I core protein prepared by incubation of apo-F_X with inorganic iron and sulfide in the presence of ß-mercaptoethanol. All measurements were performed at 5 μg Chl/ml in 50 mM Tris buffer, pH 8.3, containing 1.7 mM ascorbate and 0.033 mM DCPIP.

The ESR spectra of the native-F_X, apo-F_X and reconstituted-F_X Photosystem I core proteins are shown in Fig. 4. The light-induced spectrum of native-F_X (Fig. 4A) has resonances at $g = 2.05$, 1.86 and 1.78, and is similar to that described previously [7]. Figure 4B shows that after oxidative denaturation, little or no light-inducible F_X is present, in agreement with the optical determination of apo-F_X shown in Figure 3B. After reconstitution with inorganic iron and sulfide in the presence of ß-mercaptoethanol, the characteristic ESR spectrum of F_X is recovered (Fig. 4C).

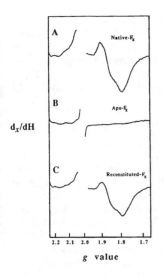

d_x/dH

g value

Fig. 4. ESR spectra of F_X in the Photosystem I core protein after illumination during freezing. (A) Light-minus-dark spectrum of native-F_X. (B) Light-minus-dark spectrum of apo-F_X. (C) Light-minus-dark spectrum of reconstituted-F_X. The samples were suspended in 50 mM Tris, pH 8.3 containing 1 mM ascorbate and 0.3 mM DCPIP at 500 μg Chl/ml. The spectra were resolved by subtracting the light-off from the light-on spectrum and amplifying 3.5-fold in software. Spectrometer conditions: temperature, 6 K; microwave power, 40 mW; microwave frequency, 9.101 GHz; receiver gain, 5 x 10^3; modulation amplitude, 40 G at 100 kHz.

2.3. Reconstitution of the F_A/F_B Iron-Sulfur Clusters in the 8.9-kDa Polypeptide with Tetemke Mehari and Kevin Parrett [ref. 17]

We found that the oxidatively-denatured F_A/F_B iron-sulfur clusters can also be reconstituted by incubating the apoprotein with $FeCl_3$ and Na_2S in the presence of ß-mercaptoethanol. The ESR spectra of the native F_A/F_B protein, the F_A/F_B apoprotein and the reconstituted F_A/F_B protein are shown in Fig. 5. The chemically-reduced spectrum of

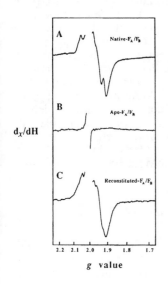

d_x/dH

g value

Fig. 5. ESR spectra of the chemically-reduced F_A/F_B proteins. (A) spectrum of the native-F_A/F_B protein. (B) spectrum of the F_A/F_B apoprotein prepared by oxidative denaturation with 3 M urea and 5 mM $K_3(FeCN)_6$. (C) spectrum of the reconstituted-F_A/F_B protein prepared by reconstitution of the F_A/F_B apoprotein with $FeCl_3$ and Na_2S in the presence of ß-mercaptoethanol. The samples were incubated 4 min with sodium dithionite and 0.033 mM methyl viologen in 0.1 M glycine, pH 10. Spectrometer conditions: temperature, 16 K; microwave power, 20 mW; microwave frequency, 9.128 GHz; receiver gain, 5.0 x 10^3; modulation amplitude, 10 G at 100 kHz.

the native F_A/F_B protein (Fig. 5A) shows principal resonances at g = 2.05, 1.94, 1.92 and 1.91, and is nearly identical to that reported previously [5,6,7]. After oxidative denaturation with urea and $K_3Fe(CN)_6$, little or no chemically-reduced F_A or F_B is observed (Fig. 5B). However, after reconstitution with Fe_3S and Na_2S in the presence of ß-mercaptoethanol, the characteristic ESR spectrum with interacting F_A and F_B is regained (Fig. 5C) with the exception of a broadening of the high- and mid-field resonances.

2.4. Rebinding of the Reconstituted-F_A/F_B Polypeptide to the Photosystem I Core Protein
with Tetemke Mehari and Kevin Parrett [refs. 12,17]

Rebinding of the native spinach F_A/F_B polypeptide to the *Synechococcus* Photosystem I core protein results in a transition in the flash-induced absorption change from a 1.2-ms optical transient due to the $P700^+$ F_X^- backreaction to a 30-ms optical transient due to the $P700^+$ $[F_A/F_B]^-$ backreaction (Fig. 6A). Attempted rebinding of the F_A/F_B apoprotein to the Photosystem I core protein results in no change in the 1.2-ms backreaction between $P700^+$ and F_X^- (Fig. 6B). However, when the spinach F_A/F_B apoprotein is incubated 12 hr with inorganic iron, sulfide and ß-mercaptoethanol and then added to the *Synechococcus* Photosystem I core protein, the 1.2-ms optical transient due to the $P700^+$ F_X^- backreaction is replaced by the 30-ms transient characteristic of the $P700^+$ $[F_A/F_B]^-$ backreaction (Fig. 3C). If the iron-sulfur clusters in the F_A/F_B apoprotein are reconstituted in the presence of the Photosystem I core protein, electron flow from P700 to F_A/F_B is also reestablished. If the F_A/F_B apoprotein and the apo-F_X Photosystem I core protein are incubated together with inorganic iron and sulfide in the presence of ß-mercaptoethanol, the 5 μs optical transient due to the relaxation of the P700 triplet is replaced by the 30-ms optical transient characteristic of the $P700^+$ $[F_A/F_B]^-$ backreaction.

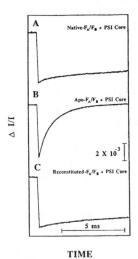

TIME

Fig. 6. Flash-induced absorption changes in the Photosystem I core protein after rebinding of the F_A/F_B polypeptide. (A) Absorption transient in the Photosystem I core protein after rebinding of the native-F_A/F_B polypeptide. (B) Absorption transient in the Photosystem I core protein after attempted rebinding of the F_A/F_B apoprotein. (C) Absorption transient in the Photosystem I core protein after rebinding of the reconstituted-F_A/F_B polypeptide. All measurements were performed at 5 μg Chl/ml in 50 mM Tris buffer, pH 8.3, containing 1.7 mM ascorbate and 0.033 mM DCPIP.

The ESR spectra of the native F_A/F_B protein, the F_A/F_B apoprotein, and the reconstituted F_A/F_B protein after rebinding to the Photosystem I core protein are shown in Fig. 7. When the native-F_A/F_B polypeptide is rebound to the Photosystem I core protein and illuminated during freezing, both F_A and F_B become photochemically reduced (Fig. 7A). This spectrum is characterized by interaction between F_A and F_B which gives rise to a slightly altered spectrum with g values of (2.05, 1.95 and 1.90) and (2.05, 1.93 and 1.90), respectively. When rebinding of the F_A/F_B apoprotein to the Photosystem I core protein is attempted (Fig. 7B) there is no evidence of photochemically-reduced F_A and F_B, thus confirming the denatured state of these clusters. However, when the F_A/F_B apoprotein is reconstituted with inorganic iron and sulfide in the presence of ß-mercaptoethanol and then rebound to the Photosystem I core protein, the characteristic spectrum of interacting F_A and F_B is recovered (Fig. 7C).

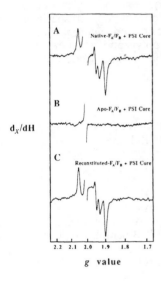

d_χ/dH

Fig. 7 ESR spectra of the F_A/F_B polypeptide after rebinding to the Photosystem I core protein and illumination during freezing. (A) Light-minus-dark spectrum of the native-F_A/F_B polypeptide after rebinding to the Photosystem I core protein. (B) Light-minus-dark spectrum of the F_A/F_B apoprotein after attempted rebinding to the Photosystem I core protein. (C) Light-minus-dark spectrum of the reconstituted-F_A/F_B polypeptide after rebinding to the Photosystem I core protein (note that F_X is difficult to observe under these conditions). The spectra were resolved by subtracting the light-off (before light on) from the light-on spectrum. The samples were suspended in 50 mM Tris buffer, pH 8.3 containing 1 mM sodium ascorbate and 0.3 mM DCPIP at 125 μg Chl/ml.

When the native-F_A/F_B polypeptide is rebound to the Photosystem I core protein, frozen in darkness, and illuminated at 16 K, F_A is 85% photoreduced (g values of 2.05, 1.94 and 1.86), and F_B is about 15% photoreduced (g values of 2.07, 1.92 and 1.89). Note that this differs significantly from the earlier reported rebinding of the spinach F_A/F_B protein to the *Synechococcus* Photosystem I core protein [9], where 50% of F_A and 50% of F_B were photoreduced. When the F_A/F_B apoprotein is reconstituted with inorganic iron and sulfide in the presence of ß-mercaptoethanol and rebound to the Photosystem I core protein, the photoreduction of F_A and F_B occur in the same amounts as the control (data not shown). Clearly, the differences in the amount of F_A and F_B photoreduced in these two experiments are not a function of the cross-species reconstitution, but instead, may be related to a time-dependent reorientation of the F_A/F_B polypeptide on the Photosystem I core protein. Experiments are now in progress to test this proposal.

The reconstitution protocol outlined here allows complete experimental control over iron-sulfur cluster denaturation and reconstitution in the F_X and F_A/F_B polypeptides, and rebinding of the reconstituted F_A/F_B polypeptide to the Photosystem I core protein to yield the intact Photosystem I complex. Studies which include chemical or genetic modification of the F_X and F_A/F_B apoproteins followed by cluster reconstitution can now be performed prior to *in vitro* reassembly of the Photosystem I complex.

3. DISCUSSION

One consequence of the finding that F_X is [4Fe-4S] cluster is that a heterodimer of the *psaA* and *psaB* polypeptides constitutes a necessary and sufficient structure for the Photosystem I core protein. A further implication is that the F_X cluster must be shared between the reaction center polypeptides, since there are an insufficient number of homologous cysteines available on either of the *psaA* or *psaB* proteins to ligate a complete iron-sulfur cluster. In this sense, the [4Fe-4S] F_X cluster in Photosystem I may share similarities with the non-heme iron in the bacterial reaction center, where the single iron atom is ligated by amino acid residues contributed by both the L and M subunits. The similarities may be extended to include the existence of two quinone molecules (only one appears to be active in Photosystem I), a chlorophyll (or bacteriochlorophyll) special pair as the primary electron donor and a monomeric chlorophyll (or bacteriochlorophyll) as the primary electron acceptor, and of course, the heterodimeric polypeptide stucture. These structural features imply that a pseudo-C_2 symmetry and a bifurcating electron acceptor chain may be common to all photochemical reaction centers.

4. ACKNOWLEDGMENTS

This material is based upon work supported by the Cooperative State Research Service, U.S. Department of Agriculture under Agreement No. 87-CRCR-1-2382.

5. REFERENCES

1. Golbeck, J.H. (1987) Biochim. Biophys. Acta 895, 167-204.
2. Golbeck, J.H. and Cornelius, J.M. (1986) Biochim. Biophys. Acta 849, 16-24.
3. Warden, J.T. and Golbeck, J.H. (1986) Biochim. Biophys. Acta 849, 25-31.
4. Golbeck, J.H., Parrett, K.G. and McDermott, A.E. (1987) Biochim. Biophys. Acta 893, 149-160.
5. Malkin, R., Aparicio, P.J. and Arnon, D.I. (1974) Proc. Natl. Acad. Sci. 71, 2362-2366.
6. Wynn, R.M., Malkin, R. (1988) FEBS Letters 229, 293-297.
7. Golbeck, J.H., Parrett, K.G., Mehari, T., Jones, K.L. and Brand, J.J. (1988) FEBS Lett. 228, 268-272
8. Parrett, K.P., Mehari, T., Warren, P. and Golbeck, J.H. (1989) Biochim. Biophys. Acta 973, 324-332.
9. Golbeck, J.H., Mehari, T., Parrett, K.P. and Ikegami, I. (1988) FEBS Lett. 240, 9-14.
10. McDermott, A., Yachandra, V., Guiles, R., Sauer, K., Klein, M., Parrett, K. and Golbeck, J.H. (1989) Biochemistry (in press).
11. Petrouleas, V., Brand, J., Parrett, K. and Golbeck, J.H. (1989) Biochemistry (in review).
12. Parrett, K.P., Mehari, T. and Golbeck, J.H. (1989) Biochim. Biophys. Acta (in review).
13. Golbeck, J.H., Lien, S. and San Pietro, A. (1977) Arch. Biochem. Biophys. 178, 140-150.
14. Golbeck, J.H. and Kok, B. (1978) Archiv. Biochem. Biophys. 188, 233-242.
15. Malkin, R and Rabinowitz, C.J. (1966) Biochem. Biophys. Res. Commun. 23, 822-827.
16. Petering, D., Fee, J.A. and Palmer, G. (1971) J. Biol. Chem. 246, 643-653.
17. Mehari, T., Parrett, K.P. and Golbeck, J.H. (manuscript in preparation).

ELECTRON TRANSFER REACTIONS OF PHOTOSYSTEM I INVOLVING THE SECONDARY ACCEPTOR A_1

Pierre Sétif[1], Hervé Bottin[1] and Klaus Brettel[2]

Dépt. Biologie, Sce Biophysique, C.E.N. Saclay, 91191 Gif sur Yvette Cedex, France[1] and Max-Volmer-Institut für Biophysik. und Physik. Chemie, T.U. Berlin, D-1000 Berlin 12[2]

1. INTRODUCTION

The electron transport chain of photosystem I (PS I) comprises the primary donor P700 and five electron acceptors : the primary electron acceptor A_0, which is a chlorophyll molecule, a secondary acceptor A_1 and 3 iron-sulfur centers $Fe-S_A$, $Fe-S_B$ and $Fe-S_X$ which act as tertiary electron acceptors. The knowledge of electron transfer pathways is far below in PS I compared to purple bacteria and PS II. Major controversial points are constituted by the electron transfer reactions concerning the secondary acceptor A_1 and moreover by the chemical nature of this acceptor, although a lot of new data have accumulated in this field during the last few years.

In accordance with the presence of vitamin K_1 in PS I reaction centers (1), recent experimental evidences strongly support the identification of A_1 with vitamin K_1 (2,3). These studies show that depletion of vitamin K_1 interrupts forward electron transfer from A_0^-. More importantly, the photoreduction of $NADP^+$ (2) and the turnover of iron-sulfur centers (3) can be restored by incubation of depleted reaction centers with vitamin K_1. This identification is supported by most spectroscopic data, obtained either by EPR (4) or by flash-absorption spectroscopy (5,6).

In a recent study, it has been reported that, under highly reducing conditions, inhibition of electron transfer from A_0^- is achieved under strong light illumination in the absence of redox mediators (7). In the same study, it was shown that this inhibition is not relaxed after dark adaptation of a preilluminated sample. These results were interpreted by a double reduction process of A_1, in accordance with the identification of A_1 with vitamin K_1. We report here that the same inhibition of forward electron transfer from A_0^- can be observed in the dark under highly reducing conditions in the presence of mediators such as methylviologen.

The kinetics of electron transfer reactions involving A_1 have been recently characterized. A recombination reaction between $P700^+$ and A_1^- to the ground

M. Baltscheffsky (ed.), Current Research in Photosynthesis, Vol. II, 539–546.

state ($t_{1/2} \approx 120$ µs) has been studied in detail by flash-absorption spectroscopy at low temperature (5). The same reaction is reported to have a halftime of 250 µs at room temperature, at least in PS I from cyanobacteria (8). However, a recombination with $t_{1/2} \approx 750$ ns between P700$^+$ and A$_1^-$ to the triplet state of P700 has been observed recently under conditions where Fe-S$_x$ is maintained in the reduced state by a weak background illumination (7). We report here more recent data obtained by flash absorption spectroscopy in the blue region with a better time resolution showing that this back-reaction has a halftime of 300 ns. These results are in contrast with previous results indicating a halftime of 30 µs for the back-reaction between P700$^+$ and A$_1^-$ in the presence of Fe-S$_x^-$ at room temperature (9). Hypothetical schemes will be given to explain these very different observations which were obtained under different experimental conditions.

2. MATERIALS AND METHODS

PS I reaction centers were obtained from spinach and from the cyanobacterium *Synechocystis* 6803 as described respectively in refs. 10 and 2. Using an absorption coefficient of 6500 M^{-1}cm^{-1} for P700$^+$ at 820 nm, the chlorophyll to P700 ratios were estimated at 65 and 120 for spinach and *Synechocystis* reaction centers, respectively.

Nanosecond absorption changes at 820 nm were measured as described in ref. 2 with one difference : the signal from the 500 MHz Nuclétudes amplifier was fed to an IN7000 oscilloscope equipped with a 1 GHz amplifier (Intertechnique). However the response lifetime of the whole set-up was limited to $\approx$15 ns presumably due to some impedance mismatch. Nanosecond absorption changes from 370 to 475 nm were measured as described in ref. 6 (time resolution of 5 ns).

When measured, the redox potential was monitored inside the cuvette, with saturated calomel and platinum-plate electrodes. The redox potential of the medium was decreased by adding sodium dithionite from a fresh stock solution and was increased by adding potassium ferricyanide or just by stirring in the presence of air. For most experiments, the redox potential had to be maintained for very long periods. Therefore, with one exception, the redox potential was maintained by adding an excess of sodium dithionite and was varied from one experiment to another by changing the pH. Unfortunately, this has the obvious disadvantage that two parameters are varying together, the pH and the ambient redox potential.

3. RESULTS and DISCUSSION

Inhibition of forward electron transfer from A$_0^-$

Incubation of PS I reaction centers in darkness, in the presence of dithionite in excess, results in the partial (pH ≤10) or complete (pH >10) reduction of the iron-sulfur centers Fe-S_A and Fe-S_B. Under these conditions, the flash-induced charge separation is stable on a nanosecond time scale (Fig. 1, left part, trace **a**, monitored in the absorption band of P700$^+$ at 820 nm). When this incubation is followed by a period of strong illumination, it has been precedingly shown that the forward electron transfer is blocked at the level of A_0 (7). This is indicated by the kinetic behavior of the reaction centers measured at 820 nm (Fig. 1, left part, trace **b**) : there is a major fast component ($t_{1/2} \approx 50$ ns) which can be ascribed to a recombination reaction between P700$^+$ and A_0^- (11). This halftime is larger than precedingly measured (30 ns). This difference is due to a change in the experimental setup (see Materials and Methods). The increase in initial signal size (compared to trace **a**) is most probably due to the contribution of A_0^-.

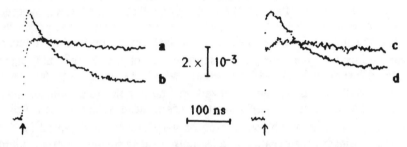

FIGURE 1 : Kinetics of absorption changes measured at 820 nm and at 293 K in PS I reaction centers from *Synechocystis* (glycine NaOH 0.2 M pH 10; DO$_{1cm}$ at 679 nm = 6.3). Left part : + DT in excess; a : dark; b : after illumination. Right part : + DT; incubation times with BV, MV, TQ, PP-670 (40 μM each) : 20 seconds and 20 minutes for c and d respectively.

A similar kinetic behavior appears when the PS I reaction centers are incubated in darkness in the presence of dithionite plus methylviologen (MV) at pH 10 (Fig. 1, right part). The appearance of the fast phase, which corresponds to the back-reaction between P700$^+$ and A_0^-, was studied as a function of time under different conditions of pHs and ambient redox potentials E_M (in the presence of an excess of sodium dithionite) and in the presence of the redox mediators MV, benzylviologen (BV), triquat (TQ) and PP-670 (12) (following table).

E_M (vs NHE)	+ MV (40 μM)	+ 4 mediators (40 μM each)
-510 mV (pH 8)	>> 600	no effect
-575 mV (pH 9)	> 60	35
-635 mV (pH 10)	5-6	12
-655 mV (pH 11)	4	6

TABLE : halftimes (in minutes) for the 50 ns phase appearance

For pH values between 9 and 11, the final kinetic trace observed in all cases was the same as trace **d** of Fig. 1 and presumably corresponds to an homogeneous state of the reaction centers. By analogy with the observations made above (dithionite + light), we propose that A_1 is entirely doubly reduced in this final state. This interpretation is sustained by the fact that under these experimental conditions, $Fe-S_x$ is essentially oxidized. Moreover, the redox potentials that are reached are not low enough to induce the reduction of A_1 to A_1^-. The relative efficiencies of the different redox mediators to promote the blocking of forward electron transfer was studied (MV > TQ > BV > PP–670; not shown) and does not appear to be related to their midpoint potentials (BV > MV > TQ > PP–670). From the results shown in the preceding table, it can be also deduced that the redox mediators may act in a competitive way for this blocking (at pHs 10 and 11, the halftime of the reaction is smaller for MV alone than for the 4 mediators together).

The double reduction of the first quinone acceptor has already been observed in PS II (13) and purple bacteria (14). In these last cases, the double reduction process was deduced by observing the disappearance of the Q^--Fe^{2+} EPR signal. This is quite different in PS I reaction centers where A_1 has a very low redox potential and possibly cannot be observed in the stable semiquinone form. Moreover, the iron-sulfur center $Fe-S_x$ must be prereduced before A_1 can trap an electron which is not an easy job considering its very low redox potential ($\approx$ -705 mV; 15). From these considerations, a hypothetical scheme for the double reduction process of A_1 is given in the following scheme, where the second electron is provided by $Fe-S_x^-$ for the double reduction of A_1 :

$$ A_1 \ Fe-S_x \underset{4}{\overset{1}{\rightleftharpoons}} A_1 \ Fe-S_x^- \underset{5}{\overset{2}{\rightleftharpoons}} A_1^- \ Fe-S_x^- \overset{3}{\longrightarrow} A_1^{2-} \ Fe-S_x $$

In the absence of mediators and under illumination, reactions 1 and 2 correspond to photoaccumulation with dithionite as electron donor and may have larger rates than reactions 4 and 5 ("leak" of electrons) when the light intensity is large enough. The reaction pathway could be the same for the formation of A_1^{2-} in darkness in the presence of mediators. In this last case, the two equilibria (1/4 and 2/5) should be displaced towards the left.

From the data of the table, it appears also that the halftime of appearance of the fast decay decreases with increasing pH from 8 to 11 and decreasing E_M. To determine which one of these two parameters controls this halftime, an experiment was conducted at pH 11 (with MV) while decreasing the E_M step by step by successive additions of dithionite : whereas no effect is observed at −455 mV, the fast phase appears with a $t_{1/2}$ of several hours at −575 mV and 15 minutes at −605 mV. These results suggest that the redox potential of the medium is the only determining factor of the fast phase appearance. It has not been possible to make a redox titration of the fast phase appearance. On the one hand, the process appears to be complete (up to 100%) for redox potentials below approximately −500 mV. On the other hand, for redox potentials higher than that value, no blocking of electron transfer is occurring after several hours.

Restoration of the electron transfer from P700 to Fe-S_A and Fe-S_B has been observed after a prolonged dialysis against fresh buffer. This was shown for samples where the fast phase had totally developped under both conditions (dithionite + strong light and dithionite + mediators in darkness) by the disappeance of the fast sub–μs phase and by the observation of the P700$^+$ - P-430$^-$ recombination reaction (data not shown).

Recombination reactions between P700$^+$ and (A$_1$ - Fe-S$_x$)$^-$

It has been described earlier that, when Fe-S_x is maintained in the reduced state by a weak illumination, the radical pair (P700$^+$ - A_1^-) decays by recombination with a $t_{1/2} \approx 750$ ns (measured in *Synechocystis* reaction centers). In the same study, it was also found that the triplet state of P700 is formed during this back-reaction with a yield approaching unity (7). Similar experiments have been repeated by measuring flash absorption changes in the region from 370 to 475 nm. A relaxation phase with $t_{1/2} \approx 300$ ns was measured in reaction centers from spinach and *Synechocystis* which presumably corresponds to the same back-reaction. This halftime is shorter than previously estimated. This is most probably due to a limited time resolution during the earlier experiments (time resolution of 5 ns in the present study versus 100 ns in 7) and a poor signal to noise ratio.

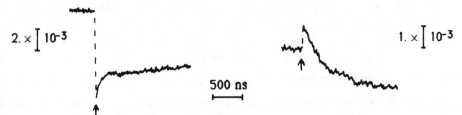

FIGURE 2 : Kinetic of absorption changes induced at 430 nm (left) and 404 nm (right) under conditions where Fe-S_x is prereduced by light (reaction centers from spinach : $DO_{1 mm}$ at 677 nm = 0.99).

These results are illustrated by two kinetic traces obtained for spinach reaction centers at 404 and 430 nm (Fig. 2). At 430 nm, the initial bleaching is followed by a fast decay ($t_{1/2} \approx 30$ ns) which can be attributed to a back-reaction between P700$^+$ and A_0^- in reaction centers where the forward electron transfer is blocked at the level of A_0 (see above). This relaxation phase is followed by a major decay with a $t_{1/2} \approx 3$ μs (not shown) which is due to the decay of the P700 triplet state. However no 300 ns phase can be detected at this wavelength, in contrast to what is observed at 404 nm. At this wavelenght, the initial positive signal, which presumably corresponds to the state (P700$^+$ - A$_1^-$) (6), is followed by a major 300 ns decay phase. The absorption change becomes negative at the end of this decay, in accordance with the (^{3}P700 - P700) spectrum (16). The absence of any detectable 300 ns phase at 430 nm agrees with a high yield of ^{3}P700 formation from the radical pair (P700$^+$ - A$_1^-$). A quantitative estimation of this yield requires the knowledge of the extinction coefficient of the P700 triplet state at this wavelength. However the spectrum of the difference (^{3}P700 - P700) in the blue region has been measured only at low temperature (16) and the extinction coefficient for the triplet state of chlorophyll a in vitro at room temperature is uncertain (from 40000 to 65000 M^{-1}cm^{-1}). Assuming an absorption coefficient of 5000 M^{-1}cm^{-1} for ^{3}P700 at 820 nm, we made a rough estimation of the differential absorption coefficient (^{3}P700 - P700) at 430 nm : 60000 ± 10000 M^{-1}cm^{-1}. Considering coefficients of 47000 M^{-1}cm^{-1} for the difference (P700$^+$ - A$_1^-$) - (P700 - A$_1$) (6) and of 60000 M^{-1}cm^{-1} for (^{3}P700 - P700), the absence of 300 ns phase at 430 nm allows to calculate a yield around 0.8 for the formation of ^{3}P700 from the pair (P700$^+$ - A$_1^-$).

As mentioned in the introduction, a sub-µs halftime for the back-reaction between P700$^+$ and A$_1^-$ in the presence of Fe-S$_X^-$ is largely different from what was found in a first study ($t_{1/2} \approx 30$ µs in 9). However, in the latter case, the experimental conditions were very different : electrons were accumulated on the acceptor side of PS I by multiple flashes in the presence of the fast physiological electron donor plastocyanin and in the presence of glycerol. During a sequence of laser flashes, Fe-S$_X$ can be reduced as plastocyanin gives rapidly an electron to P700 ($t_{1/2} \approx 12$ µs; 17). The next flash should then allow to observe the recombination reaction between P700$^+$ and A$_1^-$, provided plastocyanin is no more available. This is the case if the delay with the previous flash (here called Δt) is short enough (less than 10 ms in the presence of glycerol (9)). In a further study, it was found that when Δt is very short, a relaxation phase with $t_{1/2} \approx 8$ µs is observed after the charge separation (18). This decay phase can be also ascribed to a relaxation from the state (P700$^+$ - A$_1^-$), probably due to a recombination reaction. When Δt is increased (i. e. when the electron has stayed on Fe-S$_X$ for a longer time), the 8 µs phase disappears and is replaced by a relaxation phase with $t_{1/2} \approx 25$-30 µs. The time delay Δt necessary for the half-disappearance of the 8 µs component and for the half-appearance of the 25-30 µs component is approximately 25 µs. Thus it seems that some change different from an electron transfer reaction is occurring in the reaction center with a halftime of 25 μs. The state $(P700^+ - A_1^-)$ is relaxing with a $t_{1/2}$ of 8 μs before this change and with a $t_{1/2}$ of 25-30 μs after the change.

So this appears rather complicated as we are left with three different halftimes of 300 ns, 8 μs and 30 μs for the relaxation of absorption changes when the iron-sulfur center $Fe-S_x$ is prereduced. We will note (1), (2) and (3) the three states of the reaction center which correspond respectively to decay halftimes of 8 μs, 30 μs and 300 ns. Two different hypotheses can be put forward to account for these three states :

1. The most obvious difference between state (3) and the two other states lies in the redox state of the iron-sulfur center $Fe-S_A$. In state (3), the three iron-sulfur centers $Fe-S_A$, $Fe-S_B$ and $Fe-S_x$ are prereduced whereas only $Fe-S_B$ and $Fe-S_x$ are prereduced in states (1) and (2). This is due to the fact that the addition of glycerol inhibits the photoreduction of center $Fe-S_A$ at room temperature (9). If this difference is the only factor which determines the very different decay halftimes observed in states (1) and (2) on the one hand and in state (3) in the other hand, that would mean that the redox state of $Fe-S_A$ has a strong influence on the recombination kinetics between $P700^+$ and A_1^-, possibly through an electrostatic effect.

2. An alternative explanation is that the photoaccumulation of $Fe-S_x^-$ by itself triggers some changes in the reaction center which affect the charge recombination processes between $P700^+$ and A_1^-. In that case, some coupling has to be assumed between the two acceptors A_1 and $Fe-S_x$. Considering this coupling, we will try to give a tentative model for the different reactions without assuming a precise location of the electrons on A_1 or $Fe-S_x$. In state (3), the reaction center is maintained in the state $(A_1-Fe-S_x)^-$ by the weak background illumination in the presence of dithionite. This is different from states (1) and (2) where $(A_1-Fe-S_x)^-$ is reoxidized after a sequence of flashes (with $t_{1/2} > 1$ ms in 18). Thus the presence of an electron on (A_1-Fe-S_x) appears to trigger two different changes in the state of the reaction center, a transition from state (1) to state (2) with $t_{1/2} \approx$ 30 μs and a transition from state (2) to state (3) with $t_{1/2} > 1$ ms according to the following scheme :

Reaction center in the state	30 μs		> 1 ms	
$(A_1 - Fe-S_x)^-$	**(1)**	$\longrightarrow$	**(2)** $\longrightarrow$	**(3)**

Relaxation of the state			
$P700^+ (A_1 - Fe-S_x)^{2-}$	8 μs	30 μs	300 ns
by recombination			(formation of $^3P700$)

The first transition could correspond to a local change in the environment of $(A_1\text{-Fe-}S_x)$ whereas the longer halftime of the second transition may be due to some more global change of the protein environment. One possible physiological role for these transitions can be hypothesized. State (3) appears to be the final state under the highest reducing conditions. In this state, the recombination reaction is much faster than in states (1) and (2). So one can imagine that the transition of the reaction center to state (3) helps to avoid accumulation of electrons on $(A_1\text{-Fe-}S_x)$ when the acceptor pool of PS 1 is highly reduced. As discussed above, the accumulation of two electrons on $(A_1\text{-Fe-}S_x)$ might lead to a double reduction process of A_1, which appears to be very slowly reversible. The double reduction of A_1 could possibly be involved in PS I photoinhibition under extremely reducing conditions (19).

4. REFERENCES
1. Interschick-Niebler, E. and Lichtenthaller, H.K. (1981) Z. Naturforsch. 36c, 276-283
2. Biggins, J. and Mathis, P. (1988) Biochemistry 27, 1494-1500
3. Itoh, S., Iwaki, M. (1989) FEBS Lett. 243, 47-52
4. Stehlik, D., Bock, C.H. and Petersen, J. (1989) J. Chem. Phys. 93, 1612-1619
5. Brettel, K., Sétif, P. and Mathis, P. (1986) FEBS Lett. 203, 220-224
6. Brettel, K. (1988) FEBS Lett. 239, 93-98
7. Sétif, P. and Bottin, H. (1989) Biochemistry 28, 2689-2697
8. Brettel, K. (1989) Biochim. Biophys. Acta, in press
9. Bottin, H., Sétif, P. and Mathis, P. (1987) Biochim. Biophys. Acta 894, 39-48
10. Lagoutte, B., Sétif, P. and Duranton, J. (1984) FEBS Lett. 174, 24-29
11. Sétif, P., Bottin, H. and Mathis, P. (1985) Biochim. Biophys. Acta 808, 112-122
12. Elstner E.F., Fischer, H.P., Osswald, W. and Kwiatkowski, G. (1980) Z. Naturforsch 35c, 770-775
13. Van Mieghem, F., Nitschke, W., Mathis, P. and Rutherford, A.W. (1989) Biochim. Biophys. Acta, in press
14. Okamura, M.Y., Isaacson, R.A. and Feher, G. (1979) Biochim. Biophys. Acta 546, 394-417
15. Chamorovsky, S.K. and Cammack, R. (1982) Photobiochem. Photobiophys. 4, 195-200
16. Den Blanken, H.J. and Hoff, A.J. (1983) Biochim. Biophys. Acta 724, 52-61
17. Bottin, H. and Mathis, P. (1985) Biochemistry 24, 6453-6460
18. Bottin, H. and Sétif, P. (1988) Fifth European Bioenergetics Conference Aberystwyth, p 171
19. Inoue, K., Fujii, T., Yokoyama, E., Matsuura, K., Hiyama, T. and Sakurai, H. (1989) Plant Cell Physiol. 30, 65-71

On Isolated Complexes of Reaction Center I and X-Ray
Characterization of Single Crystals

Witt, H.T., , Rögner, M., Mühlenhoff, U., Witt, I.[*], Hinrichs, W.[*], Saenger, W.[*], Betzel, Ch.[o], Dauter,Z.[o],
Boekema, E.J.[+]
Max-Volmer-Institut, TU Berlin, Str. d. 17. Juni 135, 1000
Berlin 12, [*]Institut für Kristallographie, FU Berlin, Takustr. 3, 1000 Berlin 33, [+]Fritz-Haber-Institut, Faradayweg
4-6, 1000 Berlin 33, [o]European Molecular Biology Laboratory
(DESY), Notkestr. 85, 2000 Hamburg 52, FRG

1. INTRODUCTION
In the last years effort has been directed at the
characterization of isolated reaction center complexes of
PS I from the thylakoid membrane and particularly from
cyanobacteria (1-8). Concerning the shape, mass and antenna
size of the minimal RC I complex, differing values are
reported (see also 9-20). For a detailed discussion see
(26).
In the case of the thermophilic cyanobacterium Synechococcus sp. and Phormidium laminosum, an oligomeric structure has been detected (6,7). Both bacteria gave evidence
for a monomeric and trimeric organization of the isolated
RC I complexes (7,20,18). In vivo, however, for both bacteria a monomeric structure for PS I was reported (2,18),
questioning a PS trimer in vivo. The mass of these
monomeric complexes in vivo also is a matter of debate,
ranging from 150 kDa to 400 kDa (6,2), as well as the
amount of antenna chlorophyll per reaction center $Chl-a_I$,
ranging from 50 up to 130 (3,2). In this contribution 3
different complexes of PS I have been isolated. Similar
polypeptide composition and antenna chlorophyll per $Chl-a_I$,
etc. give evidence that the complexes represent monomers,
dimers and trimers of the same miminal RC I unit. The
size, shape, mass and activity of this unit have been
estimated.
    To get information on the inner molecular architecture,
the trimereric complex of RC I has been crystallized. On
the X-ray characterization of single crystals of this RC I
complex is reported.
2. METHODS
Growth and isolation of PS I particle was carried out as in
(21,22,19). Desaggregation of the particles was carried out
by incubation of the particles in 1 M Tris (pH 8.3) and 5%
OGP and heating at 56 °C. The protein mixture obtained

M. Baltscheffsky (ed.), Current Research in Photosynthesis, Vol. II, 547–554.
© 1990 Kluwer Academic Publishers. Printed in the Netherlands.

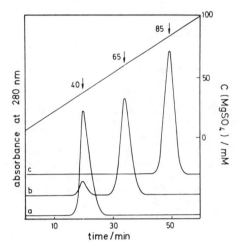

Fig. 1
Elution profiles of (a)
MQa, (b) MQb, and (c) MQc
preparation from an anion
exchange column upon
applying a MgSO$_4$ gradient
flow: 0.4 ml/min (26).

Table 1 (26)

Complex	Apparent Mass/kDa	Chl/Chl-a$_I$ Chemical Oxidation	Chl/Chl-a$_I$ Photo Oxidation
MQa	280 $\pm$ 20	68 $\pm$ 4	88 $\pm$ 5
MQb	500 $\pm$ 25	64 $\pm$ 4	87 $\pm$ 5
MQc	670 $\pm$ 35	68 $\pm$ 4	85 $\pm$ 5

was layered on a sucrose density gradient and centrifuged.
The obtained three green bands were purified by an anion
exchange column Mono Q (Pharmacia)(21).
SDS-PAGE was performed according to (24). The ratio Chl-
a/Chl-a$_I$ was determined by analysis of chemically and
flash-induced Chl-a$_I$ oxidation (25). The apparent mass was
determined by gel filtration column TSK 4000SW (Beckmann).
The ratio of chlorophyll to protein was performed with a
BCA protein-assay reagent. For more details see (26).
Electron microscopy was carried out as in (7,20). Images
were aligned and averaged in a digitizing camera.
Crystallization was performed as outlined in (28,29). X-
ray diffraction patterns were taken on the DESY Synchrotron
beam line X31 (Hamburg).
3. RESULTS
The following results are presented in detail in (26):
  Fig. 1 shows the purification of the desintegrated PS I
complexes on the HPLC anion exchange column Mono Q, yielding 3 purified complexes: MQa, -b and -c. They have the
same absorption spectra typical for PS I complexes (not
shown).

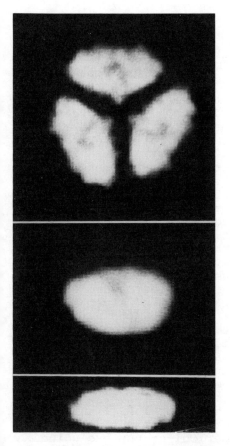

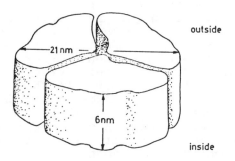

outside

inside

Fig. 2
Electron microscope images of
the MQc and MQa PS I particles solubilized with 0.02%
dodecylmaltoside. Top: Average
top view image of 120 MQc complexes. Center: Average top
view image of 160 MQa complexes. Bottom: Average side view
image of 66 MQa (26).
Right: Simplified sketch of the
size and shape of the trimer

⊢————⊣5nm

HPLC gel-filtration results in apparent masses of about
260, 500 and 670 kDa (see table 1).
The protein composition analyzed by SDS-PAGE shows for all
three complexes a similar composition of apparent mass of
64, 59, 16 and 12 kDa and smaller peptides (details see
(26)).
  The Chl-a/Chl-a$_I$ ratio for each complex, evaluated by
chemical and photo-induced Chla-$_I$ oxidation, was shown to
be as depicted in table 1. All three complexes have the
ratio of about 65 Chl-a/Chl-a$_I$. The slightly higher values
obtained by photo oxidation are probably due to some loss
of the natural acceptor components.
  The chlorophyll to protein ratio of PS I was determined
with the MQc complex. A ratio of 1:3.1 w/w was obtained.
Hence, with Chl-a/Chla$_I$ of about 65 (see table 1), the
chlorophyll mass is 58 kDa and that of the protein consequently 180 kDa per Chl-a$_I$. In total, the mass per Chl-a$_I$
is therefore 238 kDa.

Fig. 2 shows the electron microscopic picture of the isolated MQc and MQa complex. It is evident that complex MQc is
identical to the previously characterized PS I trimer
(7,20). Due to the instability of MQb, pictures could not
be taken. A comparison of Figs. 2,top, and 2,center, indicates that the dimensions of MQa, top view, corresponds
approximately to those of one third of MQc. The larger
width of MQa compared to the monomeric part of the trimer
MQc, can be explained by different contributions of the detergent boundary layer (see below).

Within the MQa and monomeric part of MQc, the heterogeneous density distribution indicates even the presence of
subunits. This can be seen much better in the original pic-
ture(20). These may be attributed to the 2 big proteins of
PS I with apparent masses of 64 and 59 kDa. Together with
the side view (not shown) one gets the dimension and
orientation of the trimer within the membrane as shown in
Fig. 2,right, similar to the result in (7), which were however solubilized in OGP. The height corresponds to the
thickness of the membrane. Obviously, larger hydrophilic
parts do not extend from the membrane. This is very
different from the architecture of purple bacteria (30).

The above characteristics of the complexes suggest that
MQb and MQc are dimers and trimers, respectively, of MQa.
The ratio of apparent mass is 1:1.8:2.5 (see table 1). The
deviation from 1:2:3 can be explained, if smaller complexes
bind more detergent than larger ones. This was shown for
monomeric and dimeric complexes from PS II (21,23).
Complex MQa obviously represents the minimal PS I unit per
oxidizable $Chl-a_I$. With the protein/Chl ratio = 3.1,
including 65 antenna chlorophyll per $Chl-a_I$ but excluding
detergent shells, an oxidizable mass of 238 kDa per $Chl-a_I$
unit was estimated (see above). The differences between
the apparent mass of MQc (280 kDa,table 1) and 238 kDa are
mainly due to the detergent shell. Our estimated weight
differs considerably from that reported as 150 kDa (6) and
300-400 kDa (2,5).

According to the electron microscopic images, the size of
this minimal PS I unit is 14.3 x 10.6 x 6.4 nm (length x
width x height). For a detailed discussion see (26).

Whether monomer or trimer represents in Synechococcus sp.
the PS I complex in vivo is open. Reassociation experients
of monomers into trimers were without success. That our
trimers are artificially induced from in vivo monomers is
unlikely, based on the fact that under the same detergent
procedure PS I from Synechocystis were exctracted as
monomers (Rögner, unpublished).

Based on the excellent homogeneity of the isolated complexes, crystallization of the trimer MQc was tried as
basis for the estimation of the RC I structure. It is
expected that the molecular architecture of the PS I center

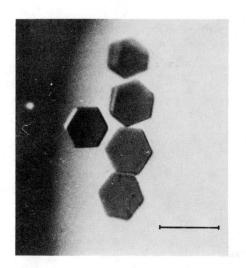
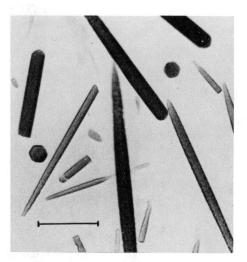

Fig. 3
Left: Hexagonal plates of green RC I crystals.
Right: Dark green needle-shaped crystals with hexagonal
cross sections (29). The bar indicates 100 µs.

is rather different from RC II and that of the reaction
center of purple bacteria. It is known that the two proteins (L- and M-subunits) of bacteria correspond in their
amino acid sequence closely to two proteins of approximately 34 and 32 kDa in RC II (D_1 and D_2 subunits)(31). It
is assumed that the organization in PS II, regarding the
photo center, might resemble that of the bacterio-chloro-
phyll center. However, no similarity in the amino acid sequence of RC I with RC II and reaction center of bacteria
does exist. Unique is also the strong reductive power
(about 500 mV) of the terminal electron acceptor in RC I,
lastly resulting in CO_2 reduction. The two big subunits of
RC I, probably span the membrane on which the photo-center
is suspended but, in addition they also are the antenna
carriers, which is different from the corresponding subunits in RC II (D_1, D_2) and RC of bacteria (L,M). With the
determination of the structure and the location and orientation of the antenna pigments it is probable that also information on the mechanism of energy migration in antenna
pigments becomes available. Ford et al. first reported on
the crystallization of PS I from the cyanobacterium
Phormidium laminosum (27). Our first crystals were
obtained from RC I complexes from Synechococcus sp. (28).
The second and third generation of crystals obtained by us
are shown in Fig. 3 (29).

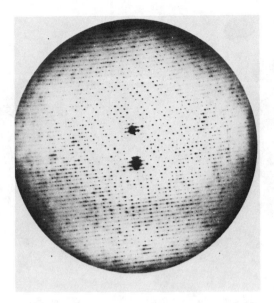

Fig. 4   X-ray diffraction pattern of a crystal showing the
         overall quality of the diffraction (29).

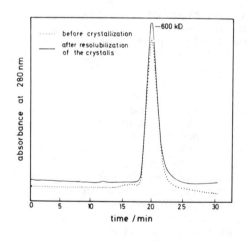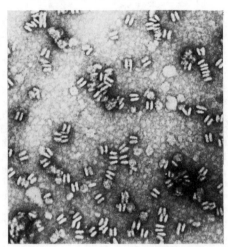

Fig. 5   Left: Elution profile on a gel-filtration column of
         the PS I reaction center protein before crystalli-
         zation and after resolubilization of the crystals
         (28).
         Right: Electron micrographs of side view projec-
         tions of trimers of RC I in solution (29).

The length of the needles is up to 1 mm, the crystals are dichroic and fully photo active. The crystals are stable in X-ray beams for several hours before the diffraction deteriorates.

The X-ray diffraction patterns are shown in Fig. 4. The patterns indicate a resolution of 4 Å. For the hexagonal unit cell dimensions it follows a = b = 285 Å and C = 167 Å, α = ß = 90° and γ = 120°. The space group of the crystal is $P6_3$ or $P6_322$.

After resolubilization of the crystals, the gel-filtration profile is exactly the same as before crystallization (see Fig. 5, left) indicating that the building blocks of the crystals probably are of trimeric structure.

With regard to the arrangement of the trimers within the crystals, a face-to-face constellation of two trimers each may be possible. This is inferred from the observation that the trimers in solution prefer a face-to-face arrangement in shape of sandwiches as shown in Fig. 5, right (29).

According to the size, shape and mass of the trimer, the unit cell probably contains as building blocks 4 trimers in two layers with 2 trimers each. From layer to layer a face-to-face arrangement of the trimers may be realized. Data collection has been started. A first evaluation indicates that the group $P6_3$ very probably is relevant to the architecture of the crystal. Determination of the amino acid sequence and heavy-atom derivates suitable for the evaluation of the phases of the reflections has begun.

REFERENCES

1 Takahashi, Y., Koike, H. and Katoh, S. (1982) Arch. Biochem. Biophys. 219, 209-218

2 Williams, R.C., Glazer, A.N. and Lundell, D.J. (1983) Proc. Natl. Acad. Sci. USA 80, 5923-5926

3 Nechushtai, R., Muster, P., Binder, A., Liveanu, V. and Nelson, N. (1983) Proc. Natl. Acad. Sci. USA 80, 1179-1183

4 Takahashi, Y., Hirota, K. and Katoh, S. (1985) Photosynth. Res. 6, 183-192

5 Lundell, D.J., Glazer, A.N., Melis, A. and Malkin, R. (1985) J. Biol. Chem.260(1), 646-654

6 Ford, R.C. (1987) Biochim. Biophys. Acta 893, 115-125

7 Boekema, E.J., Dekker, J.P., van Heel, M.C., Rögner, M., Saenger, W., Witt, I. and Witt, H.T. (1987) FEBS Lett. 217, 283-286

8 Golbeck, J.H., Parrett, K.G., Mehari, T., Jones, K.L. and Brand,J.L. (1988) FEBS Lett. 228, 268-272

9 Guikema, J. and Sherman, L. (1982) Biochim. Biophys. Acta 681, 440-450

10 Evans, E.H., Dickson, D.P.E., Johnson, C.E., Rush, J.D. and Evans, M.C.W. (1981) Eur. J. Biochem. 118, 81-84

11 Golbeck, J.H., McDermott, A.E., Johnes, W.K. and Kurtz,

D.M. (1987) Biochim. Biophys. Acta 891, 94-98

12 McDermott, A.E., Yachandra, V.K., Guiles, R.D., Britt, R.D., Dexheimer, S.L., Sauer, K. and Klein, M.P. (1988) Biochemistry 27, 4013-4020

13 Malkin, R. and Wynn, R.M. (1988) FEBS Lett. 229(2), 293-297

14 Setif, P. and Mathis, P. (1986) in Photosynthesis III Staehelin, L.A. and Arntzen, C.J. eds.), pp. 476-486, Springer Verlag Berlin

15 Rutherford, A.W. and Heathcote, P. (1986) Photosynth. Res. 6, 295-316

16 Bryant, D.A. (1986) Can. Bull. Fish. Aquat. Sci. 214, 423-500

17 Malkin, R. (1987) in The Light Reactions (Barber, J., ed.), pp.495-525, Elsevier, Amsterdam

18 Ford, R.C. and Holzenburg, A. (1988) EMBO J. 7, 2287-2293

19 Witt, I., Witt, H.T., Gerken, S., Saenger, W., Dekker, J.P. and Rögner, M. (1987) FEBS Lett. 221(2), 260-264

20 Boekema, E.J., Dekker, J.P., Rögner, M., Witt, I., Witt, H.T. and van Heel, M.C. (1989) Biochim. Biophys. Acta 974, 81-87

21 Dekker, J.P., Boekema, E.J., Witt, H.T. and Rögner, M. (1988) Biochim. Biophys. Acta 936, 307-318

22 Schatz, G.H. and Witt, H.T. (1984) Photobiochem. Photo-Biophys. 7,1-14

23 Rögner, M., Dekker, J.P., Boekema, E.J. and Witt, H.T. (1987) FEBS Lett. 219, 207-211

24 Laemmli, U.K. (1970) Nature 277, 680-685

25 Rumberg, B. and Witt, H.T. (1964) Z. Naturforsch. 19b, 693-707

26 Rögner, M., Mühlenhoff, U., Boekema, E.J. and Witt, H.T. (1989) Biochim. Biophys. Acta (in press)

27 Ford, R.C., Picot, D. and Garavito, R.M. (1987) EMBO J. 6, 1581-

28 Witt, I., Witt, H.T., Gerken, S., Saenger, W., Dekker, J.P. and Rögner, M. (1987) FEBS Lett. 221, 260-264

29 Witt, I., Witt, H.T.,DiFiore, D., Rögner, M., Hinrichs, W., Saenger, W., Granzin, J., Betzel, Ch. and Dauter,Z. (1988) Ber. Bunsenges. Phys. Chem. 92,1503-1506

30 Deisenhofer, J., Depp, O., Miki, K., Huber, R. and Michel, H. (1984) J. Mol. Biol. 180, 385

31 Trebst, A. (1986) Z. Naturforsch. 41c, 240

PHOTOSYSTEM I REACTION CENTER OF MASTIGOCLADUS LAMINOSUS: STRUCTURAL AND FUNCTIONAL ASPECTS

Gil Shoham,[1] Dorit Michaeli[2] and Rachel Nechushtai[2]
Department of Inorganic Chemistry[1] and Department of Botany[2]
The Hebrew University of Jerusalem 91904, Israel.

1. INTRODUCTION

Oxygenic photosynthesis takes place in two photochemical reaction centers: Photosystem I (PSI) and Photosystem II (PSII). While PSII is believed to be closely related to the reaction center of purple bacteria (1), PSI appears to be unique to oxygenic photosynthetic organisms. It is clear that this photosynthetic complex has no structural or functional similarities to the bacterial reaction center, nevertheless it plays a major role in the oxygenic photosynthetic process. Its function in the reducing site of the electron transfer chain enables the reduction of ferredoxin, and eventually the reduction of one of the energy components formed in the process, NADPH.

The last two decades have witnessed substantial increases in the number of studies investigating the structural, functional and molecular biology aspects of PSI. In all these studies researchers attempted to provide a better understanding of both the chemical and biological characteristics of PSI, as well as its detailed function in electron transfer within the complex and across the photosynthetic membrane.

It is commonly agreed that in higher plants, PSI is composed of two chlorophyll-protein complexes, a core complex (CCI) and a light harvesting complex (LHCI) (2). The LHCI complex which contains all the chlorophyll b of PSI, perfoms only light harvesting (3-6). The CCI complex, on the other hand, contains the reaction center of PSI (P_{700}) and both the primary photochemical process of charge separation as well as some light harvesting takes place in it (3,5,7). The CCI complex, also designated as the photosystem I reaction center (PS-I-RC), has been purified from a variety of higher plants such as maize, pea, spinach, spirodella, *lemna*, etc. (2-9). In all preparations, the PS-I-RC was found to contain seven polypeptide subunits in the range of 8-83 kDa, 40-65 chlorophyll a molecules, 1 or 2 β-carotene molecules, the primary donor (P_{700}), and all the primary and secondary electron acceptors (2-9).

Recently, all the genes coding for the different polypeptide subunits of spinach PS-I-RC have been sequenced (10-14). The primary structure of each of these polypeptides enabled a prediction of their major secondary structure elements, and a possible arrangement with respect to the lipid bilayer. This important data clarified, at least in part, the function of different parts of the polypeptide chain of each subunit. This preliminary data also contributed, to some extent, to the understanding of the spatial arrangement of the entire PS-I-RC complex. There is no doubt, however, that only a detailed, high

M. Baltscheffsky (ed.), Current Research in Photosynthesis, Vol. II, 555–562.

resolution, three dimensional structure of the PS-I-RC complex will provide complete details of the structure, function and mechanism of action of this complex. The only direct way today to get an accurate three dimensional structure of macromolecules is X-ray crystallography. This approach, although questioned substantially at the early stages, proved very useful and reliable with a number of large protein complexes. Recently the power of macromolecular crystallography has been demonstrated in the bacterial reaction center, where the X-ray diffraction information of single crystals led to the determination of the three dimensional structure of the reaction centers of *Rhodopseudomonas viridis* (15) and *Rhodobacter sphaeroidis* (16,17). These recent high resolution structural analyses brought to a real breakthrough in the understanding of the photosynthetic process. It was for the first time that both the spatial arrangement of the chromophores within the protein skeleton and the arrangement of the entire complex within the photosynthetic membrane have been directly determined. These pioneer studies demonstrated, among other things, the feasibility of both crystallization and detailed structural analysis of a complex membrane protein.

The success of these crystallographic analyses encouraged several laboratories to attempt similar studies with other photosynthetic complexes. The PS-I-RC was, of course, one of the more atractive ones and indeed several groups reported lately some success in the crystallization of PS-I-RC purified from cyanobacteria (22-24). Cyanobacterial PS-I-RC has been shown to be analogous to that of higher plants with respect to its pigment content, partial photochemical functions, and immunological cross-reactivity between some of its subunits and the analogous subunits of higher plants (18). Lately the genes coding for some of the polypeptide subunits of cyanobacteria PS-I-RC had been cloned and sequenced. The elucidation of these sequences confirmed the close relationships between these subunits and the analogous subunits of PS-I-RC in higher plants (19,20,21). These findings and the evidence that the PS-I-RC from higher plants had evolved from the cyanobacterial complex, made the latter a good candidate for crystallographic studies. Reports from Witt *et al* (22), Ford and Garavito (23) and Reilly and Nelson (24), have shown three dimensional crystals of PSI preparations purified from *Synechococcus, Phormidium laminosus* and *Synechocystis*. Witt (22) and Ford (23) showed some diffraction data, and recently Witt *et al* reported a 4Å resolution diffraction pattern from their PSI crystals (25). In the present work, we describe the crystallization of the PS-I-RC of the thermophilic cyanobacteria *Mastigocladus laminosus*. We have characterized this PS-I-RC both in its crystalline and soluble forms, and discuss these results in comparison to the characteristics of higher plant RC (spinach).

2. MATERIALS AND METHODS

2.1 *Growing the plants and the cyanobacteria:* Spinach was grown hydroponically at 25°C with 16 hour light and 8 hour dark cycles. *Mastigocladus laminosus* was grown at 55°C, under continuous illumination (30 $\mu Ei/cm^2/sec^{-1}$) as described before (18).

2.2 *Isolation of thylakoids:* Spinach leaves were ground in a blender in STN buffer (0.4M sucrose, 0.01M Tricine-NaOH, pH 8.0, and 0.01M NaCl); and their chloroplasts were pelleted at 3,500xg. *Mastigocladus* cells were passed through a French Pressure cell at a pressure of 18,000 *p.s.i.* to allow breakage. A centrifugation in 1,000xg allowed the separation of unbroken cells, and the thylakoids were recovered from the supernatant by centrifugation at 15,000xg for 15 minutes. Both the spinach and Mastigocladus thylakoids were washed in Tricine and Tricine-NaCl buffers as described before (9,18).

2.3. *Purification of PS-I-RC:* Both spinach and *Mastigocladus* PS-I-RC were purified according to published procedures based on the extraction of the PS-I-RC from the thylakoids by Triton X-100, separating it from PS II on an ion exchange column (DEAE-cellulose) and further purifing it on a sucrose gradient (9,18). The purity of the preparations was determined by SDS-PAGE, and by determining their chlorophyll to P_{700} ratios (8).

2.4. *Crystallization of PS-I-RC:* The purified PS-I-RC's were used for the crystallization experiments. In most of those studies, the PS-I-RC was applied to a DEAE-cellulose and the Triton was exchanged with Dodecyl-β-D-Maltoside as described in (26). Then, about 20-100 μl of the PS-I-RC solution, in a chlorophyll concentration of about 4 mg/ml, were placed in a crystallization dish with 1-5% PEG-6000 or 1M KPi as precipitants. The precipitant concentration in the reservoir buffer outside the crystallization wells was 2-3 times that of the concentration in the protein solution. The dishes were well sealed and crystallization was allowed to occur at 4-25°C via vapor diffusion as described by Michel et al (15).

3. RESULTS AND DISCUSSION

The PS-I-RC purified from the thermophilic cyanobacterium *Mastigocladus laminosus* differs from the PS-I-RC complex of higher plants (spinach) both in the number of the polypeptide subunits and in the molecular weight of some of them (Figure 1). While subunit I (the P_{700} apo-protein) and subunit VII (the subunit containing the Fe-S centers A&B) are identical in *Mastigocladus* and spinach, all the other subunits have different sizes. However, despite these differences in molecular weights, some of the cyanobacterial PS-I-RC subunits were shown to be analogous to the higher plants' subunits both by immunological cross-reactivity and by comparing their primary structures (18-21). In addition, the PS-I-RC from cyanobacteria shows many of the functional characteristics seen in the complex from higher plants. Using both optical spectroscopy and electron paramagnetic resonance spectroscopy, we have demonstrated that *Mastigocladus* PS-I-RC contains all the electron acceptors present in the spinach PS-I-RC (18,27). We chose, therefore, to study the cyanobacterial PS-I-RC as a general model for PS-I, since it is more amenable for use both in crystallographic analysis, and at a later stage, in molecular genetic manipulations of the complex. In the following we describe the crystallization of *Mastigocladus laminosus* PS-I-RC, and discuss typical properties of these crystals with respect to their biological relevance.

When dealing with crystals of a macromolecular complex it is critical to demonstrate that the complex has not been changed upon crystallization. Therefore we examined one of the crystal forms obtained from the *Mastigocladus* PS-I-RC, the form which will be used later for the crystallographic analysis. Both the subunit composition, pigment content, and the photochemical activity were compared to those of the soluble PS-I-RC preparations. Figure 1 compares the protein profiles detected by PAGE, of the original soluble *Mastigocladus* PS-I-RC that have been used for the crystallization experiments (lane 1) with that of the PS-I-RC from the crystals (lane 2).

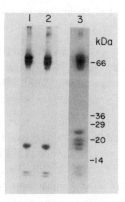

Figure 1. The polypeptide composition of *Mastigocladus* PS-I-RC before (1) and after crystallization (2), compared with the polypeptide composition of spinach PS-I-RC (3).

It is evident that the crystals obtained contain all the polypeptide subunits of the original PS-I-RC with exactly the same size and appearance in the gel. We also find that and that the stochiometry of the subunits in the crystals has not been changed. As in the native complexes (18) there are 2 copies of subunit I and one of each of the other subunits. It is very likely also that the *Mastigocladus* PS-I-RC complexes were highly monodisperse during crystallization (and obviously in the crystals). It is well known that the degree of monodispersion is an important factor in the crystallization of large multi-subunits complexes.

Crystals were obtained in periods of one day to one week. Usually, small crystals appeared initially within the first 12 hours and then kept growing over the next few days. Crystallization rate and crystal quality are very sensitive to the purity of the PS-I-RC preparation. Fresh, pure preparations yielded higher quality crystals within the first few hours. Changing the crystallization conditions resulted in the formation of several crystal forms, varying in morphology and size. All crystal forms, however, retained the native polypeptide composition of the PS-I-RC complex. Figure 2 shows three of these crystal forms. Fine tuning of the protein concentration, the salt concentration, and the PEG concentration were necessary to achieve the optimal crystallyzation conditions. In general, it was possible to increase the protein concentration with a parallel decrease in the salt concentration. In a fixed salt concentration, however, the ratio between protein concentration and PEG concentration determined the specific crystal form. For example, higher concentrations of protein (about 10 mg/ml), resulted in the formation of the needle-type crystals (2a), while lower concentrations of protein resulted in the formation of small squared crystals (2b) or long thin plates (2c).

The needle-type crystals have thus far proven to be the best ones for crystallographic analysis. These crystals usually grow to dimensions of about 1mm X 0.1mm X 0.1mm. They are birefringent when they are still 5-10 μm thick, and they turn dark green (practically no light transmittance) when they get over 20 μm thick. Small crystals of this form (70 x 20 x 20 μm) showed only low resolution diffraction when irradiated with synchrotron radiation (SSRL). However with the present size of these crystals we are confident that synchrotron X-ray diffraction will be obtained to significantly higher resolution. The small crystals examined at the synchrotron seemed to be rather sensitive to the high power X-ray beam. The short life time in the beam allowed only a rough estimate of the unit cell dimensions and space group. The low resolution diffraction patterns of these small needle-type crystals indicated

an hexagonal space group with unit cell dimensions of about 300 x 300 x 150 Å. These parameters are somewhat similar to those reported recently by Witt *et al* for the crystals of the PS-I-RC complex of *Synechococcus* (25). All the other crystal forms diffracted poorly, although some of them display sharp birefringence (see for example the thin plate form in panel c of Figure 2).

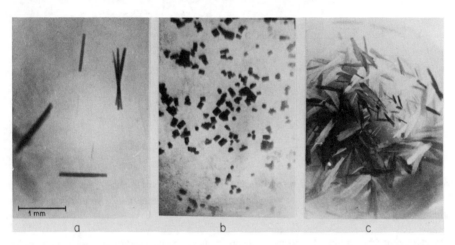

Figure 2: Several forms of *Mastigocladus* PS-I-RC crystals; **a.** Needle-type crystals formed at a protein concentration of 10 mg/ml and 1-3% PEG 6000, **b.** Square crystals formed at a protein concentration of 5 mg/ml and 100 mM KPi, **c.** Thin plates formed at a protein concentration of 5 mg/ml and 1-4% PEG (under polarized light).

All crystal forms were also tested for typical photochemical properties characteristic for PS-I-RC. Here again it is important to show that in the crystals, all the cofactors retain both their composition and function so that the complex will have a similar photochemical activity in the crystalline form as in the soluble form. When it comes to photosynthetic complexes, two major parameters regarding the unique photochemical property need to be proven: a. that indeed the pigmental content was preserved in the crystals, and b. that the crystals have the ability to carry out the photochemistry, i.e., the charge separation and electron transfer reactions.

In order to characterize the pigments in the crystals we determined the chlorophyll concentration, the chlorophyll to P_{700} ratio, and recorded their absorption spectra. Figure 3 shows the original absorption spectra of both forms (crystalline vs. soluble), together with their first- and second-order derivatives. These spectra, and especially the more sensitive first- and second-order derivatives, demonstrate clearly that the PS-I-RC in the crystals has practically an identical absorbance to that of the soluble form. Moreover, the fact that this spectrum is typical to native PS-I-RC and different from a spectrum of "free" chlorophyll *a* in solution, proves that all those pigments are tightly bound to the proteins of the complex. These pigments are definitely not associated with the crystals in a non-specific way, as might be argued on the basis of their color alone. If the latter was the case, upon resolving the crystals a typical "free" pigment spectrum, peaking at 663nm, would have been obtained.

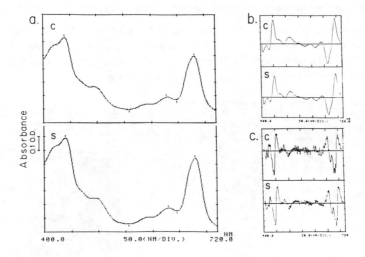

Figure 3. a. Absorption spectra of *Mastigocladus* PS-I-RC in solution (S) and in the crystal (C). b. First-order derivative of the absoption spectra of the solution (S) vs. crystal (C). c. Second-order derivative of the spectra (S and C).

In addition to demostrating that all the pigments are bound in the crystals, it is very important to show that the reaction center (P_{700}) is present in the crystals and that it displays a full oxidation-reduction activity.

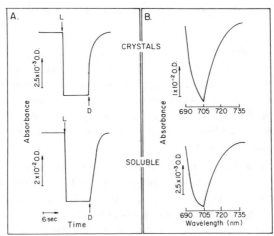

Figure 4. The P_{700} photo-oxidation of *Mastigocladus* PS-I-RC in soluble and crystalline forms: a. Oxidation and re-reduction at 700nm. b. Light-minus-dark difference spectra in the region of 690-735nm. The changes are due to the P_{700} photo-oxidation.

The results presented in Figure 4 demonstrate clearly that the crystallization of the *Mastigocladus* PS-I-RC did not affect its photochemical activity. The P_{700} reaction center in the crystals was able to undergo typical photo-oxidation and re-reduction processes. The PS-I-RC in the crystals was also fully functional in its oxidation site. It was capable in photo-oxidizing its secondary donor plastocyanin (data not shown). Unfortunately, there is no assay available as yet for demonstrating the activity of the reducing side of PS-I-RC, since no NADP photoreduction activity has been shown with any PS-I preparation of cyanobacteria. Thus, within the limits of the tests available to us, our data imply a practically full photosynthetic activity of the reaction centers of the crystals.

4. CONCLUSIONS

In the present work we characterized several forms of *Mastigocladus laminosus* PS-I-RC crystals. It has been shown that these crystalline complexes contain all the original components (both protein and pigments); that these components have not been altered by crystallization, and that the photochemical activity is retained in the crystals as well. These conclusions, although expected from previous data reported on soluble proteins, needed to be specifically shown in our particular system to provide biological significance to the ongoing crystallographic analysis. Furthermore, since this type of data has not been fully obtained for multi-subunits membranal complexes, it was necessary to demonstrate the validity of such analyses in details for such complicated system. It was certainly not obvious that the PS-I reaction center would retain full structure and activity in the crystal. It should be noted that our PS-I-RC complex has been taken out of the photosynthetic membrane and that it is crystallized in the presense of both salt, PEG and detergent. It is therefore extremely critical to ensure that despite these significant changes in the natural environment of the complex, together with the special intermolecular packing forces in the crystal, the PS-I-RC has remained practically unchanged. These data also make it more likely that the structure that will be obtained from the crystallographic analysis represent closely not only the structure in solution but also the structure of the PS-I-RC complex in the actual *in situ* lipid bilayer. We are convinced, therefore, that the X-ray diffraction data currently collected on the characterized PS-I-RC crystals will eventually lead to a high resolution structure of the native reaction center, and hence to the desired understanding of the relationships between the structure and function of photosystem I and its specific role in higher plant photosythesis.

Acknowledgements

We wish to thank Professor D. C. Rees for valuable crystallographic assistance and helpful discussions. This research was supported by a grant from the Charles H. Revson Foundation (#828/88) awarded to R. Nechushtai and G. Shoham.

5. REFERENCES

1.   Williams, J.C., Steinez, L.A. and Feher, G. (1986) *Proteins* **1**, 312-325.

2.   Thornber, J.P. (1986) *in Enc. Plant Physiol. New Series* **19**, 98-142.

3.   Mullet, J.E., Burke, J.J. and Arnzen, C.J. (1980) *Plant Physiol.* **65**, 814-822.

4.   Lam, E., Ortiz, W. and Malkin, R. (1984) *FEBS Lett.* **168**, 10-14.

5.   Nechushtai, R., Peterson, C.C., Peter, G.F. and Thornber, J.P. (1987) *Eur. J. Biochem.* **164**, 345-350.

6.   Vainstein, S., Peterson, C.C. and Thornber, J.P. (1989) *J. Biol. Chem.* **246**, 4058-4063.

7.   Malkin, R. (1987) in *The Light Reactions*, (Barber, J., ed.) pp. 495-526, Elsevier, Amsterdam, New York.

8.   Bengis, C. and Nelson, N. (1977) *J. Biol. Chem.* **250**, 2783-2788.

9.   Nechushtai, R., Nelson, N., Mattoo, A. and Edelman, M. (1981) *FEBS Lett.* **125**, 115-119.

10. Kirsch, W., Seyer, P. and Herrmann, R.G. (1986) *Curr. Genet.* **10**, 843-855.

11. Munch, S., Ljungberg, U., Steppuhn, J., Schneiderbauer, A., Nechushtai, R., Beyreuther, K. and Herrmann, R.G. (1988) *Curr. Genet.* **14**, 511-518.

12. Steppuhn, J., Hermans, J., Nechushtai, R., Ljungberg, U., Thummler, F., Lottspeich, F. and Herrmann, R.G. (1988) *FEBS Lett.* **237**, 218-224.

13. Lagoutte, B. (1988) *FEBS Lett.* **232**, 275-280.

14. Steppuhn, J., Hermans, J., Neuchushtai, R., Herrmann, G.S. and Herrmann, R.G. (1989) *Curr. Genet.*, (in press).

15. Deisenhofer, J., Epp, O., Miki, K., Huber, R. and Michel, H. (1984) *Nature* **318**, 618-624.

16. Allen, J.P., Feher, G., Yeates, T.O., Rees, D.C., Deisenhofer, J. Michel, H. and Huber, R. (1986) *Proc. Natl. Acad. Sci. USA* **83**, 8389-8593

17. Chang, C.H., Tiede, D., Tang, J., Smith, U., Norris, J. and Schiffer, M. (1986) *FEBS Lett.* **205**, 82-86.

18. Nechushtai, R., Muster, P. Binder, A., Liveanu, V. and Nelson N. (1983) *Proc. Natl. Acad. Sci. USA* **80**, 1179-1183.

19. Reilly, P. Hulmes, J.D., Pan, Y-C and Nelson, N. (1988) *J. Biol. Chem.* **263**, 17658-17662.

20. Cantrell, A. and Bryant D.A. (1987) *Plant Mol. Biol.* **9**, 453-468.

21. Chitnis, P. and Nelson, N. (1989) *J. Biol. Chem.*, in press.

22. Witt, I., Witt, H.T., Gerken, S., Saenger, W., Dekker, J.P. and Rögner, M. (1987) *FEBS Lett.* **221**, 260-264.

23. Ford, R.C., Picot, D. and Garavito, R.M. (1987) *EMBO J.* **6**, 1581-1585.

24. Reilly, P. and Nelson, N. (1988) *Photosynthesis Research* **19**, 73-84.

25. Witt, I., Witt, H.T., Di Fiore, D., Rögner, M., Hinrichs, W., Saenger, W., Granzin, J., Betzel, Ch. and Dauter, Z. (1988) *Ber. Bunsenges. Phys. Chem.* **92**, 1503-1506.

26. Nechushtai, R., Nourizadeh, S.D. and Thornber, J.P. (1986) *Biochim. Biophys. Acta* **848**, 193-200.

27. Nechushtai, R., Nelson, N., Gonen, O. and Levanon, H. (1985) *Biochim. Biophys. Acta* **807**, 35-42.

MOLECULAR WEIGHT DETERMINATION OF AN ACTIVE AND MONO-
MERIC PSI COMPLEX

M.E. Schafheutle[1], E. Šetlíková[2], P.A. Timmins[3], I. Šetlík[2] and W.
Welte[1], Institut f. Biophysik u. Strahlenbiologie, Albertstr.23, 7800
Freiburg, FRG; Mikrobiologický ústav, Československá akademie věd,
37981 Třeboň, ČSSR[2]; Institut Laue-Langevin, 156X Centre de Tri,
38042 Grenoble-Cedex, France[3].

A) Purification
The thylakoid membranes of *Synechococcus elongatus* were prepared
according to [1] and treated with the zwitterionic detergent SB12,
after centrifugation, the pellet is enriched in PSI complex. To remove
residual PSII as well as other polypeptides a two-step purification
scheme was developed.

1) Isoelectric focusing with a *Rotophor Cell* (Bio Rad):
The pellet was solubilized with Triton X-100 at 4°C for 1 hour in
the dark. After centrifugation, the supernant was mixed with a 2%
solution of Servalyt 3-6 (Serva, FRG) in 20% glycerol and brought to
0.2% final conc. of Triton X-100. Preparative isoelectric focusing was
performed at 4°C (*Rotophor Cell*) for 4 hours with 12 Watt. At
pH 4.2-4.4 a green band was focused, which consisted of PSI complexes.

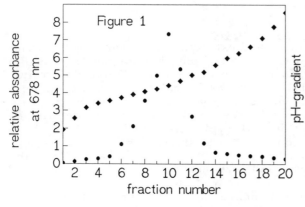

Fig. 1 shows the ab-
sorption at 678nm (•)
as well as the pH in
the fractions (♦) of the
pH gradient harvested
from the cell.

2) DEAE chromatography
After isoelectric focusing, the material was dialysed and applied to
a column filled with Q-Sepharose (Pharmacia, FRG), previously equilibrated with 20 mM Tris-HCl pH 8.0, 20% glycerol, 3 mM sodium azide

M. Baltscheffsky (ed.), Current Research in Photosynthesis, Vol. II, 563–566.
© 1990 *Kluwer Academic Publishers. Printed in the Netherlands.*

("buffer") plus 0.03% Triton X-100. Washing of the column with 4.8%
sodium-cholate in "buffer" eluted polypeptides in the region of 20-40
kDa. In this step the trimeric PSI particles were splited into monomeric PSI. After reequilibration with "buffer" plus 0.03% Triton X-100,
PSI was eluted with a linear gradient of $MgSO_4$ (0-250mM) in "buffer"
plus 0.03% Triton-X100.

B) Functional tests

By chemical redox titration, the concentration of active P_{700} was
determined. The ratio of Chl/P_{700} was calculated using an extinction
coefficient of 64 000 at 700 nm.

The formation and decay of the primary donor radical cation was
monitored at 820 nm by flash photolysis. The signal was stable upon
storage of the PSI sample at room temperature for 1 week.

The pigments were extracted in aceton and Chl-a was quantified by
using its known extinction coefficient. A ratio of 60 Chl/P_{700} was
calculated.

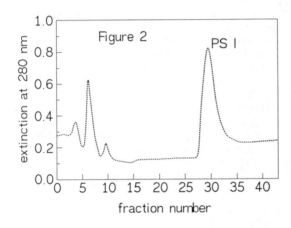

Fig. 2 shows the eluti-
on diagram. The band
at 100 mM $MgSO_4$ re-
presents the PSI com-
plex.

C) Quantitative amino acid analysis

PSI samples were precipitated and extracted three times with ether-
ethanol at -20°C to remove glycerol, lipids and pigments. The Bio
Rad protein assay showed, that the protein was precipitated quantitatively by this procedure. The pellet was hydrolysed with hydrochloric
acid in presence of norleucine as internal standard. The hydrolysate
was analysed with a Biotronik System. Amino acids were determined
fluorimetrically after reaction with o-phthalaldehyd.

In Tab. 1 the amino acid composition is shown. The protein concentration was determined by summing the amounts of the single amino
acids and correcting for the undetermined amino acids Cys and Pro
by a factor 1.09.

Chl was extracted from the original sample and determined spectroscopically. A weight ratio of protein to chlorophyll of 4.66 was estimated.

The total concentration of the PSI complex can now be calculated
by summing the protein and the Chl concentration.

Tab.1 presents the amino acid composition found by us compared with previously reported data from other PSI preparations.

Tab. 1:

	Barley[2]	Spinach[3]	Tobacco[4]	Oat[4]	Beet[4]	Phormidium[4]	Syn. el.[5]
asx	7.8	7.7	-.-	7.6	8.4	8.8	7.4
thr	6.1	5.6	4.2	4.5	5.2	5.9	7.0
ser	6.1	6.5	4.4	3.5	5.5	5.9	3.9
glx	6.8	6.9	6.6	6.6	7.8	6.5	6.9
gly	10.6	12.6	10.1	9.9	11.0	10.0	9.2
ala	10.5	9.8	9.0	9.2	9.8	10.0	10.3
cys	1.1	-.-	-.-	-.-	0.3	0.9	"0.9"
val	4.5	4.7	5.6	4.8	6.3	6.2	7.8
met	1.4	3.3	-.-	-.-	1.4	1.9	1.8
ile	8.6	5.4	6.2	6.6	6.5	6.2	6.7
leu	14.6	11.3	10.6	10.6	11.4	11.2	11.9
tyr	2.6	3.0	1.8	2.2	2.7	3.1	3.5
phe	7.2	6.1	6.8	6.2	6.8	6.2	6.8
lys	1.6	3.0	2.5	2.7	2.9	3.4	3.8
his	3.4	5.2	3.4	3.6	5.9	4.0	2.7
arg	3.5	4.0	2.4	3.3	3.6	3.4	5.1
pro	3.6	4.9	4.9	3.6	4.2	4.7	"4.8"

2-4 see references, 5 this study

D) Molecular weight determination by small angle neutron diffraction:

The molecular weight M_r of a protein is related to the normalised neutron scattering intensity at zero angle by the following formula [5]:

$$\frac{I_o(0)}{I_{inc}(0)} = f \cdot \frac{4 \cdot \pi \cdot T_s}{(1-T_w)} \cdot M_r \cdot N_A \cdot t \cdot 10^{-3} \cdot \left(\frac{1}{M_r} \cdot (\Sigma b - \rho V) \right)^2 \cdot C$$

C: concentration of the protein and chlorophyll [mg/ml] = 1.9 mg/ml determined by amino acid analysis.

$\frac{I_o(0)}{I_{inc}(0)}$: neutron scattering of the protein solution at angle $0°$

incoherent neutr. scatt. of water at $0°$

= 0.088

f: wavelength correction factor (=1 for λ=10 Å)

t: sample thickness (0.1 mm cuvettes); N_A: Avogadro's number

T_s: transmission of sample (=0.5); T_w: transmission of water (=0.46)

$(\frac{1}{M_r} \cdot (\Sigma b - \rho V))$: difference scattering length of protein and buffer per molecular weight unit

ρ: is the scattering length density of the chosen H_2O/D_2O mixture The D_2O concentration is chosen so that the detergent belt around the PSI complex does not contribute to I_o. This "matchpoint concentration" of Triton X-100 was determined in a separate experiment to be at 16% w/v D_2O.

Σb: is the sum of the scattering length of all amino acids as well as the chlorophylls in the PSI complex.

$\frac{\Sigma b}{M_r}$ was calculated from the amino acid composition and from the known Chl/protein weight ratio of 0.151.

M_r can be calculated: 217 +/- 30 kDa

E) Electron microscopy of the PSI complex

Specimens for electron microscopy were prepared and negatively stained with uranyl acetate as described by Ford and Holzenburg [6]. The long and short axis of 20 particles were measured and mean values of 14.8 nm and 9.1 nm respectively, were obtained.

Conclusions

The smallest unit of PSI, according to several studies, consists of two rather homologous polypeptides (sequenced), each of 83 kDa, one copy of a 20 kDa polypeptide and one copy of a 9 kDa, carrying two iron-sulfur complexes, which serve as terminal electron acceptors, and some 40 to 60 Chl molecules. We conclude, that our preparation is an active monomer consisting of the above mentioned polypeptides and containig one P_{700} primary donor.

1 Schatz,G.H. and Witt,H.T. (1984) Photobiochem. Photobiophys. 7, 1-14
2 Vierling,E. and Alberte,R.S. (1983) Plant Physiol. 72, 625-633
3 Setif,P. and Mathis,P. (1980) Arch. Bioch. Biophys. 204, 477-485
4 Thornber,J.P. (1969) Biochim. Biophys. Acta 172, 230-241
5 Jacrot,B. and Zaccai,G. (1981) Biopolymers 20, 2413-2426
6 Ford,R.C. and Holzenburg,A. (1988) EMBO J. 7, 2287-2293

A COMPARISON OF THE PS1 POLYPEPTIDE ORGANIZATION OF SOYBEAN AND THE CYANOBACTERIUM, ANACYSTIS NIDULANS

Ralph L. Henry, Maolin Li, and James A. Guikema, Division of Biology, Kansas State University, Manhattan, KS 66506, USA

1. INTRODUCTION

The macromolecular complexes of PS1 in cyanobacteria share many structural features with their counterparts in higher plants (1,2). As an example, there is a high degree of sequence indentity among psaA, psaB, and psaC genes from a variety of sources (3,4), underscoring an implied functional similarity. However, the periferal features of these complexes, those most susceptible to evolutionary, environmental, and stress-related constraints, are not the same. No LHC1 component has yet been resolved from cyanobacteria, for example, and it is likely that significant differences also exist in peptides which regulate the lateral interactions of the PS1 core with other membrane-bound polypeptides.

This is a preliminary report comparing the PS1 complexes of Anacystis and soybean in which we present three points: [i] PS1-enriched particles have been resolved on a high-resolution TRICINE gel system, to compare the composition of low MW polypeptides; [ii] antibodies have been prepared and assessed for crossreactivity; and [iii] antisera has been used to assess patterns of peptide crosslinking in Anacystis.

2. MATERIALS AND METHODS

PS1 particles were prepared from Anacystis nidulans (5) and soybean (6) using modifications of published procedures. In addition, particles were resolved from both organisms using a 2-dimensional maltoside-PAGE system (7). Two SDS-gel systems were employed to analyze peptide patterns: polyacrylamide gradient gels using a TRIS/glycine buffer system to visualize peptides above 15 kDa (8), and discontinuous, non-gradient TRICINE system to resolve peptides from 1.5 - 15 kDa (9).

3. RESULTS AND DISCUSSION

Fig. 1 shows the polypeptide patterns obtained from PS1 preparations of Anacystis and soybean. In each preparation, two prominent bands appeared between 62-65 kDa, as the psaA and psaB gene products. The soybean preparation (Fig. 1B) had a mimimal contamination of LHC2 polypeptides, observed also on a dodecyl-maltoside 2-dimensional gel which permits concommitant examination of PS1 and PS2 proteins (7). Three LHC1 proteins were observed (Fig. 1B), and have been isolated and injected into rabbits for antisera production.

M. Baltscheffsky (ed.), Current Research in Photosynthesis, Vol. II, 567–570.
© 1990 *Kluwer Academic Publishers. Printed in the Netherlands.*

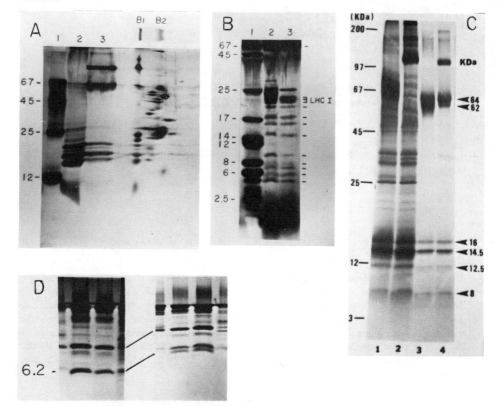

Fig. 1. Peptide patterns of PS1. A. TRIS/glycine gel of MW markers [lane 1], acetone-precipitated PS1 core [lane 2], PS1 core [lane 3], and a 2nd-dimensional analysis of a dodecyl-maltoside gel of membranes, resolving a PS1 green band (B1) and a PS2 green band (B2). B. TRICINE gel of MW markers [lane 1], NaBr-washed PS1 [lane 2], and B1 excised from a dodecyl maltoside gel. C. TRIS/glycine gel of _Anacystis_ membranes [lanes 1,2] and isolated PS1 core [lanes 3,4]. D. TRICINE gel of _Anacystis_ PS1 core in the absence [left] and presence [right] of 6 M urea.

A number of small MW polypeptides were apparent in the two preparations. For example, four proteins reproducibly appeared in PS1 from _Anacystis_ at 16, 14.5, 12.5 and 8 kDa. The 8 kDa peptide is of special interest, since it may be the Fe/S-binding protein (8) as the psaC gene product. These small polypeptides were most easily visuallized using a TRICINE-based polyacrylamide gel system (Fig. 1B,D). Interestingly, the 8 kDa peptide resolved into two proteins which differ by 1 kDa only when urea is present in the analyzing gel. In soybean, four peptides were also observed below 16 kDa.

Several of these _Anacystis_ peptides were excised from gels, and polyclonal or monoclonal antibodies were prepared. Table 1 shows selected serological preparations raised against the _Anacystis_ subunits. Crossreactivity with soybean was observed in all sera (both polyclonal and monoclonal) directed against the 62/64 kDa proteins. Experiments are underway to identify the epitopic domains which are recognized by the monoclonal antibodies.

Antibodies directed against the 8 kDa protein showed strong crossreactivity with a soybean peptide at 6 kDa. The strong crossreactivity suggests a high degree of conservation in the Anacystis and soybean peptides, and underscores the possibility that this peptide may represent the Fe/S-binding protein of PS1.

A major goal of this project will be to examine the protein/protein interactions within PS1. As a first step towards this objective, we have examined the association of each Anacystis small molecular weight subunit with the large polypeptides at 62/64 kDa. For example, Enami and colleagues (10) have shown that most PS1 subunits disappear in concert from the correct

Table 1. Reactivity of antibodies raised against Anacystis nidulans PS1 polypeptides.

Serum designation	Raised against (kDa)	Reactivity	
		Soybean	Anacystis
84-74	64/62	64/62	64/62
86-76	16	nr	14.5/16
86-77	14.5	nr	14.5
86-78	12.5	nr	12.5
86-79	8	6	8
89-F2-2(monoclonal)	64/62	62 and/or 64	62 and/or 64
89-F2-6(monoclonal)	64/62	62 and/or 64	62 and/or 64

Table 2. Effects of chemical crosslinking on peptide patterns of Anacystis PS1.

Chemical Crosslinker	Aggregations observed			
	62/64--16[*]	62/64--14.5	62/64--12.5	62/64--8
glu	+ +	88 kDa	95 kDa	-
HMDC	+ +	95 kDa	76 kDa	-
SMPB	+ +	95 kDa	125 kDa	75 kDa

[*] The antibody probe for the 16 kDa subunit showed reactivity against the 14.5 kDa subunit also. The aggregates of the 16 kDa peptide will not be further quantified until a specific antibody is isolated.

position on acrylamide gels when PS1 preparations were treated with chemical crosslinkers. Surprisingly, the 8 kDa peptide (presumptive Fe/S-binding protein) was impervious to the crosslinkers which they employed.

We screened over 15 chemicals for their ability to crosslink Anacystis PS1 proteins. From these, we chose 3 for further analysis: glutaraldehyde (glu), hexamethylenediisocyanate (HMDC), and succinimidyl 4-(p-maleimidophenyl)butyrate (SMPB). We examined the crosslinking patterns observed using a range of crosslinker concentrations in each case. After the transfer of proteins to nitrocellulose, we probed each pattern with [1] antisera against the 62/64 kDa protein and [2] sera directed against each of the small MW polypeptides. Our goal was to map the patterns of interaction between the large and small MW PS1 subunits.

Table 2 summarizes our crosslinking data. Two important facets merit emphasis. First, similar to the findings of Enami et al (10), the 8 kDa peptide was impervious to crosslinking by glu and HMDC. In contrast, treatment with SMPB yielded crosslinked aggregates at 75 and 145 kDa. Second, crosslinked products were identified between the 62/64 kDa and each of the other small MW subunits, suggesting a spacial arrangement in which the large peptides form a core, flanked by the smaller peptides.

ACKNOWLEDGMENTS

This work was supported in part by NASA (NAGW-1197) and the USDA Competitive Research Grants Program.

REFERENCES

1. Wollman F-A. Encyclopedia of Plant Physiol 1986; 19:487-495.
2. Sherman LA, Bricker TM, Guikema JA, Pakrasi HB. In: Fay P, Van Baalen C, eds. The Cyanobacteria. Amsterdam:Elsevier Science Publishers B.V., 1987:1-33.
3. Cantrell A, Bryant DA. PCC 7002. Plant Mol Biol 1987; 9:453-468.
4. Dunn PPJ, Gray JC. Plant Mol Biol 1988; 11:311-319.
5. Lundell DJ, Glazer AN, Melis A, Malkin R. J Biol Chem 1985; 260:646-654.
6. Mullet JE, Grossman AR, Chua NH. In: Cold Spring Harbor Symposia on Quantitative Biology. Cold Spring Harbor:Cold Spring Harbor Laboratory, 1982:979-983.
7. Bass WT, Bricker TM. Anal Biochem 1988; 171:320-338.
8. Guikema JA, Sherman LA. Biochim Biophys Acta 1982; 681:440-450.
9. Schagger H, von Jagon G. Anal Biochem 1987; 166:368-379.
10. Enami I, Ohta H, Miyaoka T. Plant Cell Physiol 1987; 28:101-111.

N-TERMINAL SEQUENCE OF 5 KDA POLYPEPTIDE ASSOCIATED WITH PHOTOSYSTEM I CORE COMPLEX FROM SPINACH

S.Hoshina[1], N.Kunishima[1], K.Wada[1] and S.Itoh[2]

Dept. of Biology, Fac. of Science, Kanazawa Univ., Kanazawa[1];
National Inst. for Basic Biology, Okazaki[2], Japan

1. INTRODUCTION

The reducing side of photosystem I (PS I) reaction center of oxygenic photosynthetic organisms is known to consist of five different acceptors (1,2). The primary electron acceptor, called A0, is assumed to be a monomeric chlorophyll molecule. An electron is passed from A0$^-$ to a secondary acceptor A1 which is believed to be phylloquinone. The electron transfer involves three different iron-sulfur centers, called FX, FB and FA. PS I high-molecular-mass subunits (about 82 kDa) are known to contain A0, A1, and FX as well as P700 (1,2). FA and FB are believed to be located in a small polypeptide of about 9 kDa (3,4). As we demonstrated elsewhere (5), heat treatment of spinach PS I particles in the presence of ethylene glycol (EG) caused the selective destruction of the iron-sulfur centers and led to the dissociation of polypeptides from the particles. A small subunit of about 5 kDa was closely associated with large subunits under this treatment. In this paper, we present the N-terminal amino acid sequence of the 5 kDa polypeptide.

2. MATERIALS AND METHODS

Spinach PS I particles (PS I-200) were prepared by Triton X-100 solubilization of thylakoids as previously described (6). PS I-200 (1 mg Chl/ml) was resuspended in a medium containing 50% (v/v) EG, 0.1 M sorbitol, 10 mM NaCl and 50 mM Tricine-NaOH (pH 7.8), and incubated at various temperatures for 5 min. Heat/EG-treated PS I-200 was centrifuged and resuspended in 0.8% (w/v) Triton X-100 at 800 µg Chl/ml. The PS I core complex was isolated from the resulting suspension by sucrose density gradient ultracentrifugation. Polypeptide analysis was carried out by Tricine-SDS-PAGE (7). For protein blotting, an unstained gel was equilibrated with blotting buffer A containing 25 mM Tris, 40 mM ε-aminocaproic acid (pH 9.5), and 20% (v/v) methanol for 15 min at room temperature. The gel was placed on a PVDF membrane and sandwiched between two sheets of filter paper saturated with blotting buffer A and two sheets of filter paper saturated with buffer B containing 25 mM Tris and 20% (v/v) methanol; underlying this assemblage were two sheets of filter paper saturated with buffer C containing 0.3 M Tris and 20% (v/v) methanol.

M. Baltscheffsky (ed.), Current Research in Photosynthesis, Vol. II, 571–574.
© 1990 *Kluwer Academic Publishers. Printed in the Netherlands.*

Electroblotting was conducted using a semidry-type electroblotter AE-6670 (Atto). Proteins transferred to the PVDF membrane were stained with 0.1% (w/v) Coomassie brilliant blue R-250 (CBB) in methanol/acetic acid/water (5:2:5, v/v) for 5 min and destained with 90% (v/v) methanol. The stained band was cut out, and sequence analysis was performed using Applied Biosystems Protein Sequencer 477A.

3. RESULTS AND DISCUSSION

Fig. 1 shows the effect of heat/EG treatment on PS I iron sulfur centers. Incubation of thylakoids at 58-60°C in the presence of EG destroyed all of FA and FB but caused little change

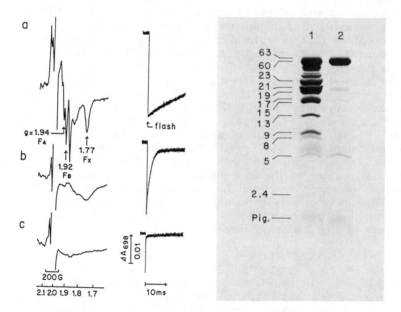

Fig. 1. EPR spectra of the iron-sulfur centers in thylakoids (left) and flash-induced absorption changes at 698 nm in PS I-200 (right). Samples were preincubated with 50% (v/v) EG at 25°C (a), 58°C (b) and 70°C for 5 min. EPR experimental conditions: temperature, 8K; microwave frequency and power of 9.69 GHz and 100 mW, respectively; gain 1.0×10^5; modulation amplitude, 20 G; Scan width, 3,200-4,200; time constant, 320 mS; reaction mixture, 0.1 M glycine-0.1 M amino methyl propanediol-NaOH (pH 10.0) 50 μM mehyl viologen, 50 μM DCPIP, 0.7% (w/v) sodium dithionite and thylakoids (2 mg chl/ml). Flash conditions: temperature, 15°C; reaction mixture, 10 μM DCPIP; 1 mM sodium ascorbate, 100 mM sorbitol, 10 mm NaCl; 50 mM Tricine-NaOH (pH 7.8) and PS I-200.

Fig. 2. Polypeptide compositions of the PS I core complex. lane 1 : PS I-200; lane 2 : 60°C/EG-core complex.

in FX level, although broadening of the FX band occurred (Fig. 1b). FX was finally lost by incubation at 70°C (Fig. 1c). In the flash-induced absorbance change of P700 measured at 698 nm, heat/EG treatment of PS I-200 led to the loss of a decay component with life time of 30 ms, reflecting the charge recombination of $P700^+$ and $P430^-$ (FA^-/FB^-). Heat/EG treatment caused the appearance of a 1 ms decay component which is thought to reflect the reduction of $P700^+$ by $A2^-$ (FX^-). The 30 ms decay component was lost almost completely at $58-60^{\circ}$C. The 1 ms decay component first appeared at temperatures above 53°C. This component decreased with elevating temperature, and it was almost lost at 70°C. A similar temperature dependence was found for the destruction of iron sulfur centers measured by both EPR signals and flash-induced absorbance changes.

The PS I core complex was isolated from PS I-200 after 58°C/EG treatment. The EPR spectrum of this preparation showed no signal arising from FA and FB but exhibited a broadened lineshape for the g = 1.77 band associated with FX, as shown in Fig. 1b (data not shown). Fig. 2 shows the polypeptide composition of the heat/EG-core complexes. Heat/EG treatment facilitated the dissociation of PS I-200, thereby removing the low molecular weight polypeptides including the 8 kDa polypeptide (FA and FB apoprotein) from the high molecular mass polypeptides (60 and 63 kDa in the gel used here) containing P700 and FX. This core complex seems to be directly comparable to the intact PS I core protein from cyanobacteria prepared by Parrett et al. (8). In our study, the 60°C/EG-core complex contained the same level of 5 kDa polypeptide as that of PS I-200 (Table 1), suggesting that the 5 kDa polypeptide is closely associated with the high molecular weight polypeptides. The content of this low molecular protein decreased when the core complex was isolated from 70°C/EG-treated particles lacking all FX (Table 1).

TABLE 1. Content of 5 kDa polypeptide in the PS I core complex.

	PS I-200	core complex from	
		60°C/EG	70°C/EG
	Ratio of 5 kDa to 82 kDa[a]		
Expt 1[b]	0.9	1.1	---
Expt 2[c]	1.3	1.6	0.7

a) Molecular weights of large subunits were estimated as 82 kDa based on DNA coding sequence instead of 60-63 kDa in our gel.
b) Calculated from the absorbance of CBB in SDS-isopropanol extracted from the gel as in (9).
c) Calculated from the area measured by densitometer after the gel was stained with CBB.

The N-terminal amino acid sequence determined for the 5 kDa polypeptide is shown in Fig. 3. This sequence did not correspond to any possible reading frame in the chloroplast DNA of liverwort or tobacco, suggesting that the 5 kDa polypeptide is encoded by the nuclear DNA. Furthermore, this protein sequence did not match any chloroplast components previously reported for higher plants and cyanobacteria, indicating that the 5 kDa polypeptide is new component. Nine of the first 21 N-terminal amino acids are hydrophobic (two Phenylalanine, two isoleucine, two leucine, two methionine and one Valine). The protein contains only one charged amino acid (Aspartic acid) and is easy to extract from the gel using SDS-isopropanol. The data indicate that the 5 kDa polypeptide is a hyrophobic protein, suggesting that this protein is not located on the surface of thylakoid membranes.

The results reported here suggest that a new protein, 5 kDa polypeptide is essential for the organization of the intact PS I core complex.

We would like to thank Dr. H. Kagamiyama for analyzing amino acid sequence; Mr. S. Sue, Miss M. Iwaki and Mr. M. Kawamoto for their technical assistance. Supported partly by a Grant on Priority area (63621003, 01621003) from the Ministry of Education, Science and Culture, Japan.

```
1                                    10
Gly Asp Phe Ile  Gly Ser Ser Thr Asn Leu
11                                   20
Ile  Met Val Thr Ser  X   X  Leu Met  X   Phe
```

Fig. 3. N-terminal amino acid sequence of 5 kDa polypeptide.

REFERENCES
1 Andreasson, L.E. and Vanngard, T. (1988) Ann. Rev. Plant Physiol. Plant Mol. Biol. 39, 379-411.
2 Golbeck, J.H. (1988) Biochim. Biophys. Acta 895, 167-204.
3 Hoj, P.B., Svendsen, I., Scheller, J.V. and Moller, B.L. (1987) J. Biol. Chem. 262, 12676-12684.
4 Oh-oka, H., Takahashi, Y., Wada, K., Matsubara, H., Ohyama, K. and Ozeki, H. (1987) FEBS Lett. 218, 52-54.
5 Hoshina, S., Sakurai, R., Kunishima, N., Wada, K. and Itoh, S. (1989) Biochim. Biophys. Acta in press.
6 Hoshina, S. and Itoh, S. (1987) Plant Cell Physiol. 28, 599-609.
7 Schagger, H. and von Jagow, G. (1987) Anal. Biochem. 166, 368-379.
8 Parrett, K.G., Mehari, T., Warren, P.G. and Golbeck, J.H. (1989) Biochim. Biophys. Acta 973, 324-332.
9 Ball, E.H. (1986) Anal. Biochem. 155, 23-27.

ORGANIZATION OF PSI SUBUNITS IN THYLAKOID MEMBRANES

APRIL ZILBER, R. MAX WYNN, ANDREW WEBBER and RICHARD MALKIN, Department of Plant Biology, University of California, Berkeley 94720 USA

The native Photosystem I complex (PSI-200) contains a light-harvesting antenna complex (LHCP I), and a core composed of ten different subunits (PSI-100). The apparent molecular mass and functions of the subunits are described in Table I.

TABLE I.   PHOTOSYSTEM I POLYPEPTIDES

SDS-PAGE	Gene	Proposed Function	Ref
62 kD	$psaA$	Bind Chl P700, A_0, A_1, Fe-S_X	1
58	$psaB$	and antenna chl	
22	$psaD$	Ferredoxin binding	2
19	$psaF$	Plastocyanin binding	3
17.8	?	Unknown	
17.3	?	Unknown	
11	?	Unknown	
10	?	Unknown	
8	$psaC$	Binds Fe-$S_{A/B}$	1
6	?	Unknown	

Our aim is to understand the organization of individual PSI subunits with respect to the thylakoid membrane. Predictions have been made on the basis of hydropathy plots for several subunits. The 62 and 58 kD subunits are each predicted to have up to eleven membrane spanning helices, connected by considerable amounts of sequence extending into the stroma and the lumen (4). The 22 kD subunit is hydrophilic and is located on the stromal side of the thylakoid (2). The 19 kD subunit has a single hydrophobic region near the C-terminal; the bulk of this subunit is probably on the lumenal side (3). The Fe-$S_{A,B}$ subunit (9 kD) is hydrophilic (5) and is probably located on the stromal side of the membrane. The orientation of the other subunits has not been extensively studied. We have used limited proteolysis and phase extraction techniques to study the organization of specific PSI subunits.

Materials and Methods
Triton X-114 phase-fractionation of spinach PSI-200 was performed following the method of Bricker and Sherman (6), except that the PSI-200 was brought to a

M. Baltscheffsky (ed.), Current Research in Photosynthesis, Vol. II, 575–578.
© 1990 *Kluwer Academic Publishers. Printed in the Netherlands.*

final chlorophyll concentration of 0.1 mg ml^{-1} for the solubilization step. The detergent and aqueous phases were re-extracted twice, and the final fractions analysed on 10-20% SDS-polyacrylamide gels.

Intact spinach thylakoids were prepared as in (7) and resuspended in blending buffer. Intact thylakoids (1 mg chl ml^{-1}) were incubated in the presence or absence of trypsin at room temperature for 30 min. The digestion was stopped by the addition of 0.2 mg soybean trypsin inhibitor per ml of sample. The samples were cooled on ice for 10 min. and pelleted at 5000 x g for 2 min. The supernatants were discarded and the pellets resuspended with blending buffer to their original volume. The samples were assayed immediately for NADP$^+$ photoreduction activity in the presence of ascorbate, DCIP and DCMU. At the same time, aliquots of the samples were added to solubilization buffer for analysis by SDS-PAGE and immunoblotting. For amino acid sequencing, trypsin-treated thylakoids were resuspended in H$_2$O and PSI-200 was prepared as described in (7). The PSI polypeptides were electrophoresed and blotted onto PVDF membrane. The band of interest was excised and submitted for gas phase sequencing.

Results and Discussion

Triton X-114 fractionation of PSI subunits is shown in Fig. 1. Only the 22, 17.3, 10 and 8 kD core subunits partitioned into the aqueous phase. The other subunits remained in the Triton X-114 phase. This result confirms the hydrophilic nature of the 22 and 8 kD subunits predicted from the amino acid sequences. The result also shows that the ~17 kD dimer is composed of two different polypeptides and that one is clearly more hydrophilic. The 10 kD subunit is also, apparently, a hydrophilic protein.

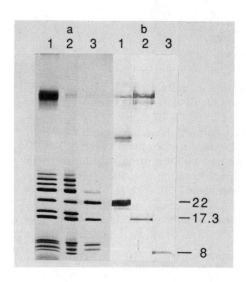

FIGURE 1. Triton X-114 fractionation of PSI-200 a) SDS-PAGE: Lane 1, control PSI-200; lane 2, Triton X-114 fraction; lane 3, aqueous fraction. b) Immunoblot of aqueous fraction probed with antibody against: Lane 1, 22 kD subunit; lane 2, 17 kD subunits; lane 3, 8 kD subunit.

Trypsin treatment of intact thylakoids results in the degradation of the 22 kD subunit to a form that migrates at 19 kD on SDS-PAGE (fig. 2. a). During trypsin treatment under these conditions the thylakoids remain intact, (fig. 2. b). as shown by the lack of degradation of the 33 kD subunit of the oxygen evolving complex (OEC). The 33 kD subunit is an extrinsic polypeptide located on the lumenal side of the thylakoid; in disrupted thylakoids it is quite sensitive to proteases (data not shown). Immunoblots shown in figure 2. c) and d) indicate that the Fe-S$_{A/B}$ protein is not detectably degraded, whereas the 62 and 58 kD dimer is degraded with increasing trypsin concentrations.

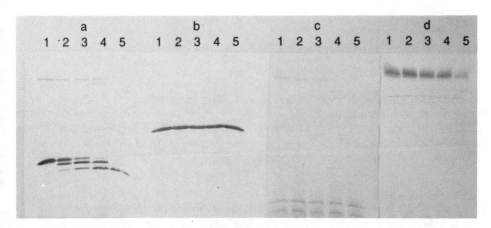

FIGURE 2. Trypsin treatment of intact thylakoids. Immunoblots with antibody against a) the 22 kD subunit, b) the 33 kD subunit., c) the Fe-S$_{A/B}$ subunit, d) the 62 and 58 kD subunits. Lanes 1-5 contain thylakoid samples treated with 0, 0.5, 1, 2, and 4 µg trypsin/mg chl, respectively.

Amino acid sequencing of the lower trypsin product (fig. 3) shows the `22 kD subunit is specifically cleaved between lysine 15 and glutamate 16. NADP$^+$ photoreduction activity of the trypsin-treated PSI is reduced to about 65% of the control. These results confirm the stromal orientation of the 22 kD subunit, and suggest that this N-terminal segment is not essential for interaction with ferredoxin. However, the decreased activity cannot be directly correlated with the degradation of the 22 kD subunit or of the 62 and 58 kD dimer.

22 kD (psaD) SEQUENCE

```
                    *         10                    ▼                    20
    Ala Ala Ala Ala Glu Gly LYS Ala Ala Thr Pro Thr Glu Thr LYS Glu Ala Pro LYS Gly

                              30                                         40
    Phe Thr Pro Pro Glu Leu Asp Pro Asn Thr Pro Ser Pro Ile Phe Ala Gly Ser Thr Gly

                              50                                         60
    Gly Leu Leu ARG LYS Ala Gln Val Glu Glu Phe Tyr Val Ile Thr Trp Glu Ser Pro LYS

                              70                                         80
    Glu Gln Ile Phe Glu Met Pro Thr Gly Gly Ala Ala Ile Met ARG Glu Gly Pro Asn Leu

                              90                                        100
    Leu LYS Leu Ala ARG LYS Glu Gln Cys Leu Ala Leu Gly Thr ARG Leu ARG Ser LYS Tyr

                             110                                        120
    LYS Ile LYS Tyr Gln Phe Tyr ARG Val Phe Pro Ser Gly Glu Val Gln Tyr Leu His Pro

                             130                                        140
    LYS Asp Gly Val Tyr Pro Glu LYS Val Asn Pro Gly ARG Gln Gly Val Gly Leu Asn Met

                             150                        *               160
    ARG Ser Ile Gly LYS Asn Val Ser Pro Ile Glu Val LYS Phe Thr Gly LYS Gln Pro Tyr

        162
    Asp Leu
```

* Possible cleavage site yielding first trypsin digestion product.
▼ Cleavage site yielding second trypsin digestion product as determined by
  amino acid sequencing.

FIGURE 3. Sequence of 22 kD subunit (8).

Treatment of intact thylakoids with 5 and 10 µg trypsin/mg chl.produced the same cleavage pattern of the 22 kD subunit. Neither the 19 kD subunit or the 33 kD OEC polypeptide were digested under these conditions. This is consistent with the proposed location of the 19 kD subunit on the lumenal side of the thylakoid membrane where it interacts with plastocyanin.

Acknowledgements
    We wish to thank Dr. Arie Admon and the Howard Hughes Foundation for amino acid sequencing. This work was supported by a grant from NSF to R.M.

References
1   Golbeck, J.H. (1987) Biochim. Biophys Acta 895, 167-204
2   Zilber, A.L. and Malkin, R. (1988) Plant Physiol. 88, 810-814
3   Wynn, R.M. and Malkin, R. (1988) Biochem. 27, 5863-5869
4   Kirsch, W., Seyer, P. and Herrmann, R.G. (1986) Curr. Genet. 10, 843-855
5   Oh-oka, H., Takahashi, Y., Kuriyama, K., Saeki, K. and Matsubara, H. (1988)
    J. Biochem. 103, 962-968
6   Bricker, T.M. and Sherman, L.A. (1982) FEBS Lett. 149, 197-202
7   Mullett, J.E., Burke, J.J. and Arntzen, C.J. (1980) Plant Physiol. 65, 814-822
8   Munch, S., Ljungberg, U., Steppuhn, J., Schneiderbauer, A., Nechushtai, R.,
    Beyreuther, K. and Herrmann, R.G. (1988) Curr. Genet. 14, 511-518

TOPOGRAPHY OF PHOTOSYSTEM 1 IN CYANOBACTERIA

J.HLADÍK, L.POSPÍŠILOVÁ and D.SOFROVÁ,

Department of Biochemistry, Faculty of Sciences, Charles University, 128 40 PRAGUE, CZECHOSLOVAKIA

1.INTRODUCTION

Photosystem 1 (PS1) of all oxygenic photoautotrophs is an integral pigment-protein complex of thylakoid membranes, the main parts of which are well known already: the core complex and internal antenna system as well as all the components essential for charge separation and electron transfer from the reaction center to ferredoxin (1,2). The polypeptide composition of cyanobacterial PS1 was likewise identified (3-5). PS1 consists of two polypeptides of molecular mass (Mr) 67-70 kDa and 4 or 5 polypeptides in the Mr range of 8 to 20 kDa. Considerable attention was recently given to crystallisation of cyanobacterial PS1 (6,7) providing new data on the arrangement of isolated PS1, which can exist in the trimeric or monomeric form. Nevertheless, the spatial arrangement of individual polypeptides in the complex remains unanswered.

2.PROCEDURE

For separation of thylakoid membrane components, thylakoid membranes of the cyanobacterium Synechococcus elongatus were solubilised by Triton X-100 (mass ratio Triton:chl = 25, final concentration of Triton 1%,v/v) or by SDS (mass ratio SDS:chl = 50, final concentration of SDS 2.5%,v/v). For details see (5). Electrophoresis on gradient polyacrylamide gel (5-10%, in case of pigment-proteins separation, 10-20% in case of polypeptide analysis) was performed in the buffer system described earlier (5,8).

For cross-linking reactions,the reversible homobifunctional agent dithio-bis(succinimidyl)propionate (DSP) and dithio-bis(sulfosuccinimidyl)propionate (DTSSP) were used. For details see (9).

For isotope iodine labelling, Iodogen (Pierce Eurochemie) was used. For details see (9).

M. Baltscheffsky (ed.), Current Research in Photosynthesis, Vol. II, 579–582.
© 1990 Kluwer Academic Publishers. Printed in the Netherlands.

3. RESULTS AND DISCUSSION

3.1. Cross-linking studies

It has been established already (3,5), that the PS 1 complex can be obtained after solubilisation of thylakoid membranes in several forms, differing on the one hand in the degree of aggregation (monomeric to trimeric forms), on the other in the low-molecular polypeptide content. The mild detergent Triton X-100 provides primarily the trimeric form, while the stronger ionic detergent SDS rather provides low-molecular PS1 forms (Fig.1.).

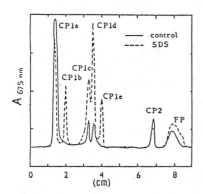

FIGURE 1. Electrophoretic separation of the Triton extract from thylakoid membranes with or without addition of SDS (50 mg SDS/mg chl).

After incubation of thylakoid membranes with the bifunctional agents DSP and DTSSP, cross-linking of nearest neighbouring proteins leads to stabilisation of some PS1-complex forms (Tab.1.).

TABLE 1. Percentual representation of individual PS1 pigment-protein complexes in SDS extract of cyanobacterial thylakoid membranes before and after cross-linking by DSP and DTSSP at pH 8.1.
Data were obtained by densitometric evaluation of respective electrophoreograms at 675 nm.

complex	control	DTSSP	DSP
CP1a	4	4	42
CP1b	3	10	19
CP1c	17	15	14
CP1d	7	30	20
CP1e	69	41	5

In the case of hydrophilic agent DTSSP, a remarkable relative increase of the proportion of the dimeric form CP1b and of the monomeric form CP1d with reduced content of low-molecular polypeptides (Mr 11, 16 and 18 kDa) is observed. Hydrophobic DSP strongly increases the proportion of the trimeric form (CP1a) at the expense of the monomeric form CP1e, which contains only two polypeptides of Mr 70 and 67 kDa.

Considering the different hydrophobicity of the two reagents, it may be assumed that the low-molecular polypeptides present in the CP1d complex form a hydrophilic domain which is accessible to water-soluble agent DTSSP. This fact most probably leads to partial stabilisation of the dimeric CP1b form, as well. For effective stabilisation of the supramolecular complex (trimeric CP1a form), the influence of DSP in the hydrophobic region is more advantageous.

3.2. Iodination studies

Separation of pigment-protein PS1 complexes after solubilisation of thylakoid membranes labelled with iodine showed radioactivity in all forms of the complex CP1 (Fig. 2.)

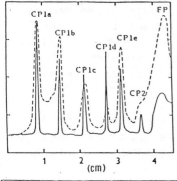

FIGURE 2. Electrophoretic separation of pigment-protein complexes obtained by SDS solubilisation of the iodinated thylakoid membranes. Full line – densitogram at 675 nm dashed line – radiogram, CPM,rel. units.

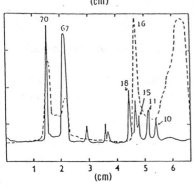

FIGURE 3. Electrophoretic separation of polypeptides of the iodinated complex CP1a.
Full line – densitogram at 650 nm dashed line – radiogram, CPM,rel. units.
Molecular weights are in kDa.

irrespective to their polypeptide composition. Since iodination using Iodogen applied in a thin layer on the test-
-tube wall can be considered to be surface-specific with
respect to the thylakoid membrane, it is highly probable
that only polypeptides common to all PS1 forms, i.e. Mr 67
and 70 kDa polypetides are exposed on the thylakoid membrane surface. This is confirmed by the separation of polypeptides of iodinated trimeric CP1a complex (Fig. 3.), because
the radioactivity was observed in the polypeptides Mr 70,
67 and 16 kDa only. The other polypetides of Mr 18, 15, 11
and 10 kDa are not accessible to iodination, more for steric reasons than due to a lack of tyrosine residues (2).

4.CONCLUSIONS
    It may be stated, on the basis of the above results as
well as some of our earlier experiments (5,9), that:
I.the pigment-protein complex PS1 of cyanobacteria is a
compact closed body composed of 5 low-molecular polypeptides surrounded by two chlorophyll-binding proteins (the
pigment antenna system) forming a protective shield which
hinders access to small polypeptides from the surface of
the complex or from the surface of the thylakoid membrane.
II.the cyanobacterial PS1 complex is present in the thylakoid membrane in the trimeric form which may be stabilised
by hydrophobic cross-linking agents and isolated after
solubilisation of the thylakoid membrane by detergents.

REFERENCES
 1 Reilly,P. and Nelson,N. (1989) Photosynth.Res. 19, 73-84
 2 Golbeck, J.H. (1988) Biochim. Biophys. Acta 895, 167-204
 3 Takahashi,Y.,Koike,H. and Katoh,S. (1982) Arch.Biochem.
   Biophys. 219, 209-218
 4 Lundell,D.J.,Glazer,A.N.,Melis,A.and Malkin,R. (1985) J.
   Biol.Chem. 260, 646-654
 5 Komenda,J., Hladik,J. and Sofrova,D. (1989) J.Photochem.
   Photobiol. in press
 6 Ford,R.C. and Holzenburg,A. (1988) EMBO J. 7, 2287-2293
 7 Boekema,E.J.,Dekker,J.P.,Rogner,M.,Witt,I.,Witt,H.T.and
   Van Heel,M. (1989) Biochim. Biophys. Acta 974, 81-87
 8 Coufal,J.,Hladik,J.and Sofrova,D., (1989)
   Photosynthetica 23, in press
 9 Pospisilova,L., Hladik,J. and Sofrova,D. J. Photochem.
   Photobiol., in press

EXTRINSIC MEMBRANE PROTEINS OF PHOTOSYSTEM I

STAFFAN TJUS AND BERTIL ANDERSSON
DEPARTMENT OF BIOCHEMISTRY, ARRHENIUS LABORATORIES,
UNIVERSITY OF STOCKHOLM, S-106 91 STOCKHOLM, SWEDEN

1. INTRODUCTION

Photosystem I is a multiprotein complex that mediates light-induced electron transport between plastocyanin and $NADP^+$. Depending on plant species and SDS-PAGE system, the number of polypeptides resolved in the photosystem I complex differs between 8-12 (1), excluding the polypeptides of the light harvesting complex I. The polypeptides have been given roman numbers I-VII. Subunits Ia, Ib and VII have been assigned direct electron transport functions. Subunit II has been shown to crosslink with ferredoxin and subunit III to interact with plastocyanin (for review see 1). The biochemical functions for the other subunits remain to be established although most of them have been cloned and sequenced. Here we have used biochemical approaches, involving alkaline salt washing and Triton X-114 fractionation, in order to identify extrinsic membrane proteins of photosystem I.

2. MATERIALS AND METHODS

Right-side out stroma lamellae vesicles were prepared from spinach thylakoids by Yeda press fragmentation and differential centrifugation (2). Photosystem I particles were isolated by solubilization of spinach thylakoids by Triton X-100 followed by sucrose density centrifugation (3). Extrinsic and integral membrane proteins were separated by Triton X-114/water phase partitioning (4). Photosystem I particles or membranes were washed by 1.0 M NaCl, 20 mM Tris-HCl (pH = 9.5) for 60 minutes at $4^{\circ}C$ followed by ultracentrifugation at 200 000 x g for 15 minutes. As control wash a buffer containing 10 mM NaCl, 100 mM sorbitol and 10 mM Tricine (pH= 7.8) was used. SDS-PAGE was performed in the buffer system of Laemmli (5) in the presence of 4 M urea. An acrylamide gradient of 12-22.5% was used. The relative amount of protein was determined by laser densitometer scanning of Coomassie-stained gels.

M. Baltscheffsky (ed.), Current Research in Photosynthesis, Vol. II, 583–586.
© 1990 *Kluwer Academic Publishers. Printed in the Netherlands.*

Photosystem I electron transport from ascorbate/DCIP to methyl-viologen was measured at saturating amounts of light as oxygen consumption using a Clark type oxygen electrode. The assay medium was composed of: 40 mM Na-phosphate (pH=7.4), 1.0 mM NaCl, 10 mM sucrose, 10 μm DCMU, 5 mM Na-azide, 1.0 mM ascorbate, 0.1 mM DCIP, 0.12 mM methylviologen and 5 μg of chlorophyll/ml. $NADP^+$ reduction was followed at 340 nm using a spectrophotometer equipped with side illumination. The assay medium contained; 40 mM Na-phosphate (pH=7.4), 1.0 mM NaCl, 2.0 mM $MgCl_2$, 10 μM DCMU, 5 mM Na-azide, 1.0 mM ascorbate, 0.3 mM DCIP 0.6 mM ADP, ferredoxin and $NADP^+$-ferredoxin reductase at saturating amounts, 0.40 mM $NADP^+$ and 5 μg of chlorophyll/ml.

3. RESULTS AND DISCUSSION

Alkaline salt wash (1.0 M NaCl, 20 mM Tris-HCl pH=9.5) of photosystem I particles released four polypeptides as revealed by SDS-PAGE (Fig. 1 lane 4, Table 1). Polypeptide bands reduced in the pellet were a 8.2 kDa band, a weak band at 10.5 kDa, a 17.2 kDa band and another weak band at 19.3 kDa. These polypeptides were all recovered in the wash supernatant (Fig. 1). Some highly resolved gels revealed that the 8.2 kDa was composed of two polypeptides out of which the upper totally disappeared after salt wash (not shown). The 17.2 and 19.3 kDa polypeptides were partly removed by the control wash indicating a very loose binding to the complex. In some salt washing experiments a total removal of a 5.0 kDa polypeptide could also be detected.

When subjecting right-side out stroma lamellae vesicles to the high salt treatment a release of polypeptides was also seen. The majority of these polypeptides belong to the CF_1 complex. However, the

TABLE 1. Properties of washed photosystem I particles.

Relative amounts of proteins:	Untreated	Controlwash	NaCl-wash
%			
kDa:			
19.3	100	58	0
17.2	100	70	42
10.5	100	100	80
8.2	100	100	0
electron transport:			
$DCIPH_2$ - M V	100	104	104
$DCIPH_2$ - $NADP^+$	100	91	96

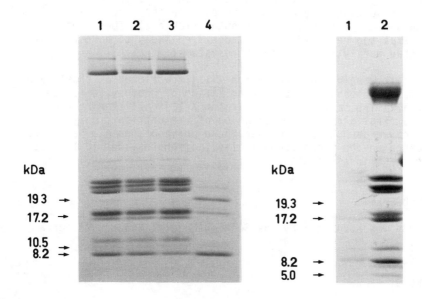

Fig   1   Fig   2

Fig. 1. SDS urea-polyacrylamide gel electrophoresis of photosystem
I particles subjected to wash treatments. (1). Native photosystem I
particles. (2) photosystem I particles after controlwash with 10 mM
NaCl, 100 mM sorbitol, 10 mM Tricine (pH=7.8). (3) photosystem I
particles after wash with 1.0 M NaCl, 20 mM Tris-HCl (pH=9.5, 20 µg
chl.). (4) supernatant from the salt wash.

Fig. 2. SDS urea-polyacrylamide gel electrophoresis of photosystem
I particles subjected to Triton X-114/water phase partitioning.
(1) Aqueous hydrophilic phase. (2) Native photosystem I particles.

8.2 kDa polypeptide was released to 50% and the 17.2 kDa polypeptide
was totally removed. Considering the right-side out sidedness of the
membrane vesicles these two proteins are proposed to be located at
the outer thylakoid surface.

Upon Triton X-114/water phase partitioning of photosystem I particles, most of the proteins that were released by the high salt
wash (5.0, 8.2, 17.2 and 19.3 kDa), all partitioned to the aqueous
phase (fig. 2 lane 1). This is in line with the washing experiment
and confirms that these photosystem I proteins are hydrophilic and
consequently extrinsic membrane proteins. In this experiment we
were not able to resolve the 10.5 kDa polypeptide.

The photosystem I particles depleted of the extrinsic polypeptides were assayed for electron transport capacity. There was no considerable reduction in electron transport neither when using methylviologen nor NADP$^+$ as electron acceptor (Table 1). These results suggest that the released polypeptides are likely to have regulatory rather than catalytic roles in photosystem I.

The salt washing and the Triton X-114 fractionation should aid in the future biochemical characterization of photosystem I. In particular alkaline salt washing or Triton X-114 partitioning could provide a first step in the isolation of the extrinsic polypeptides. At present we do not know whether these polypeptides all have a correspondence to the known subunits I-VII of photosystem I. This is under current investigation.

ACKNOWLEDGEMENT

This study was supported by the Swedish Natural Science Research Council.

REFERENCES

1. Golbeck, J.H. (1987) Biochim. Biophys. Acta 895, 167-204.
2. Andersson, B. and Anderson, J.M. (1980) Biochim. Biophys. Acta 593, 427-440.
3. Mullet, J.E., Burke, J.J. and Arntzen, C.J. (1980) Plant Physiol. 65, 814-822.
4. Bordier, C. (1981) J. Biol. Chem. 256, 1604-1607.
5. Laemmli, U.K. (1970) Nature 227, 680-685.

A PHOTOSYSTEM-1 REACTION CENTER COMPLEX CONSTITUTED ONLY BY TWO SUBUNITS

TETSUO HIYAMA,   NORIMASA YANAI,   YASUHIRO TAKANO,   HIDEO OGISO, KOICHI
SUZUKI AND KIYOSHI TERAKADO,   DEPARTMENT OF BIOCHEMISTRY,   SAITAMA
UNIVERSITY, URAWA 338, JAPAN

1. INTRODUCTION

A number of laboratories have reported on the preparation of Photosystem-1 reaction center complexes.   They differ each other mainly in their subunit compositions.   In a typical case, a complex consists of large subunits (50-70kD on SDS-PAGE) and several smaller ones (less than 20kD). It became clear that the large subunits are in fact two different polypeptides of 83 snd 82 kD's, since two kinds of genes were found on a chloroplast DNA(1). The genes were designated as psaA and psaB (2). The large subunits have been implicated by numerous workers as the sites of the Photosystem-1 reaction center pigment, P700, a yet-to-be-identified primary electron acceptor(Ao) and some other early electron acceptors (Vitamin K1 or A1, Component X or A2). One of the other smaller subunits, the 9kD polypeptide was isolated by several groups including us (3-5). From the N-terminal amino acid sequence, the gene for this subunit was identified on chloroplast DNAs and designated as either psaC(3,4) or frxA(5).   Judging from the deduced primary structure, which was later confirmed by the sequencing of the peptide itself(6), the subunit is most likely an apoprotein for iron-sulfur clusters, Centers A and B. This has been confirmed recently by measuring EPR spectra of more intact prepara-tions(7-9).   We reported earlier on a reaction center preparation which consisted of no other than the large subunits yet retained an intact P700 activity, obtained by further treating a spinach reaction center with a chaotropic agent(10). The complex showed a low temperature EPR signal due to Component X but lacked those due to either Center A or Center B.   It also showed a flash-induced absorbance change whose spectrum resembled to that of P430.   Although the P700 activity of this preparation was stable, the yield was poor, thus not suited for further chemical analysis. Recently, a similar complex prepared from cyanobacterial thylakoids that showed a clear EPR spectrum of Component X but not those of either Center A or Center B, was reported (11). They showed also a difference spectrum of a flash-induced change, which was almost identical to that of the ori-ginal P430(10), although they did not implicate it as such. Here, we re-port a stable preparation from spinach that can be prepared with a high yield simply through a short exposure to SDS followed by gel filtration, and the results of photochemical measurement and chemical analyses of this reaction center complex constituted only by the large subunits.

M. Baltscheffsky (ed.), Current Research in Photosynthesis, Vol. II, 587–590.
© 1990 *Kluwer Academic Publishers. Printed in the Netherlands.*

2. PROCEDURE
2.1. Material and Methods
  A Photosystem-1 complex preparation with the small subunits (ps1) was
prepared as described before(10) by Triton X-100 treatment of spinach
thylakoids followed by ammonium sulfate fractionation and ion exchange
chromatographies.   The photochemical activities of P700 were routinely
measured by using a home-made flash spectrophotometer equipped with a
100-μsec xenon flash. Flash-induced photooxidations of P700 were measured
as absorbance changes at 430 nm.   A set of data from   several flashes
were averaged through a home-made signal averager. The extinction coefficient to calculate a P700 concentration was 45,000 M cm (12).
Chemically induced oxidized-minus-reduced difference spectra were recorded on a Hitachi 557 spectrophotometer connected to an NEC 8801
personal computer.   The P700 concentration in this case was determined
from the peak height at 700 nm of a ferricyanide-minus-ascorbate/TMPD(N,
N,N',N'-tetramethyl-p-phenylenediamine) difference spectrum using an
extinction coefficient, 72,000 M cm according to (12).   For amino acid
analysis, a complex preparation was hydrolyzed either by using 6N HCl or
4N methane sulfonic acid. The hydrolyzate was analyzed on a Hitachi amino
acid analysis system equipped with a post-column o-phthalaldehyde
labeling system. Iron was determined colorimetrically according to (13).
Cysteine residues were determined after converted into cysteinic acid.
The acid-labile sulfur was determined according to (14).   Vitamin K1
(phyloquinone) was determined by using a reverse phase HPLC.   Protein
concentration was determined according to (15) with bovine serum albumin
as the standard. Electron micrographs were taken by using a Hitachi H700H
electron microscope.   The samples were fixed with 1% glutaraldehyde and
negatively stained with uranyl acetate.   Chlorophyll concentrations were
measured according to Arnon.
2.2. A reaction center preparation without small subunits (cp1)
  The ps1 preparation, diluted to give the chlorophyll concentration of
0.1 mg/ml was mixed with SDS (final concentration, 0.2%).   After one
minute incubation at 40 C, the mixture was quickly chilled on an ice
bath, and the aliquot was loaded on a Sephacryl S300HR column equili-
briated with 10 mM Tris-HCl, pH 8 containing 0.05% Triton X-100.   The
column was eluted with the above medium.   Among the two major 280-nm
absorbing peaks, the faster moving one was collected and loaded on a
small DEAE-cellulose column. This column was eluted with a minimal amount
of the above medium supplemeted with 0.1 M NaCl. This procedure of a gel
filtration followed by a concentration was repeated once.   The resulted
aliquot was dialyzed against 10 mM Tris-HCl, pH 8, and then 20% sucrose
was added before storage at -55 C.   No significant change in the photochemical activities was observed after more than six month under these
storage conditions. The yield of cp1 was typically more than 60% starting
from ps1.

3. RESULTS AND DISCUSSIONS
3.1. Electron microscopic observation of ps1 and cp1
  Fairly uniform round particles were observed under an electron microscope with negatively stained samples of both ps1 and cp1.   Their sizes
were not different each other and about 10 nm in diameter in both cases.

3.2. Subunit compositions

SDS-PAGE, stained with Coomassie Brilliant Blue, of cpl revealed a single intense band around 67kD with faint traces of bands at 20.5 and 19 kD's but nothing at 9kD. The 67kD band could be resolved into two bands in a high resolution gel supplemented with urea.

3.3. Photochemical activities

With a psl preparation, a flash-induced change at 430 nm in the absence of an artificial electron acceptor (e.g. methyl viologen) is typically an instant absorbance decrease followed by a monophasic recovery phase with a half time of 50-100 msec, as was documented many years ago(16). Upon the addition of methyl viologen, there appear two clearly separated recovery phases, one slow and another fast. The faster phase becomes faster by increasing the methyl viologen concentration, while the slower one becomes faster by increasing the concentration of an electron donor, e.g. TMPD/ascorbate. The faster one has been designated as P430, whereas the slower one is P700. The situation was somewhat different with cpl which lacked any smaller subunit. Without methyl viologen, the recovery had two phases, the major one with half time of a few msec, and the minor one with half time of 50-200 msec. With methyl viologen, the two phases became almost indistinguishable and equally slow, while a minor faster phase appeared. This major slow phase was now dependent on an electron donor concentration, thus identified as P700. The decay time of the minor faster phase was dependent on methyl viologen concentration. The difference spectrum of this phase was similar to that of the originl 430 in preparations similar to psl(10). At 444 nm, where the absorbance change due to P700 was null, only the faster phase was observed. Although the decay at 444 nm in cpl was much faster than that in psl in the absence of methyl viologen, the pseudofirst order rate constants for methyl viologen were close each other. A similarly obtained difference spectrum in a cyanobacterial preparation equivalent to our cpl(11) is also quite reminiscent of the P430 spectrum in (10). This strongly supports our earlier contention (17) that P430 is Component X or A2 but neither Center A nor Center B, though a different interpretation was given in (11). In psl, the amount of P700 determined by using flash spectrometry at 430 nm was consistent with that from a chemical difference spectrum around 700 nm. In cpl, a flash-photometrically determined number was somewhat smaller than that chemically determined.

3.4. Iron, acid-labile sulfur and Vitamin K1

The results are summarized in Table 1. The numbers are mol. per P700.

Table 1.	Chl a	Fe	Acid-labile S	Vitamin K	Protein	a/b ratio
psl	50	12	12	2	250000	<10
cpl	50	4	4	1	220000	<10

3.5. Stoichiometry of the two subunits

Amino acid contents of the hydrolyzate of cpl were determined quantitatively in terms of P700. The results were compared with the amino acid compositions of the large subunits, which were calculated by using the known sequences of the psaA and psaB genes of spinach chloroplast DNA(2). The result was consistent with an assumption that the ratio of the subunit A:aubunit B: P700 is 1:1:1.

3.6. A tentative model of Photosystem 1 reaction center

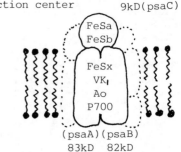

The results of cysteine content analysis of both ps1 and cp1 indicated that the 9kD subunit, which contains 9 Cys residues per mole, only one per one pair of the large subunits, which altogether contains 6 cysteines. Thus, a tentative model of Photosystem 1 reaction center can be drawn as in Fig 1.

ACKNOWLEDGEMENT: the work was partly supported by a grant from Japanese Ministry of Education, Culture and Science (No. 01621503).

REFERENCES
1 Fish, E., Kück, U. and Bogorad, L. (1985) J. Biol. Chem. 260, 1413-1421
2 Kirsch, W., Seyer, P. and Herrmann, R.G. (1986) Curr. Gen. 10, 843-855
3 Hayashida, N., Matsubayashi, T., Shinozaki, K., Sugiura, M., Inoue, K. and Hiyama, T. (1987) Curr. Gen. 12, 247-250
4 Høj, P.B., Svendsen, I., Scheller, H.V., Møller, B.L. (1987) J. Biol. Chem. 262, 12676-12684
5 Oh-oka, H., Takahashi, Y., Wada, K., Matsubara, H., Ohyama, K. and Ozeki, H. (1987) FEBS Lett. 218, 52-54
6 Oh-oka, H., Takahashi, Y., Kuriyama, K., Saeki, K. and Matsubara, H. (1988) J. Biochem., 103, 962-968
7 Oh-oka, H., Takahashi, Y., Matsubara, H. and Itoh, S. (1988)   FEBS Lett. 234, 291-294
8 Wynn, R.M. and Malkin, R. (1988) FEBS Lett. 229, 293-297
9 Golbeck, J.H., Mehari, T., Parrett, K. and Ikegami, I (1988)   FEBS Lett. 240, 9-14
10 Hiyama, T., Katoh, A., Shimizu, T., Inoue, K. and Kubo, A. (1987) in Progress in Photosynthesis Research (ed. J. Biggins) Vol II, pp.45-48 Martinus Nijhoff, Dordrecht
11 Parrett, K.G., Mehari, T., Warren, P.G. and Golbeck, J.H. (1989) Biochim. Biophys. Acta 973, 324-332
12 Hiyama, T. and Ke, B. (1972) Biochim. Biophys. Acta 267, 160-170
13 Saito, M., Horiguchi, D. and Kina, K. (1981) Bunsekikagaku(Japan), 30 635-639
14 Høj, P.B. and Møller, B.L. (1987) Anal. Biochem. 164, 307-314
15 Bradford, M.M. (1976) Anal. Biochem. 72, 248-254
16 Hiyama, T. and Ke, B. (1971) Arch. Biochem. Biophys. 147, 99-102
17 Hiyama, T. and Fork, D.C. (1980) Arch. Biochem. Biophys. 199, 488-496

ISOLATION AND CHARACTERIZATION OF cDNA CLONES ENCODING FIVE SUBUNITS OF PHOTOSYSTEM I FROM THE GREEN ALGA <u>CHLAMYDOMONAS REINHARDTII</u>

Lars-Gunnar Franzén[1], Gerhard Frank[2], Herbert Zuber[2]
and Jean-David Rochaix[1]
[1]Département de Biologie Moléculaire, Université de Genève, 30 quai
Ernest-Ansermet, 1211 Genève 4, and [2]Institut für Molekularbiologie
und Biophysik, ETH-Hönggerberg, CH-8093 Zürich, Switzerland

INTRODUCTION
The Photosystem I (PS I) reaction-centre is a multisubunit complex
consisting of two large subunits (80-85 kDa) and several smaller
subunits (3-25 kDa). The two large subunits which bind the reaction-
centre pigments and an 8-9 kDa iron-sulphur protein are encoded by
the chloroplast genome while the other subunits appear to be nuclear-
encoded. In the unicellular green alga Chlamydomonas reinhardtii six
nuclear-encoded subunits of PS I have been identified [1]: the C.
reinhardtii thylakoid polypeptides number 20, 21, 28, 30, 35 and 37
(apparent molecular masses in SDS-PAGE 18, 18, 13, 11, 5 and 3 kDa,
respectively). Here we present the analysis of cDNA clones encoding
polypeptides 21, 28, 30, 35 and 37 (P21, P28, P30, P35 and P37,
respectively). The nucleotide sequences will appear in the EMBL,
GenBank and DDBJ Databases under the accession numbers X13495 (P21),
X15164 (P28), X13496 (P30), X15165 (P35) and X15166 (P37).

MATERIALS AND METHODS
PS I-enriched preparations [1] were isolated from thylakoids of the
PS II-deficient mutant FUD7. The PS I subunits were isolated from the
PS I preparation by preparative SDS-PAGE and their N-terminal amino-
acid sequences were determined. Oligonucleotides corresponding to the
protein sequences were used to screen lambda gt10 and gt11 cDNA
libraries. In this way cDNA clones encoding polypeptides 21, 28, 30,
35 and 37 were isolated. DNA sequencing and Southern and Northern
analysis were as described in [2].

RESULTS AND DISCUSSION
The nucleotide sequences of the cDNA clones have been presented in
[2] and [3]. Figure 1 shows the deduced amino acid sequences of the
precursor polypeptides of polypeptides 21, 28, 30, 35 and 37. Except
for P30 all of the proteins contain hydrophobic domains (underlined
in figure 1). Various algoritms [4-6] were applied to estimate if
these segments span the membrane. The most C-terminal domain in P37
was consistently identified as a membrane-spanning helix by all the
algoritms used while the hydrophobicity of the other domains
indicated in figure 1 may be to low to anchor the proteins in the

M. Baltscheffsky (ed.), Current Research in Photosynthesis, Vol. II, 591–594.
© 1990 *Kluwer Academic Publishers. Printed in the Netherlands.*

P21 MALTMRNPAV KASSRVAPSS RRALRVACQA QKNETASKVG TALAASALAA AVSLSAPSAA
     MA * DIAGL TPCSESKAYA KLEKKELKTL EKRLKQYEAD SAPAVALKAT MERTKARFAN
     YAKAGLLCGN DGLPHLIADP GLALKYGHAG EVFIPTFGFL YVAGYIGYVG RQYLIAVKGE
     AKPTDKEIII DVPLATKLAW QGAGWPLAAV QELQRGTLLE KEENITVSPR

P28 MALVARPVLS ARVAASRPRV AARKAVRVSA * KYGENSR YFDLQDMENT TGSWDMYGVD
     EKKRYPDNQA KFFTQATDII SRRESLRALV ALSGIAAIVT YGLKGAKDAD LPITKGPQTT
     GENGKGGSVR SRL

P30 MQALSSRVNI AAKPQRAQRL VVRA * EEV KAAPKKEVGP KRGSLVKILR PESYWFNQVG
     KVVSVDQSGV RYPVVVRFEN QNYAGVTTNN YALDEVVAAK

P35 MQTLASRPSL RASARVAPRR APRVAVVTKA * ALDPQIV ISGSTAAFLA IGRFVFLGYQ
     RREANFDSTV GPKTTGATYF DDLQKNSTIF ATNDPAGFNI IDVAGWGALG HAVGFAVLAI
     NSLQGANLS

P37 MQALATRPSA IRPTKAARRS SVVVRA * D GFIGSSTNLI MVASTTATLA AARFGLAPTV
     KKNTTAGLKL VDSKNSAGVI SNDPAGFTIV DVLAMGAAGH GLGVGIVLGL KGIGAL

FIGURE 1. Precursor polypeptides of PS I subunits from C.
reinhardtii. The protein sequences have been deduced from cDNA
sequences. The processing sites between transit peptides and
mature proteins (*) were determined by comparing the open reading
frames of cDNAs with the N-terminal sequences of the mature
proteins. Hydrophobic domains are underlined.

membrane. Therefore, we suggest that P37 is an intrinsic membrane
protein and that P21, P28, P30 and P35 are extrinsic membrane
proteins. The properties of the proteins are summarized in Table 1.

The transit sequences (Fig. 1) share features shown by other transit
peptides of chloroplast proteins. C. reinhardtii chloroplast transit
peptides [3] are generally shorter and contain fewer hydroxylated
amino acids than the corresponding transit peptides of higher plant
proteins (e.g. [7]). The most striking feature of the transit
peptides is the presence of several positively charged amino acids.
The transit peptide of P21 is much longer than the transit peptides
of P28, P30, P35 and P37. It resembles transit peptides of proteins
found in the thylakoid lumen (e.g. [7]). Lumen-targetting transit
peptides consist of two domains. The N-terminal part is similar to
the complete transit peptides of stromal proteins. The C-terminal
part is hydrophobic and is probably involved in routing the protein

TABLE 1. Properties of nuclear-encoded Photosystem I subunits of Chlamydomonas reinhardtii[a]

	P21	P28	P30	P35	P37
Number of amino acids					
- mature protein	165	100	73	96	87
- transit peptide	62	30	24	30	26
Molecular mass					
- from SDS-PAGE[b]	18	13	11	5	3
- from sequence	17.9	11.0	8.1	10.0	8.4
Theoretical isoelectric point	9.1	9.5	9.9	4.5	10.3
Polarity index[c]	39	51	45	38	33
Possible location in the membrane[d]	lumen	stroma	stroma	stroma	int.
Corresponding PS I subunit from spinach[e]	IV	?	III	V	?

[a]The analysis is restricted to the properties of the mature proteins (except for "number of amino acids/transit peptide")
[b]Determined in the SDS-urea electrophoresis system described in [8]
[c]Polarity index = D+N+E+Q+K+R+S+T+H/total amino acids, mol % [9]
[d]lumenal side / stromal side / intrinsic membrane protein
[e]Nomenclature according to [10] and [11].

through the thylakoid membrane. Thus P21 may be an extrinsic subunit located on the lumenal side of the thylakoid membrane while P28, P30 and P35 may be located on the stromal side of the membrane.

Table 1 also shows the correspondence between PS I subunits from C. reinhardtii (this work) and spinach [10,11]. P21/subunit IV appears to be the only subunit that is located on the lumenal side of the thylakoid membrane. Possibly, it is identical to the "19 kDa subunit" [12] that binds plastocyanin. However, "subunit III" [13] seems to be involved in the electron transfer from plastocyanin to P700. It is possible that the sequenced subunit IV [10] corresponds to subunit III in [13] and that the the sequenced subunit III [11] corresponds to subunit IV in [13]; the identities of subunits III and IV of higher plants are easily confused as the positions of these proteins on SDS gels interchange depending on the buffer system used (discussed in [3]).

Fragments of the cDNAs were ^{32}P-labelled and used to probe Southern and northern blots (data not shown). In the Southern blot analysis, the cDNA probes hybridized with only one genomic DNA fragment for most of the restriction enzymes used, indicating that the proteins are encoded by single copy genes. The northern blot analysis showed that the genes are transcribed to mRNAs of 1400 (P21), 960 (P28), 740 (P30), 1120 (P35) and 790 (P37) nucleotides, respectively.

ACKNOWLEDGEMENTS
This work was supported by grant 3.328-086 from the Swiss National Foundation. LGF was supported by a Long-Term Fellowship from the European Molecular Biology Organization.

REFERENCES
1. Girard, J., Chua, N.H., Bennoun. .P, Schmidt, G. and Delosme, M. (1980) Curr. Genet. 2, 215-221
2. Franzén, L.-G., Frank, G., Zuber, H. and Rochaix J.-D. (1989) Plant. Mol. Biol. 12, 463-474
3. Franzén, L.-G., Frank, G., Zuber, H. and Rochaix J.-D. (1989) Mol. Gen. Genet. in press
4. Eisenberg, D., Schwarz, E., Komaromy, M. and Wall, R. (1984) J. Mol. Biol. 179, 125-142
5. Klein, P., Kanehisa, M. and DeLisi C. (1985) Biochim. Biophys. Acta 815, 468-476
6. Rao, J.K.M. and Argos, P. (1986) Biochim. Biophys. Acta 869, 197-214
7. von Heijne, G., Steppuhn, J. and Herrmann, R.G. (1989) Eur. J. Biochem. 180, 535-545
8. Piccioni, R.G., Bennoun, P. and Chua, N.-H. (1981) Eur. J. Biochem. 117, 93-102
9. Capaldi R.A. and Vanderkooi, G. (1972) Proc. Natl. Acad. Sci. USA 69, 930-932
10. Steppuhn, J., Hermans, J., Nechushtai, R., Ljungberg, U., Thümmler, F., Lottspeich, F. and Herrmann, R.G. (1988) FEBS Lett. 237, 218-224
11. Münch, S., Ljungberg, U., Steppuhn, J., Schneiderbauer, A., Nechushtai, R., Beyreuther, K. and Herrmann, R.G. (1988) Curr. Genet. 14, 511-518
12. Wynn, R.M. and Malkin, R. (1988) Biochemistry 27, 5863-5869
13. Bengis, C. and Nelson, N. (1977) J. Biol. Chem. 252, 4564-4569

VARIATIONS OF THE DIFFERENTIAL EXTINCTION COEFFICIENT OF P-700 AND RE-ESTIMATION OF STOICHIOMETRY OF CONSTITUENTS IN PHOTOSYSTEM I REACTION CENTER COMPLEXES FROM SYNECHOCOCCUS ELONGATUS

KINTAKE SONOIKE[*] and SAKAE KATOH
DEPARTMENT OF BIOLOGY, FACULTY OF SCIENCE, UNIVERSITY OF TOKYO, HONGO, BUNKYO-KU TOKYO 113, JAPAN

1. INTRODUCTION

Photosystem I (PS I) reaction center complex consists of two large subunits which carry antenna chlorophyll a, P-700 and early electron acceptors and several small subunits, one of which contains the iron-sulfur centers, F_A and F_B. Because the PS I complexes are usually isolated with detergents, careful evaluation of detergent-effects, such as solubilization of chlorophyll a, or inactivation of P-700, is essential for determination of stoichiometry of subunit polypeptides and functional constituents in the complex. Recently, we have shown that the differential extinction coefficient of P-700 is markedly affected by sodium dodecyl sulfate (SDS) which induces a band-shift of chlorophyll a molecules at 690 nm [1]. Herein, we report effects of other detergents on the extinction coefficient of P-700 and provide a simple method to estimate the extinction coefficient in PS I preparations treated with various detergents. Using the extinction values thus determined, stoichiometry of chlorophyll a and the two large subunits in PS I reaction center complexes were estimated.

2. MATERIALS AND METHODS

The thylakoid membranes and PS I preparations from the thermophilic cyanobacterium Synechococcus elongatus Nägeli (clonal strain BP-1) were used [2,3,4]. Digitonin PS I preparation (F3) was prepared as described by Nakayama et al. [5] and further purified by gel electrophoresis with the discontinuous buffer system of Davis [6]. PS I reaction center complexes, CP1-a and -e, were prepared by SDS gel electrophoresis as described by Takahashi et al. [2]. PS I particles were also prepared with Triton X-100 [7].

The reduced-minus-oxidized differential extinction coefficient of P-700 at the peak wavelength of the 700 nm band was determined by measuring oxidation of TMPD coupled with reduction of flash-oxidized P-700 according to the method of Hiyama and Ke [1,6]. Polypeptide compositions of PS I complexes were analyzed by SDS polyacrylamide gel

----

*Present address: SOLAR ENERGY RESEARCH GROUP, THE INSTITUTE OF PHYSICAL AND CHEMICAL RESEARCH (RIKEN), WAKO, SAITAMA 351-01, JAPAN

M. Baltscheffsky (ed.), Current Research in Photosynthesis, Vol. II, 595–598.
© 1990 *Kluwer Academic Publishers. Printed in the Netherlands.*

electrophoresis according to Laemmli [8].   Protein was determined by measuring total amino acid contents of PS I complexes with L-α-amino-β-guanidinopropionic acid as an internal standard.   For uniform labeling of cells with ^{14}C, <u>Synechococcus</u> were photosynthetically grown in a closed system with 20 or 30 mM ^{14}C-NaHCO$_3$ (0.3 or 0.5 Ci/M) as a sole carbon source.

3. RESULTS AND DISCUSSION

We have shown previously that SDS (plus methyl viologen) induces a bleaching at 695 nm and a positive band at 685 nm, in the difference spectrum of P-700 [1].   Spectral changes were ascribed to a band shift of chlorophyll <u>a</u> molecules maximally absorbing at 690 nm.   Similar changes were also induced by Triton X-100 (Fig. 1).   Experiments with various detergents and under different conditions showed that,

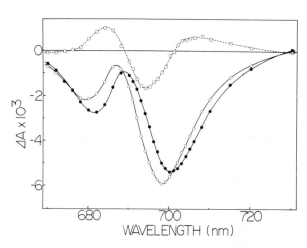

Figure 1   Effects of Triton X-100 on the difference spectrum for flash-induced absorption changes in thylakoid membranes. $\bullet$; untreated membranes. $\circ$; membranes treated with 0.25% Triton X-100 for 90 min at room temperature.   The difference between the two spectra is shown by open squares.

irrespective of the detergent used, variations of the differential extinction coefficient are well related to the bands shift of the 690 nm chlorophyll <u>a</u>.   The band shift also affected the two bleaching bands at 680 nm and 700 nm of the P-700 difference spectrum in opposite directions.   In Fig. 2, the differential extinction coefficients determined in detergent-treated preparations are plotted against the ratio of the 680 nm to 700 nm bands.   It is seen that the differential extinction coefficient of P-700 varies from 52 to 87 mM^{-1}cm^{-1} with the 680 nm/700 nm ratios and, in particular, the value steeply increases as the ratio decreases from 0.5 to 0.3.   Thus, Fig. 2 provides a simple mean to estimate the apparent differential extinction coefficient of P-700 from the 680 nm/700 nm ratios.   The extinction value determined by this method gives a much better approximation of P-700 contents in PS I preparations with the 680 nm/700 nm ratios below 0.5 as compared with the extinction coefficients in the literature.   Another advantage of the method is that the 680 nm/700 nm ratio and, hence, the extinction coefficient of P-700, is readily determined with a conventional spectrophotometer with a cross-illumination system.

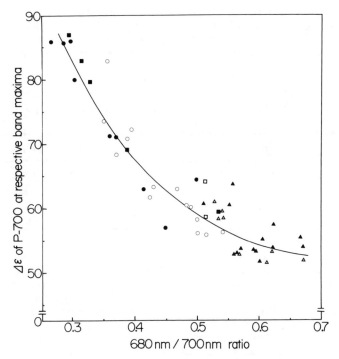

Figure 2   Relationship between the differential extinction coefficients of P-700 and ratio of magnitudes of the 680 nm band and 700 nm band. o; Triton-PS I preparations in the presence of varied concentrations of Triton X-100.   •; thylakoid membranes treated with 0.1% SDS for 1 h plus various concentrations of methyl viologen.   ■; digitonin particles treated various concentrations (0-0.1%) of SDS for 1 h plus 4 mM methyl viologen.   □; untreated thylakoid membranes.   ▲; digitonin particles. △; digitonin particles treated with 0.5 and 1% octyl-D-glucoside for 1 h.

Using the revised differential extinction values of P-700, we have determined the antenna size of PS I.   SDS and Triton X-100 liberated significant amounts of chlorophyll a from PS I complex and more or less inactivated P-700.   However, highly purified PS I reaction center complexes could be isolated with digitonin without solubilization of chlorophyll, nor inactivation of P-700.   Thus, digitonin-PS I complexes enabled us to estimate the in situ antenna size of the PS I complex. Table I compares chlorophyll/P-700 ratios of the thylakoid membranes and several PS I preparations, which were obtained with the differential extinction coefficients of P-700 determined for respective preparations. The chlorophyll/P-700 ratio of purified digitonin PS I complexes was 94. Larger values found in the thylakoid membranes and a crude digitonin preparation (F3) are ascribed to chlorophyll associated with PS II reaction center complexes because the cyanobacterium lacks light-harvesting chlorophyll protein complexes.   Because PS II reaction center have 48 chlorophyll $\underline{a}/Q_A$ [9], the PS I to PS II ratio is estimated to be 1:0.27, which agrees with the ratio of 1:0.33 estimated previously [10]. A lower chlorophyll/P-700 ratio of CP1-a, PS I complex isolated with SDS, indicates a liberation of significant amounts of chlorophyll during SDS-treatment.

Table I   Chlorophyll/P-700 Ratios of Thylakoid Membranes and PS I Preparations

Preparations	Chlorophyll/P-700
Thylakoid membranes	107
F3	104
Digitonin-PS I complex	94
CP1-a	74

Table II   Stoichiometry of the 62 and 60 kDa polypeptides in CP1-a

Polypeptides	mol/mol P-700
62 kDa	0.74 ± 0.12
60 kDa	0.76 ± 0.12

Stoichiometry and copy number of the large subunits present in PS I complexes were also determined by two different methods. The protein content of CP1-a which had been determined by measuring the total amino acid content of the complexes with L-α-amino-β-guanidinopropionic acid as an internal standard, was about 250 kDa proteins per P-700. Assuming that each one copy of the 10, 13 and 14 kDa subunits is present in the complex, the value shows that there are two or three copies of the large subunits in the PS I complexes. In the second approach, Synechococcus cells were uniformly labeled with ^{14}C and radioactivities of the subunit polypeptides separated by SDS gel electrophoresis were determined. Because samples with known P-700 contents were applied to gel, quantities of the subunits estimated from the specific activity of radioactive carbon could be related to the P-700 content. Table II shows that PS I complexes contain one copy each of the two large subunits. Thus, if chlorophyll distributes evenly between the two large subunits, one subunit carry 47 chlorophyll $\underline{a}$.

REFERENCES
1 Sonoike, K. and Katoh, S. (1988) Biochim. Biophys. Acta 935, 61-71
2 Takahashi, Y., Koike, H. and Katoh, S. (1987) Arch. Biochem. Biophys. 219, 209-218
3 Yamaoka, T., Satoh, K. and Katoh, S. (1978) Plant Cell Physiol. 19, 943-954
4 Hirano, M., Satoh, K. and Katoh, S. (1980) Photosynth. Res. 1, 149-162
5 Nakayama, K., Yamaoka, T. and Katoh, S. (1979) Plant Cell Physiol. 20, 1565-1576
6 Hiyama, T. and Ke, B (1972) Biochim. Biophys. Acta 267, 160-171
7 Lundell, D.J., Glazer, A.N., Melis, A. and Malkin, R. (1985) J. Biol. Chem. 260, 646-654
8 Laemmli, U.K. (1970) Nature (London) 227, 680-685
9 Satoh, K., Ohno, T. and Katoh, S. (1985) FEBS Lett. 180, 326-330
10 Aoki, M., Hirano, M., Takahashi, Y. and Katoh, S. (1983) 24, 517-525

CHARACTERIZATION OF P700 BY FTIR DIFFERENCE SPECTROSCOPY

E. NABEDRYK[1], M. LEONHARD[2], W. MÄNTELE[2] and J. BRETON[1]

[1] Service de Biophysique, CEN Saclay, Gif-sur-Yvette cedex, France
[2] Institut für Biophysik und Strahlenbiologie der Universität Freiburg, D-7800 Freiburg, FRG

INTRODUCTION

The primary photochemical act in photosynthesis leads to the generation of the radical cation of a specialized chlorophyll (Chl) or bacteriochlorophyll (BChl) species. For purple bacteria, the primary electron donor is a pair of BChl whose molecular structure has been extensively investigated by various spectroscopic techniques and recently elucidated by X-ray cristallography of the bacterial reaction center. In the absence of high-resolution X-ray data for green plant PS I and PS II, proposals for the structure and bonding interactions of their primary donor rely only on spectroscopy. In particular, the primary donor of PS I, P700, is probably a Chl a dimer, although several spectroscopic studies suggest that the positive charge in the $P700^+$ radical cation is localized on only one of the two Chl molecules that comprise P700 (1-3). Model studies also incorporate a possible keto-enol tautomerization of Chl a upon P700 photooxidation (4,5).

In previous work, we have shown that the nature of the bonding interactions of the primary reactants in purple bacteria and green plant photosynthesis can be investigated by Fourier transform infrared (FTIR) difference spectroscopy (6-10). In particular, the specific molecular changes associated with the photooxidation of P700 have been investigated by light-induced FTIR spectroscopy on particles enriched in PS I (8). Highly-resolved FTIR difference spectra were obtained for these particles, showing features identical to those obtained for intact thylakoids. The most characteristic differential signals were observed in the carbonyl stretching frequency region (1620-1760 cm^{-1}). However, in the absence of IR model compound studies and especially of the in vitro Chl a cation IR spectrum, the assignments proposed for the differential IR bands observed in the $P700^+/P700$ spectrum were only tentative. In particular, the frequency of the 9 keto C=O in $P700^+$ could not be unambiguously determined (8).

In order to assign and to interpret the features observed on the light-induced spectra of the photooxidation of P700, the IR spectra of isolated chlorophylls in both their neutral and ionized states have been investigated. The cation radicals of the chlorophylls, including that of pyroderivatives (lacking the 10a ester carbonyl), were generated electrochemically in a special cell suited for the visible and IR spectral regions (11). Comparison of the light-induced FTIR difference spectra associated with the photooxidation of P700 in vivo with difference FTIR spectra of the Chl a cation formation in vitro, now leads to the assignment of the frequencies of the 9 keto carbonyl in P700 and $P700^+$.

M. Baltscheffsky (ed.), Current Research in Photosynthesis, Vol. II, 599–606.
© 1990 *Kluwer Academic Publishers. Printed in the Netherlands.*

MATERIALS AND METHODS

Suspensions of thylakoids from the cyanobacteria *Spirulina geitleri* were deposited on CaF_2 windows and air–dried. Films were covered with a 5 mM, pH 7.0 Tris buffer (containing 10 mM Na ascorbate) and sealed with another CaF_2 window, constituting microcells ($\approx$10 μm optical pathlength) which were thermostatically controlled. Light–minus–dark FTIR spectra of these films, as well as the corresponding P700 absorbance changes controls in the visible spectral range were obtained as previously described (8).

Chl a was isolated from spinach and BChl a was prepared from *Rhodospirillum rubrum*. Pyro(B)Chl a were obtained by adapting a relatively mild pyrolysis method first described by Pennington et al., (12) for Chl a. The pigments were purified using HPLC (13). Solutions of chlorophylls (1–2 mM) were prepared in deuterated solvents (tetrahydrofuran, dichloromethane, methanol). The techniques used for solvent drying, for purification of the supporting electrolyte (tetrabutylammonium hexafluorophosphate) and for electrochemistry (including cyclic voltammetry, controlled potential electrolysis and coulometry), have been described in (11 and references therein). Using a transparent thin layer electrochemical cell (11), visible and IR spectra were recorded before and after cation formation.

RESULTS AND DISCUSSION

A spectrum of Chl a in deuterated tetrahydrofuran (THF), recorded in the visible spectral range using the spectroelectrochemical cell, is shown in Fig. 1 (inset), together with the spectrum obtained after several minutes of electrolysis at U = +0.8 V. At this potential the π monocation radical is generated (14). The spectrum of the Chl a cation formation shows a decrease of the main absorbance band at 665 nm (Q_y transition of the neutral Chl a) and a slight increase of absorbance in the near–IR at $\approx$ 820 nm which has been assigned to the Q_y transition of the cation. Furthermore, changes in the other spectral regions are observed. This spectrum of Chl a$^+$ is in good agreement with the ones reported in (14,5). The reaction is reversible at U = –0.5 V, with a yield of at least 90%.

The corresponding IR absorption spectra of the neutral and radical cation of Chl a in THF are shown in Fig. 1. The solvent and electrolyte bands have been subtracted using a blank spectrum taken in the same cell. The IR difference spectrum (Chl a$^+$–minus–Chl a), hereafter referred as Chl a$^+$/Chl a spectrum, is shown in Fig. 2a. Positive bands in this spectrum arise from the Chl a cation radical while the disappearing bands of the neutral Chl a are negative. The two bands at 1695 cm^{-1} and 1737 cm^{-1} in the IR spectrum of neutral Chl a (Fig. 1) have been assigned to the C=O vibration of the 9 keto and ester groups (in this solvent, the two ester carbonyls at the 7c and 10a cannot be distinguished), respectively. The frequencies are characteristic of non–interacting C=O groups as expected for a non–hydrogen bonding solvent and unaggregated pigments. Chl a cation formation results in a number of IR spectral changes, especially in the C=O frequency region (Fig. 1). The 1737–cm^{-1} ester C=O band shows a significant decrease of its absorption while a shoulder on its high frequency side appears. This change is reflected by the differential signal at 1751/1738 cm^{-1} in the Chl a$^+$/Chl a spectrum (Fig. 2a). In addition, the 9 keto C=O band at 1695 cm^{-1} disappears and a new band appears at 1719 cm^{-1} (Fig. 1), giving rise to the differential signal at 1718/1693 cm^{-1} in the Chl a$^+$/Chl a spectrum (Fig. 2a).

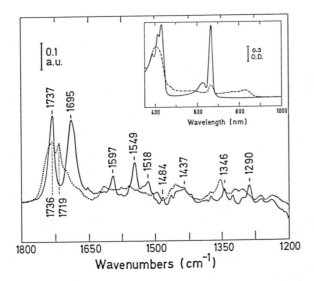

FIGURE 1 : FTIR absorbance spectra of the neutral Chl a in THF in the electrochemical cell (250 μm optical pathlength), before electrolysis (full line) and after cation formation at U = +0.8V (dashed line). T = 295K, 4-cm⁻¹ resolution. Inset: corresponding spectra in the visible spectral range.

The differential signal at 1751/1738 cm^{-1} (Fig. 2a) can be assigned in principle to either one or both of the 7c or 10a ester C=O groups. For bonds not directly involved in conjugation such as these ester C=O groups, only inductive coulombic effects from the π–electron system are expected (10). Comparing the distance of these groups to the conjugated system, the 10a ester should be predominantly affected. An almost identical feature at 1750/1737 cm^{-1} is also observed in the IR difference spectrum of the BChl a cation formation in THF (Fig. 2b) but does not appear in the pyroderivatives of BChl a (Fig. 2c) and Chl a (M. Leonhard & al., these proceedings). In pyrochlorophylls, the carbomethoxy group at C–10 is replaced by a hydrogen atom. Our data thus demonstrate that the IR absorption of the 7c ester C=O is essentially unperturbed upon chlorophyll cation formation (see also M. Leonhard et al., these proceedings). Therefore, the 1750–/1737–cm^{-1} signal in the BChl a$^+$/BChl a spectrum as well as the 1751/1738 cm^{-1} signal in the Chl a$^+$/Chl a spectrum are attributed to a shift of the only 10a ester C=O vibration after (B)Chl a cation formation. When the Chl a cation is generated in dichloromethane or in methanol, a comparable shift at 1749/1735 cm^{-1} or at 1750/1739 cm^{-1}, respectively, is observed (15). Furthermore, the large differential signal at 1718/1693 cm^{-1} in the Chl a$^+$/Chl a spectrum (Fig. 2a) is closely analogous to the ones observed at 1716/1684 cm^{-1} for BChl a$^+$/BChl a (Fig. 2b), at 1710/1679 cm^{-1} for pyroBChl a$^+$/pyroBChl a (Fig. 2c), and at 1712/1686 cm^{-1} for pyroChla$^+$/pyroChl a (M. Leonhard & al., these proceedings), respectively. The absorption change detected at 1659 cm^{-1} (1656 cm^{-1}) upon BChl a (pyroBChl a) cation formation is assigned to the 2a acetyl C=O group. For pyroderivatives, the absence of the 10a ester C=O allows the positive band at 1710 cm^{-1} in pyroBChl a$^+$/pyroBChl a and at 1712 cm^{-1} in pyroChl a$^+$/pyroChl a to be unambiguously identified to the keto C=O of the cation radical.

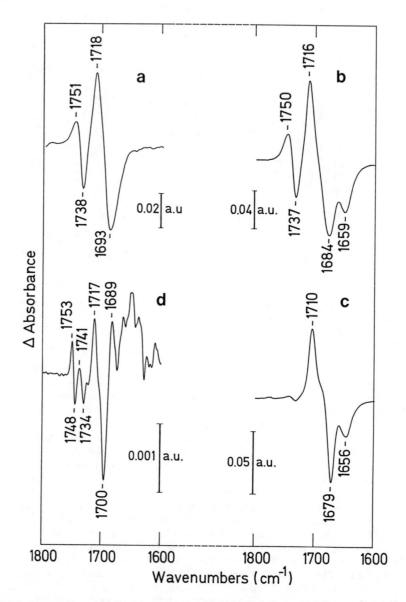

FIGURE 2 : Redox–induced FTIR difference spectra of chlorophyll cation formation in THF. a) Chl a^+–minus–Chl a at U = +0.8V; b) BChl a^+–minus–BChl a at U = +0.5V; c) pyroBChl a^+–minus–pyroBChl a at U = +0.8V; 64 interferograms co–added; d) Light–induced FTIR difference spectrum of P700 photooxidation (P700$^+$–minus–P700) in thylakoids from *Spirulina geitleri* (excitation wavelength 665 nm–1000 nm); 512 interferograms co–added. T = 295K, 4–cm^{-1} resolution.

Thus, we assign the corresponding positive band at 1718 cm^{-1} in the Chl a$^+$/Chl a spectrum (Fig. 2a) to the 9 keto C=O vibration of the Chl a radical cation. When the Chl a cation is generated in dichloromethane or in methanol, a large differential signal at 1720/1689 cm^{-1} or at 1720/1683 cm^{-1}, respectively, is observed for the 9 keto C=O (15).

Light–minus–dark FTIR spectra of the photooxidation of P700 (referred as P700$^+$/P700 spectra) obtained from hydrated films of thylakoids of *Spirulina geitleri* (Fig. 2d) are nearly identical to the ones previously reported for pea and spinach thylakoids and for PS I particles obtained from green plants and cyanobacteria at both room temperature (8,16) and low temperature (E.N., C. Berthomieu & J.B., unpublished). The largest FTIR differential signals (especially the pronounced negative signal at 1700 cm^{-1}) are observed in the C=O stretching frequency region (1620–1760 cm^{-1}) where contributions from protein, chlorophyll and lipid carbonyls as well as the OH bending vibration of water might also arise. A 44– ± 1–cm^{-1} frequency downshift upon ^{13}C substitution together with an absence of shift (± 1 cm^{-1}) upon ^{15}N substitution have been reported for all the bands in the 1620– to 1760–cm^{-1} region in both P700$^+$/P700 spectra and Chl a$^+$/Chl a spectra obtained with thylakoids and pigments extracted from cyanobacteria fed with these isotopes (15,16). This observation unambiguously demonstrates that the 1700–cm^{-1} signal of P700 is indeed a pure C=O mode. It is well–established that peptide C=O bonds absorb in the 1620– to 1690–cm^{-1} IR domain (the so–called amide I absorption band), depending on the peptide backbone conformation and a band around 1735 cm^{-1} with a higher and lower frequency component at 1744 cm^{-1} and 1716 cm^{-1}, respectively, has been shown to be associated with the two ester C=O stretching vibrations of the lipids head groups. On the other hand, the 9 keto carbonyl of chlorophylls *in vitro* covers the 1715– to 1650–cm^{-1} frequency range. Thus, the frequency (1700 cm^{-1}) of the C=O group which disappears upon P700$^+$ formation lies within the range of vibration of the 9 keto C=O group of Chl a but is outside the usual frequency range of both peptide C=O bonds and ester carbonyls from lipids and chlorophylls. The direct involvement of the 9 keto C=O of Chl a in the 1700–cm^{-1} signal appears therefore as a likely possibility. This hypothesis is further substantiated by the striking similarities found between the *in vivo* and *in vitro* data upon comparison of the P700$^+$/P700 and Chl a$^+$/Chl a spectra (Fig. 2). In particular, the large differential signal at 1717/1700 cm^{-1} in the P700$^+$/P700 spectrum (Fig. 2d) bears a close analogy with the differential signal observed at 1718/1693 cm^{-1} in the Chl a$^+$/Chl a spectrum (Fig. 2a). This striking similarity actually appears to be a general observation when comparing the light–induced difference FTIR spectra and the relevant redox difference spectra corresponding to the photooxidation (photoreduction) of a number of primary electron donors (acceptors) in both purple bacteria and PS II reaction centers (6–10,16–18). The negative component of the largest differential signal is always observed in the 1710– to 1675–cm^{-1} region and thus has been assigned to the 9 keto C=O group of the pigments in their neutral state. This group is upshifted by ≈ 30 cm^{-1} upon cation formation of the bacteriochlorophylls both *in vivo* and in THF while it is downshifted upon generation of the (bacterio)pheophytin anion. It therefore appears that the generation of chlorophyll radicals both *in vitro* and *in vivo* always leads to the detection of a large signal in the 9 keto C=O stretching region. Such large signals are not limited to free keto groups as the study of the BChl a cation generated in methanol indicates that, even when extensive hydrogen–bonding of carbonyls induces a considerable downshift in frequency of the 9 keto C=O of the neutral species, a large differential signal at 1721/1652 cm^{-1} is observed upon cation formation (10). Taking into account these IR data both *in vivo* and *in vitro*, the observations that the largest differential signal in the P700$^+$/P700 spectrum is at 1717/1700 cm^{-1}, and the fact that it is well–established that photooxidation of P700 generates a Chl a cation, we thus favor the assignment of the 1717–/1700–cm^{-1} signal observed in the P700$^+$/P700 spectrum to a frequency upshift upon primary donor photooxidation of the 9 keto C=O group(s) of the Chl a molecule(s) constituting P700. It therefore appears that the 9 keto C=O group(s) of P700 absorbing at 1700 cm^{-1} is (are) free of interaction in the neutral state of the primary donor, and upshifted to 1717 cm^{-1} in P700$^+$.

As discussed above, the high frequency region of the Chl a$^+$/Chl a spectrum is understood in terms of a shift of the 10a ester C=O from 1738 to 1751 cm^{-1}, with essentially no participation of the 7c ester. In contrast, two differential signals are present in the P700$^+$/P700 spectra at 1753/1748 cm^{-1} and 1741/1734 cm^{-1} (Fig. 2d). Both signals might have several origins. A reasonable hypothesis for the signal at 1741/1734 cm^{-1} is that it corresponds to the 10a ester C=O of the Chl molecule(s) constituting P700. Compared to the negative 1738–cm^{-1} signal detected in the Chl a$^+$/Chl a spectrum (Fig. 2a), the negative 1734–cm^{-1} signal in the P700$^+$/P700 spectrum might be assigned to a weakly interacting 10a ester C=O in the neutral state of P700. A less likely hypothesis for this signal is the involvement of the 7c ester C=O provided it is bound to the protein in the neutral P700 state and this bonding is affected by charge separation. In this respect, it can be noticed that in the latest X–ray analysis of the bacterial reaction center from *Rbodobacter sphaeroides*, the only hydrogen bond involving the BChl a special pair is a propionic 7c ester which is located at a suitable distance to interact with a Tyr aminoacid residue (19).

The presence of a higher frequency signal at 1753/1748 cm^{-1} in the P700$^+$/P700 spectrum can be interpreted in terms of a free 10a ester C=0 absorbing at 1748 cm^{-1} in the neutral state of P700 (the frequency of this signal is too high to involve a 7c ester C=O bound to the protein). The observed shift for the 10a ester C=O from 1738 cm^{-1} *in vitro* to 1748 cm^{-1} *in vivo* is comparable to the one found for the free 9 keto C=O (1693 cm^{-1} *in vitro* to 1700 cm^{-1} *in vivo*). Such an upshift by 7 to 10 cm^{-1} of the 9 keto and 10a ester groups *in vivo* compared to Chl a in THF can be rationalized in terms of the difference in dielectric constant and/or local environment effects.

Finally, the 1753–/1748–cm^{-1} and 1741–/1734–cm^{-1} signals (Fig. 2d) might also reflect the perturbation of side chain groups from the protein as possible contributions from aminoacid (Asp or Glu) carboxylic C=O groups are expected in the 1760– to 1700–cm^{-1} frequency region. However, the observed sharp differential signals exclude that carboxyl groups undergo protonation changes which would shift the bands to lower frequency ($\approx$ 1560 cm^{-1}). We have not observed any deuterium isotopic effect on the signals in the 1760– to 1600–cm^{-1} frequency region when photooxidation of P700 was performed on films of thylakoids covered with ^{2}H$_2$O buffer (15). This suggests that no carboxylic groups contribute to the spectrum, although it cannot definitely be excluded that the 1753–/1748–cm^{-1} and/or 1741–/1734–cm^{-1} signals might arise from the perturbation of the environment of a side chain carboxylic group deeply buried in the protein, with no accessibility to deuterium exchange. The assignment of the differential signals at 1753/1748 cm^{-1} and at 1741/1734 cm^{-1} (Fig. 2d) is thus still not definitive. However, we presently favor the hypothesis that both of these signals originate from 10a ester carbonyls, an assignment which would support a dimeric model for P700 (in agreement with recent resonance Raman data (RR) on P700, see ref. 20) and suggest that the large 1717–/1700–cm^{-1} signal involves the keto group(s) of either a symmetric dimer or an asymmetric dimer of Chl a with the decreased charge density localized on only one of the two Chl a molecules.

The participation of enol forms of chlorophylls in primary reactions of photosynthesis is still debated. On the basis of redox potential measurements and ENDOR spectroscopy of Chl a enol models, Wasielewski et al.,(4) favored an oxidized Chl a enol form at the C–9 of ring V for P700$^+$. Recently, from RR spectroscopy of the neutral and electrochemically–

generated cation radical of Chl a, Heald et al., (5) also raised the possibility that oxidation of Chl a might generate the enol form of the 9 keto group, both *in vitro* and *in vivo*. In agreement with our IR data, these authors observed a loss of intensity at the 9 keto C=O absorption at $1687 \, cm^{-1}$ when Chl a (in dichloromethane) is oxidized while a new peak appears at $1717 \, cm^{-1}$. In general, the 10a ester C=O cannot be observed in RR spectra of Chl a because this bond is not in conjugation with the π-electron system and therefore there is no resonance enhancement. However, Heald et al., (5) did not attribute the large upshift from $1687 \, cm^{-1}$ to $1717 \, cm^{-1}$ observed upon Chl a cation formation to the 9 keto C=O. Instead, they identify the appearing $1717\text{-}cm^{-1}$ band in the RR spectrum of the Chl a cation to a downshifted 10a ester C=O vibration consequent to the enolization of the 9 keto C=O after oxidation of Chl a. In this scenario, the resulting formation of a double bond across C–9 and C–10 on ring V concomitant with the transfer of the hydrogen at C–10 to the 9 keto function leads to a redistribution of charge, which induces a partial conjugation of the 10a ester C=O into the macrocycle. This partial conjugation of the 10a ester C=O decreases its energy (frequency) and allows it to be detected in RR experiments. On the contrary, our FTIR data on BChl a, pyroBChl a, Chl a and pyroChl a demonstrate that upon cation formation, the 10a ester C=O of Chl a is upshifted from $1738 \, cm^{-1}$ to $1751 \, cm^{-1}$ and not downshifted to $1717 \, cm^{-1}$ as proposed by Heald et al., (5). Although, to the best of our knowledge, no experimental or theoretical data are presently available to estimate the vibrational absorption frequency of a C—O enol at C–9 in a Chl a cation, it seems justified to exclude that the $1717\text{-}cm^{-1}$ positive band in the P700[+]/P700 spectrum could arise from the enol form of the Chl a cation in P700[+].

As a conclusion, the present FTIR spectroscopy study provides a solid basis for the assignment of the vibrational frequencies of carbonyl groups in Chl a[+], P700 and P700[+]. In particular, studies of the molecular interactions *in vivo* reveal free keto C=O groups in both P700 and P700[+]. Therefore, it appears that for Chl a both *in vitro* and in P700, we find no evidence in favor of the keto/enol tautomerization consequent to cation formation.

ACKNOWLEDGEMENTS

We would like to thank G. Berger, J. KLéo and S. Andrianambinintsoa for the purification and chemical modification of the pigments, B.A. Tavitian and A. Wollenweber for their help in the initial phase of this project, R. Mermet–Bouvier for his kind gift of *Spirulina geitleri* cells grown on ^{13}C and ^{15}N media. Part of this which was funded by EEC (contract # ST2J–0118–2–D).

REFERENCES

1   **Wasielewski & al.,** (1981a) *J. Am. Chem. Soc. 103*, 7664–7665.
2   **O'Malley & Babcock** (1984) *Proc. Natl. Acad. Sci. U.S.A 81*, 1098–1101.
3   **Ikegami & Itoh** (1988) *Biochim.Biophys.Acta 934*, 39–46.
4   **Wasielewski & al.,** (1981b) *Proc. Natl. Acad. Sci. U.S.A 78*, 2957–2961.
5   **Heald & al.,** (1988) *J. Phys. Chem. 92*, 4820–4824.
6   **Mäntele & al.,** (1985) *FEBS Lett. 187*, 227–232.
7   **Nabedryk & al.,** (1986) *Photochem. Photobiol. 43*, 461–465.
8   **Tavitian & al.,** (1986) *FEBS Lett. 201*, 151–157.
9   **Nabedryk & al.,** (1987) in *Progress in Photosynthesis Research* (Biggins, J. Ed.) Nijhof/Junk, Brussels, Vol.1, pp. 177–180.
10 **Mäntele & al.,** (1988a) *Proc. Natl. Acad. Sci. U.S.A 85*, 8468–8472.

11   **Mäntele & al.,** (1988b) *Photochem. Photobiol. 47*, 451–455.
12   **Pennington & al.,** (1964) *J. Am. Chem. Soc. 86*, 1418–1426.
13   **Berger & al.,** (1987) *J. Liquid Chromatogr. 10*, 1519–1531.
14   **Davis & al.,** (1979) *Proc. Natl. Acad. Sci. U.S.A 76*, 4170–4174.
15   **Tavitian** (1987) *Thesis*, Université P. et M. Curie, Paris VI.
16   **Tavitian & al.,** (1988) in *Spectroscopy of Biological Molecules–New Advances* (Schmid, E.D., Schneider, F.W., & Siebert, F., Eds.), Wiley & Sons, pp. 297–300.
17   **Nabedryk & al.,** (1988) in *The Photosynthetic Bacterial Reaction Center : Structure and Dynamics* (Breton & Vermeglio Eds.) NATO ASI Series , Vol.149, pp. 237–250.
18   **Barillot & al.,** (1989) *Biophys. J. 55*, 180a.
19   **Yeates & al.,** (1988) *Proc. Natl. Acad. Sci. U.S.A 85*, 7993–7997.
20   **Moënne-Loccoz & al.,** (1989) in *Techniques and New Developments in Photosynthesis Research* (Barber, J. Ed.) NATO ASI Series, Plenum, New York, (in press).

MULTIPLE FUNCTIONS OF ß-CAROTENE IN PHOTOSYSTEM I

INGO DAMM, DIETER STEINMETZ and L. HORST GRIMME
Dept. of Biol./Chem., Univ. of Bremen, D-2800 Bremen, FRG

1. INTRODUCTION

It is well known, that carotenoids serve as light-harvesting pigments and protect the photosynthetic apparatus against photooxidative
damage. Within the thylakoid membranes of higher plants carotenoids
show a distinct pattern in their distribution among the antenna and
reaction centre complexes (1). This specific association of the different carotenoids is not well understood with respect to their function
in photosynthesis.

In the present study we analysed the ß-carotene content of the PS I
core complex (RC I) and the PS I antenna (LHC I). Photobleaching experiments with RC I in the same way as structural investigations of
LHC I lead to the conclusion that ß-carotene has several functions in
photosystem I to maintain the structural and functional integrity
during photosynthesis.

2. MATERIALS AND METHODS

PS I-200 from spinach was fractionated by sucrose density gradient
centrifugation by the procedure of HAWORTH et al. (2). Photobleaching
of RC I was induced by a slide projector ($660W/m^2$). Pigment analysis
by reverse-phase HPLC and mildly dissociating SDS-PAGE was performed
according to KNOETZEL et al. (3). Low temperature fluorescence spectra
were obtained from an Aminco SPF-500 spectrofluorimeter.

3. RESULTS AND DISCUSSION

In Tab. 1 the pigment composition of PS I-200, RC I and LHC I is
shown. In RC I the dominant carotenoid is ß-carotene, whereas the

TABLE 1. Pigment content of photosystem I (PS I-200), a core
preparation (RC I) and the PS I antenna (LHC I)
(mol/mol P700)

	PS I-200	RC I	LHC I*
neoxanthin	1	0	1
violaxanthin	8	1	7
lutein	12	(1)	12
chl b	27	5	23
chl a	176	72	69
ß-carotene	30	15	8
P700	1	1	-

*derived from relative pigment composition assuming
lutein being localized exclusively in LHC I

M. Baltscheffsky (ed.), Current Research in Photosynthesis, Vol. II, 607–610.
© 1990 *Kluwer Academic Publishers. Printed in the Netherlands.*

xanthophylls of PS I are located in the peripheral antenna complex.

Illumination of RC I under photobleaching conditions induces a rapid decrease of pigment content (4). After prolonged photodestruction a complex with a stable pigment composition of approximately 20 molecules chlorophyll a (chl a), 2 - 3 ß-carotene and 1 chl a' per reaction centre is found, indicating a close spatial and functional relationship between these pigments (Tab. 2).

TABLE 2. Molar pigment/P700 ratio in RC I during illumination with strong white light (660 W/m²). Chl a' : C10-epimer of chl a. (N₂) : N₂-atmosphere during illumination.

pigment	pigment/P700 ratio[a] (mol/mol)							
	illumination time (h)							
	0	2	4	7	10	13	4 (N_2)	13 (N_2)
neoxanthin	0.01	-	-	-	-	-	-	-
violaxanthin	0.86	0.46	0.43	0.46	0.94	2.39	0.60	0.92
lutein	0.83	0.49	0.48	0.42	0.77	1.90	0.63	0.41
chl b	4.77	0.62	0.31	0.19	0.06	traces	1.53	0.27
chl a	72.5	25.87	22.11	18.00	19.53	16.71	35.78	20.32
chl a'	2.15	0.74	0.85	1.01	1.54	_[b]	0.91	0.91
ß-carotene	14.99	4.79	3.22	2.09	2.85	4.61	7.45	2.92

[a] photochemical assay   [b] chl a and chl a' not separated

P700 is the most stable pigment in RC I, its photodestruction starts after 4 hours of illumination. At that time only 20 % of the initial ß-carotene is present. Photobleaching under nitrogen atmosphere gives comparable results (Tab. 2). From these data we conclude, that only 2 - 3 molecules ß-carotene in photosystem I are necessary to protect P700 very efficiently from damage due to excess of light. The other 12 molecules ß-carotene in RC I (see Tab. 1) are involved in the (less effective) protection of the chl a core antenna, as we concluded from the concomitant loss of both pigments (4).

During the preparation of RC I and LHC I from PS I-200 a considerable amount of chl a (31 molecules) and ß-carotene (7 molecules) is selectively lost as free pigments, as can be deduced from Tab. 1. This specific loss of the most lipophilic pigments of the thylakoid membranes leads to the suggestion, that these pigments are involved in the binding of the peripheral antenna to reaction centre polypeptides and allow an efficient energy transfer from the peripheral antenna to the core antenna.

Mildly dissociating SDS-PAGE of the LHC I fraction recovered from the sucrose density gradient reveals 3 pigmented bands (Fig. 1).

The 77 K fluorescence emission spectrum of the upper band of the LHC I fraction in Fig. 1 shows the long-wavelength emission at 730 nm of the PS I antenna (Fig. 2 B). This pigment-protein complex is designated LHC I (730) and corresponds probably to LHC I-730 from BASSI and SIMPSON (5). The fluorescence excitation spectrum demonstrates efficient energy transfer from chl b (474 nm) and carotenoids (shoulder at 486 nm) to chl a (Fig. 2 A).

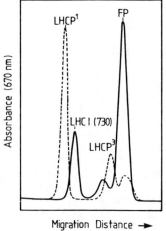

FIGURE 1. Mildly dissociating SDS-PAGE of the LHC I fraction (——) from the sucrose density gradient. For comparison, LHC II complexes (-----) are separated under identical conditions. FP = free pigments, LHCP[1] and LHCP[3] = oligomer and monomer of LHC II, respectively.

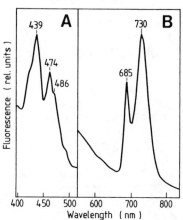

FIGURE 2. Fluorescence excitation (A) and emission spectrum (B) at 77 K of the upper band in Fig. 1 [LHC I (730)]. Excitation at 439 nm, emission wavelength 730 nm.

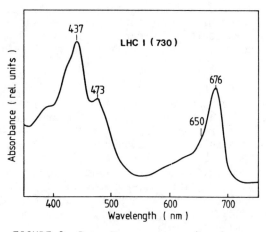

FIGURE 3. Room temperature absorbance spectrum of LHC I (730).

The absorbance spectrum of LHC I (730) is shown in Fig. 3. The maximun in the red is at 676 nm and the shoulder at 650 indicates the presence of chl b. The pigment analysis of LHC I (730) shows molar ratios of 0.5 for neoxanthin, 10.8 for violaxanthin, 17.3 for lutein, 40.5 for chl b and 2.4 for ß-carotene per 100 mol chl a. This pigment composition of LHC I (730) is different from the calculated pigment composition of LHC I in Tab. 1, probably due to the presence of a second pigment-protein complex and the large amount of free pigments (40 - 60 %) after SDS-PAGE (Fig.1). In contrast to LHC II there is still some ß-carotene bound to LHC I (730), but most of this pigment is found in the free pigment zone, indicating the sensitivity of this pigment in the isolated PS I antenna against mild detergent treatment.

The intermediate band of the electrophoretic separation of LHC I in Fig. 1 is probably equivalent to LHC I-680 (5). This is confirmed by 77 K fluorescence emission at 680 nm and an absorbance maximum at 670 nm.

Taken together, ß-carotene displays three functions in LHC I. This carotenoid is associated with the long-wavelength chl a forms (6) which act as an energy sink in LHC I upon closure of the reaction centres (7). Recently we have shown that at least some of the ß-carotene molecules in the isolated LHC I are involved in photoprotection (4). Consequently we conclude that these ß-carotene molecules shield the energy valve system of the native PS I-200 complex from excessive excitation energy.

Additionally, beside the antenna function ß-carotene is an important structural element which enables the assembly of the PS I antenna system and connection to the core polypeptides.

Further investigations are necessary to answer the question whether all molecules of ß-carotene are involved in all three functions simultaneously, or whether each individual molecule fulfills a specific role.

4. REFERENCES

1 Siefermann-Harms, D. (1985) Biochim. Biophys. Acta 811, 325-355
2 Haworth, P., Watson, J.L. and Arntzen, C.J. (1983) Biochim. Biophys. Acta 724, 151-158
3 Knoetzel, J., Braumann, T. and Grimme, L.H. (1988) J. Photochem. Photobiol. B Biol. 1, 475-491
4 Damm, I., Knoetzel, J. and Grimme, L.H. (1987) in Progr. Photosynth. Res. (Biggins, J., ed.), Vol. 2, pp. 351-354, Nijhoff, Dordrecht
5 Bassi, R. and Simpson, D. (1987) Eur. J. Biochem. 163, 221-230
6 Junge, W., Schaffernicht, H. and Nelson, N. (1977) Biochim. Biophys. Acta 462, 73-85
7 Stahl, U., Tusov, V.B., Paschenko, V.Z. and Voigt, J. (1989) Biochim. Biophys. Acta 973, 198-204

ACKNOWLEDGEMENTS
This work was supported partially by the Deutsche Forschungsgemeinschaft (DFG Gr 355/10-1). We would like to thank Erika Lorenz for technical assistence.

ENERGY TRANSFER KINETICS IN PHOTOSYSTEM I PARTICLES ISOLATED FROM SYNECHOCOCCUS sp. AND FROM HIGHER PLANTS

A.R. Holzwarth[1], W. Haehnel[2], R. Ratajczak[2], E.Bittersmann[1] and G.H. Schatz[1]

[1] Max–Planck–Institut für Strahlenchemie, D–4330 Mülheim a.d. Ruhr, FRG, and
[2] Institut für Biochemie der Pflanzen, Westfälische Wilhelms–Universität, Münster, FRG.

1. INTRODUCTION

The antenna of photosystem (PS) I in higher plants, green algae, and cyanobacteria contains various chlorophyll (Chl) pigment proteins each with characteristic absorbance and corresponding fluorescence spectra. A pigment called C695 has been held responsible for the low and room temperature fluorescence emission F720 while a pigment C705 is attributed to the low temperature emission band F730. The bulk of the PS I Chl a antenna absorbs at ~ 678 nm and generally emits with a maximum around 684 nm and sometimes up to 695 nm at room temperature (F685).

In PS I the kinetics of energy migration to and charge separation in the reaction center is only scarcely understood so far. Of particular interest is the question whether the overall exciton trapping (by charge separation) is a trap–limited or a diffusion–limited process (1). The latter suggestion has been put forward based on data from a study of PS I particles of various antenna sizes (2). From a detailed study on isolated PS II particles we concluded that in PS II the charge–separation was clearly trap–limited (3). For PS I this question has to be answered independently in view of the fact that P700 in PS I is a deeper trap than P680 in PS II with respect to the energy of their antenna Chls. In this contribution we report on the energy transfer kinetics in PS I particles at room temperature isolated from the thermophilic cyanobacterium Synechococcus sp. Studying the kinetics of these PS I particles is particularly interesting in view of the fact that their room temperature emission maximum is located at ~ 720 nm, i.e. at longer wavelength than for all previously reported PS I preparations. We also report on the fluorescence kinetics of an intact stroma thylakoid fraction from spinach chloroplasts which is highly enriched in PS I.

2. MATERIALS AND METHODS

PS I particles of the thermophilic Synechococcus sp. were isolated from thylakoids by extraction with Triton X–100 and subsequent sucrose density gradient centrifugation. The detailed isolation procedure will be described elsewhere (G.H. Schatz, to be published). The particles contain only negligible amounts of PS II. The Chl a / P700 ratio is about 100 : 1. The stroma thylakoids from spinach (PS I Y100) have been isolated without the use of detergents by differential centrifugation of Yeda press treated thylakoids. This preparation contains the PS I units in their native state. Corrected steady state emission and excitation spectra were measured on a Spex–Fluorolog instrument. Picosecond fluorescence kinetics were measured by the single–photon counting technique with 5 ps resolution employing a micro channelplate detector (model 1564U–01, Hamamatsu). Excitation occured at 670 nm with picosecond pulses of very low intensity at a repetition rate of 400 kHz. Fluorescence was resolved by a double monochromator (DH10, Jobin Yvon) with 4 nm resolution. The fluorescence lifetime measurements were carried out under magic angle polarization conditions. The sample was pumped through a flow measuring cuvette which was thermostatted at 5 °C. Decay–associated (DAS) fluorescence spectra were calculated from

M. Baltscheffsky (ed.), Current Research in Photosynthesis, Vol. II, 611–614.

each set of decays recorded over the whole emission wavelength range by using the global analysis procedure as described (4). The amplitudes of the DAS were corrected for the wavelength dependence in the sensitivity of the detector.

3. RESULTS AND DISCUSSION
PS I from Synechococcus

The room temperature absorption and corrected fluorescence emission spectra of the Synechococcus PS I particles are shown in Fig. 1. It can be clearly seen that the maximum of the steady state emission occurs at ~ 720 nm (F720) while at ~ 685 nm (F685) the emission exhibits a shoulder. Judging from the absorption spectra, the main emission of F720 must occur from a very small long–wavelength pigment pool, while the bulk of the Chl pigments emits only with low intensity (F685). The latter emission is further decreased by lowering the temperature.

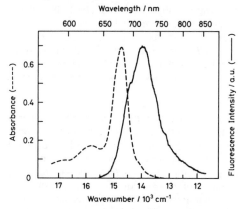

Fig. 1: Steady state absorption (dashed) and fluorescence (full) spectra of PS I particles from Synechococcus at room temperature.

Fig. 2 shows the picosecond time–resolved emission (DAS) for the PS I particles under reducing conditions (addition of ascorbate). No significant change was observed in the DAS when P700 was oxidized by ferricyanide. Generally, three and sometimes four exponential lifetime components are required for a good fit of the picosecond data. Only two of the components – the shortest–lived ones – have a substantial rel. amplitude. The fastest component τ_1 with a lifetime in the range of 10 ± 2 ps shows positive amplitude at 690 nm and is negative above 710 nm, with a negative maximum at ~ 720 nm. This behaviour clearly indicates an energy transfer process from the F685 to the F720 emitting pigments. The second lifetime component ($\tau_2 = 36 \pm 3$ ps) shows two bands in the corresponding DAS. The one with lower intensity is due to F685 while the intensity maximum is attributed to F720. In addition to these two prominent lifetime components we observe one or occasionally two components with very small rel. amplitudes ($\leq 1\%$). Their lifetimes are in the $2 - 5$ ns range. We attribute them to a small amount of uncoupled Chl. It is worthwhile to note that these long–lived contributions are much smaller ($\leq 1\%$) than observed in previously published work on PS I particles. We therefore believe that the PS I particles studied here are particularly pure and the Chls are well coupled to the reaction centers.

At this point a comparison with other measurements on cyanobacterial PS I particles is of interest. (5) reported also a very fast decay component of ~ 14 ps in a PS I particle from Phormidium which was of similar size as ours. They analyzed their decays in terms of a biexponential model with the second lifetime being as low as 84 ps. Thus, assuming a small amount of unresolved longer–lived components, their kinetics may be very similar to ours. However, since they did not wavelength–resolve the fluorescence but observed mostly the integral emission, they may have missed the rising part of the shortest–lived component at long wavelengths. This lead them to explain their data in terms of a model which is at variance with our data. They attributed the fast component to the trapping of the excitons from the core antennae by the reaction center P700. The longer–lived component is attributed to the trapping of the excitons from the peripheral antenna (5). We can clearly exclude this possibility. If it were true, the F720 band in the longer–lived (τ = 36 ps) component should be lower than the F685 band, which is clearly not the case. Provided that singlett annihilation can be excluded an indication for a rapid energy transfer component may have been observed in transient absorption experiments also (6).

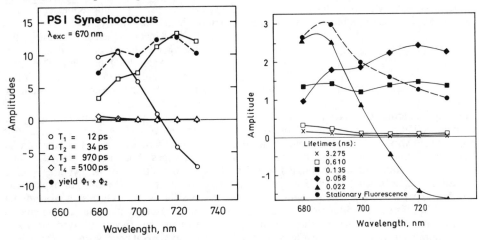

Fig. 2 (left): Decay–associated fluorescence spectra (DAS) of PS I particles from Synechococcus at 5°C upon excitation at 670 nm.

Fig. 3 (right): Decay–associated fluorescence spectra (DAS) of stroma thylakoid PS I particles from spinach (PS I Y100) at 5°C upon excitation at 670 nm. The dashed lines indicate the steady–state emission spectra.

PS I from spinach stroma thylakoids

Fig. 3 shows the DAS of the stroma thylakoid preparation from spinach. The fastest lifetime of 22 ps has dominant positive amplitude around 685 nm an turns negative above 710 nm, similar to the corresponding component in the PS I particles from Synechococcus. Two lifetime components with spectral characteristics of PS I fluorescence, showing both F685 and F720 emission, are observed with lifetimes of about 60 ps and 135 ps. The DAS of these components show quite different F685/F720 intensity ratios. We tentatively attribute these two components to PS I units of different antenna sizes. Two longer–lived components with very small amplitudes are probably due to impurities of some kind, possibly representing some PS II contaminations. Very similar lifetimes for the main components were reported for a different, detergent–isolated, PS I preparation from spinach (7). The antenna size of that preparation (~200 Chl/P700) was probably very similar to that of our PS I Y100 preparation. The major difference to the kinetics observed by us consists in the lack of a riseterm at long wavelengths, although their preparation did show a pronounced F730 band in the ~100 ps component. At low temperature such a riseterm was in fact observed (7). The reason for this unexpected difference to our results is unclear at present.

Kinetic model

Although it may eventually be necessary to analyze our data in terms of a more complex pigment organization, the simplest interpretation of our observations for both preparations is in terms of a "two pigment pool" model only (Fig. 4). Within this model the main pigment pool absorbing at 678 nm and comprizing nearly 100 Chls in the Synechococcus particles and ~200 Chls in the PS I Y100 preparation is responsible for the F685 emission. Excitons in this pool equilibrate in about 10 ps (22 ps for PS I Y100) with the small pool of pigments giving rise to F720. The equilibrated excitons in both pools – being mostly located on the long–wavelength pigments for the Synechococcus particles – decay with a lifetime of 37 ps (60 ps and 135 ps, depending on antenna size, for the PS I Y100) by trapping and charge separation in the reaction center.

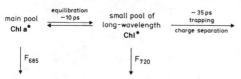

Fig. 4: Kinetic scheme explaining the picosecond fluorescence data from Synechococcus PS I particles. The same scheme holds also for PS I Y100 particles when the corresponding lifetimes are used (see text).

We may, therefore, conclude that the exciton migration in the antenna, leading to complete exciton equilibration within ~ 10 ps or ~ 22 ps, respectively, over all available Chl pigments, is very rapid as compared to the overall exciton lifetimes. Since the latter are at least 3 – 4 times longer than the antenna equilibration times, both PS I systems clearly display the features of a trap–limited kinetics. This is in contrast to the hypothesis of a diffusion–limited kinetics in PS I as proposed earlier by Owens et al. (2,8). An explanation for this apparent contradiction might consist in the possibility that Owens et al. did not resolve the fastest (equilibration) component in their measurements. Our measurements present the first case where this equilibration component has been resolved at room temperature by way of the rising (negative amplitude) component at long wavelengths, which unequivocally allows us to attribute this component to exciton–equilibration. We note that an ultrafast antenna equilibration kinetics in intact chloroplasts and green algae have recently been found by us (9,10). It therefore seems that the antenna equilibration in most Chl protein complexes of both PS I and PS II occurs in times less than ~ 25 ps.

4. ACKNOWLEDGEMENTS

We acknowledge partial financial support by the Deutsche Forschungsgemeinschaft.

5.REFERENCES

(1) Holzwarth,A.R., (1989). in: The Chlorophylls, CRC Critical Reviews, Uniscience Series (H. Scheer ed.). CRC press, Boca Raton, in press.
(2) Owens,T.G., Webb,S.P., Mets,L., Alberte,R.S., and Fleming,G.R., (1987). Proc. Natl. Acad. Sci. USA 84: 1532–1536.
(3) Schatz,G.H., Brock,H., and Holzwarth,A.R., (1988). Biophys. J. 54: 397–405.
(4) Holzwarth,A.R., Wendler,J., and Suter,G.W., (1987). Biophys. J. 51: 1–12.
(5) Wittmershaus,B.P., Berns,D.S., and Huang,C., (1987). Biophys. J. 52: 829–836.
(6) Evans,E.H., Sparrow,R., and Brown,R.G., (1987). in: Prog. Photosyn. Res. (J. Biggins ed.). Nijhoff; Dordrecht, 1: 99–102.
(7) Mukerji,I. and Sauer,K., (1989). C.S. French Symposium on Photosynthesis ; in press.
(8) Owens,T.G., Webb,S.P., Alberte,R.S., Mets,L., and Fleming,G.R., (1988). Biophys. J. 53: 733–745.
(9) Bittersmann,E. and Holzwarth,A.R., (1989). Biophys. J. in press.
(10) McCauley,S.W., Bittersmann,E., and Holzwarth,A.R., (1989). FEBS Lett. 249: 285–288.

PICOSECOND ABSORPTION MEASUREMENTS OF PHOTOSYSTEM 1 FROM THE CYANOBACTERIUM, CHLOROGLOEA FRITSCHII

E.H. Evans[1], Raymond Sparrow[1], Robert G. Brown[2]
Schools of Applied Biology[1] and Chemistry[2], Lancashire Polytechnic, Preston, Lancashire, PR1 2TQ, U.K.
Roger Chittock ande William Toner
Central Laser Facility, Rutherford Appleton Laboratory, Chilton, Didcot, Oxon, OX11 0QX, U.K.
Michael C.W. Evans
Department of Botany and Microbiology, University College, Gower Street, London, WC1

INTRODUCTION
Absorption measurements in the picosecond time scale of Photosystems 1 and 2 (PS1, PS2) have proved more difficult than those of photosynthetic bacterial reaction centres as the associated light harvesting complexes have not proved amenable to removal, rendering it necessary for the measurement of very small absorption transients with considerable background absorbance. Previous measurements on PS1 absorption transients on a picosecond timescale have been performed with excitation flashes of 10-35 ps (1-4), giving risetimes for excitation of the reaction centre of no less than 15 ps. Giorgi et al (5, 6) and our own preliminary data (5) showed that absorption transients at 670-680 nm which could be ascribed to light-harvesting chlorophylls occurred at more rapid times than the absorbance change of P700. Shuvalov et al (2) identified an absorbance change at 693 nm with a lifetime of 32 ps which they attributed to the formation of reduced acceptor A_o^-. Such an absorbance transient has been observed by Wasielewski (6).

RESULTS
The transient bleaches seen in the 675-725 nm region following excitation of PS1 particles from C. fritschii at 585 nm display a complex dependence on wavelength, probe delay, pump intensity and redox potential.

Spectra
The specta at fixed time and pump intensity have two groups of peaks at 680 to 690 nm and at 700 to 720 nm separated by a pronounced minimum at 695 nm.

Time Components
(A) In the 680 to 690 region the dominant feature at early times is a fast ($<$2 psec) rising bleach with a 10 ± 2 psec recovery time which is present in all redox conditions. (Figure 1).

M. Baltscheffsky (ed.), Current Research in Photosynthesis, Vol. II, 615–618.
© 1990 *Kluwer Academic Publishers. Printed in the Netherlands.*

(B)   In the 700 to 720 region dominant feature at early times is a fast (<2 psec) rising bleach with a $35{\pm}5$ psec recovery time which is again present in all redox conditions. (Figure 2).

(C)   At late times the main feature is a bleach at constant level over the 3n sec delay range of the experiment. This feature has a marked sensitivity to redox potential being normally present under reduced conditions and absent under conditions when P700 would be oxidised. Broad peaks in both 680-690 and 700-720 regions of the spectrum are observed.

(D)   We have recently observed a weaker feature peaking in the 680-690 region with a recovery time of the order of 200 psec.

Pump Intensity Dependence

All pump intensity dependences measured at fixed times are of the form $A = aP - b(1 - \exp - P/p_0)$ where a and b are constants (depending on wavelength, time and redox), P is the pump intensity (mJ/cm^2) and $P_0 = 0.5$ mJ cm^{-2}, for samples with 50% transmission at the pump wavelength. The equivalent saturation parameter p' for a thin sample is estimated at .35 mJ cm^{-2}, i.e. 1×10^{15} photons/cm^2 which corresponds to the value to be expected for an absorber with some twenty active antennae chlorophyll molecules. We have therefore identified all transients exhibiting strong saturation (b>>a) as due to effects in the reaction centre and the linear components (a>>b) as due to the antennae.

Components (B), (C) and (D) normally exhibit pronounced saturation behaviour in fresh samples whereas component (A) (obtained by extrapolating the later time behaviour due to (B) and (D) to early time and subtracting from the peak) is always at least linear. (Figure 3).

Rise Times

These are dominated by the prompt onset of components (A) or (B). However, a prompt onset for (C) and (D) in the 690 nm spectral region can be inferred from the fact that all early time saturation effects can be accounted for by extrapolation of the late time tail. It is not excluded, however, that the early and late features have a parent-daughter relationship, one growing in as the other decays, with the same time constant. In that case, the constant bleach, (C), is in reality two features one growing from (A) and the other from (B).

DISCUSSION

We assign the saturating long lived species with maximal absorbance at 706 nm to P700, present only in reduced samples. Preliminary redox measurements at 706 nm are consistent with this. We have previously suggested that a chlorophyll molecule on a common energy transfer pathway with P700 is responsible for the saturating absorbance transient in the 700-715 nm region with a $35{\pm}5$ psec

Figure 1   Transient at 680 nm excited at 585 nm
            Pulse width 2.53 ps
            Sample reduced by sodium dithionite

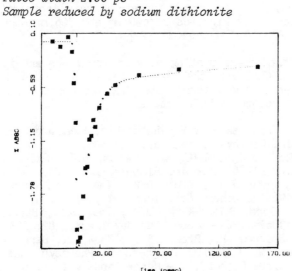

Figure 2   As Fig. 1 but transient at 706.5 nm

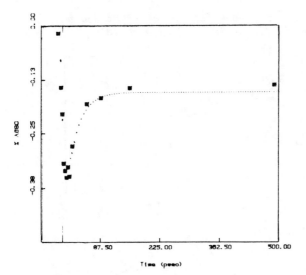

recovery time (7). It is likely that the saturating long lived components in the 680-690 nm region are related to the species observed by others (2, 6), and ascribed to the appearance of the reduced acceptor A_o^-. The prompt onset of this transient and the absence of similar decay kinetics at 690 nm and 706 nm suggests that the formation of $P700^+ A_o^-$ occurs in <2 ps.

We ascribe the fast non-saturating peak of the transient in the 680-690 nm region to LHChl, with the 10±2 ps decay time not corresponding to energy transfer to the intermediate Chl, component B, which rises in <2 ps, but to a secondary LHChl state.

1. Il'ins, M.D., Krasauskas, V.V., Rotomskis, R.R. and Borisov, Y.Y. (1984) Biochim. Biophys. Acta, 767, 501-506.
2. Schuvalov, V.A., Nuija, A.M., van Gorkom, H.J., Smit, H.W.J. and Duysens, L.N.M. (1986) Biochim. Biophys. Acta, 850, 319-323.
3. Giorgi, L.B., Gore, B.L., Klug, D.R., Ide, J.P., Barber, J. and Porter, G. (1986) Biochem. Soc. Trans. 14, 47-48.
4. Giorgi, L.B., Gore, B.L., Klug, D.R., Ide, J.P., Barber, J. and Porter, G. (1986) J. Chem. Soc. Faraday Trans., 82, 2231-2236.
5. Evans, E.H., Sparrow, R., Brown, R.G., Shaw, D., Barr, J., Smith, M. and Ronter, W. (1987). Progress in Photosyn. Res. (Ed. J. Biggins), Martinus Nijhoff, The Netherlands vol. 1, p. 99-102.
6. Wasielewski, M.R., Fenton, J.M. and Govindjee (1987) Photosyn, Res. 12, 181-190.
7. Evans, E.H., Sparrow, R., Brown, R.G., Chittock, R.S., Toner, W.T. and Evans M.C.W. (1988) EBEC Reports, 5, 174.

Figure 3 *Saturation curves for transient at 680 nm, measured 4.3 ps (○) or 159.9 ps (●)*

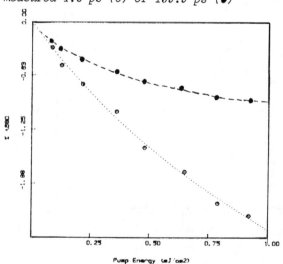

Pump Energy (mJ/cm2)

THE TRANSIENT PHOTOSYSTEM I EPR SPECTRA CORRELATED SPIN PAIR CONCEPT AND STRUCTURAL CONCLUSIONS

DIETMAR STEHLIK, CHRISTIAN H. BOCK, ARTHUR J. VAN DER EST,
FB Physik, FU Berlin, Arnimallee 14, D-1000 Berlin 33

1. INTRODUCTION

For many years it has been known that primary charge separation in photosynthetic reaction centers is associated with spin polarized EPR-signals. Such signals can be detected directly in preparations containing PS I whereas their observation in bacterial reaction centers or PS II requires removal or decoupling of the non-heme iron, which acts as a strong relaxation center. However, their usefullness has been hampered for some time by a lack of understanding of their origin. With the present knowledge of the molecular arrangement of the chromophores in the bacterial reaction center it is obvious that transient EPR-detection occurs in coupled spin pairs. With this concept /1-5/ observed transient EPR spectra can be understood satisfactorily /6/. Here, we want to address some of the questions raised in the context of this interpretation and present confirming evidence for the major conclusions reached previously /6/.

2. CORRELATED SPIN PAIR CONCEPT AND SOME CRITICAL ASPECTS

The first critical aspect we wish to address is the transfer of polarization between successive coupled spin pairs. With the time resolution of EPR experiments limited to the order of 10 ns, the earliest charge separated state detectable by EPR is $P^+Q_A^-$ in BRC or $P_{700}^+A_1^-$ in PS I. This pair is preceeded by the primary charge separated state $P_{700}^+A_0^-$ which has a lifetime of the order of 200 ps in intact PS I. Thus even singlet-triplet mixing terms corresponding to frequencies of several GHz or interaction parameters up to 100 mT would not affect the spin dynamics significantly before the observed spin pair state $P_{700}^+A_1^-$ is reached and the assumption of a pure singlet state precursor seems well justified. From the general structure of the BRC it has to be concluded that the two radical ion spins involved are coupled at least by a weak dipolar coupling of $D \sim -1.2$ G (corresponding to a distance of 28 Å). EPR detection in this spin pair under the assumption of a photo-excited singlet precursor state has been described /5,6/. With essentially independently known interaction parameters, it was possible to obtain satisfactory simulations of the observed transient EPR-spectra in X-band (9 GHz) as well as at higher spectral resolution in K-band (24 GHz) /6/. It is important to emphasize that the large reaction

M. Baltscheffsky (ed.), Current Research in Photosynthesis, Vol. II, 619–622.
© 1990 *Kluwer Academic Publishers. Printed in the Netherlands.*

center reorients slowly compared with time scale of the experiment (about 10^{-6} s) and thus no averaging of the anisotropic contributions to the spectrum occurs even at ambient temperatures.

Successive polarized transient EPR-spectra have been observed in several systems containing PS I. The spectra are interpreted as arising from the charge separated states $P_{700}^{+}A_1^{-}$ and P_{700}^{+} (FeS)$^{-}$ and a time constant of $t_{1/e}=260\pm20$ ns has been determined for the electron transfer from A_1 to FeS /7/. In order to describe the second spectrum we must take into account the singlet-triplet mixing in the $P_{700}^{+}(A_1)^{-}$ pair as well as the spin-spin coupling between the P_{700}^{+} and (FeS)$^{-}$ radical ions.

A second critical aspect concerns the influence of the microwave field on the polarization pattern observed. In the direct detection mode the microwave field is present during detection and can only be neglected if it is sufficiently small to leave the population on the spin levels unchanged within the required limits. We will describe the effects of strong microwave fields, which in turn specifies the conditions for the low power case where the B_1 field can be neglected.

3.   RESULTS AND DISCUSSION
3.1. SUCCESSIVE SPIN PAIRS
The problem of spin polarization in successive differently coupled spin pairs is approached under very simplifying assumptions. The mixing frequencies Ω (defined in /6/) are large compared to the inverse lifetime of the spin pair. Therefore, we can consider time independent relative populations on the eigenstates of each spin pair as well as on any other appropriate basis system. The transition probabilities for the electron transfer step follow the projection of the spin states in the first spin pair onto the spin states of the second pair.(A more rigorous treatment has been performed in the group of J. R. Norris.) A test of our analysis is that it yields the expression for the standard CIDEP result (see e.g. /8/) when the coupling in the second pair is set to zero. Fig. 1 shows a simulation of polarized transient X-band EPR-spectra of deuterated PS I (the experimental and simulated $P_{700}^{+}A_1^{-}$ spectrum is as shown in Fig. 7 of Ref. 6). The second pair $P_{700}^{+}A_1$(FeS)$^{-}$ produces the spectrum in the P_{700}^{+} region. If the spins are no longer coupled, the P_{700}^{+} spectrum will be completely emissive (broken line in Fig. 1), while the corresponding absorptive spectrum of (FeS)$^{-}$ is too far spread due to its large g-anisotropy. Introducing a realistic spin coupling of −0.1 mT results in the dotted line spectrum of Fig. 1, distinguished by the small absorption parts on either side of the emission. The absolute and relative amplitudes of the absorptions are dependent upon the sign and magnitude the spin interaction as well as the orientation of the two pair partners relative to the dipolar axis. This spectrum is in qualitative agreement with the observed second spin

polarized spectrum in intact PS I samples /7/. We believe it should be possible to obtain quantitative agreement by optimizing the coupling parameters and taking the hyperfine interaction into account.

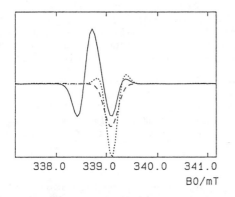

FIGURE 1.Simulation of X-band ESP spectra of the initial spin pair $P^+_{700}A^-_1$ (D=-0.12 mT, solid line) and the second pair $P^+_{700}(FeS)^-$ populated from the precursor $P^+_{700}A^-_1$ (D=0, broken line; D=-0.1 mT, dotted line).For these simulations no hyperfine inter- action has been taken into account. For details of method see /6/.

338.0   339.0   340.0   341.0
BO/mT

3.2   INFLUENCE OF MICROWAVE POWER ON A COUPLED SPIN PAIR

We have previously reported the influence of the microwave power on the transient PS I EPR-spectra (see Fig. 1 of /9/).

Spectra extracted from the complete data set of a high power (200 mW) experiment at K-band are shown in Fig. 2a. The solid line is obtained from the initial amplitudes of transient nutation signals. The broken line has been obtained from the Fourier coefficients of the nutation frequency where only times longer than 900 ns after the laser pulse have been retained in the transformation of the transients. Both spec- tra – although totally different – belong to the same spin pair $P^+_{700}A^-_1$. They can be simulated quite satisfactorily (Fig. 2b): The early

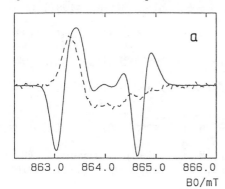
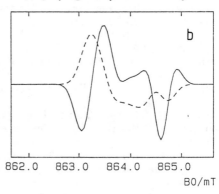

863.0   864.0   865.0   866.0
BO/mT

862.0   863.0   864.0   865.0
BO/mT

FIGURE 2.a) Experimental K-band ESP spectrum of deuterated *Synechococ- cus lividus*. Solid line: spectrum at early times. Broken line: spectrum of nutations at late times. For full data set see /10/. b) Solid line: simulation of the spectrum of the coupled pair $P^+_{700}A^-_1$ /6/. Broken line: same pair with coupling set to zero.

spectrum (solid line) is almost identical to that observed and simulated at low power (see /6/). It represents the polarization developing in the coupled spin pair $P_{700}^{+}A_1^{-}$ (D=-0.12 mT) when populated from a singlet precursor. If the microwave field amplitude (B_1=0.06 mT) becomes comparable to the spin coupling, the two oppositely polarized lines of each radical pair partner, which are split by the spin coupling, are both irradiated and their polarization cancels. What remains are the $\langle S_z \rangle$ expectation values of the respective "decoupled" radical ion species giving rise to the broken line spectrum of Fig. 2.

The successful simulations presented here provide strong support for the correlated spin pair concept and hence for the implicit conclusions with respect to structural features and electron transfer kinetics suggested in previous papers /6,7/.

ACKNOWLEDGEMENTS
We thank Marion C. Thurnauer (Argonne) for the fruitful collaboration. AvdE wishes to thank the Natural Sciences and Engineering Research Council of Canada for support in the form of a postdoctoral fellowship. This work was supported by grants from the Deutsche Forschungsgemeinschaft, Sfb 312 (A1).

REFERENCES
1 Thurnauer, M. C. and Norris, J. R. (1980) Chem. Phys. Lett. 76, 557–561; Thurnauer, M. C. and Meisel, D. J. (1983) J. Am. Chem. Soc. 105, 3729–3731
2 Closs, G. L., Forbes, M. D. E. and Norris, J. R. (1987) J. Phys. Chem. 91, 3592–3599
3 Closs, G. L. and Forbes, M. D. E. (1987) J. Am. Chem. Soc. 109, 6185–6187
4 Buckley, C. D., Hunter, D. A. and Mc Lauchlan, K. A. (1987) Chem. Phys. Lett. 135, 307–312
5 Hore, P. J., Hunter, D. A., McKie, C. D. and Hoff, A. J. (1987) Chem. Phys. Lett. 137, 495–500
6 Stehlik, D., Bock, C. H. and Petersen, J. (1989) J. Phys. Chem. 93, 1612–1619
7 Bock, C. H., van der Est, A. J., Brettel, K. and Stehlik, D. (1989) FEBS Lett. 247, 91–96
8 Hoff, A. J., (1984) Quart. Rev. Biophys. 7, 153–282
9 Bock, C. H., Stehlik, D., Thurnauer, M. C. (1988), Isr. J. Chem. 28, 177–182
10 Stehlik, D., Bock, C. H., Thurnauer, M. C. (1989) in Advanced EPR in Biology and Biochemistry (Hoff, A. J. ed.) Chap. 12, Elsevier, Amsterdam

FAST ELECTRON TRANSFER KINETICS IN PHOTOSYSTEM I FROM TRANSIENT
EPR-SPECTROSCOPY AT ROOM TEMPERATURE

CHRISTIAN H. BOCK, KLAUS BRETTEL[*], ARTHUR J. VAN DER EST, INA SIECK-
MANN, DIETMAR STEHLIK, Fachbereich Physik, FU Berlin, Arnimallee 14,
D-1000 Berlin 33, [*] Max Volmer Institut, TU Berlin, Straße des 17. Juni
135, D-1000 Berlin 12

1. INTRODUCTION

Following light excitation of the donor P_{700} and primary charge
separation electron transfer in photosystem I (PSI) is believed to
proceed via a chain of membrane bound acceptors termed A_0, A_1, F_X, F_A,
F_B /1,2/. Transient EPR-spectroscopy of spin polarized signals provides
a useful tool to study the kinetics of these processes provided the
transfer times fall within the time resolution presently approaching
the physical limit around 10 ns. Our own recent EPR results /3/ demonstrated that in intact PS I preparations at ambient temperatures the
primary subnanosecond events are followed by the electron transfer step

$$P_{700}^+ \ A_1^- \ \xrightarrow{\ \tau_1=260 \ ns\ } \ P_{700}^+ \ A_1 \ (FeS)^- \qquad (1)$$

where (FeS) represents the first iron sulfur center (possibly F_X) in
the electron transfer chain. It is important to emphasize that a common
kinetic behaviour was observed over the whole spectral range showing
development from the early spectrum of the radical ion pair $P_{700}^+A_1^-$ to
that of $P_{700}^+ \ (FeS)^-$. The signal amplitude $S(t,B_0)$ as a function of time
after the laser flash and of the magnetic field B_0 is given by:

$$S(t,B_0)= \alpha(B_0) \ exp \ (-t/\tau_1) + \beta(B_0)(1-exp(-t/\tau_1))exp(-t/\tau_2). \qquad (2)$$

The coefficients $\alpha(B_0)$ and $\beta(B_0)$ plotted as a function of the magnetic
field B_0 yield the separate spectra of the successive radical ion pairs
(see Fig.3 of ref./3/). The decay of spectrum α corresponds to the rise
of spectrum β and indicates the electron transfer time τ_1 between successive radical ion pairs (1). τ_2 is the spin relaxation time of the
second pair $P_{700}^+ \ (FeS)^-$.

Transient optical absorption difference spectroscopy performed on the
same PS I preparation /4/ led to results in full agreement with those
by transient EPR. The spectral information from both methods is compatible with the identification of A_1 as a quinonelike acceptor (presuma-

bly vitamin K_1, also termed phylloquinone). In this contribution we investigate the effect of prereduction of the iron sulfur centers F_A, F_B in PS I particles. From results with optical absorption difference spectroscopy it was concluded that in this case P^+_{700} recombines with A_1^- (and not F_X^-) with $t_{1/2}=250$ μs /5/.

2. MATERIALS AND METHODS

The procedures were identical to those mentioned before /3,4/ except that the PS I particles from *Synechococcus* sp. were suspended in 100 mM CAPS/NaOH(pH 10.2) and supplied with either 100 μM sodium ascorbate (called "intact" in the following) or 10 mg/ml $Na_2S_2O_4$ ("prereduced"). The X-band EPR techniques were described previously /3,6/. Direct detection with the overall time resolution of 50 ns was used to follow the time development of the spin polarized EPR-spectra while 100 kHz field modulation with a time resolution of 20 μs was applied to measure the kinetics of the thermalized signals. The sample was excited by a frequency-doubled Nd-YAG laser at a repetition rate of 2 Hz.

3. RESULTS AND DISCUSSION

Transient EPR signals $S(t,B_0)$ were taken as sets with full kinetic and spectral dependence for PS I particles from *Synecochoccus* sp. They were analyzed with the kinetic equation (2). The resulting early ($\alpha(B_0)$, solid line) and later ($\beta(B_0)$, broken line) spin polarized spectra are compared in Fig. 1 for intact

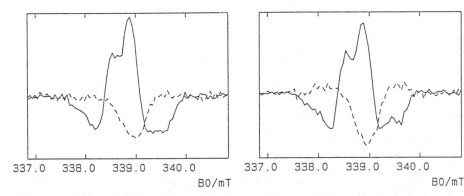

337.0	338.0	339.0	340.0

BO/mT

337.0	338.0	339.0	340.0

BO/mT

FIGURE 1. Directly detected spin polarized spectra of intact (left) and prereduced (right) PS I particles from *Synechococcus* as extracted from the full data sets $S(t,B_0)$ according to eq. (2). Solid lines: early spectra $\alpha(B_0)$; broken lines: late spectra $\beta(B_0)$. Rise/decay time $\tau_1=260$ ns for intact sample and 420 ns for prereduced sample.

(left) and prereduced (right) samples of the same PS I preparation. For

intact PS I the spectra are indistinguishable from those (Fig.3 of ref. /3/) obtained at lower pH. For prereduced PS I the early and late spin polarized spectra are observed again with comparable relative ampli- tudes and only minor differences on the low-field side of the late spectrum. However, the decay time of the early spectrum equal to the rise time of the second spectrum has lengthened from τ_1(in tact)=260±20 ns to τ_1(prereduced)=420±30 ns.

In addition, we have measured the kinetics of the unpolarized signals at lower time resolution ($\geq$ 20 μs) with 100 kHz field modulation. For the intact PS I sample, the flash induced spectrum (Fig. 3, solid line) decays essentially with a lifetime of $\sim$ 60 ms (Fig. 2, trace a, full decay not shown). This spectrum can be attributed to P_{700}^+ alone because the reduced electron acceptor, present at the same time, is an iron–sul- fur center which does not contribute in the spectral range depicted in Fig. 3. For the prereduced PS I sample the lifetime shortened to $\sim$ 310 μs ($t_{1/2}$=215 μs) (Fig. 2, trace b) which is to be compared with $t_{1/2}\approx$250 μs observed before by many research groups with flash induced absorption changes (see /5/ and ref. therein). Note that for the prere- duced sample the whole signal decays to zero with this lifetime indica- ting that the sample has been prereduced throughout. The extrapolated initial spectrum associated with this decay time is shown in Fig. 3, broken line.

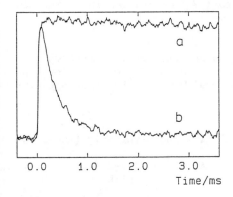

0.0   1.0   2.0   3.0

Time/ms

FIGURE 2. Transients of the un- polarized signals in the g=2 re- gion; a: intact sample; b: pre- reduced sample.

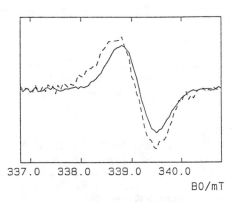

337.0   338.0   339.0   340.0

B0/mT

FIGURE 3. Solid line: derivative spectrum of the slow decay from in- tact samples (beginning shown in Fig. 2, trace a). Broken line: spec- trum of the 310 μs decay of the pre- reduced sample (extrapolated initial amplitude).

Comparing the spectral shapes in Fig. 3 one clearly notes a shift and extra contributions on the low field parts for the prereduced sample (dotted line). The added spectral contribution is fully compatible with that of a quinone-like radical ion as for instance A_1^-. Since the whole spectrum follows the 310 μs kinetics, this result would be in line with the assignment to a $P_{700}^+A_1^-$ recombination as concluded from optical results /5/. Despite this, according to Fig. 1 we observe a time development from an early to a later spin polarized spectrum in the prereduced sample as well as in intact PS I but with a slower kinetics of 420 ns as compared to 260 ns in the intact sample. While in the latter case the observed kinetics were attributed to the electron transfer from A_1 to FeS in agreement with optical results /4/, a different process must be involved in the prereduced sample, because the spectra of Fig. 3 as well as the optical data /5/ point to no electron transfer beyond A_1. As spin polarized EPR-spectra can also be affected by spin relaxation we suggest that a suitable relaxation process is operative in the prereduced sample. One possibility is a preferential relaxation in the A_1^- radical ion species (e. g. induced by a nearby iron sulfur center). This relaxation is also felt by the P_{700}^+ part but on a slower time scale due to the weak coupling in the $P_{700}^+A_1^-$ pair. A quantitative analysis of this proposal is in progress. Finally, we would like to refer to previous spin echo studies /8/ at different redox potentials. A special echo was found to disappear at lowered redox potential (prereduced F_A, F_B) but reappeared at more positive potential. This result is expected if the electron transfer past A_1^- is blocked in prereduced PS I.

ACKNOWLEDGEMENTS
AvdE wishes to thank the Natural Sciences and Engineering Research Council of Canada for support in the form of a postdoctoral fellowship. This work was supported by grants from the Deutsche Forschungsgemeinschaft, Sfb 312 (A1 and A3).

REFERENCES
1 Mathis, P. and Rutherford, A. W. (1987) in: Photosynthesis (Amesz, J. ed) pp. 63-96, Elsevier, Amsterdam
2 Golbeck, J. H. (1987) Biochim. Biophys. Acta 895, 167-204
3 Bock, C. H., van der Est A. J., Brettel, K. and Stehlik, D. (1989) FEBS Lett. 247, 91-96
4 Brettel, K. (1988) FEBS Lett. 239, 93-98
5 Brettel, K. (1989) Biochim. Biophys. Acta, in print, see also contribution in these proceedings
6 Stehlik, D., Bock, C. H., Thurnauer, M. C. (1989) in: Advanced EPR in Biology and Biochemistry (Hoff, A. J. ed) Chap. 12, Elsevier, Amsterdam
7 Stehlik, D., Bock, C. H., Petersen, J. (1989) J. Phys. Chem. 93, 1612-1619
8 Thurnauer, M. C., Rutherford, A. W., Norris, J. R. (1982), Biochim. Biophys. Acta 682, 332-338

Electron Transfer in Photosystem I from Synechococcus sp.
Under Reducing Conditions

K. Brettel, Max-Volmer-Institut, Technische Universität
Berlin, Str. d. 17. Juni 135, D-1000 Berlin 12

1. INTRODUCTION

The photochemical charge separation in photosystem I (PS I)(see (1) for a recent review), starting from the excited primary donor, P700 (a chlorophyll dimer), involves five membrane-bound electron acceptors: the primary acceptor A_0 (chlorophyll a), a secondary acceptor A_1 (presumably vitamin K_1) and three iron sulfur centers, F_X, F_B and F_A. F_B and F_A together probably constitute the terminal electron acceptor called P430.
The present contribution deals with PS I under conditions where F_A and F_B are chemically prereduced. Under such conditions, flash-induced absorption changes decaying with $t_{1/2}$ = 250 µs were observed and attributed to charge recombination between P700$^+$ and F_X^- (e.g.,2,3). This kinetic phase will be reinvestigated and now assigned to the pair P700$^+$A$_1^-$. Even more reducing conditions will also be studied.

2. MATERIALS AND METHODS

Preparation of PS I particles and absorption change measurements were performed as in (4), except that the particles were suspended in a buffer containing 200 mM glycine (pH 10.0), 20 mM MgCl$_2$, 0.04% (w/w) ß-dodecyl-D-maltoside and 5 mM Na-ascorbate. The time resolution of the conventional flash photometer was set to 30 µs.

3. RESULTS AND DISCUSSION

Fig. 1 compares the flash-induced absorption changes under conditions of normal electron transfer ("control"; presence of Na-ascorbate only, pH 10) and under conditions of prereduced F_A and F_B (addition of 5 mg/ml Na$_2$S$_2$O$_4$ to the control sample). In the control, the pair P700$^+$P430$^-$ is formed within the time resolution of this measurement (30 µs) and decays with $t_{1/2} \approx$ 50 ms (full decay not shown). The spectrum of the "initial" absorption change in the control (Fig. 1A, circles) supports the assignment to the pair P700$^+$P430$^-$ (cf. ref. 4). After addition of Na$_2$S$_2$O$_4$ to the control sample, the 250 µs kinetics appeared. The difference spectrum of the 250 µs phase (Fig. 1A, triangles), however, is strikingly different from the control spectrum between 360 and 410 and also between 450 and 490 nm (around 430 nm, both spectra are dominated by the strong bleaching

M. Baltscheffsky (ed.), Current Research in Photosynthesis, Vol. II, 627–630.

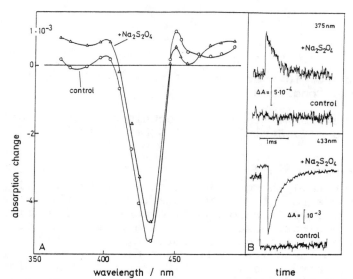

Fig. 1 A: Absorption diffference spectra deduced from
measurements like those depicted in part B. Circles:
"initial" (t = 50 μs) absorption change in control samples,
Triangles: amplitude of the 250 μs phase in the presence of
$Na_2S_2O_4$. B: Flash-induced absorption changes at 375 and 433
nm before and after addition of 5 mg $Na_2S_2O_4$ per ml. 74 μM
Chl; d = 1.1 mm; 64 averages; repetition rate, 0.8 Hz. A
fresh sample was used for each wavelength.

due to the oxidation of P700). From these spectra, it is
unlikely that the partner of $P700^+$ in the 250 μs recombination is an iron-sulfur center. Instead, the spectrum of
the 250 μs phase agrees with the difference spectrum
attributed to the pair $P700^+A_1^-$ (4). This provides strong
evidence that it is the pair $P700^+A_1^-$ (and not $P700^+F_X^-$)
which recombines with $t_{1/2}$ = 250 μs. This conclusion is
supported by the ESR spectrum of the 250 μs phase (5).
Measurements on a ns-time scale show that there is no significant forward electron transfer further than A_1^- in the
presence of $Na_2S_2O_4$ at pH 10 (see Fig. 2,bottom, for an example at 375 nm; the control (top) shows electron transfer
from A_1^- to the next iron-sulfur center with $t_{1/2} \approx 300$
ns). This is in contrast to a recent measurement at 370 nm
(6) indicating electron transfer from A_1^- to F_X with $t_{1/2} \approx$
15 ns in so-called PS I-ß particles from spinach under
conditions of pre-reduced F_A and F_B. It is not clear at
present whether this discrepancy is related to the different organisms (spinach vs. Synechococcus) or to different
preparation methods.
One might suppose that the equilibrium constant K for
$P700^+A_1^-F_X \rightleftharpoons P700^+A_1F_X^-$ is affected by the preparation

Fig. 2 Absorption changes at 375 nm before and after addition of 5 mg $Na_2S_2O_4$ per ml, time resolution 5 ns; 60 μM Chl; d = 2 mm; 256 averages; repetition rate, 1.7 Hz.

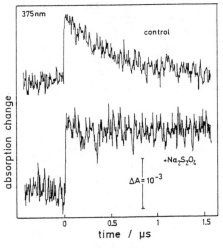 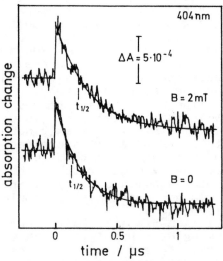

Fig. 3 Magnetic field effect on absorption changes at 404 nm during continuous white illumination in the presence of $Na_2S_2O_4$ at pH 10. Two measurements (64 averages each) with B = 2 mT were "sandwiched" by two measurements with B = 0 and - with a fresh sample - vice versa. This was repeated with another two fresh samples. Illumination started 3 min before measurements. 150 μM Chl;d = 1 mm. The solid lines are monoexponential fits, yielding $t_{1/2}$ = 185 ns (B = 2 mT) and 130 ns (B = 0).

procedure and/or depends on the organism. The signal-to-noise ratio of the results in Fig. 2 would still be compatible with an electron transfer from A_1^- to F_x in a minority (<20%) of the centers. Thus, K may be ≲0.25 in PS I particles from Synechococcus and ≳1 in PS I-ß particles from spinach. It should be mentioned that K may be smaller than the equilibrium constant K' for $P700A_1^-F_x \rightleftharpoons P700A_1F_x^-$ because the Coulomb interaction of $P700^+$ with A_1^- may be stronger than with F_x^-.

Further acceptor components (in addition to F_A and F_B) can be pre-reduced, if the sample is exposed to continuous illumination in the presence of $Na_2S_2O_4$ at pH 10. Sétif and Bottin (8) concluded that, when Fx becomes reduced, the pair $P700^+A_1^-$ recombines to the triplet state $^3P700$ with a yield close to 1 and with $t_{1/2} \approx 750$ ns (in PS I from Synechocystis). Essentially the same results were obtained here for Synechococcus, except that the rise time of $^3P700$ formation is in the order of 200 ns (measured at 1064 nm;

not shown). In the following, the effect of a weak magnetic field on this reaction will be described:

Fig. 3 shows measurements at 404 nm during continuous illumination in the presence of $Na_2S_2O_4$ at pH 10. The formation of $P700^+A_1^-$ is accompanied by an absorption increase at 404 nm (4) and subsequent formation of $^3P700$ by an absorption decrease (8). A B-field of only 2 mT slows the reaction $P700^+A_1^- \longrightarrow ^3P700$ significantly: monoexponential fits to the signals in the presence (Fig. 3, top) and absence (bottom) of the B field yield half-life times of 185 and 130 ns, respectively.

In line with ideas outlined in the literature (reviewed in (9)), this effect can be understood as follows:

(I) $P700^+A_1^-$ is a weakly coupled pair (10); its singlet state $^1(P700^+A_1^-)$ (as created from $^1P700^*$ via $^1(P700^+A_0^-)$) and all three substates of its triplet state $^3(P700^+A_1^-)$ are nearly degenerate in the absence of a B-field; these states are mixed by hyperfine interactions on a time scale of 10 ns, leading to a population of up to 75% for $^3(P700^+A_1^-)$.

(II) A B-field lifts the degeneracy of the T_+ and T_- substates of $^3(P700^+A_1^-)$ with the T_0 substate and with $^1(P700^+A_1^-)$ so that only the latter two states can be mixed. This results in up to 50% population for T_0 as the only populated substate of $^3(P700^+A_1^-)$.

(III) If the rate constant k_T for the triplet recombination path $^3(P700^+A_1^-) \longrightarrow ^3P700$ is much higher than that for the singlet path $^1(P700^+A_1^-) \longrightarrow ^1P700$, the yield of $^3P700$ should be close to 1 and fairly independent of the magnetic field, as observed in (7). The rate of $^3P700$ formation, however, should be decreased by a B-field according to the decreased population of $^3(P700^+A_1^-)$ as observed in Fig. 3.

ACKNOWLEDGEMENTS. This work was supported by the DFG.

REFERENCES
1 Lagoutte, B. and Mathis, P. (1989) Photochem. Photobiol. 49, 833-844
2 Sauer, K., Mathis, P., Acker, S. and van Best, J.A. (1978) Biochim. Biophys. Acta 503, 120-134
3 Takahashi, Y. and Katoh, S. (1982) Arch. Biochim. Biophys. 219, 219-2274
4 Brettel, K. (1988) FEBS Lett. 239, 93-98
5 Bock, C.H., Brettel, K., van der Est, A.J., Sieckmann, I. and Stehlik, D. (1989) these proceedings
6 Mathis, P. and Sétif, P. (1988) FEBS Lett. 237, 65-68
7 Sétif, P. and Bottin, H. (1989) Biochemistry 28, 2689-2697
8 Den Blanken, H.J. and Hoff, A.J. (1983) Biochim.Biophys. Acta 724, 52-61
9 Hoff, A.J. (1981) Quart. Rev. Biophys. 14, 599-665
10 Stehlik, D., Bock, C.H. and Petersen, J.(1989) J. Phys. Chem. 93, 1612-1619

DARK REDUCTION OF THE PHOTOSYSTEM–I ELECTRON ACCEPTOR A1

**Hervé Bottin and Pierre Sétif. Dépt. Biologie, Sce Biophysique
CEN de Saclay   91191 Gif sur Yvette Cedex   FRANCE**

1. INTRODUCTION

Continuous illumination of PS–I reaction centers in the presence of dithionite and at high pH is known to induce the reduction of the iron–sulfur electron acceptors $Fe–S_A$, $Fe–S_B$ and $Fe–S_X$ (1). Under such conditions, a flash induces the charge separation state $P–700^+...A_1^-$ (A_1 has been identified with phylloquinone (2)), characterized by its recombination half–time ($t_{1/2} < 1\mu s$ in spinach)(3). It has been recently shown that a strong illumination induces the stable double reduction of the acceptor A_1 (2). In the present work, it is shown that the incubation in total darkness of PS–I from the cyanobacterium Synechocystis PCC 6803 at high pH, in the presence of dithionite and electron mediators such as methylviologen, induces the inhibition of the electron transfer after the primary electron acceptor A_0. Results are interpreted as due to A_1 double reduction. The reduced reaction acceptor can be totally re–oxidized by ferricyanide or oxygen without any damage.

2. MATERIALS AND METHODS

PS–I reaction centers from Synechocystis PCC 6803 were prepared according to Biggins and Mathis (2). Flash spectroscopy measurements were done at 820 nm using a laser excitation at 532 nm, 30 ps duration as described by Sétif and Bottin (3). Potentiometric measurements were done directly in the optical cuvette, using platinum and calomel electrodes. The cuvette was continuously flushed with oxygen–free argon.

3. RESULTS AND DISCUSSION

Incubation of PS–I reactions centers in darkness, in the presence of dithionite in excess does not induce the appearance of a sub–μs recombination reaction. Depending on the pH value (between 8 and 11), this treatment results either in the reduction of $Fe–S_A$ and $Fe–S_B$ (pH > 10) or leaves these iron–sulfur acceptors partially in the oxidized state (pH < 10). Identical experiments performed in the presence of methylviologen alone or methylviologen (MV), benzylviologen (BV), triquat (TQ) and PP–670 gave the following results. For pH values >9, the absorbance changes measured at 820 nm showed the appearance of a fast decay ($t_{1/2}$ = 45–50 ns). The total amplitude of the flash induced absorbance change was also increased. This increase is attributed to the absorption of A_0^-. The amplitude of this kinetic

M. Baltscheffsky (ed.), Current Research in Photosynthesis, Vol. II, 631–634.

phase increased with incubation time as shown in figure 1. The half times of appearance of the fast decay under different conditions are summarized in the table.

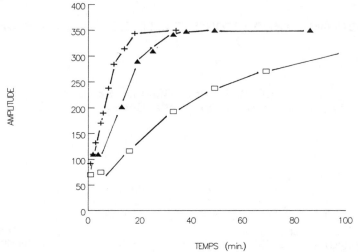

TEMPS (min.)

Figure 1: Amplitude of the fast decay ($t_{1/2}$ = 50 ns) measured at 820 nm versus the time of incubation in darkness. MV, BV, TQ and PP–670 were 40 μM; Na dithionite was 12 mM; chlorophyll: 50μg/ml; Glycine/NaOH 0.2 M. The suspension was continuously stirred and the cuvette was flushed with oxygen–free argon. Crosses: pH 11. Triangles: pH 10. Open squares: pH 9.

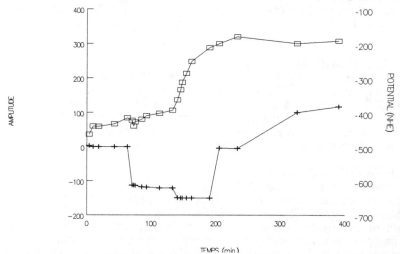

TEMPS (min.)

Figure 2: Amplitude of the fast decay ($t_{1/2}$ = 50 ns) (squares) and measured redox potential (crosses) versus time of dark incubation. Chlorophyll 50μg/ml. MV and TQ were 96 μM. Glycine/NaOH 0.2 M, pH 11. The potential was lowered or increased by addition of small volumes of concentrated dithionite or of diluted ferricyanide.

Table

pH	$t_{1/2}$	$t_{1/2}$	Em (N.H.E.)
	MV alone (40 μM)	MV + BV + TQ + PP (40 μM each)	
11	4 min	6 min	– 655 mV
10	5–6 min	12 min	–635 mV
9	> 60 min	35 min	–575 mV

Figure 2 shows the time course of a dark incubation at pH 11 as shown before, but in this case the Em has been decreased step by step, by successive additions of concentrated dithionite. It shows that the $t_{1/2}$ of appearance of the fast kinetic phase does not depend directly upon the pH but upon the Em of the suspension medium. At Em = –455 mV the fast phase is absent, at Em = –575 mV it appears with a $t_{1/2}$ of several hours and at Em = –605 mV, $t_{1/2}$ = 15 minutes.

Figure 2 also shows that after the fast phase has appeared, if the redox potential is increased to –455 mV, the amplitude of the fast phase stays at its maximum value. So the reaction responsible for the appearance of the 50 ns phase is either an irreversible process or is kinetically limited (when the Em is higher than –500 mV). A similar observation has been made on a sample in which the fast phase was induced by continuous illumination in the presence of dithionite. No decrease of the fast decay occured after 25 hours at Em $\approx$ – 255 mV.

It must be noted that the four electron mediators used here are not equivalently efficient (MV > TQ > BV > PP–670), and that their efficiency is not related to their midpoint potential (BV > MV >TQ >PP–670)(not shown).

Overnight dialysis against fresh buffer of a sample in which the fast phase has totally developped restores entirely the electron transfer from P–700 to the iron–sulfur centers Fe–S_A or Fe–S_B. Such a dialysed sample can be submitted to another dark incubation in the presence of dithionite and mediators, and then shows a behaviour similar to that of a fresh sample.

A similar mechanism has been proposed for the double reduction of Q_A in PS–II reaction centers by Van Mieghem et al.(4) and in purple bacteria by Okamura et al.(5). In the case of PS–I, the dark incubation in the presence of dithionite induces the inhibition of the electron transfer further than A_0. The potential values that are reached are obviously not low enough to promote the reduction of A_1 to A_1^- (Em A_1/A_1^- <–700 mV). Different mechanims for the inhibition of the electron transfer from A_0^- to A_1 can be proposed. As the dark reduction of A_1 to the semiquinone form is unlikely, we consider that the double reduction of A_1 is the most probable interpretation of our results. However, it cannot be excluded that electron transfer from A_0^- to A_1 can be impeded due to some other structural or chemical modifications of A_1, induced by the non–physiological experimental conditions.

II.7.**634**

4. REFERENCES

1. Evans,M.C.W., Sihra,C.K., Bolton,J.R. and Cammack,R. (1975) Nature 256, 668–670.

2. Biggins,J. and Mathis,P. (1988) Biochemistry 27,1494–1500.

3. Sétif,P. and Bottin,H. (1989) Biochemistry 28,2689–2697.

4. van Mieghem,F., Nitschke,W., Mathis,P. and Rutherford A.W. (1989), Biochim.Biophys. Acta in press.

5. Okamura,M.Y., Isaacson,R.A. and Feher,G. (1979) Biochim.Biophys. Acta 546,394–417.

NANOSECOND SPECTROSCOPY OF EARLY ELECTRON TRANSFERS IN PHOTOSYS-
TEM 1. IRON-SULFUR CLUSTER F_x IS REDUCED WITHIN 5 NANOSECONDS.

Joseph T. Warden, Center for Biophysics, Department of Chemistry, Rensselaer Polytechnic Institute, Troy, NY, USA 12180-3590

1. INTRODUCTION

The reaction-center protein complex of Photosystem 1 is comprised of the primary
photo-oxidant, P700, and a triad of non-heme iron-sulfur clusters, labeled F_x, F_A and F_B.
Clusters F_A and F_B have been assigned to a 8.9 kDa polypeptide associated with PS1 and are
(4Fe-4S) structures exhibiting reduction potentials of -540mV and -590mV respectively [1].
Recent EXAFS studies suggest that Center F_x is also a 4Fe-4S cluster [2], although the esr
spectrum and reduction potential for this species (~-720mV) is anomalous for four iron clusters.

Evidence has accumulated recently for the existence of two electron carriers intermediate between P700 and the iron-sulfur cluster acceptors [1]. The presumed primary acceptor
is designated as A0 and has been attributed to a chlorophyll [3] . Evidence for the second
intermediary acceptor, A1, in Photosystem 1 is provided by absorption changes detected in the
350-400 nm region at cryogenic and room temperature [4,5]. The chemical identity for A1 is
speculative, although a tentative assignment to phylloquinone anion has been proposed [6].
Setif and Mathis have detected a *ca*. 15 ns transient, centered about 370 nm, which is persistent
in the presence of dithionite [4]. In contrast, Brettel observes a 200 ns transient with a spectrum
similar to that reported by Setif and Mathis [5]. Both laboratories assign the decay kinetics to
forward electron transfer, presumably to Center F_x; however, the source of the discrepancy in
the temporal data between the two laboratories is obscure.

If the electron transfer sequence is linear from P700 to F_x:
$$P700 \rightarrow A0 \rightarrow A1 \rightarrow F_x$$
then a careful comparative examination of the kinetics for the formation of F_x^- and the oxidation
of the A1 anion should provide quantitative and mechanistic verification of the role of the 370-
380 nm transient in Photosystem 1 electron transport.

2. MATERIALS AND METHODS

Flash spectroscopic studies were performed with a purpose-designed instrument optimized for measurements in the wavelength range 220-600 nm with temporal duration of 5 ns-
1 μs. An EG&G FX200U UV-grade bulb flashlamp is utilized as a monitoring source. This flashlamp is powered by a 15J supply; the lamp and power supply combination permit repetitive,
kinetic measurements to be made at the 10 Hz frequency of the Nd-YAG actinic source. The
image of the arc of the lamp is focussed behind the sample cell on a 2.0 mm slit and the resulting
image is collected and refocussed on the entrance slit of a 250 mm monochromator. The
entrance slit to the monochromator is filtered by an appropriate interference filter to discriminate against the actinic flash and the accompanying fluorescence artifact. Optical transients
in the 300-500 nm region are detected with an EMI 9816 photomultiplier; the minimum
instrument response time ($t_{1/2}$) is determined to be 4 ns. Timing for the probe pulse and data
collection trigger is controlled by an SRS DG535 Programmable Pulse Generator. A Tektronix
7912AD transient recorder, controlled by a PC-AT clone, is utilized for data collection. Routines
for data collection were derived from the Tektronix Guru II package and kinetic analysis of the
experimental data was performed on a Sun 3/50 workstation.

Photosystem 1 particles with Chl/P700 ~ 120 were fractionated with Triton X-100 from

M. Baltscheffsky (ed.), Current Research in Photosynthesis, Vol. II, 635–638.
© 1990 *Kluwer Academic Publishers. Printed in the Netherlands.*

locally grown spinach[7]. These particles contain the full complement of acceptor iron-sulfur clusters: F_X, F_A and F_B. Photosystem 1 particles deficient in clusters F_A and F_B were prepared from the Triton PS1 particles by the method of Golbeck [8]. Photosystem 1 particles from Synechococcus sp. 6301, containing only Center F_X were generously provided by Kevin Parrett and John Golbeck. For analysis all PS 1 samples were suspended (Chl - 10-20 µg/mL) in Tris buffer (50 mM, pH 8.3) and supplied with 40 µM dichlorophenol indophenol and 2mM sodium ascorbate.

3. RESULTS AND DISCUSSION

The 350-450 nm region has been examined in spinach Triton and spinach or Synechococus PS1 particles depleted of the tertiary acceptors, F_A and F_B. Figure 1 presents the transient absorption spectrum at 5 ns for the Synechococcus core protein. Identical spectra (within experimental error) were obtained also from Triton PS1 particles which either contained or were deficient in Centers F_A and F_B. In the region centered about 430 nm a bleaching is observed that arises from the oxidation of P700 and the reduction of an iron-sulfur cluster. In the Synechococcus particles the extent of bleaching is comparable to that reported by Golbeck for the formation of the $P700^+F_X^-$ pair [1].

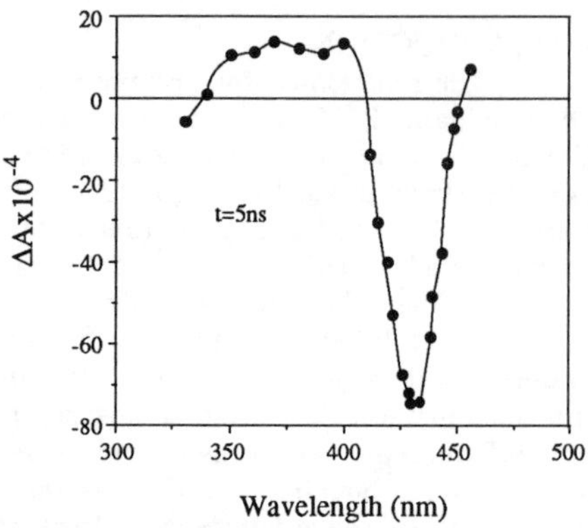

In the wavelength region below 400 nm an absorption increase is observed that is greater than that predicted (especially in the region of 370-380 nm) solely from the contribution of $P700^+$ [9]. The transient spectrum in this region is comparable to that reported by

Figure 1. Transient absorption spectrum at 5 ns for Synechococcus PS 1 particles. Each point represents the average of 256 events. Actinic illumination was provided at 598 nm with energy of 2 mJ per pulse at a repetition rate of 1.3 Hz.

Brettel et al. [6] and by Brettel [5]; a spectrum attributed to A1 anion, the secondary electron acceptor in PS 1.

Representative flash-induced kinetics at four wavelengths are presented in Figure 2. At 430 nm P700 oxidation occurs within the instrumental response time and no rereduction is observed during the 160 ns observation period following the flash. Similar oxidation kinetics are observed with Photosystem 1 particles containing or deficient in Centers F_A or F_B. In contrast to Brettel's observation there is no 200 ns bleaching component observed at this wavelength, although reduction of F_X is predicted to contribute ca. 27% to the absorption change at 430nm [1].

The kinetics at 430 nm indicate that if indeed Center F_X is reduced as suggested by the extent of the bleaching in the 425-435 nm region (Figure 1), then the reduction must occur within ca. 5ns. The difference spectrum for the $P700^+$/P700 couple contains two isosbestic wavelengths in the 400-450 nm region, one at 410 nm and the other at 445 nm (data not shown, [9]). Hence, these two wavelengths can be used as diagnostic for the kinetics and extent of reduction of the iron-sulfur acceptors in PS 1, since both F_X and F_A/F_B exhibit bleaching at these wavelengths. As Figure 2 illustrates, at 445 nm an absorbance decrease is observed which occurs within ca. 5ns. Since this preparation lacks Centers F_A and F_B, this bleaching is attributed to the reduction of F_X. Similar kinetics are observed in preparations containing Centers F_A and F_B. In no instance has a 200 ns or a 16 ns component been observed, the reduction of F_X appears to occur in tandem with the oxidation of P700! Equivalent kinetics are obtained also at the 410 nm isosbestic wavelength for P700$^+$/P700.

If the putative, intermediary acceptor, A1, functions between A0 and F_x, then the data of Figure 2 suggests that the kinetics for A1$^-$ reoxidation, monitored at wavelengths diagnostic for A1, should occur within the time resolution of the spectrometer. As a test of this premise, flash photolysis was performed at 380 nm, a wavelength reported to be indicative for A1 anion. As depicted by Figure 2, after the initial increase during the actinic flash, the absorbance exhibits a biphasic decrease with the half-life of the fast phase (accounting for 55% of the total transient absorbance) determined to be ca. 33±5 ns. The biphasic absorption kinetics at 380 nm, a wavelength at which absorbance from P700$^+$ is minimal (ca. 5 x 10^{-4}), is similar to that

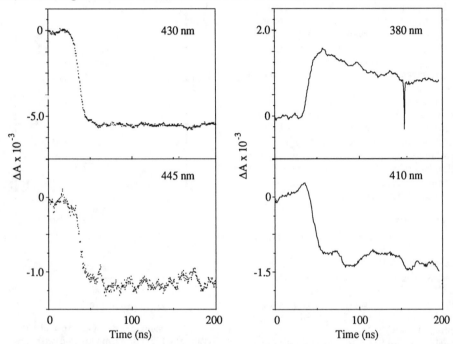

Figure 2. Transient kinetics induced by a 7 ns (FWHM) laser flash in Synechococcus PS 1 core protein at 19 °C. Data at 430 nm and 445 nm were collected with 256 averages. Data at 380 nm and 410 nm represent 512 averages.

reported recently by Setif and Mathis [4]. The slow phase which cannot be fit accurately on this time scale is estimated to have a half-life greater than 1 μs. The data of Figure 2 thus are not consistent with an assignment of the absorption change in the 350-380 nm region to an obligate electron carrier intermediate between A0 and F_x, since the decay kinetics at 380nm are slower than the observed reduction time for F_x. Rather, these data suggest, given the constraints of instrument time-resolution and sensitivity, that there is no experimental evidence for an intermediate electron acceptor, A1.

Recently we reported that inactivation of the iron-sulfur clusters during incubation of PS 1 with 8 M urea and 0.1M potassium ferricyanide correlates with the appearance of the spin-polarized, reaction-center triplet. This electron spin resonance study provided no evidence for the participation of the acceptor A1 in PS 1 electron transport, following the destruction of Center F_x [10]. Figure 3 presents the comparative kinetic study of spinach Triton PS 1 particles, following inactivation of the iron-sulfur clusters according to the protocol reported previously

II.7.**638**

[7]. The kinetics at 432 nm reveal a rapid bleaching preceding a biphasic absorption increase. The fast phase (71% of the total absorbance change) decays with a half-life of 16±5 ns and the slower phase (29%) extrapolates to a half-life of greater that 500 ns. The rapid kinetic phase is assigned to the recombination of the P700$^+$A0$^-$ radical pair [3], which has been reported to exhibit decay kinetics in the 20-50 ns domain. The slow phase has been assigned by Setif et al. to the radical-pair triplet of PS 1 [11], and the data of Figure 3 indicates that the PS 1 triplet

is formed in ca. 30% yield at room temperature in urea/ferricyanide-inactivated PS 1. Further examination of the kinetics at 370 nm for this PS 1 preparation, in which the acceptor, A1, is nonfunctional, reveals a biphasic decay similar to that observed in control samples. The fast phase (70% of the absorbance) has a half-life of 40±5 ns, similar to that observed in PS 1 preparations competent in forward electron tranport to the iron-sulfur acceptor(s). The presence of this kinetic component in inactivated samples is incongruous with the assignment of this transient to the A1 anion. Indeed, preliminary investigation of PS 1 particles depleted of phylloquinone by UV irradiation has demonstrated the existence of an analogous absorption transient centered in the region of 350-370 nm.

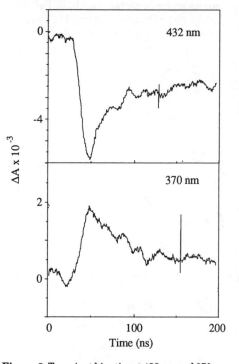

REFERENCES
1. Golbeck, J.H. (1989) Biochem. Biophys. Acta, 895. 167-204.
2. McDermott, A.E., Yachandra, V., Guiles, R., Sauer, K., Klein, M., Parrett, K. and Golbeck, J.H. (1989) Biochemistry (in press).
3. Shuvalov, V.A., Nuijs, A., van Gorkon, H., Smit, H. and Duysens, L. (1986) Biochem. Biophys. Acta 850, 319-323.
4. Mathis, P. and Setif, P. (1988) FEBS Letts., 237, 65-68.

Figure 3. Transient kinetics at 432 nm and 370 nm in Triton PS 1 particles inactivated with urea/ferricyanide. Each trace is the average of 512 flashes.

5. Brettel, K. (1988) FEBS Letts., 239, 93-98.
6. Brettel, K., Setif, P. and Mathis, P. (1986) FEBS Letts. 203, 230-234.
7. Golbeck, J.H. and Warden, J.T. (1982) Biochem. Biophys. Acta 681, 77-84.
8. Golbeck, J.H., Mehari, T., Parrett, K., Jones, K. and Brand, J. (1988) FEBS Letts., 240, 9-14.
9. Ke, B. (1972) Arch. Biochem. Biophys. 152, 70-77.
10. Warden, J.T. and Golbeck, J.H. (1987) Biochem. Biophys. Acta 891, 286-292.
11. Setif, P., Bottin, H. and Mathis, P. (1985) Biochem. Biophys. Acta 808, 112-122.

ACKNOWLEDGEMENTS
This research was supported by the National Institutes of Health (GM26133). The author acknowledges the contribution of Timothy Kohl for the development of the data analysis routines for the nanosecond spectrometer and the continued dialog and collaboration of John Golbeck in this laboratory's investigations in Photosystem 1.

FUNCTIONAL ROLE OF PHYLLOQUINONE ON THE ACCEPTOR SIDE OF PHOTOSYSTEM 1

JOHN BIGGINS and **NORMAND A. TANGUAY,** Section of Biochemistry, Brown University, Providence, RI 02912, USA; and **HARRY A. FRANK,** Department of Chemistry, University of Connecticut, Storrs, CT 06269, USA.

1. INTRODUCTION

The stabilization of charge in the primary reaction of PSI is promoted by rapid electron transfer reactions involving the five redox centers $A_0A_1F_xF_AF_B$ (1). A_0 is monomeric Chl a and $F_xF_AF_B$ are 4Fe:4S clusters. F_x is associated with the PSI core and F_AF_B are localized on an 8·9 kDa polypeptide. Provisional identification of A_1 as a quinone was based upon the EPR signal of A_1 (2,3) and comparison of the electron spin polarized flash-induced EPR K-band spectrum of the species $P_{700}^+A_1^-$ with that of $P_{870}^+Q^-$ in Fe-depleted bacterial reaction centers (4). Direct support for the participation of quinone followed a study of flash-induced optical transients at low temperature (5) and the specific reconstitution of room temperature electron transfer reactions in solvent-extracted cyanobacterial PSI using phylloquinone (vitamin K_1) (6). The reconstitution studies have been recently confirmed using an ether-extracted preparation of PSI derived from spinach (7).

Two sets of data pertaining to the involvement of phylloquinone, however, are presently controversial. Examination of preparations of PSI that were totally depleted of phylloquinone by solvent extraction showed that the terminal acceptors F_AF_B were photoreduced at low temperature (8), and preparations that were irradiated using UV to destroy the phylloquinone *in situ* still showed the room temperature recombination between P_{700}^+ and terminal Fe:S$^-$ (9) and the EPR spectrum of A_1 (10).

This reports 1) a reinvestigation of the effect of UV-irradiation on the electron transfer activities of PSI, and 2) an examination of the quinone specificity for the reconstitution of solvent-extracted preparations in primary electron transfer.

2. MATERIALS AND METHODS

2.1 Spinach D-144 preparations enriched in PSI were isolated (11) and stored at -80^0. Extraction of lyophyllized PSI, phylloquinone analysis, NADP$^+$-photoreduction and reconstitution were as reported previously (6).

2.2 The UV-irradiation of PSI was conducted at 2^0C at a Chl concentration of 10 μg/ml, incident intensity 50 Wm^{-2} and wavelengths 300-400 nm.

2.3 Flash-induced absorbance transients were detected at both 820 and 700 nm. Saturating activation flashes, 8-9 ns FWHH, were provided by a Q-switched, frequency doubled Nd:YAG laser.

2.4 EPR experiments were carried out using an X-band spectrometer employing an E102-E bridge, field modulation 100 kHz and 16G, lock-in sensitivity 100 mV, sweep time 10 min, time constant 1 s, microwave frequency 9·055 GHz and microwave power 50 mW. The temperature was maintained between 7-10K using a He-flow cryostat.

M. Baltscheffsky (ed.), Current Research in Photosynthesis, Vol. II, 639–642.
© 1990 *Kluwer Academic Publishers. Printed in the Netherlands.*

2.5 Quinones were obtained from Aldrich Chem. Co., Sigma Chem. Co., and through the kindness of Dr. Peter Rich, Bodmin, U.K.

3. RESULTS AND DISCUSSION
3.1 Effects of UV-irradiation on PSI.
3.1.1 The PSI preparations were found to contain $2 \cdot 12 \pm 0 \cdot 38$ phylloquinone/ P_{700} and upon UV-irradiation the quinone was depleted after approximately 2 hr. Figure 1 shows that the inactivation of $NADP^+$-photoreduction (- $\diamond$ -) closely follows the quinone depletion (- $\blacklozenge$ -) confirming the results observed for solvent extraction of phylloquinone in *Synechocystis* PSI (6) and that loss of physiological electron transfer parallels the removal of phylloquinone.

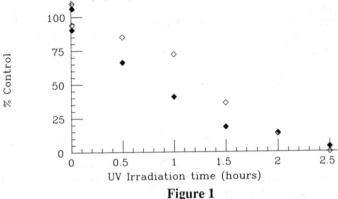

Figure 1

3.1.2 Figure 2 shows flash-induced absorbance transients due to P_{700}^+. The decay halftime in the control was ca 30 ms and assumed to reflect recombination between P_{700}^+ and $F_A F_B^-$ (1). After UV-irradiation and depletion of phylloquinone the optical transient still showed a slow recombination in confirmation of (9) but the decay halftime was longer. This behavior is different from that in solvent-extracted preparations where a fast recombination was observed between P_{700}^+ and A_0^- (6). We suggest that UV-irradiation results in extensive modification of PSI and that the optical flash transients do not support the conclusion (9) that PSI electron transfer function is unimpaired following such treatment.

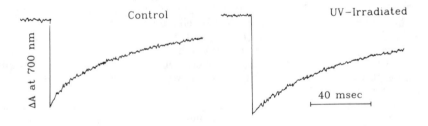

Figure 2

3.1.3   The behavior of the terminal Fe:S centers, $F_A F_B$, was investigated via EPR for control and UV-irradiated PSI preparations. Figure 3 shows that center F_A was phototrapped (15 sec light at 7K, record in darkness) in both the control and the sample depleted of phylloquinone. The samples were then continuously illuminated and Figure 4 shows that center F_B was reduced in both samples. For both light protocols, the EPR intensities arising from the $F_A F_B$ centers in control and UV-irradiated samples were comparable indicating that the terminal acceptors were photoreduced at low temperature in PSI depleted of phylloquinone. These data confirm the observations of similar experiments on solvent-extracted PSI (8), and we conclude that this anomaly results from heterogeneity introduced into PSI due to quinone removal, or to a bypass of the phylloquinone acceptor site.

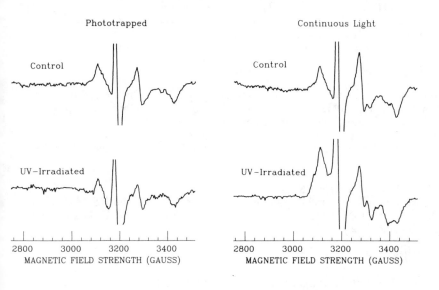

Figure 3   Figure 4

3.2 Quinone substitution studies.

3.2.1 We showed previously that vitamin K_3 (2-methyl 1-4, naphthoquinone) would not substitute for phylloquinone in the reconstitution of PSI, and concluded that the 3-phytyl tail may be essential to provide the correct interaction for binding the quinone in the active site on the PSI core (6). We have now extended this study and examined additional naphtho- and ubiquinone derivatives for possible reconstitution of phylloquinone-extracted PSI preparations. Table 1 shows the structures of the quinones tested so far.

As noted previously (6), the extracted PSI showed a very rapid recombination reaction between P_{700}^+ and A_0^-, and decay of triplet P_{700} resulting from the primary biradical as measured by room temperature flash kinetic spectroscopy. Addition of 5 μm phylloquinone restored the slow (30 ms) flash transient indicative of reconstitution

TABLE 1.   Quinones tested for reconstitution of PSI electron transfer

1-4 Naphthoquinones

	position 2	position 3	activity
K1	methyl	phytyl	+
K3	methyl	H	-
K2	methyl	[isoprenyl]4	-
	methyl	[isoprenyl]2	-
	methyl	decyl	-
	H	decyl	-
	H	H	-
ubiquinones	[isoprenyl]6		-
	[isoprenyl]10		-

of electron transfer function, and this was not radically affected by the addition of 5 mM dithionite which would reduce exogenous phylloquinone, but not that occupying the acceptor site at a redox potential more negative than -0.7 mV (12). In contrast, all the other quinones tested would not reconstitute but acted as good exogenous electron acceptors. We conclude that the acceptor site is specific for phylloquinone.

4.   ACKNOWLEDGMENTS

The research was supported by the NSF (DMB-86-03586) and USDA-CRGO (88-37130-4135) to John Biggins and the NIH (GM-30353) and USDA-CRGO (88-37130-3938) to Harry A. Frank.

REFERENCES

1. Goldbeck, J.H. (1987), *Biochim. Biophys. Acta*, **895**, 167-204.
2. Bonnerjea, J., and Evans, M.C.W. (1982), *FEBS Lett.* **148**, 313-316.
3. Gast, P., Swarthoff, T., Ebskamp, F.C.R., and Hoff, A.J. (1983), *Biochim. Biophys. Acta* **722**, 168-175.
4. Peterson, J., Stehlick, D., Gast, P., and Thurnauer, M. (1987) *Photosynth. Res.* **14**, 15-29.
5. Brettel, K., Setif, P., and Mathis, P. (1987) *FEBS Lett.* **203**, 220-224.
6. Biggins, J., and Mathis, P. (1988) *Biochemistry* **27**, 1494-1500.
7. Itoh, S., and Kwaki, M. (1989) *FEBS Lett.* **243**, 47-52.
8. Setif, P., Ikegami, I., and Biggins, J. (1987) *Biochim. Biophys. Acta* **894**, 146-156.
9. Palace, G.P., Franke, J.E., and Warden, J.T. (1987) *FEBS Lett.* **215**, 58-62.
10. Zeigler, K., Lockau, W., and Nitschke, W. (1987) *FEBS Lett.* **217**, 16-20.
11. Anderson, J.M., and Boardman, N.K. (1966) *Biochim. Biophys. Acta* **112**, 403-421.
12. Chamarovsky, S.K., and Cammack, R. (1982) *Photobiochem. Photobiophys.* **4**, 195-200.

PROPERTIES OF P700–ENRICHED PARTICLES ISOLATED FROM THE THERMOPHILIC CYANOBACTERIUM SYNECHOCOCCUS ELONGATUS

ISAMU IKEGAMI[a], SHIGERU ITOH[b] and SAKAE KATOH[c]
[a]Faculty of Pharmaceutical Sciences, Teikyo University, Sagamiko, Kanagawa 199-01, [b]National Institute for Basic Biology, Okazaki 444 and [c]Department of Biology, Faculty of Science, University of Tokyo, Tokyo 113, JAPAN

1. INTRODUCTION

By the treatment with ether containing an appropriate amount of water, antenna chlorophyll is selectively extracted from spinach PS–I particles without any loss of P700, resulting in a chl–a to P700 ratio as low as 6–9(1). Two molecules of vitamin K_1(VK_1) in PS–I are also extracted by this treatment, concomitant with a considerable decrease in electron flow from P700 to the PS–I stable electron acceptor (F_A/F_B)(2). In this work, we used the thermophilic cyanobacterium Synechococcus elongatus as a material to prepare P700–enriched particles. Because of its high thermostability as well as its far genealogical distance from spinach, it is interesting to compare the organization of chromophores around P700 between these two organisms.

2. METHODS

Spectrophotometric assay of P700 and light–induced absorption changes were carried out with a Hitachi 556 dual wavelength spectrophotometer(1,2). EPR measurements of Fe–S proteins were performed as described previously(2).

3. RESULTS AND DISCUSSION

3.1. Preparation of P700–enriched particles from cyanobacterium

Washing of lyophilized Synechococcus thylakoid membranes with diethylether containing an appropriate amount of water, extracted most of chl–a and β–carotene without loss of P700 activity. A part of phycobiliproteins, which remained tightly bound after the ether–wash, were easily removed by successive washing with water. The washed membranes were then solubilized with 0.1–0.3% Triton X–100 and insoluble brownish-red materials were removed by centrifugation. After addition of solid ammonium sulfate(0.13g/ml) to the blue–green supernatant, precipitates formed were collected and then dissolved into phosphate buffer(20 mM, pH 8) containing 0.1–0.2% Triton X–100. P700–enriched particles thus prepared had a polypeptide composition similar to that of the CP–1 complexes isolated previously from the same cyanobacterium, showing two prominent bands of 60–67 kDa and three small bands of 14, 13 and 10 kDa by SDS-PAGE.

M. Baltscheffsky (ed.), Current Research in Photosynthesis, Vol. II, 643–646.
© 1990 *Kluwer Academic Publishers. Printed in the Netherlands.*

3.2. Effect of water content in ether(TABLE 1)

As has been described with spinach PS-I particles(1), the higher the water content in ether was, the more the pigments were extracted. There was essentially no loss of photochemically active P700 with increasing water content in ether up to 70% saturation. Consequently, the ratio of the total chl-a to P700 decreased from 147 to 13. At higher levels of water content in ether, P700 was also extracted so that any further enrichment of P700 was not achieved. The absorption spectrum of the P700-enriched particles having a chl-a/P700 ratio of 13 was similar to that of spinach P700-enriched particles(3), suggesting similar chlorophyll components locating in or around the PS-I reaction center. Three VK_1 present in the Synechococcus thylakoid membranes were almost completely extracted by treatment even with dry ether.

TABLE 1 Chl, P700 and VK_1 contents in the particles extracted with diethylether containing various amounts of water

Sample	H_2O content in ether (%saturation)	Chl-a (%)	P700 (%)	Chl-a/P700 (mol/mol)	VK_1/P700 (mol/mol)
Thylakoid membranes	–	100	100	147	2.95
Ether-extracted particles	0	40.5	104	57	n.d.
	20	28.0	103	40	–
	40	16.5	106	23	–
	70	8.6	97	13	n.d.
	100	3.6	41	13	–

(n.d., not detected)

3.3. Light-induced absorption changes of P700(FIGURE 1)

Illumination of spinach P700-enriched particles with continuous light caused almost complete photooxidation of P700 in spite of the absence of vitamin K_1(2), suggesting a significant electron flow bypassing A_1. In contrast, P700 was slowly and only partially photooxidized by illumination of Synechococcus P700-enriched particles. The addition of VK_3(or VK_1) to the particles significantly increased both rate and magnitude of P700 photooxidation. Thus, the electron leakage is not significant in the cyanobacterial preparation.

3.4. EPR signals of F_A/F_B(FIGURE 2)

On illumination of the Synechococcus thylakoid membranes at 20K, one electron is transferred from P700 to F_A/F_B and the EPR signal mainly corresponding to the F_A^-/F_B state was observed. The photoreduction of F_A/F_B at 20K was diminished in the ether-extracted (i.e., VK_1-depleted) particles even after prolonged illumination, indicating a block in electron flow to F_A/F_B(cf. Fig. 1). However, on addition of VK_1(or VK_3), the photoreduction of F_A/F_B was recovered to about 80% of the original level, although F_B was preferentially reduced after ether-extraction(see ref. 2). The results suggest that externally added naphthoquinones bind to the A_1-binding site on PS-I core protein and act as an electron carrier between A_0 and the Fe-S centers, consistent with the notion that A_1 is vitamin K_1.

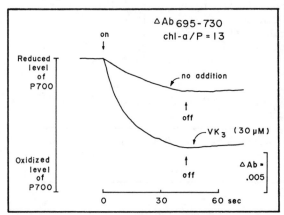

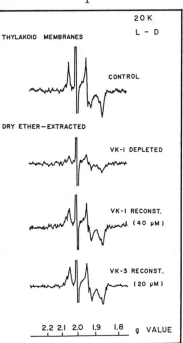

FIGURE 1(upper) Light-induced absorbance changes in P700-enriched particles(the absorbance at 675 nm = 0.200)

FIGURE 2(right) Light-minus-dark difference EPR spectra at 20K. Concentrations of P700 were adjusted to 22.5 µM in all preparations. (9.7GHz, 10mW, 10G)

3.5. Heat stability of P700(TABLE 2)

P700 was fully photoactive even after heat treatment of Synechococcus membranes at 80°C for 5 min. The heat stability of P700 was considerably diminished with decreasing antenna size. Treatment at 50°C for 5 min inactivated P700 photooxidation only by 5% in dry ether-extracted particles which had a chl-a/P700 ratio of 54, whereas the same treatment caused 40% and 70-75% inactivation in particles having a chl-a/P700 ratio of 22 and 13, respectively. Chemical determination of P700 revealed that the heat inactivation is due to destruction of P700 itself.

Interestingly, heat stability of P700 photooxidation was significantly restored by readdition of the ether extract to ether-extracted particles. Purified chl-a can rebind to ether-extracted particles without any appreciable effect on the heat stability. On the other hand, combined addition of chl-a and phosphatidylglycerol (PG), markedly increased the heat stability of P700. MGDG was less effective than PG, and other lipids, such as PC, PI and DGDG, were without effect. Addition of PG alone was ineffective, either.

4. CONCLUSION

In conclusion, Synechococcus P700-enriched particles are excellent materials for investigation on the function of VK_1 in PS-I, because there is little electron leakage from A_0 to the Fe–S centers but the electron flow is effectively restored by added naphthoquinones. Another unique feature of the cyanobacterium is an extremely high thermostability of P700 photooxidation. The present work indicates that chl-a and lipids greatly contribute to the heat stable property of the PS-I reaction center. Because P700 is associated with the two chl-containing subunit polypeptides, the deformation of the poly-peptides must result in destruction of P700. We suggest that chl-a and lipids have important structural roles to fortify the conformation of the two subunit polypeptides.

TABLE 2 Effect of chl-a and lipids on heat stability of P700 in ether-extracted particles

Preparations	Chl-a (%)	Chl-a/P700 (mol/mol)	Inactivation of P700 photoox. (%)**
Thylakoid membranes	100	147	0
Dry ether-extracted particles	40.5	57	5
Wet ether-extracted particles	4.0	13	73
Wet ether-extracted particles reconstituted with*			
Ether extract	30.4	90	55
Chl-a	12.0	40	74
PG	4.0	13	71
Chl-a + PG	27.7	65	25
Chl-a + MGDG	25.9	64	44
Chl-a + PI	24.8	68	60
Chl-a + PC	10.7	30	65
Chl-a + DGDG	13.2	36	68

*Ether extract(90 µg chl-a, equivalent to about a half of the total chl-a originally present), chl-a(50 µg) or/and a lipid(200 µg) were added back to the wet(i.e., H_2O-saturated) ether-extracted particles. For the method of the reconstitution, see ref 4. **Magnitude of P700 photooxidation after treatment at $50^{\circ}C$ for 5 min relative to that before the heat treatment.

ACKNOWLEDGMENTS
   This work was supported in part by grants from Ministry of Education, Science and Culture in Japan, and by Co-operative Research Program of NIBB in Japan.

REFERENCES
1 Ikegami, I. and Katoh, S. (1975) Biochim. Biophys. Acta 376, 588–592
2 Itoh, S., Iwaki, M. and Ikegami, I. (1987) Biochim. Biophys. Acta 893, 508–516
3 Ikegami, I. and Itoh, S. (1986) Biochim. Biophys. Acta 851, 75–85
4 Ikegami, I. (1984) Biochim. Biophys. Acta 722, 492–497

FUNCTION OF SUBSTITUTED QUINONES AS THE ELECTRON ACCEPTOR A-1 (PHYLLOQUINONE) IN PHOTOSYSTEM I REACTION CENTER

Masayo Iwaki and Shigeru Itoh
National Institute for Basic Biology, Myodaijicho, Okazaki 444, Japan

1. INTRODUCTION

In the photosystem I (PS I) reaction center of oxygenic photosynthetic organisms, absorption of light oxidizes a reaction center chlorophyll a, P700, and initiates a series of electron transfer steps as follows [1]:

$$P700 \underset{35\text{ns } [2,6\text{-}9]}{\overset{<3\text{ps } [2,3]}{\rightleftharpoons}} A_0 \xrightarrow{35\text{ps } [2,3]} A_1 \xrightarrow{15 \text{ or } 200\text{ns } [4,5]} F_X \longrightarrow F_B, F_A \; (\rightarrow \rightarrow NADP)$$

where A_0 is the electron acceptor chlorophyll a-690 [2,3,9], and A_1 the primary electron acceptor, F_X, F_A or F_B iron-sulfur center X, A or B. The chemical identity of A_1 is presumably one of two phylloquinone (2-methyl-3-phytyl-1,4-naphthoquinone, vitamin K_1) molecules contained in the PS I reaction center [1,10]. The phylloquinone binding site (Q_φ site) in the PS I reaction center gives an environment, in which E_m value for semiquinone$^-$/quinone couple is significantly lower than that in the Q_A or Q_B site in reaction center of purple bacteria. We here report that phylloquinone in PS I reaction center can be replaced by various quinones. The efficiency of quinone to function as A_1 depended on its redox property as well as its structure.

2. MATERIALS AND METHODS

Lyophylized spinach PS I particles were extracted with diethyl-ether containing 50 % saturated level of water. The obtained particles are fully depleted of phylloquinone, about 85 % of antenna chlorophylls and all carotenoids [11-14]. P700, A_0, F_X, F_B and F_A were almost unaffected [9,11-14]. The particles were dispersed in 50 mM glycine buffer, pH 10 and then diluted in 50 mM Tris buffer, pH 7.5 containing 0.3 %(v/v) Triton X-100. After 30 min incubation, undissolved materials were eliminated by centrifugation. The supernatant was diluted with 50 mM Tris buffer, pH 7.5 containing 30 %(v/v) glycerol to give a final P700 concentration of 0.25 μM.

To reconstitute quinones, the suspension of the ether-extracted PS I particles was incubated with quinones for a day at 0°C in the dark. The flash-induced absorption change was measured by a split-beam spectrophotometer [12] at 6°C. The sample was excited by the flash (532

M. Baltscheffsky (ed.), Current Research in Photosynthesis, Vol. II, 647–650.
© 1990 *Kluwer Academic Publishers. Printed in the Netherlands.*

nm, 10 ns FWHM) from a frequency doubled Nd-YAG laser. $P700^+$ was reduced by an ascorbate - dichloroindophenol couple.

3. RESULTS AND DISCUSSION

In photosystem I reaction centers in which intrinsic phylloquinone is extracted with diethylether, only a small extent of $P700^+$ was detected in a μs-ms time range (traces of no additions in Fig. 1). This is interpreted by the rapid decay of $P700^+$ ($t_{1/2}$ = 35 ns) due to the recombination reaction with A_0^- [6-9]. This reaction produces a triplet state, $P700^T$ ($t_{1/2}$ = 80 μs) also detected at 695 nm (Fig. 1). A small extent of $P700^+$ decays slowly ($t_{1/2}$= 10-100 ms), due to the reduction either by an ascorbate-dichloroindophenol couple or by photo-reduced iron-sulfur centers. The flash-induced $P700^+$ extent in the μs-ms range was increased when various naphtho- and anthraquinones were substituted for the intrinsic phylloquinone (Fig. 1) indicating that all of them can oxidize A_0^-.

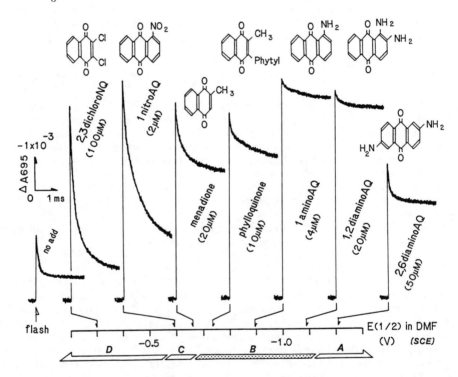

FIGURE 1. Flash-induced absorption change of P700 measured at 695 nm in the presence of substituted quinones in phylloquinone-depleted PS I particles. The concentration of each quinone was adjusted to give a saturating effect and shown in parenthesis. $E_{1/2}$ (S.C.E.) [16] can be related to $E_{1/2}$ (S.H.E.) by adding 0.24 V. NQ; 1,4- naphthoquinone. AQ; 9,10-anthraquinone.

Kinetic pattern of the flash-induced $P700^+$ seemed to vary depending on redox property, which is represented by the $E_{1/2}$ value in DMF, of reconstituted quinone. First of all, there is a group of quinones which induced the high extent of flash-oxidized $P700^+$ followed by a slow decay ($t_{1/2}$ = 10-100 ms). The slow decay time corresponds to the re-reduction of $P700^+$ by F_B/F_A [12]. Phylloquinone, 1-amino-anthraquinone and 1,2-diaminoanthraquinone belong to this group. These quinones fully mediated electron flow from A_0^- to F_X and then to F_B/F_A, i.e. replaced function of A_1. The E_m values of these quinones are, thus, expected to be intermediate between those of the A_0 and F_X. This group is regarded as type B in Fig. 2.

In the case of 2,6-diamino-9,10-anthraquinone having a lower $E_{1/2}$ value, the initial extent of $P700^+$ and the extent of the slow decay phase were low (Fig. 1). This may reflect incomplete reduction of this quinone by A_0^-. This quinone seems to belong to A type (Fig. 2), in which the E_m of the quinone is comparable or lower than that of A_0.

In the case of menadione and 1-nitroanthraquinone, the initial extent of 700^+ was high. The decay of $P700^+$ was composed of the fast ($t_{1/2}$ = 0.3-1 ms) and slow ($t_{1/2}$ = 30-100 ms) phases. This may be explained if these quinones have E_m comparable with that of F_X and can only partially reduce F_X and, therefore, F_B/F_A (type C). The remaining semiquinone$^-$ then will directly reduce $P700^+$ as the fast phase.

In the case of 2,3-dichloronaphthoquinone (Fig. 1), the high extent of flash-induced $P700^+$ decayed rapidly ($t_{1/2}$ = 300 μs) with almost no increase of the slow phase. This high potential quinone does not seem to reduce F_X. The semiquinone$^-$ formed seems to reduce $P700^+$ directly with this rate. E_m of this quinone is estimated to be too high to reduce F_X (type D).

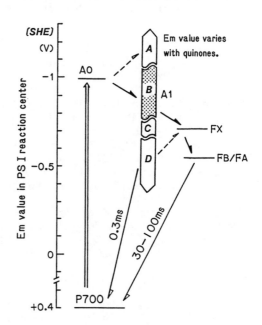

FIGURE 2.   Energy diagram and electron transfer pathways in PS I reaction centers containing various quinones with different E_m values of semiquinone$^-$/quinone couple (A, B, C and D types) in place of native phylloquinone.

4. CONCLUSION

Various quinones bind to the PS I $Q\varphi$ site in place of native phylloquinone and function as A_1. This supports that A_1 is phylloquinone and indicates that the quinone specificity of the site is not strict. Structural feature of phylloquinone such as having a phytyl group or a naphthoquinone ring, does not seem to be essential for the function as A_1, although it is important for binding to the Q_φ site. The quinones in the type B, which is characterized by the wide range of $E_{1/2}$ from -0.7 to -1.1 V (S.C.E)(Fig. 1), fully function as A_1. Benzoquinones, on the other hand, are rather unfavorable to function as A_1 because of their high E_m (data not shown).

We propose that thermodynamic relationship between the substituted quinone and its reaction partners can be grouped into four (A, B, C and D) types depending on its E_m *in situ* of the semiquinone$^-$/quinone couple in the Q_φ site (Fig. 2) with respect to E_m's of A_0 (about -1.0 V ?) and F_X (-0.705 V [15]). E_m values of the quinones in the Q_φ site seem to be almost linearly related to $E_{1/2}$ in DMF.

E_m of phylloquinone (A_1) in the Q_φ site can be estimated to be around -0.9 V (intermediate between A_0 and F_X), then it is 0.4 V lower than that in DMF, and 0.8 V lower than that of menaquinone in bacterial Q_A site [16]. Menaquinone differs only in structure of hydrocarbon tail from phylloquinone and also function as A_1 in the PS I Q_φ site (Iwaki and Itoh unpublished data). This indicates that the stability of semiquinone$^-$ is significantly lower at the Q_φ site than at the Q_A site.

5. ACKNOWLEDGMENT

The authors thank Dr. Y. Fujita of NIBB and Dr. P. L. Dutton of Univ. Pennsylvania for their stimulating discussions.

6. REFERENCES
 1. Andréasson, L.-E. and Vängard, T.(1988) Ann. Rev. Plant Physiol. Plant Mol. Biol. 39, 379-411.
 2. Shuvalov, V. A., Nuijs, A. M., van Gorkom, H. J.,Smit, H. W. J. and Duysens, L.N.M. (1986) Biochim. Biophys. Acta, 850, 319-323.
 3. Wasielewski, M. R., Fenton, J. M. and Govindjee (1987) Photosynth. Res. 12, 181-190.
 4. Mathis, P. and Sétif, P. (1988) FEBS Lett. 237, 65-68.
 5. Brettel, K.(1988) FEBS Lett. 239, 93-98.
 6. Biggins, J. and Mathis, P. (1988) Biochem. 27, 1494-1500.
 7. Ikegami, I., Sétif, P. and Mathis, P. (1987) Biochim. Biophys. Acta, 894, 414-422.
 8. Itoh, S. and Iwaki, M. (1988) Biochim. Biophys. Acta, 934, 32-38.
 9. Mathis, P., Ikegami, I. and Sétif, P. (1988) Photosynth. Res. 16, 203-210.
10. Takahashi, Y., Hirota, K. and Katoh, S.(1985) Photosynth. Res. 6, 183-192.
11. Itoh, S., Iwaki, M. and Ikegami, I. (1987) Biochim. Biophys. Acta, 893, 508-516.
12. Itoh, S. and Iwaki, M. (1989) FEBS Lett. 243, 47-52.
13. Itoh, S. and Iwaki, M. (1989) FEBS Lett. 250, 441-447.
14. Ikegami,I. and Katoh,S.(1975) Biochim. Biophys. Acta, 376,588-592.
15. Chamorovsky, S. K. and Cammack, R. (1982) Photobiochem. Photobiophys. 4, 195-200.
16. Woodbury, N. W., Parson, W. W., Gunner, M. R., Prince, R. C. and Dutton, P. L. (1986) Biochim. Biophys. Acta, 851, 6-22.

COMPETITIVE BINDINGS OF HERBICIDE AND QUINONE TO PHOTOSYSTEM I
PHYLLOQUINONE (A-1) BINDING SITE.

Shigeru Itoh and Masayo Iwaki
National Institute for Basic Biology, Nishigonaka 38, Myodaiji, Okazaki
444 (Japan)

1. INTRODUCTION
     In the reaction centers of photosystem II or purple bacteria, two
quinones function in series as the primary (Q_A) and the secondary (Q_B)
electron acceptors [1]. The Q_B sites are known to be the herbicide
binding sites [2]. On the other hand, binding of herbicide to PS I
reaction center has never been reported.
     PS I reaction center contains two molecules of phylloquinone (2-
methyl-3-phytyl-1,4-naphthoquinone=vitamin K_1)[3-5], one of which
functions as the electron acceptor A_1 [5-10] and mediates the electron
transfer between the reduced electron acceptor chlorophyll a (A_0^-) and
the iron sulfur center F_x.
     We first reported that PS I phylloquinone can be reversively
extracted with diethyl ether leaving the photochemical charge separation
activity virtually intact [5]. This enhances the rapid 35ns charge
recombination between the
oxidized donor P700$^+$ and A_0^-
[5-9]. Reconstitutions of
phylloquinone or menadione
(3-methyl-1,4-naphthoquinone)
[5-9], or other quiones [12]
suppress this recombination
reaction and restore the
electron transfer [5,7] from
A_0^- to iron sulfur centers,
as shown in Fig. 1 [9].
     In this study,
herbicide binding to the PS
I phylloquinone-binding site
(designated as the Q_φ site
[13]) was studied through
the competition between
herbicides and menadione to
the phylloquinone-extracted
PS I particles.

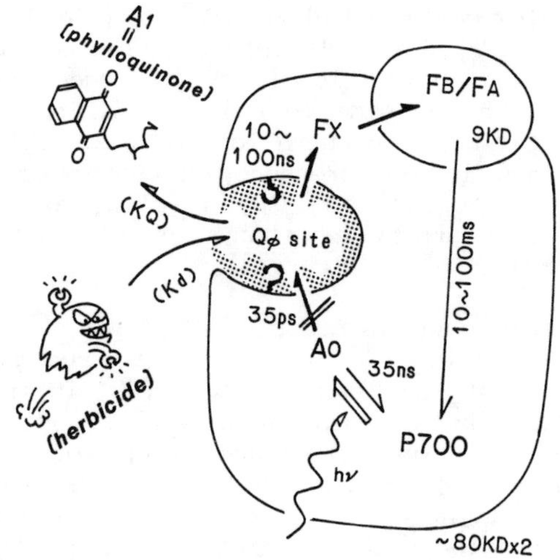

Figure 1. Quinone reconstitution and
herbicide binding to PS I reaction center

M. Baltscheffsky (ed.), Current Research in Photosynthesis, Vol. II, 651–654.
© 1990 Kluwer Academic Publishers. Printed in the Netherlands.

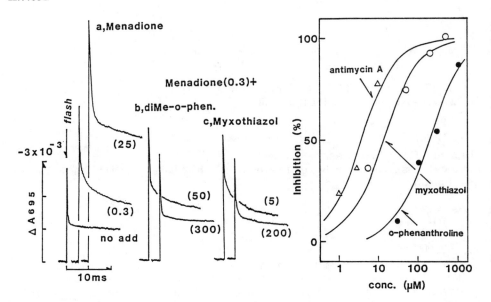

Figure 2.   Effects of menadione and inhibitors on the flash induced
oxidation of P700 in the ether-extracted PS I particles.   a, effect of
concentration of menadione. b-c, effects of inhibitors on the 0.3 µM
menadione-reconstituted P700 oxidation.
Figure 3.   Suppression of the 0.3 µM menadione-induced $P700^+$
  stabilization by inhibitors.

2. Materials and Methods.

Lyophylized spinach PS I particles were extracted twice with diethyl
ether containing a 50% saturated amount of water [5-7].   The resultant
particles contained about 20 chlorophylls/P700 and no phylloquinone and
carotenoids [5-7].   The ether-extracted particles, dissolved in a medium
containing 50 mM Tris-Cl (pH 7.5) and 0.1% Triton X-100 were diluted 50
times with the same medium   containing 30% glycerol without Triton to
give a final concentration of 0.22 µM, and   incubated with 0.3 µM
menadione in the presence or absence of inhibitors overnight at 0°.
Ten mM ascorbate and 0.1 mM dichloroindophenol were added to reduce
P700. The   absorption change of P700 induced by Nd-YAG laser flash was
measured at 6° [5,7].

3. Results and Discusion

Extraction of phylloquinone from PS I particles results in a
decrease of the flash-induced $P700^+$ in the µs-ms time range due to the
enhanced charge recombination [5-9] (see Fig. 1).   Flash excitation
induces a small rapid absorption change ($t_{1/2}$ =80µs) of the
recombination-induced $P700^T$ state   and a slow ($t_{1/2}$ =100ms) $P700^+$ decay
due to reduction by added dichloroindophenol (Fig. 2a) [7].
Preincubation with menadione enhances the $P700^+$ extent by suppressing
the charge recombination, with an apparent dissociation constant (K_Q) of
3.5×10^{-7} M.   This value   shows weaker binding of menadione than

phylloquinone ($K_Q < 10^{-8}$ M)[7]. The enhancement is interpreted by the longer stay of electrons in F_x and F_B/F_A mediated by menadione [5-7]. The extent of P700$^+$ in a μs-ms time range (Fig. 2a), thus, represents the extent of the menadione-reconstituted PS I reaction center.

Traces in Fig. 2 b and c show the P700$^+$ kinetics in the PS I particles reconstituted with 0.3 μM menadione. The reconstitution was suppressed in the presence of 4,7-dimethyl-o-phenanthroline or myxothiazol. However, higher concentrations of menadione, if added, gave the high extent of P700$^+$ even in the presence of these inhibitors indicating that the inhibitions are competitive (not shown).

The extent of flash-induced P700$^+$, supported by 0.3 μM menadione, was suppressed by o-phenanthroline, myxothiazol or antimycin A (Fig. 3). As the increase of inhibitor concetrations, the suppression became stronger. The curves are interpreted by competitive binding of these inhibitors and menadione to the Qφ site (see legend of Table 1). K_d values for antimycin A, myxothiazol and o-phenanthroline as well as other inhibitors were calculated by experiments as in Fig. 3 (Table 1).

Table I. K_d between herbicide and the PS I Q_φ site estimated in competitive inhibition of menadione reconstituion.

Additions	K_d value (M)
Q_B site inhibitors	
o-phenanthroline	1.2×10^{-4}
4,7-dimethyl-o-phenanthroline	2.4×10^{-5}
DBMIB	5.7×10^{-3}
Atrazine	$> 10^{-2}$
Prometone	5.7×10^{-3}
prometryne	1.1×10^{-3}
DCMU	1.8×10^{-4}
Inhibitors of b/c1 complex	
on the quinol-oxidase site	
Myxothiazol	9.5×10^{-6}
on the quinol-reductase site	
Antimycin A	2.8×10^{-6}
HOQNO	1.7×10^{-4}

K_d was calculated from the inhibition of the P700$^+$ extent as shown in Fig. 2 suported by 0.3 μM menadione using the equation below assuming a competitive, one-site binding.

$$R = \frac{1}{\dfrac{K_Q}{[Q]}\left(1+\dfrac{[I]}{K_d}\right)+1}$$

K_Q(menadione)=3.5×10^{-7} M. R;ratio of activities with and without herbicide. I; free herbicide concentration.

Phenanthrolines showed K_d values a little higher than those reported in the Q_B sites [2,7,14,15]. Similar or lower K_d values were estimated for HOQNO and myxothiazol. Antimycin A showed the lowest K_d value. On the other hand, atrazines, DCMU and bezoquinone analogue DBMIB, known to bind to the bacterial [2,14,15] and PS II Q_B sites [2], were rather ineffective in PS I. Similar K_d values were also estimated from the inhibitor-induced shift of the K_Q value (not shown).

The results above indicate that the PS I Q_φ site is also a herbicide binding site as the other quinone-functioning sites. However, these inhibitors are expected to show only a low inhibitory effect in the intact PS I reaction center due to the stronger binding of intrinsic phylloquinone to the Q_φ site.

The Q_φ site may have common structural features with the Q_B sites judging from the sensitivity for o-phenanthroline which is known to bind to the Q_B sites by making H-bond to histidine residue in place of the quinone carbonyl group[2]. Low sensitivity for atrazines, DCMU and

DBMIB, on the other hand, gives aother feature of the Q_φ site. The sensitivity for antimycin A, HOQNO and myxothiazol, may inidcate that the Q_φ site has some structural feature also common with the quinone binding sites in the b/c_1 complex. The results charaterize the Q_φ site since antimycin A and HOQNO are known to attack at the quinone reductase site of cytochrome b/c_1 complex which is different from the quinol-oxidase site attacked by myxothiazol [16].

Although only a low homology seems to exist between the amino acid sequences of PS I core proteins [11] and subunits of cytochrome b/c_1 complex or PSII and purple bacterial reaction centers, the results in this study suggest some structural feature common among different quinone-functioning sites. The characteristics of the PS I Q_φ site shown here will contribute to a better understanding of the structure of PS I reaction center, to the evolutional relationship between different quinone binding sites, and presumably to the design of new herbicides.

4. ACKNOWLEDGMENT

The authors thank Dr. K. Satoh of Okayama University for the kind gift of atarzines, Dr. Y. Fujita of National Institute for Basic Biology for his discussion during the work.

5. REFERENCES

1. Andréasson, L. E. and Vängard,T.(1988)Ann. Rev. Plant Physiol. Plant Mol.Biochem. 39, 379-411.
2. Trebst, A. (1987) Z. Naturforsch. 42C, 742-750.
3. Takahashi, Y., Hirota, K. and Katoh, S. (1985) Photosynth. Res. 6, 183-192.
4. Schoeder, H. E., and Lockau, W. (1986) FEBS Lett. 199, 23-27.
5. Itoh, S.,Iwaki, M. and Ikegami,I.(1987) Biochim. Biophys. Acta, 893,503-516.
6. Itoh, S. and Iwaki, M. (1988) Biochim. Biophys. Acta 984, 32-38
7. Itoh, S. and Iwaki, M. (1989) FEBS Lett., 243, 47-52.
8. Ikegami,I., Sétif, P.and Mathis, P.(1987) Biochim. Biophys.Acta 894,414-422.
9. Biggins, J. and Mathis, P. (1988) Biochem. 27, 1494-1500.
10. Brettel, K. (1988) FEBS Lett., 239, 93-98.
11. Fish, L. E., Kück, U. and Bogorad, L.(1985) J. Biol. Chem. 260, 1413-1421.
12. Iwaki, M. and Itoh, S.(1989) FEBS Lett., in press.
13. Itoh, S. and Iwaki, M.(1989) FEBS Lett., 250, 441-447.
14. Paddock, M. L., Rongey, S. H., Abresch, E. C., Feher, G. and Okamura, M. Y. (1988) Photosynth. Res. 17, 75-96.
15. Giangiacomo, K. M., Robertson, D. E., Gunner, M. R. and Dutton, P. L.(1986) in Adv.in Photosynt.Res.(Biggins, J. ed.),II,pp. 409-412. Martinus Nijhoff.
16. Cramer, W. A., Black, M. T., Widger, W. R. and Girvin, M. E.(1987) in The Light Reactions (Barber, J., ed.), pp. 447-493. Elsevier, Amsterdam.

THE SITES OF PHOTOINHIBITION AROUND PHOTOSYSTEM I IN
CHLOROPLASTS

KAZUHITO INOUE[1], TSUTOMU FUJII[2], EI-ICHI YOKOYAMA[2], NORIAKI
KUSUMOTO[2], and HIDEHIRO SAKURAI[2],
[1]Dept. Biol. Sci., Fac. Sci., Kanagawa Univ., Hiratsuka,
Kanagawa 259-12, and [2]Dept. Biol., Sch. Educ., Waseda Univ.,
Shinjuku, Tokyo 169, Japan

1. INTRODUCTION
    Illumination of chloroplasts with strong light brings
about photoinhibition of photosynthetic electron transport
around PSI as well as around PSII (1). In contrast with
photoinhibition of PSII, photoinhibition of PSI usually
requires the presence of O_2 (2). We have found that the
main cause of photoinhibition of PSI under aerobic conditions is the destruction of three Fe-S centers by some
species of active oxygen produced by illuminated broken
chloroplasts (3).
    Under strictly anaerobic conditions in the presence of
dithionite, however, Satoh and Fork (4) reported that PSI
was inhibited by illuminating intact Bryopsis chloroplasts
with strong light and that the decrease of PSI activity (MV
photoreduction) paralleled the loss of P700. We studied the
photoinhibition of PSI in the presence of dithionite using
spinach broken chloroplasts and have found that photoinhibition of PSI was not correlated with the destruction of P700
and that the efficiency of electron transport between A_o and
Fe-S X was lowered (5).
    In this paper, we further characterized electron trans-
ferring properties of these photoinhibited preparations.

2. MATERIALS AND METHODS
    Preparation of broken spinach chloroplasts, extraction
of particles with digitonin, and the conditions of aerobic
and anaerobic photoinhibition were as described (3,5).
Measurements of MV photoreduction activity by O_2 consumption
using Clark-type electrode at 25°C and spectroscopic
measurements of NADP photoreduction activity at 340 nm with
ascorbate-DPIP as electron donors in the presence of
saturating amounts of Fd and FNR were as in (3,5). P700
content was determined by the continuous light-induced absorbance change at 430 nm (6) or the ferricyanide-oxidized
minus the ascorbate-reduced absorbance at 700 nm (7). EPR

M. Baltscheffsky (ed.), Current Research in Photosynthesis, Vol. II, 655–658.
© 1990 Kluwer Academic Publishers. Printed in the Netherlands.

spectra of Fe-S centers were measured at cryogenic temperatures with a JEOL EPR spectrometer essentially as in (8).
Flash-induced absorbance changes were measured with a
laboratory-constructed single beam spectrophotometer as
described previously (5).

3. RESULTS AND DISCUSSION

When broken chloroplasts were illuminated aerobically,
NADP photoreduction activity was gradually destroyed (Fig.
1.). From EPR measurements, we found that all of the Fe-S
centers (X, B, A) were more or less destroyed. P700 was not
appreciably destroyed. The extent of photoinactivation of
any of these centers or P700 as single components could not
account for loss of NADP photoreduction activity. However,
decrease of NADP photoreduction activity was correlated with
the product of each fraction of the three Fe-S centers
remaining intact. These results suggest that the intactness
of all of the three Fe-S centers are required for NADP
photoreduction. Incubation of thylakoids in the dark with
xanthine oxidase (an active oxygen generator) led to
decrease of PSI activity as well as of Fe-S centers. It is
concluded that the main cause of photoinhibition of PSI is
the destruction of Fe-S centers by some species of active
oxygen produced by illuminated chloroplasts (3).

FIGURE 1. Time course of
photoinhibition of PSI
under aerobic conditions.
MV photoreduction activity
was measured with a Clark-
type electrode. NADP
photoreduction activity
was measured at 340 nm with
a spectrophotometer (Hitachi
557). P700 content was
determined by the ferri-
cyanide-oxidized minus
the ascorbate-reduced
absorbance at 700 nm.
MV and NADP photoreduction
activities of the control
chrloplasts were
285 μ mol $O_2 \cdot$mg chl$^{-1} \cdot$h^{-1} and
132 μ mol NADP reduced$\cdot$
mg chl$^{-1} \cdot$h^{-1}, respectively.

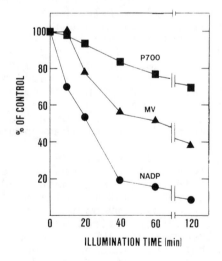

PSI appreciably is much resistant to photoinhibition under anaerobic conditions brought about by merely removing
O_2. When dithionite was added to thylakoids, however,
severe photoinhibition occurred. Although considerable
destruction of antenna chlorophylls also occurred, this
destruction could not explain the photoinhibition of PSI.
Although NADP photoreduction activity and MV photoreduction
activity were decreased to about 20% and 35%, respectively,
after 60 min illumination, none of P700, Fe-S centers, or
vitamin K1 was significantly decreased. For flash spectroscopy measurements, PSI particles were prepared with
digitonin from the control and photoinhibited chloroplasts.
On the basis of continuous light-oxidizable P700 in extracted particles, the magnitude of the flash-induced P700
changes of PSI particles from photoinhibited chloroplasts
were much smaller than those of the control particles even
in saturating actinic flash intensities (Table 1). It is
concluded that the lesion of functional link between A_o and
Fe-S X occurred, and that the back reaction between the
reduced A_o (or A_1) and $P700^+$ became non-negligible.

TABLE 1. The loss of NADP photoreduction activity and the
maximal flash-induced P700 absorption change in PSI particles prepared by anaerobic photoinhibited chloroplasts.

EX.	loss of NADP (%)	loss of flash induced P700 (%)
1	29	25
2	49	43
3	59	52
4	62	56
5	79	62

The sites of photoinhibition around PSI under variety
conditions as well as the inhibition site by $HgCl_2$ are shown
in Fig. 2.
Oxygen electrode in conjunction with MV is currently
most widely used in determining PSI activity, because the
method is convenient. However, the sites on PSI of electron
donation to MV is not fully elucidated. In $HgCl_2$-treated
thylakoids in which Fe-S center B was selectively destroyed
and NADP photoreduction was almost completely inhibited (9),
Fujii et al (10) found that these preparations were about
50% as active as untreated ones in photoinduced MV reducing
activity. In aerobic photoinhibition of 40 min illumination
(Fig. 1.), about 80% of NADP photoreduction activity was

destroyed, whereas more than 50% of MV photoreduction activity survived. On the other hand, in anaerobic photoinhibition, the decline of MV photoreduction activity almost paralleled with that of NADP photoreduction activity up to 40 min. It is clear that the assessments of PSI activities with MV may sometimes lead to erroneous conclusions.

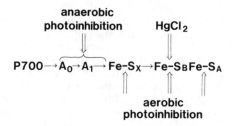

FIGURE 2. The sites of photoinhibition around PSI under variety conditions and inhibition site by $HgCl_2$.

ACKNOWLEDGEMENTS
    The authors would like to thank Professor T. Hiyama of Saitama University for EPR measurement, Professor Y. Fujita and Dr. S. Itoh of NIBB for their discussion and use of laboratory facilities. This work was carried out under the NIBB Cooperative Research Program and was supported by grants (01302064, 01304003) from the Ministry of Eduction, Science and Culture, Japan to H.S.

REFERENCES
1 Powles, S.B. (1984) Annu. Rev. Plant Physiol. 25, 15-44
2 Satoh, Ki. (1970) Plant Cell Physiol. 11, 29-38
3 Inoue, K., Sakurai, H. and Hiyama, T. (1986) Plant Cell Physiol. 27, 961-968
4 Satoh, Ka. and Fork, D. C. (1982) Plant Physiol. 70, 1004-1008
5 Inoue, K., Fujii, T., Yokoyama, E., Matsuura, K., Hiyama, T. and Sakurai, H. (1989) Plant Cell Physiol. 30, 65-71
6 Sakurai, H. and San Pietro, A. (1985) J. Biochem. 98,69-76
7 Murakami, A. and Fujita, Y. (1988) Plant Cell Physiol. 29, 305-311
8 Hiyama, T., Murakami, A., Itoh, S., Fujita, Y. and Sakurai, H. (1985) J. Biochem. 97, 89-95
9 Kojima, Y., Niinomi, Y., Tsuboi. S., Hiyama. T. and Sakurai, H. Bot. Mag. Tokyo 100, 243-253
10 Fujii, T., Yokoyama, E., Inoue, K. and Sakurai, H. Biochim. Biophys. Acta (submitted).

STRUCTURE AND FUNCTION OF FERREDOXIN–NADP REDUCTASE COMPLEX

MASATERU SHIN, Department of Biology, Faculty of Science, Kobe
University, Nada-ku, Kobe, 657, JAPAN

1. INTRODUCTION

In 1963, Shin et al. (1) first isolated ferredoxin–NADP reductase
(FNR, EC. 1.18.1.2) in crystalline form from spinach and demonstrated
that the crystallized enzyme reduced NADP when it was added back
together with ferredoxin to illuminated chloroplasts from which "built-
in" FNR had been removed. In this experiment, however, a very large
excess of crystallized FNR was required to restore the original activity.
This requirement of excess FNR indicates that membrane-bound FNR is more
functional in the NADP photoreduction than the FNR added in a soluble
state. So our recent interest has been focused on the structure and
function of membrane-bound FNR. We have found that two molecules of a
small form of FNR, FNR-S, was connected with a new thylakoid protein,
connectein, to form a large form of FNR, FNR-L. The FNR-L was anchored
on the surface of thylakoids via a base protein to constitute a
ferredoxin–NADP reductase complex.

2. LOCALIZATION OF TWO FORMS OF FNR ON THYLAKOIDS

Two molecular forms of FNR, FNR-S and FNR-L, have been isolated
from spinach (2). Purified FNR-S has a molecular weight of 33,000 and
FNR-L has a molecular weight of 75,000 (3). FNR-L consists of two
molecules of FNR-S and their connective protein, connectein (4). When
spinach chloroplasts were incubated in a diluted Tris-HCl buffer at pH
7.8, almost all FNR-L was easily released from thylakoids within two
hours. In contrast, FNR-S is rather hard to extract and remained in
thylakoids after the release of FNR-L. Therefore, it is suggested that
FNR-L is localized on the surface of thylakoids and FNR-S is localized
somewhere at an internal part of thylakoids. Our recent observation on
localization of FNR-S showed that FNR-S was bound to photosystem I
particles. Two different types of membrane-bound FNR, loosely bound and
tightly bound (5), are likely to correspond to our FNR-L and FNR-S,
respectively.

3. CONNECTEIN

Connectein has been found as a constituent of FNR-L (4). When FNR-L
was treated with 66% iso-propanol, it was separated into two fractions,

M. Baltscheffsky (ed.), Current Research in Photosynthesis, Vol. II, 659–662.
© 1990 *Kluwer Academic Publishers. Printed in the Netherlands.*

insoluble and soluble. The insoluble fraction was precipitate of FNR-S
and the soluble fraction contained connectein. The connectein could be
further purified by column chromatography with DEAE-Toyopearl or butyl-
Toyopearl (Tosoh Corporation, Tokyo). The protein had a molecular
weight of about 10,000, estimated by gel filtration analysis. It contained a large amount of proline (up to 17.5%) and no phenylalanine. It
was colorless and had no distinct absorption maximum around 280 nm.

Identification of connectein by polyacrylamide gel electrophoresis
was unsuccessful, for this protein easily diffused on the gel plate
during electrophoresis and was scarcely stained by Coomassie brilliant
blue or silver staining. When connectein was mixed with FNR-S in the
presence of high concentrations of ammonium sulfate or NaCl, it connected two molecules of FNR-S to form FNR-L within one hour. The conversion
of FNR-S to FNR-L was detectable by an aqueous two phase partition
method or by gel filtration chromatography (4). Recently, we are determining connectein by gel filtration chromatography on a TSK-gel G3000SW
column (0.75 x 60 cm, Tosoh Corporation, Tokyo) in a high-pressure
liquid chromatography system. The amount of FNR-L reconstituted was
proportional to the amount of connectein added to FNR-S.

4. RECONSTITUTION OF FERREDOXIN-NADP REDUCTASE COMPLEX ON THYLAKOIDS
The reconstitution of NADP photoreducing system of thylakoids has
been reported by Nozaki et al. (6), which was achieved by recombination
of three components isolated from spinach chloroplasts; purified FNR-S,
purified connectein, and the FNR-removed thylakoids. They extracted FNR
from spinach chloroplasts by overnight incubation in 20 mM Tris-HCl
buffer at pH 7.8 and washing with the same buffer three times at an
appropriate interval during the incubation. This prolonged extraction
resulted in release of both FNR-L and FNR-S.

Since exclusive extraction of FNR-L is more desirable for investigation on the function of connectein, we have incubated spinach whole
chloroplasts for a shorter time (60 min) in 20 mM Tris-HCl buffer at
pH 7.8 at 0° C. After the extraction, NADPH-diaphorase and NADP photoreducing activities of thylakoids decreased to about 2/3 of the original
activities. The amount of activity decreased by the extraction of
FNR was taken as 100% standard of activity restored by the rebinding
of FNR in FIG. 1. When the FNR-removed thylakoids were incubated with
purified FNR-S in an isotonic solution containing 0.35 M NaCl at pH 7.8,
roughly the same diaphorase activity was restored regardless of the
presence or absence of connectein (53 and 50%, respectively), indicating that connectein was not indispensable for rebinding FNR-S to
thylakoids. On the other hand, NADP photoreducing activity of thylakoids
was restored more remarkably in the presence of connectein (62%) than
in the absence of connectein (18%). This suggests that, of FNR-S
rebound to thylakoids, only the fraction rebound via connectein was
functional in NADP photoreduction. The most remarkable restoration was
achieved by rebinding FNR-L to the FNR-removed thylakoids. The FNR-L
was prepared by reassociation of purified FNR-S and connectein under
high salt conditions. In this case, restoration of NADP photoreduction
reached 93% while that of NADPH-diaphorase activity was merely 61%.
This indicates that FNR-L is a functional constituent of the ferredoxin-

NADP reductase complex.

As mentioned above, about 2/3 of NADP photoreducing activity remained on the thylakoids after the extraction of FNR-L. This remaining activity may be mostly ascribable to FNR-S that is buried in an internal part of thylakoids. The mechanism of NADP photoreduction by this membrane-burried FNR-S awaits further investigation.

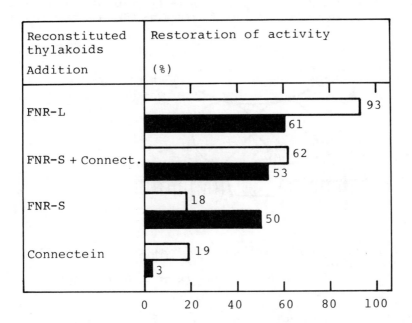

Reconstituted thylakoids	Restoration of activity
Addition	(%)
FNR-L	93 / 61
FNR-S + Connect.	62 / 53
FNR-S	18 / 50
Connectein	19 / 3

FIGURE 1. Restoration of NADPH-diaphorase and NADP photoreducing activities on reconstituted thylakoids.

The amount of activity of thylakoids decreased by the extraction (about 1/3 of the original activity) was taken as 100% standard for restoration of activity. The reconstituted thylakoids were prepared by rebinding the components indicated. The NADPH-diaphorase activity (■■■■■) was determined by measuring a decrease in absorbance at 600 nm of DCIP. The NADP photoreducing activity (▭) was determined by measuring an increase in absorbance at 340 nm of reduced NADP under illumination. Sodium ascorbate-DCIP couple was used as an electron donner system.

5. EVIDENCE FOR EXISTENCE OF A BASE PROTEIN

"Base protein" is a tentative name for an unknown protein located on the surface of thylakoids that provides a binding site for FNR. Although it has not actually been isolated from thylakoids, Nozaki et al. (6) presented evidence for its existence. When thylakoids was digested by trypsin, FNR-L was exclusively extracted to the supernatant

and the trypsinized thylakoids no longer rebound FNR-S via connectein.
The trypsin treatment should detach FNR-L by digesting the unknown
protein (or proteins).

6. STRUCTURE OF FERREDOXIN-NADP REDUCTASE COMPLEX
    Based on our recent studies, the author proposes an arrangement of
ferredoxin-NADP reductase complex on the surface of thylakoids as
illustrated in FIG. 2. Connectein connects two molecules of FNR-S and
attaches to a base protein to form ferredoxin-NADP reductase complex.

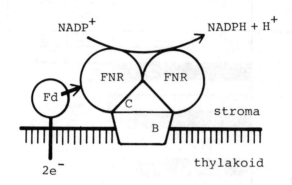

FIGURE 2. Arrangement of ferredoxin-NADP reductase complex on
          thylakoids.
              Fd, ferredoxin; C, connectein; B, base protein

REFERENCES
1 Shin, M., Tagawa, K. and Arnon, D. I. (1963) Biochem, Z. 338, 84-96
2 Shin, M. and Oshino, R. (1978) J. Biochem. 83, 357-361
3 Shin, M. and Oshino, R. (1980) in Flavins and Flavoproteins (Yagi, K.
  and Yamano, T., eds.), pp.537-541, Japan Scientific Societies Press,
  Tokyo and University Park Press, Baltimore.
4 Shin, M., Ishida, H. and Nozaki, Y. (1985) Plant Cell Physiol. 26,
  559-663
5 Matthijs, H. C. P., Coughlan, S. J. and Hind. G. (1986) J. Biol. Chem.
  261, 12154-12158
6 Nozaki, Y. and Shin, M. (1985) Physiol. Veg. 23, 627-633

REACTIVATION OF DARK-INACTIVATED *Anabaena* FNR.

M. F. Fillat   and C. Gomez-Moreno. Departamento de Bioquimica y Biologia Molecular y Celular. Universidad de Zaragoza. 50009, Zaragoza. Spain.

Ferredoxin-NADP$^+$-oxidorreductasa (FNR) is a key enzyme in the transfer of electrons from PSI to NADP$^+$ in photosynthetic organisms. This flavoprotein , which contains FAD as a cofactor , is weakly bound to the tylakoidal membrane in the presence of flavodoxin or ferredoxin across a binding peptide (3,5,6).

Carrillo et al. (5-7) have reported that photosynthetic electron transport in spinach is light-regulated at the level of the FNR. This process takes place in a few seconds, through several conformational changes of the membrane-bound enzyme that are produced by the increasing of the pH in the stroma, as well as the variation of the energy state of the tylakoidal membrane.However, the FNR from the nitrogen-fixing cyanobacterium *Anabaena variabilis* undergoes an "in vivo" deactivation/reactivation process that is regulated by the light intensity in the culture and that appears as a previous step for degradation of the enzyme (Fillat et al., submitted). This decay in all the enzymatic activities of FNR seems to be produced by unfolding of the polipeptidic chain that affects NADPH and FAD domains and the interphase for the binding to ferredoxin, which is reflected in a big increment of the disociation constant of the electrostatic complex between both proteins.

We present here studies that demonstrate the reversibility of this deactivation process, emphasizing the recovery of the activity in an "in vitro" system.

MATERIALS AND METHODS.

Anabaena variabilis 1403.4b was grown in BG-11 medium (1). Native FNR was obtained from cultures under 3500-4000 lux of light intensity, and continuosly bubbled with a mixture of 95% air and 5% CO_2.

M. Baltscheffsky (ed.), Current Research in Photosynthesis, Vol. II, 663–666.
© *1990 Kluwer Academic Publishers. Printed in the Netherlands.*

Inactive FNR was purified from cultures grown in the same conditions , but maintained in the dark during 48 hours before harvesting. Purification of FNR , and determination of DCPIP-diaphorase activity were performed according to (10). Binding constants between FNR and ferredoxin were determined spectrophotometrically using a modification of the programe designed by Duglebby (9).

RESULTS AND DISCUSSION.

"In vivo" reactivation of the FNR takes place when the light intensity on the cultures containing inactive FNR is increased until 3500-4000 lux. This can be done by two different procedures :

- Diluting a culture in the stationary phase with either fresh or reutilized medium, until the intensity of the light reaching the inner part of the culture is 3500 lux or higher.

- Irradiating a culture in the exponential phase, that was submitted to dark for 48 hours , with light intensities about 3500 to 4000 lux.

Several attempts to achieve **reactivation "in vitro"** of the homogeneous protein have been done, without noticeable changes in its turnover number:

- Irradiation of the pure protein in an open system, as well as in anaerobic atmosphere.This experiment was performed on regarding the blue-light activation of nitrate reductase from several sources (2).

- Incubation of the enzyme with different concentrations of 1,4 dithiothreitol, (DTT), in the dark or irradiating the sample. Open systems and anaerobic conditions were tested as well.

- Irradiation of photosynthetic particles containing deactive FNR , and the thiorredoxin / thiorredoxin-reductase system (4). Neither in this mixture, nor in a duplicate supplemented with DTT and illuminated changes were found in the activity of the FNR.

However, the activity of the pure FNR can be recovered when diluted prpeparations of the enzyme are frozen and thawn several times in Tris/ HCl buffer or phosphate buffer. This recovery of activity is partially inhibited in the presence of 20% glycerol in the freezing-thawing mixture (table 1).

SAMPLE	T.N.0	T.N.1	T.N.g
n-FNR 1.5 uM	6135	6017	5976
n-FNR 3.0 uM	5980	6120	5749
n-FNR 6.8 uM	6252	5980	5565
n-FNR 22.5 uM	5995	5740	6027
d-FNR 1.36 uM	2120	6147	4283
d-FNR 3.06 uM	2218	5458	2286
d-FNR 6.83 uM	2083	4641	2120
d-FNR 22.9 uM	2371	3612	1979

Table 1.- Effect of glycerol present in the "in vitro" reactivation of the FNR.(DCPIP-diaphorase activity).$T.N._0$ = T.N. of control; $T.N._1$= T.N. after freezing and thawing the FNR twice; T.N.g= After freezing and thawing the FNR in presence of glycerol.

This reactivation reminds the process described by Curti et al. (8) for the flavoprotein L-aminoacid oxidase from venom; this enzyme suffers a deactivation process by freezing that involves changes in its tertiary structure. The process is probed to be reversible in the presence of the addecuate buffer. In the case of the FNR, the decreasing in the binding constant for the electrostatic complex between the reactive FNR & ferredoxin , that resembles to the value found for the constant in the complex of the native enzyme with ferredoxin (table 2), also shows that some change in the tertiary structure of the FNR has taken place.

COMPLEX	Kd (uM)	$\Delta \epsilon$ mM^{-1}cm^{-1}
n-FNR/Fd	3.57	1.44
d-FNR/Fd	64.20	1.29
r-FNR/Fd	8.14	1.17

Table 2.- Binding constants and extinction coefficients of the electrostatic complex between ferredoxin and the different forms of FNR. n-FNR: native enzyme; d-FNR:deactive enzyme, r-FNR: reactive enzyme.

(Fd):(FNR)	TURNOVER NUMBER (uM^{-1} min^{-1})			
	n-FNR		d-FNR	
	0	1	0	1
0	5900	5950	2650	5600
0.5	4616	4650	2317	3329
1.0	4425	4440	2237	2303
2.0	3122	2900	2197	2730

Table 3.- Reactivation of FNR in the presence of different concentrations of ferredoxin. 0:FNR without freezing, 1: FNR frozen and melted twice. Final concentration of FNR is 3 uM.

Presence of ferredoxin in the reactivation mixture difficultes the refolding of FNR, giving a lower yield of reactivation (table 3). This can be due to the formation of the electrostatic complex between the inactive FNR & ferredoxin in the mixture, that increases the energy requiered for the system to produce the rearrangement of the tertiary structure of the FNR, that takes place when the enzyme is free.

4. REFERENCES

1.- Allen, M. 1968. J. Phycol. 4, p. 1-3.
2.-Azuara, M.P. and Aparicio, P. 1983. Plant. Physiol. 71.p. 286-290.
3.- Avron, M. and Jagendorf, A. 1957. Arch. Biochem. Biophys. 72.p.17-24.
4.- Buchanan, B.B. 1984. BioScience. 34. p. 378-383.
5.- Carrillo, N., Lucero, H.A. and Vallejos R.H. 1981. J. Biol.Chem. 256. p. 1058 - 1059.
6.- Carrillo, N. and Vallejos R.H.1982. Plant Physiol. 69. p. 210-213.
7.- Carrillo, N. and Vallejos R.H. 1983. TIBS. February. p. 52-56.
8.- Curty, B., Massey, V. and Zmudka, M. 1968. J. Biol. Chem. 243. p. 2306-2314.
9.- Duggleby, R.G. 1981. Anal. Biochem. 110. p. 9-18.
10.- Sancho, J., Peleato, M.L., Gomez-Moreno , C. and Edmondson, D.E. 1988. Arch. Biochem. Biophys. 260. p. 200-207.

ABSORBANCE TRANSIENTS OF FERREDOXIN:NADP$^+$ REDUCTASE IN ISOLATED THYLAKOID MEMBRANES

G. Garab[*], Y. Hong, S.J. Coughlan, H.C.P. Matthijs and G. Hind
Biology Department, Brookhaven National Laboratory, Upton N.Y.
U.S.A. and [*]Biological Research Center, Szeged, Hungary

1. INTRODUCTION

The reduction of NADP$^+$ by ferredoxin:NADP$^+$ reductase (FNR, EC 1.18.1.2) is the terminal step in the photosynthetic generation of strong reductant in chloroplasts (1). FNR, an FAD containing enzyme, also catalyzes electron flow from NADPH to ferredoxin (Fd), which supplies electrons for reduction of nitrite and sulfite (2), and may facilitate the redox poising of cyclic electron transport around PS1 (3).

Schemes of electron transfer interactions of FNR in thylakoid membranes are deduced mainly from experimental results obtained in model systems (reviewed in 1). Pioneering works by Bouges-Bocquet (4), who studied flash-induced transient of FNR in algal cells, has not been followed by systematic investigations in isolated chloroplasts and thylakoid membranes. In algal cells, ambiguity arises from intense light scattering (5). Low permeability of the cell wall also restricts the use of inhibitors, ionophores, artificial acceptors and substrates. It is consequently necessary to confirm and extend these earlier studies using isolated thylakoid membranes and/or subchloroplast particles.

This work attempts a systematic exploration of the role of FNR in thylakoid membranes. Flash induced absorbance transients linked to the electron transfer processes involving FNR have been identified in thylakoid membranes between 300 and 590 nm and its kinetics studied in the time range from about 20 us to a few sec at various experimental conditions. In this paper our attention is focussed on the mechanism of photoreduction of FNR by PS1. The absorbance transient spectra of FNR$^{\cdot}$, the neutral singly reduced form, was identified between 430 and 550 nm and the kinetics of the absorbance changes were studied in membrane preparations of different FNR and Fd content. Our results show that photoreduction of FNR to FNR$^{\cdot}$ by PS1 does not require the presence of soluble or membrane-bound Fd.

2. MATERIALS AND METHODS

Spinach chloroplasts and thylakoid membranes were isolated as previously described (6). FNR-content of membranes was determined by diaphorase activity measurements (7). Aliquots of the membrane (2-20 ug chlorophyll content) and the supernatant (5-50 ul) after various stages of the washing procedure were subjected to SDS-PAGE, electroblotting to nitrocellulose, and probing with purified rabbit IgG to FNR, Fd or plastocyanin. Blots were reacted with I^{125}-protein and autoradiographed. Radioactivity was quantified both by densitometric scanning of the autoradiograms, and by excising radioactive areas of nitrocellulose and

M. Baltscheffsky (ed.), Current Research in Photosynthesis, Vol. II, 667–670.

counting in a -counter. All values were normalized to intact chloroplasts and represent the mean values of 3 independent experiments.

Absorbance changes of thylakoid membranes induced by single turnover
flashes were measured as previously described (8). The repetition rate
of the exciting flashes was 0.5 Hz. The reaction medium consisted of
100 mM sorbitol, 30 mM tricine/KOH pH 7.8, 20 mM KCl, 5 mM MgCl$_2$ and
thylakoid membranes at a chlorophyll (a+b) concentration of 40 uM. Gramicidin and DCMU were added at a concentration of 5 uM and 20 uM,
respectively. Correction of data points and/or kinetic traces for absorbance contributions of P700$^+$, cytochrome f$^+$ and cytochrome b$_{563}^-$ was
based on published oxidized-minus-reduced difference spectra (9,10).

All preparation procedures were done at 0-4 $^{\circ}$C. Data were collected
at room temperature (18-22 $^{\circ}$C).

3.RESULTS AND DISCUSSION
Transient formation of semireduced FNR in thylakoid membranes. When
thylakoids deprived of natural or artificial electron acceptors are subjected to a brief actinic flash, a fast, gramicidin-insensitive absorbance transient is observed at all wavelengths monitored between 505 and
545 nm (Fig. 1). The qualitative consistency of kinetic traces throughout this range suggests an origin in a single absorbing species.

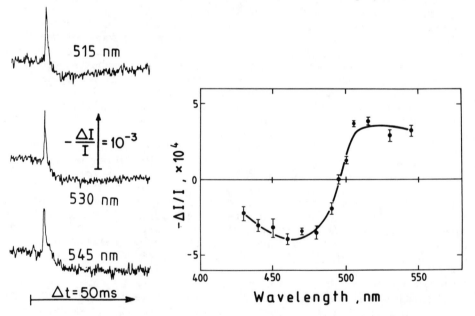

FIGURE 1. Gramicidin insensitive absorbance transients in thylakoid
membranes at 515, 530 and 545 nm; average of 32 transients.
FIGURE 2. Transient spectrum at 200 us following a single turnover
saturating flash excitation of thylakoids in the presence of gramicidin.
The contributions due to P700$^+$ and cytochrome f$^+$ have been subtracted;
mean values and standard errors from six independent experiments.

The absorbance transient can be unequivocally assigned to PS1, since it persists in the presence of DCMU under anaerobic conditions favorable for cyclic electron transport around PS1 (11) or in the presence of DCMU and 5-10 mM ascorbate (data not shown).

The transient spectrum at 200 us (Fig. 2) closely resembles that of FNR$^{\cdot}$-FNR$_{ox}$, the difference spectrum between the neutral singly-reduced and the oxidized form of the enzyme (12,13). The concentration of FNR$^{\cdot}$ was calculated from the transient spectrum using the extinction coefficients given in (13); at 200 us the mean value of concentration was 30 nM. Since the transient decays with a halftime of 400 us, the concentration of FNR$^{\cdot}$ generated by a single turnover flash could be estimated to 42 nM. This value is commensurate with the concentration of P700, 45 6 nM, determined spectrophotometrically in the same membrane preparations. Upon repeated washing of the membranes in 5 mM NaCl, EDTA or the zwitterionic detergent CHAPS (7) the amplitude of the absorbance changes which are attributed to the formation of FNR$^{\cdot}$ decreased parallel to the loss of FNR content of membranes. These data further support the notion that the absorbance transient shown in Fig. 2 originates from the generation of FNR$^{\cdot}$.

Effect of release of membrane-bound Fd. For establishing the role of Fd in the reduction of FNR by PS1, we can take advantage of the fact that the release of Fd proceeds much faster than that of FNR. After three consecutive washings in 5 mM NaCl no residual Fd can be detected in the membranes. On the other hand, more than 50 % of the FNR content of chloroplasts is retained in the membranes (Fig. 3).

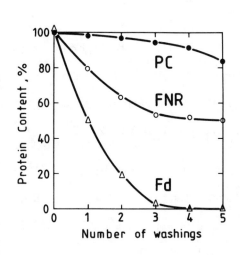 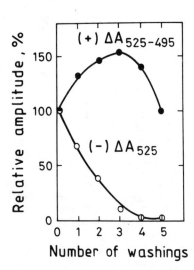

FIGURE 3. Depletion of Fd, FNR and plastocyanin (PC) from the thylakoid membranes by repeated washing of the membranes in 5 mM NaCl.

FIGURE 4. Effect of washing of membranes in 5 mM NaCl on the initial amplitude of $.A_{525-495}$ and on the amplitude of the negative absorbance change at 525 nm; 100 %, values in osmotically shocked chloroplasts.

Absence of Fd had no noticeable effect on the risetime and did not lead to a decrease in the amplitude of $A_{525-495}$ assignable to FNR$\cdot$ (Fig. 4). (The initial enhancement can be due to a kinetic competition between the rise and decay or competition between FNR and Fd for PS1 electrons.)

Upon gradual release of Fd the slow absorbance decrease at was gradually abolished (Fig. 4). This finding and data obtained in the presence of soluble Fd, inhibitors, acceptors and at different ionic strengths (not shown) suggest that this component is correlated with the formation of Fd:FNR complex or intracomplex electrostatic interactions.

According to the most widely accepted scheme, which is based mainly on data obtained in model systems, electrons from PS1 are transferred to FNR via Fd (1). However, it has been suggested that in algal cells reduction of FNR does not involve Fd. Some data in model systems also permit a direct reduction of FNR instead of a reduction via Fd (14).

4. CONCLUSION

Absorbance transients have been observed in isolated thylakoids which could be identified to originate from the reduction of FNR to the semireduced FNR$\cdot$ by PS1. Generation of FNR$\cdot$ appears to occur unperturbed in the absence of Fd. Role of Fd and the Fd:FNR complex, its dynamic properties under various experimental conditions as well as the role of ferredoxin quinone reductase (FQR) are currently investigated.

ACKNOWLEDGEMENT

This work was performed at Brookhaven National Laboratory under the auspices of the Division of Biological Energy Research, Office of Basic Energy Sciences, United States Department of Energy.

REFERENCES
1. Carrillo, N. and Vallejos, R. H. (1987) in The Light Reactions (Barber, J., ed.) pp. 527-560, Elsevier, Amsterdam
2. Guerrero, M. G., Vega, J. M. and Losada, M. (1981) Ann. Rev. Plant Physiol. 32, 169-204
3. Shahak, Y., Crowther, D. and Hind, G. (1981) Biochim. Biophys. Acta 636, 234-243
4. Bouges-Bocquet, B. (1980) Biochim. Biophys. Acta 590, 223-233
5. Garab, G., Paillotin, G. and Joliot, P. (1979) Biochim. Biophys. Acta 545, 445-453
6. Garab, G., Faludi-Daniel, A, Sutherland, J. and Hind, G. (1988) Biochemistry 27, 2425-2430
7. Matthijs, H. C. P., Coughlan, S. J. and Hind, G. (1986) J. Biol. Chem. 261, 12154-12158
8. Crowther, D. and Hind, G. (1980) Arch. Biochem. Biophys. 204, 568-577
9. Ke, B. (1973) Biochim. Biophys. Acta 303, 1-33
10. Wasserman, A. R. (1980) Methods Enzymol. 69, 181-202
11. Garab, G. and Hind, G. (1987) Progress in Photosynthesis Research (Biggins, J., ed.) Vol. II pp. 545-548, M. Nijhoff, Dordrecht
12. Shin, M. and Arnon, D. I. (1965) J. Biol. Chem. 240, 1405-1411
13. Batie, C. J. and Kamin, H. (1984) J. Biol. Chem. 259, 11976-11985
14. Bhattacharyya, A.K., Meyer, T.E. and Tollin, G. (1986) Biochemistry 25, 4655-4661

NEAREST NEIGHBOUR ANALYSIS OF THE PHOTOSYSTEM I SUBUNITS
IN BARLEY AND THEIR BINDING OF FERREDOXIN.

BIRGITTE ANDERSEN, BIRGIT KOCH, HENRIK VIBE SCHELLER,
JENS SIGURD OKKELS and BIRGER LINDBERG MØLLER, Department
of Plant Physiology, Royal Veterinary & Agricultural University, DK-
1871 Frederiksberg C, Denmark.

1. INTRODUCTION.
   Photosystem I (PS I) mediates electron transfer from plastocyanin to
ferredoxin through the reaction center P700 and the five electron
acceptors A_0, A_1, X, A and B (1). PS I preparations from barley contain
the reaction center protein P700-chlorophyll a-protein 1 (CP1) and smaller
polypeptides with apparent molecular masses of 18- (PSI-D), 16- (PSI-E),
14-, 9.5- (PSI-H), 9- (PSI-C), 4- and 1.5-kDa (PSI-I) (2). CP1 is a
heterodimer of the two homologous approximately 82-kDa polypeptides
PSI-A and PSI-B (2) and binds the reaction center P700 and the iron-
sulfur center X (3). The iron-sulfur centers A and B are located on the
PSI-C subunit (4). Iron-sulfur centers A and/or B donate electrons to
ferredoxin on the stromal side of the thylakoid membrane.
   Nearest neighbour analysis of the PS I subunits can be carried out by
chemical cross-linking. We have used the hydrophilic zero-length crosslinker N-ethyl-3-(3-dimethyl-aminopropyl)-carbodiimide (EDC) which
covalently cross-links closely positioned amino and carboxyl groups. In
studies with spinach, EDC have previously been used to cross-link
ferredoxin to a PSI subunit with an apparent molecular mass between 20
and 22 kDa (5,6). Based on the apparent molecular mass of a spinach
polypeptide, it is difficult to conclude to which of the barley PS I
polypeptides, the cross-reacting polypeptide corresponds. In the present
study we report the results of nearest neighbour analysis of the PS I
subunits of barley. We also demonstrate that it is the 18-kDa PSI-D
subunit of barley, the product of the $Psa-D$ gene, which forms the major
cross-reacting product with ferredoxin.

2. MATERIALS AND METHODS
   PS I and ferredoxin were isolated from barley as reported in (4) and
(7). Cross-linking with EDC was carried out at 20°C in the light for 30
min in 20 mM MOPS (pH 7.5) containing 5 mM EDC and 0.7 mg chl/ml.
Electrophoretic analysis was carried out using 8-25% high Tris SDS-
polyacrylamide gels (8) which were either stained directly with Coomassie
Brilliant Blue R250 or electroblotted onto nitrocellulose, incubated with
monospecific antibodies towards the individual PS I polypeptides and
visualized by use of alkaline phosphatase conjugated secondary antibodies.

3. RESULTS AND DISCUSSION
   The cross-linking experiments with EDC demonstrates the formation of

M. Baltscheffsky (ed.), Current Research in Photosynthesis, Vol. II, 671–674.
© 1990 *Kluwer Academic Publishers. Printed in the Netherlands.*

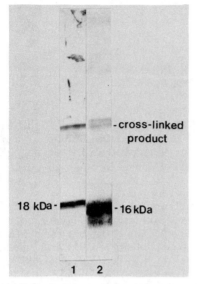

FIGURE 1: Western blot of PS I cross-linked with EDC.
lane 1: incubated with an antibody against the 18-kDa polypeptide
lane 2: incubated with an antibody against the 16-kDa polypeptide

cross-linked products between the 18- and 16-kDa polypeptides and between the 18- and the 9.5-kDa polypeptide. The composition of the cross-linked products was determined from their reaction with mono-specific antibodies towards the individual PS I polypeptides as shown for the 18- and 16-kDa product on Fig. 1. When the cross-linking is carried out in the presence of ferredoxin, two cross-linking products are formed

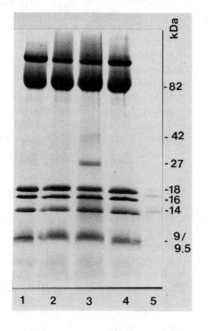

FIGURE 2: PS I cross-linked with EDC in the absence or presence of ferredoxin (Fd). The gel is stained with Coomassie Brilliant Blue R250.
Lane 1: PS I
Lane 2: PS I + EDC
Lane 3: PS I + EDC + Fd
Lane 4: PS I + Fd
Lane 5: Fd

(Fig. 2). The dominant product migrating with an apparent molecular mass of 27 kDa is composed of ferredoxin and the 18-kDa polypeptide, whereas the diffuse product migrating at 42 kDa is composed of ferredoxin and the 18- and 16-kDa polypeptides (Fig. 3). The cross-linked products are

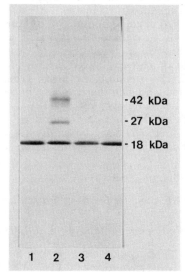

FIGURE 3: Western blot of PS I cross-linked with EDC in the absence or presence of ferredoxin (Fd). The blot was incubated with an antibody against the 18-kDa polypeptide.
Lane 1: PS I + EDC
Lane 2: PS I + EDC + Fd
Lane 3: PS I + EDC + denatured Fd
Lane 4: PS I + Fd

not observed if the reaction is carried out *(1)* in the absence of added ferredoxin, *(2)* with heat-denatured ferredoxin or *(3)* at an elevated salt concentration. The 18-kDa polypeptide has been isolated and 60% of its amino acid sequence determined (9). The amino acid sequence demonstrates that this polypeptide is the product of the *PsaD* gene (10). The PSI-D

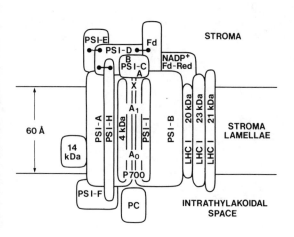

FIGURE 4: Model of PS I. The cross-linked polypeptides are indicated with ●—●

polypeptide is positively charged and its role in the docking of ferredoxin to the PSI complex could be to reduce the electrostatic repulsion between the negatively charged ferredoxin and the surface of the thylakoid membrane. The fact that the cross-linking is inhibited at high ionic strength supports the role of an electrostatic interaction. The absence of a cross-linked product when heat-denatured ferredoxin is used, indicates that the cross-linking reflects a genuine *in vivo* association of the components. Mild treatment of thylakoids with Proteinase K reveal that the 18- and 16-kDa polypeptides are susceptible for degradation and thus at least partly exposed at the the stromal side of the thylakoid membrane (data not shown). This is in agreement with the predictions made from the amino acid sequence of the transit peptides and the mature polypeptides (10). Based on *(1)* the stoichiometry of the PSI polypeptides (2), *(2)* the secondary structure predictions made from the deduced amino acid sequences of most of the PS I subunits, and *(3)* the cross-linking experiments here reported we visualize the subunit arrangement of PS I by the model shown on Fig. 4.

4. REFERENCES
1. Andréasson, L.-E. and Vänngård, T. (1988) Ann. Rev. Plant Physiol.. Plant Mol. Biol. 39, 379–411
2. Scheller, H.V., Svendsen, I. and Møller, B.L. (1989) J. Biol. Chem. 264, 6929–6934
3. Høj, P.B. and Møller, B.L. (1986) J. Biol. Chem. 261, 14292–14300
4. Høj, P.B., Svendsen, I., Scheller, H.V. and Møller, B.L. (1987) J. Biol. Chem. 262, 12676–12684
5. Zanetti, G. and Merati, G. (1987) Eur. J. Biochem. 169, 143–146
6. Zilber, A.L. and Malkin, R. (1988) Plant Physiol. 88, 810–814
7. Buchanan, B.B. and Arnon, D.I. (1971) Methods Enzymol. 23, 413–440
8. Fling, S.P. and Gregerson, D.S. (1986) Anal. Biochem. 155, 83–88
9. Scheller, H.V., Høj, P.B., Svendsen, I. and Møller, B.L. (1988) Biochim. Biophys. Acta 933, 501–505
10. Hoffman, N.E., Pichersky, E., Malik, V.S., Ko, K. and Cashmore, A.R. (1988) Plant Mol. Biol. 10, 435–445

IDENTIFICATION OF THE PLASTOCYANIN BINDING SUBUNIT OF PHOTOSYSTEM I

Michael Hippler, Rafael Ratajczak and Wolfgang Haehnel
Lehrstuhl für Biochemie der Pflanzen, *Lehrstuhl für Medizinische Cytologie,
University of Münster, D-4400 Münster, Federal Republic of Germany

1. INTRODUCTION

A photosystem (PS) I complex being competent in mediating the electron transfer from plastocyanin (PCy) to ferredoxin is assembled from more than 7 subunits [1]. The two large chlorophyll (chl) a containing subunits Ia and Ib are plastid encoded and carry the primary electron donor P700 and the electron acceptors A_0, phylloquinone and Fe-S_X. Subunit VII carries the electron acceptors Fe-S_A and Fe-S_B (reviewed in [2]). Subunit II has been shown by cross-linking to ensure the docking of ferredoxin to subunit VII [3]. Subunit III appeared to be necessary for the electron transfer from PCy to PS I [1]. This subunit does not carry a prosthetic group [4] and it is positively charged [5]. Its attribution to a band in SDS-PAGE is ambiguous because subunit III and IV alter their relative position in different gel systems [6]. Subunit III has been suggested to be identical with a subunit of 21 kDa [7] or a positively charged subunit of 9.7 kDa as deduced from the gene sequence [8]. Several authors have questioned a role of subunit III. However, in a recent study [9] PCy was cross-linked to a PS I subunit of 19 kDa. The function of this subunit and the assignment to one of the PS I subunits remains to be established.

2. MATERIALS AND METHODS

Stroma lamellae were isolated from spinach chloroplasts by Yeda press fractionation [10]. Isolation of PS I particles [9] and of PCy [5] followed given procedures. Stroma lamellae in the presence of 0.1 % (w/v) Triton X-100 [5] or PS I particles were incubated at 0.2 mg chl/ml with 5 mM N-ethyl-1-3-[3-(dimethylamino)propyl]carbodiimide (EDC) and 50 μM PCy for 15 min at room temperature. The reaction was terminated by 0.2 mM ammonium acetate and residual EDC and PCy removed by centrifugation. SDS-PAGE was carried out at 4 °C on a gradient from 10.2 to 15,4 % T at 2.6 % C [11]. Electroblotting to nitrocellulose, immuno-gold staining and characterization of the monospecific antibodies raised against PCy has been described [12]. Bands were excised after preparative SDS-PAGE [13] and extracted with 75 % formic acid. The samples were transferred to a gas-phase protein sequencer (Applied Biosystems, model 477A) or previously rerun on a gel and electroblotted to a Immobilon membrane (Millipore).

Absorbance changes of P700 were induced by repetitive flashes of 6 μs

M. Baltscheffsky (ed.), Current Research in Photosynthesis, Vol. II, 675–678.
© 1990 *Kluwer Academic Publishers. Printed in the Netherlands.*

(FWHM) duration and monitored at 703 nm [5]. Stroma thylakoids or PS I particles were suspended in a 1 x 1 cm cuvette. Details are given in the figure legend.

3. RESULTS

Incubation of stroma lamellae with EDC in the presence of externally added PCy results in the disappearance of a band of SDS-PAGE at 18.5 kDa and a new one at 31.5 kDa (Fig. 1D). The same result is found with isolated PS I as indicated by arrows in Fig. 1H.

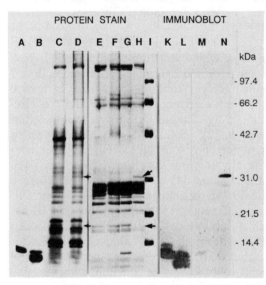

Figure 1.

SDS-PAGE analysis of stroma lamellae and PSI-particles cross-linked with plastocyanin.

Lane A-I, protein stain; lane K-N, immunoblot probed with anti-PCy antibody and stained with protein A-gold.
10 µg PCy (A, K) treated with EDC (B, L). Stroma lamellae (Y-100) were treated with PCy (C) and with EDC + PCy (D). PS I-particles (E) were treated with EDC (F), with PCy (G, M), and with EDC + PCy (H, N).
Lane I, protein markers.

Electroblotting of the gel and immuno-gold staining with antibodies to PCy shows that the new band at 31.5 kDa contains cross-linked PCy (Fig. 1N). The two large subunits of PS I are found at molecular masses of 69 and 64 kDa, the light harvesting proteins LHCI at 24 - 29 kDa, and the smaller subunits of PS I at 21.4, 18.5, 17.4, 16.9, 11.2, 10.1 and 9.1. The band at 18.5 kDa and after cross-linking of PCy with EDC that at 31.5 kDa were excised and collected from several gels. The N-terminal sequences were determined in a gas-phase sequencer (X denotes not determined positions). Table I shows the results of the cross-linked product.

By comparison with the protein sequences currently available and the translated genes of PS I subunits, subunit III is unambiguously identified with the mature protein of the nuclear encoded sequence of the *psa*F gene [14]. The the amount of the amino acids indicate that PCy is stoichiometrically cross-linked to subunit III. The flash induced reduction of $P700^+$ in PS I with cross-linked PCy show fast first-order kinetics with a halftime of 13 - 17 µs and a relative amplitude of 51 - 55 % (Fig. 2). This reaction time of cross-linked PCy is the same as that of PCy bound to PS I in the *in vivo* complex [15].

TABLE I. N-terminal sequence of the cross-linked product between a subunit of PS I and plastocyanin

Cycle #	Raw data (pmol)	Identified Amino acid of	
		Plastocyanin	Subunit III
1	D (6.5) / V (7.9)	Val	Asp
2	E (8.3) / I (7.1)	Glu	Ile
3	A (7.7) / V (6.3)	Val	Ala
4	G (8.1) / L (7.3)	Leu	Gly
5	L (13.4)	Leu	Leu
6	T (6.6) / G (10.4)	Gly	Thr
7	G (9.3) / P (4.2)	Gly	(Pro)

The background of the peaks was equivalent to 1 - 2 pmol of the amino acids.

                                               1   5   10

N-terminal amino acid residues of 18.5 kDa peptide   XI AGL XP XKE XKQF

Deduced sequence - spinach *psa*F gene product [14]   DI AGL TP CKES KQF

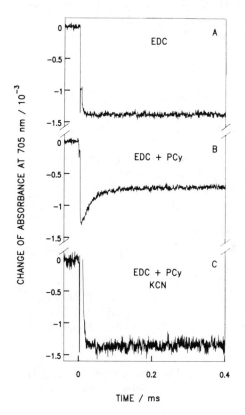

Figure 2.
Absorbance changes of P700 in PS I particles (PSI-200) at 703 nm induced by a flash of saturating intensity.
A, PS I treated with EDC;
B, PS I treated with EDC + PCy;
C, sample used for trace B after incubation with 30 mM KCN for 15 min.
The measuring solution contained 11 μM chl, 1 mM ascorbate, 0.1 mM 2,6-dichlorophenol-indophenol, 0.2 mM methyl viologen, 1 mM MgSO$_4$, 15 mM MOPS buffer, pH 7.
A, B, average of 100 signals monitored at 35 μW/cm^2; C, average of 300 signals monitored at 11 μW/cm^2.
The electrical bandwidth ranged from d.c. to 1 MHz; the dwell time of the transient recorder was 2 μs. The fluorescence artefact was subtracted.

4. DISCUSSION

The term Subunit III has been coined by Nelson for the subunit involved in the interaction between PS I and PCy [1]. Our results show that it is coded by the *psa*F gene for a mature protein of 154 amino acids with a molecular mass of 17.3 kDa [14] which was attributed to subunit IV. To avoid inconsistent nomenclature the subunit will be renamed subunit III (R. Herrmann, personal communication). The two hydrophobic domains of the predicted sequence [14] may be involved in the binding to the large subunits of PS I as suggested by the high Triton X-100 concentration needed to release subunit III [1, 5]. The excess of 7 positively charged residues may not only compensate the high negative surface charge density at the electron transfer site to P700 [5] but also provide a suitable protein environment for rapid binding [4] of the negative PCy molecule. The reaction time of cross-linked PCy is evidence that EDC conserves the conformation of the native complex probably by covalently linking a carboxyl group of PCy with a lysine residue of subunit III.

REFERENCES

[1]   Bengis, C. and Nelson, N. (1977) J. Biol. Chem. 252, 4564-4569
[2]   Malkin, R. (1987) In: The Light Reactions. Topics in Photosynthesis, Vol. 8 (Barber, J., ed.), pp. 495-525, Elsevier, Amsterdam
[3]   Zanetti, G. and Merati, G. (1987) Eur. J. Biochem. 169, 143-146
[4]   Haehnel, W., Hesse, V. and Pröpper, A. (1980) FEBS Lett. 111, 79-82
[5]   Ratajczak, R., Mitchell, R. and Haehnel, W. (1988) Biochim. Biophys. Acta 933, 306-318
[6]   Nechushtai, R., Nelson, N., Mattoo, A. K. and Edelman, M. (1981) FEBS Lett. 125, 115-119
[7]   Dunn, P. P. J., Packman, L. C., Pappin, D. and Gray, J. C. (1988) FEBS Lett. 228, 157-161
[8]   Münch, S., Ljungberg, U., Steppuhn, J., Schneiderbauer, A., Nechushtai, R., Beyreuther, K., Herrmann, R. G. (1988) Curr. Genet. 14, 511-518
[9]   Wynn, R. M. and Malkin, R. (1988) Biochemistry 27, 5863-5869
[10]   Andersson, B., Åkerlund, H.-E. and Albertsson, P.-Å. (1976) Biochim. Biophys. Acta 423, 122-132
[11]   Laemmli, U. K. (1970) Nature 227, 680-685
[12]   Haehnel, W., Ratajczak, R. and Robenek, H. (1989) J. Cell Biol. 108, 1397-1405
[13]   Chua, N.-H. (1980) Methods Enzymol. 69, 434-446
[14]   Steppuhn, J., Hermans, J., Nechushtai, R., Ljungberg, U., Thümmler, F., Lottspeich, F. and Herrmann, R. G. (1988) FEBS Lett. 237, 218-224
[15]   Haehnel, W., Pröpper, A. and Krause, H. (1980) Biochim. Biophys. Acta 593, 384-399

ACKNOWLEDGEMENT: Support by Deutsche Forschungsgemeinschaft (Ha 1084/5-2) and by Fonds der Chemischen Industrie is gratefully acknowledged.

PHOTOSYSTEM I IN BARLEY: SUBUNIT PSI-F IS NOT ESSENTIAL FOR THE INTERACTION WITH PLASTOCYANIN.

HENRIK VIBE SCHELLER, BIRGITTE ANDERSEN, SIGURD OKKELS, *IB SVENDSEN, AND BIRGER LINDBERG MØLLER.

DEPARTMENT OF PLANT PHYSIOLOGY, ROYAL VETERINARY AND AGRICULTURAL UNIVERSITY, DK-1871 FREDERIKSBERG C AND *DEPARTMENT OF CHEMISTRY, CARLSBERG LABORATORY, DK-2500 VALBY, DENMARK.

1. INTRODUCTION

Photosystem I (PS I) preparations from barley contain polypeptides with apparent molecular masses of 82 (PSI-A and PSI-B), 18 (PSI-D), 16 (PSI-E), 14, 9.5 (PSI-H), 9 (PSI-C), 4, and 1.5 kDa (PSI-I) (1, 2). The nomenclature used for the polypeptides was proposed by Schantz and Bogorad (3) and is described in detail by Møller et al. (4). One copy of PSI-A, PSI-B, PSI-C, PSI-D, PSI-E, and PSI-H is present per P700 reaction center (1). The stoichiometry of the remaining subunits has not been determined.

The chloroplast encoded PSI-A and PSI-B polypeptides are homologous and form a heterodimeric pigment-protein complex known as P700-chlorophyll a-protein 1. This complex carries P700 and the electron acceptors A_0, A_1, and X. The chloroplast encoded PSI-C polypeptide carries the remaining electron transfer components of PS I, i. e. the iron-sulfur centers A and B (2). The function of the additional polypeptides is uncertain. The PSI-D polypeptide has been implicated as involved in the reaction between PS I and ferredoxin (5). PS I preparations from Swiss chard depleted in 'subunit III' by detergent treatment were deficient in $NADP^+$-photoreduction activity (6), and subunit III has been implicated as necessary for the reaction between plastocyanin and P700 (6, 7). The decreased rate of electron transfer between plastocyanin and P700 in detergent-treated PS I could however be partly overcome by the presence of cations or low pH (8-11). The cation concentrations necessary for optimal activity varies greatly in the different studies. Subunit III corresponds to PSI-F for which amino acid sequence information is available in several species (12-14). No polypeptide homologous to PSI-F has been reported in barley PS I preparations. In this paper we report the identification of the PSI-F polypeptide in barley by amino acid sequencing and demonstrate an apparent lack of importance of this polypeptide for $NADP^+$-photoreduction activity.

2. MATERIALS AND METHODS.

Barley PS I preparations were prepared as described previously (2) or

M. Baltscheffsky (ed.), Current Research in Photosynthesis, Vol. II, 679–682.

by the method of Mullet et al. (15). NADP$^+$-photoreduction was measured essentially as described by Bengis and Nelson (6). Electroelution of PSI-F was carried out according to Dunn et al. (12). Amino acid sequencing was carried out as described previously (2).

3. RESULTS AND DISCUSSION.

Different PS I preparations were analyzed by sodium dodecyl sulfate-polyacrylamide gel electrophoresis (Fig. 1). The band corresponding to a molecular mass of 15 kDa was observed in all preparations but varied in intensity. In previously reported experiments this band was never observed (1, 2). We are not aware of any changes in our analytical and preparative procedures which could explain this variance. An antibody preparation raised against our previously obtained PS I preparations does not react with the 15-kDa component. Electroelution and subsequent amino acid sequencing of the 15-kDa polypeptide clearly identified this as homologous to PSI-F from other species (Fig. 2).

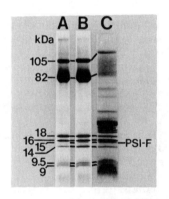

FIGURE 1. Sodium dodecyl sulfate-polyacrylamide gel electrophoresis of three different PS I preparations. Preparation A and B were prepared according to Høj et al. (2), and preparation C according to Mullet et al. (15). The preparations contained 70, 130, and 360 chlorophyll molecules per P700 reaction center, respectively.

```
Barley          D-I-A-G-L(T-P)?-K-E-S-K-A-F-A-K-R-?-K-Q(A-L)K-K-L-...
Spinach         D-I-A-G-L-T-P-C-K-E-S-K-Q-F-A-K-R-E-K-Q-A-L-K-K-L-Q-/
Pea             D-I-S-G-L-T-P-C-K-E-S-K-Q-F-A-K-R-E-K-Q-...
Chlamydomonas   D-I-A-G-L-T-P-C-S-E-S-K-A-Y-A-K-L-E-K-K-E-L-K-T-L-E-/
```

FIGURE 2. N-terminal amino acid sequence of the 15-kDa PSI-F polypeptide from barley. The sequences from spinach (13), pea (12), and Chlamydomonas (14) are shown for comparison.

PSI-F and PSI-E switch position in many electrophoretic gel systems (8) and this has caused some confusion. Münch et al. (16) have suggested that PSI-E corresponds to subunit III, but this is in disagreement with our results showing PSI-E to be located on the stromal side of the thylakoid membrane (5, 17, 18). The amino acid sequence of the transit peptide of the nuclear encoded PSI-F polypeptide suggests that this polypeptide is directed towards the thylakoid lumen (13, 14). As originally reported for subunit III (6), PSI-F is more easily dissociated from PS I than the other subunits. Hence, PSI-F is concluded to correspond to subunit III in the nomenclature of Bengis and Nelson (6).

The NADP⁺-photoreducing ability of three different PS I preparations was determined using different concentrations of MgSO₄ (Fig. 3). In all cases the optimum concentration was 10 mM MgSO₄, a value similar to the optimum in thylakoids (10). Without the addition of cations, the NADP⁺-photoreduction was barely detectable in the different preparations. This was also true for preparation C which contained the full complement of PS I polypeptides including light-harvesting complex I and II polypeptides. Similar findings have been reported by other workers (7, 9-11) and contradict the findings of Nelson and coworkers (6, 8) indicating high activity in PSI-F containing preparations even in the absence of cations. The maximum activity varied in the different preparations but the variations were not correlated with the relative amount of PSI-F present in the preparations. NADP⁺-reduction by PS I preparations depleted in PSI-F did not show a dependence on very high salt concentrations which has been reported in other studies (10, 11). Nechushtai and Nelson (8) found activation in PSI-F depleted preparations at lower concentrations and noted that the depleted preparations could be fully active at physiological conditions.

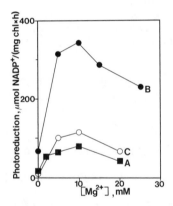

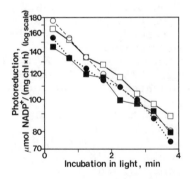

FIGURE 3. Effect of MgSO₄ on NADP⁺-photoreduction in the three different PS I preparations. The polypeptide composition of the PS I preparations is shown in Fig. 1.

FIGURE 4. Light-dependent inactivation of NADP⁺-photoreducing activity. Reaction mixtures contained 0.002% Triton X-100. Incubation with higher detergent concentrations resulted in much faster inactivation. The samples were incubated in the dark for 0 (O), 2 (●), 4 (□), and 6 min (■) prior to illumination with saturating red light.

Detergents in combination with light has a detrimental effect on PS I activity whereas no or little effect is seen in the dark (Fig. 4). Depletion of PS I with respect to PSI-F requires treatment with detergents. Lack of activity after such treatment may be more related to photooxidation than to dissociation of a subunit from PS I.

The results with the barley PS I preparations do not indicate a functional difference between PS I preparations with different amounts of PSI-F. Therefore we have no evidence for an important function of PSI-F in the reaction with plastocyanin. A spinach PS I subunit, presumably PSI-F, can be crosslinked to plastocyanin with a resulting loss of PS I activity (19). In barley, a subunit which is identified as PSI-F in preliminary studies can also be crosslinked to plastocyanin (B. Andersen, H. V. Scheller, and B. L. Møller, unpublished). Thus, it seems that PSI-F either forms a docking site for plastocyanin or at least is situated close to such a site. Nevertheless, we conclude that PSI-F is not essential for PS I activity. Due to the many adverse effects of detergent treatments used to remove PSI-F, the importance of this subunit can not be accurately quantified by analysis of depleted PS I preparations. Reconstitution studies with isolated PSI-F and PS I should allow more quantitative conclusions to be made.

REFERENCES.
1 Scheller, H.V., Svendsen, I. and Møller, B.L. (1989) J. Biol. Chem. 264, 6929-6934
2 Høj, P.B., Svendsen, I., Scheller, H.V. and Møller, B.L. (1987) J. Biol. Chem. 262, 12676-12684
3 Schantz, R. and Bogorad, L. (1988) Plant Mol. Biol. 11, 239-247
4 Møller, B.L, Scheller, H.V., Okkels, J.S., Koch, B., Andersen, B., Nielsen, H.L., Olsen, I., Halkier, B.A. and Høj, P.B., these proceedings.
5 Andersen, B., Koch, B., Scheller, H.V., Okkels, J.S. and Møller, B.L., these proceedings
6 Bengis, C. and Nelson, N. (1977) J. Biol. Chem. 4564-4569
7 Haehnel, W., Hesse, V. and Pröpper, A. (1980) FEBS Lett. 111, 79-82
8 Nechushtai, R. and Nelson, N. (1981) J. Bioenerg. Biomembr. 13, 295-306
9 Davis, D.J., Krogmann, D.W. and San Pietro, A. (1980) Plant Physiol. 65, 697-702
10 Ratajczak, R., Mitchell, R. and Haehnel, W. (1988) Biochim. Biophys. Acta 933, 306-318
11 Takabe, T., Ishikawa, H., Iwasaki, Y. and Inoue, H. (1989) Plant Cell Physiol. 30, 85-90
12 Dunn, P.P.J., Packman, L.C., Pappin, D. and Gray, J.C. (1988) FEBS Lett. 228, 157-161
13 Steppuhn, J., Hermans, J., Nechushtai, R., Ljungberg, U., Thümmler, F., Lottspeich, F. and Herrmann, R.G. (1988) FEBS Lett. 237, 218-224
14 Franzén, L.-G., Frank, G., Zuber, H. and Rochaix, J.-D. (1989) Plant Mol. Biol. 12, 463-474
15 Mullet, J.E., Burke, J.J. and Arntzen, C.J. (1980) Plant Physiol. 65, 814-822
16 Münch, S., Ljungberg, U., Steppuhn, J., Schneiderbauer, A., Nechushtai, R., Beyreuter, K. and Herrmann, R.G. (1988) Curr. Genet. 14, 511-518
17 Okkels, J.S., Jepsen, L.B., Hønberg, L.S., Lehmbeck, J., Scheller, H.V., Brandt, P., Høyer-Hansen, G., Stummann, B., Henningsen, K.W., Wettstein, D.v. and Møller, B.L. (1988) FEBS Lett. 237, 108-112
18 Scheller, H.V., Okkels, J.S., Roepstorff, P., Jepsen, L.B. and Møller, B.L., these proceedings
19 Wynn, R.M. and Malkin, R. (1988) Biochemistry 27, 5863-5869

SIMULATION OF THE FLASH INDUCED P_{700}^+ REDUCTION KINETICS USING A MODIFIED SIMPLEX METHOD
SCOPE AND LIMITATION OF THE APPROACH.

E. VANDER DONCKT[1], R. VANDELOISE[1] and S. MAURO[2].
[1] Laboratoire de Chimie Organique Physique and [2] Laboratoire de Physiologie Végétale, Université Libre de Bruxelles, 50 av. F.D. Roosevelt, B-1050 Bruxelles. Belgique.

1. INTRODUCTION

The redox reactions between PSII and PSI involve the diffusion of the electron carriers plastoquinol and plastocyanin. The cyt b_6/f behaves as a control gate with plastoquinol-plastocyanin oxydoreductase activity.
The reduction kinetics of P_{700}^+ has been intensively studied (1) as it is directly related to the rate of all preceding reactions including the long range diffusion of plastoquinol and plastocyanin.
We have previously succeeded in computing that in-series model by numerical integration (2).
Our simulation studies were extended to assess the precision and foundation of the calculated rate parameters by making use of a Modified Simplex Method (MSM).

The simplex method
The simplex method is a multivariate fitting procedure which, in our case, proceeds via a comparison between an experimental and a calculated curve. The fitting between experimental and computed data is optimized by minimizing the objective response function R_e :

$$R_e = \frac{1}{n} \sum_{t=1}^{t=n} (A_{t,exp} - A_{t,calc})^2$$

where $A_{t,exp}$ and $A_{t,calc}$ are respectively the measured and calculated absorbance changes due to P_{700}^+ reduction, n is the number of points where the comparison is performed.

The simplex is a geometric figure with one more vertex than the numbers of parameters to adjust (Fig. 1). The simplex algorithm directs the adjustment away from the combination of the rate constants yielding the poorest response (high R_e values) towards those giving a better response (lower R_e values). Reflection, expansion and contraction along the line joining the worst vertex and the centroid of the opposite hyperface of the simplex are its basic operations.

M. Baltscheffsky (ed.), Current Research in Photosynthesis, Vol. II, 683–686.
© 1990 *Kluwer Academic Publishers. Printed in the Netherlands.*

Reflection should yield a new vertex with a smaller R_e value than that calculated for at least one of the vertices of the last simplex; expansion accelerates the progression towards the optimal combination of the rate parameters. A contraction is performed if a better vertex is not found by reflection (3,4).

2. RESULTS
    We have previously shown that an adequate simulation of the P_{700}^+ reduction kinetics was critically dependant on the assumed values for the rate constants of X_{320}^- oxidation (k_1 = 1260 s^{-1}), cyt b_6/f reduction (k_7 = 516 s^{-1}) and diffusion of plastoquinols (D = 10^{-11} cm^2 s^{-1} if the distance between the 2 photosystems is taken as 100 nm).
    The simplex routine was first started with rate constants chosen far away from the values given above (Fig. 2).

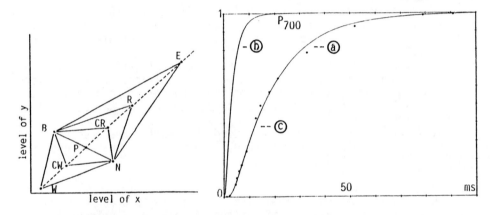

Fig. 1 Possible moves for a modified simplex in two dimensions.
       B,W and N correspond to the vertices yielding the Best, Worst and Next-to-the-worst response.

Fig. 2 Experimental and calculated time course of P_{700}^+ reduction.
       a: k_1=1260 s^{-1}, k_7= 516 s^{-1}, D=$10^{-11}cm^2s^{-1}$
       b: k_1=4040 s^{-1}, k_7=2100 s^{-1}, D=$10^{-10}cm^2s^{-1}$
       c: k_1=4022 s^{-1}, k_7=1980 s^{-1}, D= 0.58 $10^{-11}cm^2s^{-1}$
       ●●● : Experimental data

An uncertainty of 2% on the experimental data was assumed. The calculations were thus stopped when R_e reached a value of 10^{-4}. The evolution in R_e against the number of iterations is illustrated in Fig. 3. The objective function decreases rapidly and essentially reaches its minimal value after 25 iterations.

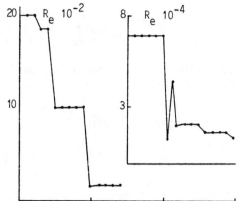

Fig. 3. Objective response function versus the number of iterations.

The corresponding variations in the rate constants are shown in Fig. 4.

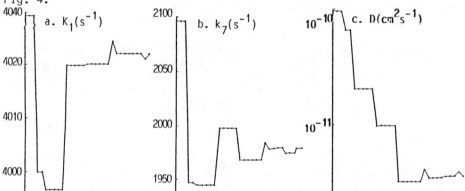

Fig. 4. Trajectories of the rate paramaters values during minimization.

The MSM yields a new set of rate constants which is equally effective in simulating the kinetics of P_{700}^+ reduction (Fig. 2).
The inability of the MSM to converge to a unique combination of rate constants is confirmed by starting the procedure with different sets of values (Table I).

Table I - MSM calculated optimal combinations of the three rate constants.

calc.	$k_1(s^{-1})$		$k_7(s^{-1})$		$D(cm^2s^{-1})$	
	initial	optimized	initial	optimized	initial	optimized
1	533	906	266	524	$1.17\ 10^{-12}$	$1.06\ 10^{-11}$
2	600	762.9	280	410.97	$11\ 10^{-13}$	$1.45\ 10^{-11}$
3	4040	4022.44	2100	1980.9	10^{-10}	$0.58\ 10^{-11}$

It also appears that if k_1 is given a sufficiently large value, a combination of D and k_7 giving a satisfactory agreement between computed and experimental data can always be obtained (Table II).

Table II - MSM calcuated optimal combinations of k_7 and D.
k_1 is kept constant at 1260 s^{-1}.

calculations	k_7 (s^{-1})		$D(cm^{-2}s^{-1})$	
	initial	optimized	initial	optimized
1	4000	3043048	$2.5 \ 10^{-14}$	$5.25 \ 10^{-12}$
2	250	410.3	$2.0 \ 10^{-9}$	$1.3 \ 10^{-11}$

3. CONCLUSION

The use of a multivariate fitting procedure shows that the shape of the experimental P_{700}^+ reduction curve can be accounted for by various sets of rate parameters and consequently cannot be employed without the greatest care to ascertain the rate constant values of the individual reactions leading to P_{700}^+ reduction.

Taking advantage of the P_{700}^+ reduction curve will thus depend on the possibility of finding and using independent kinetic information about the linking between PSII and PSI; the concentration as a function of time of plastoquinols in the region between two photosystems would possibly fulfill that purpose.

REFERENCES
1. Haehnel W. (1987) In: Proc. Int. Cong. Photosynth. (Biggins J., Ed.) Vol. 2, pp 513-520. Martinus Nijhoff, Dordrecht.
2. Mauro S., Lannoye R., Vandeloise R. and Vander Donckt E. (1986) Photobiochem. Photobiophys. 11, 83-94.
3. Parker L.R., Cave M.R. and Barnes R.M. (1985) Anal. Chem. Acta 175, 231-237.
4. Deming S.N. and Morgan S.L. (1973) Anal. Chem. 45, 278-283

LOW POTENTIAL CYTOCHROME c_{550} FUNCTION IN CYANOBACTERIA AND ALGAE.

D. W. KROGMANN and S. SMITH, DEPARTMENT OF BIOCHEMISTRY, PURDUE
UNIVERSITY, WEST LAFAYETTE, IN 47907 U.S.A.

ABSTRACT

Low potential cytochrome c_{550} has been found in a variety of
oxygenic photosynthetic organisms from aquatic habitats. The amino
acid sequence reveals regions of striking similarity to regions of
cytochrome c_{553} which has a high redox potential and functions as
an electron donor to Photosystem I. Parts of the gene for one of
these cytochromes have been used in the formation of the gene for
the other cytochrome. We have found cytochrome c_{550} to be rapidly
autooxidized at very low O_2 concentrations and, under anaerobic
conditions, to be rapidly reduced by ferredoxin II. In some genera
of cyanobacteria, cytochrome c_{550} and ferredoxin II increase in
concentration as the cell density rises to the point of limiting
the availability of light and oxygen. Evidence will be presented
which suggests that this cytochrome functions in the anaerobic
disposal of electrons from carbohydrate reserves which are dissimi-
lated to supply ATP for cell maintenance in the absence of light
and oxygen.

1. Introduction

Cytochrome c_{550} is a low potential cytochrome (E'_o =
260 mV) first described by Holton and Myers (1). This
cytochrome has been found in a variety of cyanobacteria and
eukaryotic algae but there is no report of it in higher plants.
The primary structure of the cytochrome from *Microcystis
aeruginosa* has been determined (2) and shows that regions of
amino acid sequence similarity are shared by this cytochrome
and the high potential cytochrome c_{553} that functions in the
photosynthetic process in the same organisms. The shared
region near the N-terminus contains the Cys X X Cys His heme
binding site characteristic of all c type cytochromes and the

M. Baltscheffsky (ed.), Current Research in Photosynthesis, Vol. II, 687–690.

---

longer shared region near the C terminus begins next to the amino acid that is the sixth ligand to the iron in the heme.

2. PROCEDURE

Materials and Methods. Cytochrome c_{550} and ferredoxins were purified from *M. aeruginosa* and from *Aphanizomenon flow-aquae* as described in (2). The final stages of ferredoxin purification were accomplished using chromatography on Sephacryl S-200 as described by Tan and Ho (3). Spinach ferredoxin-NADP oxidoreductase and glucose oxidase were purchased from Sigma Chemical Co. Measurements of the enzymatic reduction of cytochrome c_{550} were done in an anaerobic cuvette that had been through three cycles of flushing with argon and degassing under vacuum. Glucose oxidase and glucose were included in the reaction mixture. Reactions were initiated by the addition of NADPH from the side arm of the cuvette and the absorbance change measured at 420 nm.

3. RESULTS AND DISCUSSION

Pulich (4) had observed the autooxidation of low potential cytochrome c_{550} in extracts of Nostoc when supplied with NADPH under aerobic conditions and he suggested that cytochrome reduction was catalysed by ferredoxin-NADP oxidoreductase in his preparation. We could easily repeat Pulich's observation using purified proteins but found the rate of cytochrome reduction was very low. The addition of crude ferredoxin to the reaction mixture greatly stimulated the rate of electron transfer. When extracts of the soluble proteins of cyanobacteria are chromatographed on DEAE cellulose ion exchange columns, two forms of ferredoxin are occasionally observed. When cells are grown with sufficient iron, one finds a ferredoxin which elutes from the column al 0.4 to 0.5 M NaCl and which is usually identified with electron transfer from Photosystem I to FNR. This is called ferredoxin I. Occasionally a second ferredoxin which elutes at lower ionic strength (0.2 - 0.3 M NaCl) is observed and this is called ferredoxin II. We found that ferredoxin II was ten times as active as ferredoxin I. Hutson *et al.* (5) had found that these ferredoxins differed by a factor of two in supporting the reduction of NADP by Photosystem I and differed less in the decarboxylation of pyruvate by the phosphoroclastic system of *Clostridium pasteruanum*. We applied the ferredoxin II fraction from the ion exchange column to a hydrophobic interaction column and resolved it into three distinct isozymes. One of these was very active in the cytochrome reduction activity, the second less active and the third isozyme was inactive. This specificity of interaction of one ferredoxin with low potential

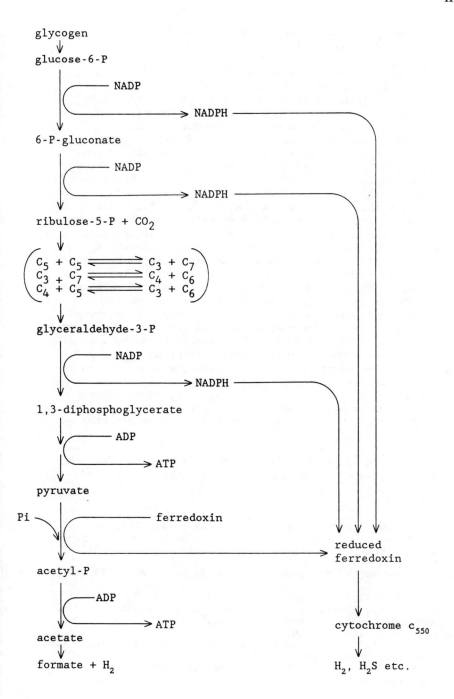

cytochrome c_{550} supports the notion of *in vivo* pathway
involving these two catalysts.

The occurrence of cytochrome c_{550} and ferredoxin in
soluble protein extracts of cyanobacteria is not regularly
observed. We found large quantities of these proteins in
M. aeruginosa and *A. flos-aquae* collected from very dense
natural blooms. Smaller amounts of cytochrome and no
detectable ferredoxin II were found in laboratory grown
M. aeruginosa and *Anacystis nidulans*. Our laboratory grown
Anabaena 7120 yielded neither the cytochrome nor the ferredoxin
II. The abundance of these catalysts in natural blooms may be
related to cell densities high enough to exclude both light and
oxygen from the environment of most of the cells. Zohary (6)
has shown that *M. aeruginosa* in a densely packed hyperscum
remains viable for three months. Heyer, Stal and Krumbein (7)
have demonstrated a fermentation of reserve glycogen in
anaerobic *Oscillatoria limosa* and van der Oost (8) has found a
fermentation pathway linked to hydrogen evolution in
Cyanothece. Other evidence suggests that oxidized sulphur
compounds can serve as terminal electron acceptors for
fermentation in dark, anaerobic cyanobacteria. We proposed
that the passage of electrons from NADPH through a flavoprotein
dehydrogenase like ferredoxin-NADP oxidoreductase to a specific
ferredox which reduces low potential cytochrome c_{550} is a
pathway for the excretion of excess reducing power needed to
sustain these fermentations. The appearance of the low
potential cytochrome in eukaryotic algae may reflect their
ability to withstand periods of anaerobic darkness such as
passing through the winter in sediments of temperate zone
waters.

Supported by grant number DCB-8722411 from the Metabolic
Biology Program of the National Science Foundation.

REFERENCES

1. Holton, R. W. and Myers, J. (1963) *Science* **142**, 1-2.
2. Cohen, C. L., Sprinkle, J. R., Alam, J., Hermodson, M., Meyer,
    T. and Krogmann, D. W. (1989) *Arch. Biochem. Biophys.* **270**, 227-235.
3. Tan, S. and Ho, K. K. (1989) *Biochim. Biophys. Acta* **973**, 111-117.
4. Pulich, W. (1977) *J. Phycol.* **13**, 40-45.
5. Hutson, K. G., Rogers, L. J., Haslett, B. G., Boulter, D. and
    Cammack, R. (1978) *Biochem. J.* **172** 465-477.
6. Zohary, T. (1985) *J. Plankton Res.* **7**, 399-409.
7. Heyer, H., Stal, L. J. and Krumbein, W. E. (1988) VI Int. Symp.
    on Photosyn. Prokaryotes, p. 247.
8. van der Ooost, J. (1988) VI Int. Symp. on Photosyn.
    Prokaryotes, p. 246.

PHOTOELECTROCHEMICAL MONITORING OF PHOTOSYSTEM I ELECTRON TRANSPORT WITH OXYGEN AS ACCEPTOR

D. Christopher Goetze and Robert Carpentier
Centre de recherche en photobiophysique, Université du Québec à Trois-Rivières, C.P. 500, Trois-Rivières (Québec), G9A 5H7, Canada

1. INTRODUCTION

In the past few years, we have used a photoelectrochemical cell first described by Allen and Crane (1) and then modified by us (2) to study the photocurrent produced by thylakoid membranes. With this type of cell, the suspension of chloroplast membranes is introduced into a small compartment (80 µl) where the reduced species produced by the photosynthetic electron transport are used to generate a photocurrent at a platinum working electrode kept under potentiostatic conditions (750 mV vs SCE). It was demonstrated that photocurrent generated by either native thylakoid membranes or isolated PSI or PSII submembrane fractions could be greatly enhanced by the addition of artificial acceptors like potassium ferricyanide, methylviologen, or 2,5-dichlorobenzoquinone (2-4). The artificial electron acceptors acted as an electroactive mediator which carry the reduced equivalents from the membranes to the platinum electrode. However, we have also reported the generation of photocurrents in the absence of any added artificial electron acceptor (2,5). It was postulated that the photocurrent could be either generated by thylakoid membranes in close contact with the platinum electrode or mediated by impurities already present in the reaction medium (4,5)

In this report, we demonstrate that oxygen can serve as an electroactive mediator through a Mehler type reaction. It is shown that the photocurrent is produced by the oxidation of H_2O_2 at the platinum electrode.

2. MATERIALS AND METHODS

Uncoupled thylakoid membranes were prepared from spinach leaves (5) and resuspended in 50 mM TesNaOH (pH 7.5), 330 mM sorbitol, 2 mM $MgCl_2$, 1 mM NH_4Cl and 2 mM EDTA to a Chl concentration of 250 µg/ml. Electrochemical measurements were performed as previously described with the cell thermostated at 20°C (2).

3. RESULTS AND DISCUSSION

Photocurrents in the order of 6-7 µA were repetitively obtained after illumination of the electrochemical cell filled with thylakoid

M. Baltscheffsky (ed.), Current Research in Photosynthesis, Vol. II, 691–694.
© 1990 Kluwer Academic Publishers. Printed in the Netherlands.

membranes (20 µg Chl) (Fig. 1). The photocurrent induction in absence of artificial donor or acceptor can be described by a first order kinetic with a rate constant of about 4.5×10^{-2} s^{-1}.

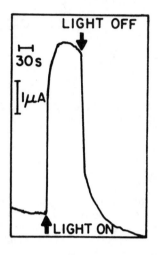

Figure 1. Photocurrent generation by the photoelectrochemical cell containing thylakoid membranes at a concentration of 250 µg Chl/ml. A potential of 750 mV (vs SCE) was applied on the working electrode. White light illumination (220 mW·cm^{-2}) was provided to the sample by a quartz-halogen lamp (250 W) though a fiber optic guide, positioned above the cell.

One possible candidate for mediation of electron transfer from thylakoid membranes to the working electrode is oxygen. The later is well known as a PSI electron acceptor and is involved in pseudocyclic electron transfer (6). In Table I, we show that removal of part of the oxygen by bubbling N$_2$ gas in the sample used for photocurrent measurements has reduced the photocurrent to 4.1 µA. However, oxygen consumption by the glucose/glucose oxidase system strongly inhibited photocurrent generation. Glucose or glucose oxidase alone were ineffective (Table I). Therefore, oxygen is certainly involved in the production of photocurrents by the thylakoid membranes.

When the specific PSII electron acceptor 2,5-dichlorobenzoquinone (DCBQ) is used, strong photocurrents are produced (Table I). Presumably, under these conditions, only PSII is participating in the photocurrent generated because DCBQ is a more favored acceptor than oxygen. Therefore, addition of glucose and glucose oxidase to samples already supplied with DCBQ does not significantly influence the extent of photocurrent generated (Table I). Thus, oxygen is not involved in the mediation of electrons between PSII and the working electrode by DCBQ. On the other hand, if the specific PSI acceptor methylviologen, is used to enhance the photoactivity, the glucose/glucose oxidase system produces a strong inhibition of photocurrent generation. In fact, methylviologen is known to reduce molecular oxygen to superoxide radical which spontaneously dismutes to hydrogen peroxyde (7).

To determine the reduced intermediate responsible for the mediation of electrons to the working electrode, three specific enzymes were used: glucose oxidase (with glucose), superoxide dismutase and catalase. As shown in Fig. 2, glucose oxidase is intermediately effective in inhibiting the photocurrent. This enzyme consumes ambient oxygen as it degradates glucose but it simultanuously produces hydrogen

TABLE I. Effect of additives on the photocurrent generated. Additive concentration: N_2, the preparation was bubbled with N_2 for 5 min before it was introduced in the cell; glucose, 4 mM; glucose oxidase, 1 500 units/ml; 2,5-dichlorobenzoquinone, 0.63 mM; methylviologen, 1.5 µM.

Additive	Photocurrent ($\mu A \cdot cm^{-2}$ 20 µg Chl^{-1})
None	7.4
N_2	4.1
Glucose	7.6
Glucose oxydase	7.4
Glucose + glucose oxidase	1.7
DCBQ	29.8
DCBQ + glucose + glucose oxidase	28.7
Methylviologen	17.4
Methulviologen + glucose + glucose oxidase	1.9

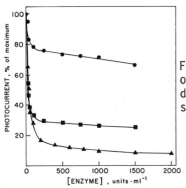

Figure 2. Inhibitory effect of enzymes on photocurrent generation: ●, superoxide dismutase; ■, glucose oxidase + 4 mM glucose; ▲, catalase.

peroxyde. Superoxide dismutase consumes superoxide radicals but in the process, also produces hydrogen peroxide. The fact that it is able to cause some degree of inhibition indicates that superoxide is being produced. The strongest inhibition of photocurrent is observed in the presence of catalase, even at relatively low concentrations. At 2 000 units/ml, more than 92% inhibition is obtained. The effectiveness of catalase is derived from its point of action in the electron flow pathway to platinum. The result show oxygen serves as the acceptor from PSI, is reduced to superoxide radical and then dismutated to hydrogen peroxide. Electrons are passed to the working electrode during the degradation of the latter product.

Hydrogen peroxyde is known to form complexes with transition metals (8). Further, platinum was used as material for the working electrode in the detection of hydrogen peroxyde under similar pH and imposed potential conditions (9). Therefore, our results indicate that the photoelectrochemical cell used could provide a new approach to monitoring pseudocyclic electron transfer, when active PSII serves as the electron donor to PSI. In this case, oxygen evolution by PSII will not be prejudicial to simultaneous monitoring of oxygen uptake by PSI since the reduced forms of oxygen, and not oxygen itself, are being monitored. Rather, oxygen evolved by PSII will be usefull in the stabilization of the dissolved oxygen concentration.

This research was supported by the National Sciences and Engineering Research Council of Canada and by the Department of Energy, Mines and Natural Resources of Canada.

REFERENCES
1   Allen, M.J. and Crane, A.E. (1976) Bioelectrochem. Bioenerg. 3, 84-91
2   Mimeault, M. and Carpentier, R. (1987) Biochem. Cell Biol. 66, 436-441
3   Lemieux, S. and Carpentier, R. (1988) Photochem. Photobiol. 48, 115-121
4   Lemieux, S. and Carpentier, R. (1988) J. Photochem. Photobiol. B2, 221-231
5   Carpentier, R. and Mimeault, M. (1987) Biotechnol. Lett. 9, 111-116
6   Robinson, J.M. (1988) Physiol. Plant. 72, 666-680
7   Lien, S. and San Pietro, A. (1979) FEBS Lett. 99, 189-193
8   Salin, M. (1987) Physiol. Plant. 72, 681-689
9   Guilbault, G.G. and Lubrano, G.J. (1973) Anal. Chim. Acta 64, 439-455

PS I PARTICLES ASSEMBLED ON CRISTA MEMBRANES CAN DRIVE ELECTRON TRANSPORT AND PHOSPHORYLATION

Li Shu-jun, Xu Ya-nan, Wang Jian, Ying Wen-long and Guo Yi-song
Shanghai Institute of Plant Physiology, Academia Sinica. Shanghai, China. 200032.

1. INTRODUCTION:
In previous papers, we proved that the photophosphorylation could be proceeded in the combination of the deficient thylakoid membranes from spinach chloroplasts with the crista membranes from mitochondria (1. 2), and that the electron transport of such combined system was linked together (2. 3), the possible electron pathways were discussed (4). The multiple sites of linkage were proved by the experiments of the reduction of cytochrome c (3). Later we found that the PS II particles could be assembled on the crista membranes of rat liver mitochondria, and showed phosphorylation activity under light (5). This means that the excited electron from PS II reaction center can drive the electron transport and phosphorylation mechanism of crista membranes. The inference of multiple sites of linkage suggests that the excited electron from PS I reaction center may also drive the electron transport and phosphorylation of crista membranes when PS I particles assembled on crista membranes. So, we conducted the experiments and the assembled system showed rather high photophosphorylation activity.

2. MATERIALS AND METHODS :
2.1. Materials : Chloroplasts and PS I particles were prepared from spinach (Spinacia oleracia L.) leaves and crista membranes were prepared from rat (Rattus norvegies) liver mitochondria.
2.2. Preparations: The preparing methods of both crista membranes and chloroplasts were as previous paper (2). The liposomes were prepared by sonication (5), and the PS I particles were prepared by digitonin treatment (6).
2.3. Examinations and determinations : The prepared PS I particles and thier assembling system were examined by electron micros-cope JEOL JEM-100 CX II. The differential spectra of P_{700} and P_{680} signals were examined by UV-3000 spectrophotometer with redox chemicals. The PS I particles were electrophorely-zed after digested by 1 % SDS in 100^0C for 2 minutes and fractionated by 0.1 % SDS-PAGE, the concentration gel was 5 % and the fractionation gel was 12 % at 30 V. for 24 hours. Stained over night by Coomassie briliant blue and decoloured by 5 % acetic acid solution. The oxygen evolution and consump-tion, phosphorylation activity, chlorophyll and protein contents were determined as previous paper (2).

M. Baltscheffsky (ed.), Current Research in Photosynthesis, Vol. II, 695–698.
© 1990 Kluwer Academic Publishers. Printed in the Netherlands.

3. RESULTS AND DISCUSSION :
3.1. PS I particles : 11 bands were obtained from the SDS-PAGE
of prepared PS I particles and thier molecular weights were
67, 55, 40, 32, 29, 24, 22, 20 18.2, 17.8 and 14.3 KD respectively. It means that the polypeptide of PS I reaction center
(67 and 55 KD) and the polypeptides of its light harvest
protein complexes (22 and 20 KD) are present, but the polypeptides of PS II reaction center (47 and 43 KD) are absent,
shown in figure 1. So, the prepared PS I particles are electrophoretically pure.

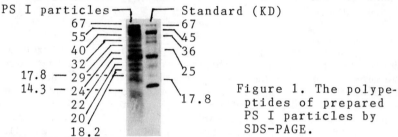

Figure 1. The polype-
ptides of prepared
PS I particles by
SDS-PAGE.

3.2. The differential redox spectra : From figure 2. we can see
that the P_{700} singnal of PS I particles is higher than that
of thylakoids and that the P_{680} signal is lower than that of
tyhylakoids. This results showed that the prepared PS I particles are richer in PS I reaction center.

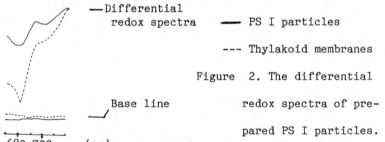

—Differential
redox spectra

Base line

680 700 (nm)

— PS I particles

--- Thylakoid membranes

Figure 2. The differential
redox spectra of pre-
pared PS I particles.

3.3. Oxygen evolution and consumption : The activity of oxygen
evolution (in FeCy system) of PS I particles was absent, and
the activity of consumption (in MV system) was obviously
higher than that of thylakoids (Table 1). It means that the
activity of PS II in the prepared PS I particles have lost.

Table 1. Comparison of evolution and consumption oxygen by
thylakoid membranes and prepared PS I particles.

Materials	A. Activity of O_2 consumption (μ mol O_2 / mg chl hr)	B. Activity of O_2 evolution	A/B
Thylakoid membranes	305	62	4.9
PS I particles	451	0	∞

3.4. Assembling condition : pH 7.2 was selected for the reaction system, because the activity of electron transport from PS I particles was decreased with the increase of the pH in reaction system (Figure 3).

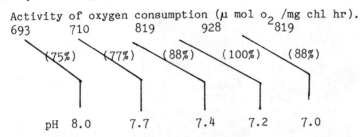

Activity of oxygen consumption (μ mol o_2 /mg chl hr).

Figure 3. Activity of oxygen consumption by PS I particles in different pH conditions.

When the PS I particles were assembled on crista membranes directly, the time required for maximum activity was 30 min. during this time the activity of crista membranes was not steady. If the assembling time was less than 10 minutes, then the assemble efficiency was very low. So, we first preassembled the PS I particles on the liposomes for 30 minutes and then combined with the fresh prepared crista membranes for 5 minutes. Such method could increase assembled efficiency near 8 times, as showm in table 2.

Table 2. Efficiency of preassembling PS I particles to liposomes.

Materials	PSP activity (CPM L-D)	Efficiency of assembling (CPM)	(%)
1. PS I particles	13		
2. 1 + crista membranes	18	139	100
3. 1 + liposomes + crista membranes	967	1088	780
4. Crista membranes	-134		

Under the suitable condition, the activity of the assembled system could reach 13 μ mol ATP synthesis per miligram per hour (Table 3).

Table 3. The combination efficiency of PS I particles with crista membranes.

Materials	PSP activity (CPM L-D)	Combined efficiency (CPM)	(μ mol ATP/mg chl hr)
1. PS I particles + Lp	-2		
2. Crista membranes +Lp	62		
3. 1 + crista membranes	886	826	13.2(15%)
4. Thylakois + Lp	5522	5522	88.0(100%)

Under the electronmicroscope the rod-like PS I particles(Figure 4-A), when assembled to the spherical liposomes (Figure 4-B) give pear shaped (Figure 4-C).They are quickly inserted into crista membrane (Figure 4-D).

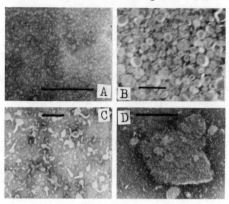

The bars are 0.2 μm.

A. PS I particles.

B. Liposomes.

C. A assembling to B.

D. C combined to crista

membranes.

Figure 4. Structures of prepared particles and thier assembled systems.

These experimental results proved both functionally and structurally that the photo-excited electron flow from PS I reaction center can be linked to the electron transport chains and phosphorylation mechanism of the crista membranes in the assembled system. The preparation of more purified PS I particles will be carried out and the transport pathways of the excited electron flow from PS I reaction center will be studied in future.

References :
1. Li Shu-jun, et al. 1981. Scientia Sinica. 24 (11) : 1575.
2. Li Shu-jun, et al. 1984. Scientia Sinica (Series B) 29 (11) : 1148.
3. Xiao Jian-ping, et al. 1986. Scientia Sinica (Series B) 29 (11) : 1157.
4. Li Shu-jun, et al. 1988. Acta Phytophysiologia Sinica. 14 (2) :145.
5. Li Shu-jun, et al. 1987. in " Progress in Photosynthesis research " II.12.657. ED : Biggins. Martinus Nijhoff Publishers. Netherlands.
6. Nelson N., in "Methods in Chloroplast Molecular Biology " pp. 907-915. 1982. Eds : Edelman K. et al. Elsevier Biomedical press.

This work was supported by National Natural Science Foundation of China.

CHARACTERISTICS OF PHOTOSYSTEM ACTIVITY OF CYANOBACTERIA IMMOBILIZED IN POLYMER FOAMS

Carlos Garbisu[1], Huang Wen[1], David O. Hall[1], and Juan L. Serra[2]. Division of Biosphere Sciences, King's College London, Campden Hill Rd. London W8 7AH, U.K.[1]; Dpto. Bioquimica y Biologia Molecular, Univ. Pais Vasco, Apdo.644, 48008-Bilbao, Spain[2]

INTRODUCTION

Phormidium laminosum is a filamentous thermophilic cyanobacterium, non-heterocystous, that can fix nitrogen under microaerophilic conditions. *Anabaena azollae* is a species of nitrogen fixing, heterocystous cyanobacterium which is usually found as a symbiont of aquatic ferns *Azolla*.

Cell immobilization appears to offer several advantages in comparison with batch or continuous culture fermentations where free cells are used (1). Polysaccharide-based gels and reticulate foams, polyvinyl(PV) and polyurethane(PU), are the preferred matrices for photosynthetic systems. When cyanobacteria are grown in foam pieces, immobilization is achieved by adsorption on the foam surface as well as by entrapment of the cells in the foam cavities.

We have studied the photosynthetic stability of *P. laminosum* cells immobilized on polyvinyl and polyurethane foams. Cells of *A. azollae* were also immobilized in polyurethane foams either by adsorption or entrapment and in polyvinyl foam by adsorption. The work on *A. azollae* has been mainly concerned with the ammonia production via nitrogenase. Scanning electron microscopy was performed to determine if such immobilization affects their structure and morphology.

MATERIALS AND METHODS

Cyanobacterial cultures and growth: *P. laminosum* was grown at 45°C in medium D of Castenholtz (2). *A. azollae* was grown in a BG-11 medium without nitrate at 28°C. Both strains were cultured as previously described (3)

Immobilization conditions: Hypol FHP 2002 (PU), and polyvinyl foams (PV 50) were kindly supplied by W. R. Grace Ltd. and Calligen respectively. Cells of *A. azollae* and *P. laminosum* were immobilized either by adsorption (PU and PV) or by entrapment in the polyurethane prepolymer followed by polymerisation as previously described (3).

Chlorophyll concentration determination: It was carried out according to MacKinney (4) and Talling *et al.* (5) for *P. laminosum* and *A. azollae* cells respectively.

Photosynyhetic electron transport activities: Photosynthesis of *P. laminosum* (free-living and cells extracted from the foams by squeezing) was measured as O_2-exchange in a Clark-type electrode at 25°C under saturating orange-red light. Photosystem (PS) II was measured by quantifying the O_2-evolution by whole cells in a volume of 3 ml of cells plus the reaction mixture containing potassium ferricyanide (4mM final concentration) and 2,6 dimethylbenzoquinone(DMBQ) (2-3 mM). O_2-uptake was used to measure PS I+II activity with the following added in sequence: 2-3 mM final concentration methylviologen(MV) and 8-13 mM sodium azide. PS I alone was measured as O_2-uptake adding the following compounds: 15 uM 3-(3,4-dichlorophenyl)-1,1-dimethylurea(DCMU), 2.5 mM glutathione(GSH), 0.3 mM 2,6 dichlorophenol-indophenol(DCPIP).

Ammonia production: Immobilized (PU and PV) and freely suspended *A. azollae* were incubated

M. Baltscheffsky (ed.), Current Research in Photosynthesis, Vol. II, 699–702.
© 1990 *Kluwer Academic Publishers. Printed in the Netherlands.*

II.7.**700**

(light/dark periods) in the growth medium in presence or absence of L-methionine sulfoximine (MSX). The determination of ammonia concentration was done according to Solorzano (6).

Scanning electron microscopy: All samples were fixed, dehydrated, dried and coated as previously described (7).

RESULTS AND DISCUSSION

Immobilization by entrapment of *P. laminosum*: When *P. laminosum* cells were entrapped in PU foams according to Brouers et al. (3), complete loss of viability was observed after 2-3 days of immobilization. Consequently, in an attempt to overcome the toxicity problems, different parameters were modified (temperature of polymerisation, prepolymer: culture medium ratio, polymerisation time, light intensity, temperature of incubation, concentration of initial cell suspension, etc.) without any success. In all cases, high toxicity was observed which lead to a rapid death of the immobilized cells. It seems that this toxicity originates in the polymerisation reaction due to a possible release of toxic compounds and local increase of temperature and pressure.

Table 1. Photosynthetic activity of free-living and immobilized *P.laminosum*.

Photosystem measured	Units	Day 26 (1)					Day 51				
		PU 1:1 (2)	PU 1:1.5 (2)	PU 1:2 (2)	PV	Free-living cells	PU 1:1 (2)	PU 1:1.5 (2)	PU 1:2 (2)	PV	Free-living cells
PS II (3)	P. a (6)	313.4 (68.1)	278.3 (82.1)	341.1 (33.2)	188.1 (16.8)	642.7 (10.0)	143.6 (0.2)	136.5 (36.4)	145.4 (24.2)	151.2 (14.3)	1066.6 (226.7)
	P. a (7)	0.273 (0.059)	0.181 (0.041)	0.228 (0.041)	0.450 (0.023)		0.126 (0.026)	0.147 (0.033)	0.105 (0.28)	0.390 (0.011)	
PS I + II (4)	P. a (6)	53.5 (7.2)	29.0 (1.6)	36.0 (10.0)	40.3 (15.9)	146.4 (0.9)	53.8 (14.2)	52.4 (3.0)	43.5 (14.3)	44.0 (3.8)	594.4 (74.9)
	P. a (7)	0.059 (0.009)	0.023 (0.002)	0.27 (0.005)	0.126 (0.092)		0.065 (0.004)	0.049 (0.002)	0.37 (0.012)	0.126 (0.014)	
PS I (5)	P. a (6)	12.8 (4.7)	12.0 (9.3)	6.9 (0.4)	20.8 (3.7)	175.7 (28.7)	28.7 (5.9)	42.2 (3.6)	44.8 (8.2)	37.4 (2.9)	323.7 (48.2)
	P. a (7)	0.014 (0.005)	0.009 (0.007)	0.005 (0.001)	0.063 (0.035)		0.036 (0.014)	0.039 (0.003)	0.038 (0.007)	0.107 (0.03)	

(1) Day 1: foams inoculation with *P.laminosum* . *(2)* Different prepolymer: medium D ratios used when preparing the PU foams. *(3)* PS II: oxygen-evolution was used to measure PS II activity adding potassium ferricyanide(final concentration 4 mM) and DMBQ (2mM: free-living cells; 3mM : cells extracted from the foams by squeezing). *(4)* PS I + II: oxygen-uptake was used to measure PS I + II activity with the following added in sequence: MV (2mM: free-living cells; 3mM: cells extracted from the foams), sodium azide (8mM: free-living cells; 13 mM: cells extracted from the foams).*(5)* For measuring PS I alone via oxygen uptake , the following compounds were added: 15 uM DCMU, 2.5 mM GSH, 0.3 mM DCPIP. *(6)* Photosynthetic activity expressed as umol O_2/h.mg chl a . *(7)* Photosynthetic activity expressed as umol O_2 /h.mg dry weight foam. In brackets, standard deviations.

Immobilization by adsorption of *P. laminosum* and photosynthetic electron transport activity: The immobilization was carried out successfully. This seems to indicate that the possible toxic compounds released during the polymerisation reaction can be removed by autoclaving the foams.

The immobilized and free-living *P. laminosum* maintained some photosynthetic electron transport activity for at least 7 weeks (table 1). The free-living cells showed a higher photosynthetic electron transport rate than the immobilized cells. No appreciable difference has been observed between the two foams (PU and PV) when the activity is expressed as umolO2 h-1 mg-1 chl a . When expressed as umolO2 h-1 mg-1 dry weight foam, PV-immobilized cells show higher values due to the lower density of the PV foam. On the other hand, PV foam can support a higher amount of cells per unit of dry weight of foam than PU foam (fig.1) due probably to the lower density of the PV foam used for these experiments.

With respect to the different PU foams the results clearly showed that the higher the density of the foam the lower amount of cells they can carry (higher proportion of medium D in the prepolymer/ medium D ratio leads to preparations with smaller pores and increasing density).

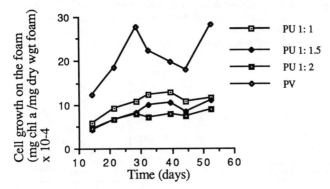

FIG.1. *P. laminosum* growth on the foams (Day 1: inoculation of foams)

Immobilization by adsorption and entrapment of A. azollae and ammonia production: The immobilization was carried out successfully using both techniques. Ammonia production by immobilized and freely suspended cultures of *A. azollae* was measured during a period of 8 hours (samples were kept under continuous illumination or darkness) with or without MSX (fig.2). The results clearly showed that ammonia production by immobilized cells was much higher than free-living cells in agreement with previous works (7). Unlike the case of immobilized cells (table 2) , no ammonia production was found in the absence of MSX with free-living cells (fig.2).

Scanning electron microscopy: SEM revealed the cells tightly adhered to the foams. The morphology was not affected by the immobilization except for the appearance, in the case of *A. azollae*, of a film covering the cell surface that is likely to be a mucilage layer (7).

Table 2. NH_4^+ production by immobilized *A. azollae* in the absence of MSX.

Sample	Time (days)	umoles NH4/mg chl.h	umoles NH4/mg dry wt. foam	ug chl/mg dry wt. foam
Foam: PV 50	5	281	48.2	0.17
	14	192.4	73.8	0.38
Immobilization technique:	19	271.1	60.2	0.25
adsorption	26	649.1	129.8	0.21
	33	523.6	190.4	0.37
	40	307.3	125.6	0.41
Foam: PV 50	85	82.6	121.8	1.47
	100	58.5	72.7	1.25
Immobilization technique:	128	89.7	142.2	1.58
adsorption	133	170.1	233.2	1.32
(different sample	140	58.7	90.6	1.54
from above)	147	188.1	205.2	1.11
	154	132.1	189.4	1.44
Foam: PU	84	32.5	155.9	4.79
	99	115.4	610.7	5.27
Immobilization technique:	127	115.1	870.3	7.56
adsorption	132	99.1	771.8	7.76
	139	39.5	341.2	7.97
	146	172.7	952.4	5.93
	153	48.2	487.4	10.12
	163	61.1	646.3	10.58
	47	84.1	73.6	0.87
Foam: PU	62	210.2	165.6	0.81
	90	183.1	112.4	0.62
Immobilization technique:	95	290.2	161.2	0.53
entrapment	102	233.1	166.5	0.71
	109	356.1	215.2	0.61
	116	386.4	125.9	0.33

CONCLUSION

Entrapment of *P. laminosum* cells in PU foams results in toxicity problems which lead to a rapid death of the immobilized cells. However, *P. laminosum* can be successfully immobilized by adsorption onto PU or PV foam, and maintains some photosynthetic electron transport activities (PSII, PS I+II, PS I) for at least 7 weeks. Free-living *P. laminosum* cells show a higher photosynthetic electron transport rate than the immobilized cells and the amount of immobilized cells attached to PU and PV foam is inversely proportional to the density of the foam. *A. azollae* cells can be successfully immobilized either by adsorption onto PU or PV foams or by entrapment in PU foams, and the ammonia production is much higher when using immobilized cells in comparison with free-living cells.

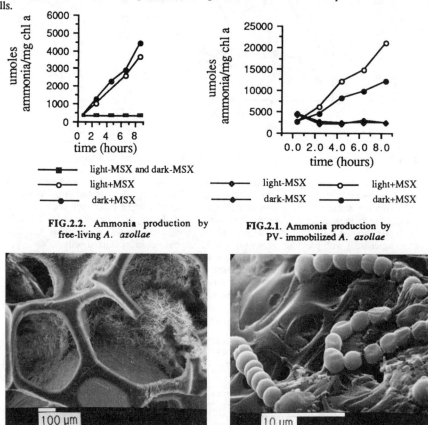

FIG.2.2. Ammonia production by free-living *A. azollae*

FIG.2.1. Ammonia production by PV- immobilized *A. azollae*

FIG. 3. SEM pictures of immobilized *A. azollae* in PU foams.

BIBLIOGRAPHY
(1) Hall, D.O. and Rao, K.K. (1989) *Chimicaoggi*, **7**, pp.41-47
(2) Castenholtz, R.W. (1969) *Bact. Rev.* **33**, 476-504
(3) Brouers, M., Shi, D.J. and Hall, D.O. (1988) in Cyanobacteria (Packer, L. and Glazer, A.N., ed.), *Methods in Enzymology* Vol.**167**, pp.629-636, Academic Press, San Diego
(4) MacKinney, G. (1940) *J. Biol. Chem.* **132**, 91-109
(5) Talling, J.F. and Driver, D. (1961) in Primary Productivity Measurement, Marine and Freshwater. *Proceedings of the 10th Pacific Science Congress.* Division of Technical Information, U.S. Atomic Energy Commission. pp.142-146
(6) Solorzano, L. (1969) *Limnol. Oceanogr.* **14**, 799-801
(7) Shi, D.J. (1987) PhD Thesis, King's College London, Univ. of London, U.K.

ISOLATION OF A REACTION CENTER PARTICLE AND A SMALL c-TYPE
CYTOCHROME FROM *HELIOBACILLUS MOBILIS*.

JEFFREY T. TROST AND ROBERT E. BLANKENSHIP
Department of Chemistry and Center for the Study of Early Events in Photosynthesis,
Arizona State University, Tempe, AZ 85287-1604, U.S.A.

1. INTRODUCTION
    The Heliobacteriaceae are the most recently isolated family of photosynthetic bacteria (1).
The main pigment in these bacteria is bacteriochlorophyll *g* (BChl *g*) which is structurally
intermediate between chlorophyll *a* found in higher plants and BChl *b* found in some purple
bacteria (2). Redox titrations and ESR measurements on isolated membranes from
Heliobacterium chlorum indicate the presence of low potential iron-sulfur centers (3,4). This
suggests that the photosynthetic reaction center (RC) is most similar to that found in green sulfur
bacteria and photosystem I. The large antenna size found in the green sulfur bacteria makes it
difficult to isolate pure RCs devoid of extraneous antenna pigments from them. By contrast, *H.
chlorum* contains only 30-60 antenna pigments per P800 (5), making it a good choice as a source
of Fe-S type RCs.
    Previously, all work reported on the Heliobacteriaceae has utilized whole cells or isolated
membranes from *H. chlorum* (3-7). *Heliobacillus mobilis*, the second isolate from this family,
(8) shows a 98% rRNA sequence identity to *H. chlorum* and apparently has an almost identical
photosynthetic system in terms of pigments and early electron acceptors. The advantages of *H.
mobilis* are faster and more robust growth than *H. chlorum* (9). We report here isolation of a
minimal reaction center complex and the major c-type cytochrome from *H. mobilis*.

2. MATERIALS AND METHODS
    Protein purification: H. mobilis was grown in medium 112 of the American Type Culture
Collection with 20 mM NaPyruvate for 12-16 hr in a 12 liter fermenter with 1200 watts of
incandescent illumination. Cells were harvested by centrifugation at 10k x g and washed once
with 20 mM Tris, 5 mM Na ascorbate, pH 8.0 buffer (2T5A8). All buffers used were
thoroughly degassed and nitrogen saturated. Membranes were isolated by sonication,
centrifugation at 10k x g for 10 min., followed by ultracentrifugation of the supernatant liquid at
200k x g for 2 hrs. The pelleted membranes were resuspended in 2T5A8 buffer to an absorbance
of 15 at 788 nm. Deriphat 160c (Henkel Corp.) was added to a concentration of 1% and the
solution was stirred for 1 hour in the dark under water aspirator vacuum. The solubilized
membranes were ultracentrifuged at 200k x g for 2 hours and the supernatant liquid was dialyzed
against 10 volumes of 2T5A8 to yield a cytochrome-containing fraction. The pellet was
resuspended in a small volume of 2T5A8 + 0.1% Deriphat, applied to a 10-60% sucrose gradient
in 2T5A8+0.1% Deriphat and centrifuged at 200k x g for 16 hours. The reaction center formed a
dark green band at 30-40% sucrose. Degraded pigment remained on top of the gradient and a
small amount of material formed a blackish pellet along with an orange band at 45% sucrose.
    The dialyzed cytochrome-containing fraction was chromatographed on a 5 x 25 cm column of
DEAE-Sephacel and eluted with 100 mM steps of KCl in 2T5A8 + 0.1% Deriphat. Cytochrome
fractions were then rechromatographed on a 2.5 x 30 cm column of DEAE-Sephacel, also eluted

M. Baltscheffsky (ed.), Current Research in Photosynthesis, Vol. II, 703–706.
© 1990 *Kluwer Academic Publishers. Printed in the Netherlands.*

with 100 mM steps of KCl. The cytochrome fractions were then chromatographed on a 2.5 x 50 cm column of High Resolution Sephacryl S-300.

SDS-PAGE: SDS-PAGE was done by the method of Laemmli (10) except samples were solubilized in 2% SDS, 100mM dithiothreitol, 3M urea and heated at 65 C for 15 minutes. Heme staining was done by the method of Thomas et al. (11).

Protein, iron and labile sulfur analysis: Protein was quantified by a modified Lowry assay (12) on triplicate samples at 3 different sample amounts. Iron was analyzed by atomic absorption using deuterium arc background correction by the method of standard additions. All samples for iron analysis were passed over Chelex resin (Bio-Rad) to remove any unbound iron. Labile sulfur analysis was done according to the method of (13) except that $CHCl_3$ was used for extraction of pigment acidification products.

P800 quantitation: Steady state photobleaching was assayed on a Varian Cary 219 spectrophotometer. Actinic illumination was from a 12V projector lamp filtered through water and a Corning 4-96 filter. The photomultiplier was protected by a Hoya R72 filter. Chemically oxidized-minus-reduced spectra were done essentially as described in (14) with the modification that samples were adjusted to +300 mV by addition of 600 mM ferricyanide to a final concentration of 11 mM (note buffer is 5 mM ascorbate) and reduced to 0 mV by addition of a 10% excess of 300 mM ascorbate. Laser flash spectroscopy was done as described in (6).

3. RESULTS AND DISCUSSION

The absorption spectrum of the enriched RC complex from *H. mobilis* at 4 K and 300 K is shown in figure 1. The major absorption bands are at 790, 671, 576, 411, 369 and 272 nm. The fourth derivative spectrum of the 4K spectrum is shown in the inset and suggests the 790 nm absorption peak is composed of 3 components with peaks at 809, 794 and 779 nm. The peak at 272 nm is fairly broad and probably has contributions from both aromatic protein residues and pigments. Laser-flash and steady-state photobleaching assays show a peak of photobleaching centered at 800 nm with an absorption increase centered at 776 nm. The decay of the 800 nm laser-flash-induced photobleaching is best fit to a single exponential decay with a time constant of 14 ms (data not shown). In contrast, the steady-state light-induced bleaching takes approximately 10 sec to decay to 1/e of its original value. Chemical and steady-state bleaching assays are in good agreement. While chemically reduced membranes show a distinct iron sulfur center ESR

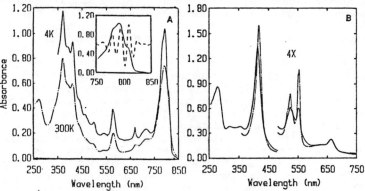

FIG 1. A) Absorption spectra of isolated RC complex at 4 K (solid line) and at 300 K (dot dash line). Inset is an expansion of the 790 nm peak (solid line) with its 4th derivative (dashed line). B) Absorption spectrum of the 16 kDa cytochrome. Solid line is with no additions and dot dash line is with added ascorbate.

signal, as described in (3,4), we have not observed such a signal in isolated RCs. Atomic absorption analysis indicates 11.5 Fe and 7-8 labile S^{2-} per P800 (assuming a $\Delta\varepsilon_{800}= 100$ mM^{-1} cm^{-1}), suggesting either the FeS centers are degraded or at a potential of less than -550 mV.

Table 1 shows the chemical analysis and spectroscopic results. Treatment of isolated membranes with 1% Deriphat releases 80% of the total protein but only 15% of the chemically assayed ΔA800. The remaining protein and 75% of the initial ΔA800 remains in the 200k x g pellet. SDS-PAGE of the pellet, after sucrose density gradient centrifugation, shows a single major band with an apparent molecular mass of 47 kDa (Fig. 2). No cytochrome is seen in the reaction center particle in either heme-stained SDS-PAGE or in dithionite-reduced minus ferricyanide-oxidized difference spectra.

Table 1	Bchl g /P800 (a)	Bchl g /P800 (b)	Fe /P800	S /P800	gm Protein /mMol P800	Proteins
Membranes	34-39	94-98	47-54	17-19	766	Many: 5 c-type cytochromes, major cytochrome at 16 kDa
Reaction Center	24-27	62-67	11-13	7-8	208	Major 47 kDa (70 kDa ?) minor doublet at $\approx$ 40 kDa

a [P800] was determined by steady state photobleaching and chemical oxidized-minus-reduced difference spectra, assuming $\Delta\varepsilon_{800} = 100$ mM^{-1} cm^{-1}. The ratio was determined by peak heights as in (16). The range represents the different results from the two assays.

b Same as a except the ratio was determined by peak areas similar to (7).

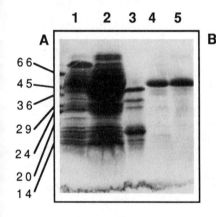
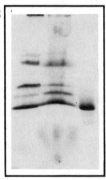

FIG 2. SDS-PAGE on 10-25% acrylamide gradient gels (see text). Panel A was stained with Coomassie Blue and Panel B stained for heme. Lanes: 1 =membranes, 2 = 1% Deriphat extract, 3 = 16 kDa cytochrome, 4 = pellet from 1% Deriphat extraction, 5 = purified reaction center.

The subunit structure of the RC is still uncertain. The inequalities from protein to protein in the Lowry assay as well as the uncertainty of the P800 differential extinction coefficient make an assignment of subunit stoichiometry difficult. The $\Delta\varepsilon_{800}$ is particularly uncertain; assuming the photooxidized cytochrome has a $\Delta\varepsilon_{800}= 20$ mM^{-1} cm^{-1}, data from figure 6 of (7) suggests an extinction coefficient of >300 mM^{-1} cm^{-1}. Additionally, Ferguson analysis of the reaction center preparation (15) indicates a molecular mass of approximately 70 kDa rather than 47 kDa for the major band in SDS-PAGE (data not shown).

In contrast to the 1% Deriphat pellet, the 1% Deriphat supernatant liquid contains many proteins including all of the c-type cytochromes found in the membranes. The major cytochrome in *H. mobilis* is found at 16 kDa. The ascorbate-reduced absorption spectrum of the 16 kDa cytochrome is shown in panel b of figure 1. The alpha peak appears to be split. The fourth derivative of the spectrum show peaks at 549.5 and 554 nm. Lane 1 in figure 2b shows 5 different c-type cytochromes in *H. mobilis* membranes at 58, 47, 28, 21 and 17 kDa.

In conclusion we have developed a method for the isolation of a photoactive RC particle from *H. mobilis*. The preparation contains a single major protein with an apparent molecular mass of 47 kDa, 20-30 BChl *g*, 11.5 Fe, and 7-8 labile sulfide per P800. A 16 kDa membrane-bound c-type cytochrome has also been purified. We are presently determining the sequence of the 47 kDa polypeptide(s). This should give us a better understanding of the relationship of the Heliobacterial RC to PS I.

4. ACKNOWLEDGEMENTS

We gratefully acknowledge Douglas E. Morrison for work on the cytochrome and Dan Brune for helpful discussions and critiques. This work was supported by a grant from the Exobiology Program of the National Aeronautic and Space Administration. This is publication #23 from the Arizona State University Center for the Study of Early Events in Photosynthesis. The Center is funded by U.S. Department of Energy grant #DE-FGO2-88ER13969 as part of the USDA/DOE/NSF Plant Science Centers program.

REFERENCES

1 Gest, H. and Favinger, J. L. (1983) *Arch. Microbiol.* <u>136</u>, 11-16.
2 Michalski, T. J., Hunt, J. E., Bowman, M. K., Smith, U., Bardeen, K., Gest, H., Norris, J. R., and Katz, J. J. (1987)*Proc. Natl Acad. Sci. USA.* <u>84</u>, 2570-2574.
3 Prince, R. C., Gest, H., and Blankenship, R. E. (1985) *Biochim. Biophys. Acta* <u>810</u>, 377-384.
4 Brok, M., Vasmel, H., Horikx, J. T. G., and Hoff, A. J. (1986) *FEBS Lett.* <u>194</u>, 322-326.
5 van Dorssen, R. J., Vasmel, H., and Amesz, J. (1985) *Biochim. Biophys. Acta* <u>809</u>, 199-203.
6 Fuller, R. C., Sprague, S. G., Gest, H., and Blankenship, R. E. (1985) *FEBS Lett.* <u>182</u>, 345-349.
7 Vos, M. H., Klaassen, H. E., and van Gorkom, H. J. (1989) *Biochim. Biophys. Acta* <u>973</u>, 163-169.
8 Beer-Romero, P. and Gest, H. (1987) *FEMS Microbiol. Lett.* <u>41</u>, 109-114.
9 Beer-Romero, P., Favinger, J. L., and Gest, H. (1988) *FEMS Microbiol. Lett.* <u>49</u> 451-454.
10 Laemmli, U. K. (1970) *Nature,* <u>227</u>, 680-685.
11 Thomas, P. E., Ryan, D., And Levin, W. (1976) *Anal. Biochem.* <u>75</u>, 168-176.
12 Peterson, G. L. (1977) *Anal. Biochem.* <u>83</u>, 346-356.
13 Golbeck, J. H. and San Pietro, A. (1976) *Anal. Biochem.* <u>73</u>, 539-542.
14 Markwell, J. P., Thornber, J. P., and Skrdla, M. P. (1980) *Biochim. Biophys. Acta* <u>591</u>, 391-399.
15 Retamal, C. and Babul, J. (1988) *Anal. Biochem.* <u>175</u>, 544-547.
16 Nuijs, A., M. van Dorssen, R. J. Duysens, L. N. M., and Amesz, J. (1985) *Proc. Natl. Acad. Sci. U.S.A.* <u>82</u>, 6865-6868.

LABELING BY A FLUORESCENT MALEIMIDE OF PEPTIDES OF CHROMATOPHORES FROM A GREENSULFUR BACTERIUM, CHLOROBIUM LIMICOLA

SEI-ICHI SHIRASAWA and HIDEHIRO SAKURAI
Dept. Biol., Sch. Education, Waseda Univ., nishiwaseda, Shinjuku, Tokyo 169, Japan

1. Introduction

Strong similarities between reaction centers of PSI and those from green sulfur bacteria have been suggested (1). Knaff and Malkin (2) observed from EPR measurements an Fe-S signal at g=1.94 with Em=-550 mV in chromatophores from Chlorobium. Nitschke et al. (3) found that isolated P840 reaction centers of Chlorobium limicola illuminated at low temperatures exhibited EPR spectra, which were very similar to those of A_1^- and A_0^- of PSI. Various methods have been successfully used to identify Fe-S peptides in PSI particles. Lagoutte et al. (4) prepared PSI particles from $[^{35}S]$-SO_4^{2-}-fed spinach, and found a $[^{35}S]$-cysteine-rich peptide of about 8 kDa. Sakurai and San Pietro (5) analyzed zero-valence sulfur(S°)-containing peptides of PSI particles, and found that P700-containing large peptides as well as a small peptide of less than 10 kDa were rich in S°. These methods do not seem to be suitable for the study of Fe-S peptides of Chlorobium chromatophore membranes, because the bacterial cells are grown in a very sulfur-rich medium. In this report, we tried to identify cysteine-rich peptides by labeling them with N-(7-dimethylamino-4-methyl-3- coumarinyl)maleimide (DACM), a fluorescent maleimide.

2. Materials and Methods

Cells of C. limicola f. thiosulfatophilum strain Tassajara were grown in 1.5-l bottles in the medium of Larsen (6) under dim light at 25-27°C, harvested by centrifugation, and stored at −70°C. The subsequent procedures were carried out below 5°C. Thawed cells were washed with 50 mM phosphate buffer (pH 6.8) containing 1 mM PMSF and 5 mM dithiothreitol (DTT), and ruptured by a French pressure cell. After centrifugation at 40,000xg for 10 min, membranes were obtained from the supernatant by centrifugation at 130,000xg for 60 min. The following extraction and chromatography were carried out in a plastic bag containing N_2 gas. The media had been bubbled with N_2 gas in order to remove O_2. For labeling with DACM, the membranes (100 μg Bchl/ml) were first incubated in 50 mM HEPES-NaOH (pH 7.0), 1 mM EDTA and 1% SDS at room temperature under N_2 gas. After 1 hr, DACM was added to a final concentration of 1 mM, and allowed to react with membranes overnight at 4°C. The membranes were separated from free DACM by passing through a Bio-gel P-4 (Bio-Rad, Richmond) column equilibrated with 50 mM Tris-Cl (pH 6.8). The membranes (30 μg Bchl/ml) were extracted with 2% octylthioglucoside, 1% sodium cholate, 5 mM DTT and 50 mM Tris-Cl (pH 7.8). After 30 min stirring, the mixture was centrifuged at 30,000xg for 15 min, and the supernatant (1 ml) was loaded on to a Toyopearl HW-65F (Toso,Tokyo) gel-permeation column (1.5x55 cm) equilibrated with 50 mM Tris-Cl (pH 7.8), 5 mM

M. Baltscheffsky (ed.), Current Research in Photosynthesis, Vol. II, 707–710.

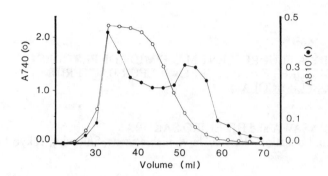

Fig.1: Elution profile of the detergent extracts from non-labeled chromatophores on Toyopearl HW65F ; A_{740} (O) use left side scale, A_{810} (●) use right side scale.

DTT, 0.05% octylthioglucoside and 0.05% sodium cholate.

3. Results and Discussion

When detergent-solubilized complexes from chromatophores were subjected to gel-permeation chromatography, Bchl-containing (A740) complexes came off as a rather broad peak (fraction A). The A810 peak (fraction B), which itself was buried in the former on A740 basis, came out later (Fig.1). The absorption spectra of fractions A and B are shown in Fig.2. The spectrum of the fraction B has some characteristics of those of the reaction center preparation reported by Fowler et al.(7), and we concluded that it is a reaction center-rich fraction.

Next, we attempted to extract a reaction center-rich fraction from DACM-labeled membranes. During DACM labeling, destruction of BChl occurred and the suspension

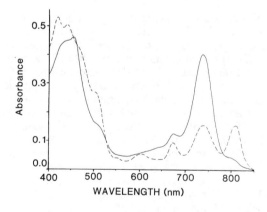

Fig.2: Absorption spectrum of "fraction A" (—) and "fraction B" (···) obtained from Toyopearl HW-65F; A_{810}=0.04 (fraction A), A_{810}=0.16 (fraction B)

turned brown in color. The DACM-labeled membranes were extracted with detergents and the supernant obtained by centrifugation was applied to the Toyopearl HW-65F gel-permeation column under the same conditions as with unmodified membranes. Instead of following A_{740} and A_{810} we followed the fluorescence intensity of each fraction (Fig.3), and found that the fluorescence peak corresponded to the fraction B peak. The fluorescence peak fractions were harvested and subjected to SDS-PAGE (Fig.4). By CBB staining (595nm), intense peaks at 42, 80 kD and dim peaks at 12, 30, 48 and 60kD were detected. By fluorescence scanning, however, we found that 12 and 42kD peptides were labeled more significantly than other peptides. These 12 and 42 kDa peptides were most abundant in the peak fraction corresponding to the fraction B in Fig.1. Thus 12 and 42kD peptides can be candidates for Fe-S containing peptides related to the reaction center.

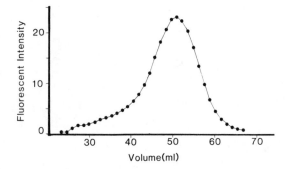

Fig.3: Elution profile of the detergent extracts of DACM-labeled chromatophores from Toyopearl HW-65F; Fluorescece intensity was measured at 470 nm for emission light and 400 nm for excitation light.

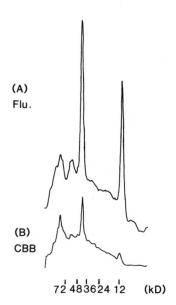

Fig.4: Resolution of DACM-labeled peptides (the peak fraction in Fig.3) by SDS-PAGE (15% gel). (A): Fluorescence (Ex=400nm, Em=500nm) (B): CBB-stained gel traced by A_{595}.

4. References

1 Clayton, R.K. (1980) in Photosynthesis: Physical Mechanisms and
  Chemical Patterns, pp.213-226, Cambridge University Press
2 Knaff, D.B. and Malkin, R. (1976) Biochim. Biophys. Acta 430, 244-252
3 Nitschke, W., Feiler, U., Lockau, W. and Hauska, G. (1987) FEBS Lett.   218,
  283-286
4 Lagoutte, B., Setif, P. and Duranton J. (1984) FEBS Lett. 174, 21-29
5 Sakurai, H. and San Pietro, A., (1985) J. Biochem. 98, 69-76
6 Larsen, H. (1953) in On the Microbiology and Biochemistry of the
  Photosynthetic Green Sulfur Bacteria, pp.1-205, Kgl. Norske Videnskab.
  Selskabs Skrifter
7 Fowler, C.F., Nugent, N.A., and Fuller, R.C. (1971) Proc. Natl. Acad. Sci. USA
  68, 2278-2282

HELIOBACTERIUM CHLORUM, AN EPR INVESTIGATION OF THE ELECTRON
ACCEPTORS

Monika R. Fischer and Arnold J. Hoff

Dept. of Biophysics, Huygens Laboratory, Leiden State University, P.O. Box 9504,
NL–2300 RA   Leiden

1. INTRODUCTION

The heliobacteria are not specifically related to any of the four other groups of
photosynthetic prokaryotes. It is therefore of interest to study the electron transfer
mechanism of these bacteria. Existing ambiguities in the organization of the electron
transport chain were the incentive to further examine this chain by low-temperature EPR
measurements under a variety of reducing conditions.

Complex EPR signals in the g= 2.00 region were detected. Spectral simulations have
been performed to identify the radicals responsible for these signals. Good agreement with
the experimental results was obtained when it was assumed that the signals result from
a convolution of EPR signals of the primary donor, a monomeric Bchl as first and a
quinone as second electron acceptor. A triplet signal was found, which was interpreted to
be a superposition of the EPR lines of an antenna- and a reaction centre triplet.

2. MATERIALS AND METHODS

All experiments were done with membrane fragments of Heliobacterium chlorum,
prepared as described elsewhere (M.R. Fischer, manuscript in preparation).

3. RESULTS AND DISCUSSION

A sample containing 10 mM ferricyanide which was illuminated during freezing to
77 K generated a gaussian EPR signal at g= 2.0027 with a linewidth of 1.05 mT, which
is attributed to the oxidized primary donor P^+ [1].

To produce different redox states the samples were treated as follows: sample
(Dith/D): frozen in the dark with 30 mM dithionite and 10 mM potassium ferrocyanide,
and sample (Dith/L): sample (Dith/D) thawed and refrozen under illumination. These
samples showed a complex behaviour in the g= 2.00 region (Fig. 1) and in order to
describe this, not only the g-values and peak-to-peak linewidths were measured, but also
the signal's double integral, which is proportional to the number of spins (Table 1). The
variety of g-values and linewidths cannot be explained with a sequence with only one

M. Baltscheffsky (ed.), Current Research in Photosynthesis, Vol. II, 711–714.
© 1990 Kluwer Academic Publishers. Printed in the Netherlands.

acceptor in addition to iron-sulphur cluster(s). Brok et al. [2] found indications for a quinone acceptor in *H. chlorum*, so it was an obvious choice to explain the observed complex behaviour by assuming two g= 2.00 acceptors, one chlorophyll-like, A_0, and one quinone-like, A_1. The acceptor complex A_0A_1 can be singly or doubly reduced, and in the latter case there may be an exchange interaction $J(A_0^-A_1^-)$. For the simulations several additional assumptions were made: (1) P^+ is a Bchl *g* dimer cation radical; (2) A_0^- is the anion radical of either a Bchl *g* monomer or dimer, a Bchl *c* monomer, or of a Bpheo *g* or *c* monomer; (3) during low-temperature illumination the iron-sulphur cluster(s) is (are) reduced reversibly, whereas A_0 and A_1 are reduced irreversibly; (4) in singly-reduced reaction centres the concentration ratio $m= I_{A0}/I_{A1}$ is variable; for every redox condition m is constant; (5) doubly-reduced reaction centres (which are exchange-coupled) are present in a fraction p of the reaction centres; p may vary between the various samples; (6) the EPR lines of the individual components are represented by symmetric gaussians with isotropic g-values. The double integrals of the g= 2.00 signals were taken as a direct measure of the total amount of all radicals. The individual contributions of P^+, A_0^- and A_1^- could be calculated from a set of linear dependent equations. Simulations of the g= 2.00 signals were carried out for various g-values and widths for the acceptors. In addition the fraction p and $J(A_0^-A_1^-)$ were varied. The calculated stick spectra were then dressed with gaussians of the appropriate linewidth. The first selection criterium for an

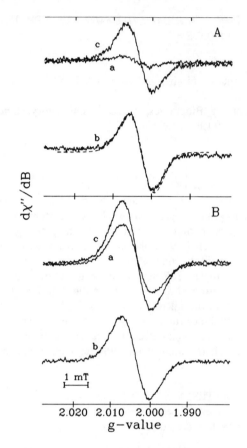

Fig. 1: A) Spectra of sample (Dith/D) in the g = 2.00 region, recorded at 8 K before (a), during (b) and after illumination (c). Modulation amplitude, 0.2 mT; microwave power, 2 μW. Dashed line : simulated spectrum for sample during illumination at 8 K. Simulation parameters: m= 1, p= 0.2, J= 0.1 mT, g(A_1^-)= 2.0054, ΔB(A_1^-)= 1.00 mT. B) Same as above for sample (Dith/L).

acceptable fit was the g-value. Acceptable fits were found only for A_0^- having a g-value of 2.0026 and a width of 1.3 mT, while A_1^- must have a g-value close to g= 2.0054 and ΔB= 0.9 to 1.0 mT (for example of fit see Fig. 1, dashed line). From a coarse-grid search, fitting *all* six spectra of Fig. 1 simultaneously, the values obtained for m, p and $J(A_0^-A_1^-)$ were 1.0 ± 0.2, 0 to 0.3 and ≤ 0.2 mT, respectively. The overall agreement between experimental and simulated spectra is satisfying. The finding that m is approximately 1 implies that, if the distribution of the negative charge over A_0 and A_1 is due to a redox equilibrium, the redox midpoint potentials should be similar. This would be surprising in a linear tranport chain. Thus, it seems that in the present membrane preparations of *H. chlorum* the reaction centres are heterogeneous in the sense that about half of them lack the quinone acceptor. In those reaction centres the backreaction between photoproduced P^+ and A_0^- is apparently inhibited. For p= 0 the fits are less good, but it cannot be excluded that none of the reaction centres is doubly reduced.

TABLE 1. g-Values and linewidths of the reduced acceptors at 8K

sample	g	ΔB^a	I^b	Fe-S	A^c
		(mT)	a.u.	g	a.u.
	± 0.0002	± 0.05	$\pm 5\%$	± 0.005	$\pm 5\%$
(Dith/D)					
dark before light[d]	2.0040	1.3	215	1.93	99
during light	2.0028	1.08	2120	1.93	143
dark after light	2.0034	1.23	1050	1.93	101
(Dith/L)					
dark before light	2.0037	1.36	920	1.93	248
during light	2.0037	1.23	1630	1.94	348
dark after light	2.0037	1.32	1380	1.93	267

[a] ΔB : peak-to-peak linewidth
[b] I : double integral of the g= 2.00 signal, corrected for temperature effects
[c] A : amplitude of the iron-sulphur first derivative signal measured at g= 1.93
[d] increased error limits (g: ± 0.0013 and ΔB: ± 0.2) due to low signal intensity (Fig. 1A(a))

A striking result is the complete reversibility of the light-induced iron-sulphur signal at 5 K. In current thinking the iron-sulphur clusters are the "last" acceptors of the electron transfer chain, and therefore it is remarkable that these clusters are reversibly reduced instead of the g= 2.00 acceptors. It is unlikely that the iron-sulphur is placed before the other acceptors, because of its relatively high redox potential. Therefore it has to be assumed that under the conditions of the experiment in part of the reaction centre population the iron-sulphur cluster is reduced instead of the A_0/A_1 acceptor complex. It is clear that further experiments are needed to shed more light on this puzzling effect.

A triplet signal was observed in the presence of dithionite (Fig. 2). The spectrum consists of two pairs of peaks centered at g= 2.00 and spaced by 51.6 mT. Each of the peaks consists of two superimposed gaussian lines, both of which are absorptive (Fig. 2, inset).

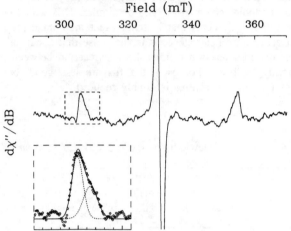

Fig. 2: *Light-minus-dark difference spectrum of a sample reduced with 30 mM sodium dithionite frozen in the dark. Inset: enlargement of the low-field triplet peak (points) with a simulation (drawn line) using two gaussian lines with midfield, peak-to-peak width and amplitude 304.95 mT, 1.47 mT, 212.3 and 306.42 mT, 1.90 mT and 109.7, respectively. Temperature, 8 K; microwave power, 0.2 mW; modulation amplitude, 1.25 mT. The spectrum is an average of 16 scans.*

The centre fields of the two superimposed gausssian lines are 1.47 mT apart, and if the two lines are attributed to two different triplet species, then $|D_1| = 241 \cdot 10^{-4}$ cm^{-1} and $|D_2| = 227 \cdot 10^{-4}$ cm^{-1}, and the $|E|$-values cannot be determined. The relatively high intensity of the z-peak of the one species overlaps with the x-peak of the other species, rendering this unobservable. Since the amplitudes of both triplets are rather small, the much less intense y-peaks could not be detected. The values of $|D|$ are very close to those found in ADMR experiments. With this technique two triplets were detected with zero-field splitting-parameters $|D| = 240$ and $226 (\pm 10) \cdot 10^{-4}$ cm^{-1}, and $|E| = 88$ and 74 $(\pm 10) \cdot 10^{-4}$ cm^{-1}, respectively (E.J. Lous and A.J. Hoff, unpublished results). These triplets were attributed to the reaction centre triplet and the triplet of an antenna pigment, respectively.

REFERENCES

1 Prince, R.J., Gest, H. and Blankenship, R.E. (1985) Biochim. Biophys. Acta 810, 377-384
2 Brok, M., Vasmel, H., Horikx, J.T.G. and Hoff, A.J. (1986) FEBS Lett. 194, 322-326

THE FLUID-MOSAIC NATURE OF THE THYLAKOID MEMBRANE

J. BARBER
AFRC Photosynthesis Research Group, Department of Biochemistry,
Imperial College, London SW7 2AY, UK

1. INTRODUCTION

In 1972 Singer and Nicolson (1) proposed that biological membranes are fluid-mosaic structures. Their model implied that the lipid bilayer acted as a two-dimensional fluid in which protein complexes and other hydrophobic components could freely diffuse, both rotationally and laterally. Evidence for such motions are numerous (2). Despite this it is also quite obvious that not all proteins in membranes are freely diffusing. Indeed the clustering of proteins to specific regions is necessary to form well known features, such as gap junctions, coated pits etc.

In the case of photosynthesis the light reactions take place in and across a membrane system. This membrane system is commonly called the thylakoids. The word thylakoid or ΘΥΛΑΚΟΕΙΔΗΣ means sac-like and originates from the description of their structure within higher plant chloroplasts (2a). Here they are observed as stacked membranes (grana) connected by intergranal membranes which are often referred to as stromal lamellae. In other organisms, e.g. green and brown algae, their organisation appears quite different (3). Nevertheless, in all chlorophyll b containing organisms the thylakoids can be distinguished by those which are in appression and those which are not. Non-chlorophyll b containing organisms (red algae, cyanobacteria) also have thylakoids but the membranes are not differentiated into appressed and non-appressed regions. Occasionally the term thylakoid is also used for the membrane systems of non-oxygenic photosynthetic bacteria (e.g. purple and green). The structure of the photosynthetic membrane in these prokaryotic organisms varies considerably and, indeed, in some cases can resemble the 'sac-like' arrangement of oxygenic eurkaryotic systems. Transmission electron micrographs of a typical higher plant chloroplast gives an impression of a static organisation which is very rigid. Such pictures also emphasise the enormous area of the thylakoid membrane. I have estimated (ref.4) that one μg of chlorophyll corresponds to 16.7 cm^2 which for a typical leaf means that the projected total surface area of the thylakoid membrane is in the region of 600 to 1000 times that of the leaf. I think there is little doubt that the thylakoid membrane is the most abundant biologically active lipo-protein structure on our planet!

Can we discuss the thylakoid membrane in terms of the fluid-mosaic model of Singer and Nicolson? The answer is yes, we can, with reservation. The first detailed discussion along these lines is to be found in an important review written by Jan Anderson and published in 1975 (5). Prior to this there were many key observations in the literature which indicated that the Singer-Nicolson concept could be applied to the thylakoid membrane of higher plant chloroplasts. Perhaps the starting point can be identified in the 1964 paper of Boardman and Anderson (6) who used the detergent digitonin to isolate lipo-protein particles enriched in photosystem one (PS1) or photosystem two (PS2). This result came somewhat as a surprise because prior to their work the 'Z-scheme' of Hill and Bendall (7) was visualized as being located in a single structure. Throughout

M. Baltscheffsky (ed.), Current Research in Photosynthesis, Vol. II, 715–724.
© 1990 *Kluwer Academic Publishers. Printed in the Netherlands.*

the sixties and seventies many groups extended this initial pioneering work, including those of Park, Vernon and Arntzen (see review 8). With advances in isolating these protein complexes came the application of freeze-fracture electron microscopy by several groups, including those of Branton, Muhlethaler and Staehelin (see review 9). By the mid-seventies it was quite clear that the chloroplast thylakoid membrane contained four major protein complexes, PS2, PS1, the cytochrome complex (isolated in a purified form by Hurt and Hauska (10) but first identified by Nelson and Neumann in 1972) and a coupling factor complex (CF_0-CF_1) which catalyses the conversion of ADP to ATP (12). Today we know a great deal about these complexes in terms of their subunit composition and structure (13).

2. SALT INDUCED CHANGES IN THYLAKOID ORGANISATION

The idea that the complexes within the thylakoid were able to laterally diffuse in the plane of the membrane came from a study by Wang and Packer (14). Using the freeze-fracture technique and electron microscopy they observed that changing the salt levels in the medium caused a dramatic reorganisation of particles within the membrane. It had previously been shown (15) that the same changes in electrolyte levels brought about changes in the degree of stacking of the thylakoids. The existence of these reversible salt induced conformational changes was also shown by others (16) and in particular by Andrew Staehelin (17). With this information, and with the data of experiments aimed at elucidating the role of salts in the control of thylakoid organisation, I developed the idea that the two phenomena (stacking and protein diffusion) were regulated by electrostatic screening and that they represented a coupled event (18-20). The arguments that the lateral diffusion of proteins and the changes in stacking were inter-related were challenged by Staehelin and Arntzen (21) but proven to be sound by Briantais et al (22). The idea that the two events were coupled stemmed from the fact that the same salt treatments which bring about the conformational changes also induced changes in chlorophyll fluorescence even when the PS2 activity was blocked by DCMU (18). The concept is simple. When the membranes are completely unstacked their is a lateral intermixing of all complexes and as a consequence good energy transfer between PS2 and PS1. This therefore is the reason why the chlorophyll fluorescence level is at a low value in this state of organisation. The randomisation and unstacking occurs in media having low levels of salts so that the electrostatic screening is at a minimum. This means that coulombic repulsive forces not only keep adjacent membranes apart but also favour randomisation of complexes within the two-dimensional fluid of the lipid matrix. On adding cations, (trivalents are more effective than divalents, which are more effective than monovalents, as would be expected from the theories of Gouy-Chapman, see ref. 20) the electrostatic screening of surface negative charges is improved so that the reduction in coulombic repulsion allows a coming together of the membrane surfaces and a concomitant phase separation of membrane complexes based on the differences in their surface charge densities. The reduction in coulombic repulsion it was argued, allows long range van der Waals forces to play a significant role in stabilizing the new conformational state. In the light of biochemical studies involving membrane fractionation, I argued that PS2 and its associated LHC-2 had a sufficiently low surface net charge density that it was able to form tightly packed domains which would also allow a strong van der Waals interaction between adjacent thylakoid surfaces, so giving rise to the appressed regions of the grana (19,20). On the other hand it was reasonable to assume that the location of PS1 in the non-stacked regions was due to the presence of significant levels of net negative charge on its surface.

Several lines of experimental evidence have emerged to support the overall concept that thylakoid membrane differentiation into stacked and unstacked regions is governed by the exposed fixed electrical charges on the surface of the intrinsic membrane protein complexes.

3. LATERAL SEPARATION OF COMPLEXES

Following the initial work of Boardman and Anderson (6) several groups used detergents (23,24), mechanical fragmentation (25) and freeze-fracture electron microscopy (26) to support the idea that PS2 and LHC-2 are associated mainly with grana while PS1 complexes were localized in both the granal and stromal membrane regions. However it was the work of Andersson, first published in his Ph.D. thesis (27), that suggested that PS2-LHC-2 complexes were located in the appressed regions of the grana and that the PS1 complexes in the grana were restricted to the non-appressed 'end' grana membranes. With his coworkers, in particular Albertsson (28) and later Jan Anderson (29), he also showed that the CF_1-CF_o complexes are located in the non-appressed regions. The restricted localization of CF_1-CF_o to the non-appressed membranes, including end granal lamellae, had been advocated earlier by Miller and Staehelin (30) based on freeze-fracture microscopy, but the extreme lateral separation of PS2 and PS1 had not been generally accepted previously. Kinetic measurements of Haehnel (31) involving flash absorption measurements indicated that the cyt b-f complexes are located close to PS1. Despite this conclusion several independent studies have consistently produced evidence that this cytochrome containing complex is evenly distributed between the appressed and non-appressed membranes (32-34).

Although appressed membranes normally contain most of the PS2 and LHC-2 complexes, a variable fraction of these two complexes can be found in non-appressed regions. In the case of PS2 units located in the stromal lamellae, their associated LHC-2 content is lower than those PS2 remaining in the appressed region. Apparently there are two main types of LHC-2 associated with the PS2 core complex, an inner more tightly bound form which, in the case of spinach, contains a 27 kD polypeptide and a 25 kD polypeptide in a ratio of 1.5 to 1 (35). The stromal LHC-2 complexes are those of the inner form and, together with the PS2 core, form independent entities with little or no energy transfer between them (36). These are known as PS2β and may not be fully functional in linear electron transport. They contrast with the PS2α units of the appressed membranes that contain both types of LHC-2 which readily undergo interunit energy transfer (36).

4. STOICHIOMETRY OF COMPLEXES

Over the past few years there has been a flush of papers which show that stoichiometry of the thylakoid complexes, particularly PS2, PS1 and LHC-2 is not fixed. Variation in the stoichiometries has usually been induced by either altering the intensity or quality of the light in which the organisms or plants are grown (e.g. 37-40). In general it seems that the level of PS2 and LHC-2 is adjusted relative to PS1 so as to reduce over excitation of the PS2 reaction centre in high intensity or in PS2-enriched light.

5. FLUIDITY

Like other biological membranes, the thylakoid membrane of oxygenic photosynthetic organisms is distinguished by its particular cocktail of lipids (see 40). The dominating species is monogalactosyldiacylgylcerol (MGDG) at about 50%. The second most important lipid class representing 30% of the total lipid is digalactosyldiacylglycerol (DGDG). The remaining classes are phosphatidylglycerol (PG) and sulphoquinovosyldiacylglycerol (SQDG). Noteworthy is the fact that when isolated the MGDG is non-bilayer forming and that the fatty acids of all the four lipid classes is dominated by α-linolenic acid which has a hydrocarbon tail of 18 carbons with three double bonds (see 40). Analyses of appressed and non-appressed membranes have not revealed any extreme lateral separation of lipid classes (41). The only consistent difference seems to be that the appressed, compared with the non-appressed, has a higher MGDG to DGDG ratio (40). The high degree of unsaturation of the fatty acids suggests that the lipid matrix of the thylakoid membrane is extremely fluid. Indeed, our measurements using the fluorescence probe 1,6-diphenyl-1,2,5-hexatriene (DPH) support this suggestion (42-43). Steady-state measurements gave polarization values (p) in the range of 0.2 to 0.25 at 25°C (42) which contrasts, for example, with 'stiff' membranes of Halobacterium halobium or human eye cortex that has p values of about 0.40 and very fluid systems, like human milk globules, where p = 0.12. Despite the fact that appressed, compared with the non-appressed, contain fatty acids which are less saturated, they seem to be more rigid than the non-appressed lamellae (43). This has been attributed to the high protein to lipid ratio of the appressed membranes (43). If the fluorescence from DPH is time resolved then additional information can be obtained that relates to the motion and ordering of the acyl chains (44,46). The dynamic component comes from the rate of rotation of the probe molecule while the order parameter is calculated from the residual anisotropy. Thus the time dependent anisotropy (r) follows an expression of the form:

$$r(t) = (r_o - r_\alpha) \exp(-t/\phi) + r_\alpha \qquad \ldots\ldots\ldots\ldots(1)$$

where r_α in the initial fluorescence anisotropy, r_α is the time-limited anisotropy, t is time and ϕ is the rotational correlation time. The latter is inversely related to the wobbling diffusion coefficient D_w which can be used to estimate the viscosity of the bilayer using the equation

$$\eta_m = kT/6D_w V_e f \qquad \ldots\ldots\ldots\ldots(2)$$

where k is the Boltzmann constant, T is absolute temperature, V_e is the volume of the probe and f is its shape factor. Using this equation a viscosity of 0.34 P was estimated for thylakoid membranes isolated from peas at 25°C (ref.44). This value contrasts with 0.42 P at 35°C for the cell membranes of human erythrocytes and 0.82 at 35°C for the purple membrane of Halobacterium halobium (47).

According to our measurements with DPH, the lipid bilayer of pea thylakoid membranes does not undergo any obvious gross phase change over the temperature range 55 to -20°C (48) but interestingly there are changes in the degree of fluidity as a result of growth temperature. We found that low growth temperatures (e.g. 7°C) gave rise to a more fluid thylakoid membrane than when plants were grown at higher temperatures (48). It is possible, therefore, that in peas (which are chill resistant) a homeostatic mechanism exists to maintain the thylakoid at an optimal level of fluidity (48). If this is so, and recognising that diffusional processes occur within the membrane in order for it to function optimally, then the ability to modify the fluidity in response to growth temperature could underlie why some plants can, and some plants cannot, survive and grow at low ambient temperatures (e.g. chill resistant verses chill sensitive).

6. DIFFUSIONAL PROCESSES
There are two types of lateral diffusion occurring in the thylakoid membrane. The diffusion of the redox active species which communicate between the membrane protein complexes and diffusion of the protein complexes themselves.

6.1. Redox active
The redox active diffusional species are plastoquinone/plastoquinol, plastocyanin and soluble ferredoxin. Only the former occurs within the membrane itself and shuttles reducing equivalents between PS2 and the cyt b-f complexes. The actual species is plastoquinone-9 (PQ-9). It is a hydrophobic molecule with two methyl groups attached to its quinone ring and has a side-chain of nine isoprenic groups. It is located evenly throughout the lipid matrix (appressed and non-appressed regions) at a level corresponding to six or seven molecules per electron transport chain (49). It seems likely that its preferred location is at the midplane of the bilayer, since the bulky isoprenoid side-chain methyl groups would not be expected to pack effectively between the acyl chains of the thylakoid lipid matrix (50). The midplane fluidity may be very high so that the diffusion coefficient for PQ-9 within the thylakoid membrane could be as large as 10^{-6} cm^2 s^{-1} (see 50). Such high values for quinone diffusion coefficients have been estimated by Lenaz and his colleagues for mitochondrial membranes (51). Using a fluorescence quenching technique, we have attempted to estimate the lateral diffusion coefficients for PQ-9 both in its oxidised and reduced forms (52). From our experiments, in which we used liposomes made from phosphatidylcholine, we obtained room temperature values ranging from 10^{-7} to 3.5×10^{-7} cm^2 s^{-1} with reduced PQ-9, being consistently slower than oxidised PQ-9.
The coefficients we obtained can be used to calculate diffusion pathlengths by applying the Einstein equation for a two-dimensional system.

$$<x>^2 = 4Dt \qquad\qquad \dots\dots\dots\dots(3)$$

where $<x>$ is the mean distance of diffusion in time t, D is the lateral diffusion coefficient and t is time. Since the oxidation of reduced PQ-9 by the cyt b-f complex is the rate limiting step of linear electron flow and has a half-time of about 20 ms we can let t = 20 ms. In this case $<x>$ is 894 nm when $D = 10^{-7}$ cm^2 s^{-1} and 836 nm when $D = 3.5 \times 10^{-7}$ cm^2 s^{-1}. These distances should be compared with the radius of a typical appressed region which is about 250 nm. It can be concluded therefore that PQ-9 in either its oxidised or reduced states can normally diffuse over long distances within the time available and that the oxidation process at the cyt b-f site is reaction, rather than diffusion limited (see also ref.53). If, however, the diffusion coefficient is reduced by a factor of ten due to the presence of proteins in the bilayer, as suggested by the recent work of Blackwell and Whitmarsh (53a), this conclusion becomes less certain.
Little is known about the diffusional properties of ferredoxin and plastocyanin along the thylakoid surface. Using lipid vesicles and applying the technique of FRAP, Fragate et al (53b) estimated a lateral diffusion coefficient of 5×10^{-8} cm^2 s^{-1} for plastocyanin. For various reasons it is problematical to apply this value to the in vivo situation as discussed in detail in ref.13.

6.2 Protein diffusion

The various studies which involved perturbating thylakoid membrane structure by changing salt levels mentioned above clearly indicated that the various protein complexes could be made to laterally diffuse along the membrane plane. This raises the question of the possibility of such movements being physiologically important. The discovery that LHC-2 could be reversibly phosphorylated (54) coupled with the concept that the differentiation of thylakoids into appressed and non-appressed regions was due to differences in surface charge properties (19) led me to propose that lateral protein movement might occur in respone to surface phosphorylation (18,20). Experimental evidence for such movements soon appeared from my own laboratory (55) and from others (56,57). It is likely that the addition of negative charges to the surface of LHC-2 (the peripheral form containing the 27 and 25 kD, see ref. 58) destabilizes the presence of the complex in the appressed regions so that it migrates to the more electrically charged non-appressed regions where it can transfer absorbed light energy to PS1 (59). This occurs when PS2 is over-excited relative to PS1 so that a build-up of reducing equivalents in the inter-system redox carriers (PQ and cyt b-f) triggers the protein kinase responsible for the phosphorylation (60,61). The function of this seems to be either to optimise the rate of electron flow under light limiting conditions (60,61) or to protect PS2 against photodamage at high light intensities (62). If on the other hand, PS1 receives more light than PS2 the kinase activity is turned off and a phosphorylase brings about the dephosphorylation of LHC-2 and, as a consequence, the complex re-establishes itself in the PS2 enriched domain of the appressed region. The argument that this shuffling of LHC-2 between the appressed and non-appressed membranes can be explained in terms of electrostatic theory was clearly shown in a paper we published in which the effects of LHC-2 phosphorylation of thylakoid structure as a function of background cation levels was studied (63).

In addition to the phosphorylation induced diffusion of the peripheral LHC-2 it has also been found that by raising the temperature of spinach thyakoids to about 40°C also brings about lateral movements (64,65). In this case the peripheral LHC-2 breaks away from PS2 and forms domains that are located in appressed regions (66). The PS2 migrate into the PS1-rich non-appressed regions and by so doing convert from α-centres to β-centres (66). The reorganisation is reversible when the temperature is lowered and has been speculated to be a genuine physiological response used as strategy to minimise photodamage of PS2. Indeed, evidence exists which shows that PS2 β-centres are more resistant to photoinhibition (67),

The diffusion of large protein complexes in the lipid matrix will be relatively slow compared with the diffusion rate of PQ-9. Using cation induced changes in chlorophyll fluorescence yield we attempted to estimate diffusion coefficients for the chlorophyll containing complexes (68). Values of 1.85×10^{-12} to 3.08×10^{-11} cm^2 s^{-1} were obtained for the temperature range from 10 to 30°C. At 25°C the estimated value was about 2×10^{-11} cm s^{-1}. These values are sufficiently low to rule out the possibility that protein diffusion controls the kinetics of electron transport as argued for the mitochondrial membrane by Hackenbrock (69). Do the diffusion coefficients given above concur with the low viscosity of 0.34 P measured using the DPH technique? The Saffman-Delbruck equation allows us to answer this question. This equation relates membrane viscosity with the lateral diffusion coefficient (D_L).

$$D_L = kT/4\pi h\eta_m \ (\ln (h\eta_m/a\eta_w) - 0.5772 \qquad \dots\dots\dots\dots(4)$$

where k is the Boltzmann factor, T is absolute temperature, η_m and η_w are viscosity coefficients of the membrane and aqueous medium surrounding the membrane respectively, h is the height of the protein and a is its radius. Taking a = 4 nm and h = 14 nm (as deduced for LHC-2 by Kuehlbrandt, ref.70) and $\eta_w = 0.01$ P and $\eta_m = 0.34$ P then the value for D_L at 25°C is approximately 2 x 10^{-11} cm^2 s^{-1} which matches very well that derived from our experiments (68).

It is now quite clear that organisation of the thylakoid membrane is easily perturbed. In order to obtain a better assessment of the energetics of these perturbations we have recently set up a model (70). The thylakoid membrane is represented as a bilayer lattice in a Monte Carlo simulation. Each 6-coordinated site can be occupied by either a species 1 or 2 representing PS1 and PS2, surrounded by lipid, and can exist in a stacked or unstacked state. The relative amounts of stacked and unstacked regions were allowed to vary by movement of a nearly linear boundary between them. We were able to show that the behaviour of this model could be characterised by four energy parameters, one representing the lateral exchange energy between species in a layer (J_{12}^h), and three others specifying the inter-layer energies in the stacked state (ε_{11}, ε_{12} and ε_{22}). Our calculations show that in order to obtain changes from unstacked mixed PS1/PS2 state to a highly segregated PS2/PS1 stacked/unstacked state requires the above parameters to have values of just a few kT. Thus our simulation model predicts that rather small energy changes can bring about the sort of reversible conformational changes observed with the thylakoid membrane in response to changes in electrolyte levels (electrostatic screening), protein phosphorylation and mild heating.

7. TURNOVER OF D1 POLYPEPTIDE

Perhaps one of the most intriguing observations which relates to thylakoid membrane dynamics is the turnover of the D1 polypeptide (71). This protein is a key component of the PS2 reaction centre (72) and turns over faster than any other protein in the membrane. It not only binds the secondary electron acceptor Q_B but also ligates (together with the D2 polypeptide) the non-haem iron and the special pair of chlorophylls that constitute P680 (73). Recently it has been shown to contain a tyrosine residue that acts as the secondary electron donor Z (74,75). There is evidence that the turnover of D1 is related to the vulnerability of the PS2 reaction centre to high light intensities and that it is the re-synthesis of the replacement D1 that underlies the recovery after the removal of photoinhibitory conditions (76). Using a pulse chase procedure, Mattoo and Edelman (77) have elegantly shown that newly synthesised D1 protein is initially inserted into the non-appressed lamellae (being the location of the chloropast ribosomes). It is then processed from a 33.5 kD to 32 kD form and then laterally diffuses to the appressed regions. The trigger for the lateral migration may be the processing itself or a post-translational palmitoylation process. The degradation presumably also requires a signal to trigger the attack of a protease which gives rise to a 23.5 kD fragment (77). We have evidence based on proteolytic mapping that the cleavage site is in the region of three glutamic acid residues at position 242-244 on the part of the D1 polypeptide that is likey to span the fourth and fifth transmembrane helices (Shipton, Marder and Barber, unpublished). The trigger for the attack could be phosphorylation of the N-terminal threonine (77-79) and indeed we have observed heavy labelling of the D1 polypeptide with ^{32}P under photoinhibitory conditions (80). When isolated, the PS2 reaction centre is highly susceptible to photo-damage in aerobic conditions (81). If, however, all oxygen is removed the isolated reaction centre becomes remarkably stable to light treatment (82). We have found that the removal of oxygen has a dramatic effect on the lifetime of the P680 triplet state generated by the recombination reaction (83), lengthening it from about 33 μs to 1 ms. This indicates that the following reaction is occurring.

$$^3P680 + {}^3O_2 \rightarrow P680 + {}^1O_2$$

where $^3O_2$ is the ground state of oxygen and $^1O_2$ is singlet oxygen. The photodamaging of isolated PS2 reaction centres is almost certainly due to the latter reactive species. Thus it is possible that singlet oxygen formation underlies the vulnerability of PS2 to high light and the necessity for the continuous replacement of the D1 polypeptide. Without any doubt the study of the mechanisms which control the disassembly and re-assembly of the PS2 reaction centre will yield valuable information about the dynamics of not only the thylakoid membrane but of all other biological membranes.

8. ACKNOWLEDGEMENTS

I would like to acknowledge the involvement of all my colleagues who have helped me develop the ideas and create the data discussed above. They are too numerous to list here but their names appear on the research papers referred to. I also wish to acknowledge financial assistance from several granting agencies but particularly the Agricultural and Food Research Council.

REFERENCES

1   Singer, S.J. and Nicolson, G.L. (1972) Science 175, 720-731
2   Barber, J. (1982) BioScience Reports 2, 1-13
2a   Mennke, W. (1962) Ann. Rev. Plant Physiol. 13, 27-44
3   Coombs, J. and Greenwood, A.D. (1976) in The Intact Chloroplast
     (Barber, J., ed.), Vol.1, pp.1-51, Elsevier, Amsterdam
4   Barber, J. (1980) in Plant Membrane Transport: Current Conceptual Issues
     (Spanswick, M., Lucas, W.J. and Dainty, J.), pp.83-84, Elsevier, Amsterdam
5   Anderson, J.M. (1975) Biochim. Biophys. Acta 416, 191-235
6   Boardman, N.K. and Anderson, J.M. (1964) Nature 203, 166-167
7   Hill, R. and Bendall, F. (1960) Nature 186, 136-137
8   Hiller, R.G. and Goodchild, D.. (1981) in The Biochemistry of Plants,
     Photosynthesis (Hatch, M.D. and Boardman, N.K., eds.), Vol.8, pp.1-49,
     Academic Press, New York
9   Staehelin, L.A. (1986) in Encycl. Plant Physiol., Photosynthesis III
     (Staehelin, L.A. and Arntzen, C.J., eds.) Vol.19, pp.1-84
10   Hurt, E. and Hauska, G. (1981) Eur. J. Biochem. 117, 591-599
11   Nelson, N. and Neumann, J. (1972) J. Biol. Chem. 247, 1917-1924
12   Pick, U. and Racker, E. (1979) J. Biol. Chem. 25, 2793-2799
13   Barber, J. (1987) in The Biochemistry of Plants, Photosynthesis (Hatch,
     M.D.
     and Boardman, N.K., eds.), Vol.10, pp.75-130
14   Wang, A.W.T. and Packer, L. (1973) Biochim. Biophys. Acta 305, 488-492
15   Izawa, S. and Good, N.E. (1966) Plant Physiol. 41, 544-552
16   Ojakian, G.K. and Satir, P. (1974) Proc. Natl. Acad. Sci. USA 21, 2052-2056
17   Staehelin, L.A. (1976) J. Cell Biol. 71, 136-158
18   Barber, J. (1980) FEBS Lett. 118, 1-10
19   Barber, J. (1980) Biochim. Biophys. Acta 594, 253-308
20   Barber, J. (1982) Ann. Rev. Plant Physiol. 33, 261-295
21   Staehelin, L.A. and Arntzen, C.J. (1979) Ciba Found. Symp. 61, 147-175

22 Briantais, J.M., Vernotte, C., Lavorel, J., Olive, J. and Wollman, F.A. (1983) Biochim. Biophys. Acta 766, 1-8
23 Vernon, L.P., Shawf, E.R. and Ke, B. (1966) J. Biol. Chem. 241, 4101-4109
24 Sane, P.V., Goodchild, D.J. and Park, R.B. (1970) Biochim. Biophys. Acta 216, 162-178
25 Michel, J.M. and Michel-Wolwertz, M.R. (1969) Prog. Photosyn. Res. 1, 115-127
26 Armond, P.A., Staehelin, L.A. and Arntzen, C.J. (1977) J. Cell Biol. 73, 400-418
27 Andersson, B. (1978) Ph.D. Thesis, University of Lund, Sweden
28 Albertsson, P.-A., Andersson, B., Larsson, C. and Akerlund, H.E. (1982) Methods in Biochem. Anal. 28, 115-150
29 Andersson, B. and Anderson, J.M. (1980) Biochim. Biophys. Acta 593, 427-440
30 Miller, K.R. and Staehelin, L.A. (1976) J. Cell Biol. 68, 30-47
31 Haehnel, W. (1982) Biochim. Biophys. Acta 682, 245-257
32 Cox, R.P. and Andersson, B. (1981) Biochem. Biophys. Res. Commun. 103, 1336-1342
33 Anderson, J.M. (1982) FEBS Lett. 138, 62-66
34 Allred, D.R. and Staehelin, L.A. (1985) Plant Physiol. 78, 199-202
35 Maenpaa, P. and Andersson, B. (1989) Z. Naturforsch. 44c, 13-16
36 Melis, A. and Homann, P.H. (1976) Photochem. Photobiol. 23, 343-350
37 Anderson, J.M. (1982) Photobiochem. Photobiophys. 3, 225-241
38 Melis, A. and Harvey, G.W. (1981) Biochim. Biophys. Acta 637, 138-145
39 Leong, T.-Y. and Anderson, J.M. (1983) Biochim. Biophys. Acta 723, 391-399
40 Chow, W.S., Anderson, J.M. and Hope, A.B. (1988) Photosyn. Res. 17, 277-281
41 Chapman, D.J., DeFelice, J. and Barber, J. (1986) Photosyn. Res. 9, 239-249
42 Ford, R.C. and Barber, J. (1981) Photobiochem. Photobiophys. 1, 263-270
43 Ford, R.C., Chapman, D.J., Barber, J., Pedersen, J.Z. and Cox, R.P. (1982) Biochim. Biophys. Acta 681, 145-151
44 Ford, R.C. and Barber, J. (1983) Biochim. Biophys. Acta 722, 341-348
45 Ford, R.C. (198) Ph.D. Thesis, Unversity of London, U.K.
46 Millner, P.A., Mitchell, R.A.C., Chapman, D.J. and Barber, J. (1984) Photosyn. Res. 5, 63-76
47 Kinosita, K., Kataoka, R., Kimura, Y., Gotch, O. and Ikegami, A. (1981) Biochemistry 20, 4270-4277
48 Barber, J., Ford, R.C., Mitchell, R.A.C. and Millner, P.A. (1984) Planta, 161, 375-380
49 Chapman, D.J. and Barber, J. (1986) Biochim. Biophys. Acta 850, 170-172
50 Millner, P.A. and Barber, J. (1984) FEBS Lett. 169, 1-6
51 Fato, R., Battino, M., Degli Esposti, M., Castelli, G.P. and Lenaz, G. (1986) Biochemistry 25, 3378-3390
52 Blackwell, M.F., Gounaris, K., Zara, S.J. and Barber, J. (1987) Biophys. J. 51, 735-744
53 Mauro, S., Lannoye, R., Vandeloise, R. and Vander Donckt, E. (1986) Photobiochem. Photobiophys. 11, 83-94
53a Blackwell, M.F. and Whitmarsh, J. (1989) in Photosynthesis: Molecular Biology and Bioenergetics (Singhal, G.S., Barber, J., Dilley, R.A., Govindjee, Haselkorn, R. and Mohanty, P. eds.) pp.225-237, Narosa Publ. House, New Delhi
53b Fragata, M., Ohnishi, S., Adada, K., Ito, T. and Takahashi, M. (1984) Biochemistry 23, 4044-4051
54 Bennett, J. (1979) Eur. J. Biochem. 99, 133-137

55 Chow, W.S., Telfer, A., Chapman, D.J. and Barber, J. (1981) Biochim. Biophys. Acta 638, 60-68
56 Andersson, B., Staehelin, L.A. and Arntzen, C.J. (1983) Arch. Biochem. Biophys. 222, 527-541
57 Kyle, D.J., Staehelin, L.A. and Arntzen, C.J. (1983) Arch. Biochem. Biophys. 222, 527-541
58 Larsson, U.K., Sundby, C. and Andersson, B. (1987) Biochim. Biophys. Acta 894, 59-68
59 Telfer, A., Whitelegge, J., Bottin, H. and Barber, J. (1986) J. Chem. Trans. 2 (Spec. Ed.) 82, 2207-2215
60 Bennett, J. (1983) Biochem. J. 212, 1-13
61 Barber, J. (1983) Photobiochem. Photobiophys. 5, 181-190
62 Horton, P. and Lee, P. (1985) Planta 165, 37-42
63 Telfer, A., Hodges, M., Millner, P.A. and Barber, J. (1984) Biochim. Biophys. Acta 766, 554-562
64 Sundby, C. and Andersson, B. (1985) FEBS Lett. 191, 24-28
65 Gounaris, K., Brain, A.P.R., Quinn, P.J. and Williams, W.P. (1983) FEBS Lett. 153, 47-52
66 Sundby, C., Melis, A., Maenpaa, P. and Andersson, B. (1986) Biochim. Biophys. Acta 851, 475-483
67 Maenpaa, P., Andersson, B. and Sundby, C. (1987) FEBS Lett. 215, 31-36
68 Rubin, B.T., Barber, J., Paillotin, G., Chow, W.S. and Yamamoto, Y. (1981) Biochim. Biophys. Acta 683, 69-74
69 Hackenbrock, C.R., Chazotte, B. and Gupte, S.S. (1986) J. Bioenergetics Biomembr. 18, 331-368
70 Nicolson, D., Zara, S.J., Parsonage, N.G. and Barber, J. (1989) J. Theor. Biol. submitted
71 Edelman, M., Mattoo, A.K. and Marder, J.B. (1984) in Chloroplast Biogenesis (Ellis, R.J. ed.), pp.283-302, Cambridge University Press, Cambridge
72 Marder,J.B., Chapman, D.J., Telfer, A., Nixon, P. and Barber, J. (1987) Plant Mol. Biol. 9, 325-333
73 Barber, J. (1987) Trends in Biochem. Sci. 12, 321-326
74 Debus, R.J., Barry, B.A., Sithole, I., Babcock, G.T. and McIntosh, L. (1988) Biochemistry 27, 9071-9074
75 Vermaas, W.F.J., Rutherford, A.W. and Hansson, O. (1988) Proc. Natl. Acad. Sci. USA 85, 8477-8481
76 Kyle, D.J., Ohad, I. and Arntzen, C.J. (1984) Proc. Natl. Acad. Sci. USA 81, 4070-4074
77 Telfer, A., Marder, J.B. and Barber, J. (1987) Biochim. Biophys. Acta 893, 557-563
78 Marder, J.B., Telfer, A. and Baraber, J. (1988) Biochim. Biophys. Acta 932, 363-365
79 Michel, H.P. and Bennett, J. (1987) FEBS Lett. 212, 103-108
80 Whitelegge, J.P. and Barber, J. (1989) Plant Physiol. submitted
81 Chapman, D.J., Gounaris, K. and Barber, J. (1989) Photosynthetica 23, in press
82 Crystall, B., Booth, P.J., Klug, D., Barber, J. and Porter, G. (1988) FEBS Lett. 249, 75-78
83 Durrant, J.R., Giorgi, L.B., Klug, D.R., Barnett, C.J., Barber, J. and Porter, G. (1989) FEBS Lett. submitted

THE STRUCTURE OF PHOTOSYSTEM I AND II.

David J. Simpson
Department of Physiology, Carlsberg Laboratory. Gamle Carlsberg Vej 10. DK-2500 Valby.
Denmark.

1. INTRODUCTION.

The thylakoid membrane is shown by electron microscopy to be differentiated into appressed and non-appressed membrane regions. Stacks of appressed thylakoid discs form grana, which in wild type barley consist of about 10 discs, approximately 0.42 μm in diameter (1). The grana have been shown by mechanical and detergent fractionation to contain mainly photosystem II and its light-harvesting chlorophyll-proteins. Grana are interconnected by non-appressed, or stroma lamellae, which contain photosystem I with its light-harvesting chlorophyll-proteins, the chloroplast ATPase or coupling factor, and ferredoxin-NADPH reductase (FNR). The location of the aforementioned components is largely restricted to one domain or the other, leading to extreme lateral heterogeneity (2). The cytochrome $b6/f$ complex is evenly distributed between appressed and non-appressed membranes (3), and while the distribution of photosystem II and FNR is highly asymmetric, there is a significant amount of photosystem II in non-appressed lamellae, and some FNR in appressed lamellae, as demonstrated by immunocytochemistry using monospecific antibodies and colloidal gold labelling (4).

Most of our knowledge about the structure and composition of photosystem I and II has come from investigations of purified complexes isolated using detergents which maintain functional properties (5,6). Many of the individual polypeptide components have now had their amino acid sequence partially determined, as well as their complete sequence deduced from the nucleotide sequence of the corresponding gene. This work has been complemented by studies of single gene mutants affected in photosynthetic capacity, particularly in *Chlamydomonas*, maize and barley. These mutants have been useful in providing independent confirmation of the composition of the different functional complexes comprising the thylakoid membrane, as well as the function of individual polypeptides. In many of these mutants, the inability to synthesize a particular polypeptide or a prosthetic group (such as chlorophyll *b*), leads to the loss of a whole functional complex. Thus, subtle genetic alterations can give rise to thylakoids with detectable changes in their structure. These may be seen by thin section electron microscopy due to the formation of giant grana, or collapsed lumen, or other abnormal morphology, but a more informative technique is freeze-fracture electron microscopy. This enables the structure of membranes to be examined at four different planes: the inner and outer membranes surfaces, and two complementary planes produced by cleaving the membrane through the lipid bilayer at low temperature (-110°C). These different planes are distinguished according to whether they are adjacent to protoplasmic or exoplasmic regions

M. Baltscheffsky (ed.), Current Research in Photosynthesis, Vol. II, 725–732.
© 1990 *Kluwer Academic Publishers. Printed in the Netherlands.*

of the cell, and whether they are true surfaces or fracture faces, and are therefore called PS, ES, PF and EF. In the case of thylakoid membranes, which are differentiated into stacked and unstacked regions, a lower case letter is added. The different planes are illustrated for the thylakoid membrane in Figure 1. The four different fracture faces are covered with small (6 -15 nm) particles, which are the structures corresponding to the multi-polypeptide functional complexes.

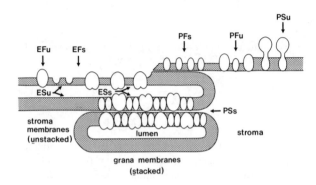

Figure 1. Diagram of the thylakoid membrane showing the four different fracture faces (EFu, PFu, EFs, PFs) and four different membrane surfaces (ESu, PSu, ESs, PSs). Each of these can be distinguished on the basis of the size and density of the particles which are found on them, as well as by their morphology.

2. RESULTS AND DISCUSSION

2.1. Location of Photosystem I and II.

Although immunocytochemistry and biochemical methods have shown that photosystem I is restricted to the non-appressed thylakoids, and photosystem II is mostly found in appressed thylakoids, a more precise localisation can only be made by freeze-fracture electron microscopy. The differences in composition of appressed and non-appressed regions is reflected in the marked differences in their freeze-fracture appearance. The identification of these particles has been made possible by comparing the freeze-fracture ultrastructure of wild type thylakoids with that of well-characterised photosynthetic mutants. Although these differences are sometimes subtle changes in the size of a population of particles on a particular freeze-fracture face, they are mostly revealed as differences in the freeze-fracture particle density, i.e., the number of particles per μm^2. Some of these are summarised for different barley mutants in Table 1. From these, and other experiments, the location of the

TABLE 1. Freeze-fracture particle density of some barley mutants.
Values are in numbers per μm^2

Mutant	Deficient in	EFu	PFu	EFs	PFs
wild type	-	347	4553	1624	6257
chlorina-f2	chlorophyll *b*	491	4092	2004	**1124**
viridis-zb[63]	photosystem I	596	4331	1455	6219
viridis-[115]	photosystem II	244	4527	**69**	6697
chlorina-[104]	LHCI + LHCII	**882**	3434	2015	**1433**

TABLE 2. Composition of freeze-fracture particles

Particle	Identity
EFs	photosystem II
PFs	LHCII
	cytochrome $b6/f$
PFu large	photosystem I
	LHCI
PFu small	coupling factor
	cytochrome $b6/f$
EFu	?
EFu pits	photosystem I
ESs	oxygen evolution
PSs	LHCII ?
PSu	coupling factor
	photosystem I

polypeptide complexes to specific populations of freeze-fracture particles has been made, as summarised in Table 2.

A correlation between the freeze-fracture data, and biochemical characterisation of thylakoid membrane complexes, has been made to produce a hypothetical model of the higher plant photosynthetic membrane, shown in Figure 2. An attempt has been made to indicate whether a polypeptide is extrinsic or intrinsic, and if extrinsic, on which side of the thylakoid it is likely to be located. For intrinsic polypeptides, the number of times they span the membrane is reflected in their width, and the stoichiometry is also indicated, where known. The organisation of the cytochrome $b6/f$ complex is based on the model of O'Keefe (7), and of the FNR1 on that of Pschorn et al. (8).

2.2. Structure of photosystem I.

The large PFu particles found in non-appressed lamellae appear to contain both the reaction centre chlorophyll-protein CPI and the LHCI antennae, based on studies with mutants of *Chlamydomonas* (9), maize (10) and barley (11). In the absence of either, the particles become smaller, and in the case of CPI, the complementary EFu pits also disappear. A functional photosystem I preparation, corresponding to these particles, can be isolated with a chlorophyll:P700 ratio of about 200:1 (PSI-200), by Triton X-100 solubilisation of de-stacked thylakoids (5,12). This can be resolved into particles with a lower chlorophyll:P700 ratio by sucrose gradient ultracentrifugation in the presence of dodecyl maltoside, or into its component chlorophyll-proteins by mild SDS-PAGE. In addition to CPI, there are two light-harvesting chlorophyll-proteins, designated LHCI-730 and LHCI-680, based on their fluorescence emission peaks at 77 K. About 90 molecules of chlorophyll *a* are non-covalently bound to CPI, which fluoresces at 720 nm at 77 K. About 90 molecules of chlorophyll *a* and *b* are associated with LHCI-730, which quenches fluorescence from the reaction centre, fluorescing at 740 nm *in vivo*, when attached to CPI. Another 30 molecules of chlorophyll *a* and *b* are non-covalently bound to LHCI-680, whose presence is required for excitation energy transfer from LHCII to CPI, for example in state 2.

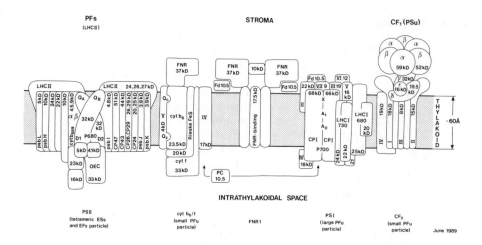

Figure 2. Model of the thylakoid membrane, correlating the freeze-fracture particles with the polypeptide components so far identified for the various structural complexes. The apparent molecular weights are indicated, along with their name, subunit designation, or gene symbol.

A model for energy transfer within photosystem I (Figure 3) has been useful in interpreting the fluorescence emission spectra of many of the barley mutants. Thus the 720 nm peak from the mutant *viridis-k*[23] can be explained by a lack of LHCI-730, which has been confirmed by immunoblot assay (13). Similarly, LHCI-730 is responsible for the 732 nm peak in the photosystem I-deficient mutant *viridis-zb*[63]. It had been thought that the chlorophyll *b*-less mutant *chlorina-f2* lacked all chlorophyll *b*-containing proteins, but the presence of a 730-740 nm fluorescence peak suggested significant amounts of LHCI, which again was confirmed by immunoblot assay (13). The presence of 60 molecules of chlorophyll *a* in LHCI in this mutant, explains why the chlorophyll:P700 ratio of photosystem I from this mutant is larger than expected (14).

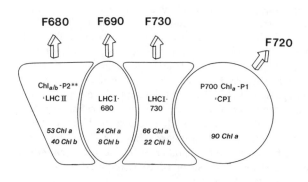

Figure 3. Model for the structure of photosystem I, showing the distribution of chlorophyll *a* and *b* between the component chlorophyll-proteins. Excitation energy transfer may occur in a linear sequence from LHCII (under state 2) to CPI. The fluorescence emission peaks for the individual chlorophyll-proteins are also shown, although are usually shifted *in vivo*, when they are associated with other chlorophyll-proteins.

The recently isolated *chlorina-104* mutant (15), which is chlorophyll-deficient when grown at 15°C due to the loss of much of its LHCI (and LHCII), has been shown to recover when the temperature is increased to 22°C. This is the first barley mutant in which existing tissue recovers after transfer from the restrictive temperature. This is the result of *de novo* synthesis and insertion of the missing chlorophyll *a/b*-proteins into the thylakoid, where they become functionally associated with their respective reaction centres, as shown by the loss of the 720 nm peak, and appearance of a 740 nm peak.

In addition to the antenna proteins, photosystem I is associated with at least 9 non-pigmented proteins with apparent molecular weights ranging from 4 to 22 kD (15-17). Six of these are shown in Figure 2, and they are all extrinsic, based on hydropathy plots, and extractibility. Subunit II is involved in binding ferredoxin, and subunit IV (which may be confused with subunit III because the two can exchange positions in SDS-PAGE) is probably located on the lumen side, where it binds plastocyanin. Subunit VII, which is coded by chloroplast DNA, contains the electron transport acceptors F_A and F_B (16). Functions for the other subunits remain to be elucidated.

The major chlorophyll-binding protein, CPI, is most likely a heterodimer (17), containing the reaction centre pigment, P700 and about 90 molecules of chlorophyll *a*. Extensive proteolysis of the isolated CPI complex results in a decrease in molecular weight from 650 to 300 kD, but none of the fragments is larger than 5 kD (18). This is accompanied by the loss of between 10-30 chlorophylls, depending on the protease used, but does not affect P700 activity, indicating that most or all of the chlorophyll is associated with hydrophobic regions of the polypeptide, resistant to protease attack. There is a loss of 720 nm fluorescence, and changes in the CD spectrum indicate that carotenoid molecules are accessible to disorganisation by protease attack. After proteolysis, the rate of P700 photo-oxidation under light-limiting conditions may decrease by a factor of 2-3, indicating a lower efficiency of excitation energy transfer to the reaction centre. There are no specific absorption changes associated with proteolysis, although the complete loss of CPI from thylakoids, results in the loss of the 691 nm peak in the fourth derivative, which by Gaussian deconvolution accounts for about 30 molecules of chlorophyll *a* per 500 chlorophyll molecules (19).

2.3. Structure of photosystem II.

The photosystem II reaction centre is located in the EFs particles in appressed grana lamellae (Figure 4a,b). The disappearance of 96% of these particles from *viridis-115* (Table 1) suggests that all the EFs particles contain photosystem II (20). These are probably the largest freeze-fracture particles known, implying a high molecular weight. Their exact composition is not known, since there is some doubt as to the location of the light-harvesting chlorophyll-proteins (LHCII, CP29, CP26, CP24), which may be exclusively in PFs particles (1), or in both EFs and PFs particles. There is some evidence now from negatively stained detergent purified photosystem II preparations, and from freeze-fractured cyanobacteria (21), that each EFs particle may contain 2 reaction centres, but this is still preliminary. In the thylakoid, the EFs particles protrude into the lumen, where they appear as tetrameric particles, containing the extrinsic polypeptides of the oxygen evolving complex (22). These are completely missing from mutants lacking photosystem II (20), and are lost from thylakoids deficient in photosystem II, in proportion to the loss of EFs particles.

The complete absence of photosystem II results in the loss of about 60 molecules of chlorophyll *a* per 500 chlorophyll molecules (20), 35 of which are associated with a component which absorbs at 683 nm at 77 K (19). The PFs face, on which LHCII is thought to be located (1), is the same as wild type, with no indication of extra particles containing LHCII derived from the EFs face.

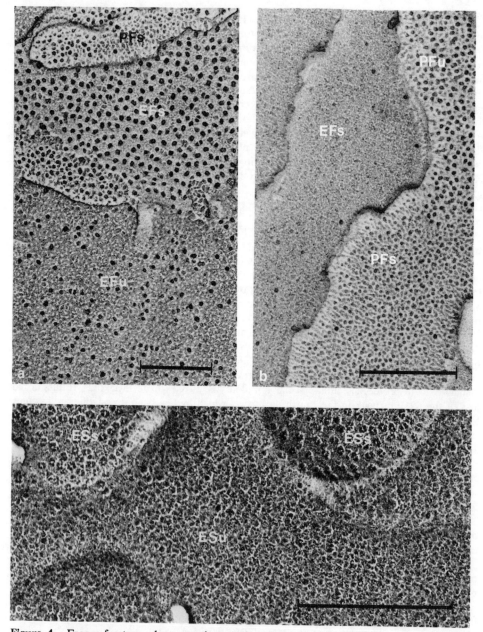

Figure 4. Freeze-fracture electron micrographs comparing (a) wild type and (b) *viridis-*[115] thylakoids. Note the loss of particles from the EFs face of the mutant, while the others look like wild type. (c) On the lumenal surface of wild type thylakoids, tetrameric particles can be seen over appressed regions, corresponding to EFs particles. The EFu particles do not appear to protrude into the lumen as tetrameric particles (ESu). Bars=0.25μm.

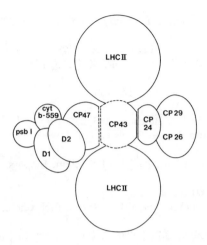

Figure 5. Model for the structure of photosystem II. LHCII transfers excitation energy via CP43 and CP47 to the reaction centre, consisting of D1, D2, cytochrome b-559 and the *psb*I protein.

Photosystem II can be isolated by detergent treatment of stacked thylakoids (6), and subjected to sub-fractionation in the presence or absence of Mg^{++} (23). The chlorophyll-protein composition of the different fractions lead to the hypothetical model of photosystem II shown in Figure 5. The simplest reaction centre preparation consists of D1, D2, cytochrome b-559 (24) and the *psb*I protein (25). These can be isolated as a complex associated with CP47 (23), and the presence of CP43 in almost all fractions suggests a central role in energy transfer from LHCII to the reaction centre. Recent results from Roberto Bassi's laboratory indicate that the minor chlorophyll a/b-proteins CP29, CP26 and CP24 mediate energy transfer between different types of LHCII (distinguished by their isoelectric points and polypeptide composition) and the reaction centre.

In spite of the loss of photosystem II, the EFu face of *viridis-[115]* contains 68% of the particles found in wild type (Table 1). These particles have been proposed as the site of photosystem II in non-appressed lamellae, but there are too few of them to account for the PSIIβ centres, since they represent only 11% of all EF particles (26). Moreover, they are found in bundle sheath thylakoids of maize (27), which lack EFs particles and photosystem II activity, and do not correlate with the amount of photosystem II activity in non-appressed lamellae, which is strongly species-dependent, accounting for 20% in spinach (28), 5% in barley (3), and less than 2% in maize bundle sheath (29). They do not have tetrameric structures associated with them in the lumen (Figure 4c), and are not affected by Mn^{++} deficiency (30) or other factors which cause a loss of EFs particles. It is possible that they represent partially assembled, non-functional photosystem II centres in the process of being transported into the appressed lamellae, to replace those with photodamaged D1 polypeptides.

REFERENCES
1. Simpson, D.J. (1979) Carlsberg Res. Commun. **44**, 305-336
2. Andersson, B. and Anderson, J.M. (1980) Biochim. Biophys. Acta **593**, 427-440
3. Vallon, O., Høyer-Hansen, G. and Simpson, D.J. (1987) Carlsberg Res. Commun. **52**, 405-421
4. Vallon, O., Wollman, F.A. and Olive, J. (1986) Photobiochem. Photobiophys. **12**, 203-220
5. Mullet, J.E., Burke, J.J. and Arntzen, C.J. (1980) Plant Physiol. **65**, 814-822

6. Berthold, D.A., Babcock, G.T. and Yocum, C.F. (1981) FEBS Lett. **134**, 231-234
7. O'Keefe, D.P. (1988) Photosyn. Res. **17**, 189-216
8. Pschorn, R., Rühle, W. and Wild, A. (1988) Photosyn. Res. **17**, 217-229
9. Olive, J., Wollman, F.A., Bennoun, P. and Recouvreur, M. (1983) Biol. Cell. **48**, 81-84
10. Miller, K.R. (1980) Biochim. Biophys. Acta **592**, 143-152
11. Simpson, D.J. (1983) Eur. J. Cell Biol. **31**, 305-314
12. Bassi, R. and Simpson, D.J. (1987) Eur. J. Biochem. **163**, 221-230
13. Høyer-Hansen, G., Bassi, R., Hønberg, L. and Simpson, D.J. (1988) Planta **173**, 12-21
14. Ghirardi, M.L., MacCauley, S.W. and Melis, A. (1986) Biochim. Biophys. Acta **851**, 331-339
15. Knoetzel, J. and Simpson, D.J. (1989) these proceedings
16. Høj, P., Svendsen, I., Scheeler, H.V. and Møller, B.L. (1987) J. Biol. Chem. **262**, 12676-12684
17. Scheeler, H.V., Svendsen, I. and Møller, B.L. (1989) J. Biol. Chem. **264**, 6929-6934
18. Hinz, U. and Simpson, D.J. (1988) Carlsberg Res. Commun. **53**, 321-330
19. Simpson, D.J. (1988) Carlsberg Res. Commun. **53**, 343-356
20. Simpson, D.J., Vallon, O. and von Wettstein, D. (1989) Biochim. Biophys. Acta **975**, 164-174
21. Mörschel, E. and Schatz, G.H. (1987) Planta **172**, 145-154
22. Simpson, D.J. and Andersson, B. (1986) Carlsberg Res. Commun. **51**, 467-474
23. Bassi, R., Høyer-Hansen, G., Barbato, R., Giacometti, G.M. and Simpson, D.J. (1987) J. Biol. Chem. **262**, 13333-13341
24. Nanba, O. and Satoh, K. (1987) Proc. Nat. Acad. Sci., USA **84**, 109-112
25. Webber, A.N., Packman, L., Chapman, D.J., Barber, J. and Gray, J.C. (1989) FEBS Lett. **242**, 259-262
26. Simpson, D.J. (1977) Carlsberg Res. Commun. **43**, 365-389
27. Miller, K.R., Miller, G.J. and McIntyre, K.R. (1977) Biochim. Biophys. Acta **459**, 145-156
28. Mäenpää, P., Andersson, B. and Sundby, C. (1987) FEBS Lett. **215**, 31-36
29. Bassi, R., Giacometti, G. and Simpson, D.J. (1988) Carlsberg Res. Commun. **53**, 221-232
30. Simpson, D.J. and Robinson, S.P. (1984) Plant Physiol. **74**, 735-741

CYCLING OF THE PHOTOSYSTEM II REACTION CENTER CORE
BETWEEN GRANA AND STROMA LAMELLAE

M. L. GHIRARDI, F. E. CALLAHAN, S. K. SOPORY[1], T. D. ELICH, M.
EDELMAN[2], and A. K. MATTOO, Plant Molecular Biology
Laboratory, USDA/ARS, Beltsville Agricultural Research Center,
Beltsville, MD 20705, USA. [1]Present address: Jawaharlal Nehru
University, New Delhi, India; [2]Present address: Weizmann
Institute of Science, Rehovot, Israel.

1. INTRODUCTION
The lateral steady-state distribution of photosystem II
(PSII) between grana and stroma lamellae in higher plant
thylakoids has been extensively investigated and documented (1-
3). The relative concentration of PSII centers in grana and
stroma lamellae has been reported to be around 80:20 in a variety
of plants. We have quantified the relative amounts of the PSII
reaction center proteins in grana and stroma lamellae of
Spirodela plants using immunoblot analysis. Our results indicate
that, while the reaction center core proteins and light-
harvesting chlorophyll a/b binding polypeptides (LHCII) are
present in both membrane regions, the other PSII-associated
proteins have an exclusive grana location.
The components of the PSII complex are known to undergo
dynamic changes, especially the 32 kDa protein of the reaction
center (also known as D1) (4). The 32 kDa protein is synthesized
on chloroplast ribosomes as a 33.5 kDa precursor which is
inserted into stroma lamellae and processed there to its mature
size (5). The processed protein is translocated to the grana
regions (6) where it is involved in mediating electron transport
from H_2O to plastoquinone . The 32 kDa protein undergoes light-
dependent degradation, yielding a membrane-bound 23.5 kDa
fragment (7). We now report the appearance of a transient form
of the 32 kDa protein that runs as a band of 32.5 kDa on SDS-
polyacrylamide gels. This short-lived protein, 32*, appears to be
present exclusively in the grana lamellae. We propose that 32* is
a modified form of the 32 kDa protein that is targeted for
degradation.
The fast turnover rate of the 32 kDa protein has been
implicated in the regulation of a number of thylakoid functions
(8). However, a perhaps more immediate consequence of its fast
turnover may be the continuous assembly and disassembly of the
PSII reaction center complex. We have isolated reaction center

M. Baltscheffsky (ed.), Current Research in Photosynthesis, Vol. II, 733–738.
© 1990 Kluwer Academic Publishers. Printed in the Netherlands.

complexes from both grana and stroma lamellae, and investigated
their PSII polypeptide composition. Based on these studies we
present a model for the dynamic flux of the PSII reaction center
between grana and stroma lamellae.

2. RESULTS

(I) STEADY-STATE DISTRIBUTION OF PSII POLYPEPTIDES BETWEEN GRANA AND STROMA LAMELLAE

Isolated thylakoids from light-grown Spirodela plants were
fractionated into grana and stroma lamellae using the dual
detergent method of Leto et al. (9). Both fractions were subjected
to immunoblot analysis using antibodies raised against the
various PSII proteins (10). The steady-state levels of the different
PSII-associated proteins were determined by densitometric
scanning of the immunoblots (Table I).

TABLE I - Quantitation of the relative distribution of the PSII
polypeptides between grana (G) and stroma lamellae (S) in
Spirodela (Adapted from ref. 10).

	% Relative Distribution		
Protein	G	S	Inferred Location
32 kDa (D1)	88	12	G + S
D2	86	14	G + S
Cyt b_{559}	88	12	G + S
LHCII	77	23	G + S
51 kDa	94	6	G
43 kDa	97	3	G

Our results reveal two classes of PSII proteins: those that
are present only in grana lamellae, and those that display lateral
heterogeneity in the thylakoids. The LHCII and the three PSII
reaction center proteins, 32 kDa, D2 and cytochrome b_{559} are
present both in grana and stroma lamellae. Such distribution is
in agreement with previous reports on the dual location of PSII
centers in the two membrane regions (1-3). In contrast, we find
that the 51 kDa and 43 kDa PSII proteins are located exclusively
in grana lamellae.

(II) DETECTION OF A MODIFIED FORM OF THE 32 kDA PROTEIN, 32*, IN THE GRANA LAMELLAE

Spirodela plants were pulse-labeled with radioactive amino acid and chased in the light for several hours. Thylakoids were isolated and proteins fractionated by SDS-PAGE (not shown). At the end of the labeling period most of the incorporated radioactivity is present in the 32 kDa band, with a smaller amount detected in the 33.5 kDa band, which corresponds to the precursor of the 32 kDa protein (11,12). After a few hours chase in the light we observe the appearance of radioactive label in a band with slower mobility than the 32 kDa protein. The relative amount of label in the new band increases during the chase, suggesting a precursor-product relationship between the 32 kDa and the newly-detected polypeptide. Immunoblot analysis indicate that the new polypeptide is immunogenically related to the 32 kDa protein. The cleavage patterns of the 32 kDa and of the novel polypeptide are indistinguishable upon partial proteolytic digestion with either Staphylococcus aureus V8 protease or papain. Given the above, we suggest that the new polypeptide is a modified form of the 32 kDa protein, referred to as 32*.

The subthylakoid location of 32* was investigated by fractionating ^{35}S-methionine pulse-labeled Spirodela into grana and stroma lamellae. Our results indicate that 32* is a product of the grana-located 32 kDa protein. It is exclusively found in the grana partitions and turns over rapidly.

Further experiments were done to determine the conditions which favor the formation of 32*. The results are summarized below:

(a) the generation of 32* is a light-dependent phenomenon; it does not occur to any appreciable extent in the dark.

(b) 32* formation is blocked by DCMU, a herbicide known to block electron transport from Q_A by competing with plastoquinone for binding to the 32 kDa protein (13);

(c) the appearance of 32* is blocked by propylgallate, a free radical scavenger which does not interfere with electron transport at PSII.

Based on these results we propose that the transient intermediate, 32*, is the light-induced modified form of the 32 kDa protein which is targeted for degradation.

(III) POLYPEPTIDE COMPOSITION OF PS II REACTION CENTERS FROM GRANA AND STROMA LAMELLAE

We used the procedure of Marder et al. (14) to isolate PSII reaction centers from purified grana and stroma lamellae samples. Granal and stroma lamellae reaction centers were collected from a Toyopearl DEAE-650S column and identified spectroscopically as containing the reaction center chromophores (15). Both granal and stroma lamellae preparations were investigated with respect to their polypeptide composition and the content of PSII core polypeptides (not shown).

The reaction center preparations had very simple polypeptide profiles. Granal PSII reaction centers were enriched in the 32 kDa protein (D1), D2 and cytochrome b559, and showed a high MW band which has been reported to be a heterodimer of the D1 and D2 core proteins (14). Stroma lamellae reaction centers showed a larger number of high MW polypeptides which were probably contaminants. The three main PSII core proteins, however, were present in the preparation.

4. DISCUSSION

Based on the results presented above, we propose a model for the dynamic flux of the PSII reaction center core in the thylakoid membrane   (Figure 1).

According to the model, the 32 kDa protein is incorporated into PSII reaction center cores in the stroma lamellae. Given the presence of a small percentage of LHCII in stroma lamellae (Table I), we propose that the PSII core complex located in that membrane region might be complexed to a small antenna of Chl a/b-containing proteins. Indeed, PSII centers with a small Chl a/b antenna have been detected in stroma lamellae of higher plants (16,17). Eventually the core complex translocates from stroma lamellae to the grana partitions forming a larger PSII complex with the remainder of the LHCII polypeptides and the 51 and the 43 kDa proteins as anchors. These anchor polypeptides are located exclusively in the grana regions of the thylakoids (10).

In the grana partitions, the 32 kDa protein undergoes a light-dependent modification which converts it into a slower-moving polypeptide, 32*. We propose that 32* is the form of the 32 kDa protein which is targeted for degradation. The nature of the modification is not known.   The 32 kDa protein has been reported to undergo light-dependent phosphorylation (18) and acylation (6). These modifications, however, have not been correlated with the turnover rate of the protein. Degradation of the 32 kDa protein, which occurs under a broad range of the spectrum, due to the action of multiple photosensitizers (19,20). One of the photosensitizers is thought to be chlorophyll; its action spectrum covers most of the red and blue regions. The second photosensitizer acts in the UV; it has been proposed to be a plastosemiquinone anion.   Both visible and UV degradation pathways may operate through a common oxygen-mediated free

radical reaction (21). Indeed, both 32 kDa degradation and 32*
formation are inhibited by propylgallate, a free radical
scavenger.

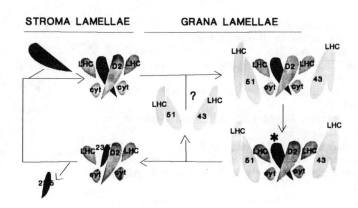

FIGURE 1 - Model for the dynamic flux of the PSII reaction center
core between the two thylakoid regions, stroma lamellae and
grana   partitions.

Cleavage of the 32 kDa protein in vivo yields a 23.5 kDa
membrane-bound fragment (7). This primary degradation
fragment has been detected mainly in stroma lamellae
(unpublished). We speculate that the PSII reaction center cycle is
completed when the 23.5 kDa fragment is replaced by a newly-
synthesized 32 kDa protein in stroma lamellae.

ACKNOWLEDGEMENTS
This investigation was supported in part by the USA-Israel
BARD grant to ME and AKM.

II.8.**738**

REFERENCES

1   Andersson, B., and Anderson, J.M. (1980) Biochim. Biophys. Acta 593, 427-440.
2   Staehelin, L.A. (1986) in Encyclopedia of Plant Physiology, New Series, Pirson, A. & Zimmerman, M.H., eds., (Springer Verlag, Berlin) vol. 19 pp 1-84.
3   Glazer, A., and Melis, A. (1987) Annu. Rev. Plant Physiol. 38, 11-45.
4   Mattoo, A.K., Marder, J.B. and Edelman, M. (1989) Cell 56, 241-246.
5   Mattoo, A.K., Callahan, F.E., Greenberg, B.M., Goloubinoff, P. and Edelman, M. (1988) in Biotechnology for Crop Protection (Hedin, P.A., Menn, J.J. and Hollingworth, R.M., eds.), pp. 248-257, American Chemical Society, Washington, DC, USA.
6   Mattoo, A.K., and Edelman, M. (1987) Proc. Natl. Acad. Sci. USA 84, 1497-1501.
7   Greenberg, B.M., Gaba, V., Mattoo, A.K., and Edelman, M. (1987) EMBO J. 6, 2865-2869.
8   Mattoo, A.K. and Edelman, M. ((1985) in Frontiers of Membrane Research in Agriculture (St. John, J.B., Berlin, E. and Jackson, P.C., eds.), pp. 23-34, Rowman & Allanheld, Totowa, USA.
9   Leto, K.J., Bell, E., and McIntosh, L. (1985) EMBO J. 4, 1645-1653
10 Callahan, F.E., Wergin, W.P., Nelson, N., Edelman, M., and Mattoo, A.K. (1989) Plant Physiol., in press.
11 Edelman, M. and Reisfeld, A. (1980) in "Genome Organization and Expression in Plants", Leaver, C.J., ed. (Plenum, New York), pp 353-362.
12 Reisfeld, A., Mattoo, A.K., and Edelman, M. (1982) Eur. J. Biochem. 124, 125-129.
13 Pfister, K., Steinback, K.E., Gardner, G. and Arntzen, C.J. (1981) Proc. Natl. Acad. Sci. USA 78, 981-985.
14 Marder, J.B., Chapman, D.J., Telfer, A., Nixon, P.J., and Barber, J. (1987) Plant Mol. Biol. 9, 325-333.
15 Nanba, O., and Satoh, K. (1987) Proc. Natl. Acad. Sci. USA 84, 109-112.
16 Anderson, J.M., and Melis, A. (1983) Proc. Natl. Acad. Sci. USA 80, 745-749.
17 Melis, A. (1985) Biochim. Biophys. Acta 808, 334-342.
18 Millner, P.A., Marder, J.B., Gounaris, K. and Barber, J. (1986) Biochim. Biophys. Acta 852, 30-37.
19 Greenberg, B.M., Gaba, V., Mattoo, A.K., and Edelman, M. (1989) Z. Naturforschung 44c, 450-452.
20 Greenberg, B.M., Gaba, V., Canaani, O., Malkin, S., Mattoo, A.K., and Edelman, M. (1989) Proc. Natl. Acad. Sci. USA 86, in press.
21 Greenberg, B.M., Sopory, K., Gaba, V., Mattoo, A.K., and Edelman, M. (1989) These proceedings.

LATERAL DIFFUSION OF PLASTOCYANIN AND PLASTOQUINOL IN THYLAKOID MEMBRANES

W. Haehnel, R. Mitchell, R. Ratajczak, A. Spillmann, and H. Robenek*

Lehrstuhl für Biochemie der Pflanzen, *Lehrstuhl für Medizinische Cytologie, University of Münster, D-4400 Münster, Federal Republic of Germany

1.   INTRODUCTION

In thylakoid membranes of higher plants the electron transport complexes are heterogeneously distributed with Photosystem (PS) II in appressed and PS I in non-appressed thylakoid membranes [1] in contrast to cytochrome (cyt) b_6/f complex, which is uniformly distributed throughout these membrane regions [2, 3]. This organization requires a long-range electron transport from PS II to PS I that is not fully understood [4]. Two electron carriers could mediate this long-range electron transport, the hydrophobic plastoquinol (PQH_2) and the hydrophilic plastocyanin. Plastoquinol diffuses in the lipid bilayer and transfers electrons from PS II to cyt b_6/f. Cyt b_6/f in stroma regions can only function efficiently in linear electron transport if PQH_2 reaches these complexes within a time considerably faster than that of the rate-limiting step. The rate, at which the PQH_2 molecule transfers electrons from PS II to the cyt b_6/f complex is determined by its diffusion coefficient and the rate of binding at the cyt b_6/f complex. Estimates of 10^{-8} and 10^{-6} cm^2s^{-1} have been made for the diffusion coefficient of PQH_2 that would be consistent with the times of electron transfer observed and the average distance between the two thylakoid regions [4-6]. Several lines of evidence indicate that the halftime of diffusion must be considerably faster than that of the oxidation of PQH_2 of about 13 ms which is the slowest step in the chain [7,8]. Direct measurements of the diffusion coefficient of ubiquinone analogs yielded 3×10^{-9} $cm^{-2}s^{-2}$ if a triplet probe was attached [9] while other studies with phospholipid liposomes reported values of 10^{-6} - 10^{-5} cm^2s^{-2} [10] and more recently 1.3 - 3.5×10^{-7} cm^2s^{-1} [11].

Plastocyanin functions between cyt b_6/f and PS I in the lumen, a continuous space inside the thylakoid membrane system. Fig. 1 illustrates the lateral differences in the membrane composition which may result in an inhomogeneous distribution of plastocyanin in stroma, grana, and exposed grana regions of the lumen. The average distance between PS I and cyt b_6/f in non-appressed and cyt b_6/f in appressed membranes is about 20 and 200 nm, respectively. The longer distance from cyt b_6/f in appressed membranes may result in a

M. Baltscheffsky (ed.), Current Research in Photosynthesis, Vol. II, 739–746.
© 1990 *Kluwer Academic Publishers. Printed in the Netherlands.*

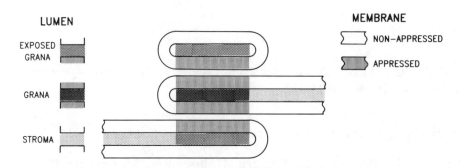

Figure 1. Scheme of lumenal regions with different properties.

considerably slower turnover of these complexes as compared to that of cyt b_6/f in non-appressed membranes at a given shuttle speed of plastocyanin. Therefore a localization of plastocyanin in the lumen of appressed grana and its fast diffusion would be essential for an efficient function of these cyt b_6/f complexes in linear electron transport. However, experimental results seem to favor a location of plastocyanin in the stromal lumen [12].

The approach to the problems of the lateral diffusion has to be different for plastocyanin and PQH_2. For plastocyanin we have used immunogold-labeling to investigate its distribution in the thylakoid lumen in the dark and during illumination. Kinetic measurements of P-700 reduction enabled us to discriminate potentially mobile and bound plastocyanin. For PQH_2 we examined the importance of its diffusion in the kinetics of linear electron transport. Our approach to this problem has been to follow the redox state of P-700 as a convenient method of accurately measuring full-chain electron transport under conditions which should vary the time for the diffusion and binding of PQH_2. We then obtained estimates for the diffusion coefficient and binding rate constant with the aid of a model which simulated these processes.

2. MATERIALS AND METHODS
2.1. Studies of plastocyanin

Intact chloroplasts were isolated from spinach on a discontinuous Percoll (Pharmacia) gradient [13]. Antibodies were raised in rabbits against spinach plastocyanin and the IgG fraction isolated on protein A-Sepharose CL4B. The amount of plastocyanin in spinach chloroplasts and thylakoids was determined by quantitative rocket electroimmunodiffusion according to the method of Laurell [14]. For immuno-cytochemical studies pieces of leaves from spinach were incubated for 15 min in 1 % glutaraldehyde and 3 % formaldehyde in the dark and during illumination. Electron micrographs were taken from Lowicryl ultra-thin sections [15] after successive incubation with the mono-specific rabbit IgG and protein A-gold. Electron micrographs with cross-sections of chloroplasts with clearly resolved grana and stroma membranes were analyzed on two sets of glossy prints at a magnification of ca. 100,000. The length of the lumen in grana stacks, exposed grana, and stroma lamellae was measured and each gold granule and its attribution to one of these regions was individually marked to minimize possible errors.

2.2. Studies of plastoquinone

Absorbance changes of P700 were induced by a flash (6 μs FWHM) of saturating blue (Schott filter BG 23/6 mm) light after oxidation of all electron carriers between PS I and PS II by the far-red monitoring light at 703 nm and measured as described [16]. The electrical bandwidth was from DC to 10 kHz. The content of the cuvette was changed every 50 flashes. The flash frequency, transient recorder dwell time and number of averaged signals used are given in the figure legends.

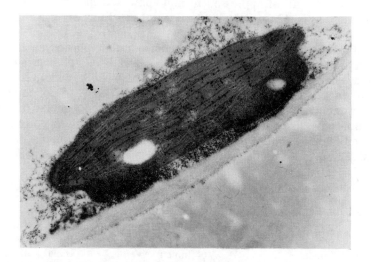

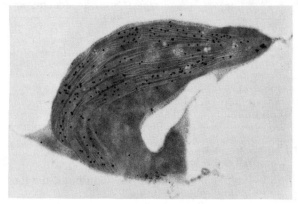

Figure 2.

Immunogold localization of plastocyanin on Lowicryl sections of spinach leaves.

Above, dark-adapted sample;

below, sample illuminated during fixation with glutaraldehyde/formaldehyde.

3. RESULTS AND DISCUSSION

3.1. Distribution of plastocyanin

The distribution of plastocyanin has been probed in thin-sections of leaves from spinach with mono-specific antibodies (IgG) in the dark and during continuous illumination and visualized by binding of colloidal protein A-gold complexes as shown in Fig.2. The analysis of the electron micrographs is shown in Table I. It indicates an inhomogeneous distribution of plastocyanin in the dark with an almost twofold concentration in the lumen between stroma as compared to that between grana membranes. Illumination decreases the labeling density in the stromal and increases that in the granal lumen. The overall labeling density is the same in the dark and light. This indicates that the binding between the antibody and plastocyanin is not different in grana and stroma and that the labeling density is proportional to the concentration of plastocyanin. The averaged ratio of the length of appressed to non-appressed membranes (cf. Fig. 1) is estimated as 58:42 from the lumenal lengths in Table 1.

Relevant for the lateral electron transport is mobile plastocyanin. Reduced plastocyanin bound to PS I reduces oxidized P-700 after a short flash with a characteristic halftime of 10-14 μs [17]. A measurement (not shown) in a dark-adapted sample indicates that to 95 % of total PS I a plastocyanin molecule is bound. We have determined a molar ratio of 205 for chlorophyll to plastocyanin by rocket immuno-electrophoresis and from the amplitude of the P-700 signal a molar ratio of 3.3 for plastocyanin to P-700. These data and the values in Table 1 suggest that in the dark

Table 1. Distribution of Gold Granules Labeling Plastocyanin in the Thylakoid Lumen

Chloroplast Sample No.	Region of lumen	Total counts	Total length of lumen (μm)	Labeling densities Average* (counts/μm)	Grana /stroma	Total counts[#] /total length of lumen (counts/μm)
spinach dark 13	grana	959	637	1.5 (± 0.2)		
	exposed–grana	444	274	1.6 (± 0.4)	0.68	1.7
	stroma	854	391	2.2 (± 0.6)		
spinach light 13	grana	1153	572	2.0 (± 0.5)		
	exposed–grana	379	206	1.8 (± 0.3)	1.25	1.8
	stroma	649	417	1.6 (± 0.5)		

*Total counts divided by total length of lumen. The mean ± SD in parentheses is given for the number No. of chloroplast cross-sections analyzed.

[#]Sum of total counts in the three regions of lumen divided by the sum of the total length of lumen in these regions.

most of the mobile fraction of plastocyanin is localized in the granal lumen. During illumination, the plastocyanin concentration in grana increases at the expense of that in the stroma regions. This is evidence for a light-induced diffusion of the negatively charged plastocyanin. The diffusion may be due to changes in the surface charge density being different in the two membrane regions during the decrease of the lumenal pH value and/or the oxidation of plastocyanin during illumination. The increase in the concentration will increase the turnover of cyt b_6/f in the grana. We conclude that the problem of the diffusion of plastocyanin across the long distances from cyt b_6/f in grana to PS I in stroma could be compensated by a high local concentration of plastocyanin in the light. The result suggests that cyt b_6/f in grana may be more efficiently connected to linear electron transport by plastocyanin in strong than in weak light.

3.2. Diffusion of plastoquinol

In a different approach we have studied the contribution of PQH_2 diffusion to linear electron transport by measuring the reduction kinetics of $P700^+$ after previous oxidation of the electron carriers between the two photosystems. The $P700^+$ reduction kinetics have been analyzed using two parameters; the halftime which is dependent mostly on the rate-determining step of linear electron transport and the initial lag which is influenced by other steps within the chain. The restriction of active PS II to grana could lead to a decrease and an increase in the contribution of a diffusional step between PS II and cyt b_6/f complex at decreasing and increasing amounts of PQH_2 produced at PS II, respectively. The P-700 absorbance change induced by two saturating flashes 2.04 ms apart is shown in Fig. 3B. When a single flash signal measured in the same sample (A) is subtracted off the two-flash signal (B), the resulting trace (B-A) represents the kinetics of full-chain electron transport of the electrons attributable to the second flash. The number of electrons produced were determined from the areas under the curves as described [18] showing that the second flash induces 85% of the electrons which are produced with a single flash. A comparison of the single and second flash signals (Fig. 3, A and B-A) after normalization to the amount of electrons produced shows that the kinetics are similar over the first 10 ms, but at longer times the second flash signal lies increasingly lower than the single flash curve, probably due to the effect of the equilibria between cyt f, plastocyanin and P-700. As a result the lag parameters of the single and second flash signals can be compared directly, but the halftime parameters can not. There is no significant difference in the lags measured in the single and second flash signals. By adding DCMU we have decreased the amount of active PS II to less than 30 % (not shown). If the curves of P-700 were scaled the signals showed also no differences.

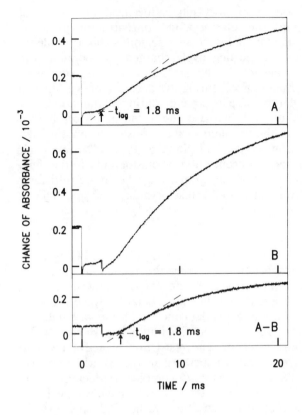

Figure 3.

A: The reduction of P-700 after a saturating flash.

B: The reduction of P-700 after two saturating flashes, 2.04 ms apart.

B-A: The result of subtracting signal A from signal B.

Average of 300 flashes with a flash frequency of 0.2 Hz.

3.3. Model of linear electron transport

The time course expected at different flash-induced amounts of PQH_2 can only be analyzed with the aid of a model which takes into account the diffusion process. The diffusion equation cannot be solved for a system with initial and boundary conditions as complex as in thylakoids. Therefore we have used the Monte Carlo algorithm to simulate the diffusional step in a model of the thylakoid shown in Fig. 4 which is based on most of the known structural details and dimensions. Most parameters of this map can interactively selected. We have chosen a stoichiometry of PS II:cyt b_6/f:PS I:CF = 1:1:1:1.5. The diffusion coefficient and the binding probability of PQH_2 at the cyt b_6/f complex have been used to characterize this step. Other electron transfer reactions have been simulated by first- and second-order reactions using known rate constants. The scheme in Fig. 5 gives an overview. We have discriminated a collisional mechanism of the oxidation of PQH_2 on encounter with the cyt b_6/f complex and a mechanism with irreversible binding of PQH_2 to the Q_Z-site of the cyt b_6/f complex before its slow oxidation where the diffusion should contribute to the rate-determining step and to a fast preceding step,

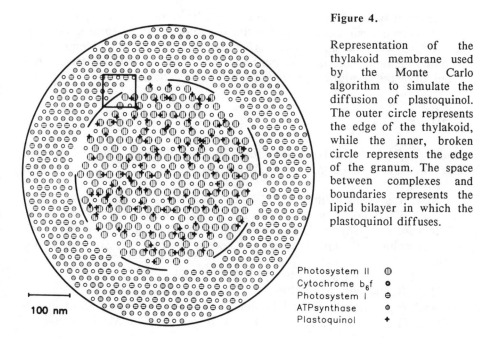

Figure 4.

Representation of the thylakoid membrane used by the Monte Carlo algorithm to simulate the diffusion of plastoquinol. The outer circle represents the edge of the thylakoid, while the inner, broken circle represents the edge of the granum. The space between complexes and boundaries represents the lipid bilayer in which the plastoquinol diffuses.

100 nm

Photosystem II   ⏀
Cytochrome b_6f   ○
Photosystem I   ⊖
ATPsynthase   ◎
Plastoquinol   +

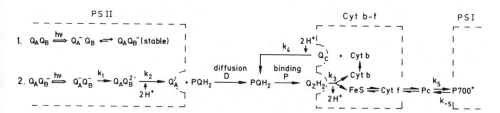

Figure 5. Scheme of reactions giving the constants used in the simulation of linear electron transport.

respectively, both using a diffusion limited and a non-diffusion limited mechanism with a high (P=0.25) and a low (P=0.005) binding probability at the cyt b_6/f complex, respectively. The diffusion of PQH_2 is simulated by a random movement in a hexagonal lattice and a step width of 1 nm, corresponding approximately to the distance between lipid molecules. Details of the model and the calculation will be published in a forthcoming paper.

In conclusion, the experimental data are best fitted by our model assuming either a very rapid tight-binding step and a value of the diffusion coefficient of PQH_2 greater or equal to $5 \cdot 10^{-7}$ cm^2s^{-1} or a non-diffusion-limited collisional mechanism for the oxidation of PQH_2 and a value of $5 \cdot 10^{-8}$ cm^2s^{-1}. The latter value is similar to diffusion coefficients determined for lipid molecules. In our view, our and other data is best accounted for by the non-diffusion-limited collisional mechanism.

REFERENCES

1 Andersson, B. and Anderson, J.M. (1980) Biochim. Biophys. Acta 593, 427-440
2 Cox, R.P. and Andersson, B. (1981) Biochem. Biophys. Res. Commun. 103, 1336-1342
3 Allred, D.R. and Staehelin, L.A. (1986) Biochim. Biophys. Acta 849, 94-103
4 Haehnel, W. (1984) Annu. Rev. Plant Physiol. 35, 659-693
5 Whitmarsh, J. (1986) In: Encyclopedia of Plant Physiology, New Ser., Vol. 19, (Staehelin, L.A. and Arntzen, C.J., eds.), pp. 508-527, Springer-Verlag Berlin
6 Millner, P. A. and Barber, J. (1984) FEBS Lett. 169, 1-6
7 Stiehl, H. H. and Witt, H. T. (1969) Z. Naturforschg. 24b, 1588-1598
8 Haehnel, W., Mitchell, R. and Spillmann, A. (1987) in Progress in Photosynthesis Research (Biggins, J., ed.), Vol. II, pp. 513-520, Martinus Nijhoff, Dordrecht
9 Gupte, S., Wu, E.-S., Hoechli, L., Hoechli, M., Jacobson, K., Sowers, A. and Hackenbrock, C.R. (1984) Proc. Natl. Acad. Sci. USA 81, 2606-2610
10 Fato, R., Battino, M., Degli Esposti, M., Castelli, G.P. and Lenaz, G. (1986) Biochemistry 25, 3378-3390
11 Blackwell, M.F., Gounaris, K., Zara, S.J. and Barber, J. (1987) Biophys. J. 51, 735-744
12 Peters, F.A.L.J., Van Wielink, J.E., Sang, H.W.W.F., De Vries, S. and Kraayenhof, R. (1983) Biochim. Biophys. Acta 722, 460-470
13 Kreimer, G., Melkonian, M. and Latzko, E. (1985) FEBS Lett. 180, 253-258
14 Laurell, C.-B. (1966) Anal. Biochem. 15, 45-52
15 Völker, W., Frick, B. and Robenek, H. (1985) J. Microscopy 138, 91-93
16 Haehnel, W. (1976) Biochim. Biophys. Acta 440, 506-521
17 Haehnel, W., Pröpper, A. and Krause, H. (1980) Biochim. Biophys. Acta 593, 384-399
18 Haehnel, W. and Trebst, A. (1982) J. Bioenerg. Biomembr. 14, 181-190

ACKNOWLEDGEMENT
Support by the Deutsche Forschungsgemeinschaft (SFB 171-A3) is gratefully acknowledged. Thanks to Richard Wagner for the measurement of the laser-induced kinetics.

REDOX CONTROL AND SEQUENCE SPECIFICITY OF A THYLAKOID PROTEIN KINASE

H. P. MICHEL, W. E. BUVINGER and J. BENNETT*, Biology Department, Brookhaven National Laboratory, Upton NY 11973, USA. *Address for correspondence: ICGEB, NII Campus, Shaheed Jeet Singh Marg, New Delhi-110067, India.

1.   INTRODUCTION

Protein phosphorylation is an important feature of the chloroplasts of green plants. Phosphoproteins have been reported in the thylakoid membranes, the stroma, the ribosomes, the inner and outer envelope membranes, and in the space between the envelopes (1-6). The most conspicuous phosphoproteins of the chloropolast are components of the thylakoid membranes, where they are associated principally with photosystem II (PS II). Among these phosphoproteins are two reaction centre proteins D1 and D2 (32 and 34 kDa), together with two additional PS II core proteins (the 43 kDa apo-protein of chlorophyll-protein complex CPa-2 and the 8 kDa psbH gene product). The phosphorylation sites of these four proteins have been sequenced: that of the psbH protein by Edman degradation (7) and those of D1, D2 and CPa-2 by tandem mass spectrometry (8). However, the major phosphoproteins of the chloroplast are the peripheral antenna proteins of PS II, namely, the light-harvesting chlorophyll a/b proteins II (LHC II, 25-28 kDa). Reversible phosphorylation of LHC II is believed to regulate the distribution of excitation energy between PS I and PS II (9).

The protein kinases which phosphorylate LHC II and the four PS II core proteins are under redox control, being activated by reduction of the intersystem electron carriers (9). However, several lines of evidence suggest that the LHC II kinase may not be identical with the PS II kinase. Firstly, inhibitors such as sulphydryl reagents (10) and the ATP analogue fluorosulphonylbenzoyladenosine (11) inhibit phosphorylation of LHC II much more effectively than phosphorylation of PS II proteins. Secondly, studies with inhibitors of the cytochrome bf complex and with mutants lacking this complex (12-17) indicate that the redox control of the LHC II kinase involves the cytochrome complex, whereas the redox control of the PS II kinase does not. Thirdly, as we now report, sequencing of the phosphorylation sites of LHC II and PS II core proteins indicate that they are phosphorylated on very different sequences. This conclusion is supported by studies with synthetic peptide analogues of the LHC II phosphorylation site; residues that are important in defining the LHC II phosphorylation site are absent from PS II core phosphoproteins.

M. Baltscheffsky (ed.), Current Research in Photosynthesis, Vol. II, 747–753.
© 1990 Kluwer Academic Publishers. Printed in the Netherlands.

2.   RESULTS AND DISCUSSION
2.1.   Sequencing of Spinach LHC II Phosphopeptides

About 30 nuclear encoded <u>cab</u> genes encoding LHC II apoproteins have been sequenced in green plants. Strong sequence
conservation is observed at the protein level, particularly in the
first and third of the three membrane-spanning segments proposed for
LHC II (18). Molecules of LHC II are synthesized as precursors prior
to import into the chloroplast, and the N-terminal extention of each
protein (known as the transit peptide) is required for targetting the
protein to the chloroplast (19). The transit peptide is one of the
most variable segments of pre-LHC II molecules but the actual site of
cleavage is believed to lie within a quite highly conserved segment
of consensus sequence: GRATMRKTAGK. This sequence is located about 35
residues from the N-terminus of the pre-LHC II molecules. Most
authors have assumed that the cleavage occurs immediately prior to
the conserved methionyl residue, but this assumption is not supported
by any evidence.

We have resolved this question and obtained additional data on
the sequence specificity of LHC II phosphorylation by isolating and
sequencing phosphopeptides representing the N-termini of four apoproteins of spinach LHC II. Although the N-terminus of LHC II is
known to be cleaved from the membrane by trypsin, we decided against
use of this enzyme in removing the phosphopeptide because we did not
want to introduce a cleavage between the phosphorylation site and the
N-terminal residue (20). Accordingly we investigated the suitability
of other proteases and found thermolysin and proteinase K
satisfactory. Thermolysin released three phosphopeptides which
appeared to derive from the 27-28 kDa forms of LHC II while a single
additional phosphopeptide was released from thermolysin-treated
thylakoids by digestion with proteinase K, this fourth peptide
deriving from the 25 kDa form of LHC II. Purification of these
phosphopeptides for sequencing was achieved by the same protocol
which we had found successful for isolation of tryptic
phosphopeptides from PS II core particles, namely, affinity
chromatography on ferric ion/iminodiacetyl-substituted agarose,
followed by C18 reverse phase HPLC (8). And, as previously, N-
terminal blocking of the peptides made it necessary to use tandem
mass spectrometry for sequencing. All four peptides began with an N-
acetyl-arginyl residue and contained eight additional residues
(Michel et al., manuscript in preparation). Although the presence of
this blocking group created problems with sequencing, it served to
prove that each peptide was derived from the N-terminus of LHC II;
internal proteolytic fragments would not have been blocked.
Furthermore, differences in sequence elsewhere in the peptides
establish that they derived from four distinct gene products.

Thirdly, the data strongly suggest that the site of cleavage is between the conserved methionyl and arginyl residue. Fourthly, the fact that PS II core proteins are acetylated on N-terminal threonyl residues raises the possibility that there are at least two acetyltransferases in the chloroplast. Finally, all four peptides were phosphorylated on the third residue (threonine in three cases and serine in the fourth).

The first N-terminal sequencing data for LHC II were obtained by Mullet (20) for a pea LHC II and are presented in Fig. 1. The sequence begins with a dipeptide consisting of arginine and lysine but the order of these two residues could not be determined because the dipeptide did not yield to Edman degradation, suggesting that it was blocked at the N-terminus.

Sequence from ref. 20:
          *(lys,arg)-ser-ala-(P?)thr-(P?)thr-lys-lys
   (* = blocked tryptic dipeptide)

Intrepretation:
          Acetyl-arg-lys-ser-ala-(P)thr-thr-lys-lys

FIGURE 1. N-terminal sequence of pea LHC II and our interpretation in the light of data presented in this paper.

The sequence contained also three hydroxy amino acids (potential phosphorylation sites). It was clear that the serine was not phosphorylated but Mullet was unable to determine whether thr-5 or thr-6 or both were phosphorylated. Concerning the N-terminal blockage, we suggest (Fig. 1) that the sequence of pea LHC II begins with N-acetyl-arg-lys. This is consistent with both our data and the sequence of cloned pea cab genes (21). Thus, in pea also, cleavage would appear to occur at the conserved met-arg bond. In the next section we consider the question of the phosphorylation site of LHC II.

2.2. Studies with Synthetic Peptide Analogues of LHC II
Phosphorylation Site

We have studied the sequence requirements for the
phosphorylation of LHC II by pea and spinach chloroplasts using
synthetic peptide analogues. Some of the data were obtained prior to
the above finding that methionine is not the N-terminal residue of
LHC II and consequently the first peptide analogues were synthesized
to include an N-terminal methionyl residue. This additional residue
does not in fact alter the results or the conclusions significantly.
We are confident that the synthetic peptides were being
phosphorylated by LHC II kinase because their phosphorylation showed
the same sensitivity to inhibitors such as diuron and DBMIB as LHC II
phosphorylation itself (12). Incorporation of radioisotope from ATP
was linear for at least 30 min in most cases whether catalyzed by
spinach thylakoids (22) or pea thylakoids (Fig. 2).

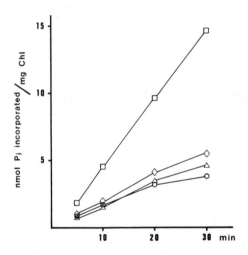

FIGURE 2. Time course of phosphorylation of five synthetic peptide
analogues of the N-terminus of a pea LHC II by isolated pea
thylakoids. See (22) for methods. Square: MRKSATTKKAVC; triangle:
MRKSASSKKAVC; circle: MRKAAATKKAVC; diamond: MRKAATAKKAVC.

We found that both spinach and pea thylakoids phosphorylated the peptide corresponding to the Mullet (20) sequence mainly, if not exclusively, on thr-5 (counting arginine as residue 1). Thr-6 may also have been phosphorylated but to a minor extent. In contrast, ser-3 was not phosphorylated at all, again in agreement with (20). When ser-3 and thr-5 were replaced by alanines, thr-6 was heavily phosphorylated, and when the two threonines at positions 5 and 6 were replaced by two serines, ser-3 was preferentially phosphorylated. Thus, we can say that the LHC II kinase can phosphorylate a serine or a threonine in position 3, 5 or 6 but the extent of phosphorylation depends on the precise nature and location of the hydroxyamino acids. Our data suggest that the phosphopeptide derived from pea LHC II (20) was probably phosphorylated mainly on thr-5 (Fig. 1). On the other hand, the synthetic peptide data support our finding that the four spinach peptides can be phosphorylated on ser-3 or thr-3: these residues are phosphorylated when there is no thr-5. Our sequence data for spinach LHC II shows clearly that in none of the four peptides was there a ser or thr at residue 4,5 or 6.

The significance of these results lies in the fact that the spinach sequences are much more typical of the large number of LHC II sequences deduced from clones than is the pea sequence. With the exception of one tomato cab gene (23), all sequenced cab genes encode ser or thr at residue 3, whereas only a minority of cloned cab genes encode thr at position 5 or 6. We conclude that almost all known cab genes encode phosphorylatable LHC II molecules.

We have now synthesized a larger set of peptide analogues which are based on the spinach sequence data but contain only one hydroxyamino acid to simplify the analysis. A key point to emerge from this study was that the basic residues on either side of the phosphorylation site are important for the kinetics of the kinase reaction. (Table I). When the lysyl residue on the C-terminal side of the phosphorylated threonine or the arginyl and lysyl residues on the N-terminal side are replaced by alanine, there is an increase in Km (decreased affinity between enzyme and substrate) and a decrease in Vmax. The conserved N-acetylarginine is clearly important for binding between enzyme and substrate but the acetyl group itself does not appear to contribute significantly. Mammalian protein kinase C is another protein kinase which requires basic residues on both sides of

TABLE 1. Kinetic constants for the phosphorylation of synthetic peptide analogues of the N-terminus of spinach LHC II by isolated spinach thylakoids.

Peptide	Km (uM)	Vmax (nmole/mg Chl/h)
Acetyl-R-K-T-A-A-K-P-A	0.32	43
Acetyl-R-K-T-A-A-A-P-A	0.91	26
Acetyl-A-K-T-A-A-K-P-A	1.51	32
Acetyl-A-A-T-A-A-K-P-A	> 3	< 5
Amino-R-K-T-A-A-K-P-A	0.31	47

the residues on both sides of the hydroxyamino acids (24). Protein kinase C also resembles the LHC II kinase in being membrane-bound and regulated in part by lipoidal molecules (phospholipid and plastoquinone, respectively) (25).

2.3.   Site-Directed Mutagenesis around the Cleavage and Phosphorylation Sites of LHC II.
The above data suggest that the invariant N-terminal arginyl residue of higher plant LHC II is required for its contribution to the protein kinase recognition site. But is it also required for recognition by the protease which cleaves between that residue and the adjacent methionyl residue? We have conducted site-directed mutagenesis of several residues in and around the cleavage site. While replacement of the conserved methionine by valine forces the protease to cleave at an as yet unidentified site slightly downstream, replacement of the conserved arginine by either histidine or leucine has no discernible effect on processing. We conclude that the arginyl residue is conserved more for its role in kinase recognition than for its role in protease recognition.

ACKNOWLEDGMENTS
This work was performed under the auspices of the US Department of Energy, Division of Biological Energy Research (Office of Basic Energy Sciences), with additional support from the Competitive Grants Program of the US Department of Agriculture.

REFERENCES

1 Bennett, J. (1977) Nature 269, 344-346.
2 Foyer, C. H. (1985) Biochem. J. 231, 97-103.
3 Guiton, C. and Mache, R. (1987) Eur. J. Biochem. 166, 249-254.
4 Guitton, C., Dorne, A.M. and Mache, R. (1984) Biochem. Biophys. Res. Commun. 121, 297-303.
5 Soll, J. (1988) Plant Physiol. 87, 898-903.
6 Soll, J. and Bennett, J. (1988) Eur. J. Biochem. 175, 301-308.
7 Michel, H.P. and Bennett, J. (1987) FEBS Lett. 212, 103-108.
8 Michel, H.P., Hunt, D.F., Shabanowitz, J. and Bennett, J. (1988) J. Biol. Chem. 263, 1123-1130.
9 Bennett, J. (1984) Physiol. Plant. 60, 583-590.
10 Millner, P.A., Widger, W.R., Abbott, M.S., Cramer, W.A. and Dilley, R.A. (1982) J. Biol. Chem. 257, 1736-1742.
11 Farchaus, J., Dilley, R.A. and Cramer, W.A. (1985) Biochim. Biophys. Acta 809, 17-26.
12 Bennett, J., Shaw, E.K. and Bakr, S. (1987) FEBS Lett. 210, 22-26.
13 Bennett, J., Shaw, E.K. and Michel, H.P. (1988) Eur. J. Biochem. 171, 95-100.
14 Gal, A., Shahak, Y., Schuster, G. and Ohad, I. (1987) FEBS Lett. 221, 205-210.
15 Wollman, F.-A. and Lemaire, C. (1988) Biochim. Biophys. Acta 933, 85-94.
16 Gal, A., Schuster, G., Frid, D., Canaani, O., Schweiger, H.-G. and Ohad, I. (1988) J. Biol. Chem. 263, 7785-7791.
17 Coughlan, S. J. (1988) Biochim. Biophys. Acta 933, 413-422.
18 Chitnis, P.R. and Thornber, J.P. (1988) Photosynth. Res. 16, 41-63.
19 Keegstra, K., Olsen, L.J. and Theg, S.M. (1989) Annu. Rev. Plant Physiol. Plant Mol. Biol. 40, 471-501.
20 Mullet, J.E. (1983) J. Biol. Chem. 258, 9941-9948.
21 Cashmore, A.R. (1984) Proc. Natl. Acad. Sci. USA. 81, 2960-2964.
22 Michel, H.P. and Bennett, J. (1989) FEBS Lett. (in press).
23 Pichersky, E., Bernatsky, R., Tanksley, S.D., Breidenbach, R.B., Kausch, A.P. and Cashmore, A.R.(1985) Gene 40, 247-258.
24 House, C., Wettenhall, R.E.H. and Kemp, B.E. (1987) J. Biol. Chem. 262, 772-777.
25 Edelman, A.M., Blumenthal, D.K. and Krebs, E.G. (1987) Annu. Rev. Biochem. 56, 567-613.

MOLECULAR ORDER AND DYNAMICS IN MEMBRANES CONTAINING α-TOCOPHEROL, (trans 16:3)-PHOSPHATIDYL-GLYCEROL AND OTHER THYLAKOID LIPIDS

G. VAN GINKEL, L.J. KORSTANJE, R. MOORMANS, G. PRUIJSEN, M. VAN ZANDVOORT, A.A. VAN 'T VELD, Y.K. LEVINE
Department of Molecular Biophysics, Buys Ballot Laboratory, University of Utrecht, Princetonplein 5, Utrecht 3584 CC, The Netherlands.

INTRODUCTION

The photosynthetic membranes of higher plant chloroplasts have an unusual lipid composition: 60 - 80 % galactolipids (MGDG, DGDG), approx. 10 % sulfolipid (SQDG), approx. 10 % (trans 16:3) phosphatidyl-glycerol (PG), 5 - 10 % phosphatidylcholines (PC) and hardly or no sterols. The majority of the lipids is highly unsaturated (1). According to current ideas these lipids play a vital role as structural lipids for stabilising the structure of the thylakoid membrane (1). Besides these structural lipids, other lipid components are present in fairly high amounts. Among these components β-carotene and α-tocopherol may play an important role in protecting the unsaturated thylakoid lipids against free radicals, which are generated during photosynthesis (2,3). The special features of these lipids must be reflected in their molecular organisation (order) and their dynamics upon their inter-action in membranes.

We therefore have investigated the molecular order and dynamics of model membranes consisting of different thylakoid lipids. β-Carotene and α-tocopherol both absorb light while α-tocopherol is also fluores-cent. These properties are particular suitable for studies of their interactions with membrane lipids using polarized light. In this way both compounds act as probe molecules reporting on their interaction with their environment.

Spin probes (like cholestane) and conventional fluorescent probes, like diphenylhexatriene (DPH) and analogs, can be also used to investigate the molecular order and dynamics of (model)membranes.

EXPERIMENTAL APPROACH

1. Measurements of angle-resolved fluorescence depolarization (AFD) of fluorescent compounds embedded in macroscopically oriented lipid bilayers, see ref. 4 and fig.1, yield information about
   a) the molecular order (order parameters), for example:
   $$<P_2> = 1/2 \ (3\cos^2\beta - 1)$$
   $$<P_4> = 1/8 \ (35\cos^4\beta - 30\cos^2\beta + 3)$$
   β = the angle between the molecular symmetry axis and the bilayer normal,

b) and about their rate of reorientational motion in the membrane (rotational diffusion constant $D_\perp$ or rotational correlation time τ_c).
Photophysical information about the orientation of absorption and transition moments in the molecular frame can also be extracted from the results.

2. Angle-resolved depolarized Resonance Raman scattering measured by excitation of pigments within their absorption bands also yield the order parameters $\langle P_2 \rangle$ and $\langle P_4 \rangle$ of the pigments in the membranes (5).

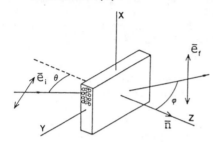

FIGURE 1. Experimental geometry of an angle-resolved fluorescence depolarization experiment. Excitation is horizontally polarized and incident on the sample at an angle θ. Emission is measured at an angle φ to the membrane director. $\bar{e}_i$ and $\bar{e}_f$ define the polarization directions of the light.

3. Analysis of time-resolved fluorescence anisotropy measurements yields information about the molecular order, the reorientational dynamics and the photophysical properties of the fluorescent molecules in membranes (4).

4. ESR spectra of the rigid spin probe cholestane embedded in model membranes yield information about the molecular order (order parameters $\langle P_2 \rangle$ and $\langle P_4 \rangle$ and about the rate of motion of the probe molecules in the membranes (rotational diffusion constants $D_\parallel$ and $D_\perp$). For a correct analysis of the ESR lineshapes in the slow motion regime ($10^{-9} < \tau_r < 10^{-7}$s), however, the spectra have to be described in terms of the stochastic Liouville Equation (SLE) formalism.
The motional narrowing assumption seriously overestimates the molecular order and dynamics (6).

RESULTS
ESR and AFD measurements show that α-tocopherol does not affect the molecular order of diphenylhexatriene (DPH) or trimethylammonium-DPH (TMA-DPH) in dioleoylphosphatidylcholine (DOPC) bilayers to a measurable extent, see table 1. However the molecular dynamics is affected in a concentration-dependent way. AFD measurements also indicate (data not shown) that α-tocopherol itself does not reorientate within the time-window of its fluorescence decay (about 1.5 - 2 ns) at lipid:tocopherol ratio's of (100:1) and (50:1). The chromophore of α-tocopherol is biaxial and is oriented preferentially with its plane perpendicular to the DOPC-bilayerplane, see figure 2.

Angle-resolved Raman spectra of β-carotene (using the vibrational enhanced peaks at 1158 cm^{-1}) in planar membranes of soybean lecithin and digalacatosyldiglyceride (DGDG) yield the following order parameters:

soybean lecithin : <P2> - 0.49   <P4> - 0.47
DGDG   : <P2> - 0.12   <P4> - 0.10

The orientational distribution functions reconstructed from these values (figure 3) show that β-carotene in soybean lecithin membranes orients preferentially parallel to the lipid chains (β - 0°), whereas in DGDG membranes a fraction of the β-carotene molecules also orients parallel to the bilayer plane(β - 90°).

TABLE 1

Molecular order and dynamics of tocopherol, DPH and TMA-DPH in planar bilayers of DOPC measured at 25 °C with AFD. The ESR measurements on liposomes of DOPC were done at 35 °C.

	<P2>	<P4>	τ_c (ns)	$D_\perp$(ns^{-1})
DOPC-α-toc(50:1)	-0.30	0.08		
DOPC-α-toc(100:1)	-0.31	0.09		
DOPC-α-toc(50:1)-DPH	0.31	0.31	4.4	
DOPC-α-toc(100:1)-DPH	0.29	0.29	3.5	
DOPC-DPH(250:1)	0.30	0.31	5.3	
DOPC-α-toc(50:1)-TMA-DPH	0.40	0.11	9.2	
DOPC-α-toc(100:1)-TMA-DPH	0.51	0.23	6.4	
DOPC-α-toc(250:1)-TMA-DPH	0.51	0.23	4.4	
DOPC-TMA-DPH(250:1)	0.54	0.21	5.9	
DOPC-cholestane(100:1)	0.50	0.25		0.10
DOPC-α-toc(5:1)-cholestane	0.50	0.25		0.08
DOPC-β-toc(5:1)-cholestane	0.50	0.25		0.06

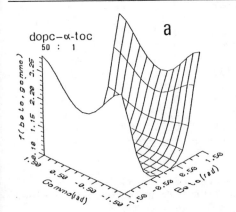

dopc–α-toc
50 : 1

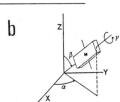

FIGURE 2a Orientational distribution function of the chromophore of α-tocopherol in planar membranes of DOPC at 25°C (DOPC:α-toc - 50:1) reconstructed from AFD measurements. FIGURE 2b Definition of the Euler angles α, β and γ.

Analysis of FA, ESR and AFD measurements, see table 2, shows that:
- (16:3 trans) PG does not measurable affect the molecular order, but decreases the rate of reorientational motions
- increasing unsaturation decreases the order parameter <P2>, does not affect the order parameter <P4> and increases the rate of reorientational motions in lipid vesicles
- stigmasterol increases the molecular order in DOPC and in DGDG bilayers, but its effects on the rate of reorientational motions depend on the lipid and the type of probe molecule used.

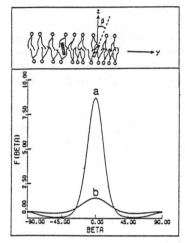

FIGURE 3. Orientation distribution function of β-carotene in planar membranes of soybean lecithin (a) and DGDG (b). The lipid to water ratio was 70:30 (wt/wt). Temperature 18 °C.

TABLE 2

Molecular order and dynamics in thylakoid lipids obtained form measurement of time-resolved fluorescence anisotropy (FA) of TMA-DPH in lipid vesicles, ESR spectra of cholestane in liposomes and AFD of DPH in planar oriented membranes.

Lipid	$\langle P2 \rangle$	$\langle P4 \rangle$	$D_\perp (ns^{-1})$	°C	Source
POPC	0.54	0.44	0.09	21	FA
DOPC	0.42	0.45	0.16	21	FA
DLPC	0.39	0.47	0.27	21	FA
DGDG	0.43	0.52	0.17	21	FA
SQDG	0.51	0.48	0.15	21	FA
POPC + (16:3 trans) PG	0.55	0.39	0.07	21	FA
DLPC + (16:3 trans) PG	0.39	0.45	0.16	21	FA
DOPC	0.50	0.25	0.10	35	ESR
DOPC + stigmasterol (5:1)	0.58	0.32	0.06	35	ESR
DGDG	0.30	0.12	0.07	35	ESR
DGDG + stigmasterol (5:1)	0.34	0.14	0.07	35	ESR
DGDG	0.43	0.21	0.006	21	AFD
DGDG + stigmasterol (5:1)	0.50	0.24	0.24	21	AFD

REFERENCES
1. Murphy, D.J. (1986) Biochim Biophys Acta, 864, 33-94
2. Halliwall, B. and Gutteridge, J.M.C. (1985) Free radicals in biology and medicine, Clarendon Press, Oxford
3. Biochemistry of chloroplasts part I and II (1966,1967) (Goodwin, T.W. ed) Academic Press, New York
4. Van Ginkel, G, van Langen, H. and Levine, Y.K. (1989) Biochimie 41, 23-32
5. Van de Ven, M., Kattenberg, M., van Ginkel, G. and Levine, Y.K. (1984), Biophys. J., 45, 1203-1210
6. Korstanje, L.J., van Faassen, E.E. and Levine, Y.K. (1989) Biochim. Biophys. Acta, 980, 225-233

EFFECTS OF BICARBONATE ON THYLAKOID PHOSPHORYLATION AND ON PHOTOINHIBITION

CECILIA SUNDBY, ULLA K. LARSSON AND TOMAS HENRYSSON, DEPARTMENT OF BIOCHEMISTRY, UNIVERSITY OF LUND, P.O. Box 124, S-221 00 LUND, SWEDEN

1. INTRODUCTION

We here report on the discovery /1/ of two new effects of bicarbonate on PS2, namely (i) that $NaHCO_3$ increases the phosphorylation of LHC2 but decreases that of the 9 kDa protein; phosphorylation of the latter can even be stimulated by $NaHCO_3$ depletion, and (ii) that in the presence of $NaHCO_3$ there is no photoinhibition upon illumination.

2. PROCEDURE

Preparation of spinach chloroplasts, or isolated thylakoid membranes, their phosphorylation with 200 $\mu E/m^2 xs$ red light in presence or absence of 20 mM $NaHCO_3$ and subsequent analysis of the (^{32}P)-incorporation into the thylakoid polypeptides is described in /1/, as is the bicarbonate depletion treatment with 20 mM sodium formate at pH 5.8. PS2 activities of thylakoid membranes were determined as the PpBQ-dependent oxygen evolution in saturating red light.

3. RESULTS AND DISCUSSION

3.1 Bicarbonate effects on phosphorylation of LHC2.

The presence of added $NaHCO_3$ gives a positive effect on the phosphorylation of the 25 kDa, but not the 27 kDa, apopolypeptide of LHC2. In the case of phosphorylation of thylakoid membranes (Table 1), the $NaHCO_3$ increased phosphorylation of the 25 kDa polypeptide with 44% compared with 4% for the 27 kDa polypeptide. The same pattern was seen when phosphorylation was induced using intact chloroplasts (Table 2).

TABLE 1 Effect of bicarbonate on light induced phosphorylation of isolated thylakoid membranes.

	Total incorp. of (^{32}P)phosphate (cpm)		
	25 kDa	27 kDa	9 kDa
Cl II control	21 903	49 681	15 259
Cl II $NaHCO_3$	31 620	51 934	13 674
Effect of $NaHCO_3$	+44%	+4%	-10%

M. Baltscheffsky (ed.), Current Research in Photosynthesis, Vol. II, 759–762.

TABLE 2 Effect of bicarbonate on light induced phosphorylation of intact chloroplasts.

Light intensity		Total incorp. of (^{32}P)phosphate (cpm)		
		25 kDa	27 kDa	9 kDa
200 uE/m^{2}xs	Cl I control	12 276	16 791	6 373
	Cl I NaHCO$_3$	17 239	16 881	4 808
	Effect of NaHCO$_3$	+40%	0%	-24%
1000 uE/m^{2}xs	Cl I control	13 281	17 058	7 852
	Cl I NaHCO$_3$	18 008	17 007	5 866
	Effect of NaHCO$_3$	+36%	0%	-25%
4000 uE/m^{2}xs	Cl I control	12 008	15 548	6 870
	Cl I NaHCO$_3$	15 400	17 194	5 578
	Effect of NaHCO$_3$	+28%	+12%	-19%
15000 uE/m^{2}xs	Cl I control	12 488	15 142	8 266
	Cl I NaHCO$_3$	16 326	17 548	6 197
	Effect of NaHCO$_3$	+31%	+16%	-25%

In this case the bicarbonate stimulation of the phosphorylation of the
25 kDa protein was 40% when illuminated with 200 uE/m2s. Note that
neither phosphorylation nor its bicarbonate stimulation can be increased by using light intensities higher than this. Again phosphorylation
of the 27 kDa polypeptide was not affected by the presence of NaHCO$_3$
during illumination, at least not at lower light intensities. At higher light intensities a small stimulation was seen, but this was rather due to a decrease in the (^{32}P)phosphate incorporation in control
chloroplasts than to a positive effect by NaHCO$_3$.
    Thus, although both the 27 and 25 kDa LHC2 polypeptides become
phosphorylated it is only the phosphorylation of the 25 kDa polypeptide that is bicarbonate stimulated. An important conclusion is therefore that it is only the phosphorylation of the 25 kDa containing pool
peripheral pool of LHC2 that is under the regulation of bicarbonate,
and not the tightly bound pool of LHC2 from which the 25 kDa polypeptide is absent /2,3/. That the phosphorylation of the 27 kDa polypeptide of LHC2 is not affected by bicarbonate may also hint that the
phosphorylation of the 27 kDa polypeptide may serve another purpose
than phoshorylation of the 25 kDa containing variable part of LHC2.

3.2. Bicarbonate effects on phosphorylation of the 9 kDa protein.
    The effect of bicarbonate on the phosphorylation of the 9 kDa PS2
phosphoprotein is quite opposite to that of the 25 kDa LHC2 polypeptide. Upon phosphorylation of thylakoid membranes (Table 1), the phoshorylation of the 9 kDa protein was rather hampered by the supply of

TABLE 3   Effect of bicarbonate depletion by sodium formate on light induced phosphorylation of isolated thylakoid membranes.

	Total incorp. of (^{32}P)phosphate (cpm)	
	25 kDa	27 kDa 9 kDa
Cl II control	1 299	1 778 231
Cl II formate	1 469	1 765 364
Effect of formate	+13%	-7% +58%

extra NaHCO$_3$ (-10%). Also upon phosphorylation of intact chloroplasts (Table 2), addition of NaHCO$_3$ had a negative influence on the phosphorylation of the 9 kDa protein (around -25%).

The classical bicarbonate effect /4/ is a stimulation of electron flow by bicarbonate seen upon prior depletion of bicarbonate by formate. In order to optimize the bicarbonate effect that we saw on thylakoid phosphorylation, we incubated the thylakoid membranes with sodium formate at low pH to obtain bicarbonate depletion. After depletion treatment (withdrawn samples were stimulated 2-3 fold by the addition of 2 mM NaHCO$_3$ to the assay medium, whereas control thylakoids were not) the thylakoids were phosphorylated in the absence or presence of NaHCO$_3$. We then found that the negative influence of bicarbonate on the phosphorylation of the 9 kD polypeptide was seen even clearer with this approach. While previous data (Table 1 and 2) already indicated a negative influence of added NaHCO$_3$ phosphorylation was increased with 58% compared to the control (Table 3) by the formate treatment that removed endogenous bicarbonate. Readdition of NaHCO$_3$ to the depleted thylakoid membranes again showed a negative effect on the phosphorylation of the 9 kDa polypeptide (data not shown). The phosphorylation of the two LHC2 polypeptides was not much affected by the NaHCO$_3$ depletion. Thus, we have an increased phosphorylation of the 9 kDa protein without a concomitant decrease in LHC2 phosphorylation, as is the case when the 9 kDa protein is much phosphorylated in mutants lacking LHC2, at early developmental stages when LHC2 is not yet present or by the use of reagents that preferentially inhibit phosphorylation of LHC2.

3.3. Bicarbonate prevents photoinhibition.

An other unexpected but highly interesting observation is that NaHCO$_3$ protects against photoinhibition. This we happened to observe as data were collected to see whether there was any change in PS2 activity resulting from the increased phosphorylation of the 9 kDa protein (which there was not). To distinguish an effect of phosphorylation from direct effects of formate/bicarbonate on the PS2 activity, the different samples, all supplied with NaF to prevent dephosphorylation, were spun down and resuspended in an assay medium containing neither formate nor bicarbonate. From these data it is obvious that the 10 min illumination used to induce phoshorylation causes a decrease in PS2 activity with 65% for the thylakoid membranes that are illuminated in absence of any electron acceptor (Table 4, compare phosphorylated samples with nonphosphorylated). However, such a photoinhibi-

TABLE 4 Effects of light induced phosphorylation on the PS2 dependent electron flow of intact chloroplasts and isolated thylakoid membranes.

| | PS2 activity (umol O_2/mg chl x h) | |
	Nonphosphorylated	Phosphorylated
Cl I control	266	270
Cl I NaHCO$_3$	275	273
Cl II control	102	68
Cl II NaHCO$_3$	114	112
Cl II formate	118	76
Cl II formate/NaHCO$_3$	114	119

tion is fully prevented in the samples to which NaHCO$_3$ was added before the illumination. This holds for both the control thylakoids and the formate treated thylakoids. The bicarbonate protection against photoinhibition is a noteworth and new finding and the phenomenon is presently under more detailed investigation.

4. CONCLUDING REMARKS

Two types of bicarbonate binding sites on the thylakoid membrane have previously been described, a high affinity site in close proximity to the Q_B-binding site and a low affinity site of unknown location /5/. Phosphorylation of LHC2 is mainly affected when the bicarbonate level is raised from endogenous level up to 20 mM and should be correlated rather with a low affinity type of site. The site could even be localized on the 25,but not the 27, kDa polypeptide.Since the phosphorylation of the 9 kDa protein is affected pronouncedly by the bicarbonate depletion treatment, its phosphorylation may be connected to a high-affinity site. Very recent suggestions are that bicarbonate is liganded to the non-heme iron between Q_A and Q_B /6,7/ or bound in a second high-affinity site to an arginine residue in the D_1-protein /8/. The effects on 9 kDa phosphorylation could mean that a high-affinity binding site also is on the 9 kDa protein. Interestingly, close to the threonine residue that becomes phosphorylated in the 9 kDa there is a sequence of basic aminoacids, Arg-Pro-Arg-Pro-Lys-Arg-, that could form a HCO$_3$- binding pocket. Removal of bicarbonate anions from this pocket might stimulate phosphorylation simply by increasing the attraction of anionic phosphate ions.

REFERENCES
1 Sundby C,Larsson UK and Henrysson T (1989) BBA 975, 277-282
2 Larsson UK, Sundby C and Andersson B (1987) BBA 894, 59-68
3 Spangfort M, Larsson UK, Anderson JM and Andersson B (1987) FEBS Lett 224, 343-347
4 Van Rensen JJS and Snel JFH (1985) Photosynthesis Res 6, 231-246
5 Stemler A (1977) BBA 460, 511-522
6 Michel H and Deisenhofer J (1988) Biochemistry 27, 1-7
7 Van Rensen JJS,Tonk WJM and deBruijn SM(1988)FEBS Lett 226,347-351
8 Blubaugh DJ and Govindjee (1988) Photosynth Res 19, 85-128

INORGANIC PYROPHOSPHATE (PPi) DEPENDENT LHCII AND PSII PROTEIN PHOSPHORYLATION

ALAUDDIN PRAMANIK, SOPHIE BINGSMARK, HERRICK BALTSCHEFFSKY, MARGARETA BALTSCHEFFSKY AND BERTIL ANDERSSON

DEPT. OF BIOCHEMISTRY, ARRHENIUS LABORATORIES, UNIVERSITY OF STOCKHOLM, S-106 91 STOCKHOLM, SWEDEN

1. INTRODUCTION

LHCII and several PSII thylakoid proteins are phosphorylated by an ATP dependent protein kinase (1,2), which is under control of the redox state of the PQ pool (3). This protein phosphorylation leads to rearrangements in the lateral organization of the thylakoid membrane (4). As a consequence, it is postulated that LHCII protein phosphorylation regulates excitation energy distribution between PSI and PSII (5); protects PSII against photoinhibition as well as regulates protein turnover (for a review, see ref. 6).

In general, ATP is used as phosphate donor in phosphorylation reactions of thylakoid proteins. This report for the first time will demonstrate that also inorganic pyrophosphate (PPi) can be used as phosphate donor for thylakoid protein phosphorylation.

2. MATERIALS AND METHODS

Protein phosphorylation was carried out by a standard method as described in (7) with the exception that $(^{32}P)PPi$ was used as phosphate donor instead of $(\gamma\text{-}^{32}P)ATP$. Isolated thylakoids were phosphorylated by illumination (500 $\mu E \cdot m^{-2} \cdot s^{-1}$) in the presence of 0.4 mM $(^{32}P)PPi$ (300 000 cpm/nmol PPi). Phosphorylation was terminated by adding 10% cold TCA. Thylakoids were washed, solubilized in SDS at 70°C, and fractionated by SDS-PAGE using a 12-22.5% acrylamide gradient (8). The thylakoid proteins were detected by staining the gel with Coomassie brilliant blue and radioactivity was located by autoradiography.

M. Baltscheffsky (ed.), Current Research in Photosynthesis, Vol. II, 763–766.
© 1990 *Kluwer Academic Publishers. Printed in the Netherlands.*

3. RESULTS

LHCII and several PSII proteins become phosphorylated with ATP as phosphate donor (1,2). Here we confirm our preliminary indications that also PPi can be used as phosphate donor for the LHCII and PSII protein phosphorylation (9). If thylakoids are illuminated in the presence of radioactive PPi ((^{32}P)PPi) instead of (γ-^{32}P)ATP, LHCII and PSII proteins are found to be labelled (Fig. 1). If thylakoids are illuminated for 1 or 2 min, only the 25 kDa polypeptide of LHCII is phosphorylated (Fig. 1, lanes B, C). When time for light incubation is increased, both the 25 kDa and the 27 kDa polypeptides of LHCII are phosphorylated, in addition to some PSII polypeptides (Fig. 1, lanes D, E).

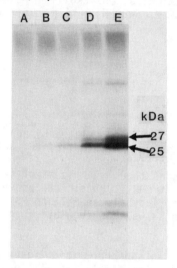

Fig. 1. Labelling of LHCII and PSII proteins with radioactive PPi ((^{32}P)PPi) in light. Experimental conditions were the same as reported in Methods. A - 10 min incubation in dark. B, C, D and E - 1, 2, 5 and 10 min incubation in light respectively.

As shown in Fig. 2 (lanes B, D) DCMU (3-(3',4'-dichlorophenyl)-1,1-dimethylauria) and PρBQ (phenyl-p-benzoquinone) completely abolish PPi dependent protein phosphorylation. Inhibition by the PSII inhibitor DCMU confirms that this phosphorylation is electron transport dependent. Inhibition by PρBQ is consistent with its role as an artificial electron acceptor, leaving the plastoquinone in an oxidized state. This indicates that PQ has to be reduced for the activation of the PPi dependent protein kinase, as is known to be the case with ATP.

As PPi dependent protein phosphorylation is light induced and electron transport dependent, and ATP dependent kinases exist in thylakoids (1,2), it is obligatory to check the possibility that Pi might be produced from hydrolyzed PPi and coupled to endogenous ADP to synthesize ATP by photophosphorylation in remaining intact chloroplasts. However, venturicidin, DCCD (N,N-dicyclohexylcarbodiimide) and Dio-9, which all inhibit ATP synthesis in thylakoids (10), do not affect the PPi dependent protein phosphorylation (Fig. 3, lanes C-E).

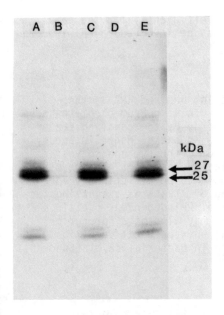

Fig. 2. Effects of DCMU, PρPQ, NH₄Cl and added ATP on PPi dependent light induced thylakoid protein phosphorylation. Experimental conditions were the same as in Methods. Thylakoids were illuminated for 10 min. A - no additions; B - 10 μM DCMU; C - 1 mM NH₄Cl; D - 400 μM PρBQ and E - 0.4 mM added ATP.

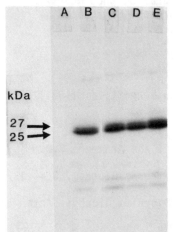

Fig. 3. Effects of inhibitors of ATP synthase on PPi dependent protein phosphorylation. Experimental conditions were the same as in Methods. A - 10 min incubation in dark. B, C, D and E - 10 min incubation in light; B - no additions; C - venturicidin (1 μg/ml); D - 100 μM DCCD; and E - Dio-9 (25 μg/ml).

Thus, no ATP is produced in our reaction conditions, and consequently photophosphorylation of any endogenous ADP is not involved in the PPi dependent protein phosphorylation. In addition, the existence of PPi dependent protein phosphorylation in the dark with reductants such as dithionite and ferredoxin/NADPH (not shown) clearly excludes any significant contribution of photophosphorylation. PMS (phenazine methosulfate) which strongly stimulates photophosphorylation decreases PPi dependent protein phosphorylation (not shown). Also NH₄Cl, which inhibits photophosphorylation, does not affect PPi induced protein phosphorylation (Fig. 2, lane C). Finally, added cold ATP in equivalent concentration does no inhibit the radioactive labelling of proteins by PPi (Fig. 2, lane E). This lack of inhibition by added ATP suggests that PPi and ATP do not compete efficiently for the same active site and that a specific kinase may be involved in PPi induced protein phosphorylation.

DISCUSSION

PPi is produced as a by-product in protein, DNA and RNA synthesis, and several other biosynthetic reactions. In R. rubrum chromatophores PPi is formed at the expense of light energy by the coupling factor PPase (inorganic pyrophosphatase). PPi is an energy donor in energy requiring reactions in chromatophores from R. rubrum and serves as phosphate and energy sources in fermentation reactions of some other bacteria. PPi and PPase have been proposed to be evolutionary "precursors" of ATP as an energy carrier and of ATPase as a coupling factor respectively (11). Possibly, the novel PPi dependent protein kinase, found by us in spinach thylakoids, may also be a "precursor" for ATP dependent kinases. Under special environmental conditions, for example under energy stress, as when in bacterial chromatophores, PPi may substitute for ATP (12).

ACKNOWLEDGEMENTS

This study was supported by the Swedish Natural Science Research Council, the Swedish Institute and Wenner-Grenska Samfundet.

REFERENCES

1   Bennett, J. (1977) Nature 269, 344-346
2   Bennett, J. (1979) FEBS Lett. 103, 342-344
3   Horton, P., Allen, J.F., Black, M.T. and Bennett, J. (1981) FEBS Lett. 125, 193-196
4   Andersson, B., Åkerlund, H.-E., Jergil, B. and Larsson, C. (1982) FEBS Lett. 149, 181-185
5   Allen, J.F., Bennett, J., Steinback, K.E. and Arntzen, C.J. (1981) Nature 291, 25-29
6   Anderson, J.M. and Andersson, B. (1988) Trends Biochem. Sci. 13, 351-355
7   Larsson, U.K. and Andersson, B. (1985) Biochim. Biophys. Acta 809, 396-402
8   Laemmli, U.K. (1970) Nature 227, 680-685
9   Pramanik, A., Bingsmark, S., Baltscheffsky, H., Baltscheffsky, M. and Andersson, B. (1988) Physiol. Plant 73 (2): A6
10 Baltscheffsky, M., Nyrén, P., Strid, Å. and Pramanik, A. (1988) Biochem. Biophys. Res. Commun. 151, 878-882
11 Baltscheffsky, H. (1971) in Chemical Evolution and the Origin of Life (Buvet, R. and Ponnamperuma, C., eds.) pp. 466-474, Amsterdam, London, North Holland Publ. Co.
12 Nyrén, P., Nore, B.F. and Baltscheffsky, M. (1986) Biochim. Biophys. Acta 851, 276-282

INVESTIGATION OF THYLAKOID PROTEIN KINASE SUBSTRATE SPECIFICITY
USING SYNTHETIC PEPTIDES.

Ian R. White, Paul A. Millner and John B.C. Findlay.
Department of Biochemistry, University of Leeds, Leeds, West Yorkshire,
LS2 9JT, U.K.

1. INTRODUCTION
    Illumination of thylakoid membranes in the presence of Mg^{2+} and
[^{32}P]- γATP results in the incorporation of [^{32}P] orthophosphate into
a distinct subset of thylakoid membrane polypeptides. Under these
conditions the greatest labelling is observed in the light harvesting
chlorophyll a/b binding polypeptides of PSII (LHCII), although other
PSII polypeptides of molecular mass 8 kDa, 32-35 kDa and 40-43 kDa
are also phosphorylated. The reversible phosphorylation of LHCII
is known to underpin the physiological mechanism responsible for
controlling light energy input into the two photosystems [1], via
lateral migration of phospho LHCII away from PSII in the appressed
thylakoid membranes with a subsequent decrease in PSII light harvesting
capacity. The kinase activity(s) responsible for catalysing thylakoid
protein phosphorylation is known to be regulated by the redox state
of the plastoquinone pool [2,3] and most likely interacts with a
subunit of the cytochrome b_6f complex [4].
    To date, three candidate thylakoid protein kinases have been
isolated, of 23 kDa and 38 kDa [5,6] and of 64 kDa [7]. Of these
only the 64 kDa protein was able to phosphorylate exogenous LHCII.
In addition the ability of anti 64 kDa kinase IgG to specifically
inhibit LHCII phosphorylation strongly implies that the 64 kDa kinase
is the physiological kinase.
    With the intention of characterising more stringently the LHCII
kinase we have synthesized peptides corresponding to the N-terminal
region of LHCII which contain the Thr residues ($T_{6,7}$) that are
phosphorylated in vivo. Additionally, analogues of the LHCII
phosphorylation sequence have been synthesized for which single
amino acid changes, N-terminal to the phosphorylated Thr residues
have been made.
    In this communication we present data demonstrating the
relationship between synthetic peptide charge and efficiency as
thylakoid protein kinase substrates.

2. MATERIALS AND METHODS
    2.1 Peptides were synthesized using FMOC chemistry on a MilliGen
9050 peptide synthesizer and purified by reverse phase HPLC. All
sequences were verified by solid phase protein sequencing.
    2.2 Thylakoid membranes were isolated from 14 day old Pisum
sativum (var. Feltham First) seedlings and resuspended in Buffer
A consisting of 25 mM Tricine NaOH pH 8.0, 330 mM sorbitol and 1mMMgCl$_2$.
    2.3 Phosphorylation assays (0.2 mg chlorophyll/ml) were carried
out at 25°C for 10 min in the presence or absence of synthetic
peptides, in buffer A plus 10 mM NaF and 200 µM ATP (0.1 µCi [^{32}P]-
ATP/nmole). Reactions were initiated by addition of sodium dithionite

M. Baltscheffsky (ed.), Current Research in Photosynthesis, Vol. II, 767–770.

to a final concentration of 5mM, or by illumination with white light.
Control incubations were carried out in the presence of 5μM DCMU.
Kinase activity was quenched by the addition of an equal volume
of ice cold 75mM phosphoric acid saturated with EDTA.
    2.4 Protein phosphorylation was examined in two ways.
2.4.1 SDS-PAGE - Aliquots of quenched reaction mix were separated
by electrophoresis on linear 10 to 30% (w/v) polyacrylamide gels
using the buffer system of Laemmli [8]. Gels were then autoradiographed
wet, immediately following electrophoresis to minimise peptide loss,
or dry following staining with Coomassie blue. Protein phosphorylation
was then quantified by linear densitometry.
2.4.2 Filter paper assays. Phosphorylated membranes were pelleted
by centrifugation at 12000 g for 3 min and aliquots of the peptide
containing supernatant spotted onto 2 cm x 1 cm Whatman P81 paper
strips. After drying at room temperature the strips were washed for
4 x 5 min in 1M phosphoric acid/10% (w/v) trichloroacetic acid and
1 x 5 min in absolute ethanol. The strips were dried again at room
temperature and counted for radioactivity in 2 ml Optiphase Safe
(LKB) liquid scintillation cocktail.

3. RESULTS AND DISCUSSION
    The synthetic peptides used in this study are all based on
the amino acid sequence of pea LHCII deduced by Cashmore [9]. The
sequences listed in Table 1 with substituted or additional residues
underlined, carry differing net charges of +2 (LHCIIa) through to
+5 (LHCIIb).

TABLE 1 Synthetic peptide structures
Peptides were synthesized and characterized as described in section 2.1

Peptide	Sequence	Charge
LHCIIa	MRDSATTKKVAC	+2
LHCIIn	MRNleSATTKKVAC	+3
LHCIIs	MRKSATTKKVAC	+4
LHCIIb	MRKKSATTKKVAC	+5

The effect of incubation of thylakoid membranes with synthetic peptides
in the presence of Mg^{2+}, ATP and reductant over a peptide concentration
range of 10μM to 5 mM is shown in Fig. 1 Fig. 1a is a short exposure
time autoradiograph of LHCII phosphorylation following SDS-PAGE
and Fig. 1b an autoradiograph of the same gel exposed for a longer
period to highlight modification of less phosphorylated polypeptides.
Quantitation of the data in Fig. 1a by densitometry (Fig. 1c) shows
elevation of endogenous LHCII phosphorylation in all cases in response
to an increase in peptide concentration from 10 μM to 100 μM. (Note
that the high level of inhibition of LHCII phosphorylation at low
LHCIIa concentrations is usually much less pronounced. At present
we are unable to explain this inhibition). Above 100 μM, LHCIIn,
LHCIIs and LHCIIb all significantly inhibit LHCII phosphorylation
in a manner dependant on concentration and net positive charge.
In addition to LHCII phosphorylation a number of other peptide related
effects are noticeable (Fig. 1b). Phosphorylation of polypeptides

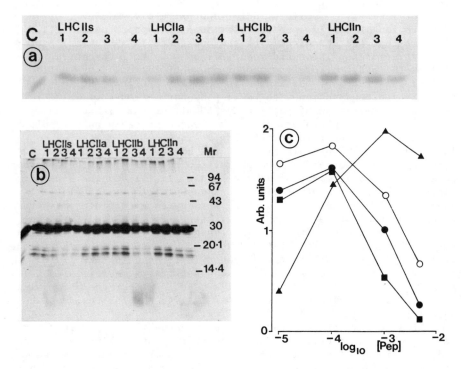

Figure 1   Thylakoid phosphorylation in the presence of synthetic
peptides (see 2.3 and 2.4.1) a) 2h autoradiograph of LHCII region
and b) 48h autoradiograph of the whole gel.   Peptide concentrations
were: 1, 10μM; 2, 100μM; 3, 1mM; and 4, 5mM. c) densitometric analysis
of (a) [LHCIIa;   LHCIIn;   LHCIIs;   LHCIIb].

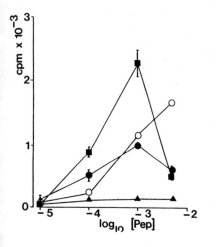

Figure 2.   Peptide phosphorylation.
Quantitation of peptide phosphorylation was carried out as 2.4.2.
Each point represents the mean
and standard error of three
determinations (symbol designation
is the same as for Fig. 1c).

of approximately 17-20 kDa and 58 kDa in molecular weight is inhibited by increasing concentrations of LHCIIn, LHCIIs and LHCIIb whereas increasing concentrations of LHCIIs and LHCIIb apparently stimulate phosphorylation of a polypeptide of approximately 40 kDa. Quantitation of peptide phosphorylation by P81-paper assay (Fig. 2) shows that the charge held by the substrate is a critical factor in substrate recognition and modification. Up to a concentration of 1 mM the order of preference for phosphorylation of synthetic peptide substrates by the kinase is LHCIIa < LHCIIn < LHCIIs < LHCIIb, and taken in conjunction with LHCII phosphorylation data (Fig. 1c) indicated competition of peptide and LHCII for the kinase. Above 1mM, LHCIIs and LHCIIb phosphorylation is reduced probably as a result of non-specific charge related effects.

The requirement of protein kinase C for basic blocks of amino acids flanking both sides of the phosphorylated residue [10], the C-terminal acidic block requirement of casein kinase II [11] and the N-terminal basic block requirement of cAMP dependant protein kinase [11] all show the value of synthetic peptide strategies in defining structural requirements of protein kinase substrates. In this study we have shown the beneficial effect of increasing positive charge N-terminal to the phosphorylatable Thr residues. The presence of basic residues immediately C-terminal to the phosphorylation side of LHCII also suggests possible similarities between substrate specificities of protein kinase C [10] and the LHCII kinase. Further analyses using analogues with residues altered C-terminal to the Thr residues should shed further light on this possibility.

Presently we are proceeding to use the synthetic peptides for cross linking studies, in order to identify protein kinases present, and as affinity ligands in protein kinase purification. The use of peptides that are somewhat longer (20-40 residues) than the short peptides used in this study should allow an assessment of the contribution made by secondary structure to substrate phosphorylation efficiency.

REFERENCES
1. Bennett, J. (1983) Biochem. J. 212, 1-13.
2. Allen, J.F. et al., (1981) Nature, 291, 25-29.
3. Millner, P.A. et al.,)1982) J. Biol. Chem. 257, 1736-1742.
4. Bennett, J. et al., (1988) Eur. J. Biochem. 171, 95-100.
5. Lin, Z.F. et al., (1982) Chem. 257, 12153-12156.
6. Lucero, H.A. et al., (1982) J. Biol. Chem. 257, 12157-12160.
7. Coughlan, S and Hind G. (1987) J. Biol. Chem. 262, 8402-8408.
8. Laemmli, U.K. (1970) Nature 227. 680-685.
9. Cashmore, A.R. (1984) Proc. Natl. Acad. Sci. USA 81, 2960-2964.
10. Woodgett, J.R. et al (1986) Eur. J. Biochem. 161, 177-184.
11. Pinna, L.A. et al (1984) FENS Lett. 210, 22-26.

REGULATION OF PHOTOSYNTHESIS: α- TO β- CONVERSION OF PHOTOSYSTEM *II* AND THYLAKOID PROTEIN PHOSPHORYLATION

MARK TIMMERHAUS & ENGELBERT WEIS,
Botanisches Institut, Univ. Düsseldorf, D-4000 Düsseldorf, FRG

1. INTRODUCTION

In thylakoid membranes of higher plants light is absorbed by three major pigment complexes: 1. the core antenna of photosystem (PS) *II*, mainly located in the *stacked* region; 2. the light-harvesting complex *II* (LHC*II*), mostly forming the complex [PS*II*•LHC*II*]; 3. the core antennae of PS*I*, located in the *non-stacked* region. A certain fraction of low-efficient PS*II* (PS*II_β*) is disconnected from LHC*II* and located in non-stacked membranes. This basic distribution of complexes can be modulated by either enzymatic protein phosphorylation-dephosphorylation [1,2] or by environmental parameters. In the phosphorylated state, LHC*II* is disconnected from PS*II*. This reversible dissociation controls the relative absorption cross section of PS*I* and PS*II* and 'initial' energy distribution (*state 1 - state 2* regulation). However, the relationship between *protein-phosphorylation* and PS*II_α*-PS*II_β heterogeneity* and also its possible effect on *spillover* of energy from PS*II* to PS*I* is not yet fully understood. Functional α- to β-conversion may occur upon protein phosphorylation, but also when the grana structure is physically affected [3, and others]. In this study we take advantage on the fact, that α- to β-conversion is stimulated by mild heating. We demonstrate that protein-phosphorylation stimulates *spillover* of energy from PS*II* centers to PS*I*, perhaps mediated by a *tripartite complex* [PS*II_b*•LHC*II*-*P*•PS*I*]. We discuss its implication for regulation.

2. MATERIALS AND METHODS

Broken spinach chloroplasts were illuminated (7 µE m^{-2}s^{-1}) in presence of 0.3 mM sorbitol, 5 mM MgCl$_2$, 10 mM KCl, +/- (0.4 mM ATP and 10 mM NaF), pH 7.6 at the indicated temperatures. P$_{700}$- photo-oxidation was followed at 20° C as absorbance increase at 820 nm in presence of 20 µM DCMU, 10 µM DBMIB and 100 µM methylviologen. Actinic light: 60 µE m^{-2}s^{-1}, 630-680 nm. Fluorescence induction was measured at 20° C in presence of 20 mM DCMU and 0.1 mM ferricyanide.

3. RESULTS AND DISCUSSION

We exposed isolated thylakoid membranes in weak light to different temperatures under conditions where protein phosphorylation was either activated (addition of ATP plus NaF) or not activated. In the non-phosphorylated state, the (normalized) yield (0<φ<1) of maximal variable fluorescence (when all Q$_A$ is re-

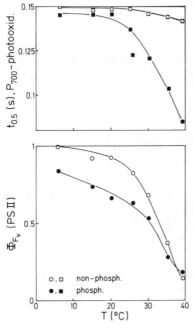

Fig. 1: *Dependence of* $t_{0.5}$ *for* P_{700} *photooxidation and quantum yield for maximal var. PS II-fluorescence,* $\dot{\phi}_{Fv}$ *on the temperature of a 20 min incubation. To activate 'protein phosphorylation' thylakoids were pre-incubated in presence of ATP and NaF.*

duced), $\dot{\phi}_{Fv}$ decreased (Fig.1) while the initial level, F_o was not affected. The decline in $\dot{\phi}_{Fv}$ was accompanied by a decline in the fast, sigmoidal α-phase in the fluorescence induction and an increase in the slow β-phase. This is demonstrated in the semi-logarithmic plots (first-order analysis) of the area over fluorescence induction, revealing the well known biphasic nature of Q_A-photo-reduction in membranes pre-adapted to moderate temperature, and an almost monophasic nature in membranes pre-adapted to elevated temperature. We relate this to a high-temperature-induced conversion of the photochemically efficient and high-fluorescent α-state to the low-efficient and low-fluorescent β-state of PSII [3]. Obviously, at 35°C almost all PSII $_α$were converted to PS$II_β$. As a consequence of this conversion, the net quantum yield for PSII- dependent e⁻-transport was lowered (about 35% after pre-adaptation at 35°C; not shown). We also examined the photochemical yield of PSI by measuring photooxidation of P_{700} (under conditions where the acceptorside of PSI was kept oxidized and re-reduction of P_{700} was blocked). In a first approximation the first-order analysis revealed a monophasic photoconversion of P_{700} (Fig. 2). Since we used non-saturating actinic light the slope of this plot should be proportional to the quantum yield for PSI activity. In Fig. 2, the half-time ($t_{0.5}$) for P_{700}-photooxidation (calculated from semilog. plots) is plotted vs temperature of pre-incubation. We found that in the non-phosphorylated state, temperature-induced α-

to β-conversion of PSII and related decline in $\dot{\phi}_{Fv}$ was accompanied by only minor stimulation of P_{700}- photooxidation (Figs. 1-2; see also Fig. 3). Between 6°to 20°C, protein-phosphorylation caused a moderate decline in $\dot{\phi}_{Fv}$ (Fig. 1). little change in fluorescence-induction (Fig. 2). In that range, we found only minor enhancement of P_{700} photooxidation (≤10%) related to protein-phosphorylation. (Figs. 1-2). This agrees with results by others [4] and it means that under such conditions the mobilized LHC-P may not attach to PSI. At elevated temperature, activation of protein phosphorylation had no effect on the slope of the semilog. analysis of fluorescence induction (Fig. 2, 35°C), however, the intercept with the Y-axis was shifted to lower values and $\dot{\phi}_{Fv}$ declined by about 25%, relative to non-phosphorylated membranes (Fig. 1). Obviously, the fluorescence yield of PS$II_β$ has declined. In this state, however, P_{700} photooxidation was enhanced (50% at 35°C; Figs. 1-2) and the decline in $\dot{\phi}_{Fv}$ was then highly cor- related with PSI-enhancement (Fig. 3). When we used farred actinic light (710-720 nm), which is exclusively absor-

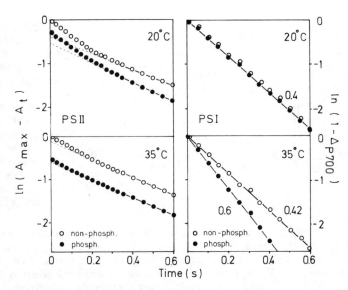

FIG. 2: Semi-logarithmic plots of the area over fluorescence (indicating photoconversion of QA; left) and of photoconversion of P_{700} (calculated from absorbance at 820 nm; right side). Temperature of pre-incubation as indicated. Measurements at 20°C.

bed by 'special' PS*I* pigments, we could not detect any significant enhancement in P_{700}- photooxidation under conditions where more than 50% enhancement was seen with red-actinic light (not shown). It indicates that in the range of conditions used here, the photochemical yield of PS*I* centers itself is not significantly affected.

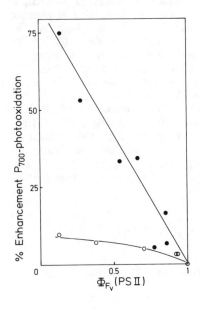

4. CONCLUSIONS

Protein phosphorylation at moderate temperature causes detachment of LHC*II* from PS*II* and LHC*II*-P is then migrating into exposed membranes [3, and others]. However, it may not form a complex with PS*I* (see scheme in Fig 4). Since P_{700}- photooxidation is not or only little stimulated (Fig. 1- 2; see also [4]), formation of the complex [LHC*II*-P•PS*I*] is unlikely to occur. α- to β-conversion of PS*II* also causes disconnection

FIG. 3: Relationship between ϕ_{Fv} and % enhancement in P_{700} photooxidation for the phosphorylated and non-phosphorylated state.(Data obtained from Fig. 1.)

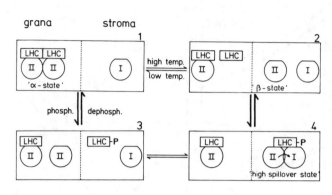

FIG. 4:
Model for distribution and conversion of pigment complexes. Explanations in the text. Any shift from state No. 1 towards states No. 2, 3 and 4, as defined in the model, may represent a "state I - state II' shift in the classical terminology.

between LHC*II* and PS*II*, however, PS*II* is now migrating out of the grana leaving LHC*II* behind (Fig. 4; see [3]). Since no significant stimulation of PS*I* activity was seen in that state (Figs. 1-2), we assume that PS*II*$_\beta$ and PS*I* remain functionally separated. A new state is achieved when α-to β-formation occurs under conditions where protein-phosphorylation is activated. In that case loss in PS*II* fluorescence (caused by α-to β-formation) is accompanied by an enhancement in PS*I* activity (Fig. 4). It is best explained by the assumption that a complex [PS*II*$_\beta$•LHC*II*-P•PS*I*] is formed, similar as already proposed in [5]. For thermodynamic reasons, in this complex excitation energy is spilled over from LHC*II*-P to PS*I* and from closed PS*II*$_\beta$-centers to PS*I*, i.e., basically all energy absorbed by the complex is delivered to PS*I*, at the expense of PS*II*. Here, we take advantage from the fact, that at elevated temperature the concentration of the proposed complex could be high and its effect on PS*I* photochemistry was expected to be large. But the *high spillover state* proposed here could also been formed under moderate physiological conditions. We assume that under physiological conditions the two states '2' and '3' as defined in the scheme (Fig. 4), though often examined in literature, may only be intermediary state. From work with intact leaves, it has been proposed that in the high-spillover state a cyclic reaction around PS*I* is favoured [6]. The role of protein phosphorylation in regulating cyclic e⁻-transport has already been discussed [7]. Dependent on the metabolic control of phosphorylation-dephosphorylation and the physical state of the membrane, an optimal balance between the high-spillover state (supporting a cyclic H⁺-pump) and the state with separated PS*II*$_\alpha$ and PS*I* (supporting linear e⁻-transport) may be established.

REFERENCES
1   Allen JF & Bennett J (1981) FEBS Lett 123, 67-70
2   Horton P & Black MT (1983)
    BIOCHIM BIOPHYS ACTA 722, 214-218
3   Sundby C, Melis A, Mäenpää P & Andersson B. (1986)
    BIOCHIM BIOPHYS ACTA 851, 475-483
4   Haworth P & Melis A (1983) FEBS Lett. 160, 277-280
5   Wendler J & Holzwarth AR (1987) BIOPHYS J 52, 717-728
6   Weis E (1985) BIOCHIM BIOPHYS ACTA 807, 118-126
7   Allen J (1983) TRENDS BIOCHEM SCI 8, 369-373

ON THE PHOSPHORYLATION AND DEPHOSPHORYLATION OF LHC-II AND OF THE PROTEIN KINASE OF SPINACH THYLAKOIDS

GIORGIO FORTI,CESARE RESTA AND ALESSANDRA SANGALLI, Centro CNR Biologia Cellulare e Molecolare delle Piante,Dipartimento di Biologia,Universita di Milano,Via Celoria 26,MILANO,ITALY

1.INTRODUCTION

A thylakoid bound protein kinase,activated when PQH_2 and/or cyt.b563 are extensively reduced, phosphorylates LHC-II and a thylakoid bound phosphatase dephosphorylates it (1,2,3).The phosphorylation-dephosphorylation of LHC-II is considered to be a mechanism for regulating energy distribution between the two photosystems (1,2,3),and to be the biochemical mechanism of the Bonaventura and Myers state 1-state 2 transitions (4).

The thylakoid protein kinase is a 64kDa polypeptide capable of autophosphorylation on a serine residue and of phosphorylating histones (5).The physiological significance of autophosphorylation is obscure. We report here the kinetics of these three activities and of the dephosphorylation of LHC-II and of the kinase itself.We also report evidence obtained by mild trypsinization of the thylakoids that the phosphorylated residue of the kinase must be on a terminal sequence.Trypsin inactivates all activities of the kinase,and the kinetics of the inactivation are faster than those of the release of the phosphorylated peptide from LHC-II.

2.METHODS

Thylakoids were isolated as previously described (6) from freshly harvested spinach leaves stored 2 hrs in darkness.The thylakoid polypeptides were extracted according to (7) and separated by PAGE on 8% polyacrylamide slab gels, run at 70 V. This procedure allows to resolve the 64kDa polypeptide into a 64 and a ca.62kDa polypeptides.The activation of protein kinase was performed by incubating 3 min the thylakoids (500 ug chl/mL) with ferredoxin 5 uM and NADPH 1mM in a buffer containing tricine 30 mM,NaCl 10 mM,5mM MgCl2 and 0.1 M sucrose. The same buffer with the addition of 10 mM NaF was used during the phosphorylation reaction in the presence of 1 mM ATP-γ-^{32}P,containing 400 to 600 cpm/picomole.Fluorescence was measured as previously described(6).

3. RESULTS AND DISCUSSION

Fig.1 shows the identification of the "62"kDa polypeptide as the autophosphorylating kinase;an extract obtained from the thylakoids with the zwitterionic detergent CHAPS phosphorylated added histone

M. Baltscheffsky (ed.), Current Research in Photosynthesis, Vol. II, 775–778.

(see the autoradiography,fig,1B lane 1) and the endogenous 62 kDa polypeptide (fig.1B,lanes 1,2,and 3),identified by comparing with the Coomassie staining of thylakoid polypeptides (lane 1,fig.1A),the histone marker (lane 6) and the molecular weight marker polypeptides (lane 5).

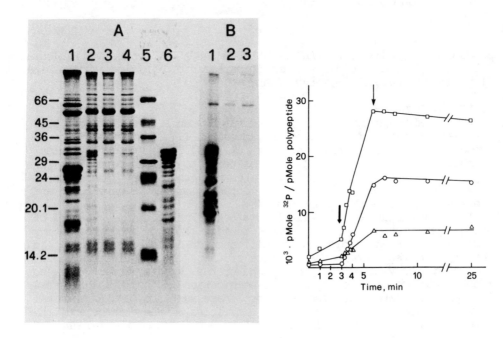

FIGURE 1   FIGURE 2

FIGURE 1A) Phosphorylation of histone III S and autophosphorylation of the 62kDa kinase by a thylakoid extract. Thylakoids (500 ug chl/mL) were extracted for 60 min at $0^{0^{-}}$ with constant shaking in the preparation buffer containing in addition 10 mM 3-(3-cholamidopropyl)dimethylammonio-1-propanesulfonic acid (CHAPS).The thylakoids were sedimented at 45,000 rpm in a Spinco ultracentrifuge for 90 min;the yellow extract was dialyzed in a 12,000-14,000 MW cut-off dialysis bag against 4 changes of CHAPS-free buffer.The extract containing 140 ug of protein/mL was incubated 30 min at 25^{0} in the presence of 250 uM gamma-labelled ATP containing 600 cpm/picomole,in a final volume of 125 uL.The reaction was stopped by TCA and the peptide phosphorylation determined as under "Methods".Lane 1,thylakoid proteins as markers;lane 2,extract plus histone;lane 3,extract plus dithiothreitol 10 mM;lane 4,extract,no additions;lane 5,molecular weight markers;lane 6,histone as a marker. Fig.1B:autoradiography of the gel.The lanes 1,2 and 3 correspond to lanes 2,3 and 4 in Figure 1A.

FIGURE 2.Kinetics of phosphorylation of LHC-II and the 62 and 64 kDa polypeptides by thylakoids upon light activation.
Light was turned on at the first arrow; DCMU 10 uM and methylviologen 100 uM were added at the second. Squares, 62kDa polypeptide; triangles,64kDa polypeptide; circles,LHC-II.

Fig.2 shows the kinetics of phosphorylation of LHC-II,the 62kDa kinase and the 64kDa polypeptide by thylakoids upon activation by illumination, and deactivation upon addition of DCMU and methylviologen, a condition where PQH2 and cyt.b563 are rapidly oxidized. It can be seen that the inactivation of the kinase is immediate, as it is upon addition of ferricyanide when the activation is performed with the ferredoxin-NADPH system as described under "Methods"(not shown). The dephosphorylation of the proteins was inhibited by NaF 10 mM;in the absence of this inhibitor both proteins are dephosphorylated by the thylakoid bound phosphatase with no lag, with half times of ca. 20 and 40 min,respectively, for LHC-II and the kinase (fig.3).

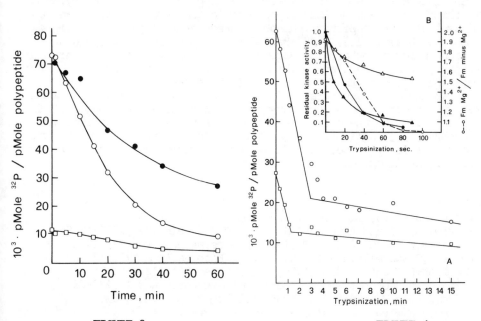

FIGURE 3   FIGURE 4

FIG.3. Dephosphorylation of LHC-II and the 62 and 64 kDa polypeptides by thylakoids. Phosphorylation was performed for 20 min (without NaF) as described in Methods, when ferricyanide (2,5 mM) was added.Samples were taken for PAGE analysis as indicated. Closed circles, 62kDa polypeptide; open circles, LHC-II; squares, 64kDa polypeptide.
FIGURE 4.Release by trypsin of the phosphorylated peptides and inhibition of kinase activity. Conditions as in "Methods". A:

Phosphorylation for 20 min, then addition of 2.5mM ferricyanide and trypsin (1ug/100ug of chl.). Samples taken for PAGE analysis at the times indicated. Circles,LHC-II; squares, 62+64 kDa polypeptides.B: Thylakoids were trypsinized (1ug trypsin/100ug chl.) for the times indicated, when samples were treated with 100-fold excess soybean trypsin inhibitor and their kinase activity measured for 4 min. Fluorescence was measured after a 100-fold dilution plus or minus 5mM MgCl2. Open circles, fluorescence ratio (+ Mg/-Mg); black circles,LHC-II; open triangles, histone; black triangles, 62kDa kinase.

The phosphorylated polypeptides of LHC-II and the 62kDa kinase are released from these proteins by a mild trypsinization of the thylakoids, with biphasic kinetics (fig.4A). In the case of LHC-II the phosphorylated peptide is the N-terminal sequence of 2kDa containing the phosphorylated threonine residue (8).In the case of the kinase,it must be a small terminal peptide, because no change in the location of the 62kDa band on the gels was observed after trypsin release of the phosphate-carrying aminoacid (not shown).
    The initial rates of inactivation by trypsin of autophosphorylation of the kinase and of LHC-II phosphorylation are faster than the release of the respective phosphorylated terminal peptides (fig.4B, compare with fig. 4A), and preceed the suppression by trypsin of the Mg ion stimulation of fluorescence. The observation that histone phosphorylation was also inhibited (fig.4B) rules out the possibility that inhibition of the other two activities was due to the digestion by trypsin of the substrates (LHC-II and the kinase itself) rather than to inactivation of the enzyme. These observations suggest that trypsin action on the enzyme may be dual: a first hit would inactivate the enzyme by splitting at a site terminal with respect to the phosphorylated residue, and a second hit would hydrolyse off the phosphorylated peptide.

REFERENCES
1 Bennett,J.(1983) Biochem.J. 212, 1-13
2 Staehelin,L.A.and Arntzen,C.J.(1983) J.Cell Biol.97, 1327-1339
3 Williams,W.P.and Allen,J.F.(1987) Photosynthesis Res.13, 19-45
4 Canaani,O.and Malkin,S.(1986) Biochim.Biophys.Acta 177,513-524
5 Coughlan,S.J.and Hind,G.(1986) J.Biol.Chem.261,11378-11385
6 Forti,G. and Grubas,P.M.G.(1986) Photosynthesis Res.10,277-282
7 Islam,K. and Jennings,R.C.(1985) Biochim.Biophys.Acta 810,
8 Mullet,J.E.(1983) J.Biol.Chem.258,9941-9948

SPECIFIC LOSS OF LHCII PHOSPHORYLATION IN A *CHLAMYDOMONAS* MUTANT LACKING THE CYTOCHROME b_6/f COMPLEX

A. Gal[1], L.J. Mets[2], and I. Ohad[1]

[1]Dept. of Biological Chemistry, The Hebrew University, Jerusalem, Israel
[2]Dept of Molecular Genetics, Chicago University, Chicago, USA

INTRODUCTION

Recent studies in our laboratory have indicated that the cytochrome b_6/f (cyt.b_6/f) complex is involved in the light induced phosphorylation of LHCII polypeptides in *Acetabularia* and *Lemna* (1,2). Similar data have been obtained with several cyt.b_6/f deficient *Chlamydomonas* (3) and maize mutants (4,5). To further ascertain that indeed the cyt.b_6/f complex is required for the activation of the redox controlled LHC II kinase, the activity of this enzyme(s) was assayed in another *Chlamydomonas* mutant lacking the complex components.

RESULTS AND DISCUSSION

The mutant, B6, was obtained following FdUrd treatment of wild type cells (6). Genetic analysis indicated that B6 is a chloroplast mutant (Roitgrund and Mets, in preparation). Measurements of fluorescence induction showed typical fluorescence rise kinetics as expected for cells possesing an active photosystem II, but impaired in the oxidation of reduced plastoquinol (*Fig. 1*). To test the possibility that the cytochrome subunits are present but inactive, cyt. b_6/f components were assayed by TMBZ heme staining and by immunoblotting with specific antibodies.

The results demonstrate that both the chloroplastic encoded subunits, cyt.b_6 and cyt.f, as well as the nuclear encoded Rieske subunit, are not detectable by antibodies raised against spinach cyt.b_6/f complex, which recognized these components in thylakoids of the y-1 *Chlamydomonas* cells, used here as a control. Both thylakoids from y-1 and mutant cells reacted with antibodies against the D1 protein of reaction center II, (*Fig. 2*).

Heme staining which identified both the intact complex in non-denaturing PAGE, or its dissociated subunits in SDS-PAGE in thylakoids from y-1 cells, did not react positively with thylakoids of the mutant cells (data not shown).

Based on these results one can conclude that the B6 mutant does not contain an assembled functional cyt.b_6/f complex.

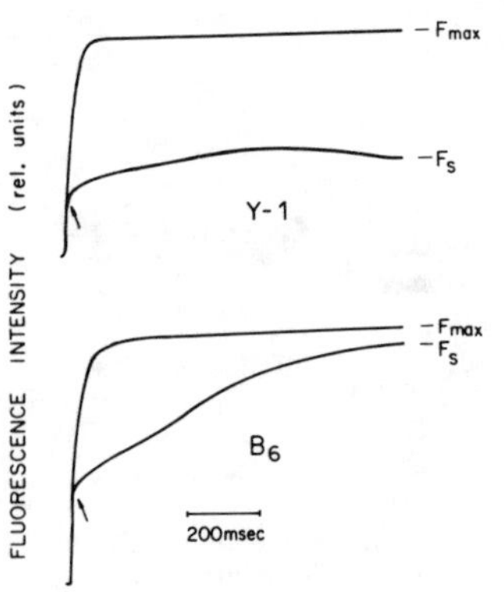

Fig. 1. Fluorescence induction of y-1 and B6 mutant cells. Tracings were recorded using a computer assisted fluorimeter as described (8). Arrow, Fo; Fm was recorded in the presence of 5 μM DCMU.

M. Baltscheffsky (ed.), Current Research in Photosynthesis, Vol. II, 779–781.

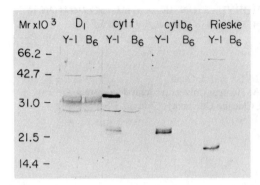

Fig. 2. Absence of cyt. b₆/f polypeptides in thylakoids of the B6 mutant cells. The D1 polypeptide used as a marker of reaction center II is present in both y-1 and B6 thylakoids. Immunodetection was carried out using antibodies prepared against the cyt. b₆/f complex polypeptides, kindly provided by Dr. G. Hauska.

Assay of thylakoid phosphorylation *in vivo* showed that the LHCII polypeptides 13 and 17 are not phosphorylated in the dark nor in light incubated cells, while LHCII polypeptides 11 and 12 as well as the 32-35 kDa polypeptides are weakly phosphorylated (*Fig. 3*). These results are in agreement with previously published data using a different cyt.b₆/f -less chloroplast mutant (3). Since *in vivo* redox controlled phosphorylation of thylakoid polypeptides in *Chlamydomonas* cells may be influenced by the chlororespiration pathway affecting the redox state of the chloroplast membranes (7), it was of interest to test the kinase(s) activity in isolated thylakoids *in vitro*. Results of such an experiment, shown in Fig.4, demonstrate that the LHCII polypeptides 13 and 17 are not phosphorylated even if reductants known to activate the redox controlled kinase were present. However no difference was found in the phosphorylation pattern of all other thylakoid polypeptides as compared with that of y-1 membranes.

The properties of the chlorophyll-protein complexes containing non-phosphorylated polypeptides in mutant thylakoids could be different from those of y-1 cells. To test this possibility chlorophyll-protein complexes of *in vitro* phosphorylated membranes were resolved by non denaturing PAGE and their polypeptide composition and phosphorylation was detected by denaturing second dimension SDS-PAGE.

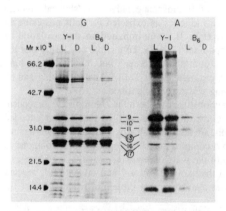

Fig 3. The LHCII polypeptides of B6 mutant thylakoids are not phosphorylated *in vivo*.
Cells were incubated in the light or dark with addition of ³²Ortophosphate for 3 hours as described (2). G, stained gel (10-17% acrylamide); A, autoradiogram; L, D, light or dark incubated cells.

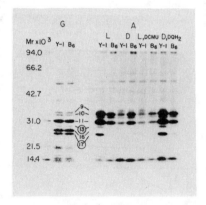

Fig 4. The LHCII polypeptides 13 and 17 in thylakoids of the B6 mutant are not phosphorylated irrespective of the redox conditions. Thylakoids were phosphorylated *in vitro* in the light (L), light with addition of 5uM DCMU (L,DCMU), in the dark (D), or in the dark with addition of 1mM Duroquinol (D, DQH₂). Assay conditions were as described (2). Analysis of the phosphorylated polypeptides was carried out using 7.5-15% acrylamide SDS-PAGE followed by autoradiography.

The results show the same chlorophyll-protein migration in the first dimension (data not shown), and a similar phosphorylation pattern, *(Fig. 5, 1D)*. The phosphorylation of the chlorophyll-protein complexes polypeptides, resolved in the second dimension of both y-1 and B6 mutant thylakoids is also similar except for the LHCIIa+b complex in which one polypeptide is not phosphorylated *(Fig. 5, 2D)*. Absence of this LHCII phosphorylation might affect the light induced state transition (7).

The results presented in this work are in agreement with previous reports (2-5), and demonstrate that the absence of the cyt.b₆/f complex results in the inability of specific LHCII polypeptides to be phosphorylated irrespective of the redox conditions of the assay.

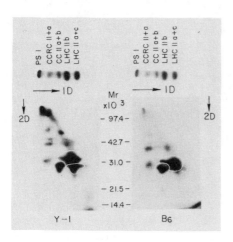

Fig 5. In vitro phosphorylation pattern of the chlorophyll- protein complexes and their constituent polypeptides of B6 and y-1 thylakoids. Phosphorylation was carried out in the light as in Fig. 4, and the chlorophyl-proteins were resolved by nondenaturing PAGE in presence of Deriphat (9), (horizontal strips,1D, 6% acrylamide); the resolved complexes were run in the second dimension using denaturing SDS-PAGE (14% acrylamide, 2D). Note the difference between the y-1 and B6 phosphorylation pattern appearing in the 2D panel (white circles);chlorophyll- protein complexes nomenclature, as in (9).

ACKNOWLEDGEMENTS

This work was supported by a grant awarded to R. Herrmann, Munchen University, and I. Ohad, by Sonderforschungsbereich, SFB, no.184.

REFERENCES

1 Gal, A., Schuster, G., Frid, D., Canaani, O., Schweiger, H.G.and Ohad, I. (1988), J.Biol.Chem. 263, 7785-7791
2 Gal, A., Shahak, Y., Schuster, G.and Ohad, I. (1987), FEBSLett. 221, 205-210
3 Wollman, F.A. and Lemaire, C. (1988), Biochim. Biophys. Acta. 933, 85-94
4 Bennett, J., Shaw, E.K. and Michel, H. (1988), Eur.J.Biochem. 171, 91- 100
5 Coughlan, S.J. (1988), Biochim.Biophys.Acta. 933, 413-422
6 Wurtz, E.A., Sears, B.B., Rabert, D.K., Shepherd, H.S., Gillham, N.W. and Boynton, J.E. (1979), Mol.Gen.Genet. 170, 235-242
7 Wollman, F.A. and Delepelaire, P., (1984), J.Cell.Biol. 98, 1-7
8 Ohad, I., Koike, H., Shochat, S. and Inoue, Y. (1988) Biochim. Biophys. Acta. 933, 288-298.
9 Peter, G.F., Machold, O. and Thornber, P. (1988), Plant membranes-Structure,Assembly and Function: J.L.Harwood and T.J. Walton eds. London, The Biochemical Society, 17-13

LHCII KINASE ACTIVITY ASSOCIATED WITH
ISOLATED CYTOCHROME b₆/f COMPLEX

A. Gal[1], T.S. Mor[1], G. Hauska[2], R. Herrmann[3], and I. Ohad[1]
[1]Dept. of Biological Chemistry, The Hebrew University, Jerusalem, Israel
[2]Dept. of Botanics, Regensburg University, Regensburg, West-Germany
[3]Botanisches Institüt, München, West-Germany

INTRODUCTION

It has been proposed before that the cytochrome b_6/f (cyt.b_6/f) complex is involved in the activation of the redox controlled LHCII kinase (1-5). Cytochrome b_6/f-less mutants did not phosphorylate the LHCII polypeptides (2-5). The putative enzyme was isolated and its properties characterised (6). However, the activity of the isolated enzyme was not increased by addition of reductants, such as duroquinol, known to activate the kinase in situ (6). To verify that the cytochrome complex is required for the activation of LHCII kinase, we attempted to reconstitute isolated cyt.b_6/f complex into thylakoid membranes of mutants lacking this complex and thus restore kinase activity. For this purpose, the complex was isolated as reported before (7). However, preliminary assays demonstrated that a highly enriched cyt.b_6/f preparation exhibits kinase activity. The properties of this kinase, including a residual response to redox control, have been investigated.

RESULTS AND DISCUSSION

Isolation of the cyt.b_6/f complex from spinach chloroplasts was carried out using the detergent MEGA-9 as previously reported (7). Analysis of the polypeptide pattern of such a preparation showed in addition to the four major subunits of the complex, the presence of several minor polypeptide bands, including one of about 64 kDA which could be the putative LHCII kinase (6). Protein kinase activity assays of this preparation showed phosphorylation of added LHCII (*Fig 1*.) and histone s-III, (*Fig. 2*), and to a lesser extent of two polypeptides corresponding to the 64kDa and the cytb₆ subunit respectively (*Figs. 1 and 2*). The phosphorylation of these intrinsic polypeptides was slightly stimulated by addition of either LHCII or histone (data not shown). These results suggest the possibility that at least part of the cytochrome complex *in vivo* may contain phosphorylated cyt.b₆ subunits. The kinase activity towards histone (*Fig. 2*) was 5-10 fold higher than that towards added LHCII. Similar results were reported for the purified kinase (8).

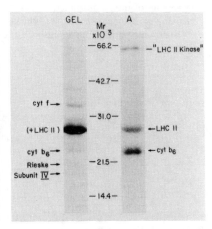

Fig 1. Phosphorylation activity of isolated cyt.b_6/f complex. The 27 kDa polypeptide of pea LHCII is phosphorylated by the enriched cyt.b_6/f preparation along with cyt.b₆ and a 64 kDa polypeptide ("LHCII kinase"). A, autoradiogram. LHCII Phosphorylation was carried out as previously described (6).

M. Baltscheffsky (ed.), Current Research in Photosynthesis, Vol. II, 783–785.
© 1990 *Kluwer Academic Publishers. Printed in the Netherlands.*

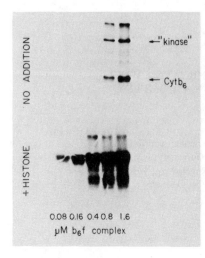

0.08 0.16 0.4 0.8 1.6
µM b₆f complex

Fig 2. Phosphorylation of histone and autophosphorylation as a function of added cyt.b₆/f complex. The complex was incubated under phosphorylation assay conditions (2) with (lower panel) or without added histone (upper panel), followed by SDS-PAGE, and autoradiography.

The higher phosphorylation of histone could be due to both the presence of a larger number of phosphorylation sites per histone molecule as compared to LHCII, and possible improper orientation of the detergent solubilised LHCII, added as a substrate (9).

The kinase activity present in the cyt.b₆/f enriched preparation could be tightly associated with the complex or only co-purifying with it. To distinguish between these possibilities, cyt.b₆/f enriched fractions obtained by ammonium sulfate precipitation (7), were purified by sucrose density gradient centrifugation in the presence of the nonionic detergent MEGA-9, used as a control, and compared to CHAPS, an ionic detergent previously used to purify the LHCII kinase (6). The results (*Fig. 3*) demonstrate that the kinase activity was associated with the cytochrome complex in the presence of the detergent MEGA-9, but separated from it when the ionic detergent was used. In the latter case the complex migrated to a higher density region of the gradient, while the kinase activity was found in the same fractions of both gradients. Co-purification of kinase activity with the cyt.b₆/f complex in the presence of octyl-glucoside was also reported for *Chlamydomonas* thylakoids (3).

Since the presence of the cytochrome complex was implied in the process of kinase activation it was of interest to test whether the fraction containing both the cytochrome and the kinase activity is affected by addition of reductants or oxydants known to activate or inhibit the thylakoid bound kinase. To this aim the kinase enriched fractions were reconstituted into asolectin liposomes and histone phosphorylation was tested. The kinase specific activity increased 2-3 fold when reconstituted into liposomes as compared to that of the detergent solubilized enzyme (data not shown). The activity of the reconstituted enzyme obtained by isolation in the presence of MEGA-9 and thus containing the cytochrome complex, increased significantly when assayed in presence of duroquinol (*Fig. 4*). The enzyme purified in the presence of CHAPS had a higher basal activity but was not stimulated by

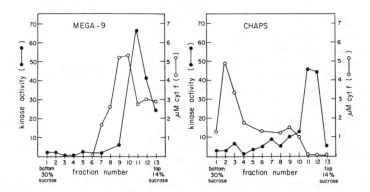

Fig 3. Migration pattern of cyt.b₆/f complex and kinase activity following sucrose gradient centrifugation in the presence of CHAPS or MEGA-9. ● pmoles ³²P incorporated into histone/10µl fraction/30 min. ○ µM cyt f was measured according to (7).

addition of reductants. These results suggest that the preparation, containing both the kinase and cytochrome complex reconstituted into liposomes, retains at least part of its response to reductants, while the enzyme preparation separated from the complex may be in the activated state. In agreement with this interpretation, Ferricyanide inhibited the activity of both enzyme preparations (data not shown). Preliminary data obtained, with the reconstituted enzyme preparation containing the cytochrome complex, using isolated LHCII as substrate, showed similar results. Data presented here do not allow yet to conclude that the stimulation of the liposome reconstituted kinase activity by duroquinol is due to a direct association of the cytochrome complex with the kinase nor that the former is solely responsible for this effect. One could consider that other polypeptides, contaminating in small amounts these preparations participate in the kinase activation. It was

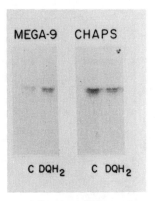

Fig 4. Histone phosphorylation (2) by cyt.b$_6$/f enriched fractions obtained by sucrose density centrifugation in the presence of either CHAPS or MEGA-9 followed by their reconstitution into asolectin liposomes. C, Control, no addition, DQH$_2$, addition of 1mM duroquinol.

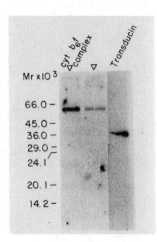

Fig 5. Antibodies against the β subunit of the G-binding protein, (transducin, 36kDa) cross react with a polypeptide of about 64 kDa in a cyt.b$_6$/f enriched preparation. Immunoblotting was carried out as described in (12).

reported before that kinase activation processes in eukaryotic systems are mediated by G-binding proteins (10). Possible involvment of G-proteins in LHCII-kinase activity was also suggested (11). Indeed, antibodies raised against a peptide containing the consensus sequence of the beta-subunit of G-binding protein (transducin) reacted with the isolated cyt b$_6$/f complex containing also the kinase activity (*Fig. 5*). Further experimental work, now in progress, is aimed at the elucidation of these findings.

ACKNOWLEDGEMENTS
This work was supported by a grant awarded to R.H. and I.O. by Sonderforschungsbereich, SFB, No 184, F.R.G.

REFERENCES

1 Gal, A., Schuster, G., Frid, D., Canaani, O., Schweiger, H. G. and Ohad, I. (1988), J. Biol.Chem. 263, 7785-7791
2 Gal, A., Shahak, Y., Schuster, G., and Ohad, I. (1987), FEBS. Lett. 221, 205-210
3 Wollman, F. A. and Lemaire, C. (1988), Biochim. Biophys. Acta. 933, 85-94
4 Bennett, J., Shaw, E.K., and Michel, H. (1988), Eur. J. Biochem. 171, 91-100
5 Coughlan, S. J. (1988), Bichim. Biophys. Acta. 933, 413-422.
6 Coughlan, S. J., and Hind, G. (1986), J. Biol. Chem. 261, 11378-11385
7 Hauska, G. (1986), Methods. in Enzymol. 126, 273-285.
8 Coughlan, S. J., Kieleczawa, J. and Hind, G. (1988), J. Biol. Chem. 263, 16631-16636
9 Mullet, J. E. and Arntzen, C. J. (1980), Biochim. Biophys. Acta. 589, 100-117
10 Edelman, A. M., Blumenthal, D. K., and Krebs, E. G. (1987), Ann. Rev. Biochem. 56, 567-614
11 Millner, P. A., (1987), FEBS.Lett.226, 155-160
12 Gershoni, J. M. and Palade, G. E. (1983), Anal. Biochem. 131, 1-15

CHARACTERISATION OF A GUANINE NUCLEOTIDE BINDING PROTEIN ASSOCIATED
WITH THE THYLAKOID MEMBRANE

Paul, A. Millner, Klaus-Dieter Hinsch[1] and Joan Clarkson[1], Department
of Biochemistry, University of Leeds, U.K. and [1] Institute für
Pharmakologie, Freie Universität, Berlin, FRG.

INTRODUCTION
     The guanine nucleotide binding regulatory proteins (G-proteins)
comprise a superfamily of signal transducing proteins that in animal
cells couple cell surface localized receptors with a variety of
effector systems [1]. The external signals percieved by the receptors
are of diverse nature and include light, hormones and odorants whilst
effector systems discovered include ion channels, nucleotide cyclases
and phosphodiesterases and the enzymes of phosphatidylinositol
metabolism. The family of G-proteins that are coupled to the rhodopsin
family of receptors display a heterotrimeric structure [2], consisting
of a α, β and γ subunits. The subunit binds GTP and interacts
with the receptor and effector, whilst the subuniit complex appear
to be responsible for attachment of the heterotrimeric complex to
the membrane. Both α and β subunits display a high degree of amino
acid sequence homology between G-protein subtypes [1,2]. Antibodies
raised to synthetic peptides which correspond to highly conserved
domains have been utilised to identify candidate G-proteins in animal
cells [3] and plant cell microsomal membranes [4]. Other G-proteins,
including the ras proteins [5] and other small (< 30 kDa) G-proteins
[6] appear to possess a single subunit. The catalytic cycle of the
heterotrimeric G-proteins is summarised in Fig. 1 and can be seen
to have a number of features of practical significance.

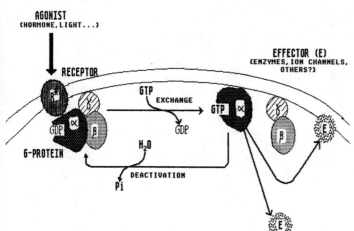

Fig. 1. G-protein catalytic cycle.

Note that GTP is bound when the G-protein interacts with its receptor. Deactivation occurs due to a slow GTP-ase activity.

Firstly, the high affinity binding (Kd $\approx 10^{-9}$ M) of GTP can be
monitored - conditions that promote binding give an indication of
the receptor species. In addition, non hydrolysable GTP analogues

(e.g. GTPγS, GppNHp) enhance G-protein mediated effects since the
activated G subunit cannot be deactivated. Finally, a number of
bacterial exotoxins, e.g. cholera toxin, act by transferring an ADP-
ribosyl moiety from NAD to the Gα subunit. This modification leads
to inhibition of GTPase activity, superactivation of the G-protein,
and if [^{32}P]-NAD is used, radiolabelling of the Gα subunit. Previously,
it was shown that pea and spinach thylakoids bound GTP and GTPγS
in a light-stimulated fashion [7]. Subsequent work [8] revealed
that a 60 kDa polypeptide was ADP-ribosylated by cholera toxin and
that ADP-ribosylation was modulated by the redox state of the thylakoid
membrane. Finally, the extent of ADP-ribosylation was correlated
with the inhibition of GTPase activity and protein kinase activity
associated with the thylakoid membrane. In this communication we
have further characterised the 60 kDa putative thylakoid G-protein
by means of salt and detergent treatment and immunolabelling using
an antibody panspecific for Gα subunits.

2. MATERIALS AND METHODS
    2.1 Cholera toxin was purchased from Sigma whilst [^{32}P]-NAD
        was from New England Nuclear. The anti-α_c antibody was raised
        as described in [3].
    2.2 ADP-ribosylation of pea thylakoid membranes was carried
        out as in [8] using thylakoids equal to 12.5 ug chl. in
        50 μl of 0.22 M sorbitol, 33 mM tricine pH 7.5, 3.3 mM MgCl$_2$,
        10 mM plus 10 μM triphenyltinchloride, 20 μM GTP, 100 μM
        NAD and 75-150 kBq of [^{32}P]-NAD.
    2.3 [^{32}P]-ADP-ribosylated thylakoids were resuspended to 0.5
        mg (chl.) ml^{-1} in 250 mM sucrose, 25 mM tricine pH 7.5 plus
        octylglucoside or CHAPS at 0.1, 0.3, 0.5, or 1% (w.v)
        respectively. Alternatively, the radiolabelled thylakoids
        were resuspended to 50 μg (chl.) ml^{-1} in 0.2 M sorbitol,
        10 mM tricine pH 7.5 plus NaCl or NaBr at 0.5, 1.0 or 2.0 M,
        or CaCl$_2$, 0.2 or 1.0 M respectively. After incubating the
        samples for 1 h on ice, the membranes were harvested at
        10,000 xg for 5 min. Thylakoid proteins present in the
        supernatants and membrane pellets were separated by SDS-
        PAGE (see 2.4).
    2.4 Thylakoid polypeptides were solubilized in sample buffer
        containing 5% (w/v) SDS and electrophoresed on 8 - 18% SDS-
        polyacrylamide gels [8]. [^{32}P]-labelled polypeptides were
        visualised by autoradiography of the dried gels.
    2.5 Immunolabelling of thylakoid polypeptides was carried out
        following SDS-PAGE (see 2.4) and electroblotting of proteins
        to nitocellulose paper [9]. The protein blots were incubated
        with anti- antibody at 1:400 dilution and immune labelled
        bands visualised with peroxidase-second antibody conjugate
        plus diaminobenzidine/H$_2$O$_2$ as substrate.

3. RESULTS AND DISCUSSION
    In order to investigate whether the putative thylakoid G-protein
was truly membrane associated or merely bound by electrostatic

interaction the ability of high ionic strength media to release the putative thylakoid G-protein was tested. The data in Fig. 2 shows that concentrations of NaCl and NaBr up to 2 M and of $CaCl_2$ to 1 M were ineffective in releasing the 60 kDa [^{32}P]-ADP-ribosylated polypeptide from the membrane. Since a number of extrinsic thylakoid proteins, e.g. CF_1-ATP synthetase and the polypeptides of the water splitting complex would be easily released by these concentrations of mono- or divalent cations [10,11], the data imply that the thylakoid G-protein is membrane associated.

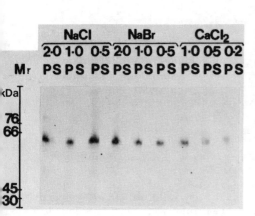

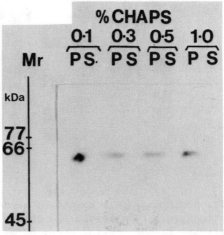

Fig. 2.   Effects of salts on [^{32}P]-ADP-ribosylated thylakoids. Salt concentrations are M; P, pellet; S, supernatant.

Effects of CHAPS on [^{32}P]- ADP-ribosylated thylakoids. CHAPS concentrations are w/v P, pellet; S, supernatant.

Subsequently, the ability of various detergents to release the 60 kDa G-protein from the thylakoid membrane was investigated. CHAPS concentrations up to 1% (w/v) (Fig. 3) and octylgucoside concentrations up to 0.5% (w/v) (Fig. 4b) were ineffective in releasing the 60kDa polypeptide from the membrane. However, 1% (w/v) octylglucoside, i.e. above the critical micellar concentration, almost quantitatively released the 60 kDa thylakoid G-protein (Fig. 4b), strongly supporting the conclusion that this polypeptide is either intrinsic or membrane anchored. It should be noted that the data in Fig. 4A and 4B also show that the 60 kDa protein crossreacts with the anti-$_{32}$antibody. Identical data to that in Fig. 4b were obtained if the [^{32}P]-ADP-ribosylated polypeptide was monitored rather than immune-reacting material.

   In summary, the thylakoid membranes of Pisum sativum and a number of other higher plant species (data not shown) possess a 60 kDa intrinsic polypeptide that can be ADP-ribosylated by cholera toxin and that is recognised by an antibody which cross reacts with animal G-protein α- subunits. Preliminary experiments indicate that this polypeptide is not present in photosystem II enriched membrane fractions, which would suggest its location to be on the upappressed thylakoid membranes. We are presently proceeding to isolate this polypeptide for protein microsequencing and subsequent cloning studies.

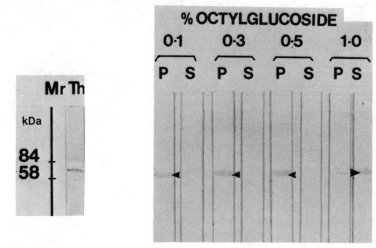

Fig. 4   Immunolabelling of thylakoid polypeptides blots with anti-antibody.   (a) Untreated pea thylakoid; Th, thylakoids. (b) Thylakoid pellets, P; and supernatants, S, after treatment with octylglucoside at the concentrations (w/v) indicated.

4.   REFERENCES
1.   Gilman, A.G. (1887) Ann. Rev. Biochem. 56, 615-649.
2.   Lochrie, M.A. and Simon, M.I. (1988) Biochemistry 27, 4957-4965.
3.   Mumby, S. et al. (1986) Proc. natl. Acad. Sci., 83, 265-269.
4.   Blum, W. et al. (1988) Biochem. Biophys. Res. Commun., 156, 954-959.
5.   Barbacid, M. (1987) Ann. Rev. Bioche,. 56, 779-827.
6.   Drobak, B.K. et al (1988) Biochem. Biophys. Res. Commun., 150, 899-903.
7.   Millner, P.A. (1987) FEBS Lett. 226, 155-160.
8.   Millner, P.A. and Robinson, P.S. (1989) Cell. Signal. - in press.
9.   Towbin, H. et al (1979) Proc. Natl. Acad. Sci., 76, 4350-4354.
10.   Kamienietzky, A., and Nelson, N. (1975) Plant Physiol. 55, 282-287..
11.   Murata, N. and Miyao, M. (1985) TIBS 10, 122-124.

DYNAMIC REARRANGEMENTS IN DIFFERENT PHOTOSYNTHETIC MEMBRA-
NES INDUCED BY PHOSPHOPROTEINS

SVETLANA M. KOCHUBEY, OLGA I. VOLOVIK, INSTITUTE
OF PLANT PHYSIOLOGY AND GENETIC, ACADEMY OF SCIEN-
CES OF THE UKRAINIAN S.S.R., KIEV, U.S.S.R.

1. INTRODUCTION

The phosphorylation of chloroplast membrane proteins
plays important role in regulating the energy distribution
between photosystems 1 and 2 (PS 1 and PS 2). The physiological role of phosphoproteins might be connected with enhancing the rate of a cyclic electron flow to maintain a
correct ATP/NADPH stoichiometry for carbon assimilation
(1,2). We have already shown that the relation between the
rates of cyclic and noncyclic electron flows is different
for plants grown under differing irradiance levels (9 and
30 W/m^2). The aim of the present study was, therefore, to
elucidate the peculiarities of the regulation of electron
transport by phosphoproteins in chloroplasts of such plants and to study unduced changes of membrane system.

2. MATERIALS AND METHODS

The chloroplasts were isolated from 12-day old pea plants grown in a climatic chamber under irradiance 9 and 30
W/m^2 (LL and HL variants) and at 15°C. The isolation medium contained 50 mM trycin buffer, pH 7.5, 0.4 M sucrose
and 5 mM MgCl$_2$. The chloroplast sediment was resuspended
in an isolation medium that contained 0.1 M sucrose used
instead of 0.4 M one. The chloroplasts were phosphorylated
by incubation in white light (70 W/m^2) in the presence of
0.2 mM ATP and 10 mM NaF. The degree of chloroplast protein phosphorylation was tested by radioactive labelling and
the spectral methods as described earlier (3).

The rate of a noncyclic electron transport was determined by the reduction of NADP from a reduced dichlorphenolindophenol in the presence of ferredoxin and monuron.
The intensity of a cyclic electron transport was determined by the rate of photophosphorylation in the presence of
phenazine methosulphate. The medium for these photoreactions contained: 1) 50 mM tris buffer pH 7.8, 5 mM MgCl$_2$,
0.5 mM NADP, 30 mkM DCPIP, 5 mM ascorbat Na; 2) 50 mM tris

M. Baltscheffsky (ed.), Current Research in Photosynthesis, Vol. II, 791–794.

buffer pH 7.8, 5 mM $MgCl_2$, 0.5 mM ADP, 5 mM K_2HPO_4, 3 mM ascorbat Na, 10 mkM PMS.

The fluorescence emission and fluorescence excitation spectra (77 K) were measured using a unit assembled in the laboratory (4). The passband was 2 nm for measurements of the fluorescence spectra, and 6 nm for the exciting and measuring monochromators in measurements of the fluorescence excitation spectra. The spectra were corrected for the sensitivity of a photomultiplier.

3. RESULTS AND DISCUSSION

The phosphorilation of membrane proteins result in changed chloroplast fluorescence spectra. The ratio of the intensities of short-wavelength and long-wavelength bands is changed more appreciably for the LL variant (Fig.1). A minor short-wavelength shift in F735 is observed for HL. The difference spectra of phosphorylated and non-phosphorylated samples show that the relative increase in F735 intensity observed for the HL variant is caused by an increased short-wavelength component F723 of this band. The intensities of both components of F723 and F733 seem to rise almost in the same way for the LL variant. We have already shown that the transfer of phospholHC2 from PS2 and its incorporation into PS1 are observed in the membrane system od chloroplasts of both types (LL and HL) (3), but

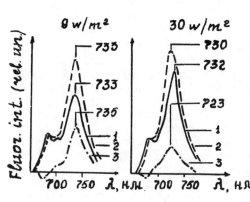

FIGURE 1. Fluorescence spectra of control (1) and phosphorylated (2) chloroplasts and their differences (3).

the prosses may be different. Measurements of the chloroplasts fluorescence spectra (Fig.1) make it possible to assume that the differences result from the different interactions of phosphoLHC2 with two long-wavelength antennae of PS1, F723 and F733. To check the assumption, we have measured the excitation spectra for fluorescence detected at 723 and 733 nm. The spectra show that when phosphorylated chloroplasts are excited in the short-wavelength region, also including the absorption region of Chl b (650 nm), a relatively higher emission at 723 nm is observed for both variants LL and HL (Fig.2). A similar increase in the emission at 733 nm is observed only for the LL variant. This implies that phosphoLHC2 is really incorporated into PS1 for both variants of chloroplasts, because the energy is

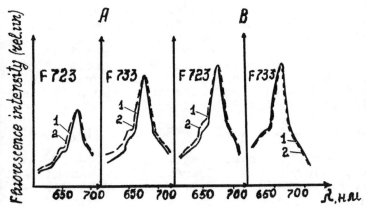

FIGURE 2. Fluorescence excitation spectra of control (1) and phosphorylated (2) chloroplasts. A and B correspond to 9 and 30 W/m² irradiance, respectively.

transferred from it toPS1 antennae. For LL phospho-LHC2 interacts with both long-wavelength antennae of F723 and F733, and for HL, it interact only with F723.

These data may be compared with the changes in the rates of cyclic and noncyclic electron flows induced by the phosphorylation of the membrane proteins in chloroplasts of two variants. The table shows that increased of both flows are observed for LL, whereas only the rate of a cyclic flow rises for HL.

TABLE. Changes in the rates of PS1 photochemical reactions induced by the phosphorylation of membrane proteins

Type of photoreaction	Ratio of the rates of reactions in phosphorylated and control samples	
	LL	HL
Noncyclic flow	1.28 ± 0.07	1.05 ± 0.04
Cyclic flow	1.23 ± 0.12	1.35 ± 0.04

This means that the transfer and incorporation of phospho-LHC2 into PS1 accelerates in different ways the cyclic and noncyclic electron flows in chloroplast membranes formed under different irradiance. Consequently, our data confirm the assumption that the phosphorylation of membrane proteins can regulate the ATP/NADPH ratio (1,2). In the LL variant, phosphoLHC2 interacts with two antennae of F723 and F733 and the rates of both electron flows are changed. The interaction with the antenna of F733 in the HL variant is concerned with an increased rate of only a cyclic flow. We conjectured earliear that each of the antennae of PS1,F723 and F733, is related to its own type of reaction centers (5). If we now assume that one type of reaction centers

with F723 antenna is included in the electron chain of a
cyclic transport, and the other type in a noncyclic one,
then the regulation of the relative rates of the two electron flows in PS1 will be effected depending on which of
the centers phosphoLHC2 interacts with. The concept of different types of reaction centers of PS1 incorporated into
the electron chains of cyclic and noncyclic transport has
already been discussed in the literature (6).

REFERENCES

1 Horton, P. and Black, M.T. (1980) FEBS Lett. 119, 141-
  144
2 Allen, J.F. (1983) Crit. Revs. Plant. Sci. 1, 1-22
3 Kochubey, S.M., Volovik, O.I., Zhuravel, T.T., Ruban, A.
  V., Samokhval, E.G. (1988) Physiol. rast. (USSR) 35, 5-
  13
4 Kochubey, S.M., Samokhval, E.G., Klimusheva, G.V., Delu-
  kov, A.A. (1980) Arch. Biochem. Biophys. 200, 65-71
5 Kochubey, S.M. and Ruban, A.V. (1988) Biofizika (USSR)
  23, 258-264
6 Setif, P., Mathis, P., Vanngard, T. (1984) Biochim. Biophys. Acta 767, 404-414

THE PARTICIPATION OF LHCP II IN ADAPTIVE REORGANIZATION OF PHOTOSYNTHETIC MEMBRANES

OLGA I. VOLOVIK, TAMARA T. ZHURAVEL, SVETLANA M. KOCHUBEY, INSTITUTE OF PLANT PHYSIOLOGY AND GENETIC, ACADEMY OF SCIENCES OF THE UKRAINIAN S.S.R., KIEV, U.S.S.R.

1. INTRODUCTION

The conditions for plant growth such as irradiance and temperature have been found to influence the structure of photosynthetic apparatus and its functional characteristics. As is known, the relative size of electron carrier pools in the electron transport chain and the pigment apparatus composition undergo a change due to low irradiance (1). The rate of linear electron transport decreases resulting thus in a decreased NADPH production (2). In chloroplasts of plants grown at high temperatures the disturbances occur in functions of the coupling apparatus leading to a decreased ATP production (3).

Thus the ATP/NADPH ratio may be altered in relation to the conditions of plant growing. Since this ratio must be maintained within certain values for the sake of a normal functioning of plants, one can suggest the existence of some mechanisms enabling the control of these values. In recent years, wide discussions are being held as regards the mechanisms of regulation of linear and nonlinear electron transport by means of phosphoproteins (4,5). A variety of changes in the relative rates of these phosphoproteins-induced photoreactions must be influencial upon the ATP/NADPH ratio value.

The main objectives of this investigation was to study the phosphorylation and lateral migration of membrane pigment-proteins in chloroplasts of plants grown under various conditions and to analyze the changes occurring in photochemical PSI and PS2 reactions due to phosphoproteins.

2. MATERIALS AND METHODS

Chloroplasts were isolated from 12-day pea plants grown in a clima chamber under the following conditions: irradiance 30 W/m^2, temperature 15°C(HL variant); 9 w/m^2,15°C(LL); 30 w/m^2, 28°C (HT). The method of isolating chloroplasts and phosphorylating membrane proteins in white lig-

M. Baltscheffsky (ed.), Current Research in Photosynthesis, Vol. II, 795–798.

ht (70 w/m^2) in the presence of ATP and NaF was described previously (6). The level of protein phosphorylation was tested by the incorporation of ^{32}P in chlorophyll-protein complexes.

PSI particles were produced by digitonin fragmentation of chloroplasts (7). The measurements were made using a 145 000 x g fraction precipitated after 100 000 x g. SDS-PAG electrophoresis of pigment-protein complexes of chloroplasts and PSI particles was performed by the method described (8). The radioactivity of the bands was measured on "Rackbeta" scintillation counter (LKB). The densitograms of separated chlorophyll-proteins were recorded by a DU-8 spectrophotometer (Beckman) at 675 nm.

The photochemical activity of PS2 was determined according to the reduction of dichlorphenolindophenol (DCPIP) from H$_2$O in white light, 70 W/m^2 (saturating) and 4 W/m^2 (limiting). The rates of noncyclic and cyclic electron transport in PSI were determined with whole chloroplasts by the reduction of NADP from DCPIPH in the presence of monuron and by the photophosphorylation in aerobic conditions in the presence of phenazine methosulphate (PMS) in white light (70 W/m^2). The methods used are described elsewhere (6). The Chl a/Chl b ratio was determined following the described procedure (9).

3. RESULTS AND DISCUSSION

It appears from the autoradiograms that oligomeric and monomeric forms of LHCII (LHCP I and LHCP III bands) were the most heavily phosphorylated for all variants. A slight labelling was also observed in the CPa band (PS2 reaction centers) and low-molecular proteins that contained no chlorophyll. The incorporation of ^{32}P into LHC II proteins

TABLE 1. Incorporation of ^{32}P into chloroplast LHC II (LHCP I + LHCP III).

Phosphorylation conditions	Radioactivity, cpm		
	HL	LL	HT
dark	1879 ± 41	2267 ± 59	2204 ± 63
light	3445 ± 173	4850 ± 211	4507 ± 225

(LHCP I + LHCP III) for LL and HT variants was 1.2 to 1.4 times higher as compared that for HL (Table 1). In the PSI phospho-particles of LL and HT, there was a greater decrease in the Chl a/Chl b ratio as well as a more pronounced increase in the areas of LHCP I and LHCP III bands (Tables 2,3). It appears thus that LL and HT variants exhibited the transfer of a greater pool of phosphoLHCII to PSI.

The rates of PSI and PS2 photochemical reactions were

measured in control and phosphorylated chloroplasts. To

TABLE 2. Changes in the Chl a/Chl b ratio in PSI particles by LHC II phosphorylation

Variant	Control	Phosphorylation	%
HL	5,9	4,8	81
LL	5,8	4,3	74
HT	5,8	4,0	69

correct the results for the photoinhibition effect, the control (nonphosphorylated) chloroplasts were exposed to actinic light in the absence of ATP during the time taken by the protein phosphorylation reaction. The PS2 activity was decreased in the phosphorylated samples. With limiting

TABLE 3. Redistribution of chlorophyll in chlorophyll-protein complexis of PSI particles as a consequence of protein phosphorylation (P, phosphorylated; C, control).

Chlorophyll-protein complex.	The percentage of the total chlorophyll on the gel in the green bands								
	HL			LL			HT		
	C	P	P/C	C	P	P/C	C	P	P/C
CPI	47,9	45,5	0,95	53,3	48,2	0,90	46,0	43,2	0,94
LHCP I	3,1	4,2	1,35	4,4	6,9	1,57	1,0	1,6	1,60
LHCP II	10,0	9,3	0,93	9,4	7,6	0,81	12,2	8,9	0,74
LHCP III	10,6	16,1	1,52	10,4	18,2	1,75	10,8	20,1	1,86
Free pigment	28,7	25,0	0,87	21,8	18,7	0,86	30,4	26,2	0,86

light, it was 73, 51 and 65% as compared to control samples (for HL, LL and HT variants, respectively),while with saturating light, it was 84, 63 and 76%. This implies that the variants differed not only in the amount of LHC II pool transferred, but also in the magnitude of changes in the vicinity of PS2 reaction centers, which are known to be induced due to membrane protein phosphorylation (10,11).

The rates of PSI photochemical reactions changed in different ways. The cyclic flow rate thus increased by 35, 23 and 19% for HL, LL and HT, respectively. However, the noncyclic flow did not display the increase in all study variants, it was only observed in LL and HT, with the increase being equal to 28 and 36%, respectively.

The changes seen in the rates of PSI photoreactions evidenced for an interaction between phospho-LHC and PSI in all cases examined, but the effects produced by such an interaction were dissimilar, resulting in different changes in the ATP/NADPH ratio. The data obtained show that the phosphorylation of membrane proteins may play a regulatory role in optimizing ATP/NADPH stoichiometry under unfavourable conditions.

REFERENCES

1 Leong, T.V., Anderson, J.M. (1983) Biochim. Biophys. Acta 723, 391-399
2 Shmeleva, V.L., Ivanov, B.N., Akulova, E.A. (1976) Fiziol. Rast. 23, 869-876
3 Volovik, O.I., Ruban, A.V., Polishchuk, A.I., Kochubey, S.M. (1988) Fiziol. Biochim.Kul't. Rast. 20, 42-46
4 Horton, P., Lee, P. (1984) Biochim. Biophys. Acta 767, 563-567
5 Fernyhough, P., Foeyr, C.H., Horton, P. (1984) FEBS Lett. 176, 133-138
6 Kochubey, S.M., Volovik, O.I., Zhuravel, T.T., Ruban, A. V., Samokhval, E.G. (1988) Physiol. Rast. (USSR) 35, 5-13
7 Photochemical systems of chloroplasts (1975) Kiev, "Naukova Dumka" Publichers, 206p.
8 Anderson, J. (1960) Biochim. Biophys. Acta 591, 113-126
9 Vernon, L.P. (1960) Analyt. Chem. 32, 1144-1150
10 Hodges, M., Packham, N.K., Barber, J. (1985) FEBS Lett. 181, 83-87
11 Kyle, D.J. and Arntzen, C.J. (1983) Photobiochem. Photobiophys. 5, 5-11

PHOSPHORYLATION OF LHCII AT LOW TEMPERATURES

SOPHIE BINGSMARK[1], ULLA K. LARSSON[2] AND BERTIL ANDERSSON[1]
DEPARTMENTS OF BIOCHEMISTRY, [1]UNIVERSITY OF STOCKHOLM AND
[2]UNIVERSITY OF LUND

1. INTRODUCTION

Higher plant thylakoids are differentiated in the lateral plane
of the membrane in that photosystem II and its light-harvesting apparatus are confined to the appressed membrane regions while photosystem I and CF_1/CF_0 are located in the stroma exposed regions (1).
However, more and more evidence are now accumulating demonstrating
the dynamic nature of the thylakoid membrane. Controlled lateral movements of components between the two thylakoid regions have been reported in connection with light and heat stress (1), biosynthesis (2)
and biodegradation (3). Thus, dynamic changes in the organization of
the thylakoid membrane are essential for both long and short term acclimation of the photosynthetic apparatus (1).

Cold stress can be quite severe for plants in particular in combination with high light (4). In this study we have investigated to
what extent the lateral rearrangements of thylakoid component are
restricted when the thylakoid membrane becomes less fluid. This was
done by studying changes in the mobility of phosphorylated LHCII at
low temperatures using a subfractional approach.

2. MATERIALS AND METHODS

Phosphorylation of spinach thylakoid proteins was performed at
0°C. Stroma thylakoid vesicles were isolated directly after the phosphorylation was terminated or after incubation of the sample at a
higher temperature for a certain time period.

Spinach thylakoids suspended in 15 mM Tricine pH 7.5, 0.1 M sorbitol, 5 mM $MgCl_2$ and 20 mM NaCl were kept in darkness for 10 min at
20°C prior to being cooled to 0°C. The sample (400 μg chl/ml) was
supplied with 10 mM NaF, and 0.4 M ATP ($\gamma-^{32}P]ATP$ 0.067 mCi/mg chl)
and illuminated (500 μE/m^2·s) at 0°C for 10 min. The temperature was
then kept at 0°C or raised to a higher temperature prior to thylakoid

M. Baltscheffsky (ed.), Current Research in Photosynthesis, Vol. II, 799–802.
© 1990 *Kluwer Academic Publishers. Printed in the Netherlands.*

fractionation by digitonin. This was performed for 2.5 min at 20°C. The homogenate was centrifuged for 40 000 xg for 30 min. The stroma thylakoids were obtained from the supernatant by centrifugation at 100 000 xg for 30 min.

3. RESULTS

The phosphorylation of LHCII at 0°C was investigated. In many experiments the ^{32}P labelling of LHCII at the low temperature was almost as high as at room temperature. However, the extent of phosphorylation at low temperature was variable depending on preparation and occasionally only 25% of the phosphorylation capacity remained as compared to room temperature conditions.

Protein phosphorylation under normal temperatures leads to migration of a subpool of LHCII from the appressed thylakoids to the stroma exposed membrane regions. This can be demonstrated by subfractionation of phopshorylated thylakoids into stroma lamellae vesicles which show high ^{32}P-labelling, increased amounts of LHCII and decreased chl a/b ratio (Tables I and II).

TABLE 1

Specific [γ-^{32}P]phosphate incorporation of LHCII at 0°C and 22°C in intact thylakoids and stroma lamellae vesicles isolated after protein phosphorylation.

	cpm/relative amount of protein	
	0°C	22°C
Intact thylakoids	5300	5565
Grana	5150	5500
Stroma	285	4730

TABLE 2

Chlorophyll a/b ratios and relative amount of LHCII in stroma exposed thylakoids isolated from unphosphorylated (control) and phosphorylated thylakoids.

Control		Phosphorylated			
		22°C		0°C	
chl a/b	% LCHII	chl a/b	% LHCII	chl a/b	% LHCII
6.8	11	4.2	25	6.6	11

In order to investigate to what extent such a lateral migration can occur at lower temperatures, thylakoids phosphorylated at 0°C where subfractionated into grana and stroma lamellae. In contrast to the room temperature control sample the stroma lamellae vesicles showed the same relative amount of LHCII and chl a/b ratio as unphosphorylated samples (Table II). Moreover, the amount of phospho-LHCII was very low as judged by a low radioactive labelling (Table I). These results clearly show that there is no lateral migration of phospho-LHCII at 0°C and that the kinase activity is restricted to the appressed thylakoid regions.

The possibility to create a situation with phospho-LHCII remaining in the grana appressions permits a study on the temperature and time dependence of the lateral migration of LHCII. This was done by raising the temperature for a certain time prior to the fractionation followed by analyses of the isolated stroma thylakoid vesicles. As can be seen in Figure 1 there is virtually no migration of LHCII into the stroma thylakoids below 10°C within 10 min of incubation. At 12°C there is a rather sharp increase in the level of phospho-LHCII as judged from measurements of ^{32}P radiolabel relative amounts of LHCII and decrease in the chlorophyll a/b ratio. As expected at higher temperatures the increase of LHCII is even more pronounced. Figure 2 gives the result of an experiment were the temperature was kept con-

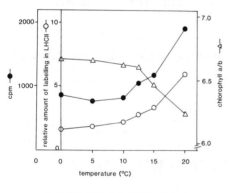

Figure 1. Temperature dependent appearance of phospho-LHCII in stroma thylakoids after phosphorylation of thylakoids at 0°C.

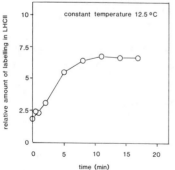

Figure 2. Time dependent appearance of phospho-LHCII in stroma thylakoids at 12.5°C after phosphorylation of thylakoids at 0°C.

stant at 12.5°C for varying time between phosphorylation and fractionation. The migration of phospho-LHCII is terminated within 10 minutes and the first phospho-LHCII units in the stroma thylakoids can be detected already within 30 sec.

4. DISCUSSION

One suggestion of the role for protein phosphorylation is protection against photoinhibition (5). Moreover, it is well established that light stress to plants is aggrevated at low temperatures (4). In this study we show that below 10°C there is virtually no migration of phospho-LHCII away from the grana partitions. The lack of LCHII migration in the thylakoid membrane may be one reason for the more pronounced photoinhibition observed at lower temperatures. It will be of interest to see if the "critical migration temperature" will differ between plant species i.e. being higher in a chilling sensitive plant than a chilling tolerant plant. The reason for the rather sharp change in mobility at 12°C is not clear but cannot be ascribed to any phase transition of the bulk membrane lipids which takes place at much lower temperatures.

The lack of migration below 10°C will probably not only affect phospho-LHCII but also other photosystem II proteins. In that case this will influence the turnover of the D1-protein and consequently the repair of photosystem II after photoinhibition has occurred.

ACKNOWLEDGEMENTS

This study was supported by the Swedish Natural Science Research Council.

REFERENCES

1   Anderson, J.M. and Andersson, B. (1988) Trends Biochem. Sci. 13, 351-355

2   Matoo, A.K. and Edelman, M. (1987) Proc. Natl. Acad. Sci. USA 84, 1497-1501

3   Virgin, I., Hundal, T., Styring, S. and Andersson, B. (1990) These proceedings.

4   Öqvist, G., Greer, D.H. and Ögren, E. (1987) in Photoinhibition (Kyle, D., Osmond, B. and Arntzen, C.J., eds.) pp. 67-87, Elsevier, Amsterdam

5   Horton, P. and Lee, P. (1985) Planta 165, 37-42

THE GRANAL MARGINS OF PLANT THYLAKOID MEMBRANES : AN IMPORTANT NONAPPRESSED DOMAIN

Jan M. Anderson[a], David J. Goodchild[a+] and William W. Thomson[b]
[a]CSIRO, Division of Plant Industry, GPO Box 1600, Canberra, ACT 2601, Australia, [b]Department of Botany, University of California, Riverside, CA 92521, USA

1. INTRODUCTION

The thylakoid membranes of mature higher plant chloroplasts show a remarkable structural and functional differentiation into appressed and nonappressed domains (Fig. 1). The closely appressed membranes of the granal compartments (whose outer surfaces do not have direct contact with the stroma) contain the PSIIα units consisting of core PSII complexes surrounded by heterogenous Chl a/b-proteins of LHCII (1,2). The planar nonappressed domains of the interconnecting stroma thylakoids and the end-grana membranes have direct access to the stroma: they contain PSI complex (1), ATP synthase (3) and few PSIIβ complexes (2) with smaller light-harvesting antennae. Only the Cyt b/f complex is thought to be present in both membrane domains (4). However, a nonappressed domain, the margins of the granal compartments (Fig. 1), has until recently been ignored. We suggest the granal margins form an important functional and structural domain.

2. GRANAL MARGINS

Structurally, the thylakoid membrane continuum is composed of three primary domains: the appressed granal membranes, the planar, nonappressed interconnecting stroma and end granal membranes, and the highly curved, nonappressed granal margins. The granal margins are interrupted by the fret junctions that interconnect the grana-stroma network. Most biochemical studies have focussed on the planar nonappressed and appressed membrane domains. Indeed Murphy (5) suggested that the granal margins would be too curved to accommodate thylakoid protein complexes. However, immunocytochemical studies have shown that some ATP synthase is localized along the margins (3), and some Cyt b/f and PSI complexes appear to be located at the periphery of the grana (6). Further, Thomson et al. (7) reported that low concentrations of Tween 20 preferentially removed the curved granal margins to reveal open granal compartments (Fig. 2). After centrifugation of this Tween-20-treated material, the supernatant contained Cyt b/f, PSI and ATP synthase complexes (8). Since Tween 20 structurally disrupted the margins, the simplest conclusion is that these protein complexes were located in the margins.

Are the granal margins a significant structural domain? To answer this question we need to consider the three-dimensional organization of the membrane continuum. Unfortunately there is no consensus as to how many fret regions there are per granal compartment (two to sixteen), how wide the fret regions are, or whether the interconnecting stroma thylakoids are broad continuous sheets (9) or narrow anastomosing, thin-flattened tubules (10). Often the thylakoid membrane network is viewed as a rigid static system which is not true. Recent electron microscopic analyses

+We sadly report that our true friend and colleague, Dr David J. Goodchild, died on May 16, 1989.

M. Baltscheffsky (ed.), Current Research in Photosynthesis, Vol. II, 803–808.
© 1990 *Kluwer Academic Publishers. Printed in the Netherlands.*

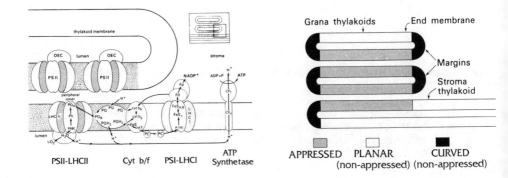

Fig. 1. Functional and structural domains of photosynthetic membranes.

(8,11,12) strengthen the idea of Weier et al. (10) that the stroma thylakoids are rather narrow; this means the area of nonappressed membrane is much less than that of the appressed membrane. Further the number of fret regions per granal compartment is likely to be low. We suggest that the granal margins could comprise some 11-30% of the nonappressed domain (5,13).

If indeed the granal margins form a significant nonappressed domain and contain Cyt *b/f*, PSI and ATP synthase complexes, this has profound consequences for the mechanisms of light-harvesting, electron transport and photophosphorylation.

3. THYLAKOID FUNCTION AT MODERATE AND SATURATING LIGHT
3.1. *Linear electron transport*: The transfer of electrons between thylakoid complexes is mediated by the mobile electron carriers, plastoquinone, plastocyanin and ferredoxin. With the lateral segregation of PSII to appressed domains and PSI to nonappressed domains, rapid lateral diffusion over very large areas might be required, since granal diameters are 500 nm or more. Since the concept of lateral heterogeneity was introduced (1), several authors have suggested that the rates of lateral diffusion might be inadequate (15,16). Perhaps the hydrophobic plastoquinone molecules would be restricted both by the "immobilized" protein complexes located in appressed domains and also by the narrow fret regions leading out from granal compartments (16). Even greater constraints for lateral diffusion over long distances have been placed on the large plastocyanin molecules due mainly to the narrow lumenal channels (15,16). Yet, we know that very good interphotosystem coupling occurs with high rates of electron flow, even at high light intensity.

We suggest that this is so because linear electron transport at high irradiance will occur only in the granal compartments (13,14). The PSIIα units in the appressed domains provide electrons to plastoquinones which will diffuse to the Cyt *b/f* complexes in *either* the nonappressed domains *or* the margins. In turn, plastocyanin will not have such long distances to laterally diffuse before reaching the marginal PSI complexes. If this is so, there will be many more PSIIα complexes than PSI complexes for linear electron transport. This is not a problem because the turnover capacity of PSI not only is very high and never rate-limiting, but also is greater than the turnover of PSII which may be colimiting (14).

3.2. *Photophosphorylation*: Flexibility in the amounts of ATP versus NADPH depends on the relative rates of noncyclic and cyclic photophosphorylation. This flexibility is needed for cells to adapt appropriately to environmental and developmental changes, particularly when the demand for ATP is high (17). Under saturating light with noncyclic photophosphorylation confined to the granal compartments, the protons generated will quickly reach the marginal ATP synthases. On the other

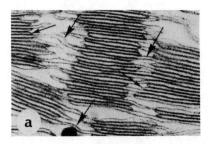 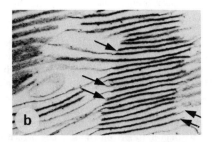

Fig. 2. Thin cross-sections of the grana-stroma network showing the fret junction (➔) and granal margins (➔) before (a) and after Tween-20 treatment (b) with granal margins absent (➔) (Ref. 8).

hand, cyclic photophosphorylation under non-limiting irradiance will occur mainly in the planar, nonappressed domains (13,14). This has several advantages for the function of the photosynthetic membrane under saturating light: (1) *in vivo* proton coupling can be localized (14); (2) the pools of plastoquinone in the granal compartments need not be in equilibrium under saturating light conditions; (3) both NADPH and ATP will be generated around the granal stacks, but only ATP on the nonappressed domains; (4) changes in the amount of membrane stacking induced by short-term or long-term regulation will permit adjustment of the ATP/NADPH ratio (see Section 5).

4. LIGHT-HARVESTING AND ELECTRON TRANSPORT UNDER LIMITING LIGHT

It is remarkable that all vascular C_3 plants have constant quantum yields, irrespective of their high or low photosynthetic rates at light saturation. Measurements of quantum yields (18) confirm earlier results, and show that 37 C_3 species representing widely different taxa, life forms and habitats all have quantum yields of 0.106 mol O_2 (mol photons)$^{-1}$, consistent with the effective utilization of 8-9 quanta for O_2 evolution. Thus, despite the higher Chl a/Chl b ratios, PSII/PSI stoichiometry, Cyt b/f complex and ATP synthase content, and greater photosynthetic capacity, on a chlorophyll basis, in sun and high-light-grown plants compared to shade and low-light-grown plants, their quantum yields are identical. For this to be true: (1) the effective absorbing cross-section of both photosystems must be equal; (2) the effective number of pigments serving each photosystem must be comparable; and (3) only a few PSI complexes will be able to participate in cyclic phosphorylation under limiting light, since the high quantum yields will allow no more than ~20% imbalance of linear electron transport by cyclic photophosphorylation operating with the Q cycle.

One can account for the high quantum yields under limiting light by the involvement of both the marginal and the nonappressed PSI complexes participating in linear electron transport. At low light there will be adequate time for the lateral diffusion of plastoquinone molecules from the appressed PSIIα complexes to the Cyt b/f complexes in the appressed, marginal or nonappressed domains. With the placement of some PSI complexes in the granal margins, plastocyanin will be relatively close to *all* PSI complexes. Thus under limiting irradiance, all PSI complexes participate in linear electron transport. Under medium and saturating irradiance, the PSI complexes of the nonappressed domains will participate mainly in cyclic photophosphorylation, while those of the marginal domains will participate in linear electron transport.

It is likely also that some marginal PSI complexes will be close to some of the PSIIα complexes that are located around the outer circumference of both the upper and lower appressed membranes. In this way, there will be opportunity for limited spillover between the peripheral LHCII of these "outer" PSIIα and marginal PSI complexes (13,14). We suggest that the location of some Cyt b/f, PSI and ATP synthase complexes in the marginal domains accounts for the constant high quantum yield of sun and shade plants, which due to modulations in the composition of their thylakoids have different degrees of membrane stacking, varying PSII/PSI stoichiometries and varying light-harvesting antennae for PSII and PSI.

5. DYNAMIC MOLECULAR ORGANIZATION

5.1. *Short-term regulation*: The molecular organization of thylakoid membranes is extraordinarily dynamic and never static. This highly mobile architecture of each membrane is vital for plants which cannot escape from their surroundings. Each chloroplast, within each cell, within each leaf, within each plant, is subject to rapid fluctuations in light intensity and quality due to momentary changes in leaf movements, sunflecks and sun angle. Dynamic rapid responses elicited by such environmental fluctuations slightly alter the existing molecular organization of some components, thereby influencing light-harvesting and electron transfer characteristics. Although there is no way to demonstate these many rapid short-term regulatory responses, they finetune the overall organization of the membrane network to function optimally regardless of the light environment. Far from being the static organization of two-dimensional electron micrographs (instant snapshots in time), there is a continuum of dynamic movements in all granal compartments, and stroma thylakoids, from the rapid conformational changes of protein complexes to the slight lateral movements (sec to min) of some existing components. There is an array of energy dissipative processes where changes in $(\Delta)pH$, $(\Delta)g$, $(\Delta)E$ and $[Mg^{++}]$ cause subtle conformational changes of the pigment beds of both photosystems, particularly PSII.

One of the main rapid regulatory responses is the reversible State I/State II transition mechanism which ensures an even distribution of light excitation energy between PSII and PSI (19). It is believed that the reversible phosphorylation of peripheral LHCII of some PSIIα units occurs when the kinase is activated by over-reduction of the plastoquinone pool (20). The introduction of the negatively-charged phosphate groups causes the phosphorylated LHCII to dissociate from PSIIα units and forces the appressed membranes apart, allowing the phosphorylated LHCII to laterally migrate to the nonappressed domain (21). When phosphorylation occurs *in vitro*, there is an increase in the surface area of nonappressed membranes (22). Even a small decrease in membrane stacking due to the phosphorylation would cause a decrease in granal diameter, and a concomitant increase in nonappressed stromal membranes. If the number of granal compartments is unaltered, as is likely, the relative proportion of marginal domain would be increased compared to that of the appressed region. Concomitantly, the proportion of marginal domain would decrease relative to the nonappressed domain. Thus, if the marginal domain is important in the interplay between PSII and PSI, slight changes in the area of this domain relative to those of the appressed and nonappressed domains must be functionally significant under light-limiting conditions in the State I/State II transition mechanism.

Indeed, even under moderate and saturating light there may be short-term regulatory mechanisms that permit reversible changes in membrane stacking which would also influence the amounts of marginal versus appressed and nonappresssed domains (14). Such a high light "stacking/destacking" mechanism could allow modulations in the amounts of cyclic and noncyclic photophosphorylation, thereby allowing the ratio of ATP/NADPH to be modulated. A slight decrease in membrane stacking would decrease the marginal domain relative to the nonappresssed domain. This should force some marginal complexes to laterally migrate from the margins to the nonappressed domain thereby, simultaneously, increasing cyclic and decreasing noncyclic photophosphorylation. On the other hand, a slight increase in membrane stacking would slightly increase noncyclic and diminish cyclic photophosphorylation. We suggest that even slight changes in membrane stacking, together with the relocation of a few PSI and ATP synthase complexes, could modulate the two types of photophosphorylation under high light conditions.

5.2. *Long-term acclimation*: The structural and functional changes elicited by the short-term responses are ineffective in coping with long-term environmental changes, particularly light, on a daily and seasonal basis. With acclimation, there are changes in the rates of synthesis and degradation of thylakoid components which modulate the actual membrane composition, function and overall membrane architecture (4). In general, plants grown under low irradiance have more granal compartments per granum and broader grana than plants grown under high light (4,22). Shade plants may have up to a hundred or more compartments per granum (23). Further, shade plants have a higher ratio of appressed to nonappressed membranes. Clearly this increase in both granal width and membrane stacking would be expected to increase proportionally the amount of membrane in the marginal domains relative to that in the nonappressed domains. We propose that these differences in the relative proportions of the three primary membrane domains between sun and shade plants could also have functional significance. Although their overall photosynthetic capacities at saturating light are very different, as expected from their varying compositions, we suggest that the sun and high-light have the *capacity for higher ATP/NADPH ratios* than shade and low-light grown species. This follows, if our proposal is correct that the granal compartments themselves are mainly the site of linear electron transport, and the nonappressed domains are the main sites of cyclic photophosphorylation. The capacity to enhance ATP relative to NADPH would be needed to maintain high rates of protein synthesis, enzyme catalyses and polypeptide transport in the sun and high-light chloroplasts which are functioning at very high turnover rates.

6.   CONCLUSION

A better knowledge of the three-dimensional architecture of the membrane network and its highly dynamic organization is vital if we are to understand function. This seems particularly true now that the lateral heterogeneity of function in the membrane continuum appears to be related to its remarkable structrual differentiation into appressed, nonappressed and marginal domains. Both structurally and functionally, *lateral heterogeneity is a three-dimensional situation*. Implicit in any short-term responses or long-term acclimation (such as wider grana or higher degrees of stacking) are the related dynamic changes in the three-dimensional architecture of thylakoid membranes. The concept that the nonappressed granal margins contain Cyt *b/f*, PSI and ATP synthase complexes provides a new framework to understand the constant quantum yields of C_3 plants regardless of their composition and membrane architecture, and to explain how the capacity to modulate the ATP/NADPH ratio may be regulated by small reversible changes in the amounts of marginal domain relative to appressed and nonappressed domains. These ideas need to be tested, particularly by structural studies.

REFERENCES
1   Andersson, B. and Anderson, J.M. (1980) Biochim. Biophys. Acta 593, 427-440
2   Anderson, J.M. and Melis, A. (1983) Proc. Natl. Acad. Sci. USA 80, 745-749
3   Miller, K.R. and Staehelin, L.A. (1976) J. Cell Biol. 68, 30-47
4   Anderson, J.M., Chow, W.S. and Goodchild, D.J. (1988) Aust. J. Plant Physiol. 15, 11-21
5   Murphy, D.J. (1986) Biochim. Biophys. Acta 864, 33-94
6   Vallon, O., Wollman, F.A. and Olive, J. (1986) Photobiochem. Photobiophys. 12, 203-220
7   Thomson, W.W. and Moeller, C.H. (1983) Protoplasma 114, 173-178
8   Webber, A.N., Platt-Aloia, K.A., Heath, R.L. and Thomson, W.W. (1988) Physiol. Plant. 72, 288-297
9   Paolillo, D.J. (1970) J. Cell Sci. 6, 243-255
10 Weier, T.E., Stocking, C.R., Thomson, W.W. and Drever, H. (1963) J.Ultrastruct. Res. 8, 122-143
11 Brangeon, J. and Mustardy,L. (1979) Biol. Cell. 36, 71-80
12 Barnes, S.H. and Blackmore, S. (1984) Micron Micros. Acta 15, 187-194
13 Anderson, J.M. and Thomson, W.W. (1989) in Towards a broad understanding of Photosynthesis (Briggs, W. ed.) Alan Liss, New York, in press
14 Anderson, J.M. (1989) Physiol. Plant. 76, 243-248
15 Haehnel, W. (1984) Ann. Rev. Plant Physiol. 35, 659-693
16 Whitmarsh, J. (1986) in Encyclop. Plant Physiol., Photosynthesis III (Staehelin, L.A. and Arntzen, C.J., eds) Vol.19, pp.508-527, Springer-Verlag, Berlin
17 Horton, P. (1985) in Progress in Photosynthesis Research (Biggens, J., ed.) Vol.II, pp.681-688, Martinus Nijhoff, Dordrecht
18 Björkman, O. and Demmig, B. (1987) Planta 170, 489-504
19 Chow, W.S., Tefler, A., Chapman, D.J. and Barber, J. (1981) Biochim. Biophys. Acta 638, 60-68
20 Bennett, J. (1983) Biochem. J. 212, 1-13
21 Barber, J. (1985) Plant Cell Environ. 6, 311-322
22 Staehelin, L.A. and Arntzen, C.J. (1983) J. Cell Biol. 97, 1327-1337
23 Goodchild, D.J., Björkman, O. and Pyliotis, N.A. (1972) Carnegie Inst. Wash. Yearbk. 71, 102-107

THE SPECIFIC SURFACE OF THYLAKOID MEMBRANES AS DETERMINED BY ABSORPTION
SPECTROSCOPY OF SINGLE BLEBS

BEAT STOLZ and DIETER WALZ, Biozentrum, University of Basel,
CH-4056 BASEL, SWITZERLAND

1. INTRODUCTION
    The specific surface $\bar{o}$ is defined as the area of one surface of the
thylakoid membrane per total chlorophyll contained therein. By means of
this quantity the specific volume of the membrane from its thickness or
the average distance between the plane thylakoid membranes from specific
volumes can be estimated. Such distances are required for the computa-
tion of the electrical potential profile across thylakoid stacks (1,2).
The specific surface has not yet been measured but only inferred from
indirect evidence. The value most frequently used is 1.5 m^2/μmol as
estimated by Barber (3).
    Blebs are spherical vesicles bounded by a single membrane with dia-
meters of several micrometers. They are formed when thylakoids are
subjected to an osmotic shock. Due to its size a bleb is visible in the
light microscope which allows us to determine its surface area and the
chlorophyll content of its membrane by means of its absorption spectrum.
The ratio of these two quantities yields the specific surface.

2. PROCEDURES
2.1. Materials and methods
    Lettuce and spinach were purchased from local sources; peas were
    grown under day light and harvested after 16 to 20 days. Thylakoids
    (class C chloroplasts) were isolated as described (4), then resus-
    pended and assayed in 250 mM KCl, 10 mM Hepes pH 7.5. Blebs were
    prepared by adding 0.2 ml of the thylakoid suspension (chlorophyll
    concentration between 2 and 4 mM) to 25 ml of a vigorously stirred
    solution containing 0.5 mM $MgSO_4$, 0.5 mM Hepes pH 7.5, and 1.5 g
    glass beads (diameter 0.8 mm). They were collected on 0.6% Dextran
    500 as described (5), then resuspended and assayed in the same
    medium (without glass beads).
    Chlorophyll was determined according to Arnon (6) and proteins
    according to Lowry et al. (7) using bovine serum albumin as stan-
    dard. Separation of lipids into monogalactosyl (MGDG), digalactosyl
    (DGDG) and sulfoquinovosyl diacyl glycerol (SL) was performed as
    described (8). Phospholipids (PL) were assayed according to
    Bartlett (9). Uncoupled electron transport rates under saturating
    light conditions were calculated from oxygen consumption with
    methylviologen (MV) as electron acceptor and either water or
    dichlorophenol indophenol (reduced with ascorbate, $DCPIPH_2$) as
    donors. ΔpH was determined with 9-amino acridine (10) using
    pyocyanine (pyo) as electron mediator.

M. Baltscheffsky (ed.), Current Research in Photosynthesis, Vol. II, 809–812.
© 1990 *Kluwer Academic Publishers. Printed in the Netherlands.*

2.2. Determination of the specific surface

The procedure was as described (5,11,12). In short, the absorption spectrum of a bleb suspension was measured, and the overall extinction coefficients were calculated by dividing the absorbances by the total chlorophyll concentration. The absorption spectrum of single blebs was recorded in a Zeiss microscope spectrophotometer. The chlorophyll content of a bleb was estimated by fitting its spectrum to the overall extinction coefficients. Its membrane surface was calculated from its diameter, and the specific surface was obtained as ratio of surface to chlorophyll content.

3. RESULTS AND DISCUSSION

3.1. Characterization of the blebs

The bleb preparations for all three species consisted of single vesicles and did not contain grape-like structures as reported for other procedures (13,14). However, a fraction of blebs displayed dark spots, so-called patches, which are considered as still stacked thylakoid membranes (13).

Data on the molecular composition of bleb membranes are compiled in Table 1 together with the corresponding data for the thylakoids from which the blebs were formed. For all species the composition

TABLE 1. Membrane composition and light reactions at pH 7.5 for thylakoids and blebs prepared from different species. Standard deviations are given in parenthesis, "nd" means not detectable, and x denotes the molar ratio of chlorophyll a to b.

	Lettuce		Pea		Spinach	
	thyl	bleb	thyl	bleb	thyl	bleb
protein/chl	3.67	4.06	4.58	3.99	4.43	4.23
	(0.18)	(0.24)	(0.28)	(0.27)	(0.26)	(0.11)
lipid/chl	4.57	4.07	3.85	3.98	3.77	3.53
	(0.34)	(0.30)	(0.17)	(1.08)	(0.13)	(0.35)
MGDG	41%	43%	57%	61%	53%	54%
DGDG	28%	26%	27%	30%	31%	30%
SL	19%	19%	2%	nd	nd	nd
PL	12%	12%	14%	9%	16%	16%
x_{thyl}/x_{bleb}	1.02 (0.05)		1.02 (0.08)		0.99 (0.05)	
$H_2O \rightarrow MV$ [*]	170	68	394	35	854	nd
	(22)	(11)	(44)	(3)	(19)	
$DCPIPH_2 \rightarrow MV$ [*]	217	139	407	302	940	159
	(55)	(18)	(75)	(30)	(106)	(10)
ΔpH (pyo)	2.9	0.9	2.6	1.1	2.8	0.6
	(0.1)	(0.3)	(0.1)	(0.3)	(0.1)	(0.2)

[*] Rates in electrons per chl per hour

of the bleb membranes is almost identical to that of thylakoids. In addition, SDS polyacrylamide gel electrophoresis yielded essentially the same polypeptide pattern for bleb and thylakoid membranes of a given species.

Blebs still perform electron transport (see Table 1) though on a reduced level (particularly for spinach) due to the low salt conditions (4). Electron transport from water through photosystem II seems to be more affected by a low ionic strength than that through photosystem I. ΔpH set up in the light was smaller in blebs than in thylakoids (Table 1), in line with the reduced electron transport rates. In addition, the permeability of bleb membranes for H^+-ions could be increased e.g. due to a partial loss of CF_1 from the H^+/ATP-synthase (0.5 mM $MgSO_4$ in the medium may not be sufficient to fully prevent this dissociation).

In view of the above data we conclude that bleb membranes can serve as faithful representatives for the parent thylakoid membranes.

3.2. Specific surface

It was shown that the measurement of the absorption spectrum of a single bleb in the microscope spectrophotometer is reproducible and free of artifacts (5,11,12). The absorption spectra of several patch free blebs with different diameters were measured for each preparation. In all cases the fit between spectra and overall extinction coefficient was as good as previously reported (5,11,12)

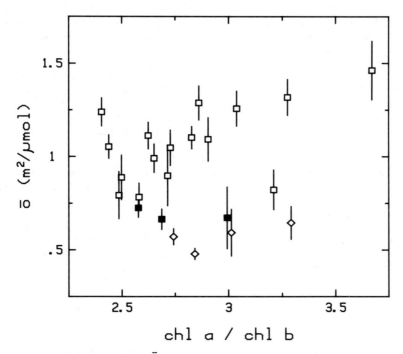

FIGURE 1. Specific surface $\bar{o}$ for thylakoids of lettuce (□), pea (■) and spinach (◇). The bars indicate standard deviations.

thus indicating that each bleb had essentially the same proportion of chlorophyll a to chlorophyll b to carotenoids as the corresponding collective of blebs. It then appears that the bleb population is fairly homogeneous with each bleb originating from grana and intergrana membranes (in contrast to a mixed population with blebs arising predominantly either from stacked or unstacked membranes).

The values for the specific surface obtained with the blebs of one preparation agreed within experimental error, and Fig. 1 then presents the mean value for each preparation, plotted as a function of the molar ratio of chlorophyll a to b. There is no clear-cut correlation between the two parameters yet a tendency of larger values for $\bar{o}$ with increasing chlorophyll a/b may exist. Taking the latter ratio as indicator for the relative abundance of photosystem I and II one can conclude that it is of little importance for the membrane area which photosystem prevails. In view of the relatively small range of variation for $\bar{o}$ it is more likely that the number of light-harvesting pigment proteins is a determining factor.

Assuming an average value of 7 nm for the thickness of the thylakoid membrane, the data for $\bar{o}$ shown in Fig. 1 yield a specific volume for this membrane which ranges between 3.5 and 10 liter/mol. These values are comparable to the specific volumes found for the lumen of thylakoids and the space between stacked thylakoids (2). This is not surprising since electronmicrographs of thin sections of chloroplasts show that the distances between the membranes are of the same order of magnitude as the thickness of the membranes.

REFERENCES

1 Walz, D. (1984) in Advances of Photosynthesis Research (Sybesma, C., ed.) Vol. 2, pp. II.4.257-260, M.Nijhoff/W.Junk Publ., The Hague
2 Walz, D. (1986) EBEC reports 4, 341
3 Barber, J. (1972) Biochim. Biophys. Acta 275, 105-116
4 Walz, D., Schuldiner, S. and Avron, D. (1971) Eur. J. Biochem. 22, 439-444
5 Stolz, B. (1988) The specific surface of thylakoid membranes as determined by absorption spectroscopy of single blebs, and the degree of stacking in lettuce thylakoids. PhD Thesis, University of Basel, Basel
6 Arnon, D.I. (1949) Plant Physiol. 24, 1-15
7 Lowry, O.H., Rosebrough, N.J., Farr, A.L. and Randall, R.J. (1951) J. Biol. Chem. 193, 265-269
8 Roughan, P.G. and Batt, R.D. (1968) Anal. Biochem. 22, 74-88
9 Bartlett, G.R. (1959) J. Biol. Chem. 234, 466-468
10 Schuldiner, S., Rottenberg, H. and Avron, M. (1972) Eur. J. Biochem. 25, 64-70
11 Stolz, B. and Walz, D. (1988) Mol. Cell. Biol. (Life Sci. Adv.) 7, 83-88
12 Stolz, B. and Walz, D. (1988) EBEC reports 5, 169
13 Barber, J. and Malkin, S. (1981) Biochim. Biophys. Acta 634, 344-349
14 Farkas, D.L., Korenstein, R. and Malkin, S. (1984) Biophys. J. 45, 363-373

SURFACE CHARGE DENSITIES, LIPID COMPOSITIONS AND FLUIDITIES
OF THYLAKOID MEMBRANES SHOWING DIFFERENT DEGREES OF
STACKING

CLAS DAHLIN[1], IAN M. MØLLER[2], HANS RYBERG[1], ANNA STINA
SANDELIUS[1], [1]Dept of Plant Physiology, University of
Göteborg, Carl Skottsbergs Gata 22, S-413 19 GÖTEBORG;
[2]Dept of Plant Physiology, University of Lund, PO Box
7007, S-220 07 LUND, SWEDEN.

1. INTRODUCTION
    Formation of thylakoid appressions occurs between
regions of the membrane where the Coulombic repulsive forces between two adjacent membrane surfaces are decreased.
This has been suggested to occur through lateral segregation of thylakoid components, such as displacement of negative surface charges to membrane regions not involved in
stacking, and/or through cations screening negative membrane surface charges in the areas involved in stacking
(1). The light-harvesting complex of photosystem II (LHC
II) may partake in the stacking process (2) and phosphatidylglycerol (PG) acylated with trans-hexadecenoic acid
[16:1(trans)] has been implicated to be involved in the
organization of LHC II (3). Chloroplasts of plants grown
with different concentrations of the herbicide SAN-9789
(Norflurazon, an inhibitor of carotenoid biosynthesis),
contain thylakoids with different degrees of stacking. In
this plant material the degree of thylakoid stacking is
correlated with the amount of LHC II (4). We here report
the surface charge densities of these membranes, correlated
to lipid composition and fluidity, as measured with the
fluorescent probe 1,6-diphenyl-1,3,5-hexatriene (DPH).

2. MATERIALS AND METHODS
    Grains of wheat (Triticum aestivum L. cv. Walde) were
    soaked in 0 or 28 mg l^{-1} SAN-9789 and grown in a
    greenhouse (without SAN-9789 only) or under weak red
    light (16 mW m^{-2}) as previously described (5). W, no
    SAN-9789 treatment and white light; R, no SAN-9789
    treatment and red light; SAN-R, SAN-9789 treatment and
    red light. Thylakoid fractions were isolated (5) and
    aliquots of the suspended membranes were analyzed for
    protein, lipid composition (6; for description of gas
    chromatography, see 7), membrane fluidity or surface

M. Baltscheffsky (ed.), Current Research in Photosynthesis, Vol. II, 813–816.

charge density. The fluidity of the membrane fractions was measured with DPH (8). The surface charge density was measured by using 9-aminoacridine (9-AA) fluorescence (9), using an exact mathematical solution (A. Bérczi and I.M. Møller, unpublished; see ref. 10 for more details). Both fluidity and surface charge density was measured using destacked thylakoid membranes.

3. RESULTS

W chloroplasts contained large grana, R chloroplasts had fewer thylakoids per granum, while SAN-R chloroplasts only contained stroma lamellae (Fig. 1). The fatty acid/protein ratio was the same for all three treatments whereas the negative surface charge density and the fluidity (high DPH fluorescence polarization indicates high order of the acyl chains i.e. low fluidity) was highest in W and similar in R and in SAN-R (Table 1). The only major lipid class to be significantly affected by the treatment was PG which constituted a lower proportion of the thylakoid lipids after treatment with SAN-9789; within the PG class, the PG-16:1(trans) was in both R and SAN-R around 50% of that in W (Table 2). The proportion of charged lipids (SQDG + PG) was also lower after SAN-9789 treatment (Table 2).

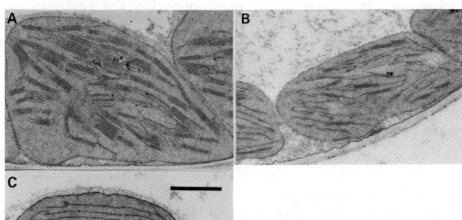

Figure 1. Electron micrographs of wheat leaves. A) Untreated, white light; B) Untreated, weak red light; C) SAN-9789, weak red light. The bar represents 1 μm.

Table 1. Thylakoid stacking, lipid/protein ratios, surface charge densities (σ) and fluidity of thylakoid membranes isolated from leaves of wheat grown with or without treatment with SAN-9789 during seed imbibition. The fluidity is expressed as steady-state DPH fluorescence polarization (p). a, $F/F_{max} = 0.70$ (9,10).

Treatment	Stacking (Fig. 1)	Fatty acid/protein (μmol/mg)	σ[a] (mC m^{-2})	p
W	+++	0.91	−47	0.215
R	+	0.95	−20	0.241
SAN-R	−	1.03	−23	0.239

Table 2. Lipid composition (major acyl lipids) of thylakoids isolated from leaves of wheat, grown with or without SAN-9789 during seed imbibition. The values are the means ± SD, n denotes number of independent experiments. MGDG, monogalactosyldiacylglycerol; DGDG, digalactosyldiacylglycerol; SQDG, sulfoquinovosyldiacylglycerol; PG, phosphatidylglycerol.

Treatment (n)	mol% lipid				
	MGDG	DGDG	SQDG	PG	PG-16:1(trans)
W (2)	49±1	26±1	15±1	11±0	5.2
R (3)	48±2	28±1	14±3	10±2	2.6
SAN-R (3)	53±6	29±5	12±1	6±1	2.6

4. DISCUSSION

4.1. W versus R chloroplasts

Higher degree of stacking is associated with higher average surface charge density, higher average fluidity and higher PG-16:1(trans) content (Tables 1 and 2), and also with higher carotenoid and LHC II contents (5). The higher surface charge density would make stacking more difficult even if the stromal lamellae carry most of the negative charges. On the other hand, the higher PG-16:1(trans) and LHC II contents are consistent with the proposed role of these components in stacking (2,3). The difference in fluidity of the membranes must be due to differences in protein-lipid interactions since the lipid/protein ratio as well as the overall lipid and fatty acid composition (11) are unchanged.

4.2. R versus SAN-R chloroplasts

A higher degree of stacking is associated with a higher content of total PG but not of PG-16:1(trans) (Table 2) and much higher carotenoid and LHC II contents (5). All other parameters are similar. Thus, also in this case stacking is associated with the presence of specific components, e.g. LHC II and total PG.

4.3. Overall conclusion

Stacking of the thylakoid membrane is not associated with average physical properties of the membrane, such as surface charge density and fluidity of the hydrophobic region, but rather with the presence of specific components and their interactions.

Acknowledgements: Financial support was from the Swedish Natural Science Research Council.

REFERENCES
1 Barber, J. (1982) Annu. Rev. Plant Physiol. 33, 261-295
2 Mullet, J.E. and Arntzen, C.J. (1980) Biochim. Biophys. Acta 589, 100-117
3 Trémolières, A., Dubacq, J.-P., Ambard-Bretteville, F. and Remy, R. (1981) FEBS Lett. 130, 27-31
4 Dahlin, C. (1989) Physiol. Plant. 76, 438-444
5 Dahlin, C. (1988) Physiol. Plant. 74, 342-348
6 Sandelius, A.S. and Sommarin, M. (1986) FEBS Lett. 201, 282-286
7 Selstam, E. and Sandelius, A.S. (1984) Plant Physiol. 76, 1036-1040
8 Barber, J., Ford, R.C., Mitchell, R.A.C. and Millner, P.A. (1984) Planta 161, 375-380
9 Møller, I.M., Lundborg, T. and Bérczi, A. (1984) FEBS Lett. 167, 181-185
10 Dahlin, C. (1989) PhD Thesis, Univ. of Göteborg, Sweden, ISBN 91-86022-41-5
11 Sandelius, A.S., Dahlin, C. Submitted

THE ROLE OF ELECTRICAL POTENTIAL IN LIGHT-INDUCED SWELLING AND SHRINKAGE OF THYLAKOID MEMBRANES

Huan-gen Ding and Yun-kang Shen, Shanghai Institute of Plant Physiology, Academia Sinica. 300 Fenglin Road, Shanghai, China, 200032

1. INTRODUCTION

Light-induced conformational change of thylakoids was widely studied in the 60'-70's[1][2]. Recently, the curiosity to understand the regulatory process of photosynthesis in vivo[3] has led people to work on this topic again[4][5]. It has been demonstrated that the shrinkage of thylakoids is induced by ΔpH and osmotic movement of weak organic acids across thylakoid membrane[2][6]. However, it has not been reported hitherto that the electrical potential involves in the light-induced conformational change of thylakoids. Electrical potential formation of thylakoid membranes under light has been studied for many years[7]. But the regulation of photosynthetic electron transport by electrical potential was not identified until 80's[8][9]. In this paper, we studied the effects of electrical potential on light-induced conformational change of thylakoids, and found that a decline of electrical potential will induce or increase the light-induced shrinkage of thylakoid in medium without or with weak organic acids.

2. MATERIALS AND METHODS

2.1. Thylakoids (Class D)were isolated from freshly harvested leaves of Spinacia oleracea L. according to the method of [6].

2.2. Reagents: FCCP, Nigericin and Valinomycin were dissolved in 95% ethanol. Final concentration of ethanol in reaction mixture is not higher than 1.5%.

2.3. Basic solution: 20mmol/l Tricine, 20mmol/l NaCl, 20mmol/l KCl, 2mmol/l $MgCl_2$, 0.1mmol/l MV, 10ug/ml Chl, pH7.8.

2.4. Flash-induced ΔA_{515} was measured as described in [6]. Nuetral red absorbance change was obtained as different in absorbance at 547nm with or without 30μmol/l neutral red in medium as in [6].

2.5. Light-induced apparent absorbance change at 540nm (ΔA_{540}): UV-3000 spectrophotometer was used to detect the time course of 548nm change of thylakoid suspension. A broad red light (half width from approx. 670nm to 690nm, and an intensity of $4.5 \times 10^3 erg/cm^2/s$) was used for excitation. The scattered light of excitation was removed by green glass.

M. Baltscheffsky (ed.), Current Research in Photosynthesis, Vol. II, 817–820.
© 1990 Kluwer Academic Publishers. Printed in the Netherlands.

3. RESULTS AND DISCUSSION
3.1. The swelling of thylakoid under light

Light-induced shrinkage of thylakoid membrane has been found in vivo[3], intact chloroplast[4] and in some media[6]. In the 60's. Packer and his coworkers [1] reported the slow swelling of thylakoid. Light stimulated the swelling process of thylakoid [1], but the mechanism of the stimulation was not quite clear. As the reverse process of thylakoid shrinkage, we think that the study on light-induced swelling of thylakoid will give some idea to understand the mechanism of light-induced shrinkage of thylakoid.

As thylakoids were suspended in pH7.8 medium without weak organic

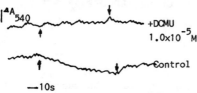

Fig.1 The inhibition of DCMU on light-induced swelling of thylakoid membranes in medium without weak organic acids (pH7.8).

acid, it could be found that light-induced ΔA_{540} decreased (Fig.1), which indicated the swelling of thylakoid[1]. DCMU inhibited the light induced ΔA_{540} change. So it could be said that the light-induced swelling of thylakoid is related to some events in the electron transport.

3.2. The relationship between electrical potential and light-induced conformational change of thylakoids

The electrical potential can be conveniently observed with electrochromatic absorbance change(ΔA_{515}). Although there were some debates on ΔA_{515}[10][11], it was still considered to be reflecting the electrical potential change across thylakoid membrane.

Fig.2 showed that both FCCP and Val. accelerated the decay of flash-induced ΔA_{515}; but the effects of them on ΔA_{540} were different. ΔA_{540} was decreased gradually in the control, and FCCP abolished any change in ΔA_{540}, while Val. increased ΔA_{540}. FCCP is considered as a lipophilic uncoupler, which may lower the pH difference and electrical potential across the thylakoid membrane[11]. If both electrical potential and ΔpH were diminished with FCCP, light-induced ΔA_{540} would be no longer observable. While only electrical potential was eliminated by Val., ΔA_{540} was increased rather than decreased.

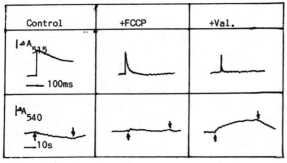

Fig.2 The effect of FCCP and Val. on the decay of ΔA_{515} and light-induced conformational change of thylakoid membranes (ΔA_{540}).

FCCP:5.0×10^{-7}M, Val.1.0×10^{-7}M

↑,light on   ↓,light off

The effect of electrical potential on the light-induced shrinkage of thylakoid membrane suspended in a medium containing different concentration of acetate was shown in Fig.3. Under this condition, electrical potential also had great effect on light-induced conformational change. If electrical potential was removed with Val., ΔA540 increased significantly. Thus it seems that electrical potential acts not only as an active force to induce the swelling of thylakoids in a medium without weak organic acid, but also as a resistance limiting the shrinkage of thylakoid in a medium with weak organic acids.

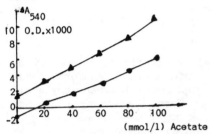

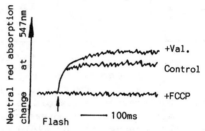

Fig.3 Light-induced ΔA_{540} change in medium with (▲) or without (●) Val. 1.0×10^{-7} mol/l, containing acetate as indicated in fig.

Fig.4 The increase of H^+ influx induced by Valinomycin
Val.:1.0×10^{-7} mol/l, FCCP:5.0×10^{-7} mol/l

3.3. The relationship between electrical potential and H^+ pump

The above results showed that the decline of electrical potential increased the shrinkage of thylakoid. It has been found that [8] H^+/e ratio increased with diminishing electrical potential; and the effect of electrical potential was located in the Cyt_{b-f}-PQ cycle[9]. In our experimental system, similar results was obtained. Fig.4 showed the effect of Val. on pH change across the thylakoid membranes as indicated by flash-induced neutral red absorbance change at 547nm. The slow phase(related to H^+ release from PQH_2)became higher in the presence of Val. As pH change is connected to the shrinkage of thylakoid membrane, H^+ accumulated inside the thylakoid membrane enhanced by the decline of electrical potential should account for part of the light-induced shrinkage of thylakoids.

3.4. The effect of electrical potential under coupling condition

It is a very interesting to know the role of electrical potential under conditions in which ΔpH across the thylakoid membrane is removed and electrical potential is not damaged, so as to eliminate the enhancement of ΔpH induced by a decline of electrical potential. Such a condition was obtained by the addition of Nig. or NH_4Cl. The result was shown in Fig.5. Nigericin, at such concentration that electron transport is uncoupled from phosphorylation, enhanced the light-induced swelling of thylakoid membrane significantly. This effect was inhibited by Val. It could be deduced that in addition to the H^+ accumulated inside the thylakoid membranes enhanced by decline of electrical potential, electrostatic repulsion between membranes should play an important role in light-induced conformational change.

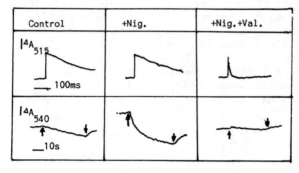

Fig.5 The effect of electrical potential on swelling of thylakoid membranes (ΔA_{540}) under uncoupled conditions with Nig.

Nig.:1.0×10^{-7}M, Val.:1.0×10^{-7}M

$\uparrow$,light on $\downarrow$,light off

It is reasonable to think that the electrostatic force caused by an electrical potential can regulate light-induced conformational change of thylakoid membranes. The repulsion between thylakoid membranes may prevent thylakoid membranes from the strong shrinkage induced by ΔpH and osmotic movement of weak organic acids under light, and keep volume change of thylakoid membrane to some range.

The relationship between electrical potential and ΔpH across the thylakoid membrane is complicated. Electrical potential affected the H^+ pump in Cyt_{b-f}-PQ cycle[8][9][10], and inversely, ΔpH was thought to influence the electrical potential[12]. Such a relation might be necessary for the regulation of conformational change of thylakoids under light. From the results presented above, we postulated that light-induced conformational change of thylakoid is related to both electrical potential and ΔpH across the thylakoid membrane.

REFERENCES
1 Packer L., Siegenthaler P.A. and Nobel P.S. (1965) J. Cell Biol. 26,593-599
2 Krause G.H. (1973) Biochim. Biophys. Acta 292,715-728
3 Dietz K.J.,Neimani S. and Heber U. (1984) Biochim. Biophys. Acta 767,444-450
4 Köster S and Heber U. (1982) Biochim. Biophys. Acta 680,88-94
5 Coughlan S.J. and Pfanz H. (1986) Biochim. Biophys. Acta 849,32-42
6 Ding Huan-gen and Shen Yun-kang (1989) Science Bulletin 17, 1345-1348
7 Witt H.T. (1979) Biochim. biophys. Acta 505,355-427
8 Graan T. and Ort D.R. (1983) J.Bio. Chem. 258,2831-2836
9 Rich P.R. (1988) Biochim. Biophys. Acta 932,33-42
10 Hope A.B. and Matthews D.B. (1987) Aust. J. Plant Physiol. 14, 29-46
11 Peters R., van Kooten O. and Vredenberg W.J. (1984) FEBS Letters 177,11-16
12 Remis D., Bulychev A.A. and Kurella G.A. (1986) Biochim. Biophys. Acta 852,67-73

EXPERIMENTAL INVESTIGATION OF ENERGY TRANSFER PROCESSES IN
THE MODEL PHOTOSYNTHETIC SYSTEMS I.

PETR PANČOŠKA, MARIE URBANOVÁ, LUCIE BEDNÁROVÁ AND
KAREL VACEK, CHARLES UNIVERSITY, FACULTY OF MATHEMATICS
AND PHYSICS, Ke Karlovu 3, 121 16 PRAGUE 2, CZECHOSLOVAKIA

1. INTRODUCTION
    The presented study is designed to evaluate the role of
structure and conformation of pigment-protein complexes in
the determination of the spectral properties of the complexed
porphyrin. The protein environment is simulated by the well-
-defined polypeptides with variable primary structures.
The discussed experimental results provide a basic insight
into the physical mechanism of the porphyrin electronic
structure alternation by protein in a pigment-protein complexes.

2. MATERIALS AND METHODS
    α, β, γ, δ -tetrakis (4-carboxyphenyl) porphyrin (TPPC)
is used as the model pigment. Synthetic sequential polypepti-
des (PP) /1/ composed from Lys, Leu, Ala, Gly are used as model part of complexes:
poly (L-lysyl-L-alanine) (LA), m.w.=6500,
poly (L-lysyl-L-alanyl-L-alanine) (LAA), m.w.=6900,
poly (L-lysyl-L-alanyl-L-alanyl-L-alanine) (LAAA), m.w.=7500,
poly (L-lysyl-L-alanyl-glycine) (LAG), m.w.=7500,
poly (L-lysyl-L-Leucyl-L-alanine) (LLA), m.w.=7900.
Complex formation occurs spontaneously in the 0.02 M phosphate buffer, pH=7.2. Constant porphyrin concentration
(c(TPPC)=5.10^{-5}) and pigment to polypeptide ratios c (TPPC)/c
(PP) from 1/1 to 15/1 were used. Absorption, circular dichroism (CD) and fluorescence spectra were measured as in ref./2/,
time resolved fluorescence experimental set-up is described in
/3/.

3. RESULTS AND DISCUSSION
    The proof of the formation of TPPC-PP complexes with rela-
tively well-defined structure is the observation of intense
induced CD for originally achiral TPPC. The intensity and
sign pattern of this induced CD depend critically on the pigment and peptide structures and the study of this aspect is

presented elsewhere /4,5/.
We were able to generate two types of structural changes by
our model PP matrices:
a) gradual change of secondary structure of (LLA) in the
complex with TPPC,
b) variability of distance of cationic groups in the amino
acid side chains given by the changes of PP primary structures ((LA), (LAA), (LAAA)) with the constant backbone secondary structure which was found to be α-helical according to
characteristic UV CD spectra in amide region.
Both above types of PP structural features were found to have large and specific effects on the studied properties of
the complexed pigment.
3.1. <u>TPPC - (LAA) - complexes</u>
  We see from the dependence of the CD spectra in amide
  UV region on the TPP/PP molar ratio that the mainly non-
  regular conformation of free peptide is gradually converted into more regular α-helical structure in complexes (Fig.1.a). Simultaneously, in the time resolved
  fluorescence experiment the nonexponential fluorescence
  decay observed for the free (aggregated) pigment is replaced by the two exponential decay kinetics with components of 240 ps and 2.4 ns. The contribution ot the

a   b

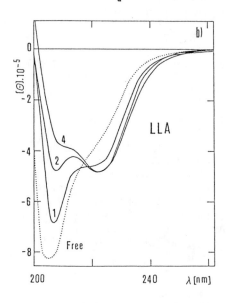 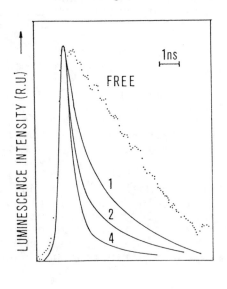

FIGURE 1.a) UV circular dichroism spectra of free(LLA) and
            those after complexation of the TPPC. The curves
            are identified by c(TPPC)/c(PP) molar ratio.
         b) Fluorescence decay curves of TPPC-(LLA) complexes,
            identification as above.

short component to the sum decay fluorescence curve progressively increases with the increasing fraction of
polypeptide α-helical conformation (Fig.1.b). The conformational regularity of our PP matrix therefore seems
to be in a direct relation to the creation of pigment
form with significantly shortened fluorescence lifetime.
As a basis for the explanation we note that conversion
of PP into α-helical conformation minimize the distance
between ε-NH$_3^+$ groups. These charges are obviously the
source of the largest - i.e. Coulombic component of PP
molecular field, so the perturbational influence on the
the fixed porphyrin increases with the observed conformational change of the peptide. For confirmation of this
hypothesis second group of model PP matrices is ideal.

3.2. TPP - (L(A)) - complexes
As well as in case a) we found that fluorescence kinetics
of complexes can be deconvolved into ns and short living
ps components. The contribution of short component to
the global quantum yield depends linearly on the positive charge density in polypeptides (decay curves see
Fig.2.). Simultaneously, in this series of model complexes the porphyrin S_1 energies (frequencies of fluorescence maxima) depend linearly on the positive charge density on corresponding polypeptide (Fig.3.).

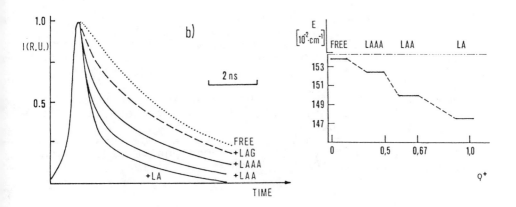

FIGURE 2. Fluorescence decay curves of TPPC-PP complexes with
          molar ratio c (TPPC) /c(PP) = 1/1

FIGURE 3. Correlation of frequencies of fluorescence maxima
          with polypeptide charge density.

II.8.**824**

4. CONCLUSIONS
   Presented results contribute to discussion of two fundamental questions:
1. How sensitive can be response of pigment observables differences in conformation of porphyrin-protein complexes?
2. Can the perturbational theory be used for theoretical explanation of protein influence on porphyrin?
We concluded that:
1. The geometry of the porphyrin-protein complex can influence the bonded pigment electronic levels in two ways - a) By
changes of protein conformation the intensity of the matrix
perturbational field is modified., which can affect the
"first-order" properties (energy related observables).
b) For observables directly depending on geometrical factors
as rotational strength, discussed effect is huge and much more complex. Nevertheless, the possibility of induction of
optical activity in achiral pigment by protein confirms the
mixing of pigment electronic states in such systems with the
possibility to change the selection rules by loss of symmetry etc. as an important and overlooked consequence.
2. Our polypeptides represent the upper limit of molecular
fields, which can be bound in photosynthetic pigment-protein
complexes. The experimental results still confirm the applicability of the perturbational theory for induced energy changes. We can therefore conclude that this theoretical approach
can be safely used for the studies of related problems in vivo.

REFERENCES
1 Pirkova, J., Churkina, S., Gut, V., Fric, I. and Bláha, K.
  (1988) Collect. Czech. Chem. Commun. 53, 145-156
2 Pančoška, P., Urbanová, M., Korvatovsky, B.N., Paschenko,
  V.Z. and Vacek, K. (1987) Chem. Phys. Letters 139, 49-54
3 Paschenko, V.Z. and Rubin, I.B. (1981) Kvant. Electron. 8,
  2569-2574
4 Urbanová, M., Pančoška, P., Bednárová, L., Naether D. and
  Roeder B.,VI. International Conference on Energy and Electron Transfer, Prague, August 14-18, 1989
5 Bednárová, L., Sopková, J., Urbanová, M., Pančoška, P.,
  Maloň, P. and Král, V., III. International Conference on
  Circular Dichroism, Prague, August 21-25, 1989.

THEORETICAL INVESTIGATION OF ENERGY TRANSFER PROCESSES IN
THE MODEL PHOTOSYNTHETIC SYSTEMS II.

L. SKÁLA, V. KAPSA and K. VACEK, FACULTY OF MATHEMATICS
AND PHYSICS, CHARLES UNIVERSITY, Ke Karlovu 3, 121 16
PRAGUE 2, CZECHOSLOVAKIA

All the so far investigated theoretical models of
the excitation energy transfer in the primary processes of
photosynthesis have only limited range of validity. For this
and other reasons we suggested a model of the transfer
processes (1,2) which is quite general as far as the intermolecular transfer it is concerned and allows to obtain the
first principle answers to the following questions. 1) What
are physical reasons of the high value of the quantum yield
of the transfer to the charge transfer state of the
reaction center? 2) What information of the intermolecular
transfer may be obtained from the experimental observables?
3) What is the effect of a finite experimental resolution
and other experimental conditions on the attainability of
this information? 4) What is the mutual relation of the
experimental observables? 5) What is the importance of different transfer regimes - coherent, intermediate and incoherent? In this contribution, some of the most important
results in this respect are summarized.
 After the photon absorption, the exciton moves co-
herently till time ~0.1-1 ps. The contribution of this
regime to the quantum yield of the excitation transfer to
the reaction center (RC) charge transfer state η_{CT} is less
than a few per cent. From this point of view, the role of
the coherent motion is insignificant. Due to averaging over
different configurations of the photosynthetic unit and
other experimental conditions, however, the coherent effects
are not observable for t > 0.1 ps. The intermediate regime,
10 ps > t > 0.1-1 ps contributes to η_{CT} also a few per cent.
The incoherent transfer for t > 10 ps has first a multi-
-exponential character which becomes at t ~25 ps a single-
-exponential one. The single-exponential transfer for
t > 25 ps is the most important one as it gives the most
significant contribution to η_{CT} (about 90 %). In this regime,
the fluorescence intensity and other observables have single-
-exponential character. The corresponding life time equals

M. Baltscheffsky (ed.), Current Research in Photosynthesis, Vol. II, 825–826.
© 1990 Kluwer Academic Publishers. Printed in the Netherlands.

$\tau_F \sim (\nu +1)/k_{CT}$, where k_{CT} is the RC trapping rate and ν is the ratio of the probabilities of finding the exciton in the antenna system and RC. It can be shown that from nine experimental observables (fluorescence and phosphorescence intensities and quantum yields, η_{CT}) only one is independent. In all the transfer regimes, the observables depend only on ν which is in general a function of time, **intra-molecular** rate constants, size of the photosynthetic unit and initial conditions. Therefore, $\nu(t)$ is the maximum information obtainable from the observables. These and further results representing general theoretical answers to problems 1)-5) were illustrated on the case of the bacterial photosynthesis (Rhodopseudomonas viridis) where they are valid for the whole range of the physically acceptable values of the Förster radius.

REFERENCES
1 Skála, L. and Kapsa, V., Chem. Phys., to be published.
2 Skála, L. and Jungwirth, P., Chem. Phys., to be published

CYTOCHROME F AS INDICATOR FOR THE INTERACTION OF THE TWO PHOTOSYSTEMS IN THE STATE 1 AND STATE 2.

W. RÜHLE, A. WEINZETTEL, P. BAUR, and A. WILD
INST. F. ALLGEM. BOT., JOHANNES GUTENBERG-UNIVERSITY MAINZ
SAARSTR. 21; D 6500 MAINZ, FRG

INTRODUCTION:

The transition of plants into a State 1 or a State 2 by an excess of PS I or PS II excitation was described by BONAVENTURA and MYERS [1]. Since the time of their investigations fluorometric methods gained increasing importance in analyzing the distribution of energy between the two photosystems [2]. It was possible to correlate the altered energy balance to the phosphorylation of LHCII and it's migration into non-appressed thylakoid membranes [3]. However fluorescence measurements can give only indirect evidences that also changes in the activity of the two photosystems are produced by the changed energy distribution. A direct assessment of the photochemical variations during state transitions was demonstrated by measuring partial reactions of PS I and PS II [4] or by tracing the behaviour of redox components located between both photosystems [5,6]. There are only a few studies with intact cells e.g. those of SATOH and FORK [7] who describe a 'State 2 – State 3 transition' with the red alga *Porphyra perforata*. Recently REHM et al. [8] have studied state transitions with intact cells of red algae by means of cytochrome f kinetics. They described a drastic decline of the apparent quantum yield of PS I under State 1 conditions. This study confirms their finding also for higher plants. It uses the absorption changes of cytochrome f but considers the influences of activation/inactivation processes which are possible in an intact leaf.

MATERIAL AND METHODS:

Cytochrome f was measured in the dual-wavelength mode (560–554 nm) with an AMINCO–DW2 or a SIGMA–ZWS11 spectrophotometer as described previously [9]. The spectrum of these signals is typical for cytochrome f and it is not significantly influenced by cytochrome b components. The measuring beams of the photometer were directed to the attached leaf with a multibranched fiberoptics which allowed additional application of actinic light. PS I was excited by a cut-off filter RG 715 (Schott). An interference filter 657 nm in combination with a RG 630 (Schott) was used to excite predominantly PS II. In the following these actinic lights will be called light 1 and light 2, respectively. State 2 was induced by a 20 minutes excitement with light 2. A corresponding illumination with

M. Baltscheffsky (ed.), Current Research in Photosynthesis, Vol. II, 827–830.
© 1990 *Kluwer Academic Publishers. Printed in the Netherlands.*

light 1 resulted in a State 1. However, during the induction of State 1 a slight amount of light 2 was added to allow linear electron flow which activates the FNR and Calvin cycle. After transferring the leaves into State 1 or State 2 cytochrome f was reduced by giving 2 seconds light 2 followed by a dark phase of 6 seconds. Then the cytochrome f kinetics was released by varying intensities of light 1 and a constant background of light 2. The intensity of light 2 used for the registration of the cytochrome f signal was the same as for the induction of the states. In this way activation processes of the electron transport and the Calvin-Benson cycle can be eliminated to a large extent.

Chlorophyll fluorescence was measured with a PAM fluorometer (Walz, Germany) under similar conditions. The fluorescence parameters F_0, q_E and q_Q were calculated according to SCHREIBER [10]. The fluorescence quenching q_T due to the changed energy distribution was taken into account when calculating the q_E values.

RESULTS AND DISCUSSION:
The decrease of F_0 fluorescence is used as indicator for a decrease in the antenna size of photosystem II by detachment of phosphorylated LHCII in State 2. Even 1 Wm^{-2} light 2 are able to induce a State 2. The maximal difference in F_0 is about 9% between State 2 and State 1 conditions. By giving additional 26 Wm^{-2} light 1 the decrease is diminished but not completely inhibited. Therefore an extreme State 1 is not reached under the conditions of 6 Wm^{-2} light 2 described in figure 1 but there remains a difference of about 5% between both conditions. Light 2 is quite effective in producing a non-photochemical fluorescence quench q_E especially at low quantum flux densities. A background of 18 Wm^{-2} light 1 reduces q_E remarkably and leads to a more linear relationship between q_E and light 2 intensity.

The cytochrome f oxidation is analyzed for increasing intensities of light 1 at a constant background of PS II excitation. With increasing PS I excitation the initial linear part of the kinetics accelerates. Especially in State 1 it may exhibit an induction effect if dark intervals longer than 1 minute preceeded the measurement. It has been demonstrated that such an induction kinetics indicates a limitation of the electron flow at the acceptor side of PS I [9]. Preillumination with the same intensity of light 2 as during the measurement avoids the induction effect. The dependence of the steady state level of cytochrome f oxidation on the intensity of light 1 is depicted in figure 1 for leaves in both states. There is a clear difference in the course of the curves for State 1 and State 2 reflecting a more oxidized cytochrome f pool in State 2. More than twice the intensity of light 1 is needed under State 1 conditions compared to State 2 to compensate for the constant background of light 2. The increase to the maximum level is also influenced by the intensity of PS II background light. If the intensity of light 2 is decreased less light 1 is necessary for its compensation, but the differences between State 1 and State 2 are similar. This effect is too big to be explained merely by the 5-9 % decreased antenna size of PS II in the State 2.

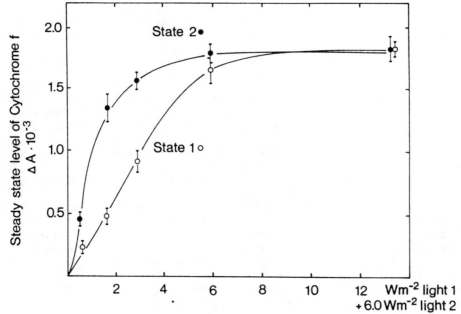

Fig 1: Dependency of the steady state level of cytochrome f oxidation on the intensity of light 1 at a constant background of 6 Wm⁻² light 2. Means and standard deviation of 8 leaves.

When the oxidation of cytochrome f is induced by 700 nm light without light 2 background the rate of photooxidation is accelerated in State 2 compared to State 1 [11]. The slope of the linear initial rise is proportional to the intensity of light 1 under both state conditions. This behaviour can be explained by a decrease in the apparent quantum yield of PS I under State 1 conditions. Its increase in the State 2 cannot be interpreted as an increased PS I antenna, because the 700 nm light of our measurements did not excite the light-harvesting complex. The same effect has been described recently by REHM et al. [8] for red algae. Our results suggest that it is not restricted to phycobilisome containing organisms but has a more general importance for state transitions.

A lower quantum efficiency of PS I may result from
- a cyclic electron flow around PS I that reduces cytochrome f simultaneously to it's oxidation by PS I.
- an impaired PS I photochemistry by a photosynthetic control at the donor side [12] or an excess of electrons at it's acceptor side.

REHM et al.[8] could exclude the contribution of a cyclic electron flow that includes plastoquinone by use of DBMIB. The quantum yield of PS I shows drastic changes during the period of preillumination. It declines to 20% of a dark adapted control within the first minute of preillumination. Only under State 2 conditions it rises again within the next 20 minutes, whereas under State 1 conditions it remains low. This can also be established with isolated intact chloroplasts. The addition of PS I electron acceptors like methylviologen or nitrite can overcome the drop in the quantum yield. A potential limitation of electron flux by the Calvin-Benson cycle was discussed by CEROVIC et al.[13]. They demonstrated a simultaneous increase in the level of cytochrome f oxidation and the rate of oxygen evolution during the first minutes of illumination.

Although the mechanism of this change in quantum yield is not clear until now, it is a fact that should be considered within the concept of state transitions. With the discovery of LHII phosphorylation the regulation during state transitions was thought to consist in a mutual change of the antenna size of both photosystems. An appropriate enhancement in the PS I absorption cross section was recently excluded at least for Scenedesmus and the effect of LHCII phosphorylation resulted only in a decreased antenna size of PS II [14]. According to WEISS and BERRY [15] the decrease in non photochemical quenching in the State 2 should be accompanied by a loss in quantum efficiency of PS II. Simultaneously the quantum yield of PS I is enhanced. We don't want to exclude the contribution of protein phosphorylation to state transitions but it's effect may be primary and has to be amplified much to bring about the observed differences. The result compensates the unequal excitation as the original hypothesis postulated but more by regulation of electron transport activity rather than by energy distribution.

This work was supported by the Deutsche Forschungsgemeinschaft.

REFERENCES
1 Bonaventura, C. and Myers, J. (1969) Biochim. Biophys. Acta 189, 366–383.
2 (1543). Chow, W. S., Telfer, A., Chapman, D. J., and Barber, J. (1981) Biochim. Biophys. Acta 638, 60–68.
3 Allen, J. F., Bennett, J., Steinback, K., and Arntzen, C. J. (1981) Nature 291, 21–25.
4 Farchaus, J. W., Widger, W. R., Cramer, W. A., and Dilley, R. A. (1982) Arch. Biochem. Biophys. 217, 362–367.
5 Biggins, J. (1983) Biochim. Biophys. Acta 724, 111–117.
6 Horton, P. and Black, M. T. (1981) FEBS Lett. 132, 75–77.
7 Satoh, K. and Fork, D.C. (1983) Photosynth. Res. 4, 61–70
8 Rehm, A.M., Gülzow, M., and Ried, A. (1989) Biochim Biophys Acta 973, 131–137
9 Rühle, W., Pschorn, R., and Wild, A. (1987) Photosynth. Res. 11, 161–171.
10 Schreiber, U. (1986) Photosynthesis Research 9, 261–272.
11 Weinzettel, A., Rühle, W., Marzinzik, K., and Wild, A. (1989) Photosynth. Res. (in press)
12 Weis, E. and Lechtenberg, D. (1988) in: Applications of chlorophyll fluorescence.(Lichtenthaler, H.K. ed.), Kluwer Acad. Publ., Dordrecht
13 Cerovic, Z. G. and Plesnicar, M. (1982) Planta 156, 249–256.
14 Allen, J. F. and Melis, A. (1988) Biochim. Biophys. Acta 933, 95–106
15 Weis, E. and Berry, J. A. (1987) Biochim. Biophys. Acta 894, 198–208.

HETEROGENEITY OF THE FUNCTIONAL ANTENNA SIZE OF PHOTOSYSTEM I FROM
SPINACH THYLAKOIDS

EVA ANDREASSON, PER SVENSSON AND PER-ÅKE ALBERTSSON
Department of Biochemistry, University of Lund, P.O. Box 124, S-221 00,
LUND, SWEDEN

1. INTRODUCTION
    We have recently fractionated the thylakoid membrane from spinach
chloroplasts into two well separated vesicle populations (1). This was
achieved by sonication and aqueous two-phase partitioning. A counter-
current distribution diagram after such a fractionation is shown in
Fig.1 . The left peak comprises the grana derived α-vesicles while the
right peak comprises the stroma derived β-vesicles. In this study we
focused on examining the light harvesting properties of PSI of the two
vesicle populations (PSIα and PSIβ respectively). We find different
functional antenna sizes of PSI. PSIα has an antenna size about 30 %
larger than PSIβ. Our results imply that this heterogeneity in antenna
size reflects the situation in the thylakoid membrane in vivo and is
not due to any spill-over from PSII.

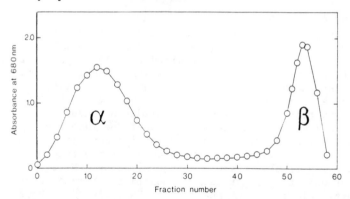

FIGURE 1. Countercurrent distribution diagram of sonicated stacked
        thylakoid membranes. The α-peak comprises vesicles origi-
        nating from the grana membrane and the β-peak comprises
        vesicles originating from the stroma membrane. From ref.(1).

2. PROCEDURE
2.1. Materials and methods
    2.1.1. The α- and β-vesicle preparations were made by sonication of
        thylakoids followed by partitioning of the material in an

M. Baltscheffsky (ed.), Current Research in Photosynthesis, Vol. II, 831–834.
© 1990 Kluwer Academic Publishers. Printed in the Netherlands.

aqueous two-phase system by a batch procedure as described in (1). The α-vesicle preparation is denoted B3 and the β-vesicle preparation is denoted T3.

2.1.2. The Yedapress homogenate, the YPH fraction, was prepared by press treatment of whole thylakoids as in (2).

2.1.3. A fraction enriched in PSIα, 120S, was prepared from grana membranes by sonication followed by aqueous two-phase partitioning of the B3 fraction. Two portions of B3 were made in the same way as in (1) but the last step, the removing of the thylakoid vesicles from the polymers of the bottom phase, was not done. Instead the two bottom phases containing B3 vesicles were combined and 10 ml of pure top phase was added. The final volume was 30 ml. The phase system containing the B3 fraction was sonicated in a Vibra-cell ultrasonic processor, Model VC 500, equipped with a 3/4 inch "High Gain" horn for 4 x 30 s with resting intervals of two min under continuous cooling. Afterwards the phase system was mixed thoroughly and separated under low speed centrifugation (1000 x g for 3 min). The top phase was collected and the PSIα-enriched vesicles (120S) were removed from the polymers by a 3-fold dilution in a suitable buffer and pelleted at 100000 x g for 90 min.

2.1.4. The absorbance difference measurements for the quantification of P-700 were made as described earlier (1).

2.1.5. Kinetics of the P-700 photooxidation of potassium cyanide treated vesicles were measured as in (1) using the method described by Melis (3).

3. RESULTS AND DISCUSSION

After disintegration of stacked thylakoid membranes by sonication followed by partitioning in an aqueous two-phase system two well-separated vesicle populations are obtained (Fig.1). Both the grana derived fraction, the α-vesicles, and the stroma derived fraction, the β-vesicles, contain PSI (Table 1, P-700 content). In fact, the P-700 of the grana derived fraction comprises 35 % of the total P-700 (1). We compared the kinetics of the P-700 photooxidation under weak illumination for the two vesicle populations. The rate constant (k) for P-700 photooxidation is proportional to the incident light and the antenna size of PSI and should be independent of the rate of electron transport to P-700 if plastocyanin is inhibited by KCN (3).

If the photooxidating light is kept constant the rate constant is solely proportional to the antenna size of PSI. Fig. 2.a shows kinetic traces of the time-course of P-700 photooxidation in fractions B3 (α-vesicles) and T3 (β-vesicles) at constant incident light. The semilogarithmic plots for B3 and T3 are shown in Fig. 2.b. The plots fit straight lines but the slopes of the lines are different and B3 displays a 28 % faster photooxidation than T3; the rate constant for B3 is 28 % larger than for T3 (Table 1). This implies that the antenna size of PSI in the grana derived fraction, PSIα, is about 30 % larger than the antenna size of PSI in the stroma derived fraction, PSIβ.

TABLE 1. Chlorophyll a/b ratio, P-700 content and rate constant (k) of
the kinetics of the P-700 photooxidation in thylakoid membrane
fractions. The k values can be compared only within each of
the pairs of experiments. (DCMU, 3-(3,4-dichlorophenyl)-1,1-
dimethylurea)

Fraction	Chl a/b	P-700/Chl (mmol/mol)	k (s^{-1})
B3	2.3	1.5	5.5
T3	5.0	4.7	4.3
YPH	2.9	2.6	6.3
120S	2.9	2.4	7.5
B3	2.3	1.5	4.6
B3(-DCMU)	2.3	1.5	4.7

Heterogeneity of the antenna size has also been shown when light-
saturation curves for PSI activity were compared for B3 and T3 (1).
Also in that investigation PSIα showed a larger antenna size than PSIβ
(30-100 %).

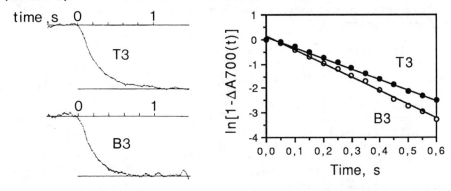

FIGURE 2. a) Kinetic traces of the time-course of P-700 photooxidation.
The trace of T3 is the mean of 6 individual measurements,
while the trace of B3 is the mean of 24 individual measurements. b) First-order kinetic analysis of the traces in
Fig.2.a, B3 gives a higher rate constant (5.5 s^{-1}) than T3
(4.3 s^{-1}).

Are the results we find really evidences of different antenna sizes
of PSI and not due to spill-over from PSII? The grana derived vesicle
population is enriched in PSII compared to the stroma derived vesicles.
If over-excitation of PSII leads to spill-over to PSI the enrichment of
PSII in the α-fraction could be the reason for PSIα showing a larger
antenna size than PSIβ. Yet, when DCMU was omitted from the medium no
significant change in the rate of photooxidation of P-700 was observed.
Thus, the rate constants for P-700 photooxidation with and without DCMU

were practically the same (Table 1). One would have expected an
enhanced degree of spill-over from PSII to PSI when DCMU is included in
the medium and thereby a change in the functional antenna size of PSI.
This change in antenna size was not observed and we interpret that the
differences in antenna size that we find for PSIα and PSIβ is not the
result of any spill-over between the two different photosystems.

The grana and stroma derived fractions have different PSI contents
and different Chl a/b ratios (Table 1). To make sure that these
differences do not affect the rate of photooxidation of P-700 under the
light conditions used we studied two fractions with about the same
P-700 content and Chl a/b ratio but with different PSIα and PSIβ
concentrations. The YPH fraction is prepared by disintegration by press
treatment of whole stacked thylakoid membranes while the 120S fraction
is prepared by sonication and aqueous two-phase partitioning of B3. The
YPH fraction should have the same concentration of PSIα and PSIβ as the
thylakoid membrane; 35 % PSIα and 65 % PSIβ, while the 120S fraction on
the other hand should consist solely of PSIα. One would therefore
expect an about 17 % larger average antenna size of PSI in the 120S
fraction than in the YPH fraction. Fig.3 shows the semilogarithmic
plots of the time-courses of the P-700 photooxidation in fractions YPH
and 120S. The rate constant (k) for 120S is 18 % larger than for YPH
(Table 1) which agrees with the result expected. The content of PSI or
the Chl a/b ratio in the samples does not therefore affect the rate of
P-700 photooxidation.

We conclude that in the spinach
thylakoid membrane there are two
different populations of PSI with
respect to antenna size, PSIα and
PSIβ. PSIα has the larger antenna
and resides in the grana membrane
region, while PSIβ with its smaller
antenna is located in the stroma
membrane. We have shown before that
the PSI of inside-out vesicles most
probably is localized in domains
separate from PSII (4). Our results
therefore suggest that the PSIα
units of the grana membrane reside
in domains separate from PSII, such
as the end membranes and the
margins of the grana and even in
domains in the partition region.

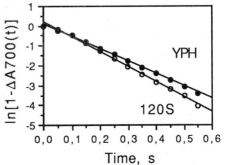

FIGURE 3. First-order kinetic
analysis of traces of the
time-course of P-700
photooxidation. 120S gave
a higher rate constant
than YPH (Table 1).

REFERENCES
1. Andreasson, E., Svensson, P. Weibull, C. and Albertsson, P.-Å.
   (1988) Biochim. Biophys. Acta 936, 339-350
2. Melis, A., Svensson, P. and Albertsson, P.-Å. (1986) Biochim.
   Biophys. Acta 850, 402-412
3. Melis, A. (1982) Arch. Biochem. Biophys. 217, 536-545
4. Albertsson, P.-Å. (1988) Q. Rev. Biophys. 21, 61-98

HETEROGENEITY OF PSIIα

PER-ÅKE ALBERTSSON, SHI-GUI YU and ULLA K.LARSSON, Department of
Biochemistry, University of Lund, P.O. Box 124, S-221 00 LUND, SWEDEN

1. INTRODUCTION

Classification by antenna size gives two classes of PSII in
chloroplasts from higher plants.The main part of PSII is located in the
grana in the form of PSIIα (1). We have previously shown that there are
subclasses of PSIIα (PSIIα$_1$, PSαII$_2$, PSIIα$_3$ etc) having different
antenna sizes (2). Sonication of inside-out thylakoid vesicles - which
originate from the grana partitions and harbour PSIIα - followed by
phase partition separated vesicles into different populations of
vesicles having different functional antenna size of PSIIα. The functional antenna size was determined from light saturation curves of the
oxygen evolution with phenylparabenzoquinone (1) or ferricyanide (P.Å
Albertsson and S.G. Yu, unpublished) as electron acceptors. We now
report data on the heterogeneity of PSIIα obtained by two additional,
independent methods, fluorescence spectroscopy and gel electrophoresis.

2. PROCEDURE

2.1. Isolation of inside-out thylakoid vesicles (B3) from spinach and
     their subfractionation by sonication and phase partition was done
     essentially as previously described (2,3). The fractions named
     180s, 540s and BS according to the nomenclature described in (2,3)
     were obtained. All these fractions derive from the B3 fraction,
     and hence from the grana partitions, and have a high PSII activity
     (2,3). Their chlorophyll a/b ratios are given in Table 1.

2.2. Fluorescence induction was measured at room temperature with a
     modified Aminco spectrophotometer. Actinic light of uniform field
     was provided in the blue-green region of the spectrum.
     Fluorescence emission at 685 nm was detected at right angles to
     the direction of the actinic beam. Integration of the area over
     the fluorescence induction curve and semilogarithmic plots were
     analysed according to Melis and Homann (4,5). The reaction mixture
     contained 50 mM Tricine, pH 7.8, 400 mM sucrose, 10 mM NaCl, 5 mM
     MgCl$_2$ and membrane vesicles (5μM Chl/ml). Fluorescence was
     measured in the presence of 20 μM DCMU and after 5 min for dark
     adaption.

2.3. Electrophoresis. For analysis of chlorophyll-protein complexes
     (Table 2) a mild SDS-DAGE method (6) was used. Two dimensional gel
     electrophoresis (7) was used for analysis of 25 and 27 kDa
     polypeptides (Fig.1).

M. Baltscheffsky (ed.), Current Research in Photosynthesis, Vol. II, 835–838.
© 1990 *Kluwer Academic Publishers. Printed in the Netherlands.*

3. RESULTS AND DISCUSSION
   The kinetics of the variable fluorescence of the different
fractions show that the BS fraction needs the shortest time to reach
half maximal rise in variable fluorescence, and also have the largest
kinetic constant for the increase of the area over the fluorescence
induction curve (Table 1). From the data of Table 1 one can conclude
that the functional antenna size of all the three fractions originating
from B3 differ in the same order as was found by measuring the light
saturation curves (2).

TABLE 1. The half-rise time ($t_{1/2}$) and the velocity constant (k) of the
area growth over the fluorescence induction curve of different
thylakoid membrane fractions in the presence of DCMU. The
value of k and the inverse value of t 1/2 are proportional to
the functional antenna size. $K\alpha$ is the constant for the fast
component representing PSIIα and $K\beta$ is the constant for the
slow component representing PSIIβ. No PSIIβ component could be
detected in the 540S, B3 and BS fractions.

	Chl a/b	$t_{1/2}$ of F_v (ms)	$K\alpha$ (s^{-1})	$K\beta$ (s^{-1})
Thylakoid	2.7	62.4	10	4.5
180S	3.3	57.3	10	4.6
540S	2.3	51.0	13	-
B3	2.3	51.0	14	-
BS	1.9	47.4	18	-

The proportion of the different light harvesting pigment proteins
of PSII and of the PSII core complex are given in Table 2. The BS
fraction has the highest ratio LHCH per PSII core complex and there is
a correlation between the ratio of LHCII per PSII core complex (Table
2) and the kinetics of the variable fluorescence (Table 1).

Table 2. Relative proportion of light-harvesting pigment proteins of
PSII (LHCII) and PSII-core complex proteins, (CP_a, including
CP43 and CP47) in different thylakoid membrane fractions.

Fraction	LHCII %	CP_a %	$\dfrac{LHCII}{CP_a}$	Free Chl %
Thylakoid	42.6	18.5	2.3	3.7
180s	53.3	18.9	2.8	4.7
B3	55.6	19.6	2.8	3.6
720s	62.2	21.4	2.9	4.6
BS	68.7	21.6	3.2	3.1

There is also a qualitative difference between the antenna systems of the different PSIIα membrane vesicles. This could be demonstrated by two dimensional gel electrophoresis which separates the two poly-peptides, 25 kDa and 27 kDa, of LHCII. The fractions which have the largest antenna size, also contain more of the 25 kDa polypeptide (Fig. 1).

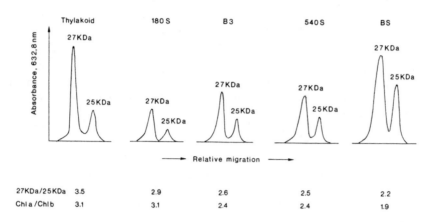

FIGURE 1. The relative content of the 25 and 27 kDa polypeptides of LHCII of different thylakoid membrane fractions.

In summary we have demonstrated by 3 independent methods, the determination of the light saturation curve for O_2-evolution, the variable fluorescence, and gel elctrophoresis, that the subclasses of PSIIα-vesicles differ in the size of their antennae. The order of antenna size within the different fractions is the same when determined by all the three methods, BS having the largest antenna. Such PSII units can be built by adding to the antenna more of the LHCII poly-peptides, whereby the functional antenna will be augmented by discrete increments. In addition there is also a qualitative difference between the fractions, in that BS has a relatively larger content of the 25 kDa polypeptide. Recent studies have shown that LHCII consists of an inner part, which contains only the 27 kDa polypeptide, and a peripheral part which contains both the 25 kDa and the 27 kDa polypeptides (7,8). All our PSIIα membrane vesicles contain both polypeptides, but those having a larger functional antenna are more enriched in 25 kDa. This shows that the stepwise increase in the antenna size is accomplished by increasing the peripheral part of the LHCII.

The inside-out vesicles (B3), which contain 75-85 per cent of the PSII of the thylakoid in the form of PSIIα, originate from the grana partitions (9). Sonication of these vesicles produces new vesicles which are smaller in size than the B3 vesicles (10). While the average diameter of the thin sections of the B3 vesicles is 0,3 μm, this

diamter is reduced to 0,1-0,2 μm after sonication (10). By phase
partition these vesicles are separated into populations of vesicles
with different average antenna sizes. Note that the material is in a
vesicle from and has not been treated by detergents. We therefore
conclude that these subclasses of PSIIα vesicles originate from
separate domains in the native thylakoid membrane.

Recently it has been shown that thylakoids from "low light"
spinach have a larger LHCII/PSII core ratio and a smaller 27 kDa/25kDa
ratio of the LHCII than thyalkoids from medium or high light spinach
(11,12). It was concluded that the LHCII of the "low light" chloroplast
contains more of the peripheral, 25 kDa rich, pool of LHCII. Since the
BS fraction contains the largest relative amount of the 25 kDa polypeptide, our results suggest that chloroplast from leaves grown under
low light conditons contain more of those grana domains from which the
BS fraction originates. Our results also suggest that these
"BS domains" may be more abundant in the interior or on the lower side
of a leaf where the light intensity is lower.

REFERENCES
1 Anderson, J.M. and Melis, A. (1983) Proc. Natl. Acad. Sci. 80,
  745-749
2 Albertsson, P.Å. and Yu, S.G. (1988) Biochim. Biophys. Acta 936,
  215-221
3 Svensson, P. and Albertsson, P.Å. (1989) Photosynth. Res. 20, 249-259
4 Melis, A. and Homann, P.H. (1975) Photochem. Photobiol. 21, 431-437
5 Melis, A. and Homann, P.H. (1976) Photochem. Photobiol. 23, 343-350
6 Anderson. J.M., Waldron, J.C. and Thorne, S.W. (1978) FEBS Lett. 92,
  227-233
7 Larsson, U.K. and Andersson, B. (1985) Biochim. Biophys. Acta 809,
  396-402
8 Spangfort, M., Larsson, U.K., Anderson, J.M. and Andersson, B. (1987)
  FEBS Lett. 224, 343-347
9 Andersson, B., Sundby, C., Åkerlund, H.E. and Albertsson, P.Å.
  (1986) Physio 1. Plkant (1985) 65, 322-330
10 Albertsson, P.Å. (1985) Physiol. Veg. 23, 731-739
11 Larsson, U.K., Anderson, J.M. and Andersson, B. (1987) Biochim.
   Biophys. Acta 894, 69-75
12 Mäenpää, P. and Andersson, B. (1989) Z. Naturforsch. 44 C, in press.

PROPERTIES OF A NON-DETERGENT PS II MEMBRANE PREPARATION

Per **Svensson**, Shi-Gui **Yu**, Ulla K. **Larsson**, Eva **Andreasson** and Per-Åke **Albertsson**.
Dept. of Biochemistry, University of Lund, P.O. BOX 124, S-221 00 Lund, Sweden.

1. INTRODUCTION

Preparation of photosystem (PS) II enriched membrane vesicles is of great interest in order to study the function of PS II in a form which resembles the situation in vivo. PS II particles, originating from the appressed regions of the thylakoid, can be obtained by treatment with the detergent Triton X-100 (1). The suspicion that the detergent could solubilize some components originally present in this membrane region suggests the search for alternative preparations. PS II preparations using mechanical disintegration procedures e.g. inside-out vesicles (2) have the drawback of relatively high content of PS I, presumably originating from the non-appressed regions of the thylakoid membrane.

Recently we have demonstrated that pure PS II vesicles can be obtained by mechanical fragmentation (3) and a preparative procedure for obtaining these vesicles has also been presented (4). The starting material for the preparation is inside-out vesicles. These vesicles are sonicated and separated by aqueous two-phase partition. The PS II vesicles, named BS, which are obtained by this non-detergent procedure have a high oxygen evolving capacity and a very low content of P700 (4). The vesicles have now been further characterized. Light saturation curves showed that the PS II is in the form PS IIα. Two-dimensional gel electrophoresis of the LHC-II polypeptides demonstrated that the ratio 27/25 kDa for BS is lower than for previous PS II membrane vesicle preparations, indicating a large peripheral subpopulation of LHC-II.

2. PROCEDURE

2.1. Materials and methods

2.1.1. Isolation of inside-out vesicles, B3, was performed according to (2) using a phase system with 5.7% (w/w) of each Dextran 500 and Polyethylene glycol 3350. The final lower phase, B3, was used directly for the sonication experiments.

2.1.2. Fractional sonication - phase partition. Twenty ml of the lower phase B3 and 10 ml of fresh upper phase was sonicated 4 x 30 s with 2 min resting intervals under continuous cooling using a Vibra-cell ultrasonic processor, Model VC 500, equipped with a 3/4 inch "High Gain" horn. The output was set at 7 with 20% duty pulses. The phases were separated by low speed centrifugation and the upper phase was removed and stored separately.

M. Baltscheffsky (ed.), Current Research in Photosynthesis, Vol. II, 839–842.

This procedure was repeated three times. The remaining material
in the in the lower phase was named BS, "bottom sonicated".

2.1.3. Light saturation curves for thylakoids and the BS fraction were
obtained as in (5). The relative functional antenna size was
determined from the slope of the plot of V/I versus V (6), where
V is the oxygen evolution in moles O_2 x (mg Chl)$^{-1}$ x h^{-1} and I
is the light intensity in mE x m^{-2} x s^{-1}.

2.1.4. Two-dimensional gel electrophoresis. The first-dimension
electrophoresis was performed as in (7). The green bands
resolved corresponding to the monomeric (LHCP 3) and trimeric
(LHCP 1) forms of LHC-II were excised from the gel. For the
second dimension these gel pieces were reelectrophoresed under
more denaturating conditions according to Laemmli (8), using a
12-22.5% gradient gel. The second dimension gels were stained
with Coomassie brilliant blue and scanned using a laser densitometer. The polypeptides were quantified from their peak areas.

2.1.5. The concentration of cytochrome (Cyt) f was determined from the
reduced-minus-oxidized absorbance change at 554.5 nm (9).

3. RESULTS AND DICUSSION

To show the reliability of the procedure three independent preparations were made (data shown in table 1). The standard deviation was
0.01-0.07 for the chlorophyll a/b ratios and 0.4-1.4 for the yields.
Note that the yield of BS is about six per cent of the thylakoids which
is a two-fold increase compared to the earlier preparartion (4). The
relatively low yield of inside-out vesicles, B3, is due to that it
otherwise would be a very tedious preparation. Yield of B3 in the range
of 30 to 40% can easily be obtained but is time-consuming when large
quantities are needed. The fact that the yield of BS is always about
one third of B3 implies that the BS fraction represents a considerable
large domain of the appressed part of the thylakoid membrane.

Table 1. Chlorophyll (Chl) a/b-ratios and yields from the PS II vesicle
preparation named BS. The data represents mean values from three
independent preparations.

	Thy	B3	BS
Chl a/b	3.0	2.3	1.9
Yield (%)	100	21	6

In order to investigate the type of PS II antenna in the BS
fraction, light saturation curves of the PS II-activity were made (Fig.
1a.). It was earlier shown that analysis of such curves by V/I versus V
plots give slopes whose inverses are proportional to the antenna size
of PS II (10). Such plots of thylakoids and BS are shown in Fig. 1b.
The thylakoids give rise to an upward concave curve demonstrating
heterogeneity in the antenna size among the PS II units. The curve can
be divided into two parts, a steep one corresponding to PS IIα and a
less steep one corresponding to PS IIβ. The BS plot, on the other hand,
fits fairly well a straight line with a steepness like that of PS IIα.

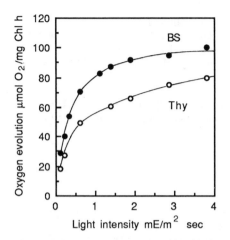

Fig. 1A. *PS II-activity of thyla-koids and BS as a function of light intensity. The activity was meas-ured as oxygen evolution using phenyl-p-benzoquinone (PpBQ) as electron acceptor. Thylakoids o, BS ●.*

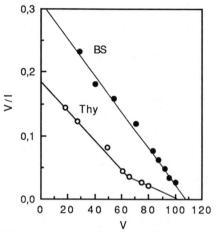

Fig. 1B. *V/I vs. V plot of the data shown in Fig. 1a. The slope is -1/Km where Km is the light inten-sity that gives half-maximum activ-ity, its inverse value is propor-tional to the functional antenna size of PS II. Thylakoids o, BS ●.*

The presence of PS IIα in the BS preparation was also demonstrated by analysis of the kinetics in variable fluorescence (P.-Å. Albertsson and S.-G. Yu, to be published).

In an attempt to further investigate the light harvesting antenna of the BS fraction two-diminsional gel electrophoresis was used. In the first dimension the chlorophyll protein complexes were resolved by mild SDS-PAGE (7). From this gel the bands that contain the oligomer and momomer of LHC-II were cut out and applied on a denatura-ting Laemmli gel (8). Laser densi-tometer scans of such gels stained with Coomassie brilliant blue are shown in Fig. 2. Note the large proportion of the 25 kDa poly-peptide in the BS fraction compared to thylakoids. It has been shown that the ratio between the 27 kDa and the 25 kDa polypeptides is different in the peripheral and the

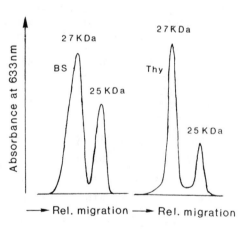

Fig. 2. *Gel scans of the 27 and 25 kDa apopolypeptides of LHC-II of thylakoids and the BS fraction after two-dimensional gel electrophoresis. The second dimension gels were stained with Coomassie brilliant blue and scanned with a laser densitometer.*

tightly bound LHC-II (11). The tightly bound LHC-II has almost exclusively the 27 kDa polypeptide while the peripheral LHC-II has an almost equal amount of the two polypeptides. Table 2 shows that BS has a substantially lower 27/25-ratio than the thylakoids indicating large amount of the peripheral antenna (11).

Table 2. Ratio between the 27 kDa and 25 kDa polypeptides from the gels shown in Fig. 2. The relative amount of the two apopolypeptides were quantified from their peak areas.

	Chl a/b	27/25-ratio
Thy	3.1	3.5
BS	1.9	2.2

Cytochrome f determinations (Table 3.) show that the BS fraction has a substantial enrichment (about 30%) compared to thylakoids. This support earlier results from measurements made in our laboratory where we find Cyt f somewhat enriched in the appressed region of the thylakoid membrane (5). For comparison an ordinary inside-out vesicle preparation, B3, was measured. As B3 shows an intermediate value for both Cyt f content (about 15% enrichment) and for PS II content (4) it is reasonable to conclude that PS II and the cytochrome b_6-f complexes are in close contact in the appressed membrane region.

Table 3. Cytochrome f distribution in spinach subchloroplast fractions. The concentration of Cyt f was determined from the reduced-minus-oxidized absorbance change at 554.5 nm.

	Thy	B3	BS
Cyt f/Chl (mmol/mol)	1.3	1.5	1.7

REFERENCES
1 Berthold, D.A., Babcock, G.T. and Yocum, C.F. (1981) FEBS Lett. 134, 231-235
2 Åkerlund, H.-E. and Andersson, B. (1983) Biochim. Biophys. Acta 725, 35-40
3 Albertsson, P.-Å. and Svensson, P. (1988) Mol. Cell. Biochem. 81, 155-163
4 Svensson, P. and Albertsson, P.-Å. (1989) Photosynth. Res. 20, 249-259
5 Albertsson, P.-Å. and Yu, S.-G. (1988) Biochim. Biophys. Acta 936, 215-221
6 Mäenpää, P., Andersson, B. and Sundby, C. (1987) FEBS Lett. 215, 31-36
7 Andersson, B. and Anderson, J.M. (1980) Biochim. Biophys. Acta 593, 427-440
8 Laemmli, U.K. (1970) Nature 227, 680-685
9 Bendall, D.S., Davenport, H.E. and Hill, R. (1972) Methods Enzymol. 23,327-344
10 Andreasson, E., Svensson, P., Weibull, C. and Albertsson, P.-Å. (1988) Biochim. Biophys. Acta 936, 339-350
11 Larsson, U.K. and Andersson, B. (1985) Biochim. Biophys. Acta 809, 396-402

PHOTOSYNTHETIC CHARACTERIZATION OF THYLAKOID MEMBRANE PREPARATIONS
ISOLATED FROM SPINACH GROWN UNDER DIFFERENT LIGHT CONDITIONS

SHI GUI YU, EVA ANDREASSON AND PER-ÅKE ALBERTSSON
Dept. of Biochemistry, University of Lund, P.O.Box 124, 221 00 Lund,
Sweden

1. INTRODUCTION

The quality and quantity of light during plant growth determine
photosynthetic structural and functional properties of higher plants.
Light environment varies not only on a large scale, such as, seasonally,
diurnally, and spatially, but also at the level of micro-circumstances of
the chloroplasts. Our previous experiments have shown that in vivo
there are different domains in the thylakoid membranes, which have
different Chla/b ratios and different average antenna sizes of
photosystem IIα (PSIIα), the dominating form of PSII(1). For optimal
photosynthesis a battery of photosynthetic units with different antenna
sizes and pigment contents might be beneficial to the plant to adapt to
changes in its light environment and to efficiently utilize the light
quanta.

In this communication we present a series of data on structural and
functional characterization of thylakoids and highly enriched PSII
membrane vesicles(named BS) isolated from spinach grown under different
light conditions. The experimental approach involved different kinds of
gel electrophoresis, spectrophotometric and kinetic analyses as well as
basic biochemical methods.

2. PROCEDURE

2.1. The thylakoids and highly enriched PSII-membrane vesicles(BS) were
isolated from spinach grown under low light and higher (ordinary)
light intensities (1). The light irradiance was 400 for ordinary
light(OL) and 50uE.m^{-2}.s^{-1} for low light(LL).

2.2. Fluorescence induction kinetics was measured at room temperature
with a modified Aminco spectrophotometer in the presence of 20 mM
DCMU after 5 min of dark adaptation. Relative rate of pheophytin
anion photoaccumulation in PSII was estimated from the analysis
of the fluorescence quenching curve in the presence of 20 mM
dithionite (in 50mM Tricine, pH 7.8).

2.3. For analysis of relative contents of chlorophyll protein
complexes, SDS-PAGE was used as reported in (2,3,4). The bands
were scanned at 632.8 nm by a laser densitometer.

2.4. The absolute content of PSII-core complexes was determined as the
concentration of atrazine-binding sites. The concentration of
PSI-core complexes was estimated from quantitative measurements of
the light induced absorbance change at 700 nm.

M. Baltscheffsky (ed.), Current Research in Photosynthesis, Vol. II, 843–846.
© 1990 *Kluwer Academic Publishers. Printed in the Netherlands.*

1. RESULTS AND DISCUSSION

Analyses of fluorescence induction kinetics show that, compared with the thylakoids isolated from ordinary light plants, the thylakoids from low light had a shorter time of the rise of Fv and an equally increased Fo and Fm, indicating an enhancement of the absorption cross section of PSII. Calculation from the semilogarithmic plots revealed that the relative content of PSIIα and its rate constant (Kα) of area growth over the fluorescence curve were higher for low light thylakoids (Table 1). These data support the notion that there is a larger average antenna size of PSIIα units in the low light plants.

TABLE 1. Comparison of the fluorescence induction curve parameters measured from thylakoids isolated from spinach grown at ordinary light (Thyl.OL) or low light (Thyl.LL).

	$t_{1/2}$ of Fv (ms)	Kα (s-1)	Kβ (s-1)	PSIIα (%)	PSIIβ (%)	Fo	Fm
Thyl.OL	62	10	4.5	63	37	14	36
Thyl.LL	57	11	3.8	68	32	18	45

Table 2 shows the fluorescence induction curve parameters for PSIIα membrane vesicles (BS) obtained from spinach grown at different light irradiation. It seems that there is a similar tendency towards the changes of the fluorescence parameters, compared with those for the thylakoids. However, the kinetic constants of PSIIα (Kα) are closer each other. This may just fit with the postulation that BS-domains in vivo might be more abundant in the interior or on the lower side of a leaf where light intensity is lower. In this case, the light environment for BS and BS in low light could be very similar.

TABLE 2. Fluorescence induction curve parameters measured on different thylakoid membrane fragments isolated from spinach grown under different light conditions.

	$t_{1/2}$ of Fv (ms)	$Kα_1$ (s^{-1})	$Kβ_1$ (s^{-1})	Fo	Fv	Fm
Thyl.OL	56	15	11	17	44	61
Thyl.LL	32	18	9	28	44	72
BS.OL	42	18	x	40	78	118
BS.LL	25	18	x	83	67	150

In order to quantitatively estimate the content of pigment protein complexes, the chlorophyll-proteins were resolved by mild SDS polyacrylamide gel electrophoresis. As seen in Table 3, there is a remarkable increase in LHCII/CPa ratio in low light thylakoids. Compared with the control, this increase is accompanied by a decrease in chlorophyll a/b ratio (Table 5). This result is in a good agreement with the results of the fluorescence measurements.

Table 4 demonstrates the polypeptide composition of LHCII for the thylakoids and BS derived from plants grown under different light conditions. It is evident that the higher ratio of LHCII/CPa was accompanied by a lower ratio of 27/25 kDa polypeptide of LHCII for the samples in low light. This means that the larger antenna size of PSII

which the low light plants have,contains relatively more 25 kDa
polypeptide,suggesting that the modification in antenna size during
plant light acclimation is accomplished by a change in the relative
content of the peripheral population of LHCII (5,6).

TABLE 3. Relative proportion of light harvesting chlorophyll a/b
protein complexes and PSII core complex in thylakoids isolated
from spinach grown at different light conditions. The results
shown are expressed as a percentage of the total absorption of
a scanned gel.

	CPa (%)	LHCII (%)	LHCII/CPa
Thyl.OL	12	51	4.2
Thyl.LL	10	55	5.5

TABLE 4. The ratio between the 27 and 25 kDa polypeptides of LHCII in
the thylakoids and PSII-membrane vesicles (BS) isolated from
spinach grown at different light conditions. The amount of
each polypeptide was quantified from its peak area after two
dimensional gel electrophoresis.

	Ratio of 27/25kDa	
	Ordinary light	Low light
Thylakoid	3.1	2.4
BS	2.4	2.2

It is well known that if Q is chemically reduced by a strong
reductant, an intensive actinic illumination will induce a fluorescence
quenching,attributed to the photoaccumulation of pheophytin anion. This
decline of fluorescence yield is accompanied by optical absorbance
changes (7). Based on this postulation we have evaluated the primary
photochemistry of PSII by fluorescence decline in the presence of
dithionite. As shown in Fig.1, this fluorescence decline is much more
evident for the PSII-membrane vesicles than that for the thylakoids.
Analysis of the fluorescence quenching kinetics by a semilogarithmic
plot shows that there is a very small difference in the rate constants
between BS from ordinary light and low light, compared with those for
thylakoids (Fig.2).

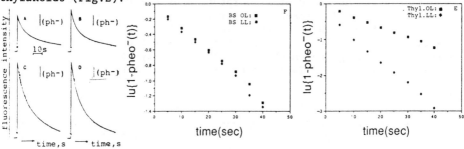

FIGURE 1. Fluorescence yield kinetics of thylakoids(A),thylakoids from
low light (B), BS (C) and BS from low light (D), incubated
for 10 min in the dark with 20 mM dithionite.

FIGURE 2. Semilogarithmic plots of pheo⁻ photoaccumulation kinetics in
the presence of 20 mM dithionite.E: for thylakoids,F: for BS.

In order to confirm directly, whether the content of PSII core
Chla-protein complex varies, depending on the light conditions, the
amount of Qb was quantified by determination of the number of atrazine
binding sites. As seen in Table 5, low light thylakoids have a lower
content of Qb than ordinary light thylakoids. This fits well with the
results from gel electrophoresis. The other electron-transfer
components, such as Cytf also become less abundant for low light
thylakoids. On the contrary, the amount of P-700 per protein increased
slightly.

TABLE 5. Comparison of chlorophyll a/b ratio, yield, the concetration
of core Chla-proteins of PSI and PSII and Cytf content
between"low light" and "ordinary light" membrane preparations.

	Chla/b	Yield (%)	P-700/prot. (nmol/g)	Atrazine-bind prot. (nmol/g)	Cytf (nmol/g)
Thyl.OL	3.1	x	1.2	1.10	0.61
Thyl.LL	2.5	x	1.3	0.75	0.42
BS,OL	1.9	30 of B3	n.d.	n.d.	n.d.
BS,LL	1.75	60 of B3	n.d.	n.d.	n.d.

This is in agreement with several other similar studies. This
pigment composition change between "high light" and "low light "
preparations also accurs in PSII-enriched membrane vesicles (BS) but to
a lesser extent (Table 5). This means that under low light conditions
it is the BS domains of the grana which increase. This conclusion is
supported by the data of Table 5 which show that the yield of BS
vesicles increases from 30 to 60 percent of the grana derived
inside-out vesicles (B3), from which BS is prepared.
In addition, the BS of low light differ qualitatively from the BS
of ordinary light both with respect to fluorescence characteristics and
polypeptide composition.To cope with low light conditions the plant
both produces more of the BS domains in the grana and modifies the
PSIIα antenna of these domains.
The fact that the ratio of P-700/protein of the thylakoids does not
decrease, but rather increases slithtly (Table 5) under low light
conditions,together with the often described observation that the grana
become larger at low light, suggests that, at low light, it is the P700
associated with the grana which increase relatively to the stroma
membrane P700, i.e. the PSIα could be expected to increase relatively
to PSIβ.

REFERENCES
1. Albertsson,P.Å and Yu,S.G.(1988) B.B.A., 936,215-221.
2. Anderson,J.M. Waldron;J.C.and Thorne,S.W.(1978)FEBS Lett,92,227-233.
3. Camm,E.L.and Green,B.R.(1980) Plant Physiol.,66,428-432.
4. Laemmli,U.K.(1970) Nature,227,680-685.
5. Larsson,U.K.,Anderson,J.M.and Andersson,B.(1987)B.B.A.894,69-75.
6. Mäenpää,P. and Andersson,B.(1989) Z.Naturforsch.44 C, in press.
7. Klimov,V.V.,et al.(1977),FEBS Lett,82,183-186.

EFFECTS OF ACRIDINE DERIVATIVES ON ENERGY TRANSDUCTION IN THYLAKOID MEMBRANES OF ANABAENA sp.

H. Agudo Simoes, C. B. C. Silva & R. M. Chaloub
Dept. of Biochemistry, Chemistry Institute, Federal University of Rio de Janeiro - 21910 - Rio de Janeiro - Brazil

1. INTRODUCTION

Since 1970 (1), the fluorescence properties of the acridine derivatives have been utilized to detect the energization state of biological membranes. On the other hand, these compounds have been pointed out as uncoupling agents in chromatophores membranes (2,3), spinach thylakoids (4,5) and submitochondrial particles (6). However, their mechanism of action remains to be fully clarified. The results reported here are the initial part of the study of this action on thylakoid membranes of <u>Anabaena sp.</u> 7119.

2. EXPERIMENTAL PROCEDURE

Cells were colected in the early stationary growth phase, washed with fresh medium and with a solution at pH 7.8 containing sucrose 0.2 M, EDTA 0.5 mM and tricine 10 mM at room temperature. After resuspention in a cold buffer at pH 7.8 containing sucrose 0.2 M, magnesium chloride 10 mM, sodium phosphate 5 mM and tricine 50 mM, they were disrupted at 12000 psi with the aid of a chilled French press. After remove unbroken cells and cell debris, the membranes were pelleted by 45 minutes centrifugation at 48000 g, resuspended in the same cold buffer (1.0 to 2.5 mg Chl/ml) and stored in liquid nitrogen. Chlorophyll was estimated spectrofotometricaly in methanolic extracts (7).

The electron transport through PS-I was measured at 25º C with a Clark type electrode device as described elsewere (8). Reaction mixtures at pH 7.8 and 8.5 were constituted by the same final buffer and HEPES was utilized instead tricine when the pH was 7.0.

3. RESULTS AND DISCUSSION

The rate of photosynthetic electron transport was stimulated by quinacrine (QA) and 9-amine acridine (9-AA) in concentrations up to 1 mM at pH values of 7.0, 7.8 and 8.5 (Fig. 1). This effect was increased by the addition of ammonium chloride 5 mM at pH 7.8, but only in the presence of low acridine derivatives concentrations. It is noteworthy that it was observed an inhibition by this salt when high concentrations of the compounds were already included (Fig. 2). Besides, quinacrine and 9-amine acridine concentrations up to 0.1 mM showed an increase of the electron transport velocity in a stepwise fashion with a plateau in the range of 0.02 to 0.05 mM, independently

M. Baltscheffsky (ed.), Current Research in Photosynthesis, Vol. II, 847–850.

of the external pH value (Fig. 3). Subsequent addition of the ammonium salt at pH 7.8 did not alter this pattern, as well the inversed order of aditions (results not shown).

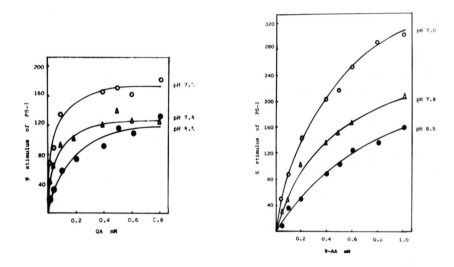

FIGURE 1: Effect of high concentrations of quinacrine (left) and 9-amine acridine (right) on the electron transport rate at different pH values.

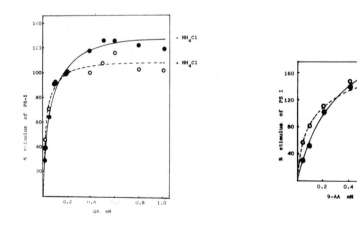

FIGURE 2: Ammonium effect on the electron transport rate in the presence of quinacrine (left) and 9-amine acridine (right) at pH 7.8

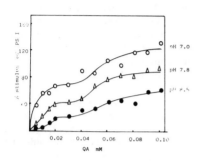 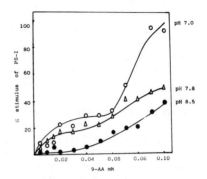

_FIGURE 3: Effect of low concentrations of quinacrine (left) and 9-amine acridine (right) on the electron transport rate at differet pH values.

The electron transport through PS-I seems to be influenced by the pH of the medium as shown at Fig. 4. In order to verify how coupled was the membrane ADP 2 mM was added. This resulted in a 12% stimulation of the electron transport velocity at each pH value. When gramicidine D (4 ug/ml) was utilized instead of ADP, it was noted that the stimulation of the electron transport decreased progressively with the increase of the external pH.

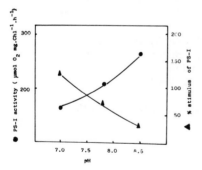

FIGURE 4: Electron transport rate at different pH values and its stimulation by gramicidine D.

It has been noticed that stimulation of the electron transport rate by quinacrine and 9-amine acridine had an inverse relationship to the pH values studied, as seen at the Fig. 1. Taking in account the pK of dissociation of the utilized acridines (9-AA: 10.0; QA: 7.9 and 10.4), with both compounds the increase of the electron transport velocity presented a saturation behavior which reached higher values when the more protonated forms were present. Thus, the reported effect could not be explained by permeation of the unprotonated form to the vesicle lumen in a similar mechanism concerned to the ammonium uncoupling.

Otherwise, the observed plateau could suggest an association of these aromatic amines with membrane components. In fact, it was shown that azido acridines do interact with proteins of submitochondrial particles (9) and that an acridine derivative covalently bounded to impermeable molecules did retain the uncouling property (10). Moreover, quinacrine is an inhibitor of the F1 ATPase solubilized from bovine heart mitochondria (11) and this property can be extended to other kind of ATPase, like the calcium dependent enzyme purified from sarcoplasmic reticulum (12).

4. REFERENCES

1. Kraayenhof R. (1970) FEBS Lett. 6, 161-165
2. Baltscheffsky H. (1960) Biochim. Biophys. Acta 40, 1-8
3. Gromet-Elhanan Z. (1972) Eur. J. Biochem. 25, 84-88
4. Baltscheffsky H. (1960) Acta Chem. Scand. 14, 264-272
5. Fiolet J.W.T., van der Erf-Ter Haar L., Kraayenhof R. & van Dam K. (1975) Biochim. Biophys. Acta 387, 320-334
6. Lee C.P. (1971) Biochemistry 10, 4375-4381
7. MacKinney G. (1941) J. Biol. Chem. 140, 315-322
8. Santos C.P. & Hall D.O. (1982) Plant Physiol. 70, 795-799
9. Mueller D.M., Hudson R.A. & Lee C.P. (1982) Biochemistry 21, 1445-1453
10. Kraayenhof R. & Fiolet J.W.T. (1974) in Dynamics of Energy Transduction Membranes (Ernster, Estabrook & Slater, eds.) pp 355-364, Elsevier, Amsterdam
11. Laikind P.K. & Allison W.S. (1983) J. Biol. Chem. 258, 14700-14704
12. Lobo G.F.V., Chaloub R.M. & Verjovski-Almeida S. (1988) Arq. Biol. Tecnol. 31, 10

THE INFLUENCE OF THE TEMPERATURE IN THE SOLUBILIZATION BY SDS   OF   THE
CHLOROPHYLL-PROTEIN COMPLEXES OF Anabaena variabilis.

M A Rodrigues and C P Santos
Dept. of Biochemistry, Chemistry Institute, Federal University of Rio
de Janeiro - CEP 21910- Rio de Janeiro - Brasil

1.   INTRODUCTION

The knowledge of how pigments and polypeptides interact with
each other in the membranes allows the construction of basic models of
the photosynthetic systems. In the biochemical   methodology   SDS-PAGE
analysis is the most important technique used both for the   polypetide
pattern   determination   and   the   characterization   of   the
chlorophyll-protein complexes (in mild denaturing conditions). It   is
well   known   that   depending   on   the   conditions   employed   for
solubilization of the membranes certain polypeptides can vary their
mobility. For the complexes however even the   composition can vary.
This work aims to study the   influence of the temperature in the
solubilization of the complexes from the photosynthetic   membranes   of
the cyanobacteria Anabaena variabilis .

2.   METHODS

Anabaena   variabilis, ATCC 29413, were grown at 30º C in
continuous fluorescence light and collected in late log phase at   room
temperature. Thylakoid membranes were   obtained   by   chilled   french
press treatment at 12000 psi in HEPES buffer (pH=7.5), with   sorbitol
0.2 M and MgC12 10 mM. The homogenate was centrifugated at   2000   x   g
for 5 min. and the supernatant was spun down at 50000 x g for 15   min.
The pellet was resuspended in the same buffer. All   procedures   were
done at low temperature
Electron transport activities of the cells and   membranes   were
determined as previously described (1). All temperature   treatments
were performed for 10 min and controls were treated at 25 ºC in the
start, middle and at the end of the experiments.   Chlorophyll
concentration was estimated using acetone 100% with the   extinction
coefficient of Arnon (2)
Electrophoresis were carried out in slab gel or   in tubes (9%
acrylamide) using the discontinuos system of Depelaire and Chua (3)
and run overnight at 10 ºC. Membranes were treated with DTT during 10
min. and then solubilized with SDS in a ratio of 20:1 (w/w) in a
protein basis for the same time, at different   temperatures. No DTT
treatment was utilized for the PAGE-tube gels
Room temperature visible absorption and fluorescence spectra
were taken in a Cary 16 spectrophotometer, and in a fluorometer

M. Baltscheffsky (ed.), Current Research in Photosynthesis, Vol. II, 851–854.
© 1990 *Kluwer Academic Publishers. Printed in the Netherlands.*

developed by Dr. G Weber, respectively. The gel slices were aligned in the beam path in order to obtain the best yield.

3.   RESULTS AND DISCUSSION

Wada et al (4) had determined by ESR spectrum of 16-SAL that the onset of phase transition of Anacistis nidulans was near 14ºC for cells grown at 28ºC. Murata et al (5) obtained similar results making use of Arrhenius plot of photosynthetic oxygen evolution. He found break points at 7º C and at 15ºC for Anabaena variabilis grown at 22 and 38ºC respectively

The Arrhenius plot of photosynthetic oxygen evolution of (isu)A. variabilis grown at 30ºC , showed break points around 14ºC and 37ºC, the first represents the apparent onset of phase transition and the latter might represent the begining of destruction of the phycobilisomes once they are sensitive to thermal denaturation (6). Although apparently the results herein presented are different from those obtained by Murata et al, the strain, the growth medium are different and the precision of the methodology might account for the differences

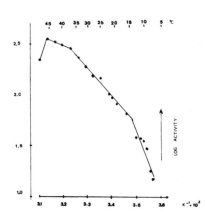

The Arrhenius plot of the electron transport activity from water to M.V. (PSI+PSII) showed a break point with inhibition at around 12.6ºC. The same plot for the activity DCPIP reduced to M.V. (PSI), exhibited break points near 12ºC and 37ºC, with no inhibition

Treatment of the membranes at temperatures higher than 30ºC resulted in loss of chlorophyll and phycocyanine, being the latter more pronounced (fig.2), in accordance with the results of Papageorgiou et al (6). In spite of this, neither the membranes nor the complexes separated by SDS-PAGE (CP1a, CP1 and CP2), displayed spectral variations in the visible absorption range.

PAGE-SDS showed a disappearence of CP2 in temperatures above 30ºC and a increment in the content of the CP1 with concomitant decrease of CP1a as can be seen in fig.3. The gels stained with coomasie blue repeated the above pattern , except for CP2 that did not disappear with the temperature, rather the bands became sharper at higher temperatures. These results seem to depend upon the centrifugal force used to pellet the membranes, as there is a clear difference in the CP1 behaviour between the 20.000 and the 50.000 fraction (fig.4). This may indicate a possible heterogeneity in the distribution of the complexes in the membrane

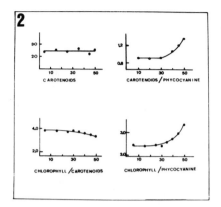

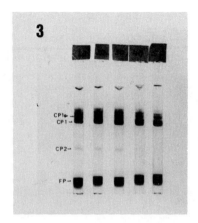

Fig.2-Pigment relations in membranes treated at different temperatures.

Fig.3-SDS-PAGE of the Chlorophyll-protein complexes of membranes solubilized at different temperatures.

Oquist et al (7), found similar results studing thylakoid membranes of a thermophilic cyanobacteria Synechococcus lividus. They found that CPa1, named here as CP1, was better extracted in temperatures above phase transition up to 60ºC, in contrast , CPa2, named here as CP2, was efficiently extracted even at 0ºC, but started to decrease if the solubilization was done at temperatures above 30ºC for cells grown at 38ºC. Guikema and Sherman (8) showed a dependence of the tempeature in the extraction of chlorophyll protein complexes. They found that the solubilization of band IV was optimal at 30-35ºC, with decreasing of the amount of bands I and III. Bruce and Malkin studing thylakoid membranes of Lemma chloroplasts (9), found that the best condition for solubilization of PSI was at 50º C during 20 min.

These results can be explained by the fluidity of the membrane. Above the phase transition the membrane become more fluid and the extraction of the comlexes by SDS is more efficient. If the pigments are bound really weaker in CP2 than in CP1 (7), a preferencial disappearance of the former is expected. Our results seems to support this hypothesis.

No variations were detected for CP2 in the emission maxima at temperatures above 10ºC. Only a small red shift was found in relation to the 5ºC treatment. Relating the loss of pigments with these data seems to indicates that there is only a progressively destruction of this complex in temperartures above its phase transition with no alterations in its environment. The fluorescence spectra of CP1 complex presented a continuos red shift with the increase of the temperature. Besides, a 686 nm emission band was observed at 5ºC together with the 722 nm one. This may indicates an alteration in the complexes with the increase in the temperature of solubilization.

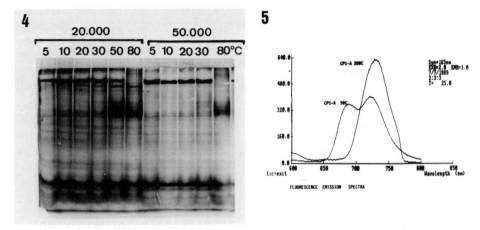

Fig.4-Protein band paterns of membranes solubilized at different temperatures im 20.000 and 50.000 x g membrane fractions.

Fig.5-**Fluorescence Spectra of the CP1 band after SDS-PAGE**

One possible reason could be its dissociation and the consequent exposition of chlorophyll molecules to water (10). Or just an PS 1 antenna component as shown by Mukerji in this congress.

Acknowledgments- This work has been supported by FINEP and CNPq in Brasil. The cells were a kind gift of Dr. Guerrero. We wish to thank Dr. Lima Silva for the use of the spectrofluorometer.

4.   REFERENCES

1. Santos C.P. & Hall D.O. (1982) Plant Physiol. 70, 795-799
2. Arnon D.I. (1979) Plant Physiol. 79, 552-560
3. Depelaire P & Chua N. H. (1979) Proc. Natl. Acad. Sc. USA vol 76, 111-115
4. Wada H. Hirasawa R., Omata T. & Murata N. (1984) Plant & Cell Physiol. 25, 907-911
5. Murata N., Wada H. & Hirasawa R. (1984) Plant & Cell Physiol. 25, 1027-1032
6. Papageorgiou G. & Lagoyani T. (1986) Appl. Microbiol. Biotechnol. 23, 417-423
7. Oquist G., Fork D. C., Schoch S & Malmberb G. (1981) B.B.A. 638, 192-200
8. Guiguema J. A. & Sherman L. A. (1983) Arch. Biochem. Biophys. 220, 155-166
9. Bruce B. B. & Malkin R. (1988) J. Biol. Chem. 263, 7302-7308
10.Tabata K., Itoh S., Sugawa M. & Nishimura M. (1983) Plant & Cell Physiol. 24, 987-994

RECONSTITUTION OF THE LIGHT-HARVESTING CHL a/b PROTEIN COMPLEX OF THE
CHL b-LESS MUTANT cbn1-48 OF CHLAMYDOMONAS REINHARDTII WITH A PIGMENT
EXTRACT DERIVED FROM WILDTYPE

Dieter Steinmetz, Ingo Damm and L.Horst Grimme
Dept. of Biology/Chem., Univ. of Bremen, D-2800 Bremen 33, FRG

1. INTRODUCTION

In the photosynthetic membrane of green algae and higher plants the
most abundant pigment-protein complex (PPC) is the light-harvesting
chlorophyll a/b complex (LHC II) which is associated with PS II. The
LHC II is known to be heterogeneous with respect to polypeptides, which
show molecular weights in the range of 23-29 kDa. LHC II contains about
50% of total chl a, most of chl b and significant amounts of the
xanthophylls of the thylakoid membrane. Pigment composition of the
LHC II preparations from green algae vary in respect to light-intensity
(1) and developmental stage (2).
In the present study we have used the chl b-less mutant of Chlamydomonas
reinhardtii strain cbn1-48 to clarify the role of chl b and carotenoids
in the assembly of LHC II. The thylakoids of the chl b-less mutant
present a distinct pigment composition and a specific LHC II
polypeptide pattern. LHC II from thylakoid membranes of the mutant
could not be resolved by mildly dissociating SDS-PAGE. However we
reconstituted the LHC II from delipidated chl b-less mutant thylakoids
with the pigment extract derived from wildtype thylakoids. Similar to
the native LHC II this reconstituted LHC II bind chl b and transfer
light energy from chl b to chl a.

2. MATERIALS AND METHODS

Chlamydomonas reinhardtii wildtype (strain 137c) and the chl b-less
mutant cbn1-48 (both cultures from Chlamydomonas Genetic Center,Durham,
USA) were cultivated autotrophycally at 21°C. The preparation of
thylakoid membranes in low salt media was done according to KNOETZEL
et al.(2). The pigment content of the thylakoids was determined by
reversed-phase HPLC (3).Polypeptides were analyzed by SDS-PAGE on a
linear 7.5-15% polyacrylamide gel (4).The in-vitro reconstitution of the
LHC II was carried out according to PLUMLEYand SCHMIDT (5), however the
solubilization of the delipidated polypeptides was performed with
0.6% SDS/0.6% TritonX-100 instead of 2% LDS (w/v). The reconstituted
LHC II were resolved by mildly dissociating SDS-PAGE with a 10% polyacrylamide gel (1). Absorption and fluorescence excitation spectra were
measured at room temperature with the spectrophotometer DW 2 and
spectrofluorometer SPF-500 (both Aminco, USA). Emission and excitation
bandpass for fluorescence measurements were 4nm.

M. Baltscheffsky (ed.), Current Research in Photosynthesis, Vol. II, 855–858.
© 1990 *Kluwer Academic Publishers. Printed in the Netherlands.*

3. RESULTS AND DISCUSSION

In TABLE 1 the relative pigment composition of thylakoids isolated from C.reinhardtii chl b-less mutant and wildtype thylakoids are compared.

TABLE 1 Relative pigment composition of thylakoids isolated from Chlamydomonas reinhardtii wildtype (WT) and the Chl b-less mutant (cbn1-48). Data represent the means of five experiments + standard deviation. Neo=neoxanthin, Tri=trihydroxy-α-carotene, Vio=violaxanthin, Ant=antheraxanthin, Lut=lutein, Chl b=chlorophyll b, α-Car=α-carotene, ß-Car=ß-carotene.

	Neo	Tri	Vio	Ant	Lut	Chl b	α-Car	ß-Car
	moles / 100 moles Chl a							
WT	6.7 +1.6	5.0 +1.2	6.6 +0.5	0.7 +0.4	10.2 +2.4	42.7 +5.2	0.5+0.1	6.5 +3.7
cbn1-48	2.1 +1.0	3.5 +1.6	18.3 +3.9	1.3 +0.3	3.6 +1.3	-	16.9+3.2	7.6 +1.3

Along with the absence of chl b the relative carotenoid composition of the mutant is drastically modified. Beside the known reduction of neoxanthin (6) the content of lutein is significantly reduced and violaxanthin is enriched. The most striking difference is the increase of the α-carotene content in the mutant thylakoids.

To obtain more information about the organization of the LHC II in the chl b-less mutant the polypeptides of the thylakoids have been isolated by SDS-PAGE (Fig.1).In the 23-29 kDa region, where LHC II polypeptides are assumed, in the mutant a large reduction of the 23 kDa polypeptide was observed, whereas the 26 kDa and mainly the 29 kDa polypeptides are not diminished. The 23, 26 and 29 kDa polypeptides can be assumed to correspondend to the three immunologically cross-reacting LHC II-apoproteins of about 24, 25 and 29 kDa recently found in C.reinhardtii (7).

FIGURE 1 Densitometric tracing of polypeptide profile of thylakoid membrane samples.
A. C.reinhardtii wildtype
B. Chl b-less mutant cbn1-48
SDS-PAGE on a 7.5-15% gel stained with Coomassie Brilliant Blue.
Numbers are molecular weights (kDa).
Both samples contained 10 µg chl.
Note the deficiency in 23 kDa polypeptides in sample B.

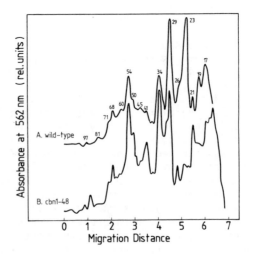

SDS-PAGE of SDS/Triton X-100 solubilized thylakoid membranes from
C.reinhardtii revealed eight PPC, designated CP1a, CP01, CP02, CP1,
LHCP1, CPa1, CPa2, LHCP3 and free pigment (Fig.2 A). Thylakoids from
the chl b-less mutant do not show CP1a, CP01 and the light-harvesting
complexes LHCP1 and LHCP3 (data not shown).

On the basis of these results we reconstituted the LHC II from chl b-
less mutant thylakoids by mixing an extract of pigments derived from
wildtype thylakoids. Mildly dissociating SDS-PAGE of this combination

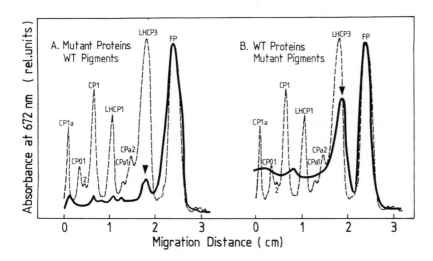

FIGURE 2   Densitometric tracing at 672 nm of chlorophyll containing bands
isolated by mildly dissociating SDS-PAGE from aceton extracted C.reinhardtii
chl b-less mutant thylakoids with pigment extract of wildtype thylakoids (A)
and acetone extracted wildtype thylakoids with pigment extract of the
chl b-less mutant (B). For comparison PPC from thylakoids of wildtype are
shown (- - -). The tracings are normalized to the absorption of free
pigment (FP). Arrows indicate reconstituted PPC.

resolved a small band with electrophoretic mobility comparable to
LHCP3 (Fig.2 A).
Additionally we added the pigment extract from chl b-less mutant
thylakoids to the delipidated thylakoids from wildtype. Here we
obtained a band with the mobility characteristics of LHCP3 with high
yield. This reveals that chl b is not a prerequisite for PPC assembly.

Spectral properties of the reconstituted complex derived from mutant
thylakoids give evidence for chl b binding (shoulder at 652 nm in
Fig.3 B) and also energy transfer from chl b to chl a, indicated by the
peak at 472 nm in the fluorescence excitation spectra (Fig.3 A).
However, the absorption and fluorescence excitation spectra of the
reconstituted PPC derived from wildtype thylakoids (Fig.3) were not
distinquishable from the spectra of free pigment (data not shown).

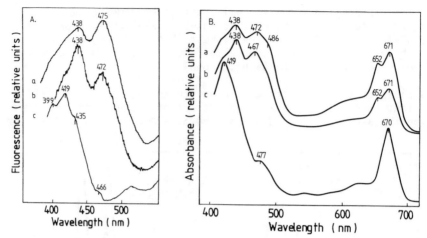

FIGURE 3 Absorption spectra (B) and fluorescence excitation spectra at
room temperature (A)of native LHCP3 (curve a) and reconstituted PPC
(curves b,c). Curves b, acetone extracted thylakoids derived from
C.reinhartii chl b-less mutant combined with pigment extract from
wildtype thylakoids. Curve c, acetone extracted thylakoids from wildtype
with the pigment extract from chl b-less mutant thylakoids. Spectra were
obtained from gel slices in situ. Emission wavelength was 680 nm.

The molecular weight of the main LHC II polypeptides in the mutant
obtained in this study was 29 kDa. Recently it was shown that the
chl a/b complex with the molecular weight of 29 kDa (CP29) is closely
associated with the photosystem II reaction centre core (8). The
apoprotein of CP29 was immunologically detected in significant amounts
in a chl b-less barley mutant (9). Whether the reconstituted LHC II
from acetone-extracted chl b-less mutant thylakoids is related to CP29
or other subpopulations of LHC II,as well as the analysis of its
pigment composition is under investigation.

REFERENCES
1 Grimme, L.H., Damm, I., Steinmetz,D., Scheffczyk,B. (1987) in Prog.
   in Photosynth.Res. (Biggins,J.,ed.), Vol.II, 347-350, Dordrecht
2 Knoetzel, J., Braumann, Th., Grimme, L.H. (1988) J.Photochem.
   Photobiol.,B., 1, 475-491
3 Braumann, Th. and Grimme, L.H. (1981) Biochim.Biophys.Acta,637,8-17
4 Delepelaire,P. and Chua,N.-H. (1979)Proc.Natl.Acad.Sci.USA,76,111-15
5 Plumley, F.G. and Schmidt, G.W. (1987) Proc.Natl.Acad.Sci.,84,146-50
6 Chunayev,A.S., Ladygin,V.G., Gavrilenko,T.A., Krela,L.P.,
   Korniushenko, G.A. (1981) Genetika,17, 2013-2024
7 Sigrist,M., Zwillenberg,C., Giroud,Ch., Eichenberger,W.,
   Boschetti,A. (1988) Plant Science, 58, 15-23
8 Camm, E.L. and Green, B.R. (1989) Biochim.Biophys.Acta, 974, 180-84
9 White, M.J. and Green,B.R. (1987) Eur.J.Biochem., 167, 531-535

TURNOVER OF LHC-I AND LHC-II APOPROTEINS IN CHL B-DEFICIENT MUTANTS OF RICE AND BARLEY.

Tomio Terao[1]) and Sakae Katoh[2])
1) Dept. of Applied Physiology, Natl. Inst. Agrobiol. Resources, Tsukuba, Ibaraki, 305 and 2) Dept. of Biology, Fac. of Science, Univ. of Tokyo, Hongo, Bunkyo-ku, Tokyo, 113, Japan

1. Introduction

Chl b is an important photosynthetic pigment which is exclusively present in light-harvesting Chl a/b-proteins, LHC-I and LHC-II[1)]. LHC-I and LHC-II are totally absent from mutants which lack Chl b[2)3)4)]. A Chl b-less barley mutant, 'chlorina f2', has the capability of synthesizing precursors of LHC apoproteins and assembling them into thylakoid membrane[5)]. However the mutant thylakoids contain very low levels of LHC-I and LHC-II apoproteins and one or two of major apoproteins have been reported to be missing[6)7)8)]. We also showed that Chl b-less rice chlorina mutants contained mRNA for apoprotein of LHC-II. All the five proteins related to LHC-I and LHC-II are present but in reduced amounts[9)]. These observation led to a suggestion that newly synthesized apoproteins are stabilized only when they are associated with Chl b[5)]. To examine this possibility, we have measured the synthesis and turnover of the apoproteins of LHC-I and LHC-II in Chl b-less mutants of rice and barley.

2. Materials and Methods

Seedlings of rice (Oryza sativa L. cultivar Norin No.8) and a Chl b-less mutant chlorina 2 derived from this cultivar, and a barley mutant (Hordeum vulgare L. chlorina f2) and a wild type strain related to chlorina f2, were grown for about 30 days in greenhouse.

Immunological blotting were carried out with antiserum raised against rice LHC-II apoproteins, which cross-reacts with the apoproteins of LHC-I[9)]. For labelling, young leaf segments were incubated with 0.2 μM [^{35}S]methionine (200 μCi/ml) at 25°C in light (120μE$\cdot$s$^{-1}\cdot$m^{-2}) for various periods of time[10)]. The thylakoid membranes were collected and subjected to SDS-polyacrylamide gel electrophoresis[11)] and labelled proteins were detected by fluorography. Protein turnover was measured by pulse-labelling leaves for 30 min with radioactive methionine and chasing in a medium containing 10 mM cold methionine for indicated periods of time[10)].

3. Results and Discussion

Fig. 1 compares immunoblotting of the apoproteins of LHC-I and

M. Baltscheffsky (ed.), Current Research in Photosynthesis, Vol. II, 859–862.

LHC-II in the thylakoid membranes of wild type and Chl b-less mutant
strains of rice and barley with the antiserum against rice LHC-II.
Five major apoproteins were detected in the normal strains of rice and
barley. Three bands in the molecular mass region of 26 kDa, 25 kDa
and 24 kDa are the apoproteins of LHC-II and two or three bands of 20-
21 kDa correspond to the apoproteins of LHC-I. All the five apoproteins were detected but in reduced amounts in the rice and barley
mutants (Table 1). The barley mutant was particularly deficient in
the 25 kDa apoprotein[8].

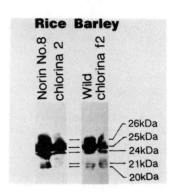

Fig. 1   Western blotting of LHC
apoproteins of the wild and Chl b-less
mutant strains of rice and barley.
Thylakoid membranes containing 3.2 μg
Chl were applied to each lane.

Table 1   Relative abundances of LHC apoproteins in rice and barley
mutants determined on the basis of thylakoid membrane proteins.

| | | LHC-II apoproteins | | LHC-I apoproteins |
		25 kDa (%)	24 kDa (%)	20-21 kDa (%)
Rice	Norin No.8	100	100	100
	chlorina 2	4.5	8.5	20
Barley	Wild	100	100	100
	chlorina f2	1-2	25-50	25-50

      The two Chl b-less mutants synthesized the five apoproteins as
rapidly as the corresponding wild type plants (Fig. 2).   However,
the accumulations of the 25 kDa apoprotein were significantly slowed
down at the late stage of labelling time in rice and barley mutants.
      Pulse-chase experiments showed that the 25 kDa apoproteins of
LHC-II are unstable in mutant leaves (Fig. 3).   In normal leaves of
rice and barley, all the newly synthesized apoproteins related to LHC-
II and LHC-I were stable.   Only the D1-protein was rapidly degraded
in the light.   On the contrary, a rapid breakdown of the 25 kDa apoprotein occurred in the two mutants.   Time-dependent changes in the
band intensity of the 25 kDa apoproteins are illustrated in Fig. 4.
Note that newly synthesized 25 kDa apoproteins in mutant leaves were
degraded very rapidly but not completely, leaving a small fraction of
the apoproteins as stable as that of the normal leaves.   The results
suggest that Chl b is important for stabilization of the 25 kDa proteins but a small proportion of the newly synthesized apoprotein is

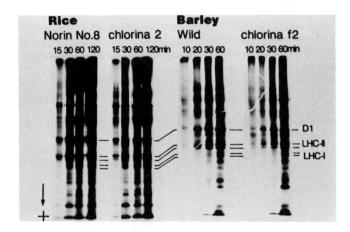

Fig. 2 Synthesis of the apoproteins in leaves of the wild-type and Chl b-less mutant strains of rice and barley. Proteins labelled with [^{35}S]methionine for the indicated periods of time were detected by fluorography. The amount of each sample applied to the gels was adjusted on the basis of fresh weight of leaf segments.

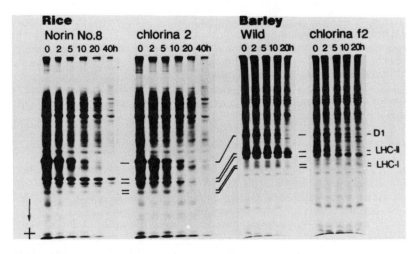

Fig. 3 Breakdown of the newly synthesized apoproteins in wild and Chl b-less mutant strains of rice and barley. Samples were pulse-labelled for 30 min with [^{35}S]methionine.

protected by a factor(s) other than Chl b. It is also seem that the amount of the stable 25 kDa protein was lower in the barley mutant than in the rice mutant. This may explain why the apoprotein content is low in the barley mutant.

The 24 and 26 kDa apoproteins of LHC-II and the 20-21 kDa apoprotein of LHC-I were also degraded in the rice mutant, whereas these

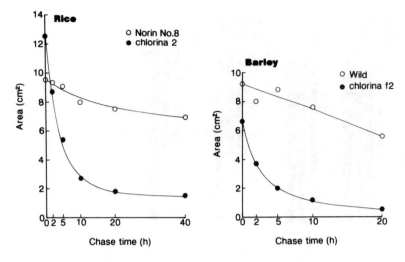

Fig. 4   Turnover of the 25 kDa apoprotein in wild-type and Chl b-less mutant strains of rice and barley.   The peak area of the 25 kDa protein band determined from densitometric tracings of fluorogram were plotted against the chase time.

apoproteins were stable in the barley mutant.   The results are consistent with the higher abundance of those proteins in the barley than in the rice mutant.   Thus, the stability of newly synthesized apoprotein are differently affected by the absence of Chl b[8)9)].   It is concluded therefore that, although newly synthesized apoproteins of LHC-I and LHC-II are mainly stabilized by Chl b, other factors such as integration of the apoproteins into thylakoid membrane, or association of Chl a or carotene also affect the stability of the proteins.

References
1 Thornber, J. P. (1975) Ann. Rev. Plant Physiol. 26, 127-158.
2 Machold, O., Simpson, D. J. and Møller, B. L. (1979) Carlsberg Res. Commun. 44, 235-254.
3 Waldron, J. C. and Anderson, J. M. (1979) Eur. J. Biochem. 102, 357-362.
4 Terao, T., Yamashita, A. and Katoh, S. (1985) Plant Cell Physiol. 26, 1369-13774 Terao
5 Bellemare, G., Bartlett, S. C. and Chua, N.-H. (1982) J. Biol. Chem. 257, 7762-7767
6 Henriques, F. and Park, R. (1975) Plant Physiol. 55, 763-767.
7 Burke, J. J., Steinback, K. E. and Arntzen, C. J. (1979) Plant Physiol. (1979)
8 White, M. J. and Green, B. R. (1987) Eur. J. Biochem. 165, 531-535
9 Terao, T., Matsuoka, M. and Katoh, S. (1988) Plant Cell Physiol. 29, 825-834
10 Terao, T. and Katoh, S. (1989) Plant Cell Physiol. 30, 571-580
11 Laemmli, U. K. (1970) Nature 227, 680-685

LIGHT AVAILABILITY INFLUENCES psbA EXPRESSION AND THE RATIO OF TWO FORMS OF D1 IN CYANOBACTERIAL THYLAKOIDS

Michael R. Schaefer[1], Silvia A. Bustos[2] and Susan S. Golden[2]
Department of Biochemistry[1] and Department of Biology[2], Texas A&M University, College Station, TX 77843

INTRODUCTION

Cyanobacteria carry out photosynthesis using a two-photosystem, oxygen-evolving photosynthetic apparatus which is structurally and functionally similar to the thylakoid membrane system of higher plant chloroplasts. At the reaction center core of PSII, a dimer of two structurally similar proteins, termed D1 and D2, houses the photoreactive chlorophylls, primary electron acceptor, and other cofactors involved in photosynthetic electron transport through PSII. D1 is encoded by the psbA gene, which is highly conserved among plants and cyanobacteria. In higher plants, the psbA gene is present as a single copy in the chloroplast genome, whereas cyanobacteria possess small psbA multigene families in the bacterial chromosome. The chromosome of Synechococcus sp. strain PCC 7942 contains three distinct copies of the psbA gene encoding two forms of D1 (1). The psbA genes predict that form I (the product of psbAI) differs from Form II (the product of both psbAII and psbAIII) at 25 residues, 12 of which are located in the first 16 amino acids of the protein.

We are interested in the functional significance of maintaining multiple psbA genes and expressing two forms of D1 in Synechococcus. An efficient transformation system for Synechococcus made it possible to insert translational gene fusions between each of the psbA genes and the lacZ gene of E. coli into the chromosome of wild-type cells at their native loci to serve as in vivo reporters of psbA activity. β-Galactosidase activities measured in the Lac+ strains indicated differential expression of the psbA genes in response to light availability (2). Using D1 form-specific antisera, we determined that light availability alters the ratio of two forms of D1 in thylakoid membranes as predicted by the psbA-lacZ reporters (3). We investigated the effect of rapid changes in light intensity on individual psbA transcript levels. Here we report dramatic changes in mRNA levels from the three psbA genes within five minutes of transfer of cells to a different light environment. Additionally, psbA-inactivated mutants indicate that loss of one form of D1 influences expression of psbA gene(s) encoding the alternate form.

M. Baltscheffsky (ed.), Current Research in Photosynthesis, Vol. II, 863–866.

1. Members of the *psbA* multigene family in *Synechococcus* are differentially expressed in response to light availability.

Strains of *Synechococcus* carrying individual *psbA-lacZ* reporter gene fusions were assayed for β-galactosidase activity along a time course of decreasing culture PPFD (2; Golden *et al.*, this volume). Expression of *psbAI* was high and inversely related to light availability; as PPFD decreased from 600 μE·m^{-2}·s^{-1} to 20 μE·m^{-2}·s^{-1}, β-galactosidase activity in strain AMC051 (Table I) increased 8-fold, suggesting a greater need for D1 form I in a low light environment. In contrast, expression of *psbAII* and *psbAIII* was low and directly related to light availability; the same decrease in culture PPFD resulted in a 10-fold reduction in β-galactosidase activity in both strains AMC052 and AMC053, suggesting a greater need for D1 form II in a high light environment.

2. Differential expression of the *psbA* family in response to light alters the ratio of two forms of D1 in thylakoids.

Thylakoids from wild-type cells adapted to different light intensities in a time course experiment were analyzed for their D1 composition (3; Golden *et al.*, this volume). Western analysis using D1 form-specific antisera showed that the D1 composition of the membrane matched predicted ratios of the two forms based on differential gene expression; form I was highest in membranes from cells adapted to low light, whereas form II was highest in membranes from cells adapted to high light. Western analysis using antisera raised against D1 from spinach (4) indicated that total D1 in thylakoids remained constant along the time course.

3. Expression of *psbAI* is enhanced at low light, whereas expression of both *psbAII* and *psbAIII* is enhanced at high light.

Transfer of wild-type cells to different light environments resulted in dramatic changes in *psbA* transcript levels within 5 minutes. Transcripts from *psbAI* decreased in cells transferred to 500 μE·m^{-2}·s^{-1} and 250 μE·m^{-2}·s^{-1}, and increased 2-fold in cells transferred to 125 μE·m^{-2}·s^{-1} and 50 μE·m^{-2}·s^{-1} (Fig. 1). In contrast, transcripts from *psbAII* and *psbAIII* increased 12-fold and 2-fold, respectively in cells transferred to 500 μE·m^{-2}·s^{-1}, and proportionately decreased at lower PPFD.

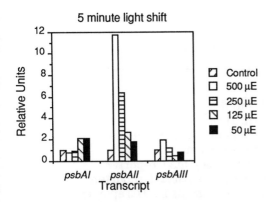

Fig. 1. Histogram showing relative levels of individual *psbA* transcripts in wild-type cells following transfer to different culture PPFD for 5 minutes. For each gene, the amount of mRNA in the control sample was given a value of 1.0. Data was obtained by densitometric scanning of autoradiograms and normalized to 16s rRNA in each sample.

4. *psbA* transcripts of *Synechococcus* mutants deficient in one form of D1 respond differently to rapid changes in the culture light environment.

Individual *psbA* transcript levels in strains R2K1 and R2S2C3 (Table I) were compared with those of wild-type cells in a 15 minute light shift assay (Fig. 2). In the absence of D1 form II (strain R2S2C3), levels of mRNA for *psbAI* appeared to remain fairly constant at all PPFD, suggesting an uncoupling of *psbAI* expression from light availability (left panel). Loss of D1 form I (strain R2K1) resulted in elevated levels of mRNA for both *psbAII* and *psbAIII* (middle and right panels, respectively) with *psbAIII* transcript levels showing some similarity to those of *psbAI* in wild-type cells under similar conditions.

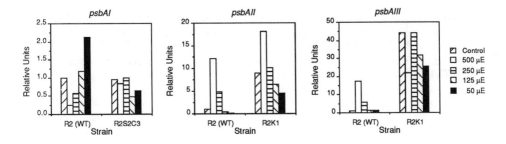

Fig. 2. Histograms showing relative levels of individual *psbA* transcripts in wild-type and mutant strains of *Synechococcus* following transfer of cells to different culture PPFD for 15 minutes.

TABLE I. *Synechococcus* **strains used to study** *psbA* **expression**

Strain	Description
R2	Wild-type
R2K1	*psbAI* gene inactivated Only D1 form II present
R2S2C3	*psbAII* and *psbAIII* genes inactivated Only D1 form I present
AMC051	*psbAI-lacZ* gene fusion as *psbAI* reporter
AMC052	*psbAII-lacZ* gene fusion as *psbAII* reporter
AMC053	*psbAIII-lacZ* gene fusion as *psbAIII* reporter

CONCLUSIONS

Differential expression of multiple copies of *psbA* encoding two forms of D1 may be related to adaptation of *Synechococcus* to different light environments. At low light, enhanced expression of *psbAI* results in an increased ratio of form I to form II in the thylakoid. In contrast, enhanced expression of both *psbAII* and *psbAIII* at high light gives rise to an increased ratio of form II to form I in the membrane. The functional difference between the two forms remains unknown.

REFERENCES

1. Golden, S.S., Brusslan, J. and Haselkorn, R. (1986) EMBO J. 5:2789-2798.
2. Schaefer, M.R. and Golden, S.S. (1989) J. Bact. 171:3973-3981.
3. Schaefer, M.R. and Golden, S.S. (1989) J. Biol. Chem. 264:7412-7417.
4. Vermass, W.F.J., Ikeuchi, M., and Inoue, Y. (1988) Photosynth. Res. 17:97-113.

CHARACTERISATION OF A TEMPERATURE-SENSITIVE MUTANT OF BARLEY.

Juergen Knoetzel and David Simpson.
Department of Physiology, Carlsberg Laboratory. Gamle Carlsberg Vej 10. DK-2500 Valby.
Denmark.

1. INTRODUCTION
Chlorina mutants are defined as being visually different from wild type, either in the concentration of chlorophyll, or the amount of chlorophyll *b*, or both, but are viable. One of the most extensively studied higher plant mutants is the chlorophyll *b*-less mutant of barley, *chlorina-f2*. This mutation was invaluable in demonstrating, among other things, that the chlorophyll *b*-containing chlorophyll-proteins were not essential for photosynthesis, but played an ancillary, light-harvesting role.
Of the first 31 *chlorina* mutants characterised in the Copenhagen mutant collection, 9 were found to be characterised by unusually high F680/F740 and Fm/Fo ratios, when examined by low temperature fluorescence emission spectroscopy and room temperature fluorescence induction kinetics (1). Of these nine, four showed these properties when grown in the glasshouse at 17°C, but not at 22°C. This paper describes one of these temperature-sensitive mutants, *chlorina-104*, which is the first barley mutant in which mutant leaf tissue returns to normal as the result of being shifted from the restrictive temperature.

2. MATERIALS AND METHODS
Seeds of wild type barley (*Hordeum vulgare L.* cv. Svalöfs Bonus) were germinated in tap water-moistened vermiculite, and grown for 7 days at 22°C under continuous illumination, as previously described (2). Seeds of the mutant *chlorina-104* were germinated and grown for 14 days at 15°C, and were either harvested, or transferred to 22°C for a further 5 days.
Low temperature fluorescence emission spectra were recorded according to (1), and SDS-PAGE under non-denaturing conditions at 4°C and the re-electrophoresis of CPI* was performed according to (3-5). Denaturing SDS-PAGE was done according to (6) and immunoblot assays as described in (7,8). PSI-200 was prepared by sucrose gradient ultracentrifugation of Triton X-100 solubilised thylakoid membranes as described in (9). Reverse-phase HPLC analysis of the chlorophyll and carotenoid composition of thylakoids and pigment-protein complexes was done according to (10).

3. RESULTS AND DISCUSSION
3.1. Biochemical characterisation
Thylakoids from *chlorina-104* grown at 15°C, with and without transfer to 22°C, were analysed for their chlorophyll-protein composition and polypeptide patterns, using non-denaturing and denaturing SDS-PAGE, and immunoblot assay using monoclonal antibodies against the chlorophyll *a/b*-binding proteins CP29 and LHCI. Non-denaturing SDS-PAGE showed that *chlorina-104* grown at 15°C contained very low amounts of the chlorophyll-protein complexes CPI* and LHCII**, while the levels of these complexes recovers to near wild type levels when the plants are transferred to 22°C. Re-electrophoresis of CPI* from wild type, and *chlorina-104* after transfer to 22°C, showed the presence of CPI, LHCI-730 and LHCI-680, which are also com-

M. Baltscheffsky (ed.), Current Research in Photosynthesis, Vol. II, 867–870.

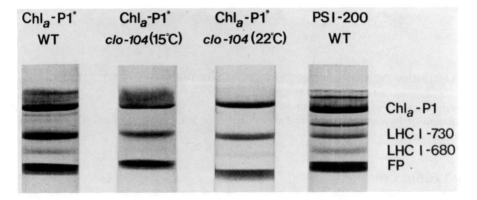

Figure 1. Composition of chlorophyll-proteins of Chl$_a$-P1* (=CPI*) isolated from wild type and *chlorina-104* grown at 15°C and 22°C, compared with PSI-200 from wild type thylakoids.

ponents of the PSI-200 preparation (Figure 1). LHCI-680 could not be detected as a chlorophyll-protein in *chlorina-104* grown at 15°C, and the level of LHCI-730 was very low. These low levels of LHCI were reflected in the relatively low amount of CPI* in *chlorina-104* grown at 15°C, since most of the CPI migrated as a chlorophyll-containing band at 110 kD.

These results were confirmed by immunoblot assay of both thylakoids and CPI*. The level of LHCI in CPI* from *chlorina-104* grown at 15°C was less than 5% of that in wild type, and returned to normal levels after 5 days at 22°C (Figure 2). In contrast, the chlorophyll *a/b*-binding protein CP29 was present in near normal levels in thylakoids, and was absent from the CPI* and PSI-200 preparations.

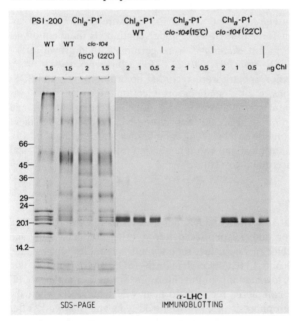

Figure 2. SDS-PAGE of PSI preparations from wild type and chlorina-^{104} grown at 15°C and 22°C. Different amounts of chlorophyll were loaded onto each track and separated on 8-25% acrylamide gels. After transfer to nitrocellulose filters, the amount of LHCI was analysed using the monoclonal antibody CMpLHCI:2.

Analysis of the pigment composition of thylakoids (Table 1), shows that the mutant grown at 15°C contains only about half as much chlorophyll *b* per 100 molecules of chlorophyll *a*, as the wild type. This is largely due to the loss of most of the LHCII, which contains large amounts of chlorophyll *b* and xanthophylls, thus explaining the higher chlorophyll *a*:xanthophyll ratio, while the chlorophyll *b*:xanthophyll ratio remains constant. Transfer of *chlorina-104* to 22°C results in a nearly wild type pigment composition.

TABLE 1.
The pigment composition (moles per 100 moles of Chl *a*) and ratios between chlorophylls and carotenoids (mole per mole) in thylakoid membranes and PSI preparations (Chl$_a$-P1*, PSI-200) of wild type barley and *chlorina-104* grown at 15°C or 22°C.

	Thylakoid membranes				Chl$_a$-P1*			PSI-200
	wild-type	*clo-104* (15°C)	*clo-104* (22°C)	wild-type	*clo-104* (15°C)	*clo-104* (22°C)	wild type
Neoxanthin	4.35	1.98	2.90	0.16	-	0.33	0.37
Violaxanthin	5.17	4.94	4.80	2.26	1.56	2.17	2.56
Lutein	12.28	6.57	8.56	3.47	1.52	3.57	4.80
Chl *b*	29.43	15.59	24.03	10.42	8.88	11.08	16.54
β-Carotene	6.12	6.90	8.14	9.47	7.24	9.93	8.12
Chl *a/b*	3.40	6.41	4.16	9.60	11.26	9.03	6.05
Chl *a/β*-Car	16.34	14.49	12.29	10.60	13.81	10.07	12.32
Chl *a*/Xan	4.59	7.41	6.15	16.96	32.47	16.47	12.93
Chl *b*/Xan	1.35	1.16	1.48	1.10	1.23	1.16	2.04

Data from two experiments. The standard deviation was better than 15%. Abbreviations: Chl, chlorophyll; *β*-Car, *β*-carotene; Xan, xanthophylls.

3.2. Spectroscopic characterisation

The fluorescence emission spectra of *chlorina-104* leaves grown at 15°C showed a strong reduction in the intensity of the long wavelength peak, and a concomitant increase in the contribution of a 720 nm component, resulting in a double peak (Figure 3). We interpret this as fluorescence arising from two different types of PSI centres. Those which lack LHCI fluoresce with a low yield at 720 nm, while a small number of PSI centres are quenched by LHCI, and fluoresce at 740 nm. The spectrum of *chlorina-104* at 22°C resembles that of wild type leaves.

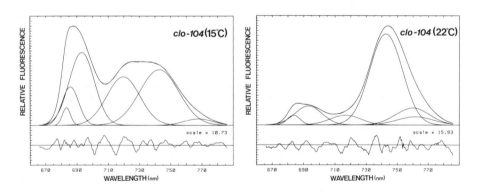

Figure 3. Fluorescence emission spectra at 77 K of leaves of *chlorina-104* grown at 15°C and 22°C, resolved into component Gaussians.

3.3. Freeze-fracture electron microscopy.

The lower chlorophyll content of seedling leaves from *chlorina-104* grown at 15°C is seen in a lower number of discs per granum. The average grana diameter, at 0.47 μm, is similar to wild type, although the variation in size is much greater, and the average number of discs per granum (3.9) is half that found in wild type (10.4). Examination of these thylakoids by freeze-fracture electron microscopy revealed several significant changes. Quantitation of the density of particles (number of particles per μm^2), revealed a loss of PFs particles, which can be correlated with the loss of LHCII, and an increase in EFs particle density, which has previously been reported for the chlorophyll *b*-less mutant *chlorina-f2* (11). PFu particle density was not changed, while the EFu particle density increased by a factor of 2 (Table 2). Quantitation of freeze-fracture particle size showed that EFs and PFu particles were smaller than wild type. We interpret the smaller PFu particle size as resulting from the loss of LHCI from the large PFu particles, which contain the PSI reaction centre (12), and which cause the holes in the EFu face. After 5 days at 22°C, both particle size and particle densities of *chlorina-104* approach the values measured for wild type thylakoids. This is the first report of a barley mutant in which the EFu particle density is significantly higher than wild type. The exact nature of these particles is still a matter of speculation, although they have been suggested to be the location of photosystem II centres in the stroma lamellae. As well as a high number of EFu particles *chlorina-104* also has a high Fm/Fo ratio, which is also a very unusual property, implying as it does, that the utilisation of absorbed energy is more efficient than in wild type.

TABLE 2. Freeze-fracture particle density data.
Numbers are particles per μm^2

Face	chlorina-104 15°C	chlorina-104 15→22°C	wild type	*chlorina-f2*
EFu	882	392	358	558
PFu	3434	3457	4729	3902
EFs	2015	1816	1622	2103
PFs	1433	4627	6525	1337
PFu large	2089	2280	3290	
EFu holes	2228	2389	3262	

REFERENCES
1. Simpson, D.J., Machold, O., Høyer-Hansen, G & D. von Wettstein. (1985) Carlsberg Res. Commun. **50**, 223-238.
2. Machold, O., Simpson, D.J. & Møller, B.L. (1979) Carlsberg Res. Commun. **44**, 235-254.
3. Bassi, R., dal Belin-Peruffo, A., Barbato, R. & Ghisi, R. (1985) Eur. J. Biochem. **146**, 589-595.
4. Bassi, R. (1985) Carlsberg Res. Commun. **50**, 127-143.
5. Bassi, R., Machold, O. & Simpson, D.J. (1985) Carlsberg Res. Commun. **50**, 145-162.
6. Fling, S.P. & Gregerson, D.S. (1986) Anal. Biochem. **155**, 83-88.
7. Høyer-Hansen, G., Hønberg, L.S. & Simpson, D.J. (1985) Carlsberg Res. Commun. **50**, 23-35.
8. Høyer-Hansen, G., Bassi, R., Hønberg, L.S. & Simpson, D.J. (1988) Planta **173**, 12-21.
9. Steinback, K.E., Mullet, J.E. & Arntzen, C.J. (1982) in Methods in Chloroplast Molecular Biology (Edelman, M., Hallick, R.B & Chua N-H., eds), pp. 863-872.
10. Knoetzel, J., Braumann, T. & Grimme, L.H. (1988) J. Photochem. Photobiol. (B) **1**, 475-491.
11. Simpson, D.J. (1979) Carlsberg Res. Commun. **44**, 305-336.
12. Simpson, D.J. (1983) Eur. J. Cell Biol. **31**, 305-314.

BIOSYNTHESIS AND DISTRIBUTION OF THE FERREDOXIN-NADP OXIDOREDUCTASE
BINDING PROTEIN

RUBEN H. VALLEJOS, RAQUEL L. CHAN AND FERNANDO C. SONCINI
CENTRO DE ESTUDIOS FOTOSINTETICOS Y BIOQUIMICOS (CONICET, F.M.LILLO,
U.N.R.), Suipacha 531, 2000 ROSARIO, ARGENTINA

1. INTRODUCTION

Ferredoxin-NADP$^+$ oxidoreductase is the final enzyme of the photosynthetic electron transport chain (for a review see Ref. 1). This flavoprotein was isolated from spinach and lettuce chloroplasts closely
associated with a trimer of a 17.5 kDa polypeptide (2,3). The purified
complex showed some of the allotopic properties of the membrane-bound
enzyme like pH and temperature profiles of diaphorase activity (2,4,5).
Immunological evidence indicates that the binding protein protrudes
from the thylakoids into the stroma (6) and that it is affected by the
extent of thylakoids energization, suggesting that it may be the regulatory subunit of the reductase.

In this paper we present evidence that this complex is widely distributed in higher plants and that there is a high degree of conservation of antigenic determinants in both polypeptides. We also analyze
the biosynthesis of the binding protein. The results obtained show that
this polypeptide is a nuclear gene product and synthesized in cytoplasmic ribosomes as a precursor of approximately 20 kDa.

2. EXPERIMENTAL PROCEDURES

Spinach ferredoxin-NADP$^+$ oxidoreductase (7), reductase binding
protein (2), total RNA and poly(A)-rich-mRNA from spinach (8) were prepared as described. Western blotting (9) and immunoprecipitation experiments (6) were carried out as in previous papers. Diaphorase activity
was measured as described (7). *In vitro* translation experiments were
carried out as described (10), and the newly synthesized protein mixture was treated with antibodies against the binding protein and the
immunoprecipitates were analyzed by SDS-PAGE (11) followed by fluorography.

3. RESULTS AND DISCUSSION

Thylakoid extracts of different higher plant species including
Beta vulgaris Cicla, *Beta vulgaris* Esculenta, *Chenopodium ambrosioides*,
Chenopodium album (Chenopodiaceae family), *Cucurbita andreana*, *Lycopersicon esculentum* (other C_3 plants), *Amaranthus viridis*, *Zea mays*, *Sac-
charum officinarum* (C_4 species) and *Kalanchoë daigremontiana* (CAM
plant) were obtained with the purpose of looking for the presence of

M. Baltscheffsky (ed.), Current Research in Photosynthesis, Vol. II, 871–874.

reductase and its binding protein by Western blotting. Figure 1A shows
the result obtained using antibodies against reductase. A cross-react
band with similar molecular weight was found in all the species analyzed. Similar results were obtained using Ouchterlony tests with fusion
of the precipitin lines (data not shown). These results indicated that
the reductases from all the species tested are antigenically identical
to the enzyme from spinach.

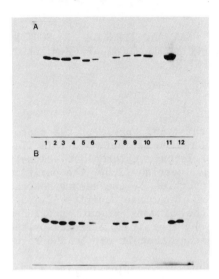 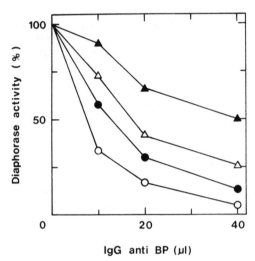

FIGURE 1. Detection of reductase (A) and its binding protein (B) from
different plant species by immunoblotting. Thylakoid extracts
were from *B. vulgaris* Cicla (1); *B. vulgaris* Esculenta (2);
C. ambrosioides (3); *C. album* (4); *C. andreana* (5); *L. esculentum* (6); *A. viridis* (7); *Z. mays* (8) ; *S. officinarum* (9);
K. daigremontiana (10); *S. oleracea* (11); and spinach reductase binding protein (12).

FIGURE 2. Immunoprecipitation of the diaphorase activity of thylakoids
from *S. oleracea* (O-O); *L. esculentum* (●-●); *B. vulgaris*
(△-△); and *Z. mays* (▲-▲) by antibodies against reductase
binding protein.

Figure 1B shows the result of probing the blotting with antibodies
against spinach reductase binding protein. Like reductase, in all the
species analyzed, a similar molecular weight band immunoreacts with
the antibodies, except for *K. daigremontiana* which gave a higher molecular weight (19 kDa).
Figure 2 shows an immunoprecipitation test in order to determine
if both polypeptides are forming a complex in other species as in spinach (2). When thylakoids extracts from *S. oleracea*, *B. vulgaris* Cicla,
L. esculentum and *Z. mays* were incubated with antibodies against the

binding protein of spinach, the diaphorase activity of the supernatants
decreased with the amount of added antibodies. The coprecipitation of
the reductase with its binding protein suggests a close interaction
between both polypeptides. We conclude that the interaction of the
ferredoxin-NADP$^+$ reductase with the thylakoid membrane through a specific polypeptide is a common mechanism in the plants tested and we can
speculate, taking into account the variety of plants analyzed, that
this mechanism is a general one to all higher plants.

The reductase is nuclear encoded and is synthesized as a larger
precursor that is imported by the chloroplast (12). It was interesting
to determine if the gene for the binding protein is nuclear or chloroplast. For this purpose we isolated RNA from spinach leaves and separated it in poly(A)-containing and unadenilated fractions. Both samples
were translated in a cell free system derived from wheat germ. Exogenous stimulation of protein synthesis, as defined by Erickson and Blobel (10) was 50 times for poly(A) mRNA and 15 times for unadenilated
RNA. When both fractions were immunoprecipitated with antibodies against reductase binding protein only the mixture containing poly(A) mRNA
showed a single band of approximately 20 kDa in a fluorography of the
SDS-PAGE indicating that the binding protein is encoded in the nucleus
and synthesized as a precursor of 20 kDa (Fig. 3).

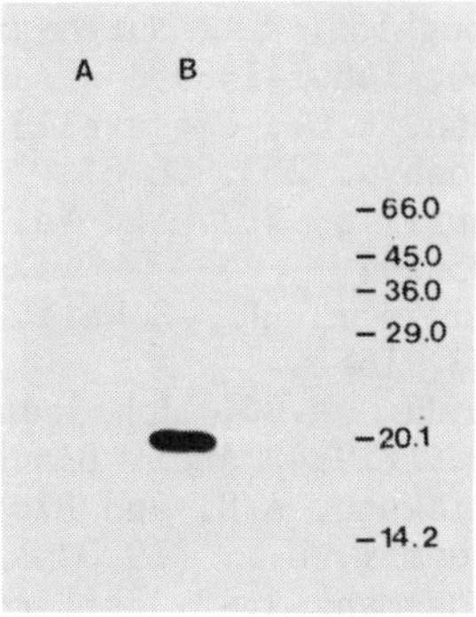

FIGURE 3. Fluorography of the immunoprecipitates obtained with specific antibodies against the reductase bin-
din protein of the *in vitro* synthesis mixture after translation
of spinach RNA. A: unadenilated
mRNA; B: poly(A)-rich mRNA. Marks
indicate molecular weight standards.

No synthesis of the binding protein
was observed in intact chloroplasts (data
not shown) supporting the suggestion that
the binding protein gene is nuclear. No
homology was observed between the N-terminal sequence fragment of 28 amino acid re-
sidues from the binding protein and the tobacco chloroplast open reading frames (unpublished results).

Most thylakoid protein complexes described so far are composed
of some polypeptide(s) encoded in the nucleus and other encoded in the
chloroplast genome. The reductase/binding protein complex seems to be
the only chloroplast protein complex whose two known components, reductase, which is synthesized in the cytoplasm as a precursor of 43 kDa
(12) and its binding protein are encoded in the nucleus, and they bind
spontaneously in their nature form when Mg^{2+} is present (2).

After the experiments described above were finished, it was found
that the N-terminal sequence of the spinach chloroplast reductase binding protein (F.C. Soncini and R.H. Vallejos, submitted for publication) is the same one of a 16.5 kDa polypeptide described as a compo-

nent of the oxygen-evolving system (13-15). Antibodies against both proteins are equivalent as shown by immunoblots, Ouchterlony assays, precipitation of reductase-binding protein complex and agglutination of thylakoids partially depleted of reductase suggesting that both polypeptides are identical. Accordingly, the biosynthesis of the putative 16.5 kDa component of the oxygen-evolving complex was previously shown (16) to be in the cytoplasm although the molecular weight of the precursor seems higher than that reported here. The discrepancy may be due to different electrophoretic conditions.

ACKNOWLEDGEMENTS

This work was supported by Consejo Nacional de Investigaciones Científicas y Técnicas (CONICET), Argentina. RHV is a member of the Investigator Career, FCS and RLC are Fellows of the same Institution.

REFERENCES

1 Carrillo, N.J. and Vallejos, R.H. (1987) in Topics in Photosynthesis (Barber, J., ed.) Vol. 8, pp 527-560, Elsevier, Amsterdam
2 Vallejos, R.H., Ceccarelli, E.A. and Chan, R.L. (1984) J. Biol. Chem. 259, 8048-8051
3 Ceccarelli, E.A., Chan, R.L. and Vallejos, R.H. (1985) FEBS Lett. 190, 165-168
4 Serrano, A., Soncini, F.C. and Vallejos, R.H. (1986) Plant Cell Physiol. 27, 1141-1146
5 Coughlan, S., Matthijs, H.C.P. and Hind, G. (1985) J. Biol. Chem. 260, 14891-14893
6 Chan, R.L., Ceccarelli, E.A. and Vallejos, R.H. (1987) Arch. Biochem. Biophys. 253, 56-61
7 Carrillo, N.J. and Vallejos, R.H. (1983) Biochim. Biophys. Acta 742, 285-294
8 Longeman, J., Schell, J. and Willmitzer, L. (1987) Anal. Biochem. 163, 16-20
9 Blake, M.S., Johnston, K.H., Russell-Jones, G.J. and Gotschlich, E.C. (1984) Anal. Biochem. 136, 175-179
10 Erickson, A.H. and Blobel, G. (1983) Methods Enzymol. 96, 38-50
11 Laemmli, U.K. (1970) Nature 227, 680-685
12 Grossman, A.R., Bartlett, S.G., Schmidt, G.W., Mullet, J.E. and Chua, N.-H. (1982) J. Biol. Chem. 257, 1558-1563
13 Kubawara, T., Murata, T., Miyao, M. and Murata, N. (1986) Biochim. Biophys. Acta 850, 146-155
14 Vater, J., Salnikon, J. and Jansson, C. (1986) FEBS Lett. 203, 230-234
15 Jansen, T., Rother, C., Steppuhn, J., Reinke, H., Beyreuther, K., Jansson, C., Andersson, B. and Herrmann, R.G. (1987) FEBS Lett. 216, 234-280
16 Westhoff, P., Jansson, C., Klein-Hitpa β, L., Berzborn, R., Larsson, C. and Bartlett, S.G. (1985) Plant Mol. Biol. 4, 137-146

THE ATP-DEPENDENT POST TRANSLATIONAL MODIFICATION OF FERREDOXIN : NADP+ OXIDOREDUCTASE

M. HODGES, M. MIGINIAC-MASLOW, P. LE MARECHAL AND R. REMY*, Laboratoire de Physiologie Végétale Moléculaire (UA1128) and *Laboratoire de Génétique Moléculaire des Plantes (UA115), Université de Paris Sud, 91405 ORSAY CEDEX, FRANCE.

INTRODUCTION

The FNR is a nuclear encoded protein located in the chloroplasts of higher plants and algae. It has a molecular weight of between 33 and 38 kDa depending upon species and has been shown to exhibit multiple forms (1). It is localised mainly in the non-appressed regions of the thylakoids although approximately 20% has been shown to be in the granal stacks (2). Two pools of FNR appear to exist in vivo: a loosely bound and a tightly bound pool (3). It is believed that the FNR interacts with certain membrane proteins via electrostatic forces (4). This key photosynthetic enzyme is activated in the light by a process requiring a pH gradient (5) and which leads to a conformational change (6). A tightly bound phosphate associated with the FNR has been mentioned in the literature. The question arises whether the FNR is subject to post translational phosphorylation control. Protein phosphorylation of thylakoids mainly concerns photosysytem II (reaction centre and antenna) proteins. The consequences of this extensive phosphorylation are still poorly understood except for the State transition mechanism. We report, for the first time, the phosphorylation of the FNR and the possible consequences on photosynthetic functioning.

MATERIALS AND METHODS

Pea chloroplasts were washed after osmotic shock in low salt and EDTA to remove the thioredoxin enzyme activation system. Spinach FNR was purified using ferredoxin-sepharose and 2',5'-ADP-sepharose affinity chromatography.

Protein phosphorylation was carried out in the presence of 200 μM ATP for 15 minutes either in the light or in the dark with 10 mM DDT. Control thylakoids were those left in the dark in the absence of DDT.

Phospho-amino acid analyses were carried out after acid hydrolysis and 2D separation on cellulose plates of repurified FNR which had been incubated with thylakoids either in the dark or in the light in the presence of ^{32}P-ATP.

SDS-PAGE was carried out on thylakoids and supernatants, the resulting gels were stained with Coomassie blue, dried and the phosphorylated proteins detected by autoradiography. Western blots were carried out on proteins transferred to nitocellulose sheets and incubated with spinach leaf FNR.

Diaphorase activity was measured at 600 nm by the reduction of DCPIP in the presence of NADPH. Light-saturated NADP+ reduction was measured at 340 nm with thylakoids supplemented with 5 μM ferredoxin. PSI dependent activities were measured with 20 μM DCMU, 100 μM DCPIP, 10 mM ascorbate and 5 μM nigericin either in the presence of 200 μM NADP+ or 100 μM methyl viologen (MV) as terminal electron acceptors.

M. Baltscheffsky (ed.), Current Research in Photosynthesis, Vol. II, 875–878.
© 1990 *Kluwer Academic Publishers. Printed in the Netherlands.*

RESULTS
Figure 1 shows the localisation of the thylakoid–bound FNR as a single band of approximately 34 kDa as judged by its migration on SDS–PAGE gels. When thylakoids were incubated for 15 minutes in the presence of 50 mM EDTA (–) and 5 mM CHAPS (+) and centrifuged at 12000 xg for 10 minutes the FNR was no longer attached to the thylakoids (T) but it was located in the supernatant (S) (Fig 1.A). This was confirmed by the changes in diaphorase activity (% total) associated with T and S (T– 67%, S– 33%; T+ 7%, S+ 93%).

It can be seen that the pea FNR migrates as a single band which is between the two bands associated with purified spinach leaf FNR. The protein band associated with the pea thylakoid FNR was confirmed by a western blot using spinach leaf FNR antibodys (Fig. 1.B).

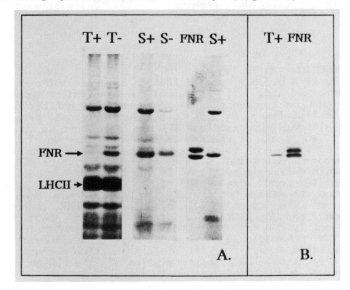

Figure 1. The localisation of FNR on SDS–PAGE gels (A) and by Western blot (B). The lanes correspond to thylakoids (T) which have been washed in the presence of EDTA (–) and CHAPS(+) and the corresponding supernatants (S) after centrifugation. The lane labelled FNR shows the migration of purified spinach leaf FNR.

When thylakoids are incubated for 15 minutes under phosphorylating conditions and submitted to a CHAPS/EDTA wash, the FNR band incorporated ^{32}P (Fig. 2.A.). This was also the case for the purified spinach FNR when it was incubated with pea thylakoids (Fig. 2.B). It was found that the FNR phosphorylation was inhibited by the addition of either FSBA (an ATP analog), NEM (an inhibitor of thiol reactions) or 5 mM $CaCl_2$,as was the case for the LHCII.

To be sure that the FNR was truely phosphorylated and that the labelling was not due to a strong binding of ^{32}P-ATP (as FNR reacts with azido–ATP (7)), phospho-amino acid analyses were carried out (Fig. 3). It was found that the FNR which had undergone a phosphorylation treatment in the presence of thylakoids (as in Fig. 2.B) and then repurified by affinity chromatography showed the presence of phosphoserine when incubated in the dark (Figure 3.A) and also phosphothreonine when treated in the light (Figure 3.B).

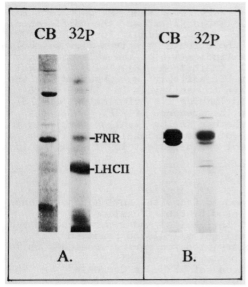

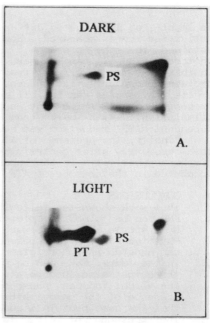

Figure 2. SDS-PAGE gels (CB) and corresponding autoradiograms (³²P) of the supernatants of EDTA/CHAPS washed thylakoids incubated in the presence of FNR (B) under phosphorylating conditions.

Figure 3. 2D-separation of the phospho-amino acids of FNR which had been incubated in the dark (A) or in the light (B) in the presence of thylakoids and ³²P-ATP.

The possible physiological consequences of this phosphorylation were investigated by measuring light saturated FNR-dependent (NADP⁺ photoreduction) and FNR-independent (methyl viologen) PSI activities.

TABLE 1. The effect of light and ATP on the light saturated photoreduction of $NADP^+$ (μmole $NADP^+$ reduced mg Chl^{-1} h^{-1}).

TREATMENT	No Adds (Whole chain)	Nigericin/DCMU (PSI only)	Nigericin/DCMU antimycin a
+ATP Light	63.0±9	42.6±3	62.9±9
−ATP	75.8±10	74.7±14	52.2±6
	−17%	−20%	+20.4%
+ATP Dark	88.9	74.2	n.d.
−ATP	84.4	60.9	n.d.
	+5%	+21.8%	−

No light- or ATP-induced differences were found when MV-dependent PSI activities were measured. However, Table 1 shows the differences obtained in the presence of ATP and/or light for the NADP$^+$ photoreduction. It can be seen that whole chain electron flow was only inhibited by the ATP/light treatment (indicative of the well-documented protein phosphorylation-induced PSII inhibition (8)). In the light-treated thylakoids an inhibition of PSI activity was observed in the presence of ATP which was sensitive to antimycin a (leading to a stimulation). With dark treated thylakoids, a stimulation of PSI-dependent NADP$^+$ reduction was seen in the presence of ATP.

Finally, the presence of ATP (whether in the light or dark) led to the recovery, after centrifugation of the thylakoids, of 17% more diaphorase activity in the supernatant with respect to the thylakoids incubated in the absence of ATP.

CONCLUSIONS

This work shows the following :
1. FNR can be almost completely removed from the thylakoid membranes by a single EDTA/CHAPS wash followed by centrifugation.
2. Purified FNR (in the presence of thylakoids) and membrane-bound FNR can undergo phosphorylation in a light-stimulated reaction.
3. In the dark, FNR can be phosphorylated on serine residues while threonines also incorporate phosphate in the light.
4. The light-induced phosphorylation of FNR is decreased in the presence of the same inhibitors of LHCII phosphorylation suggesting that the same protein kinase is involved in both cases.
5. The presence of ATP leads to a weakening of FNR-thylakoid interactions and modifications in PSI-dependent electron transfer reactions to NADP$^+$. The light-stimulated phosphorylation leads to an antimycin a sensitive inhibition of light saturated NADP$^+$ photoreduction.

These observations suggest that FNR phosphorylation could play an important role in the control of cyclic electron transfer around PSI by modifying specific FNR-protein interactions (perhaps between PSI and the cytochrome b$_6$/f complex). This could involve changes in the electrostatic forces involved in different FNR-protein associations by the addition or removal of negatively charged phosphate groups.

REFERENCES
1 Carrillo, N.and Vallejos, R.H. (1987) in Topics in Photosynthesis (Barber, J., ed.), Vol. 8, pp. 527-560, Elsevier
2 Vallon, O., Wollman, F-A. and Olive, J. (1986) Photochem. Photobiophys. 12, 203-220
3 Matthijs, H.C.P., Coughlan, S.J. and Hind, G. (1986) J. Biol. Chem. 261, 12154-12158
4 Carrillo, N. and Vallejos, R.H. (1982) Plant Physiol. 63, 210-213
5 Pschörn, R., Rühle, W. and Wild, A. (1988) Z. Naturforsch 43c, 207-212
6 Carrillo, N., Lucero, H.A. and Vallejos, R.H. (1980) Plant Physiol. 65, 495-498
7 Coughlan, S.J. and Hind, G. (1986) in Progress in Photosynthesis Research (Biggins, J., ed.), Vol. 2, pp. 797-800, Nijhoff
8 Hodges, M., Boussac, A. and Briantais, J-M. (1987) Biochim. Biophys. Acta 894, 138-145

ACKNOWLEDGEMENTS
M.H. would like to thank the Royal Society (London, U.K.) for financial support during a part of this work. We also acknowledge the support of the C.N.R.S. (France).

ORGANIZATION OF THE PLASTOQUINONE POOL IN CHLOROPLASTS : EVIDENCE FOR
CLUSTERS OF DIFFERENT SIZES.

P. Joliot, J. Lavergne and D. Béal. Institut de Biologie Physico-
Chimique, 13, rue Pierre et Marie Curie, 75005 Paris, France

1. INTRODUCTION

The purpose of this work is to examine the relationship between
the primary quinonic acceptor of PS II, Q_a, and its pool of secondary
acceptors (plastoquinones). Basic established features are : (i) There
are about 8 PQ per PS II (this part of the chain can accept 16 e-).
(ii) Several PS II centers share a common PQ pool (indeed, PQ reduction
is slower when a fraction of PS II centers is inhibited [1-2]).(iii)
The midpoint potential of $Q_a/Q_a^-(H^+)$ is about 0 mV, that of PQ/PQH_2
110 mV (pH 7). The equilibrium constant, (Qox/Qred)/(PQox/PQred),
should thus be about 70, or greater if non-protonated Q_a^- is involved.
(iv) e--transfer from Q_a to PQ occurs in the ms range.

Accordingly, one expects that, past the first few ms following photochemical turnover of PS II, an equilibrium should be attained, with
Q_a about totally oxidized as long as PQ is not totally reduced.
However, it has been known for long [3-5] that this is not actually
observed, unless the system is allowed to equilibrate for much longer
times (tens of seconds). In the 10 ms - 1 ms time-range following
illumination, a large fraction of reduced Q_a coexists with the partially
reduced pool: an apparent equilibrium constant of 1-5 is observed
instead of the large value deduced from thermodynamic data.

The interpretation we propose here is that long-range thermodynamic
equilibrium between Q_a and PQ is not achieved in the 10 ms - 1 s time-
range, but rather, local equilibrium within isolated regions.

2. RESULTS

Fig. 1 shows the progressive reduction of Q_a accompanying pool
reduction upon a series of saturating flashes. The C-550 change was
monitored at 100 ms after each flash. Curve A was obtained with a
dark-adapted sample, curve B after a preillumination of 25 flashes
followed by 25 s darkness. Although little PQH_2 has reoxidized in 25 s
(as may be estimated from area computations), a large reoxidation of
Q^- has taken place, followed by a steeper reduction when resuming the
flashing regime. If equilibrium were achieved, a unique Q_a-PQ relationship should be obtained : clearly, such is not the case.

Fig.2 shows oxygen evolution upon a series of flashes. The solid
line is a plot of the average yield on groups of 4 flashes. It expres-
ses again the reduction of Q_a accompanying that of the pool, and is
similar to curve A in Fig.1. Almost identical results were obtained
with a flashing period of either 40 ms or 160 ms, confirming the
absence of rate-limitation in this time-range.

M. Baltscheffsky (ed.), Current Research in Photosynthesis, Vol. II, 879–882.
© 1990 *Kluwer Academic Publishers. Printed in the Netherlands.*

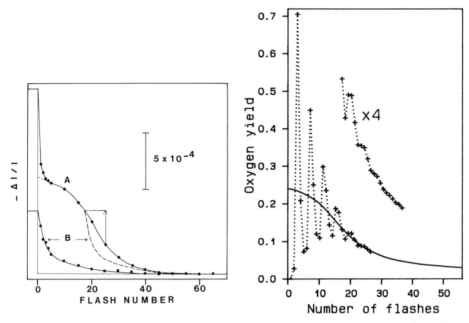

Fig.1. Absorption changes of C-550 (550 nm - 540 nm), during a series
of 70 saturating flashes (150 ms apart). p-Benzoquinone - treated algae
(mutant strain of Chlorella Sorokiniana, lacking PS I and LHC).
Anaerobic conditions, with 5 mM NH_2OH. The horizontal segments on the
left indicate the baselines of the curves, that were arranged at a
common final level. Curve A : dark-adapted sample. The Q_a - formed on the
first flash is due to centers impaired on the Q_b site (see [6]).
Curve B : same as A, after a 25 flashes preillumination followed by 25 s
darkness. The vertical arrow indicates Q_a reoxidation in the 25 s interval, during which about 7% of the PQH_2 have reoxidized (from area
calculations).

Fig.2. Flash-induced oxygen yield with dark-adapted, anaerobic spinach
chloroplasts (part of the data plotted on an expanded scale). The solid
line was obtained by computing the average yield on groups of 4 flashes,
giving an estimate of the amount of active centers.

A remarkable feature is the persistence of the period-4 oscillatory
pattern even when a large fraction of Q_a is reduced. The 8th oscillation
is still detectable, while there remains only 25% active centers. This
is in dramatic contradiction with Kok's model predictions if the
increase of inactive centers is assumed to imply an increased "miss-
coefficient" (α). Indeed, a value of α=50% is amply sufficient to cause
total damping of the oscillations. This suggests that, for O_2-emitting
centers, α remains unmodified, whereas an increasing fraction of the
centers becomes totally blocked. This conclusion is strengthened by noticing the absence of a progressive phase shift in the oscillations

(the successive maxima keep occuring every 4 flashes). In contrast, an increase of α by as little as 4% causes a one-flash phase shift over 3 periods in simulated sequences. Therefore, for those centers that still emit O_2 at, say, the 7th period, the increase of α must not exceed 4%, while an important fraction of the pool has become reduced. This implies that the Q_a/PQ equilibrium constant felt by each center is actually a large one : the reduced Q_a's are those associated with a totally reduced pool. Thus, the progressive appearance of such fully reduced pools implies isolated regions with a distribution of pool sizes. Upon illumination, the smaller pools get totally reduced earlier.

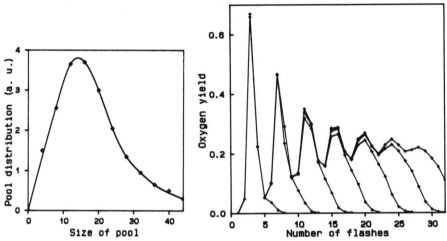

Fig.3. A plot of the derivative (with sign inversion) of the solid line in Fig.2., expressing the distribution of centers associated with pools of a given size, on an electron basis (thus twice the PQ/Q_a stoichiometry). This assumes an infinite value of the equilibrium constant.
Fig.4. Computed sequences, using Kok model, and assuming an equilibrium constant of 70 between Q_a and pools of variable size. On an electron basis, the pool sizes are : 4,8,12,...28. Other parameters : S0=0.1, S1=0.9 (initially), 0.08 misses, and 0.03 double hits.

In this framework, the curves of Fig.1 (A) or 2 (solid line) give the distribution of the pool sizes, simply by plotting the increment of Q_a^- upon each flash. This yields the bell-shaped curve of Fig.3, that was used for weighting the simulated sequences with various pool sizes shown in Fig.4. The reconstituted sequence (not shown) simulates satisfactorily the main features of the experimental sequence of Fig.2 : low "apparent equilibrium constant", absence of increased damping accompanying pool reduction. The effect of a partial reduction followed by a dark period (curve B in Fig.1) can now be interpreted as indicating the slow redistribution of PQ among the regions, in the tens of seconds time-range.
So far, we have brought no information on the size of the isolated regions, in terms e.g., of the number of PS II centers present in each one. The experiment of Fig.5 suggests that this number is actually

rather small. The time course of PQ reduction was monitored through its U-V absorption change, using a continuous illumination of high intensity (≈ 1 hν per center per 2 ms). In the presence of non-saturating concentrations of DCMU, inhibiting part of the centers, the kinetics is slowed down (in agreement with earlier results [1-2]). A new finding, however, is that the amount of photoreducible PQ also decreases when increasing the fraction of inhibited centers, meaning that in some of the isolated regions, all the centers are inhibited (as a result of the statistical distribution of DCMU). Analysis of these results suggests that the isolated regions involve 5-7 centers, and perhaps less, if DCMU happens to bind preferentially in regions with a small pool size (because of competition with PQ for binding to the Q_b site).

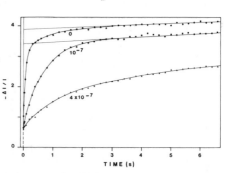

Fig.5. Time course of PQ reduction induced by a saturating continuous illumination, with DCMU as indicated. Spinach chloroplasts. The ordinate is the difference of absorbances (265nm-285nm). The dashed-line indicates the initial offset caused by the contribution of Q_a^- at this pair of wavelengths (because of saturating illumination, total reduction of Q_a is achieved in a few ms after the onset of light). The fraction of inhibited centers at 10^{-7} M DCMU was estimated about 70% (from O_2 measurements).

3. CONCLUSION

On a sub-second time-scale, equilibration of PS II with plastoquinones occurs within isolated regions, whereas global, long-range equilibration requires more than 10 s. The Q_a/PQ stoichiometric ratio is not a constant among all regions, but follows a wide distribution. Each region contains a small number of PS II centers (<7).

A structural interpretation of these results would be premature. On the other hand, they do suggest that the diffusion of plastoquinones cannot be involved in the long-range communication between PS II in stacked regions, and PS I in unstacked regions, leaving this role to plastocyanin.

REFERENCES
1 Joliot, A. (1968) Physiol. Vég. 6, 235-254.
2 Siggel, U., Renger, G., Stiehl, H. and Rumberg, B. (1972) Biochim. Biophys. Acta 256, 328-335.
3 Joliot, P. (1965) Biochim. Biophys. Acta 102, 116-134.
4 Joliot, P., Joliot, A. and Kok, B. (1968) Biochim. Biophys. Acta 153, 635-652.
5 Forbush, B. and Kok, B. (1968) Biochim. Biophys. Acta 162, 243-253.
6 Lavergne, J. (1987) Biochim. Biophys. Acta 894, 91-107.

FLASH-INDUCED ABSORBANCE CHANGES IN THYLAKOID MEMBRANES IN THE 490-550 nm WAVELENGTH REGION. THE GRAMICIDIN-INSENSITIVE COMPONENT.

Wim J. Vredenberg, Wilma Versluis and Jaap J.J. Ooms
Department Plant Physiological Research, Wageningen Agricultural University, Gen. Foulkesweg 72, 6703 BW Wageningen, the Netherlands.

1. INTRODUCTION
    In the flash-induced electrochromic bandshift measured at 518 nm four different components can be distinguished in intact chloroplasts [1]. Reaction 1/RC reflects the primary charge separation in the reaction centra, it has an instrument-limited rise-time of 0.5 ms and a single exponential decay with a half time of 50-100 ms. Reaction 1/Q reflects an electrogenic secondary charge separation due to a Q-cycle with a rise time of 10-20 ms and decay kinetics equal to those of reaction 1/RC. Reaction 2, a third component, reflects a non-electrogenic phenomenon. It has been suggested that reaction 2 is associated with the liberation and stabilization of protons in inner membrane domains [2,3,4]. The fourth component, which is neglected in most experimental work is the gramicidin insensitive component. It has an amplitude of only 5-10% of the over-all P515 signal, decays slowly (2-5 sec.) and has a broad spectrum different from P515 [5,6]. This component, was either called phase d [7] or reaction 3 [6]. Reaction 3 has been suggested to be due to scattering changes [6]. This view is supported by its broad spectrum in the wavelength range 490-540 nm which shows similarities with the spectrum of scattering changes induced by continuous illumination [8]. In this work we studied the effects of DCMU, DQH_2, DBMIB and ferricyanide on the amplitude of reaction 3 and on the turn-over of cytochrome f and P700.

2. MATERIALS AND METHODS
    In all experiments we used fresh intact isolated spinach chloroplasts broken prior to the experiment. All measuring conditions and media are as described in [1] with the supplementary addition of 60 µM methylviologen and 5 µM gramicidin. The turn-over of cytochrome f was monitored as the difference in absorbance change at 554 and 540 nm and P700 was monitored as the absorbance changes around 830 nm. Measurements were carried out with a modified pulse modulation fluorometer as described by Schreiber et al.[9] in the reflection mode. In order to conduct all measurements under same conditions, we removed the photomultiplier and positioned the light fiber directly against the cuvetteholder of the spectrophotometer.

3. RESULTS AND DISCUSSION
    Figure 1 shows the spectrum of reaction 3, defined here as the absorbance change 500 ms after a series of six flashes fired at a frequency of 5 Hz. It is likely that in the wavelength range 490-540 nm also flash-induced absorbance

M. Baltscheffsky (ed.), Current Research in Photosynthesis, Vol. II, 883–886.

changes from other components, e.g. cytochromes b and f, P700, plastocyanin and ferredoxin, contribute to the signal [10]. However it is known that the signals from these components decay within 100 ms after the flash. The amplitude of the signal 500 ms after the flash is considered to be mainly, if not completely due to reaction 3. At 490 nm contributions to the flash-induced absorbance change from the afore mentioned components are minimal and at this wavelength there is no interference with the P515 signal. Hence we have chosen 490 nm for further experiments on reaction 3.

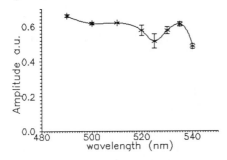

Figure 1: Spectrum of reaction 3, under control conditions (see fig 2a) defined as the absorbance change after a series of six flashes.

Figure 2 shows in the left column measurements of reaction 3 at 490 nm and the effects of the addition of DCMU, DCMU+DQH$_2$ and DCMU+DQH$_2$+DBMIB respectively. The middle column shows the same experiments monitoring the effects of the different additions on cytochrome f. The right column shows the same experiments monitoring the redox state of P700. All measurements were carried out under the same conditions.

From figure 2a it is clear that reaction 3 accumulates on every flash and shows slow decay kinetics. Under the same conditions cytochrome f and P700 show a turn-over on each flash. The spike measured in the P700 signal is due to a flash artefact. The turn-over of P700 is too fast to be monitored with our measuring equipment so only the redox state of steady state levels can be compared.

DCMU severely inhibits reaction 3, cytochrome f and P700 on the second flash, whereas on the third flash full inhibition is accomplished (fig 2b). In figure 2c reaction 3 and the turn-over of cytochrome f and P700 are fully restored by the addition of DQH$_2$. This suggests that the appearance of reaction 3 parallels the possibility to oxidize P700 by a flash. Figure 2d shows that this restoration can be inhibited by DBMIB. The second flash hardly oxidizes cytochrome f, while P700 is making a full turn-over. After the second flash P700 is only partly rereduced, diminishing further turn-over of P700 on the third flash. This correlates well with the lower amplitude of reaction 3 on the third flash. The correlation between the extent of reaction 3 and the redox state of P700, suggest a direct involvement of electron transport in or beyond photosystem 1.

Schreiber et al.[10] have reported binary oscillations in the extent of rereduction of P700 in the presence of ferricyanide. We found a small oscillation in the rereduction of P700 and a highly damped oscillation in the extent of reaction 3 (figure 3).

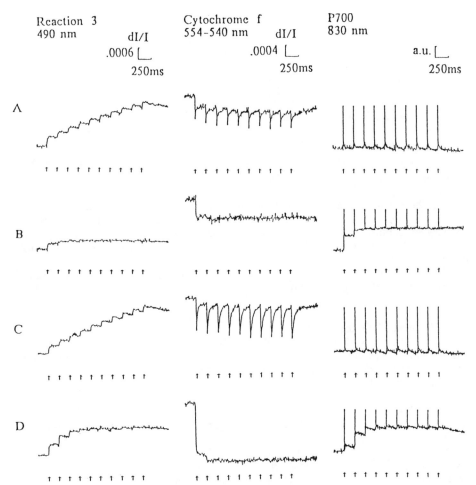

Figure 2: Flash-induced absorbance changes of reaction 3, cytochrome f and P700 of freshly broken spinach chloroplasts, in the presence of 60 μM MV and 5 μM gramicidin. A: control without further additions, B: with 10 μM DCMU, C: with 10 μM DCMU and 450 μM DQH_2, D: with 10 μM DCMU, 450 μM DQH_2 and 1.5 μM DBMIB. All signals are averages of 20 flash trains.

With far-red background illumination in the presence of p-benzoquinone as electron acceptor of photosystem 2 and DBMIB to inhibit electron transport through photosystem 1, we demonstrated a nearly full inhibition of reaction 3 and under the same conditions a normal turn-over of photosystem 2 (data not shown). This experiment clearly indicates that photosystem 2 is not involved in the appearance of reaction 3.

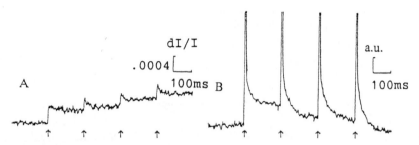

Figure 3: Flash-induced absorbance changes of reaction 3 (A) and P700 (B). Conditions as in fig 2A, where 60 μM MV is replaced by 5 mM ferricyanide.

From these results we conclude that reaction 3 is directly related to electron transport in PS1. It suggestive to think that the reduction of the primary or secondary acceptors of PS1 cause slowly relaxing conformational changes in proteins at the outside of the thylakoid membrane, which may cause scattering changes.

It is clear that one should take care in interpreting the P515 signal. Small changes in the P515 signal might be due to non-electrochromic phenomena, like reaction 3.

ACKNOWNLEDGMENT

We thank Drs J. Snel and O. van Kooten for helpful discussions and technical advises. This research was in part supported by the Stichting Scheikundig Onderzoek Nederland (SON), financed by the Nederlandse organisatie voor Wetenschappelijk Onderzoek (NWO).

REFERENCES

1 Ooms, J.J.J., Vredenberg, W.J. and Buurmeijer, W.F. (1989) Photosynth. Res. 20, 119-128
2 Schapendonk,A.H.C.M. and Vredenberg, W.J. (1979) FEBS-lett. 100, 325-330
3 Vredenberg, W.J. (1981) Physiol. Plant. 53, 598-602
4 Schreiber, U. and Rienits, K.G. (1982) Biochim. Biophys. Acta 682, 115-123
5 Junge, W. (1977) Ann. Rev. Plant. Physiol. 28, 503-536
6 Vredenberg, W.J., Van Kooten, O. and Peters, R. (1983) in Advances in Photo-synthesis Research (Sybesma, C., ed.), Vol 2, pp. 241-246
7 Schapendonk, A.H.C.M., Vredenberg, W.J. and Tonk, W.J.M. (1979) FEBS-lett. 100, 325-330
8 Coughlan, S.J. and Schreiber, U. (1984) Z. Naturforsch. 39c, 1120-1127
9 Schreiber, U., Klughammer, C.and Neubauer, C. (1988) Z. Naturforsch. 43c, 686-698.
10 de Wolf, F.A., Krab, K., Vischers, R.W., de Waard, J.H. and Kraayenhof, R. (1988) Biochim. Biophys. Acta 936, 487-503

EFFECT OF PHOSPHONIC ACID ESTER PAE-6 ON ELECTRON TRANSPORT IN
THYLAKOID MEMBRANES OF WHEAT AND BROAD BEAN

OLGA GÓRNICKA and KAZIMIERZ STRZAŁKA
Jan Zurzycki Institute of Molecular Biology, Jagiellonian University
Al. Mickiewicza 3, 31-120 Kraków, Poland

1. INTRODUCTION

Phosphonic acid dialkyl esters (PAE) are a group of compounds
exhibiting biological activity as herbicides, defoliants, insecticides
etc. (1). They are relatively large and non-rigid molecules described
by a general formula $RP(O)(OR')_2$. For most PAE, molecular shape and
structure as well as order parameters are known not only from
experimental work but also from theoretical studies (2 - 4). Such data
are very useful for the interpretation of molecular arrangement,
elastic deformation, domain formation and molecular anisotropy of
these compounds. Independently of the mechanism of their action in the
cell, PAE have to penetrate through or to be incorporated into the
membranes, so that investigations on these compounds are focused on
the motional behaviour of PAE in membranes and their influence on
model and biological membranes (3). The aim of this study was to
investigate the effect of PAE-6, i.e. phosphonic acid ester having
substituted C_6H_{13} for R and C_2H_5 for R' on electron transport chain
activity of thylakoid membranes of wheat and broad bean.

2. MATERIALS AND METHODS

2.1. Plant material and thylakoid membrane isolation.

Wheat and broad bean seedlings were grown for 6 and 14 days,
respectively on liquid Hoagland medium at $25°C$ and continuous
illumination with white light of the intensity of 20 W m^2. Thylakoid
membranes used for measurement of photosynthetic activity were
isolated by homogenization of leaves in 0.067 M phosphate buffer pH
7.3 containing 0.4 M sucrose, 1.8 mM $MgSO_4$ and 50 mM KCl. The
homogenate was filtered through four layers of cheese-cloth and the
filtrate was centrifuged for 4 min at 600 x g. The resulting
supernatant was centrifuged again for 10 min at 2900 x g. The pellet
obtained was subjected to osmotic shock by suspending it in 10 mM
$MgCl_2$. Thylakoid membranes were pelleted by centrifugation for 5 min
at 6000 x g and then resuspended in isolation buffer. For measurement
of membrane fluidity, where a higher degree of purity is needed,
thylakoid membranes free of stroma proteins were isolated in glycerol
density gradient as described previously (5).

M. Baltscheffsky (ed.), Current Research in Photosynthesis, Vol. II, 887–890.
© 1990 *Kluwer Academic Publishers. Printed in the Netherlands.*

2.2. Measurement of electron transport activity.

Activity of electron transport within PSII was determined by measuring oxygen evolution using conventional Clark-type electrode and potassium ferricyanide as exogenous electron acceptor. PSI activity was measured as methyl viologen-mediated oxygen consumption in the presence of DCMU.

2.3. Measurement of thylakoid membrane fluidity.

The fluidity of thylakoid membranes was measured using 5-doxylstearic acid as a spin probe (final conc. 0.1 mM) and ESR spectrometer Varian working in X band, as described previously (6).

2.4. Incorporation of PAE-6 into thylakoid membranes.

An appropriate amount of PAE-6 dissolved in methanol was evaporated in a glass tube under nitrogen stream to form a thin film of the ester on the bottom of the tube. Then a suspension of thylakoid membranes was added and shaken vigorously for 2 min in darkness.

3. RESULTS AND DISCUSSION

PAE-6 exerts an inhibitory effect on photosynthetic oxygen evolution by wheat and broad bean thylakoid membranes over a broad range of concentrations (Fig. 1, A and B). The degree of inhibition, however, depends on the actual PAE-6/chlorophyll ratio. Below the value of 0.001 μM PAE-6 per μg of chlorophyll no inhibitory effect is observed. From this value to the value of c. 0.050 there is linear

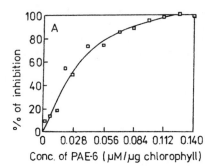 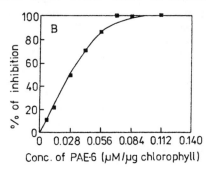

FIGURE 1. Effect of PAE-6 on the inhibition of oxygen evolution by wheat (A) and broad bean (B) thylakoids.

dependence between the PAE-6 to chlorophyll ratio and the inhibition of oxygen evolution. Above the value of 0.050 the slope of the inhibition curve changes and eventually it reaches 100% of inhibition at the PAE-6/chlorophyll ratio close to the value of 0.140 for wheat and 0.070 for broad bean.

PAE-6 also inhibits PSI activity, though the shape of the inhibition curve differs from that for PSII (Fig. 2, A and B). For wheat thylakoids, between PAE-6/chlorophyll ratio of 0.001 and 0.015 there is linear proportionality between the amount of PAE-6 per chlorophyll unit and inhibition of methyl viologen-mediated oxygen consumption. For the range of PAE-6 concentration from 0.028 up to

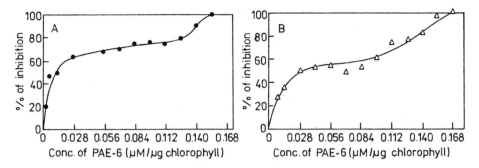

FIGURE 2. Effect of PAE-6 on the inhibition of methyl viologen mediated oxygen uptake by wheat (A) and broad bean (B) thylakoids.

about 0.126 the shape of the curve is a kind of plateau and above the latter value again a rise is observed in the curve. Similarly to PSII, at PAE-6 concentrations above the value of 0.140 - 0.160 µM/µg 100% of inhibition was always obtained. The inhibition curve for broad bean thylakoids also exhibits a three-phase shape, but the shape at respective stages shows some differences in comparison with that found for wheat thylakoids.

In order to correlate the inhibitory effect of PAE-6 on PSII and PSI activity and the changes it causes in thylakoid membrane

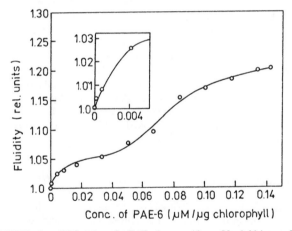

FIGURE 3. Effect of PAE-6 on the fluidity of thylakoid membranes of wheat. All measurements were normalized to the fluidity of control membranes taken as 1.

properties, measurements of membrane fluidity were performed using 5-doxylstearic acid as a probe. As shown in Fig. 3 an initial fast rise in membrane fluidity is followed by a slow phase, related in shape to a plateau about the values 0.02 - 0.04, and then again a rise in spin label mobility is observed, though the increase is slower than that in the initial phase.

PAE-6 due to its shape of an inverted cone is incorporated preferentially into membrane regions of large curvature (3). Therefore it may be assumed, that PAE-6 initially is incorporated mainly into the outer leaflet of the thylakoid membrane within the region of the margin. In this initial stage the incorporation of PAE-6 is accompanied by a relatively fast rise in thylakoid membrane fluidity. After saturating the curved marginal regions subsequent PAE-6 molecules must be localized in planar regions of the thylakoids, especially in lipid domains enriched with monogalactosyldiglyceride. This predominant thylakoid lipid resembles a cone in shape (7), thus for sterical reason it should be a good candidate for the accomodation the inverted cone of PAE-6. The incorporation of PAE-6 into monogalactosyldiglyceride-rich lipid domains may correspond to the slow phase in the increase in membrane fluidity. At still higher concentrations of PAE-6 it is most probably incorporated unspecifically into different regions of the thylakoid membranes, again increasing its fluidity and finally disorganizing the membrane structure.

The initial fast rise in thylakoid membrane fluidity at low PAE-6 concentrations correlates well with the inhibition of PSI activity. The onset of the slow phase in membrane fluidity increase also coincides well with the plateau in PSI activity of wheat thylakoids. At still higher concentrations of PAE-6, however, the rise in membrane fluidity precedes that of PSI further inhibition. In the case of PSII there is a correlation between membrane fluidity changes and the inhibition of oxygen evolution only at a low range of PAE-6 concentrations. Above PAE-6/chlorophyll ratio of 0.015 a further decrease in oxygen evolution is observed, while the fluidity of thylakoid membrane does not change much. It is therefore plausible to assume that PAE-6 affects electron transport chain activity within PSII not only through changes in thylakoid membrane fluidity but also through interactions of another type, most probably with hydrophobic portions of integral membrane proteins.

4. REFERENCES

1 Kramer,W., Gûnther,E., Löttge,W., Bech,R. and Kochmann,W. (1975) Congress of Pesticide Chemistry, Proc. pp. 686-689, Helsinki.
2 Klose,G., Hentschel,M., Bayerl,T. and Strobel,U. (1984) Seventh School on Bioph. of Membr. Transport, Proc. pp.185-210, Zakopane.
3 Hentschel,M. and Klose,G. (1985) Biochim.Biophys.Acta 812,447-452.
4 Bilke,S. and Klose,G. (1985) Coll.Polym.Sci. 263, 1031-1040.
5 Strzałka,K. and Subczyński,W. (1980) Photosynthetica 14, 575-579.
6 Strzałka,K. and Subczyński,W. (1981) Photobiochem.Photobiophys. 2, 227-232.
7 Murphy,D.J. and Woodrow,I. (1983) Biochim.Biophys.Acta 725, 104-112.

This study was carried out under the Polish Academy of Sciences project CPBP 05.02.

STATE TRANSITIONS IN PHOTOMORPHOGENETIC MUTANTS OF TOMATO.

Willem F. Buurmeijer, Jeannette H.A.M. Wonders and Wim J. Vredenberg.
Dept. of Plant Physiological Res., Agric. Univ. Wageningen, Gen. Foulkesweg 72, 6703 BW Wageningen, The Netherlands.

1. INTRODUCTION

The distribution of light energy between photosystem (PS) I and II in higher plants can be regulated by changing the relative sizes of the antennae pigment complexes associated with the photosystems. State transitions occur when the light quality of the absorbed light induces an imbalance between the turn-over rate of both PS's. This imbalance will be counterbalanced by migrations of antennas. It is generally accepted that the Chl b containing antennae pigment complex of PS II, (LHC II) plays a major role in this regulation (1). The mechanism of regulation of the excitation energy distribution is based on a balance between phosphorylated and dephosphorylated LHC II, with the redox-state of the plastoquinone as a modulator of kinase/phosphatase activity.

We have used two photomorphogenetic tomato mutants: *aurea* (*au*) and *yellow green-2* (*yg-2*) (2,3). They have a chlorophyll a/b ratio of 4-6, with the largest a/b ratio for *au*. The decreased LHC II content of

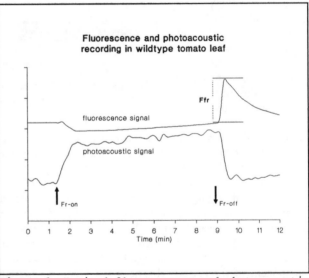

Figure 1. Typical fluorescence and photoacoustic signals of a wildtype tomato leaf during a state II-state I transition. See text for further explanation.

the mutants makes them a valuable tool for investigating state transitions. We report here results on photoacoustic and the more 'classic' chlorophyll (Chl) fluorescence measurements with leaves of wildtype and the mutants during state-II state-I transitions. Photoacoustic spectroscopy (PAS) promises to be a valuable tool for investigating state-transitions (4,5).

2. MATERIALS AND METHODS

Material: Tomato leaves of wildtype (WT) (*Lycopersicon esculentum* Mill cv. Mon-

M. Baltscheffsky (ed.), Current Research in Photosynthesis, Vol. II, 891–894.
© 1990 *Kluwer Academic Publishers. Printed in the Netherlands.*

eymaker) and the long hypocotyl mutants *yg-2* and *au* have been used (2).

Instrumental setup: Figure 2 represents a schematic drawing of the combined Chl fluorescence and PAS instrumental setup. The fluorescence of the plant leaf was determined with a Pulse Amplitude Modulation fluorometer (PAM chlorophyll fluorometer, Walz, Effeltrich, Germany) as described in (6). Excitation and emission light passed through the fiberoptics, consisting of four separate bundles, which merge

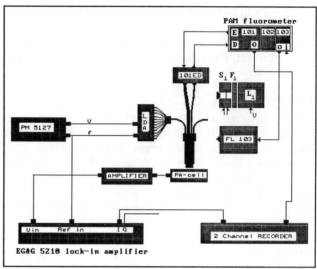

Figure 2. Instrumental setup of a combined Chl fluorescence and photoacoustic measurement. See text for further explanation.

into one joint bundle, over a 400 mm pathway. Two bundles are used for the modulated fluorescence measuring light beam (pulsed LED) and the fluorescence detector (photodiode). The modulated PA measurement light came from a laboratory build voltage controlled Light emitting Diode Array (LDA). The LDA was connected to a multibranched lightguide which was in turn connected to one of the four central fiber arms. The energy fluence rate of the LDA (wavelength approx. 660 nm) at the PA-cell (JEDA) was 6 $W \cdot m^{-2}$. The voltage (V) (intensity) and frequency (f) of the modulated light was controlled by a function generator (PM 5127, Philips). A high intensity lightsource (FL 103) (KL 1500, Schott) was used to optimize the photobaric component of the PA-signal. The signal from the microphone in the PA-cell was preamplified and fed to a 2 phase lock-in amplifier (EG&G 5210). The in-phase (I) or quadrature-component (Q) of the PA-signal was recorded by a paper-recorder. The halogen lightsource (L_1) with manual shutter (S_1) and a Schott 694 nm cut-off filter (F_1) was used as a far-red (FR) lightsource. The energy fluence rate of the FR was approx. 15 $W \cdot m^{-2}$. The fluorescence signal from the PAM fluorometer was recorded on the second channel of the recorder.

The experimental procedure: A leaf was placed in the PA-cell with a wet paperfilter, to prevent closure of the leaf stomata. The photobaric component was adjusted with modulated red light with a frequency of 68 Hz. After 30 min adaption in the cell the maximal fluorescence (Fmax) was determined with a 1 sec saturating light pulse of the FL103. After that the leaf was irradiated with increasing time periods of FR. The time between the FR-treatments was 5 min, to reverse the state transition. The change in fluorescence intensity after switching off the FR (Ffr) (see Figure 1) was normalized with respect to the Fmax.

The setup described above was hampered by a relatively poor signal/noise ratio of the fluorescence signal and strong oscillatory patterns at the decline of the Ffr (not shown) which prevented a good approximation of the maximal Ffr level. This problem was circumvented by using a special leafcuvette for the fluorescence measurements. It should be noted that both experiments (PAS + fluorescence) and only fluorescence gave comparable results. Reproducibility of the single fluorescence measurements in general was higher.

3. RESULTS AND DISCUSSION

Figure 1 shows a typical recordings of state II-state I transitions in the WT of tomato. It can be seen that the oxygen evolution (the photobaric component) increases when the FR is switched on. This is known as the Emerson enhancement. The fluorescence signal shows a fast increase in the fluorescence (Ffr) when the FR is switched off. This is caused by a transient over-excitation of PS II, resulting in a highly reduced PQ-pool, hence high fluorescence intensity. Figure 3 sho-

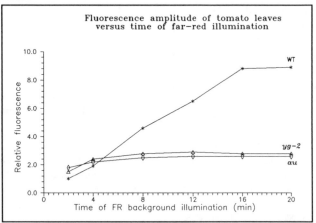

Figure 3. The relative fluorescence level after switching of the far red background light in the 3 tomato genotypes. The fluorescence is normalized at the Fmax.

ws the change in the fluorescence intensity after adaption to increasing FR-illumination times. The WT signal indicates the largest adaptation to state I, while the mutants show a small adaption. The adaption is however faster in the mutants. The halftime of the full response in the mutants is approx. 2 min and in WT 8 min. Figure 4 shows the Emerson enhancement during a state I-state II transition in the tomato plants. The WT shows the highest Emerson enhancement, which is maximal after 20 min FR. The mutants require less time of FR illumination to reach maximal enhancement. The mutant *yg-2* shows the lowest enhancement. The relaxation time of the response in *au* and *yg-2* are about the same.
From the results it is clear that the mutants can perform state transitions. The Ffr and Emerson enhancement is smaller in the mutants as we would expect on basis of the LHC II content. This is in agreement with findings with other Chl *b* mutants (4). It is however not clear why the *au* has a higher Emerson enhancement than the *yg-2*, because *au* has less LHC II.
The faster adaption to state I in the mutants can possibly explained by i) a LHC II pool size effect, ii) a shorter diffusion path for LHC II, iii) a lower resistance to lateral diffusion of LHC II, or iv) a higher protein-kinase activity in the mutants.

The pool size effect would mean that a certain change in the size of a small LHC II pool (which is the case for the mutants) has relatively more effect then the same change in a large pool. The total response after completion of the state transition then will be still smaller with a lower LHC II content. A shorter lateral diffusion path for the antennae is likely on basis of electron micrographs which show smaller grana structures in the chloro-

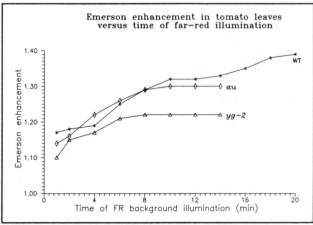

Figure 4. The Emerson enhancement in the 3 genotypes of tomato versus time of far red illumination.

plasts of the mutants (2). A lower diffusion resistance could be expected on basis of the lower LHC II content which would decrease self-hindrance during diffusion. Protein kinase activity has not been determined in the mutants as yet.

ACKNOWLEDGEMENTS

This research was supported in part by the Foundation for Biophysics, with financial aid from the Netherlands Organization for Scientific Research (NWO).

REFERENCES.

1) Williams, W. and Allen, J.F. (1987) Photosynth. Res 13, 19-45
2) Koornneef, M. et al. (1985) J. of Plant Physiol. 120, 153-165
3) Buurmeijer, W.F. et al (1987) in Progress in Photosynthesis Research (Biggins, J., ed.), Vol. 2, pp. 383-386, Martinus Nijhoff Publishers, Dordrecht
4) Canaani, O. and Malkin, S. (1984) Biochim. Biophys. Acta 766, 513-524
5) Canaani, O. et al. (1989) Photosynth. Res. 20, 129-146
6) Schreiber, U. et al. (1986) Photosynth. Res. 10, 51-62

SERINE PROTEIN PHOSPHORYLATION IN THE NON-APPRESSED (STROMA)
THYLAKOID MEMBRANES.

Eleonora Garcia-Véscovi and Héctor A. Lucero

Area Biología, Facultad de Ciencias Bioquímicas
y Farmacéuticas, Universidad Nacional de
Rosario. Suipacha 531. 2000 Rosario. Argentina.

1. INTRODUCTION

Thylakoid protein phosphorylation occurs in the light (1) and
in the dark (E. Garcia-Vescovi and H. Lucero, unpublished).
Light phosphorylation takes place mostly at threonine
residues (1), is related to the state transition mechanism
(2) and is catalyzed by a 64 K protein kinase (3) that is
localized in the appressed thylakoid (4) where it
phosphorylates LHC II (1) and some PS II core complex
proteins (5). It is accepted that a single protein kinase is
involved in the light phosphorylation of thylakoid proteins
since the purified 64 K kinase reconstitutes *in situ* the
light phosphorylation pattern which is inhibited by
antibodies against 64 K protein (6). We have purified from
thylakoid two serine protein kinases, ChlPK 1 (25 K) and
ChlPK 2 (38 K) (7,8). While ChlPK 1 was predominant, ChlPK 2
contribution was substantially smaller (7). Later we observed
that ChlPK 2 activity was barely detectable or even absent in
some purifications (H. Lucero, unpublished) suggesting that
ChlPK 2 is sensitive to the detergent extraction. Neither
ChlPK 1 nor ChlPK 2 phosphorylate LHC II (8). Using lysine-
rich histone we have showed that a dark protein serine
kinase is functionally distinguished from the light-activated
threonine protein kinase (9). Recently, (E. Garcia-Vescovi
and H. Lucero, unpublished) we have observed in thylakoids a
distinct pattern of endogenous protein serine phosphorylation
in the dark which is impaired by illumination and mostly
localized in the non-appressed thylakoid. Here we show
evidence suggesting that ChlPK 1 catalyzes the dark, serine
phoshorylation of some of the proteins of thylakoids. Using
polyclonal antibodies against ChlPK 1 we detected a 25 K
protein in thylakoids and in PS I and PS II particles.

2. MATERIALS AND METHODS

Preparation of thylakoids (7) and subthylakoid particles (10,
11) from spinach, purification of prothylakoid membranes from

M. Baltscheffsky (ed.), Current Research in Photosynthesis, Vol. II, 895–898.
© 1990 *Kluwer Academic Publishers. Printed in the Netherlands.*

etiolated wheat leaves (12), purification of ChlPK 1 (7), Cybacrom-blue affinity chromatography (3), antibodies in rabbit (13), phosphoamino acid analysis (7), gel electrophoresis (7) and autoradiography were done as described (7). 5mM NEM treatment of thylakoids (25μg Chlorophyll), PS I particles (25μg Chlorophyll) and ChlPK 1 (5μg) was carried out in a medium (50μl) containing 70 mM Tricine pH 7.8, 10 mM MgCl2 at 27°C for 10 min in the dark. The excess of NEM was quenched by addition of 5μl 1 M DTT to the samples including the controls that were not exposed to NEM. After 5 min at 27°C, ChlPK 1 (5μg) was added where indicated. 20μl of (γ32P-ATP) (2,000 cpm/pmol) - 5μM final- was then added to start the kinase reaction for 15 min at 27°C. The reaction was terminated by addition of an equal volume of SDS-PAGE sample buffer. 15% SDS-PAGE and autoradiography were carried out as described (7).

3. RESULTS AND DISCUSSION

Polyclonal antibodies against ChlPK 1 react with three proteins of 34 K, 25 K and 14 K in thylakoids and in PS II particles (Fig. 1, lanes 1 and 2). In PS I particles the 34 K band was barely observed while the 14 K band was absent (Fig.1, lane 3). Purified ChlPK 1 showed mostly a 25 K band with a very weak signal at around 34 K (Fig. 1, lane 4). Our antibody is not monospecific for a control blot without anti ChlPK 1 treatment did not show any band (Fig. 1). However the 25 K band was consistently observed in thylakoids and in subthylakoid particles as well as in purified ChlPK 1, suggesting that ChlPK 1 is homogenously distributed within the thylakoid disk.

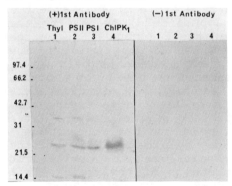

Figure 1: Immunoblot of thylakoids, PSI particles, PSII particles and ChlPK1 with rabbit anti-ChlPK1

The majority of the dark-phosphorylated proteins in thylakoids are in the non-appressed region (E. Garcia-Vescovi and H. Lucero, unpublished). Dark phosphorylated proteins in thylakoids and in PS I particles are 80-90% inhibited by NEM treatment (Fig.2, lanes 2 and 6). ChlPK 1 partially restores the phosphorylation of proteins of 42 K ("a"), 16 K ("e"), 14 K ("f") and 8 K ("g") in NEM-treated thylakoids and of 42 K ("a"), 25 K ("b"), 23 K ("c"), 19 K ("d"), 16 K ("e") and 8 K ("g") in NEM-treated PS I particles. The presence of ChlPK 1 in the phosphorylation of the control membranes had no detectable effect (Fig. 2, lanes 4 and 8). NEM-treated ChlPK 1 was inactive and failed to reconstitute phosphorylation (not shown). This *in situ* reconstitution of dark-phosphorylated membrane proteins by purified ChlPK 1 together with the immuno detection of ChlPK 1 antigen in the thylakoid and in the non-appressed membranes strongly suggests the involvement of this kinase in the serine dark phosphorylation of thylakoids.

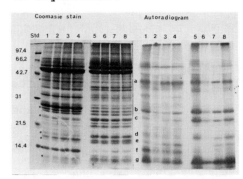

Figure 2: Resconstitution of dark phosphorylation in NEN-treated thylakoids and NEM-treated PS I particles. Lanes:1,Control thylakoids; 2, NEM-thylakoids;3,NEM-thylakoids+ChlPK1;4, Control thylakoids+ChlPK1;5, Control PSI particles; 6, NEM-PSI particles;7,NEM-PSI particles+ChlPK1;8, PSI particles+ChlPK1

Light independent protein phosphorylation occurs in prothylakoid membranes (12). Such phosphorylation takes place in serine residues of endogenous prothylakoid membranes as well as in histone catalyzed by these membranes (Fig. 3, lane 1). Mature thylakoids and to a lesser extent PS II particles catalyze protein threonine phosphorylation in endogenous substrates (Fig. 3, lanes 2 and 3). These results suggest that while the light-activated, protein threonine phosphorylation is restricted to photosynthetically mature thylakoids, a thylakoid-bound protein serine kinase activity seems to be present at early stages of thylakoid development. Serine protein phoshorylation in thylakoid could be related to the biogenesis and/or to some of the biological activities of mature chloroplast. The latter possibility is particularly attractive since illumination impairs the serine phosphorylation of dark-phosphorylated thylakoids (E. Garcia-Vescovi and H. Lucero, unpublished).

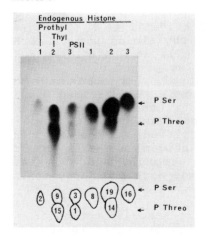

Figure 3: Phosphoamino acid Analysis of endogenous substrates in prothylakoids, thylakoids and in PS II particles and in lysine-rich histone phosphorylated by these membranes. Figures in the profile spots are cpm x 10^{-3}.

Acknowledgements
This work has been supported by grants from the Argentinian National Research Council (CONICET: Consejo Nacional de Investigaciones Cientificas y Tecnicas) and from the Third World Academy of Science (TWAS). We thank Karlie Riess and Vicki Shaff for mastering the computer format of this paper.

REFERENCES
1. Bennett, J. (1977) Nature 269, 344-346
2. Bennett, J., Steinback, E.and Arntzen, C.J.(1980) Proc. Natl. Acad. Sci. 77, 5253-5257
3. Coughland, S.J. and Hind, G. (1986) J. Biol. Chem. 261, 11378-11385
4. Coughland, S.J. and Hind, G. (1087) Biochemistry 26, 6515-6521
5. Millner, P.A., Marder, J.B., Gournaris, K. and Barber, J.(1986) Biochim. Biophys. Acta 852, 30-37
6. Coughland, S.J. and Hind, G. (1987) J. Biol. Chem. 262, 8402-8408
7. Lin, Z.F., Lucero, H.A. and Racker, E.(1982) J. Biol.Chem. 257, 12153-12156
8. Lucero, H.A., Lin, Z.F. and Racker, E.(1982) J. Biol. Chem. 257, 12157-12160
9. Lucero, H.A., Cortez, N. and Vallejos, R.H.(1987) Biochim. Biophys. Acta 890,77-81
10. Peters, F.A.L., Van Wielink, J.E., Wong Fong Sang, H.W., Deuries, S. and Kraayenhoff, R. (1983) Biochim.Biophys. Acta 722, 460-470
11. Berthold, D.A., Babcock, G.T and Jocum, C.F. (1981) FEBS Lett.134, 231-234
12. Covello, P.S., Webber, A.N., Dankos, S.J., Marwell, J.P. and Baker, N.R. (1987) Photosynthesis Res. 12, 243-254
13. Winston, S.E., Fuller, S.A. and Hurrell, J.G.R (1989) in "Current Protocols in Molecular Biology" Vol.2, 10.8.1-10.8.6, (Ausuber, F.M. et al. Eds.) Greene Publishing Associates and Wiley-Interscience

THE ROLE OF LHCII PHOSPHORYLATION AND D1 TURNOVER IN THE
STRUCTURE AND FUNCTION OF PSII

CHRISTA CRITCHLEY, Department of Botany, The University
of Queensland, ST LUCIA, QLD, 4067, AUSTRALIA

1. INTRODUCTION
        Photosynthesis proceeds in chloroplasts of higher plant
leaves with very high quantum conversion efficiency and at maximal
rates, although conditions of light quantity and quality can be
extremely variable. This variability can be long term and
dominated by diurnal changes, as would be the case in an overall
bright light, open habitat, or short term, an example here being
understory shade punctuated by sunflecks of variable duration and
intensity. In many plants, and perhaps even most, the range of
response to light conditions of the photosynthetic apparatus is
extremely large [1]. Not only can many species adapt to quite low
or very high intensities or anything in between over a longer
term, but some can also change photosynthetic rates upwards or
downwards within seconds without apparent reduction in quantum
yield [2]. Furthermore, quantum yields remain high in many plant
species even under conditions of significant environmental stress
such as salinity or drought while photosynthetic rates can be very
low. How is this achieved? What is the mechanism for the short
term adjustment process? What role does the three-dimensional
thylakoid membrane structure play?
        I have recently proposed a hypothesis [3] that describes
a possible mechanism for rapid change in photosynthetic rate and
maintenance of high quantum yields. Its central point is the
functional role of the rapid turnover rate of the PSII reaction
centre protein D1. The overall concept is one of constant dynamic
movement changing the three-dimensional thylakoid membrane system
through unstacking and restacking of lamellae with only limited
lateral movement of pigment/protein and redox complexes. In the
dark the dynamic movement is extremely slow, the system idles as
it were. With increasing light intensity this motion becomes
faster, leading to a more rapid rearrangement of the thylakoid
membranes.

2. THE ROLE OF D1 PROTEIN TURNOVER
        When it became apparent that two polypeptides of PSII,
D1 and D2, showed extensive amino acid sequence homology with the
bacterial reaction centre proteins L and M, and when X ray
crystallography revealed the detailed molecular architecture of

M. Baltscheffsky (ed.), Current Research in Photosynthesis, Vol. II, 899–902.
© 1990 *Kluwer Academic Publishers. Printed in the Netherlands.*

the bacterial reaction centre, it also became obvious that the reaction centre of PSII may be constructed in a similar, if not the same, way [4]. In this context, the extensively documented, light dependent, rapid turnover of the D1 protein became an even more puzzling feature of PSII than it had hitherto been. Clearly, the continuous degradation and resynthesis of D1, and with it the core of PSII, had to be a significant functional feature of PSII, perhaps even the entire thylakoid membrane system. In [3] I suggested a role for light driven D1 protein turnover in PSII and for the whole of the green membrane system. Here I wish to refine that part of the hypothesis by extending my considerations to the roles that D1 phosphorylation and D1 acylation play.

The kinase which phosphorylates D1 is controlled by factors other than those that control LHCII phosphorylation [5]. Although we do not yet have any definitive experimental evidence to suggest that D1 in the phosphorylated state may also be the target for the specific protease, and hence 'active' in turnover, I would like to propose a regulatory role for D1 phosphorylation in D1 protein turnover. This regulatory function is in addition to that exerted by the occupation of the Q_B binding site [3].

I do not share the general enthusiasm for the existence of a 'pool' of newly synthesized D1 protein in the stromal membranes which finds its way eventually into the heart of a PSII complex, nor for the notion that extensive lateral movement of multisubunit protein complexes takes place in the thylakoid membrane system. (This, I hasten to add, however, does not entirely discount the concept of 'lateral heterogeneity' recently espoused by many in the field). In the absence of any evidence that indicates total PSII reaction centre turnover and resynthesis or disassembly and reassembly, I favour the view that newly synthesized D1 protein is inserted directly into pre-existing PSII reaction centre shells [3]. This view is consistent with at least two observations; (i) Murphy [6] calculated that very little lipid, if any, is present between multimeric protein complexes in the thylakoid membrane, hence lateral movement would be very unfavourable energetically if not impossible physically; and (ii) association between D1 and D2 is very intimate, if the PSII reaction centre is anything like the bacterial one, which would suggest a rather more sophisticated assembly process than random collision. Acylation (palmitoylation) of the mature D1 protein has been reported [7] and has been suggested to assist with functional integration of the protein into the complex. This would appear to agree well with recent reports of nuclear gene products that are involved in the continued synthesis, stability and assembly of PSII reaction centre components [8,9]. The acylation enzyme may be just such a nuclear gene product, as may be the specific kinase that phosphorylates D1.

3. THE ROLE OF LHCII PHOSPHORYLATION

The rapid adjustment of the quantum capturing and excitation energy transfer capacity must be a key element in the maintenance of optimal quantum yields under variable light conditions. The regulatory mechanism underlying this adjustment in capacity would have to involve the molecular structure of the two photosystems, the architecture of the entire thylakoid membrane system, the positioning of the chloroplasts and the orientation of the leaf. Any adjustments in the long term would presumably involve all of these levels to some degree dependent on plant species and other factors. Very short term changes, however, may not extend beyond the level of the thylakoid membrane system, if that, and it is the very rapid changes in molecular structure that I wish to address here.

Given that the rate of turnover of the D1 protein is proportional to light intensity, and assuming that the remaining shells of PSII created even only for a very short period, are nonfunctional, it follows that temporarily depleted PSII units would have to be rendered as non-absorbing as possible to maintain a high quantum yield. Differential phosphorylation of polypeptides of the light harvesting complex of PSII, among them CP29 and CP24, and instant detachment of light harvesting units from the reaction centre would do just that. It does presumably not require a large distance to be created between LHCII units and PSII reaction centres to prevent excitation energy transfer to the core. A more tricky question is how to minimize absorption by temporarily detached LHCII units as well. The solution here may lie in the architecture of the thylakoid membrane system and the way it changes in response to D1 degradation and simultaneous LHCII phosphorylation. It may be possible that localized unstacking events and the subtle alterations that this would cause in the overall membrane organization lead to shading of unstacked areas. This kind of three-dimensional phenomenon requires a much better understanding of the thylakoid membrane folding than we have at present. However, it is very likely that the prime supramolecular mechanism involved is localized but multiple unstacking events leading to subtle changes in the structure of the membrane system. It would be consistent with the notion that the thylakoid membranes are continuously changing while at the same time they seem to stay the same.

4. CONCLUSION

The two-dimensional view of the thylakoid membrane system with which electron microscopic pictures have presented us has, I believe, limited and perhaps even misdirected our concepts and ideas about why the thylakoid membrane system looks the way it does and how it works. A new, more sophisticated model is required that encompasses the molecular structure of multisubunit membrane complexes as well as the three-dimensional architecture of the entire membrane system in a chloroplast. This paper, and the one already published [3] offers a beginning.

REFERENCES
1   Lichtenthaler, H.K. et al. (1982) Z. Naturforsch. Teil C 37,
    464-475
2   Pearcy, R.W. et al. (1985) Plant Physiol. 79, 896-902
3   Critchley, C. (1988) Photosynth. Res. 19, 265-276
4   Michel, H. and Deisenhofer, J. (1988) Biochem. 27, 1-7
5   Bennett, J. et al. (1987) FEBS Lett. 210, 22-26
6   Murphy, D.J. (1986) Biochim. Biophys. Acta 864, 33-94
7   Mattoo, A.K. and Edelman, M. (1987) Proc. Natl. Acad. Sci.
    USA 84, 1497-1501
8   Klein, R.R. and Mullet, J.E. (1987) J. Biol. Chem. 262, 4341-
    4348
9   Gamble, P.E. and Mullet, J.E. (1989) J. Biol. Chem. 264,
    7236-7243

Note added in proof:
While it may have been more in keeping with convention to present
some experimental evidence to support this hypothesis, the
acquisition of such data has proven to be hampered by a lack of
research funding for the purpose. In my defense I draw to your
attention a paper that appeared in Nature this year: 'The
hypothetical way of progress' by V.A. Huszagh and J.P. Infante.
Vol 338, p.109

A NEW GREEN GEL SYSTEM THAT RESOLVES UP TO TWENTY CHLOROPHYLL-PROTEIN COMPLEXES FROM *CHLAMYDOMONAS REINHARDTII* THYLAKOIDS.

Keith D. Allen, and L. Andrew Staehelin. Dept of MCD Biology, University of Colorado, Boulder, Colorado 80309-0347 USA.

Introduction.   We are interested in the relationships between assembly, composition and ultrastructure of the thylakoid membrane in higher plants and algae. As part of this interest, we have investigated means for improving the resolution of available methods for the separation and analysis of chlorophyll-protein complexes. The result of this work is a new native green gel system that resolves up to twenty chlorophyll-proteins from *Chlamydomonas reinhardtii* thylakoids with very little release of free pigment. Although developed for *Chlamydomonas*, this system resolves similar numbers of chlorophyll-proteins from a variey of higher plant species (see Allen, *et al.*, these Proceedings). We report here the general characteristics of this system and its application to the chlorophyll b-deficient cbn1-48 mutant of *Chlamydomonas*.

Materials and Methods. Thylakoid membranes were isolated from wild type (strain 137c) and cbn1-48 *Chlamydomonas* and purified on sucrose step gradients as described by Chua and Bennoun (1975). Details of the green gel technique will be dealt with in detail in an upcoming paper (Allen and Staehelin, manuscript in preparation).

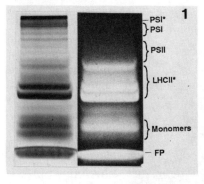

Results and Discussion. Figure 1 shows an example separation of *Chlamydomonas* chlorophyll-protein complexes solubilized with a mixture of octyl glucoside, decyl maltoside, and lithium dodecyl sulfate. The left hand panel shows the unstained green band pattern, while the right hand panel shows intrinsic room temperature chlorophyll fluorescence with excitation at 365 nm. This technique allows for the rapid assignment of antenna complexes, which fluoresce brightly, and reaction center complexes which are non-fluorescent or only weakly fluorescent at room temperature.

The green band pattern may be divided into four zones of increasing electrophoretic mobility based on spectral properties, chlorophyll a/b ratios, and polypeptide compositions. The slowest migrating zone contains PSI-LHCI complexes. A set of these bands, designated PSI*, are apparently PSI dimers or trimers based on their extremely low electrophoretic mobility. The next set of four bands, designated PSI A-D are PSI-LHCI complexes which differ from each other with respect to chlorophyll a/b ratios, fluorescence emission spectra, and polypeptide compositions. The PSI-LHCI region overlaps somewhat, depending on the specific acrylamide mixture used, with a region of at least four PSII-LHCII bands, designated PSII A-D. These bands also differ from each other with regard to chlorophyll a/b ratios, fluorescence emission spectra, and polypeptide compositions. Specifically, the PSII-LHCII complexes may be differentiated based on the amount of bound LHCII, the specific LHCII polypeptides bound to each complex, and the presence of lower molecular weight components. The third zone contains four peripheral light harvesting antenna complexes of PSII, designated LHCII* A-D. Specific differences between these complexes, their presence in stacked *versus* unstacked membranes, and their order of appearance during greening of a *Chlamydomonas* mutant that fails to make chlorophyll in the dark, will be dealt with in a future paper (Allen and Staehelin, manuscript in prep.). The fourth zone contains monomeric complexes, such as LHCII monomers and the *Chlamydomonas* equivalent of CP29.

It is important to note that the small amount of free pigment released during this electrophoretic procedure is mainly carotenoid rather than chlorophyll. The small amount of free pigment released and the high degree of membrane solubilization, as judged by sedimentation experiments, indicates that this proceedure yields an accurate representation of the total membrane and maintains complexes in a more native state than most conventional green gel systems. However, due to the unexpected complexity of the green band pattern resolved by this new gel system, the relationship of these *in vitro* complexes to in vivo membrane complexes is not immediately clear. To clarify this point, we are currently investigating changes in the banding pattern in response to solubilization conditions, gel and running buffer compositions, growth conditions of *Chlamydomonas* cultures, and a variety of mutations affecting different aspects of thylakoid assembly.

As an example of one of the several parameters we have tested with this gel system, Figure 2 shows the effect of divalent cation concentration, in this case Mg^{++}, on the stability of chlorophyll-protein complexes. In this experiment, a range of Mg^{++}

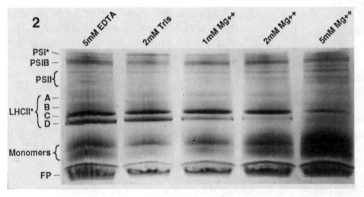

concentrations, from near zero (5mM EDTA) to 5mM $MgCl_2$, were present in both the wash buffers and in the final detergent solution. The most striking result from this experiment is that increasing Mg^{++} concentrations not only have a destabilizing effect on LHCII*, as evidenced by the transfer of chlorophyll density from the LHCII* region to the monomer region but that the different LHCII* complexes are also differentially sensitive to increasing Mg^{++} concentrations, with LHCII* C being the most resistant, and LHCII* D the most labile. This pattern of differential stability of LHCII* complexes, which is a significant extension of earlier work on cation effects on the stability of LHCII oligomers (Argyroudi-Akoyunoglou, 1980) has also been observed in experiments with different detergent mixtures (data not shown).

We have found the chlorophyll b-less cbn1-48 mutant of *Chlamydomonas* to be particularly helpful in highlighting some of the unique features of our new gel system, and in demonstrating how specific chlorophyll-protein complexes may relate to structural parameters of chloroplast membranes (Chunayev, et al., 1984).

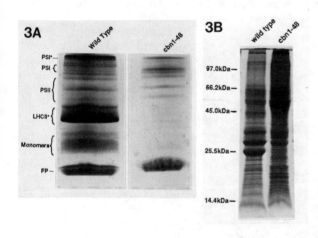

As shown in Figure 3a, the cbn1-48 green band profile is substantially simplified relative to the wild type, with the complete or nearly complete loss of all chlorophyll b-containing antenna complexes. The non-fluorescent PSI bands all show an increase in electrophoretic mobility relative to the corresponding wild type bands, consistent with the loss of LHCI. The faintly fluorescent PSII bands show an analagous increase in electrophoretic mobility, consistent with the loss of LHCII from these complexes. The LHCII* complexes are almost completely absent, though some faint, fluorescent bands are visible ahead of the LHCII* region. There is almost no chlorophyll density in the monomer region, indicating an almost complete loss of these complexes.

Several hypotheses would account for the absence of chlorophyll b-containing complexes from the green band profile. First, these complexes could be present at normal levels in the membrane, binding chlorophyll a at sites which would normally bind chlorophyll b, but these resulting chlorophyll a complexes are labile to detergent extraction and are thus not visible in the green gel pattern. Alternatively, the apoproteins of LHCI and LHCII may fail to accumulate in the membrane at normal levels in the absence of chlorophyll b, as is the case in higher plants (see, for example, Allen, et al., 1988). Finally, these apoproteins may be present in the membrane but fail to bind chlorophyll, and thus do not appear as green bands. The polypeptide profile shown in figure 3b shows a dramatic reduction of LHCII apoproteins #11 (29kDa), #13 (27.5kDa) and

#17 (26kDa), as well as LHCI apoproteins #17.2 (24kDa) and #22 (20kDa). We conclude that in the absence of chlorophyll b biosynthesis LHC apoproteins fail to accumulate in the membrane or are present at drastically reduced levels.

Previous studies of the wild type ultrastructure of *Chlamydomonas* (see, for example, Ohad, et al., 1967)have demonstrated a clear differentiation between appressed, grana lamellae and unstacked, stroma lamellae, similar to that seen in higher plants.

As illustrated in Figure 4, the mutant cbn1-48 shows a dramatically altered thylakoid morphology relative to the wild type. Although thylakoids may run closely parallel to each other in some regions (arrow, Fig. 4), unambiguously identifiable grana stacks are never seen in these cells. Whether or not these occasional, closely spaced membranes represent rudimentary grana stacks, it is clear that the loss of chlorophyll a/b-binding proteins in this mutant is accompanied by dramatic changes in chloroplast membrane ultrastructure. This would suggest that LHCII plays a role in grana formation in *Chlamydomonas* as has been shown in higher plants. Supported by NIH grant GM22912 to LAS.

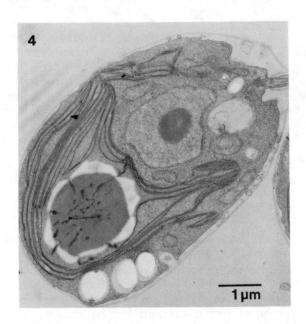

References.

Allen, K.D., Duysen, M.E., and Staehelin, L.A. (1988) J. Cell Biol. **107**:907-919.
Argyroudi-Akoyunoglou, J.H. (1980) Photobiochem. Photobiophys. **1**:279.
Chua, N.-H., and Bennoun, P. (1975) PNAS USA **72**:2175-2179.
Chunayev, A.S., Ladygin, V.G., Mirnaya, O.N., Semyonov, E.P., Gayevsky, N.A., and Boldina, O.N. (1984) Genetika **20**:775-781.
Ohad, I., Siekevitz, P., and Palade, G.E. (1967) J. Cell Biol. **35**:521-552.

SURFACE-ENHANCED RESONANCE RAMAN SCATTERING (SERRS) SPECTROSCOPY OF BACTERIAL MEMBRANES: THE FLAVOPROTEINS.

R. Picorel[a,c], T. Lu[b], R.E. Holt[b], T.M. Cotton[b] and M. Seibert[c]. [a]E. E. Aula Dei, CSIC, Apdo. 202, 50080-Zaragoza; [b]University of Nebraska, Lincoln, NE 68588-0304, USA; [c]Solar Energy Res. Inst., Golden, CO 80401, USA.

INTRODUCTION

The importance of biological membranes for cellular function is unquestionable. Membranes provide the structural framework for anchoring proteins and liposulable cofactors. The membranes also provide for compartmentation and spatial separation of different parts of the cell. In bacteria these functions are supported by the cytoplasmic membrane which becomes highly invaginated when the oxygen tension in the growth medium decreases to certain limits. The invaginations, called chromatophores, contain the photosynthetic apparatus. Flavoproteins are essential components of photosynthetic and respiratory electron transfer systems. We used SERRS spectroscopy to study the location of flavoproteins on the membrane of **R. rubrum**. The unique feature of SERRS spectroscopy is the fact that the resonance Raman signal from a scattering molecule is greatly enhenced when the molecule is on or close to the surface of a potentiostated electrode (1). The effect is extremely distant sensitive. Then, we applied SERRS technique to probe for the location of flavoproteins on the surface of chromatophores (cytoplasmic side out) and spheroplasts (periplasmic side out).

PROCEDURE

Rhodospirillum rubrum G9, a carotenoidless mutant, was grown photosynthetically at 32 °C. Cells were harvested in exponential phase, washed once, resuspended in 200 mM Tris-HCl (pH 8.0) and divided in two halves. One half was used to isolate chromatophores and other half to prepare spheroplasts. To isolate chromatophores the cells were broken by two passages through a precooled French pressure cell at 20,000 pounds per square inch. The homogenate was centrifuged at 20,000 x g for 20 min and the resultant supernatant pelleted at 120,000 x g for 90 min. Chromatophore pellet was resuspended in 10 mM Tris-HCl (pH 8.0) and kept in the dark at 4 °C until use. To prepare spheroplasts the cells were resuspended to a final optical density of 10 at 660 nm in 200 mM Tris-HCl (pH 8.0), 10% (w/v) sucrose, 2 mg/ml egg lysozyme and 6 mM EDTA previously neutralized at pH 7.3

M. Baltscheffsky (ed.), Current Research in Photosynthesis, Vol. II, 907–910.
© 1990 Kluwer Academic Publishers. Printed in the Netherlands.

with NaOH. At the end of a 2-h incubation at 35 °C MgSO$_4$
crystals up to a final concentration of 50 mM were added to
the spheroplast suspension and incubated for 15 min at room
temperature with gentle stirring. The suspension then was
centrifuged at low speed (7,000 x g) for 20 min and the
pellet (spheroplast fraction) carefully resuspended in 10
mM Tris-HCl (pH 8.0), 10% (w/v) sucrose, and 50 mM MgSO$_4$
using a soft paint brush. The spheroplast fraction was
washed three times in the same buffer.

SERRS spectra were recorded using the 488.0 nm line (50
mW) of an Ar ion laser. The geometry and the characteristics of the spectrometer is described in Picorel et al.
(2). Spectra were taken and manipulated using OMA II software. Single scans were collected using 60 delays and 16
scans accumulated per spectrum. The electrochemical cell
used in this work was the same as described previously (3).

RESULTS AND DISCUSION

Excitation of a spheroplast suspension with the 488.0 nm
line (50 mW) of an Ar ion laser induced a distinct SERRS
spectra with major peaks at 1630, 1344, 1279 and 1090 cm
(Fig. 1). The signal cannot be due to the carotenoids of
the photosynthetic apparatus that usually dominate this
region of the spectrum using this excitation wavelength
(2,4) because spheroplasts were prepared from R. rubrum G9,
a carotenoidless mutant. Normal resonance Raman signal
was barely detectable (lower trace of Fig. 1) at the concentration used in this experiment emphasizing the extreme
sensitivity associated with the SERRS technique. Similar
spec-tra, although somewhat less intense, were detected in
a suspension of chromatophores isolated from the mutant.
This figure also shows a SERRS spectrum of FAD in solution.
All three spectra have similar characteristics.

Figure 2 shows that the intensity of spheroplasts SERRS
signal varied with the potential applied to the active Ag
electrode. A maximum intensity was observed at about -0.3 V
and a minimun at about -0.6 V vs SCE. Similar behavior was
found with the chromatophore sample (not shown).

The results of this work strongly indicate that the observed SERRS spectra arises from the prosthetic group (FAD)
of flavoproteins bound to the bacterial membrane. Because
the signal was detected in both spheroplasts (periplasmic
side out) and chromatophores (cytoplasmic side out) we can
conclude that the prosthetic group of flavoproteins is
located on or near the surface of both sides of the cytoplasmic

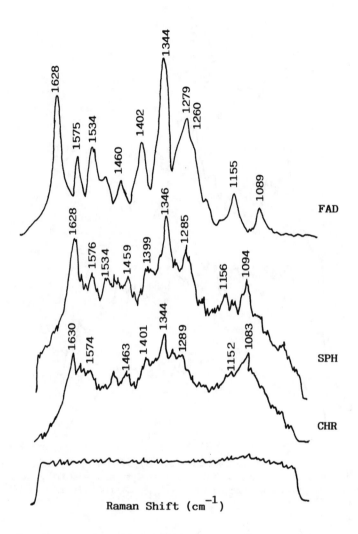

Fig. 1.   SERRS spectra of FAD in solution, spheroplasts (SPH) and chromatophores (CHR).   The frequencies of the peaks are reported in cm^{-1},
and the lower trace is a spectrum of the SPH sample on the polished elec
trode prior to anodization. λ_{ex} = 488.0 nm (50 mW); Bchl = 1.24 µg/ml.

membrane of photosynthetic bacteria. This work also demonstrates that SERRS technique can be used to detect and
locate redox components of biological membranes.

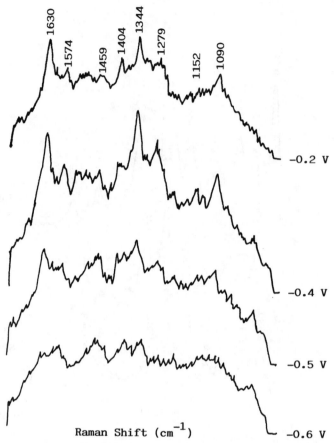

Fig. 2.   SERRS spectra of spheroplasts at different potentials applied
to the Ag working electrode in the electrolytical cuvette. The frequencies of the peaks are reported in cm^{-1}. λ_{ex}= 488.0 nm (50 mw); Bchl=1.24
µg/ml.

1.   Cotton, T.M. (1988) in Advances in Spectroscopy (Clark,
     R. J. H.,and Hester, R. E., eds) Vol.15, John Wiley and
     Sons, New York.
2.   Picorel, R., Holt, R. E., Cotton, T. M. and Seibert, M.
     (1988) J. Biol.   Chem. 263: 4374-4390.
3.   Seibert, M. and Cotton, T.M. (1985) FEBS Lett. 182: 34-
     38.
4.   Picorel, R., Lu, T., Holt, R. E., Cotton, T. M. and
     Seibert, M. Submitted.

ACKNOWLEDGMENT
   This work was supported by the US National Science
Fundation and the CSIC of Spain.

COMPLETE SUPPRESSION OF OXYGEN EVOLUTION IN OPEN PS2
CENTERS BY NON-PHOTOCHEMICAL FLUORESCENCE QUENCHING ?

Jan F.H. Snel, Wim van Ieperen and Wim J. Vredenberg,
Department of Plant Physiological Research, Wageningen Agricultural University,
Gen. Foulkesweg 72, NL-6703 BW Wageningen, The Netherlands

1. INTRODUCTION

The relation between the quantum yield of electron flow in open PS2 reaction centers (Φ_p) and non-photochemical quenching (q_{NP}) during steady state photosynthesis has been shown to be linear (1). Two qantum yield parameters Φ_{PO} and Φ_{PE} were proposed: the quantum yield of electron flow in open PS2 reaction centers in the non-energized and in the energized state respectively. Φ_{PO} and Φ_{PE} were determined by linear extrapolation of Φ_p to $q_{NP}=0$ and $q_{NP}=1$ respectively (1). The rate of electron flow (J_E) was then calculated from chlorophyll fluorescence using the following equation:

$$J_E = I^*q_p^*(\Phi_{PO}^*(1-q_{NP})+\Phi_{PE}^*q_{NP}) \qquad \text{eq. [1]}$$

with: I, light intensity ($\mu mole.m^{-2}.s^{-1}$); q_p, photochemical quenching)

At low oxygen concentrations J_E has been shown to be correlated with steady state electron flow calculated from gas exchange measurements (1). Here we investigate the validity of this relation during photosynthetic induction in dark adapted spinach leaves. Photosynthetic electron flow was estimated from measurements of the rate of oxygen evolution with the photoacoustic technique (2,3,4). Our results indicate that equation [1] holds during induction, but that Φ_{PE} is very small compared to Φ_{PO}, i.e. electron flow is almost completely suppressed in "energized" open PS2 reaction centers.

2. MATERIALS AND METHODS

Photoacoustic transients were measured by illuminating Spinach (Spinacia oleracea) leaf discs (9mm diameter) from 2-3 weeks old plants in a setup slightly modified from (2). Sinusoidally modulated red light (660 nm) from 10 light emmitting diodes (Stanley H-3000) was transmitted through 10 arms of a 12 armed fiberoptic lightguide to the photoacoustic cell (average intensity 30 W/m²). Chlorophyll fluorescence was excited and detected with a PAM fluorometer via the two remaining arms of the lightguide. The leaf disc was illuminated from the backside with non-modulated, saturating white light to remove photochemical quenching (5) and to suppress modulated oxygen evolution (3,4). The initial CO_2 concentration was adjusted by including a filter paper disc wetted with 10µl $Na_2CO_3/NaHCO_3$ (0.1M) buffer. Although the small amount of CO_2 buffer is exhausted during illumination with a concomitant decrease in CO_2 concentration, the initial CO_2 concentration stimulates the steady state photoacoustic oxygen signal (data not shown). The phase of the lock-in amplifier was set perpendicular to the photothermal signal to exclude thermal contributions and measure only signals related to oxygen evolution. The timeconstant of the lock-in amplifier was 130 ms. All experiments were carried out at room temperature. Chlorophyll fluorescence was measured and the quenching parameters q_p and q_{NP} were determined as in (5). The amplitude of the PA-signal was determined from the PA-signal immediately before each of the saturating light pulses (700 ms duration) which were given every 30 s.

3. RESULTS and DISCUSSION

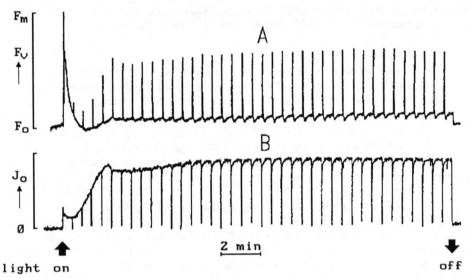

FIGURE 1. Chlorophyll fluorescence (A) and photoacoustic oxygen signal (B) transients from a dark adapted spinach leaf disc. Initial CO_2 concentration: 1260 ppm. Further conditions: see materials and methods.

Figure 1 shows typical chlorophyll fluorescence (A) and photoacoustic transients from a dark adapted spinach leaf disc at an initial CO_2 concentration of 1260 ppm. The kinetics of oxygen evolution can be resolved as a result of the high time resolution (130 ms) of the photoacoustic technique. Fig.1A indicates that some quenching of F_o may have occured during part of the induction transient; no correction for F_o quenching was applied in the calculation of q_p and q_{NP} since the kinetics of F_o quenching could not be resolved. A small error in the determination of F_o would mainly influence the value of q_p at the conditions used here (high q_p, moderate q_{NP}, see Fig.2). Figure 2D shows the relation between the quantum yield of electron flow in open PS2 reaction centers and non-photochemical quenching during the dark-light transition. The relation between Φ_p and q_{NP} appears to be linear. Extrapolation by means of linear regression yields $\Phi_{po}= 25.0$ and $\Phi_{PE}=1.0$. These data show that the method developed by Weis and Berry (1) for the steady state can also

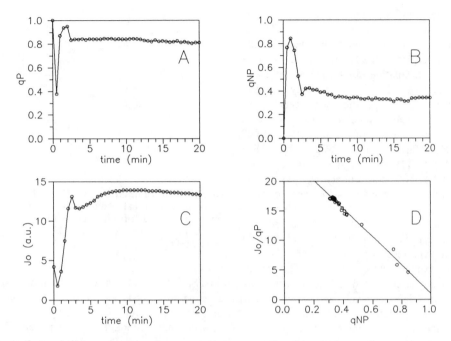

FIGURE 2. Timecourse of q_P (A), q_{NP} (B) and the amplitude of the photoacoustic signal (C) calculated from Fig.1. The relation between the quantum yield of electron flow and nonphotochemical quenching is shown in Fig.2D.

be applied to induction transients if the detection of electron flow or oxygen evolution is fast enough to detect the transients. In contrast to the value reported for the steady state (1), the ratio Φ_{PE}/Φ_{PO} appears to be extremely small during induction. According to the model proposed by Weis and Berry (1), this would imply that the quantum efficiency of electron flow in energized open PS2 reaction centers is practically zero. The consequence of neglecting Φ_{PE} is that equation [1] simplifies to: $J_E = I^*\Phi_{PO}{}^*q_P{}^*(1-q_{NP})$. This implies that chlorophyll fluorescence transients, measured and analyzed using the saturating light pulse technique (5), might suffice to estimate the kinetics of oxygen evolution in intact spinach leaves.

The results given in Fig.2D seem to be at variance with experiments on isolated chloroplasts, where a poor correlation between Φ_P and nonphotochemical quenching was found (7). Perhaps a different form of nonphotochemical quenching might be involved. But also the rate constant of the dissipative process in the reaction center might be different in leaves and chloroplasts; this could have a strong influence on the relation between Φ_P and q_{NP}. This is illustrated in Figure 3, which shows a simulation of the relation between Φ_P and q_{NP} at different redox states of Q_A at a moderate rate constant for the dissipative process in PS2. The simulation model is based on a combination of a model of energy conversion in PS2 (6, bipartite version) and a model of regulation of Φ_P by q_{NP} (1). Chlorophyll fluorescence is assumed to originate solely from the antennas of the two types of PS2 described in (1): non-energized (PS2$_O$) and energized (PS2$_E$, increased non-radiative dissipation in RC). Energy transfer between PS2 units is only possible between units of the same type. Non-photochemical quenching was simulated by conversion of PS2$_O$ (Φ_{PO}:=1.000, F_V/F_M:=0.847) into PS2$_E$ (Φ_{PE}:=0.837, F_V/F_M:=0.111) and assumed to be absent at 100% PS2$_O$. The quenching parameters q_P and q_{NP} at a given state were calculated as in (5) using the fluorescence intensity with Q_A fully oxidized/reduced as an estimates for $F_O/(F_V)_s$ and the maximal fluorescence from 100% PS2$_O$ as the maximal fluorescence F_M. The increa-

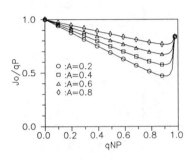

FIGURE 3: Simulation of the effect of non-photochemical quenching on the quantum yield of electron flow in PS2 at different redox states of Q_A. (A= $Q_A/(Q_A+Q_A^-)$).

se in q_{NP} is simulated by converting PS2$_O$ into PS2$_E$. As in closed PS2$_E$ reaction centers backflow of excitation energy to the antenna proceeds with lower efficiency due to nonradiative dissipation in the reaction center, variable fluorescence is lowered and q_{NP} is increased. Figure 3 shows clearly that, although a linear relation between Φ_P and q_{NP} is observed when q_{NP} is smaller than 0.9, this relation is redox-state dependent and extrapolation to q_{NP}=1 gives a erroneous estimate of Φ_{PE}. The error is caused by the fact that in contrast to PS2$_O$ units, where excitation energy transfer between units is normal, PS2$_E$ units show much less energy transfer via their own antenna as a result of dissipation in the reaction center. This will lead to a misleading value for q_P since fluorescence yield is mainly determined by the fluorescence contribution of the antenna associated with PS2$_O$. Therefore q_P may overestimate the amount of energy available to open PS2$_E$ reaction centers, except when the number of PS2$_E$ units is much larger than those of PS2$_O$, which occurs only at q_{NP} values close to the maximum. Thus, if Φ_P is only slightly affected by the dissipative process, large errors in the determination of Φ_{PE} can result.

REFERENCES

1 Weis E and Berry JA (1987) Biochim Biophys Acta 894: 198–208
2 Bicanic D, Harren F, Reuss J, Woltering E, Snel J F H et al., (1989) In: P Hess, ed.; Photoacoustic, Photothermal and Photochemical Processes in Gases, Topics in Current Physics, Vol. 46, Springer, Heidelberg, pp. 213–253
3 Bults G, Horwitz BA, Malkin S and Cahen D (1982) Biochim Biophys Acta 679: 452–465
4 Poulet P, Cahen D and Malkin S (1983) Biochim Biophys Acta 724: 433–446
5 Schreiber U, Schliwa U and Bilger W (1986) Photosynth Res 10: 51–62
6 Strasser RJ (1981) in: Proc. 5th Intern. Photosynth. Congr., Vol.III, Balaban Intern. Science Services, Philadelphia, pp. 727–737
7 Oxborough, K and Horton P (1988) Biochim Biophys Acta 934:135–143

HOW DOES PROTEIN PHOSPHORYLATION CONTROL PROTEIN-PROTEIN INTERACTIONS IN THE PHOTOSYNTHETIC MEMBRANE?

JOHN F ALLEN, Department of Pure and Applied Biology, University of Leeds, Leeds LS2 9JT, England

1.   THE STRUCTURE AND PHOSPHORYLATION OF LHC II

The light-harvesting chlorophyll a/b complex (LHC II) of green plant chloroplasts accounts for about half the chlorophyll and a third of the protein of the thylakoid membrane (1,2). For each polypeptide of between 24 and 27 kDa, the complex contains 4 chlorophyll a molecules, 3 chlorophyll b molecules and 1-2 xanthophyll molecules. Each polypeptide is encoded by one of a family of nuclear genes.

The consensus view of the membrane disposition of the LHC IIb polypeptide is three membrane-spanning alpha-helices (3,4), with an extensive amino-terminal sequence on the stromal side of the membrane and a shorter carboxy-terminal sequence on the inside thylakoid surface. The amino-terminal structure on the outside is most likely the one contributing to the larger, 20 A surface-exposed extension, with a smaller, 7 A surface-exposed extension on the inside.

It is thought that the amino-terminal surface-exposed regions of the complex are sites of membrane adhesion that cause thylakoid stacking (5). This is consistent with the three-dimensional structure proposed by Kuhlbrandt on the basis of electron microscopy of two-dimensional crystals (6). This structure has three-fold rotational symmetry and a platform at one surface that could provide for interaction with a neighbouring platform through van der Waals' forces.

Proteolysis of thylakoid membranes shows that phosphorylation of LHC II polypeptides (7) occurs on the amino-terminal surface-exposed segment that is also required for membrane stacking, at one or both of adjacent threonines in positions six and seven in pea (8).

It is widely held (5,7,9) that phosphorylation alters the net electrical charge of LHC II at the membrane surface, causing a change leading to electrostatic repulsion that can overcome the resultant of van der Waals' and other forces otherwise holding neighbouring LHC IIs at 180^0 to each other on a common axis perpendicular to each membrane plane. This may be described as the "surface charge" hypothesis. It states that inter-

M. Baltscheffsky (ed.), Current Research in Photosynthesis, Vol. II, 915–918.
© 1990 *Kluwer Academic Publishers. Printed in the Netherlands.*

<u>molecular</u>, <u>inter-membrane</u> forces control the LHC II-PS II interaction and it is these that are modified, directly, by protein phosphorylation. This model takes cation effects on stacking and on excitation energy transfer as a model for effects of phosphorylation.

An alternative suggestion (10) is that electrostatic repulsion between phosphorylated LHC II and a phosphorylated intermediate light-harvesting complex of PS II serves to detach the mobile LHC II pool from the PS II core and thereby functionally to disconnect PS II centres. This may be termed the "mutual electrostatic repulsion" hypothesis. It states that <u>inter-molecular</u>, <u>intra-membrane</u> forces control the LHC II-PS II interaction and are modified by protein phosphorylation. This model has the advantage over the surface charge hypothesis that thylakoid lateral heterogeneity in distribution of PS I and PS II is no longer a necessary condition for effects of phosphorylation on energy transfer and cooperativity. Unlike the surface charge hypothesis, the mutual electrostatic repulsion hypothesis can accommodate effects of phosphorylation in prokaryotic and other membrane systems devoid of lateral heterogeneity (10).

2.   HYPOTHESIS: MOLECULAR RECOGNITION
     I now propose a third possibility. I suggest that phosphorylation itself has a negligible direct effect on the electrical interactions of neighbouring membrane proteins, and that it is the sum of individually weak inter-molecular forces that is disrupted by phosphorylation at an allosteric site. I therefore suggest that the direct effect of phosphorylation is on <u>intra-molecular</u> forces in the hydrophilic domain of membrane proteins. The electrical effects of altered cation concentration may thus have served as a rather misleading model for phosphorylation effects.

     I propose that the predominantly hydrophilic surface-exposed structures assumed in vivo by the 20 A amino-terminal segments of LHC II<u>b</u> and by similar segments of other membrane-intrinsic proteins of PS II possess complemetary recognition and docking structures that determine their respective interactions in the aqueous phase. Recognition and docking of these complementary surfaces above the membrane surface will serve to guide the interaction of each protein's hydrophobic structures buried in the membrane. By this means phosphorylation of surface-exposed amino acids will control the function of the proteins' hydrophobic domains in inter-molecular excitation energy transfer.

     This "molecular recognition" model for structural and functional effects of protein phosphorylation does not require direct control by phosphorylation of forces

holding   neighbouring   complexes   together.   The
electrostatic effect of the phosphate group may be exerted
purely   on   amino   acid   side   chains   within   the   same
polypeptide, and may alter molecular recognition by steric
effects   that   distort   the   docking   surface   otherwise
complementary to that of the neighbouring protein complex.
    This   hypothesis   is   testable.   It   specifically
predicts   a   three-dimensional   structure   for   the   20   A
stromal-surface   extension   of   LHC   II<u>b</u>   that   includes   a
docking   surface   for   a   neighbouring,   complementary
structure.   It also predicts a conformational change upon
phosphorylation that distorts the docking surface, thereby
changing the binding constant of the two polypeptides and
hence   also   of   the   two   complexes   of   which   each   forms   a
part.
    Conformational   changes   have   lost   some   of   their
mystical   associations   in   recent   years.   From   X-ray
crystallography there is now an atomic-level resolution
model   for   both   the   active,   phosphorylated   and   inactive,
dephosphorylated   forms   of   the   enzyme   glycogen
phosphorylase (11).   From comparison of these structures,
it is seen that the effect of phosphorylation of serine-14
of   each   subunit   is   to   create   an   ordered   helical
conformation at each amino-terminus which in consequence
binds   more   closely   to   the   surface   of   the   glycogen
phosphorylase   dimer.   This   produces   rotation   of   each
subunit   about   an   axis   perpendicular   to   the   axis   of
symmetry of the dimer.   This structural change clearly
alters   substrate   binding   at   the   catalytic   site,   even
though the catalytic pyridoxal phosphates are located more
than 30 A from the phosphoserine (12).

3.   PREDICTIONS
    Phosphorylation of LHC II and of other thylakoid and
chromatophore membrane proteins does not have to work in
the   same   way   as   that   of   the   soluble   enzyme   glycogen
phosphorylase.   Nevertheless, I should like to suggest
that the eventual solution of the structure of an antenna
complex will show a docking surface for a reaction centre
core component, and that the structure of this surface
will be altered by covalent modification at a site remote
from   both   the   docking   surface   itself   and   the   site   of
excitation   transfer   between   chromophores.   Complementary
docking   surfaces   on   the   same   protein   are   also   to   be
expected,   since   their   modification   by   phosphorylation
would   then   permit   altered   connectivity   between
photosynthetic   units   (10).   As   allosteric   proteins,
antenna complexes will always be oligomeric (12).
    It   is   possible   in   the   case   of   purple   bacterial
reaction centres that a docking surface could be capable
of   resolution   in   the   existing   X-ray   crystal   structures

(13,14). From the above considerations one would predict its location in the large cytoplasmic-surface-exposed domain of the H-subunit.

The "molecular recognition" hypothesis proposed here for control of photosynthetic unit function by protein phosphorylation is testable in principle, but probably not in practice on data available at the present time. In this event I should like to recommend an aphorism of Myers, who also helped cause all these problems (15), and whose view is amply demonstrated by developments subsequent to the paper in which it is stated (16). "The test of a concept, like the question of pregnancy in the human female, is not current majority opinion but the test of time".

ACKNOWLEDGEMENTS

I should like to acknowledge SERC for existing research grants and my current colleagues Alan Cox, Michael Harrison and Nicholas Tsinoremas for many helpful discussions.

REFERENCES
1 Thornber, J.P. et al (1988) in Light-energy Transduction in Photosynthesis: Higher Plant and Bacterial Models (Stevens, S.E. and Bryant, D.A., eds.), pp.137-154, American Society of Plant Physiologists
2 Peters, G.F. and Thornber, J.P. (1989) in Photosynthetic Light-Harvesting Systems (Scheer, H. and Schneider, S., eds.), pp.176-186, Walter de Gruyter & Co., Berlin
3 Karlin-Neumann, G.A. et al (1985) J. Molec. Appl. Genet. 3, 45-61
4 Burgi, R. et al (1987) Biochim. Biophys. Acta. 890, 346-351
5 Staehelin, L.A. and Arntzen, C.J. (1983) J. Cell. Biol. 97, 1327-1337
6 Kuhlbrandt, W. (1984) Nature 307, 478-480
7 Bennett, J. (1983) Biochem. J. 212, 1-13
8 Mullet, J.E. (1983) J. Biol. Chem. 258, 9941-9948
9 Barber, J. (1982) Annu. Rev. Plant Physiol. 33, 261-295
10 Allen, J.F. and Holmes, N.G. (1986) FEBS Lett. 202, 175-181
11 Sprang, S.R. et al (1988) Nature 336, 215-221
12 Perutz, M.F. (1988) Nature 336, 202-203
13 Deisenhofer, J. et al (1985) Nature 318, 618-642
14 Feher, G. et al (1989) Nature 339, 111-116
15 Bonaventura, C. and Myers, J. (1969) Biochim. Biophys. Acta 189, 366-383
16 Myers, J. (1975) Plant Physiol. 54, 420-426

P-700 PHOTOOXIDATION IN STATE 1 AND IN STATE 2 IN CYANOBACTERIA UPON FLASH ILLUMINATION WITH PHYCOBILIN AND CHLOROPHYLL ABSORBED LIGHT.

Nicholas F. Tsinoremas, Julia A. M. Hubbard*, Michael C. W. Evans* and John F. Allen

Department of Pure and Applied Biology, University of Leeds, Leeds LS2 9JT and *Biology Department, University College London, Gower street, London WC1E 6BT, U.K.

1. INTRODUCTION
Photosynthetic organisms that contain two photosystems have the ability to vary the distribution of excitation energy between the photosystems and thereby maximize the overall efficiency of photosynthesis under any given light conditions. Bonaventura and Myers [1] and Murata [2] showed that selective excitation of PS I causes the transition to state 1 and selective excitation of PS II causes the transition to state 2.
The mechanism in phycobilisome-containing organisms by which the excitation energy is redistributed in state transitions remains controversial. Ley and Butler [3] suggested a spillover model by which energy is transferred from PS II to PS I but not vice versa. However Allen et al. [4] proposed that in state 2 the phycobili- some is detached from PS II and becomes attached to PS I, causing a decrease of the absorption cross-section of PS I and an increase in the absorption cross-section of PS I. Mullineaux and Allen [5] more recently suggested a model by which the detached phycobilisome does not couple to PS I but instead the PS I and the detached PS II reaction centre cores associate more closely.
Here we report results of experiments designed to address the question of the pathways of excitation energy transfer in the two light states in cyanobacteria.
2. MATERIALS AND METHODS
Nostoc MAC and Synechococcus 6301 were grown as in [6]. Fluorescence measurements were made in a stirred cuvette at 22 °C as in [7]. Absorption measurments at 820 nm were made using a laser flash spectrophotometer as described in [8], except that the measuring device was a large area silicon photodiode type UDT 10D. Samples were excited at either 337 nm with a 800 ps flash supplied by a N_2 laser or 532 nm with 6 ns flash using a Nd:YAG laser.

M. Baltscheffsky (ed.), Current Research in Photosynthesis, Vol. II, 919–922.
© 1990 *Kluwer Academic Publishers. Printed in the Netherlands.*

3. RESULTS AND DISCUSSION

The fluorescence emission of PS II is dependent in part on the absorption cross-section of PS I and hence can be used as an indicator of light state transitions.

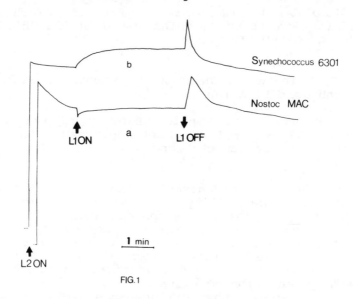

FIG. 1

Fig. 1a shows characteristic state 1 and state 2 transitions in Nostoc MAC using a modulated fluorescence measurement system as described in [6]. Light 1 induces a fast fluorescence decrease and a slow rising phase which are characteristic of the state 1 transition [2]. When light 1 is extinguished there is a rapid rise of fluorescence followed by a slow falling phase and these are interpreted as the state 2 trasition [2].Fig. 1b shows characteristic state transitions in Synechococcus 6301.

The light absorbed by PS I is proportional to the incident light intensity and to the effective absorption cross-section of PS I reaction centres [9]. We have measured the flash-induced absorbance change at 820 nm which in microsecond time range has been attributed essentially to P-700$^+$ [10]. Fig. 2 shows absorption changes at 820 nm following laser excitation at 337 nm in Nostoc MAC in state 2 (a) and in state 1 (b) and for Synechococcus 6301 in state 2 (a) and state 1 (b). These data demonstrate that in state 2 there is an increase in the absorption cross-section of PS I for light at 337 nm.

Fig. 3 shows that when using a 532 nm laser (light predominantly absorbed by the phycobilisome) in Nostoc MAC in state 2 (a) and state 1 (b) and in Synechococcus 6301 in state 2 (c) and in state 1 (d), the absolute yield of P-700 photooxidation is increased in state 2.

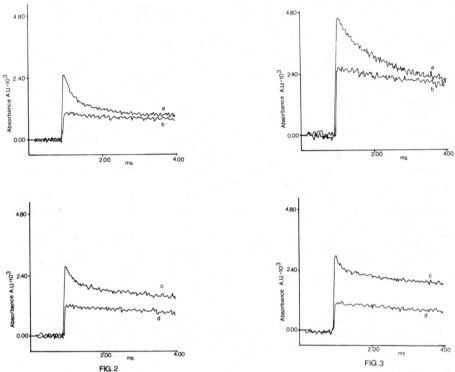

FIG.2

FIG.3

These results suggest that there is an increase in the absorption cross-section of PS I for phycobilisome-absorbed light. The absorption decay after the 337 nm and 532 nm flashes is the same for both species. Thus, the absorption decay is monophasic during state 1 ($t_{1/2}$= 8-10 ms) but multiphasic kinetics in state 2 ($t_{1/2}$= 100-150 us and $t_{1/2}$ = 8-10 ms).

Using 337 nm and 532 nm laser flashes an increase in the absolute yield of P-700[+] in state 2 in both species was observed. At 532 nm only phycobilins can absorb and the increased P-700 photooxidation is therefore consistent with a mobile phycobilisome being transferred to PS I in state 2. At 337 nm chlorophyll a absorbs as well as phycocyanin, so this wavelength is not very specific for excitation of chlorophyll a. Thus our results at this wavelength could also be explained by the mobile phycobilisome model [4].

The differences in kinetics of P-700 re-reduction that we have observed between state 2 and state 1 allow us also to draw conclusions about the mechanism that drives state transitions in cyanobacteria as follows. Our data show that in state 1 the P-700 re-reduction kinetics are biphasic while in state 1 they are monophasic, with no fast phase (figs 2,3). DBMIB (5 uM) also removes the fast phase in state 2 (data not shown). This difference in kinetics could be due to the redox state of an electron carrier which is located at the donor site of PS I: reduction of this carrier in state 2 causes the biphasic kinetics, while oxidation of this carrier causes the monophasic kinetics. Haehnel et al. [11] also observed biphasic kinetics of P-700 re-reduction in intact chloroplasts upon pre-illumination at 655 nm and monophasic upon far-red pre-illumination. Finally we conclude that state transitions in cyanobacteria are regulated by the redox state of plastoquinone [7]. The reduction of this electron carrier may trigger activation of a protein kinase causing the phosphorylation of light harvesting-polypeptides [12-13]. Whatever the biochemical basis for redistribution of excitation energy in phycobilisome-containing organisms, it is now likely that it involves redox control of the absorption cross-section of PS II and PS I by detachment of PS II from the phycobi-some and reattachment of the phycobilisome to PS I.

ACKNOWLEDGEMENTS
     We thank Alan Cox, Michael Harrison and Conrad Mullineaux for helpful discussions. This work was supported by SERC grants to JFA and MCWE.

REFERENCES
1. Bonaventura, C. and Myers, J. (1969) Biochim. Biphys. Acta 189, 366-383.
2. Murata, N. (1969) Biochim. Biophys. Acta 172, 242-251.
3. Ley, A.C. and Butler, W.L. (1980) Biochim. Biophys.Acta 592, 349-363.
4. Allen et al. (1985) FEBS Lett. 193, 271-275.
5. Mullineaux, C.W. and Allen, J.F. (1988) Biochim. Biophys. Acta 934, 96-107.
6. Tsinoremas et al. FEBS Lett. submitted.
7. Mullineaux, C.W. and Allen, J.F. (1986) FEBS Lett. 205, 155-160.
8. Mansfield et al. (1987) FEBS Lett. 220, 74-78.
9. Melis, A. (1982) Arch. Biochem. Biophys. 217, 536-545.
10.Van Best, J.A. and Mathis, P. (1978) Biochim. Biophys. Acta 503, 178-188.
11.Haehnel et al. (1971) Z. Naturforsch. 26b, 1171-1174.
12.Allen, J.F. and Holmes, N.G. (1986) FEBS Lett. 202, 175-181.
13.Harrison, M.A. and Allen, J.F. these proceedings.

ORGANIZATION OF THE THYLAKOID MEMBRANE WITH RESPECT TO THE FOUR
PHOTOSYSTEMS, PSIα, PSIβ, PSIIα AND PSIIβ.

PER-ÅKE ALBERTSSON, EVA ANDREASSON, AGNETA PERSSON and PER SVENSSON
Department of Biochemistry, University of Lund, P.O. Box 124, S-221 00
LUND, SWEDEN.

1. INTRODUCTION
    The thylakoid membrane is an extremely complicated structure with
several different domains having specialized functions. There is a
heterogeneity among the photosystems. Of the two classes of PSII the
main, PSIIα, with its larger antenna is localized in the grana, while
the other, PSIIβ, with its smaller antenna is localized in the stroma
membrane. Recently we presented evidences that showed that also among
PSI there is heterogeneity (1). One form, PSIα, is localized in the
grana and has a larger antenna than the other form, PSIβ, which is
localized in the stroma membrane. In this paper we calculate how much
chlorophyll is associated with the four photosystems. Two alternative
and partly independent approaches are used.

2. EXPERIMENTAL
    Sonication of spinach chloroplasts followed by partition with an
aqueous polymer two-phase system separates the thylakoid membrane
vesicles into two well defined vesicle populations (Fig. 1). One

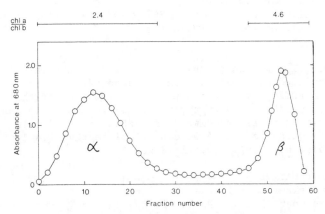

FIGURE 1. Separation of sonicated, stacked, thylakoids from spinach by
counter-current distribution. The α peak originates from the
grana and the β peak from the stroma membranes. From ref (1).

population (α) originates from the grana and contains 63% of the
chlorophyll while the other population (β) originates from the stroma

M. Baltscheffsky (ed.), Current Research in Photosynthesis, Vol. II, 923–926.
© 1990 *Kluwer Academic Publishers. Printed in the Netherlands.*

membranes and contains 37 % of the chlorophyll. 85 % of the PSII is in the α vesicles in the form of PSIIα while the remaining 15 % is in the β vesicles in the form of PSIIβ. 36 % of PSI is in the α vesicles in the form of PSIα and the remaining 64 % is in the β vesicles in the form of PSIβ. The antenna size of PSIIα is about two times larger than that of PSIIβ and the antenna size of PSIα is about 30 % larger than that of PSIβ (1). The PSIα and PSIIα are probably segregated into different domains of the grana (2,3).

TABLE 1. Distribution of components between the two vesicle populations of Fig. 1. Data from reference 1.

	Chl a/b	Chl %	P700 %	PSII activity %	Cyt. f %
α	2.4	63	36	85	57
β	4.6	37	64	15	43

3. CALCULATION, ALTERNATIVE A.
3.1. Assumptions and experimental data
  3.1.1. Chlorophyll/P700 for PSIβ = 190. This is based on experimental values for stroma membrane preparations which give Chl/P700 values of 210 (4) and assuming that 10 % of this Chl is associated with PSIIβ.
  3.1.2. The antenna size of PSIα is 28 % larger than that of PSIβ. This is based on experimental data on the kinetics of P700 photooxidation (1). This gives a value of Chl/P700 of 243 for PSIα.
  3.1.3. For the α peak i.e. the grana derived membranes Chl/P700 = 625 (data from ref. 1).
  3.1.4. 15 % of PSII is in the form of PSIIβ and the antenna size of PSIIβ is half of that of PSIIα (5).

3.2. Calculation
  From 3.1.2 and 3.1.3 we can calculate that 39 % of the Chl of the α peak is associated with PSIα and the remainder, 61 %, is associated with PSIIα. Since the α peak contains 63 % of the chlorophyll of the thylakoid we arrive at 25 % of the chlorophyll of the thylakoid which is associated with PSIα and 38 % with PSIIα. From the values of 3.1.4 we can calculate that 3.4 % of the Chl is associated with PSIIβ (0.5x15/85x38=3.4).

4. CALCULATION, ALTERNATIVE B
4.1. Assumptions and experimental data
  4.1.1. We assume that PSIα and PSIIα are segregated in the grana and that a pure PSIIα membrane has a Chl a/b value of 1.8 and a pure PSIα membrane a Chl a/b value of 5. These values are based on isolated, highly enriched PSII membrane vesicles (2,3) and on PSI membrane preparations (4).
  4.1.2. The α fraction, i.e. the grana derived fraction has a Chl a/b ratio of 2.4 (Table 1).

4.2. Calculation
    Based on the assumption of 4.1.1 and the data of 4.1.2 the α
    fraction, i.e. the grana derived fraction, consists of 33 % PSIα
    membrane and 67 % of PSIIα membrane. Since the α peak contains
    63 % of the total chlorophyll we arrive at 21 and 42 % of the
    chlorophyll of the thylakoid associated with PSIα and PSIIα
    respectively. The distribution of chlorophyll among PSIIα and
    PSIIβ is calculated in the same way as for alternative A. The
    results are summarized in Table 2.

TABLE 2. Distribution of chlorophyll, in %, among the 4 photosystems.

	PSIα	PSIIα	PSIβ	PSIIβ	PSI	PSII
Alternative A	25	38	34	3	59	41
Alternative B	21	42	33	4	54	46

5. ANTENNA SIZE
5.1. Assumptions and experimental data
    5.1.1. Thylakoids have 385 Chl/P700 and 36 % PSIα and 64 % PSIβ
        (data from ref. 1).
    5.1.2. Thylakoids have 400 Chl/atrazine binding site (measured in
        our laboratory) and 85 % PSIIα and 15 % PSIIβ.

5.2. Calculation
    With the assumptions above and the distribution of chlorophyll
    between the photosystems (Table 2) we can calculate Chl/P700 or
    atrazine binding site, Table 3. Note that in Alternative B the
    antenna size of PSIα is larger than PSIβ which is an additional
    evidence for the heterogeneity of PSI.

TABLE 3. Antenna sizes of the 4 different photosystems expressed as
       moles Chl/P700 (PSI) or Chl/atrazine binding site (PSII)

	PSIα	PSIβ	PSIIα	PSIIβ
Alternative A	260	200	180	90
Alternative B	230	200	200	100

6. DISCUSSION
    The results of Table 2 are interesting for two reasons. First, for
both alternatives, there is, in the chloroplast, more chlorophyll
associated with PSI than with PSII. This is in contradiction with
published data on the chlorophyll distribution between PSI and PSII
based on gel electrophoresis (5). Estimation of chlorophyll in the
various gel bands point to a greater fraction of chlorophyll associated
with PSII than with PSI. Such data may be uncertain, however, because
of difficulties in identification and quantification of gel bands. If
our results are correct it means that we do not have to worry about

overexitation of PSII if we consider the whole chloroplast.

Second, 33-40 % of the chlorophyll in the α vesicles, i.e. those
originating from the grana, is associated with PSIα. This substantial
amount of PSIα in the grana suggest that PSIα and PSIIα may function
together in non cyclic electron transport. Although there is an excess
of PSII chlorophyll in the grana this is not as effective in light
absorption as the PSI chlorophyll because of the larger amount of Chl b
in the PSIIα antenna. Chlorophyll b absorbs less red light per mole
than Chl a. Also, the carotenoids of PSIα may increase the functional
antenna size of PSIα compared to PSIIα (5). With these arguments we
claim that PSIα and PSIIα might well function together in non cyclic
electron transport with a balanced turn over rate of the two photosystems, while the main function of the stroma membrane is to carry out
cyclic electron transport.

Our results therefore agree with a model (Fig. 2) where the grana
carry out non cyclic electron transport using the two α-systems while
the stroma membrane carries out cyclic electron transport using the two
β systems. Since the β systems have a smaller respective antenna these
would contribute relatively more at hight light intensities when
relatively more ATP is needed by the chloroplast for the synthesis of
proteins from amino acids, starch from glucos, repair of the photosynthetic apparatus and other ATP requiring processes in the chloroplast.

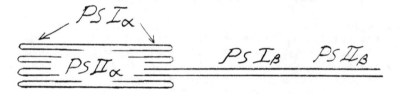

FIGURE 2. Model for the localization of the four photosystems. The two
α systems PSIα and PSIIα with their larger respective antennae are
localized in the grana while the β systems PSIβ and PSIIβ are
localized in the stroma membranes. PSIα and PSIIα are segregated;
PSIIα being confined to the central core of the grana partitions
and PSIα in the margins and end membranes. It is not known whether
PSIβ and PSIIβ are mixed or segregated in the stroma membranes.

REFERENCES
1 Andreasson, E., Svensson, P., Weibull, C. and Albertsson, P.-Å.
  (1988) Biochim. Biophys. Acta 936, 339-350
2 Albertsson, P.-Å. and Svensson, P. (1988) Mol. Cell. Biochem. 81,
  155-163
3 Svensson, P. and Albertsson, P.-Å. (1989) Photosynth. Res. 20,
  249-259
4 Melis, A., Svensson, P. and Albertsson, P.-Å. (1986) Biochim.
  Biophys. Acta 850, 402-412
5 Melis, A., Spangfort, M. and Andersson, B. (1987) Photobiochem.
  Photobiol. 45, 129-136

CHLOROPHYLL FLUORESCENCE QUENCHING AND PROTEIN PHOSPHORYLATION IN RICE
MUTANTS WITH DIFFERENT CONTENTS OF CHLOROPHYLL B

Y. KOBAYASHI, K. CHYAEN, T. YOSHIHIRA, K. YAMAMOTO, N. IWATA and T. OKU
FACULTY OF AGRICULTURE, KYUSHU UNIVERSITY, FUKUOKA, 812 JAPAN

1. INTRODUCTION
    Chlorophyll(Chl) b-less and Chl b-deficient mutants of green plants
have been useful to elucidate the role of Chl a/b protein complexes.
Biochemical studies on the mutants have led to the conclusion that the
primary function of the genetic block is attributed to the synthesis of
Chl b, not to the Chl a/b binding polypeptides(1, 2). Evidence has been
accumulated for the presence of a pleiotropic gene on the content of
Chl b(3, 4). These studies showed that the deficiency of Chl b in barley
and Chlamydomonas was due to a single recessive gene. The present communication reports that the shortage of Chl b in rice mutants was owing
to intragenic mutations occured in one gene locus, pgl. The gene locus
seems to be crucial in regulating the accumulation level of Chl b. Upon
illumination of dark-adapted leaves, there is a decrease in the yield of
chlorophyll fluorescence. It has been proposed that the quenching of
chlorophyll fluorescence can be due to i) the oxidation of Q at PS II,
ii) an increased rate of radiationless de-excitation by the formation of
transmembrane ΔpH, iii) the distribution of excitation energy between
PS II and PS I effected by phosphorylation of light-harvesting Chl a/b
protein complexes(5). We produced F1 rice plants which have different
Chl a/b ratios over a wide range. The quenching of chlorophyll fluorescence and light-induced phosphorylation of Chl a/b protein complexes
were analysed in regard to the ratio of Chl b/a+b. The extent of quenching changed in a specific manner with increase in the content of Chl b.

2. MATERIALS AND METHODS
    Wild type of rice(Oryza sativa L. var. Kinmaze) and ten Chl b
mutants derived from vars. Kinmaze, Okayama-kibiho, Taichyu No. 65 and
Norin No. 8 were grown for one month in a green house. The mutants(CHL
1, 2, 11, 14 and 15) from var. Norin No. 8 were received from Dr. T.
Terao. Planting of the seedlings was made in a pot per one seedling, and
the plants were cultivated for 5 months under field conditions to be
crossed. Seeds of F1 generation were sawn in soil and grown for 3-10
weeks at 25°C under low light(85 μE/m²·s) with a photoperiod of 12 h in
a growth chamber or under high light(ambient light conditions) in
phytotron. The contents of Chl a and Chl b were determined with HPLC
equipped with a reverse phase column and a fluorescence detector.
Chlorophyll fluorescence from the surface of a detached leaf was monitored at 695 ± 10 nm by the excitation with blue light or at 740 ± 10 nm
with red light.

M. Baltscheffsky (ed.), Current Research in Photosynthesis, Vol. II, 927–930.
© 1990 *Kluwer Academic Publishers. Printed in the Netherlands.*

3. RESULTS AND DISCUSSION

Ten strains of the mutants were divided into three groups on the basis of their Chl a/b ratio which was attained after 3 weeks of germination under low light. Five strains(Group A; KL 218, CM 1545, CM 1552, CHL 1 and CHL 2) were Chl b-less mutants, one strain(Group B; HO 775) which has been proved to carry pgl gene on the 7th chromosome was about 6 in the ratio, and four strains(Group C; 87M$_3$ 1003, CHL 11, CHL 14 and CHL 15) had the ratio in excess of 10. All F$_1$ plants obtained by fifty reciprocal crosses between the Chl b-less mutants assigned to Group A did not form Chl b. Hybrids obtained by the control crosses between wild type and each of the mutants belonging to Groups A, B and C accumulated Chl b to the same level as the wild type. These results indicate that the allelic recessive mutations occured in the gene locus pgl.

TABLE 1. Mean value of Chl a/b ratios in hybrids obtained from the mutants of three groups(A, B and C) differing in Chl a/b ratio.

Combination	Supposed intra-genic mutation sites in pgl	Growth conditions	
		low light	high light
		Chl a/b ratio	
A x A	($\bullet$-B-C / $\bullet$-B-C)	Chl b-less	Chl b-less
A x C	($\bullet$-B-C / A-B-$\bullet$)	21.6	27.1
C x C	(A-B-$\bullet$ / A-B-$\bullet$)	11.3	13.8
A x B	($\bullet$-B-C / A-$\bullet$-C)	6.9	13.7
B x B	(A-$\bullet$-C / A-$\bullet$-C)	6.0	12.7
B x C	(A-$\bullet$-C / A-B-$\bullet$)	4.7	4.4
wild t. x wild t.	(A-B-C / A-B-C)	3.1	2.9

The ten mutants were crossed each other, and the resulting information on the pgl was analysed on the basis of the Chl a/b ratio determined in the 4th leaf at 5-leaf stage of the F$_1$ generation grown under low light or high light. The results are summarized in Table 1, where for clarity an average of the Chl a/b ratios in each hybrid group is shown. The most significant feature appeared in the F$_1$ generation was that the hybrids of B x C(e.g., all the hybrids obtained by the crosses between the mutants assigned to Groups B and C) accumulated Chl b upto higher level than these of B x B and C x C. The results can be explained in terms of "cis-dominance" if we assume that the pgl has three functional regions, A, B and C, being responsible for the synthesis of Chl b. In the case, the region A is able to control the expression of structural genes in the two regions of B and C. The assumption may be supported by the fact that the hybrids of A x A did not accumulate Chl b at all. At higher light intensity the accumulation level of Chl b was reduced particularly in the hybrids of A x B and B x B, while the accumulation level in these of B x C became rather high as well as the level in wild type. However, one should notice that the light intensity was not a primary factor governing the accumulation level of Chl b.

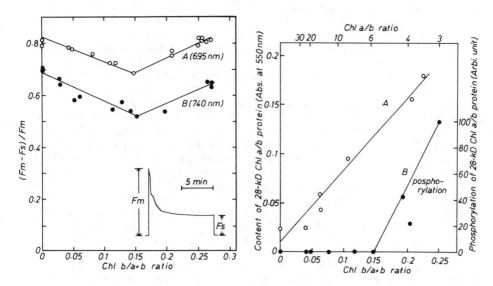

FIGURE 1(left). Correlation between the extent of fluorescence quenching and the ratio of Chl b/a+b in rice mutants.
FIGURE 2(right). Content(A) and light-induced phosphorylation(B) of 28-kD Chl a/b binding polypeptide in the mutants.

The hybrids and the homozygotes of mutants were employed to appraise the fluorescence quenching being responsible for Chl a/b protein complexes. Trace in Fig. 1 shows a typical time course of fluorescence change observed in dark-adapted Chl b-less mutant at 740 nm by the excitation with red light(25 W/m^2). Surprisingly, the extent of fluorescence quenching in Chl b-less mutants was similar to that in wild type when the extent of quenching was measured as (Fm − Fs)/Fm, where Fm and Fs are the fluorescence intensity before quenching and the intensity at a steady state reached during illumination for 10 min, respectively. The smallest extent of quenching was obtained in Chl b-deficient mutant which was about 6 in the ratio of Chl a/b. The values of (Fm − Fs)/Fm, plotted as a function of Chl b/a+b, at 695 nm by the excitation with blue light(50 W/m^2) and at 740 nm with red light(25 W/m^2) are shown by Curves A and B, respectively, in Fig. 1. The values decreased linearly with increase in the ratio to 0.15 from 0, but increased with rise in the ratio from 0.15 to 0.27 in turn. There was a linear correlation between the content of 28-kD Chl a/b binding polypeptide and the ratio of Chl b/a+b, when the peak height of absorption at 550 nm of the polypeptide band in Coomassie blue-stained gel after SDS-PAGE of thylakoid membranes(3.5 μg Chl) was taken(Curve A in Fig. 2). An appreciable amount of 28, 27 and 26-kD Chl a/b binding polypeptides was found in Chl b-less mutant by Western blot(data not shown). The fluorescence quenching is believed to be closely related to the phosphorylation of light-harvesting Chl a/b protein complexes(6). Light-induced phosphorylation

of the Chl a/b protein complexes was, therefore, examined. A leaf
segment was pre-incubated with ^{32}P-phosphate(0.5 mCi/ml) for 2 h in the
dark, and the dark-adapted sample was illuminated for 10 min. The
reaction was stopped in hot methanol, and the sample was homogenized
three times in dissolving solution(150 μl) containing 2 % SDS to
extract leaf protein. Phosphorylated polypeptides were detected by autoradiography after electrophoresis of the leaf extract(3.4 μg Chl).
Under these conditions, light-induced phosphorylation of 28 and 27-kD
Chl a/b binding polypeptides was readily detectable only in the leaves
which have the ratio of Chl b/a+b above 0.15, but not at all in the
leaves with the ratio less than 0.15. The amount of phosphorylated 28-kD
polypeptide evaluated from the densitogram of X-ray film is shown by
Curve B in Fig. 2. There was no significant difference in light-intensity curves for CO_2-uptake activity measured in intact leaves of Chl b-
less mutant and wild type. The observation suggests that Chl b-less
mutant has the least antenna unit which is needed to drive photosynthesis efficiently. Two conclusions were deduced from the data under the
assumptions; the mutants and wild type have an equivalent antenna unit
of Chl-a molecules bound to reaction center of PS II, and fluorescence
emitted from the Chl-a molecules is able to be quenched by photochemical
and non-photochemical manners such as the oxidation of Q and the
formation of ΔpH. i) In the leaves with low Chl b/a+b ratio(< 0.15),
light-harvesting Chl a/b protein complexes are unable to transfer its
excitation energy to reaction center. This results in apparent decrease
of variable fluorescence by overlapping of the emission originated from
the Chl a/b protein complexes. ii) In the leaves with high Chl b/a+b
ratio(> 0.15), light-harvesting Chl a/b protein complexes are partly
phosphorylated and turned into non-fluorescent form being capable of
transferring excitation energy. Consequently, variable fluorescence is
enhanced with increase of the phosphorylated Chl a/b protein complexes.
The fluorescence quenching derived from Chl a/b protein complexes was
estimated as 30 and 38 % of overall quenching at 695 and 740 nm, respectively, in wild type(Chl b/a+b = 0.27) grown for 10 weeks under low
light when the rate was calculated from the values of (Fm - Fs)/Fm
obtained by the extraporation of the V-shaped curves in Fig. 1.

REFERENCES
1 Michel, H., Tellenbach, M. and Boschetti, A.(1983) Biochim. Biophys.
  Acta 725, 417-424
2 Terao, T., Matsuoka, M. and Katoh, S.(1988) Plant Cell Physiol. 29,
  825-834
3 Machold, O., Meister, A., Sagromsky, H., Høyer-Hansen, G. and
  Wettstein, D., von(1977) Photosynthetica 11, 200-206
4 Chunaev, A. S., Ladygin, V. G., Kornyushenko, G. A., Gaevskii, N. A.
  and Mirnaya, O. N.(1987) Photosynthetica 21, 301-307
5 Briantis, J. M., Vernotte, C., Krause, G. H. and Weis, E.(1986)
  in Light Emission by Plants and Bacteria(Govindjee et al., eds.), pp.
  539-583, Academic Press, New York
6 Horton, P. and Black, M. T.(1981) Biochim. Biophys Acta 635, 53-62

THE EFFECT OF VARIOUS DETERGENTS ON THE FRAGMENTATION
OF THYLAKOID MEMBRANES DURING LEAF ONTOGENY

NAĎA WILHELMOVÁ and ZDENĚK ŠESTÁK
Department of Physiology of Photosynthesis and Water Relations,
Institute of Experimental Botany, Czechoslovak Academy of Sciences,
Na Karlovce 1a, CS-160 00 PRAHA 6, CZECHOSLOVAKIA

1. INTRODUCTION
    Detergents are commonly used as a useful tool in studies of
thylakoid membrane architecture and composition and for the isolation
of highly purified particular chlorophyll-protein complexes, showing
photochemical activities. An empirical knowledge is usually exploited
in these attempts but the exact nature of the interactions of
detergents with thylakoid membranes is not known (1). It is also not
clear whether the physiological state of the used leaves and
chloroplasts, e.g. their age, does affect the fragmentation efficiency
of a given detergent. Therefore we have investigated the effects of
various types of detergents on the fractionation of thylakoid membranes
prepared from French bean leaves of different ages.
    We have selected a group of detergents according to their
physico-chemical properties. We employed the non-ionic detergents
digitonin (Dg) and Triton X-100 (TX) differing in size and shape of
their molecules, the cationic detergent cetylpyridinium chloride (CPC),
the anionic detergent sodium dodecylsulphate (SDS), and the
zwitterionic detergents Zwittergent 3-12 (Z-12), 3-14 (Z-14) and 3-16
(Z-16), with 12-, 14- and 16-C long acyl chains, respectively.

2. PROCEDURE
2.1. Materials
    French bean plants (*Phaseolus vulgaris* L. cv. Jantar) were grown
in sand cultures in the growth chamber (Kovodružstvo, Kladno)
under constant temperature 25/16 °C, air humidity 60/80 %, and
fluorescence tubes irradiance 300/0 μmol m^{-2} s^{-1} (PAR)
(day/night). Plants were twice a week supplied with an IBP
nutritive solution, on the other days with distilled water.
Primary leaves were used for analysis, buds of other leaves were
continuously removed.
2.2 Methods
    From 14 - 45 d old bean leaves class II chloroplasts were isolated
according to Jursinic and Govindjee (2). They were resuspended
in 0.05 M Tricine with 5.10^{-3} M MgCl$_2$, and incubated for 30 min
at 20 °C in the dark in a thermostated shaker with a particular
detergent (for concentrations see Table 1). Membrane fragments
were separated on Percoll gradients (35 % Percoll in 0.25 M
sucrose with the same detergent concentrations) in the Beckman
J2-21 M/E centrifuge for 50 min at 39 000 *g* in 20 °C. The sigmoid

M. Baltscheffsky (ed.), Current Research in Photosynthesis, Vol. II, 931–934.

shape of Percoll gradient was selected which facilitated a separation of particles with close buoyant densities. Membrane fractions were detected in a flow cell placed in the spectrophotometer Philips PU 8800 adjusted to 678 nm, and subsequently collected as 1 cm^3 fractions with a fraction collector. Green fractions were characterized by their chlorophyll (chl) and protein contents, chl a/b ratios, and absorption and fluorescence emission spectra. The chl a and b amounts were determined according to Arnon (3), protein amounts according to Miller (4). Absorption spectra were measured with the PU 8800 spectrophotometer at room temperature. Fluorescence emission spectra excited at 470 nm were measured with the Perkin-Elmer LS-5 fluorimeter at 77 K. Buoyant density of membrane particles was determined by a comparison with the density marker beads (Pharmacia).

TABLE 1. Fractionation patterns of subchloroplast particles during onto-geny of primary French bean leaves. For each detergent the fractions were independently marked starting with I according to increasing density (1.041 to 1.138 g cm^{-3}). The letters a to t represent individual ranges of density (a = 1.041 – 1.045, b = 1.046 – 1.050, etc.) and enable a comparison of individual detergents.

Leaf age [d]	Dg 0.3 mM	TX 0.03mM	CPC 0.3 mM	SDS 0.03 mM	Z-12 0.03 mM	Z-14 0.03 mM	Z-16 0.03 mM
14	b I 1.049	aI 1.042	aI 1.042	a I 1.042	aI 1.042	aI 1.042	aI 1.043
	cII 1.053	dII 1.056	dIV 1.060	aII 1.045	dV 1.060	dIII 1.056	bII 1.048
	dIII 1.060			cIII 1.055			
21	b I 1.048	aI 1.043	a I 1.043	aII 1.045	a I 1.043	a I 1.041	a I 1.045
	fIV 1.070	eIII 1.062	f VI 1.069	dIII 1.057	b II 1.050	dIII 1.058	b II 1.048
		fIV 1.069	qVIII 1.122		f V 1.068	fVI 1.070	oIX 1.113
		o V 1.114			qIX 1.121		
28	b I 1.048	c II 1.054	dIII 1.056	b II 1.049	cIII 1.052	b II 1.050	bII 1.049
	b II 1.050	eIII 1.064	f V 1.066	d IV 1.060	f VI 1.070	e IV 1.062	cIII 1.054
		g IV 1.071	gVI 1.071	f V 1.066	1VIII 1.098	1VII 1.097	
		s VI 1.132		1 VI 1.097			
33	b I 1.048	d II 1.056	cII 1.053	a I 1.042	c IV 1.055	bII 1.049	bII 1.049
	fIV 1.069	e III 1.063	gVI 1.071	e IV 1.061	g VII 1.072	dIII 1.056	cIII 1.054
	t VI 1.138	f IV 1.069	iVIII 1.084	f V 1.066	q IX 1.121	f V 1.066	
		1 V 1.096		p VI 1.116		g VI 1.074	
						1VII 1.097	
45	b I 1.048	a I 1.041	c II 1.051	b II 1.050	bII 1.049	b II 1.050	b II 1.050
	f IV 1.069	eII 1.061	cIII 1.055	dIII 1.057	hVII 1.077	dIII 1.057	cIII 1.053
	i V 1.085	g V 1.073	fVI 1.070	f V 1.069		f V 1.069	
	tVI 1.137						

3. RESULTS AND DISCUSSION

As the goal of this study was to determine the interaction of thylakoid membranes with the selected detergents, the maximum concentration of each detergent was chosen for analyses that did not yet induce a complete membrane solubilization but produced a broken thylakoid material. TX was about 10 fold more efficient in chloroplast solubilization than Dg and CPC, all the other detergents had a similar potency like TX. Hence the charge or chain length of the detergent molecule was not a critical factor influencing its efficiency.

Various amounts of subchloroplast particle types were produced by using different detergents: three in Z-16, six in Dg, TX and SDS, eight in CPC, and nine in Z-12 and Z-14. The particle types were marked with Roman numerals starting with I according to increasing density independently for each detergent. The comparison of various detergents was enabled by labelling each range of density (in 0.005g cm^{-3} steps) with letters from a (lowest density) to t (Table 1).

By using Dg the lightest fraction a was absent, but the fraction b was formed by fragmenting chloroplasts from leaves of all age groups (marked as 14 d, 21 d, etc.). Fraction d was found only at 14 d and fraction i only at 45 d. By using TX the number of fractions grew from 2 (14 d) to 4 (21d to 33 d), the lightest fraction a was absent at 28 d and 33 d. In CPC always three fractions were formed (with the exception of the 14 d leaves), the fraction a was present only at 14 d and 21 d. In SDS 3 to 4 fractions were formed (four at 28 d and 33 d). In Z-12 the amount of fractions grew with leaf age from 2 to 4 (at 21 d), in Z-14 from 2 to 5 (at 33 d), and then declined in old leaves. In Z-16 at every leaf age only two types of fragments were produced: the fractions a and b at 14 d and 21 d, and the fractions b and c in preparations from older leaves.

The changes in general characteristics of fractionation patterns during leaf ontogeny were as follows:
1) An increase in amount of fractions (to 28 d or 33 d) was followed by a decline. The least changes in amount and density of fragments were found by using Z-16.
2) The predominance of light fractions in young leaves disappeared during leaf ageing and was replaced by a formation of more dense fragments. This agrees with the results of Šesták (5,6) who fragmented the French press particles from young and old spinach and radish leaves on linear and step sucrose gradients.

In individual fractions the relative content of chl was determined (% of total) as well as chl a/b and chl/protein ratios, and the positions of red absorption peak and fluorescence emission maxima. The results may be summarized as follows:
a) In young leaves relatively more chl was contained in the light fractions, and during leaf ontogeny the amount of chl in dense fractions increased. An exception was a high portion of the b fraction at 45 d when Dg was used. The shift to higher amount of dense particles during leaf ageing agrees with that obtained for French press particles (5,6).
b) The chl a/b ratio was lower in all fractions than in the chloroplasts. The reason might be a preferential liberation of chl

a from subchloroplast particles in the course of fragmentation. The free chl a formed mixed micelles with the detergents that were evident as a green background in the analyses. The chl a/b ratio mostly increased with fragment density, only exceptionally extremely low ratios were found in the densest fraction (e.g., 45 d leaves with Dg). The smallest changes in the chl a/b ratio were found by using CPC.
c) In young leaves a preponderance of protein was found in the densest fraction. With leaf ageing the maximum chl/protein ratio shifted to middle fractions and the differences between fractions were smaller. In senescent leaves the highest protein amount was in the upper fraction (using TX, CPC, and Z-12) or in the bottom fraction (Dg, SDS and Z-14). In the Z-16 preparations rather low relative amounts of protein were found in all cases.
d) With the increase in fraction density from 1.041 to ca. 1.100 g cm^{-3} the position of the red absorption peak (A_{max}) shifted to a longer wavelength (in the range of 673.2 to 680.6 nm) but a further increase in the fraction density (up to 1.125 g cm^{-3}) was accompanied with a return of A_{max} to the shorter wavelength range. These changes were independent of the type of detergent or leaf age. At the plant age of 14 d the fragment densities were lower than 1.060 g cm^{-3} and the maximum wavelength of A_{max} was only 678.9 nm. The only exception was Dg for which such dependence was not found.
e) In the low temperature fluorescence emission spectra three peaks, at 680 – 690, 703 – 718 and 727 – 740 nm, could have been distinguished, with eventual shoulders. Their shape depended on the type of fraction, its density, the used detergent and leaf age.

4. CONCLUSIONS

The amount and quality of subchloroplast fractions obtained during chloroplast fragmentation depends not only on the detergent used but also on the age of leaves from which the chloroplasts were isolated. The number of fractions obtained increased with leaf age to a maximum and then declined. Fractions of low densities, low protein content and high relative chlorophyll content prevailed in preparations from young leaves. With leaf ageing more dense fragments appeared and their chlorophyll content increased. The chlorophyll a/b ratio increased with fragment density. The position of the red absorption peak was independent of detergent used or leaf age, but depended on the fraction density. The largest variance was found in the shapes of fluorescence emission spectra. The lowest number of fractions of rather steady properties was obtained by using Z-16, while the highest diversity of fragments and their properties was obtained with digitonin.

REFERENCES
1 Markwell, J.P., Thornber, J.P., Reinman, S., Satoh, K., Bennett, J., Skrdla, M.P. and Miles, C.D. (1981) in Photosynthesis (Akoyunoglou, G., ed.), Vol. III, pp. 317 – 325, Balaban Int. Sci. Serv., Philadelphia
2 Jursinic, P. and Govindjee (1977) Biochim. Biophys. Acta 461, 253 – 267
3 Arnon, D.I. (1949) Plant Physiol. 24, 1 – 15
4 Miller, G.L. (1959) Anal. Chem. 31, 964
5 Šesták, Z. (1969) Photosynthetica 3, 285 – 287
6 Šesták, Z. (1970) Carnegie Inst. Year Book 68, 572 – 574

LIGHT REGULATION OF THE PHOTOSYSTEM II AND PHOTOSYSTEM I REACTION
CENTRES OF PLANT THYLAKOID MEMBRANES

W.S. CHOW and JAN M. ANDERSON
CSIRO Division of Plant Industry,
Canberra, ACT 2601, Australia

1. INTRODUCTION
    The light environment (intensity and quality) has a profound
influence on the composition, function and structure of thylakoid
membranes resulting in coordinated changes in both the light-
harvesting antennae of photosystem(PS) II and PSI, and the amounts of
thylakoid protein complexes(1). It is well established that the
photosystem stoichiometry is rarely unity: higher plants have
variable PSII/PSI reaction centre ratios of 1.2 - 2.0, and this ratio
is influenced by both light intensity and quality (1-3). Our aim in
this study is threefold: to ensure accurate determinations of
functional PSII reaction centres by an *in vivo* assay; to compare the
photosystem stoichiometries in sun and shade plants, and in sun
species grown under high and low light; and, to provide a rational
explanation for the marked variation of PSII/PSI reaction centre
ratios.

2. METHODS
    Shade leaves were collected from a shade gully in the Australian
National Botanic Gardens. Thylakoid membranes were gently isolated by
a rapid procedure designed to preserve PSII function as in (4). The
functional PSII reaction centres *in vivo* were determined from the O_2
yield per single turnover xenon flash given to leaf discs at 4 Hz
with background far-red light to ensure no limitation by PSI turnover
(5). DCMU-binding was performed on freshly isolated thylakoids (4).
P700 was assayed by the light-induced absorbance change at 703 nm in
a flash photometer made by Prof. Haehnel (4).

3. RESULTS AND DISCUSSION
3.1 *Oxygen yield per flash for direct assay of PSII in vivo*
    The estimation of functional PSII centres on a Chl basis in
isolated thylakoids is controversial with different labs reporting
different values for the same species, and some authors advocating
large pools of inactive PSII units. As part of the discrepancies may
be due to varying degrees of inactivation of PSII function during
thylakoid isolation and storage, we have developed a method to
quantify functional PSII in leaves directly by the oxygen yield from
leaf discs exposed to 1% CO_2 and repetitive flashes with far-red
background light to keep the plastoquinone pool oxidised (5).

    To test the validity of the oxygen yield in leaves, we also
determined the DCMU-binding capacity of thylakoids isolated from
leaves comparable to those used in the O_2 electrode. As shown in Fig.

M. Baltscheffsky (ed.), Current Research in Photosynthesis, Vol. II, 935–938.
© 1990 *Kluwer Academic Publishers. Printed in the Netherlands.*

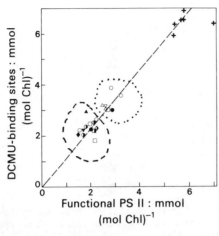

Fig. 1. Correlation between functional [PSII] *in vivo*, determined in leaf discs by the O$_2$ yield per flash in the presence of far-red light with the DCMU-binding sites of thylakoids isolated from the same leaves.
Shade plants (---)
Sun plants (....)
Chl b-less barley mutant (+).

1, the functional [PSII] of leaves of different species correlates very well with the concentration of the DCMU-binding sites of isolated thylakoids. The linear regression through the origin fitted to those points has a slope of 1.14, partly attributible to the miss-factor in the flash-induced O$_2$ evolution (4). Hence this leaf disc method provides a convenient, direct measure of the functional PSII in leaves, without artifacts due to inactivation of PSII during thylakoid isolation and measurement. These results demonstrate clearly the range of PSII concentrations in different species, and the values obtained are close to those of Melis (2) who assayed PSII in thylakoids by a light-induced absorbance change at 325 nm. Note also that the close correlation between functional concentration with the DCMU-binding sites of thylakoids demonstrates clearly that most of the PSII centres are connected to the plastoquinone pool, contradicting conclusions of Graan and Ort (6) that 40% of the PSII centres are non-functional.

3.2 *Variable PSII/PSI reaction centre stoichiometries in plants grown in natural habitats or varying light intensities*
As shown in Table 1, on a chlorophyll basis, the amount of P700 is rather constant in sun species with Chl/P700 ratios of 600. However, shade species have substantially lower P700 concentrations as noted earlier (7). Variations in growth irradiance do not produce substantial changes in the Chl/P700 ratios of sun species. The amount of functional PSII per unit chlorophyll shows a much greater variation between sun and shade plants, with sun plants having more PSII than most shade plants. Variations in growth irradiance also markedly alter [PSII] with low-light plants having only ~70% of the [PSII] of high-light acclimated plants.

Our results (Table 1) show that the PSII/PSI reaction centre ratios are variable with sun species having substantially larger ratios than most shade species. The Chl b-less barley mutant with no LHCII and hence decreased light-harvesting capacity in PSII, has more PSII units relative to PSI units to help balance light absorption, as noted earlier (8). This adjustment of photosystem stoichiometry is dynamic; when pea plants grown in low light were transferred to moderate light, the PSII/PSI ratio changed from 1.25 to 1.7, respectively (9).

Table 1. Chl a/Chl b ratios and photosystem reaction centre ratios of sun and shade plants, and plants grown in high and low light.

	$\dfrac{\text{Chl a}}{\text{Chl b}}$	PSII mmol	PSI (mol Chl)$^{-1}$	$\dfrac{\text{PSII}}{\text{PSI}}$
Species grown in glasshouse				
spinach	3.3	2.98	1.71	1.74
pea	3.3	2.93	1.64	1.79
barley, wild type	3.1	2.89	1.53	1.89
Chl b-less barley	-	5.99	1.94	3.09
Species grown under canopy shade				
Dicksonia antarctica	1.8	1.79	1.51	1.19
Pollia crispata	2.0	2.14	1.14	1.88
Tasmannia purpurascens	2.0	1.88	1.46	1.29
Aristotelia australasica	1.9	2.15	1.27	1.69
Species grown in low fluorescent light				
spinach	2.7	2.39	1.81	1.32
pea	2.6	2.12	1.69	1.25
Alocosia	2.5	2.00	1.43	1.40

3.3 *The light-regulated adjustment of photosystem stoichiometries increases the efficiency of photosynthesis*
It is well known that sun and high-light grown plants have higher Chl a/Chl b ratios than shade and low-light grown plants (1) (Table 1). These variations elicited in the sun/shade response result in variations in the distribution of total chlorophyll between the light-harvesting Chl a/b-proteins, LHCII and LHCI, versus the core Chl a-proteins of PSII and PSI (3). This results in modulations of both the stoichiometries of P680 and P700, and the number of light-harvesting molecules associated with each reaction centre, i.e. the photosynthetic unit size of PSII and PSI.

What is the purpose of these light-regulated changes in photosystem reaction centre stoichiometry which are regulated by the interplay of both light intensity and quality? From our growth irradiance studies, it is clear that low-light plants have a PSII/PSI ratio of 1.1 - 1.3 compared to 1.7 - 2.0 in high-light plants (Table 1). In contrast, light quality also influences photosystem stoichiometry: the PSII/PSI reaction centre ratio of peas grown in light absorbed mainly by PSI was 2-fold greater than that of peas grown in mainly PSII-sensitising light (10). In this case the plants respond to the prevailing light quality, so that the relative concentrations of PSII and PSI minimize the imbalance in light absorption. Shade plants receive less than 0.5% of the irradiance at the top of the forest canopy: 40% of this continuous diffuse radiance is greatly enriched in far-red PSI light and 60% is direct, intermittent sun-flecks (11). We suggest that the regulation of photosystem stoichiometry is thus an opposing interplay of both *very low intensity and altered quality*. In most cases, the resultant balance of photosystem ratios of shade plants is generally lower than that of sun species indicating that it is controlled more by *intensity than by quality*.

Table 2. Estimation of apparent antenna sizes of PSI and PSII[*]

Irradiance	Spinach		Alocasia	
	High	Low	High	low
PSI/(1000 total Chl)	1.6	1.6	1.5	1.5
PSII/(1000 total Chl)	3.0	2.0	3.0	1.8
PSII/PSI	1.8	1.2	2.0	1.2
PSI antenna size (Chl)	303	303	333	333
PSI antenna size (Chl)	167	250	167	278
Ratio of PSII antenna sizes high-light/low-light	0.67		0.60	

[*]The estimation of apparent antenna sizes is based on the assumption that, because the quantum yield of O_2 evolution is close to theoretical expectations, energy distribution between PSII and PSI is balanced; i.e. for 1000 total Chl molecules, ~500 serve PSII's, and ~500 serve PSI's. The antenna size of PSI or PSII is calculated as 500 divided by the no. of reaction centres per 1000 total Chl molecules.

In Table 2, we have estimated the antenna size of PSII and PSI. The PSII antenna size of high-light/low-light spinach is 0.67; thus, low-light plants have less PSII and their PSII unit size is larger than high-light spinach. This is true also for a shade-tolerant species, *Alocasia*. So light acclimation to both shade and low irradiance gives fewer, but larger PSII units, relative to PSI. Sun species and high-light plants have more, but smaller PSII units which are less readily photoinhibited.

It is remarkable that despite the altered composition, function and structure of shade and low-light chloroplasts compared to sun and high light chloroplasts, all C_3, non-stressed plants have the same quantum yields of O_2 evolution under light-limiting conditions. We suggest that this remarkable constancy of quantum yield is achieved by the light regulation (the interplay of quality and quantity) of both the relative amounts of P680 and P700, and the light-harvesting antenna size of PSII and PSI.

REFERENCES
1 Anderson, J.M. (1986) Annu. Rev Plant Physiol 37: 93-136
2 Melis, A. and Brown J.S. (1980) Proc Natl Acad Sci USA 77: 4712-16
3 Anderson, J.M., Chow, W.S. and Goodchild, D.J. (1988) Aust J Plant Physiol. 15: 11-26
4 Chow, W.S. and Hope, A.B. (1987) Aust J Plant Physiol 14: 21-28
5 Chow, W.S., Hope, A.B. and Anderson, J.M. (1989) Biochim Biophys Acta 973: 105-108
6 Graan, T. and Ort, D.R. (1986) Biochim Biophys Acta 582: 320-330
7 Boardman, N.K., Anderson, J.M., Thorne, S.W. and Björkman, O. (1972) Carneg Instit Wash Yearbook 71: 107-114
8 Ghirardi, M.L., McCauley, S.W. and Melis, A. (1986) Biochim Biophys Acta 851: 331-339
9 Chow, W.S. and Anderson, J.M. (1987) Aust J Plant Physiol 14: 9-19
10 Glick, R.E., McCauley, S.W., Gruissem, W. and Melis, A. (1986) Proc Natl Acad Sci USA 83: 4287-4291
11 Björkman, O. and Ludlow, M.M. (1972) Carneg Instit Wash Yearbk 71: 85-94
12 Björkman, O. and Demmig, B. (1987) Planta 170: 489-504

STRUCTURE OF AN AMINOGLYCOSPHINGOLIPID FROM CHLOROBIUM

M.T. JENSEN, J. KNUDSEN AND J.M. OLSON, INSTITUTE OF BIOCHEMISTRY, ODENSE UNIVERSITY, CAMPUSVEJ 55, DK-5230 ODENSE M, DENMARK

INTRODUCTION
   Chlorobium limicola f. thiosulfatophilum is known to contain several unusual glycolipids (1). One of these has been purified and characterized as an aminoglycosphingolipid. This type of lipid with a sphingosine backbone is seldom found in bacteria. The lipid was estimated to be a major component of the total lipid pool (2) and was shown to be confined to the plasma membrane (3). An unusual feature of this lipid is that it is a zwitterion at physiological pH.

MATERIALS AND METHODS
   The lipid was extracted with chloroform and methanol, and then precipitated with acetone 3 times. The lipid was purified by isocratic and gradient HPLC, using solvent systems composed of hexane, isopropanol and water.

RESULTS AND DISCUSSION
   The IR-spectrum of the purified lipid is identical to that of the "fluorescent" aminolipid of (2). The "fluorescence" ascribed to this lipid was an artifact due to contamination by fluorescent components which can be separated from the lipid by careful chromatography. The IR-spectrum shows the absence of ester bonds but the presence of at least one amide bond (1610 cm^{-1}). The carbon-13 NMR spectrum (Table 1) shows good agreement with the structure of the sphingosine and fatty acid parts of the glycosphingolipid of (4). In the aminolipid there is one mole of myristic acid per mole of sphingosine. When the sugar part of the molecule was derivatized and purified, the purified derivative was found to be identical to the derivative of sialic acid (5). The part of the carbon-13 NMR spectrum due to the sugar part is similar but not identical to the spectrum of sialic acid (6). The proton NMR spectrum in chloroform/methanol, 1/1 (v/v) with 0.12 M DCl (Table 2), does not support the sialic acid structure, because there is no singlet at 2 PPM from an acetic acid residue. However the proton NMR-spectrum in DMSO shows two broad peaks at 7.6 and 7.1 PPM which indicate a protonized primary amine. If one removes the acetic acid residue in sialic acid leaving a primary amino group, one obtains a sugar structure, which when derivatized according to (5), gives exactly the same derivative as does sialic acid. These results together with the molecular weight of 760.58 (FAB/MS) lead to the proposed structure in Fig. 1 - that of an aminoglycosphingolipid.

M. Baltscheffsky (ed.), Current Research in Photosynthesis, Vol. II, 939–941.
© 1990 *Kluwer Academic Publishers. Printed in the Netherlands.*

TABLE 1. Carbon-13 NMR spectrum of approx. 1 mg lipid in DMSO

PPM	Interpretation
0.2	TMS internal standard
5.9	impurity
14.0	methyl groups
22.2-35.4	carbons in fatty acid and aliphatic part of sphingosine
40	DMSO
41.6 }	{ deoxycarbon in sugar
42.5 }	{ impurity
51.0	sugar carbon vicinal to nitrogen
54.0	sphingosine carbon vicinal to nitrogen
64.0	primary alcohol in sugar
68.9	sphingosine carbon bound to sugar via glycosidic bond
69.6	sugar carbon
70.4	sugar carbon
71.0	sphingosine carbon with hydroxygroup
73.1	sugar carbon
101.5	anonmeric carbon in sugar
129.5	double bond in sphingosine
171.5 }	{ carboxylic acid group in sugar
172.0 }	{ secondary amide in sphingosine

TABLE 2. Proton NMR spectrum of 10 mg lipid in chloroform/methanol 1/1 (v/v) with 0.12M DC1

PPM	Area	Interpretation
0.88	9.070	triplet, methyl groups
1.28	95.333	peak complex, methylene groups
2.0	0.726	impurity
2.35	2.853	triplet, methylene group vicinal to carbonyl
2.6	1.485	quartet
3.1	1.643	quartet
3.3-4.1	18.595	peak complex, sugar protons
3.35		quartet, methanol (solvent)
5.35	0.190	double bond
5.7	23.030	singlet, HOD in acid solvent
7.7		singlet, chloroform (solvent)

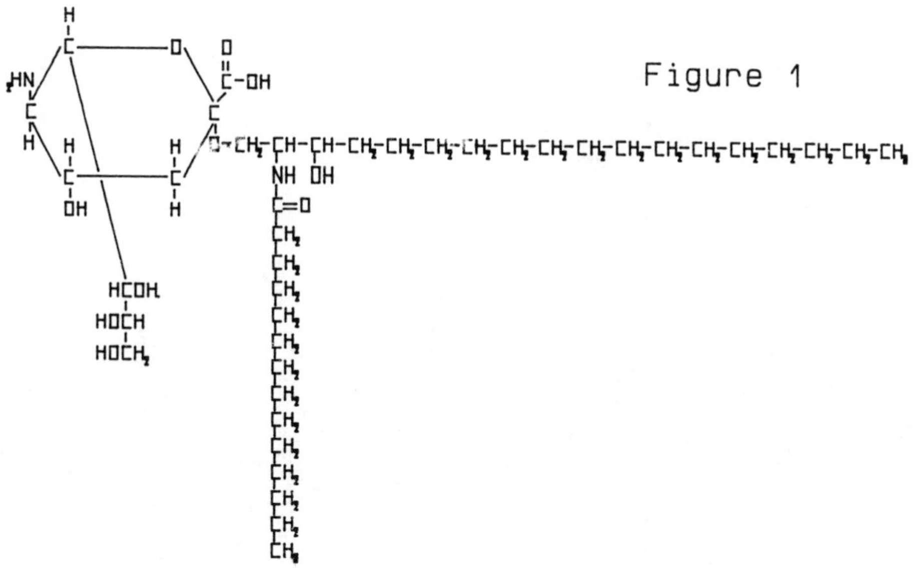

Figure 1

```
    H
    |
    C——O   O
  HN/ \     ‖
  C    \   C-OH
  H  H  H \ /C
   \C----C/ O-CH₂-CH-CH-CH₂-CH₂-CH₂-CH₂-CH₂-CH₂-CH₂-CH₂-CH₂-CH₂-CH₂-CH₂-CH₂-CH₂-CH₃
    |    |        NH OH
    OH   H        C=O
                  CH₂
                  CH₂
       HCOH       CH₂
       HOCH       CH₂
       HOCH₂      CH₂
                  CH₂
                  CH₂
                  CH₂
                  CH₂
                  CH₂
                  CH₂
                  CH₃
```

To our knowledge this is the first example of an aminoglycosphingolipid in a procaryote. It may be significant that this lipid is found
in green sulfur bacteria which are related to the bacteroides/
flavobacteria by the criterion of 16S rRNA structure (7). These are
the only two groups of bacteria known to contain sphingolipids.

Because the aminolipid is a zwitterion at physiological pH, it may
act as a membrane anchor for proteins with negatively and positively
charged groups. The water-soluble bacteriochlorophyll a-protein (8)
found only in green sulfur bacteria might be bound in this way.

REFERENCES
1 Kenyon, C.N. (1978) in The Photosynthetic Bacteria (Clayton, R.K.
  and Sistrom, W.R., eds.), pp. 281-313, Plenum Press, New York
2 Olson, J.M., Shaw, E.K., Gaffney, J.S. and Scandella, C.J. (1983)
  Biochemistry 22, 1819-1827
3 Olson, J.M., Shaw, E.K., Gaffney, J.S. and Scandella, C.J. (1984) in
  Advances in Photosynthesis (Sybesma, C., ed.), Vol. 3, pp. 139-142,
  Nijhoff/Junk, The Hague
4 Dabrowski, J., Egge, H. and Hanfland, P. (1980) Chem. phys. lipids
  26, 187-196
5 Jentoft, N. (1985) Anal. Biochem. 148, 424-433
6 Vliegenthart, J.F.G., Dorland, L., van Halbeek, H. and Haverkamp, J.
  (1982) in Sialic Acids (Schauer, R., ed.) Springer, Wien
7 Woese, C.R. (1987) Microbiological Reviews 51, 221-271
8 Olson, J.M. (1978) in The Photosynthetic Bacteria (Clayton, R.K. and
  Sistrom, W.R., eds.), pp. 161-178, Plenum Press, New York

THE INTERACTION OF STATE TRANSITIONS AND CHLORORESPIRATION IN THE XANTHOPHYCEAN ALGA PLEUROCHLORIS MEIRINGENSIS

C. BÜCHEL AND C. WILHELM
INSTITUT FÜR ALLGEMEINE BOTANIK
JOHANNES-GUTENBERG UNIVERSITÄT D-6500 MAINZ, FRG

1. INTRODUCTION

Wavelength dependent State I-State II-transitions have been shown to exist in chlorophytes and red algae. Little is known about the regulation of energy distribution between the photosystems of chlorophyll c-containing plants. Previously it was shown that in the xanthophycean alga Pleurochloris meiringensis two states of energy distribution could be established [1] : In state "D" light is preferentially transferred to PS II, whereas in state "L" PS I is favoured. These state regulations strictly depend on the intensity and not on the wavelength of preillumination. In this paper we give new evidence that chlororespiration is involved in the mechanism of state "L"-state "D"-transitions.

2. PROCEDURE

Pleurochloris meiringensis (Culture collection Göttingen 860-3) was homocontinuously cultured under 16 W/m^2 as previously described [1] . Fluorescence emission spectra at 77K and the F II/F I values were measured according to [1]. For the detection of the fluorescence kinetics at room temperature the PAM 101 [2] was used. Cells were stirred in a cuvette under physiological conditions. The cells were kept in the dark or illuminated with 64 W/m^2 for 20 min to adjust different states. The intensities of actinic illumination given in tab. 1 did not produce photoinhibition [1] . Fmax was determined by the application of saturating flashes (400 W/m^2, 700 msec lifetime, 1/30 s frequency). Inhibitor concentrations were as follows. DCMU: 10^{-2} mol m^{-3}; antimycin A: 3×10^{-4} mol m^{-3}; NH$_4$Cl: 20 mol m^{-3}. Anaerobiosis was obtained by adding 40 units/ml of glucose-oxidase, 20 mol m^{-3} glucose and 600 U/ml catalase.

3. RESULTS AND DISCUSSION

Pleurochloris meiringensis reversibly changes the states of energy distribution (Fig. 1). State "L" is characterized by

M. Baltscheffsky (ed.), Current Research in Photosynthesis, Vol. II, 943–946.
© 1990 *Kluwer Academic Publishers. Printed in the Netherlands.*

a low F II/F I ratio, whereas in state "D" the PS II-emis-
sion is enhanced. The $t_{1/2}$ of the state "L"-state "D"-tran-
sition is 3,5 min, the reverse reaction is three times faster. In order to characterize the different states, the
photochemical (qQ) and non-photochemical (qE, qI, qT) quenching coefficients were determined. Because photoinhibition
did not occur, qI was neglected. The state "D"-state "L"-
transition coincides with a decrease of Fo during the illumination of dark adapted cells (data not shown). The non-
photochemical quenching was corrected by Fo-changes leading
to qE values which depend mainly on the formation of a pH-
gradient.

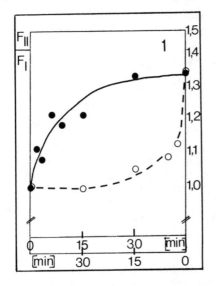
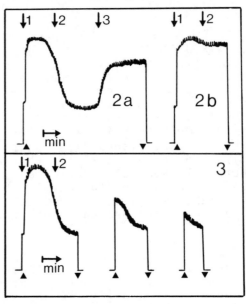

Fig. 1
Reversibility of the state
"L"-state "D"-transitions

Fig. 2 a/b
Fluorescence induction curve of dark adapted, DCMU (↓1)
treated cells under the influence of antimycin A (↓2),
NH_4CL (↓3) (2a) or
anaerobiosis (2b)

Fig. 3
Fluorescence induction
as Fig. 2a interrupted by
short period of darkness.
▲ actinic on
▼ actinic off

As given in tab. 1, the qE values are unusually low in Pleurochloris, nearly at zero level under low actinic intensities. This phenomenon is enhanced in state "D" adapted
cells. The low qE values can be explained only by this exis-

tence of a pH-gradient in the dark induced by light-independent electron transport, a so-called chlororespiration
[3,4,5]. This pathway is controlled by light intensity to
maintain a pH-gradient strong enough for ATP synthesis. Under anaerobic conditions the acceptor side of the chlororespiration, the cyt c oxidase, is blocked but also the PQ-
pool (besides other components of the electron transport
chain) is reduced leading to decreasing qQ values (Tab. 1).
In case of a strong reduction of the PQ-pool and an inhibition of the cyt c oxidase by O_2-deficiency a stronger pH-
gradient can be seen (Tab.1). The low qE values of dark adapted cells together with the effect of anaerobiosis give
evidence for the existence of a cyt c oxidase which is more
active in state "D".

The fluorescence induction of dark adapted, DCMU poisoned
cells (Fig.2) shows after the addition of antimycin A a
strong quenching, which could be cancelled in some extend
by uncouplers. Antimycin A blocks the cyclic flow around PS
I by inhibition of the ferredoxin-PQ-oxidoreductase leading
to a strongly oxidized

TABLE 1

state	inhibitor	actinic light intensity (W/m^2)	qE	qQ
D		5	0.009	0.977
D		13	0.000	0.918
D		34	0.005	0.833
D		61	0.065	0.065
D		115	0.210	0.731
L		5	0.004	0.975
L		13	0.016	0.930
L		34	0.011	0.891
L		61	0.224	0.807
L		115	0.453	0.686
D	antimycin A	13	0.230	0.845
D	antimycin A	61	0.548	0.946
D	anaerobiosis	61	0.570	0.515

PQ-pool. Assuming that under DCMU, uncouplers and antimycin
A qQ and qE are set to zero, the remaining quench is either
caused by state transitions (qT) or the oxidation of the
PQ-pool (qP), which has been shown in Mantoniella previous-

ly[3] . The importance of the redox state of the PQ-pool is supported by the fact that the quenching does not occur under the influence of a strong reductant (glucoseoxidase). qP can be cancelled by short periods of darkness (Fig.3). The influx of electrons during the dark gives a hint for the activity of a plastoquinone-NADPH-oxidoreductase. The activity of the cyt c oxidase depends on light intensity and oxidation of the PQ-pool. When antimycin A is added alone, the PQ-pool becomes oxidized and qE increases due to the inhibition of the cyt c oxidase activity (Tab.1).

In the light of the given results the two states can be described as follows: State "D" is characterized by a high absorption capacity of PS II, a reduced PQ-pool and a high chlororespiration activity generating a pH-gradient in the dark. In state "L" adapted cells the chlororespiration is inhibited, the PQ-pool is more oxidized and the absorption cross section of PS I is enhanced. From our data we propose that the thylakoid membrane of Pleurochloris is mainly used to control the energy charge, even in the dark. If ATP synthesis is saturated under high irradiances the membrane function is altered in order to optimize the production of reduction equivalents.

ACKNOWLEDGEMENTS
This work was supported by the DFG (Wi 764/1-6) and is part of the first authors PhD-Thesis.

REFERENCES
[1]   Büchel, C., Wilhelm, C. and Lenartz-Weiler, I. (1988) Botanica Acta 101, 283-365
[2]   Schreiber, U., Schliwa, U. and Bilger, W. (1986) Photosyn. Res. 2, 261-272
[3]   Wilhelm, C. and Duval, J.C. (1989) BBA submitted
[4]   Bennoun, P. (1982) Proc. Natl. Acad. Sci. USA 79, 4352-4356
[5]   Caron, L., Berkaloff, C., Duval, J.C. and Jupin, H. (1987) Photosynth. Res. 11, 131-139

Index of Names

950

952